WHY COMPETITION?

Voices from the Antitrust Community and Beyond

Concurrences

Paris - New York - London

106 West 32nd Street, Suite 144 New York, NY, 10001, USA
www.concurrences.com
book@concurrences.com

First Printing, November 2024
978-1-954750-66-1 (Hardcover)
Library of Congress Control Number: 2024949667

Cover Design: Yves Buliard, www.yvesbuliard.fr
Book Design and Layout implementation: Nord Compo

Concurrences Books

Tributes

James F. Rill – A Life in Antitrust, *John Taladay, Paul Lugard (eds), 2024*

Eleanor M. Fox – Antitrust Ambassador to the World, *2021*

Herbert Hovenkamp – The Dean of American Antitrust Law, *2021*

Frédéric Jenny – Standing Up for Convergence and Relevance in Antitrust, (Vol. I & II), *2019 & 2021*

Albert Foer – A Consumer Voice in the Antitrust Arena, *2020*

Richard Whish – Taking Competition Law Outside the Box, *2020*

Douglas H. Ginsburg – An Antitrust Professor on the Bench (Vol. I & II), *2018 & 2020*

Wang Xiaoye – The Pioneer of Competition Law in China, *A. Emch, W. Ng (eds.), 2019*

Ian S. Forrester – A Scot without Borders (Vol. I & II), *A. Komninos (eds.), 2015*

William E. Kovacic – An Antitrust Tribute (Vol. I & II), *2013 & 2014*

Practical Books

The DMA and more – Future application and margin of manoeuvre for national jurisdictions, *G. Muscolo & A. Massolo (eds.), Forthcoming 2024*

Artificial Intelligence and Competition Policy, *A. Abbott, T. Schrepel (eds.), Forthcoming 2024*

State Aid & National Enforcement, *J. Derenne, D. Jouve, C. Lemaire, F. Martucci (eds.), Forthcoming 2024*

The 2023 U.S. Merger Guidelines: A Review, *Sean Sullivan (ed.), 2024*

Competition Inspections in 25 Jurisdictions 2nd Edition – A Practitioner's Guide, *N. Jalabert-Doury (ed.), 2024*

EU Antitrust Enforcement – Law, Economics, History, *Policy & Practice, Wouter P. J. Wils, 2024*

The EU Foreign Subsidies Regulation, *Andreas Reindl, Isabelle Van Damme, 2024*

Compendium of Antitrust Damages Actions – ICC – 2nd edition, *J. W.H. Denton AO, F. Brunet, S. Williams, C. Inthavisay (eds.), 2023*

Pharmaceutical Antitrust: An Analysis of US and EU Law, *M. Thill-Tayara, G. Gordon (eds.), 2023*

Innovation Paradox in Merger Control, *G. Gurkaynak, 2023*

Antitrust and the Digital Economy, *Y. Katsoulacos (ed.), 2023 (in collaboration with CRESSE)*

Judicial Review of Competition Cases, *D. Ginsburg, T. Eicke (eds.), 2023*

Competition Law Treatment of Joint Ventures, *B. Bleicher, N. Campbell, A. Hamilton, N. Hukkinen, A. Khan, A. Mordaunt (eds.), 2022 (in collaboration with the IBA)*

Information Exchange & Related Risks, *Z. Marosi, M. Soares (eds.), 2022 (in collaboration with the IBA)*

Rulemaking Authority of the US Federal Trade Commission, *D. Crane (ed.), 2022*

The International Competition Network at Twenty, *D. Anderson & P. Lugard (eds.), 2022*

Competition Case Law Digest – 5th Edition, *F. Jenny, N. Charbit (eds.), 2022*

Competition Inspections in 21 Jurisdictions – A Practitioner's Guide, *N. Jalabert-Doury (ed.), 2022*

Perspectives on Antitrust Compliance, *A. Riley, A. Stephan, A. Tubbs (eds.), 2022 (in collaboration with the ICC)*

Turkish Competition Law, *G. Gürkaynak, 2021*

Competition Law – Climate Change & Environmental Sustainability, *S. Holmes, D. Middelschulte, M. Snoep (eds.), 2021*

Merger Control in Latin America – A Jurisdictional Guide, *P. Burnier da Silveira, P. Sittenfeld (eds.), 2020*

Competition Inspections under EU Law – A Practitioner's Guide, *N. Jalabert-Doury, 2020*

Gun Jumping in Merger Control – A Jurisdictional Guide, *C. Hatton, Y. Comtois, A. Hamilton (eds.), 2019 (in collaboration with the IBA)*

Choice – A New Standard for Competition Analysis? *P. Nihoul (ed.), 2016*

PhD Theses

The Economics of Digital Markets – Essays in Theoretical and Empirical Industrial Organization, *E. Arnaud-Joufray, 2024, Forthcoming 2024*

Abuse of Platform Power, *F. Bostoen, 2023*

Reform of Chinese State-Owned Enterprises, *X. Bai, 2023*

Competition & Regulation in Network Industries – Essays in Industrial Organization, *J-M. Zogheib, 2021*

The Role of Media Pluralism in the Enforcement of EU Competition Law, *K. Bania, 2019*

Buyer Power, *I. Herrera Anchustegui, 2017*

General Interest

Why Competition? Voices from the Antitrust Community and Beyond, *D. Crane, D. Gerard, R. Tritell (eds.), 2024*

Competition Law Dictionary, *D. Healey, R. Whish, W. E. Kovacic, P. Trevisán (eds.), 2024*

Great Antitrust Enforcers, *W. E. Kovacic, 2023*

Competition – How to Speak Like an Expert, *E. Combe , 2023*

Women and Antitrust – Voices from the Field (Vol I & II), *E. Kurgonaite & K. Nordlander, 2020*

WHY COMPETITION?

Voices from the Antitrust Community and Beyond

Foreword by Frédéric Jenny

Editors

Daniel A. Crane

Damien Gérard

Randolph Tritell

Concurrences Editors

Nicolas Charbit

Tudor N. Pana

Margaux Seager

Sébastien Gachot

Foreword

Twenty years ago, in July 2004, the WTO General Council decided to drop the issue of competition policy from the agenda of the Doha Round of negotiations. This decision, prompted by the difficulties of the negotiations regarding the other, more traditional, items on the agenda of the Doha Round, marked the end of an era for both trade and for competition.

The 1990s had been characterized by a rapid expansion of bilateral and regional trade agreements (such as the Mercosur Agreement in 1991 or Nafta in 1994), the increasingly frequent adoption of competition chapters in such agreements (requiring trading nations to have a competition law (to ensure that the elimination of their governmental trade barriers to trade would not be compensated by the rise of private barriers making entry in their markets difficult or even impossible), the multiplication of national competition laws across the world and the successful completion of a 14 years negotiation between China and the WTO culminating with China joining the WTO in December 2001. Trade liberalization and the adoption of competition laws were seen as complementary, to a large extent. The most frequently discussed issue in international competition circles was whether sufficient convergence existed between the various laws around the consumer welfare protection paradigm, which had become dominant, first in the US and the rest of the world.

The debates around trade liberalization, competition, and competition law became much more complex, first in the aftermath of the 2008 financial crisis and later during the aftermath of the Covid-19 pandemic in 2020-2022. Both events suggested that competitive markets could fail (in the case of the mortgage market in the US) or work too slowly (in the case of the market for vaccines against Covid 19) and that regulation (in the case of financial sectors) or cooperation between competitors (in the case of pharmaceutical firms) could, in some instances, lead to faster results and fewer negative externalities for society. In addition, both events changed the perspective on trade liberalization. Several countries realized that efficiency benefits obtained thanks to trade liberalization also meant that the resilience of their economy could be threatened when their trading partners were affected by an exogenous shock. This led to a reappraisal of the benefits expected from trade liberalization and a more cautious attitude toward open trade policies.

The realization that trade liberalization and competition could have downsides was reinforced by the rapid rise of China in international trade. China was the world's sixth largest economy, with 1.3 billion people at the time of its accession to the WTO. Over the following 20 years, China grew from the sixth to the world's second-largest economy, with its GDP increasing 11-fold to almost USD 15 trillion. Thanks to its participation in the WTO, its ability to export was one of the crucial factors of this economic expansion. This came at a cost to Chinese competitors in developed countries. The feeling that international competition was unfair because of the vast subsidies that made Chinese exporters so successful brought home the idea that international competition could be unfair. Indeed, the reallocation mechanism which makes competition theoretically a win-win policy assumes perfect mobility of labor across economic activities and regions, which is a fiction for many reasons:

- There are few programs to help displaced labor find new technical skills in demand.
- The fact that several family members may be employed means that relocation could be more complex than if only one family member were employed.
- The fact that an entire industrial areas, can be wiped out by international competition means that local workers in such areas may end up without any realistic hope of selling their assets to start a new life in an area where, furthermore, the same kind of asset will be much more expensive because of the dynamic development of the region.

The unfairness of (international) competition became a popular theme of populist movements and parties, attracting large followings in economically depressed areas.

This issue was compounded by the insolent success of a few entrepreneurs in the digital sector. Successful startups were sold for amounts that defied the imagination, and fortunes were made seemingly overnight by a few. This contributed to an increase in wealth and income inequality without competition authorities seemingly able or willing to intervene and curb the excesses. Competition seemed an unfair lottery, with a few becoming all-powerful and the share of labor earnings in the GDP decreasing significantly. Thomas Piketty's internationally successful book "Capital in the 20th Century" argues that because the rate of return on capital is greater than the rate of economic growth over the long term, wealth becomes more concentrated and the distribution of wealth becomes more unequal, causing social and economic instability. Its international success was partly due to being published at a time when workers felt displaced. Reducing growing inequalities was perceived as a more worthy goal than promoting competition or efficiency at all costs.

The question of why competition law seemed unable to control concentration in the digital sector and to sanction abuses by large platforms became a subject of discussion. Competition authorities in all countries became aware of the necessity of developing new theories of harm to deal with competition issues in the digital sector between diversified ecosystems. In the US, the Neo-brandeisians also called for a return to the original goal of the 1890 Sherman Antitrust Act, which was, according to their reading of history, to fight economic power rather than promote consumers' welfare. Europeans asked themselves whether the competition law instrument was adequate to deal with competition issues in dynamic hi-tech markets and whether ex-ante regulation of the gatekeepers in the digital sector designed to keep markets contestable and fair was a necessary complement to competition law.

Finally, there is a growing awareness that competition must be thought about in a longer-term and more dynamic perspective than what the static microeconomic theory framework has so far suggested. This new awareness results from three factors: the rapid development of the digital sector, the intensified technological competition between Western countries and China, and increasing concerns about climate change. The rapid development of the digital sector, with the rise of new innovative and sometimes disruptive services by large platforms, raised the question of the relationship between competition (or market power) and innovation, a relationship that economists have not yet fully understood. In the context of the perceived technological race between Western countries and China, whether we need a more assertive industrial policy and the relationship between such an industrial policy and competition policy are hotly debated. Finally, the concern with climate change raises both the issue of whether we should use a longer time frame and broader perspective in merger control to assess the potential anticompetitive and efficiency effects of a transaction and the problem of the development and the introduction of products made using new technologies designated as clean technologies, and whether the risk of first-mover disadvantage justifies some cooperation between competitors.

Overall, the vibrant debate about competition over the last twenty years has been characterized by the emergence of several new perspectives on the goals of competition law, new issues on the competition analysis of conduct and transactions of undertakings, and new instruments at the disposal of competition law enforcers. We are still in the experimental phase of a number of these developments. More than ever, competition law is a vital and exciting field.

Frederic Jenny
Emeritus Professor of Economics, ESSEC Business School
Chairman OECD Competition Committee

Editors' Note

Why Competition? Voices from the Antitrust Community and Beyond is a landmark publication celebrating 20 years of Concurrences' dedication to advancing thought leadership in competition law and economics. This collection of no less than 100 essays reflects two decades of rigorous scholarship, and dynamic debate on the ever-evolving challenges facing competition policy across the globe.

This volume explores the central question: Why competition? As the various contributors demonstrate, the answers are far-reaching. Competition ensures that markets remain open and fair, drives innovation, and enhances consumer welfare. However, achieving effective competition requires constant reassessment and adaptation, especially as economies grow more digital and experience multiple geo-economic crises.

The diverse voices – leading figures in competition law, economics, and policy – gathered in this volume provide nuanced perspectives on these critical issues. In doing so, contributors offer insights on a broad range of contemporary competition policy issues and enforcement challenges, including the fundamental relationship between antitrust enforcement, competition, competitiveness, trade and welfare, both in developed and developing economies, particular concerns arising in the digital, agri-food or sports sectors, as well as views of the current enforcement landscape from the consumer or particular territorial perspectives, be it the EU, the Americas, Asia or Africa. Hence, this book offers a comprehensive exploration of the core tenets of competition policy from various vantage points, fields, and geographies.

The breadth and depth of the contributions also underscore the global relevance and interdisciplinary nature of competition law. As the challenges facing markets become more complex, Why Competition? aims to bring clarity, share knowledge, stimulate new ideas, and foster further debate within the antitrust community, while ensuring that the discussion remains attuned with the shifting global landscape.

As editors, we are deeply grateful to the team at Concurrences and to all the contributors who have made this publication possible. As Concurrences celebrates two decades, we look forward to continuing to support scholarly dialogue that not only responds to today's challenges facing competition policy but also shapes its future.

Randy Tritell
Former Director, Office of International Affairs, Federal Trade Commission

Daniel Crane
Frederick Paul Furth Sr. Professor of Law, University of Michigan

Damien Gerard
Prosecutor General, Belgian Competition Authority

Publishers' Note

As we celebrate 20 years of promoting dialogue and scholarship in competition law and antitrust economics, Concurrences is proud to present Why Competition? Voices from the Antitrust Community and Beyond. This anniversary book reflects on two decades of contributions to the global conversation on antitrust issues, marked by the publication of insightful essays and analyses from leading experts.

Founded in 2004 with the invaluable support of Professors Laurence Idot and Frédéric Jenny, Concurrences has grown from a vision into a leading independent publisher with offices in Paris, London, and New York. Our mission has always been clear: to provide a platform for legal and economic experts to explore and debate the challenges and developments in competition law. Throughout the years, we have consistently upheld our commitment to academic rigor, independence, and objectivity.

The growth and success of Concurrences have been made possible by the expertise of our Scientific and Steering committees and Editorial boards, which have ensured the highest standards in every publication. From legal professionals to economists, from policymakers to academics, we have attracted a broad and diverse audience that shares our passion for antitrust law and competition economics. Our work spans various topics – regulatory frameworks, market structures, enforcement policies, and beyond – connecting legal theory with real-world applications.

This focus on competition and antitrust has made Concurrences a pivotal influence in shaping policy discussions and fostering intellectual exchange. Over the past two decades, we have expanded our reach and solidified our position as one of the world's most influential think tanks in the antitrust field.

Why Competition? celebrates these efforts by bringing together a collection of diverse essays that examine the essential role competition plays in driving innovation, ensuring market fairness, and enhancing consumer welfare. The insights presented here reflect the depth of expertise that has defined Concurrences for 20 years, offering readers a comprehensive look at the evolving landscape of antitrust law and competition policy.

As we mark this milestone, we extend our heartfelt thanks to our contributors, readers, and the entire antitrust community who have supported Concurrences's journey. Together, we have built a foundation of scholarship and discourse that will continue to shape the future of competition law and economics for many years.

Nicolas Charbit
Founder and CEO
Concurrences

Tudor N. Pana
Associate Editor
Concurrences

Margaux Seager
Associate Editor
Concurrences

List of Contributors

Alden Abbott
Sia Aik Kor
Giuliano Amato
Reiko Aoki
Rana Aref
David Bailey
Caron Beaton-Wells
Jean-Francois Bellis
Pascal Belmin
Matthieu Blayney
Jan Blockx
Christian Bovet
Paulo Burnier Da Silveira
Darren Bush
Luis Cabral
Gina Cass-Gottlieb
Nadia Calvino
Rodrigo Cárcamo-Díaz
Jean Cattan
Samuel Chan
Jean-Pascal Chazal
Elie Cohen
Anthony Collins
Alexandre Cordeiro Macedo
Nuno Cunha Rodrigues
Josef Drexl
Ariel Ezrachi
Jonathan Faull
Cani Fernandez
Ian Forrester
Eleanor Fox
Jens-Uwe Franck
Peter Freeman
David Gerber
Calvin Goldman
Olivier Guersent
Gönenç Gürkaynak
Deborah Healey
Andreas Heinemann
Simon Holmes
Mina Hosseini
Edward M. Iacobucci
Marcela Iacub
Felipe Irarrázabal
Marc Ivaldi
Frederic Jenny
Francis Wang'ombe Kariuki
Krisztian Katona
Han Ki Jeong
Gaspard Koenig
Ioannis Kokkoris
Haïm Korsia
Pierre Larouche
Bruno Lasserre
Connie Lee
Hubert Legal
François Lévêque
Abbott B. Lipsky
Philip Lowe
Barry Lynn
Imelda Maher
Petros C. Mavroidis
Andrea Marván Saltiel
Michelle Meagher
Martin Merlin
Mahmoud Momtaz
Maria Teresa Moreira
Andreas Mundt
Willard Mwemba
Darren Brady Nelson
Damien Neven
Phedon Nicolaides
Philip E. Ogden
Ulf Öberg
Jorge Padilla
Nicolas Petit
Martin Peitz
Étienne Perrot
Salvatore Piccolo
Jean Pisani Ferry
Rupprecht Podszun
Aurelien Portuese
Alejandra Palacios Prieto
Stephane Retterer
Agustin Reyna
Cyril Ritter
Nicole Robins
Barry Rodger
Alexander Rose
Lilian Santos Marques Severino
Andreas Schwab
Thibault Schrepel
Fiona M. Scott-Morton
Rod Sims
Martijn Snoep
Jacques Steenbergen
Matt Stoller
Alexandre de Streel
Marisa Tierno
Laurent Truchot
Pablo Trevisan
Vanessa Turner
Nicolas Véron
Anne Wachsmann
Florian Wagner-von Papp
Nils Wahl
Spencer Waller
Alexis Walckiers
Xiaoye Wang
Diane Wood
Marc van der Woude
Angela Zhang
Huang Yong

Summary

PART II: Global Competition Challenges and Opportunities

PART III: Enforcement and Market Regulation

PART IV: The Digital Age: Competition and Innovation

PART VI: Sector-Specific Insights and Emerging Trends

PART VII: Personal Reflections and Regional Experiences

PART I

Foundations and Philosophical Insights on Competition

What is Competition? – The Meanings and Usefulness of "Competition" as the Measure of Legality

ELEANOR M. FOX*
New York University

I. Introduction

1. What is competition? How useful is the concept as the principal metric to determine the permissibility of market acts and transactions?

2. In this chapter, I note the changing meanings of the concept "competition" over time in US antitrust law; I compare the meaning conveyed by current US Supreme Court case law with that accorded by the Biden Agencies; and I consider the place of the word internationally by reference to applications in Europe and Africa. I conclude that "competition" has held up well as the guiding concept for controlling market power and its abuse. While it has an elasticity that could impugn it as ambiguous or unworkable,[1] that elasticity has proven to be a virtue that allows it to interact with different norms and changing market realities and to withstand the tests of time and place.

---

* Eleanor Fox is Professor of Law Emerita and Walter J. Derenberg Professor of Trade Regulation Emerita at New York University School of Law. She thanks Randy Tritell for his valuable suggestions.

1 See Daniel Francis, *Antitrust Without Competition*, 74 Duke L.J. _ (forthcoming), available at SSRN: https://ssrn.com/abstract=4734468.

II. The Meaning of "Competition"

3. "Competition" is a process of rivalry. It is defined in the definitions from *Oxford Languages* as "an event or contest in which people compete."[2] It is defined in the *Cambridge Dictionary* as "a situation in which someone is trying to win something or be more successful than someone else… ."[3] It is defined in the *Dictionary Britannica* as "the act or process of trying to get or win something (such as a prize or a higher level of success) that someone else is also trying to get or win: the act or process of competing… ."[4]

4. The word "competition" was not always the descriptor behind antitrust or competition law. Industrializing Britain used the phrase "restraint of trade." In 1890, "restraint of trade" and "monopolization" were enshrined in the US Sherman Act. Justice Oliver Wendell Holmes slyly observed, in defense of the big railroad merger (albeit in dissent), that "the [Sherman] Act says nothing about competition."[5] But the Sherman Act case law virtually always used the language of competition to describe the process to be preserved, as in the big railroad merger itself.[6] By the time of the Progressive Movement in the United States, "competition" became the key word of the Clayton Act of 1914 which prohibited firms from merging where the effect of their merger "may be to substantially lessen *competition* between [them]… ."[7] The consequential amendment of 1950 (the Celler-Kefauver Act) widened the scope to prohibit mergers whose "effect may be substantially to lessen competition" in any market.[8] "Restraint of trade" in the Sherman Act became universally understood to mean "anticompetitive."[9]

5. By the time I began practicing law in January 1962, there was no doubt that the US antitrust laws meant to protect competition; that the Sherman Act prohibited anticompetitive agreements and anticompetitive acts of monopolists; and that the Clayton Act prohibited potentially anticompetitive mergers. Almost the entire weight of the law was on: what is the meaning of "anticompetitive?"

---

2 Oxford Languages, https://languages.oup.com/google-dictionary-en/ (last visited Oct. 15, 2024).

3 Cambridge Dictionary, https://dictionary.cambridge.org/us/dictionary/english/competition (last visited Oct. 15, 2024).

4 Dictionary Britannica, https://www.britannica.com/dictionary/competition (last visited Oct. 15, 2024).

5 Northern Securities Co. v. United States, 193 U.S. 197 (1904), replying to Justice Harlan's statements in his majority opinion that the object of the combination was: "competition between the constituent companies would cease …" "If such a combination be not destroyed, all the advantages that would naturally come to the public under the operation of the general laws of competition, as between the Great Northern and Northern Pacific Railway companies, will be lost …" *Id.* at 327.

6 *Id.*

7 Clayton Act, Oct. 15, 1914, ch. 323, 38 Stat. 730, 731 (emphasis added).

8 Celler-Kefauver Act of 1950, Pub. L. No. 81-899, 64 Stat. 1125 (codified as amended at 15 U.S.C. § 18).

9 *See e.g.*, National Society of Professional Engineers v. United States, 435 U.S. 679 (1978).

III. Evolution and Revolution in the United States

6. In the 1960s in the United States, the application of "anticompetitive" was relatively clear but the category was expanding. Eliminating competition between major rivals – as in the railroad merger – was clearly anticompetitive because it eliminated the rivalry between them and thus eliminated an important force for better performance in the market. Tying and other exclusionary agreements imposed by a major firm were anticompetitive because (and if) they foreclosed smaller challengers from succeeding on their merits; the conduct clogged open markets by introducing elements foreign to competition on the merits and thus prevented challengers' products from reaching consumers, harming the competition of the smaller firms against the incumbent. Vertical mergers of big players at each of two functional levels were often anticompetitive because – by threatening to foreclose needed inputs or outlets to unintegrated rivals – they diminished the competitive forces that would otherwise be wielded by the firms that became beholden to the leading player. Resale price maintenance agreements were anticompetitive because they stopped the distributor from competing on price, raising prices to consumers. (Most of these generalizations would later come under attack as simplistic and one-sided, and as demonstrating why "competition" was a useless or at least indeterminate metric.)

7. Six months after I began practicing law, the Supreme Court handed down *Brown Shoe Co. v. United States*.[10] At stake was a district court decision condemning a 4 percent shoe manufacturer's acquisition of a popular shoe retailer where each had a foot in the market of the other and there was a trend towards consolidation of the hundreds of market participants. The Supreme Court affirmed, stressing that small independent stores may be excluded from access to outlets by the growing, large, national chain. Famously, the Court said, by Chief Justice Warren:

> "Of course, some of the results of large integrated or chain operations are beneficial to consumers. Their expansion is not rendered unlawful by the mere fact that small independent stores may be adversely affected. *It is competition, not competitors, which the Act protects. But we cannot fail to recognize Congress' desire to promote competition through the protection of viable, small, locally owned business.* Congress appreciated that occasional higher costs and prices might result from the maintenance of fragmented industries and markets. It resolved these competing considerations in favor of decentralization. We must give effect to that decision."[11]

---

10 370 U.S. 294 (1962). No Justices dissented on the merits. Justice Harlan dissented on jurisdiction and concurred in the substantive result.

11 *Id.* at 344. Emphasis added.

8. We, the antitrust lawyers, pored over these words. What did they mean? What was "competition that the law protected?" Given Congress' desire, it was, among other things, competition among viable, small, local firms. Congress favored decentralization, even if it meant occasional higher prices. This interpretation was woven into the advice that antitrust lawyers gave their clients for the next two decades. In all events (whether or not the law could protect inefficiencies), the law protected the process of competition. It gave particular regard to the competition of the underdog and of firms without power. It protected competition on the merits of firms without power and condemned exclusionary practices that threw roadblocks in their path.[12]

9. The Court made course corrections in the mid to late 1970s to guard against market-harming results, but it was not until the start of the Reagan Administration in 1981 that the fight to overthrow Warren Court antitrust took root. The "Chicago School" – which symbolized faith in the self-correcting power of markets and concern that regulatory intervention would chill competition and outlive its utility – had been pounding on the door, and at last the door flew open. The attacks came through various projects and modes. Strong leadership at the antitrust agencies, and the appointment of hundreds of judges, were critical to the cause. Two particular methods of attacks were notable. One: introduction and constant repetition of the phrase: the Warren Court protected competitors. The law must protect consumers, not competitors. Two: introduction of a pathway; take the stress off competition as a process and put it on outcomes. Reconceptualize antitrust to condemn nothing at all unless its result is to lessen output and raise prices, and add the neoliberal presumptions that lessening output is hard to do; markets are inherently efficient.

10. For the rhetoric, the movement got help from, of all places, the opinion in *Brown Shoe*. It lifted out of context the now very famous words, quoted above: "It is competition, not competitors, which the Act protects."[13] This was the greatest word heist in lexicology. *Brown Shoe*, of all cases, did not turn its back on helping small and middle-sized firms. The ploy worked. The citers got away with it. In US parlance and case law, the modern meaning of the *Brown Shoe* phrase is: we must not concern ourselves with protecting opportunities or opening markets for competitors, for that will inevitably protect inefficient small competitors, raise prices, and hurt consumers. This is not at all what *Brown Shoe* meant.

11. For the pathway – shifting from a focus on the competition process to outcomes, condemning nothing unless its result was allocatively inefficient (limiting output), and assuming that markets are efficient: The 1982 Merger Guidelines produced a roadmap. They essentially approved mergers unless the transaction would congeal an industry cartel or the structure that conduces

---

12 *See*, Eleanor Fox, *Tilting the Law Towards a More Competitive Economy*, 37 WASH. & LEE L. REV. 49 (1980).

13 *See*, Address by William Kolasky, Deputy Assistant Attorney General, Antitrust Division, U.S. Dep't of Justice, "What Is Competition?" (The Hague, Oct. 28, 2002); Eleanor Fox, *We Protect Competition, You Protect Competitors*, 26 WORLD COMPETITION 149 (2003), https://kluwerlawonline.com/journalarticle/World+Competition/26.2/WOCO2003002.

to cooperation without an agreement. Their corporation-friendly influence lived on[14] until December 2023 when the Biden Administration introduced new merger guidelines that took the focus off outcomes and put it back on competition and the competitive process.[15]

12. The Supreme Court case law has today, and it has had for the last two decades, a fairly clear notion of: what is competition that the law protects? Past the cartel offense, the category is narrow. The *Trinko* case[16] is a good example, and indeed is the principal case that shrank the law. Under *Trinko* and its progeny, in unilateral conduct cases, what (even monopoly) firms do is presumed efficient. Their freedom to act as they choose is emphasized as important to give them the incentive to invent and invest. Conduct is impugned only if it successfully passes through a narrow gateway. In the case itself, the Court ruled that it was not anticompetitive for the purposes of the Sherman Act for the incumbent telecom provider and controller of the local loop to create noise and interruptions in the systems of its new competitors in order to keep its customers from shifting to the new suppliers.[17] *Trinko* and its philosophy has been entrenched in subsequent cases.[18]

13. The Biden Justice Department and the Federal Trade Commission (FTC) have brought a number of cases, now pending. They are striving to push out the narrowing circle of what is anticompetitive that the law condemns. They are trying to reclaim ground for competition by litigation,[19] policy statements,[20] and guidelines.[21] The Merger Guidelines of 2023 are a significant accomplishment in providing a framework that could help reset the stage to protect competition.[22]

---

14 The document was, however, updated from time to time and each update made the guidelines more realistic and more modern.

15 Fed. Trade Comm'n. & U.S. Dep't of Justice, *Merger Guidelines (2023)*, (Dec. 18, 2023), https://www.ftc.gov/system/files/ftc_gov/pdf/P234000-NEW-MERGER-GUIDELINES.pdf

16 Verizon Communications v. Law Offices of Curtis V. Trinko, 540 U.S. 398 (2004), see James E. Scheuermann & William D. Semins, *The US Supreme Court introduces a new method for regulatory antitrust analysis (Trinko / Verizon)*, E-COMPETITIONS Jan. 2004, art. No. 43984.

17 In context, the market had recently become liberalized by legislation. The new competitors included AT&T, which was now allowed to enter the northeast market. The challenged conduct of the incumbent monopolist was limited to about two months, for the Federal Communications Commission had already ruled that the conduct violated the Federal Communications Act. The antitrust case was before the Supreme Court on a motion to dismiss, so the Court was obliged to accept the facts pleaded as true. Nonetheless, it did not do so and speculated that the interruptions of service to the competitors might have been inadvertent adjustment pains.

18 *See e.g.*, Pacific Bell Telephone Co. v. linkLine Communications, Inc., 555 U.S. 438 (2009); Ohio v. American Express Co., 585 U.S. __ (2018). See William Kovacic, *Root and Branch Reconstruction: The Modern Transformation of U.S. Antitrust Law and Policy?*, 35 ANTITRUST MAG. 46 (ABA, Summer 2021); Carl Shapiro, *Antitrust: What Went Wrong and How to Fix It*, 35 ANTITRUST MAG. 33 (ABA, Summer 2021).

19 Cases are pending against Google, Meta, and Amazon, among others. In United States v. Bertelsmann SE & Co., the Department of Justice succeeded in blocking the Penguin Random House/Simon & Schuster merger, validating the use of antitrust to protect market harms to the supply side (D.D.C. Oct. 31, 2022). In Illumina v. FTC, No. 23-60167 (5th Cir. 2023), the FTC succeeded against Illumina's acquisition of Grail, affirming its ability to prove a significant vertical acquisition anticompetitive.

20 *See, e.g.*, Fed. Trade Comm'n, *FTC Policy Statement Regarding the Scope of Unfair Methods of Competition Under Section 5 of the Federal Trade Commission Act*, (Nov. 10, 2022).

21 *See, Merger Guidelines, supra* note 15.

22 *See*, Fiona Scott Morton, *The New and Improved 2023 Merger Guidelines*, PROMARKET (Dec. 18, 2023), https://www.promarket.org/2023/12/18/the-new-and-improved-2023-merger-guidelines/.

IV. Europe

14. The shifting winds on the meaning and application of the concepts "competition" and "competition that the law protects" are uniquely American. The European competition law project was first and foremost based on the goal of market integration. Thus, European competition law was always guided by a goal of open markets and contestability of markets – a perspective that tends to favor more rather than fewer players in a market and not to embrace output theory as the North star,[23] much less output theory with neoliberal presumptions. European law prioritizes "competition on the merits," and therefore is likely to condemn dominant firm conduct that excludes worthy (efficient or potentially efficient) competitors for no good pro-market reason.[24] Conscious in the last two decades that its broad attention to market foreclosure of rivals may have led to overbroad condemnations, it adopted a "more economic approach," elevating consideration of market effects.[25] What is necessary and sufficient to prove anticompetitive effects is a question of great moment and debate, with hints in the case law giving guidance but remaining elusive. The DG-COMP is preparing guidelines on exclusionary abuses of dominance to reflect the recent CJEU judgments and to clarify the law.[26]

15. If there is a significant, growing tension in Europe, it is not so much between a decentralized vision (competition among the many) and a laissez-faire one (if concentration happens, it is probably efficient). Rather it is between sticking with competition as the metric for governing the economy or treating it as an obsolescing tool, to be readily supplanted by industrial policy. The DG-COMP has thus far been reliably for competition, but the balance in the institutions could shift.[27] This, indeed, is a risk generally in the world.

---

23 *See*, Eleanor Fox, *Monopolization and Abuse of Dominance: Why Europe is Different*, 59 Antitrust Bull. 129 (2014); Eleanor Fox, *The Decline, Fall, and Renewal of U.S. Leadership in Antitrust Law and Policy*, CPI Antitrust Chron. (Apr. 2022), https://papers.ssrn.com/sol3/papers.cfm?abstract_id=4097141.

24 *See*, Case C-680/20, Unilever Italia Mkt Operations Srl v. Autorita Garante della Concorrenza e del Mercato, ECLI:EU:C:2023:33, see Claire Mongouachon, *Imputability criteria : The Court of Justice of the European Union specifies the criteria for imputability to the dominant producer of acts committed through its distributors and clarifies the scope of the "competitor as effective as" test for exclusivity clauses (Unilever Italia)*, Concurrences No. 2-2023, art. No. 112510 76-78; Case C-377/20, Servizio Elettrico Nazionale SpA v. Autorita Garante della Concorrenza e del Mercato, ECLI:EU:C:2022:379. It may be necessary to prove also that the conduct is capable of having anticompetitive effects by excluding equally efficient undertakings or hindering their growth. Case C-333/21, European Superleague Company SL v. Federation internationale de football association (FIFA), ECLI:EU:C:2023:1011, ¶129.

25 See e.g., Case T-286/09, Intel Corp. v. Eur. Comm'n, ECLI:EU:T:2014:547, see Albert Sánchez Graells, *The EU General Court upholds the Commission's decision in consideration of two exclusionary practices on the market for the supply of CPUs, opening the door to a further appeal to the Court of Justice and a possible application before the ECtHR (Intel)*, e-Competitions June 2014, art. No. 67162; Case T-286/09 RENV, Intel Corp. v. Eur. Comm'n, ECLI:EU:T:2022:19.

26 See European Commission, *Competition Policy Application of Article 102 TFEU*, https://competition-policy.ec.europa.eu/antitrust-and-cartels/legislation/application-article-102-tfeu_en (last visited Oct. 15, 2024).

27 *See*, The Draghi Report, The Future of European Competitiveness, https://commission.europa.eu/topics/strengthening-european-competitiveness/eu-competitiveness-looking-ahead_en; Leigh Thomas, *France, Germany step up pressure over Alstom-Siemens deal, Reuters*, Reuters (Jan. 21, 2019, 2:26 PM GMT), https://www.reuters.com/article/us-alstom-m-a-siemens-idUSKCN1PF0PK/ (France and Germany trying, unsuccessfully, to defeat big rail rolling stock merger on grounds of need for European champion to take on China). See also Hans Kundnani, *Europe May Be Headed for Something Unthinkable*,

V. Developing Countries

16. Like other jurisdictions, developing countries imbue the word and concept "competition" with a unique character to fit with their cultures. The African countries are good examples. In general, they adopt inclusiveness as a value in their competition laws – not a surprise for peoples who have endured brute exclusion by colonizing forces and are continuingly vulnerable to exploitations. The new African Continental Competition protocol, now pending ratification, expressly includes the value of inclusive growth alongside market efficiency, and, inferentially, conceives of competition as rivalry on a level playing field free of abuses not only of traditional economic market power but also of economic dependence.[28]

17. South Africa has the most developed competition regime in Africa. Blighted by apartheid, South Africa enacted its modern competition law to transform the society, as well as to control market power and prime an efficient economy. South Africans hoped that the market capped by the Competition Act[29] would integrate the society; that open market competition would naturally result in an economy that, demographically, mirrored the people. That did not happen. Path dependency and the stubborn strength of hierarchy perpetuated the old economic order. The need to accelerate transformation led to the 2018–2019 amendments to the Competition Act, which mandate positive action to advance the ownership and participation of historically disadvantaged persons and SMEs in the economy.[30]

18. The South African Constitutional Court has had the opportunity to engage with the South African Competition Act, and, doing so, has construed it as a human rights act to uphold the dignity of the people. Validating competition means construing the Act to protect human rights, including access to health care, of the poorer, left out, and (especially) historically disadvantaged people.[31]

N. Y. Times (Dec. 13, 2023).

28 *See, AfCFTA Protocol on Competition Policy: Factsheet*, Tralac (Oct. 5, 2023), https://www.tralac.org/resources/infographic/16150-afcfta-protocol-on-competition-policyfactsheet.html.

29 Competition Act (South Africa) No. 89 of 1998, later amended by The Competition Amendment Act, No. 18 of 2018. See text at note 31.

30 See Eleanor Fox, *South Africa, Competition Law and Equality: Restoring Equity by Antitrust in a Land where Markets were Brutally Skewed*, CPI Antitrust Chron. (Fall 2019), https://papers.ssrn.com/sol3/papers.cfm?abstract_id=3876527.

31 Competition Comm'n S. Afr. v. Mediclinic S. Afr. (Pty) Ltd. (CCT 31/20) [2021] ZACC 35; 2022 (5) BCLR 532 (CC); 2022 (4) SA 323 (CC) (Oct. 15, 2021). See especially ¶¶ 2-4.

VI. Conclusion

19. "Competition" means rivalry. Competition law protects competition. But it does not protect ALL rivalry. It allows partnerships.[32] It allows many, even most, acquisitions. It allows conduct such as low pricing and innovation that shuts out less attractive competitors. In other words, competition of the sort that the law protects needs to be defined.

20. Where the lines are drawn is generally a matter for case law. In the United States, there have been significant swings of the line between the poles of competition among the many, with antitrust having a long reach, and laissez faire, with business having generous latitude. While there are many points between the poles,[33] it is fair to say that modern US Supreme Court case law tends to reflect the latter perspective. The Biden Administration enforcers tend to embrace the former perspective, and they are counting on heavily fact-based cases, as well as policy pronouncements and guides, to move the line. The EU and developing countries, likewise, deal with their version of the same challenge – to define what is competition that the competition law should preserve – through case law and guidance.

21. Despite its elasticity, the concept "competition" is quintessentially useful. It is central to an understanding of governance of markets. It is, however, important to know how the law uses the term, which is often not obvious. In this chapter, I have tried to advance the project of discerning meaning. Awareness is the first step towards transparency.

---

32 See Mitchel v. Reynolds, 1 P. Wms. 181 (1711). See also Sanjukta Paul, *On Firms*, 90 U. CHI. L. REV. (forthcoming), available at https://papers.ssrn.com/sol3/papers.cfm?abstract_id=4188190; Francis, *supra* note 1.

33 See Justice Breyer's dissenting and concurring opinions in Ohio v. American Express Co., *supra* note 18, and Cal. Dental Ass'n v. FTC., 526 U.S 756 (1999), and Fox, *supra* note 23, at IV. *A Way Forward.*

"The tool is the message: Time to improve the antitrust toolbox"*

Michelle Meagher**
University College London

1. In the 1960s, communications theorist Marshall McLuhan coined the phrase "the medium is the message." McLuhan's point was that the medium through which a message is communicated itself forms part of the message conveyed. I was reminded of this concept during a conversation on the role of politics in competition policy with a competition enforcer. In this foreword, I observe that the analytical tools of antitrust, in particular industrial organisation (IO) economics, appear to contain an implicit message – a political message – resulting in a limited role for competition law as a tool of economic policy. This political message has contributed to the challenges of today and constrains the ability of competition policy to address them. A policy tool is only as good as the analytical tools it can deploy. The politics of today may require a different message to that which IO delivers.

2. The tools of IO economics – a subset of neoclassical economics – have profoundly shaped the practice of EU competition law and policy. The EU Courts initiated a shift towards a "more economic approach" in the early 2000s, demanding that the Commission provide weightier evidence to back up complex theories of harm in EU competition cases. The context was a diplomatic fallout with

* This article has been previously published in Concurrences, and it might have been edited for clarity and cohesion. Michelle Meagher, The tool is the message: Time to improve the antitrust toolbox, May 2024, Concurrences N° 2-2024, Art. N° 118015.

** Some of the observations in this article are based on exchanges and discussions with practitioners and experts, economists and lawyers, both enforcers and those in private practice, who spoke on condition of confidentiality. I would also like to thank Diane Coyle, Simon Holmes, Helena Malikova, Maria Luisa Stasi, and Jonathan Todd for continuing conversations on this topic and their useful comments on this piece. All errors remain my own. I would like to thank the Centre for Research on Multinational Corporations (SOMO) for its support.

the US, which had accused the EU of overzealous competition enforcement. Under the new approach, policy and political choices were to be undergirded by scientific rigour and by neutral IO analysis. The establishment of the Chief Economist Team in 2003 ensured that every complex case ran through the filter of IO. The courts have since underscored the role that economic evidence must play in the Commission's decision-making, partly based on the understanding that economics can give a fuller picture of corporate conduct.

3. IO economics is built on a particular "theory of the firm," centred on the presumptive efficiency of companies. Market intervention by the state should be required only rarely, to correct for minor deviations from the competitive norm. Much has been written about the flaws of neoclassical economics and neoliberalism more broadly, in particular how the reductive assumptions of the underlying models lead, in fact, to an incomplete picture of the world. These deficiencies have proven to be problematic in the operationalisation of neoclassical theory in real-world economic policy, including in relation to IO.

4. We can begin to discern the message conveyed by the tools of IO by investigating the track record of competition enforcement. Ironically, even with its focus on price (and output), it is nevertheless difficult to build a case of excessive pricing using IO economics. The Commission appears to be unable or unwilling to bring exploitative abuse cases in the form of excessive prices. It may be that such cases are difficult to construct using IO because the monopoly price of a dominant firm is the only output of the model. Reconstructing a price that would prevail in a non-monopoly situation is not IO's forte.

5. Along with excessive high prices, Lina Khan, now chair of the Federal Trade Commission, famously pointed out that antitrust using IO fails to diagnose excessively low (predatory) prices. More generally, IO sees size and market power as going hand in hand with efficiency, whether or not lower costs are achieved through a better product and more innovative, cost-effective production processes. Assumed efficiencies count as a defence for big firms whether, in practice, they are passed on to consumers in the form of low prices or to shareholders in the form of dividends and stock buybacks. This is despite Big Tech firms ostensibly not claiming these sorts of efficiencies anyway.[1] Meanwhile, such production efficiencies generally cannot count as a defence for agreements between unions of small independent businesses.[2]

6. IO embodies a preference for corporate bigness. Mergers are welcome because they are generally assumed to bring even more efficiencies in the form of cost savings. Under the IO paradigm, the Commission should in principle

1 See H. Malikova et al., Elusive Efficiencies in Digital M&A, forthcoming.

2 See S. Paul, Antitrust as Allocator of Coordination Rights, *UCLA L. Rev.*, Vol. 67, Issue 2, 2020, pp. 378–431 https://www.uclalawreview.org/ antitrust-as-allocator-of-coordination-rights.

refrain from robbing consumers of these efficiencies. Undue intervention is seen as the ultimate evil.

7. Cumulatively, this has resulted in timid, almost performative enforcement against mergers, niche enforcement against dominant firms, and a fixation with certain forms of coordination (cartels) but not others (mergers). For many commentators, this is as it should be. This sentiment is embodied in the frequently repeated refrain in competition circles that antitrust should not be used as an "axe" or "sledgehammer" but rather as a "scalpel" – surgical, precise, cautious, economical.

8. The Chief Economist Team was established by Director General Philip Lowe and Competition Commissioner Mario Monti in part to improve the perception that the Commission's cases were "*not as thorough and comprehensive as on the other side of the Atlantic*".[3] The intention was to meet the criticism from the courts with robust evidence. Fifteen years later, in 2018, Lowe reminisced that the Chief Economist Team had "*had the refreshing approach in bringing a solution to your problems rather than a problem to your solution.*"

9. But the political and economic context has now changed. The evidence is growing that markets have become highly concentrated across many sectors, across much of the world. Antitrust enforcement (or lack of) under the "more economic approach," which waved through successive consolidations and failed to target abuse, is part of that story. As I wrote in my book, *Competition Is Killing Us: How Big Business Is Harming Our Society and Planet – and What to Do About It* (Penguin Business, 2020), it is as if antitrust "*donned a pair of anti-competition infrared goggles*" but switched the detection mode so that it could not see concentrated power.

10. As has been widely documented, the biggest and most powerful firms engage in actively terraforming the planet and our digital and social spaces in ambiguous ways. This, in turn, shapes our world, and how we live in it, impacting a number of health and social indicators, the geographical spread of supply chains, trade patterns, distribution of information and capital, collective decision-making processes, which forests are felled and which are spared, our built and natural environment.

11. This was the ultimate political message of IO and efficiency in competition policy, with outsized consequence; a message with which policymakers must now contend. Given this policy and political backdrop, and the growing sense of crisis – climate change, pandemic, war, and democratic dissolution – we must ask ourselves: What good, in such times, is a scalpel?

12. Putting aside the neoliberal principle of state non-interventionism, governments around the world are today seeking to actively shape markets and outcomes through industrial policy, aiming at a wide agenda of economic

3 P. Lowe, The Origins of the Chief Economist Team: Mission, early achievement and challenges, Speech at the DG Competition Workshop, 26 June 2018, https:// ec.europa.eu/competition/compat60/memories/pdf/019-lowe.pdf.

objectives, including innovation, security, competitiveness, resilience, justice, distribution, growth, employment, and just transition.

13. As a former director general, Lowe's remarks ("*bringing a solution to your problems*") express a sense of empowerment – the hope and promise – that the Chief Economist Team brought to the enforcement possibilities of a Commission mired in the reputational damage of a series of very public defeats in the early 2000s. Twenty years later, things do not seem to have turned out as expected.

14. The current director general, Olivier Guersent, for example, brings a very different perspective. Guersent caused controversy in January 2024 by stating at a conference titled "Antitrust, Regulation and the Next World Order" that in his view competition policy is a "side dish," meaning an incidental or ancillary instrument to other more substantial tools of economic policy. This sentiment reflects a chilling effect on enforcement, a result that would be very much in line with the initial political objective of laissez-faire economics. Today, this objective is no longer explicitly championed at the highest political level, but it is nevertheless coded in the analytical tools of competition policy via IO economics and is still the approach endorsed by the courts. Guersent does not want to get anyone's hopes up: there are serious limits to what competition policy can do, in his view. Using the tools of IO, this is necessarily the case.

15. Efficiency or power: which is the more relevant message for the competition policy of our times? It is understandable that Guersent might be resigned to the limits of competition policy using the analytical tools of IO. After twenty years of enforcement under the "more economic approach," competition policy has found itself less and less empowered and indeed increasingly limited by the straightjacket of IO economics, operating with self-restraint that can no longer be entirely commended. But IO – and the core concept of efficiency – is not the neutral tool that its adopters thought it was, as demonstrated by the political economic consequences of its application: highly concentrated markets and powerful firms. As I wrote in my book, "*The politics is already baked into the economics.*" In other words, the tool has taken on a life of its own – and may no longer be serving the Commission in its mandate.

16. This has led policymakers – in the EU and in other similarly challenged jurisdictions – to reach for different policy tools to fill in the gaps left by a hamstrung competition policy. One example of this is the new Digital Markets Act (DMA). Another is the use of consumer protection competencies to bring price gouging and corporate profiteering investigations in the UK following on from the pandemic – rather than bringing excessive pricing competition cases more generally. Yet another is the introduction of excess profits taxes for oil and gas companies.

17. But it is also possible to improve the existing policy tool by upgrading the analytical tools – and there is room for improvement. As the controversy of

his "side dish" comment spilled over onto the pages of the *Financial Times*,[4] Guersent emphasised the Commission's track record of enforcement.[5] It is true this has been better than the US authorities' for the last thirty years. It still, however, leaves much to be desired. For example, new research shows that the Commission prevented only 0.7% of mergers between 2005 and 2023.[6]

18. The tools of economics outside competition are in the throes of overhaul. As the political context has changed for the Commission, so can its analytical tools – indeed, they must, as the tools are not neutral and instead continue to proliferate messages that are increasingly out of step.

19. Rapid technological change not only renders the existing toolkit less relevant, it also raises political questions about the structure of markets and normative questions about the proper role of antitrust.[7] IO economics speaks to a particular political economic context – one that no longer holds.

20. Guersent said in a recent interview: "[G]*ood economic analysis does not give you answers but forces you to ask the questions that common sense would not*".[8] The Chief Economist's Team was established to play devil's advocate to the Commission's case team. The impact has been to limit the enforcement of the European Commission. Increasingly, this appears to be leading to "*internal strife*" and "*friction*" inside the Commission, as reported in relation to the *Booking/eTraveli* merger prohibition.[9] Commentators are also asking questions about conflicts of interest,[10] lobbying in the form of gifts and expenses,[11] and the tactic of external economic experts "spamming" the Commission with economic evidence.[12]

21. IO is useful in generating the sorts of questions that can be used to challenge the Commission internally. But the toolbox has not shown itself to be up to the task of enabling the Commission to build cases that can deal with the political economy of today.

---

4 R. Foroohar, The great US-Europe antitrust divide, 5 February 2024.

5 Letter: Europe has an unrivalled record on antitrust, 6 February 2024.

6 See B. Rock, Merger intervention rates in the EU, Hertie School Centre for Digital Governance, *Student Working Paper Series*, 17 January 2024, https://hertieschool-f4e6. kxcdn.com/fileadmin/2_Research/2_ Research_ directory/Research_Centres/Centre_for_Digital_ Governance/5_Papers/Student_publications/ Student_working_paper_series/2024_Rock_ Merger_intervention_rates_in_the_EU__final_.pdf.

7 See D. Coyle and H. Dahmen, The Political Economy of Competition Policy, in Elias Deutscher, Justin Lindeboom, and Stavros Makirs (eds), *Cambridge Handbook on the Theoretical Foundations of Antitrust and Competition Law*. Cambridge: Cambridge University Press, forthcoming.

8 D. Foster, Interview with Olivier Guersent (Part 2), The Role of Economics and New Developments in Competition Policy, Competitive Tension, https:// thecompetitivetension.com/new-developments-in-competition-policy.

9 N. McNelis, Exclusive: 'Ecosystem' concerns behind Booking-Etraveli veto sparked friction inside EU Commission, MLex, 10 October 2023, https://mlex.shorthandstories.com/ecosystem-concerns-behind-booking-etraveli-veto-sparked-friction-inside-eu-commission.

10 N. Shaxson, The Scott Morton affair: anatomy of a democratic victory, The Counterbalance, 26 July 2023 https:// thecounterbalance.substack.com/p/the-scott-morton-affair-anatomy-of.

11 E. Hancock, Consultants showered EU antitrust enforcers with free flights and hotels, *Politico*, 19 December 2023, https:// www.politico.eu/article/consultants-shower-eu-antitrust-watchdog-free-flights-hotels/.

12 M. Jugl et al., Spamming the regulator: exploring a new lobbying strategy in EU competition procedures, *Journal of Antitrust Enforcement*, Vol. 12, Issue 1, 2024, pp. 7–28, https://academic.oup.com/ antitrust/ article-abstract/12/1/7/7128249.

22. What new analytical tools can be used to empower the Commission to better understand business conduct and build robust and evidence-based cases in areas where IO cannot deliver? One starting point may be to use the same tools that companies use themselves to manage their businesses: financial analysis.

23. Analysis using IO starts from abstract economic models and asks the investigated parties to generate data inputs the companies do not compute in the ordinary course of business, which can then be plugged into the mathematical formulae on which those models are based. These models tend to spit out one answer: leave the market alone. In 2018, *The Economist* dissected the sorts of input data that competition authorities use and found it wanting: marginal cost is "*undetectable in the real world*"; gross margins "*are not statutorily defined by American or European accounting regulators and are arbitrarily computed by each firm at its discretion*"; "*Sometimes* [antitrust] *experts discuss absolute profits, but rarely the capital used to create them*".[13] The article notes that the excessive profitability of Standard Oil relative to its capital base was a relevant factor in assessing its monopoly position in the early 1900s; today such an approach "*would be viewed as risqué.*"

24. By contrast, financial analysis of conduct might start with how the business sees itself, using information from management reporting and internal key performance indicators (KPIs), looking at how a particular business line compares in terms of performance and profitability to other business lines within the company, to other geographies, and to other companies, across time. This builds a picture of how that product sits within the market, and whether there is any market power at play, including exploitative abusive power.

25. Financial analysis can be introduced as a complement to other economic evidence in building competition cases, and such data already plays a big role in particular aspects of competition law, such as the failing firm defence and when devising remedies. "Accounting data" appears to have been central in building the excessive pricing story in *Aspen* – an exceptional exploitative case from the last few decades.[14] Whereas in *Apple music streaming*, another exploitative case, it appears that the Commission does not (or perhaps cannot, using the tools of IO) take a view on the level of the price – namely, the fee charged by Apple.

26. Institutionally, the Chief Economist Team could be complemented by a chief financial economist, heading up a Chief Financial Economist Team, building on the model of the Remedies, Business and Financial Analysis team introduced by the UK's Competition and Markets Authority in 2018.[15] The FTC also has several financial analysts working within the Bureau of Economics.

---

13 Regulators across the West are in need of a shake-up, *The Economist*, 15 November 2018, https://www.economist.com/ special-report/2018/11/15/regulators-across-the-west-are-in-need-of-a-shake-up.

14 Eur. Comm., press release IP/21/524 of 10 February 2021, Antitrust: Commission accepts commitments by Aspen to reduce prices for six off-patent cancer medicines by 73% addressing excessive pricing concerns, https://ec.europa.eu/commission/presscorner/detail/en/ip_21_524.

15 A. Land, Introducing our Remedies, Business and Financial Analysis team, CMA Blog, 17 August 2018, https://competitionandmarkets. blog.gov.uk/2018/08/17/introducing-our-remedies-business-and-financial-analysis-team.

27. As opposed to the scalpel of IO, financial economics, and other complementary analytical tools such as behavioural economics, data science, labour and environmental economics, can be used to switch the Commission's market-vision goggles to "on," offering a new lens through which to detect harm deriving from power, size and concentration, currently imperceptible within the frame of IO economics. This would also help support the enforcement of other tools, including the DMA and the Foreign Subsidies Regulation. An expanded analytical toolbox may also assist the Commission in its work on sustainability, looking beyond "green collaborations" under Article 101 of the Treaty on the Functioning of the European Union and into mergers and dominance cases, as detailed in an article co-authored with Simon Holmes, "A sustainable future: how can control of monopoly power play a part?".[16]

28. A better understanding of the implicit messages embedded in the tools we use would help us understand the economic realities they are bound to create. We can also then attempt to reconcile those messages with the mandate of the European Commission – and the current economic and political context. The Commission has a task on its hands to correct for the biases of prior enforcement, and to tackle the market structures that have emerged in the meantime. We must give it the right tools for the job.

16 https://www.balancedeconomy. org/wp-content/uploads/2023/06/A-sustainable-future_Parts-I-to-III-1.pdf.

The Prime Objective of Competition Laws

GÖNENÇ GÜRKAYNAK*
ELIG Gürkaynak Attorneys-at-Law

1. As competition law continues to evolve and expand its boundaries, a crucial debate has resurfaced concerning its prime objective. The effective use of competition law is essential in maximising social welfare, and safeguarding economic efficiency is a crucial step towards achieving this objective.[1]

I. Understanding the Prime Objective of Competition Laws

2. It is imperative that the free-market mechanism operates competitively, in order to achieve an efficient distribution of resources for the highest level of social welfare. However, the natural course that the free-market mechanism takes, may sometimes weaken this competitive process. In such a case, it is necessary for the law to intervene so as to protect the competitive process. In order to effectively identify, control and manage the interventions to this process, there can be no doubt that defining the prime objective of competition law takes priority.

---

* Founding Partner of ELIG Gürkaynak Attorneys-at-Law (Istanbul); Professor of Practice at University College London (UCL) Faculty of Laws; Senior Research Fellow at the Center for Law, Economics & Society (CLES) at UCL Faculty of Laws; Member of Faculty at Bilkent University Faculty of Law (Ankara); gonenc.

1 Roger D Blair and D Daniel Sokol, 'Welfare Standards in U.S. and E.U. Antitrust Enforcement' (2013) 81 Fordham L Rev 2497.

3. However, what the prime objective of competition law is a controversial point. Some consider the prime objective of competition law as 'maintaining and encouraging the process of competition in order to promote efficient use of resources while protecting the freedom of economic action of various market participants, across the most jurisdictions'.[2] The EU focuses on 'consumer welfare',[3] whereas the United Nations Conference on Trade and Development (UNCTAD) sets the objective as '*promoting efficiency and enhancing economic growth and consumer welfare*'.[4] In this context, new academic and policy discussions primarily focus on two objectives: overall welfare, which relates to the surplus for both producers and consumers; and consumer welfare, which specifically pertains to the surplus gained by consumers.[5]

4. Today, 'ensuring total welfare'[6] is largely acknowledged as the prime objective in the doctrine.[7] In this context, competition law is well-positioned as a 'tool' to attain a greater 'social welfare' by first achieving 'economic efficiency'. Nevertheless, the idea of 'enhancing social welfare', as an objective, is not readily amenable to direct targeting, due to the fact that it is less manageable, goal-oriented, quantifiable or identifiable compared to 'ensuring economic efficiency'. Thus, the concept of 'attaining economic efficiency' stands as a way station for achieving social welfare, in terms of our approach to establish the objective of the competition laws. On the other hand, considering the purpose of the social welfare function within the realm of competition law, it is imperative to focus on attaining those elements endowed with a 'guiding' characteristic and aiming to maximise social welfare. These elements comprise 'dynamic efficiency',[8] 'cost efficiency' and 'allocative efficiency'. For this

---

2 OECD, 'The Objectives of Competition Law and Policy – Note by the Secretariat' (2003) 2 <https://one.oecd.org/document/CCNM/GF/COMP(2003)3/en/pdf> accessed 12 October 2024.

3 Svend Albæk, 'Consumer Welfare in EU Competition Policy' in *Aims and Values in Competition Law* (DJØF Publishing 2013).

4 United Nations, Intergovernmental Group of Experts on Competition Law and Policy, 'Examining the interface between the objectives of competition policy and intellectual property' (Fifteenth Session, Geneva, 19–21 October 2016) (Note by the UNCTAD secretariat) <https://unctad.org/system/files/official-document/ciclpd36_en.pdf> accessed 12 October 2024.

5 Blair and Sokol (n 1).

6 'Total welfare' refers to the sum of consumer surplus and producer surplus (which is 'the difference between the price producers are paid for what they sell and the cost of production') (Louis Kaplow, 'On The Choice Of Welfare Standards In Competition Law' (2011) Harvard University John M Olin Center For Law, Economics and Business, Discussion Paper 693, 3)

7 ibid.

8 Dynamic efficiency is recognised as a pivotal factor contributing significantly to economic growth (Edward F Denison, *Accounting for United States Economic Growth 1929–1969* (Brookings Institution 1974); Lester C Thurow, 'A Weakness in Process Technology' (1987) 238 *Science* 1659–63; Zvi Griliches, 'R&D and Productivity: Econometric Results and Measurement Issues' in Paul Stoneman (ed), *Handbook of Economics of Innovation and Technological Change* (Blackwell 1995) 53–89; Bruno Crepon, Emmanuel Duguet and Jacques Mairesse, 'Research Innovation and Productivity: An Econometric Analysis at Firm Level' (1998) NBER Working Paper No. 6696; FM Scherer, *New Perspectives on Economic Growth and Technological Innovation* (Brookings Institution 1999); and Tor Klette and Zvi Griliches, 'Empirical Patterns of Firms Growth and R&D Investment: A Quality Ladder Model Interpretation' (2000) 110 *The Economic Journal* 363–87). In this respect, according to Rowe, a competition policy that neglects to acknowledge the significance of dynamic efficiency may risk overlooking one of the most substantial objectives available for enhancing social welfare. (Frederick M Rowe, 'The Decline of Antitrust and the Delusions of Models: The Faustian Pact of Law and Economics' (1984) 72 *Georgetown LJ* 1553–59.)

reason, 'ensuring economic efficiency'[9] is used as the 'target' term for the objective of competition laws.

5. All in all, by using the competition law framework which serves to safeguard the competitive process as an invaluable instrument, the ultimate objective can only be defined as achieving social welfare by actively fostering economic efficiency.[10]

6. Ordinarily, the implementation of competition law is aimed at boosting economic efficiency, consequently leading to improvements in both social and consumer welfare. However, under specific circumstances, this assumption does not hold true.[11] In light of this, it becomes evident that a more effective approach would involve using competition law for 'economic efficiency' in order to enhance social welfare.

7. In this sense, if there is an analysis to be made under competition law, it should not only consider how prices will be affected in the short run, but also how economic efficiency and social welfare will fare in the long run. For example, even if one approaches the issue from a purely 'consumer welfare' perspective, one cannot ignore the fact that consumers' long-term benefit may be greater than a benefit from a decrease in prices in the short term.[12]

8. As we further explore in the next section on the diversified objectives of competition law, it becomes evident that the war on inflation, or the protection of small businesses, while important in their own right, do not constitute the prime objective of competition law. Instead, competition law's pivotal role is to create an environment where competition thrives, promoting efficient resource allocation, cost-efficient production and ultimately enhancing social welfare. In this context, competition law serves as the guardian of a competitive marketplace, ensuring that the benefits of competition are harnessed for the long-term benefit of both consumers and society at large.

---

9 As explained, promoting economic efficiency is generally acknowledged as one of the principal goals of competition law. As a matter of fact, it is our understanding that this general acknowledgement is primarily influenced by significant rulings in the US (*United States v General Dynamics Corp* 415 US 486 (1974); *Continental TV Inc v GTE Sylvania Inc* 433 US 36 (1977); *Brunswick v Pueblo Bowl-O-Mat* 429 US 477 (1977); *National Society of Professional Engineers v United States* 435 US 679 (1978); *Broadcast Music Inc v Columbia Broadcasting Sys Inc* 441 US 1 (1979); *Reiter v Sonotone Corp* 442 US 330 (1979); *Leegin Creative Leather Prods Inc v PSKS Inc* 551 US 877 (2007)), see Tyler M Cunningham and Don T Hibner, 'The Kansas Supreme Court holds that the district judge erred in his demand for proof of a "concrete injury" in the price fixing of women's accessories (O'Brien / Leegin Creative Leather Prods)' (2012) e-Competitions art. No. 66498. concurrences.com/66498

10 Gönenç Gürkaynak, *Türk Rekabet Hukuku Uygulaması İçin 'Hukuk ve İktisat' Perspektifinden 'Amaç' Tartışması* (*A Discussion on the Prime Objective of the Turkish Competition Law from a Law & Economics Perspective*) (The Turkish Competition Authority Press 2003).

11 For example, in the *Broadcast Music Inc* decision, the blanket license granted by the American Society of Composers, Authors, and Publishers (ASCAP) and Broadcast Music Inc (BMI) to Columbia Broadcasting System Inc (CBS) served as a powerful tool for price discrimination. This arrangement led to an increase in the output, allowing producers to capture consumer benefits entirely. In the ensuing legal dispute, where CBS alleged that the blanket license involved an unlawful pricing agreement and bundling of products, the US Supreme Court ultimately ruled that the license promoted economic efficiency. The court reasoned that it constituted a distinct and original product, leading to a decision not to impose any sanctions. Another scenario is the collaborative efforts between competing initiatives aimed at cutting down production expenses, concurrently providing an opportunity for participants to raise their prices. In such instances, although there might be a reduction in the consumer's share of welfare, there is potential for an overall increase in social welfare.

12 *United States v Corn Products Refining Co* 234 F 964 (SDNY 1916).

II. Diversified Objectives of Competition Law: A Critical Analysis

9. In this section, we delve into the multifaceted objectives of competition law, scrutinising the viability of certain proposed aims. Another noteworthy perspective within competition law acknowledges that there are values that lie beyond the scope of economic modelling. As a result, it incorporates objectives beyond the principle of 'upholding economic efficiency' in the analysis of competition law, while also adopting a somewhat circumscribed view of the role of economics in this domain. This viewpoint considers elements such as 'safeguarding small businesses',[13] 'consumer protection', 'preventing the consolidation of economic and political influence',[14] 'facilitating equitable income distribution',[15] 'preserving market accessibility' and 'promoting fairness in commercial conduct'[16] as legitimate 'objectives' in competition law.[17]

10. First, in this regard, we challenge the notion that combating inflation should be a primary objective of competition law. We assert that the true objective of competition law should be a guiding principle that gives purpose to the field and that 'fighting inflation' does not align with this fundamental purpose. Then, we scrutinise the idea that safeguarding small businesses should be a primary goal of competition policy. Finally, we analyse how safeguarding consumers sits apart from the consumer welfare objective.

1. War on Inflation: Why it Cannot be the Objective of Competition Law

11. No matter how strong the belief that 'creating a competitive environment will bring down inflation' may be, bringing down inflation cannot be an 'objective' of competition law in the sense specified here. Instead, it may be one of the 'outcomes', albeit indirectly, of competition law. Indeed, if the fight against inflation is positioned as an objective in competition law, one can expect the prospect of conducting a sound and complete competition law analysis to be jeopardised, as the competition law analyses will focus only on price hikes.

12. On the other hand, there is no doubt that the phenomenon of inflation is related to the enforcement of competition law, among many others. In point of fact,

---

13 Laura Parret, 'Shouldn't We Know What We Are Protecting? Yes We Should! A Plea for A Solid and Comprehensive Debate About the Objectives of EU Competition Law and Policy' (2010) 6 ELJ 339, 346–358.

14 Ariel Ezrachi, 'EU Competition Law Goals and the Digital Economy' (2018) Oxford Legal Studies Research Paper 17/2018.

15 Ioannis Lianos, 'The Poverty of Competition Law: The Long Story' (2018) CLES Research Paper Series No. 2/2018 <www.ucl.ac.uk/cles/sites/cles/files/cles_2-2018.pdf> accessed 12 October 2024.

16 Adi Ayal, *Fairness in Antitrust* (Hart Publishing 2016) 207–212.

17 See for example, Lawrence A Sullivan, 'Book Review' (1975) 75 CL Rev 1214; Kenneth G Elzinga, 'The Goals of Antitrust Other Than Competition and Efficiency, What Else Counts?' (1977) 125 UPL Rev 1191; Louis B Schwartz, '"Justice" and Other Non-Economic Goals of Antitrust' (1979) 127 UPL Rev 1076; Robert Pitofsky, 'The Political Content of Antitrust' (1979) 127 UPL Rev 1051; Herbert Hovenkamp, 'Distributive Justice and the Antitrust Laws' 51 (1982) GW L Rev 1, 24–26.

there is a correlation between inflation and the enforcement of competition law, particularly when competition law is applied with the secondary goal of reducing inflation. Nevertheless, this relationship does not constitute an aspect of competition law which would render the reduction of inflation as its 'objective'. Indeed, the 'objective of competition law' ought to be a principle that shapes and guides this legal discipline, rendering the competition policy meaningful. However, an objective such as 'fighting inflation' would not serve such a role.

2. Protecting Small Businesses: A Fundamental Divergence

13. Competition policy, in general, cannot be constructed with the 'objective' of 'protecting the small businesses'. This is because there is a fundamental divergence between the objectives of competition law and small businesses. One economic rationale for this phenomenon can be illustrated through the example of a cartel. Even though smaller businesses incur higher costs compared to the larger enterprises that constitute the cartel, the larger entities deliberately create a greater disparity between their costs and prices. This manoeuvre enables the smaller businesses to maintain their presence in the market.[18]

14. Similarly, the US. Supreme Court did not recognise the objective of safeguarding the undertaking, as it mandated a complainant to assert and substantiate that the grievance adversely impacts not only their own competitive standing, but also the broader competitive process.[19] The aim of competition law was articulated as preserving competition, rather than the individual competitors,[20] in the Supreme Court decisions.[21]

15. In summary, the protection of small and medium-sized businesses is neither one of the 'objectives' of competition law, nor is it a result or function of it.

3. How 'Protecting the Consumer' Differs from the 'Consumer Welfare' as an Objective of the Competition Laws

16. In the context of social welfare, an objective of competition law is to enhance consumer welfare, a goal intrinsically linked to the objective of 'attaining economic efficiency'. The enhancement of consumer welfare is fundamentally an economic notion contingent on the level of economic efficiency achieved. Maximising consumer welfare and economic efficiency go hand to hand. However, the approach that delineates and endorses the objective of 'consumer

---

18 Richard A Posner, *Antitrust Law* (2nd edn, University of Chicago Press 2001); (*Antitrust Law: An Economic Perspective* (1st edn, 1976).

19 *Nynex v Discon* 119 S Ct 493 (1998), see James Burling, Michelle D Miller and John Christie, 'The US Supreme Court unanimously agrees that an agreement between a single supplier and single customer does not constitute a per se illegal refusal to deal (NYNEX / Discon)' (1998) e-Competitions art. No. 120234.

20 *Brown Shoe Co v United States* 370 US 294, 320, 344 (1962).

21 Prior to these rulings, which did not recognise the protection of the undertaking as the primary goal of competition law and referred to the preservation of the 'competitive process' as the paramount value, there were verdicts that expressly dismissed the objective of protecting small undertakings and prioritised the preservation of competition as the main concern, instead. The most prominent ruling among such decisions is the *Topco* decision (*United States v Topco Associates* 405 US 596 (1972)).

protection' as separate from the pursuit of 'achieving economic efficiency', positions its aim under the social realm.[22] This defined objective deviates from the goal we define in the field of economics as the 'improvement of consumer welfare'. In *Reiter*[23] the US Government asserted that the Sherman Act's main intent was to safeguard consumers and thus the Supreme Court adopted 'consumer welfare'[24] as the updated criterion in the realm of competition regulation, effectively supplanting the initial standard of competition.[25]

17. When 'consumer protection' is considered as an objective independent from the objective of 'ensuring economic efficiency' and 'increasing consumer welfare', there may be a conflict between the short-term interests of the consumer and the objective of ensuring economic efficiency, and in such cases, the objective of 'consumer protection' may prevail.

18. In the author's view, competition law does not have a general 'consumer protection' objective directly in the social plane, other than 'ensuring social welfare and consequently consumer welfare through the protection of economic efficiency'.[26] The societal aim of 'consumer protection' can influence competition law in a limited, specific scenario. However, this does not imply that the application of competition law is primarily for safeguarding consumers. In this context, 'consumer protection' may serve as a facet of competition law, but it does not constitute its fundamental 'objective'.

III. Intersection between the Objective of Competition Law and Sustainability

19. Sustainability has elicited various perspectives, as it emerged as a captivating subject in the realm of competition law.[27] The sustainability initiatives contend

22 Competition law has no 'consumer protection' objective, although it may occasionally borrow the 'consumer protection' objective in the societal sense on a case-by-case basis. On the other hand, 'consumer protection' is mostly a derivative function which competition law serves to, when enforced to achieve the objective of economic efficiency. Consumers benefit from competition because it leads to lower prices and better-quality goods and services. For example, if undertakings holding a dominant position in a market do not conduct research and development activities in that market within the framework of a deliberate policy and prevent such activities of other undertakings that may enter that market or increase their share in the market through horizontal agreements or concerted practices, they should be held responsible for these actions and practices under competition law. At this point, the 'objective' is not the protection of consumers, but the protection of competition and thus economic efficiency.

23 *Reiter v Sonotone Corp* 442 US 330, 343, 99 S Ct 2326, 2333, 60 L Ed 2d 931 (1979).

24 However, Blair and Sokol argue that the 'consumer welfare' reference in *Reiter* was made quoting Bork who actually used 'consumer welfare' in lieu of 'total welfare' by associating this criterion with total welfare. This, in turn, brought ambiguity on whether the following rulings of the courts mean consumer welfare in its literal sense or the way Bork intended. (Roger D Blair and D Daniel Sokol, 'The Rule of Reason and the Goals of Antitrust: An Economic Approach' (2012) 78 *Antitrust LJ* 471-504.)

25 Barak Orbach, 'How Antitrust Lost Its Goal' (2013) 81 *Fordham L Rev* 2253, referencing Robert H Bork, *The Antitrust Paradox: A Policy at War with Itself* (Basic Books1978).

26 Also see, Konstantinos Stylianou and Marios Iacovides, 'The Goals of EU Competition Law: A Comprehensive Empirical Investigation' (2022) 42 LS 620–648.

27 Hungarian Competition Authority, *Sustainable Development and Competition Law Survey Report* (2021) (Special Project for the 2021 ICN Annual Conference – Survey) 7.

that sustainability goals are inherently intertwined with the non-price aspects of competition. Like most other government policies, both the environmental and the competition policies have the shared aim of safeguarding and optimising social welfare, albeit via different measures.[28]

20. In this context, it is anticipated that the public entities involved in competition law forums will adopt an approach that is both comprehensive and cautious, and which prioritises prompt action. This is important and time sensitive; any delay would likely result in a failure to realise both the sustainability agenda and the goals of competition law. Putting an end to unfulfilled objectives requires proactive public intervention in market dynamics and the pursuit of sustainable development. The shift towards a sustainable economy will thrive with the collective backing of both public and private entities. The latter necessitates not only legal assurance, but also a multifaceted framework of incentives to incorporate sustainability goals into their business strategies. It is the role of competition authorities to ease this transition towards a greener economy.[29]

IV. Conclusion

21. In conclusion, the prime objective of competition law is to maximise social welfare by fostering economic efficiency. The intricate interplay between economics and law within the competition law framework highlights the significance of prioritising the evaluation of dynamic efficiency and innovation.

---

28 Nordic Competition Authorities, *Report from the Nordic competition authorities – Competition Policy and Green Growth – Interactions and Challenges* (2010) 15.

29 Hellenic Competition Commission, 'Draft Staff Discussion Paper on Sustainability Issues and Competition Law' (2020) 45.

Viewing Competition: Power As a Lens

David J. Gerber*
Chicago-Kent College of Law

1. The title chosen for this volume is intriguing. "Why Competition?" can lead to explorations and comments in many directions. For some, the issue is why we should have competition; others see it as a question of why there is competition; and there is no lack of other directions. This brief chapter focuses on a fundamental relationship that is central to thinking about most, perhaps all, of the other topics – i.e., the relationship between power and competition.

2. Power has long been either explicitly or implicitly part of thought and discussion relating to competition. Typically, however, it is treated in ways that are either too vague to be of significant analytical value or too narrow to capture important dimensions of the subject. As a result, discussions often obscure power's relationships to competition and impede effective responses to its potential harms. In this contribution I suggest that identifying and analyzing the lenses used to view the relationship between power and competition can provide valuable insight into the issues and the discussions surrounding them.

3. For our purposes here, a lens on power can be described simply as the way we think about it. As with eyeglasses or telescopes, the lens we use determines what we "see," how we perceive the external world. For example, are the elements noticed large or small, distant or near, blurred or clear, and how are they related to other elements. A lens on economic power shapes what we see when we think about markets and other economic relationships. It identifies features of the perceptual field such as whether power is central to thinking about markets or merely peripheral; and how is it related to competition.

---

* Distinguished Professor, Emeritus, and Distinguished Professor of Law, Emeritus.

It foregrounds some elements and marginalizes or excludes others. A lens on markets is shaped by factors such as its historical contexts, contributing ideologies, and shared experiences of power.

4. The basic scenario is familiar. Competition has many potential economic, social, and even political benefits, but it can break down and generate forms of economic power that destroy or hobble competition itself which can entrain potential social, economic and political harms. Communities are then faced with the issue of whether to intervene in the competitive process in order to limit such power or control its abuse. Recognizing the lenses used in viewing power can be of value in responding to this issue.

5. Lenses on economic power shape responses in numerous ways. For example, they filter the arguments that have weight in discussions, validating some and rejecting others as irrelevant. They can also shed light on the goals that discussants pursue and the strategies they employ. A lens may simply exclude some forms of power from view; more often it influences how much attention is paid to a particular form of power. Identifying the operative lenses is particularly useful in assessing whether competition harms exceed its benefits in a specific market.

6. Although lenses on power play important roles in the perception and assessment of competition, relevant discussions in policy and legal circles seldom reflect awareness of the lenses or of their importance. This can blur, disguise, and potentially distort the issues. In this chapter I highlight the potential value of paying closer attention to the lenses themselves as a means of clarifying key issues surrounding "why competition."

7. My main aims here are to identify prominent lenses used in viewing economic power; sketch for each lens its potential relevance for viewing competition; provide a few insights into the kinds of factors that have shaped it; and point to some of the potential consequences of using it.

8. Three main themes guide us: (1) images of economic power frame the way competition is understood and evaluated; (2) these images are critical in shaping public responses to competitive harms; and (3) conceptions of economic power often shift, making analysis particularly important, but also especially difficult.

9. The space limit for contributions to this volume restrict the scope of the discussion in both coverage and in depth. For example, important lenses such as those that have been crafted in the process of European integration have had to be omitted. Similarly, lenses used by cultures and systems with limited experience of a market economy receive little attention. I plan therefore to expand into these important issues in a book-length project soon.

I. Framing the Chapter

10. Several points are necessary for framing this chapter. First, here I use the term "power" to refer to the capacity of an individual or institution to cause another to decide in a way or ways other than those that it would have chosen in the absence of that power. "Economic power" refers to this capacity when it is based on private economic resources. Second, the discussion assumes the context of a market economy – i.e., an economy in which in which market transactions by private persons generally guide economic outcomes. For most of history, the areas of an economy that operate on market principles have been few or of local importance only. Political, bureaucratic, or personal (autocratic) decisions have played greater roles. Third, official public responses to economic power – e.g., in the form of laws and government actions – are intertwined with public opinion and views. Each influences the other in a variety of ways only a few of which we can touch on here. Fourth, my primary concern here is competition as a "public good" – i.e., a social process that has value for societies or communities in which it operates. I do not focus on its roles in the creation of private resources. Fifth, the chapter pays particular attention to competition law (i.e., antitrust law) and policy, primarily because this is the arena in which these issues play a central role.

II. A Cartel-Centered Lens

11. A cartel lens has long played a central role in thinking about economic power. This lens recognizes power only where it is based on collaboration among independent firms. "Cartel" here refers to coordinated relationships among firms for the purpose of increasing profits and/or stabilizing markets. Cartels in their modern form emerged in Europe and the US during the late nineteenth century, leading many states and communities to respond through administrative action and/or the development of competition law (aka antitrust law) or "competition policy."

12. We focus here on Europe, because for decades the cartel lens played a central role in shaping responses to economic power. It became a central lens on economic power in the context of a wave of cartelization that spread across the continent around the turn of the twentieth century. Many large cartels took control of markets, excluding competitors and raising prices to consumers, so they became an obvious focus of concerns about harm from economic power. This historical context shaped a lens on competition that focuses on harm from competitor collaboration and that became embedded in thinking about economic power. It demonstrates the role that historical context plays in shaping lenses on power.

13. Other factors strengthened the lens in Europe. I note two of the more important ones. First, responses to economic power in European countries were – and

to some extent still are – predominantly administrative, and administrators have had incentives to leverage state power against cartels rather than against powerful individuals, families, and firms. Moreover, the obvious harms associated with coordinated conduct tend to be a more attractive target than the more vague claims of harm attributable to the conduct of single firms acting alone. Second, long-standing civil law principles have constrained courts and commentators from attending to power wielded by firms acting alone.

14. Using the cartel lens by itself focuses attention on a particular form of power and excludes from view or marginalizes concerns about other forms of economic power. It also focuses attention on other issues specifically related to this form of power. For example, it foregrounds the issue of whether concerted action actually exists, which, in turn, requires attention to issues of proof and procedure necessary to establish such collaboration. In the European context, these effects kept attention focused on cartels while diverting attention from single-firm powerholders. This effect can also be seen in many other countries.

15. Lenses on power changed in Europe later in the twentieth century, but the cartel focus has remained a key component of the lens used in viewing economic power and competition.[1]

III. The Monopoly Lens

16. The monopoly lens plays a different but similarly important role in shaping images of economic power. The term "monopoly" was originally used to refer to a market in which there was only one seller. Early Romans and others before them recognized that where there is only one seller on a market, the seller holds much power vis-à-vis both potential competitors and buyers on the market. This has often generated fear that the powerholder would use its power in ways that caused societal harm.

17. This fear remains powerful, and it has nurtured an image of economic power in which monopoly and competition are seen as opposites. The opposition is attractive, not least because it is easily perceived and seems obvious to many. Nevertheless, it has significant consequences for thinking about markets. At least implicit in this opposition is an either–or proposition: if you have one, you don't have the other. Consequently, if monopoly isn't present, we can assume that there is sufficient competition and thus no basis for concern about harms from economic power.

18. Non-local markets in which there is only one seller are not common, however, and the definition of monopoly gradually expanded to include markets

1 I follow European developments in detail in David J. Gerber, Law and Competition in Twentieth Century Europe (Oxford Univ. Press 1998), (2001). For additional background and explanation, see David J. Gerber, Global Competition: Law, Markets and Globalization (Oxford Univ. Press 2010), (2011) and David J. Gerber, Competition Law and Antitrust: A Global Guide (Oxford Univ. Press 2020).

where a single firm has a high degree of economic power. What that means is seldom clear, however, creating much uncertainty about the need to respond to its potential harms. This "either-or" image of economic power continues to influence thinking about how to respond to it. Expansion of the concept of monopoly also reflects the continuing political and conceptual force of the monopoly lens.

IV. Monopolization and the Power Bifocals of US Law

19. The static image of economic power created by the monopoly lens and the uncertainties about what constitutes monopoly fostered the development of a related lens on power – "monopolization." Through this lens harms from single-firm economic power derive not from "having" monopoly, but from seeking to attain or maintain it. The noun "monopoly" becomes the verb "monopolize." This perspective constricts the area of concern about economic power and may weaken its perceived importance. Not only is there uncertainty about what the concept of monopoly itself means, but there is also uncertainty about what forms of conduct constitute "monopolization."

20. The monopolization lens entered US law in the Sherman Act of 1889, which remains the basic text of US antitrust law. It is there presented as one of two main concepts intended to treat harm from economic power (hence the "bifocal" label). The law makes illegal both conduct "in restraint of trade" (concerted action) and "monopolization" (single firm conduct). The statute was basically a response to pressures on Congress from companies and consumers who were harmed by the power of the called "trusts" – i.e., large economic entities that controlled key segments of the US economy around the turn of the twentieth century. Trusts operated as single entities, but they were formed by combining ownership of independent firms, so they also had some cartel characteristics. These two basic concepts were drawn from English and US cases dealing with other kinds of legal problems and not based on careful consideration of the potential consequences of using them. The importance of the legislation itself and the many well-publicized cases implementing it have made it an important lens on economic power in the US.

21. These two lenses have had very different trajectories and differ significantly in strength. "Restraint of trade" has long been central to US antitrust law and to thinking about power. Courts, commentators, and public discussions use it frequently to deal with power based on coordinated conduct. Monopolization, on the other hand, has not proven as attractive. Courts and commentators have struggled for more than a century to give it a convincing meaning. These differences in strength and scope between the two forms of economic power highlight the potential value of paying close attention to the lenses being used. This type of analysis reveals relationships between the two forms

of economic power that often go unnoticed. As with wearing bifocal lenses, awareness of the lenses being used can be of much value in understanding a specific situation or discussion.

V. The Lens of Neo-Classical Economics

22. Beginning in the 1980s dissatisfaction with the uncertainties of American antitrust law led economists and others associated with the "Chicago School" of economics to promote a narrower and more precise lens on economic power. This lens recognizes economic power only where it takes the form of "market power" as defined by neo-classical economics. At its most basic, "market power" is the capacity of a firm or firms to increase market price above a competitive level. From this perspective other images of power are too vague to be effective as tools of thought and policy.

23. Use of this lens constricts thinking about economic power to a terrain defined by neo-classical economics. It has the advantage of being conceptually precise, so that the language of those using it tends to be consistent, thereby avoiding or reducing uncertainty about how to address the issues. It also limits interventions in the economy to those that can be justified by this conceptual framework. These factors have made it attractive to many.

24. The lens also excludes or marginalizes, however, many forms and elements of economic power as well as their social and political consequences. As a result, it often encounters significant resistance. The lens itself provides little or no room for consideration of factors such as social justice and economic inequality. Outcomes produced by using the lens may yield benefits in these areas, but the lens itself focuses attention on a narrower vision of economic power and competition. Moreover, appropriate use of the lens requires professional economic analysis. It is a matter of scientific argument within the vocabulary of neo-classical economics, so only professional economists with a particular set of analytical tools can make legitimate claims about it. Judges, bureaucrats, and lay people must rely on these experts in considering issues of economic power.

25. This lens on power has become central to thinking about power and competition in the US, and it has often been influential elsewhere.

VI. The Social Embeddedness Lens and Abuse of a Dominant Position

26. A quite different lens relates economic power to its social contexts. Through this lens economic power appears as a component of the social relationships in which it is embedded and which it influences. This view generates questions about competition's capacity to support effective social relationships and the

capacity of economic power to disrupt those relationships. The embeddedness lens is necessarily less precise than the economic lens, because it creates a broader range of images and takes into account a larger set of factors. It relies less on economic science and more on the capacity of individuals and communities – e.g., judges, bureaucrats, political and community leaders, to promote fairness and social welfare.

27. This lens on power is most closely associated with efforts to rebuild German society after the disastrous experiences of Nazism and war. For German leaders of the postwar period the goal was to create and maintain a more democratic, inclusive, and fair society, and they viewed economic power from that perspective. They envisioned competition as a central feature in the so-called "social market economy" that is widely credited with rebuilding both the German economy and its social and political systems after the Second World War. Controls on the abuse of power were seen as a companion to competition that was necessary to assure members of society that the economy was contributing to a more inclusive society.

28. Recognizing the role of this lens on power illuminates the development of the concept of "abuse of a dominant position" as a response to concerns about economic power. According to the German competition law enacted in 1957, the conduct of firms acting alone was not to be measured by economic concepts alone or by the idea of monopolization contained in US law, but rather by how a firm used its economic power in relation to other competitors and in relation to consumers. This generated the idea that a firm with a dominant position has a special duty not to abuse its power.

29. This lens and many of the related ideas and concerns have found their way into the competition laws of the European Union and into national laws in Europe and elsewhere.

VII. Using Power as a Lens on Competition

30. This brief overview reveals the potential value of identifying and analyzing the lenses used to view economic power and its relationship to competition. Policy discussions and legal arguments are driven and shaped by the lenses that participants use in them, which means that recognizing the lens can give powerful insights into the arguments themselves as well as into the motivations supporting them. In particular, we have seen that specific ways of viewing power shape views of competition, influence responses to harms from competition, and relate competition issues to contemporary political and ideological agendas. This chapter only scratches the surface of the potential value of this type of analysis.

31. These distinct and varied lenses on economic power often function as part of a composite lens in which each component has differing roles, strengths,

and areas of application. As with multi-focal eyeglasses, one lens identifies and draws attention to one part of the visual field while others focus on and highlight other areas. Identifying which lens is being used for which purpose in a given situation can be of much analytical and practical value.

32. The digital economy – and AI, in particular – will undoubtedly test the capacity of these lenses to provide value for thinking about the relationship between competition and economic power. It is also likely to generate new lenses for viewing that relationship, because AI represents new forms of power. These elements are likely to be incorporated together with existing lenses into new composite lenses that will shape discussions and decisions far into the future.

Some Reflections from Last Century

Ian S. Forrester*
Ian Forrester Consulting

1. My career as a competition lawyer started in Brussels in 1972, where I had the great advantage of three talented teachers: Donald Holley who was quiet, academic, gently expert; Richard Webster, robust, exigent, clear in exposition; and Walter Oberreit, practical and positive. I was meant to be doing something to do with Euro dollars but as tax law changed to close that fiscal niche, my specialties became customs, trade and thence competition.

2. This was very long ago, legally and procedurally speaking. There were few formally adopted competition decisions from the European Commission, maybe ten in a year. Officials were a conservative, purist, prudent caste. German scholarly analysis predominated. It was much easier to derail an innovative decision than to press it on to adoption by the College of Commissioners. The judgements of the Court of Justice of the European Union (CJUE) were so infrequent that a study lunch would be dedicated to squeezing out all the juicy goodness of the (then) quite brief judgements. The European Court Reports were the thickness of a novel. The law on mergers was almost non-existent; aspirational would be a better word. The most commonly prosecuted infringements were contractual bans or practical bans on the export to other Member States of goods in order to protect resellers who had been allocated exclusive territories.

3. The legal framework was distinctive, not to say improbable: the prohibition of Article 85(1) of the EC Treaty, the core of the competition section of the Treaty caught not just 'bad' agreements but any agreement which contained restrictive features such as an exclusivity provision. In theory, a deal which contained restrictive elements, but which could be justified on balance as

* King's Counsel at the Scots Bar; Judge of the General Court of the European Union 2015 2020; Honorary Professor and Doctor of Laws.

pro-competitive needed an exemption, which the Commission and no one else was empowered to issue. To alleviate the obvious uncertainty associated with a broad prohibition of commonly found agreements and limited manpower to issue exemptions, the Commission adopted 'block exemption' regulations which provided an automatic blessing for certain categories of agreement. Predictably, administrations being cautious, these regulations were tightly framed and had numerous conditions. They became mini regulations, in practice compelling certain patterns of behaviour. Regulation 67/67 was broadly respected. They constituted useful guidance, notably with respect to the sensitive topic of the exclusive distribution of physical goods, which had traditionally been organised on a national territorial basis, a tradition which the business community was reluctant to discontinue.

4. Although the procedure appeared rational, it functioned irrationally. There was in theory the need to file a 'notification' to the Commission seeking either its confirmation that there was no problem at all (negative clearance) or that the restrictions in the agreement were justifiable and matched the criteria of Article 85(3) (indispensability and least restrictive solution, essentially). But in reality, the Commission's nervous and conservative approach to the reach of Article 85(1) created a huge need for exemptions under Article 85(3) which the Commission's resources could never deliver. So, the availability in theory of a truly unavailable exemption created opportunities for gaming the system. Those who wanted not to comply with the agreement might file a notification in the expectation that questions might be posed. The absence of a response to a notification could be said to show approval, or non-opposition or doubt. Great effort was devoted to extracting 'informal' 'comfort letters' from the Commission staff which could be said to show the view of the institution, albeit not the formal exemption contemplated by the regulations. Thus, the notification and exemption system came to be a source not of legal certainty but of the opposite.

5. A notification could be a means of burying a controversial clause and trying to enforce before challenges arose. In the matter of *DCL v European Commission*, Bulloch intervening, a differential pricing scheme was intended to impose a surcharge on UK parallel exporters of Johnnie Walker and other whiskies. If a case were resold in Scotland, the price was about £7. If exported to Belgium, the price was increased to £12.20. This was to deter 'freeriding' by independent traders and protect local resellers who had the job of building up demand. The notification of the dual pricing system was less than candid, supposedly, in that the prices were not revealed. The Commission subsequently 'refrained' from imposing a fine. DCL was threatening to ruin a Glasgow grocer, Mr Sandy Bulloch. He had exported cases of whisky to Belgium at the lower, UK price. He received a demand for a huge surcharge and challenged the legality of the surcharge by complaining to the Commission. After the hearing before the EC Directorate General for Competition (DGIV) (the first for which I was responsible), the decision condemned DCL, which appealed to

the CJUE. Professor Michel Waelbroeck (no less!) acted for DCL. Mr Bulloch was represented by Mario Siragusa and myself (no more!). He and his sister came to court dressed in humble sober tweeds, modestly seeking their rights as EC economic operators. The kind registrar Van Houtte helped us to get properly robed. Counsel were invited to drinks in the *salle des délibérés* after the argument. Val Korah (the unquenchable) felt DCL was correct in their approach, as did AG Warner, whose opinion favoured annulment, but Michel Waelbroeck privately predicted the outcome, which upheld the Commission's findings and reasoning.

6. And Mr Bulloch, when asked on television if he was pleased about his victory, replied that it was not a victory, just a wrong being put right. The moral? The complaint offered DGIV a vehicle to make new law, not very surprising law, but rather a refinement of existing doctrine. And it showed that having a nice client helps.

7. Some while later came *Magill*. The BBC, ITN and RTE in Ireland each published lucrative single broadcaster weekly programme guides. (The BBC's Radio Times was the best-selling magazine in the UK). TV addicts in Ireland had to buy three guides to be fully informed of what was coming the week ahead. Daily lists of forthcoming programmes were sent to every newspaper free of charge, for publication on a daily *not* weekly basis. Magill TV Guide was launched in Ireland. It offered in a single magazine a multi-channel weekly guide which thus threatened the single channel guides of BBC, RTE and ITN, respectively. Magill was stifled at birth by litigation in Ireland, after only one issue, on the grounds that the lists of programmes were covered by copyright. A complaint was made to the Irish Member of the Commission, Peter Sutherland. There was intense debate inside the Commission over whether it could be an abuse to refuse to license copyrighted material. On the one hand, a listing consisting of 20:30 News; 21:00 Sport; 21:30 Dallas, does not seem worthy of protection; but indeed utilitarian materials (maps, timetables, etc.) can enjoy copyright protection. And both Irish and English judges in separate cases had decided that copyright did attach to the listings of forthcoming programmes, as skill was involved when deciding what programme to broadcast and when. The decision was greatly delayed by internal debate within the Commission; and possibly not unconnected with this fact was the Commission's decision to entrust the defence of the decision in court to outside counsel (myself) under the instructions of Jacques Bourgeois. The decision merely ordered the broadcasters to start negotiations, but even that (arguably modest) demand was suspended by the President of the Court, Koopmans J, who asked pertinent questions about the Commission's theory of the case and got (from myself) only mushy answers. The appeal proceeded before the newly created Court of First Instance (CFI).

8. At the hearing, I produced a pile of multi-channel guides from all over Europe, including countries which respected copyright principles. Why should Ireland be so different? Was classic copyright really threatened by a battle about

retaining a triple monopoly of weekly publicity guides? But the materials had been found to be copyrighted by an Irish and one English judge. Were they wrong or was the Commission wrong to disparage the copyright? Did the Commission have the right to uphold some IP laws but not others? Why should a publisher not aggregate freely available advertising material and re-publish it in a new format? Does that apply to other compilations, maybe of literary works? But what were the limiting principles? Why was a compulsory license not available for all utilitarian material? How to distinguish a bad refusal to license from a good one? The broadcasters had the right to refuse to publish: did that principle apply without dilution to copyright over utilitarian publicity data? What was the limiting principle?

9. Just before the start of the oral argument (on appeal to the CJUE from the CFI, where the Commission had won heavily), the juge-rapporteur caused eyebrows to rise when he said that in his view there was no need even to hold an argument, as the case was easy. Counsel had no idea which way the Court was leaning. The Commission's team echoed Robert Clive who said at his trial for corruption that he 'stood amazed by his own moderation'. The facts were bizarre; the law was uncertain. What were the limiting principles? It was the Court which discovered the distinguishing principle: the broadcasters were preventing the emergence of a new product which consumers wanted but which the broadcasters would not themselves supply. The judgement was greeted with consternation ('the end of copyright' said one Professor) but it lay quietly for several years until *IMS/NDC*, which confirmed that a new product (eligible for a compulsory license) had to be not a mere copy with a few tweaks, but something really new. The moral? In the field of abuse of dominance, good facts can overcome strict IP theory if sympathetically presented.

The Litigant as Martyr

10. Professional sports leagues present unusual competitive characteristics. Quite apart from the fanatic enthusiasms football generates, there is a degree of interdependence in that the most successful team has an interest in maintaining the validity of the weakest club in the league. Every club needs good players. Wealthy clubs can buy the best. Small clubs must develop them. It is in that context that the case of Jean-Marc Bosman arose. The practice in dispute was the so-called *indemnité de formation*, applicable to young players when they moved on out of contract from their first club to a more distinguished club. This was a payment payable by the hiring club to the club which had found the young talent, trained him technically, sportively and physically. The amount of the payment was objectively based on goals scored, placed in international youth team, number of games, etc., and disputes whether inside one country or cross-border were settled by arbitration.

11. Bosman was a promising young player with a Liège club. He had a falling out, after being told his salary would sharply fall in the next season. He got

a new job with Olympic Dunkerque. But the transfer fell through because the Belgian football association failed to send to the French football association an international certificate of transfer. The failure was because the two clubs were arguing about the amount of the *indemnité de formation*. Yet the sporting regulations were clear: the player should start playing whether or not the amount had been settled. So, Bosman lost his job, was unemployed for a while, and his career did not prosper. His case was taken up by professional players unions and enormous press attention ensued.

12. On the one hand the football authorities contended that the system worked well and gave needed revenue to small clubs which were rarely financially comfortable. It was part of the solidarity expected in a professional league. The system applied to domestic and international transfers equally. Arbitration settled disagreements about amounts, and the player should always be able to play at his new club, regardless of any disagreement. On the other hand, it was clear that Bosman had been grievously prejudiced. He argued that the whole system was unfair, even corrupt, and reflected a wish to deter player movements on the part of the football establishment. Did the failure of the system on this occasion justify condemning it altogether? Litigation started before a Liège court, and the judge posed questions to the Court of Justice as to the interpretation of Article 85 (competition) and 48 of the EC Treaty (free movement of workers).

13. The parties focused on Article 85, but that presented the problem that collective bargaining agreements involving concertation between enterprises and workers' representatives might by implication be vulnerable.

14. So, the rules on freedom of movement for workers became the relevant principle. The Court found that the transfer rules constituted an obstacle to freedom of movement. Could they be justified by 'pressing reasons of public interest'? But the Court found that the fees earned by *indemnités de formation* were 'contingent and uncertain'. It therefore reached the conclusion that the transfer system as established was precluded by Article 48. It was not necessary to consider the applicability of Article 85. I wish that the Court had left it to the Belgian court to decide whether the functioning of the transfer system actually hindered the free movement of workers, players across frontiers, or whether on balance it was a proportionate measure of pursuing a legitimate goal. The Court made that factual determination, declaring – curiously – that uncertainty rendered the system unacceptable. Is uncertainty a bad thing in the context of the organisation of sport?

15. In any event, profound changes ensued in the world of football. I respectfully doubt that small clubs and moderately promising players are better off. Sadly, Mr Bosman got very little benefit from the case. Moral of the case? A well-funded attempt to change the situation can succeed if there is human interest as well as a legal theory.

16. I have had the immense privilege of serving as a practising lawyer, as an author and as a judge; and now as a lawyer again. In the early days, Brussels

practitioners were part of the movement: there was sympathy for the notion of building an alliance between nine Member States. Our parents' generation had known the war. (Two members of the Court of Justice had been on opposite sides at a battle in Italy: another spoke of hearing the young soldiers under his command weeping during the night.) So, each of these early Commission decisions was noted with sympathy, interest, curiosity, yet from a technical point of view, rigorously. They were quite short, ten or twenty pages long, by comparison to four hundred pages today. That is a consequence of the greater complexity of the facts, but not only that, the process of determining the facts by the European Commission's DG COMP is flawed. The procedure is a mixture of quasi-criminal prosecution and administrative rulemaking. There is no determination of facts by a neutral or independent person. The Hearing Officer is a senior, well-respected, well-experienced official. But the Hearing Officer's function is to ensure that the hearing proceeds in an orderly manner and that proper access is accorded to the file, not to decide as a fact whether Mr Smith was present at the Hilton Hotel in Zurich at a meeting of widget manufacturers' delegates. And last but not least the Courts have repeatedly found the process to be not illegal. That doesn't exclude reform, of course.

17. The Commission is an incorrupt, zealous, diligent institution, qualities which have been repeatedly recognised. Its staff are creative, keen, receptive to new theories, but not foolishly so. And the case team knows that it is by no means certain that a draft decision will get through the complex internal procedural path to adoption. True, but it is much more difficult for skilled, honest, careful officials to carry through to the end a novel theory of infringement in the United States. Private litigation is far more significant in shaping the law in the US. Hence, especially in periods when there is a Republican White House, Brussels promises a better reception for legal creativity.

18. That is a separate phenomenon than deference: the notion that a properly functioning administration deserves to be given leeway, a right to make choices and make policy, without being micro-managed. This is especially so where the administration makes what Laitenberger J calls a 'normative choice'. Accused companies of course have the right to be represented by counsel, to call experts, to get diplomatic support (rare but not unheard of), and trade association input. The possibility of an immense fine is these days more akin to a cost of doing business than a carefully calibrated punishment imposed after close study of the sentencing guidelines. But whatever label is used to describe the proceedings, they are not structured so as to stop or to go depending on whether the crucial facts have been proven to the satisfaction of an independent trier of facts. This I suggest has a relevance to the problem of prolixity. In any large case there will be numerous minor arguments and a small number of big points of principle. The Commission team wishes not to be reproached for omitting any relevant issue, so it includes and includes and includes. The ultimate decision is fattened and fattened to hundreds and hundreds of paragraphs. And judicial review beckons. But counsel have to

draft the appeal within about 70 days. And, just to be safe, nothing is omitted from the appeal. An application of 250 pages ensues. The judge and the judge's cabinet sigh and start to plod through the morass of accusatory language, trying to show persistent bad faith. And the juge-rapporteur will try to produce a draft for colleagues which omits nothing. If there has been a procedural weakness that is a convenient basis for criticism. But such a disposition leaves undisturbed (sometimes) the big intellectual principle which the decision advances. Putting it differently, genuine but minor problems access to the file, failure to respond to an argument, time limits) may be the basis for annulment, while big principles may be addressed properly.

19. It has to be recognised that there is almost universal (maybe very 'widespread' is better) acceptance that huge technology companies have vast power, are indispensable, and very aggressively competitive. It is equally true that by good luck and by talent they have mastered their own destiny. The competition agency (regardless of where located) may be entrusted with pursuing (as well as cartels and monopolistic practices) consumer protection, class or mass litigation, and other policies which are not classical 'antitrust' policies. Instead of considering whether a breach of the competition rules occurred in the past, the enforcer is often acting as a regulator prescribing new norms of behaviours. In former days, the complainant would fit its case into established principles; with the advent of the Digital Markets Act, new norms of affirmatively pro-competitive conduct have been prescribed. The danger is the aphorism that 'America innovates; China imitates; and Europe regulates'. Everyone recognises that embarrassing reproach: and says that the world is better off with some restraints on corporate power, I record the debate but cast no vote.

20. As EU competition law, and more broadly competition enforcement broadens, I commend the goal and salute the institution. But I persist in suggesting that its reputation would be enhanced, and its output more respected, if it took a fresh look at the adequacy of the fairness of its procedures. Perfect process implies delay, even paralysis and wonderful procedural games. We cannot help competition by according the same amount of time to reaching a conclusion or procedural rights as for a murder.

21. What could be done without delaying excessively the enforcement process? One big step would be earlier testing of facts before by an independent, skilled, person like an 'administrative law judge' in Brussels. Wahl J and I have commended such an idea. Maybe it is worth not being forgotten.

The Law's Answers to the Question: "Why Competition?"

EDWARD M. IACOBUCCI*
University of Toronto

I. Introduction

1. In order to understand why competition law exists, and how it ought to be applied, it is fundamentally important to answer the prior question, "Why do we care about competition?" It is remarkable that competition law has existed in one form or another for over a century without a clear answer, or even a clear cluster of answers, to this question. The crescendo of debate in recent years about the appropriate purpose of antitrust law is entirely unsurprising in a world in which foundational questions have gone largely unanswered.[1] In this chapter I explore the uncertainty underlying competition law.

2. Section II of the contribution identifies the root of the problem: while promoting "competition", or its companion, "competitive process", sounds pleasing, these objectives are themselves normatively empty. For its successful implementation, it is essential for competition law to have a self-conscious understanding of *why* competition matters. As Section II discusses, the law does not have such a self-understanding, and instead offers a large, and growing, variety of objectives that may or may not be consistent with one another.

---

* TSE Chair in Capital Markets, Faculty of Law, University of Toronto. The author thanks Anthony Niblett and Ralph Winter for helpful discussions.

1 See, e.g., Carl Shapiro, "Antitrust in a Time of Populism" (2018) 61 *International J Industrial Organisation* 714; Daniel Crane, "The New Crisis in Antitrust (?)" (2020) 83 *Antitrust LJ* 253.

3. Section III identifies the critical problem with antitrust law that fails to identify clearly its normative foundation. Because the competitive effects of conduct are highly context-specific, the law necessarily relies not on trans-contextual legal rules that proscribe or allow specific actions, but rather on general standards and principles that authorities apply in a given case to a particular constellation of facts.[2] Without an understanding of why competition matters, authorities (agencies, courts) and the public do not have a guide for the appropriate application of standards and general principles to the facts of a given case, indeterminacy may result.
4. Section IV identifies indeterminacy in practice in Canadian experience. The failure to identify the normative basis for antitrust is manifest in confused doctrine and enforcement, and the potential for more of such outcomes in the future.
5. Section V concludes, observing that the goal of this volume to canvass responses to "why competition?" is a welcome one. It would be problematic, however, to keep adding to the list of why competition, and thus competition law matters; rather, it would be better for the law to start narrowing the list.

II. Competition as an Objective

6. Competition law, presumably tautologically, adopts as a central purpose the promotion of competition. But competition is itself a normatively empty goal. As a general proposition, the idea that one person ought to behave so as to realize gains for herself at the expense of others is not something that society consistently regards favourably; it is not, for example, the motto for living taught in kindergarten. Even in market settings, there is no inherent reason why society ought to encourage firms to attract buyers from other firms through pricing, quality or other choices. To be sure, there are good reasons to care about pricing, quality, and other features of the market, but any outcome of a competitive market can be replicated in principle by an omniscient social planner. A social planner could in principle achieve allocative efficiency simply by ordering optimal production and allocating the products optimally to consumers with greater demand for the product.
7. Of course, competition in markets is socially valuable. But the reason why competition matters is not because it is good in itself, but rather because competition promotes normatively attractive outcomes, such as (but not limited to) allocative efficiency.

---

2 For example, the law does not say something like, "the firm with the fifth most sales in the market cannot purchase the firm with the fourth most sales in the market"; rather, the law says something like, "mergers cannot substantially lessen competition".

8. Similarly, promoting the "competitive process" is normatively empty, despite growing support for it as an objective.[3] Again, in theory any outcome resulting from the "competitive process" could in theory be replicated by an omniscient social planner without losing anything normatively meaningful. It is not the competitive process that is intrinsically valuable, rather, for antitrust law to have a compelling foundation, it must be that competition, or the competitive process, leads to something that society values.

9. The law does not fail to identify normatively valuable objectives that competition may help achieve. Indeed, competition law around the world identifies an enormous variety of normatively meaningful values that competition may promote.[4] The problem, however, with the normative underpinnings of competition law is not that the law never identifies relevant values that competition advances, but rather that it identifies too many.

10. Canada's competition statute provides an example. Its purpose clause provides:

> "1.1 The purpose of this Act is to maintain and encourage competition in Canada in order to promote the efficiency and adaptability of the Canadian economy, in order to expand opportunities for Canadian participation in world markets while at the same time recognizing the role of foreign competition in Canada, in order to ensure that small and medium-sized enterprises have an equitable opportunity to participate in the Canadian economy and in order to provide consumers with competitive prices and product choices".[5]

11. Appropriately, the Competition Act does not identify "competition" as its objective, full stop – this would improperly elevate a means to an end to an end in itself – but rather identifies competition as a means to various ends, namely, efficiency, Canadian participation in world markets, an equitable opportunity for SMEs to compete, and competitive prices and quality. These goals are not always consistent with one another. Efficiency is often associated with competitive prices, for example, but not always: a merger may lower costs efficiently, but raise prices. Anticompetitive exclusion of SMEs may be inefficient and is presumably inequitable, but ruthlessly competitive markets may also exclude inefficient SMEs, which presumably could be inequitable depending on one's conception of "equitable".

12. While there has been consistent criticism of this incoherence in the Competition Act s. 1.1 (at least by me[6]), a recent sweeping government review of the Act

---

3 For discussion of the elusive significance of "competitive process", see Francesco Ducci, "Consumer Welfare and the Competitive Process" (2023) (conference paper, unpublished).

4 See, e.g., Eleanor Fox and Michael Trebilcock (eds), *The Design of Competition Law Institutions: Global Norms, Local Choices* (OUP 2013).

5 Competition Act (Canada) RSC, 1985, ch C-34, s 1.1.

6 See, e.g., Edward Iacobucci, "The *Superior Propane* Saga: The Efficiencies Defence in Canada" in Barry Rodger (ed), *Landmark Cases in Competition Law: Around the World in Fourteen Stories* (Kluwer International 2013); Edward Iacobucci, "Examining the Competition Act in the Digital Era" (2021) <https://sencanada.ca/media/368377/examining-the-canadian-competition-act-in-the-digital-era-en-pdf.pdf> accessed 15 October 2024; Edward Iacobucci, "Is the Canadian *Competition Act* Fit for Purpose in the Digital Era? What Purpose(s)?" (2023) 67 *Canadian Business LJ* 7.

explicitly chose not to open debate on the purpose clause.[7] While politically understandable, perhaps, given the range of objectives that various actors would propose in these unusually politically active days for competition law discourse, the decision leaves untouched a jumbled grab-bag of motivations that fails to provide a coherent foundation for the Act.

13. Canada is far from unique in its failure to identify clearly and consistently why competition matters. There is a wide range of objectives for competition law around the world, extending well beyond the largely economic criteria outlined in s. 1.1 to matters such as Black empowerment in South Africa, and political integration among the Members of the European Union.[8] And the list of possible objectives for competition law is growing. While the mantra in US practice for some time is that antitrust law protects competition, not competitors,[9] US political and enforcement agency leaders are increasingly expressing concern about protecting SMEs. Amazon, for example, is criticized in recent years for providing intense competition against firms that sell on its site.[10] Privacy is another, relatively novel potential value in antitrust litigation.[11] For example, the *Google/Fitbit* merger involved complementary products, not competitive substitutes, but was only approved in Europe on the condition that Google and Fitbit were to keep data separate to protect privacy.[12]

14. In summary, the problem at present with competition law's answers to "why competition?" and its companion "why competition law?" is not that the law naively understands competition to be an end in itself. Competition is not normatively meaningful, and the law does not generally treat it as such, rather, the problem is that the law supplies too many reasons why we ought to take competition seriously. As the next section elaborates, the law's attempt to advance several, often internally conflicting, objectives at once risks pursuing none of them well, and instead creating indeterminacy in the law.

7 While the Department of Innovation, Science and Economic Development (ISED) indicated that it would accept submissions on the purpose clause when initiating a consultation on reform to the *Competition Act*, in its framework discussion paper it took the purpose clause as given and did not propose potential amendments to it, stating, "For ease of discussion, this paper assumes that the objectives of the Competition Act have for the most part not changed, and focuses on how the substantive provisions of the law could be improved to better achieve them in the current environment". ISED, "The Future of Competition Policy in Canada" (2022) <https://ised-isde.canada.ca/site/strategic-policy-sector/sites/default/files/attachments/2022/The-Future-of-Competition-Policy-eng_0.pdf> accessed 15 October 2024.

8 Fox and Trebilcock (n 4).

9 *Brown Shoe Inc v United States* 370 US 294 (1962).

10 See, e.g., discussion in Anthony Niblett, "The Competition Act, Not the Competitors Act" (2023) 67 *Canadian Business J* 83.

11 See, e.g., Erika Douglas, "The New Antitrust/Data Privacy Interface" (2020–2021) 130 *Yale LJ Forum* 647.

12 Google maintained that the merger was not motivated by access to data, but rather devices, and was therefore content to hold the data separate: see Rick Osterloh, "Google Completes Fitbit Acquisition" (14 January 2021) <https://blog.google/products/platforms-devices/fitbit-acquisition/> accessed 15 October 2024.

III. Rules, Standards and Multiple Objectives

15. Many areas of law have multiple, sometimes contradictory goals. For this reason, one might reasonably ask why we should be concerned about multiple, contradictory goals in antitrust. While perhaps not unique to antitrust, there are particular features of competition law that make multiple and internally inconsistent goals problematic. At root, the problem is that, because specific, nuanced context is essential to understand the competitive effects of conduct, the law requires reliance on standards, not specific rules; and applying standards based on a menu of inconsistent, legally relevant objectives creates too much discretion on the part of enforcement authorities and adjudicators. A law based on a list of potentially contradictory values risks indeterminacy.

16. In elaborating the reasons for this conclusion, it is helpful to consider different contexts where a multiplicity of goals does not compromise the determinacy of the law. Take speed limits, for example, there are undoubtedly multiple considerations that are relevant to speed limits on roads and highways: the opportunity cost of time is clearly relevant; as is safety, and the cost of accidents. The wear and tear on the road may also be relevant. Some factors point to a higher speed limit, others to a lower limit. These considerations can be weighed by the legislature and a compromise speed limit identified. This limit will reflect a trade-off between the different values at stake, but at the same time provides specific guidance to enforcers and adjudicators in applying the law, and thus guidance to the public.

17. The critical reason why these varying objectives can be weighed against one another to produce a single speed limit is that the optimal speed limit is not especially context specific. That is, for a given stretch of road, the optimal speed limit does not depend on innumerable or unstable factors; a single speed limit remains suitable across a wide range of conditions for the road. This may not always be entirely true, and there may be nuances. For example, a school zone may have a lower speed limit or could have a lower limit only during certain times when children are more likely to be around. Or a blizzard may result in road closure out of safety concerns. In general, however, the fact that the speed limit is robustly applicable to varying conditions allows the adoption of a single limit that is easily operationalized, yet reflects multiple objectives.

18. Consider now competition law. Certainly, in light of conventional objectives for antitrust, it is not possible generally to craft sensible, easily operationalized rules that reflect a compromise between a wide variety of goals and that are robust to a wide variety of contexts. This is because competitive effects of conduct are heavily context specific, and nuances may be dispositive in a given case. It is therefore unsurprising that competition law instead relies on standards that invite authorities and adjudicators to apply general principles to a given set of facts, not fully articulated rules, to determine the legal status of the conduct in question.

19. A counterexample illustrates the problems with attempts to make rules in antitrust. US antitrust law treats price-fixing as a per se criminal offence, which sounds rule-like. But even here context has assumed importance, sometimes overwhelming importance. In *BMI* the US Supreme Court observed that "easy labels do not always supply ready answers" and concluded that before concluding that horizontal price-fixing, in that case by a copyright collective, is per se illegal, the Court ought to take a "quick look" to determine whether there are redeeming features of the arrangement that invite rule of reason scrutiny.[13] This illustrates the point: that even in a relatively straightforward area of law, price-fixing, context matters in antitrust and rules are generally unsuitable.

20. Reliance on standards in turn requires guidance to adjudicators about how to apply standards. For example, US antitrust law condemns contracts in restraint of trade, but all contracts restrain trade; more is needed to separate improper restraints of trade from proper restraints. To conduct this separation, it is necessary to have a sense of the values that competition law is intended to promote. Similarly, many laws call for an assessment of whether conduct substantially lessens competition. Applying this standard requires an understanding of why competition matters. To take a Canadian example, a substantial lessening of competition might mean one thing if efficiency motivates competition law, but something rather different if the law is motivated to ensure that SMEs participate in a market. Standards that allow adjudicators to pick and choose from a list of possible objectives do not provide meaningful guidance.

21. To the extent that a legal system relies on precedent to govern judicial decision-making, it could be that doctrine will narrow the scope of relevant values over time. There are two problems with this response to concerns about indeterminacy. First, precedent is always vulnerable, and there is the possibility that future cases will resurrect long-thought irrelevant values; that is, uncertainty remains even in the presence of clarifying precedent.

22. Second, and more fundamentally, there is a question whether it is institutionally appropriate to ask adjudicators to balance the kinds of values at stake in competition law. Consider the speeding example again. Safety and convenience are values that are widely recognized as important, but preference for one or the other will tend to reduce to a political choice; it cannot be dictated by the outcome of an uncontroversial calculus. As a consequence, it makes sense for the appropriate speed limit to be chosen by political representatives who are accountable to the electorate, not by the judiciary.

23. Asking competition adjudicators to make a choice between, for example, economic equality and efficiency, is to ask them to conduct a political trade-off, something that they are not obviously suited to do. Consider again the goals of antitrust in the Canadian example. It is not at all clear what value is furthered by providing SMEs equitable access to markets (or what "equitable" means).

---

13 *Broadcast Music Inc v CBS Inc* 441 US 1 (1979).

If it is about the inherent value of small business that we must respect, how does a judge begin to think about the trade-off with other values, competitive prices, or efficiency for example? This is a political question, and it is not obvious where to begin as a matter of principle.

24. There is a corresponding issue with relying on the judiciary and precedent to clarify the importance of different goals for competition law: it will result in considerable path-dependence and arbitrariness. The path of the law will depend on the preferences of those who decide initial cases, which amongst other things may lead to extreme outcomes not reflective of a reasonable legislature's preferences.[14]

25. In summary, by setting out a variety of goals for competition law in answering the question, "why competition?", legislatures avoid the mistake of treating competition as an end in itself, but instead create uncertainty, and indeed indeterminacy, in the application of standards that govern antitrust by adopting a range of conceptually disconnected goals that often point in different directions.

IV. Indeterminacy Matters

26. The challenges that result from too many goals are not merely theoretical. Canada provides an example of why concerns about indeterminacy matter. First, there are questions about how the law has been applied. Second, there are questions about how the law will be applied.

27. Enforcement of the Competition Act in Canada from its passage in 1986 to date has largely, but not entirely, sidestepped questions of the appropriate goals of the law by unselfconsciously pursuing efficiency over other concerns.[15] For example, when cases have involved allegations of anticompetitive exclusion by a dominant firm, the Competition Bureau in bringing enforcement actions, and adjudicators in ruling on them, have not asked whether conduct has denied SMEs "equitable" access to markets, but rather whether there has been inefficient exclusion of economically viable entrants.

28. Another example is that the Bureau, when crafting its Merger Enforcement Guidelines, initially took an efficiency approach to the s. 96 efficiencies defence to mergers. Section 96 of the Act, which was recently repealed, allowed anticompetitive mergers if efficiency gains offset the anticompetitive effects. The provision left anticompetitive effects undefined, however, which begged the following question: were only deadweight efficiency losses to be considered anticompetitive effects, or were higher prices on goods that were sold without deadweight losses also problematic because they

14 See Anthony Niblett, "Case-by-Case Adjudication and the Path of the Law" (2013) 42 JLS 303.

15 See, e.g., Edward Iacobucci, "The Competition Bureau's Rejection of Efficiency as the Key Criterion in Competition Policy: A Critique" (2022) 35 CC L Rev 1.

would benefit shareholders at the expense of consumers? Illustrating the prevailing approach to enforcement, the original Guidelines focused only on deadweight losses.

29. To be clear, s. 1.1 of the Competition Act does not require such an efficiency focus, but rather its inclusion of other objectives for competition law, including competitive prices and SME welfare, suggests the legitimacy of broader considerations. This was put to the test in a merger case that turned on the interpretation of the efficiencies defence, *Superior Propane*.[16] Largely because of the breadth of s. 1.1, the Federal Court of Appeal rejected the narrow efficiency approach to the defence, and instead invited the Tribunal to weigh deadweight losses, efficiency savings, and consumer losses in applying the defence. It did not provide guidance on how to do so, however, and indeed observed that the appropriate weighting of efficiency and harms to consumers may vary on a case-by-case basis. This case illustrates that a multiplicity of inconsistent goals can lead to indeterminacy in practice.

30. While the government recently abolished the efficiencies defence to mergers in Canada, it committed to retain s. 1.1. This leads to a second question: how will competition law be applied in the future? There is always the possibility that future enforcement agencies, and future adjudicators, will shift emphasis in s. 1.1 away from the conventional emphasis on efficiency and towards one of the other objectives.

31. Consider again the example of exclusion. While the focus in practice in Canada has been on anticompetitive, inefficient exclusion, it is not a foregone conclusion that that focus will continue to prevail, rather, following similar populist thinking in the US, there has been a push to treat harms to competitors as a key foundation of an abuse claim. For example, without considering evidence of competition in insurance and body shop markets, and without taking seriously benign explanations for the practice, a commentator has suggested that insurance companies that operate their own body shops are improperly harming independent body shops, and that such vertical integration ought to be prevented by the Competition Act.[17]

32. Much of the push to protect competitors under abuse has focused on statutory reform. Judicial interpretation has (unfortunately) characterized acts that harm competitors, even if they ultimately promote competition, as anticompetitive acts for the purposes of an abuse of dominance case.[18] Fortunately, at present the statute also requires that an abuse of dominance prevents or substantially lessens competition. There is, however, a proposed private member's bill

16 *Canada (Commissioner of Competition) v Superior Propane Inc* [2000] CCTD No 15 (Comp Trib); [2001] FCJ No 455 (F.C.A.); *Canada (Commissioner of Competition) v Superior Propane Inc* [2002] CCTC No 10; *Canada (Commissioner of Competition) v Superior Propane Inc* [2003] 3 FC 529.

17 Vass Bednar, "Self-Preferencing is Cannibalizing Canada's Auto Repair Industry" *Financial Post* (25 August 2022), <https://financialpost.com/transportation/autos/vass-bednar-self-preferencing-is-cannibalizing-canadas-auto-repair-industry> accessed 15 October 2024.

18 *Canada (Commissioner of Competition) v Canada Pipe Company Ltd* 2006 FCA 233.

to amend the statute to allow orders against dominant firms if they engage in anticompetitive acts without requiring analysis of harms to competition. This would allow orders against acts that harm competitors, even if they are pro-competitive.[19]

33. Even if there were no statutory amendment, the push to protect competitors could already fit within the statute because of s. 1.1. The purposes of promoting competition, according to s. 1.1, include providing SMEs with equitable access to markets. Even if there remained a test that conduct must prevent or substantially lessen competition, the authorities could argue that a dominant firm's practice of certain acts harms competitors by, say, limiting their pool of customers, and *therefore* harms competition. For example, it could be argued that when an insurance company forecloses access to its customers by independent body shops, the inability of the independent competitors to compete with the insurance company for these customers ought to be understood as a legally cognizable harm to competition because of s. 1.1, regardless of the intensity of remaining competition. Such an outcome may have very little connection to conventional economic efficiency understandings of exclusion and a substantial lessening of competition, but that does not mean that it is foreclosed by the statute.

34. While I have focused on Canada, what I describe is a common phenomenon, at least at the level of principle. Debates have intensified in the US and elsewhere about the appropriate goals for antitrust, with potentially profound implications for the enforcement of antitrust law. For example, labour welfare has gained support as an objective of US antitrust law, with potentially far-reaching implications. This raises potential conflict with other objectives, including the conventional focus on consumer welfare. Suppose that a merger would result in lower prices, but lower employment: should this be stopped to protect labour welfare? Given the variety of answers to "why antitrust" that exist, it may be difficult to know how competition law will evolve in the coming years.

V. Conclusion

35. This volume is framed around the fundamentally important question for competition law, "why competition?" At present, the law on this question has not one but many answers, and as a consequence, no practical answer. The question of what the answer ought to be is beyond the scope of this chapter, but I will close with this; whatever the answer to "why competition?", it is imperative to view competition law as only one arrow in the government's

19 The leader of the New Democratic Party has proposed a private member's bill that would amend the Competition Act in a variety of ways, including by abolishing the competitive effects test in abuse cases: <www.parl.ca/DocumentViewer/en/44-1/bill/C-352/first-reading> accessed 15 October 2024.

legal quiver. A variety of legal policies, from free trade to tax policy to campaign finance laws (and more), are relevant in promoting the values that burden antitrust law at present. Antitrust law wobbles and sometimes falls under the weight of divergent and sometimes inconsistent expectations, and would be better off with a lighter load.

20 Years of Changes

Olivier Guersent[*]

European Commission's Directorate-General for Competition

I. Introduction

1. In this contribution, I will offer my personal perspective on why competition policy remains as relevant today as it was two decades ago, when Concurrences started its journey. Having spent a large part of my career with the Commission's antitrust enforcement arm, I will share my views on the role and mission of our competition policy, how it has fulfilled its role in changing times, what this entailed and what it still requires going forward, in order to ensure that competition policy continues to play a key role in supporting a thriving and innovative internal market that serves EU companies and citizens.

II. Twenty Years of Changes, Creating Challenges and Opportunities

2. It is not an exaggeration to say that over the last 20 years our markets and societies have undergone one of the biggest transformations in the modern era. This transformation has created great opportunities for economic growth, but also significant challenges, including for competition policy and enforcement in Europe but also more widely.

3. This transformation has been driven by two main forces: globalisation and digitalisation.

---

[*] Director-General, DG-Competition. With special thanks to Pinelopi Stamou, Paul Bridgeland, Joanna Kay, Franziska Rupp-Solaroli and Natacha Callens of DG Competition for their contribution in preparing this chapter.

4. The early twenty-first century witnessed a surge in globalisation, characterised by rapid economic development in Asia, increased international trade, cross-border investments, and interconnected supply chains across geographies. While recent years have seen a rollback in certain aspects of globalisation, we undoubtedly live in a much more economically integrated world than we did two decades ago. Overall, this has contributed to faster deployment of technologies and better access to a wider choice of products for consumers, in some cases even at lower prices.

5. Concurrently, the last two decades have seen the digitalisation of the economy, with technology playing a transformative role across industries. The rise of digital platforms, e-commerce giants and data-driven business models has re-shaped market structures. Digitalisation has brought opportunities even for smaller businesses to extend their reach and to remain resilient in the face of economic disruption, by, for instance, relying on the growth of e-commerce.

6. But the increase in cross-border trade and digitalisation have not only created opportunities; they have also created challenges when it comes to keeping markets open and maintaining a level playing field. They have, for instance, facilitated the rise of digital behemoths, which have benefitted from first-mover advantages and gained market power through strong network effects and the accumulation of data. Digitalisation and market integration have also coincided with increasing industry concentration, even in traditional or established industries.

7. These developments have made vigorous antitrust enforcement even more critical. When I started my career at the Commission's Directorate-General for Competition, one of the big challenges for competition in Europe was to loosen the grip of national statutory monopolies and "liberalise" key sectors of the economy. Nowadays, digital gatekeepers create different, but in some ways similar, challenges: while these digital giants are not a legacy of the former State monopolies, the markets in which they flourish have some common features with the national markets of the 1990s: high barriers to entry and entrenched dominant players. And of course, increasing market concentration calls for merger control intervention, especially – but not only – when it comes to horizontal consolidation.

8. But the last 20 years were not only about challenges brought about through gradual transformations. They also included major shocks and crises. If we think about the global financial crisis of 2008, and, more recently, the Coronavirus pandemic and the Ukraine war, it is hard to imagine what bigger shocks we could administer to our economies and societies to test their resilience.

9. However, these crises also created opportunities, including for competition policy. By that, I certainly do not mean only opportunities to tighten competition enforcement, but also to rethink it. In the last two decades, competition law enforcement has confirmed its importance in keeping markets working well and creating stable business environments that foster investment in innovation, even during times of crisis. At the same time, such challenges also force us to revisit our tools and practices and identify areas for improvement.

10. All in all, when looking back at the last 20 years, I see a world that has undergone a deep transformation that created opportunities for growth and technological progress, but at the same time risks of market power being abused to the detriment of EU consumers. And in this fast-paced reality, the challenge for competition policy and enforcement was to remain relevant and preserve our industries' competitiveness.

11. In the following section I will seek to explain how EU competition policy and enforcement has risen to the challenge of remaining relevant. Our enforcement work has contributed not only to the protection of the competitive process but also to other EU political objectives, such as the green transition. Importantly, our policy and enforcement work has also helped to create a "competition culture" that has accelerated antitrust enforcement at national level across EU Member States, thereby also contributing to the smooth functioning of our internal market in a decentralised way. But remaining relevant does not happen automatically – it requires revisiting our tools and approach, where appropriate, and being creative and open-minded.

III. Competition Policy: Steady Relevance and Fitness through Adaptation

1. The Key Role of Competition Policy and Enforcement for the EU's Internal Market

12. In view of the transformation that I have described, we should not lose sight of the important role that competition policy and enforcement continue to play in our market economy, ensuring a properly functioning EU internal market, and how they have achieved that.

13. Think, for example, about the Commission's decision in the *AB InBev* case, concerning the limitation of imports by a dominant beer producer, and the *Valve* case where the Commission took issue with the geo-blocking practices put in place by the owner of a gaming platform and its videogame publishers. In both cases the message was clear: cross-border sales cannot be hindered in breach of competition rules. These examples show that competition law enforcement can have a direct impact in safeguarding the internal market by removing obstacles to trade between Member States.

2. The Core Mission of Competition Policy and its Contribution to Further Objectives

14. While competition policy has been a stable pillar of the internal market, this does not mean that it has stood still for the last 20 years. Competition policy, by its very nature, cannot be designed or enforced in a vacuum. It needs to stay close to market developments and constantly reflect wider

policy objectives as these evolve over time. This has been a guiding principle for the Commission, and for me personally, in all the posts I have held at DG-Competition.

15. Of course, the core mission of EU competition law enforcement has always been to ensure the proper functioning of markets, so that scarce resources are allocated efficiently, resulting ultimately in the protection of consumer welfare. This explains why the notion of consumer welfare in Europe has always been – and blessed by the EU Courts as such – broad, in the sense that it has a focus beyond price effects. Notably, we would also be concerned about negative impact on choice, quality and innovation. Take for example our merger control decisions *Dow/Dupont* or *Bayer/Monsanto* in the agrochemicals sector, where we looked at the competitive impact of a merger on incentives to innovate or to engage in R&D.

16. One could say that our approach is not so far from the neo-Brandeisian approach in the US, however this is only partially true. Our assessment indeed usually includes some of the factors considered important for the neo-Brandeisian school, such as innovation, buyer power and data. However, we would not include other factors, or at least not directly, as standards by which to judge companies' behaviour.

17. To the extent allowed by its core mandate, competition policy can and should also contribute to the pursuit of other policy objectives. First of all, a healthy competitive environment produces a variety of positive side-effects beyond the strictly economic sphere. Take the example of the market for general online search services in the EU, which is dominated by Google. Competition enforcement in this market is important not only to ensure that competition remains possible in online search services as such, but, as the General Court stated in its recent *Android* judgment, also for the positive impact it has on our democratic society, by ensuring that multiple sources of information are available online. So, there are very real and positive side-effects of competition enforcement for other public policy objectives.

18. This takes me to another important point: as competition law enforcers, we work as part of the Commission and use our tools to support, whenever possible, the EU's wider goals. If we look at the current green transition objectives of the EU, it is clear that our competition policy and case practice is geared to also – albeit indirectly – facilitate the achievement of the European Green Deal. Competition ensures an efficient allocation of resources, it drives innovation that leads to the new technologies needed for the green transition, and it keeps prices down, so we can more easily afford to invest in sustainable processes. If we take our recent initiatives in antitrust, our new Horizontal Guidelines explain how sustainability goals can be taken into account in the assessment of agreements between competitors, to enable procompetitive green initiatives while preventing "greenwashing". The Commission is also applying innovation theories of harm in merger cases to prevent the loss of "green" innovation. For example, last year we conducted a Phase II investigation into

Norsk/Hydro Alumetal – a merger of two producers of low-carbon aluminium. And we also conditionally cleared the purchase of MBCC by SIKA, both of which play a crucial role in developing chemical admixtures to make “greener” cement.

19. What has been particularly important in recent years is that the EU competition rules have been proven to have a lot of in-built flexibility to cope with new market realities and crises. In both the Coronavirus pandemic and the Ukraine war – which quickly turned into an energy crisis – our competition tools have proven apt to deliver quick solutions and to contribute to limiting repercussions on European businesses and the EU economy as a whole. Through the temporary frameworks introduced during the Coronavirus pandemic and the Ukraine war, the Commission adapted its rules to allow, under an exceptional framework, financial aid to businesses affected by the pandemic or by the energy crisis. And the Antitrust Temporary Framework adopted in April 2020 provided guidance and legal certainty to companies when, for example, they wished to cooperate to address shortages of critical hospital medicines and medical equipment or bottlenecks in vaccine production.

20. Naturally, there are obvious limits. Competition policy and enforcement are first and foremost about the functioning of markets and consumer welfare. They cannot necessarily contribute to all the objectives of other policy areas. As a competition law enforcer, we do not have the mandate – especially in terms of democratic legitimacy – to balance all possible public interest goals against harm to competition.

3. The European Competition Network and the Advancement of an EU Competition Culture

21. One of the success stories of the last 20 years has been the creation of a strong competition law culture across the Union, and this is thanks in large part to the competence and dynamism of the National Competition Authorities (NCAs). The successful decentralisation of antitrust enforcement in 2004 depended on the NCAs stepping up and using their new powers. This is a story of competition authorities running ground-breaking cases, taking on their national champions and getting concrete results for their consumers. Over 80% of the more than 3000 investigations conducted by the European Competition Network (ECN) have been national investigations. It is also a story of NCAs developing their rulebook: in the last two decades many NCAs have developed a merger control regime where there used to be none.

22. Of course, the decentralisation of competition law enforcement required teamwork – NCAs finding new ways of working together and doing so more and more frequently. For example, we see NCAs conducting joint inspections, exchanging evidence, negotiating commitments together, publishing joint reflection papers, and helping to enforce each other’s decisions. DG-Competition has also played its part: we devote significant time and resources to preparing and

running the ECN meetings at which we share knowledge and discuss policy. The regularity of these contacts – at all levels – has allowed us to build relationships of openness and trust. And these achievements have recently been reinforced by the ECN+ Directive, which aimed to "level up" the NCAs in terms of independence, resources and enforcement powers.

23. As the NCAs have gradually embraced the EU competition tools as our common good, the ECN has evolved towards a less Commission-centric model and towards one in which all members own, manage and develop EU competition rules in a cooperative way.

4. Keeping our Antitrust Tools Sharp

24. As markets, technology and society evolve, so too must our enforcement tools, if they are to remain effective.

25. In antitrust, we recently renewed our main block exemption regulations and guidelines, updating them to reflect the latest market developments and case law. For agreements between companies at the same level of the supply chain (horizontal agreements), we added guidance on data sharing agreements and sustainability agreements, amongst others, and for agreements between companies operating at different levels of the supply chain (vertical agreements), we added new rules and guidance covering restrictions on online sales and agreements with online platforms. In 2022, we also revised our Informal Guidance Notice, to make it easier for companies to approach us with agreements that raise novel or unresolved issues.

26. And we are not stopping there. We are currently systematising into Guidelines our by now extensive enforcement experience on abusive practices by dominant companies that exclude actual or potential competitors from the market. The Guidelines will reflect the rich case law from the EU Courts that has resulted from our numerous decisions in recent years.

27. In addition, there has of course been another important twentieth birthday recently – our antitrust implementing regulation: Regulation 1/2003, turned twenty in 2023. This cornerstone of our procedural set-up has achieved its key objectives, one of which was to decentralise enforcement, thereby allowing us to focus resources on cases best dealt with at EU level. But "Reg 1" is also starting to show some signs of age – for one thing, it was designed in and for a world of paper documents. Digitalisation has not only changed the way companies handle and store information and reduced the boundaries between professional and private life, but it has also increased the amount of information that we have to process in our enforcement work. These are some of the reasons why we are evaluating Regulation 1/2003 to enable us to decide whether and how it should be revised.

28. If we turn to merger control, our tools are of course inter-connected with those of the Member States, as embodied in the referrals system under the Merger Regulation. Together with the Member States, we have been on a learning curve

as to how best ensure that transactions that merit review do not fall through the cracks. That is why, from a jurisdictional perspective, the Commission has sought to reinvigorate Article 22 of the Merger Regulation. Article 22 allows Member States to refer "any" concentration to the Commission that threatens to significantly affect competition in its territory and that has an impact on trade between Member States, but this power had not been used to its full potential until recently. We revised our approach to empower Member States to refer concentrations to the Commission irrespective of whether national merger control thresholds are met, provided the conditions of Article 22 are met and the turnover of at least one of the parties does not reflect its actual or future competitive potential. their It should be noted that the Commission's interpretation of Article 22 was confirmed by the General Court in the *Illumina* judgment of 2022, but, at the time of writing, we are still waiting for the final word on this matter from the Court of Justice. At EEA Member State level, several initiatives have also been undertaken to close the enforcement gap. Countries that revised their merger control thresholds include Germany and Austria, where subsidiary notification thresholds based on the value of the transaction were introduced in recent years. Countries that have introduced, so-called "call-in" provisions include Latvia, Ireland, Norway, Italy, Slovenia and Sweden. One thing is clear, transactions that may raise significant competition concerns should not escape all scrutiny.

29. All these initiatives show that we have not shied away from revisiting our tools, where necessary, and this stems from our conviction that competition enforcement needs to have teeth to fulfil its purpose.

5. Staying Creative: New Theories of Harm in Antitrust and Merger Control

30. As you will have gathered, one recurring lesson from my long career in DG-Competition is that competition policy and enforcement cannot stand still. They need to evolve and adapt. This is not only a matter of ensuring that our tools remain fit-for-purpose. It also requires being creative and thinking openly when actually applying the rules that govern our action and making full use of the tools in our enforcement arsenal.

31. If we take merger control, the EU framework of review is proving resilient and flexible. Based on this framework, we have been able to apply theories of harm that reflect the evolving economic reality. *Meta/Kustomer*, *Amazon/MGM*, *Microsoft/Activision* and *Google/Photomath* are all recent examples of cases where we considered the impact of interrelated market realities, sometimes referred to as digital "ecosystems". Our more recent *Booking/eTraveli* decision is also a testament to the ability of our existing tools to capture new theories of harm, including those focusing on a merger complementing, extending or reinforcing an existing ecosystem and its knock-on effect on competition.

32. In antitrust as well, we have found that our general framework is sufficiently flexible to allow us to capture concerns about new ways of distorting

competition in evolving markets. In this regard, it is worth recalling that the Commission was among the first to run antitrust cases in the digital sphere, such as the *Google Shopping*, *Google Android* and *Google AdTech* cases. In these cases, we have applied "classic" theories of harm, such as tying, in the context of the specific features of the digital sector: network effects, zero-pricing and two-sided markets. We have also been "creative" by adapting our theories of harm to the digital sector and the practices of digital players, while maintaining the general principles of competition law that underpin those theories. The *Google Shopping* decision, for instance, focused on concerns around Google's "self-preferencing" conduct, whereby Google was favouring its own comparison-shopping service to the detriment of competitors.

6. Competition Law and Regulation: Complementarity and Cross-Fertilisation

33. Finding the right balance and interplay between sector-specific ex ante regulation and competition enforcement is not a new issue, but this question is still as relevant today as it was 20 years ago, and this is certainly something that we keep in mind in our day-to-day work as enforcers.

34. Of course, competition law enforcement is not a panacea, and its achievements over the last 20 years have not removed the need for specific regulation, in particular, in network industries. The need to specify upfront some rules of the game became clear most recently in the digital sector, where a few players on tipped platform markets had become so powerful that they reminded me quite a bit of the incumbents in liberalised markets a few decades ago.

35. Naturally, our experience in antitrust was an effective and rich source of inspiration for the Digital Markets Act (DMA) and enabled the legislator to identify the types of practices that are so systemic and so generally problematic if adopted by so-called "gatekeepers" that it would be appropriate to regulate them ex ante. The aim is to achieve through the enforcement of the DMA real change on the ground, to the benefit of those who seek to enter or grow in these markets, and ultimately of all of us who are digital consumers. At the same time, the introduction of regulation does not mean that competition enforcement becomes impossible or unnecessary, quite the contrary. The instruments of competition law and the applicable regulatory instruments operate in complementarity; they are not mutually exclusive. One can inspire the other, and one should certainly complement the other. In other words, the existence of regulation certainly does not prevent the competition law instruments from being applied where needed. Specifically with regard to the DMA, just like for other sectors where regulation was introduced, ie banking, telecoms or energy, the DMA will not "cut out" competition law in digital. The rules of antitrust and merger control will continue to apply, including to gatekeepers, and we will not shy away from enforcing them if that is what is needed to keep digital markets competitive.

IV. Concluding Remarks

36. In conclusion, today just as 20 years ago, the protection of competition remains a core policy of the EU. It is key to a well-functioning market economy and remains an essential component of our internal market. It is still the most powerful autonomous power of the Commission, acting as a referee in its function as Guardian of the Treaties. In other words, it has been and will remain a key pillar of the European project. Over the last two decades, globalisation and digitalisation have transformed our economies and societies and created unique challenges for competition policy. EU competition policy has proved capable of navigating these challenges, and I am confident that our adaptive and proactive approach will allow us to keep markets fair, open and working for consumers in the decades to come.

An Analysis of Why Competition

DIANE P. WOOD*
The University of Chicago

1. Every now and then, it is a good idea to step back and re-examine basic assumptions. Those assumptions typically operate at a variety of levels: personally, philosophically, empirically, and morally, to name only a few. Economics has not been exempt from the re-examination and adjustment to which this process leads: the world has seen many economic systems, beginning with primitive hunting and gathering, moving along much later to feudal systems, mercantilism, the laissez-faire period, and landing today (for much of the world) with market economies – that is, structures in which there is a great deal of freedom for individual firms, but at the same time there are restrictions designed to prevent distortions or abuse of that freedom.

2. Competition, in the sense of rivalry among economic actors, has played a central role in the history of the United States. Today, there is a broad consensus for the proposition that competition among market participants assures the greatest number and quality of goods and services at the lowest possible price. Many people believe that this is the exclusive role for competition. Others, however, see broader purposes. They would add that properly bounded competition creates a market economy that is open to new market entrants. Implicit in this is the further idea that those new entrants are entitled to a fair chance of entering the market and establishing themselves. The latter goal raises the question whether competition itself may be carried on using whatever tactics the individual firm chooses – fair or unfair, moral or amoral – at least from the standpoint of core competition law. That idea is more controversial.

3. Adherents to the Chicago School do not agree that the "competition" to which the antitrust laws refer comes along with behavioral expectations.

---

* Director, American Law Institute Senior Lecturer in Law, The University of Chicago Circuit Judge (ret.), U.S. Court of Appeals for the Seventh Circuit.

They concede that it is not permissible to eliminate a rival from the market by blowing up its plant, but that is not because antitrust law addresses such behavior. It is instead because that tactic is prohibited by tort, and criminal law. The same argument applies to other business torts. More traditional competition scholars, looking at the history of the US antitrust laws (as well as the scope of the competition laws in many other jurisdictions), contend that an essential part of the concept of "competition" is that it be accomplished using ethical (even if tough) methods. Interestingly, however, neither side goes so far as to advocate for unfettered competition. Hard-core agreements among competitors to fix prices, allocate markets, restrict quantity, and the like, must be off the table, because they harm consumers (or in the monopsonist situation, producers) and impose a deadweight loss on the economy. Logically, monopolies should suffer the same fate, but at the same time, antitrust courts do not want to become price-control boards for individual firms. In the final analysis, US law eschews both extremes – unregulated competition, or state-controlled markets – and it strives to find the right scope for competition somewhere in the middle. The optimal spot within that middle range, however, is impossible to pinpoint without first knowing why we have competition laws and what the realistic alternatives would be.

4. The spot one chooses is important. It dictates the degree of freedom that rivals in the relevant market are permitted to enjoy. Those economic actors might use that freedom to engage in tough competition, but experience shows that they may also use it to suppress or even eliminate competitors and ultimately achieve a monopolistic position. Most countries today have competition laws (dubbed "antitrust law" in the United States for historical reasons) that attempt to encourage the former and to ban, or at least discourage, the latter. But society's expectations for competition have varied over time, and the ultimate goal of the laws has changed both across the years and across the globe.

5. A brief look at the history of US law in this area illustrates this point. What did society hope to gain from legal doctrines addressed to monopolies and restraints of trade during the common-law period, before laws such as the Sherman Act came into being? What competitive regime did the Sherman Act and subsequent legislation contemplate? And what has the U.S. Supreme Court made of all this over the years? The answers to those questions shed light on what we mean by "competition," why it is (or is not) a desirable model for national or global markets, and what can be done to achieve the goals a given society has set for itself.

I. Common-Law Antecedents

6. The common-law judges who developed the original laws against monopolies and restraints of trade did so in the context of an economic setting that was markedly different from today's. Freedom of trade and freedom

of contract, as those terms are now understood, were at best highly qualified – at worst, non-existent. Tradespeople belonged to a myriad of guilds – mandatory associations that restricted membership, set prices, and generally regulated the way one could carry on a business.[1] Nothing like the modern business organization existed. Instead, there were "patents," "monopolies," and charters for companies, granted first by the Crown and later by Parliament.

7. William Letwin identified four distinct branches of the English law governing economic organization: "[T]he law [1] on monopoly power, whether by patent, charter, or custom; [2] on forestalling, engrossing, and regrating; [3] on contracts in restraint of trade; and [4] on combinations in restraint of trade".[2] In other words, English common law addressed exclusive rights granted by a public authority; it addressed various types of evasions of organized markets, such as refusals to confine trades to permitted hours, places, quantities, and times (i.e., forestalling, regrating, and engrossing); it forbade some contracts in which one person promised not to compete with another (so-called contracts in restraint of trade); and it barred certain combinations of companies. One would be hard-pressed to find, among these creatures of the old English writ system, anything resembling an interest in the modern consumer welfare standard, let alone a single-minded focus in that direction.

8. That is not to say that modern concerns were entirely lacking in the precursor era. The famous *Case of Monopolies*,[3] also known as *Darcy v. Allin*, represented Allin's effort to set aside a Crown-bestowed monopoly on the manufacture, import, and distribution of playing cards. The court agreed with him that the Queen's grant was void. Along the way, it highlighted

> "three inseparable incidents to every monopoly against the commonwealth, [namely,] 1. That the price of the same commodity will be raised (…). 2. (…) that after the monopoly granted the commodity is not so good and merchantable as it was before: for the patentee having the sole trade, regards only his private benefit, and not the common wealth. 3. It tends to the impoverishment of divers artificers and others, who before, by their labour of their hands in their art or trade, had maintained themselves and their families, who now will of necessity be constrained to live in idleness and beggary." (77 Eng. Rep. at 1263).

9. The first two bear a family resemblance to today's antitrust law. But the third – depriving former market participants of a job and the wherewithal to support their families – would be seen as grist for the social welfare system, not a problem for antitrust to solve.

---

1 See generally M. Cartwright, "Medieval Guilds," *World History Encyclopedia*, November 14, 2018, https://www.worldhistory.org/Medieval_Guilds/.

2 W. L. Letwin, "The English Common Law Concerning Monopolies," *University of Chicago Law Review* 21, no. 3, (1954): 355–85, at 356.

3 11 Coke 87, 77 Eng. Rep. 1260 (K.B. 1602).

10. Another early case, *Mitchel v. Reynolds*[4] has often been hailed as the forebear of today's ancillary restraints analysis, but it too rested on more than welfare concerns. The facts were simple: D conveyed an interest in a bakery to P for a five-year period. As part of the deal, D promised not to open a competing business in the parish during the five years that the conveyance was in effect. Later, D seems to have had second thoughts about the deal, and so he sued to set aside the covenant not to compete as void. The court held for P.

11. Today, this would have been a simple matter: any court would hold that D's promise not to compete was reasonably ancillary to the temporary transfer of the business, was reasonable in both scope and time, and thus was not one that was "in restraint of trade." The King's Bench, however, did not see the matter so simply. Instead, it devoted some time to the difference between voluntary and involuntary restraints, as well as to the distinction between "general" restraints covering all of England and "particular" restraints supported by consideration and a good reason. Only the latter were sustainable. Significantly, the judges agreed that "no man can contract not to use his trade at all".[5] They went on to deplore "the mischief which may arise from [a covenant not to compete], 1 st, to the party, by the loss of his livelihood, and the subsistence of his family; 2 dly, to the publick, by depriving it of an useful member".[6] Those concerns would have been entirely absent from a modern opinion discussing the validity of a non-compete clause, limited, as this one was.

II. The Sherman Act

12. It should be no surprise that the themes one finds in the common-law cases make an appearance in the national conversation that led Senator John Sherman to introduce his path-breaking legislation in 1888. The public was already hostile to government-granted monopolies, and it saw no meaningful difference between that older business form and the new privately created "trusts" that seemed to be swallowing up more and more industries. Traces of the earlier concern about government action still existed, to be sure – the agricultural movement objected vociferously to tariffs on manufactured goods that it saw as protecting domestic manufacturers at the expense of farmers. But private power seemed to be slipping out of control. Sector after sector was falling under the control of the trusts, and the railroads were another concern. Economic abuses abounded, at least in the popular understanding. Although some state attorneys general were trying to rein in the authors of those abuses, the sense was growing that nothing but federal regulation would suffice.

---

4 1 P. Wms. 181, 24 Eng. Rep. 347 (K.B. 1711).

5 1 P. Wms. 187.

6 Ibid., 190.

13. Once again, William Letwin provides a concise summary of the situation.[7] He catalogued at least six objections that the public had with respect to the trusts:

- Threats to liberty because of outsized influence;
- Corruption of civil servants and bribery of legislators;
- Unjustified privileges granted by law, such as tariff protection;
- Predatory pricing to force competitors from the market;
- High prices, made possible by their monopolistic position;
- Watering of stock, which defrauded investors; and
- Loss of worker jobs, from closing plants and reducing supply.[8]

14. No one was sure what to do about all this, or whether any legal rule that could be imagined stood a chance of making a difference. Some economists were persuaded that the trusts had grown so large because they were, in their respective sectors, natural monopolists. If that were the case, then the answer lay in some form of public regulation, but it was not at all clear who should be doing the regulating, and what they ought to be ordering.

15. As we know, what emerged from all this was the Act of July 2, 1890,[9] popularly known for its original sponsor, Senator Sherman. But the early cases decided under the newly minted statute reflect a similar ambivalence about what type of business behavior was protected, what was forbidden (and even criminal, though at the time the violation was defined only as a misdemeanor), and what distinguished one from the other. One of the first cases that reached the Supreme Court was *United States v. Trans-Missouri Freight Association*, 166 U.S. 290 (1897), in which the government was trying to break up a railroad cartel. Easy, today's antitrust lawyer would think. Simple application of the consumer-welfare model would lead to the condemnation of the association. But, in a famous passage, Justice Peckham returned to the populist roots of the law:

> "It is true, the results of trusts, or combinations of that nature, may be different in different kinds of corporations, and yet they all have an essential similarity, and have been induced by motives of individual or corporate aggrandizement as against the public interest. In business or trading combinations they may even temporarily, or perhaps permanently, reduce the price of the article traded in or manufactured by reducing the expense inseparable from the running of many different companies for the same purpose. Trade or commerce under those circumstances may nevertheless be badly and unfortunately restrained by

7 See W. L. Letwin, "Congress and the Sherman Antitrust Law: 1887–1890," *University of Chicago Law Review* 23, no. 2, (1956): 221–59.

8 Ibid., 235.

9 26 Stat. 209.

> driving out of business the small dealers and worthy men whose lives have been spent therein, and who might be unable to readjust themselves to their altered surroundings. Mere reduction in the price of the commodity dealt in might be dearly paid for by the ruin of such a class and the absorption of control over one commodity by an all-powerful combination of capital".[10]

16. Since the 1970s, generations of antitrust scholars and students have chuckled at Justice Peckham's reference to, and concern for, the "small dealers and worthy men." But in singling them out, he was only being true to the common law and the background of the statute he was construing. He would have been startled by the proposition that the Sherman Act is indifferent to the distributional consequences of a business arrangement, or that it has nothing to say about exclusionary practices. The small dealers were surely competing in the markets they served. It is just that they predictably lacked the economies of scale available to their larger rivals. Yet to be determined, was whether society was prepared to do without competition from small (and arguably less efficient) businesses and cede the market to a few giants. Add to this the fact that the Sherman Act was also understood as a statute that empowered the "little guys" to fight a rearguard action against predatory and exclusionary practices, and the complexity of the conditions for healthy competition becomes more apparent.

III. Development of Antitrust Doctrine

17. Later decisions of the Supreme Court flipped and flopped about the meaning of competition. The *Trans-Missouri Freight* decision had firmly rejected the idea that the reasonableness of a price could excuse price-fixing:

> "It is now, with much amplification of argument, urged that the statute, in declaring illegal every combination in the form of trust or otherwise (…) does not mean what the language used therein plainly imports, but that it only means to declare illegal any such contract which is in unreasonable restraint of trade, while leaving all others unaffected by the provisions of the Act; that the common law meaning of the term 'contract in restraint of trade' includes only such contracts as are in unreasonable restraint of trade; and, when that term is used in the federal statute, it is not intended to include all contracts in restraint of trade, but only those which are in unreasonable restraint thereof".[11]

18. The Court's answer was unambiguous: "The term is not of such limited signification".[12] It also rejected the railroads' argument that "competition,

---

10 Ibid., 322–23.

11 Ibid., 327–28.

12 Ibid., 328.

while perhaps right and proper in other business, simply leads in railroad business to financial ruin and insolvency".[13] The only "refuge" from that ruinous competition, they contended, was to permit agreements to maintain reasonable rates. The Court was unmoved by these contentions: all contracts meant all, not just the reasonable ones.

19. That literalism did not last. Approximately 15 years later, the Court took a more nuanced approach – to be honest, an approach that repudiated *Trans-Missouri Freight*'s rejection of a "reasonableness" gloss on the prohibitions of Sherman Act section 1 in favor of an overarching "rule of reason" to guide statutory interpretation. I am referring, of course, to the decision in *Standard Oil of New Jersey v. United States*, 221 U.S. 1 (1911). Even though the ultimate judgment of the Court was to uphold the government's antitrust challenge to the Standard Oil Trust, its rationale opened the door to a reasonableness gloss on its prohibitions. The Court's central concern was that the *Trans-Missouri Freight* approach left insufficient room for legitimate business arrangements (i.e., for competition), and so, without specifically overruling *Trans-Missouri*, it softened that decision at the edges. The result may not have been what it expected. In an era where "trust-busting" was a popular political stance, Congress responded to *Standard Oil* with legislation designed to reinforce the Sherman Act, the Clayton Act[14] and the Federal Trade Commission Act.[15]

20. In the years that followed, the Court sometimes lent a sympathetic ear to industries that pleaded for more freedom of contract (and less antitrust intervention), and sometimes it refused to do so. Think, for example, of *Appalachian Coals v. United States*, 288 U.S. 344 (1933). which arose in the midst of the Great Depression, and which permitted a large group of coal producers to use a common selling agent (a common cartel device). Bouncing back to the other side seven years later, the Court in *United States v. Socony-Vacuum Oil Co.*, 310 U.S. 150 (1940) found that it was a per se violation of the Clayton Act for a group of oil producers to coordinate purchases of gasoline designed to prevent a feared market collapse.

21. Perhaps even more notable has been the Court's willingness to tolerate ever-larger concentrations of economic power resulting from mergers. The Clayton Act makes illegal any merger or acquisition "in any line of commerce (…) in any section of the country" where "the effect of such acquisition may be substantially to lessen competition, or to tend to create a monopoly".[16] Here, the trajectory is easiest to see if one begins in the early 1950s, after the Clayton Act had been amended to include both stock and asset acquisitions,[17] with the

---

13 Ibid., 330.

14 Pub. L. No. 63-212, 38 Stat. 730 (1914).

15 Pub. L. No. 63-203, 38 Stat. 717 (1914).

16 15 U.S.C. § 18.

17 See Cellar-Kefauver Act of 1950, Act of Dec. 29, 1950, c. 1184, 64 Stat. 1125.

case of *Brown Shoe Co. v. United States*, 370 U.S. 294 (1962). Brown Shoe, the number three seller of shoes in the country, wanted to acquire Kinney, the number eight seller. But those numbers do not tell the whole story. Brown Shoe, the Court noted, was responsible for only "4% of the Nation's total footwear production",[18] while Kinney's share was a measly 1.2 percent.[19] It is safe to say that no Administration from the Reagan group to the present would bring such a case.[20]

22. Indeed, the interesting fact about modern merger enforcement is how concentrated a post-merger market can become before the transaction is blocked by the courts. In *Hospital Corporation of America v. Federal Trade Commission*, 807 F.2d 1381 (7th Cir. 1986), the court upheld the FTC's decision to block a merger that left only four significant competitors in the area. But in *United States v. Baker Hughes Inc.*, 908 F.2d 981 (D.C. Cir. 1990), a different court of appeals rejected the government's challenge to a merger in the oil field drilling equipment market between firms with a combined 76 percent of the market – one that brought about an astronomical increase in concentration as measured by the Herfindahl-Hirschman Index.[21]

23. This would not be as consequential if it were easier to use the antitrust laws to reach single-firm behavior, called "monopolization" or "attempt to monopolize" in section 2 of the Sherman Act, or "abuse of a dominant position" in the European Union and many other jurisdictions. But section 2 cases are notoriously difficult to prosecute and win, whether by the government as plaintiff or by a private party. Yet time and again, individual firms have grown, either through internal efforts or through mergers, to the point of market dominance. In the iconic *Alcoa* case, the court thought it obvious that 90 percent of a relevant market was enough to constitute a monopoly.[22] The court regarded the 90 percent figure as accurately depicting Alcoa's power on the record before it. It also indicated, in dicta, how it might characterize smaller market shares: "The percentage we have already mentioned – over ninety – results only if we both include all 'Alcoa's' production and exclude 'secondary.' That percentage is enough to constitute a monopoly; it is doubtful whether sixty or sixty-four percent would be enough; and certainly thirty-three per cent is not."[23] But that was just the beginning. The court recognized that the very competitive process the Sherman Act is designed to foster holds within it the seed of its own destruction – the creation of a monopoly.

---

18 Ibid., 303.

19 Ibid.

20 See, e.g., Department of Justice and the Federal Trade Commission, "Merger Guidelines" (December 18, 2023). Earlier versions of these Guidelines, going back to 1982, were, if anything, more skeptical about merger challenges. Thus, if no challenge is likely under the 2023 version, a fortiori, nothing would have happened under the earlier editions.

21 From 2878 to 4303, where the Merger Guidelines define 1800 as highly concentrated (ibid., 224n3).

22 *United States v. Aluminum Co. of America*, 148 F.2d 416, 424 (2d Cir. 1945).

23 Ibid.

24. It is worth taking a moment to review the reasons the *Alcoa* court gave for its disapproval of monopoly. First, it highlighted the legal and economic reasons for that outcome. Legally speaking, the court acknowledged that "at least as to § 1, that there are some contracts restricting competition which are unlawful, no matter how beneficent they may be; no industrial exigency will justify them; they are absolutely forbidden".[24] And the same result followed, the court reasoned, for section 2, because "the vice of restrictive contracts and of monopoly is really one, it is the denial to commerce of the supposed protection of competition".[25] But the court did not stop there. It went on to list noneconomic reasons for forbidding monopoly, such as Congress's "desire to put an end to great aggregations of capital because of the helplessness of the individual before them",[26] and its intent "to perpetuate and preserve, for its own sake and in spite of possible cost, an organization of industry in small units which can effectively compete with each other".[27]

25. But it is not so easy to protect competition and prohibit monopolization at the same time. As *Alcoa* pointed out, a single producer might emerge from a market "merely by virtue of his superior skill, foresight, and industry. (...) The successful competitor, having been urged to compete, must not be turned upon when he wins".[28] The Supreme Court tried to provide a test that would distinguish between a monopolist whose position does not violate the law from one that has committed the offense of "monopolizing" in *United States v. Grinnell Corp.*, 384 U.S. 563 (1966), but it is not clear how well it succeeded. The Court identified two elements of the offense, as follows: "The offense of monopoly under § 2 of the Sherman Act has two elements: (1) the possession of monopoly power in the relevant market, and (2) the willful acquisition or maintenance of that power as distinguished from growth or development as a consequence of a superior product, business acumen, or historic accident".[29]

26. In other words, if the monopolist acquired its monopoly power through impermissible means (that is, exclusionary or other unfair practices), or if it became a monopolist lawfully but then maintained that monopoly power through similar forbidden means, then the offense has been established. One way of refuting the charge that the power was unlawfully acquired or maintained is to show that it resulted from competition on the merits or historic accident.

27. The dearth of successful section 2 cases, especially over the last couple of decades, is a testament to how hard it is to thread the *Grinnell* needle. What, then, is one to do if the idea that monopolization has been forbidden by statute is accepted, yet at the same time, it is clear that a showing of monopoly power

24 Ibid., 427.

25 Ibid., 428.

26 Ibid.

27 Ibid., 429.

28 Ibid., 430.

29 Ibid., 570–71.

alone is legally insufficient to state a claim. And to make matters worse, how should we think about the risk of error in these cases: is it more costly to err by condemning a firm for monopolizing, to intervene perhaps by breaking the firm up, or demanding that it make its technology available as a quasi-public utility (i.e., to commit a Type 1 error – a false positive); or is it more costly to err by failing to punish something that is actually anticompetitive (i.e., to commit a Type 2 error – a false negative)? Underlying this debate is an empirical question – which type of error tends to occur more frequently, and how quickly can it be corrected (either by the market or by regulatory intervention) when it does arise?

IV. Can Competition Do the Job?

28. Modern market economies have placed their eggs in the competition basket, in the hopes of achieving the healthiest and most productive markets possible. Indeed, in a rhetorical burst, Justice Thurgood Marshall once said that "[a] titrust laws in general, and the Sherman Act in particular, are the Magna Carta of free enterprise".[30] And, reflecting the broader view of antitrust that prevailed as late as the 1970s, he explained that analogy as follows:

> "[The antitrust laws] are as important to the preservation of economic freedom and our free-enterprise system as the Bill of Rights is to the protection of our fundamental personal freedoms. And the freedom guaranteed each and every business, no matter how small, is the freedom to compete – to assert with vigor, imagination, devotion, and ingenuity whatever economic muscle it can muster. Implicit in such freedom is the notion that it cannot be foreclosed with respect to one sector of the economy because certain private citizens or groups believe that such foreclosure might promote greater competition in a more important sector of the economy".[31]

29. This reflects the broader purposes of antitrust that the Court recognized until the Chicago School rethinking took place, beginning with *Continental T.V., Inc. v. GTE Sylvania Inc.*, 433 U.S. 36 (1977) and continuing to the present day. But broad or narrow, there are three questions that proponents of competition must answer: when should firms be left entirely free to choose their strategies on the market? What restrictions on that autonomy can be imposed that will protect the competitive process? What alternatives to competition are available if the cost or ineffectiveness of antitrust enforcement seems prohibitive?

30. Taking these inquiries in turn, the first issue relates to such fundamental notions as freedom of contract and personal autonomy. If a person – call her Alpha – decides to open up a restaurant in Chicago, she is entitled to decide what theme the restaurant will have, how it will be decorated, whether to sign up with an

---

30 *United States v. Topco Associates, Inc.*, 405 U.S. 596, 610 (1972).

31 Ibid.

online booking service, from whom she wants to order supplies, and so on. Normally, there is no need whatsoever for antitrust intervention in her business, unless she is foolish enough to enter into an agreement with other restaurants in the area for a fixed wage scale for the cooks, waitstaff, and hosts. But we can assume that she has been advised not to take such a step. At a broader level, we might ask whether it is possible to identify a set of characteristics for firms that require no intervention at all from competition law. (This is just the exercise in which many competition law agencies engage when they issue enforcement guidelines, and as part of those guidelines they describe "safe harbors" where firms can be assured that their actions will fall within permissible limits.)

31. Experience has shown that there are several situations where minimal, or even non-existent, intervention is needed. In these situations, the natural competitive process will work as it should. Consumers will have the benefits of efficiently low prices and a variety of options, there will be no incentive to engage in impermissibly exclusionary conduct, and the market will hum along. Here are some such situations:

- The firms in a defined product and geographic market, taken as a whole, have a low enough market share that it is reasonable to conclude that their collective market power is insignificant. One could argue about the best place to put that threshold, but 10 percent seems reasonable, if not conservative.

- Any effective competition is going to have some exclusionary effect. If Alpha's restaurant serves excellent food and has a cheerful and efficient waitstaff, her competitor down the street, Beta, may lose business. If the difference is great enough, Beta may even go out of business. Literally, then, Alpha engaged in a practice that wound up by excluding Beta from the market. But the outcome of tough competition is not what antitrust law means by "exclusionary effects." The classic list of exclusionary acts i.e., tying arrangements, refusals to deal, group boycotts, bundling, predation of various kinds, includes only practices that are somehow outside the boundaries of fair business behavior. With that in mind, this part of the safe harbor would include the requirement that any exclusionary effect that results from the practices used occurs only because of consumer choice. It would not occur because consumers are somehow forced through an exclusionary device to choose the firm's product or services.

- Another area in which nonintervention may be all that is necessary is more controversial. It covers markets that are changing so rapidly that any attempt at competition law enforcement would automatically be outdated. As Judge Richard Posner put it in 2001,

  > "[t]he mismatch between law time and new-economy real time is troubling in two respects. First, an antitrust case (…) may drag on

for so long relative to the changing conditions of the industry as to become irrelevant, ineffectual. (…) Second, even if the case is not made obsolete by passage of time, its pendency may cast a pall over parties to and affected by the litigation, making investment riskier and complicating business planning".[32]

In that situation, correction of any deviations from the competitive norm may be more likely to be fixed by the market than by any intervention.

- Finally, there may be vigorous international competition over which the existing market participants have no control. Indeed, in today's world, global competition can arise overnight from cyberspace – think, for instance, of artificial intelligence models that are being developed everywhere, launched everywhere, and are almost entirely outside the realm of geographic restrictions.

32. The next question to consider is whether there are any situations in which it is better simply to give up on competition and acquiesce in monopoly. For years, the answer would have been yes, and perhaps that is still the case (though likely not to the same degree, and not in the same markets).

    - The first example is one that even Senator Sherman would have recognized: natural monopolies. The classic example is the firm whose marginal costs go down with greater quantities, and relative to market demand that never stops. People used to point to electric utilities, for example, which required huge capital expenditures to construct generating plants and distribution networks. Duplicating those facilities was not an efficient response, and so what happened instead is that the utilities were regulated by administrative bodies. Things have changed now in the electric market, but a modified version of the theory may still have some life. Network effects may result in something like a natural monopoly in the big internet businesses (think of Meta and Alphabet), even though entry is technically quite open in that sector. The expected duration of a monopoly may also influence the assessment of whether intervention is possible or desirable, though durational predictions can be wildly off, and path-dependence means that yesterday's monopoly power may be leveraged into the future more effectively than one might think at first glance.

    - A true patent monopoly (i.e., one in which not only is the product or process patented, but it has no economic substitutes in the market) has always been understood to lie beyond the reach of competition laws. But even that statement requires some qualification. Standard essential patents may be subject to compulsory licensing regimes requiring fair, reasonable, and nondiscriminatory (FRAND) terms. There is also a

32 R. A. Posner, Antitrust in the New Economy, *Antitrust Law J*ournal 68, No. 3, (2001): 925–43, at 939.

residual interest (especially outside the United States) in monopolies held by firms that are "essential facilities." Whether that label adds any analytical heft to the normal rules for monopolies is a topic beyond the scope of this paper, but at a minimum, section 2 analysis would apply.

33. Another question for the situations in which normal competition does not seem to be possible is whether there are aspects of the competitive regime that should be replicated somehow, via administrative regulation or litigation. Which is worse: leaving alone a firm that meets the *Alcoa* 90 percent market-share threshold; bringing a lawsuit against it in which the only meaningful remedy would be either dismemberment of the firm or a court order requiring certain business practices; or a full-blown administrative remedy, placing the firm under the supervision of either the competition enforcement authority or a sectoral agency and giving up on the market altogether? None of those options is attractive. It is no accident that the last time the United States tried divestiture was 40 years ago, in the 1982 Modified Final Judgment that terminated the AT&T litigation.[33] That is not because the government was unaware of other monopolists; it is because the remedy toolbox has not proven to be up to the task.

V. Conclusion

34. The question "Why Competition?" proves to be much easier to answer than the follow-up inquiry is – "How to achieve competition?" That is partly because our expectations of competition have evolved over the last 135 years – hardly surprising, given the changes in both the US and the global economy over that period. It is also partly because of the tensions we observe: we want firms to compete vigorously, but we do not want them to engage in the "wrong" kind of exclusionary behavior. And we do not want the end result of the competitive process to be the elimination of all competitors save the surviving monopolist. One way that happens is through the exit of firms that cannot stand the competitive heat. Another way – perhaps more significant in today's economy – is through mergers and acquisitions. If we care about tomorrow's competition, we may wish to be more wary of transactions that leave us with an oligopolistic market structure of three, four or five survivors. The antitrust laws are notoriously unable to deal with oligopolies, and as we have seen, they are not so great with monopolies either. Although, as the Supreme Court likes to remind us, the antitrust laws protect competition, not competitors, the converse is also important: there will be no competition without competitors.

35. The challenge for the future will be to find agile ways to address new forms of market power, and to the greatest extent possible, continue to enjoy the benefits of competition. It won't be easy.

---

33 See *United States v. American Telephone & Telegraph Co.*, 552 F. Supp. 131 (D.D.C. 1983).

The Goals of Competition Law: Is "Consumer Welfare" Really Better Defined Than "Competition as Such"?

FLORIAN WAGNER-VON PAPP*
Helmut Schmidt University
University of the Federal Armed Forces in Hamburg (HSU)

1. The debate about the goals of competition law is once again high on the agenda on both sides of the Atlantic. Of course, the controversy never really went away completely ever since the debates in the run-up to the Sherman Act some 135 years ago,[1] but there are ebbs and flows. In the US, there is a trend away from the Chicago School's exclusive focus on total welfare (mislabeled as "consumer welfare") towards a more "Neo-Brandeisian" framework, at least in academia and at the level of the antitrust authorities.[2] In the EU, the original ordoliberal process-oriented concept of "competition as such" based

---

* This contribution is dedicated to my academic teacher and mentor, Wernhard Möschel, who passed away on Feb. 9, 2024, and whose views on the concept of competition and its relationship to efficiencies and consumer welfare (*see, e.g.*, the works cited in notes 4, 5, and 19) have heavily influenced my own. I would like to thank Giorgio Monti, Stavros Makris, and Wouter Wils for helpful comments.

1 *See, e.g.*, Charles A. Boston, *The Spirit behind the Sherman Anti-Trust Law*, 21 YALE L.J. 341 (1912); Robert H. Bork, Legislative Intent and the Policy of the Sherman Act, 9 J. L. & ECON. 7 (1966); Harvey J. Goldschmid, H. Michael Mann & J. Fred Weston (eds), INDUSTRIAL CONCENTRATION: THE NEW LEARNING (Little Brown and Company 1974); Christopher Grandy, *Original Intent and the Sherman Antitrust Act: A Re-examination of the Consumer-Welfare Hypothesis*, 53 J. ECON. HIST. 359 (1993); ROBERT PITOFSKI, HOW THE CHICAGO SCHOOL OVERSHOT THE MARK (Oxford Univ. Press 2008); for an extensive discussion from a European angle Ioannis Lianos, *Some Reflections on the Question of the Goals of EU Competition Law*, *in* 1 HANDBOOK ON EUROPEAN COMPETITION LAW: SUBSTANTIVE ASPECTS (Ioannis Lianos & Damien Geradin eds., Edward Elgar 2013); see also the contributions *in* ECONOMIC THEORY AND COMPETITION LAW (Josef Drexl, Laurence Idot & Joël Monéger eds., Edward Elgar 2009).

2 *See, e.g.*, Tim Wu, *The Utah Statement: Reviving Antimonopoly Traditions for the Era of Big Tech*, MEDIUM (Nov. 18, 2019), https://onezero.medium.com/the-utah-statement-reviving-antimonopoly-traditions-for-the-era-of-big-tech-e6be198012d7.

on an individual freedom to compete[3] was challenged by DG IV/Competition at the end of the 1990s, who preferred an effects-based, so-called "more economic" approach,[4] and the high tide of this effects-based approached has now reached the Court of Justice, influencing its recent judgments especially on abuses by undertakings in dominant positions. At the same time, however, the Commission now realizes that it may have bitten off more than it can chew and is trying to row back with a Policy Brief,[5] the revision of the Priority Paper,[6] and the plans for Article 102 TFEU Guidelines. Commission officials take great pains to emphasize that the Commission does not want to distance itself from the effects-based approach, and only wants to make it more "dynamic and workable,"[7] "taking into account administrability, legal certainty and the risk of false positives and negatives."[8] Overall, however, it becomes clear that the Commission (as I will argue: rightly) considers the effects-based approach actually not to be the more economically sensible approach and that the competitive process (under certain circumstances including competition from less efficient competitors) should play a greater role, possibly even in a framework with a pluralistic set of goals. The Policy Brief quotes Vice President and Competition Commissioner Margrethe Vestager's statement that "[E]U competition policy is able to pursue multiple goals, such as fairness and level-playing field, market integration, preserving competitive processes, consumer welfare, efficiency and innovation, and ultimately plurality and democracy."[9] It would appear that the emphasis on the "effects-based approach" in the titles[10] of the contribu-

3 For a recent extensive qualitative and quantitative analysis, see ANSELM KÜSTERS, THE MAKING AND UNMAKING OF ORDOLIBERAL LANGUAGE (Vittorio Klostermann 2023); similarly, Wernhard Möschel, *The Proper Scope of Government Viewed from an Ordoliberal Perspective: The Example of Competition Policy*, 157 J. INST. THEORETICAL ECON. 3 (2001) considers the founding treaties of the European Community to reflect the ordoliberal approach. Wouter Wils's description of the Treaties' concept of undistorted competition (Wouter P.J. Wils, *The Judgment of the EU General Court in Intel and the so-called 'more economic approach' to abuse of dominance*, 37 WORLD COMPETITION 405 (2014)) perfectly describes the essence of the ordoliberal approach (without explicitly attributing it to ordoliberalism). Pinar Akman denies the ordoliberal influence on the basis that the drafters frequently mentioned efficiency and consumer welfare (PINAR AKMAN, THE CONCEPT OF ABUSE IN EU COMPETITION LAW 49 (Hart Publishing 2015); Pinar Akman & Hussein Kassim, *Myth and Myth-Making in the European Union: The Institutionalization and Interpretation of EU Competition Policy*, 48 J. COMMON MKT. STUD. 111 (2010)); however, no-one denies that Walter Eucken, the foremost economist of the ordoliberal Freiburg School, also considered efficiency to be important – it is just that efficiency is generally one of the desirable *effects* of protecting competition, and not the goal of antitrust (see Peter Behrens, *The Ordoliberal Concept of Abuse of a Dominant Position and its impact on Article 102 TFEU*, *in* ABUSIVE PRACTICES IN COMPETITION LAW 5, 22–23 (Fabiana di Porto & Rupprecht Podszun, eds., Edward Elgar 218)).

4 For a critical discussion from an ordoliberal perspective *see, e.g.*, WERNHARD MÖSCHEL, WIRTSCHAFTSRECHT IM WANDEL 124–134 (Nomos 2011); see also Wils, *supra* note 3; Jürgen Basedow, *Konsumentenwohlfahrt und Effizienz – Neue Leitbilder der Wettbewerbspolitik*, 57 WIRTSCHAFT UND WETTBEWERB 712 (2007).

5 Linsey McCallum et al., *A Dynamic and Workable Effects-Based Approach to Abuse of Dominance*, COMPETITION POL'Y BRIEF No. 1/2003 (Mar. 2023).

6 European Commission – Guidance on the Commission's enforcement priorities in applying Article 82 of the EC Treaty to abusive exclusionary conduct by dominant undertakings, 2023, O.J. (C 116) 1.

7 McCallum et al., *supra* note 5.

8 Massimiliano Kadar & Johannes Holzwarth, *Effects-Based Approach? Effects-Based Approach! The European Commission's "Article 102 Package"*, NEUE ZEITSCHRIFT FÜR KARTELLRECHT 333 (2023).

9 See McCallum et al., *supra* note 5, at 1, quoting EVP Margrethe Vestager, Keynote Speech, *A Principles Based approach to Competition Policy*, (Competition Law Tuesdays, Oct. 22, 2022); *see also*, European Commission, *supra* note 6, at 1, ¶ 1, noting that the competition rules are "instrumental in protecting the competitive process," contribute "to a level playing field where markets serve consumers" and "contribute to achieving objectives that go beyond consumer welfare, such as plurality in a democratic society."

10 See McCallum et al., *supra* note 5 and Kadar & Holzwarth, *supra* note 8.

tions accompanying the reform agenda is primarily due to the recognition by Sir Humphrey Appleby that one should "always dispose of the difficult bit in the title. It does less harm there than in the text."[11]

I. Relationship between Competition and Consumer Welfare

2. A fundamental question when it comes to the question of the goal(s) of competition law is the relationship between the competitive process on the hand and welfare or efficiency on the other. There are two extreme positions.

3. At one end of the spectrum is the view that consumer welfare is the exclusive goal of antitrust law.[12] Proponents either equate competition with efficiency and consumer welfare or consider competition at best as one of many interchangeable methods to achieve this goal. Over the past four decades, this view was predominant in the US antitrust debate,[13] and gained ground in the EU in the guise of the "more economic approach" since the late 1990s.

4. At the opposite end of the spectrum lies the ordoliberal approach.[14] It is a liberal approach in the sense of valuing *libertas*, freedom, as such: competition is a value in itself, instead of being merely instrumental to achieving efficiency or consumer welfare (or indeed any other outcome), because it allows individuals to exercise their freedom to compete[15] – just like other fundamental rights such as free speech are valued as such and not only as a means to a particular end. The ordoliberal approach is based on Kantian philosophy, in stark contrast to the utilitarian, effects-based and therefore outcome-oriented approach of the Chicago School.

5. Outside the ordoliberal school, libertarians influenced by Austrian economics have tried to take this approach to the extreme: in their view, *any* interference with markets, including antitrust intervention, is impermissible, with the result that *laissez-faire* liberalism is considered to be the truest form of liberalism.[16] However, this approach is only seemingly more

---

11 "Yes Minister," Episode 1: Open Government, at 17:20.

12 Robert H. Bork, The Antitrust Paradox: A Policy at War with Itself 81–89, 405 (The Free Press, 1978) (1993), and throughout the book.

13 See *id.*, in addition, *e.g.*, Richard A. Posner, Antitrust Law 29 (Univ. Chicago Press 2nd ed. 1976) (2001) ("Efficiency is the ultimate goal of antitrust [...]"); Lawrence H. Summers, *Competition in the New Economy*, 69 Antitrust L.J. 353, 358 (2001) ("[T]he goal is efficiency, not competition. The ultimate goal is that there be efficiency"); Address by William J. Kolasky, *Conglomerate Mergers and Range Effects: It's a long way from Chicago to Brussels,* (George Mason University Symposium, Nov. 9, 2001), https://www.justice.gov/atr/speech/conglomerate-mergers-and-range-effects-its-long-way-chicago-brussels.

14 For a good introduction in English see Möschel, *supra* note 3, at 157.

15 *See, e.g.*, Ernst-Joachim Mestmäcker & Heike Schweitzer, Europäisches Wettbewerbsrecht 67–68, § 3 ¶¶ 9–12 (C.H. Beck, 3rd ed. 2014); Möschel, *supra* note 4, at 103, 119, 131.

16 For this extreme position see Edwin S. Rockefeller, The Antitrust Religion (Cato Institute 2007); Dominick T. Armentano, Antitrust: The Case for Repeal (Ludwig von Mises Institute, rev. 2nd ed. 1999).

consistent in its quest to protect freedom. Its mistake is to overlook the "paradox of freedom."

6. The paradox of freedom is a shorthand for the endogeneity problem of freedom, namely that freedom has a well-known tendency to cannibalize itself. The paradox of freedom is, according to Karl Popper, "a paradox that can be expressed by saying that unlimited freedom leads to its opposite, since without its protection and restriction by law, freedom must lead to a tyranny of the strong over the weak."[17] Applying this insight to competition law, Wernhard Möschel posited: "A further condition [for maintaining a system of freedom of trade and competition] is the protection of the individual's freedom to participate, the attempt to protect market rationality against its endogenous perversion: market participants leave the legitimizing basis of their freedom when the effects of their free actions destroy the very conditions necessary for the exercise of these freedoms."[18] Contrary to the extreme libertarian, Austrian view, *laissez-faire* liberalism does not maximize *overall* freedom: it maximizes freedom for the strongest, but at the price of denying an equal freedom to other market participants, namely the freedom to compete and to participate in the market on equal terms.

7. The individual's freedom to compete must be protected not only from restrictions imposed by the state, but also from restrictions imposed by those who, having exercised their freedom to compete, have achieved market power and now exercise it to the detriment of others.[19] This view is captured in Senator Sherman's famous statement that "[i]f we will not endure a King as a political power we should not endure a King over the production, transportation, and sale of the necessaries of life. If we would not submit to an emperor we should not submit to an autocrat of trade with power to prevent competition and to fix the price of any commodity."[20]

---

17 Karl Popper, The Open Society and Its Enemies, Vol. 2: Hegel and Marx 48 (Routledge 1945) (1995) with endnote 41 to Chapter Twelve, tracing the statement of the paradox back to Plato and Rousseau (Jean-Jacques Rousseau, Du Contrat Social (1762) Livre Premier, Chapitre VIII: "[I]l faut bien distinguer la liberté naturelle qui n'a pour bornes que les forces de l'individu, de la liberté civile qui est limitée par la volonté général") and crediting Immanuel Kant with its resolution, namely that freedom is to be protected only insofar as it does not interfere with an equal degree of freedom of all (Immanuel Kant, *Die Metaphysik der Sitten*, in 6 Kants Werke 210, 230 (Königlich Preußische Akademie der Wissenschaften, ed., 2nd ed. 1798) (1914), Einleitung in die Rechtslehre § C: "Eine jede Handlung ist recht, die oder nach deren Maxime die Freiheit der Willkür eines jeden mit jedermanns Freiheit nach einem allgemeinen Gesetze zusammen bestehen kann.").

18 Wernhard Möschel, Recht der Wettbewerbsbeschränkungen 3, ¶ 2 (Carl Heymanns 1983) (my translation); see also Möschel, *supra* note 4, at 104. Similarly, Aaron Edlin & Joseph Farrell, *Freedom to Trade and the Competitive Process*, *in* 1 The Oxford Handbook of International Antitrust Economics 298, 299 n6 (Roger D. Blair & D. Daniel Sokol eds., Oxford Univ. Press 2015), call it "a shallow paradox to observe that laws protecting freedom can take the form of prohibitions." See also the discussion of the freedom of contract in a competitive order by Walter Eucken, *Die Wettbewerbsordnung und ihre Verwirklichung*, 2 ORDO 1, 56–57 (1949); *id.*, Grundsätze der Wirtschaftspolitik 266–267, 276–279 (Edith Eucken & K. Paul Hensel eds., JCB Mohr 6th ed. 1990).

19 Eucken, *supra* note 18, at 38–39.

20 21 Cong. Rec. 2457 (Mar. 21, 1890).

8. Given the paradox of freedom, it is necessary to restrict the freedom of those with market power to maximize freedom overall. As with other fundamental rights, the freedom to compete is to be protected only "insofar as it does not interfere with an equal degree of freedom of all."[21] Franz Böhm, one of the founding fathers of ordoliberalism, stated in the parliamentary debates that led up to the German Act against Restraints of Competition that: "Those who have power have no right to be free, and those who want to be free should have no power, at least no typical and widespread power that makes them masters of fate over any given number of individuals' professional opportunities."[22] The resolution of the paradox of freedom is the essence of the dominant undertaking's "special responsibility not to allow its behaviour to impair genuine, undistorted competition on the internal market:"[23] with great power comes special responsibility.

9. When ordoliberals seek to protect the freedom to compete "on equal terms," equality is to be understood as equality *of opportunity*, not equality *of outcomes*. This is the basic misunderstanding of those who believe that "we [the US] protect competition, you [the EU] protect competitors."[24] European competition law – from an ordoliberal perspective – seeks to keep access to market opportunities open for all. This does not mean that those who fail to succeed in the marketplace, despite having had an equal opportunity to compete, have a right to remain in the market: "Competition on the merits may, by definition, lead to the departure from the market or the marginalization of competitors that are less efficient and so less attractive to consumers from the point of view of, among other things, price, choice, quality or innovation."[25]

---

21 Kant, *supra* note 17.

22 Franz Böhm, *Protocol of the 76th meeting of the 2nd German Bundestag*, 4217(C) (Mar. 24, 1955), https://dserver.bundestag.de/btp/02/02076.pdf (in the German original: "Wer Macht hat, der hat keinen Anspruch darauf, frei zu sein, und wer frei sein will, der sollte keine Macht haben, wenigstens keine typische und weit ausgebreitete Macht, die ihn zum Herrn des Schicksals über soundso viele Berufschancen von Individuen erhebt"; my translation).

23 Consistent case law since Judgment of the Court of Justice, Nov. 9, 1983, Case 322/81, Nederlandsche Banden-Industrie-Michelin v. Eur. Comm'n, ECLI:EU:C:1983:313, ¶ 57, *see, e.g.*, Judgment of the Court of Justice (Grand Chamber) of Sept. 6, 2017, Case C-413/14 P, Intel Corp. v. Eur. Comm'n, ECLI:EU:C:2017:632, ¶ 135; Judgment of the Court of Justice, Jan. 19. 2023, Case C-680/20, Unilever Italia Mkt Operations Srl v. Autorita Garante della Concorrenza e del Mercato, ECLI:EU:C:2023:33, ¶ 28.

24 This was the title of an excellent article by Eleanor M. Fox in 26 WORLD COMPETITION 149 (2003); see also Florian Wagner-von Papp, *Comparative Antitrust Federalism and the Error-Cost-Framework or: Rhetoric and Reality: You Protect Competitors, We Protect Competition – Except When We Protect Competitors*, *in* WILLIAM E. KOVACIC: AN ANTITRUST TRIBUTE, LIBER AMICORUM VOL. II, 23, 30 (Nicolas Charbit & Elisa Ramundo eds., Institute of Competition Law 2014).

25 Judgment of the Court of Justice, March 27, 2012, Case C-209/10, Post Danmark v. Eur. Comm'n, ECLI:EU:C:2012:172, ¶ 22, see Wessel Geursen, *The EU Court of Justice endorses an effects-based approach on the assessment of low pricing policy under Article 102 TFEU (Post Danmark)*, E-COMPETITIONS Mar. 2012, art. No. 57395. Similarly, MESTMÄCKER & SCHWEITZER, *supra* note 15, at § 3, ¶ 9; MÖSCHEL, *supra* note 4, at 125.

II. Is an Equal Claim to the Freedom to Compete "Nonsense on Stilts"?

10. From a utilitarian perspective, the freedom to compete, like other natural and imprescriptible rights, is likely to appear – in the words of Jeremy Bentham – as "nonsense upon stilts."[26] Similarly, proponents of the effects-based approach have ridiculed "competition on the merits," "competition as such," "freedom to compete," and the "special responsibility of the dominant undertaking" as vacuous concepts.

11. There is a kernel of truth in this: invoking these concepts, without more, rarely allows an unambiguous disposition of a case. When is an action by a dominant undertaking "competition on the merits" and when is it abusive? Whose freedom is to be attributed more weight when deciding whether suppliers may restrict their distributors' conduct – the suppliers' freedom to structure the distribution of their products as they see fit or the distributors' freedom to determine the way in which they market the goods?

12. Deciding a case requires a balancing of the rights of various market participants, and the exact point where the exercise of a freedom is no longer compatible with "an equal degree of freedom for all" is impossible to pinpoint without difficult value judgments. The disposition of a case regularly depends on questions of degree. For example, we may give more weight to the suppliers' freedom to structure the distribution system as they see fit where distributors have a realistic choice between different suppliers, that is, where there is competition on the upstream market, while we may give more weight to the distributors' freedom not to be restricted in their own activity where they are facing a supplier with substantial market power. This need for a balancing of competing claims to the exercise of freedoms, however, is hardly unique to competition law: it is necessary in nearly all legal disputes.[27]

III. Is the Effects-Based and (Allegedly) "More Economic" Approach the Solution?

13. Proponents of an effects-based, allegedly "more economic" approach ridicule the rights-based approach as unscientific and vague. In its place, the effects-based approach is lauded as bringing scientific rigor into antitrust.

---

26 Jeremy Bentham, *Anarchical Fallacies, in* 2 The Works of Jeremy Bentham 501 (John Bowring ed., William Tait 1843), facsimile version available at: https://oll.libertyfund.org/titles/bowring-the-works-of-jeremy-bentham-vol-2. For a nuanced discussion of Bentham's views, see Philip Schofield, *Jeremy Bentham's "Nonsense on Stilts"*, 15 Utilitas 1 (2003).

27 Mestmäcker & Schweitzer, *supra* note 15, at § 3, ¶ 9.

14. There are, however, several problems with the more economic approach. The first is a conceptual one. In principle, the economic approach seems to share the methodological individualism of the rights-based approach. It is the individual's utility that lies at the heart of the analysis, and preferences are subjective, need not be of a pecuniary nature, may possibly even be altruistic or other-regarding, and include preferences about the present and future states of the world. Interpersonal utility comparisons are impermissible because there can only be an ordinal ranking of preferences, not a cardinal quantification. Up to this point, each individual is assessed purely on the basis of their own preferences. This is compatible with a rights-based approach, but it does not allow statements about the aggregate. Welfare theory overcomes this obstacle by relying on preferences revealed in the marketplace, on the choices actually made by the market participants, assuming they rationally maximize their utility and generally assuming perfectly competitive (partial) markets to achieve a general equilibrium. This allows statements about the aggregate, but it is no longer compatible with a rights-based approach. According to welfare theory, these revealed preferences should be satisfied efficiently, in terms of productive efficiency (using a minimum of inputs to achieve a given level of output or alternatively achieving a maximum level of output by using a given amount of input), allocative efficiency (an efficient distribution so that resources move to those who value them most highly), and dynamic efficiency (such as efficient investments and technological progress).

15. If all present and future states of the world and preferences were known, competition would be a tremendously wasteful way to achieve consumer welfare.[28] A planned economy with an omniscient and benevolent economist's king (replacing Plato's philosopher's king) at its helm would achieve the result with much less friction. I do not, however, know any living economists who think such a centrally planned economy would be either feasible or desirable. The suggestion is not meant to be a realistic option but an *argumentum ad absurdum*: if the economics of a market were as calculable on the basis of available data as the effects-based approach suggests, central planning should not be an impossible task. In reality, central planning is not feasible because the centralization of dispersed knowledge creates insurmountable obstacles.[29] The closest equivalent to an attempt to anticipate society's future preferences and demand in real life, namely communist five-year plans, are not generally considered to have been a particularly successful experiment. Nor would such a calculus, even if it were feasible, be desirable – at least not from a rights-based perspective. If a pre-definition of future preferences were possible,

---

28 Friedrich August von Hayek, *Competition as a Discovery Procedure*, *in* THE ESSENCE OF HAYEK 254 (Chiaki Nishiyama & Kurt R. Leube eds., Hoover Institution Press repr't. 1984).

29 Friedrich August von Hayek, *The Use of Knowledge in Society*, *in* THE ESSENCE OF HAYEK 211 (Chiaki Nishiyama & Kurt R. Leube eds., Hoover Institution Press repr't. 1984); *id.*, *The Pretence of Knowledge*, (Nobel Memorial Prize lecture, Dec. 11, 1974), https://www.nobelprize.org/prizes/economic-sciences/1974/hayek/lecture/; *id.*, *Competition as a Discovery Procedure*, *supra* note 28).

there would not be any individual freedom; if there is individual freedom, the pre-definition of future preferences and states of the world is impossible.

16. Accordingly, even the most hardened proponents of the total welfare approach do not suggest doing the welfare calculus *ab ovo*. Instead, they – just like proponents of the rights-based approach – generally rely on competition: "Efficiency is the ultimate goal of antitrust, *but competition a mediate goal that will often be close enough to the ultimate goal to allow the courts to look no further.*"[30] Only once the process of competition is restricted do they reach for the total welfare yardstick to determine whether the restriction is an unreasonable (inefficient) one. While this may substantially reduce the information requirements, the difficulties in principle remain. A true calculation would still require information about the current and future states of the world and the preferences of its inhabitants, and its complexity exceeds the capabilities of any central planner.

17. Instead, any "effects-based calculation" can only be an approximation on the basis of the facts that happen to be available. Sometimes, this is the only viable option (even for those who prefer a rights-based, process-oriented concept of competition), for example, when in a private damages claim the quantum has to be calculated on the basis of a counterfactual analysis, or when an abuse of a dominant position is claimed to lie in the price level (be it an exclusionary abuse in the form of predatory prices or an exploitative abuse in the form of excessive prices). The experience with these outcome-oriented calculations has not generally been one to inspire much confidence. Let us take the quantification of a damages claim as an example. The uncertainties in this calculation are legendary. Estimates of expert witnesses frequently range from damages of zero (indeed, listening to defendants' expert witnesses one might occasionally be tempted to wish that all industries were cartelized) to damages in the 25-45 percent region – in the same case, on the basis of largely the same facts. Nor is it only the parties' strategic interests that result in this wide range; competition authorities are not keen on calculating the quantum of damages, either, and court-appointed experts also get to a wide range of possible counterfactuals.[31] This wide range of estimates in cartel damages cases is all the more astonishing because the analysis is *backward*-looking: the analysis has the distinct advantage that actual market developments in the relevant timeframe are known. If the analysis of *past* competitive developments is difficult, one would expect the prediction of the effects of future conduct to be even more difficult. After all, "predictions are difficult, especially

30 POSNER, *supra* note 13, at 29.

31 See also the analysis of the Joint Executive Committee, a historical railroad cartel which (because it was legal at the time) left very detailed records. On the one hand, Robert H. Porter, *A Study of Cartel Stability: The Joint Executive Committee, 1880–1886*, 14 BELL J. ECON. 301, 309–310 (1983), finds conduct that approximated "Cournot behavior in cooperative periods;" on the other hand, Glenn Ellison, *Theories of Cartel Stability and the Joint Executive Committee*, 25 RAND J. ECON. 37, 56 (1994), finds, on the same set of data, "prices much closer to the monopoly level."

about the future."[32] And yet, some economists display greater confidence in predicting future competitive effects of conduct than in assessing the effects of conduct in the past; a cynic might add that they share this predilection for predictions about the future with psychics.

IV. Dynamic Efficiency in Particular

18. As Hayek stated 50 years ago, "in economics and other disciplines that deal with essentially complex phenomena, the aspects of the events to be accounted for about which we can get quantitative data are necessarily limited and may not include the important ones. […] [I]n the social sciences *often that is treated as important which happens to be accessible to measurement.*"[33] While this is already a problem regarding productive and allocative efficiencies, the impact of this problem increases exponentially when it comes to dynamic efficiencies. Productive and allocative efficiencies in a static setting are at least to some extent predetermined by the market structure and observable conduct. Where an undertaking is productively or allocatively inefficient, it will not in the long run survive competition. Data on production and distribution costs is accessible, allocative inefficiencies may be approximated by the market structure and the elasticities of demand and supply (and off-set by cost advantages, e.g., deriving from efficiencies of scale or scope).

19. Dynamic efficiencies, in particular innovation, are not similarly predetermined. The size of effects based on innovation often exceeds by magnitudes the effects of cutting the costs of production on the basis of existing technologies and the effects of a more efficient allocation of existing products.[34] The reason why dynamic efficiencies hardly play any role in most antitrust assessments is not that they are unimportant. On the contrary, there is widespread consensus that the effects of innovation are the greatest driver of both competition and welfare. Marginal improvements in productive and allocative efficiencies can be important, but real advances in the welfare of societies generally depend on innovation. The reason why dynamic efficiency is not often factored into the analysis is that the data for calculating the dynamic efficiency effects are not "accessible to measurement."

20. David Teece has identified the problem of the neglect of dynamic efficiencies with great clarity.[35] He considers the difficulties in assessing dynamic efficiencies to split those who recognize the problem into two camps: optimists, who

32 The attribution of this quotation is uncertain; it has been variously attributed to Niels Bohr, Samuel Goodwyn, Mark Twain, and Yogi Berra; it appears to have Danish origins.

33 von Hayek, *supra* note 29. Bork, *supra* note 12, at 127 agrees: "Economists … will measure what is susceptible of measurement and will tend to forget what is not, though what is forgotten may be far more important than what is measured."

34 *See, e.g.*, Eleanor M. Fox, *The Efficiency Paradox*, *in* How the Chicago School Overshot the Mark 77, 78 (Oxford Univ. Press 2008).

35 David J. Teece, *The Dynamic Competition Paradigm: Insights and Implications*, Colum. Bus. L. Rev. 373 (2023) with further references at 381–382 in n20. *See also*, Möschel, *supra* note 4, at 130.

"believe that the right frameworks and tools coupled with the investigative powers of regulators can lead to better insights if not predictions" and pessimists, who "are skeptical about how much we can understand about markets and business evolution because of deep uncertainty and the complexity of interactions in the economy."[36] His own "optimistic" response is to identify factors that allow the assessment of (ordinary and dynamic) "capabilities" derived from strategic management theory and evolutionary as well as complexity economics in order to enable a fact-based assessment of dynamic efficiencies.[37] The tendency of his conclusions is placing "minimal weight on traditional structural criteria,"[38] a recommendation to look forward instead of challenging past conduct "unless that conduct continues to threaten the innovation that is capable of disciplining it in the future,"[39] and pursuing a "long-run consumer welfare standard," for which "[c]ultivating robust and innovative and competitive ecosystems is a good proxy."[40]

21. While I agree with Teece's analysis in so far as it points out the glaring omission of dynamic efficiencies in an effects-based approach, my conclusions are very different. This is partly because, as a gloomy German, I fall into Teece's camp of complexity pessimists (and consider myself in excellent company with Friedrich August von Hayek,[41] Ernst-Joachim Mestmäcker and Heike Schweitzer,[42] Wernhard Möschel,[43] Peter Behrens,[44] Jürgen Basedow,[45] Erich Hoppmann,[46] and implicitly in their Ordo idea Franz Böhm,[47] and Walter Eucken,[48] to name but a few from my Teutonic bubble, but also authors from outside this bubble, such as Eleanor M. Fox,[49] Wouter Wils,[50] Joseph F. Brodley,[51] or Harry S. Gerla[52] – not to mention the Neo-Brandeisians). The outcomes in a dynamic setting depend on a wide variety of factors, future

36 Teece, *supra* note 35, at 389.

37 *Id.* at 389, 400 et seq.

38 *Id.* at 387.

39 *Id.* at 392.

40 *Id.* at 388

41 von Hayek, *supra* note 29.

42 Mestmäcker & Schweitzer, *supra* note 15, at § 3.

43 Möschel, *supra* note 4, at 130.

44 Behrens, *supra* note 3.

45 Basedow, *supra* note 4.

46 Erich Hoppmann, *Kulturelle Evolution und ökonomische Effizienz*, *in* Festschrift für Ernst-Joachim Mestmäcker zum siebzigsten Geburtstag (Ulrich Immenga, Wernhard Möschel & Dieter Reuter eds., Nomos 1996) 177; *id.*, *Workable Competition als wettbewerbspolitisches Konzept*, *in* Theoretisch und institutionelle Grundlagen der Wirtschaftspolitik: Theodor Wessels zum 65. Geburtstag 145, 148 (Hans Besters ed., Duncker & Humblodt 1967).

47 Cf. Franz Böhm, Wettbewerb und Monopolkampf 127 (Carl Heymanns 1933).

48 Eucken, Grundsätze, *supra* note 18, at 241.

49 Fox, *supra* note 34, Fox, *supra* note 24, and Eleanor M. Fox & Lawrence A. Sullivan, *Antitrust – Retrospective and Prospective: Where Are We Coming From? Where Are We Going?* 62 N.Y.U. L. Rev. 936 (1987).

50 Wils, *supra* note 3.

51 Joseph F. Brodley, *The Economic Goals of Antitrust: Efficiency, Consumer Welfare, and Technological Progress*, 62 N.Y.U. L. Rev. 1020 (1987).

52 Harry S. Gerla, *Restoring Rivalry as a Central Concept in Antitrust Law*, 75 Neb. L. Rev. 209 (1996).

developments in the state of the world and the market participants' reaction to these developments (and, *horribile dictu*,[53] changing preferences). These are far too complex for any central planner to predict – Adam Smith's invisible hand cannot easily be replaced or anticipated by the economist's or strategic manager's notepad. The advances of economics are undeniable, but the pretense that complex phenomena can be reduced to a number of measurable factors that is large enough to feed a model that is sufficiently representative of the complexity of the system, yet small enough to fit into a parsimonious model is no truer today than it was in Adam Smith's, von Hayek's or Erich Hoppmann's times.

22. It may sound less exciting to admit that we cannot grasp the complexity of human interactions in the marketplace, to be "pessimistic," than to claim that it is possible to define the preconditions for innovation and that by adding them to the welfare analysis we can anticipate the good results we expect from the process of competition, and by taking this shortcut make competition as a process superfluous. But this is just a result of the framing of the issue.

23. I prefer a different framing. How sad would it be if the results of the exercise of human freedom and ingenuity were predictable? We can predict everything only if freedom is eliminated from the equation. That seems to me to be the truly pessimistic view. If we acknowledge that we cannot know what the results of the exercise of human freedom will be, that we prefer the sometimes-wasteful evolutionary struggle of competition that results from the exercise of the freedom to compete by individual market participants, and that, as a pattern prediction, results in progress, that seems to me the genuinely optimistic outlook.

V. What is Competition on the Merits?

24. Even if one does not value the freedom to compete and the institution of competition as such but merely wants to ensure good outcomes in the long run, it is preferable to entrust this task to an evolutionary process of competition. This brings us back to the accusation that "competition as such" is supposedly not sufficiently well defined. As with any evolutionary process, the starting point is variation: only where there is variety can a selection mechanism (here: the consumer's autonomous choice) determine the best fit to the environment; and only where sufficient variation and variability persists can there be adaptation to a changing environment.[54] As mentioned above, the evolutionary process does not prevent – indeed, it requires – that undertakings lose market share or leave the market entirely if they cannot

53 George J. Stigler, *The Conference Handbook*, 85 J. Pol. Econ. 441, 442 (1977), comment 31.

54 See in particular Hoppmann, *Kulturelle Evolution*, *supra* note 46.

succeed in attracting consumers; this is the selection mechanism at work.[55] What is important is that markets remain contestable so that the better fit prevails even when the environment changes.

25. For horizontal cooperation, this need for variation means that there is a preference for market participants to find their own way respectively. Hence the requirement of independence, that is, the "concept inherent in the provisions of the Treaty relating to competition that each economic operator must determine independently the policy which he intends to adopt on the [...] market."[56] When there are contacts between competitors that jeopardize this independence (and thus reduce variation), this is generally an interference with the competitive process.

26. There are cases that may at first glance look like cooperation between competitors where in reality none of the "competitors" could offer the product in question by themselves, so that the contributions of each competitor are complements rather than substitutes; in these cases, the product can only be offered through cooperation, so that in these cases cooperation does not decrease, but increases variation.[57]

27. If that is not the case, there is still the possibility that *the competitive process* works better despite a reduction of the independence between competitors if the conduct is ancillary to a scheme that is not in itself anticompetitive and increases the evolutionary potential of the process. For example, some forms of information exchange increase vertical transparency so that customers or suppliers can more easily identify the best alternative (but also increase horizontal transparency between competitors). In these cases, the variation of available options may be slightly reduced (because of the increase in horizontal transparency) but if the improvement of the selection mechanism more than neutralizes this effect (because the market becomes more transparent for customers or suppliers so that the selection mechanism works more smoothly), then this is still an overall improvement of the competitive process. This is a balancing of *pro- and anti-competitive* factors as parts of the *competitive process*; it has nothing to do with a balancing between competition as process and resulting efficiencies. There is an unfortunate tendency in Europe to import the US terminology "pro-competitive" to denote merely *efficient* conduct.

---

55 See, *supra* note 26.

56 Consistent jurisprudence since Judgment of the Court of Justice of Dec. 16, 1975, Cases 40–48, 50, 54–56, 111, 113 and 114/73, Suiker Unie v. Eur. Comm'n, ECLI:EU:C:1975:174, ¶ 173, *see, e.g.*, Judgment of the Court of Justice of July 14, 1981, Case 172/80, Züchner v. Bayerische Vereinsbank, ECLI:EU:C:1981:178, ¶ 13; Judgment of the Court of May 28, 1998, Case C-7/95 P, Deere v. Eur. Comm'n, ECLI:EU:C:1998:256, ¶ 86. While this concept is often used in the context of differentiating between concerted practices and mere tacit collusion, it is a wider principle to ensure the variation of approaches.

57 *See, e.g.*, Judgment of the Court of First Instance of May 2, 2006, Case T-328/03, O2 (Germany) v. Eur. Comm'n, ECLI:EU:T:2006:116, ¶¶ 77–79, see Marc van der Woude, *Restriction of competition: The European Commission failed to demonstrate why the notified agreement restricted competition in the telecommunications sector (O2)*, CONCURRENCES, No. N 3-2006, art. No. 12008 87; European Commission – Guidelines on the applicability of Article 101 of the Treaty on the Functioning of the European Union to horizontal co-operation agreements, 2023, O.J. (C 259/1), ¶¶ 33, 138–139, 227(b), 260, 352.

In the US, there is little need to distinguish between pro-competitive (in the sense of: improving the competitive process) and efficient conduct: as all unreasonable restraints of competition are prohibited under § 1 Sherman Act, there is only one step: balance anticompetitive with procompetitive and efficiency factors (and usually, efficiency factors are subsumed in the term "procompetitive"). In contrast, in the EU Article 101 TFEU requires a two-step process. Under Article 101(1) TFEU, only anticompetitive and procompetitive factors – in the narrow sense, that is, excluding efficiency considerations – may be balanced in order to find out if the conduct restricts competition. There is no rule of reason in Article 101(1) TFEU that would allow a balancing of a restriction of competition against efficiencies. Nor is there a need for such a rule of reason: where the conduct restricts the competitive process in the meaning of Article 101(1) TFEU, a balancing with resulting efficiencies is still possible under Article 101(3) TFEU. The difference is that the result-oriented efficiency analysis under Article 101(3) TFEU is the clear exception to the rule: the burden of proof lies with the undertaking to prove that the four conditions apply, namely that the efficiencies outweigh the restrictive effect, that the consumers receive a fair share of the gains, that the restriction is indispensable to achieve the efficiencies and that the undertakings do not have the possibility of eliminating competition for a substantial part of the market. In other words: for pragmatic reasons, a result-oriented shortcut to an efficient result may exceptionally be permissible, but only under the very restrictive condition that it can be proven that the result – not only the one for society, but also for the consumers in the market – is no worse than if the process of competition had remained unrestricted; and only if there is sufficient residual competition to allow the evolutionary process of competition to provide a check on the meme of "managed efficiency."

28. For the most part, EU practice with regard to horizontal cooperation still conforms to the desirable primacy of competition as a process. However, there are some signs that the effects-based approach is undermining the system that clearly underlies the structure of Article 101(1) vs. 101(3) TFEU. First, there is the tendency of the European institutions to use "pro-competitive," both when they mean efficient *and* when they mean beneficial to the competitive process. Second, there is an increasing willingness to incorporate efficiency reasoning into Article 101(1) TFEU, for example when efficiency aspects are considered to determine if conduct is restrictive by object. The treatment of purchasing cooperation in the Guidelines in particular erases the dividing line and, conversely, results in a tortuous attempt to differentiate buyer cartels to limit the damage. A clear conceptual distinction between competitive and efficiency arguments would bring much more clarity, although it would also (and rightly) subject many more purchasing cooperation agreements to an analysis under Article 101(3) TFEU.

29. With regard to vertical agreements, the ordoliberal approach is less definitive from the outset,[58] because – as indicated above – both parties can invoke a credible claim to freedom: the supplier who wants to be free to determine the distribution system and the distributor who wants to be free from being told by the supplier how to increase sales. The supplier's freedom to determine the distribution system may further the competitive process (not only efficiency) because there can be competition between suppliers competing on the form of their distribution system. Indeed, some have argued that because the clash of the two freedoms leads to an indeterminate result, the only criterion resolving the stand-off is efficiency.[59] However, even in these cases a balancing of the freedoms is generally sufficient,[60] because the comparative assessment of freedoms is not usually a zero-sum game, so that tipping the scale in one or the other direction will allow the finding of a joint maximum. For example, the greater the market foreclosure in the specific case, the less weight the supplier's interest deserves. Nevertheless, in the vertical context, the ordoliberal and the effects-based approach generally are not too far apart. Indeed, the predominantly ordoliberal German Act against Restraints of Competition of 1957 introduced a significantly more liberal regime for vertical distribution agreements than GTE Sylvania did twenty years later in the US: under the German Act, with the exception of the vertical fixing of prices and conditions, vertical distribution restraints were generally legal, although they could be prohibited *ex nunc* by the competition authorities if they resulted in unfair restrictions of the economic freedom of one of the parties or other undertakings *and* competition on the market was substantially impeded.[61] The ordoliberal approach may, however, explain the particular aversion to vertical price fixing, because this practice not only eliminates the distributor's freedom to determine a central competitive parameter, but also reduces the responsiveness of the competitive process to consumer reactions to different prices and therefore restricts the competitive feedback mechanism that allows a flexible adaptation.[62]

30. From the perspective of ordoliberalism, merger control plays a particularly important role. The question of an efficiency defense is quickly answered by going back to first principles. Why do we not prohibit *all* horizontal mergers, even though they clearly eliminate competition between the merger parties? In other words, why do we privilege concentrations in comparison to agreements

---

58 MÖSCHEL, *supra* note 18 at 215, ¶376.

59 Dieter Schmidtchen, *Der "more economic approach" in der Wettbewerbspolitik*, 56 WIRTSCHAFT UND WETTBEWERB 6, 12 (2006); C. Christian von Weizsäcker, *Konsumentenwohlfahrt und Wettbewerbsfreiheit: Über den tieferen Sinn des "Economic Approach"* 57 WIRTSCHAFT UND WETTBEWERB 1078 (2007).

60 MESTMÄCKER & SCHWEITZER, *supra* note 15, at § 3, ¶ 63.

61 § 18 of the Act against Restraints of Competition, BUNDESGESETZBLATT 1957 I 1081 (Aug. 9, 1957). Equivalent provisions remained in force until 2005, when Germany adopted the European scheme.

62 But see Edlin & Farrell, *supra* note 18, at 306, who, on the basis of a freedom-to-trade and process-oriented approach which has some similarities with the ordoliberal approach, conclude that vertical price fixing does not harm the competitive process because it does not restrict a trade (between the distributor and the customer) that would happen but for the agreement between the supplier and the distributor – because without that latter agreement, the distributor would have nothing to trade.

to restrict competition? The answer is that we accept that merging parties will, after the merger, plan for one single unit and will therefore achieve efficiencies (whether this is empirically true is a separate matter), even without all merging parties proving that the merger creates efficiencies.[63] In other words: the legislator has already taken the potential for efficiencies into account by raising the threshold from the one applicable to agreements, namely a merely "appreciable" restriction, to – initially – the threshold of the creation or strengthening of a dominant position and now a significant impediment to effective competition. Below this threshold, parties may merrily merge and enjoy their efficiencies. Once this higher threshold is exceeded, however, there is no reason for double counting by taking efficiencies into account yet again, this time in an efficiency defense. Not only does the merger regulation not have an "Article 101(3)"; even if it had one, its conditions would by definition never be met, because where the merger results in the creation or strengthening of a dominant position (or otherwise in a significant impediment to effective competition), by definition the last of the four conditions of Article 101(3) TFEU cannot be satisfied.

31. The differences between the ordoliberal and the effects-based approach are the starkest when it comes to the abuse of dominant positions. Here, there is a need to decide where the unilateral exercise of a freedom degenerates into the cannibalization of the equal freedom of others. This is the true battleground of the paradox of freedom: in how far do we need to constrain the freedom of the strongest player to ensure an equal freedom for all?

32. This raises difficult questions, for example, the question whether predatory pricing should only ever apply where an as-efficient competitor would be excluded. There are some good arguments for this proposition: the dominant undertaking has its own costs as an available yardstick, and competing on price is generally competition on the merits unless prices fall below an appropriate measure of cost (be it marginal cost (MC), average variable cost (AVC) or average avoidable cost (AAC)); after all, we generally do not want to force dominant undertakings to raise price above cost. Nevertheless, it seems to me that we do not want to exclude categorically the possibility of above-cost predation. Here, the distinction between "price levels" and "price patterns" introduced by Edlin and Farrell appears helpful.[64] Generally predation should only be considered abusive where an as-efficient competitor would be excluded. However, above-cost pricing that targets the customers of particular competitors selectively, especially competitors that are perceived as a threat because they may become an as-efficient competitor in the future, demonstrates that the dominant undertaking is not competing

63 Möschel, *supra* note 4, at 114.

64 Edlin & Farrell, *supra* note 18, at 303–306. The German Bundeskartellamt and Monopolies Commission had previously drawn a similar distinction between "price level abuses" and "price structure abuses" in the context of exploitative price abuses: Bundeskartellamt, Tätigkeitbericht 1976, Bundestags-Drucksache 8/704, 27; Monopolkommission, Hauptgutachten 1976/77: Fortschreitende Konzentration bei Grossunternehmen ¶ 388 (Nomos 1978).

on the merits but is investing into preventing its competitors to exercise their freedom to compete on equal terms.

33. The fiercest debate today rages about exclusivity agreements and loyalty rebates. If there were space, much could be said about these practices. Unfortunately, there is no space. Fortunately, however, Wouter Wils has already said everything, and said it better than I could have done.[65] While these may be efficient practices in some circumstances, they are practices that should be allowed for non-dominant undertakings but not for dominant undertakings: *quod licet bovi, non licet Iovi*. At a minimum, it should be for the dominant undertaking to prove the existence of any efficiencies sufficient for the purpose of objective justification.[66]

34. The *Intel* case demonstrates particularly well how illusory the "calculability" of complex market interactions is. The Commission's Chief Competition Economist clearly thought that this would be a particularly well-suited case for demonstrating the feasibility of an effects-based approach. Nevertheless, the Commission admitted that it "assessed the Intel conditional rebates to NEC in the fourth quarter of 2002 (*as that is the only quarter where sufficient data are available for the Commission to perform an analysis of the capability of the rebates to foreclose an as-efficient competitor*)." This is precisely the danger of which von Hayek had warned when he said that "they thereupon happily proceed on the fiction that the factors which they can measure are the only ones that are relevant;"[67] indeed, the General Court's assessment in the Renvoi judgment mirrors von Hayek closely: "It [...] follows [...] that the Commission appears to have relied on the example of NEC and on one single quarter *not simply because of its relevance, but because it was the only quarter for which it had been able to obtain information* in order to carry out the AEC analysis for MSH."[68]

35. A second danger of which von Hayek warned is also well illustrated by the *Intel* case: the allure of a mathematically *precise* calculation regardless of its *accuracy* (or *trueness*), that is, closeness to the true value. The Commission

---

65 Wils, *supra* note 3; *see also*, Edlin & Farrell, *supra* note 18, at 305–306.

66 Wils, *supra* note 3 accepts the current availability of an efficiency defense. I agree that efficiencies may be a factor in deciding whether conduct constitutes an abuse or is objectively justified. However, just like the merger regulation, Article 102 TFEU does not contain an equivalent to Article 101(3) TFEU (Basedow, *supra* note 4, at 57 Wirtschaft und Wettbewerb 712, 714 (2007)), and just like in the case of the merger regulation, even if it did, the fourth condition would by definition not be satisfied. Therefore, while efficiencies may be taken into account, there cannot be a defense once an abuse is demonstrated. In cases of loyalty rebates, there is the curiosity that now we possibly have an AEC test in Article 102 TFEU. However, in *Hoffmann-La Roche*, the Court gave the Commission the option to pursue such arrangements under either Article 101 or 102 TFEU (Judgment of the Court of Feb. 13, 1979, Case 85/76, Hoffmann-La Roche v. Eur. Comm'n, ECLI:EU:C:1979:36, ¶ 116. An assessment of the same loyalty rebate under Article 101 TFEU would result in the finding of an agreed vertical restriction of competition; both the vertical BER and Article 101(3) TFEU would be inapplicable because dominance is incompatible with the fourth condition. In other words, the Article 101 TFEU analysis, which does not require dominance, would result in stricter obligations than Article 102 TFEU. This shows that requiring an AEC test in Article 102 TFEU for loyalty rebates is misguided.

67 von Hayek, *supra* note 29.

68 Judgment of the General Court of Jan. 26, 2022, Case T-286/09 RENV, Intel Corp. v. Eur. Comm'n, ECLI:EU:T:2022:19, ¶ 476, see Jens Munk Plum & Sonny Gaarslev, *The EU General Court sets aside a €1.06B fine imposed on a semiconductor chip manufacturer over an alleged abuse of dominance by offering fidelity rebates to manufacturers and distributors (Intel)*, e-Competitions Jan. 2022, art. No. 115859.

had calculated the contestable share precisely to one decimal place, namely 7.1 percent. Even under its own calculations, it was actually somewhere between 5.6 percent and 10.4 percent, and at least over time increased to more than 24 percent.[69] What is the point of giving the result down to a tenth of a percentage point if the estimate may be off by a factor of three – except to suggest (pseudo-) scientific exactness?

36. Here, von Hayek's statement is apposite: "I prefer true but imperfect knowledge, even if it leaves much indetermined and unpredictable, to a pretence of exact knowledge that is likely to be false,"[70] paraphrasing Carved Read's pithier "[i]t is better to be vaguely right than exactly wrong."[71]

VI. Some Conciliatory Remarks

37. Is the contrast between the two approaches, the process-oriented ordoliberal approach and the effects-based approach always as stark as it has been painted above? Fortunately not, and for several reasons.

38. First, ordoliberals do not deny that they value competition not only for its liberty-preserving aspect of ensuring an equal freedom to compete, but also because *as a pattern prediction* competition leads to good results in the form of higher social welfare and efficiency, and usually also to other beneficial aspects such as dispersed political power. It is just that they perceive these good results as a welcome by-product, not as the goal of antitrust.

39. Second, at least when it comes to Article 101 TFEU, the purity of the freedom- and process-oriented approach is limited by the result-oriented justification in Article 101(3) TFEU. As a matter of positive law, there is no question that in exceptional cases we are asked to pretend to have the knowledge that allows us to decide that the resulting efficiencies outweigh the negative effects of agreed restriction of competition. As indicated above, the exceptional nature of this departure from the principle of reliance on the competitive process comes with strings attached, in particular the shifting of the burden of proof to those relying on the exception and the (distributive) requirement of proving the full compensation of consumers. Ordoliberals will be much more wary of such a "pretense of knowledge" than those who pursue an effects-based approach, but this is only a matter of degree; the "if" has been decided by the Treaty.

40. Third, even those who see efficiency and welfare as the (exclusive) ultimate goal, consider "competition a mediate goal that will often be close enough to

69 Case T-286/09 RENV, *Intel Corp.* ¶¶ 202–256.

70 von Hayek, *supra* note 29.

71 Carveth Read, Logic – Deductive and Inductive 351, ch XXII § 2 (Simkin, Marshall, Hamilton, Kent & Co., 4th ed. 1914).

the ultimate goal to allow the courts to look no further."[72] In many antitrust cases, both a process-of-competition and an efficiency analysis reach the same result, be it that certain conduct both impedes the competitive process and is inefficient, or that it is pro-competitive and efficient. The rarity with which the efficiency defense in merger analysis becomes relevant is an indication that the two forms of analysis often are "in sync."

41. Fourth, even among those who prefer an effects-based approach, not all call for an efficiency analysis in the individual case. Many consider it sufficient to consider the economics at a more abstract level. There is a wide range of views at what level of abstraction the analysis should consider efficiencies, but an uncontroversial example are hardcore cartels: Here, it is common ground that an efficiency analysis would only increase administrative costs, that very few efficiencies are ever forgone by a per se rule (note that in contrast to the per se rule in the US, the EU in theory allows efficiency arguments even here, although the practical difference is zero), and that the signal to market participants that hardcore cartels are always prohibited is clear and deterrent. This is a "form-based approach." The debate is only about the level of abstraction at which this categorization should take place. Proponents of effects-based approaches are wary of forgoing efficiencies, while proponents of the ordoliberal approach are willing to sacrifice a few more efficiencies in order to have the advantage of justiciable (form-based) rules that provide legal certainty to undertakings and reduce administrative costs in their application.[73] There is a debate to be had about "optimally differentiated rules,"[74] and in the drafting of these, economic expertise is more than welcome: at the abstract level at which rules are drafted, economists can supply valuable insights into pattern predictions, and of course it is desirable that rules to be used in a form-based approach be economically sensible.

42. A debate about optimally differentiated rules is likely to bring the two camps closer together. On a philosophical level, such an approach may be likened to "rule utilitarianism," under which an action is right if it conforms to a rule, with the rule being drafted with a view to maximizing utility in general. Just as rule utilitarianism does not completely satisfy either Kantians pursuing the categorical imperative free from shabby considerations of utility or act utilitarians pursuing the maximum of utility in every case, a form-based approach on the basis of economically sensible rules may not satisfy everyone in all cases; but it is likely to reduce disagreements to a much smaller set of cases.

---

72 Posner, *supra* note 13, at 29.

73 *See e.g.*, Möschel, *supra* note 4, at 113–114.

74 See Arndt Christiansen & Wolfgang Kerber, *Competition Policy with Optimally Differentiated Rules Instead of "Per Se Rules vs Rule of Reason"*, 2 J. Competition L. & Econ. 215 (2006).

Competition Policy, Anticompetitive Market Distortions, and Economic Welfare

ALDEN F. ABBOTT*
Mercatus Center at George Mason University

I. Introduction and Overview

1. Competition policy has received increased public attention in recent years, as multiple governments have sought to attack allegedly abusive business practices of the great "big tech" companies (such as Google, Amazon, Facebook, and Apple) through antitrust lawsuits and regulation.[1] Mere headlines, however, may tend to obscure the broader significance of competition policy for the general welfare. A properly designed competition policy should do far more than focus merely on anticompetitive private conduct. It also should seek to eliminate government-fomented distortions of competition that severely burden domestic and international commerce. A two-pronged competition policy centered on combating both private *and public* restraints will be far

---

* Senior Research Fellow, Mercatus Center at George Mason University, and former General Counsel, Federal Trade Commission.

1 *See, e.g.*, CONGRESSIONAL RESEARCH SERVICE, ANTITRUST AND BIG TECH FIRMS (updated Nov. 21, 2023), for a discussion of antitrust enforcement and regulatory proposals aimed at big tech companies in the United States. For a brief description of new big tech regulations in the European Union, *see, e.g.*, Jeremiah Johnson, *Europe's Tech Curbs Are a Double-Edged Sword*, FOREIGNPOLICY.COM (Oct. 23, 2023), https://foreignpolicy.com/2023/10/23/metaverse-europe-uk-us-big-tech-regulation-innovation/#cookie_message_anchor. Laws directed at anticompetitive behavior are referred to as antitrust laws in the United States, and as competition laws elsewhere in the world. The term "competition laws" is employed in this chapter.

more effective in enhancing consumer welfare[2] and, what's more, in significantly promoting economic growth.

2. This article describes obstacles that stand in the way of implementing optimal competition policy, and suggests methods by which governments may seek to overcome them. In particular, competition policy should be reformed by adopting a new emphasis on combating government-generated anticompetitive market distortions (ACMDs) that undermine global economic well-being. Such a change will require a "whole of government" approach, featuring greater cooperation between competition enforcers and trade officials, as well as the involvement of other branches of government. The adoption of new international trade enforcement instruments targeted at ACMDs should be a key element in a multilateral strategy designed to curb those restraints. Finally, competition enforcement must have advancement of consumer welfare as its overarching goal, if it is to contribute to the ACMD solution, rather than being part of the problem.

II. The ACMDs Problem and Its Impact

3. Anticompetitive market distortions, or ACMDs, are government-imposed restrictions that distort market-based competition, domestically or internationally. They "involve government actions that empower certain private interests to obtain or retain artificial competitive advantages over their rivals be they foreign or domestic."[3] ACMDs comprise "[g]overnment laws, regulations, or practices that eliminate competition completely; … practices that lessen competition; … [l]aws or regulations that are applied differently among firms, or regulatory exemptions given to some firms; … [competitive] [d]istortions caused by state-owned enterprises; … action or inaction by competition agencies; and … anticompetitive state aid or support."[4]

4. Because they frequently distort the treatment of different competitors engaged in international commerce, ACMDs are a major impediment to international trade as well as to domestic competition.[5] Nevertheless, most ACMDs fall

---

2 Then Federal Trade Commission Chairman Timothy J. Muris emphasized this point in a major 2003 speech. *See* Timothy J. Muris Remarks, Chairman, Fed. Trade Comm'n, State Intervention/State Action – A U.S. Perspective, Remarks Before Fordham Annual Conference on International Antitrust Law & Policy (New York, Oct. 24, 2003), https://www.ftc.gov/sites/default/files/documents/public_statements/state-intervention/state-action-u.s.perspective/fordham031024.pdf.

3 Alden F. Abbott & Shanker A. Singham, *Enhancing welfare by attacking anticompetitive market distortions*, Concurrences No. 4-2011, art. No. 39546.

4 Shanker A. Singham et al., Introduction to Anti-Competitive Market Distortions and the Distortions Index 1, 5 (Sept. 2016).

5 *See* Shanker A. Singham & Alden F. Abbott, Trade, Competition and Regulatory Policy 102–112 (2023) for an overview of the theory of anticompetitive market distortions. *See also*, Shanker A. Singham, Freeing the Global Market: How to Boost the Economy by Curbing Regulatory Distortions (Oct. 2012). Post-World War II international trade liberalization under the auspices of the General Agreement on Tariffs and Trade (GATT) and its successor, the World Trade Organization (WTO), eliminated or reduced many trade restrictions at the border, but did not cope with the even more serious problem of restrictions within the border, stemming from ACMDs.

outside the scope of current competition laws and international trade laws,[6] complicating potential multilateral efforts that might be undertaken to rein them in. Indeed, because they are imposed and maintained by government authority, ACMDs are more pernicious and long-lasting than purely private restrictions, that are disciplined by market forces and government prosecution.

5. Anticompetitive market distortions are recognized to be a serious global economic problem. Two major international economic organizations, the OECD and the World Bank, have spotlighted ACMDs and have encouraged governments to avoid and dismantle them.[7] In a similar vein, the International Competition Network (ICN), established in 2001, provides support for "competition advocacy" initiatives by its member competition agencies, aimed at encouraging national governments to avoid anticompetitive public policies.[8]

6. Despite this institutional attention, however, ACMDs remain pervasive, due in no small part to the fact that their costs to the general public and competitors are hidden from sight. The development of measures to estimate the costs of ACMDs could strengthen the case for rooting them out. Even more significantly, cost measures could be used to develop targeted trade sanctions calibrated to counteract specific ACMDs. The threat of sanctions and the publicized scale of the ACMD problem could also facilitate multilateral efforts to incentivize the phasing out of these pernicious restrictions.

7. Fortunately, since 2014 research to estimate the economic impact of ACMDs is being carried out. In 2016 Singham and Rangan published a basic econometric model for estimating the cost of ACMDs.[9] That model included a

---

6 *See id.* at 4–5. One slight qualification should be noted. European Union competition law does sanction certain anticompetitive government subsidies (state aids) and abuses of monopoly power by state-owned companies. There are, however, significant limitations to the coverage of the relevant legal provisions, found in Articles 107 (state aids) and 106 (exclusive right) of the Treaty on the Functioning of the European Union. *See* Andreas Heineman, *Exclusive Right (Art. 106 TFEU)*, *Global Dictionary of Competition Law*, Concurrences, art. No 86073. Moreover, there are many other ACMDs employed by European Union countries that are not related to state aids or abuses by state-owned monopolies.

7 Beginning in 2007, the Organization of Economic Cooperation and Development (OECD) developed and subsequently has continued to refine a Competition Assessment Toolkit. The Toolkit identifies many types of ACMDs to assist governments in applying less competitively objectionable methods to advance their policy objectives. *See* OECD, *Competition Assessment Toolkit*, https://web-archive.oecd.org/temp/2024-03-12/66941-assessment-toolkit.htm (last visited Dec. 28, 2023). The World Bank also has focused on government-imposed regulatory distortions in addition to private anticompetitive behavior in working with governments on economic reform. According to the World Bank, "[a]t the regional, national, and subnational levels, sector-specific rules and regulations frequently limit market entry or reinforce the dominance of a few firms … Regulatory frameworks often fail to ensure that more efficient market players can compete on a level playing field. State-owned enterprises (SoEs) tend to be more significant market participants in developing countries and to benefit from undue competitive advantages." World Bank, *Markets and Competition Policy*, https://www.worldbank.org/en/topic/competition-policy (last visited Dec. 28, 2023).

8 The ICN is an informal voluntary network of competition agencies and non-governmental advisers that promotes "soft convergence" toward "sound competition policies across the global antitrust community." As the ICN explains, competition advocacy directed at government restrictions on competition "refers to those activities conducted by the competition agency, that are related to the promotion of a competitive environment by means of non-enforcement mechanisms, mainly through its relationships with other governmental entities and by increasing public awareness in regard to the benefits of competition." International Competition Network, *Advocacy*, https://www.internationalcompetitionnetwork.org/working-groups/advocacy/ (last visited Jan. 2, 2024).

9 *See* Singham et al., *supra* note 4. For an updated published discussion of that model and its broad implications for public policy analysis, *see* The Growth Commission, The Growth Budget 2023 71–83 (Nov. 2023), https://assets-global.website-files.com/646a30e30500c46bb82472c0/65534d5cc6f65dfbfcca6752_FINAL%20Growth%20Budget%202023%20DIGITAL%20SPREAD%20(1).pdf. Projections based on that model "suggest

metric that estimated the negative impact on economic welfare stemming from ACMDs' harmful effects on property rights, domestic competition, and international competition. The authors applied that model to estimate the impact of ACMDs in India,[10] and found "that if all ACMDs in India were replaced with truly pro-competitive policies, then the productivity of the Indian economy [and its]... GDP would rise [dramatically,]... making India the fourth-biggest economy in the world behind only the EU, US, and China."[11] [This makes the point in a simpler more direct fashion.] A subsequent 2019 study prepared by the Centre for Economics and Business Research (Cebr)[12] found that a within-country trade distortion (ACMD) of 25 percent (where ACMDs prohibit one-fourth of beneficial commercial transactions between companies and consumers) reduces global output relative to the benchmark case with no distortions by around 14 percent. Research along these lines continues.

8. Studies finding dramatic ACMD-specific welfare losses are generally consistent with other recent quantitative research finding a strong relationship between a growth in regulation and a major decline in economic growth.[13] Although certainly not definitive (the research deals with regulations in general, which may include some non-ACMDs), this research clearly bolsters the case for combating ACMDs as a key element of competition policy.

---

that a reduction in ACMDs does lead to a significant increase in GDP per capita in line with the projections ...from other sources, such as OECD and other figures on the impact of anti-competitive regulation on growth." *Id.* at 82.

10 *See* Shanker A. Singham et al., Anti-Competitive Market Distortions and Their Impact: A Case Study of India (May 2016), https://shankersingham.com/wp-content/uploads/2023/08/LIACMDIndia.pdf.

11 *Id.* at 2.

12 Institute of Economic Affairs, An agent-based model of trade: Market distortions and output 5–6 (Feb. 2019), https://img1.wsimg.com/blobby/go/bf4d316c-4c0b-4e87-8edb-350f819ee031/downloads/Cebr%20Market%20Distortions%20Trade%20Report.pdf.

13 For example, an economic growth model based on a textual analysis of federal regulations affecting 22 major industries between 1977 and 2012 concluded that had regulation been held constant at 1980 levels, the US economy would have been nearly 25 percent larger by 2012. See Bentley Coffey, Patrick McLaughlin & Pietro Peretto, *The Cumulative Costs of Regulations*, 18 Rev. Econ. Dynamics 1 (2020). Stated differently, the study found that regulatory growth between 1980 and 2012 cost the US economy $4 trillion in 2012, or roughly $13,000 per capita. Another economic study found that a 36 percent decline in the stock of British Columbia regulations between 2001 and 2006 (due to the adoption of a "regulatory growth budget") was responsible for a one percent rise in the economic growth rate. See Patrick McLaughlin & Bentley Coffey, *Regulation and Economic Growth: Evidence from British Columbia's Experiment in Regulatory Budgeting* (Mercatus Ctr George Mason Univ., Working Paper, June 1, 2021). And the 2020 Economic Report of the President assessed the economic benefits of reductions in regulatory output and the promulgation of new rules having a regulatory focus under the Trump Administration. See Economic Report of the President, Together with the Annual Report of the Council of Economic Advisers: Chapter Six, Empowering Economic Freedom by Reducing Regulatory Burdens 173–198 (Jan. 2021), https://trumpwhitehouse.archives.gov/wp-content/uploads/2021/01/Economic-Report-of-the-President-Jan2021.pdf. The Report estimated that Trump deregulatory policies, if continued, would raise US real income by $3,100 per household per year after five to ten years. (This did not happen, due to the election of the Biden Administration.)

III. Competition Policy Directed at Private Conduct

9. We turn now to a brief examination of the state of competition policy directed at private conduct, a topic which recently has become a source of some concern.

10. Prior to 2021, United States federal antitrust enforcement agencies, the Federal Trade Commission (FTC) and the US Department of Justice (DOJ), supported a "consumer welfare" standard in antitrust enforcement. This standard has been characterized by the leading American antitrust treatise writer as promoting "maximum output [including quantity, quality, and innovation enhancement] that is consistent with sustainable competition."[14] The DOJ and the FTC had worked to advance this standard around the world since the 1990s, with a substantial degree of success. According to a 2011 ICN report on competition enforcement and consumer welfare, "the promotion of consumer welfare is a common theme for most [Competition] Authorities throughout the world, regardless of whether or not it plays a formal role in their legal framework."[15]

11. The consumer welfare standard is largely congruent with definitions of economic welfare applied in studies estimating the negative effects of ACMDs and excessive regulation, summarized above. In other words, to the extent it is aimed at consumer welfare enhancement, competition enforcement works in tandem with the elimination of ACMDs to raise economic growth and economic welfare.

12. Competition enforcement that lacks a consumer welfare focus, however, cannot be counted on to have this beneficial effect. Indeed, to the extent competition enforcement is transmogrified into a form of business regulation not focused on consumer welfare, but rather on the advancement of other social goals (such as, for example, protecting smaller competitors, advancing social equity, or favoring workers' rights), it may distort marketplace competition on the economic merits. To the extent it does, such an alternative version of "competition policy" may well qualify as an ACMD. If it does, it will prove economically counterproductive, reducing the magnitude of the welfare gains that can be achieved through the elimination of other ACMDs.

13. Unfortunately, the prior widespread support for a consumer welfare focus recently has been attenuated, if not entirely abandoned, by major jurisdictions. Beginning in 2021, the FTC and DOJ renounced primary reliance on the consumer welfare standard, indicating that various other considerations would be weighed as part of a far more aggressive antitrust enforcement policy.[16]

---

14 Herbert Hovenkamp, Federal Antitrust Policy 102 (6th ed. 2020).

15 International Competition Network, *Competition Enforcement and Consumer Welfare: Setting the Agenda*, 7 (2011), https://www.internationalcompetitionnetwork.org/wp-content/uploads/2019/11/SP_CWelfare2011.pdf.

16 *See generally* Alden Abbott, *The FTC, DOJ, and International Competition Law: Convergence Away from the Consumer Welfare Standard?*, Truth on the Market (Sept. 15, 2023), https://truthonthemarket.com/2023/09/15/the-ftc-doj-and-international-competition-law-convergence-away-from-the-consumer-welfare-standard/.

14. The European Commission, the other international "thought leader" in competition enforcement, also has been moving in an increasingly interventionist direction.[17] Particularly in abuse of dominance cases, it is placing increasing emphasis on protection of competitors, with consumer welfare (at least implicitly) playing a less central role. Furthermore, through the new Digital Markets Act (DMA), the European Commission has adopted a regulatory overlay on top of competition enforcement applicable to big digital platforms.[18] This new regulatory scheme threatens to distort competitive forces and therefore may amount to a substantial ACMD.

15. The regrettable recent policy turn by American and European competition authorities is likely to weaken support for a consumer welfare standard in other jurisdictions, given the historic leading role of the United States and the European Union in setting the global competition policy agenda. At least for the time being, this places a partial obstacle to international agreement on all aspects of a pro-economic growth anti-ACMD strategy.

16. In short, consumer welfare-centric competition enforcement complements an economic growth strategy focused on dismantling ACMDs. It is to be hoped that competition authorities will come to recognize that fact and, as such, revert to endorsement of the consumer welfare standard as their competition enforcement lodestar.

IV. A Multilateral Strategy to Rein in ACMDs

17. Anticompetitive market distortions and their baleful economic effects constitute a global problem. To be effective, an anti-ACMD strategy must come to grips with the fact that many of these distortions exist due to the lobbying of powerful organized special interest "rent-seekers," that manipulate government processes to gain competitive advantage.[19] Accordingly, any effort to rein in ACMDs must involve international cooperation. Such cooperation must include agreements embodying robust enforcement mechanisms with credible commitments[20] that induce like-minded market-centered nations to eliminate

---

17 *See, e.g.*, Alden Abbott, *What the European Commission's More Interventionist Approach to Exclusionary Abuses Could Mean for EU Courts and for U.S. States*, Truth on the Market (Apr. 5, 2023), https://truthonthemarket.com/2023/04/05/what-the-european-commissions-more-interventionist-approach-to-exclusionary-abuses-could-mean-for-eu-courts-and-for-u-s-states/.

18 *See, e.g.*, Lazar Radic, *Gatekeeping, the DMA, and the Future of Competition Regulation*, Truth on the Market (Nov. 8, 2023), https://truthonthemarket.com/2023/11/08/gatekeeping-the-dma-and-the-future-of-competition-regulation/.

19 *See* Alden F. Abbott, *Anticompetitive Market Distortions as an Ungoverned Space, and Prospects for Reform*, 36 SAIS Rev. Int'l Affs. 87 (Summer–Fall 2016), https://www.jstor.org/stable/e27001427.

20 For a discussion of the concept of credible commitments and its key role in promoting successful agreements, *see* Douglass C. North, *Institutions and Credible Commitments*, 149 J. Inst. & Theoretical Econ. 11 (1993).

specific ACMDs – and to act in concert to counteract ACMDs imposed by third party nations, such as China.[21]

18. ACMD trade remedies may be unilateral or multilateral. For example, a nation unilaterally may assess a duty equivalent to the size of a distortion (tariffication) on imports that artificially benefit from a foreign ACMD and harm domestic producers. A tariffication-based trade remedy may also be imposed more broadly on a multilateral basis, and included in free trade agreements (FTAs) with like-minded nations, as detailed in a 2021 United Kingdom Trade and Agriculture Commission (TAC) report:

> "*Tariffication of the distortion* is a mechanism, which could be used in trade policy to deal with situations where countries have agreed to lower tariffs in an FTA but then go on to protect their markets and give their producers an artificial edge by distorting their markets.
>
> The result of the mechanism is a tariff based on the scale of the distortion, which operates as a trade remedy. The mechanism can be used offensively, where a country is preventing market access by the UK by means of the market distortion, or defensively where a distortion in a foreign market leads to excess exports from that market ... Offensively, we envisage provisions on distortions in trade agreements that discipline their use, and allow dispute resolution when they are applied in violation of the agreement."[22]
>
> "[Defensively,] [a]n aggrieved country would have to show:
>
> 1. a market distortion (deviation from an agreed standard in an FTA or an internationally agreed norm, rule or standard at large ...). In addition to the cases above, an anti-competitive market distortion (ACMD) could result from the deliberate derogation from a country's own law in order to promote trade or competitive advantage;
> 2. impact on competition;
> 3. excess exports as a result of the distortion; and
> 4. damage to its producers."

21 The following discussion of trade remedies for dealing with ACMDs draws heavily upon unpublished materials developed by (and my conversations with) Shanker Singham, a co-author and friend of mine who is one of the world's leading trade experts. More information on Singham and his work may be found at https://shankersingham.com/. China's pervasive use of ACMDs to distort international trade flows for the benefit of Chinese enterprises is well-documented and is a source of major concern for other trading nations, including the United States. *See, e.g.*, White House Press Release, Office of Trade & Manufacturing Policy, *How China's Economic Aggression Threatens the Technologies and Intellectual Property of the United States and the World*, (June 2018), https://trumpwhitehouse.archives.gov/briefings-statements/office-trade-manufacturing-policy-report-chinas-economic-aggression-threatens-technologies-intellectual-property-united-states-world/.

22 UK Trade and Agriculture Commission, Final Report 136 (March 2021), (emphasis in the original), https://assets.publishing.service.gov.uk/media/636cedd7e90e076199296338/trade-and-agriculture-commission-final-report-march-2021.pdf. The TAC Final Report anticipates that ACMDs can be quantified, which will require additional work by economists on refining ACMD metrics. Such work should seek to minimize errors of estimation in measuring ACMDs, in order to maximize the welfare benefits of tariffication.

19. Other potential unilateral remedies for ACMD violations may include, among others, penalties and fines; withdrawal of licenses in the case of licensed or regulated services; disciplines of domestic firms that receive government distortion benefits from a foreign government (China being a prime example); prohibitions on investments in domestic firms by foreign ACMD beneficiaries; and applications of surcharges to government procurement bids by companies that benefited from a foreign ACMD.[23]

20. Dealing with ACMDs that a nation uses to protect its domestic industries from foreign competition may be more complicated than imposing defensive measures, especially when the favored industries export little or nothing. In such cases, it would be vital to ensure that trade agreements included disciplines on those ACMDs. Failure to unwind or modify ACMDs could lead to dispute settlement and the potential for retaliatory tariffs on sectors that do export.

21. Domestic antitrust remedies may occasionally prove helpful in combating ACMDs.[24] For example, ACMD subsidies enjoyed by an exporter are likely to justify findings that below cost pricing of imports is predatory (sales below private costs can be maintained for the long term when the ACMD frees the exporter from normal financial constraints). Blocking a merger can prevent future harm when one of the parties benefits from a foreign ACMD that would enable the merged entity to predate against other competitors post-acquisition.

22. Finally, trade remedies will be far more effective when ACMDs are simultaneously being weakened and phased out on the domestic plane. That will require a multi-faceted domestic government strategy. It will entail cooperation between a nation's competition authorities and international trade negotiators, to identify the country's significant ACMDs (in addition to the major ACMDs of other jurisdictions). Domestic competition advocacy efforts, which already receive the approbation of international organizations,[25] should be supported and linked to a commitment by central governments to subject proposed and existing regulations (and, to the extent possible, laws) to regulatory review. Ideally regulatory review, honed to spotlight ACMDs (perhaps as an adjunct to existing cost-benefit analyses),[26] would lead to the full elimination or reduction in the number of ACMDs, over time if not immediately.

---

23 A surcharge would be calibrated to reflect the size of the ACMD distortion benefiting a bid. In cases of a huge distortion that was hard to measure accurately, an ACMD beneficiary might be barred from bidding for a government procurement.

24 *See* OECD, *Subsidies, Competition, and Trade*, (Nov. 2022), https://one.oecd.org/document/DAF/COMP/GF/WD(2022)65/en/pdf.

25 *See* text accompanying *supra* notes 7–8.

26 In 2023, the US Office of Management and Budget issued a directive requiring federal agencies to account for competitive effects in developing and analyzing regulatory actions. *See* US Office of Information and Regulatory Affairs, Office of Management and Budget, *Guidance on Accounting for Competition Effects when Developing and Analyzing Regulatory Actions*, (Oct. 2023), https://www.whitehouse.gov/wp-content/uploads/2023/10/RegulatoryCompetitionGuidance.pdf.

23. Domestic political considerations, affected by special interest pleading,[27] undoubtedly will constrain national governments' efforts to eliminate their ACMDs. As such, the rapid adoption of international trade agreements providing for effective ACMD countermeasures could prove quite valuable in strengthening the hand of reform-minded governments as they seek to dismantle problematic competitive distortions.

V. Conclusion

24. Attention directed to competition policy by the mass media has centered largely on big antitrust cases affecting large high-tech firms. But relatively little notice has been given to government-imposed anticompetitive market distortions, which are pervasive in the modern global economy and are hard to root out. Empirical work on ACMDs is growing. Studies to date indicate that ACMDs not only undermine efficiency and harm competition, but they also substantially slow economic growth and significantly reduce economic output.

25. The lack of attention to ACMDs should be remedied. An economically sound competition policy should target both private anticompetitive restraints and ACMDs. Specifically, competition law challenges to private conduct should center on consumer welfare enhancement. ACMDs should be combated on the domestic plane through competition advocacy and robust regulatory review, and on the global plane through international agreements that establish targeted measures to counteract the harmful effects of ACMDs.[28]

26. In sum, optimal global competition policy requires an appropriate melding of consumer-centered antitrust enforcement, regulatory reform, and international trade cooperation to eliminate ACMDs – an "all of governments" approach. Developing and implementing this agenda will be a complicated long-term project, but it is well worth the effort, given the major economic benefits at stake. Accordingly, this project merits the close attention of governments worldwide, as a top economic policy priority.

---

27 *See* text accompanying *supra* note 20.

28 It follows, of course, that support for economists' development of metrics to quantify ACMDs should be an important government policy task. See note 22, *supra*.

Why is Competition a Good Thing?

LUIS CABRAL*
New York University

I. Introduction

1. Why is competition a good thing? This may seem an obvious question – until you start comparing notes and realize that different people suggest different answers. My goal in this contribution is to go over a list of possible reasons why competition matters, hoping to contribute to a better understanding of the pros and cons of a market-based economy.

II. The Fundamental Theorem

2. The Economics 101 approach to the benefits of markets and competition is based on the so-called law of supply and demand and the associated fundamental theorem of welfare economics. In a competitive market, one with many small buyers and sellers – one where competition is intense – the equilibrium price exactly balances out supply and demand. This is more than an equilibrium: it is an outcome whereby the buyers who buy the various units of a good are precisely those who value the good the most – by which we mean the buyers who are willing to pay the most.

3. But there is more: To the extent that a voluntary transaction between two well-informed agents leads to a mutual gain (were that not the case, the agents would not accept the deal), we say that markets lead to gains from trade. And it can be shown that the above market equilibrium maximizes the potential

---

* Professor of Economics, Stern School of Business, New York University.

gains from trade: all transactions leading to gains from trade take place, and no transaction takes place that would imply a loss to any of the parties.

4. This result, hinted at by Adam Smith and formalized with increasing precision throughout the nineteenth and twentieth centuries, is still the most frequent answer you will get when you ask an economist why competition is good.

5. The fundamental theorem seems reasonable – until you push it with the intensity that die-hard economists are wont to. One case in point is what is usually referred to as price gouging. Suppose there is an unexpected shock to supply or demand so that a particular good is in excess demand. Left to its own devices, the market will push prices to very high levels. Most non-economists would deem this unfair – and would normally label the increase as price gouging. When surveyed, most economists counter that it is simply the market mechanism at work. Moreover, they will stand by the opinion that a price increase is the best that can happen at the time.

6. How can different people hold such disparate views? One thing that non-economists frequently fail to appreciate is the supply incentive created by high prices. Take for example Hurricane Sandy, which disrupted the supply of gas to the greater New York area in 2012. Were prices allowed to freely increase, one might reasonably expect enterprising agents to procure gas in different places not affected by Sandy (say, Philadelphia), thus increasing gasoline supply in the greater New York area. In other words, the price increase that non-economists decry may actually have a positive effect.

7. By contrast, one thing that economists frequently fail to appreciate is the rather limited nature of the fundamental theorem. The market equilibrium maximizes total surplus assuming that a dollar of willingness to pay is the right measure of value created. But that is a strong assumption. Take for example price gouging during the Covid-19 pandemic. The online price of 3M masks increased by a factor of 20 or more relative to pre-pandemic levels. An economist might say that, in this way, the buyers who are willing to pay the most are the ones who are allocated the masks: an efficient outcome. But take the case of nurses taking care of Covid-19 patients. They might have an enormous value for a mask but might simply not be able to afford it at a price of hundreds of dollars per piece (as was the case at times).

III. Competition is Good for Buyers

8. A related approach to the ideas in the previous section is the principle that competition between sellers is good for buyers (and competition between buyers is good for sellers). Let us look specifically at the latter. Suppose I have an object that I would like to sell. I would like to sell it for as much as possible and have a choice between two different strategies: (a) negotiate with a potential buyer; (b) auction the object.

9. Some businesspeople who consider themselves "masters of the deal" would likely choose direct negotiation. However, in a mathematically challenging but nicely written paper (*Auctions Versus Negotiations*), Jeremy Bulow and Paul Klemperer show that, under reasonable and broad assumptions, a seller is better off running an auction rather than going through a bargaining process, even if the latter is optimally structured from the seller's perspective. In other words, competition works better than negotiation skills.

10. As a specific example, consider the case of Olympic Games TV broadcasting rights. The Montreal 1976 rights were directly negotiated by the organizers with one of the networks, ABC, who paid the games' organizers $25 million. In 1980 dollars, this corresponds to $36.25 million (remember, these were years of high inflation rates). In 1980, the Moscow games organizers decided to run an auction instead of directly negotiating with a network. The rights were sold for $87 million. In real terms, this is more than twice the price of the previous games, which is particularly impressive considering that many Western countries boycotted the 1980 games (to protest against the Soviet Union's invasion of Afghanistan).

11. The idea that competition is good for consumers is, so to speak, the foundation of antitrust and competition policy. One economic argument that helping consumers is a good thing is that a dollar in the hands of a consumer is better than a dollar in the hands of a corporation (it saves the government the hassle of redistributing income and wealth). Firm owners typically belong to a higher echelon of the income distribution than consumers, and so lower prices indirectly amount to a transfer from the wealthier to the poorer.

IV. Productive Efficiency

12. Economist John Hicks famously noted that "the best of all monopoly profits is a quiet life," meaning that, if you don't have any competitor to deal with, then there is little pressure to become more efficient. By contrast, when firms compete, it's sink or swim: either you are efficient, or you are out. In fact, as economist Robert Frank and others have noted, while we cite Adam Smith as the source for the benefits of competition, we should also cite Charles Darwin: competition is a process of "natural" selection.

13. A specific example is given by the airline industry, in particular the different paths followed in Europe and the US in the past 30 years or so. Until the early 1990s, European airline markets were highly regulated. For example, if you wanted to travel from Rome to Paris, you only had two options: Alitalia or AirFrance. Moreover, there was no competition between these state-owned airlines: fares were set by an open agreement between the governments of Italy and France. As a result, airfares were expensive, very expensive. Europeans had to pay between 34 and 65 cents per mile, about three times as much as Americans (controlling for flight distance).

14. In 1992, the European Union Regulation 2408/92 on access for Community air carriers to intra-Community air routes, dictated that, by 1997, any European carrier could offer service on any intra-European route. Once the cartel agreements were gone, the number of airlines and flights expanded. By 1990, the number of European flights per week was just under 60,000. By 2000, that number was already greater than 100,000. Inevitably, the supply expansion had an effect on prices. By 2010, for similar 600-mile flights, Europeans were paying 11 cents per mile, whereas Americans were paying 23 cents per mile. A quarter of a century earlier (in 1986, to be precise) these fares were 52 and 15 cents per mile, respectively.

15. To summarize, in the 24 years from 1986 to 2010, we estimate European fares (for 600-mile flights) dropped from about 52 to about 11 cents per mile, whereas in the US the fares increased from 15 to 23 cents per mile! Since 2010, matters have become even worse for Americans, on account of a major consolidation of US airlines.

16. One of the channels that led to this gigantic turnaround was the process of "natural selection" among European airlines. Once competition set in, underperforming airlines such as Sabena or Swissair were replaced by low-cost carriers such as easyJet and Ryanair.

17. In sum, Hicks' pithy quote might well be rephrased as "the best of all cartel profits is a quiet life." And once Regulation 2408/92 busted the cartel, that was the end of the quiet life and the beginning of Darwinian survival of the fittest at work, with significant gains in terms of productive efficiency (and consumer prices).

V. Innovation

18. Fun fact: the average height of Chinese men is 5' 6.5'" (169.5cm), whereas the average height of Dutch men is 5' 11'" (180.8cm). However, in 2019 the top five players on China's 2019 men's national basketball team was 6' 10.6'" (2.098m), whereas the corresponding value for the Dutch men's team was a mere 6' 9.9'" (2.08m). In other words, the average Dutch man is taller than the average Chinese man, but the Chinese men's basketball team is taller than the Dutch men's basketball team.

19. How do we get a reversal in order as we move from the population average to the average of the top 5? The key is that, in 2019, there were about 700 million Chinese males but only 9 million Dutch males. As we pick the top 5 from a larger pool, we get a larger average. That is what order statistics do for you.

20. What does this all have to do with competition? Let's start with a widely accepted proposition: innovation is the primary factor leading to economic growth. What then causes innovation? Basically, ideas. And here's the analogy with height: the "tallest" idea among a certain number of ideas is "taller" the

greater the number of ideas. In other words, the best idea out of 1000 ideas is normally better than the best idea out of 100 ideas, which in turn is normally better than the best idea out of 10 ideas. This is where competition comes in: to the extent that competition induces a "race" between a larger number of independent ideas, the best ideas will be very good indeed, resulting in a faster pace of innovation.

21. There has been a long debate in economics regarding the advantages of large corporations and large government programs as a force pushing innovation. We have not been able to settle the discussion definitively, and I do not claim the ability or the intention of doing so here. But it is fair to say that, all things considered, competition remains an important contributor to innovation.

22. It is remarkable (in a negative sense) that most economics textbooks (and most economics instructors) spend most of their time praising the benefits of competition in terms of allocation efficiency (each unit of each good is allocated to the agent willing to pay the most) but relatively little time on the effects of competition on innovation. Schumpeter may be an exception, but not many people understand Schumpeter well (myself included), and even fewer teach his work in the classroom.

VI. Rent-Seeking Behavior

23. One of the many challenges faced by some developing countries stems from the so-called "resource curse." Take Nigeria, for example, a country rich in oil. Partly due to the lack of competition in oil extraction, the government-owned oil company earns considerable profits. Everyone wants a share of this "pie." As a result, a disproportionate share of Nigerian talent flocks to the oil sector, to the detriment of other sectors of the economy. If the oil sector were sufficiently competitive, then no excessive profits (rents) would be available, and the "gold rush" we observe in these situations would not take place. In sum, the case can be made that absence of competition leads to the creation of "artificial" rents, which in turn lead to rent-seeking behavior, which in turn represents an economic loss for the economy.

VII. Concluding Remarks

24. In the above sections, I presented the four main categories that economists list when describing the benefits of competition. But the economics perspective is obviously not exhaustive. Particularly important, though not frequently discussed, is the importance of competition for a well-functioning democracy. In 1804, while representing an editor accused of libeling then-President Thomas Jefferson, Alexander Hamilton argued that one must have "the liberty

of publishing truth, with good motives and for justifiable ends, even though it reflect on government, magistrates, or private persons." This freedom is enshrined in the US Constitution, as it should be, but it is of little value if it is not accompanied by a variety of sources, which ultimately requires some degree of competition.

25. Lack of competition is also a threat to democracy when a few corporations garner a disproportionate degree of market power – even if such market power cannot be measured by common market share indexes – due to political pressure, media control, or control of personal information. I don't have the space here or the ability to delve into these issues. Let us just say that a considerable number of industrial organization economists, traditionally more interested in "conventional market competition," have become increasingly interested in the economics of media, a field where the focus goes well beyond the traditional microeconomics approach to competition and welfare. Long live media economics for the service it provides to democracy.

26. To conclude, there are indeed many reasons why competition is a good thing.

A Return to 1912: The Antitrust Center Will Not Hold*

Matt Stoller**
Open Markets Institute

1. In the crises of the 1930s, one of the great investigations in American history was done by a pugnacious working-class lawyer, Ferdinand Pecora, who embarrassed the lords of Wall Street in 1933 as the lead counsel for the Senate Banking Committee. A few years later, as a judge, Pecora observed why countries all over the world were taking the road to fascism or Communism. "In other lands democratic government has abdicated to dictatorship," he said, "not because men no longer wished to be free, but because democratic governments become impotent to deal with economic problems."

2. Today, we are in a similar situation as those who, from the late nineteenth century until World War II, were engaged in a set of violent political struggles to figure out how to manage the power of industrialization. Indeed, the current debate over antitrust policy and enforcement is linked to the broader crisis of liberal democracy around the world.

3. That there is a crisis is undoubtable. In Hungary, Viktor Orbán has imposed an autocratic regime. Rodrigo Duterte in the Philippines is running an increasingly authoritarian state. In Brazil, Israel, and India, nationalists with authoritarian tendencies are winning. And the center left is collapsing. Angela Merkel in Germany and Emmanuel Macron in France are politically weak. Democracy, meaning self-government, is retreating, all over the world.

---

* This article has been previously published in Concurrences, and it might have been edited for clarity and cohesion. Matt Stoller, A return to 1912: The antitrust center will not hold, November 2019, Concurrences N° 4-2019, Art. N° 90939.

** Fellow, Open Markets Institute, Washington DC.

4. What does this have to do with antitrust? Antitrust is one of the key bodies of law that is intended to constrain corporate power, from addressing restraints of trade and monopolization to mergers.

5. And if you are looking at a global problem, you have to look at a global cause. The institutions that stretch all over the world and touch each of our lives are corporations and banks. In Brazil, Israel, Hungary, the Philippines, and India, people search for information using Google and communicate with each other through Facebook subsidiary WhatsApp, and often get seeds and chemicals from Bayer-Monsanto. More fundamentally we live in societies increasingly structured by powerful global corporations that corrupt our politics. Democracy is under threat because we have allowed the concentration of power in our industrial and financial sectors to rival, and exceed, the power of democratic institutions themselves. All over the world.

6. The current neoliberal system, half-democratic and half-corporatist, has failed to offer an answer to the problem people have in their lives, which is a lack of control over our communities. Instead, political leaders have allowed the monopolization of markets and said "let them eat charity." The far right is offering drama and power, and pointing the finger at corporate power as enabling both plutocracy and multiculturalism. They are offering a false idol, but such tricksters are always present. The difference is, today they are, as John Kenneth Galbraith said of all successful revolutions, pushing at a rotten door.

7. The debate in the US over how to address industrial power began in the late 1880s, and crystalized in the 1912 election. Teddy Roosevelt suggested a model he called The New Nationalism, concentrating power in the hands of the state, public masters over private monopolies, in which Roosevelt sought to aid American national champion style monopolies to compete with foreign goliaths. Taft had a mild laissez-faire technocratic approach, a status quo adherence, private masters over private monopolies. Woodrow Wilson, backed by Louis Brandeis, suggested The New Freedom, or regulated competition, to break the role of both public and private masters, and to encourage global free trade without barriers from either protectionist public rules or private monopolies and cartels. Despite Wilson's victory in the election, and an aggressive policymaking regime, the debate was cut short by World War I. Wilson brought forth half a revolution, with the other half left undone until the Great Depression collapsed the rickety structure of concentrated finance.

8. In the 1930s, different countries went down different paths to address burgeoning industrial power. In Germany and Eastern Europe, fascists responded most effectively and potently to a social crisis, in Russia it was the Communists who centralized power, and in the US it was populists in the form of New Dealers who resurrected liberal democracy through assertive anti-monopoly rules. New Dealers, and then their post-war allies in Europe, ended up winning

the war in the West, and structured a liberal international order that held the peace for decades. For roughly forty years, antitrust, and a whole suite of anti-monopoly laws and institutions, were oriented around constraining concentrations of power.

9. In the 1970s, the New Deal fell into crisis. There were insolvencies among companies like Franklin National Bank, Penn Central, Pan Am and Con Edison; even New York City nearly went bust. The problem was inflation, not fascism, and baby boomers then coming into politics did not think inflation was related to corporate concentration or banking power. A series of technocrats, some from the law and economics school centered at the University of Chicago, and planner liberals influenced by socialist John Kenneth Galbraith argued that limiting corporate concentration with democratic institutions was foolish. Concentrating that power, as Teddy Roosevelt might have, was the way to address the crises of the 1970s.

10. George Stigler, the law and economics scholar in Chicago, argued the victory over New Dealers happened by the end of the decade. "Indeed," he wrote, "it can be said that they conquered the field; by 1980 there remained scarcely a trace of the" old anti-monopoly framework in the economic literature. This victory, in time, would be as total in Europe and globally as it was in the United States.

11. The resolution of the debate in the 1980s was to shield questions of political economy from democratic forces. No longer was unregulated monopoly or concentration a problem, it was just natural forces at work. Instead, the focus was on consumer welfare, or low prices. The rights of producers in markets, whether workers, suppliers, rivals, farmers, authors, engineers, became irrelevant in service to the rights of consumers in markets.

12. Corporate concentration, which has accelerated rapidly since the early 1980s, has induced a host of problems all over the world, from lower productivity growth to higher regional inequality to income inequality. The number of public companies in the US, for instance, has dropped from roughly 7,000 in the 1990s to 3,500 today, largely through mergers. While every country has its own cultural and legal fabric, there's no reason to assume the trend lines point in a different direction than they do in America. The neoliberal revolution was global, and its effects are everywhere.

13. But now, what is happening in the US and Europe is a fast-moving debate over the nature of corporate power, and democracy.

14. There will be suits, big suits, very soon. Sure, the US federal government seems irrelevant, with the Federal Trade Commission abdicating leadership to enforcement agencies around the world. But the politics are heating up. Antitrust is now a part of presidential politics, with Elizabeth Warren leading the way with a bold plan for break-ups across the economy in everything from technology to agriculture, but virtually every other candidate also discussing the need for hard looks at reviving antitrust enforcement. State attorney

generals are circling big tech giants with potential suits. An intra-corporate war is brewing; 50 percent of Fortune 500 CEOs, for instance, think Facebook needs to be regulated more assertively, and Google and Amazon aren't far behind. Less than 10 percent feel that way about AT&T or Microsoft.

15. Congress is considering privacy crackdowns, passing bills to address price gouging by pharmaceutical companies, and holding hearings on monopolies in the military defense base. Just last week, a monopolist called TransDigm voluntarily gave back $16 million to the Pentagon in response to a House Oversight hearing; Chairman Elijah Cummings said that monopolies would be a focus for the committee going forward. Senator Josh Hawley of Missouri has resurrected the Do Not Track bill to address the use of data in anti-competitive ways. This restructuring of political economy thinking maps to Trump's new trade policy framework, an assertive use of state power to address anti-competitive mercantilist behavior by China and Germany.

16. Addressing monopolies through state power is back. But it's not just a question of when. It's also a question of how. In Europe, the mirage of assertive regulation and enforcement is being unmasked as a holding pattern. European privacy regulators are simply not enforcing the General Data Protection Regulation, and Google and Facebook are retaining their power as a result. European Competition Commissioner Margrethe Vestager, despite a flurry of suits against Google, has failed to meaningfully restructure the online advertising or search market in the EU. EU enforcers, imitating their flaccid American cousins, even allowed Facebook to lie about its privacy settings in its WhatsApp acquisition with a "parking ticket" level fine.

17. Despite statements of assertiveness, Europeans, with the exception of the German Federal Cartel Office, are often leery of wielding power. In an interview with Kara Swisher, Vestager made it clear that she is philosophically opposed to break-ups, and deeply in thrall to Google's way of thinking about the world. "We're dealing with private property," she said. Companies like Google, she asserted, are "businesses that are built and invested in and become successful because of their innovation. So to break up a company, to break up private property, would be very far-reaching." There is a clear choice facing Vestager, to truly enforce the laws and break Google's power, or to make the laws a mere public relations façade.

18. But even Vestager is too strong for many of the politicians in the EU. Earlier this year, German Chancellor Angela Merkel and French President Emmanuel Macron began a campaign to weaken Europe's antitrust rules after Vestager blocked a high-speed rail merger between Alstom and Siemens. Macron and Merkel believe that "European champions" are essential for competing on the world stage between China and America. The French are largely focused on the use of tax policy to structure big tech, with Macron attempting global and largely meaningless bromides about ending hate speech online, without a coherent understanding of the incentives that underpin the velocity of such speech.

19. There will be a radical restructuring of how we do antitrust. It's not a question of if, it's a question of when, and a question of how. We are now back in the intellectual world of the early twentieth century, with different philosophies of how to address corporate power manifesting themselves through dangerous and fascinating political movements. The status quo will not hold. The two remaining paths are an authoritarian approach – regulated monopoly similar to that of Teddy Roosevelt in 1912 and Trump, Macron, Merkel, and China today – or a democratic approach – regulated competition, similar to that of Wilson and Brandeis in 1912, and Warren, Mundt and Hawley today. And which we choose will be a function not just of debates among economists and experts, but among voters and politicians.

20. Each of these philosophies shapes the kind of societies we live in, and whether we can do politics as a collective act of self-governance. But the debate is no longer solely among the lawyers and economists. They have failed to bring meaningful cases or show that they are interested or willing to stop authoritarians in commerce. It is not too late; real cases to break up concentrations of power can help citizens regain confidence in their institutions and experts. But if they do not, the antitrust establishment will become irrelevant, sidelined, appropriately, by the ballot box.

No Need to Bang on the Table*

Anthony M. Collins**
General Court of the European Union

1. The General Court's jurisdiction to review Commission decisions in the field of competition law may be analysed under three headings:
   - First, review by reference to the jurisdictional and procedural rules that govern the exercise of the Commission's powers.
   - Second, review on grounds of compliance with the applicable substantive legal rules, usually whether the Commission applied the correct legal test to the circumstances of the case.
   - Third, examining whether the evidence upon which the Commission relied is factually accurate, reliable and consistent, whether it contains all of the information necessary to assess the situation in question and whether it is capable of sustaining the conclusions drawn from it.

2. Criticism of the General Court in the field of competition law tends to be levelled at the exercise of its jurisdiction under the second and third of these categories, rather than the first. In this context, it may be observed that the General Court is generally bound to respect the adversarial principle strictly. That respect automatically limits the scope of any adjudication to the issues raised by the parties in the course of the procedure and the evidence adduced in support thereof. No argument and/ or no evidence = no case! The burden of proof imposed upon applicants and the standard to which facts are to be proved of its nature afford the respondent an inbuilt advantage when defending

---

* This article has been previously published in Concurrences, and it might have been edited for clarity and cohesion. Anthony M. Collins, No need to bang on the table, November 2020, Concurrences N° 4-2020, Art. N° 96683, pp. 2-4.

** President Third Chamber, General Court of the European Union, Luxembourg. This foreword is written in a purely personal capacity. It does not purport to represent the views of the General Court as a body or of its members.

actions for annulment. Moreover, it has been said that at times the General Court has deferred to the Commission's assessment of the facts rather than adjudicating upon them objectively.

3. Two recent judgments of the General Court show that, when presented with rigorous argument and convincing evidence to challenge the factual basis for Commission decisions, it will adjudicate on those issues, to the point where the Commission is driven to convince the General Court of the merits of both its findings of fact and of the conclusions that it drew therefrom. On 28 May 2020, the enlarged formation of its First Chamber delivered judgment in Case T-399/16, *CK Telecoms UK Investments Ltd v. European Commission* (hereinafter "*CK Telecoms*"), whereby it annulled a Commission decision of 11 May 2016 declaring the acquisition of Telefónica Europe Plc by Hutchison 3G UK Investments Ltd incompatible with the internal market. About one and a half months later, on 15 July 2020, an enlarged formation of the Seventh Chamber annulled the Commission's decision of 30 August 2016 that Ireland had granted State aid to subsidiaries of Apple Inc. by way of various tax rulings in Cases T-778/16 and T-892/16, *Ireland v. European Commission* (hereinafter "*Apple*").

I. Exhibit I: *CK Telecoms*

4. The decision challenged in *CK Telecoms* in effect found that the acquisition of one mobile network operator by another would have reduced competition in the United Kingdom retail mobile telecommunications market, leading to higher prices, limited choice and reduced quality for consumers. The Commission took the view that the two mobile network operators involved in the acquisition exerted an important competitive constraint in the market and that one of them, Three, was an "important competitive force". The Commission also relied on evidence that the two mobile network operators competed closely with each other.

5. The General Court interpreted Article 2(3) of Regulation No. 139/2004, which provides that the Commission may prohibit a transaction where it was found to "significantly impede effective competition (…) in particular as the result of the creation or strengthening of a dominant position", as requiring two conditions to be satisfied. First, the transaction eliminates important competitive constraints that the parties had exerted upon each other. Second, the transaction reduces competitive pressure on the operators remaining on the market. Having established the test, the General Court held that the burden of proof to establish that state of affairs lay with the Commission. As for the standard of proof, since merger control procedures necessarily relied upon prospective analyses, the less discernible the chains of cause and effect and the less certain the analysis, the greater the quality of the evidence the Commission was required to produce to support its position. Moreover, since it is for the

Commission to show that the significant impediment to effective competition it had identified was the direct and immediate effect of the transaction, it must produce evidence sufficient to demonstrate a strong probability of the existence of such impediments.

6. The General Court accordingly fixed the standard of proof demanded of the Commission as higher than the balance of probabilities but not as strong as that of beyond reasonable doubt. Thereafter the General Court's judgment explains in considerable detail why, upon a close examination of the facts in the light of the parties' arguments and evidence, it concluded that the evidence in support of the Commission's analysis, and the various theories of harm invoked in its support, did not meet the test that it had established.

II. Exhibit II: *Apple*

7. Apple challenged a Commission decision that had found that two tax rulings Ireland had made in respect of two branches of Apple subsidiaries operating, but not tax resident, in Ireland, had enabled these subsidiaries to reduce the amount of tax for which they were liable, thus constituting an advantage as compared with other companies in a comparable situation. The Commission also found that the allocation of profits agreed by the Irish authorities did not correspond to economic reality because the subsidiaries, as distinct from its branches, did not have any physical presence of employees.

8. In *Apple* the General Court reiterated the legal principles governing the review of Commission decisions on the presence of State aid in tax rulings made by Member States' competent authorities. The judgment confirmed the Commission's jurisdiction to investigate tax rulings by reference to the rules on State aid, the test for the existence of a selective advantage and the Commission's recourse both to the arm's length principle to establish the existence of an advantage and to the authorised OECD approach for the allocation of profits.

9. Nevertheless, the General Court found that the Commission had erred in its assessment of the requirements of both the applicable Irish tax law, which required an objective analysis of the activities or functions of the Irish branch of a non-resident company, and the authorised OECD approach for the allocation of profits. The General Court likewise rejected the alternative basis for the Commission's decision – namely, that the methodology used to allocate profits to the subsidiaries understated the taxable profits that ought to have been attributed thereto. It held that the Commission could not limit itself to pointing to methodological defects in the profit allocation or profit calculation method used in the rulings but had to positively demonstrate that that method reduced the subsidiaries' tax burden as compared to what would have been the case had those tax rulings had not been issued. The General Court also found that neither the Commission's criticism of the choice of operating

costs, as opposed to revenues or total costs as a proxy for the calculation of taxable profit, nor its comparability analysis, which sought to benchmark the estimated profit in the rulings with that of a sample of companies, proved that the subsidiaries' Irish tax liability had been reduced as compared to what it ought to have been.

III. Keep to the Facts

10. Decisions of the General Court in actions for the annulment of Commission decisions are subject to a right of appeal to the Court of Justice on points of law only. Save in highly exceptional cases, no appeal lies against the General Court's determination of issues of fact, which of their nature include questions of national law. This allocation of jurisdiction follows from the rationale for the establishment of the precursor of the General Court in order, inter alia, to hear actions that require the close examination of complex facts.

11. In *CK Telecoms* and in *Apple* the General Court makes it clear that where an applicant challenges the facts the Commission relied upon in order to reach a decision in a given set of circumstances, the Commission must prove those facts to the satisfaction of the General Court on pain of the annulment of that decision. In discharging that responsibility, the General Court cannot afford the Commission any margin of discretion or deference: the Commission has no right to go wrong as to the facts or, indeed, the law.

12. In approaching challenges to Commission decisions in this way, the General Court reinforces the authority of the Union's decision-making processes. Nonetheless it ought not to be overlooked that, in a legal system grounded on the adversarial principle, it is always a matter for the parties to marshal and to present the requisite factual and legal elements in support of their case. There is an adage amongst practitioners that when the facts are against your client, you bang on the law; when the law is against your client, you bang on the facts and that when the facts and the law are against your client, you bang on the table. *CK Telecoms* and *Apple* show that persuasively argued cases grounded upon sound factual evidence will succeed before the General Court without their being any requirement to bang on the table

Both Private and Public Powers Are Going Beyond Their Bounds – Let's Keep an Eye on Both*

Giuliano Amato**
Constitutional Court of Italy

1. Twenty-five years ago, when I wrote *Antitrust and the Bounds of Powers* (Hart Publishing), my purpose was to remind the antitrust community, at the time absorbed in the thousand technicalities of our discipline, that the discipline itself was not only about efficiency and consumer welfare; it had to do with something much more substantial. It had to do with power and with the abuses of it that endanger freedom and, ultimately, democracy. I do not know how many of my colleagues found my appeal convincing and decided to raise their eyes above the technicalities. For sure nowadays, in the world of Big Tech and Big Data, which the New Brandeis movement is exploring with meticulous attention, that antitrust is, first of all, antitrust – in other words, a fight against power – is an undisputable truth for everybody. If a problem exists, this refers to the limits antitrust meets in this fight – namely, which conducts its toolbox allows it to reach and to curb and whether it is being stretched beyond its limits towards manifestations of power to be restricted by other means.

2. It is a serious problem (in Germany, a decision is pending on Facebook precisely in relation to it, and it is not by chance that the ECJ has been requested from the Oberlandesgericht Dusseldorf to issue a preliminary ruling that for now has received the opinion of AG Rantos). However, it is a well-known one, and there is no reason to return to it once more in this foreword.

---

* This article has been previously published in Concurrences, and it might have been edited for clarity and cohesion. Giuliano Amato, Both private and public powers are going beyond their bounds – let's keep an eye on both, February 2023, Concurrences N° 1-2023, Art. N° 110213.

** Former President Italian Constitutional Court, Rome.

3. What I want to do here is to examine the other side of the coin, namely, the side of the excess not of private power, but of public power, which is the other enemy a balanced antitrust policy should keep under control. Eleanor Fox has recently noticed (in her contribution to the volume *Antitrust and the Bounds of Powers: 25 Years On*, edited by Oles Andriychuk, to be published by Hart Publishing) that lately, both private and public powers have gone far beyond their bounds. I had warned against an excess of public powers in terms of antitrust over-reaction, while public power – she writes – is trespassing its limits in another direction, namely, becoming authoritarian, as it has already happened in some European countries. I share this remark, which receives further evidence in our post-globalisation time, due to the other numerous public interferences with the market that have supervened.

I. Market Competitiveness Has Always to be Protected, Whatever the Legal Means

4. What is happening in economic markets where states or supranational regions (such as Europe) have decided to achieve "strategic autonomy" in relation to the production of goods previously coming from other parts of the world that might be suddenly precluded due to pandemics or wars? What, again, if a state does not want its national companies to merge with certain foreign companies or, even more, to have such companies among their shareholders? Aren't the powers consequently exercised public disturbances to the competitiveness of the relevant markets, either in the form of State aid or in other forms? Do the public interests that are pursued supply a reasonable ground for such disturbances? Does a border exist here too, beyond which they are unjustifiably intrusive?

5. One might argue that, from an antitrust angle, this is not another side of the same coin, for not necessarily all these public interferences with the competitiveness of the market fall under the scrutiny of antitrust. It certainly would be a good argument, in parallel with what we have already assessed in relation to the manifestations of private power. However, it would not be a good reason not to examine this area, where some of the interferences might fall themselves under antitrust prohibitions (State aids), while the rules applicable to others represent a relevant question. After all, market competitiveness is and remains a unitary concept, whatever the legal means by which it has to be protected.

II. When Do State Aids and Special Powers Illegally Affect Trading Conditions?

6. Upon this premise, two points I want to make. The first one is that we should more thoroughly study State aids – both their structure and their functioning – in relation to competition. As we know, in the US, they are considered

a matter for member states' legislation, rarely relevant at the federal level. In the European Union, they actually are a significant chapter of antitrust itself. However, the language of the treaty offers a plurality of windows of flexibility that transparently demonstrate how easily State aid can be justified under the light of other European policies. The fact of the matter is that Member States have always considered their industrial and regional policies above antitrust, the rules of which, in their view, should always adapt to their needs. The Commission has defended its competences and, on the whole, has not allowed antitrust to be submerged by suspensions of its rules or exceptions to them. What may happen nowadays, with new industrial policies that are officially more European than national? The documents state that such policies aim at making European industry more competitive, but the general aim they are part of is to achieve "strategic autonomy" in several sectors. Are the two goals really compatible? As long as the instruments are structural reforms and, therefore, simplifications of official rules and formalities, it is fine. As long as new and more efficient public infrastructures are provided for, it is equally fine. What about access to the financial markets when it is made easier by privileged bonds or grants-in-aid? Can we be satisfied as long as there are no discriminations nor privileged areas inside the European integrated market, but discriminations and privileged areas necessarily are produced in the wider markets? Article 107 TFEU says that aids which contribute to the development of activities are admissible when they do "not adversely affect trading conditions". Does this clause also apply to trading conditions outside the EU market? We know well that no global antitrust authority exists to give us an answer. But the WTO does exist and we, the antitrust community, should offer keys useful to its work. Let me also add that strategic autonomy may also conflict with other European policies, such as support for developing economies, which does not mean that it should not be pursued. It simply means that from every angle, it should be handled with care – with great care.

7. I briefly examine my second point, namely, the power several states are equipping themselves with to interfere with their national companies in their relationships with foreign companies. It is the so-called golden power. In principle, such power has a solid legitimacy based on the strategic interests of the state. The sectors where it was initially adopted were defence and security. It is very difficult to imagine any external control on the use of it, when this is the reason. For sure, defence and security are outside the reach of antitrust. However, the magic of the adjective "strategic" has widened the sectors where the golden power can be exercised: any other "strategic sector". Therefore – I take the case of my country – the government is now entitled to intervene in finance, banking, energy, transport, food, artificial intelligence, digital equipment (and others). Sometimes the reason is no less compelling than in defence: so is the case of the foreign company that has become a shareholder, which is legally obliged to transmit to its government all the information it has acquired in such a role. However, the strategic implications are not always

equally perceptible. Furthermore, there have been cases in which the golden power of a Member State of the EU has been used vis-à-vis a company of another Member State, which is per se inadmissible.

III. The Excesses of Public Powers Are No Less Harmful Than the Growth of Private Powers

8. It is quite unlikely that the scrutiny on the use of this power (when admissible) falls under the jurisdiction of antitrust. First of all, antitrust deals with private conduct, not with public measures, unless explicitly stated by law, as in the case of State aid. Furthermore, several measures adopted under the golden powers affect the freedom of choice, not the competitiveness of the companies involved. However, competitiveness itself may be affected and, independently of it, this is a new public power that is expanding itself over the economy.

9. Here we are now. Antitrust – and not only antitrust – is based on an appropriate balance that prevents and, if necessary, prohibits the growth of private powers on the one side and the excesses of public powers on the other. As Eleanor Fox has rightly noticed, both have gone too far, whatever their directions. Hundreds of reasons explain why it has happened. No reason prevails on the need to restore, with all the necessary means, the balance we have lost.

About Competition Jurisdictional Control*

Hubert Legal**
Council of the European Union

1. The time is not yet far off when the Court of Justice of the European Communities and the Court of First Instance considered that they had amply fulfilled their duty of review of the Commission's competition decisions when they had generally verified that the institution had not committed a manifest error in its economic assessments – which are always complex – and, in the event of some marginal defect affecting the decision, reduced the fine – if there was one – to an amount slightly lower than the initial amount, fixed by approximation at a round figure. This at least had the merit of honesty.

2. It was not a happy time for Community economic law because its concepts were poor and its procedures opaque; in this context of legal vagueness, the fear of being suspected of arbitrariness inhibited the Commission's action. The active implementation of the regulatory function and the deepening of its contentious control, facilitated by the transparency effort undertaken by the Commission on its own initiative, have taken place at a contemporary date. These complementary phenomena are only apparently contradictory.

---

* This article has been previously published in Concurrences, and it might have been edited for clarity and cohesion. Hubert Legal, About competition jurisdictional control, May 2005, Concurrences N° 2-2005, Art. N° 96, pp. 1-2.

** Director-General of the Council Legal Service. Council of the European Union, Brussels. The author of the review would like to make it clear that, although not expressly stated, the comments contained in this article are his own and not those of the institution of which he is a member. Moreover, since the foreword has been interpreted in the press in a manner far removed from the author's intentions, the author points out that his intention was to identify, in a subjective manner, some of the aspects underlying a specific theoretical problem and not to offer a critical assessment of the work of the Court of First Instance; consequently, none of the terms of the foreword should be understood as relating to an objective assessment of the current functioning of the institution.

3. The present moment, though less dull, is no more satisfying – so much so that one wonders whether one has fallen from the Charybdis to the Scylla. The discovery by the Community courts, and more particularly by the Court of First Instance (which now has jurisdiction at first instance for all direct actions concerning competition), of its prerogatives of full jurisdiction is the cause of a worrying lack of clarity in the case law. Filled with the zeal of the converted and assured by the intention affirmed by the Court of Justice in its judgments in *Commission v Tetra Laval* of 15 February this year not to interfere, on appeal, in their sovereign jurisdiction to verify economic analyses, the judges – and I know that they are – sometimes feel like censors who are teaching censors and want to go over everything from A to Z in each appeal in order to write the final judgment which will set the law by example as to what is appropriate in the field of cartels or abuses of dominant positions.

4. However, we must remember the logic of our institutional system. The regulatory authority is the Commission; it takes decisions that are administrative acts, which are considered to be almost entirely unjustified in terms of criminal law, except for the procedural guarantees that must accompany a repressive intervention with pecuniary effect. Judicial review is a review of legality that in principle excludes any consideration of the appropriateness of the measure; it is not for the judge, according to the terms enshrined, to substitute his assessment for that of the administration unless, since the latter has misinterpreted or misapplied the rule of law, the circumstances make it possible to judge the dispute by setting the sanction without referral.

5. The shortcut, however, is tempting. One can discern a tendency of the Tribunal to take itself for a judge of appeal seized by the devolutive effect, reforming from the outset the operative part before it without first identifying what was censured, for illegality, in the reasons for the initial decision.

6. There are several reasons for this. Among these, the limited conception of the judge of the appeal of the control of the legal classification in economic matters has already been pointed out.

7. A second cause is to be found in the highly articulated and detailed nature of the Commission's decisions and their voluntary submission to guidelines which must be respected; the more one says, the more one is exposed to the risk that documentary or logical imperfections in the administrative investigation will come to light – and there are almost inevitably some.

8. The third factor prompting reconsideration is sociological. Much of the real decision- making power of the Court of First Instance lies in the hands of the referendaries, who are collaborators of the judges and are increasingly young since enlargement, fresh from the European colleges and without judicial, administrative or diplomatic experience. Brilliant minds wishing to assert their hold, some, Community by ambition, nourished by the doctrine of precedent, see the public interest only as an abstract, even suspicious notion, and believe

in their duty to act towards their judge, sometimes handicapped by a limited mastery of the language of deliberation, in the ayatollahs of free enterprise.

9. However, the Court of First Instance does not have the means to carry out a systematic recasting of the Commission's decisions. Its constraints in terms of staff numbers, deadlines, language and knowledge also impose self-limitations on it if it wishes to remain credible. Moreover, duplication between the administrative authority and its judge makes no sense from the point of view of institutional rationality.

10. Finally, I believe that there are only two coherent and convincing organisational models in this area. The current Community model is one of them. It presupposes at judicial level a review of legality, possibly supplemented, if the case permits, by the exercise of powers to reverse the contested decision. The other model is one in which the administration investigates the case and the decision is taken by a judicial body. Its merits should not be overlooked. Not least of all is the avoidance of a duplication of the review of the facts at intervals of several months or years and the full use of the administration's means of investigation and analysis, free from the pressure induced by the responsibility to punish, and the judge's powers of appreciation.

11. Nothing is as distressing as the demonstration of arbitrariness that can be represented by the substitution of a new assessment, not necessarily better in opportunity or in law, made by persons who, with few exceptions, are less familiar with the case, for the assessment made by persons who know the situation in depth.

Competition Law in Question: Putting It into Perspective*

FRÉDÉRIC JENNY**
Organisation for Economic Co-operation and Development (OECD)

1. In recent years, competition law in both the United States and Europe has given rise to a number of questions concerning its purpose, raison d'être and effectiveness.

2. Various aspects of competition law have given rise to controversy. Some felt that competition law had lost sight of what its purpose should be; others argued that the growing role of economics in the implementation of competition law had distorted it and made it so complex as to threaten legal certainty; still others considered that what they perceived as the failure of competition law implementation in the digital sector needed to be corrected by the adoption of ex-ante regulations complementary to competition law, as the only way to effectively combat anticompetitive practices and transactions in this sector. These controversies have frequently pitted economists and lawyers against each other.

3. I'd like to put these controversies into perspective by addressing three issues: the question of the purpose of competition law, the question of the test in the implementation of competition law, and finally the question of the effectiveness of the implementation of competition law.

---

* This article has been previously published in Concurrences, and it might have been edited for clarity and cohesion. Frédéric Jenny, Competition law in question: Putting it into perspective, May 2024, Concurrences N° 2-2024, Art. N° 118053.

** Professor of Economics ESSEC Business School and President of the International Committee of Concurrences Review.

I. The Aim of Competition Law

4. As far as the purpose of competition law is concerned, a twofold observation is in order. Firstly, there are many different conceptions of competition; secondly, most national competition laws do not clearly state which conception of competition they refer to, nor what the precise purpose of competition law is.

5. As far as competition is concerned, we need to distinguish between different conceptions. Take, for example, sporting competition, which is highly regulated and in which a single winner emerges, with the other competitors defeated. This form of competition is far removed from economic competition, which, on the contrary, places the freedom of players rather than their regulation at the heart of the market process, and aims to ensure that economic agents benefit overall from an efficient allocation of resources, in the form of an increased collective surplus. But this economic form of competition is itself different from that underlying ordoliberal thinking, for which the purpose of competition policy is not the maximization of consumer welfare, but the imperative of allowing economic agents free access to the market and thus preserving the structure of competition.[1] These notions of competition are also different from the notion of fair competition, which aims to establish ethical rules of behavior between economic agents independently of their effects on markets. All these notions are also different from the notion of "fair and equitable" competition, which aims to enable balanced competition between market players. We could go on with this list of different notions of competition, but there's no need to prolong it here. What we must remember is that the first step is to clarify the notion of competition, which lies at the heart of competition law.

6. Competition laws rarely spell out the notion of competition they are intended to promote. This imprecision gives rise to controversy as to what their purpose should be. And yet, as we shall see, determining this purpose is crucial in determining the substantive test that must be applied to distinguish prohibited practices or transactions from those that are permitted.

7. European competition law is no exception to the vagueness of its purpose. A reading of the European treaties suggests that the purpose of competition law is to be a means to the undistorted functioning of the internal market.

8. This internal market is provided for in Article 3(3) of the Treaty on European Union, which states: "The Union shall establish an internal market. It shall work for the sustainable development of Europe based on balanced economic growth and price stability, a highly competitive social market economy, aiming at full employment and social progress, and a high level of protection and improvement of the quality of the environment. It shall promote scientific and technical

---

1 V. F. Marty: Politiques européennes de concurrence et économie sociale de marché, in *Les valeurs communes dans l'Union européenne*, L. Potvin-Solis (dir.), Bruylant, Brussels, 2014, pp. 341-377.

progress," and Protocol No. 27 on the internal market and competition, which states that "the internal market as defined in Article 3 of the Treaty on European Union includes a system ensuring that competition is not distorted."

9. However, in 2001, Mario Monti, then European Commissioner for Competition, gave a much more economic definition of the purpose of European competition law, stating: "The purpose of competition law, in all its dimensions, is to protect consumer surplus by maintaining a high degree of competition in the common market. Competition should lead to lower prices, wider choice and the benefit of technological innovation, all in the interests of consumers".[2]

II. European Competition Law Pursues a Variety of Objectives

10. In 2018, Ariel Ezrachi,[3] based on an analysis of the decisions of the Court of Justice of the European Union, showed that European competition law pursues a variety of objectives such as consumer welfare (a notion broader than consumer surplus and incorporating consideration of personal data protection or a fair distribution of resources), efficiency and innovation, the maintenance of an effective structure of competition,[4] economic freedom, pluralism and democracy,[5] fairness in economic relations[6] or the completion of the single market.[7]

11. In the United States, a vigorous intellectual battle was waged between the Chicago School, for whom competition law was designed to protect consumers' economic surplus, and the neo-Brandesians, for whom the Sherman Act had a broader ambition, namely to combat economic power, which is a threat to democracy.

III. The Purpose of Competition Law and the Substantive Test for Prohibited Practices

12. In Europe, unlike in the United States, we have been able to live with a degree of vagueness about the objectives of our competition law, and have so far avoided trench warfare over the purpose of this law. However, we have not

---

2 M. Monti, The Future for Competition Policy in the European Union, speech, Merchant Taylor's Hall, London, July 9, 2001.

3 EU Competition Law Goals and the Digital Economy, *Oxford Legal Studies Research Paper* No. 17/2018.

4 E.g. in the *T-Mobile* judgment, June 4, 2009, aff. C-8/08, EU:C:2009:343, paras 31, 36, 38-39, or the *GlaxoSmithKline Services Unlimited v Commission* judgment, October 6, 2009, Case C-501/06 P, EU:C:2009:610, para. 63.

5 E.g. in the *TeliaSonera* judgment, February 17, 2011, Case C-52/09, EU:C:2011:83.

6 E.g. in the judgments concerning *General Motors Continental*, November 13, 1975, Case 26-75, EU:C:1975:150, or *United Brands*, February 14, 1978, Case 27/76, EU:C:1978:22; Case C-177/16.

7 E.g. in *GlaxoSmithKline Services Unlimited.*

escaped guerrilla warfare over the tests to be applied to determine whether a practice is anticompetitive, particularly with regard to abusive practices that exclude companies in a dominant position.

13. This intellectual guerrilla war pits economists in favor of an "effects-based" approach against a number of legal experts who, put off by the complexity of this approach and concerned about the legal uncertainty it is likely to generate, are in favor of a broader recourse to the notion of infringement by object or to presumptions.

14. The stages leading up to the outbreak of this guerrilla war are well known.

15. The aforementioned statements by Mario Monti in 2001 testify to a shift in DG Competition's thinking, aimed at fostering convergence with the practices of North American competition authorities by introducing a more economic approach to the implementation of competition law than had hitherto prevailed.

16. In 2005, the Economic Advisory Group on Competition Policy (EAGCP), made up of economists selected by DG Competition's Chief Economist and appointed by the Commissioner, published a note entitled "An economic approach to Article 82," which stated:

> "European competition policy has recently been reformed and now follows a more economic approach in the implementation of Article 81 on anti-competitive agreements and in merger control; we will argue here for a similar approach to the application of Article 82 on abuse of dominance. In particular, we will argue that the competition authority should adopt an effects-based rather than a form-based approach to competition policy. (…) [N] efirst review the net benefits of such an approach, then make a few remarks on how to implement it." (Free translation)

17. In 2009, the Commission published a communication entitled "Guidance on the Commission's priorities for the application of Article 82 of the EC Treaty to abusive exclusionary conduct by dominant undertakings," in which it endorsed the economic approach advocated a few years earlier by the EAGCP, and set out the substantive test on which it intended to base its assessment of anticompetitive exclusionary conduct by dominant undertakings. According to recital 23 of this communication, the Commission stated: "To avoid anticompetitive foreclosure, the Commission will normally intervene only where the practices in question have already impeded or are likely to impede competition from undertakings considered to be as efficient as the dominant undertaking."

18. In the Commission's view, this test for eliminating an equally efficient competitor had the dual advantage of making economic sense and being understandable to European jurists and courts, since in *AKZO Chemie v Commission*,[8]

8 Judgment of July 3, 1991, aff. C-62/86, EU:C:1991:286, para. 72.

followed an approach close to this test, stating (with regard to prices below costs): "Such prices may (…) drive out of the market undertakings which may be as efficient as the dominant undertaking but which, because of their lesser financial capacity, are unable to withstand the competition which they face."

19. However, two events thwarted the evolution of competition law towards a more economic approach.

20. First, the Commission and the national competition authorities of the Member States, with the support of the Court of First Instance, chose to considerably broaden the scope of infringements considered to be infringements of competition law by object, i.e. infringements whose degree of harmfulness was supposed to be so obvious that it was superfluous to demonstrate their effects.

21. For competition authorities, the existence of an infringement by object offers a considerable procedural advantage. This allows them to dispense with defining the relevant market and demonstrating the anticompetitive effects of the disputed practice (and, therefore, to apply the economic test requiring an equally efficient competitor).

22. The question arises as to why the Commission, which was itself at the origin of a more economic approach to competition law, chose in a number of cases to resort to the notion of infringement by object rather than implement the economic test it had itself defined. Several factors seem to have contributed to this evolution. First, this test is fairly permissive in that it allows dominant companies to exclude their less efficient competitors (only the exclusion of an equally efficient competitor is prohibited), and it can be assumed that in a number of cases the Commission was unable to demonstrate the exclusion of equally efficient competitors. Second, the economic test, by its very nature based on a number of assumptions, could easily be called into question before the referring courts, which could appear to weaken the Commission's decisions.

23. In 2014, the Court of Justice framed this jurisprudential development in its *Groupement des cartes bancaires* judgment.[9] In this judgment, the Court of Justice criticizes the General Court for deciding that the existence of a restriction of competition by object should not be analyzed "*restrictively*," a conclusion that the General Court had believed it could draw in view of the "non-exhaustive" nature of the examples given by Article 101(1) of the Treaty on the Functioning of the European Union (TFEU). The Court also held that the "*essential*" legal criterion for establishing an infringement by object is "a finding that such coordination is in itself sufficiently harmful to competition." Such a finding must be apparent from the content of the provisions of the agreement in question (e.g. its "very terms"), its objectives, and the economic and legal context in which it operates.

---

9 Judgment of September 11, 2014, aff. C-67/13 P, EU:C:2014:2204.

24. Second, the application of the equally efficient competitor exclusion test in cases of conditional rebates granted by dominant undertakings has been the subject of particularly vigorous challenges in two cases before the Court of Justice: the *Post Danmark II*[10] and *Intel*[11] cases.

25. In the *Post Danmark II* case, the Danish Post Office had been condemned by the Danish competition authority for abusing its dominant position on the bulk mail market by applying a system of loyalty discounts on direct mail ranging from 6 to 16 percent, which did not distinguish between mail falling under Post Danmark's monopoly and that falling under the market open to competition. The Danish Maritime and Commercial Court made a reference for a preliminary ruling under Article 267 TFEU, putting three questions to the Court of Justice concerning, firstly, the criteria or "guidelines" to be applied under Article 82 EC in assessing discount schemes granted by undertakings in a dominant position, and in particular whether an "equally efficient competitor" cost test should be applied to demonstrate the foreclosure effect.

26. In this case, Ms Kokott delivered conclusions[12] that have remained, like many of her conclusions, famous. It states:

> "3. In this case, the Court will have to determine in particular whether, in order to assess the anticompetitive nature of rebate schemes within the meaning of Article 82 EC, it is legally necessary to carry out an analysis of prices and costs by comparing the commercial practices of the undertaking in a dominant position with those of an equally efficient competitor ('As efficient competitor' Test). In addition, the question arises as to whether the foreclosure effect produced by the rebate system practiced by a company in a dominant position must exceed some threshold of sensitivity (de minimis threshold) in order to be classified as anticompetitive.
>
> 4. At a time when calls for a 'more economic approach' to European competition law are becoming increasingly frequent, these questions take on particular importance. In providing answers to its questions, whose impact should extend far beyond the present case, in our view the Court should not allow itself to be overly influenced by the spirit of the age or passing fashions, but rather return to the legal foundations on which the prohibition of abuse of a dominant position in Union law is founded."

27. In this passage, Advocate General Kokott did more than express her reticence towards the economic approach of European competition law. She also pointed out that the substantive test for distinguishing the anticompetitive practices of

---

10 Judgment of October 6, 2015, Case C-23/14, EU:C:2015:651.

11 Judgment of September 6, 2017, Case C-413/14 P, EU:C:2017:632.

12 Conclusions AG Kokott, May 24, 2015, Case C-23/14, EU:C:2015:343.

dominant companies from those that are not prohibited must be aligned with the objectives of competition law. In other words, discussion of the substantive test to be applied is meaningless without consideration of the purpose of competition law. But, as we have seen, this purpose is itself open to debate.

28. It is clear, however, that if we consider that the purpose of competition law is to protect consumer surplus, the use of presumptions of illegality and the scope of practices by dominant firms that can be considered as infringements by object can only be limited. Indeed, economic analysis suggests that most practices by dominant firms can be either pro or anticompetitive, depending on the context in which they are implemented. Consequently, the only way to determine whether a practice is prohibited is to apply an economic analysis and place it in the context in which it was implemented. Conversely, if the aim of competition law is to ensure fair trade or the unification of the single European market, the number of practices that can be qualified as infringements by object can be much greater.

29. The *Post Danmark II* judgment, in which the Court of Justice largely followed Ms Kokott's opinion, states:

> "59. (…) [D]n a situation such as that in the main proceedings, where the undertaking in a dominant position holds a very large market share and enjoys structural advantages conferred in particular by the legal monopoly of that undertaking, which applied to 70% of shipments on the market concerned, application of the criterion of an equally efficient competitor is irrelevant insofar as the structure of the market makes it practically impossible for an equally efficient competitor to emerge.
>
> 60. Moreover, in a market such as the one at issue in the main proceedings, where access is protected by high barriers, the presence of a less efficient competitor could contribute to intensifying competitive pressure on the market, thereby constraining the behavior of the company in a dominant position.
>
> 61. The criterion of an equally efficient competitor must therefore be considered as one instrument among others for assessing the existence of abuse of a dominant position in the context of a rebate system."

30. Answering one of the questions referred to it for a preliminary ruling, the Court of Justice concluded (para. 62) that "[i]t is therefore appropriate to reply to the first question, third and fourth paragraphs, that application of the criterion of an equally efficient competitor is not an essential condition for establishing the abusive nature of a rebate system under Article 82 EC. In a situation such as that in the main proceedings, application of the "equally efficient competitor" criterion is irrelevant."

31. This judgment was followed by the annulment of the Court's decision confirming the Commission's decision in the *Intel* case.

32. It should be noted that the Court of Justice's ruling can only be understood if we accept that the object of competition law is not the protection of consumer surplus or the pursuit of economic efficiency, but, as the Court of Justice implicitly states, the protection of the competitive structure of markets. As indicated above, there is a close link between the object of competition law and the substantive test to be employed in its implementation.

IV. It Is Abusive to Identify the Economic Approach of Competition Law and the Test of Exclusion of the Competitor as Effective

33. This development in case law has had two main effects. Firstly, it has led the European Commission to amend its 2008 guidelines on exclusionary abuses.[13] Among other changes, the Commission broadens the scope of prohibited exclusionary practices by a dominant undertaking, indicating that it will intervene more often even in cases where the abuse in question affects only less efficient competitors than the dominant undertaking (for example, in cases of high barriers to entry, opportunities for economies of scale or network effects to the advantage of the dominant undertaking), thus drawing the consequences of the *Post Danmark II* ruling. The Commission also points out, in line with the case law of the European Court of Justice, that competition authorities are under no legal obligation to apply the efficient competitor test. This test may be relevant, particularly in the case of exclusivity clauses, or it may be inappropriate as unnecessarily complex for the analysis of exclusivity rebates in particular, given the high probability of competition being harmed by such rebates. In the Commission's view, the "equally efficient competitor" test should now be used as one of several tools for analyzing the anticompetitive effects of a price-based predatory practice. In other words, the Commission is retreating from the effects-based approach advocated in 2008, and from the usefulness of the equally efficient competitor test for implementing this practice.

34. The second effect of this ruling was a renewed challenge by legal experts to the economic approach to competition law enforcement, on the grounds of the legal uncertainty this approach would imply, given the complexity of implementing the test for excluding such an effective competitor. Strong arguments have been put forward in favor of abandoning this approach in favor of a more legal approach, which favors the prosecution of practices considered restrictive of competition by object (and, correlatively, an extension of this category of infringement).

---

13 Communication from the Commission, Amendments to the Communication from the Commission entitled "Guidance on the Commission's priorities for applying Article 82 of the EC Treaty to abusive exclusionary conduct by dominant undertakings," C(2023) 1923 final, March 27, 2023.

35. Suffice it to say that it is a misnomer to identify the economic approach to competition law and the competitor exclusion test as equally effective. It should be noted in this respect that the EAGCP, while advocating a more economic approach to abusive exclusionary practices by companies in a dominant position, in no way suggested that the equally efficient competitor test was the only possible test for analyzing such practices. Numerous economic tests have been proposed in economic literature to establish the anticompetitive nature of exclusionary practices, such as the "sacrifice of profit" test, the "absence of economic sense" test, the "Elhauge test," etc.[14] Each economic test has its limitations, and it is important to choose the most appropriate economic test given the nature of the practices under scrutiny. The fact that the test of exclusion of the most efficient competitor has proved highly complex in cases of conditional rebates in no way indicates that the economic method is in itself unsuitable for the application of competition law, but simply indicates that each type of exclusionary practice by dominant undertakings must be examined in the light of an appropriate economic test.

V. The Purpose, Substantive Test and Effectiveness of Competition Law

36. A final word on the notion of the effectiveness of competition law. Neither economists nor lawyers question the fact that the implementation of competition law must enable it to achieve its objective, which is to eliminate practices considered anticompetitive.

37. Arguing that the implementation of competition law through economic analysis of the effects of practices or transactions was ineffective in punishing those practices or transactions that were anticompetitive, particularly in the digital sector, neo-Brandesians in the USA argued for a revision of the purpose of competition law to enable the fight against abuse of economic power rather than simply the fight against abuse of market power. Similarly, it is on the grounds that the implementation of competition law is too complex and uncertain that some European jurists are arguing for an extension of the use of the notion of infringement by object.

38. What is striking, however, is that economists and lawyers each have a partial view of the problem of the effectiveness of competition law. Economists favor an approach based, on the one hand, on implementing the law in such a way as to minimize the cost of errors of economic judgment (by avoiding condemning practices that are nonetheless pro-competitive, or not condemning practices that are nonetheless anticompetitive) and, on the other hand, on deterrence, arguing that sanctions must be sufficient to

14 See in this respect Competition Committee, *OECD Reference Note, Policy Roundtables, Competition on the Merits 2005, DAF/COMP(2005) 27*, March 30, 2006.

render anticompetitive practices unprofitable. Lawyers, for their part, insist on the "administrable" nature of the substantive test and on the predictability of competition law. Unlike economists, they argue that a test that is too complex to implement loses its usefulness, even if it is theoretically well-founded, because it does not enable litigants to predict with sufficient confidence the prohibited or tolerated nature of their practices or transactions, and consequently does not serve as a guide for economic players in determining their conduct.

VI. Effective Competition Law Requires Both Discernment and Dissuasive Sanctions, As Well As Legibility and Predictability

39. The concerns of lawyers and economists are equally well-founded. The effectiveness of competition law requires both discernment and dissuasive sanctions, as well as readability and predictability. However, in adopting a more economic approach to competition law in 2008, the European Commission did not concern itself with the "manageability" of the test it was proposing, and it took almost fifteen years to realize that this test, which was perfectly simple to use for certain practices such as *margin squeezes*, was unbearably complex in the case of certain other potentially anticompetitive practices (such as conditional rebates).

40. Let's hope that future discussions on the future of competition law will be more holistic, bringing together economists and legal experts for joint reflection. The debate will gain in clarity and depth.

The Theory of the Free Market of Ideas*

MARCELA IACUB
French National Centre for Scientific Research

1. In 1917, the United States entered the war. President Woodrow Wilson immediately announced that "disloyalty" was not a subject that could be freely debated. Those who would be guilty of it would lose "the right to enjoy civil liberties." In this spirit of patriotic fanaticism, the Espionage Act of 1917 was enacted. It punished anyone who would report false news or make false statements in order to interfere with war operations, promote the success of the enemies of the United States, incite insubordination, disloyalty, obstruct recruitment, or insult military service. Penalties could reach up to twenty years in prison. This law resulted in over 2,000 prosecutions – most of which concerned individuals who made statements deemed unpatriotic – and was applied in an arbitrary and paranoid manner. For instance, a jury convicted an individual who stated that the financial interests of capitalists were responsible for America's involvement in the armed conflict. Another convicted a pastor who distributed a pamphlet claiming that Christ would not have killed during the war. Twenty-seven German farmers, members of the Socialist Party, were sentenced because they had submitted a petition to the governor of South Dakota to reverse his decision exempting certain counties from military service.

2. In 1918, an amendment to this law was passed, driven by the same oppressive spirit. Its purpose was to combat the momentum generated by the Bolshevik revolution, the creation of the Third International, Red Syndicalism, socialism, and anarchism. Based on this amendment, Rosa Pastor, the editor of

* This article has been previously published, in French, in Concurrences' book "A quoi sert la concurrence", it has been translated and edited for clarity and cohesion.

the Jewish Daily, was sentenced to ten years in prison for stating in a public speech, "I am for the people while the government is for the profiteers." D.T. Blodget, another activist, received a twenty-year sentence for distributing flyers encouraging Iowa voters not to re-elect a Congressman who supported conscription. The Supreme Court upheld all these convictions...

3. It was during one of these infamous decisions that Justice Oliver Holmes (a Supreme Court Justice from 1902 to 1932), in the Abrams case (1919), formulated a dissenting opinion that laid the first foundations of the theory of the free market of ideas. For a detailed study of the theory in the Supreme Court's jurisprudence, see M. Iacub, *On Pornography in America: Freedom of Speech in the Age of Deliberative Democracy*, Fayard, Paris, 2010. Countering the position adopted by the Supreme Court at the time, this foundational opinion was joined by Justice Louis Brandeis, another fervent advocate of freedom of expression.

The Competition of Ideas and Democratic Debate

4. "The persecution of the expression of opinions," Holmes wrote, "seems perfectly logical if you have no doubts about your premises (...) But when men come to understand that time has overturned so many belligerent beliefs, they will come to believe (...) that the ultimate good will be more easily reached through the free trade of ideas than through the best test of truth, which is the power to be accepted through market competition (...) It is an experimentation, as all life is an experimentation (...) Since this experimentation is part of our system, I think we should be eternally vigilant against any attempt to suppress the expression of opinions that disgust us and that we consider dangerous, unless they threaten so imminently to thwart the legitimate objectives of the law that an immediate sanction is required to save the country."

5. The theory of the free market of ideas rests on two theses that are not empirical but transcendental. Their function is not to describe a proven reality but to produce rules capable of structuring democratic debate. The first states that in matters of opinion, no truth can be taken for granted. The second asserts that all men will one day agree on a common truth. Holmes describes the latter as "the ultimate good" because it is "the only ground upon which their desires can be safely realized." This theory opposes established consensus by highlighting their lack of foundation – no truth is guaranteed once and for all – and the relativity of explicit disagreements – since a common truth remains the ultimate horizon. Therefore, in Holmes's view, "the best test of truth is the power of thought to be accepted through market competition."

6. The theory of the free market of ideas modifies the classical conception of democratic debate in several respects. It implies a theory of the public space. The public space becomes a properly transcendental condition of democratic truth. This truth is immanent to the debate and never transcendent. It is not decreed; it is born from the confrontation of ideas. If the public space is a

laboratory of truth, it is because it functions like a market. Truth, both indispensable and impossible, precarious and absolute, can only emerge through the “free trade of ideas.” State sanctions must not disrupt their free competition by claiming to set the value of ideas. Intervening in this game, favoring certain ideas at the expense of others, endangers this mechanism that supports the very possibility of democratic debate. This is why there are no false or aberrant ideas in light of the First Amendment. Public speech must not be accountable to any state authority, any doctrine, any lesson drawn from the past, or any responsibility towards the future. This leads to the establishment of a discussion space independent of power, ideologically neutral, allowing everyone to step outside their own community and values.

7. Another consequence of this theory is to distinguish men from their ideas. In intellectual or ideological matters, it is not men who fight, but their ideas. The democratic society has no enemies who can be defined as such due to their opinions. Men are dissociable from their ideas; these are not consubstantial to their situation, interests, or subjectivity. There are in the ideas that human beings formulate collective and impersonal processes that will gain value independently of their will. Ideas are collective resources that can potentially change the lives of all.

8. To achieve such a result, it seems essential to protect the speaker. The important aspect of Holmes’s theory is to be able to derive from freedom of expression messages freely produced whose value is constantly subjected to the test of the market. This is why the intentions, whether good or bad, of those who speak do not matter. Even the most malevolent speaker is likely to produce messages that, in association, opposition, or complementarity within the collective flow of all messages, will take on a value independent of their intentions. In practice, such a model of democratic debate leads to the protection of rare, marginal, and minority ideas against the will of majorities to crush them. This has nothing to do with the classical notion of tolerance. On the contrary, without these thoughts, those of the majorities would impoverish.

9. This theory poses a new dimension of politics in public speech. Typically, war is considered the end of politics, whereas here the public debate is a battlefield that the free competition of ideas both allows and wards off. War becomes moral and no longer physical and deadly. We kill with words rather than with bombs or machine guns. We bet that the harder and more violent the words, the less we will resort to the latter.

10. It is not very difficult to understand how this theory opposes the way freedom of expression is conceived in Europe. European judges believe there are official truths to defend and thus deem it essential to sanction certain opinions. By not protecting minority ideas, the European model also impoverishes the ideas of the majority. Moreover, democratic debate is not seen in Europe as a means of warding off war. On the contrary, moral violence is perceived there as something to be excluded from public debate. According to Europeans,

there would only be a difference of degree between this violence and that of bombs and machine guns.

11. The theory of the free market of ideas will only triumph in the jurisprudence of the Supreme Court from the 1950s onward, transforming the United States into undisputed champions of freedom of expression. Perhaps on the occasion of the centenary of Holmes's dissenting opinion, Europeans will also want to think that competition is not only good for goods but also for ideas.

The Market of Ideas*

Gaspard Koenig
GenerationLibre

1. Competition is not the monopoly of economists. Ever since the disputes between Socrates and the sophists to conquer the minds of the young men of Athens, it exercises its ambiguous virtues in the most evanescent field of all, that of thought.

2. However, it was not until the day after the First World War that the now common concept of a "market of ideas" developed. It was born under the pen of *Justice* Oliver Holmes, judge at the Supreme Court of the United States. Russian activists were sentenced to heavy prison terms for distributing leaflets denouncing American capitalism and calling for socialist revolution in the midst of the war. The case was referred to the Supreme Court in 1919 as *Abrams v. United States*. The court upheld the sentence, finding that the authors and distributors of the leaflets were intended to hinder the American war effort. But Justice Holmes, in a famous dissenting opinion, expressed his disagreement in the name of freedom of expression guaranteed by the First Amendment. It is natural, he explained, to want to suppress opposing opinions, especially when one is convinced of the truths one is defending. And indeed, who has never wanted to prohibit the absurd, erroneous or unpleasant words we hear every day? But, Holmes continues, "when men realized that time had invalidated many fervent beliefs, they came to believe, beyond even their own values, that the greatest good comes from the free exchange of ideas – and that the best test of truth is to accept the competition of the marketplace. "*Free trade in ideas, competition of the market*: the words are out. The truth cannot accept the ease of monopoly. It is by being constantly exposed to disruption that it can strengthen and progress.

* This article has been previously published in Concurrences, and it might have been edited for clarity and cohesion. Gaspard Koenig, The market of ideas, November 2016, Concurrences N° 4-2016, Art. N° 81712.

If capitalism wants to demonstrate its superiority over socialism, Justice Holmes tells us in substance, let it do so with its own methods: competition rather than repression.

I. "The best test for the truth is to accept the competition of the market."

3. Although Justice Holmes was the first to use this vocabulary, his reasoning is rooted in John Stuart Mill's seminal text for freedom of speech: *On Liberty* (1859), particularly the second chapter. In it, the utilitarian philosopher defends the plurality of opinions in the name less of tolerance, as was still the case with Voltaire, for example, than of the search for truth itself. First of all, because no one is infallible and knowledge advances by trial and error. But above all because the truth must be able to emerge strengthened from the most extreme counter-argument: what the Church itself had understood well when it put on stage the "devil's advocates" during the canonization trials. Failing to accept these trials, the most irrefutable truth becomes, according to Mill's superb expression, a "dead dogma". Contradiction is essential to the advancement of knowledge as much as to its vitality.

4. While this logic works for scientific truths, it applies even better to political values, which are by nature less definitive. This is why Mill encourages party pluralism and alternating governments, which have the merit of maintaining "a hard fight between combatants fighting each other under hostile banners". Even though the market of ideas is not yet explained as such in Mill's writings, its characteristics are meticulously detailed. Unsurprisingly, Mill was also a strong proponent of free trade. The market shakes up dead dogmas as well as inefficient monopolies…

5. The marketplace of ideas is not just a metaphor. Or rather, this metaphor is only possible insofar as the two phenomena are profoundly similar, rooted in the ultimate expression of individual genius: innovation, whether economic or intellectual.

6. In this sense, it would be instructive to reread the history of ideas in the light of competition theory. Let's give it a try, before I hope others pursue it more scientifically.

II. "It would be instructive to reread the history of ideas in the light of competition theory."

7. One might suppose, for example, that Western thought was marked, for the longest part of its history, by the existence of a fiercely protected monopoly, that of Judeo-Christian dogma. Centralized in Rome, this monopoly captured

the national regulators, as our Kings could hardly do without the Pope's anointing. Any attempt to introduce competitors was mercilessly repressed: thus the Cathar heretics, having been convinced of their error by the Cistercian monks, were exterminated during bloody crusades; any persistence was pursued by the Inquisition, created on that occasion. The Church took care to preserve its monopoly by controlling the entire chain of teaching. So the innovators had to multiply the tricks, taking the monopoly at its own game. Thus Spinoza and his ingenious *Dive sive Natura*, identifying God and Nature so as not to confess his atheism (he was nevertheless excommunicated by the Jewish authorities). A bit like Amazon charging a cent for his deliveries so as not to contravene the law on the unique price of a book…

8. The Enlightenment opened a period of all-out competition. At a time when the precursors of political economy were beginning to theorize the benefits of competition in the creation of wealth (such as Pierre de Boisguilbert in his *Dissertation on the Nature of Wealth, Money and Tributes*, 1707: "reciprocal utility can only be brought about through competition and the freedom of producers"), the literate enjoyed an almost total laissez-faire attitude. One could think of a radical amoralism and imagine absolute sexual freedom, like the one Diderot describes with appetite in the *Supplement to the Voyage of Bougainville*. Or, conversely, one could fantasize a universe romantically designed by God to satisfy our every need, to the point of claiming with Bernardin de Saint-Pierre that "the melon has been divided into slices by nature in order to be eaten as a family". Or even deny religion with an open face, like Baron d'Holbach. But the competition quickly attacked the innovators themselves. John Stuart Mill analyzes the emergence of Rousseau through this prism, whose paradoxes "exploded like bombs, dislocating the compact mass of received ideas, and forcing their elements to recombine into a superior form, incorporating new ingredients. Rousseau disrupted the disrupters by questioning the progress of civilization, which was itself achieved through hard struggle against the Thomistic idea of a fixed social order.

9. In this blessed and effervescent century, no thought remains dominant for long. All the writings, all the theses are questionable and contested. Faced with this ultra-competitive profusion, the consumer of ideas is sometimes as discouraged as a buyer in front of the shampoo shelf of a hypermarket. Some are tempted by scepticism… before being refuted in turn by the Savoyard Vicar: "How can one be sceptical by system and in good faith? I cannot understand it. "The refusal of competition is itself put in competition…

10. Since then, the competition of ideas has undoubtedly become less intense, regulated and self-censored. Today, I have the feeling of being confronted with a strongly oligopolistic field: between the neo-Foucaldian progressives and the Finkielkrautian identities, between Michel Onfray's militant atheism and the revival of religious idolatry, between redistributive socialism and employer productivism, alternative thoughts are having a hard time making a breakthrough. Above all, in the face of threats to our security, the authorities

are tempted to punish not men, but ideas ("banning Salafism", for example). This would be a very unfortunate step backwards, against which Justice Holmes, who wrote in times of war that were far more deadly, warned us almost a century ago. Bad ideas should not be prohibited by law, but should be driven out by the market!

11. This market of ideas could probably be analysed in more detail by borrowing sophisticated concepts from economic theory.

12. Consider, for example, the three main benefits that Jean Tirole attributes to competition in his *Economie du bien commun* (PUF, 2016):

13. The first benefit is affordability. Just as the price of a product decreases as more firms compete for a market, a theory is more likely to be disseminated and popularized the more it is threatened. The principle of affordability would explain the impetus for the Catholic Counter-Reformation, which sought to make its dogma more popular in reaction to the spread of Protestantism – hence the opening of many universities or the revival of religious art with the emergence of the Baroque.

14. The second benefit is innovation. Competition encourages individual creativity. The disappearance of the great philosophical schools in the second half of the twentieth century was accompanied, around the Free University of Vincennes, by the appearance of original thinkers (Foucault, Lyotard, Deleuze, Serres, Derrida…) that cannot be grouped under the catch-all category of "post-modern". In Vincennes, no more masters or disciples, but thoughts rubbing up against each other in a campus open to the whole world.

15. The third benefit is integrity (in the sense of the disappearance of the annuity). Does competition make one intellectually honest? Hypothesis as another: it was the strong pressure exerted by Keynesian thought that forced liberalism to reform, recognizing at the famous Lippmann colloquium (1938) that laissez-faire had shown its limits, and that the state could play a legitimate role in regulating… competition!

16. We could go on.

17. Are there unquestionable, natural monopolies in the ideas? If we follow Francis Fukuyama, this would be the case of democracy among political systems.

18. Are there common goods, basic infrastructure that the state should provide? Undoubtedly: a shared vocabulary, uniformly taught at school, and allowing the communication of ideas (what the educationalist E.D. Hirsch calls "cultural literacy"). Conversely, if everyone reinvented their own language, we would find ourselves in a situation as absurd as when buses were racing in London after the botched privatization of the 1980s… The Tower of Babel, in short, is a case of wild competition.

19. What would be the role of a competition authority? To ensure that new ideas can enter the market, in a function quite similar to that of the CSA to ensure diversity in media space.

III. "Rather than suing fools, let's tax them!"

20. Is it possible to imagine an industrial policy on the part of the State? It's called the Académie Française, which is as effective in promoting new thinkers as the BPI is in discovering digital nuggets.

21. Will we one day establish an exchange of ideas, where we could bet on some and shorten others? A few years ago, I had imagined setting up this new kind of financial centre, but the administration kindly replied that the betting legislation prohibited me from doing so… CQFD

22. My favourite question remains: what to do with negative externalities? Should we, in good logic, create a tax on ideas that are harmful to ideas? Rather than suing fools, let's tax them! This would be a quick way of bailing out the Treasury…

23. Nothing could happen to the competition worse than to become, in turn, a dead dogma. Let us rejoice that so many intellectuals and politicians condemn it, for the pleasure of praising its merits!

PART II

Global Competition Challenges and Opportunities

Why Competition in Developing Countries? Key Challenges from the Latin American experience

PAULO BURNIER DA SILVEIRA*
Organisation for Economic Co-operation and Development (OECD)

I. Introduction

1. The benefits of competition between market players are well known including the positive effects that it can bring to the overall economy, economic growth, productivity, and consumers who may benefit from lower prices, better products and services, and more innovation.
2. In developing countries, competition can be particularly helpful in two additional ways. First, it may contribute to addressing competition issues in highly concentrated markets, frequently present in smaller economies, which may increase the risk of market failures. Second, competition can also help the poorest population, who are often the main victims of anti-competitive practices and represent a large share of developing countries' inhabitants, for instance by providing greater opportunity for mobility.[1]
3. Despite the clear benefits of competition law and policy, competition principles are often challenged in many countries around the world including

---

* Paulo Burnier da Silveira is a Senior Competition Expert at the OECD, Professor at University of Brasilia (on leave) and Visiting-Professor at Sciences-Po Paris. He is also a former Commissioner at the Brazilian Competition Authority (CADE) and has several publications in the area of competition including *Merger Control in Latin America: a Jurisdictional Guide* (2020). The opinions expressed in this chapter are personal and do not necessarily reflect the official views of the OECD, its Member Countries, or any other institution to which the author is affiliated.

1 Frédéric Jenny, Keynote Speech on Peer Review on Competition Law and Policy in Dominican Republic (OECD-IDB Latin American and Caribbean Competition Forum (LACCF) Santo Domingo, Jan. 22, 2024).

in developing countries: government price controls, state subsidies to promote national champions, and certain provisions to protect local small and medium-size enterprises – to name a few examples. While this may seem like a paradox, given the well-known benefits of competition, it reflects the complexity in the implementation of competition policy, which is not an island and should constantly interrelate to other public policies such as foreign trade, employment, and poverty reduction.

4. This short paper aims to address this false paradox between competition policy and other public policies that can limit competition, hopefully adding insights to the question: "why competition in developing countries?" For this purpose, it will focus on three specific challenges for developing countries from a Latin American perspective: one related to the goals of competition policy and its interplay with other public policies, a second that concerns a lack of competition culture in the region, and a third regarding the need to work in an environment of constant political instability.

II. Challenge 1: Integrating Competition Policy into a Set of Social Constitutional Goals

5. Over the last years, competition experts and policy makers have discussed the goals of competition policy, including in recent OECD Roundtables at the Global Forum on Competition.[2] The main discussion refers to the scope of competition policy objectives, namely if the traditional standard of consumer welfare should be maintained, or rather a broader scope should be justified to capture other policy goals, such as poverty reduction, sustainability, and gender equality.[3] Moreover, the institutional setups, levels of economic development and political contexts in different countries may also influence the extension of the goals of competition policy, which adds another layer to the complexity of the discussion. One example is South Africa: "(…) South Africa's political and economic history underpins the manner in which the Act was drafted. One need only look to the preamble and other parts of the Act in which themes of equity and justice run like a common golden thread. For example, the preamble refers to the political background and motivations for the Act, including policies of equity, distribution and efficiency."[4]

6. In Latin America, competition policy is often placed at the constitutional level alongside other public policies and objectives, many related to the social

---

2 OECD, *Competition Under Fire*, (2019), https://www.oecd-ilibrary.org/finance-and-investment/competition-under-fire_8b573de7-en; and OECD, *Goals of Competition Policy,* (2022), https://one.oecd.org/document/DAF/COMP/GF/WD(2022)1/en/pdf.

3 OECD, *Advantages and Disadvantages of Competition Welfare Standards*, (2023), https://one.oecd.org/document/DAF/COMP/WD(2023)28/en/pdf.

4 South Africa's written contribution to the OECD Roundtable, *Advantages and Disadvantages of Competition Welfare Standards*, (2023).

inequalities present in the region. For instance, the Brazilian Constitution 1988 establishes poverty eradication as a fundamental objective of the Republic (Article 3) and indicates competition protection in a section related to economic principles (Article 170); the Colombian Constitution 1991 has several guiding principles related to social justice and fairness, which guides the application of the entire legal framework; and the Mexican Constitution 1907 has a provision that combines both competition and fairness considerations (Article 26).

7. While this constitutional set-up proposes an integrated approach of public policies, with close coordination of important policy goals such as promoting economic growth, poverty reduction, and protecting consumers,[5] it has also led to certain criticisms specially from those who argue that a "de-constitutionalism" of competition policy would favor a greater legal certainty on the application of competition law including a clear use of the consumer welfare standard for this purpose.[6]

8. Competition authorities have indeed tried to better integrate at least some of these broader constitutional goals in their work, for instance by prioritizing markets that have a greater proportional impact in the low-income population.[7] This may include a focus on products and services that affect mostly the poorest part of the population, but also a more holistic view in which competition policy integrates a set of public policies that incorporate key objectives such as poverty reduction.[8]

9. Professor Eleanor Fox proposes the expression "pro-poor competition policy" to advocate for competition laws that consider poverty reduction at the heart of its enforcement actions. This should not be seen as a "silver bullet" to alleviate poverty, but rather an approach that could open more channels, facilitating the work of competition authorities, and gradually delivering better outcomes.[9] In this sense, competition authorities seeking to reduce inequality may adjust their priorities and target markets that are disproportionately important to low-income people – for instance agriculture and health care, since food and medicine compose a large share of their budget. Certain authors even suggest that it would be appropriate to introduce distributional weights into antitrust analysis by sacrificing economic efficiency for key distributional goals such as inequality issues.[10]

---

5 Daniel Bonilla, Constitutionalism of the Global South: The Activist Tribunals of India, South Africa, and Colombia (Cambridge Univ. Press 2013).

6 Luis Fernando Schuartz, *A desconstitucionalização do direito de defesa da Concorrência*, (FGV Direito Rio, 2008), https://revista.ibrac.org.br/index.php/revista/article/view/296.

7 OECD, *Competition and Poverty: The Role of Competition Authorities*, (2023), https://www.oecd-ilibrary.org/finance-and-investment/competition-and-poverty-the-role-of-competition-authorities_69813097-en#:~:text=The%20final%20remarks%20point%20that,of%20essential%20goods%20and%20services).

8 Further experiences from competition authorities are available in the related materials discussed in OECD, *supra* note 2.

9 Eleanor Fox, *Imagine: Pro-Poor(er) Competition Law*, (OECD Roundtable on Competition Policy and Poverty Reduction 2013).

10 Eric A. Posner & Cass R. Sunstein, *Antitrust and Inequality* (Working Paper, 2022).

10. Indeed, competition policy has important synergies with other public policies such as poverty reduction. However, the perception that competition law has been unable to properly contribute to these broader goals has fueled a debate about whether public interest considerations should play a role in competition law enforcement, a perspective that tends to be rejected by competition authorities.[11] In this context, the constitutional law element in Latin America represents an additional challenge as it encompasses several public interest considerations, which competition authorities should be ready to address, for instance in broader public policy debates on how to integrate constitutional goals to competition policy.

III. Challenge 2: Overcoming Barriers Related to a lack of Competition Culture

11. Historically, Latin American economies have often been characterized by concentrated market structures and a prevalence of monopolies or oligopolies in various sectors. Professor Patricio Meller employs the term "pattern of industrial concentration" in this context, arguing with empirical evidence about the high concentration levels in the region, covering various industries and countries.[12] These historical structures have resulted in limited competition, hindering the growth of dynamic markets and contributing to a culture where businesses are less inclined to compete vigorously, perpetuating a cycle of inefficiency and stifled innovation.[13]

12. Professor Juan Pablo Herrera Saavedra reminds that the challenges in fostering a competition culture in the region concern a diverse spectrum of stakeholders including business, government, and civil society.[14] In the private sector, business needs to overcome years of a culture used to protectionist measures, subsidies, and preferential treatment. The public sector also has a vital role to play in addressing this challenge, embedding competition principles as a positive feature and accepting letting go of traditional state-owned or state-controlled companies, particularly in non-strategic areas, such postal services.

13. Julian Peña highlights the influence that religion can play in this matter, arguing that Catholic values and tradition, for instance the concepts of the social function of property, theory of fair price and fair wage, have also contributed to the lack of competition culture in Latin America.[15] Indeed, religious values may play a role in the way business practices evolve including those

---

11 Frédéric Jenny, *Competition under Fire*, (Briefing Note by Chairman, 2019).

12 Patricio Meller, *The Pattern of Industrial Concentration in Latin America*, 27 J. Ind. Econ. 41-47 (1978).

13 Calixto Salomão Filho, Direito Concorrencial (2021).

14 Juan Pablo Herrera Saavedra, *América Latina y el Caribe y sus desafíos para promover cultura de libre competencia*, LR Republica (Oct. 5, 2023), https://www.larepublica.co/analisis/juan-pablo-herrera-saavedra-401993/america-latina-y-el-caribe-y-sus-desafios-para-promover-cultura-de-libre-competencia-3720738.

15 Julian Peña, *Cultural Challenges to Competition Law Enforcement in Latin America*, J. Antitrust Enf't (2023), https://academic.oup.com/antitrust/advance-article-abstract/doi/10.1093/jaenfo/jnad041/7240554.

related to competition, for instance the morality of competition for Christianity as explored by Kenneth Elzinga and Daniel Crane who argue for a "deep interconnectedness – historically, thematically, and contemporarily – of the Christian faith with antitrust as a discipline".[16]

14. The presence of a large share of informal economy is also a particularity of developing countries, being estimated at around 50 percent of the economy in Latin America adding to the challenge of overcoming barriers related to a lack of competition culture.[17] Indeed, informality often thrives in an environment with weak competition enforcement, hindering the growth of formal businesses and preventing fair market competition. At the same time, formal markets offer better conditions to workers, including social protection coverage, access to essential health care and basic income security. In this sense, reducing informality rescues poor workers from vulnerable situations and contributes to the overall economic stability of the country. In this context, competition authorities can help to reduce the size of informal economy by enforcing competition laws in this sector, particularly in markets where formal and informal firms compete. In these markets, informal firms gain an undue competitive advantage over formal firms by reducing supply costs in ways that have nothing to do with market efficiencies (e.g., evading taxes and reducing labor costs) and which would be desirable from a competitive market. As a result, formal firms may be unable to enter or expand into a market if they cannot offer attractive prices to consumers.[18]

15. In other words, the lack of competition culture emerges as a key challenge for competition policy, particularly in Latin American countries for historical and cultural reasons. Various stakeholders such as governments, businesses and civil society can work together to foster a culture that values and encourages competition, helping to build a sound competition policy and better address the question "why competition."

IV. Challenge 3: Ensuring Continuity of Competition Policy in an Environment of Constant Political Instability

16. Latin American countries also face the challenge of ensuring the continuity of competition policy in an environment of constant political instability. Continuity is indeed key to explaining and to maintaining the benefits of competition in the longer term. The overall policy effects can

---

16 Kenneth Elzinga & Daniel Crane, *Christianity and Antitrust* in CHRISTIANITY AND MARKET REGULATION: AN INTRODUCTION (2021).

17 WORLD BANK, WORLD DEVELOPMENT REPORT: TRADING FOR DEVELOPMENT IN THE AGE OF GLOBAL VALUE CHAINS (2020), https://www.worldbank.org/en/publication/wdr2020.

18 OECD, *supra* note 7.

be significantly affected if a given competition authority performs well for a number of years, then stops or reduces considerably its activities for another set of years.

17. Two recent examples, from Argentina and Mexico, illustrate this challenge.

18. In 2023, in the context of the new elected government in Argentina, competition policy seems to have re-gained track after oscillating between periods of more and less active enforcement including legislative improvements. Pablo Trevisán argues that political influence over the competition authority has been the "Achilles heel" of competition policy in the country since 1999 when the current competition law was enacted.[19]

19. In 2024, the President of the Republic in Mexico proposed draft legislation to extinguish regulators including both competition authorities, the *Comisión Federal de Competencia Económica* (COFECE) and the *Instituto Federal de Telecomunicaciones* (IFT).[20] Their roles would be transferred to governmental bodies, such as the Ministry of Finance and the Ministry of Communications, with clear changes in the institutional set-ups including their autonomy to handle competition enforcement matters.

20. Ensuring continuity of competition policy in an environment of constant political instability requires a strategic and adaptable approach. A key element to address this challenge is establishing a solid legal framework, containing comprehensive and clear legislation that define the roles, responsibilities, and powers of the competition authority. The legal framework should not be subject to changes due to new political initiatives and should involve multiple stakeholders in the legislative process to help to build consensus and to reduce the likelihood of abrupt policy shifts. Likewise, having an independent competition authority, insulated from political interference (e.g., in specific enforcement matters), with autonomy in decision-making and budgetary matters, seems an essential element. In other words, strengthening institutions is crucial for effective competition policy implementation.[21]

21. Finally, frequent engagement with stakeholders and regular review of the competition policy framework, in particular to adapt to changing economic conditions and to address emerging challenges, points to a proactive approach and helps preventing the need for sudden and disruptive changes during times of political instability.

---

19 Pablo Trevisán, *Libre Competencia: Dentro de la ley, todo; fuera de la ley, nada*, Centro Competencia (2023), https://centrocompetencia.com/libre-competencia-dentro-todo-fuera-nada/.

20 Draft Executive Decree Feb. 5, 2024 (*Gaceta Parlamentaria*, XXVII, n. 6457, Annex 18).

21 OECD Roundtable, *Key Points on Changes in Institutional Design,* (2015).

V. Final Remarks

22. In conclusion, the Latin American experience sheds light on the relevant question of "why competition," which presents specific challenges for developing countries. This contribution focuses on three key challenges: integrating competition policy with social constitutional goals, overcoming barriers related to a lack of competition culture, and ensuring continuity amid political instability.

23. The first challenge emphasizes the call for a competition policy that aligns with broader constitutional objectives in Latin American countries. While integrating competition policy with social goals may introduce complexity, the concept of "pro-poor competition policy" emerges as an example of a concrete avenue for competition authorities to help in addressing inequality issues.

24. The second challenge highlights the lack of a competition cultures in Latin American countries, stemming from concentrated market structures, protectionist policies, and the influence of cultural and social values. Overcoming this challenge requires concerted efforts from both the private and public sectors, emphasizing the importance of dismantling ingrained beliefs, fostering a competitive mindset, and reducing informality.

25. The third challenge addresses the necessity of ensuring continuity in competition policy amidst constant political instability. The paper underscores the importance of a solid legal framework, an independent competition authority, and stakeholder engagement. These elements collectively contribute to building resilient institutions capable of withstanding political shifts and ensuring the sustained benefits of competition over the long term.

26. In summary, addressing these challenges requires a multifaceted and adaptive approach, involving cooperation among government, businesses, and civil society. By navigating the complexities inherent in integrating competition policy with broader societal goals, fostering a competitive culture, and maintaining policy continuity, developing countries in Latin America can unlock the full potential of competition for economic growth, innovation, and social welfare while benefiting final consumers with better products and services at lower prices.

The Indispensable Role of Antitrust Enforcement in Less Developed Countries

WILLARD MWEMBA*
The COMESA Competition Commission[1]

1. Competition law has one fundamental objective: the preservation of democratic and contestable markets for the benefit of consumers. Competition laws create an environment in which enterprises are free to enter, expand and exit the market. In so doing, they engage in rivalry to outdo each other through legitimate means like enhancing dynamic and static efficiencies. Dynamic efficiency implies being innovative which results in the production of a variety of new and better products, thereby resulting in wider choices for consumers. Static efficiency relates to the production of goods and services at lower costs and transferring this to lower prices for consumers. The illegitimate ways of enterprises outdoing each other are what are termed as anticompetitive conduct. These include anticompetitive mergers and acquisitions, cartels, abuse of dominance and anticompetitive vertical and horizontal agreements.

2. The indispensability of the role of competition law is universal as it applies to both developed and less developed countries (LDCs). A plethora of authorities support this view. For example, Joseph Stiglitz[2] aptly observed that: "Strong

* Dr Willard Mwemba is the Chief Executive Officer of the Common Market for Eastern and Southern Africa Competition Commission (COMESA).

1 COMESA comprises of twenty-one (21) Member States namely: Burundi, Comoros, Democratic Republic of the Congo, Djibouti, Egypt, Eritrea, Eswatini, Ethiopia, Kenya, Libya, Madagascar, Malawi, Mauritius, Rwanda, Seychelles, Federal Republic of Somalia, Sudan, Tunisia, Uganda, Zambia and Zimbabwe.The COMESA Competition Commission is a regional competition authority with a mandate of regulating competition and consumer matters in 21 African countries. It is based in Lilongwe, Malawi.

2 Joseph E Stiglitz is a Nobel laureate in economics and a former chief economist of the World Bank (1997–2000)

competition policy is not just a luxury to be enjoyed by rich countries, but a real necessity for those striving to create democratic market economies". Nevertheless, it can be argued that it is more indispensable in LDCs for a number of reasons, some that are discussed in the sections that follow.

I. Highly Concentrated Markets

3. Market concentration refers to the number and size of firms operating in a market. Generally, the fewer the number of dominant firms in a market, the more highly concentrated it is likely to be.[3] The converse is to a very large extent true. The level of economic development and degree of market liberalisation in an economy are partly reflected in the number of firms that operate in that economy. It is a notorious fact that markets in most LDCs are highly concentrated because of several factors among them, ie. the command nature of their economies, their countries and economies are not as old as developed countries which have had long periods of allowing their markets to grow, and low levels of disposable income among consumers that do not support the establishment of many firms in LDCs.

4. Highly concentrated markets are very prone to anticompetitive conduct such as abuse of market power and cartel conduct among others. Abuse of market power is more likely to occur in markets dominated by one or few firms because the consumers have no alternatives should these firms engage in anti-competitive conduct. Further, the firms are not fettered in their anticompetitive behaviour because of lack of sensitivity to the reaction of competitors who are conspicuously absent in such markets. That dominant firms, or those with market power, have the capability of engaging in anticompetitive conduct was neatly laid down in the case of *Europemballage Corp v Commission of the European Communities*. In the aforementioned case, dominance was defined as:

> "Undertakings are in a dominant position when they have the power to behave independently, which puts them in a position to act without taking into account their competitors, purchasers or suppliers. That is a position when, because of their share of the market, or of their share of the market combined with the availability of technical knowledge, raw materials or capital, they have power to determine prices or to control production or distribution for a significant part of the products in question".[4]

5. Referring to the above definition, it is apparent that the characteristics elucidated therein are present in most markets and economies in LDCs. As a

---

3 It should be noted that this supposition may not always hold in all circumstances as market concentration does not just depend on the number of firms operating in the market but also their dispersion which may reflect in their size. Nevertheless, with respect to LDCs a general trend of highly concentrated markets can be observed as there are fewer firms operating therein, which largely dominate the markets.

4 Case 6/72 *Europemballage Corp v Commission of the European Communities* ECLI:EU:C:1973:22.

matter of fact, the abuse of dominance does not need to completely eliminate competition, neither does it only occur in markets completely devoid of competition, but it also occurs in markets with some degree of competition but insufficient to constrain the behaviour of a dominant firm. This observation is supported by the ruling in the seminal case *Hoffmann La Roche v Commission of the European Communities* that:

> "Such a position does not preclude some competition … but enables the undertaking which profits by it, if not to determine, at least to have an appreciable effect on the conditions under which that competition will develop, and in any case to act largely in disregard of it so long as such conduct does not operate to its detriment".[5]

6. Abuse of dominance may also result in market foreclosure of other firms desiring to enter the market, therefore perpetuating the status quo of dwarfed economies and markets. Observable also is that in highly concentrated markets, firms are more likely to coordinate their behaviour in the market to the detriment of consumers. The coordination of such behaviour is more sustainable in markets with fewer firms because it is easy to implement the rules of coordination and any deviation from these rules is easily detectable.

7. The foregoing is more injurious to markets and consumers in LDCs than in developed countries due to the high poverty levels in LDCs. Such conduct therefore aggravates the poverty situation. In such markets, it should not be expected that these types of firms are operated in the interest of consumers and the economy. The overriding objective of firms is the maximisation of profits and if left unchecked, any means could be used to achieve this objective. Engaging in progressive competition may be the least consideration to achieve the objective of profit maximisation in such an environment because competition may threaten the existence of those firms that are not innovative. Professor W Lachmann observed in 1999 that: "[C]ompetition is always in danger. Since it is uncomfortable or even threatening, business tries to avoid it. To use a metaphor: competition is not a weed that grows even if left alone; rather it is a cultural plant that needs constant government attention".[6] Such government attention would and should manifest through the effective and efficient implementation of a well drafted competition law. It is this law that would constrain the anticompetitive behaviour of firms in such markets. The result of this would be market growth through healthy competition in which firms strive to win consumers' patronage. Rivalry in the market puts pressure on businesses to constantly innovate to attract and retain consumers by offering a better and wider range of products at more competitive prices. The

---

5 Case 85/76 *F Hoffmann La Roche & Co AG v Commission of the European Communities* ECLI:EU:C:1979:36, see European Court of Justice, "The EU Court of Justice clarifies the criteria for determining dominance and the types of conduct that constitute abuse (Hoffman-La-Roche)" (1979) e-Competitions art. No. 105107.

6 Werner Lachmann, *The Development Dimension of Competition Law and Policy* (UNCTAD 1999) <https://unctad.org/system/files/official-document/poitcdclpm9.en.pdf> accessed 29 October 2024.

more developed countries have seen the dangers of concentrated markets and the benefits of competition and competition laws a long time ago. For example, in the United States, which is arguably the most liberalised economy in the world, the risks and dangers to markets and society posed by trusts and large corporations were observed, culminating in the enactment of antitrust laws in 1890. With these laws, markets expanded, levels of concentration declined, and it became increasingly difficult for firms to engage in anticompetitive conduct as they would only do so at their own peril because consumers would have other alternatives. This notion is largely absent in LDCs. Therefore, the indispensable role of competition laws in LDCs should not be in dispute as it contributes significantly to economic development and the alleviation of poverty. For example, there is evidence that the enforcement against the fertiliser cartel in Zambia in 2012 revealed that the Government of Zambia was losing about US$20 million per annum as a result of the cartel, which could have been channelled to other sectors of the economy.[7]

II. Difficulties in Accessing Capital

8. Basic economic theory avers that in competitive markets, there are firms that strive to attract consumers in orthodox ways, information is readily available, and no single market player dictates how conditions will develop in that market. In such markets, entry and exit is relatively easy because information asymmetry is not a concern. Herein lies the underlying assumptions that in a competitive market, any distortions in the market would be corrected by the market itself. For example, where there is an abuse of dominance through excessive pricing and the earning of supra-normal profits, it is expected that this will attract the entry of new firms and ultimately the price will fall, and market equilibrium will be restored. But this assumption is based on the *ceteris paribus* (all other things being equal). Further, it is not any potential entry that may be admissible as defence. To be admissible as defense, ntry, should be likely, sufficient and timely to diminish the egregious effects of an anticompetitive conduct.

9. For new firms to enter easily and promptly, there should not be high barriers to entry and capital should be readily available to support such entry. However, access to capital and funding is notoriously difficult in LDCs, making it unlikely that new firms can enter in time to curtail the anticompetitive conduct of the incumbents. In addition, where such entry occurs, it is insufficient and takes an inordinately long time and as such, consumers would continue experiencing from the effects of anticompetitive conduct for a long time.

7 The author was the lead investigator in this case and made these computations.

10. One of the characteristic features of LDCs is the prevalence of high interest rates, ranging typically from 24% to 50% per annum.[8] Further, those who are able to access this credit are also faced with short repayment periods, making it very difficult to embark on any developmental or expansion projects.[9] This situation does not prevail in a number of developed countries. It therefore means that in developed countries, there is a higher likelihood that markets will correct themselves through easy entry and exit compared with LDCs, necessitating the indispensable role of competition law in the latter.

III. Lack of Appreciation and Awareness on the Benefits of Competition Laws

11. Competition law is a relatively new development in most LDCs and therefore there is less appreciation of the benefits of competition law by governments, consumers, businesses and other stakeholders. In most LDCs, governments are preoccupied with laws and policies that have a direct impact on the majority of the poor. It is difficult to sell the story of how competition law contributes to economic development and poverty alleviation in LDCs. As a result, most governments in these countries have not given competition law the required attention. Even in those countries where laws were enacted and enforcement institutions created, a regression has been witnessed in recent times. Two such countries are Ethiopia and Uganda.

12. The United Nations Conference on Trade and Development (UNCTAD) and the COMESA Competition Commissionwere central in developing and strengthening the capacity of the Trade Competition and Consumer Protection Authority, an institution that was charged with the responsibility of implementing competition and consumer laws in Ethiopia. However, circa 2021, the Ethiopian Government abolished this institution and transferred this role to the Ministry of Trade and Regional Integration (MoTRI). One of the elements of effective competition law enforcement is to have an independent and effective competition authority. Placing the implementation of competition laws in a government ministry is more likely to produce sub-optimal outcomes because government ministries are more skilled at policy formulation and not the enforcement of laws. This development in Ethiopia signalled the lack of importance and priority attached to competition law implementation for it may have been considered secondary such that it could be handled as an incidental matter by MoTRI. Another example is Uganda. The COMESA Competition Commission n and other stakeholders have been instrumental in

---

8 Anand G Chandavarkar, "Some Aspects of Interest Rate Policies in Less Developed Economies: The Experience of Selected Asian Countries" (*IMF*, 1971) <www.elibrary.imf.org/view/journals/024/1971/001/article-A003-en.xml> accessed 29 October 2024.

9 John Ackah and Sylvester Vuvor, "The Challenges faced by Small & Medium Enterprises (SMEs) in Obtaining Credit in Ghana" (MA thesis, KTH Royal Institute of Technology 2011) <www.diva-portal.org/smash/record.jsf?pid=diva2%3A829684&dswid=-7185> accessed 29 October 2024.

promulgating competition legislation in Uganda. While a lot of progress has been recorded and the law was been assented to by the President, its enactment stalled for a long time because the Competition Bill provided for the creation of an independent competition authority. However, there was no appetite by the executive to establish this institution. Instead, the government's preference was to give the responsibility of implementing the competition law to the Ministry of Trade, Industry and Cooperatives. A word of caution here is that this chapter is not advocating for a blanket condemnation of countries that have chosen to have competition law implemented by a division in a government ministry, this contribution however unequivocally argues that such an approach is not the most effective.

13. The lack of knowledge and the benefits of competition law by governments compound this problem. There is empirical evidence that most competition authorities in LDCs are poorly funded because governments think that it is better to channel the meagre resources to other government endeavours that will directly result in economic growth and development. Therefore, competition authorities are poorly funded such that they cannot effectively implement their mandate. Thomas Cheng observed that having recently adopted competition law, many developing countries still need to decide how much resources they want to devote to its enforcement. Given the dearth of public funding, precious resources need to be deployed to maximise the prospects for growth and potential for development.[10]

14. Further, we have also observed governments in some LDCs blatantly remarking that competition authorities are a hindrance to market development and growth as they frustrate business. In some LDCs, governments have sided with firms who have lobbied for the circumvention of the application of competition law. This is a clear demonstration of ignorance on the importance of competition law because if properly implemented, competition law would yield market development and growth which is so critically needed in LDCs. Governments should not entertain firms that lobby for the circumvention of competition law as it should be clear from this behaviour that the firms are more concerned about their interests and not necessarily the interests of society. Competition authorities should also be well versed with the principles and practical application of competition law to thwart anticompetitive conduct. Absent this, anticompetitive conduct is likely to continue with clearance from competition authorities. For example, in one of the cases involving single branding and resale price maintenance handled by the COMESA Competition Commission, the respondents argued that such conduct was permissible in competition law because the restriction in intra-brand competition would enhance inter-brand competition. However, the Commission observed that there was no effective inter-brand competition in the first place. This was clearly an attempt to evade

10 Thomas Cheng, "Why Competition Law Is So Important for Developing Countries" (14 July 2020) <www.promarket.org/2020/07/14/why-competition-law-is-so-important-for-developing-countries/> accessed 29 October 2024.

the application of competition law and where ignorance on the benefits of competition law exists, such an argument by the respondents may prevail. If inter-brand competition was not effective for whatever reason hitherto, then the argument that a restriction of intra-brand competition through single branding would enhance inter-brand competition is not only a fallacy, but wicked.

15. The lack of knowledge and awareness of the importance and benefits of competition law and sometimes of its existence by consumers, businesses and other stakeholders exacerbate the problem. Where consumers have an appreciation of competition law and their rights within the competition framework, they are likely to report instances of misconduct of firms to competition authorities who would then act to remedy the situation and deter would-be offenders and recidivism. Similarly, businesses with an understanding that anticompetitive conduct is outlawed would report exclusionary anticompetitive conduct by other firms. Such conduct perpetuates high levels of market concentration which ultimately does not support the growth of dwarfed economies and the alleviation of poverty. Further, consumers, businesses and other stakeholders who appreciate the importance of competition law would demand the enactment of competition legislation in countries where this is absent. This has been witnessed in Burundi where stakeholders have been vocal in calling for the implementation of competition legislation in order to contribute to economic development.

16. Competition does indeed contribute to economic growth, and thus promoting competition law enforcement will enhance the growth prospects of developing countries. Therefore, LDCs should take competition enforcement seriously. It is important that proponents of competition law at various levels and institutions such as the COMESA Competition Commission, UNCTAD, ICN, OECD and the World Bank, among others continue to advocate for the effective implementation of competition law and raise awareness to stakeholders on its indispensable role in economic development. A clear case should be made on how it contributes to economic growth and how its absence may have opposite effects.

IV. Competition Laws Address Public Interest Issues

17. In LDCs competition laws are designed to address challenges and problems that go beyond a purist approach to competition law application; namely the substantial prevention and/or lessening of competition. Aspects such as jobs, entrepreneurship, protection of small and medium enterprises, historically disadvantaged people and supply and distribution contracts may be addressed by competition law in LDCs. For example, in Kenya, Malawi and Zambia among other countries in the less developed world, it has become fashionable for competition authorities to authorise merger transactions subject to conditions that no jobs would be lost and that all supply contracts concluded by the merging

parties prior to the merger shall subsist and shall not be terminated as result of the merger transaction. In countries like South Africa, competition law has been used to address other public interest issues, eg addressing the plight of historically marginalised people. In South Africa therefore, the implementation of competition law is not just about the prevention of a substantial lessening of competition but also about achieving social and economic equity as it is believed that this is the only way economic growth and development will be guaranteed and sustained in South Africa. This supposition is supported by some distinguished practitioners and scholars like Hardin Ratshisusu[11] and Liberty Mncube[12] who remarked that:[13]

> "Competition law is not just about the efficiency goal. Placing value on opportunities for black owned businesses to enter, expand, and participate in markets is likely to be a key element in South Africa's route to become an efficient, competitive economic environment focused on development and ultimately benefiting all South Africans.... In South Africa, equity is a recognized goal and a permissible consideration of competition law and a key driver of inclusive markets, economic development and, ultimately, empowerment of black people".

18. It is in the public domain that South Africa has sometimes been heavily criticised for its public interest approach in competition law enforcement especially when it relates to merger control. However, South Africa should not be unreservedly criticised. Competition law should address the economic fundamentals of a country and economic and social inequality are among those fundamentals. A competition law that is severed from the realities of its economy would be irrelevant and may not be taken seriously. For example, COMESA in its draft amendments to the COMESA competition regulations has proposed environmental considerations in its competition law enforcement as a public interest matter in the wake of climate change. Therefore, views on the South African public interest approach in its implementation of competition law should focus on how this approach can be perfected to achieve the desired goals. The question that should be posed is, to what extent has South Africa achieved these desired goals and if not, how can this approach be designed to achieve the intended goals? It should be incontrovertible that the bespoke design and application of competition law in LDCs is advocated if competition laws are to make a meaningful contribution to economic growth and development.

---

11 Deputy Commissioner, Competition Commission of South Africa.

12 Associate Professor of Economics, University of Witwatersrand.

13 Liberty Mncube and Hardin Ratshisusu, "Competition Policy and Black Empowerment: South Africa's Path to Inclusion" (2021) SCIS Working Paper 22 <https://wiredspace.wits.ac.za/server/api/core/bitstreams/2f3322b5-a274-48f9-9644-50dc71225307/content#:~:text=Competition%20Amendment%20Act%20and%20black%20empowerment&text=The%20main%20focus%20of%20the,owned%20by%20black%20South%20Africans> accessed 29 October 2024.

V. Conclusion

19. This chapter has put forward a case that the role of competition law in LDCs is indispensable and more so than it may be in developed countries. The underlying fundamentals behind this supposition are the differences in economic and social development between LDCs and developed countries. LDCs are characterised by high market concentrations, barriers to entry, lack of or costly capital and low competition culture. Given these unique features, it is important that the design and application of competition law is aligned to the economic and social realities of the LDCs, otherwise these laws may not achieve the desired objectives. The purist approach of only considering the substantial lessening of competition test should be reconsidered as competition laws are used to address other public interest considerations in LDCs.

20. The indispensable role of competition law enforcement in LDCs should be indisputable. It is important therefore to raise the awareness of many stakeholders including governments, consumers and businesses among others to ensure that these laws contribute to economic development and growth, and the alleviation of poverty which is the greatest concern in LDCs.

Amazon's Pricing Algorithms and the Enforcement Response in the US and Europe*

Fiona M. Scott-Morton
Yale University

1. In the US there are several antitrust cases against Amazon currently in litigation, including those brought by the state of California[1] and the Federal Trade Commission and seventeen states[2]. European regulators have also been busy: an antitrust case against Amazon by the European Commission was resolved with commitments in December 2022[3]. In addition, Amazon's e-commerce business was designated a core platform service by the European Commission[4] and therefore it will have to comply with the Digital Markets Act beginning in March of 2024. Both sets of regulators can learn from, and leverage, the enforcement of the other.

---

* This article has been previously published in Concurrences, and it might have been edited for clarity and cohesion. Fiona M. Scott-Morton, Amazon's pricing algorithms and the enforcement response in the US and Europe, March 2024, Concurrences N° 1-2024, Art. N° 116147.

1 *California v. Amazon*, case No. CGC-22-601826 (Sept. 14, 2022), https://oag.ca.gov/system/files/attachments/press-docs/2022-09-14%20California%20v.%20Amazon%20 Complaint-redacted.pdf ("California complaint").

2 *FTC et al. v. Amazon*, W.D. Wash., case No. 2:23-cv-01495 (Sept. 26, 2023), https://www.ftc.gov/system/files/ftc_gov/pdf/1910134amazonecommercecomplaintrevisedredactions.pdf ("FTC complaint").

3 https://ec.europa. eu/commission/presscorner/detail/en/ip_22_777.

4 https://ec.europa.eu/commission/presscorner/detail/ en/ip_23_432.

I. How Amazon's alleged conduct controls prices on rival marketplaces

2. Both the California and FTC complaints explain that Amazon operates what are effectively platform MFNs ("most favored nation" commitments, a term borrowed from international trade) for third-party marketplace sellers and the brand representatives. Platform MFNs are requirements that third-party sellers on a platform, in this case a marketplace, set prices for the good on competing marketplaces that are at least as high as those found on the platform requiring the MFN. The MFN controls prices on the seller's own website as well as competing marketplaces. These contracts end price competition between marketplaces because all prices for the good are the same. Furthermore, a merchant selling on a marketplace with lower fees cannot pass those lower fees through to consumers in the form of lower prices without – under the terms of the MFN – also lowering the price of the good on the primary platform, in this case Amazon, which has higher fees. Therefore, the lower-priced entrant has no way to attract customers with lower prices if it wants to sell the products of merchants covered by the Amazon platform MFN and the MFN thus limits competition between marketplaces. A paper I wrote with Jon Baker in 2018 explains how these platform MFNs are anticompetitive and likely a violation of competition laws[5]. A large economics literature supports this conclusion: sellers will choose to set high prices on all competing sites to match those on a large platform with an MFN. This harms competition in goods. Secondly, the competing marketplace now has no reason to lower its fees, since it cannot gain more business that way. This harms competition between the marketplaces themselves and disincentivizes entry of more efficient marketplaces.

3. This economic logic is well-known among enforcers, and MFN contracts have therefore been a frequent target of enforcement efforts in many industries. Indeed, in 2013 the German competition authority opened an investigation of Amazon's MFN contracts, which caused the company to abandon them in Europe. In 2019, at the instigation of Senator Richard Blumenthal (not the FTC), Amazon announced that it was voluntarily ending its MFN contracts in the United States. Observers might well have thought, therefore, that the anticompetitive effects of these contracts were gone.

II. *De jure* versus de facto MFNs

4. However, we learn from these lawsuits about the steps Amazon took to recreate the effects of the MFN contracts after it formally ended them. Both

5 Antitrust Enforcement Against Platform MFNs, *Yale Law Journal*, Vol. 127, No. 7, 2018, pp. 2176–2202, https://www.yalelawjournal.org/pdf/BakerScottMorton_trhf5iiv.pdf.

the California and FTC complaints describe the replacement tactics Amazon has used to control prices off its platform through a number of policies. If a seller's prices are lower on a rival site, Amazon downgrades the listing of the good, and removes it from eligibility for the "Buy Box" or "featured offer." (The "Buy Box" is the familiar box on the top right of the Amazon page that appears after the user selects a product. It shows one seller that Amazon has chosen and, by virtue of the design of the box, made more prominent than any other seller.) Given Amazon's large base of consumers, and the fact that 98% of purchases occur through users choosing the seller in the Buy Box, the merchant will lose most of their sales with this downgrade. Furthermore, the complaints are detailed in their evidence that Amazon's managers were aware of the purpose of the programs. For example, the program "SC-FOD" was designed to enforce the contractual MFN's "*expectations and policies*," which "*ha*[d] *not changed*." The FTC complaint states: "*According to a senior Amazon executive, Amazon expanded th*[e] *designation* [of 'Select Competitors'] *to make 'the punitive aspect' of SC-FOD 'more effective.'*"

5. Both complaints explain that "Amazon's Standards for Brands" or "ASB" program contractually requires certain third-party sellers to "*ensure that their products' prices on other online stores are as high or higher than their prices on Amazon at least 95% of the time*" and imposes additional restrictions on sellers' inventory and Prime membership so they effectively cannot sell anywhere but on Amazon. As with the SC-FOD program, Amazon was clear about the reasons it penalized ASB sellers who did not meet the program's requirements: "*Amazon told those punished ASB sellers that they were being sanctioned because 'customers considering your products could have easily found your products cheaper at another major retailer, and may have chosen to shop elsewhere.'*" These statements demonstrate how an MFN contract can be effectively replaced with an algorithm when managers design it to achieve the same objectives.

III. How Amazon's alleged conduct controls prices on rival retail sites

6. Turning to Amazon's retail operation, the California complaint describes behavior that creates an effective MFN in that business also. Recall that the retail business of Amazon differs from the marketplace business because Amazon itself buys goods at wholesale prices, owns those goods, and then retails them on its own website at prices it chooses. A marketplace, by contrast, hosts independent merchants who control what they sell, how it is delivered, and set their own prices. As described in the complaint, brands that sell directly to Amazon at wholesale fare even worse than resellers because of an equivalent MFN-like scheme. Amazon requires brands to agree to a contract called a "Minimum Margin Agreement." Amazon uses an algorithm to match

its retail prices if it finds a lower price for the same product on a rival website such as Walmart.com. But at the same time that Amazon is lowering its retail prices to match rivals, it holds the brand on which it is price matching (e.g., Tide) responsible for maintaining Amazon's profit margin. The brand must make up the difference between the price that Amazon initially set and the lower price on Walmart.com that Amazon then matched. This is true even though in neither setting is the brand itself choosing the retail price; the online stores have that responsibility.

7. The result of this scheme is that when Walmart. com has a sale on Tide, Amazon matches that price, and Amazon's profit margin on Tide may fall below its target level. If so, Amazon requires Tide to make Amazon whole with a payment that compensates Amazon for Tide's new low price. Naturally, this penalty causes Tide to want to sell to Walmart.com at a high enough wholesale price so that Amazon's retail price will be lower than Walmart's. In general, a brand does not want to offer any discounts to Walmart because that might encourage a sale that would cause the brand to suffer. Indeed, the brand might withdraw from Walmart.com altogether if such sales cause it to owe Amazon large sums. The anticompetitive incentives of the scheme are the same as those in an MFN: they create higher prices at rival stores.

IV. What remedies would restore vigorous price competition?

8. Assuming that these facts just described are proven, the agency or court will be faced with the need to impose a remedy to restore the lost competition. The simplest remedy is to ban MFNs entirely, both wide MFNs (that cover prices in rival e-commerce stores), narrow MFNs (that cover prices on the website of the brand itself), and any conduct that creates the same incentives as an MFN such as that described above. Europe has already banned MFNs in Article 5(3) of the Digital Markets Act, which comes into full force in March of 2024.

9. To explain the impact of the remedy of an MFN ban on the strategies of all parties, it is useful to consider two questions. First, for the MFN to be triggered, a rival must have a lower price.

10. Why is a rival e-commerce store setting a retail price that is lower than Amazon's price?

    1. The rival store has lower costs of operation than Amazon;
    2. The rival platform bought the good for a lower price from its manufacturer; or
    3. The rival platform has a different strategy or weaker market position than Amazon so that lower prices are the best way to attract consumers.

These answers are standard manifestations of competition that benefits consumers. If prices are lower on a rival e-commerce site for any of these reasons, consumers gain, and the law should not permit Amazon to suppress that competition through its contracts or policies. If Amazon wishes to retain customers after this MFN is banned, it can bring down its fees or raise its value. Likewise, Amazon can bargain for a lower price from the manufacturer or possibly lower its costs by making its own private-label version of the product.

Why is a third-party reseller setting a price on Amazon that is higher than on other platforms?

4. It thinks Amazon shoppers are inattentive and not price responsive and is exploiting them with a high price; or

5. Its costs are lower on rival platforms because those platforms' fees are lower.

11. A reseller is not violating competition laws if it chooses to set different prices in different distribution channels for reasons such as differences in cost or demand. But, of course, this conduct hurts Amazon shoppers and Amazon's brand. A remedy that restores the lost competition in fees (5) should ideally allow Amazon to protect its own consumers from any possible exploitation in (4).

12. Amazon has already built the tool needed to combat the possible exploitation in (4): the Buy Box. When third-party sellers list on Amazon, the firm's algorithm evaluates their offers and puts the one that meets its criteria into the Buy Box. If Amazon's algorithm weights high prices negatively, a third-party seller engaging in the exploitation in (4) would be expected to sell very little because it is not in the Buy Box, and if any diligent consumers search the listing, they will find an exploitative price.

13. The design of the Buy Box means it can legitimately be used by Amazon to defend consumers on Amazon Marketplace from exploitation by high-priced sellers. Thus, it duplicates the pro-competitive impact of the MFN without the anticompetitive element and can be used to replace it when the MFN is banned. Because the Buy Box concerns itself only with prices on the Amazon platform, it does not duplicate the restraint on horizontal competition that characterizes an MFN.

14. Now consider the case where a product is only carried by one reseller on Amazon, and that reseller is pricing in an exploitative manner. The Buy Box cannot fix this problem. However, Amazon has the incentive and ability to recruit another reseller to the platform. Entry will be attractive for this new seller because undercutting the incumbent's exploitative price still allows for a healthy margin. Thus, both Amazon and a rival third-party seller have

the incentive to defeat the conduct described in (4), while Amazon has the information to identify the opportunity and the ability to facilitate entry of lower-priced rivals.

15. If there is only one original seller of the product, such as the brand itself, there is also no competition from resellers and nothing for the Buy Box to leverage. However, Amazon has pro-competitive tools to combat exploitative brand pricing. For example, the brand's listing on the search results page could truthfully explain to the customer what the brand's regular list price is and recommend substitute products on Amazon that are not overpriced – all without removing the ability to buy the brand if the consumer so chooses.

16. An Amazon price premium could occur because of an exploitative strategy or because the cost of selling is higher on Amazon. These costs could be driven by advertising that is effectively required or high fees charged by the platform. High costs that are built into a higher price are a normal feature of a competitive economy. Customers will evaluate the benefits of the Amazon platform (one-click purchasing, fast delivery, saved addresses) and compare them to the price difference. If the latter outweighs the former, the customer will leave Amazon to buy the brand for a lower price elsewhere.

17. A reasonable concern is that a ban on MFNs will lead to inefficient free riding (showrooming). This occurs when sellers use the dominant platform to display their product and attract buyers, but then encourage those buyers to purchase off the platform, thereby avoiding the platform's fees. This can reduce the incentive to build and invest in a platform below the optimal level. However, a consumer who sees a product on Amazon and searches for the seller's page to buy it at a lower price is giving up all the services of Amazon: saved payment, saved addresses, and quick delivery times. Amazon itself touts the superiority of its services and the stickiness it creates with time- and attention-strapped consumers. The government complaints contain quotations from managers at the company that acknowledge high switching costs for consumers. Amazon's business model and competitive advantage suggest free riding will be minimal.

18. All of these factors combine to make an MFN ban likely an easy as well as effective policy response to both the FTC and California *Amazon* cases. In addition, since the European Union is also adopting this policy in March 2024, Amazon will incur minimal incremental engineering cost to implement it in the United States.

Financial Stability and Competition in the Single Market*

NADIA CALVIÑO
European Investment Bank

MARTIN MERLIN
European Commission

1. Since the summer of 2007 and the onset of the financial crisis, the European Union has embarked on a profound reform of its financial sector regulation. This reform, aligned with the guidelines developed by the G20, has three main components: the strengthening of banking prudential regulation, a sector where the crisis exposed serious deficiencies; the extension of regulation to areas that were previously not subject to European standards, such as credit rating agencies and alternative investment funds; and finally, the creation of a new financial sector supervisory structure, with the establishment of three European supervisory authorities (for banking, insurance/occupational pensions, and securities markets) and a European Systemic Risk Board. The aim is for this reform process, comparable in scope and content to the Dodd-Frank Act passed in the United States, to be completed by 2013.

2. The reform's primary goal is to enhance financial stability in Europe. It is designed to protect European citizens and the European economy from the disastrous consequences of a new financial crisis. Even though it would be unrealistic to prevent every future crisis, the measures being adopted are aimed at reducing the risk of crises, limiting their severity if they do occur,

---

* This article has been previously published in Concurrences, and it might have been edited for clarity and cohesion. Nadia Calvino, Martin Merlin, Financial stability and competition in the European Union, February 2011, Concurrences N° 1-2011, Art. N° 33958, pp. 1-3.

and putting in place the mechanisms needed to respond effectively and in a coordinated way if necessary.

3. In light of the events that have unfolded since 2007, and the continuing tensions in sovereign debt markets, it is legitimate for public authorities to prioritize the lasting restoration of financial stability. However, achieving this objective should not come at the expense of other key public policy goals. In particular, it is important to ensure that public authorities' actions and the new financial sector regulations do not distort competition among financial institutions. This is especially critical, as one of the lessons learned from the 1929 crisis is that maintaining free and fair competition is a key condition for economic recovery. For this reason, the Commission has ensured that the public support provided to troubled banks during the crisis in the name of financial stability does not create undue competition distortions.

4. The interactions between financial stability and competition have been the subject of numerous studies. Some have argued that very stringent regulation could limit the degree of competition, particularly by hindering providers' ability to offer innovative services. However, in general, strong financial sector regulation, primarily focused on stability, does not necessarily have a negative impact on competition among operators. A clear regulatory framework, based on a good understanding of economic realities, and focusing on the operating conditions of different financial businesses, rather than regulating the services offered by providers, can actually stimulate competition. This is especially true when it comes to European financial regulation, whose historical goal, as enshrined in the treaties, is to foster and enhance cross-border competition within the single market.

5. In fact, the current regulatory developments in Europe aim to deepen this single market by equipping it with European institutions and common rules that guarantee equal treatment for all economic operators. Several examples can illustrate this.

6. First, the deepening of EU regulation in sectors such as banking and insurance goes hand in hand with the gradual elimination of national regulatory specificities, allowing companies to compete based on the quality of services provided and pricing, rather than differences in prudential and conduct rules. This trend should culminate, in line with a direction set by the European Council in June 2009, with the gradual development of a single European rulebook applicable to all financial operators. Where technically feasible, directly applicable European regulations would replace directives. Moreover, national exemptions or exceptions would be kept to a strict minimum.

7. European regulation also seeks to ensure equal treatment between different types of institutions offering products that perform equivalent functions for consumers or investors. This is the case in the area of retail investment products, where the Commission will propose in 2011 a common regulatory framework for investment funds, life insurance companies, and banks offering

such products. It is also the case for funded occupational pensions, where the Commission is expected to make proposals aimed at avoiding competition distortions between life insurance companies and pension funds.

8. Regulation can also, of course, aim to modify or prohibit practices in certain markets that distort competition. The Commission recently proposed a regulation that sets a deadline for the creation of a single European area for credit transfers and direct debits (SEPA) and clarifies the regime applicable to multilateral interchange fees agreed upon between banks for direct debits.

9. Other regulatory initiatives are directly and explicitly aimed at stimulating competition, particularly by addressing information asymmetries between providers and clients. For example, the legislative proposals in preparation in the areas of mortgages and savings will aim to strengthen consumers' ability to compare available products on the market and choose the one that best suits their situation. In the same vein, the Commission aims to increase price transparency in securities markets through the revision of the Markets in Financial Instruments Directive (MiFID), for which a public consultation has recently been launched.

10. Moreover, the extension of the scope of European regulation opens new markets for the operators concerned. The regulation of alternative investment funds and credit rating agencies, already adopted by the Council and Parliament, will lead to the granting of single passports to these operators, allowing them to freely conduct their activities throughout the single market. In 2011, the Commission intends to make a similar proposal for credit intermediaries.

11. Finally, the establishment of European supervisory authorities as of January 1, 2011, should also promote competition. It is indeed essential to have strong, competent, and credible supervisory authorities alongside effective competition authorities. These authorities must ensure the strict, fair, and uniform application of prudential rules in force. This will be the precise role of the European supervisory authorities, which will ensure that all competitors in the single market are treated equally, without preferences being granted to "national champions." To achieve this, the new authorities will be given significant powers, such as the ability to issue legally binding decisions to national authorities and, in some cases, to financial institutions themselves.

12. The increased involvement of states in the ownership of certain banks following the crisis must be acknowledged. It is crucial that national authorities remain completely neutral between public and private banks; the European supervisory authorities will ensure this neutrality in terms of European rules. Furthermore, the exceptional state aid provided to the financial sector due to the crisis should be gradually phased out.

13. Nonetheless, the need to reconcile financial stability and competition will present numerous challenges in the coming years.

14. While the relevant market dimension may still be national for retail services, it is increasingly global for wholesale markets. Therefore, it is essential to

ensure that new regulations are defined and implemented at the global level, so that European operators are not disadvantaged compared to their competitors. International convergence is a major priority for the Commission, which is playing an increasingly important role in various international bodies, such as the G20 and the Financial Stability Board, where these issues are discussed.

15. The implementation of all the measures adopted following the crisis will undoubtedly have a significant impact, particularly on the banking sector. The cumulative impact of new regulations will need to be continuously assessed over the coming years to ensure that they do not, in particular, create barriers to entry for small and medium-sized operators.

16. This raises the issue of concentration in the financial sector, both at the European and global levels. The crisis has led to greater concentration in the banking sector. This process could accelerate in the coming years, driven by the necessary restructuring of fragile institutions and increased capital rules, exacerbating the risks posed by systemically important institutions that are "too big to fail," but also posing a potential problem for market structure from a competition perspective. This issue is on the agenda of the Financial Stability Board in 2011. It is an area where the concerns of supervisory and competition authorities converge, and where useful synergies could emerge in the use of their respective tools.

17. The same could be true for credit rating agencies and auditing. The Commission has indeed launched two consultations asking stakeholders how European regulation could contribute to stimulating more competition in these oligopolistic markets, particularly by reducing barriers to entry and exit costs.

18. Financial stability and competition are not mutually exclusive goals. On the contrary, well-designed financial regulation can both enhance financial stability and stimulate competition. To achieve this, it must avoid excessive intrusion into operators' individual decisions or business models, keep in mind the need for "contestability" of markets, and, of course, remain neutral regarding the public or private ownership of financial institutions.

19. It is also essential that regulatory authorities and competition authorities establish and maintain a close dialogue. This will enable them to better define and implement policies that will allow them to serve a common cause: the well-being of consumers and investors.

Why Competition?
Case for Japan and Asia

REIKO AOKI*
Japan Fair Trade Commission

I. Introduction

1. The Japanese Antimonopoly Act (AMA) Article 1 states that its purpose is "to promote the democratic and wholesome development of the national economy as well as to assure the interests of general consumers."

2. The Japanese AMA was established in 1947 as part of the democratization of society including establishment of competitive, and thus free and fair markets. One of the three pillars of democratization was the dissolution of Zaibatsus. Zaibatsus, such as Mitsubishi, Mitsui, Sumitomo, and Yasuda were firm groups typically consisting of a bank, firms in mining, chemical, heavy and light manufacturing, and a trading company. AMA made sure that such firm groups with market power would never emerge again.

3. This was over 70 years ago, but this aspect of AMA has become relevant again with the emergence of new conglomerates and digital ecosystems. A competitive market is necessary to ensure that innovative firms with new products and services will continue to enter existing markets or invent new markets.

4. Looking back over the past 20 years, the adoption of competition policy and competition laws has accelerated as more countries join the global market. A competitive domestic market is essential for domestic firms to be globally competitive, to attract foreign investment, and for its citizens to benefit from the best products and services from around the world. On the other hand, the

---

* Commissioner Japan Fair Trade Commission. The views expressed here are those of the author and do not necessarily represent those of Japan Fair Trade Commission.

emergence of global firms and global ecosystems based on new technologies, particularly digital technologies (hardware and algorithms), is posing a challenge to competitive markets.

5. In this chapter, I first answer the question "Why competition?" with economic reasoning and the Japanese point of view. While the basic principle does not change, antitrust has become global in the last 20 years as new challenges to competition emerge. I suggest that antitrust in the last 20 years has been shaped by economic globalization under the World Trade Organization (WTO, established in 1995) and the information and communication technology (ICT) revolution, i.e., the so called "second unbundling."[1] Free trade under the WTO and ICT has unbundled production and consumption by eliminating barriers to the movement of goods, services, and information. (The first unbundling was the introduction of steam locomotives which eliminated barriers to transporting goods.) This led to international cartels and accumulation of market power by innovators of integrated circuit (IC) chips, computers and other hardware, operations systems (OS), and software. Most recently, there is concern about the market power of digital platforms. I will look at examples of responses to the second unbundling in Japan, a mature antitrust agency, and then in Southeast Asia, where there are many young agencies.

II. What is a Competitive Market?

6. A perfectly competitive market is defined in economics as a market where everyone is a price taker (everyone must sell or buy at the prevailing market price), has perfect information (relevant attributes of a product, and price is known to all participants), and has free entry and exit. This leads to the question of how the prevailing market price is determined? It is determined by supply and demand. Supply is the aggregation of the quantity every producer is willing to supply at the prevailing price, and demand is the aggregation of quantity every consumer (firms, in the case of intermediate goods) is willing to buy at the prevailing price. There is no real market that is perfectly competitive, but it is a useful benchmark concept.

7. If there is perfect information, all consumers and producers can make consumption and production decisions that are best (optimal) for that individual with free will. If the market sets the prevailing prices, prices signal social scarcity (abundance or shortage) of goods. So, perfectly competitive markets have a very desirable welfare characteristic: social surplus (the sum of producer and consumer surplus) is maximized.

8. If a market is perfectly competitive, socially optimal allocation is achieved by individuals producing and consuming on their own, based on price. Prices

1 Richard Baldwin, The Great Convergence: Information Technology and the New Globalization (Belknap Press 2016).

convey all the information necessary to make the decision. Of course, product and services information must be perfect (public), but there is no need for consumers to reveal their preference or for producers to reveal cost or production information.

9. With free entry and exit, whenever there is positive profit to be made, new firms will enter the market, increasing supply and reducing the prevailing price. This will reduce profit. A firm that makes a loss at this new price (high production cost) will exit the market. Thus, in the long run, firms make zero (excess) profit in a perfectly competitive market. (In perfectly competitive markets, producer surplus is zero in the long run, so social surplus is equal to consumer surplus.)

10. Market power is the ability not to be a price taker, i.e., the ability to set a price. (Market power also means the ability to choose output or consumption at will. A seller choosing a price is equal to that seller choosing the corresponding point on the demand curve.) A monopolist or monopsonist is able to set the selling or buying price at will. The buyer must buy or the seller must sell at whatever price the monopolist or monopsonist sets. Prices in this case will not reflect social scarcity. The monopolist price is too high and the monopsonist price is too low, leading to transacted quantity being less than optimal.

11. In the real market, it is not possible for a producer or consumer to have information about every product (including intermediate goods) and services. Economic agents having access to better information about prices and quality of goods and services should make the market closer to perfectly competitive markets, which is a good thing. In the beginning of the internet, this was the belief. This is probably true if everyone has the same information. However, an agent possessing better information (finer or more data) than others will be able to effectively control prices or outputs, which is market power. I say effectively, because it may not look like they are controlling. For instance, a firm may display a higher priced item that a consumer likes on the first page of a search result knowing consumer preferences. If a consumer were able to see all combinations of product and price, they would have chosen another product with a different price.

12. Allocation that is optimal or close to optimal could be achieved by matching markets. Matching markets typically do not post price but reveal some other form of preference revelation. Digital technology makes matching feasible because more information or agent attributes can be processed. Matches are determined by a centralized mechanism. Agents will reveal more information, and they will be rewarded with better matches. There is a trade-off that is non-necessary when allocating goods and services using only price. This is the advantage of a competitive market.

13. Competitive markets face a trade-off when it comes to decisions across time. Economics has a framework for this called dynamic decision-making. In reality, dynamic decision-making means deciding what to do in the future, which

means there will be uncertainty. Innovation, for example, becomes difficult because the outcome of innovation, such as what new knowledge is acquired and when, is uncertain.

14. Again, it is possible to leave innovation decisions to the market or to have some centralized allocation mechanism. In the case of innovation, centralized or coordinated mechanisms can have advantages by internalizing spillovers.

III. Globalization and Second Unbundling

15. Reducing the cost of trade, physical or institutional, allows production and consumption to be unbundled. Steam engines lowered the cost of trade by reducing transportation costs. Thus, the invention of the steam engine and advances that followed comprise the "first unbundling." But cost of communication and face-to-face interactions still remained high.

16. The Uruguay Round agreement reduced the institutional cost of trade by reducing trade barriers such as tariffs. The World Trade Organization (WTO) was established in 1995 to maintain the free global trade environment. The WTO began with 76 members, and currently there are 164 member states.[2] Competition policy was not included in the Uruguay Round commitments.

17. The ICT revolution reduced the cost of communication and made virtual face-to-face communication possible. This advance made trade in services cheaper. It also helped trade in information, such as know-how and intellectual property. Many advances occurred around 1990. The Global System for Mobile Communications (GSM) was launched in 1991. The World Wide Web was proposed in 1990. The Pentium chip was introduced, and NVIDIA was founded, both started in 1993.

18. The WTO regime and the ICT revolution reduced trade and communication costs and effectively reduced the cost of face-to-face interaction. Baldwin[3] called this the "second unbundling." Increased global trade led to international cartels. Citric acid, vitamins, and lysine cartels involving the US, Europe, and Japan were fined in the late 1990s. ICT markets with network effects and two-sidedness resulted in concentration very quickly. The US Federal Trade Commission (FTC) in 1992 and the US Department of Justice in 1993 started investigating Microsoft's integration of accounting, word processing, and internet browsing software into their Windows operating system. In 2009 the FTC filed a complaint against Intel. In the most recent decade, there have been various cases brought against digital platforms in multiple jurisdictions. The OECD's Competition Committee and the International Competition Network (ICN) became important fora for global competition policy convergence.

---

2 WTO, Members and Observers, https://www.wto.org/english/thewto_e/whatis_e/tif_e/org6_e.htm (last visited Oct. 22, 2024).

3 Baldwin, *supra* note 1.

IV. Examples from Japan

19. In Japan, where AMA already existed, the law evolved to accommodate both the domestic and the international post second unbundling economic environment.[4]

1. Amendments to AMA

20. The 2009 AMA Amendment Bill (effective January 1, 2010) included the expansion of types of conduct subject to surcharges to exclusionary types of private monopolization, and certain types of unfair trade practices (concerted refusal to trade, discriminatory pricing, unjust low-price sales, resale price restriction, and abuse of superior bargaining position). Maximum jail terms for cartels and bid-rigging were extended from three years to five years. Provision of conditions to be satisfied when the JFTC exchanges information with foreign competition authorities was also included in the bill.[5] The bill came into effect in January 1, 2010.

21. In the 2013 AMA Amendment Bill (effective April 1, 2015), the hearing procedure for appealing administrative orders such as cease and desist orders and surcharge payment orders was abolished. The first instance of appeals became the Tokyo District Court. The old process had been criticized by both domestic and foreign firms.[6]

22. Commitment procedures were introduced as amendments to AMA and incorporated into the Comprehensive and Progressive Agreement for Trans-Pacific Partnership (CPTPP). The CPTPP was signed by 11 countries on March 28, 2018 and was promulgated in 2020.[7] The first commitment application was made by Rakuten, Inc. in response to a JFTC inquiry of suspected violation of Article 19 (paragraph 12 [Trading on Restrictive Terms]) of July 23, 2019. The JFTC approved their commitment plan on October 25, 2019.[8]

23. The AMA Revision Bill of 2019 introduced system surcharge reduction from leniency filing according to the extent of cooperation in providing information to the JFTC to help with a case. This amendment also introduced the Determination Procedure. The Determination Procedure provides the protocol for legal counsel and client to maintain confidentiality. This was introduced to help make the new leniency system function effectively. Both additions were

4 JFTC, *Dokkin Seisaku no Ayumi Heisei 19 nen – Reiwa 4 nen* (Evolution Competition Policy 2007–2022).

5 JFTC, *Summary of the Antimonopoly Act Amendment Bill,* (2009), https://www.jftc.go.jp/en/pressreleases/yearly-2009/mar/2009-Mar-4.html.

6 JFTC, *Enactment of the Bill to Amend the Antimonopoly Act*, (2013), https://www.jftc.go.jp/en/pressreleases/yearly-2013/Dec/individual131209.html.

7 JFTC, *Enactment of the Act for Partial Amendment of the Act on the Development of Related Legislation Following the Conclusion of the Trans-Pacific*, (2018), https://www.jftc.go.jp/en/pressreleases/yearly-2018/June/180629.html.

8 JFTC, *Approval of the Commitment Plan submitted by Rakuten, Inc.,* (2019), https://www.jftc.go.jp/en/pressreleases/yearly-2019/October/191025.html.

made to make the Japanese system consistent with global practices. Japan does not have plea bargaining or client–lawyer privilege.[9]

2. New and Revised Guidelines

24. The JFTC produced new and revised guidelines in the past 20 years in response to globalization and new technologies. Economic activity was global as were firms. In 2007, Guidelines for the Use of Intellectual Property under the Antimonopoly Act were published extending the scope of technology to "any technology protected under the Patent Act, the Utility Model Act, the Act Concerning the Circuit Layout of a Semiconductor Integrated Circuit, the Plant Variety Protection and Seed Act, the Copyright Act and the Design Act and to any technology protected as know-how"[10] from the Guidelines for Technology Licensing (1999) (i.e., patents, utility model, and know-how). This was in response to a call for clarification of software licensing and EU changes to technology transfers and publication of technology transfer guidelines. The Guideline were revised in 2016 to address fair, reasonable, and non-discriminatory (FRAND) licensing of standard essential patents (SEP). For example, a FRAND-encumbered SEP owner refusing to license (hold-out) or filing for injunction against a willing licensee can violate the AMA as private monopolization.

25. The JFTC revised its Merger Guidelines in December 2019, clarifying its approach to merger reviews based on the characteristics of digital services, such as the evaluation of data accumulation and consideration of indirect network effects. At the same time, to appropriately deal with so-called "killer acquisitions," the JFTC clarified that merger reviews would be conducted in cases where the acquisition amount was large, even if it does not meet the standards for notification. Although the case of Google's acquisition of Fitbit did not meet the standards, the JFTC conducted a review under this policy and completed the review in January 2023.

3. Abuse of Superior Bargaining Position

26. There is a type of unfair trade practices that the AMA called "abuse of a superior bargaining position" (ASBP), which regulates that a party that has a superior bargaining position against the other transacting party makes use of such position to impose a disadvantage on the transacting party, unjustly in light of normal business practices. The JFTC has utilized ASBP to deal with the conduct of digital platforms.

27. Amazon Japan, a Japanese subsidiary of Amazon, was suspected of ASBP by unjustly demanding its suppliers to reduce the price or pay fees, and in

---

9 JFTC, *Amendment to the Antimonopoly Act*, (2019), https://www.jftc.go.jp/en/policy_enforcement/210413.html.

10 JFTC, *Guidelines for the Use of Intellectual Property under the Antimonopoly Act*, (2016), https://www.jftc.go.jp/en/legislation_gls/imonopoly_guidelines_files/IPGL_Frand.pdf.

September 2020, the JFTC resolved this case through a commitment procedure. Furthermore, there is also the case where Rakuten, a Japanese operator of an online retail platform, forced merchants to apply a common free shipping threshold which could be ASBP. The JFTC reviewed Rakuten's proposal to take voluntary measures, and announced closing the investigation of this case after the JFTC confirmed the proposed measures had been taken by Rakuten.

28. An important aspect of digital platforms is that consumers are in direct contact with it. Often consumers can obtain services in return for giving information about themselves. Consumers are individuals and have a very weak bargaining position. JFTC held a study group and conducted interviews to consider how the AMA could be applied to abusive behaviors concerning the use of personal information by digital platforms. Based on these studies and discussions, Japan published the new Guidelines in 2019, which clarify what kinds of conduct to acquire, possess, or use personal information could be regarded as ASBP under the AMA.

29. The Guidelines point out that if a digital platform puts consumers in a disadvantageous position by making use of a superior bargaining position, such conduct will not only impede the free and independent judgment of such consumers, but it is also likely to give such platforms a competitive advantage over their competitors. In short, a digital platform has superior bargaining position over consumers who provide personal information when the consumers are compelled to accept detrimental treatment for using the services.

30. The Guidelines also describe several examples of determining what kind of unjustifiable acquisition or use of consumers' personal information may constitute ASBP by digital platforms. For example, it may constitute abusive behavior when a digital platform acquired information which was beyond the necessary scope to achieve the purpose of the use, without obtaining the consent of consumers or by compelling consumers to consent.

V. Evidence in Asia

1. Adoption of Competition Law

31. The WTO was established in 1995 and many Asian countries such as Japan, India, Hong Kong, Indonesia, Bangladesh, Brunei, Singapore, Malaysia, Pakistan, Thailand, Philippines, and Korea were the original members. Others such as Mongolia (1997), People's Republic of China (2001), Cambodia (2004), Nepal (2004), Chinese Taipei (2002), and Vietnam (2007) followed.[11]

---

11 WTO, WTO Accessions, (2024), https://www.wto.org/english/thewto_e/acc_e/acc_e.htm.

Table 1: Timing of competition law adoption and regulatory body establishment[12, 13]

	Competition Law	Regulatory Body
1947	Japan	
1949		Japan
1974	Australia	
1980	South Korea	
1981		South Korea
1986	New Zealand	New Zealand
1991	Taiwan	
1992		Taiwan
1993	Mongolia	
1995		Australia
1999	Indonesia, Thailand	Indonesia, Thailand
2002	India	
2003	Sri Lanka	India, Sri Lanka
2004	Singapore, Vietnam	Mongolia
2005		Singapore
2006	Nepal	Vietnam
2007	China, Pakistan	China, Pakistan
2010	Malaysia	
2011		Malaysia
2012	Bangladesh, Hong Kong	Bangladesh
2014		Hong Kong
2015	Phillipines , Brunei, Lao PDR, Myanmar	
2016		Phillipines
2017	Thailand (amended)	
2018		Lao PDR, Myanmar
2021	Cambodia	
2022		Cambodia

32. Table 1 shows the timing of competition law adoption and agency establishment. We see that many countries adopted competition law around the time of the establishment of the WTO and expectation of world trade expansion, and the realization of that followed. Nations wanting to join the global supply chain did not want local tycoons to amass market power. There might even have

12 Ravago et al., Adapting *Competition Law* and *Policy* for *Economic Development:* Asian *Illustration* (U. Haw. Dep't Econ., Working Paper No. 21-01, 2021).

13 Cambodia Ministry of Commerce (2021), https://www.ccfdg.gov.kh/en/pdf-view/?filename=https://www.ccfdg.gov.kh/wp-content/uploads/2021/11/Final-08112021ENG_CAM_Law-on-Competition.pdf.

been pressure from developing countries (and technical assistance) to developing countries to guarantee a fair market. There was also the need to fight cartels at the global level. Another source of change was the Asian Financial Crisis (AFC) of 1997. Collapse of the old financial institutions required and was an opportunity for the introduction of new regulations and laws.

2. Empirical Evidence

33. The relationship between globalization of domestic markets and competition policy can be verified empirically.[14][15] We regressed year (and forward lags) of WTO accession, Asian financial crisis and aggregated governance level[16] of each country to three competition policy adoption variables. The three dependent variables reflect the year of competition law adoption,[17] year of violation fine adoption,[18] and competition policy enforcement budget size.

34. THe regression results using global data show that before accession to the WTO, countries tended to enact competition law. In an adaptation of competition policies, market-oriented reforms, triggered by AFC, seem to play a critical role. Both the years leading to accession and the years following crisis variables are significant. We also found, using variables that measure perceived government effectiveness and corruption eradication, that governance level matters in adopting competition laws and policies.

35. Furthermore, a robust correlation between the perceived effectiveness of competition policy and the level of local competition was identified by

---

14 Reiko Aoki et al., *Diffusion and Adaptation of Competition Policy in Asia*, *in* Designing Competition Policy for Economic Development in Asia (Arsenio Balisacan et al eds., forthcoming 2024).

15 Data sources (see Section 3.3.2, Aoki et al (2024) for details)

1) Overall competition law characteristics, Comparative Competition Law (CCL) data (Bradford et al (2019) years 1945-2019 for selected countries, and Ravago et al (2021) years1947-2018 for Asia. Global Competition Review (GCR) data set for budget data.

2) Governance variables: Worldwide Governance Indicators (WGI) project database

3) Economic crises: global crises data constructed by Carmen Reinhart with her coauthors Kenneth Rogoff, Christoph Trebesch, and Vincent Reinhart.

4) Macroeconomic variables: Penn World Tables (Feenstra et al. 2015),World Development Indicators of the World Bank.

Bradford, A., A. Chilton, C. Megaw, and N. Sokol. (2019) "Gone Global: The Comparative Competition Law and Enforcement

Datasets". *Journal of Empirical Legal Studies* 16(2): 411–443.

Ravago, M-L., J. Roumasset, and A. Balisacan.(2021). Adapting

Competition Law and Policy for Economic Development: Asian Illustration. University of Hawai'i Manoa Department of Economics Working Paper No. 21-01,

Feenstra, R. C., R. Inklaar and M. P. Timmer. 2015. The Next Generation of the Penn World Table. American Economic Review. 105(10): 3150–3182. www.ggdc.net/pwt

16 Daniel Kaufmann et al., *The Worldwide Governance Indicators: Methodology and Analytical Issues* (World Bank Pol'y Rsch., Working Paper No. 5430, 2010).

17 Indicator function indexed by year that takes 1 for years competition law is in place and 0 for years that the law does not exist.

18 Indicator function indexed by year that takes 1 for years fines are in place and 0 for years that the fines do not exist.

constructing a variable from questions from the World Economic Forum's Global Competitive Report for the years 2017-2018. The first variable is the effectiveness of the "competition policy" that is based on a question: "In your country, how effective are anti-monopoly policies at ensuring fair competition?" with answer choices ranging from 1= not effective at all, to 7= extremely effective. The second variable is a composite index of "local competition," combining two variables of (1) intensity of local competition based on a question: "In your country, how intense is competition in the local markets?" with answer choices ranging from 1= not intense at all, to 7= extremely intense, and (2) extent of market dominance based on a question: "In your country, how do you characterize corporate activity?" with answer choices ranging from 1= dominated by a few business groups, to 7= spread among many firms.

36. This analysis shows that there is a robust positive correlation between these two variables across the entire spectrum of their values. This finding underscores the notion that effective competition policies exert a favorable influence on market competition dynamics. This empirical observation lends support to the proposition that the efficacy of both de jure and de facto competition policies, both in terms of adoption and adaptation, can significantly contribute to the enhancement of overall market competition.

VI. Concluding Remarks

37. The WTO trading regime and the ICT revolution reduced the physical and institutional cost of trading and communication dramatically. This happened in the 1990s. In the last 20 years, we have seen competition concerns, such as international cartels and accumulation of market power by ICT-related firms, and most recently, digital platforms.

38. Japan amended its AMA and Guidelines to accommodate this change. Japan has yet to resort to the introduction of new ex-ante regulation as in the EU and other mature agencies. The JFTC uses guidelines to signal competition concerns, which function as a kind of light-handed or nudging ex-ante regulation.

39. Many countries in South and Southeast Asia adopted competition law and competition policy regimes in anticipation of globalization. Globalization gives consumers access to foreign products and services and allows producers to join the global supply chain. A domestic competitive market is necessary for a domestic market conducive to foreign investment and to climatize domestic firms to the competitive international market. These economies are still in the process of joining the global network of competition enforcers.

Why Competition?
Voice from China

XIAOYE WANG*

Chinese Academy of Social Sciences

1. I am very pleased to be invited to join Concurrences' Book Project to talk about Why Competition from the point of view of China's Anti-Monopoly Law (AML). I also would like to talk a little about the current situation and problems of the anti-monopoly enforcement in China.

I. The Goal of The AML Is to Protect Competition

2. China's AML was promulgated in 2007 and came into effect in 2008. In 2022, the law underwent its first amendment. Setting out its legislative purposes, Article 1 of the AML states that: "This Law is enacted for the purpose of preventing and stopping monopolistic behavior, protecting fair competition in the market, encouraging innovation, improving the efficiency of economic operation, safeguarding the legitimate rights and interests of consumers and the social public interests, and promoting the healthy development of the socialist market economy." Although this article shows the diversified purpose of China's anti-monopoly legislation, there is no doubt that "preventing and stopping monopolistic behavior and protecting fair competition in the market" stands as the primary purpose and motivation of this legislation.

3. Why does China's AML oppose restricting competition and protect fair competition? The answer to this question is nothing more than hundreds of years' experience of the market economy, that is, the market competition mechanism

---

* Distinguished Professor at Shenzhen University, and Law Professor at Chinese Academy of Social Sciences.

can bring at least two desired efficiencies, one is the efficiency of resource allocation, the other is production efficiency, both of which are instrumental to improving consumer social welfare.

4. To begin with, market competition can improve the efficiency of resource allocation. Different from the planned economy such as the one implemented before the reform of China's economic system, the allocation of resources under the market economy does not rely on the administrative orders of the government but is rather determined by market players according to various variable factors in the market, among which the pricing factor plays a decisive role in business activities. That is, rising prices are signals that encourage companies to invest in some markets; and conversely, falling prices will lead them to transfer their capital to other markets. However, to allow price mechanism to perform the function of adjusting market supply and demand, and optimize resource allocation, at least two preconditions have to be met: one is free pricing, and the other is market opening, which means that the market has to be competitive.

5. Second, competition mechanism can help improve production efficiency. In a competitive market, in pursuit of a monopoly position and an extra profit at least for a period of time, enterprises inevitably strive to reduce costs, enhance quality, and constantly develop new technologies, new products, and improve management. Market competition is a vigorous process, where once an enterprise gains a competitive advantage because of the development of new products, other enterprises will imitate or develop new products. As Schumpeter pointed out, "Under the influence of competition, the energetic entrepreneur is like a trailblazer." "[1]

6. Third, even though the realization of the two aforesaid efficiencies is through methodological individualism, just as Adam Smith pointed out, market competition is like an invisible hand that creates wealth for individuals as well as for social welfare at same time.[2] That is to say, the most important function of market competition is to improve consumer social welfare, because competition can direct business operators to satisfy the requirements of consumers as much as possible in terms of product quality, quantity, specifications, varieties, etc., and out of competitive pressure, they dare not to set the price of their products too high, so that the mass products can reach an appropriate pricing point. In this case, we can say that competition makes consumers "Gods" and brings them great social welfare.

7. According to the experience of market economy, competition is always associated with the restriction of competition. In order to protect competition and oppose restrictions on competition, the substantive content of the AML

---

1 *See*, E. Kantzenbach & H.H. Kallfab, Das Konzept des funktionsfähigen Wettbebwerbs § 108 (H. Cox, U. Jens & K. Markert eds., Franz Vahlen 1981).

2 *See*, Peter Foster, *Adam Smith's Invisible Hand,* AdamSmithWorks **(Nov. 30, 2018), https://www.adamsmithworks.org/documents/adam-smith-peter-foster-invisible-hand.**

includes three pillars: prohibiting monopoly agreements, prohibiting abuse of dominant position, and merger control.[3] Additionally, today China still remains in transition from a planned economy to a market economy, the AML also prohibits the administrative organs from abusing administrative power to eliminate or restrict competition,[4] The most notable revision of the AML is that it emphasizes "the State adheres to the principles of marketization and rule of law, and strengthens the foundational position of competition policy"[5] and introduces the fair competition review system, that is, "administrative organs and organizations authorized by laws and regulations to manage public affairs shall conduct fair competition review before publishing any legal document impacting the economic activities of market entities."[6] With the implementation of the AML, in order to refine the enforcement principles, ideas and standards, the Anti-Monopoly Commission under the State Council issued eight anti-monopoly guidelines,[7] the State Administration for Market Regulation (SAMR) issued six revised regulations,[8] and the Supreme People's Court is currently revising its judicial interpretation on anti-monopoly civil litigation issued in 2012.[9]

II. The Indirect Purposes of Anti-Monopoly Will Not Affect the Primary Purpose

8. In addition to the primary purpose of "preventing and prohibiting monopolistic conduct and protecting fair market competition ", China's AML also has diversified indirect purposes, including "encouraging innovation, improving economic operation efficiency, safeguarding the legitimate interests of consumers and societal public interests, and promoting the healthy development of the socialist market economy." Because these various indirect purposes derived from the benefits of market competition, they generally do not affect the direct purpose of the AML's protection of competition. The following

3 Anti-Monopoly Law (AML) chs. 2–4.

4 *Id.* at ch. 5.

5 *Id.* at art. 4.

6 *Id.* at art. 5.

7 *See*, *Guidelines for Defining Relevant Markets,* (May 24, 2009); *Guidelines for Anti-monopoly in the Automotive Industry*, (Jan. 4, 2019); *Guidelines for Undertakings in Monopoly Cases*, (Jan 4, 2019); *Guidelines for the Application of Leniency Systems in Horizontal Monopoly Agreement Cases*, (Jan 4, 2019); *Guidelines for Antimonopoly Enforcement in the Intellectual Property Sector*, (Jan 4, 2019); *Guidelines for Anti-monopoly Compliance of Operators*, (2020); *Guidelines for Anti-monopoly in Platform Economy*, (Feb.7, 2021); *Guidelines for Anti-monopoly in Bulk Drug Field*, (Nov. 15, 2021).

8 SAMR, Provisions on the Prohibition of Monopoly Agreements, on the Prohibiting the Abuse of Dominant Market Position, on the Review of Concentration of Undertakings, on Stopping the Abuse of Administrative Power to Eliminate or Restrict Competition (Apr. 15, 2023) and Provisions on Prohibiting the Abuse of Intellectual Property Rights to Eliminate or Restrict Competition (Aug. 1, 2023). SAMR issued also the Provisions on behalf of the State Council on the Criteria for Notification of Concentration of Undertakings (under revision).

9 *See*, Draft Judicial Interpretation of the Supreme People's Court on Anti-Monopoly Civil Litigation (Nov. 2022).

part of this chapter briefly discusses " social public interest" and " innovation encouragement" as two indirect purposes of the AML.

1. Social Public Interest

9. The AML contains some provisions related to "social public interest," Article 20 AML stipulates that the parties may require the anti-monopoly enforcement agency to grant exemptions to monopoly agreements that eliminate or restrict competition on the grounds of achieving social public interests such as energy saving, environmental protection, disaster relief and so on. Article 34 stipulates that where undertakings can prove that the concentration "conforms to the public interest," the enforcement agency may make a decision not to prohibit.

10. However, social public interest is a controversial concept. Some people may believe that it refers to the interests of consumers; others may think that it refers to national interests. However, social public interest should not be motivated by an individual person, enterprise, or group, but rests with a general or integral interest, which can be economic or non-economic such as political interests. In any case, considering that public interest is a relatively vague and flexible concept, this provision will inevitably grant discretion to the enforcement agencies. However, the majority of monopolies, including the administrative monopolies, are unreasonable phenomena, which essentially hinder the competition mechanism from adjusting supply and demand to the detriment of resource allocation optimization. In the short run, monopoly leads to the rise of prices and the decline of quality, which damages the interests of consumers, and in the long run, monopoly results in low production efficiency of enterprises and the shortage of national economy. Therefore, I believe that "social public interest" is not a very important legislative purpose of the AML, and so far, there has been no anti-monopoly case exempted on the ground of "social public interest."

2. Encouraging Innovation

11. Article 1 of the amended AML added "encouraging innovation" as a new legislative purpose. Many scholars have questioned this purpose because competition protected by the AML can put business operators under competitive pressure, so that they will strive to reduce prices, improve quality, and develop new technologies and products, which is actually innovation. In short, "encouraging innovation" is already covered by the purpose of "economic efficiency" and therefore not necessary to set it as a separate and special purpose of the AML.[10] However, some people believe that to add "encourage innovation" is in line with the development of the digital economy, and the enforcement agency should "shift from static efficiency and price changes to emphasizing

---

10 *See*, Ni Tai, *Experts Discuss Highlights and Key Points of the Draft Amendment of the AML*, China Mkt. Regul. News (Dec. 11, 2021).

dynamic efficiency and encouraging innovation."[11] Some even argue that "encouraging innovation" is as important as "protecting competition," or even more important than the former.[12] My question here is that if "encouraging innovation" is not deemed as an indirect purpose, i.e. a benefit derived from protecting competition, a question may arise as to which legislative purpose, i.e. "protects competition" or "encourages innovation," takes precedence. On the other hand, if "encouraging innovation" becomes the direct purpose of anti-monopoly, it should be not only a slogan, but it also calls for legislator's real efforts to incentivize innovation. For example, innovation requires massive investment and may carry great risks, so should the government grant competition exemption to the enterprises involved in innovation? Or should governments adopt industrial policies, such as financial subsidies, to boost innovation? In my view, even if "encouraging innovation" is set as an direct purpose of a legislation, the relevant legal system should be that aimed at protecting intellectual property, otherwise no one will be motivated to innovate. Therefore, "encouraging innovation" in Article 1 of the AML should be an indirect purpose derived from the protection of competition, and in case of conflict between protecting competition and encouraging innovation, the protection of competition should be given priority.

3. Protection of Competition of the AML Based on National Conditions

12. There has always been a dispute about the goals of anti-monopoly legislation internationally. The New Brandeis School recently emerging in the United States argues that the Sherman Act condemns all economic forces and inequalities, even if they do not unreasonably raise prices, reduce output or harm innovation, because their existence is a threat to social democracy and justice.[13] However, given that the legal systems including the anti-monopoly regimes take root in the history of each country, their legislative purposes should allow for different interpretations. As far as China's AML is concerned, it was promulgated after more than 40 years' implementation of a planned economic system, and its designer realized that market competition is an indispensable propeller for increasing efficiency and improving consumer welfare, so the goal of the AML is undoubtedly concerned with economic, but not political issues.

13. China's planned economy has made achievements in the past few decades, especially at the beginning of the founding of the PRC, when it played a positive role in restoring production and promoting economic development. However, over time, the inefficiency and bureaucracy that prevailed in the

11 Shi Jianzhong, Detailed Description of the Expert Revised Draft of the AML of the PRC 4 (China Univ. Pol. Sci. & L. Press 2020).

12 *See*, *How Does Antitrust Encourage Innovation?*, Southern Metropolis Daily (June 10, 2021), https://news.qq.com/rain/a/20210610A04PFS00.

13 Richard J. Gilbert & A. Douglas Melamed, *Innovation: A Bridge to the New Brandeisians?*, CPI (Feb. 21, 2022), https://www.pymnts.com/cpi-posts/innovation-a-bridge-to-the-new-brandeisians/

planned economy became more and more intolerable. It is generally recognized that enterprises under the planned economic system are part of the big state apparatus, have no operational autonomy, face minimal competition among themselves, and thus lack the initiative and innovative spirit of production and operation. To address the innate defect of the planned economy, at the end of 1978, the Third Plenary Session of the 11th CPC Central Committee proposed that the focus of the work of the Party and the State should be shifted to economic construction, and the policies concerning reforming the domestic economic system and opening to the outside world should be implemented.[14]

14. In October 1980, the State Council promulgated the Interim Provisions on Launching and Protecting Socialist Competition (the "Provision"), a landmark government policy which, for the first time, set up the task of anti-monopoly, especially against administrative monopoly. The Provisions pointed out that: "To carry out competition, we must break regional blockades and sectoral divisions, and no region or economic department is allowed to block the market; it is not allowed to prohibit the sale of goods from other regions in local markets or in their own departments."[15] That meant that the great function of competition had begun to be recognized in China, and " competition," which is traditionally regarded as "flood and beast" of capitalism in this country, had become an "unstoppable torrent," and entered into economic life under China's socialist system.[16]

15. It is notable that the 1984 Decision of the Central Committee of the CPC on Economic System Reform affirmed the positive role of competition in economic development for the first time. It states: "The founders of Marxism predicted that socialism, on the basis of the abolition of the system of exploitation, would inevitably create higher productivity and enable the productive forces to advance at a higher speed. The profound changes taking place in our country over the past 35 years since the founding of the PRC have initially demonstrated the superiority of the socialist system. However, it must be pointed out that this superiority has not yet been exploited as it should. In addition to historical, political, and ideological reasons for not achieve superiority, an important economic reason in the is that a rigid pattern has been formed in the economic system that is incompatible with the requirements of the development of the socialist productive forces.[17] The Report of the 14th Congress of the CPC in 1992 stated:

> "The socialist market economic system we want to establish is to enable the market to play a basic role in the allocation of resources under

---

14 *See*, Communist Party of China, Communiqué of the Third Plenary Session of the 11th Central Committee (Oct. 13, 2009), https://www.gov.cn/test/2009-10/13/content_1437683.htm.

15 *See*, China State Council, Interim Regulations of the State Council on Carrying out and Protecting Socialist Competition (1980), https://law.lawtime.cn/d658413663507.html

16 *See*, Wang Xiaoye, *The Prospect of Antimonopoly Legislation in China*, 1 Wash. U. Glob. Stud. L. Rev. (2002); Wang Xiaoye, *Issues Surrounding the Drafting of China's Anti-monopoly law*, 3 Wash. U. Glob. Stud. L. Rev. (200)4.

17 *See*, CPC, Decision of the Central Committee of CPC on the Reform of the Economic System (June 26, 2008), https://www.gov.cn/test/2008-06/26/content_1028140.htm.

> the macro-control of the socialist state,… Through the function of price leverage and competition mechanism, resources are allocated to the links with better benefits, and enterprises are given pressure and motivation to achieve survival of the fittest. Take advantages of the market's sensitive response to various economic signals to promote timely coordination of production and demand."[18]

16. This fully affirms that the market, price, and competition mechanisms are also the integral components of the socialist market economy, and thus affirms the great significance of protecting competition to deepen the reform of the economic system and to establish the socialist market economic system.

17. Here, I in particular, would like to mention the important role played by Mr. Deng Xiaoping in reforming China's economic system. Deng Xiaoping repeatedly talked about the development of the Chinese market economy, such as "a planned economy is not equal to socialism, because capitalism also has a plan; a market economy is not equal to capitalism, because socialism also has a market. Planning and the market are both economic means, and whether there is more planning or more market is not the essential differentiator between socialism and capitalism."[19] This incisive expression is very helpful to free people's minds, that is, no longer bound by the debate over whether "planning" and "market" implicate "capitalism" or "socialism", and therefore also helpful in formulating thoughts and theories on establishing a socialist market economy in China.

18. In short, the formulation and implementation of the China's AML stemmed from the recognition by the legislator of the unparalleled superiority of a market economy, i.e. it does not depend on government's self-righteous plans aimed at boosting enterprise's global development or business scale. On the contrary, a market economy rests on sticking to market competition. No matter what the enterprise, their market development is an unknown trajectory, so they should flexibly adapt themself to the changing market. As Von Hayek noted, competition is "systematically as a procedure for discovering facts which, if the procedure did not exist, would remain unknown or at least would not be used."[20] That means that information on the market can only be transmitted with the help of competition, the production capacity of enterprises can be adjusted according to market demand, market power can be constrained, and various interests and decisions of enterprises can be coordinated. Although individuals inevitably make mistakes in the market their mistakes do not affect the whole process of social and economic development. Therefore, protection of competition,

---

18 *See*, Jiang Zemin, Report at the 14th National Congress of the Communist Party of China (Oct. 12, 1992), https://fuwu.12371.cn/2012/09/26/ARTI1348641194361954.shtml

19 *See*, CPNN, *Deng Xiaoping, Why Can't Socialism Have a Market Economy?*, (Jan. 17, 2020), http://cpc.people.com.cn/n1/2020/0117/c69113-31553563.html

20 *See*, Fiedrich A. von Hayek, *Der Wettbewerb als Entdeckungsverfahren*, *in* Freiburger Studien, Gesammelte Aufsätze § 249 (1969).

as a discovering procedure, should be regarded as an indispensable part of market economic order.[21]

4. Two Focal Points in the Current Enforcement of the AML

19. Why should competition also be explained through the lens of the AML's implementation? As of August 2023, 339 investigations involving monopoly agreements and abusive behaviors have been closed with pecuniary fines and confiscation of illegal gains amounting to RMB37.9 billion, and 5,409 concentrations of undertakings have been concluded. According to the statement of the SAMR, "many significant monopolistic behaviors incurring strong reactions from the people have been effectively contained, and the position and role of the AML in the national economic and social development have become more prominent."[22] However, in my view, there are at least two focal points which are also difficult issues facing the SAMR: one is anti-monopoly in the digital economy, and the other is how to counter administrative monopoly.

A. *Strengthening Anti-Monopoly in the Digital Economy*

20. China is the second largest digital economy in the world. At present, its internet users has reached 1.079 billion, and the internet penetration reached 76.4 percent.[23] Although digital platforms such as search engines, social networks, and e-commerce bring people a lot of conveniences, due to obvious direct and indirect network effects of the platforms, and their business model which rely heavily on data collection and integration, the large platform enterprises are keen to expand their market power through M&A,[24] and various restrictions on competition, in particular the "either/or" strategy, have emerged in the e-commerce sphere. That is, the larger platforms force their suppliers not to sell goods or services on other platforms, thereby restricting fair competition among platform operators.[25] Given the fact that successful enterprises in the platform sector have left less and less space for competition, as in the US and EU, in China there have also been calls in recent years to strengthen anti-monopoly in the digital sector.

---

21 *See*, Ernst-Joachim Mestmäcker, *Wirschatsrecht in* RabelsZ 54 409–430 (1990).

22 *See*, SAMR, Report on the 15th Anniversary of the Implementation of the AML (Aug. 11, 2023), https://www.samr.gov.cn/xw/zj/art/2023/art_101af9a1c3d945b09284acdb5b46ddef.html

23 *See*, CN News Agency, *52nd Statistical Report on China's Internet Development released by the China Internet Network Information Center*, (Aug. 28, 2023), https://www.thepaper.cn/newsDetail_forward_24391842.

24 For example, in 2019 Tencent participated in 121 cases, Alibaba 81, Baidu 45, and JD.com 32, respectively, and these cases concentrated in the fields of technology, finance, e-commerce retail and entertainment. *See*, CN News Agency, *M&A Report 2019 – Internet Giants are Cautious*, https://m.pedaily.cn/news/451967 (last visited Oct. 30, 2024).

25 *See*, SAMR, Decision on Administrative Penalties for Alibaba's Two-Choice Behavior No. 28 (2021) State Municipal Supervision Office.

21. Along with this trend, controversy has also arisen on how to carry out reasonable anti-monopoly regulation in this field. Some scholars borrowed FTC Chair Lina Kahn's idea[26] noting that digital platforms should be regulated as new utilities in order to achieve social goals beyond competition policy, namely, to extend from purely economic antitrust to broader social regulation.[27] There are also scholars suggesting that China should learn from the EU's Digital Market Act (DMA) and implement "ex-ante regulation" against large platform enterprises.[28]

22. In my view, although strengthening anti-monopoly in the digital economy is obviously a focal point, following the New Brandeis Doctrine in the US or the EU approach to regulating digital "gatekeepers," is not necessarily in line with the trend of China's AML enforcement, because the Chinese legislator attaches equal importance to both "regulation" and "development," particularly in the digital sector.[29] Recently at a symposium with large platform enterprises, Premier Li Qiang stressed that "governments at all levels should strive to create a fair market environment, improve investment access and security assessment, increase transparency and predictability, reduce compliance costs for enterprises, in order to promote the benign development of the industry."[30] Some scholars articulate that the AML enforcement should be precise, which means, that to relax anti-monopoly in the digital economy is wrong, but an over and excessive implementation at the other extreme is also wrong, because it will harm innovation and development of enterprises.[31] Taking the public utility theory advocated by the New Brandeis School as an example, if one does not distinguish between natural monopoly and competitive activity, this theory will no doubt lead to the expansion of the scope of economic regulation and inhibit the vitality of market competition.[32] The set of quantitative criteria for digital gatekeepers in the EU Digital Markets Act is also very problematic. Taking China's big digital platforms as an example, Baidu, which has a market share of more than 70 percent in the search engine sector, may have a lower market capitalization than JD.com, which has a market share of less than 30 percent in the e-commerce sector. This example shows that if the relevant market is not defined and the specific market behavior is not

26 *See*, Lina M. Khan, *Amazon's Antitrust Paradox*, 126 Yale L.J. (2017), https://www.yalelawjournal.org/note/amazons-antitrust-paradox.

27 *See*, Gao Wei, *New Utility Theory of Platform Regulation* (Legal Rsch., Working Paper No. 3, 2021).

28 *See*, Zhou Hanhua, *On the Binary Separation of Anti-monopoly and ex ante Regulation in the Platform Economy*, 1 China L.J. (2023). *See also*, Regulation (EU) 2022/1925 of the European Parliament and of the Council of Sept. 14, 2022 on contestable and fair markets in the digital sector and amending Directives (EU) 2019/1937 and (EU) 2020/1828 (Digital Markets Act), 2022, O.J. (L 265) 1.

29 *See*, People's Daily, *Adhere to Regulation and Development with Equal Emphasis*, (Sept. 8, 2021), https://www.gov.cn/xinwen/2021-09/08/content_5636122.htm.

30 *See*, CN News Agency, *Li Qiang Presided over a Symposium for Platform Companies*, (July 12, 2023), https://www.gov.cn/yaowen/liebiao/202307/content_6891546.htm.

31 *See*, Wang Xianlin, *International Observation and Domestic Thinking on Antitrust on Digital Platforms*, 5 J. U. Chinese Acad. Soc. Sci. (2022).

32 *See*, Li Jian, *Digital Platform Regulation: Reflection on Public Theory and Application of Economic Regulation* (Legal Rsch., Working Paper No. 5, 2023).

concretely analyzed, mere reliance on quantitative criteria and across-the-board prohibitions are very likely to result in problems in practice. Therefore, in my view, instead of rushing to impose ex-ante regulation on digital platforms, Chinese lawmaker should still apply the AML on a regular case-by-case basis, and let the bullets fly for a while, whilst waiting for the experience or lessons to be drawn from the implement of the EU Digital Market Act.[33]

B. *Strengthening Anti-Administrative Monopoly*

23. Opposing abuse of administrative power to eliminate and restrict competition is an important part of China's AML. Administrative monopolies normally take the forms of prohibiting forced transactions, obstructing the free movement of goods or services, and excluding or restricting non-local operators from participating in local bidding activities and so on. The revised AML also introduced a fair competition review system, under which the administrative agencies must conduct fair competition review before issuing rules or regulations impacting business activities of market entities.[34] Theoretically, these provisions should play an important role in promoting a unified national market. However, since administrative restrictions on competition are still relatively serious, especially in the market segmentation across regions where the differential treatment between enterprises is more obvious, the AML has limitations in protecting competition.[35]

24. For example, China organizes and manages its economy to a considerable extent according to administrative divisions. With the central and local governments "eating separately" financially, regional protectionism has become the main sticking point in market segmentation across China. Considering that the promotion of local leading enterprises is closely tied with the GDP performance of their regions, it is not very realistic to expect local governments to completely eliminate local protections merely through the fair competition review system.

25. The differential treatment across enterprises is mainly manifested in their ownership. According to statistics, China's private economy contributes more than 50 percent of the tax revenue, more than 60 percent of GDP, more than 70 percent of technological innovation achievements, more than 80 percent of urban jobs, and accounts for more than 90 percent of the total number of various enterprises in China.[36] Despite the great contribution, and the 16th National Congress of the CPC's determination to "unswervingly encourage, support and guide the development of the non-public economy," many private

---

33 *See*, Wang Xiaoye & Gao Yajie, *China's Antimonopoly Law Enforcement in the Digital Economy*, 4 ANTITRUST BULL. (2022).

34 *See*, Anti-Monopoly Law (AML), art. 5.

35 *See*, Wang Xiaoye, *Highlights and Issues Concerning the Amendment of China's AML*, CPI ANTITRUST CHRON. (Mar. 2023).

36 *See*, People's Daily, *The Private Economy Steadily Moving Towards High Quality*, (May 31, 2023), https://www.gov.cn/yaowen/liebiao/202305/content_6883880.htm.

enterprises believe that their living space is shrinking and their business environment is not good. There may be many reasons explaining the situation of private enterprises, one of which is that some government departments have not achieved competitive neutrality in terms of the equal treatment of enterprises of different ownership. That is, private enterprises have institutional obstacles such as market access, qualification review, and administrative approval of business activities; to a considerable extent, the private economy and the state-owned economy are only equal in form, but in fact they are not equal. Therefore, in recent years, the State has strongly emphasized optimizing and improving the business environment of the private economy, and the CPC Central Committee and the State Council have recently issued the "Opinions on Promoting the Development and Growth of the Private Economy," which clearly stresses "equal treatment of enterprises of all types of ownership" and "stronger AML enforcement to stop the abuse of administrative power to eliminate restrictions on competition."[37]

26. There is no doubt that the anti-administrative monopoly and fair competition review system of the AML should play a key role in breaking down local protection and eliminating differential treatment of enterprises under different ownership. However, administrative monopolies and differential treatment across enterprises of different ownership are not only economic issues, but also involve the political and social systems of the State. Therefore, the solution to these problems also requires the State to further deepen the reform of the economic system.[38]

III. Conclusion

27. China's AML protects the right of enterprises to participate in fair and free competition in the market, and therefore its goal is to protect market competition, but not the competitor. Along with the digital economy becoming a focal point of anti-monopoly, improving social welfare should still be the fundamental goal of anti-monopoly in this sector, regardless of the different characteristics of this sector from traditional economy. Administrative monopoly is still a huge obstacle to the economic system reform in China today, so anti-monopoly enforcement should still focus on breaking administrative monopoly and strive to enable all forms of ownership economies to use production factors equally, participate in market competition fairly, and enjoy equal legal protection in accordance with the AML. Finally, I would like to repeat the provision of Article 4 of the AML, that is: "The State

37 *See*, Lester Ross & Kenneth Zhou, *China Issues New Policy to Boost Private Economy*, WilmerHale (Aug. 11, 2023), https://www.wilmerhale.com/insights/client-alerts/20230811-china-issues-new-policy-to-boost-private-economy

38 *See*, Wang Xiaoye, *Optimizing the Business Environment of the Private Economy is Inseparable from Fair Competition*, Chinese Soc. Sci. Today (Sept. 27, 2023).

adheres to the principle of marketization and rule of law, and strengthens the fundamental position of competition policy." This provision is not only the core of the first amendment of the AML, but also the correct direction towards which China needs to make unremitting efforts in order to strengthen anti-monopoly, improve the market competition environment, and establish a sound unified national large market.

Competition Policy in Progressive Economic Transition Nations: A Perspective from China

HUANG YONG*
University of International Business and Economics

I. Introduction

1. Understanding China's competition policy not only requires recognizing China as a transition economy but also requires noting the fact that China adopts a progressive economic transition approach rather than the "shock therapy." This context makes China unique and often leads to new developments in the implementation of its competition policy.

2. Observing China's competition further requires identifying a central theme, which is the special mission of China's antitrust laws to actively expand the scope of competition mechanisms during the progressive transition. With such perspective in mind, this chapter explores how competition policy has gradually moved from the background to the forefront alongside the implementation of antitrust laws, giving rise to new policies and systems, and subsequently driving the next wave of reforms. It is evident that approximately every two to three years, China's economic system reforms and its competition policy moves up to a new level.

3. As China has become the world's second-largest economy, sustaining high-speed growth has become increasingly difficult, and economic system reforms

* Professor Huang Yong, University of International Business & Economics (UIBE), member of the Expert Advisory Committee under the Anti-Monopoly Commission of China's State Council, and an elected deputy of the Beijing Municipal People's Congress.

have entered a "deep-water zone." The impact of the pandemic on economic recovery has also led to a greater inclination of governmental intervention in the market. Given these multiple contexts, for China's competition policy to better respond and support economic system reform, it must establish a rule-of-law system to effectively safeguard existing reform achievements while pursuing new reform and development. This presents a unique challenge for China's leadership, legislators, scholars, and practitioners alike.

4. Fortunately, China has long been deeply integrated into the global economy and continues to reap the benefits of economic globalization. Therefore, maintaining the direction of progressive market-oriented reform aligns with China's own interests and demands.

5. From the perspectives of scholars and practitioners, it may seem easy to identify shortcomings in China's competition policy; but it is also important to recognize that China is both a relatively nascent jurisdiction in terms of antitrust law and a developing market economy that is still in the process of progressive transition. Regardless, with the further strengthening of competition policy language and provisions in China's new antitrust laws, the country's reform efforts now have a stronger foundation than ever before. Coupled with the gradual accumulation of enforcement and judicial experience, China's competition policy will possess a more international perspective and more coordinated approach, playing a greater role in responding and supporting future economic reforms.

II. Progressive Economic Transition: The Overall Context of Introducing and Implementing China's Competition Policy

6. As is well-known, China is a transitioning economy that has shifted from a command economic system to a market-based economic system. However, the description of a transitioning economy alone does not fully illustrate the background of implementing China's competition policy. It is essential to consider the specific manner in which this transition is undertaken. In the context of China, what needs to be taken into account is the impact of the progressive transition process on the establishment and implementation of competition policy.

7. Since the late 1980s, following the disintegration of the former Soviet Union, some countries opted for the "shock therapy" system to transition from command economies to market economies. However, the outcomes of shock therapy varied across different nations. For instance, Poland experienced rapid development after a brief period of pain, whereas Russia plunged into turmoil following shock therapy. In contrast, China adopted a progressive transition approach. During this progressive transition, China's leadership and society

went through the process of "exploring reform limit, forging political consensus, formulating policy documents, and pushing for legal revisions."

8. In 1978, China initiated the reform and opening-up policy. In the 1982 Chinese Constitution of People's Republic of China, it was stipulated that China's economic system was based on "socialist public ownership" and that market regulation played only a "supplementary role."[1]

9. In 1984, China's Central Committee of the Communist Party issued a significant document on economic system reform, proposing the implementation of a "planned commodity economy." Deng Xiaoping once remarked on this, saying: "In the past, we couldn't have written such a policy document." At that time, the introduction of the concept of a commodity economy was already a major breakthrough, highlighting the formidable challenges China faced in its economic system reform.

10. In 1993, a significant transformation occurred in China's economic system. The constitutional amendment of that year explicitly stated that China would implement a "socialist market economy."[2] From that point onwards, the concept of the "market" began to enter the public consciousness in China, quietly bringing about changes.

11. Even though the term "market economy" had been written into the Chinese Constitution, the timing for enacting the Anti-Monopoly Law was still not mature. This was because the mechanisms, frameworks, and foundations of the market had not yet been fully established, and the systemic mechanisms and ingrained mindset of the planned economy still dominated the national and societal discourse. However, starting from that moment, several scholars began to contemplate the legislative goals of China's Anti-Monopoly Law and how it would regulate administrative monopolies, state-owned enterprise monopolies, and economic monopolies in the future. These topics were increasingly mentioned and discussed.

12. In 2005, four years after China's accession to the WTO, the anti-monopoly legislation plan was officially listed on the national legislative agenda. Questions arose regarding whether this law should apply to state-owned enterprises and whether provisions regulating administrative monopolies were appropriate for inclusion in this legislation. Such questions sparked intense debates. At the same time, one influential suggestion gained prominence: that the text of China's Anti-Monopoly Law must explicitly incorporate "competition policy." In this suggestion, competition policy was no longer narrowly referred to the antitrust legal system but instead broadly represented a collection of policies, laws, and practices guided by the principles of "respecting the market" and "prioritizing competition."[3]

---

1 Constitution of the People's Republic of China (1982) art. 15, http://www.npc.gov.cn/zgrdw/npc/zt/qt/gjxfz/2014-12/03/content_1888093.htm (in Chinese).

2 *Id.*

3 Huang Yong, *On the System and Implementation Mechanism of Legal Protection for Competition Policy in China*, 16 Tsinghua U. L.J. 28-42 (2022).

13. In 2007, China's legislative body passed the Anti-Monopoly Law of the People's Republic of China, which concluded the previous debates. First, this law explicitly stipulates that state-owned enterprises and industries with statutory monopolies shall not use their positions to harm consumer interests. This implies that the Anti-Monopoly Law will be applied to state-owned enterprises and industries with statutory monopolies, just as it will be applied to the private sector. Second, the Anti-Monopoly Law of China includes a dedicated chapter on: "Abuse of Administrative Power to Exclude or Restrict Competition," providing China with the legal mechanisms to address administrative monopolies for the first time in history. Third, it designates the State Council's Anti-Monopoly Commission as responsible for "formulating relevant competition policies," explicitly incorporating competition policy into the law and leaving room for further development in the future.

14. It is important to note that at this point, the Anti-Monopoly Law in China does not have the status of a true "economic constitution" and is not yet the most crucial reference book for China's economic operation and administrative management. However, the market-oriented concepts and competitive thinking inherent in the Anti-Monopoly Law can serve as a probe and microscope in China's economic system reform, helping China to better define reform objectives from the perspective of market competition. Therefore, completing the anti-monopoly legislation marks a new starting point for China's progressive market-oriented reform instead of the endpoint, and is certainly not time for a break, but rather an opportunity to push forward with economic system reform.

III. Responding and Supporting Economic System Reform: The Synergy between Anti-Monopoly Law and Competition Policy

15. The dedicated chapter on administrative monopolies and the inclusion of competition policy, coupled with the economic system reform tasks facing China, have made China's Anti-Monopoly Law a legal framework that differs significantly from those in western countries, appearing similar in form but diverging in spirit. Market economies in mature western countries tend to evolve spontaneously from the bottom up, while China's market has gradually taken shape as governmental authority continuously makes room for the private sector, expanding the scope of competition mechanisms. Therefore, in China, the Anti-Monopoly Law not only aims to prevent economic monopolies but also to dismantle administrative monopolies. It is not merely about safeguarding competition mechanisms from distortion but actively expanding the reach of competition mechanisms.

16. However, in many aspects, the role that the Anti-Monopoly Law could play at that time was relatively limited. For instance, when it comes to administrative

monopolies, even after a significant revision of China's Anti-Monopoly Law in 2022, the new legal provisions still merely specify that the superior authority of the agency responsible for implementing administrative monopoly behavior should order corrective measures and impose penalties on relevant personnel. It does not directly empower the antitrust enforcement agency to make decisions or their execution; instead, the antitrust enforcement agency is limited to investigative and advisory roles. Furthermore, when the Anti-Monopoly Law applies to state-owned enterprises, it often faces an awkward situation: senior executives of state-owned enterprises hold administrative rank similar to antitrust enforcement officers, and the former's ranks are often higher, making it challenging for the antitrust enforcement agency to assert its authority effectively.

17. Despite numerous challenges, China's Anti-Monopoly Law fulfilled its mission effectively during its initial years of implementation. On August 1, 2008, the very first day the law came into effect, four anti-counterfeiting companies in Beijing sued the former General Administration of Quality Supervision, Inspection and Quarantine, accusing it of administrative monopoly. The reason behind this lawsuit was the agency's involvement in the establishment of the "Zhongxin Guojian" company while promoting the electronic monitoring network. It also required companies to obtain electronic monitoring code authorization exclusively from this company.[4] This case, being China's first antitrust case, quickly shifted public attention towards concerns about administrative monopolies.

18. In 2011, the National Development and Reform Commission (NDRC), one of China's antitrust enforcement agencies at the time, disclosed an investigation into suspected price-fixing practices by China Telecom and China Unicom.[5] The case was ultimately resolved with commitments from the telecom companies to rectify their behavior.

19. In 2013, antitrust enforcement agencies in Guizhou and Sichuan provinces, imposed fines of 247 million RMB and 202 million RMB, respectively, on China's largest liquor companies, Maotai and Wuliangye, for maintaining resale prices.[6] This action demonstrated a clear stance that even large state-owned enterprises could not be exempt from antitrust enforcement.

20. As anti-monopoly enforcement and terms such as "breaking administrative monopolies" and "preventing state-owned enterprise monopolies" became more prominent in the public discourse, the opportunity for "competition policy" to enter the societal discourse began to mature. In 2015, a central policy document

4 *See*, *Four anti-counterfeiting companies sued the General Administration of Quality Supervision, Inspection and Quarantine for administrative monopoly*, ChinaNews (Aug. 6, 2008, at 08:26 AM CST), https://www.chinanews.com/cj/gncj/news/2008/08-06/1336931.shtml.

5 *See*, *Editor's Note*, http://www.china.com.cn/v/zhuanti/node_7142578.htm (last visited Oct. 14, 2024).

6 *See*, *Moutai and Wuliangye's share prices continue to fall. It is reported that they were fined 450 million yuan for price monopoly*, ChinaNews (Feb. 19, 2013, at 13:32 AM CST), https://www.chinanews.com/stock/2013/02-19/4576663.shtml.

of the Communist Party of China introduced the phrase "gradually establish the foundational status of competition policy."[7] This marked the first appearance of the term "competition policy" in the party's documents. In nearly 70 years from the founding of the People's Republic of China and nearly 40 years of reform and opening-up, policy documents had more commonly used keywords such as "industrial policy," "fiscal policy," "investment policy," "trade policy," and "consumer policy." The emergence of this new phrase in the documents of a state led by the Communist Party of China quickly garnered attention and sparked discussions throughout Chinese society.

21. On one hand, as discussions became more widespread and in-depth, people began to realize that, in addition to familiar policies like industrial and fiscal policies, there was also a role for competition policy within the economic policy framework. On the other hand, as globalization brought about more benefits to China and the country surpassed Japan in GDP in 2010 to become the world's second-largest economy, people also became more aware of the advantages that marketization and competition can bring.

22. As competition policy gained visibility in the public eye and garnered more consensus, the new task for China's competition policy was to promote institutionalization and legalization, ultimately creating a more instrumental legal environment to advancing economic system reform in China. At this point, the initial mission of China's competition policy remained focused on breaking administrative monopolies, countering state-owned enterprise monopolies, and creating more space for the market. Therefore, between 2016 and 2017, China's competition policy saw further developments.

23. First, in 2016, the State Council officially implemented the Fair Competition Review Mechanism.[8] This system was based on the provision in China's Anti-Monopoly Law, which stated that government departments should "not abuse administrative power to formulate provisions that exclude or restrict competition." Drawing on the experiences of the Australian Fair Competition Assessment System and the OECD competition assessment tools, and taking into account China's specific circumstances, this system required policy-making agencies to conduct self-assessments against review criteria when formulating economic policies and drafting legislative documents.[9]

24. Second, in 2017, the Market Regulation Roadmap for the Thirteenth Five-Year Plan period proposed the implementation of a "competition neutrality system." If established, this system would effectively constrain the government and state-owned financial institutions to maintain neutrality when dealing with

---

7 China State Council, *Several Opinions of the CPC Central Committee and the State Council on Promoting the Reform of the Price Mechanism*, State Council Gazette (Oct. 12, 2015), https://www.gov.cn/gongbao/content/2015/content_2953936.htm.

8 China State Council, *The State Council's decision on the construction of a market system Opinions on Establishing a Fair Competition Review System*, State Council Gazette (June 14, 2016), https://www.gov.cn/zhengce/content/2016-06/14/content_5082066.htm.

9 Li Qing, *A Review and Outlook on China's Competition Policy*,.2 Competition Pol'y Rsch. 5–15 (2018).

both public and non-public enterprises, preventing state-owned enterprises from enjoying unfair competitive advantages in the market.

25. In 2019, as a result of deeper theoretical and practical exploration, China's competition policy experienced significant progress. A document passed during the Fourth Plenary Session of the Nineteenth Central Committee of the Communist Party of China explicitly called for the "strengthening of the foundational status of competition policy." Documents passed during the Central Committee Plenary Sessions represent the highest-level of practical guidance and enforcement in China, and the new wording elevated China's competition policy from a "foundation-like status" to a "foundational status." This implies that competition policy now has a more significant opportunity to interact on an equal footing with industrial and fiscal policies in China. Building upon this, a 2022 document from the Central Committee of the Communist Party of China proposed the "establishment of a coordinated safeguard mechanism for fair competition policy and industrial policy,"[10] providing new space for competition policy to operate.

26. All in all, China's Anti-Monopoly Law has consistently adhered to its original mission of actively expanding the scope of competition mechanisms. With its growing influence, it has continuously pushed competition policy from behind the scenes to the forefront, elevating its importance. Furthermore, it is fortunate that the amended Chinese Anti-Monopoly Law which was completed in 2022 includes provisions emphasizing the principles of marketization and the rule of law, while strengthening the foundational status of competition policy. Compared to the past, these new provisions place China's competition policy on a new starting point with legal safeguards. Although in the past, merely incorporating "competition policy" into the law had already brought about significant changes and developments, it is reasonable to believe that the new Anti-Monopoly Law will bring even more promising outcomes for competition policy in China.

IV. Transitioning from Reaction and Support to Building a Legal Safeguarding System: The New Historical Mission of China's Competition Policy

27. After strengthening the foundational status of competition policy incorporated into China's Anti-Monopoly Law, how should this be utilized as an opportunity to further advance economic system reforms? What aspects of the

---

10 China State Council, *Opinions of the CPC Central Committee and the State Council on Accelerating the Construction of a National Unified Market,* Xinhua News Agency (Apr. 10, 2022, at 19:20 PM CST), https://www.gov.cn/zhengce/2022-04/10/content_5684385.htm.

implementation of the Anti-Monopoly Law should be prioritized for improvement? This contribution believes that these considerations are closely tied to China's current stage of development, the overall economic environment, and key reform directions.

28. First, China's economic system reform has entered a "deep water zone," which imposes new and higher demands on competition policy.

29. In pursuit of further development through deepening economic system reform, these reforms will increasingly challenge the current distribution of interests. Unlike in the past when China's economy experienced rapid growth and reforms progressed swiftly, competition policy mainly needed to respond and support the rapid reform process to yield significant results. However, in the current context, it is essential to emphasize the establishment of a legal framework and the implementation of a legal safeguard system. This will enable competition policy to protect existing reform achievements within a framework of rule of law and to continue advancing new reforms.[11]

30. Second, China's current economy is facing downward pressure, making it even more crucial to emphasize the role of competition policy and related institutions.

31. Experience has shown that during times of economic uncertainty, governments tend to intervene more extensively. Therefore, it is essential to highlight the role of competition policy and related institutions such as anti-administrative monopoly measures and fair competition reviews. This helps prevent undue interference by public authorities that can harm market competition. In particular, while ensuring a foundational legal framework, it is necessary to promote the top-level design in competition policy, allowing it to influence public policy decisions in China from the outset. Specifically, this involves clarifying the coordination of relationships and mechanisms between competition policy and other policies such as industry, finance, currency, finance, investment, trade, employment, consumption, environment, and regional policies.[12]

32. Third, from the perspective of industrial development stages, China is actively transitioning from a manufacturing powerhouse to an innovation-driven economy. This transition will drive the evolution and advancement of China's anti-monopoly enforcement and judicial processes, particularly in terms of legal technology and due process.

33. The platform economy that leads China's digital economic development is posing challenges to anti-monopoly enforcement agencies, and China is responding with a long-term view and international perspective. China's platform companies have a significant presence domestically and have their unique

---

11 Huang Yong & Tang Jinglun. *Implementing Competition Policy and Ensuring the Rule of Law, Consolidating and Promoting Deepening Reform and Opening Up*, 12 China Dev. Observation 68–73 (2023), https://cdo.develpress.com/?p=15176.

12 Huang Yong. *On the System and Implementation Mechanism of Legal Protection for Competition Policy in China*, 16 Tsinghua U. L.J. 28–42 (2022).

characteristics, though they may lack a comprehensive global reach like some of their American counterparts. However, these platforms often attract global investments. Therefore, China's regulatory approach towards platform companies should be designed to attract foreign investment, indirectly introducing international competition mechanisms into China's platform economy and making Chinese regulatory rules more internationally oriented and predictable. For instance, alongside the amendment of China's Anti-Monopoly Law, revisions to related supporting rules have also been initiated. One of the most important rules is the provision of notification thresholds by the State Council. From the previous draft of the consultation document, one controversial proposal was added to address the so-called "killer acquisitions," which required companies with revenues exceeding CNY 100 billion to make voluntary notifications when acquiring companies with market values or valuations exceeding CNY 800 million. This proposal sparked debates due to the uncertainty surrounding valuations, as these can vary depending on the evaluator and methodology used. Finally, in the adopted version of the "State Council Provisions on Notification Thresholds," this provision was discarded by China's legislative authorities.[13]

34. There are new considerations in the application of anti-monopoly laws in the field of intellectual property rights (IPR). In the past, China's industrial landscape was primarily focused on manufacturing, and reducing the cost of IPR licensing that would promote competition in China. After years of business practice and development, the number of standard essential patents (SEPs) owned by Chinese entities has significantly increased in the 5G era. Lowering the cost of IPR can have a dual effect – promoting both competition and innovation while potentially hindering it. As long as China continues to adhere to its strategy of becoming a technology powerhouse and places importance on protecting intellectual property rights, this factor will have an increasingly significant role to play in relevant anti-monopoly cases.

35. Last but not the least, antitrust litigation may drive advancements in the legal technicalities and due process implementation of China's antitrust laws. In the new Anti-Monopoly Law of China, the legal responsibilities for monopolistic behaviors have been significantly strengthened, greatly enhancing the deterrent power of this law. Simultaneously, China's Administrative Procedure Law stipulates that individuals or entities subject to administrative penalties have the right to file administrative lawsuits in accordance with the law if they are dissatisfied with the penalty decision made by administrative authorities.[14] With the strengthened legal responsibilities, parties involved in cases may have a greater incentive to engage in the administrative litigation system and

13 China State Council, *The State Council's Provisions on the Reporting Standards for Concentration of Operators*, State Council Gazette (Jan. 26, 2024), https://www.gov.cn/zhengce/zhengceku/202401/content_6928388.htm.

14 National People's Congress, Administrative Litigation Law of the People's Republic of China (June 27, 2017), https://flk.npc.gov.cn/detail2.html?MmM5MDlmZGQ2NzhiZjE3OTAxNjc4YmY4NTg1NTBhMGY%3D.

challenge administrative penalty decisions. The emergence of such scenarios will also compel antitrust enforcement agencies to continuously enhance their legal expertise and due process standards.

V. The Outlook for China's Competition Policy

36. China is both a nascent jurisdiction in the field of anti-monopoly laws and a young market economy. Therefore, it is essential to observe the development of China's competition policy from a more rational and comprehensive perspective, considering the historical perspective of "institutional change."

37. In the first 15 years of implementing the Anti-Monopoly Law, China underwent two significant reforms in its enforcement agencies. The first occurred in 2018 when the State Administration for Market Regulation (SAMR) was established, taking over and consolidated the enforcement power from the National Development and Reform Commission (NDRC), the Ministry of Commerce (MOFCOM), and the State Administration for Industry and Commerce (SAIC), respectively. SAMR was tasked with unified enforcement of anti-monopoly laws. The second reform happened at the end of 2021 when SAMR expanded its single enforcement bureau into three bureaus, strengthening its anti-monopoly regulatory capacity. These reforms illustrate that China's competition policy has frequently achieved new accomplishments and developments in the context of gradual, rather than revolutionary, economic transformation. This dynamic nature of competition policy in China adds complexity to observing and participating in the practice of China's anti-monopoly law.

38. Nevertheless, the authors believe that the fundamental principles of competition policy remain unchanged. While the emergence of a unified international competition law may be unlikely and challenging, competition law continues to exhibit convergent tendencies on a global scale. The values of free competition in the market and shared institutional frameworks increasingly underpin competition law, despite occasional conflicts arising from different countries and regions due to factors such as industrial development stages, economic maturity, and judicial systems, which lead to diverse interests.

39. Although further deepening economic system reforms presents challenges to China's governance techniques and artistry, China's unwavering commitment to gradual market-oriented reforms remains constant. China's economic growth experience has unequivocally demonstrated that China's continued development is inseparable from global markets and proactive institutional openness. Today, China's competition policy is grounded in a more solid political and legal foundation than ever before. Coupled with the accumulation of enforcement and judicial experience, China's competition policy rules and implementation will continue to play an increasingly pivotal role from a new starting point.

Competition Policy Objectives and Beyond: The Case of Egypt

Mahmoud Momtaz* and Rana Aref**
Egyptian Competition Authority

I. Introduction

1. In an attempt to modernize and strengthen their economies, the majority of Arab countries have adopted competition legislation since the 1990s.[1] The objective was to encourage economic liberalization and competitiveness, embrace an open market economy, attain economic integration, draw in more foreign and domestic investments, and especially lessen the role of the State as a major market participant.[2]

2. Although most of the Arab States possess a competition law that includes key components of competition following the United States or the European Union models,[3] this remains insufficient in order to achieve the desired economic

---

* Head of the mergers and acquisitions department at the Egyptian Competition Authority

** Chairman of the Egyptian Competition Authority and Lecturer of Competition Law and Economics. The views represented in this article are those of the authors and do not reflect the opinion of the Egyptian Competition Authority or any of its officials.

1 According to the United Nations Economic and Social Commission for Western Asia (ESCWA), Algeria adopted its competition law in 1995; Bahrain in 2018; Comoros in 2023; Djibouti in 2008; Egypt in 2005; Iraq in 2010; Jordan in 2004; Kuwait in 2007; Lebanon in 2022; Libya in 2010; Mauritania in 2000; Oman in 2014; Qatar in 2006; Saudi Arabia in 2004; Sudan in 2009; the Syrian Arab Republic in 2008; Tunisia in 1991; the United Arab Emirates in 2012; and Yemen in 1999.

2 Note by the secretariat, OECD, *The Objectives of Competition Law and Policy*, (2003). Note by the secretariat, UNCTAD, *The Role of Competition Policy in Promoting Economic Development: The Appropriate Design and Effectiveness of Competition Law and Policy*, (2010).

3 ESCWA, Report on Arab Business Legislative Framework (2021).

goals. Indeed, a considerable number of Arab countries have ranked relatively low in global indicators on competition.[4]

3. This can be explained by the adopted legislation's inability to fulfil Arab countries' objectives for economic growth and development. The primary objective of most of these instruments is the protection of competition as a way to improve consumer welfare.[5] However, this has been demonstrated to be insufficient to address the needs of Arab nations.[6] Consequently, the divergence between the intended goals and those specified in the legislation, combined with the limited competition policy experience of Arab authorities, has pushed them to largely rely on the experiences of competition legislation in developed countries, and has resulted in a number of cases of ineffective enforcement of competition law and policy.

4. As a result, in Egypt, significant efforts were and will continue to be pursued through a whole government approach in the area of competition in order to lay the groundwork for policies and practices that aim to improve the business climate, entice more foreign and domestic investments, increase intra- and inter-market competition, and thus ultimately enhance consumer welfare.

5. The following sections summarize some of the major developments in competition law and policy in Egypt. Following this introduction, Section II illustrates the objective of competition policy in Egypt, which goes beyond the mere protection of competition. Section III shows the advocacy efforts that have been pursued in Egypt, specifically the Egyptian government's efforts towards enhancing competitive neutrality in order to foster a competitive climate. Section IV sheds light on how the objectives pursued under the competition law and policy have influenced the enforcement activity of the Egyptian Competition Authority (ECA) in both areas of prohibition of anticompetitive practices and merger control, and Section V offers the concluding remarks.

II. The Objective of Competition Policy in Egypt: Towards a More Holistic Approach

6. The objective of competition policy varies across different countries.[7] A significant number of developed countries have set their competition law objective to protect competition in order to improve consumer welfare. This stance

---

4 The World Economic Forum publishes the Global Competitiveness Index (GCI), defined as "the set of institutions, policies, and factors that determine a country's level of productivity," in order to quantify the competitiveness level of each country. The index relies on 12 pillars, namely, institutions, infrastructure, macroeconomic environment, health and primary education, higher education and training, goods market efficiency, labor market efficiency, financial market development, technological readiness, market size, business sophistication, and innovation. See, Klaus Schwab, World Economic Forum, Global Competitiveness Index Report (2019).

5 Thomas Cheng, Competition Law in Developing Countries (Oxford Univ. Press 2020). David J. Gerber, After Convergence: Competition Law in Emerging Markets (2019).

6 *Id.*

7 OECD, *supra* note 2.

was following primarily either the models of the EU or the US, a number of countries, especially developing ones, tend to include broad public interest objectives in their competition laws that go beyond the mere protection of competition process and consumer welfare.[8] South Africa is an example where the purpose of its Competition Act is to promote and maintain competition in order to: (1) promote the efficiency, adaptability and development of the economy, (2) provide consumers with competitive prices and product choices, (3) promote employment and advance the social and economic welfare of South Africans, (4) expand opportunities for South African participation in world markets and recognize the role of foreign competition in the Republic, (5) ensure that small- and medium-sized enterprises have an equitable opportunity to participate in the economy, and (6) promote a greater spread of ownership, in particular to increase the ownership stakes of historically disadvantaged persons.[9]

7. In Egypt, Law No. 3/2005 on the Protection of Competition and the Prohibition of Monopolistic Practices (ECL) was enacted in 2005. According to Article 1 of ECL, the objective of competition law in Egypt is to ensure the freedom of competition in the different markets.[10] Notwithstanding the apparent limited scope of the objective stated in Article 1 of ECL, recent developments show that competition policy should not be considered as a standalone policy, on the contrary it should be considered as part of the whole economic policy in Egypt, and thus is intended to have serving the economic growth and development as its ultimate goal. This has been illustrated clearly in the ECA's Strategy for the years 2021–2025 which is developed within the framework of Egypt's Strategy for Sustainable Development (Egypt's Vision 2030). In this context, the strategy delineates the mission dedicated to the ECA as the establishment of competition policy and elimination of anticompetitive practices through reducing barriers to entry and promoting competitive neutrality, hence ensuring competitive markets for the benefit of consumers, businesses, and the national economy.[11] By the same token, the strategy states that it aims to promote competition in markets and grant their openness to all market players, including domestic and foreign investors, in order to support economic growth and stability as well as increased diversity and competitiveness. It could be argued that the objective is to play an active role in enhancing Egypt's competitiveness in the international economy, to create employment opportunities for its people, improve their standard of living, and foster greater creativity and knowledge, and in turn, assisting in achieving Egypt's vision 2030.[12]

8 *Id.*

9 Competition Act No. 89 of 1998, ch 1(2), Purpose of Act.

10 According to ECL art. 1 "Economic activities shall be undertaken in a manner that does not prevent, restrict or harm the freedom of competition in accordance with the provisions of the Law."

11 ECA, Strategy 2021–2025.

12 Egypt's Vision 2030.

8. Hence, it is evident that Egypt's competition policy is an integral part of the country's broader economic policy, aiming to contribute to the achievement of sustainable development through protecting competition.

III. The Egyptian National Strategy for Competitive Neutrality

9. The ECA issued its National Competitive Neutrality Strategy in 2022. The Strategy aims at creating a competitive climate, removing barriers to entry and expansion, and ensuring that all market players compete on a level playing field under the same regulatory framework.[13]

10. In applying the Strategy, the Egyptian government has undertaken the following measures:

(1) The High Committee on Competition Policy and Competitive Neutrality, headed by the Prime Minister has been established in order to take the necessary corrective measures in case of existence of anticompetitive State measures;[14]

(2) The Competition Policy and Competitive Neutrality Department has been established at the ECA. The Department is entrusted to receive complaints from citizens and investors and initiate studies concerning anticompetitive State measures in light of Article 11(5) of ECL.[15] The findings are then submitted to the High Committee on Competition Policy and Competitive Neutrality;

(3) The ECA's Guidelines on Assessing the Impact of State Measures have been disseminated via a circular issued by the Cabinet of Ministers among all State authorities. The Circular required State agencies to consult the ECA before issuing any measures that may impact competition in the application of Article 11(5) of ECL;

(4) The ECA has hosted more than 50 workshops in different regions across the country in order to raise awareness among State agencies on the importance of competition and competitive neutrality; and

(5) The ECA is working on developing a competitive neutrality index, aiming to quantitatively measure the degree of competitive neutrality in different sectors and assesses the impact of High Committee decisions on competitive neutrality.

---

13 ECA, National Strategy on Competitive Neutrality 2022.

14 *Id.*

15 According to Law No. 3/2005 on the Protection of Competition and the Prohibition of Monopolistic Practices (ECL) art.11(5), the ECA has the power to give "its opinion, voluntarily or upon the request of the Cabinet of Ministers, Ministries or concerned entities, on legislations, policies, or decisions that would harm competition, and the concerned Authorities shall be obliged to take the opinion of the Authority with regard to draft laws, and regulations relating to the regulation of competition.

11. As a result, the ECA's advocacy activity has significantly increased since 2022. Indeed, in 2022, it has issued 15 opinions in State measures. In 2023, this number increased by 49 percent.

12. Furthermore, it is worth mentioning that, in Egypt, there are no exemptions in ECL that make state-owned enterprises (SOEs) immune from the enforcement of the Law. Indeed, the ECA has recently issued decisions in cases where SOEs were among the infringers, along with some private firms.

13. For instance, in 2021, the ECA initiated an investigation concerning the tenders issued by the electricity distribution companies (9 companies) in Egypt in order to purchase galvanized steel lamp posts. The initiation resulted in detecting anticompetitive practices by several market players including SOEs. Specifically, the ECA discovered that 10 of the companies operating in the lamp posts market were colluding by offering identical price offers, besides dividing the quantities among them in some of the tenders, in violation of Article 6(c) of ECL.[16]

14. More recently, in 2023, the ECA initiated an investigation into two SOEs, which operate in the petroleum sector. The ECA's investigation revealed that two public petroleum distribution companies violated Article 8(d) of ECL, through tying the sale of bitumen 70/60 (market where the companies are dominant), which is the basic material in the composition of the asphalt mixture, to emulsions and highly volatile bituminous solutions, which are the materials used for adhesive and wetting of the asphalt mixture.[17]

15. Thus, the Egyptian government has adopted a "Whole Government Approach" in order to ensure that State measures are in conformity with the competition policy and competitive neutrality.

IV. Competition Enforcement

16. This section illustrates how the objectives of competition policy in Egypt, have influenced the ECA's enforcement activity in both merger control and prohibition of anticompetitive practices, through adopting legislative reforms and refining the ECA's enforcement capacity.

1. Legislative Reforms

17. In Egypt, on December 29, 2022, Law No. 175/2022, which introduced amendments to ECL, was published in the *Official Gazette*. The provisions of Law No. 175/2022, provide the ECA with the power to conduct ex-ante review of economic concentrations.[18]

---

16 ECA, Press Release, (Jan. 30, 2023).

17 ECA, Press Release, (Jan. 20, 2024.

18 Law No. 175/2022 amending the provisions of Law No. 3/2005 (ECL), published in the *Official Gazette* (Dec. 29, 2022).

18. Three special elements of the new merger control regime may illustrate that the objective of competition policy goes beyond the protection of consumer welfare: (a) the introduction of material influence in the definition of economic concentration, (b) the introduction of ex-post assessment of economic concentrations that do not meet the notification thresholds set forth in the Law, and (c) the exemptions that could be granted by the ECA in case of anticompetitive economic concentrations.

A. *The Introduction of Material Influence in the Definition of Economic Concentration*

19. Pursuant to Article 2(g) of ECL, an economic concentration is any change of control or material influence over one or more persons. According to Article 2(i) of ECL the material influence is defined as the ability to influence, directly or indirectly, the policy of another person, including its strategic decisions or commercial objectives.[19] "Material influence" as a lower level than "control" has been included in the definition of economic concentration to prevent the adverse effect on competition in particular and the economy in general that may result from the acquisition of minority shareholdings.

20. Indeed, the ECA has practical experience when it comes to the effect that acquisition of non-controlling minority shareholdings may have on the market. In 2019, the ECA found that Glovo and Delivery Hero SE – two companies that operate in the online food delivery market – had agreed on Glovo's exit from the Egyptian market in breach of Articles 6(b) and (d) of ECL. The ECA established that Delivery Hero entered into a Shareholders' Agreement with Glovo by acquiring 16 percent of Glovo's shares. The Shareholders' Agreement between the parties conferred on Delivery Hero certain corporate rights that allowed the company to access commercially sensitive information of its competitor operations in the Egyptian market and to influence Glovo's strategic business decisions, particularly, through conferring on Delivery Hero a veto right concerning the approval of new financing rounds and thus Delivery Hero had the ability to block any investment round, preventing Glovo from expanding its business. Therefore, the acquisition of non-controlling minority shareholding may have led to a significant loss in jobs (3000 employees) and investment, as well as the exit of an efficient and innovative market player that was rapidly growing in the Egyptian market and offering innovative solutions to Egyptian consumers.[20]

---

19 ECL art. 2(i).

20 ECA, Press Release, (May 28, 2019).

B. *The Introduction of Ex-post Assessment of Certain Non-notifiable Economic Concentrations*

21. The second paragraph of Article 19 bis of ECL provides the ECA with the power to review transactions that do not meet the prescribed thresholds, on the ECA's Board of Directors' approval, if there was circumstantial evidence that the economic concentration might lessen, restrict or harm the freedom of competition, within one year of its implementation. Additionally, Article 19 bis of ECL specifies the circumstantial evidence that can be considered as follows: (1) restriction of technological development and innovation, (2) controlling the market by any act that may lead to an increase or decrease in prices, (3) reducing the quality of products, and (4) creation of entry or expansion barriers in the market.

22. Enabling the ECA to conduct an ex-post review of non-notifiable economic concentrations would enable the authority to step in when small- and medium-sized businesses are acquired by larger firms with the intention of stifling their innovative products or putting them under the exclusive control of the larger firm. This could potentially jeopardize market competition, and innovation.[21]

C. *Possible Exemptions*

23. According to Article 19 bis (b) of ECL, an economic concentration shall be prohibited if it is likely to lessen, restrict, or harm the freedom of competition in the market. The Executive Regulations of ECL shall indicate the elements to be taken into consideration when assessing the effects of the economic concentration on the freedom of competition in the market. During its appraisal, the ECA shall take into account defenses submitted by the concerned persons, notably claims related to economic efficiencies, failing firms, and public security.[22] Exemptions shall be granted after approval of the Cabinet of Ministers.

2. Enforcement Capacity

24. The ECA has focused its enforcement capacity on the high-priority sectors for the Egyptian government, which are healthcare, education, and food. In 2023, the number of issued decisions in both areas of merger control and prohibition of anticompetitive practices has increased. The ECA has issued 351 decisions in various sectors: 280 decisions in the healthcare sector, 19 decisions in

---

21 Note by Egypt, OECD, *Start-Ups, Killer Acquisitions and Merger Control,* (2020).

22 According to ECL art. 19 bis (b), the economic concentration shall be prohibited if it lessens, restricts or harms the freedom of competition. ECA may authorize the implementation of an economic concentration after the approval of the Cabinet of Ministers in any of the following cases: (1) if the non-implementation of the economic concentration may cause the exit of a person from the market, in other terms failing firm, (2) if the implementation of the economic concentration will generate efficiencies that outweigh the anticompetitive effects, (3) if the economic concentration is subject to national security considerations.

the education sector, and 5 decisions in the food sector. Concerning merger control, the ECA has issued 278 clearance decisions on submitted notifications. As for the prohibition of anticompetitive practices, the ECA has issued 35 infringement decisions, representing an increase of 32 percent over the previous year.[23]

25. Particularly, the education sector has been given special attention by the ECA. Indeed, in February 2023, the ECA found that representative offices of two publishing houses, in cooperation with their authorized distributors, had engaged in anticompetitive agreements that aimed to increase the prices of educational books that are exported from abroad by agreeing upon an exchange rate that exceeded the official exchange rate of the Egyptian Central Bank by 80 percent, in violation of Article 6(a) of ECL. Additionally, they engaged in market allocation agreements by dividing schools among authorized distributors in violation of Article 6(b) of ECL. The anticompetitive agreements have resulted in increasing financial burdens on Egyptian families and limiting school choices, in addition to creating barriers to entry for distributors aiming to enter the market.[24]

26. Furthermore, in December 2023, the ECA found that 33 printing companies had agreed to set the minimum bid prices for the various items of the tender issued by the Central Administration for Book Affairs at the Ministry of Education to print and supply schoolbooks for the academic year 2022–2023. The ECA found that the companies had violated Article 6(c) of ECL. It is worth noting that such practices negatively affect the effectiveness of government spending and could result in a waste of public money.[25]

27. Moreover, the ECA found that 8 schools had breached the provisions of ECL in the market for school uniforms. On the one hand, a number of schools had infringed Articles 8(a) and (d) of ECL by abusing their dominant position in the market by restricting the sale of their school uniforms through exclusive outlets and preventing competing companies from entering or expanding in the market, while suspending the sale of school uniforms by purchasing them from the school's own outlets and not other stores. On the other hand, certain schools had breached Article 7 of the ECL by engaging in exclusive dealings with certain school uniform stores. In response to the recurrent infringements in the market for school uniforms, the ECA has issued guidelines for the school uniform sector in order to raise awareness on competition rules among the different stakeholders in this sector.[26]

28. The enforcement activity of the ECA reflects that the objective of competition policy in Egypt is wider than the mere protection of competition. Through its

---

23 ECA, Press Release, (Dec. 26, 2023).

24 ECA, Press Release, (Feb. 25, 2023

25 ECA, Press Release, (Jan. 3, 2024).

26 ECA, Press Release, (Sept. 5, 2023

enforcement activity, the ECA intends to ensure competitive markets for the benefit of consumers, businesses, and the national economy.

V. Conclusion

29. No one size fits all; and the objectives of competition policy differ from one country to another. In Egypt, the objective of competition law and policy goes beyond the mere protection of competition. Competition policy should be considered as an integral part of the wider economic policy and contribute to achieving economic growth and development through protecting competition in markets. This approach has been reflected in both the enforcement and advocacy of competition law and policy in Egypt.

Competition in Small Island Economies in Oceania: What Regulatory Tools?*

STÉPHANE RETTERER
New Caledonia Competition Authority

1. The South Pacific small island economies, with their marvelous lagoons such as the ones in New Caledonia, are not a paradise for competition law. Indeed, New Caledonia's Island economy, with only 270,000 inhabitants and the third-highest GDP per capita in the region after Australia and New Zealand, faces the challenges of anti-competitive practices (high degree of concentration of companies' market power, "collusive practices," etc.) and regulatory measures (legal monopolies, protectionist measures, price regulation, etc.) that undermine the principles of free competition and free pricing.
2. Within their own unique context, the young competition authorities in Micronesia, Melanesia and Polynesia are considering which types of tools and regulations are best suited for their economies. Local competition law practitioners are seeking to develop a tailored competition framework for their territory, inspired by foreign laws yet adapted to the specific characteristics of local insular economies.
3. They seek to improve existing competition tools, while developing market structure regulation.

---

* This article has been previously published in Concurrences, and it might have been edited for clarity and cohesion. Stephane Retterer, Competition in small island economies in Oceania: What regulatory tools?, September 2024, Concurrences N° 3-2024, Art. N° 119106.

I. Improving existing tools

4. In New Caledonia, the New Caledonia Competition Authority (NCCA) is constantly searching for ways to improve its competition tools and adapt them to the local context, and render market regulations more effective. Similarly to Malta's legislative framework, for example, the NCCA wishes to introduce in its legislation a specific provision regarding the enforcement against abuse of dominance for excessive prices and margins. This addition to the classic European definition of abuse of dominance in New Caledonian law would provide a clear framework in order to define abuse via excessive prices and margins and provide more legal certainty for undertakings, thereby promoting compliance.

5. Also, French and New Caledonian competition law guarantees fair and balanced commercial relations between enterprises by prohibiting certain practices per se. The NCCA is the only independent administrative authority in France with the power to condemn these practices. This allows it, while considering local specificities, to determine which practices restrictive of competition are the most relevant for the territory and to improve their legal framework. Hence, the NCCA, by setting up proper conditions for free commercial negotiation, will be able to bring an end to certain prohibitions per se (prohibition of deferred and year-end discounts and resale at a loss) and fight the high cost of living.

II. Regulating market structure

6. Small island economies are characterized by narrow, naturally concentrated markets. Therefore, the implementation of economies of scale meant to improve efficiency (e.g., through vertical integration) may, in fact, create problematic structural competitive situations instead.

7. The merger control regime mechanism, which in New Caledonia and French Polynesia also includes the review of retail business creations or expansions, allows these authorities to review *ex ante* the potential anticompetitive effects of transactions, evaluate whether efficiency gains can be derived from them, and obtain behavioral and/or structural remedies if applicable.

8. This type of regulation involves anticipating companies' anti-competitive behavior regarding the examined market structure. The efficiency of *ex ante* regulation highlights the shortcomings of antitrust law.

9. In a small island economy and its eventual protective barriers, the ultra-concentration of markets and their transparency can encourage "tacit collusion" between companies that are motivated by their search for commodities. In such cases, the law on anti-competitive agreements cannot be used to establish an infringement.

10. In French overseas departments and territories (except for French Polynesia), the so-called structural injunction tool theoretically allows intervention in market structures by the French Competition Authority (Autorité de la concurrence or ADLC) for the overseas departments and regions, and by the NCCA for its own territory.

11. This intervention, justified on competition concern grounds, is carried out by means of injunctions (behavioral in principle and structural in exception) rather than penalties, when a company in a dominant position or companies in a collectively dominant position charge high prices or markups. To use this tool more effectively, the NCCA wishes to remove the condition requiring that high prices and margins be identified "*by comparison with the averages usually observed in the economic sector concerned*." This would allow the Authority to assess the structure of prices and margins based on the concerned company's data without necessarily having to apply the comparison method.

12. A stronger paradigm shift would be to implement the UK "market investigation" tool, which is being extended to other countries.

13. This notion goes beyond "structural injunction" by allowing the Authority's intervention solely based on proof of market structure dysfunctions, markets which are often oligopolistic in small island economies. Its application does not require that a company hold a dominant position along with the existence of high prices or margins. While it is aware that the procedure can be cumbersome and requires a high degree of expertise for its implementation, the NCCA wishes nevertheless to examine integrating such a tool into its legal framework.

III. Regulations, legal monopoly and regulation

14. Advocacy, backed by advisory opinions, may convince public authorities to deregulate in favor of free competition, but efficacy may remain limited. Therefore, the question of setting up independent sectoral regulation (of energy, telecommunications or other sectors) arises acutely in small island economies. Indeed, regulatory law allows for the control of the market structure (market entrants, resource allocation, price regulation, etc.), defines what activity belongs to the public service and what belongs to competitive markets, organizes access to essential infrastructure, and prevents the risks of cross-subsidies, for example.

15. Most Pacific authorities, such as Australia, New Zealand, Fiji and Papua New Guinea, have chosen to combine competition and sectoral regulation in one sole authority. This choice promotes cost-sharing benefits and multi-functionality. Therefore, the possible and future opening of the legal mobile telephony monopoly to competition in New Caledonia should, according to the advisory opinion of the NCCA issued on 11 March 2024, involve the creation of an independent sector regulator that may be attached to the NCCA.

Similarly, the Polynesian Competition Authority (Autorité polynésienne de la concurrence or APC) also considers it necessary to have an independent telecommunications regulator for Tahiti and its islands, as stated in its advisory opinion of 29 April 2024.

16. Bearing this in mind, the Pacific Island Network of Competition, Consumer and Economic Regulation (PINCCER), launched in 2023, brings together all the Pacific authorities and is strongly supported by the Australian Competition and Consumer Commission (ACCC), the New Zealand Commerce Commission and the APC. One of the aims of the network is to help develop the younger authorities' "laboratories," some of which are still under construction, and to exchange ideas on appropriate competition tools and regulatory models.

17. Finally, as a final thought, a simple and appropriate law on State aid to businesses must be seriously considered in highly administered economies such as New Caledonia, to preserve the competitive model.

18. In conclusion, 20 years ago, Michal S. Gal, in her book *Competition Policy for Small Market Economies*, already explained "*the need to tailor competition law to economic size*"; "[t]*his* [would] *require*[s] *small economies to change the focus of their competition laws to regulate such markets efficiently*," where "*a total welfare over a consumer welfare approach*" should be privileged. These are the issues that still prevail today in small island economies.

Creating and Promoting Competitive Markets in Singapore – Perspectives from a Small and Open Economy

SIA AIK KOR*
Competition and Consumer Commission of Singapore

I. Overview

1. A country's economic landscape plays a pivotal role in shaping its policies, strategies and overall trajectory. As a small and open economy without natural resources, Singapore's approach in implementing and enforcing competition law provides a unique perspective on how it works to create and promote competitive markets.

II. Singapore's Economic Landscape

2. Singapore's journey towards a robust competition policy began in the early 2000s as an increasingly globalised world underscored the importance of safeguarding market competition and creating a level playing field for existing market players and new entrants. To ensure that markets in Singapore functioned efficiently and that businesses and consumers were protected from anticompetitive practices, national competition policy was introduced in 2004 as a fundamental component of Singapore's economic strategy. The introduction of the Competition Act 2004 was a landmark moment and signalled Singapore's commitment to a competitive market landscape. Prior to the

---

* Former Chief Executive, Competition and Consumer Commission of Singapore.

enactment of the Act, there were only rules against anticompetitive conduct in specific sectors such as energy and telecommunications.

3. To establish an effective competition regime, it is necessary to implement and enforce competition laws in a manner that reflects and aligns with the unique context of the country. Being a small and open economy without a natural hinterland, Singapore's economic strategy over the years has been founded on a strong adherence to free market principles and international best practices adapted to local conditions. Singapore's policymakers recognised that liberal trade policies and low regulatory barriers allow non-domestic firms to impose competitive discipline on domestic firms while also allowing domestic firms to access global markets to compete with their non-domestic counterparts on an equal footing.

III. Competition Framework in Singapore

4. At the core of Singapore's competition framework is the Competition Act 2004, which was enacted in 2004. The Act aims to maintain and enhance efficient market conduct and promote the overall productivity, innovation and competitiveness of markets in Singapore. As highlighted in the second reading of the Competition Bill:

> "Instead of attempting to catch all forms of anti-competitive activities, our principal focus will be on those that have an appreciable adverse effect on competition in Singapore or that do not have any net economic benefit. In assessing whether an action is anti-competitive, we will also give due consideration to whether it promotes innovation, productivity or longer-term economic efficiency. This approach will ensure that we do not inadvertently constrain innovative and enterprising endeavours".

5. The Competition Act 2004 provides a comprehensive legal framework to address anticompetitive conduct, mergers and acquisitions, and other practices that could harm competition in Singapore. The Act provides for the establishment of a body, the Competition and Consumer Commission of Singapore (CCCS) to administer and enforce the Competition Act 2004. Among others, CCCS is empowered to investigate and adjudicate anticompetitive activities, issue directions to stop or prevent anticompetitive activities and to impose financial penalties.

6. While the Act covers Singapore's entire economy, there are several sectors that are excluded from the law, particularly those that are regulated by other existing competition laws. These sectors include telecommunications, electricity, gas and media.

7. Three key prohibitions are covered under the Competition Act 2004:

   – Anticompetitive Agreements

   Agreements or practices that prevent, restrict, or distort competition in Singapore are prohibited. This includes price-fixing, market-sharing, bid-rigging, and other collusive behaviour among competitors. However, vertical agreements, which are agreements between undertakings operating at different levels of the production or distribution chain, are excluded.

– Abuse of Dominance

Firms are not prohibited from being dominant or striving to achieve dominance, but dominant firms are restricted from engaging in practices that protect, enhance or perpetuate their dominance in ways that are unrelated to competitive merit, thereby harming competition.

– Merger Control

Mergers or acquisitions that substantially lessen competition in Singapore are prohibited. However, it is not mandatory to seek CCCS' clearance for a merger or acquisition in Singapore. Rather, businesses are required to carry out self-assessments of their transactions and seek approval from CCCS should there be competition concerns.

IV. Some Features of Singapore's Competition Regime

8. While Singapore's competition regime shares many similarities with those of the European Union and United Kingdom upon which it is based on, there are certain distinctions which arise due to Singapore's unique characteristics as a small and open economy. For example, Singapore adopts a total welfare standard instead of focusing only on consumer welfare. In Europe and the United Kingdom, the economic benefits exemption only applies to agreements that, among other factors, allow consumers a fair share of the resulting benefit. This requirement was not adopted in the agreements with net economic benefit exclusion in paragraph 9 of the Third Schedule of the Singapore Competition Act 2004. This approach which focuses on the total welfare of both producers and consumers, rather than on the distribution of welfare between them, has been applied in the context of airline alliance agreements that involved the coordination of capacity, scheduling and pricing. Benefits from such agreements such as an increase in capacity, frequencies, destinations or higher passenger traffic which may strengthen Singapore's position as an air hub can be found to outweigh the harm to competition in the relevant markets.

9. Another example is how vertical agreements are treated in Singapore. Vertical agreements cover a range of arrangements between businesses at different levels of the supply chain. In certain jurisdictions, some vertical agreements have been made per se illegal, such that these agreements are considered inherently anticompetitive without the need for in-depth analysis of their impact. Rather than subjecting vertical agreements to competition law, Singapore has excluded vertical agreements from the scope of competition law in the first instance. This approach reflects Singapore's stance that many vertical agreements have procompetitive effects that outweigh their potential anticompetitive effects.

Intra-brand restraints have little anticompetitive impact if there is sufficient inter-brand competition. In cases of vertical agreements where the potential anticompetitive effects outweigh the procompetitive effects, the Minister may issue an order to declare that the competition law will apply to a certain type of vertical agreement. Vertical agreements involving a dominant undertaking will be covered by the prohibition against abuse of dominance. Such an approach ie exclusion subject to the safeguard clawback provision, will reduce regulatory costs.

10. Another difference between Singapore's competition legislation and that of the UK Competition Act relates to the examples of an abuse of dominance listed in the statute. Out of four examples stated, three are identical but the first differs. Section 47(2)(a) of the Competition Act 2004 lists predatory behaviour towards competitors as an example of an abuse. Section 18(2)(a) of the UK Competition Act, on the other hand, lists as an abuse, directly or indirectly imposing unfair purchase or selling prices or other unfair trading conditions.

11. Another feature of Singapore's competition regime is a voluntary merger notification regime to reduce the regulatory and administrative burden on businesses. Under this system, merging entities may conduct their own self-assessment and may proceed with the transaction if there are no competition concerns. Should entities have concerns or are unsure about whether the transaction would infringe the law, they should then notify CCCS which will assess the transaction. CCCS also retains the right to review and unscramble the transaction if it finds that competition concerns would result. While Singapore has a voluntary merger notification regime, this does not mean that there are no risks to parties proceeding with a merger without first notifying CCCS. Parties run not just the risk of infringing the law but also the further risk that any commitments they may subsequently offer may be rejected. In 2020, the Competition Appeal Board (CAB) dismissed an appeal by Uber, upholding CCCS' decision that Uber's sale of its Southeast Asian business to Grab had resulted in a substantial lessening of competition (SLC) in the ride-hailing platform market in Singapore which infringed the Competition Act 2004. Significantly, the CAB held that CCCS could, when exercising its discretion whether to accept commitments, consider the need to deter businesses from engaging in anticompetitive practices and decide, instead, to issue directions to the merger parties, including imposing financial penalties. The CAB made clear that this option was open to CCCS even if the commitments offered by the merger parties are in fact sufficient to remedy or prevent any SLC arising from the merger. In this regard, Singapore's voluntary merger notification regime strikes a balance between being pro-business and ensuring that competition is not harmed, which is in line with Singapore's core economic objectives of creating a business-friendly environment anchored in free market principles.

12. Singapore's open economy creates opportunities for cartels to infiltrate its borders and impact the local market. Indeed, CCCS has uncovered several

international cartels that had operations in Singapore. However, cartels are secretive by nature and therefore, difficult to detect. International experience has shown that leniency programmes are effective in incentivising businesses that have participated in cartel activities. As such, CCCS has put in place a leniency programme so that cartel members are incentivised to proactively come forward with information and evidence on the cartel. Companies that come forward and cooperate with CCCS before or during investigations may receive immunity from or reduced financial penalties. Since its establishment to FY2022, CCCS has undertaken 36 leniency cases.

V. Challenges in Promoting Competition in Singapore

13. As a small country, Singapore's limited domestic market may limit the number of market players in a specific industry, with market players also facing greater difficulties to achieve economies of scale. This can be detrimental to businesses and consumers alike. A certain degree of collaboration among competitors may therefore be necessary or even beneficial to the economy. CCCS is keenly aware of these domestic constraints and takes the necessary measures to account for these considerations in its enforcement work. For example, when CCCS assesses airline alliances, it considers whether there are net economic benefits rather than focusing on whether the conduct is per se anticompetitive in nature. Where behavioural commitments address the competition concerns which have been identified, CCCS is open to accepting such commitments. CCCS has also issued a guidance note to clarify its position on seven common types of business collaborations so that businesses can collaborate more confidently for better and more efficient outcomes without harming competition.

14. In the face of technological innovation, cases have become increasingly complex. Rapid advances in technology, particularly in the digital economy, have introduced complexities that many competition authorities, including CCCS, must address. The digital economy has transformed the way businesses operate, and the way that consumers engage with products and services. E-commerce, digital platforms and data-driven business models have disrupted traditional industries, creating new opportunities for businesses. However, the digital economy has also brought to the forefront implications from network effects and data dominance. Firms with extensive user data and powerful digital ecosystems can leverage their position to maintain and expand their dominance. For competition authorities, evaluating the impact of these network effects and data-driven advantages on market competition becomes a complex task. Assessing the competitive effects of mergers involving digital firms is also a multi-faceted challenge that requires a deep understanding of the industry's dynamics.

VI. CCCS' Approach to Enhance and Promote Competition

15. CCCS' mission is to make markets work well to create opportunities and choices for business and consumers in Singapore. To this end, it has employed various strategies to achieve its mission.

1. Advocacy and Stakeholder Engagement

16. In administering and enforcing the Competition Act 2004, CCCS adopts a two-pronged approach of enforcement and advocacy. CCCS enforces the Act by taking action against anticompetitive activities, particularly those that have a significant adverse impact on the economy. At the same time, CCCS also works with government agencies, businesses, and the public to advocate pro-competition practices. Through regular public engagement, seminars to university students, targeted workshops and collaboration with industry associations, CCCS reaches out to educate businesses, consumers and stakeholders about the benefits of competition and the importance of competition compliance. In the long term, CCCS believes that increasing awareness of competition policy would foster a culture of competition as the public becomes more informed and the business community enlightened. As competition becomes "part of life", businesses would strive to deliver products and services with better value and through innovative ways. Consumers would also recognise anticompetitive practices and be inclined to report such practices to CCCS, which could deter businesses from engaging in such conduct in the first place. CCCS has also adopted a proactive approach in identifying issues and clarifying its position to encourage compliance and promote a strong competitive culture and environment. One example in which CCCS has done so is in respect of environmental sustainability collaboration. CCCS recognises that efforts to realise Singapore's climate change goals may involve businesses, including competitors, engaging in collaboration in existing, emerging or even new markets. As such, CCCS published for consultation the Environmental Sustainability Guidance Note to clarify how it will assess such business collaboration in addressing any concerns of compliance with competition law. Another example in which the CCCS has leaned forward is in revising its Competition Guidelines after its e-commerce platforms market study. With the rise of the digital economy, the revisions aim to provide greater clarity on issues related to market definition, assessment of market power, types of potentially abusive conduct and the relevance of proprietary rights and data in the digital era.

17. On a biannual basis, CCCS also conducts a Stakeholder Perception Survey which is an initiative designed to gather valuable insights from various stakeholders, ranging from businesses and competition law practitioners to consumers. Each stakeholder brings with it a different perspective that sheds light

on how CCCS can move towards a more competitive market in Singapore. Businesses, for instance, are able to express their views on how their operations are impacted by competition law and the challenges associated with competition compliance, while competition law practitioners are able to share their perspectives on the legal framework and enforcement practices, and how these may be improved. Surveying consumers also provides a measure of how informed they are with regard to competition issues and the areas that CCCS can work on to improve their understanding of competition law. Taken as a whole, the results from the survey shape CCCS' decision-making and allow it to make informed, evidence-based policy choices. In addition, the survey highlights areas where stakeholders may need additional education and outreach. CCCS can then focus its efforts on addressing these gaps to promote a culture of competition in Singapore.

2. Whole-of-Government Approach

18. A key stakeholder in CCCS' advocacy efforts is the government and other public authorities. One of CCCS' statutory roles is to advise the government or any public authority on national needs and policies in respect of competition matters generally. CCCS therefore takes proactive steps to advise other government agencies on how policy and regulatory decisions can affect competition in markets. This helps to ensure that government actions do not inadvertently hinder competition, and that competition policy considerations are integrated into broader economic and regulatory policies. In FY2022, CCCS completed a total of 35 advisories to 19 government agencies on their initiatives which may involve industry collaboration or consolidation. In each case, CCCS advised the government agency on the competition impact of their initiatives and suggested practical ways in which competition concerns can be mitigated while still achieving the policy intent.

19. CCCS regularly engages government agencies through the Community of Practice for Competition and Economic Regulations (COPCOMER) which is an inter-agency platform for government agencies to learn about the latest local and overseas market developments and share best practices and experiences on competition, consumer protection and regulatory issues. By providing an opportunity for CCCS to engage other government agencies, COPCOMER also allows CCCS to advocate for government policies that promote competition across various markets at an early stage of the policy-making process. This allows CCCS to address potential upstream competition issues before any serious harm to competition occurs.

20. To better address complex challenges, CCCS participates in cross-agency workgroups to harness the collective expertise and resources of different government agencies. This enables CCCS to address "wicked problems" that may extend beyond the scope of competition law. For example, to tackle increasingly complex cases involving data and privacy issues, CCCS collaborates closely with the Personal Data Protection Commission, Singapore, to resolve

tensions and reap synergies between these two policy areas. Collaboration includes a joint published paper on data portability which has since been legislated, joint market studies, cross-participation in each other's international fora and joint protocols for determining the lead agency in respect of intersecting cases or matters. These steps enable both agencies to jointly advocate and adopt a considered policy that promotes secure data sharing practices, allowing companies to harness big data while also facilitating competition and preventing data misuse.

3. International Collaboration

21. In today's global economy, competition cases have increasingly transcended national boundaries. With businesses expanding internationally and markets becoming more intertwined, the need for international collaboration in the area of competition law has become critical, especially for a small and open economy. Recognising the significance of global and regional partnerships, CCCS regularly engages its overseas counterparts through various platforms.

22. CCCS actively participates in the International Competition Network (ICN), the dedicated international body for competition law enforcement. Among others, the ICN develops recommended best practices, manuals and frameworks to guide competition authorities on various issues such as competition enforcement, advocacy and agency effectiveness. The ICN also holds an annual conference and regular workshops which provide opportunities for discussions on various working group projects and their impact on competition enforcement. These initiatives allow the formation of a dynamic dialogue that is consensus driven to facilitate convergence towards the adoption of best practices. The ICN's work is guided by a Steering Group which is elected by its members every two years, and CCCS is a member of the Steering Group.

23. As part of the Association of Southeast Asian Nations (ASEAN) community, Singapore works regularly with other ASEAN members to develop sound competition policies and best practices for the region. Under the ASEAN Economic Community (AEC) Blueprint 2025, ASEAN Member States, including Singapore, aim to provide a level playing field for all firms through effective implementation and enforcement of competition policy and law in the region. The ASEAN Experts Group on Competition (AEGC) is the official platform looking into competition policy and law issues in ASEAN and comprises representatives from the competition authorities and agencies responsible for competition policy and law in ASEAN Member States. It oversees cooperation activities relating to competition policy and law in ASEAN as well as the implementation of measures under the AEC Blueprint. CCCS represents Singapore and has been an active contributor to the various initiatives and activities at the AEGC. For example, in 2022, Singapore led the development of an ASEAN Investigation Manual on Competition Policy and Law for the Digital Economy. The manual provided guidance for ASEAN competition authorities on how to investigate anticompetitive activity in the context of the digital economy.

24. CCCS also actively participates in other platforms that discuss competition policy and law issues, such as the Organisation of Economic Cooperation and Development (OECD), and the Asia Pacific Economic Cooperation (APEC) Competition Policy and Law Group, among others. In addition, CCCS has signed cooperation agreements with the Japan Fair Trade Commission (JFTC), the Indonesia Competition Commission (ICC), the Competition Bureau Canada (CBC), the Philippine Competition Commission (PCC), and the State Administration for Market Regulation (SAMR) of the People's Republic of China.

25. CCCS' active participation in various international and regional collaborations underscores its commitment to promoting competition policy and law not only within its borders but also in the global arena. This contributes to the development of a more integrated and competitive global economy, benefiting both businesses and consumers.

VII. Conclusion

26. Singapore's approach of implementing and enforcing competition law reflects its unique situation as a small and open economy. Singapore has a conducive regulatory ecosystem that stems from government agencies' capabilities in identifying and understanding the impact of their policies and regulations on competition and taking such impact into due consideration in their policy formulation or decision ensures that markets remain open and contestable. Regulatory burden for businesses is reduced while compliance with competition law is not compromised. Other features of Singapore's competition law regime which are distinctive to its context include a voluntary merger notification regime and the exclusion of vertical agreements.

27. As with any competition authority, CCCS faces its own set of challenges. Through regular stakeholder engagement, whole-of-government collaboration, international engagements, and robust staff training, CCCS has adopted a multi-faceted response to addressing these challenges and to achieving its mission of making markets work well to create opportunities and choices for business and consumers in Singapore.

Competition Law in an Era of Deglobalization*

JAN BLOCKX
University of Antwerp

1. After a long period in which economies became increasingly integrated across the globe, we are currently experiencing a period of deglobalization. A pivotal year was probably 2016, when UK voters decided to exit the European internal market and US elections resulted in a victory for isolationist candidate Donald Trump. But the slowdown of globalization was already apparent before, for example in the United States in the form of increased scepticism about China's place in the World Trade Organization (WTO) and increasingly strict foreign investment review under the CFIUS (Committee on Foreign Investment in the United States) regime. In Europe as well, Chinese investments peaked in 2017 to subsequently decline, a process that reflects stricter foreign investment regimes in EU Member States, but also Chinese restrictions on capital outflows.

2. What may have looked like a temporary slump became a full-scale crisis of internationalism when the Covid-19 pandemic all but halted intercontinental air traffic. Two years later, Russia's invasion of Ukraine and the sanctions many countries imposed in response have further severed economic ties. According to the DHL Global Connectedness Index, the world's interconnectedness never returned to its peak in 2017. And next steps to decouple some of the world's economies may be on the horizon, for example, with Chinese shareholders putting pressure on HSBC to split its Western and Asian businesses.

---

* This article has been previously published in Concurrences, and it might have been edited for clarity and cohesion. Jan Blockx, Competition law in an era of deglobalization, November 2022, Concurrences N° 4-2022, Art. N° 108953.

3. Obviously, this process of deglobalization, just like the process of globalization, is not unavoidable nor irreversible. However, as it is ongoing, the question arises as to what impact it may have on competition policy. Indeed, competition policy as we know it today has developed in parallel with the globalization of the world economy. In fact, competition policy itself became globalized: while in 1970, only a dozen jurisdictions had competition legislation, now more than 125 jurisdictions have such laws. Competition authorities from different countries regularly work together to investigate international cartel agreements and cross-border mergers and acquisitions, and they coordinate their policies in international fora such as the International Competition Network (ICN), the Organisation for Economic Co-operation and Development (OECD) and others.

4. So: what will happen to competition policy if the decade-long process of globalization is (temporarily or permanently) halted or even reversed? As the saying goes, it is difficult to make predictions, especially about the future. However, with this process already ongoing for a few years now, some developments can be spotted on the horizon.

I. Legal impediments to international trade

5. First of all, various legal measures may directly affect the competitive environment in which businesses operate and in which agencies enforce competition law. Economic sanctions against foreign businesses will naturally affect the ability of these businesses to operate in other markets and also the ability of non-sanctioned businesses to engage in transactions with the sanctioned operators. Foreign direct investment screening increases the hurdles for foreign businesses to make investments in the countries that introduce such rules. And these barriers arise before and even without any actual intervention based on these new regimes: legal and compliance costs increase, and companies may shy away from situations that expose them to sanctions or foreign investment screening.

6. In Europe, a particularly important legal instrument that is being considered at the moment is a regulation on foreign subsidies distorting the internal market, which was proposed by the European Commission in May 2021 and on which political agreement was reached in June 2022. This proposal aims to partially extend the existing system of screening of State aid granted to businesses by EU Member States to also cover subsidies granted by foreign governments (at least to the extent that these subsidies may affect European markets). The new system is meant to avoid competitive distortions in the European market but will mainly affect how non-EU businesses can operate in Europe. Because the proposal is a response to the lack of a robust subsidy screening system at the WTO level, it is also a symptom of the deadlock of globalization.

7. Many other legal interventions can be mentioned that may negatively affect global commerce, including measures as simple as increased tariffs, which, of course, will increase the cost of imports and therefore affect the incentives of foreign businesses to be active in the market.

II. The withdrawal into more localized markets

8. Secondly, whether because of the existence of legal impediments to cross-border commerce or because of purely economic reasons for reshoring or nearshoring, the fragmentation of markets will reduce the presence of businesses across different geographic markets and, in turn, reduce competitive pressure in some of these markets. One of the virtues of globalization was precisely that it exposed domestic firms to competition from foreign firms, thereby forcing the former to become more efficient and innovative. In the European Union, one of the purposes of the creation of the European internal market was precisely to enhance competitiveness and innovation by breaking down national monopolies. If this process is reversed by deglobalization, the competitive benefits are likely to disappear as well.

9. Furthermore, if businesses are active across several geographic markets, they may be able to achieve economies of scale without necessarily taking up significant market power in each of these markets. If this process is reversed, consumers may suffer from higher prices, lower quality and less innovation.

10. From a competition perspective, more localized markets are more likely to give rise to monopolies and other forms of market power. Furthermore, if localized markets contain fewer players, this may facilitate the formation of cartels. Global fragmentation may therefore increase the need for stricter competition enforcement on all fronts.

III. The intertwining of local business and local politics

11. Thirdly, the two previous processes may have feedback effects. In particular, legal barriers to international trade and the withdrawal of businesses into domestic markets risk concentrating national markets, thereby facilitating domestic lobby efforts. More consolidated industries indeed suffer less from collective action problems and can therefore be expected to result in more aligned industry positions towards governments. Furthermore, in a more antagonistic international environment, these governments may be more inclined to create or protect domestic industries and national or regional champions. That Siemens tried to acquire Alstom's train business to effectively create a European high-speed train monopoly in response to the merger of the two Chinese train manufacturers is an obvious example of this, which was only narrowly averted when the European Commission blocked the acquisition in 2019.

12. These lobby efforts may be propelled by the increased politicization of competition policy over the last few years. Indeed, after two decades of strong technocratic enforcement based purely on efficiency considerations, policy-makers are aiming to increase the societal relevance of competition law. In my view, this broader perspective on competition policy must be welcomed to prevent competition enforcement from taking place in an ivory tower. However, by definition, it opens up that policy to broader political influences and interest groups (for better or worse).

13. In some instances, deglobalization may go hand in hand with the nationalization of businesses, as is happening in part of the energy sector in Germany (Gazprom Germany, Rosneft refineries, Uniper). This will further increase ties between businesses and governments and align their incentives.

IV. Reduced international cooperation in competition policy

14. Finally, the effects of deglobalization on legal barriers, market developments and political interests may be combined with direct effects on competition policy itself. If fragmentation leads to reduced coordination of policies in international fora, it is likely to result in greater divergence in competition policies in different jurisdictions, even in areas where no specific domestic interests are at stake.

15. The decision by the chair of the ICN of 2 March 2022 to suspend the participation of the Federal Antimonopoly Service of the Russian Federation in ICN activities will have the direct consequence of reducing coordination with that competition authority. Incidentally, the Chinese State Administration for Market Regulation is not (nor have its predecessor agencies ever been) a member of the ICN. But also amongst authorities that are members of the ICN or other organizations, divergences may increase. There are, of course, fields in which there appears to be increased alignment amongst authorities in recent years, for example, the US agencies' increased willingness to pursue monopolization cases, which seems to come closer to the European Commission's approach in the field of abuse of dominance. These instances may, however, be informed more by comparable economic developments in these jurisdictions (e.g. the increasing digitization of the economy) than by conscious decisions to align. If economic developments become less aligned, the same may happen to economic policies, including competition law.

16. Deglobalization may also exacerbate the differences in the values that underpin some economic policies and, therefore, competition enforcement. The interest in the interplay between competition law and sustainability in Europe, which does not seem to be present in other jurisdictions, could be an example of this.

V. Conclusion

17. That more fragmentation in competition policy and enforcement is a realistic possibility becomes apparent when looking at the development of the Internet in recent years. While it was hailed upon its creation as facilitating the creation of a global village, it has increasingly become a "splinternet," as various countries restrict their citizens' access to certain websites. While this phenomenon may have started with the Great Firewall in China more than twenty years ago, the idea that citizens should be protected from unpleasant opinions is now also spreading to jurisdictions that pride themselves on the freedom of expression and information. An obvious example is the decision by the Council of the European Union of 1 March 2022 to ban certain Russian propaganda outlets from the European Internet (and television).

18. More fragmented competition policies and enforcement will arise much more easily than a fragmented online space. For those who, like myself, study competition law academically, this may make this field of law even more interesting. And, in the grand scheme of things, more divergent competition policies and enforcement may well be a small price to pay to ward off some of the perceived ills of globalization or to obtain greater geopolitical security.

19. However, for legal advisors of businesses, the situation is likely to become more complex. Rather than applying certain general and uniform principles, they will need to adjust to multiple interpretations of what competition means and entails. *Concurrences* (in plural) indeed.

Competition Policy in Mexico: A New Chapter

ANDREA MARVAN SALTIEL*
Mexican Competition Authority (COFECE)

1. The conversation surrounding the objectives of competition policy has recently gained momentum as academics, practitioners, governments and even civil society are increasingly advocating for a revaluation of competition policy goals. It seems that the traditional focus on market efficiency to guide competition law in the future is becoming inadequate to address the complexities of today's economy.

2. The active participation of civil society in this debate marks a significant departure from the past. For far too long, major discussions and decisions about public policy, including competition policy, were confined to a highly technical and hermetic environment, which meant that little or no explanation was given to the general population. However, there is a palpable shift towards a more inclusive conversation, with the public keen on engaging in these discussions and understanding the policies that affect their daily lives. In a world characterized by growing inequality, this shift seems not only natural but necessary.

3. Integrating competition policy into the democratic fabric will become crucial in these times. By doing so, we ensure that there is a balanced system where competition policy does is not just the purview of technical experts but reflects collective societal knowledge and engagement. This approach enhances transparency and accountability, making competition policy more responsive to the needs of the public.

4. In this chapter, my aim is to contribute to this ongoing debate by delineating the fundamental principles that underpin competition policy, how has

* Andrea Marván Saltiel, Chairwoman of the Mexican Economic Competition (COFECE).

competition improved the Mexican economy and how we have decided to reinvigorate competition enforcement to show people the real benefits of competition in their daily lives.

I. The Roots of Competition Policy – Why Was Competition Policy Created?

5. In the early years of the twentieth century, competition policy emerged as a response to unchecked growth of economic power. At its core, competition policy was tied to the economic freedom of individuals, as it was a tool crafted to foster prosperity, freedom and well-being. The notion that power – be it economic or otherwise – must be curtailed so that no entity or individual stands beyond the reach of law, finds its roots deep in democratic thought. Competition policy, in that regard, plays a pivotal role in promoting a pluralism of economic actors and interests, thwarting the concentration of economic power.

6. With this foundational principle, competition policy evolved over the years, growing in sophistication and complexity alongside the economy and the society. While originally conceptualized as a tool to ensure the well-being of the population through competitive outcomes in the markets, competition policy quickly turned into a public policy goal to promote economic growth as it revealed its capacity to foster innovation.

7. By the end of the twentieth century, competition policy had been adopted by a significant number of countries worldwide and cemented itself as a policy aimed at ensuring that market economies functioned openly. Thus, a process of competition policy consolidation started throughout the world and with the passing of years, competition policy increasingly required more technical, specialized, sophisticated, and complex economic knowledge and, as a result, it also increasingly disconnected itself from its original stakeholders: the general population.

II. Competition Policy in Mexico

8. In the early 1990s, Mexico witnessed the emergence of competition policy amid aspirations for economic growth and negotiations for the North American Free Trade Agreement (NAFTA) with the United States and Canada. In this context, it was crucial to have a policy that promoted free competition and to create an institution that would enforce it, providing certainty to new players interested in entering traditionally closed markets.[1]

---

1 Juan Carlos Moreno-Brid, *La Comisión Federal de Competencia y la agenda de desarrollo de México: orígenes macro de una gesta micro*, in La Política De Competencia Económica En México: Retrospectiva, Balances Y Retos (2023), https://www.cofece.mx/wp-content/uploads/2023/11/Libro_aniversario_Cofece_vf.pdf.

9. In 1992, the Mexican government established the former Federal Competition Commission (CFC) and enacted the first competition law. The primary goal of the law was to create a "fair and equitable" business environment among companies, ensuring a "level playing field" with minimal distortions in the competition process that would guarantee fair treatment regardless of investors' origins. Two decades later, a constitutional amendment in 2013 brought profound structural changes to the Mexican economy and resulted in the enactment of the new Federal Economic Competition Law and the creation of the Federal Economic Competition Commission (Cofece).[2]

10. Whilst Mexico has achieved significant success in bolstering economic development through robust enforcement of competition law over the past decades, Mexicans are still grappling with a pressing question they seem to share with the rest of the world: *What has competition policy done for me?*

11. This question highlights a significant gap between the theoretical benefits of competition policy and its tangible impact on the everyday lives of individuals. Despite the considerable achievements in economic growth through competition policy in Mexico and globally, it seems that a large segment of the population feels disconnected from this success. Perhaps, the disconnection we are now seeing can be explained by the fact that Mexico, akin many other nations around the globe, embraced and developed competition policy in an era where market efficiency was seen as the ultimate goal, inadvertently sidelining the very people these policies were originally intended to benefit.

12. This situation represents a significant challenge for enforcers, but it is also a unique opportunity to redefine and reinvigorate competition policy to bring it closer to the people. Ultimately, if our goal as enforcers or policymakers is to make of competition not a mere policy but a culture, we need people to start caring about it.

13. That is why Cofece has decided to open on a new stage of competition policy in Mexico, aiming to close the gap between public policy and public engagement. By leveraging the achievements of the past and reinvigorating enforcement and advocacy through an innovative approach, we are committed to demonstrating the real benefits of competition policy to the Mexican people.

14. As we move forward into the second decade of the twenty-first century, competition policy must evolve to address the dynamic and changing needs of the society. This evolution entails not only a reassessment of policy objectives to prioritize societal well-being over abstract economic metrics but also a shift in how we communicate these public policies. By making competition policy more accessible and understandable, and by showcasing its direct benefits to the public, Cofece aims to cultivate a deeper appreciation and engagement with competition policy among Mexicans.

---

2 Josefina Cortés Campos, *Reflexiones sobre la autonomía constitucional*, in La Política De Competencia Económica En México: Retrospectiva, Balances Y Retos (2023), https://www.cofece.mx/wp-content/uploads/2023/11/Libro_aniversario_Cofece_vf.pdf.

III. Competition Policy with a Social Vision

15. Competitive markets have been consistently recognized not only for their potential to improve economic development, but also for their capacity to be engines for economic revitalization in countries, offering solutions to social challenges that impair the economic prosperity of citizens. Evidence from the Organization for Economic Cooperation and Development (OECD) underscores the disproportionate impact of unjustified price increases on those living in poverty.[3] For instance, a study conducted in 2018 revealed that Mexican families spend an average of 15.7 percent of their yearly income on overprices charged upon basic goods.[4]

16. Hence, Cofece has recognized the necessity to refine our competition policy priorities and focus its enforcement and advocacy actions in sectors that significantly impact household budgets in Mexico, such as food, energy, transportation, healthcare, and financial services.

17. For example, last year Cofece took decisive action against several individuals and undertakings engaged in price-fixing and output-restriction conduct of corn tortillas in the municipality of Huixtla in the state of Chiapas. On a macroeconomic level, this might not seem a very big or relevant case, but the people that live in one of the most marginalized municipalities in Mexico would disagree. Corn tortillas are a staple food item for Mexican families, with lower-income households allocating more than 8 percent of their food budget to this essential product.[5] Indeed, big cases are important for the economy and the population, but "small" cases also have the capacity to bring meaningful impact to consumers lives, which is what competition policy was originally intended to do.

18. Similarly, in 2022 Cofece levied significant fines to several LP gas distributors that engaged in price manipulation and market allocation agreements across the national territory, highlighting Cofece's commitment to ensuring that essential goods remain affordable and accessible for all Mexicans. According to official statistics, LP gas is the primary domestic fuel in Mexico, relied upon by eight out of ten families for cooking and heating purposes.[6]

19. Considering that some of the conduct lasted over a decade and their significant impact on the welfare of the most marginalized sectors of the population,

---

3 Jeremy K. West & Zsofia Tari, *Competition and Poverty Reduction*, OECD Glob. F. Competition (2013), https://one.oecd.org/document/DAF/COMP/GF(2013)1/En/pdf.

4 Cofece, Poder de Mercado y Bienestar Social (2018), https://www.cofece.mx/wp-content/uploads/2018/10/Libro-CPC-PoderyBienestar-ver4.pdf.

5 Cofece, *Cofece sanctions several persons and economic agents for more than 2 million pesos and disqualifies natural persons for manipulating the price of tortillas and limiting their sale in Huixtla, Chiapas*, (June 21, 2023), https://www.cofece.mx/wp-content/uploads/2023/06/Cofece-017-2023_ENG.pdf.

6 Cofece, *Cofece imposes fines of more than 2.4 billion pesos on LP gas distributors for manipulating prices and dividing up the market to the detriment of consumers*, (Nov. 9, 2022), https://www.cofece.mx/la-cofece-impone-multas-a-distribuidores-de-gas-lp-por-manipular-precios-y-repartirse-el-mercado/.

Cofece decided to impose a historically high fine of US$140 million[7] and disqualified several directors to send a strong signal to undertakings and to deter future anticompetitive conduct.

20. This kind of action underscores Cofece's renewed commitment in focusing its enforcement actions on sectors that will have a tangible impact on Mexican families and on making competition policy a tool that will help achieve a fairer and more inclusive economic landscape. And although there is still much to be done to further enhance people's lives through competition, we have estimated that Cofece's endeavors have returned approximately US$441,000 dollars per day to Mexican society since December 2018.

21. Even though this approach represents a new era in the application of competition policy for Mexico, it also represents a return to the foundational principles upon which competition policy was established. We stand upon a moment that calls us to remember that fostering competitive and efficient market conditions was never meant to be a goal by itself, it was always about population welfare.

22. This recent surge in societal engagement and dialogue around competition policy does not entail, as some may say, the denaturalization or creation of a radically new framework. On the contrary, it serves as a powerful reminder that, for competition policy to evolve towards new horizons, it must remain close to the people.

IV. New Boundaries of Competition Policy

23. As we move forward, we must reinvigorate our commitment to a competition policy that is deeply interconnected with the society in which it operates. In that regard, we can no longer ignore that competition policy has the capacity to enhance a wide array of public policy goals, transcending its traditionally economically enclosed boundaries. From narrowing gender gaps and improving working conditions to promoting environmental sustainability and investment, competition policy can play a pivotal role in driving society towards more inclusive and fairer economic outcomes.

24. Labor markets are a clear illustration of how competition policy can tangibly enhance people's lives as competition encourages employers to compete for talent by offering more attractive wages and working conditions. Conversely, restrictions that artificially constrain labor mobility undermine the very essence of competition, severely damaging not just workers and their families, but the broader economic landscape.

25. In a landmark case from 2021, Cofece fined seventeen football clubs US$10 million dollars[8] for colluding in the signing of professional football players.

7 MXN$2,400 million pesos at MXN$17.02 pesos per dollar exchange rate.

8 MXN$177 million pesos at MXN$17.02 pesos per dollar exchange rate.

By means of this agreement, the clubs agreed that they would not hire contract-free players from other clubs unless they had explicit consent from the former club, often subject to the payment of a financial compensation.[9]

26. Additionally, the investigation found that the clubs and the Mexican Football Federation had agreed upon salary caps on professional female players based on age and status. Therefore, players over 23 years old had their salary capped at US$120 dollars per month; players under 23 years old, had their salary capped at US$30 dollars per month; and players under 17 years old would not be entitled to any salary, but would be eligible for transportation, education, and food assistance.

27. This case illustrates the broader implications of competition policy beyond traditional market dynamics, demonstrating the potential of competitive markets to address issues such as gender inequality in the workforce. By penalizing conduct that restrict labor mobility, competition policy fosters a more equitable economic landscape. This approach not only serves to dismantle barriers to competition but is also a significant step towards closing the gender gap, setting a precedent for how competition policy can be leveraged to promote parity and fairness across all sectors of the economy. Competition agencies play a crucial role in eliminating regulatory barriers to ensure that all individuals, regardless of gender, have equal opportunities to contribute to and benefit from economic activities.

28. Finally, there is an expanding worldwide interest in the intersection between competition policy and environmental sustainability, reflecting a growing recognition of the need to align market dynamics with ecological objectives. This emerging focus is being reflected in an increasing number of competition agencies that are issuing policies or guidelines to evaluate corporate strategies aimed at implementing collaboration agreements on projects with sustainability objectives that seek to eliminate environmentally harmful products, circular economy enterprises or various forms of voluntary sustainability standards.

29. Such initiatives may eem like a paradigm shift towards integrating sustainability into the core objectives of competition policy. However, competition policy has always demonstrated its capacity to foster and drive innovation. In an era where society faces significant environmental challenges, leveraging the benefits of competition policy as a mechanism to encourage the adoption of innovative sustainable practices represents a logical and necessary evolution. The premise behind this rationale is simple: for sustainable solutions and products to gain widespread acceptance, they must be affordable to consumers, a condition best fulfilled in a competitive marketplace.

---

9 Cofece, *Cofece sanctions 17 Liga MX clubs , the Mexican Football Federation and 8 individuals for colluding in the football players "transfer market"*, (2021), https://www.cofece.mx/cofece-sanciona-a-17-clubes-de-la-liga-mx-a-la-federacion-mexicana-de-futbol-y-8-personas-fisicas-por-coludirse-en-el-mercado-de-fichaje-de-las-y-los-futbolistas/#:~:text=El%20Pleno%20de%20la%20Comisi%C3%B3n,a%20la%20Federaci%C3%B3n%20Mexicana%20de.

30. Considering the above, in 2021 Cofece issued a policy document, "Transition into Competitive Energy Markets," where they addressed the topic of clean electric energy and had several recommendations to promote competition conditions in the sector that had the potential to help the environment.[10] Additionally, Cofece is currently working on a comprehensive policy document that will address various sustainability challenges within Mexican markets from a competition standpoint.

31. As we move forward, the role of competition policy in fostering more efficient market structures, whether that means cost-efficient or environmentally efficient products cannot be ignored. As there is a growing consumer demand for products that minimize ecological footprint, companies are now trying to win consumer preference by incorporating sustainability factors into their products and that is competition at its finest.

V. Competition Policy as a State Matter

32. While competition agencies are responsible of enforcing competition laws, fostering and implementing a culture of competition requires a collaborative effort across public institutions, private entities and civil society. For this exact reason, renewed public interest in competition represents an exceptional opportunity for competition authorities and policymakers to strengthen advocacy and outreach efforts to spearhead the development of a united stance for competition culture.

33. As part of this new stage in competition policy, Cofece has adopted a whole-of-government approach to make competition policy a national priority in Mexico. To achieve the goals of competition policy and fully leverage its benefits, a concerted effort from every sector of the economy is required, underscoring the importance of collaboration between governmental bodies, business leaders, entrepreneurs, academic circles, and the broader community to succeed in enhancing public welfare through competitive markets.

34. The significance of a well-established competition policy transcends its immediate impact on product diversity, pricing, and general welfare. It also plays a pivotal role in supporting public institutions by stimulating investment and protecting public entities against anticompetitive conduct.

35. On the investment side, a cornerstone of competition policy is its capacity to dismantle barriers to entry that otherwise hinder small- and medium-sized enterprises from entering markets and competing on an equal footing with larger corporations. This approach will allow us to fully harness the role of competition policy in fostering entrepreneurship and investment, especially by

10 Cofece, *Cofece publishes the document "Transition towards competed energy markets: The Clean Energy Certificates in the Mexican electric industry"*, (May 18, 2021), https://www.cofece.mx/wp-content/uploads/2021/05/COFECE-016-2021_ENG.pdf.

leveraging investment opportunities such as those presented by the nearshoring trend. While attracting investment is a crucial initial step, maintaining a conducive economic climate to retain these investments is equally vital, and this is where competition policy plays a major role. This will not only facilitate market entry but also promote a dynamic and inclusive economic landscape where innovation and competition thrive.

36. In a significant case we recently addressed, Cofece identified the presence of various barriers to competition in the card payment processing market.[11] These barriers predominantly impact micro-, small- and medium-sized businesses, as they have little incentives to accept card payments due to the high costs associated with maintaining a POS (Point of Sale) terminal. According to our findings, the fees paid among banks for operating the card payment system average 1.36 percent, while fees paid in European countries are of approximately 0.2 percent. This means that Mexico pays fees that are six-times higher.

37. This discrepancy leads to a systemic effect. If small retailers do not accept card payments, the population will not use them. Mexico remains one of the countries where a considerable portion of the population (around 15 percent) reported preferring cash as it is the payment method accepted at the establishments they visit. Therefore, the Commission has made several regulatory recommendations and closely collaborated with financial regulators to make various adjustments to the regulatory framework to foster competition in this sector, promoting financial inclusion and increasing the acceptance of card payments. This collaborative approach is a step towards amplifying the inclusivity and accessibility of financial services, thereby democratizing the benefits of economic participation across all society.

38. Additionally, Cofece has prioritized collaboration with state governments, institutions, and various local organizations to ensure that the benefits of the competition policy have a broader impact across the entire population. Encompassing over 125 million inhabitants and even two different time zones, Mexico has a complex variety of economic challenges, and it has become clear that while certain national challenges persist, the economic realities of the different regions differ from each other.

39. To address this reality, we launched a pivotal initiative, "Competition in Your State" last year, which is designed to foster cooperation between Cofece and local governments by focusing on the most significant economic sectors of each state, ensuring that localized benefits of competition can be leveraged by the local population.[12] Through this initiative we seek to foster collaboration with local public officials by establishing capacity-building programs that provide the tools to scrutinize local regulations for competition barriers.

11 Cofece, *Cofece identified barriers to competition in the card payment processing market*, (Sept. 14, 2023), https://www.cofece.mx/wp-content/uploads/2023/09/Cofece-025-2023_ENG.pdf.

12 Cofece, *Expanding enforcement and advocacy tools to a state level*, (2023), https://awards.concurrences.com/IMG/pdf/initaitive-cofece-state-1.pdf?117439/521eef7bc659af0ff3f0f78f396afeec4e4d07d78eec19bd1165b4719c8bf54b.

Furthermore, we engage directly with small- and medium-sized companies to grasp their unique challenges, identify regulatory barriers, and guide them on how to report anticompetitive conduct.

40. As we step into this new economic landscape of digital markets and novel business models, we must not forget the potential of outreach strategies to implement measures that bolster the well-being of its inhabitants. Through this lens, competition policy transcends its conventional boundaries, emerging as a keystone for progress in our quest for a more inclusive economy.

VI. Moving Forward into the New Era of Competition Policy

41. As we draw this discussion to a conclusion, it is especially important to recognize and build upon the experience and success competition policy has had throughout this last century, both in Mexico and around the world. However, we are now embarking upon a new era in which society is reminding enforcers and policymakers of its original purpose and stakeholders. In response, Cofece has embarked upon a new era of competition policy in Mexico, where we aim to make competition a powerful tool to enhance people lives and create a more inclusive economy.

42. This commitment is evidenced by our concerted efforts to make the benefits derived from competitive markets more tangible to the population and to make competition policy a national priority, reinforcing the idea that it is not a distant concept from the public.

43. We are now faced with a moment where the evolution of competition policy is not only possible but essential. The time has come to demystify competition policy, making it accessible and beneficial for the very people it was designed to protect. By doing so, we not only honor its original intent but also unlock its full potential to enhance the population's well-being through competitive and fair markets. This new era of competition policy in Mexico, marked by tangible benefits and broad-based collaboration, is a testament to our dedication to embark on this journey towards a future where competition policy becomes a cornerstone for a more inclusive, dynamic, and prosperous society.

Argentine Competition Policy: A Matter of Faith

PABLO TREVISÁN*
Instituto de Derecho de la Competencia (IDC)

I. Introduction

1. Having already traveled a century-old path, it would not be wrong to affirm that Argentine competition law is enjoying good health. Paradoxically, nothing similar could be said about competition policy in our country, which has long suffered from serious chronic health problems. Politics and law are not going hand in hand. And that is perceived in the markets, it is felt in SMEs and it is suffered in *Doña Rosa*'s pocket.
2. Law and policy have been on opposite paths in our country for decades on the antitrust field. The legal side is very well nourished, with a modern act in force and an active and informed antitrust community of professionals and academics. To close this virtuous circle, all that remains is (i) for universities to include the subject in their undergraduate courses, and not limit their teaching to postgraduate studies, and (ii) even more importantly, that the issue ceases to be an exclusive topic of some professionals and academics, and be well known by all citizens.
3. Since the beginning of this millennium, competition policy has been on a roller coaster. Its evolution has been like an electrocardiogram, with very marked ups and downs, which prevent the defense of competition from becoming, once and for all, a long-term public policy, as ordered by our Argentinian National Constitution. Let us see why.

---

* Partner, Estudio Trevisán Abogados, Buenos Aires. Founder and Director, IDC – Instituto de Derecho de la Competencia. Co-author of the Argentine Competition Act.

4. From 1999 to date, all and each of the national governments have been of the most diverse political and ideological overtones, but what they all have in common is that none of them has had the firm will to fully comply with the institutional design established by the legislators. That is to say, including the current one, the last twelve presidents of the Argentine Republic have failed to comply with the written law and the constitutional mandate. Politics interfering with policy, again and again.Paradoxically, these days the Nobel Prize in Economics was announced to Daron Acemoglu, Simon Johnson and James Robinson "for their studies on how institutions are formed and how they affect prosperity." Their insights into how institutions influence prosperity demonstrate that working to support democracy and inclusive institutions is an important way forward to promote economic development. Any similarity with the reasons that motivate the fragile enforcement of Argentine competition law is not a mere coincidence.

5. We wonder if competition policy has any hope of surviving in our country. In this context, although we could analyze whether we are dealing with a terminally ill patient or a patient in a coma, it seems more appropriate to conclude that we are dealing with a question of faith. That is why we choose to believe.

6. In this present contribution, we analyze the consequences of this anomie, starting from the systematic lack of compliance with the institutional design provided under the applicable legislation, and focusing fundamentally on some of its harmful consequences and, in particular, with respect to three of the core institutes incorporated by the competition act that, several years after its sanction, are still pending to be fully applied, namely: premerger control, the leniency program, and private enforcement. We will close our work with brief conclusions and a proposal for change, in the event that in the short term it is not possible to comply with the institutional design created by law.

II. Achilles Heel

7. The Achilles Heel of our competition policy has been, and continues to be to date, the systematic lack of implementation of the independent authority created by law (both in the previous law of 1999, and in Law 27,442 (LDC) of 2018). *Silly anomie* (i.e., "*anomia boba,*" in Spanish), to which Carlos Nino referred, in his book *A Country on the Margins of the Law* ("*Un País al Margen de la Ley,*" the original title in Spanish);[1] is a situation that arises when as a society we deviate from the norms, even when it is not convenient for us.

8. The lack of constitution of the National Competition Authority (ANC) implies that the current enforcement authority continues to be the Secretary

1 Carlos Nino, Un País al Margen de la Ley (Editorial Ariel 1992) (2011).

of Commerce and Industry (SCI), with prior intervention by the National Commission for the Defense of Competition (CNDC). This competition authority scheme, which the 2018 legislator ordered to be transitory, has become permanent, and is, unfailingly and continuously, at the mercy of the political pressures of the governments in power.

9. During the entire validity of the law prior to the LDC, as the authority created by law had never been put into operation, there was – in the words of the different Courts of Appeals[2] and even the Supreme Court of Justice of the Nation (CSJN) – a legal scandal.

10. Unfortunately, this legal scandal has been renewed and maintained in recent years, after the enactment of the LDC in 2018. These and other factors clearly indicate that the mere existence of a good antitrust legal regime does not guarantee the effective application of antitrust policy.[3]

11. What are the consequences of this scandal? Among others: (i) the enforcement authority lacks internal procedural rules, which is why very few cases are resolved, and too many are closed due to the expiration of the statute of limitation or other similar reasons; meaning that while some cases accelerate, others fall asleep; (ii) since there are few sanctions for anti-competitive practices, there are not enough fingers on one hand to count the cases of private enforcement; (iii) the time taken to conduct investigations and merger control cases is excessively long; (iv) there is no subsequent review or analysis of the impact that the cases resolved by the authority have in practice; (v) core

2 There have been several jurisprudential precedents that referred to this situation. To name a few:

- CNCont. Fed. Adm., Chamber III, Apr. 16, 2007, in the *Multicanal* ruling, when analyzing and resolving whether the CNDC had the power to issue precautionary measures, held that this does not arise from art. 35 nor of art. 58 LDC, concluding that "until the TNDC is established, the issuance of precautionary measures finds coverage only in the aforementioned art. 24 inc. m) LDC, according to which the competent judge may be requested to take the precautionary measures that are deemed pertinent … it cannot be accepted that in the administrative procedure the administrative body – due to lack of constitution of the TNDC – is at the same time a party and a judge within a same cause. Pretending that the administrative body has jurisdictional powers and can issue precautionary measures violates the republican principle of separation of powers, and the entity that does so would incur excess power."
- CNCiv. and Com. Fed., Chamber II, on July 27, 2009, in the *Telefónica/Telecom* case, held a criterion similar to that of Chamber II in *Multicanal*: that "…power… art. 35 LDC… is attributed to an administrative court that has not yet been established and that has certain guarantees of independence regarding its constitution and operation."
- CNAPE, Chamber A, on Oct. 21, 2009, also within the framework of *Telefónica/Telecom*, held that "… the exercise of a judicial function by an EP body, transgresses the provision of article 109 of the CN (…) the delay incurred in the integration of the administrative court constitutes a 'legal scandal.'"
- CNCiv. and Com. Fed., Chamber II, on Feb. 19, 2010, in the *Cablevisión S.A.* case. held that "in accordance with the criteria established by the Chamber in other cases, the CNDC would not have the power to issue precautionary measures under the terms of art. 35 of the LDC (conf. Telecom Italia SpA and other) (…). The CNDC has not received all the powers that law 25,156 places at the head of the TNDC." Adding that "this Chamber has recently highlighted the omission incurred by the Executive Branch in establishing the TNDC – over ten years, which is why it brought this circumstance to the attention of the president of the Supreme Court of Justice of the Nation in order to that measures or efforts that it deems pertinent be considered, aimed at favoring the constitution of the aforementioned court (Agreed conf. No. 16/09, of 12.2.09). Similarly, Chamber A of the CNAPE sent a communication to the High Court of similar tenor (conf. Telefónica de España, Olimpia and others.)."
- Cam. Nac. Civ. and Com. Fed., Room 2, Feb. 25, 2010, in the proceedings *Direct TV*, insists on emphasizing the obligation to establish the TNDC.

3 Michal Gal, *The Ecology of Antitrust – Preconditions for Competition Law Enforcement in Developing Countries*, *in* Competition, Competitiveness and Development 20–58, 21 (UNCTAD 2004).

institutes incorporated by the 2018 law, are still pending to be fully applied. We will delve into this last point in this work.

12. As we mentioned above, Argentina has a centuries-old tradition of antitrust legislation, although it has a huge debt related to the vigorous enforcement of its policies and the correct execution of its written rules.

13. One of the main causes of this situation is due to the permanent lack of impartiality and independence of its enforcement authority.

14. When we talk about an independent authority, we are not referring to an organization that acts in a vacuum, but to an authority with a certain autonomy from the central power, its own budget, stability of its members – who must be eminently technical and suitable for the position and, definitely, with sufficient powers and essential capabilities that allow it to combat anticompetitive behavior and promote the benefits of free competition.[4]

15. The institutional system envisaged in the LDC was one of its main innovations, as confirmed by the recent UNCTAD Voluntary Peer Review,[5] as well as by many other organizations, authorities, bar associations, academics and professionals, nationally and internationally, commenting on the then-LDC draft bill.

16. And why is this question so important? Because the legislator provided for a specific institutional design, granting the enforcement authority the powers, guarantees, and sufficient tools to be able to ensure compliance with the constitutional mandate and, based on that institutional design, established the different gears that make up the engineering to the full exercise of its powers, which allow it to ensure the correct functioning of the markets and the competition system therein.

17. That is, it is through that design that the legislator considered that he was establishing the means to achieve the ends. He could have considered other models, without a doubt, such as, a more adversarial model, without an administrative agency that acts as an enforcement authority, turning the resolution of cases to the judicial branch, as happens in several jurisdictions. It was not the case, although, if this situation of permanent anomie persists, it would not be crazy, but quite the opposite, to consider whether Argentina should definitely move towards an adversarial or accusatorial model.

18. As a necessary consequence of not fully complying with the institutional design provided for by the legislator, other institutes established under the LDC have also remain unrealized, such as: (i) continuing to deal with an ex-post merger control system, postponing (once again) the entry into force of the premerger control system, (ii) the lack of incentives and sufficient case law that would allow the full development of a solid private enforcement system for the compensation and reparation of damages caused by anti-competitive

4 William E. Kovacic & David A. Hyman, *Competition Agency Design: What's on the Menu?*, (GW L. Fac. Publ'n, Paper No. 628, 2012).

5 Luis Berenguer, *Voluntary Peer Review of Competition Law and Policy – Argentina,* UNCTAD 28 (2017), https://unctad.org/publication/voluntary-peer-review-competition-law-and-policy-argentina.

conducts, and (iii) the lack of effective implementation of the leniency program that, as a tool, would allow the detection and sanction of a greater number of cases of cartelization.

19. Let us see now what each of these three questions implies.

III. Dealing with the "Transitory" Ex-Post Merger Control System, while postponing the implementation of the Premerger Control provided under the LDC

20. The ex-post control of economic concentrations is a total nonsense when the procedure, as happens from time to time in our country, presents huge delays that sometimes exceed a decade.

21. For its part, premerger control requires greater speed of approval from the implementing authority, at the risk of becoming a true limit to the speed of trade.

22. Successful cases from neighboring countries with similar backgrounds, such as Brazil, show that it is possible to manage a system of prior notification of concentrations efficiently and in a timely manner, without stopping the progress of business, in particular by establishing special simplified procedures for cases that, given certain objective characteristics, do not present competition concerns.

23. In this sense, the LDC sought to increase the efficiency of the procedure, for which it significantly increased the notification thresholds of the previous law, which had become completely outdated,[6] and which had forced the agency to examine irrelevant concentrations, increasing costs to the agency and the economy in general.

24. The basis of merger control consists of preventing mergers or transfers of shares or assets that could, with a high probability, result in harm to the general economic interest, through a decrease in the levels of rivalry in the markets. The central idea is that blocking or restoring competition once an anticompetitive concentration has been carried out is too complex.

25. While it consists of a preventive procedure, the ideal of the merger control procedure would be that it operates prior to the consummation of the economic concentration and not a posteriori, as to a large extent, happens under the conduct regime. The costs that are desired to be avoided, associated with ex-post control, are too high for society when it is determined that a certain operation must be blocked or conditioned after its consummation.

---

6 At the time of the enactment of Law 25,156, the volume threshold was, in pesos, equivalent to 150 million US dollars and, due to the mere effect of inflation, at the time of the sanction of the new LDC it represented slightly more than 7.5 million dollars.

26. The problem with a control system that works ex-post is that it introduces a good part of the costs and largely eliminates the benefits of a preventive or prospective procedure, making the procedure less attractive and inefficient (and, in many cases, useless).

27. Under a genuine ex-ante control system, the parties have important incentives to cooperate since the delay in providing the relevant information to the agency is at their expense, since until the competition authority issues its opinion, the transaction in question cannot be closed or, even less, consummated. That is, the delay produced as a result of lack of information and full collaboration with the enforcement authority is paid by the company.

28. In an ex-post control system, the delay is paid by society and probably, through agency costs, in some cases, by companies, which must face higher costs (for example, higher fees for their lawyers and consultants). In this way, costs increase and delays in procedures tend to be frequent, largely because there are no necessary incentives for the procedure to be completed in a short time, thus increasing private costs and, even worse, the social costs of the ex-post procedure.

29. One of the main benefits, then, is to prevent anticompetitive concentrations by preserving the status prior to the operation of the concentration, a situation that is not verified with the possible high costs that the adoption of structural remedies would imply – after the consummation of the concentration operation in question, which can be too costly for the parties and society in general. After the firms are integrated, it may be very costly, if not unfeasible, to impose a structural remedy, after, for example, the closure of a factory, the discontinuation of production of certain products, the joint use of distribution networks or any other of these measures that can be highly costly to roll back.

30. Likewise, we consider that under the new LDC, prior to the establishment of a full ex-ante merger control, two serious avoidable errors have been committed.

31. The first, in our opinion, consists of the introduction of a temporary scheme for the subsistence of the – confusing – system of the previous Law 25,156 on the matter, until one year after the start of operation of the ANC.[7]

32. In this regard, at the time[8] we stated that there were no sufficient or found reasons to incorporate such nonsense into the new LDC. During the discussion of the LDC project, some voices argued that the inclusion of said transitional regime was necessary, due to the enforcement authority's long resolution times of merger control cases under the previous Law 25,156. On the contrary, we always maintained that it was important to make an immediate change, leaving aside the harmful ex-post control, to move to a true ex-ante control, considering that the conditions were absolutely right for it.

---

7 LDC art. 81: "The regulations will establish the conditions under which the processing of files initiated under the terms of what is established in Chapter III of Law 25,156 will continue."

8 Pablo Trevisán, Desafíos Presentes y Futuros en Defensa de la Competencia (La Ley 2019).

33. In maintaining this, we indicated two absolutely verifiable factual arguments: first, what happened in Brazil, whose economy is significantly larger than Argentina and which, at the time of the reform of its merger control system in 2012 towards an ex-ante one, had statistics and experiences very similar to those of Argentina in 2015; and, mainly, what happened in Argentina between the end of 2015 and May 2018, when the new law was passed.

34. In Brazil, despite the bad omens of the Brazilian business sector at that time, from 2012 onwards the competition authority of that country managed to significantly reduce the times of its merger control processes, to the point that – to date – Brazil has an average end-to-end review of these types of cases of no more than 25 days, falling short of international best practices.

35. For its part, in our country, and even under the validity of Law 25,156, whose thresholds were completely outdated, the application authority managed to significantly reduce the review periods of these procedures; specifically, from an average of more than three and a half years, as of December 2015, to an average of just over three months, as of May 2018.

36. That is, like Brazil in 2012 but with the advantage that in our country the indicators had already improved significantly at the time the new LDC was sanctioned, Argentina was already prepared to go directly to an ex-ante control, without the need for a regime transient.

37. Second, unnecessarily complicating things even more, Decree 480/2018 introduces through the last sentence of its Article 84 a change that may have gone unnoticed by some, but that deepens the issue even further, by suspending the application of the third paragraph of Article 9 of Law 27,442. Beyond considering that at this point Decree 480/2018 seems to have gone too far by modifying a law issued by the National Congress, in practice, it means that in Argentina – and until a year has passed after the implementation functioning of the ANC – we have an ex-post concentration control system like never before seen in our country, with all the "contraindications" previously mentioned about it. Based on the provisions of Article 84 of Decree 480/2018, the notifying parties, without any doubt, from then, will be able not only to close the transactions, but also to consummate them, prior to the intervention of the regulatory authority. An unnecessary mischief.

38. Under the previous legislation, Law 25,156, it was provided that the merger notification could be made after (up to one week) the takeover of the company in question. Contrary to the recurrent interpretation made by the enforcement authority on this point, we have repeatedly[9] maintained that the wording of the first paragraph of Article 8 of Law 25,156 was procedural in nature and indicated when the procedural formality must be complied with to notify a concentration operation. However, the second sentence of Article 8, which was of a substantial nature, provided that the transaction brought to the attention of

9 Pablo Trevisán, Merger Control in Latin America, Concurrences (2020), p. 7.

the enforcement authority could not have effects between the parties and with respect to third parties until the authority has resolved on the matter. That is, although under an unfortunate wording, the old Law 25,156 allowed closing or perfecting the transaction prior to notification, but – in light of the second sentence of its Article 8 – it did not allow the consummation of the operation, until the authority resolved.

39. Unfortunately, even though the intention of the LDC is clearly to move towards ex-ante concentration control, during the transition stage much more ex-post concentration control will be applied than that which existed during the validity of Law 25,156.

IV. Implementation of the Leniency Program

40. The leniency program incorporated into the LDC attempted to be a relevant milestone in the evolution of competition law in our country. The challenge was – and continues to be – to make it work in practice, something very complex within the framework of a "transitional" and non-independent authority. The fact that after several years since its creation, there is no known case of requesting acceptance of the leniency program established by the LDC, speaks clearly about the importance of having a relatively independent authority that can provide the guarantees of full confidentiality that this type of tool requires.

41. Companies participating in cartels are generally aware that their conduct is illegal, and, through all types of maneuvers, they try to keep it secret and avoid being detected by antitrust authorities. An important tool for competition authorities is the possibility of granting leniency to "whistleblowers."

42. The leniency program generates incentives for defection and therefore modifies the cost-benefit ratio of remaining in the anticompetitive arrangement, increasing the risk of being denounced. For this reason, in addition, the risks increase and it becomes less attractive to be part of a cartel. Meanwhile, the main reason for benefiting from a leniency program, after all, is that the probability, the sanction or both are great enough to induce the denunciation and breakup of the cartel.[10]

43. Chapter VIII of the LDC establishes a modern leniency program. Since the mid-1990s to date, anti-cartel policy in the European Union and the United States owes part of its success to the leniency programs in force in those two jurisdictions.

44. When a company applies to the program and provides information about a cartel, it increases the marginal or incremental cost of the other members

10 Theoretical studies are (with limits) conclusive that leniency programs generate incentives to destabilize cartels and that they constitute effective tools to deter the formation of cartels. Motta & Polo (2003), and Spagnolo (2003), Aubert, Kovacic & Rey (2006), Chen & Harrington (2007), Harrington (2008) and Hinloopen & Soetevent (2008). See also, Jeroen Hinloopen & Adriaan R. Soetevent, *Laboratory Evidence on the Effectiveness of Corporate Leniency Programs*, 39 RAND J. Econ. 607-616 (2008).

of the cartel since it imposes on them the payment of the fine. Given this, naturally, the leniency program has or should have deterrent effects.

45. Article 60 of the LDC establishes the essential conditions for the operation of the leniency program, which is largely in line with the similar program in force in the EU. Likewise, the same Article 60 establishes "leniency plus," a mechanism that does not exist in the EU, but does exist in the US and the United Kingdom, through which a company that is under investigation in relation to a certain cartel and informs about the existence of another cartel, could obtain a reduction of up to a third of the fine in relation to the first company.

46. Article 61 of the LDC provides that individuals can benefit from a company's requests for leniency, in cases where personal liability may exist in accordance with Article 58 of the LDC. Something similar happens in the United Kingdom, where individuals can be protected by their employer's request for immunity.[11]

47. The introduction of the leniency program is accompanied by a much needed and increase in sanctions, one of the conditions for its effectiveness. Cultural tradition and the quality of institutions in general can affect the effectiveness of the program, but with respect to the former, the success of these programs is at least auspicious for most countries and particularly for those that have the same tradition and similar business cultural values, such as Mexico, Chile or Brazil.

V. Developing a Private Enforcement System

48. As mentioned above, the principles of the defense of competition have received constitutional status in our country in the last reform of 1994. In this sense, Article 42[12] of the National Constitution constitutes a clear limit to the autonomy of the will of the contracting parties and, therefore, is an obligation that does not require an express contractual agreement.

49. The sanctions and corrective measures applied by the competition authority – which respond mainly to the general interest of society – provide a certain degree of deterrence against current and potential offenders, although they are clearly not sufficient – on their own – to achieve, and at the same time, protect private interest within the framework of antitrust law.

---

11 See, OFT, *Applications for Leniency and No-Action in Cartel Cases*, (July 2013), https://assets.publishing.service.gov.uk/media/5a7b9fec40f0b62826a04c65/OFT1495.pdf.

12 National Constitution art. 42: "Consumers and users of goods and services have the right, in the consumer relationship, to the protection of their health, safety and economic interests; to adequate and truthful information; to freedom of choice, and to conditions of equitable and dignified treatment. The authorities will provide for the protection of these rights, for consumer education, for the defense of competition against all forms of market distortion, for the control of natural and legal monopolies, for the quality and efficiency of public services, and the constitution of consumer and user associations. The legislation will establish effective procedures for the prevention and resolution of conflicts, and the regulatory frameworks for public services of national jurisdiction, providing for the necessary participation of consumer and user associations and interested provinces in the control bodies."

50. In this context, and without losing sight of the fact that the main objective of actions for damages in competition matters pursue a fundamentally individual interest in compensation for damages, suffered as a consequence of an anticompetitive conduct, it is important to consider the important deterrent effect that these actions also present.

51. This is one of the most important contributions of the new LDC, through the establishment of new guidelines and tools, which, undoubtedly, will contribute to ensuring that the repair of damages, caused as a consequence of anti-competitive acts, ceases to be a chimera and becomes a reality.

52. Thus, the combination and interaction of a renewed execution – public and private – of the LDC will contribute to maintaining and restoring the integrity of the market, to prevent artificial forces influencing prices, to the optimal provision of goods and services, to the elimination of entry barriers to markets, in the innovation of competitive products, and in the better general well-being of consumers.

53. The principle of civil liability by which damage must be repaired is fully applicable to compensation for anticompetitive offenses. The latest reform of the Civil and Commercial Code even expands this principle, as jurisprudence had previously accepted, establishing that there is not only the duty to repair, but also the obligation to avoid damage. In previous works we have referred to the prevention of harm and the defense of competition, to which we refer the reader,[13] since the topic exceeds the scope of this chapter.

54. In practice, it will be the parties and the judges who must carry out a process of adapting the general principles and rules of civil liability to the specific situations that may arise as a consequence of anticompetitive behavior. In this process, the principles and objectives of the competition defense regulations must be respected. Consequently, the scenario is presented from a general perspective with the structural elements of civil liability, and from a more specific perspective, sifting that responsibility through the guiding principles and specific regulations of the area of antitrust defense.[14]

55. Along these lines, Article 62 of the LDC states that: "Human or legal persons affected by the acts prohibited by this law, may exercise an action for compensation for damages in accordance with the rules of common law, before the judge competent in that matter." That is, the right of those affected by acts prohibited by the LDC will be governed by the general civil liability regime of the Civil and Commercial Code (*cf.* Articles 1708 to 1780).

---

13 Pablo Trevisán, *Acción Preventiva de Daños y Defensa de la Competencia*, 63 (Apr. 15, 2016), https://pablotrevisan.wordpress.com/?s=Acci%C3%B3n+Preventiva+de+Da%C3%B1os+.

14 Fernando De La Vega, Responsabilidad Civil Derivada del Ilícito Concurrencial, Resarcimiento del Daño Causado al Competidor 56 (Civitas 2001). This author maintains that "(…) civil liability for damages caused by illicit acts of competition should not be considered, therefore, as a sanction specific to Competition Law, it is a legal consequence that derives from behavior carried out in a market area with a competitive purpose and whose essential and primary normative element is the rules of civil liability, leaving the legal organization of competitive activity in the background (…)."

56. On the other hand and although the LDC only includes express provisions referring to the nullity of the legal acts prohibited by it under the new Article 2, we consider that the terms of the LDC (Article 1) are sufficient grounds to cause the nullities provided in the Civil and Commercial Code in relation to said acts.[15]

57. Among other important reforms introduced by the LDC on this issue, the so-called "follow-on actions" stand out, that is, those actions that derive from final resolutions on cases in which the enforcement authority has previously resolved, as provided for in Article 63[16] of the new LDC.

58. Along these lines, and without prejudice to the foregoing, taking special consideration of the essentially economic nature implicit in antitrust issues, we also consider that in those cases in which there is no prior resolution from the enforcement authority, the judges involved in the hearing of causes for reparation of damages due to anticompetitive offenses, may request that the LDC enforcement authority issue an opinion.

59. In this case, it will be important to coordinate judicial actions with administrative actions. In this sense, the provisions of Articles 1774 to 1780 of the Civil and Commercial Code are fully applicable when before – or during – the judicial process, administrative action is initiated before the LDC enforcement authority. Consequently, with rare exceptions, if the administrative action had been initiated, a civil decision could not be issued until there was one under the administrative process. On the other hand, if there is an administrative conviction, the existence of the infraction or the guilt of the defendant cannot be discussed in the civil process. On the contrary, if there is an administrative acquittal, the existence of the main fact on which the acquittal occurred cannot be argued.

60. The new LDC has taken a significant step in the right direction, by establishing that the resolutions of the Competition Defense Court that rule on violations of the LDC will become *res judicata* on the matter, so that they can later serve as a basis for the judges and the parties to the process (we are referring here to the aforementioned "follow-on actions" of comparative law). This, as we have been demanding for a long time, in addition to lightening the burden of proof on the victims, will also mean the processes to will no longer proceed through ordinary means – as was the case before the sanction

15 Guillermo Cabanellas De Las Cuevas, II Derecho Antimonopólico y de Defensa de la Competencia 393 (Heliasta 2022). In the same sense, and even when referring to the old Civil Code of Velez Sarfield, this author maintains that "(…) the terms of the prohibition included in article 1 of the LDC are broad enough to give rise to the nullity provided for in articles 953 and 1,044 of the Civil Code, in a manner consistent with the provisions of article 18 of the same Code."

16 LDC art. 63: "The resolution of the Competition Tribunal on the violation of this law, once it is final, will become res judicata on this matter. The action for reparation of damages that takes place due to the final resolution issued by the Court for the Defense of Competition, will be processed in accordance with the summary process established in chapter II of title III, of the second book of the Code of Civil Procedure and Commercial of the Nation. The competent judge, when ruling on the reparation of damages, will base his ruling on the conduct, facts and legal classification of the same, established in the resolution of the Court for the Defense of Competition, issued on the occasion of the application of this present law."

of the LDC – but in a more expeditious way by the summary route. The European Commission decided something similar in a matter analogous to the one mentioned here, through the scope established on the matter by the Antitrust Damages Directive.[17]

VI. Conclusion

61. The greatest challenge in the medium and long term is to ensure that competition law and policy are consolidated as public policy.

62. The political and social reality of our country has reflected a serious lack of institutions in matters of competition defense, while a significant degree of general misinformation and lack of knowledge on the matter is perceived, both among consumers, businessmen, and public officials.

63. In the immediate term, as we have said, the greatest challenge will be the institutional one, since much of the intrinsic benefits that the LDC presents will depend to a large extent on the institutional context that contains and promotes them in the future. Continuing on the path of repeating the mistakes of the past is unforgivable. Sooner rather than later, the institutional design devised and created by the legislator must be put into full operation.

64. We have seen throughout this contribution, how three of the most important institutes incorporated by the LDC are still pending application, several years after the enactment of the LDC (i.e., pre-merger control, leniency program, private enforcement). As long as the institutional framework designed by the 2018 legislator is not respected, there is little that the members of the CNDC will be able to do, no matter how much effort they make. Commendable indeed, although the problem exceeds them.

65. The current composition of the CNDC is made up of technical professionals, all of whom have solid backgrounds and experience in the field. Something similar applies to the permanent staff of the CNDC, which in general terms is made up of very good professionals, who over the years have acquired valuable expertise in the matter. But both, unfortunately, must work in a fragile context that is permeable to political interference in the investigation of the cases before the CNDC.

66. The current Secretary of Commerce and Industry (SCI), responsible for leading the call for public competition for the formation of the ANC, has said publicly and repeatedly that, if deregulated markets are to be achieved, it is very important to have a robust and independent competition authority. Impeccable.

67. However, a reasonable amount of time has passed for the Milei government, and there are no concrete signals of the call for the public tender, although

17 Directive 2014/104/EU of the European Parliament and of the Council of 26 November 2014 on certain rules governing actions for damages under national law for infringements of the competition law provisions of the Member States and of the European Union, 2014, O.J. (L 349) 1.

direct sources from the SCI report that the tender would soon be called. If that happens, the Milei government will have fulfilled the constitutional mandate that none of its predecessors from the last quarter of a century managed to fulfill.

68. Should the ANC fail to be formed during the Milei government, we would have to seriously consider whether Argentina should not renounce the enforcement scheme of administrative application, to definitively go to a more adversarial system, with less intervention from the central administration and greater prominence of the judicial power and *Doña Rosa*.

69. We are facing a historic opportunity in the evolution of Argentinian competition law and policy. I choose to believe.

Why Competition? A Review of Competition Regulation in Africa: Focusing on Key Competition Regimes in Sub-Saharan Africa

FRANCIS WANG'OMBE KARIUKI*

Bowmans

1. Overview, Scope and Institutions Dispensation

1. Africa has experienced growth in development and enforcement of competition policy and law over the last 15 years. This development is at national, regional levels and at the continental level. Forty-two countries in Africa have promulgated competition laws, while at the Continental level, COMESA, EAC, WAEMU and ECOWAS have regulations governing competition. Among the Regional Economic Communities (RECs) competition agencies, COMESA Competition Commission (CCC) is the most visible in terms of enforcement.
2. At Continental level, 54 African Countries have developed, and ratified a Competition Protocol to guide competition enforcement under the Africa Continental Free Trade Area (ACFTA). In terms of agencies' enforcement capacity, there is evidence of expansion, albeit slow, from advocacy and mergers determination towards the more egregious competition infractions such as cartels and abuse of dominance (AoD). In addition, over the last

---

* Senior Consultant, Competition and Trade Policy, Bowmans Law.

few years, enforcement boundaries have expanded to encompass emerging areas such as digital economy and platforms and even beyond the traditional competition law realms such as abuse of buyer power/superior bargaining position.[1]

3. The development and provisions of the competition laws in Africa have generally been driven by the respective national economic agenda and the national/regional experiences while the drafting been greatly motivated by inputs from African Competition Forum (ACF) members, International Competition Network (ICN) and OECD Global Competition Forum outputs. The Concurrences antitrust events/workshops agenda primarily on developing economies competition enforcement, has consequently informed this development too.

4. These forums, in summary, aim at informing international best practices to deepen effective competition law enforcement especially in novel areas, across the globe. However, we should be alive to the fact that although these forums formulate *best* practices, it should not be forgotten that different economies' market challenges are not congruent across the world nor are they homogeneous, especially between the Global North and South.

5. Hence, each country has been customizing the specific outputs to attend to their peculiar national needs; balancing the substantial lessening of competition criteria and public interest criteria. In addition, law development and reviews, including institutional development,[2]have been informed by enforcement challenges and as a result of market inquiries findings.

6. Despite this seemingly positive growth, the African Continent presents a scenario of dissymmetry in the status of competition policy and law development across the countries. Specifically, competition agencies can be categorized as being in one of following four levels of maturity:

    1. Operational and fully functional competition agencies;
    2. Operational but not yet fully functional agencies;
    3. Competition laws in place but no operational agency;
    4. Competition laws in development, and/or dispersed across mandates of sector regulators.[3]

7. The uneven growth has generally has been caused by budgetary constraints and lack of appreciation of the clear role of competition policy in supporting the always demanding governments priority economic agenda, within a very short space of time. Competition law enforcement results tend to take longer time compared to public interest interventions. However, this does not mean

1 South Africa and Kenya.

2 The Competition Authority of Kenya (CAK) organizational structure was changed after the Competition Act was revised to provide for abuse of buyer power.

3 Wang'ombe Kariuki & Rafe Mazer, *Digital Platforms and Competition Policy in the African Continental Free Trade Area*, (May, 2024).

that these public interest interventions present optimal market results. On the positive side, the uneven development creates opportunities for the upcoming agencies to learn from the more mature agencies, offering African solutions and approaches to African competition regulation problems.

8. A quick review of the laws, both at national and regional level, depicts a general motivation to enact regimes[4] with the objective, inter alia, of promoting and safeguarding effective competition, fostering national and international competitiveness, support of micro, small, and medium enterprises, promoting economic efficiency, supporting inclusivity including to 'regulate the transfer of economic ownership.'[5]

9. The enforcement of the laws is generally aimed at eliminating the competition risks posed by unilateral and concerted antcompetitive practices. The enforcement is through control of mergers and acquisitions that may result in dominance and the subsequent potential of its abuse. On the other hand, competition agencies enforcement powers include advocacy, informed by market inquiries and investigations targeting concerted and unilateral infractions of anti-competitive practices. Over time, the enforcement scope has been expanding in various economies to include other emerging competition risks such as economic dependence.[6]

10. The most applied assessment criteria in analyzing competition effects have been the substantial lessening of competition (SLC) and public interest criteria (PIC), while tethering it to the ex-post approach. Nonetheless, with increased digitization of markets, informed by the dynamism experienced in this economy, including the need to balance benefits of markets transformation while minimizing competition risks, competition agencies are applying their market inquiry provisions to attend to market failures in these markets, in a faster and non-adversarial process.[7]

11. Most African competition agencies, seem to be increasing overzealousness in the application and interpretation of the PIC *in lieu* of competition concerns to achieve other government economic policies such as employment[8] and inclusivity agenda especially after the Covid-19 pandemic. The COMESA Competition Commission (CCC), in the draft amendments to its competition regulations is also proposing to expand its public interest provisions.[9]

---

4 Kenya, Angola, Mozambique, Zambia, South Africa, COMESA.

5 CCSA Competition Act No. 89 1998, https://www.compcom.co.za/wp-content/uploads/2021/03/Competition-Act-A6.pdf (last visited Oct. 30, 2024).

6 The recent enacted laws such as Mozambique and Angola.

7 See, https://www.cak.go.ke/sites/default/files/USSD%20Service%20Provision%20Market%20Inquiry.pdf. and https://www.compcom.co.za/wp-content/uploads/2024/08/booking-com-and-competition-commission-reach-settlement-on-online-intermediation-platforms-market-inquiry-appeal-1.pdf

8 Joyce Karanja, *Saving Jobs is a Priority for African Competition Authorities*, Bowmans (May 18, 2018), https://bowmanslaw.com/insights/saving-jobs-is-a-priority-for-african-competition-authorities/.

9 Draft COMESA Competition and Consumer Protection Regulations (as amended Nov. 2023), https://comesacompetition.org/wp-content/uploads/2024/01/CCC-Draft-Proposed-Amendments-the-Regulations-shared_stakeholders.pdf (last visited Oct. 30, 2024).

12. As indicated earlier, RECs have created competition agencies to regulate competition at regional level aimed at facilitating regional/cross-border trade integration and to encourage investments. The CCC, with a membership of 21 Member States, has been the most visible and active REC competition agency. The CCC's enforcement of competition regulation has created awareness and is also driving the advocacy initiatives over the last decade of its existence since January, 2013. Although at the initial stage it focused more on mergers regulations, of late it is not only approving mergers with conditions but also directing its efforts to anticompetitive practices infractions.

13. The other RECs agencies, WAEMU and ECOWAS are yet to establish credible enforcement machinery, although ECOWAS has recently developed regulations to operationalize its enforcement, despite the fact they were established over 20 years ago. The East Africa Community Competition Authority was created under the East Africa Competition Act,[10] assented in 2007, with the '… objective of enhancing the welfare of the people in the Community…' The authority has a skeleton staff and it is yet to embark on its enforcement mandate. Nevertheless, it has developed various subsidiary legislation and guidelines to manage mergers analysis, investigations, among others.

14. The African Continental Free Trade Area (ACFTA) came into force in March, 2019 and '… aims at accelerating intra-African trade and boosting Africa's trading position in the global market by strengthening Africa's common voice and policy space in global trade negotiations….' The Agreement establishing the ACFTA is to be actualized through various protocols including the Competition Protocol.[11] The Protocol envisages, among others, the creation of an African continental competition agency by 2034. This creates another layer in competition regulation in the continent and hence the optimal interfacing for the agencies at different levels should be established.

15. The continental agency will have powers to enforce competition, on matters with a *continental dimension,* in regard to mergers approvals, anticompetitive business practices including cartels and AoD. It goes further in providing for the regulation of economic dependence and gatekeeping, which is a novel area in competition regulation across the globe. The Protocol will be guided by regulations which will determine and define the thresholds for dominance, continental dimension matters, market definition, and analysis, including acting as the interface between the National Competition Agencies, Regional Agencies, and the Continental Competition body.

16. The African Competition Forum (ACF)[12] has informed competition regulation in Africa through joint research and capacity-building initiatives since its

---

10 East Africa Competition Act 2006, https://www.eacompetition.org/laws/category/competition-act (last visited Oct. 30, 2024).

11 Draft Protocol to the Agreement Establishing the African Continental Free Trade Area on Competition Policy 2023, https://www.bilaterals.org/IMG/pdf/en_-_draft_afcfta_protocol_on_competition_policy.pdf (last visited Oct. 30, 2024).

12 African Competition Forum (ACF), *About ACF*, https://www.cak.go.ke/acf (last visited Oct. 30, 2024).

establishment in 2014. The ACF is a voluntary informal network to progress regional integration through enforcement of competition policy and law among the forum members. The research is especially on politically sensitive sectors such as agriculture, telecommunications, and airlines. The ACF's main objective is to build capacity to regulate competition and also to inform the removal of government induced regulatory obstacles, through market studies and inquiries.

17. Further, ACF's joint capacity-building initiatives are aimed at not only deepening case analysis but also minimizing individual agency costs, through cooperation. The forum has also been a critical interface with the ICN, leading to more inclusivity at the international competition forums, in terms of the topics discussed but also the panelists representation.

18. Concurrences' Antitrust for Developing and Emerging Economies Conference focus has added a voice, perspective and appreciation to Africa's competition enforcement approach. The forum has managed to minimize the North-South chasm especially in appreciation and deployment of PIC to attend to market failures.

Table 1: Summary of the Sampled Agencies

Country	**Enactment**	**Operational Year**	**Competition Law Amended? (Y/N)**		**Scope**					
				Horizontal Agreements	Vertical Agreements	Abuse Of Dominance	Abuse Of Buyer Power	Abuse Of Economic Dependence	Merger control	Market Inquiry
Angola[13]	2018	2018	N	✔	✔	✔	X	✔	✔	X
COMESA[14]	2004	2013	N	✔	✔	✔	X	X	✔	✔
Kenya[15]	2010	2011	Y	✔	✔	✔	✔	X	✔	✔
Mozambique[16]	2013	2021	N	✔	✔	✔	X	✔	✔	X
South Africa[17]	1998	1998	Y	✔	✔	✔	✔	X	✔	✔
Zambia[18]	1994	1995	Y	✔	✔	✔	X	X	✔	✔

13 See, ARC, https://arc.minfin.gov.ao/PortalARC/#!/controlo-de-concentracoes/decisoes-da-arc (last visited Oct. 30, 2024).

14 COMESA, Competition Regulations (Jan. 25, 2023), https://comesacompetition.org/resources/regulations/comesa-competition-regulations-english/.

15 Competition Act No. 12 2010, https://www.cak.go.ke/sites/default/files/Competition_Act_No._2012_of_2010.pdf (last visited Oct. 30, 2024).

16 Mozambique Law no. 20/2013, https://osall.org.za/docs/2011/03/Mozambique-Competition-Law-10-of-2013-Eng-Unofficial-version-as-at-2-July-2013.pdf (last visited Oct. 30, 2024).

17 CCSA Competition Act No. 89 1998.

18 Zambia Competition and Consumer Protection Act 2010, https://www.ccpc.org.zm/media/policy/CCPC-ACT-2010.pdf (last visited Oct. 30, 2024).

II. Enforcement

19. As depicted in Table 1 above, the commonality provisions under the laws of the sampled competition agencies are horizontal agreements, vertical agreements, abuse of dominance and merger control. It is interesting to note that South Africa and Kenya, which are among the most mature competition regimes in Africa have same provisions, while Mozambique and Angola, Portuguese speaking countries, and relatively younger agencies have the same provisions and have gone further to include regulation in novel areas such as economic dependence. Kenya[19] and CCC have already initiated proposals to expand their capacity to regulate digital economy and platforms.

20. The enforcement approach is diverse but it can be collapsed into two approaches: soft enforcement, and hard enforcement. Market inquiries are the bedrock of the soft enforcement limb. South Africa and Kenya have employed this approach extensively to attend to competition risks in the new economy, which have not been understood fully. The approach has been preferred because it is non-adversarial, consultative and generally targeting removal of regulatory obstacles while at the same time balancing regulatory interventions and motivating innovation.

21. On the other hand, hard enforcement is guided by investigation powers and procedures, under the law. It is usually applied in alleged concerted practice infractions, mainly horizontal actions and unilateral conduct. Investigations are also initiated to unearth gun-jumping in mergers. Merger determinations have also been used to deter market concentration, although this has not been common, but it is on the increase. The CCC in 2023 rejected a merger in some of its Member States,[20] the first rejection since the CCC was established a decade ago.

22. The agencies' enforcement priorities have also been wide-ranging from manufacturing, construction, agriculture, personal preventive equipment/garments (PEPs), telecoms including its infrastructure, and sports advertising industry. This has been resolved with a cocktail of remedies, depending on the provisions of the law, its interpretation, and the process applied, as to whether penalties/fines or settlement, commitment decisions and also the agency's flexibility are implemented, as we shall see in the following section.

23. Competition enforcement through the traditional competition law provisions.

1. Concerted and Unilateral Conduct, the Ultimate *Sin*!

24. The Competition Regulatory Authority of Angola (*L'Autorité de Régulation de la concurrence* (ARC)) in December 2023 imposed a fine of 3.2 percent

---

19 Keyna Competition (Amendment) Bill 2024, https://bowmanslaw.com/wp-content/uploads/2024/06/THE-COMPETITION-AMENDMENT-BILL-2024.pdf (last visited Oct. 30, 2024).

20 CCC Merger Decision (Sept. 2, 2023), https://comesacompetition.org/wp-content/uploads/2022/09/CID-Decision-CCC-MER-09-45-2023_Redacted.pdf.

of Castel Group's turnover,[21] amounting to approximately. USD 129,693, and ordered Castel Group to adopt a competition compliance program on terms acceptable to the ARC.

25. The ARC found that the Castel Group had engaged in recommendation and enforcement of resale price maintenance (RPM) in the channel of the Angolan beverages market. The ARC indicates that enforcement mechanism for the RPM included: (i) threatening to terminate contractual relationships with distributors where distributors were found to charge retailers prices other than the recommended resale price; (ii) sanctioning distributors for on-selling the products to retailers at prices other than the recommended resale price; and (ii) offering distributors a bonus discount of approximately 12 percent for products sold at the recommended resale price.

26. Premised on this, the ARC concluded that distributors were not free to independently determine their commercial policies or to determine the price at which products were sold to retailers.

27. The ARC has a choice of remedial measures to cure competition infringements. These include penalties and commitment decisions which may include developing and adopting a compliance program. This not only shifts the regulatory burden to the regulated but also creates explicit monitoring parameters for the agency. The bonus discount of up to 12 percent offered to parties that sold at recommended price meant that the recommended price was very high and hence deprived the consumers of the benefit of market prices signaled by market forces. The intervention by the ARC, and especially within a year of its operation, reflects the importance of competition enforcement and second, irrespective of the agency's maturity, their interventions are critical in facilitating consumers choice and welfare.

28. The COMESA Competition Commission (CCC) fined the Confédération Africaine de Football (CAF) and beIN Media Group LLC (beIN) USD 300,000 each for breach of the COMESA competition regulations in December, 2023.[22]

29. The CCC ruled that the lack of an open tender process for the award of the pay-tv broadcast rights for CAF competitions resulted in a significant prevention, restriction or distortion of competition within the Common Market. Additionally, the CCC stated that having regard to the fact that the CAF competitions were held annually or bi-annually, the duration of the exclusive beIN agreements was disproportionately long and increased the likelihood of market foreclosure. This is the first matter in which the CCC imposed a financial penalty for an anticompetitive business practice since it was operationalized in 2013.

---

21 *Castel Group fined by the Competition Regulatory Authority*, VERANGOLA (July 28, 2023), https://www.verangola.net/va/en/072023/Trade/36571/Castel-Group-fined-by-the-Competition-Regulatory-Authority.htm.

22 COMESA, Press Release, CAF Fined for Breach of Regional Regulations (Jan. 29, 2024), https://www.comesa.int/caf-fined-for-breach-of-regional-regulations/.

30. It is expected that expunging of exclusivity clauses, which favors only one market and thereby creates monopoly in the relevant market with the concomitant loss of consumer welfare, will ultimately create competition for the market with its resultant benefits.

31. In 2022, The Competition Regulatory Authority of Mozambique (CRA) found the recommendation of rates for driving lessons by driving schools by Associação das Escolas de Condução de Moçambique (AECOMO) tantamount to fixing prices in breach of prohibitions against agreements and decisions of associations of undertakings directly or indirectly fixing prices.[23] Although this was found to be a horizontal agreement, CRA issued an interim measure/cease-and-desist order ordering the immediate suspension of the prices.

32. The CRA chose not to apply any fine, stating that the prices in question had not been implemented and the association cooperated with the CRA during the administrative procedure. The CRA nevertheless expressly warned the association to refrain from further anticompetitive practices under penalty of incurring severe sanctions. Prohibited horizontal agreements are punishable by a fine of up to 5 percent of the infringing companies' annual turnover.

33. It is interesting to note that cartel infringements attract 5 percent of the annual turnover, compared to the other countries which apply a 10 percent penalty. Also, it is defensible if price recommendations have not been actualized and cooperation is also a defense.

34. One year after the operationalization of the Competition Act in Kenya, the Competition Authority of Kenya (CAK) issued an advisory opinion to the Tea Board of Kenya (TBK), the sector regulator. CAK advised the sector regulator to revise a provision under the Tea Act that provided that for any new entrant in the growing and processing of tea, the incumbent/s had a right to object or accept their entry. A new entrant, Njeru Industries (NI) alleged that Kenya Tea Development Agency (KTDA), Michimikuru Tea Factory Ltd, Kiegoi Tea Factory Co. Ltd, and Igembe Tea Factory Co. Ltd were jointly restricting market entry by opposing the construction of a Specialty Tea Factory by NI.

35. Cognizant that the 'no objection' provision was anchored in an existing statute governing the sector, CAK applied its advisory mandate. The case was resolved on the basis that the tea growing and processing market is contestable and hence more investors should be licensed.

36. The advisory opinion pursuant to this matter informed the liberalization of the growing and processing of the market for specialty teas in Kenya.[24]

---

23 *Legal alert: Mozambique: First Infringement Decisions of the Competition Regulatory Authority*, MDR Advogados (Aug. 10, 2022), https://insights.afriwise.com/blog/legal-alert-mozambique-first-infringement-decisions-of-the-competition-regulatory-authority.

24 *Creating Kenya's Purple Tea Market – Markets and Competition Policy in Action*, World Bank Grp. (Aug. 29, 2017), https://www.worldbank.org/en/news/feature/2017/08/29/creating-kenyas-purple-tea-market---markets-and-competition-policy-in-action.

37. The opening up of the tea sector, did not only increase investments through entry of four new investors but also increased consumers' choice through availability of specialty tea, created employment of approximately 2,500 people, and also enhanced farmers' earnings (generally small scale farmers), through increased producer prices for the specialty tea compared to orthodox tea. This intervention, expounds the benefits of a flexible competition law in terms of approach and remedial measures alive to the realities of markets, especially the historically controlled and favored sectors by the government through sector regulators.

38. In 2021, Zambia's Competition and Consumer Protection Commission (Commission) fined Lafarge Zambia plc (Lafarge) and Mpande Limestone Ltd (Mpande) 10 percent of their annual turnovers in 2019 and 2020, following findings that these companies, together with Dangote Cement Zambia Ltd (Dangote), fixed prices and divided markets in the local cement industry.[25]

39. The investigation was triggered by the sustained increase in prices of cement. The investigations concluded that the parties shared price adjustment proposals seeking approval for price changes before the implementation date and in some cases before they were approved by their respective management. The exchange of commercially sensitive information on future prices and rebates demonstrated that there was a 'meeting of minds.'

40. Cement is a critical, major and non-substitutable input in the construction industry, from construction of roads and homes, to public utilities. These factors also act as drivers on the other sectors of the economy. Hence, this intervention extinguished distortion of the cement prices by about 90 percent from the market prices and mitigated the snowballing effect it would have ignited to the whole economy.

2. Controlling Concentration, through Mergers

41. The CCC prohibited Amsterdam-based AkzoNobel N.V.'s (AkzoNobel's) acquisition of the decorative coatings business of Kansai Plascon Africa Ltd (Kansai) in Eswatini, Zambia, and Zimbabwe. The merger was prohibited based on a substantial lessening of competition. This is the first merger case to be prohibited by the CCC since it became operational in 2013.[26] In addition, the CCC has penalized parties for gun-jumping.[27] The CAK has never rejected a merger but it has also penalized parties for gun-jumping in various instances. The CAK has also been applying its PIC in approving mergers with conditions.

25 Zambia Summary of Cement Cartel Case in South Central Africa, https://unctad.org/system/files/information-document/ccpb_Summary_Cement_Cartel_Case_South_Central__Africa_Zambian_en.pdf (last visited Oct. 30, 2024).

26 Joyce Karanja & Xolani Nyali, *COMESA: Competition Commission partially prohibits AkzoNobel's acquisition of Kansai Plascon*, Bowmans (Sept. 4, 2023), https://bowmanslaw.com/insights/comesa-competition-commission-partially-prohibits-akzonobels-acquisition-of-kansai-plascon/.

27 Nazeera Mia & Tamara Dini, *COMESA: Penalty Imposed for Failure to Timeously Notify a Proposed Merger*, Bowmans (Sept. 7, 2021), https://bowmanslaw.com/insights/comesa-penalty-imposed-for-failure-to-timeously-notify-a-proposed-merger/.

The conditions include retention of employees and also support to SMEs. This case applied in the acquisition of a controlling stake in Almasi Beverages Ltd by Coca-Cola Sabco (East Africa) Ltd, subject to several conditions[28] where Coca-Cola Sabco was ordered to reserve 25 percent, of the coolers it supplies the small retail shops, to beverages supplied by its SME competitors.

42. The Competition Tribunal (Tribunal) of South Africa concurred with the Competition Commission of South Africa (CCSA) and issued an order prohibiting the proposed merger involving Akzo Nobel N.V.'s (AkzoNobel) acquisition of the majority of the issued ordinary shares of Kansai Plascon Africa Ltd (KPAL) and all the issued ordinary shares of Kansai Plascon East Africa (Pty) Ltd (KPEA) from Kansai Paint Co. Ltd (Kansai Paint). It found that the transaction would likely result in a substantial prevention or reduction of competition in the market for the manufacture and supply of decorative coatings. According to the Commission, the merger would combine the largest and second-largest manufacturers of decorative coatings, i.e. the Dulux and Plascon brands manufactured by AkzoNobel and KPAL respectively.[29]

3. Collaboration in Enforcement, through Market Inquiries

43. As highlighted above, African competition agencies have been collaborating in conducting studies under the African Competition Forum (ACF). The ACF conducted a market inquiry, the Cross-Country Study on International Roaming Charges[30] on cost of mobile phone call roaming. The objective was to appreciate the market structure, identify state imposed regulatory obstacles, and the regulatory setting of the telecommunications industry in some COMESA economies, specifically DRC, Egypt, Kenya, Uganda, and Zambia, with a particular focus on the determination of roaming charges that impact on regional trade and tourism. The study also aimed to identify the competition concerns and policy recommendations aimed at promoting competition in the telecommunications sector.

44. The mobile services market in the Common Market was dominated by MTN, Vodafone, Orange, and Airtel. These four MNOs operated in 13 of the 21 Member States of the Common Market, accounting for about 75.7 percent of the total population. Competition enforcement was embedded by some sector regulators despite the fact that all the countries had operational competition agencies save for DRC and Uganda.

---

28 CAK, *Proposed Acquisition of a Controlling Stake in Almasi Beverages Limited by Coca-Cola Sabco (East Africa) Ltd*, https://cak.go.ke/sites/default/files/2019-10/CAK%20Decision%20on%20Proposed%20Acquisition%20of%20a%20Controlling%20Stake%20in%20Almasi%20Beverages%20Ltd%20by%20Coca-Cola%20Sabco%20(East%20Africa)%20Limited.pdf (last visited Oct. 30, 2024).

29 COMESA, *Notice of Inquiry into the Proposed Merger involving AkzoNobel N.V, Kansai Plascon East Africa Proprietary Limited and Kansai Plascon Africa Ltd*, (2022), https://comesacompetition.org/notice-of-inquiry-into-the-proposed-merger-involving-akzonobel-n-v-kansai-plascon-east-africa-proprietary-limited-and-kansai-plascon-africa-limited/

30 ACF, Cross-Country Study on International Roaming Charges, https://www.compcom.co.za/wp-content/uploads/2023/08/ACF-roaming-Study-Final-Book-print-3.pdf (last visited Oct. 30, 2024).

45. The cost of roaming for subscribers in the countries under examination was high. However, MNOs with extensive networks within the Common Market charged much lower prices compared to other MNOs for subscribers' roaming using partner operators in their network, such as Airtel and Vodafone. Countries with special regional or bilateral arrangements for roaming enabled their consumers to benefit from lower roaming costs. There was lack of transparency in wholesale agreements between MNOs and their roaming partners, with prices influenced by the volume of roaming traffic. Additionally, the demand for roaming services was inelastic, and the market was characterized by high barriers to entry. Consumers lacked countervailing power, leading to a lack of effective competition in the market. These factors were identified as potential contributors to the behavior of existing MNOs in the market.

46. Despite new technological developments and the availability of services such as WhatsApp, Messengers, Facetime, and Skype that could offer competition to mobile roaming, their usage was affected by high charges for mobile data roaming, restrictions on use in some countries, and inadequate access to the internet in certain regions.

47. The study recommends governments to encourage entry through relaxing the regulatory barriers to entry such as the issuing of licenses and allocation of spectrum to new market players. Also, governments should encourage the development of infrastructure that increases access to mobile and fixed internet. Such developments are necessary for the increased use of technologies such as WhatsApp, Messenger, Skype, and Facetime among consumers as they provide an alternative to mobile roaming and if well-developed could offer competition to MNOs offering mobile roaming services. In addition, the study recommended that competition authorities should require MNOs to provide greater transparency in their cost structure in providing roaming services, to ascertain the margins attained and reasonableness of the margins. This could ensure protecting consumers from excessive pricing.

48. Competition enforcement in the new frontiers.

A. *Supporting Sustainability – Control of Abuse of Buyer Power*

49. Over the years, the National Competition Agencies (NCAs) have revised their laws to empower them to extinguish risks which affect markets negatively not necessarily extinguishing competition but affecting the supply chain or jeopardizing the sustainability of SMEs in the markets. A good example is informed by the collapse of a major retail stores while owing suppliers and SMEs. The Competition Act of Kenya was revised to have powers to deal with abuse of buyer power.

50. The provisions aim at ensuring the contracts between buyers and suppliers, especially the SMEs, are *fair* in terms of payment terms, rebates, managing

disputes, among others. The CAK has been visible in enforcing these provisions.[31] The CCSA, informed by the provisions under the Kenyan regime, has also expanded its mandate to control abuse of buyer power.

B. *Regulating the Digital Economy*

51. The 2024 ICN Annual Conference in Brazil,[32] depicts that the developed countries competition agencies have moved from mere appreciation of the digital platforms to diving deep into endeavors to regulate artificial intelligence and algorithmic competition. On the other hand, most of the African competition agencies' focus, understandably, is still at the stage of identification of the key risks and formulating solutions, including the regulatory approach while at the same time deepening their existing human and legal capacity. This means there exists a regulatory development chasm not only in regard to priorities but also in the resources to deal with the emerging regulatory issues between the North and the South.

52. Nonetheless, some competition agencies, specifically CAK and CCSA have undertaken successful enforcement interventions in the digital markets, through investigations and market inquiries, leading to securing commitment decisions. For example, CAK ordered the dominant mobile money payment and transfer firm to expunge self-preferencing clauses in its contracts with the Mobile Money Agents. This led to increased competition for the agents leading to more commissions while mobile money transfer fees, especially the lower bands, commonly helpful to the vulnerable members of society were revised downwards.[33] Through market inquiries findings, CCSA has procured some commitments by Booking.com which include the removal of wide and narrow price-parity and '... substantial programme to provide funding... to grow accommodation establishments, activities and experiences provided by small to medium enterprises that are owned by historically disadvantaged persons (HDPs) or... communities.'[34] The removal of the price parities is expected to offer consumers better price options while the funding requirement is aimed at supporting the achievement of the public interest objective of the South African Competition Act.

---

31 CAK, Press Release, The Competition Authority of Kenya Sanctions Majid Al Futtaim Hypermarkets Limited (Carrefour) for Abuse of Buyer Power (Dec. 19, 2023), https://cak.go.ke/sites/default/files/2024-01/PRESS%20RELEASE%20-%20CAK%20Sanctions%20Carrefour%20for%20Abuse%20of%20Buyer%20Power.pdf.

32 ICN Annual Conference (2024), https://icn2024sauipe.cade.gov.br/program/.

33 CAK, 11 Years of Competition Law in Kenya, https://cak.go.ke/sites/default/files/2023-01/11%20Years%20of%20Competition%20Law%20Enforcement%20in%20Kenya_Final.pdf (last visited Oct. 30, 2024).

34 CCSA, Press Release, Booking.com and Competition Commission Reach Settlement on Online Intermediation Platforms Market Inquiry Appeal (Aug. 13, 2024), https://www.compcom.co.za/wp-content/uploads/2024/08/booking-com-and-competition-commission-reach-settlement-on-online-intermediation-platforms-market-inquiry-appeal-1.pdf.

III. Conclusion

53. As highlighted above, Africa has experienced growth in competition enforcement over the last two decades, in the following ways:

   - Promulgation of competition laws, at national and regional levels and expanding to continental level. As Buthe & Kigwiru note[35] 'competition law used to be very uncommon in Africa, but in the last two to three decades has rapidly spread throughout most of the continent.' Specifically, the number of countries with competition laws has grown from three in the late 80s early 90s to the current 42 laws.

   - Not only has the number of NCAs increased but also competition agencies to support competition at Regional Economic Communities such as East Africa Community, COMESA, ECOWAS and WAEMU have been established. The ACFTA is in the process of establishing a continental competition authority. The ACFTA will be actualized under the *acquis principle* and therefore the current NCAs, RECs will be interfaced through a correct framework with the authority at continental level in order to manage information sharing and coordinate investigations.

54. The ICN, OECD, UNCTAD and Concurrences outputs have greatly influenced the contents of these African competition laws. It is evident these outputs have shaped the laws. However, the subsequent revisions have largely been influenced by local national needs. Kenya and South Africa are classic examples of how amendments have been driven by the need to attend to larger public interests using competition law.

   - The laws have also expanded in terms of the provisions and scope. We have experienced extension of mandate beacons to encompass non-traditional competition mandates such as control of abuse of buyer power, including vigorous implementation of public interest provisions especially on protecting the sustainability of SMES. These provisions were applied successfully during the Covid-19 pandemic period to ensure continued supply and accessibility of the essentials.

   - Enforcement has progressed from mergers control and advocacy to complex and the more demanding enforcement terrains of cartels and abuse of dominance. Competition agencies in Africa, just as in the Global North, have also started focusing on regulating the emerging areas such as the digital economy. This is being established through building of human capacity and critical mass including MoUs to manage cooperation and collaboration.[36]

35 Tim Buthe & Vellah Kedogo Kigwiru, *The Spread of Competition Law and Policy in Africa: A Research Agenda*, African J. Int'l Econ. L. (Dec. 18, 2020), https://papers.ssrn.com/sol3/papers.cfm?abstract_id=3901690.

36 Joint Statement of the African Heads of Competition Authorities Dialogue on Regulation of Digital Markets (Feb. 8, 2023), https://comesacompetition.org/wp-content/uploads/2023/02/Joint-Statement-of-the-Africa-Heads-of-Competition-Dialogue-08-Feb-2023-Cairo83561.pdf.

- There is increased cooperation in areas of research through the ACF, bilateral MoUs to inform capacity-building while the CCC is taking a leading role in advancing advocacy initiatives among its 21 Member countries. This is expected to lead towards convergence, of case analysis, and law in the future. African competition agencies participation in international forums including CAK and CCSA being members of ICN Steering Group Committee has created a dependable path towards ICN outputs in the continent.

55. As highlighted in this chapter, competition enforcement has opened up markets in key sectors such as agriculture in Kenya, supported the achievement of the inclusivity agenda in South Africa, blocked increased cement prices in Zambia hence helping the population to meet one of their basic needs, and housing, at affordable costs. Competition plays a role in enhancing regional integration and trade ,through minimized roaming charges in the COMESA. In addition, the protection of consumers from RPM in Angola of more than 12 percent, ensured the consumers' welfare was increased.

56. These highlighted developments place Africa on a trajectory path in competition enforcement, albeit some challenges remain with regard to speed, however, this may due to resources constrains, contradicting national government policies leading to creation or maintenance of regulatory obstacles, the need to balance the transformative benefits of digital economy while minimizing potential competition risks, while at the same time aligning their enforcement priorities with their government's national economic agenda.

Competition Law in Need for Speed*

Andreas Heinemann
University of Zurich

1. According to widespread opinion, competition law is not up to the challenges of the digital economy because undesirable developments happen faster than competition law can correct them. This may be the case, for example, if anti-competitive behavior cannot be stopped before markets have tipped and the winner has taken it all. Even if competition persists, the rent of anticompetitive behavior may be higher than the sanctions since fines are not necessarily linked to illegal gains, and in many jurisdictions, private enforcement has to be further developed so that an efficient breach of competition law is still possible. In any event, the general principle is that damages should better be prevented than repaired. And this is where competition law in its current shape shows deficiencies.

2. In the EU, a completely new body of law is supposed to fix these shortcomings. The Digital Markets Act (DMA), proposed by the European Commission, is supposed to introduce a specific regulation for gatekeeper platforms. In spite of the emergence of conglomerate ecosystems, markets shall remain contestable and fair. The instrument to achieve this goal is *ex ante* regulation that – in contrast to traditional competition law enforced *ex post* – intervenes before harmful behavior is enacted. The new platform regulation is based on a system of notification and designation and establishes a list of specific obligations that are much more detailed than the examples given in many jurisdictions for the abuse of a dominant position. The overall goal of the new mechanism is to guarantee immediate compliance. Behind this is the assessment that classical competition law often comes into play

* This article has been previously published in Concurrences, and it might have been edited for clarity and cohesion. Andreas Heinemann, Competition law in need for speed, November 2021, Concurrences N° 4-2021, Art. N° 102814, pp.2-4.

too late. Therefore, straightforward rules shall make it possible to intervene more quickly. The new rules are not supposed to replace existing competition rules but to complement them.

I. The duration of procedures as a general problem of competition law

3. While the DMA is a promising proposal to limit market concentration and to guarantee contestability in the digital economy, the underlying problem is of a more general nature and not restricted to specific economic sectors. In many jurisdictions, competition law procedures take too much time. This is a threat not only to the effectiveness of competition policy and its reputation by the public, but to the legitimacy of the economic system in general. Without effective competition, the market economy cannot achieve its goals satisfactorily, neither optimal factor allocation nor the generation of innovation. Excessively long procedures prevent the swift restoration of competition and impair the deterrent effect of sanctions. Of course, the reasons for long procedures may be manifold, for example, the lack of resources, the intricacy of procedural steps or the duration of court proceedings. However, it is often overlooked that the design of substantive and procedural law in itself can also be responsible for lengthy procedures.

II. Form-based and effects-based elements

4. Starting in the US and inspired by the Chicago School, competition law has been consistently based on economic analysis. The more economic approach has been adopted in many other jurisdictions including the EU, albeit not always to the same extent. Even in US antitrust law, the effects-based approach has not completely eliminated form-based elements. For example, hardcore cartels remain subject to a per se ban. The US Supreme Court has given the reason for the necessity of per se prohibitions in *Northern Pacific Railway Company v. US* (1958): An "*incredibly complicated and prolonged economic investigation*" is not indicated if economic experience tells us that the behavior in question lacks "*any redeeming virtue*." Hence, in order to avoid unnecessary procedural costs and delays, the analysis of effects is dispensable in cases where pernicious effects on competition follow from the form of the behavior. This is an important insight: A comprehensive economic analysis has to take into consideration not only substantive law but also enforcement costs. For the same reason, EU competition law distinguishes between restrictions by object and by effect. If an agreement "*reveals in itself a sufficient degree of harm to competition*," it is "*not appropriate to assess its effects*" (ECJ, 26 November 2015, *Maxima Latvija*, case C-345/14, pt 20).

The deeper reason for form-based elements is therefore precisely an economic one: Effective competition can only be maintained if enforcement costs remain manageable and procedures do not take too long. In EU competition law, coherent results are achieved because the efficiency justification always applies, also with respect to restrictions by object.

5. With respect to unilateral behavior, the proper balance between form-based and effects-based elements has not been found yet. In the EU, the *Intel* case on conditional rebates is the most prominent example. The case started with the formal complaint of the main competitor in 2000, followed by the decision of the European Commission in 2009, of the General Court in 2014 and of the European Court of Justice (ECJ) in 2017, which remanded the case to the General Court where it is still pending. The ECJ has basically requested a stronger substantiation of foreclosure effects. It has to be emphasized that the *Intel* case does not raise new questions of the digital economy (as it is the case for example in some of the *Google* cases) but regards a classic problem of competition law, i.e., fidelity rebates granted by dominant firms. Hence, the long duration of the procedure is not based on latest developments that make completely new approaches necessary. It is rather due to the uncertainties concerning the right balance between form-based and effects-based elements in dominance cases. It is obvious that procedural durations of more than two decades miss the purpose of competition law enforcement.

6. As already mentioned, the idea behind the DMA is to escape from the difficulties of traditional competition law by listing specific obligations applying to designated gatekeepers. While the obligations in Article 5 of the DMA proposal are self-executing, the obligations in Article 6 DMA have to be further specified. From a competition law perspective, both groups of rules are to be qualified as form-based. Apparently, exaggerations of the effects-based approach have led to an unsatisfactory situation that has to be fixed by new rules based on a radically different approach. The DMA particularly stresses that the new rules – while providing for some flexibility in exceptional circumstances – renounce on an assessment of effects and even on an efficiency defense. Thus, the discontent with the cumbersome and lengthy procedures in traditional competition law has led to an initiative that makes the pendulum swing in the direction of a pure form-based approach. This is in radical contrast to the decades-long efforts in favor of a more economic method of analysis. In our view, such pendulum swings could be avoided if a better balance of form-based and effects-based elements were sought from the outset. In particular, the category of restrictions by object for particularly dangerous forms of behavior should also be introduced into the prohibition of abusive behavior by dominant firms. The goal is not to take an "object shortcut" but to complete the economic analysis by including enforcement costs and duration.

III. Interim measures

7. Besides a rebalancing in substantive law, competition law procedures could be accelerated by more frequent use of interim measures. In many jurisdictions, such measures are in principle available. But they are rarely used in practice. In the EU for example, interim measures imposed on Broadcom in 2019 have been the first example since the interim measures imposed on IMS Health in 2001 (successfully challenged in court). The *Broadcom* case demonstrates the potential of interim measures: One year after the adoption of interim measures, the procedure was closed by commitments restoring competition. As in the *Intel* case, the focus was on a well-known group of cases – namely, exclusivity arrangements by a dominant firm. However, the outcome was completely different. Whereas the *Intel* case is still pending, the competition law problem could be swiftly solved in *Broadcom*.

8. Of course, interim measures do not bar parties from lodging an appeal (see *IMS Health*). But they may create an incentive to find a quick and sustainable solution (*Broadcom*). The legal prerequisites should be adapted to the important role of interim measures. As noted by the Furman Report, the requirements for interim measures should be designed in a way that makes interim measures more practicable. For this purpose, the preventive character of interim measures has to be kept in mind, and hindsight biases have to be avoided. Certainly, legal cultures are different when it comes to interim measures. It will therefore be important to compare the different experiences in the world in order to improve the practicability of interim measures. The OECD Competition Committee could play a major role in this respect as always when it comes to the search for best practices on a global level.

IV. Perspectives

9. Lengthy procedures may cause irreparable damage to competition and therefore constitute a risk for the efficacy of competition law at large. A basic condition for speedy procedures is certainly that competition authorities and courts are adequately equipped and that the enforcement mechanism is appropriately shaped. This is not sufficient, though. Substantive law and procedural instruments have to be designed in a way that does not inhibit speedy proceedings. The discussion on the effects-based vs. form-based approach has not led to a satisfying result. Exaggerations of the effects-based analysis are responsible for protracted procedures. This problem has become most apparent in the digital economy. In the EU, the DMA is a promising project to guarantee the contestability of markets in timely procedures. At the same time, it must be borne in mind that small or medium-sized jurisdictions do not have the capacity to set up a completely new system that requires significant personal and material resources. In these jurisdictions, the number of employees of

the entire authority is often smaller than the staff that will be responsible for the application of the DMA alone.

10. This makes it particularly clear that a new platform regulation does not obviate the need for a better articulation of traditional competition law. Finding the right mix between form-based and effects-based elements does not contradict the economic approach but follows from it. Moreover, it would speed up procedures with respect not only to the digital economy but to all economic sectors. The better balancing of substantive law should be complemented by appropriate procedural instruments. An example is the availability of interim measures, not only in theory but also in practice. All measures together have a common goal: Competition law should ensure good solutions in good time. Otherwise, it will lose its importance and will be gradually superseded by specific regulations that are more effective and can intervene more quickly. Given the fundamental importance of competition law for the market economy, the resulting loss of orientation should definitely be avoided.

Bureaucratic Politics in China's Antitrust Enforcement*

Angela Zhang**
King's College London

1. In a recent paper, I investigated Chinese bureaucratic politics in-depth in order to analyse how these dynamics affect the outcome of antitrust enforcement in China. Bureaucratic politics are ubiquitous. Why do they matter particularly in the Chinese context? The answer lies in the quality of judicial supervision of administrative behaviour. China's Administrative Litigation Law of 1989, which allows citizens to bring lawsuits against government agencies, has not proven to be effective for the establishment of rule of law in China. Indeed, since the enactment of the Anti-Monopoly Law (AML) in 2008, no single appeal has been lodged against any antitrust enforcement agency in a Chinese court. This absence of judicial review thus turns administrative enforcement of the AML into what is essentially a political process. Therefore the study of the bureaucratic structure, the policy process, as well as the incentives and the constraints faced by the enforcement agencies becomes essential to understanding the enforcement outcome.

2. While Chinese enforcement agencies have not been subject to judicial oversight, it would be naïve to conclude that they are free from any constraints and thus can enforce the AML at will. The Chinese Communist Party (CCP), which maintains supreme authority over every apparatus of the country, has established an

* This article has been previously published in Concurrences, and it might have been edited for clarity and cohesion. Angela Huyue Zhang, Bureaucratic politics in China's antitrust enforcement, May 2014, Concurrences N° 2-2014, Art. N° 65564.

** Lecturer in Competition Law & Trade, King's College London. This foreword is a summary of my article "Bureaucratic Politics and China' Anti-Monopoly Law" (2014) 47 Cornell Intl LJ <https://scholarship.law.cornell.edu/cilj/vol47/iss3/6/> accessed 1 November 2024.

elaborate control mechanism to govern its huge bureaucracy. For instance, political scientists have long observed a method of decision-making called "delegation by consensus" within Chinese government bureaucracy.[1] At each government bureaucratic level, agency representatives make decisions by a rule of consensus. If they all agree, the decision is automatically ratified. Otherwise the decision will be referred to authorities at a higher level, who will either step in to make the decision or allow the matter to be dropped until consensus can be reached. The rationale behind such a procedure is two-fold: First, it provides some checks and balances among the agencies. Chinese ministries are organized by either function (e.g. education, culture, finance) or economic sector (e.g. agriculture, telecommunication, transportation). This complex structure gives virtual representation to all those economic groups and interests on whom the CCP leadership depends for political support. Second, it alleviates information asymmetry between the superior and the subordinate agency. When consensus can't be reached, the issue is pushed to the top and the superior can exploit the information advantage it obtains through different subordinate agencies.

3. Upon extensive interviews with government officials working at central ministries, I realized that Chinese antitrust enforcement is no exception in this regard. For instance, it has been widely known among experienced practitioners that the Anti-Monopoly Bureau at the Ministry of Commerce (MOFCOM) regularly confers with other government departments and organizations during merger review, particularly those bureaus in charge of industrial policy at the National Development and Reform Commission (NDRC) and the Ministry of Industry and Information Technology. While this consulting practice has struck many outsiders as "unusual", it is in fact a customary procedure for economic policy and decision-making for central ministries. Since large merger transactions often have an impact on the competitive structure of domestic industries, a merger review will inevitably involve the functions of other government departments such as those responsible for industrial policy or those in charge of overseeing certain economic industry sectors. Accordingly, even if the consulting process constrains MOFCOM's discretion to some extent, it also mitigates the risk that a decision will be problematic – that it will negatively impact the interests of the other government agencies at play.

4. One direct consequence of the requirement of consensus building within government bureaucracy is that power becomes fragmented when it comes to policymaking and implementation.[2]

5. As each of the three main antitrust enforcement agencies is nested within ministries working like large conglomerates, they have divergent responsibilities and missions. The endless struggle among these government actors for

---

1 See e.g., Susan L Shirk, *The Political Logic of Economic Reform in China* (University of California Press 1993) 116–117.

2 See generally Kenneth Lieberthal and Michel Oksenberg, *Policy Making in China: Leaders, Structures, and Processes* (Princeton University Press 1988).

control of policy therefore accounts for the heterogeneity of China's antitrust enforcement outcome. For instance, in recent years that NDRC has appeared particularly aggressive in tackling price-related behaviour in certain industrial sectors. So far it has investigated a number of high-profile cases and imposed remedies and hefty fines on a variety of influential economic actors. To understand what has motivated NDRC to establish such an enforcement priority, we need to closely examine its mission and incentive structure. The predecessor of NDRC was the State Planning Commission, which was primarily in charge of macroeconomic management and industrial planning. Although it went through several restructurings and reorganizations over the years, it continues to rely on direct government intervention to solve most economic problems. This is not surprising since promoting government intervention is directly related to its own bureaucratic interests.

6. In recent years, NDRC has started to appreciate the AML as a powerful tool for fulfilling its original mission of "price control", but without being seen as in contradiction with the market. Indeed, almost all the large cases NDRC has brought (or actively cooperated with local authorities to bring) in recent years have involved basic daily consumption goods that have been subject to its price monitoring, including pharmaceutical products, dairy products, liquor, broadband access and consumer electronics.

7. Meanwhile, the central government's attempt to use the AML as a tool to police the internal common market seems unlikely to be successful. While local enforcement agencies clearly desire to increase their antitrust policy control, they are faced with constraints imposed by local governments, whose preference takes priority over that of the central ministries. As regional governments compete fiercely for economic growth within their own jurisdictions, they have the incentives to erect trade barriers and ban imports from other regions. This has created market conditions conducive to the rise of monopolies at the local level, which are often deemed local champions and are important contributors to local GDPs. Accordingly, unless central ministries intervene, the reliance on local enforcement is unlikely to be effective in tackling local monopolies, particularly those that are supported by strong political ties with local governments.

8. Upon opening the black box of the political decision-making process, we find that antitrust enforcement in China is in fact a highly pluralistic process involving officials from various central government ministries and local government agencies with overlapping functions and divergent missions and objectives. Their incentive structure and the formal and tacit rules of the Chinese bureaucracy shape the enforcement outcome of the AML. Indeed, in the absence of effective judicial supervision, Chinese government agencies have essentially monopolized the public enforcement of the AML and subjected it to an elusive political process. This also suggests that without addressing the fundamental institutional problem – the lack of an independent judiciary – any proposal to reform AML enforcement is likely to generate only cosmetic results.

Possible Reform of Competition Law: Food for Thought to Improve the Interplay between Merger Control and Other EU Policies*

PASCAL BELMIN**
Airbus

1. The debate over the need to reform European competition law rules has been developing and intensifying over the last months. It has notably been fuelled by a clear evolution in the EU institutions' perception of the challenges facing the Union and of the appropriate answers.

2. The official declaration adopted in December 2018 by no less than 18 EU Member States at ministerial level (the Friends of Industry, among which France, Germany, Austria, Spain, the Netherlands, and Italy) provides some particularly clear and relevant statements, which also show that this thinking line is by no means limited to France or Germany.

3. The declaration made it clear that the

> "European Union must build a European industrial policy that encourages the creation of major economic players capable of facing global competition on equal terms while protecting European consumers. While the major powers do not hesitate to defend their national champions, Europe must take account, in its competition policy, the evolution

* This article has been previously published in Concurrences, and it might have been edited for clarity and cohesion. Pascal Belmin, Possible reform of competition law: Food for thought to improve the interplay between merger control and other EU policies, September 2019, Concurrences N° 3-2019, Art. N° 90980.

** Vice-President, Head of EU Regulatory Affairs, Airbus Group, Brussels. This contribution is personal. Views and opinions expressed belong solely to the author.

> of the global competitive environment in terms of investment, trade and industry".

4. The declaration further stressed the need for the EU to

> "carry out by the first half of 2020 a comparative assessment of competition policies and State aid control mechanisms of third countries with a view to (…) [e]xplore the adaptations to be made to European competition policy so that it allows European players of international scale to emerge [and] [s]trengthen rules in free trade agreements with the aim to limit subsidies and anticompetitive practices by third countries, which can be harmful to European companies".

5. The European Council (heads of state or government level) was also very clear in the conclusions reached further to its 22 March 2019, summit:

> "[I]n view of the importance of a globally integrated, sustainable and competitive industrial base, the Commission is invited to present, by the end of 2019, a long-term vision for the EU's industrial future, with concrete measures to implement it. It should address the challenges European industry faces, touching upon all relevant policy areas".

6. "[F]air competition should be ensured within the Single Market and globally, both to protect consumers and to foster economic growth and competitiveness, in line with the long-term strategic interests of the Union. We will continue to update our European competition framework to new technological and global market developments. The Commission intends to identify before the end of the year how to fill gaps in EU law in order to address fully the distortive effects of foreign state ownership and state-aid financing in the Single Market".

7. EU Member States expressed in the abovementioned Friends of Industry declaration the need to "mobilise all European policies contributing to industrial competitiveness", which "should incorporate: policies in the areas of competition, research and innovation, digital, defence, the Single Market, the elaboration as well as the promotion of European norms and standards, regional development, international trade, energy and sustainable development, taxation and skills".

8. This is fully echoed by the Council of European Council 27 May 2019 conclusions on an "EU Industrial Policy Strategy: a Vision for 2030", reiterate "the call by the European Council for a strong economic base that is of key importance for Europe's prosperity and competitiveness, and for its role on the global stage, which should be achieved through an integrated approach addressing the current and emerging global, technological, security and sustainability challenges and connecting all relevant policies and dimensions". In this perspective, the Council

> "stresses the importance of mobilising all relevant EU and Member State policies and instruments, applying the better regulation principles

and continue the work on fostering an innovation and growth-friendly regulatory environment and ensuring fair competition within the Single Market and globally, both to protect consumers and to foster economic growth and competitiveness, and continuing to update our European competition framework to new technological and global market developments".

I. A Revitalised EU Political Agenda on Strategic Issues

9. These are not just words. These statements concur with the acceleration and intensification of the political and regulatory EU production, particularly on European strategic issues and industrial policy. Among other initiatives, the following very recent examples can be underlined:

   - The emergence of a European Defence Fund, built around the core concept of EU strategic autonomy;
   - The wide EU Strategic Value Chain initiative, a starting point to be further deepened and enlarged;
   - The launch of wide European projects in the field of electrical batteries and microelectronics;
   - Important achievements and political statements regarding the space sector industrial policy, such as the partial adoption of the EU Space Programme Regulation and the May 2019 Council conclusions on "Space as an enabler";
   - The adoption of the EU regulation on screening of foreign direct investments;
   - The adoption of an updated EU Blocking Statute Regulation in August 2019, in response to the US withdrawal from the Iran-related JCPOA agreement;
   - The adoption of numerous policies and regulations relating to the Digital Single Market;
   - The development of a proposal of International Procurement Instrument, in relation to public procurement (not adopted yet).

10. EU institutions have therefore evolved over the last months, both in their perception of and attitude towards external challenges and in their commitment to adopt EU policies and regulations on particularly strategic issues – including but not limited to industrial policy.

11. Against this background, any reform of competition policy should be aimed at improving and deepening the alignment and consistency between competition policy and other EU policies.

12. As further explained below, one tool already exists, which would constitute a very relevant source of inspiration for the field of merger control: the State aid concept of Important Projects of Common European Interest (IPCEI).

13. The proposal set out below would by no means exclude other consistent ideas, for instance seeking to better factor in longer-term perspectives, subsidies received by non-EU competitors, or to bring simplification or flexibility (for instance regarding remedies) to existing processes.

14. In essence, the IPCEI regime explicitly allows the Commission to factor in its competition analysis positive contributions that a given project brings

15. "in a concrete, clear and identifiable manner to one or more Union objectives [with] a significant impact on competitiveness of the Union, sustainable growth, addressing societal challenges or value creation across the Union. The project must represent an important contribution to the Union's objectives, for instance by being of major importance for the Europe 2020 strategy, the European Research Area, the European strategy for KETs, the Energy Strategy for Europe, the 2030 framework for climate and energy policies, the European Energy Security Strategy, the Electronics Strategy for Europe, the Trans-European Transport and Energy networks, the Union's flagship initiatives such as the Innovation Union, Digital Agenda for Europe, the Resource Efficient Europe, or the Integrated Industrial Policy for the Globalisation Era" (Commission's 2014 IPCEI Communication).

16. Drawing inspiration from this precedent, the EU Merger Control Regulation could be amended to explicitly allow the Commission to take into account, as efficiencies, positive contributions that a merger transaction could bring to such EU objectives and policies.

17. Such modification would lead to significant benefits:

    - The scope would be clear and defined, since only elements relating to adopted EU rules and policies could be invoked.
    - Focusing on EU policies and regulations would guarantee a strong democratic legitimacy and ensure that EU long-term interests remain centre stage.
    - This would already contribute to better factor in the external competitive landscape and the predicted evolution of industries or sectors, since these elements would normally be well reflected in the EU policies concerned.
    - This would avoid process disruptions and loss of expertise: DG-COMP would remain in charge of the assessment of the merger case, while the parties and other Commission directorates would become explicitly entitled to put forward positive contributions to other EU policies. This would trigger intra-Commission discussions very early on and contribute to forging an iterated and substantiated collegial approach

within the Commission. Appropriate confidentiality obligations or reassurances could be put in place.

- Although it may be true that the existing merger control framework can sometimes prove flexible enough to reach case-by-case solutions which also take into account other EU policies, the existing legal test does not incorporate contributions to the latter. And, ultimately, this test is the only one that EU courts are authorised to rely upon in order to assess the legality of a Commission decision.
- Arguing that a wider welfare concept could already be relied upon in practice to reach a de facto similar result would in our view not be sufficient. Allowing to demonstrate contributions to precisely defined and drafted policies would be much more specific, relevant and respectful of the democratic process having led to the adoption of these policies and regulations.
- Last but not least, this would contribute more generally to placing a stronger emphasis on the analysis of efficiencies, an area which is often regarded as being insufficiently taken into account in the assessment.

18. Of course, the modification of the European Merger Control Regulation could be accompanied by other amendments to lower-level texts, for instance to improve the appraisal of longer-term effects or simplify processes.

II. Some Useful Adaptations to State Aid Rules

19. Looking beyond merger control, a final element could be added with respect to State aid rules.

20. Although the State aid modernisation initiative has already significantly improved the situation, it would appear important to make a specific effort to further facilitate research, development and innovation activities, notably when it comes to close-to-market stages.

21. Similarly, the regime applicable to IPCEIs could be pushed one step further. This could be done by simplifying the process and alleviating requirements, for instance on spillovers and in relation to the counterfactual scenario condition, notably with a view to allow downstream research industrial projects to also be labelled as IPCEIs.

22. This would significantly increase the incentive for Member States to invest jointly rather than separately and to channel their support towards high TRL R&D projects, which would bring strong and concrete contributions to EU objectives and policies.

PART III

Enforcement and Market Regulation

Enforcing Competition Law – Finding the Right Balance between Structure and Effect

ANDREAS MUNDT*
Federal Cartel Office (Bundeskartellamt)

1. The right course of action for competition enforcement has been discussed for decades. Today, cases are spiked with economic and legal hurdles in an ever more complex economy. The debate on how to enforce competition law is in full swing.

2. In Europe, in the early 2000s, the debate centred around the role of economics in applying competition law. At the time, three lost merger prohibitions by DG-COMP marked a turning point as the courts criticised a lack of sound economic reasoning in *Airtours/First Choice*,[1] *Schneider/Legrand*[2] and *Tetra Laval/Sidel*.[3] An international debate triggered a broader rethinking. As a result, the so called "more economic approach" led to a more effects-based antitrust enforcement with a stronger focus on economic principles and economic evidence including the introduction of an as-efficient-competitor test (AEC test) in appropriate cases. The more effects-based approach was never a solo effort by DG-COMP but carried by a broad international debate that more economic assessment was needed in enforcement. Already by that time though, there was an intensive debate

---

* Bundeskartellamt President. Kaiser-Friedrich-Str. 16, 53113 Bonn, Germany, Tel: 0228 94 99 – 0.

1 Judgment of the Court of First Instance of 6 June 2002 in Case T-342/99 *Airtours Plc v Commission of the European Communities* ECLI:EU:T:2002:146.

2 Judgment Court of First Instance of 22 October 2002 in Case T-310/01 *Schneider Electric SA v Commission of the European Communities* ECLI:EU:T:2002:254.

3 Judgment Court of 15 February 2005 in Case C-13/03 P *Commission of the European Communities v Tetra Laval BV* ECLI:EU:C:2005:88.

about the right balance between an economic effects-based approach in an attempt to predict the actual market outcome, and a more structural approach, focusing on the market conditions as such. DG-COMP and the Bundeskartellamt were not always on the same page. The main argument was that focusing too much on effects might risk a less effective enforcement and a general loss of legal certainty. Tools like the AEC test were seen as quite complex, leading to heavy legal and economic obstacles. However, there is also a tension between over and underenforcement. In a nutshell the debate was not so much about if competitive analysis should put greater emphasis on economic effects, instead it was a question of the dose, of how much economic assessment was needed.

3. The challenge is to minimise the risk of incorrect decisions under competition law considering the associated administrative costs (or error costs).[4] For instance, structural or form-based approaches in abuse control attempt to focus on specific behaviours that are considered anticompetitive with little requirement to demonstrate effects. From an economic perspective, this approach increases the risk of so-called type-1 errors (or false positives). On the contrary, an effects-based analysis might lead to more type-2 errors (false negatives) if more resources are required and fewer cases are carried out.[5] A compromise between structure and effect on both ends of the spectrum would be working with strong (but rebuttable) legal presumptions.[6]

I. Where Do We Stand?

4. It seems, the pendulum has been swinging back to a less effects-based approach recently. Antitrust enforcement suffers from long proceedings both in abuse cases and merger control. It has become apparent that cases tend to be highly complex both from a legal and an economic point of view.

5. The European Courts play an important role: In 2000, chip-manufacturer AMD filed a complaint regarding Intel's rebates to computer producers and a retailer. The Commission conducted an AEC test, but the decision did not rely on this test. This seemingly followed a general economic experience that exclusive rebates granted by a dominant company are anticompetitive per se referring

4 Arndt Christiansen and Wolfgang Kerber, "Competition Policy with Optimally Differentiated Rules Instead of 'Per Se Rules vs Rule of Reason'" (2006) 2 J Competition L & Economics 215-244.

5 Rupprecht Podszun and Tristan Rohner, "Making Article 102 TFEU Future-Proof – Learnings from the Past" (24 April 2023) <https://papers.ssrn.com/sol3/papers.cfm?abstract_id=4428170> accessed 29 September 2024. Comments for the European Commission's 2023 Call for Evidence regarding Guidelines on Article 102 TFEU are also quoted in Wagner-von Papp's analysis of the enforcement of Article 102 and the AEC test at the meeting of the Bundeskartellamt's Working Group on Competition Law. See Florian Wagner-von Papp, "Moving away from the AEC Test: 'It is Better to be Vaguely Right Than Exactly Wrong'" (29 September 2023), <www.bundeskartellamt.de/SharedDocs/Publikation/DE/Diskussions_Hintergrundpapier/AK_Kartellrecht_2023_vonPapp.html?nn=294276> accessed 29 September 2024.

6 In the US also referred to as "quick look" – analyses depending on "evidentiary shortcuts", see Herbert Hovenkamp, "The Rule of Reason" (2018) 70 Florida L Rev 121 (direct quotes at 126).

to the *Hoffmann-La Roche* judgment of the Court of Justice of the European Union (CJEU).[7] After the case was referred back by the CJEU,[8] the General Court ruled in 2022 that the AEC test – if conducted – was important evidence when assessing the ability to foreclose and found that the Commission's analysis did not determine the anticompetitive effects. The decision was annulled in part.[9] In October 2024, the CJEU upheld the annulment by the General Court of the Commission's decision.[10] Last year, the Court decided in *Unilever Italia* that the relevance of an AEC test could not be ruled out even in the case of non-pricing practices like exclusivity clauses.[11] This means that if a company provides an AEC analysis, the competition authority cannot disregard that evidence without examining its probative value. The Commission has amended its priority paper to bring it in line with recent case law and has launched the process to adopt guidelines on exclusionary abuse of dominance.[12]

6. The main argument for the introduction of the SIEC (significant impediment to effective competition) test in the EC Merger Regulation in 2004 (later also in the German Competition Act – (*Gesetz gegen Wettbewerbsbeschränkungen* – GWB) was to improve the accuracy and effectiveness of merger control. The SIEC test advances the preceding dominance test which it maintains as a presumptive example. In comparison to the dominance test, it also enables enforcement in cases which do not lead to the creation or strengthening of a dominant market position, but nonetheless to significantly negative effects on competition (so called gap cases). From the Bundeskartellamt's perspective, the SIEC test is a good compromise between a structural and an effects-based approach. On the one hand, by maintaining the dominance test remedial action can largely be based on structural parameters (such as market shares) when the resulting market structure strongly indicates that effective competition cannot be sustained or is already impaired. Enforcement in such cases is further facilitated by strong (rebuttable) legal presumptions (according to Section 18(4)–(6) GWB). On the other hand, in cases where structural parameters are less indicative of the competitive effects, enforcement is still possible based on an economic assessment that finds strong adverse impacts on competition.

7. Only recently, jurisprudence on the application of the SIEC test in gap cases evolved. In the *CK Telecoms* saga, the CJEU in its referral of the case back to the General Court supported the Commission in applying

7 Judgment of the Court of 13 February 1979 in Case 85/76 *F Hoffmann La Roche & Co AG v Commission of the European Communities* ECLI:EU:C:1979:36, para 89.

8 Judgment of the Court of 6 September 2017 in Case C-413/14 P *Intel Corp Inc v European Commission* ECLI:EU:C:2017:632.

9 Judgment of the General Court of 26 January 2022 in Case T-286/09 RENV *Intel Corp Inc v European Commission* ECLI:EU:T:2022:19.

10 Judgment of the Court of 24 October 2024 in Case C-240/22 P | *Commission v Intel Corporation* ECLI:EU:C:2024:915.

11 Judgment of the Court of 19 January 2023 in Case C-680/20 *Unilever Italia Mkt Operations Srl v Autorita Garante della Concorrenza e del Mercato* ECLI:EU:C:2023:33.

12 European Commission Press Release, "Antitrust: Commission Announces Guidelines on Exclusionary Abuses and Amends Guidance on Enforcement Priorities" (27 March 2023) <https://ec.europa.eu/commission/presscorner/detail/en/IP_23_1911> accessed 29 September 2024.

the SIEC test in oligopolistic markets as well as the applicable standard of proof under which the Commission has to show that a SIEC is "more likely than not".[13] It, thus, did not agree with the much disputed ruling of the General Court which set out high standards of proof for the SIEC test in gap cases.

8. In a German case from 2020, which dealt with a merger of retail chains in the furniture sector, the Bundeskartellamt cleared the transaction subject to the condition to disinvest outlets in several regional markets. Following an in-depth examination, it identified unilateral effects leading to a SIEC in some of the many regional markets affected, because the Bundeskartellamt considered the merging parties particularly close competitors in a market for differentiated goods. Following an appeal, the Higher Regional Court in Düsseldorf ruled that the conditions of the clearance were unlawful. In general, the court confirmed the Bundeskartellamt's market definition but adopted a different definition of the market segments and held that a specific large competitor belongs to another market segment. Moreover, in this SIEC case based on unilateral effects, the court defined two general structural thresholds which the Bundeskartellamt decision – according to the court – did not meet: a SIEC based on a theory of harm regarding closeness of competition had to meet an "oligopolistic market structure-test" as well as a "monopolistic segment structure test" (i.e., the merger eliminates a close competitor and no other is left in the market segment).[14] The Federal Court of Justice (BGH) did not grant leave to appeal. The Bundeskartellamt therefore received no clarifying jurisprudence on the application of the SIEC test from the court of last instance.[15] Nevertheless, it gained some important insights from *CK Telecoms* and its reception in German case law with respect to assessing unilateral effects and their complex nature: the CJEU reaffirms that a number of factors are relevant for establishing a SIEC in oligopolistic markets while holding that a SIEC can occur even if the merging parties are not particularly close competitors.[16]

9. Notable developments are taking place in the US as well. With the New Brandeis Movement, calls for structural remedies against monopolies are becoming louder. These calls are resounding in Europe as well. Recently, the Department of Justice (DOJ) and Federal Trade Commission (FTC) updated their Merger Guidelines setting out how the US agencies intend to assess the material test of US merger control. The 2023 Merger Guidelines announce rigorous enforcement standards (to some extent surpassing European enforcement standards), while appearing to turn away from a purely effects-based

---

13 Judgment of the Court of 13 July 2023 in Case C-376/20 P *European Commission v CK Telecoms UK Investments Ltd* ECLI:EU:C:2023:561.

14 OLG Düsseldorf (Higher Regional Court Düsseldorf), Beschluss (Decision) of 9 March 2022 Kart 2/21 (V), paras 60 ff., paras 74 ff. and paras 236 ff.

15 Bundesgerichtshof (BGH, Federal Court of Justice) Beschluss vom 27 Juni 2023, KVZ 33/22.

16 *CK Telecoms*, para 189, see also Bah and Tayar (n 12).

merger control. In particular, market shares and other structural concentration measures are presented as core evidence, while a minor role is ascribed to efficiency claims.[17]

II. Structure and Effect in Practice

10. In the debate between structure and effects, the Bundeskartellamt has always tried to combine the best of both worlds. Over the last two decades, there have been no dramatic changes in posture. The Bundeskartellamt uses economics in a way so that its cases benefit the most from economic assessment. Furthermore, the Bundeskartellamt has always seen and appreciated the opportunity to refine its economic toolkit.

1. Recent Merger Control Examples

- In 2022, the Bundeskartellamt decided that the *acquisition of the OMV petrol station network by EG Group (Esso)* could only be cleared under the condition that 48 service stations be sold to third companies. A central result of the investigation was that there would have been the risk of the merger creating or strengthening a joint dominant position of the leading fuel companies BP/Aral, Shell and EG Group in several regional markets. Besides looking at market shares, the Bundeskartellamt assessed all relevant factors for coordinated effects amongst the key players, including symmetry, stability, market entry barriers, market transparency, effective deterrence and possible outsider reactions considering the actual market behaviour.[18]
- In 2023, the Bundeskartellamt cleared plans by *Theo Müller Group (UTM) to acquire brands and production sites for a number of dairy products from Royal Friesland Campina (RFC)* subject to commitments. For defining the relevant markets, the Bundeskartellamt surveyed market players and conducted an empirical analysis (event analysis). Data on price changes and discounts for specific products were examined to check how consumers respond to them and to find out whether the products are actually substitutable. Separate product markets for rice pudding, fresh dairy drinks and basic dairy drinks were defined. Further investigations had shown that UTM clearly dominates the markets with market shares of over 60% in all three

---

17 US Department of Justice and the Federal Trade Commission, "Merger Guidelines 2023" (18 December 2023). See also FTC and DOJ Press Release, "Federal Trade Commission and Justice Department Release 2023 Merger Guidelines" (18 December 2023) <www.ftc.gov/news-events/news/press-releases/2023/12/federal-trade-commission-justice-department-release-2023-merger-guidelines> accessed 29 September 2024.

18 Bundeskartellamt Press Release, "Acquisition of OMV Petrol Station Network by EG Group (Esso) Cleared under the Condition that 48 Service Stations Be Sold to Third Companies" (11 February 2022) (full decision B8-77/21) <www.bundeskartellamt.de/SharedDocs/Meldung/EN/Pressemitteilungen/2022/11_02_2022_EG_OMV.html> accessed 29 September 2024.

problematic areas. The takeover of Friesland Campina brands, despite adding little market share, would have strengthened Theo Müller's market dominance even further. To address the serious competition concerns, UTM committed itself to selling parts of its business to an independent third party dairy on the one hand and to grant brand licenses on the other.[19]

– In food retailing, the Bundeskartellamt examined the *sale of "Real" retail stores* over recent years in several extensive proceedings (in particular merger projects by EDEKA and Kaufland). It intensively examined the sales and procurement side and used an analysis of loyalty/bonus-card data for defining the geographic markets complemented by a consumer survey to also measure closeness of competition. Several structural criteria were used for capturing unilateral effects in regional markets precisely to the level of postal codes. As a result, the acquisition of a considerable number of stores was prohibited. For the supply-side, "Real" stores with a total food purchase volume of at least EUR 200 million had to be sold to medium-sized food retailers.[20]

2. Navigating Abuse Proceedings

11. Abuse control is clearly one of the difficult challenges in antitrust practice. In recent years, lengthy proceedings as well as subsequent court proceedings have given rise to debates about its complexity, duration and effectiveness. The above-mentioned case *Commission v Intel* goes back to a complaint from the year 2000.[21] This legal battle came to an end, some 24 years later, with a final decision by the CJEU.[22] The Bundeskartellamt's *Facebook* case was initiated in 2016 and the prohibition decision was issued in 2019.[23] Meta appealed the decision, leading to several years of legal proceedings. After successful negotiations about concrete measures to implement the Bundeskartellamt's decision and Meta's withdrawal of the appeal pending before the Düsseldorf Higher Regional

---

19 Bundeskartellamt Press Release, "Following Commitments Theo Müller Group Can Acquire Parts of the Dairy Business of Royal Friesland Campina" (22 February 2023) (full decision B4-90/22) <www.bundeskartellamt.de/SharedDocs/Meldung/EN/Pressemitteilungen/2023/22_02_2023_Mueller_Friesland_Campina.html> accessed 29 September 2024.

20 Bundeskartellamt, "Annual Report 2020/21" (2021) 45 (full decisions in cases B2-83/20 – Kaufland and B2-85/20-EDEKA also published) <https://www.bundeskartellamt.de/SharedDocs/Publikation/EN/Jahresbericht/Jahresbericht_2020-2021.pdf?__blob=publicationFile&v=4> accessed 15 October 2024.

21 Bundeskartellamt, "Guidelines on Article 102 TFEU – New Standards for Abuse Control?" (28 September 2023) Bundeskartellamt Working Group on Competition Law <www.bundeskartellamt.de/SharedDocs/Publikation/EN/Diskussions_Hintergrundpapiere/2023/Working_Group_on_Competition_Law_2023.pdf?__blob=publicationFile&v=2> accessed 29 September 2024.

22 CJEU Press Release, "The Court of Justice upholds the annulment by the General Court of the Commission's decision finding an abuse of a dominant position on the part of Intel and imposing a fine of €1.06 billion on Intel" (24 October 2024) <https://curia.europa.eu/jcms/upload/docs/application/pdf/2024-10/cp240185en.pdf>.

23 Bundeskartellamt, "Case Summary – Facebook, Exploitative business terms pursuant to Section 19(1) GWB for inadequate data processing" (15 February 2019) (full decision B6-22/16) <www.bundeskartellamt.de/SharedDocs/Entscheidung/EN/Fallberichte/Missbrauchsaufsicht/2019/B6-22-16.pdf?__blob=publicationFile&v=3> accessed 29 September 2024.

Court, the proceeding has finally been concluded in 2024.[24] The case also led to the CJEU landmark decision that clarified that competition authorities can also look into a company's compliance with data protection rules in order to determine whether it is abusing its market power.[25] Both German and European competition law include examples of practices by dominant companies that are prohibited (eg discrimination, impairing business opportunities or exploitation). Still, an effects-based analysis can and sometimes must complement a structural or form-based approach to discern abusive conduct from acceptable conduct under competition law (including possible objective justifications as noted in the GWB). An example from the Bundeskartellamt's case practice illustrates how this approach combines both worlds:

12. In 2017, the Bundeskartellamt concluded the abuse proceeding against CTS Eventim, Germany's largest ticketing system operator. It assessed adverse competitive effects caused by exclusive contracts used by CTS Eventim with organisers of live entertainment events and advance booking offices. Both the exclusive agreements of CTS with promoters and advance booking offices had been classified by the Bundeskartellamt as abusive and as such prohibited under competition law.[26] However, the Bundeskartellamt also assessed the actual market foreclosure effect which can be attributed to the exclusivity agreements. In a market characterised by indirect network effects, extensive exclusivity agreements reinforce the foreclosure effect and encourage a general trend towards further monopolisation (so-called tipping).[27] Our approach and the prohibition of specific clauses was later confirmed by the Federal Court of Justice.[28]

III. Dealing with (New) Challenges and Refining our Toolbox

13. As competition agencies we always need to be consistent while dealing with present and future challenges. How fit is our toolbox in dealing with these challenges?

24 Bundeskartellamt, "Case summary – Facebook; Implementation of the Bundeskartellamt's decision of 6 February 2019 (Abusive business terms due to inappropriate data processing)" (10 October 2024) <https://www.bundeskartellamt.de/SharedDocs/Entscheidung/EN/Fallberichte/Missbrauchsaufsicht/2024/B6-22-16.pdf?__blob=publicationFile&v=8> accessed 15 October 2024. See also Bundeskartellamt Press Release, "Facebook proceeding concluded" (10 October 2024) <https://www.bundeskartellamt.de/SharedDocs/Meldung/EN/Pressemitteilungen/2024/10_10_2024_Facebook.html?nn=48916> accessed 15 October 2024.

25 Judgment of the Court 4 July 2023 in Case C-252/21 *Meta Platforms Inc v Bundeskartellamt* ECLI:EU:C:2023:537.

26 Bundeskartellamt, decision of 4 December 2017 B6-132/14-2 *CTS Eventim Exklusivitätsvereinbarungen* <www.bundeskartellamt.de/SharedDocs/Entscheidung/EN/Entscheidungen/Missbrauchsaufsicht/2019/B6-132-14.pdf?__blob=publicationFile&v=4> accessed 29 September 2024.

27 Bundeskartellamt Press Release, "Bundeskartellamt Prohibits Exclusive Contracts between CTS Eventim and Event Organisers and Advance Booking Offices" (4 December 2017) <https://www.bundeskartellamt.de/SharedDocs/Meldung/EN/Pressemitteilungen/2017/04_12_2017_CTS_Exklusivit%C3%A4t.html> accessed 29 September 2024>.

28 Federal Court of Justice (BGH) KVZ 44/19, paras 6-9.

14. The most prominent example is the digital economy where competition authorities and legislators have so far focused on addressing new competition problems mostly in abuse control. The EU Digital Markets Act (DMA) is a new regulatory tool, enforced by the Commission, with norms that are strongly inspired by cases based on competition law. It applies regardless of the effects of the respective conduct on competition on a given market.[29] But needless to say, the enforcement of the DMA is complemented by the enforcement of competition law. Starting in 2021, the Bundeskartellamt has applied Section 19a of the GWB – the extended abuse control for the digital economy.[30] The main purpose of Section 19a is to capture special positions of power and their possible anticompetitive effects on and threats to competition in the area of "digital ecosystems". Whether an undertaking in the digital economy is in a position of "paramount significance for competition across markets" is determined by an overall economic assessment of all circumstances relevant in the individual case. Once the Bundeskartellamt has established that a company holds such a position of power, which gives rise to a scope of action across markets that is not sufficiently controlled by competition, it can prohibit the respective undertaking from certain types of conduct, building on the respective designation decision. Section 19a, as part of competition law, offers great flexibility and the Bundeskartellamt benefits from a shift in the burden of proof when objective justification arguments are brought forward by companies. Besides a set of specific rule examples meant to contribute to greater effectiveness and legal certainty by illustrating which potential harm the more general prohibition principles can in particular cover, the Bundeskartellamt also benefits from shortened judicial review as all appealed cases are brought directly before the Federal Court of Justice. So here we see a new legal tool aimed at combining the best of two worlds: it has become easier to address abusive conduct by powerful digital ecosystems, while allowing objective justification where appropriate.

15. The Bundeskartellamt's most powerful tool is still merger control. It is easier to prevent market power upfront than to curb it later. For a long time, there has been the perception of significant underenforcement in the digital sector.[31] This is to some extent because a large number of merger projects involving major digital companies were not subject to merger control. To address this issue the German legislator introduced a transaction value threshold in 2017,

---

29 Regulation (EU) 2022/1925 of the European Parliament and of the Council of 14 September 2022 on contestable and fair markets in the digital sector and amending Directives (EU) 2019/1937 and (EU) 2020/1828 (Digital Markets Act) [2022] OJ L265/1.

30 An overview of Section 19a cases is available on Bundeskartellamt, "Proceedings against large digital companies" (2024) <https://www.bundeskartellamt.de/SharedDocs/Publikation/EN/Downloads/List_proceedings_digital_companies.pdf?__blob=publicationFile&v=12> accessed 15 October 2024.

31 An overview of the discussion and relevant literature can be found in: Bundeskartellamt, "Merger Control in the Digital Age – Challenges and Development Perspectives" (29 September 2022) Working Group on Competition Law 6 <https://www.bundeskartellamt.de/SharedDocs/Publikation/EN/Diskussions_Hintergrundpapiere/2022/Working_Group_on_Competition_Law_2022.pdf?__blob=publicationFile&v=2> accessed 15 October 2024.

so that merger control also applies to transactions that do not fully meet the turnover thresholds.[32] The transaction value threshold can help to catch acquisitions of young innovative startups that have not yet achieved considerable revenue streams, but that exhibit strong competitive potential. In practice, the Bundeskartellamt finds that the transaction value threshold often applies to mergers in digital markets and pharmaceuticals. It, thus, strengthens merger control in innovative sectors. Of the approximately 130 cases since 2017 that were notified to the Bundeskartellamt according to the transaction value threshold, so far just one merger project – Thermo Fisher / Olink – has triggered an in-depth investigation (and was ultimately cleared[33]). This is also due to the fact that the Bundeskartellamt referred several concerning mergers to the European Commission, for instance *Booking/eTraveli* or *Adobe/Figma*. The recent interventions at EU level, including *Amazon/iRobot* and *Microsoft/Activision Blizzard*, could indicate a shift towards more consistent enforcement. Scrutiny can also be warranted with respect to projects that fall somewhere between cooperations and acquisitions, particularly in the field of AI: the Commission, for example, has looked into the cooperation between Microsoft and OpenAI to clarify whether the transaction could be subject to merger control (and came to the conclusion that Microsoft did not acquire lasting control over OpenAI).[34] For Germany, the Bundeskartellamt had already conducted a thorough examination with the result that the project is currently not subject to German merger control.[35]

16. Another question is how to prohibit harmful mergers beyond the established theories of harm including those in multi-layered ecosystems in dynamic stages of development. The Bundeskartellamt's thinking on how to strengthen merger control with regard to big tech is part of being an advocate for competition. Balancing structure and effect will probably not be enough, it needs to think about a refined set of rules and approaches to be able to prohibit projects whenever necessary while providing companies the greatest possible legal certainty. In 2022, the Bundeskartellamt's Working Group on Competition Law looked into possible solutions for merger control in the digital age. The Association of German Jurists and others have proposed the introduction of stricter merger control rules for companies to be of paramount significance for competition across markets (companies being subject to extended abuse control pursuant to Section 19a German Competition Act). This could be

32 German Competition Act (*Gesetz gegen Wettbewerbsbeschränkungen* – GWB) s 35(1a).

33 Bundeskartellamt, "Case summary – Bundeskartellamt clears acquisition of Olink Holding AB by Thermo Fisher Scientific Inc." (26 August 2024) (full decision B3-25/24) <https://www.bundeskartellamt.de/SharedDocs/Entscheidung/EN/Fallberichte/Fusionskontrolle/2024/B3-25-24.pdf?__blob=publicationFile&v=2> accessed 16 October 2024.

34 Speech by EVP Margrethe Vestager at the European Commission workshop on "Competition in Virtual Worlds and Generative AI" (28 June 2024) <https://ec.europa.eu/commission/presscorner/detail/en/speech_24_3550> accessed 16 October 2024.

35 Bundeskartellamt Press Release, "Cooperation between Microsoft and OpenAI Currently Not Subject to Merger Control" (15 November 2023) <www.bundeskartellamt.de/SharedDocs/Meldung/EN/Pressemitteilungen/2023/15_11_2023_Microsoft_OpenAI.html> accessed 29 September 2024.

achieved by reducing the standard of proof in establishing a SIEC, shifting the burden of proof or establishing a new criterion for prohibiting a merger aimed at the expansion or strengthening of an ecosystem as well as corresponding positions of power.[36]

17. Also, in other areas, the Bundeskartellamt strives to strike a balance between structure and effects. The 11th amendment to the GWB dated November 2023 introduced as a key element a German "new competition tool". This tool enables the Bundeskartellamt to impose remedies following a sector inquiry (similar to the UK's market investigation), and after having determined a significant and persistent malfunctioning of competition with regard to specific companies. While remedies can be imposed on companies without first having to demonstrate a violation of the law, the procedural and substantive legal requirements for such an intervention are quite demanding.

IV. The Best Way Forward

18. The stakes for competition are high in all sectors of the economy. The Bundeskartellamt is part of a very dynamic economic, geopolitical and legal environment. We need instruments which are nuanced, practical and can respond to changes in the economy. In the EU, the consultation of Guidelines on exclusionary abuses of dominance under Article 102 TFEU has started and the Commission has concluded the evaluation of Regulation 1/2003. In Germany, the GWB is being reviewed and updated on a regular basis.

19. For the Bundeskartellamt, there is no single way of enforcing competition. Our way of enforcement has had much success in the past. It has always been put to the test and therefore the Bundeskartellamt can never stand still. There is much to suggest that future challenges will require no less effort. So, the Bundeskartellamt's north star will always be to keep markets open, serve consumer welfare and promote competition as the fundamental pillar of the social market economy. At its core, limiting economic power serves freedom and our democracy.

---

36 Ibid. Bundeskartellamt (n 31) 34.

Why Competition and Competition Law Enforcement

Jacques Steenbergen*
KU Leuven

1. In a market economy with free enterprise, undertakings and markets determine what will be available to whom and at what conditions to satisfy the needs and preferences of citizens, unless goods and services are offered as decided by public authorities. It is, at least among economists and other experts, widely assumed that competition on the supply side of markets in interaction with pressures from the demand side offers the best chance that stakeholders can find and offer what they need or want at a reasonable cost to themselves and society.[1]

2. It follows that societies that opted for a market economy and free enterprise need to protect themselves against forms of market failure. This is necessary in order to see the expected allocation and distribution benefits, and thus to maintain the confidence in and ultimately the legitimacy of the option for a market economy, and of the institutions that defend the market economy model.

I. A Bumpy Ride

3. The belief in the relative efficiency of a market economy and free trade has since the Second World War been stimulated by the failures of state planned economies.

---

* Professor Emeritus, Dr Steenbergen is former President of the Belgian Competition Authority.

1 See e.g. Richard Wish and David Bailey, *Competition Law* (10th edn, OUP 2021) 5–10, but also 10–14 on limits to the benefits of competition.

4. But successive crises, especially since 2007, as well a lack of expectation management, have shaken the confidence in free trade and competition in a globalised market economy[2] searching for economic efficiencies. Many distrust both markets and technocrats.[3] They question the added value of competition authorities, while others tend to expect too much from them.

5. We must face the fact that what the competition community sees as a contribution to society by making markets work more efficiently, is perceived by others as the source of their problems. Globalisation greatly contributed to growth. But as eg Frederic Jenny pointed out,[4] we were wrong in assuming that growth would benefit to all. Factors such as rigidities in labour markets make that significant groups do not benefit and feel excluded. This puts our legitimacy to the test. And it is difficult to be effective when not seen to be legitimate.[5]

6. There is also more at stake than the legitimacy of the pursuit of free trade and competition law enforcement. Societies risk disintegration and destructive behaviour when many feel at the mercy of developments that they can no longer control. Protectionism and militant nationalism are logical defence strategies in societies that hope to restore or preserve control. Also reasonable people risk being tempted by populism and extremist views at either end of the political spectrum. We receive moreover from psychiatrists the warning that a culture of efficiency is self-destructive.[6] I cannot assess these views. I can only see that they have an impact on groups of intellectuals who

2 It may be useful to recall that global trade, challenges and challengers are not new. Europeans tend to forget that China is said to have had the highest *per capita* income in the world in the fifteenth century, and to have accounted for one third of the world's GDP as recently as 1820, at a time that the US only accounted for 2%. See for a succinct survey e.g. Stephen Green, *Good Value: Reflections on Morals, Money, Morality and an Uncertain World* (Allen Lane 2009) 52 et seq. If global trade was seen in the nineteenth and first half of the twentieth century as less threatening in Europe, it was largely because European powers could to a significant extent control it as 'domestic' trade within colonial empires. I developed this further in Jacques Steenbergen, 'Competition and Trade Policy and the Challenge of Globalisation' in Inge Govaere, Reinhard Quick and Marco Bronckers (eds), *Trade and Competition Law in the EU and beyond, Liber Amicorum Jacques Bourgeois* (Edward Elgar 2011) 3–17.

3 This holds even true in the more market-oriented jurisdictions such as the UK: see e.g. CMA, 'Lord Tyrie's letter to the Secretary of State for Business' (21 February 2019) <https://assets.publishing.service.gov.uk/government/uploads/system/uploads/attachment_data/file/781151/Letter_from_Andrew_Tyrie_to_the_Secretary_of_State_BEIS.pdf> accessed 18 October 2024. And in some Member States people have historically been more sceptical about the merits of competition than in others. See e.g. concerning France, Bruno Lasserre, 'French Competition Authority' in William E Kovacic (ed), *Great Antitrust Enforcers* (Concurrences 2023) 203–214.

4 See eg Frederic Jenny, 'How Can Competition Contribute to Fairer Societies?' (November 2018) OECD Global Forum on Competition <www.slideshare.net/slideshow/how-can-competition-contribute-to-fairer-societies-jenny-november-2018-oecd-gfc-discussion/124381108> accessed 19 October 2024. See also Y Van Gerven, 'Editoriaal' (2018) *Competitio* (formerly *Tijdschrift voor Belgische Mededinging*) 217. And on the impact of globalisation on inequality also e.g. Zaki Laïdi, *La Grande Perturbation* (Flammarion 2004) 321 et seq. and 385–402.

5 I developed this further in Jacques Steenbergen, 'Some Thoughts on Legality and Legitimacy' in David Edwards, Jacquelyn MacLennan, Assimakis Komninos (eds), *Ian Forrester, A Scott Without Borders, Liber Amicorum* (Concurrences 2015) vol II, 329–336.

6 See e.g. Paul Verhaeghe, 'De effecten van een neoliberale meritocratie op identiteit en interpersoonlijke verhoudingen' in Martine Groen en Paul Kuypers (eds), *Woorden breken, het democratisch tekort* (Garant 2018) 119–136. Foqué has however emphasised the distinction between the impact of liberal and of neo-liberal market thinking on the relation between 'the market' and society: Rene Foqué, 'Vrije mededinging in rechtstatelijk perspectief' in Dirk Arts et al. (eds), *Liber Amicorum Jacques Steenbergen* (Larcier 2014) 44 et seq.

were already suspicious of markets. They attack not only a dis-functioning of markets but also the legitimacy and the intellectual framework of the efforts to make them work better.

7. Enlargement has moreover 'imported' the anti-globalisation tendencies into the EU as it has fuelled intra-European relocation.[7] Enlargement has thus increased the tendency to see the European institutions as one of the driving forces of globalisation, rather than as a European response. And all who are more easily impressed by threats than motivated by opportunities can therefore be expected to see the European construction, open market and competition policies as a cause of their problems and not as a solution.

II. Restoring Confidence: The Fairness Debate

8. The public, on whom competition authorities depend in order to be perceived as legitimate enforcers of rules their stakeholders want to see enforced, tends to insist more on fairness than on efficiency.[8] But seen from a legitimacy perspective, it can be quite unfair to be inefficient. It is therefore most welcome that EU Executive Vice-President Vestager helps to reframe the fairness debate by insisting that it is not competition, but a lack of competition that is unfair to consumers, starters, SMEs and all who risk being the victim of cartels and abuse of dominance. And that competition law enforcement is not about losing control over one's life but aims at protecting the right to choose and to give back control when necessary.[9] The Commission's digital strategy[10] with the DMA, DSA, Data Act, Data Governance Act as well as eg the GDPR Regulation not only aim at facilitating market entry for new and innovative competitors. They give the control over data back to citizens, enable them to make better informed choices and protect them against abusive practices and misleading information.[11] We must ensure that this message comes across.

---

7 I developed this further in Rene Foqué and Jacques Steenbergen, 'The Limits of the Law and the Development of the EU' in Erik Claes, Wouter Devroe and Bert Keirsbilck (eds), *Facing the Limits of the Law* (Springer 2009) 205–236.

8 See e.g. Jenny (n 4).

9 See e.g. Margarethe Vestager's contribution on 'Competition and Europe's digital future' (14 March 2019) Bundeskartellamt Conference Berlin; and in the enforcers panel (29 March 2019) ABA Spring Meeting Conference Washington. And more recently also in respect of state aid 'Remarks by Executive Vice-President Vestager following the Court of Justice rulings on the Apple tax State aid and Google Shopping antitrust cases', (10 September 2024)(https://ec.europa.eu/press corner).

10 European Commission, A Europe Fit for the Digital Age, <https://commission.europa.eu/strategy-and-policy/priorities-2019-2024/europe-fit-digital-age_en> accessed 18 October 2024.

11 Regulation (EU) 2022/1925 of the European Parliament and of the Council of 14 September 2022 on contestable and fair markets in the digital sector and amending Directives (EU) 2019/1937 and (EU) 2020/1828 (Digital Markets Act) [2022] OJ L 265/1; Regulation (EU) 2022/2065 of the European Parliament and of the Council of 19 October 2022 on a Single Market For Digital Services and amending Directive 2000/31/EC (Digital Services Act) [2022] OJ L 277/1. Regulation (EU) 2023/2854 of the European Parliament and of the Council of 13 December 2023 on harmonised rules on fair access to and use of data and amending Regulation (EU) 2017/2394 and Directive (EU) 2020/1828 (Data Act) [202] OJ L Series. Regulation (EU) 2022/868 of the European Parliament and of the Council of 30 May 2022 on European data governance and amending

9. And while the antitrust community analyses in minute detail every case in order to predict future decisions, we cannot expect all stakeholders to share our fascination for every change in a turn of phrase. Expert reports on the way to deal with digital markets recommend therefore a two-track approach.[12] Some digital transformation challenges can be addressed more effectively by regulation, if only because regulations apply *erga omnes* and *ex ante*.[13] It is now generally accepted that competition law enforcement and (pro competitive) regulation can be complementary tools with shared objectives. And we must of course also continue to improve the policing of markets by competition authorities and to foster a competition culture[14] in order to demonstrate credibly that, provided market failures are addressed, competition makes markets more and not less fair.

III. The Legal Environment and Challenges to the EU

10. In democratic societies based on the rule of law, a key option such as the reliance on a market economy, can be expected to be enshrined in law. Looking at national law, its legal basis is found more often in a set of laws and regulations enacted in a national constitutional system, rather than in the system's constitution. It is sometimes enacted as a basic principle of economic law, as in the Belgian Code of Economic Law,[15] or only implicitly presumed as a context without which secondary law such as the freedom to contract in the civil code or competition law are more difficult to understand. Questions about the legitimacy of the market economy do therefore not necessarily affect the legitimacy of the national state.

Regulation (EU) 2018/1724 (Data Governance Act) [2022] OJ L152/1. Regulation (EU) 2016/679 of the European Parliament and of the Council of 27 April 2016 on the protection of natural persons with regard to the processing of personal data and on the free movement of such data, and repealing Directive 95/46/EC (General Data Protection Regulation) [2016] OJ L119/1.

12 See e.g. the report by the experts appointed by Commissioner Vestager: Jacques Cremer, Yves-Alexandre de Montjoye and Heike Schweitzer, *Competition Policy for the Digital Era* (DG-Comp, 2019) 9, 10, 82, and esp. 87 and 107 (the Experts' Report) <https://op.europa.eu/en/publication-detail/-/publication/21dc175c-7b76-11e9-9f05-01aa75ed71a1/language-en>accessed 19 October 2024.

13 See e.g. Regulation (EU) 2017/920 of the European Parliament and of the Council of 17 May 2017 amending Regulation (EU) 531/2012 as regards rules for wholesale roaming markets [2017] OJ L147/1; Regulation (EU) 2018/302 of the European Parliament and of the Council of 28 February 2018 on addressing unjustified geo-blocking and other forms of discrimination based on customers' nationality, place of residence or place of establishment within the internal market and amending Regulations (EC) 2006/2004 and (EU) 2017/2394 and Directive 2009/22/EC [2018] OJ LI60/1; Regulation (EC) 924/2009 of the European Parliament and of the Council of 16 September 2009 on cross-border payments in the Community and repealing Regulation (EC) 2560/2001 [2009] OJ L266/11 and Regulation (EU) 260/2012 of the European Parliament and of the Council of 14 March 2012 establishing technical and business requirements for credit transfers and direct debits in euro and amending Regulation (EC) 924/2009 [2012] OJ L94/22 and Case C-382/12 P *MasterCard Inc v European Commission* ECLI:EU:C:2014:2201 on cross-border payments and interchange fees, the Directive (EU) 2015/2366 of the European Parliament and of the Council of 25 November 2015 on payment services in the internal market, amending Directives 2002/65/EC, 2009/110/EC and 2013/36/EU and Regulation (EU) 1093/2010, and repealing Directive 2007/64/EC [2015] OJ L337/35.

14 See Jacques Steenbergen, 'Concurrence: Effet utile sans culture de la concurrence?' in Martine Behar-Touchais, Nicola Charbit and Rafael Amaro (eds), *A quoi sert la concurrence* (Concurrences 2014) 727–733.

15 CEL art II.2-4. See E Pieters, 'La place et le rôle du droit de la concurrence dans la codification du droit économique' in Arts et al. (eds), *Liber Amicorum Jacques Steenbergen* (Larcier 2014) 141–152.

11. In the EU's multi-layered legal system, the TEU and TFEU have, however, priority over national law and they are not policy neutral. The EU legal order is based on the option in favour of an internal market (ie internal free trade) and a free competition model. This has been confirmed in the Lisbon Reform Treaty.[16] Since the Amsterdam Treaty, social and environmental policies gradually found their way into the Treaties.[17] But the provisions of what are now Article 3 TEU, Article 9 and Title IX TFEU on employment, Article 11 and Title XX TFEU on the environment as well as other provisions in the Treaties did, notwithstanding Article 7 TFEU, not put significant constraints on competition policy makers (they are eg convinced that they ultimately act in the interest of employment). The inclusion of additional substantive law provisions in institutional treaties(emphasised even that the institutions are not free to develop policies. The restructuring of the treaty provisions in the TEU and the TFEU by the Lisbon Reform Treaty has helped to disentangle the institutional and substantive elements in the EU's construction. And the successive reforms of the Treaties from EEC to EC to EU and the case law of the CJEU also significantly broadened the scope of the Union that can no longer be said to be almost exclusively focussed on trade in goods and services.[18] But given the priority of both Treaties on national institutional as well as substantive law, this has not (yet) significantly altered the fact and the perception that the EU institutions have been established and have received delegated powers to pursue specified policies.[19] That makes it likely that all who are opposed to such policies reject the institutions which became painfully clear with Brexit.

12. A competition based open market policy is moreover (rightly) considered to require the enforcement of competition rules by autonomous agencies.[20] These autonomous competition authorities (and other market regulators) increasingly operate in networks that bring together the European Commission and national agencies.[21] The networks help to create a link between 'Brussels'

16 The new TEU art 3 stipulates that the 'Union shall establish an internal market. It shall work for the sustainable development of Europe based on balanced economic growth and price stability, a highly competitive social market economy (…)'. This text is not significantly weaker than the reference to competition policy in the EC Treaty arts 3(g) and 4(1). It is strengthened further by Protocol 6 to the Reform Treaty and the references to the '*social market economy*' and '*aiming at full employment and social progress*' in the same provision.

17 See Stéphane Van Raepenbusch, 'Les services sociaux en droit communautaire ou la recherché d'un juste équilibre entre l'économique et le social' in Jean-Victor Louis and Stéphane Rodriques (eds), *Les Services d'intérêt économique général et l'Union européenne* (Bruylant 2006) 107 et seq. and 161. See also TFEU arts 7, 9 and 11.

18 See e.g. Koen Lenaerts et al., *European Union Law* (3rd edn, Sweet & Maxwell 2011) 177–193 and 309–343.

19 See on the nature of the EU's delegated powers, id. 112–140. I developed this further in Foqué and Steenbergen (n 7), 205–236

20 This is e.g. clearly illustrated by the OECD criteria for the assessment of competition laws and authorities. See e.g. OECD, 'The Optimal Design, Organization and Powers of Competition Authorities' (December 2023). The Competition Committee is a committee of OECD Member States unlike a more self-regulatory organisation such as the ICN. See for the EU Directive (EU) 2019/1 of the European Parliament and of the Council of 11 December 2018 to empower the competition authorities of the Member States to be more effective enforcers and to ensure the proper functioning of the internal market [2019] OJ L11/3, art 4.

21 See for the competition authorities the Council Regulation (EC) 1/2003 of 16 December 2002 on the implementation of the rules on competition laid down in Articles 81 and 82 of the Treaty [2003] OJ L1/114, art 4 and Council Regulation (EC) 139/2004 of 20 January 2004 on the control of concentrations between undertakings (the EC Merger Regulation) [2004 OJ L24/1, art 19. See also the Commission Notice on

and the Member States – but because the national agencies also need to be independent from national governments, some may say that they only add to the democratic deficit.

IV. The Way Forward

13. Autonomous agencies need in a democratic system[22] to respect both the scope and the limits of their delegated powers. One can hardly argue that concepts in Articles 101 and 102 TFEU and the Merger Regulation 139/2004 are well defined. I submit that attempts to define them usually rely on a specific school of economic thinking. But the Treaties do not require competition authorities and courts to decide for or against the teachings of the Chicago School, ordo-liberalism or any other economic doctrine. The CJEU did eg not endorse an *exclusive* focus on consumer welfare,[23] And the Commission also referred in its notice on priorities for the enforcement of Article 102 TFEU to the protection of the competitive process.[24] The many discussions on the goals of competition policy and (non-economic) public policy considerations at various levels[25] should therefore be welcomed.

---

cooperation within the Network of Competition Authorities OJ 2004 C101/43. See on the appreciation on what already been achieved and convergence and complementarity of the views for further developments of two key actors Bruno Lasserre, 'Le Réseau européen de concurrence: entre réussites et défis' and Andreas Mundt, 'Ten years of ECN – Cooperation at it best' in Arts et al. (eds), *Liber Amicorum Jacques Steenbergen* (Larcier 2014) 475–482 and 503–514. The abovementioned ECN+ Directive (EU) 2019/1 answered some of these suggestions. See for electronic communications Directive 2002/21/EC of the European Parliament and of the Council of 7 March 2002 on a common regulatory framework for electronic communications networks and services (Framework Directive) [2002] OJ L108/33, art 22. There are similar networks e.g. for the energy sector, for financial and for postal services, etc.

22 See for the TEU EU art 2 and Title II.

23 See e.g. Case C-501/06P *GlaxoSmithKline Services Unlimited v Commission of the European Communities* ECLI:EU:C:2009:610, para 63. Contrary to what is sometimes argued, the Court did not decide in the *MasterCard Inc* judgement (11 September 2014) that only in-market benefits can be taken into account and only when they fully compensate affected consumers: '(they) cannot, in themselves, (…) compensate (…) in the absence of any proof of appreciable objective advantages (…) in the relevant market' ie. the affected consumers should also benefit (and receive a fair share), but the Court did not add that the affected consumers should be fully compensated. See further e.g. Ioannis Lianos, 'Some Reflections on the Question of the Goals of EU Competition Law' (2013) CLES Working Paper Series 3/2013. See earlier on EU competition law theories of harm and economic doctrine Philip Marsden and Simon Bishop 'Intellectual Leaders Still Need Ground to Stand On' (2007) 3 ECJ 315. See Cyril Sarrazin, 'Exemption: The ECJ upholds the analysis of the CFI on restrictions of parallel trades in medicines and restriction of competition by object (GlaxoSmithKline)' (6 October 2009) 1 Concurrences 30307 89-90.

24 European Commission, Guidance on the Commission's enforcement priorities in applying Article 82 of the EC Treaty to abusive exclusionary conduct by dominant undertakings. See also paragraph 5 of the draft Guidelines on the application of Article 102 of the TFEU to abusive exclusionary conduct by dominant undertakings (opened for public consultation). [2009] OJ C45/02. See in the same sense the Experts' Report (n 11), 40–41.

25 See e.g. the OECD, 'The Goals of Competition Policy' (December 2022) Global Forum on Competition Round Table; and the OECD, 'Public Interest Considerations in Merger Control' (June 2016) Competition Committee Round Table. See also the discussions following the *Siemens/Alstom* decision of the Commission of 6 February 2019. See further e.g. JW van de Gronden, 'Europees mededingingsrecht en niet-economische belangen' [2016] SEW 472–483; and with focus on agriculture, the *GIG economy* and sports: ME Litjes and HHB Volder, 'Als de pen machtiger is dan het zwaard – over de noodzaak goed na te denken over de verhouding tussen mededinging en andere belangen en dit goed te verwoorden' [2022] SEW 432–441.

14. With regard to the legitimacy of autonomous authorities with delegated powers we need in principle to make a transparent distinction between decisions taken because of the limits of these powers (for which one can hardly blame the authority), and decisions taken within their margin of appreciation for which they can be held accountable. Ensuring the legitimacy of autonomous authorities always requires a delicate balance between the safeguarding of their independence and democratic accountability. The distinction between the limits and the scope of their powers is, however, not really helpful in respect of EU competition law enforcement because the margin of appreciation of competition authorities results primarily from the interpretability of the concepts that define the limits of their mandate.[26] But if the competition law provisions are not read in isolation, more guidance can be found in the context of the Treaties and eg in the Articles 3(3), 4(3) TEU and 9, 11, 14 and 26 TFEU.[27] The interaction between these provisions and the rules of competition help to define both the limits and the scope of the competition authorities in the Union. And by a transparent fulfilment of their delegated task, ie by making a clear distinction by what they must and what they cannot do pursuant to the Treaties and what they decide to do using the margins of interpretation the Treaties require them to use, they strengthen their own legitimacy and help to fight the perception that the Union institutions are only there to impose rigidly defined policies.

15. As you can expect from a former head of a competition authority, I firmly believe that not notwithstanding but because of the abovementioned challenges, the way forward is not to have less but to have ever better competition law enforcement. Competition authorities need to listen to stakeholders. And the scope of their mandate is defined by their duty to make markets work better in the interest of a 'sustainable development of Europe based on balanced economic growth and price stability, a highly competitive social market economy (…)'.[28] The Treaties thus offer a framework for a competition policy that continues to foster innovation[29] and to support sustainable growth.[30] They do so without creating a slippery slope allowing competition authorities to give way to any general policy concern: competition

26 See e.g. 'restriction of competition', 'abuse', 'dominance' in the TFEU arts 101 and 102 and the concepts in TFEU art 101(3).

27 See further e.g. W Devroe, 'Waardenvol Europees mededingingsrecht en interne markt recht' in Arts et al. (eds), *Liber Amicorum Jacques Steenbergen* (Larcier 2014) 636–653.

28 TEU art 3.

29 See eg. the Commission Decision of 27 March 2017, case M7932, *Dow-Dupont*. With regard to telecoms consolidation. I may eg add that competition authorities have in my experience facilitated innovative cross border consolidation, but acted against anti-competitive transactions on purely national markets. See eg Commission decisions of 17 July 1996 on case No IV/35.617 - Phoenix/GlobalOne; and of 29 October 1997 on case No IV/35.830 – Unisource. See further e.g. Jacques Steenbergen, "(Geliberaliseerde) openbare diensten en EU-reglementering", in *Liber amicorum Walter van Gerven*, Story-Scientia, Antwerpen, 2000, 427-447.

30 Competition policy has thus and can continues to contribute to the policies advocated by Mario Draghi: Mario Draghi, *The future of European Competitiveness*, (EU Commission 2024), eg pp. 15 and 65.

authorities can only be concerned with what is relevant to the functioning of markets and do what is also in the interest of consumers in the broad meaning of that concept.[31]

16. There is no contradiction between a rigorous enforcement of competition law and an interpretation of competition law rules such as Article 101(3) TFEU, taking into account the impact of decisions on sustainability when its purpose is to contribute to the *sustainable* development. There is no contradiction between rigorous enforcement in the Union in the interest of its consumers and the creation of undertakings that are fit to compete on world markets because it is difficult to see how undertakings can compete effectively abroad when they are not competitive on their home market. And there is no contradiction between rigorous enforcement of competition law and the stakeholders' search for fairness when we can demonstrate the unfairness of a lack of competition. But rigorous enforcement of the rules of the Articles 101 and 102 TFEU and the Merger regulation requires a continued effort of all concerned to give guidance to undertakings in ever faster developing markets and to decide cases when decisions can still produce the intended benefit for the stakeholders.

---

31 See n23.

A '*General*' Court in Name Only?[*]

ULF ÖBERG[**]

General Court of the European Union

1. The recent reform of Protocol No. 3 of the Statute of the Court of Justice has renewed the debate on specialization at the General Court.
2. The purpose and the *raison d'être* of the General Court are defined in the Council Decision establishing a Court of First Instance[1]. The original purpose of attaching the General Court to the Court of Justice and introducing two levels of jurisdiction was, first, to improve the judicial protection of individual interests, in particular in proceedings necessitating close examination of complex facts. Second, it was to maintain the quality and effectiveness of judicial review in the EU legal order, by enabling the Court of Justice to concentrate on its essential task – namely, to ensure that in the interpretation and application of EU law, the law is observed[2].
3. In this respect, the EU Courts have confirmed that the action for annulment provides a particularly appropriate procedural framework for the thorough examination, both parties being duly heard, of legal and factual questions, particularly in technical and complex fields such as State aid[3] and competition law[4].

---

* This article has been previously published in Concurrences, and it might have been edited for clarity and cohesion. Ulf Öberg, A 'General' Court in Name Only?, September 2024, Concurrences N° 3-2024, Art. N° 119191, pp. 2-6.

** This foreword is an expanded version of my personal views already expressed at the Closing Discussion of The Tech Antitrust Conference held in Palo Alto on January 11th, 2024. The usual disclaimer applies. I am grateful for the assistance of Mrs Nathalie Leyns, legal secretary at my chambers the General Court, and of Mrs Raluca Sbîrnea, former legal assistant in my chambers, for conducting research and for reviewing earlier versions of this editorial.

1 Council Decision 88/591/ECSC, EEC, Euratom of 24 October 1988 establishing a Court of First Instance of the European Communities, OJ L 319, 25.11.1988, p. 1.

2 See, to that effect, CJEC, 17 December 1998, *Baustahlgewebe v. Commission*, case C-185/95 P, EU:C:1998:608, para. 41.

3 CJEU, 25 July 2018, *Georgsmarienhütte and Others*, case C-135/16, EU:C:2018:582, para. 19.

4 GCEU, 28 May 2020, *CK Telecoms UK Investments v. Commission*, case T-399/16, EU:T:2020:217, reversed and remanded on appeal by CJEU, 13 July 2023, *Commission v. CK Telecoms UK Investments*, case C-376/20 P, EU:C:2023:561.

4. In order to achieve the goals of the EU legislator, specialization at the General Court can occur at multiple levels:
   - by creating specialized courts attached to the General Court under Article 257 of the Treaty on the Functioning of the European Union (TFEU);
   - by specializing chambers of the General Court in certain areas;
   - or by specializing individual judges through the allocation of cases to reporting judges[5].

5. Generally speaking, specialized courts are recognized as particularly cost-efficient, being able to produce cases rapidly and qualitatively. It is a fact that in several Member States, competition law cases, trade protection cases, value-added tax (VAT) cases, as well as more straightforward intellectual property law cases are often heard by specialized courts or by specialized chambers. With the reform of the General Court in 2016, a first attempt to set up specialized courts within the EU judicial system was abandoned at the request of the Court of Justice. The Civil Service Tribunal, recognized for the efficiency with which it operated, was in practice merged with the General Court. An alternative option to create specialized courts in more complex economic matters was never seriously considered and was thus not taken up by the EU legislator.

6. In order to at least partially heed the calls of its external stakeholders, the General Court decided in 2019 to introduce two main areas of specialization for four chambers hearing civil service cases and six chambers hearing intellectual property cases, which form the bulk of less complex cases on the docket and which can be heard by a single judge. The formal assignment of cases to chambers and of formation of specialized chambers was in practice made on the basis of the preferences of the Presidents of chambers and, to the extent possible, of the individual Members of the Court[6].

7. In principle, the General Court maintained a rota system of random allocation of complex economic cases among all chambers and reporting judges by the date of the lodging of a case for competition law, State aid, trade protection, foreign subsidies distorting the internal market, rules on digital marketing and services as well as for all other cases.

8. Nevertheless, under the current system of allocation of cases, the President of the General Court may derogate from the method of allocating cases by rota on the ground that cases are related or with a view to ensuring an even

---

5 U. Öberg, M. Ali and P. Sabouret, On Specialisation of Chambers at the General Court, in *The Court of Justice of the European Union: Multidisciplinary Perspectives*, M. Derlén and J. Lindholm (eds.), Hart Publishing, Oxford, 2018, pp. 211–224.

6 Decisions of the plenums of General Court of 3 July 2019 and of 4 October 2019 on *Criteria for the assignment of cases to* Chambers (OJ 2019 C 246, p. 2 and OJ 2019 C 372 p. 2) and decisions of 30 September 2019 and, latest, of 19 September 2022 on *Formation of Chambers and assignment of Judges to Chambers*, OJ 2019 C 372 p. 3 and OJ 2022 C 398, p. 6.

spread of the workload, which leaves room for discretion in the interest of good administration of justice[7]. In practice, this has led to an increased ad hoc specialization of certain chambers and of certain judges according to the priorities of the President and of the Presidents of Chambers of the General Court by means of an interpretation of the legal concept of "*connexité*," taken in a wide sense ("*connexité au sens large*").

9. According to Laurence Boisson de Chazournes, "*connexité*" is originally a concept of French law that regulates a conflict of jurisdiction where two cases are pending that are not identical (so *lis pendens* does not apply) but are similar enough that they should be consolidated into one case, assigned to the same chamber or, as has been a common feature in recent years at the General Court, to increasingly specialized reporting judges. This doctrine is discretionary in nature, and so it would appear to be a close cousin of *forum non conveniens*. The discretion in connecting proceedings may be exercised where it is expedient to do so, and where there is a risk that two judgments may be irreconcilable[8].

I. Will the transfer of competence of "lesser tasks" to the General Court transform the Court of Justice from a Supreme Court into a Constitutional Court of the European Union?

10. The reform will deepen the process of specialization in the General Court, confirming, if maintained, the existence of a specialized jurisdiction in areas such as staff cases and intellectual property cases. From October 2024 onwards, the General Court has decided to specialize two further chambers in the "specific areas" in which the General Court may hear requests for preliminary rulings[9]. The reform provides for the transfer of competences from the Court of Justice to the General Court, upon an examination of whether the cases concerned come within the following areas: (i) the common system of value-added tax; (ii) excise duties; (iii) the Customs Code; (iv) the tariff classification of goods under the Combined Nomenclature; (v) compensation and assistance to passengers in the event of denied boarding or of delay or cancellation of transport services; (vi) the system for greenhouse gas emission allowance trading).

7 CJEU, 2 October 2014, *Strack v. Commission*, case C-127/13 P, EU:C:2014:2250, para. 50.

8 See L. Boisson de Chazournes, Plurality in the Fabric of International Courts and Tribunals: The Threads of a Managerial Approach: A Rejoinder – Fears and Anxieties, *European Journal of International Law*, Vol. 28, Issue 4, 2017, pp. 1275–1281, https://doi.org/10.1093/ejil/chx081.

9 Art. 1(4) of the Regulation of the European Parliament and of the Council amending Protocol No. 3 on the Statute of the Court of Justice of the European Union.

11. One of the main rationales underlying the transfer of preliminary rulings in certain specific areas to the General Court is the gradual transformation of the Court of Justice into a constitutional court, exclusively or mostly entrusted with the resolution of disputes of constitutional relevance[10].

12. Indeed, in the words of the current President of the General Court, Marc van der Woude, the conceptual model underpinning the reform is one where the Court of Justice would increasingly act as the Union's Constitutional Court and transfer the "lesser task" and responsibilities to the General Court. Under his vision, the General Court would thus become the Union's *Conseil d'État*, controlling the conduct of the EU institutions when they act directly or indirectly in close cooperation with national administrations[11].

13. From a theoretical point of view, the conceptual distinction between the objective of the Court of Justice to evolve from its current role as a supreme court of the European Union to become a constitutional court raises questions about which competencies the Court of Justice should have, which tasks should it be charged with fulfilling, and which matters should be brought before the Court of Justice rather than the General Court. Indeed, while a supreme court is competent to hear cases on all legal issues and is charged with the task of maintaining legal unity, a constitutional court addresses a limited number of cases on questions of fundamental importance[12].

14. This gradual transformation of the mission of the Court of Justice is confirmed in the preamble of the Regulation of the European Parliament and of the Council amending Protocol No. 3 on the Statute of the Court of Justice of the European Union. Under the first recital of the regulation, the objective of the reform is twofold, namely, "*to allow the Court of Justice to continue to fulfil its mission of safeguarding and strengthening the unity and consistency of Union law*" and "*to ensure that the decisions of the Court of Justice are of the highest quality*." The transfer to the General Court of part of the jurisdiction to give preliminary rulings should, according to its second recital, "*enable the Court of Justice to devote more time and resources to examining the most complex and sensitive requests for a preliminary ruling*." Under the fourth recital, the Court of Justice is increasingly required, in preliminary ruling cases, to "*rule on matters of a constitutional nature or related to human rights and the Charter of Fundamental Rights of the European Union*."

10 D. Sarmiento, Editorial Note: On the Road to a Constitutional Court of the European Union: The Court of Justice After the Transfer of the Preliminary Reference Jurisdiction to the General Court, *Croatian Yearbook of European Law & Policy*, Vol. 19, 2023, pp. VII–XVII.

11 M. van der Woude, The Place of the General Court in the Institutional Framework of the Union, *EU Law Live*, Weekend Edition, No. 81, 27 November 2021, pp. 20–26, https://eulawlive. com/weekend-edition/ weekend-edition-no81/.

12 S. Kirchner, Conference Report – Legal Unity Through Specialized Courts on a European Level?, *German Law Journal*, Vol. 6, Issue 1, 2005, pp. 217–226, at 222, doi:10.1017/S2071832200013584.

II. Will the increased specialization of the chambers of the General Court in more "simple cases" come at the expense of its original mission in complex economic cases?

15. Under this constitutional court conceptual model, it is only logical that the Court of Justice retains jurisdiction to hear and determine requests for a preliminary ruling that raise independent questions relating to the interpretation of primary law, public international law, general principles of Union law or the Charter of Fundamental Rights of the European Union.

16. The institutional balance between the Court of Justice and the General Court is thus poised to shift: the Court of Justice will be in charge of interpreting primary law and the EU Charter of Fundamental Rights under requests for preliminary rulings, while the General Court will only be competent to hear less complex and less sensitive requests pursuant to a prior evaluation of the Court. This reform creates a new institutional balance and entrusts a new function to the General Court.

17. As already stated, in order to ensure the success and the legitimacy of the reform, the General Court has decided to dedicate, at least at an initial stage of the reform, two full chambers and two advocates general to primarily hear requests for preliminary rulings. This new equilibrium brings to the forefront some novel (and some age-old) questions of allocation of cases to chambers and to reporting judges.

18. Indeed, specializing and dedicating a fifth of the members of the General Court to decide "more simple" and "less sensitive" requests for preliminary rulings in specialized chambers will necessarily have the collateral effect of drawing judges and resources from the instruction of more complex economic cases in direct actions. If left unaddressed, it will further concentrate the current formal specialization of chambers of the General Court to the "simple cases," namely staff cases and trademark cases, which, according to the Rules of Procedure, can be heard by a single judge. The General Court will in that case end up with an equal number of judges as during the second phase of the reform of the General Court (during the years 2016–2019), but with significantly fewer legal secretaries per judge in order to instruct and adjudicate direct actions in complex economic cases.

19. Upon consultation with some of its main external stakeholders, the General Court has therefore recently adopted informal guidelines on the proactive case management of complex economic cases, or what in the common parlance of the Court is identified as "Very Big Cases."

III. The principle of the lawful judge sets limits to informal *ad hoc* specialization of judges and chambers

20. Nevertheless, unless clearly provided by law, the principle of legality and the respect of the principle of the lawful judge (de. *Grundsatz des gesetzlichen Richters,* fr. *principe du juge légal,*) set clear and binding limits to informal *ad hoc* or even fully discretionary specialization of chambers or judges[13].

21. Indeed, it is settled case law that the guarantees of access to an independent and impartial tribunal previously established by law, and in particular those that determine what constitutes a tribunal and how it is composed, represent the cornerstone of the right to a fair trial. That right means that every court is obliged to check whether, as composed, it constitutes such a tribunal where a serious doubt arises on that point. That check is necessary for the confidence that the courts in a democratic society must inspire in those subject to their jurisdiction. In that respect, such a check is an essential procedural requirement, compliance with which is a matter of public policy and must be verified on the court's own motion. Indeed, the Court must raise on its own motion an irregularity in the composition of the panel of judges, which is a matter of public policy that the General Court must examine on its own motion[14].

22. According to the Council of Europe's Sofia Action Plan "*[t]he allocation of cases within a court should follow objective, pre-established criteria in order to safeguard the right to an independent and impartial judge. There are various systems to organise the distribution of cases. What is important is that the actual distribution is not subject to external or internal influence and is not designed to benefit any of the parties. Several member states have adopted measures in this direction and have secured that exceptions to the rule of random allocation of cases are admitted only in exceptional cases, are made in a transparent manner and duly motivated*"[15].

23. Indeed, systems of random case allocation "*protects judges from arbitrary case assignments decisions that can serve to reward or punish them. The random allocation of cases also helps ensure fair and equitable workloads and reassure the public that cases are heard by an impartial judge*"[16].

24. In this respect, upholding the "*luck of the draw*" is essential to ensure the confidence of the public in the proper administration of justice under a formally

---

13 T. Rönnau and A. Hoffmann, Vertrauen ist gut, Kontrolle ist besser: Das Prinzip des gesetzlichen Richters am EuGH, *Zeitschrift für Internationale Strafrechtsdogmatik*, No. 7–8, 2018, pp. 233–248.

14 See CJEU, 26 March 2020, *Review Simpson v. Council* and *HG v. Commission*, joined case C-542/18 RX-II and C-543/18 RX-II, EU:C:2020:232.

15 Review of the implementation of the Council of Europe Plan of Action on Strengthening Judicial Independence and Impartiality – Report (November 2022), point 76.

16 See Council of Europe Draft detailed outline ("Implementation of the Sofia Action Plan CDCJ written contribution to Secretary General's report"), 29 April 2021, CDCJ-BU(2021)9, p. 4; see also P. Butler, *The Assignment of Cases to Judges* (2003) 1 NZJPIL, Available at SSRN: https://ssrn.com/abstract=2718772.

adopted and published rota system based on the principle of randomized allocation of cases. Sometimes, in fact, we want to exclude reasons from decision-making entirely, and for good reason[17].

IV. The General Court at a crossroads in the debate on specialization

25. The General Court is therefore at a crossroads, where it will sooner rather than later have to make some difficult choices. Does it make sense to maintain over time a formal specialization of chambers in cases of preliminary rulings purportedly of "lesser importance and complexity," as well as more simple direct actions that can be heard by a single judge? Alternatively, should we instead change our underlying philosophy on specialization, and formally specialize our chambers in more complex economic cases? How does the method of allocating cases to chambers and reporting judges play into this? Should the General Court make use of the individual expertise of judges in the triennial composition of chambers, with the risk of capturing institutional and individual interests? Would an increased specialization at the General Court alter the profile in the appointment of its judges and in their recruitment of legal secretaries to their chambers to assist them?

26. Or is it preferable to maintain the status quo, on the basis of the prevailing assumption that justice is best served by predominantly generalist judges, capable or even entitled to adjudicate all types of cases on the docket during the comparatively short mandate of a judge at the General Court[18]?

27. A final option would be to simply abandon the current formal published rota system and opt for a more hierarchical and discretionary system, in order to ensure coherence and efficiency through a managerial approach of adjudication[19]. According to Krenn, this risks, however, favouring the emergence of an "elite group" of judges who write the bulk of the most important decisions of the Court[20].

28. Unless exercised with utter caution and a sophisticated *Fingerspitzengefühl*, one could however fear that a fully discretionary system would open the

---

17 See P. Stone, *The Luck of the Draw: The Role of Lotteries in Decision Making*, Oxford Academic, 2011 online ed., 1 May 2011, https://doi.org/10.1093/ acprof:oso/9780199756100.001.0001, accessed 30 May 2024.

18 For a comparative study, see M. Fabri and P. Langbroek, Is There a Right Judge for Each Case? A Comparative Study of Case Assignment in Six European Countries, *European Journal of Legal Studies*, Vol. 1, No. 2, 2007, pp. 1–292–315.

19 Boisson de Chazournes, *supra*.

20 See C. Krenn, A Sense of Common Purpose: On the Role of Case Assignment and the Judge-Rapporteur at the European Court of Justice, in *Researching the European Court of Justice: Methodological Shifts and Law's Embeddedness*, M. R. Madsen, F. Nicola and A. Vauchez (eds.), Cambridge University Press, 2022, pp. 187–208; see also S. S. L. Hermansen, (2020). Building legitimacy: strategic case allocations in the Court of Justice of the European Union. *Journal of European Public Policy*, 27(8), 1215–1235. https:// doi.org/10.1080/13501763.2020.1714697.

door to the allocation of decisions as an instrument of power, which could potentially even influence the outcome of cases. Krenn nevertheless argues that the Court of Justice's discretionary case assignment system is an important mechanism for its institutional success, since it has allowed the Court to maintain a sense of common purpose in the idea of its mandate as guardian of the effectiveness and primacy of EU law or – as it may be after the latest reform of EU's judicial architecture – the EU legislator's apparent ambition to transform the Court into a Constitutional Court of the European Union.

29. As I have previously suggested, it would therefore be helpful to undertake a formal impact assessment of the formal specialization undertaken to date in staff cases and intellectual property cases, in particular in the light of the aggregated rate of appeal and rate of overturn by the Court of Justice in more complex cases. If carried out and made available to the public, such an analysis could perhaps be subject to a public consultation and to a debate with external stakeholders on the various options, subject matters and forms of specialization to be considered. This would enlighten the Members of the General Court and help us reach an informed decision on a contentious and potentially divisive issue.

V. Keep it simple!

30. On a final note, not every competition, State aid, trade defence or Digital Markets Act/Digital Services Act (DMA/DSA) case necessarily raises complex legal or economic questions. Allocating increased resources to applicants and defendants who may be tempted to draw out the length of the proceedings is, in my view, not the way forward. A more proactive case management recently decided by the General Court will hopefully deter parties from trying to overwhelm the bench by throwing spaghetti at the wall, hoping that at least some plea or argument will stick. Indeed, adding further complexity in litigation in order to challenge already complex and, at times, lengthy and excessively evidence-burdened Commission decisions, in order to divert attention from the core issue at hand, may be one of the oldest tricks in a litigator's toolbox. Keeping it simple, and assisting the Court in making timely, informed and well-reasoned judgments will, on the other hand, always be appreciated by any judge.

31. It remains to be seen how the debate will evolve in practice. Until then, one thing is certain: specialization is neither intrinsically good nor bad, nor a solution to all the challenges the General Court is currently facing. Quite the contrary. It is a means to achieve a goal.

32. In my personal view, a degree of increased specialization in complex economic cases would undoubtedly increase the quality and effectiveness of judicial review in the EU legal order, improve the judicial protection

of individual interests, ensure the rule of law is observed and increase the general court's productivity and the consistency of our case law. At the end of the day, it is the manner in which specialization occurs at the General Court which will be essential to ensure the public's trust in our independence and impartiality.

Back To Basics: The Fight Against Cartels

Alexandre Cordeiro Macedo*,
Lílian Santos Marques Severino**
Administrative Council for Economic Defense (CADE)

I. Introduction

1. A cartel is an antitrust violation that causes serious damages to the economic order and is considered "the most harmful of all anticompetitive conducts".[1] In the context of government procurements, these consequences are even more harmful, since the procurement involves government goods and services, bringing consequences to the society as a whole.

2. In the last decades, several international organisations have joined forces to present recommendations to the antitrust authorities for an effective fight against cartels. For instance, an effective leniency programme; the use of pro-active tools for detecting cartels, especially in government procurement cases; the use of the competition authority's full powers to conduct the investigations; the possibility of cooperation between the authorities and institutions; incentives for quick solutions through agreement negotiations; the use of

---

* CADE President since July 2021. Alexandre Cordeiro Macedo is the President of the Administrative Council for Economic Defense (CADE) since July 2021. Prior to becoming the head of CADE, Cordeiro was the Superintendent General of CADE for four years. He also previously served as a Commissioner at CADE. President Cordeiro holds a PhD in Law from the University of Minas Gerais (UFMG).

** CADE Chief Economist since October 2023. Lílian Santos Marques Severino is the Chief Economist of CADE, she is a former Head of the Advisory Unit, former Coordinator-General of Antitrust Analysis at the Office of the Superintendent General, and former Assistant Chief Economist of the Department of Economic Studies, at CADE. Lílian Marques holds a PhD in Economics from the Catholic University of Brasília.

1 OECD, *Fighting Hard Core Cartels: Harm Effective Sanctions and Leniency Programs*, (2002) <www.oecd-ilibrary.org/governance/fighting-hard-core-cartels_9789264174993-en> accessed 26 September 2024.

mechanisms to compensate for damages; advocacy efforts to prevent collusive conducts; and mainly the use of effective penalties (administrative and/or criminal, pecuniary or non pecuniary), so that the competition authority can achieve the adequate deterrent level.[2]

3. In accordance with the OECD's recommendations,[3] and with the objective of making decisions and actions more transparent, the Brazilian antitrust authority recently published the Guide for Cartel Penalties, which is complementary to a series of guidelines.[4]

4. In this context, it is worth noting that CADE must ensure transparency and proportionality of the penalties, thus providing greater legal certainty for its decisions. Concerning fines, it is also important to be transparent about the criteria adopted, especially for the basis of calculation and tax rates. In addition, the fines must be dissuasive, adequate, and sufficient to remove the incentives for economic agents to perform the anticompetitive conduct. The authorities must also weigh up the aggravating and mitigating factors when calculating the penalty, to achieve the elements of adequacy of the penalty to the specific conduct, respecting the principle of equality in the strict sense. Another important factor to consider is the duration of the conduct, which reflects the severity of the violation.

5. Based on these parameters, this discussion will address the concurrences book "Why Competition?". Some topics will be addressed in the following sections: (1) the experience of the Brazilian antitrust authority regarding the methodology for calculating fines in cartel cases in the last ten years; (2) the importance, in quantitative terms, of the benefits expected from CADE's performance in the fight against cartels; and (3) the need for continuous improvement of the policy for fighting cartels, emphasising the importance of "going back to basics" which is the fight against cartels, paying attention to the whole administrative proceeding process, from the investigation to the imposition of the fine.

II. Definition of Cartel Penalties: Analysis of the Brazilian Case Law

6. Law 12529/2011 structures the Brazilian Competition Defense System (SBDC) and sets forth the prevention and suppression of violations against

---

2 OECD, *Recommendation of the Council concerning Effective Action against Hard Core Cartels*, (2023) <https://legalinstruments.oecd.org/en/instruments/OECD-LEGAL-0452#supportDocuments> accessed 26 September2024. See also, International Competition Network, *Anti Cartel Enforcement Manual* <www.internationalcompetitionnetwork.org/working-groups/cartel/investigation-enforcement/> accessed 26 September 2024.

3 OECD, 'Peer Reviews of Competition Law and Policy: Brazil' (2019) <https://web-archive.oecd.org/2019-04-17/505848-oecd-peer-reviews-of-competition-law-and-policy-brazil-ENG-web.pdf> accessed 26 September 2024.

4 CADE, *supra* note 1.

the economic order. Legal persons, either governed by public or private law, as well as associations, are all accountable for these types of violations.

7. One of the conclusions from the OECD[5] was that "CADE should clarify the methodology for calculating fines. For instance, by setting an approach that relies on readily identifiable data and avoids having to engage in complex calculations regarding the profit derived by a company from its competition law infringement". CADE made an assessment of all the information on the convictions given by the authority in hardcore cartel cases, bid rigging, and international cartels in the first decade the new law came into force (2012-2022), substantiating the design of the Guide for Cartel Penalties.

8. The assessment includes 490 convictions[6] involving individuals, companies and other legal persons,[7] in 59 administrative proceedings (See Figures 1 and 2 below).

9. The research showed that 60% of the convictions were related to cartel conducts (hardcore or softcore cartels), 37% of them were bid rigging, and a remaining 3% of the convictions were classified as international cartels (Figure 3). Regarding the basis of calculation for the definition of fines to be applied, when it comes to companies (Figure 4), the gross turnover (73%) is prevalent, followed by the virtual turnover (16%). Although Article 37, Item 1, of Law 12529/11, determines that the fines will not be inferior to the accrued benefits, whenever possible to estimate them, as the OECD has already stated, it is not simple to use the accrued benefits (7%) as the basis of calculation, especially since this information involved complex calculations with great deviation of estimates. These can be questioned by the judiciary, putting in check the desired dissuasive effect.

---

5 OECD, *supra* note 5.

6 Moreover, according to Article 37 of Law 12529/2011, committing an antitrust violation subjects the liable parties to the following penalties:

1. in the case of a company, a fine of 0.1% to 20% of the gross sales revenue of the company, group, or conglomerate earned in Brazil in the field of the activity affected by the conduct in the year before the proceedings were initiated, which should never be less than the accrued benefits, whenever possible to estimate them;
2. a fine amounting to between BRL 50,000 and BRL 2,000,000,000 is applied when impossible to use the gross sales revenue criterion in the case of individuals and legal persons governed by public and private law, or associations of entities or individuals, whether de facto or de jure, even if temporarily established, incorporated or not, which do not perform a business activity;
3. in case an administrator is directly or indirectly liable for a violation committed intentionally or negligently: a fine of 1% to 20% of the fine levied on the company, in the case of Item 1 of the head provision of this Article, or of the fine levied on the legal persons or entities, in the case of Item 2 of the head provision of this Article.

Paragraph 1: Fines are doubled for repeat violations.

Paragraph 2: In calculating the fine described in Item 1 of the head provision of this Article, CADE may consider the total turnover of the company or group of companies, whenever information on the turnover linked to the field of economic activity in which the violation occurred as defined by CADE, is unavailable or whenever the information presented is incomplete, not entirely clear or appropriate, or both.

7 The term "other legal persons" refers especially to unions and business associations.

Figure 1. Quantity of administrative proceedings per year and conduct

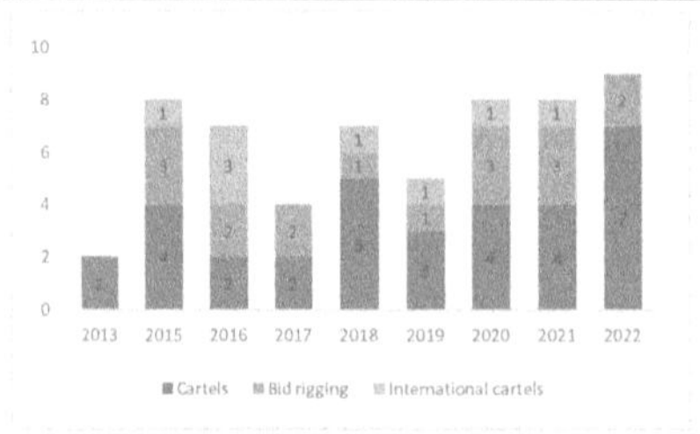

Figure 2. Quantity of convicted respondents per year and type

Source: CADE.

Note: The years 2012 and 2014 did not have cases heard under the Law 12529/2011, as it was beneficial to some defendants to apply the Law 8884/1994 to the violations that happened when this law was in force.

Figure 3. Convicted sample by conduct

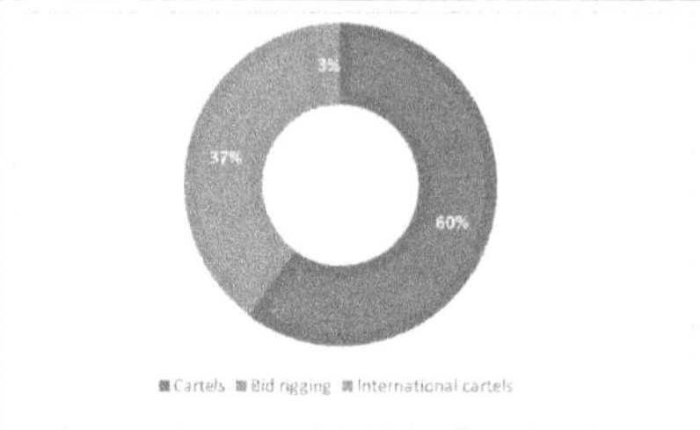

Figure 4. Companies convicted sample by basis of calculation

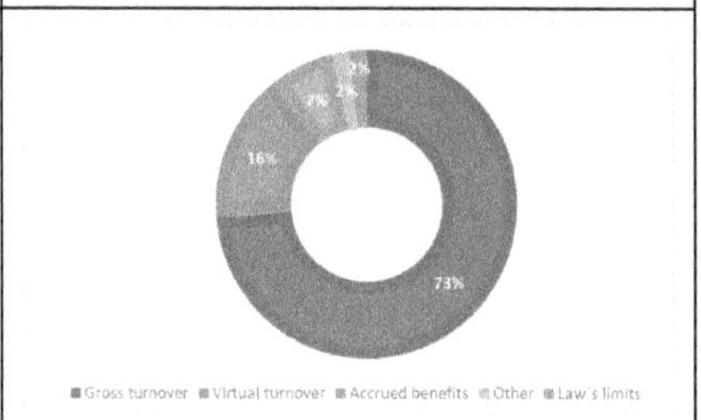

Source: CADE.

10. One of the main points of the Guide for Cartel Penalties is the presentation of the field of activity followed by a series of examples. CADE Resolution 3/2012, as modified by Resolution 18/2016, also refers to the competition law and lists the fields of economic activity to be considered for calculating penalties (Article 1). Furthermore, Article 2(a) of Resolution 3/2012 states that CADE "may adapt the field of activity according to the specificities of the practice, whenever the parameters set in Article 1 are found to be grossly disproportionate, upon a reasoned decision by the Tribunal". Thus, depending on the circumstances of the case, if the Brazilian authority understands that the field of activity mentioned in CADE Resolution 3/2012 is found to be "grossly disproportionate", the agency may consider adapting that field in which the violation occurred, such as the "subfields of economic activity" or the "affected market". Therefore, the orientation of the guide for the use of the gross turnover in the field of activity, in fact, represents what already has been done in 90% of the sanctions imposed by CADE during that period (2012–2022).

11. After understanding the basis of calculation, it is necessary to go to the next phase, which is the definition of the tax rate to be applied. Based on the data from Table 1, it is possible to conclude that CADE has not only followed the orientation of the Guidelines: Cease and Desist Agreement for cartel cases

(TCC)[8] – document which presents effective tax rates to calculate the fine for companies in hardcore and softcore cartel cases – but also that there is a possibility of improvement with parameters appointed for tax rates in cases of bid rigging. This possibility occurred due to the considerable size of the samples for individuals and companies in the bid rigging cases.

Table 1. Descriptive statistics for tax rate by conduct and classification (2012–2022)

	Companies			Individuals		
	Bid Rigging	Cartels	International Cartels	Bid Rigging	Cartels	International Cartels
Average	0.1610	0.1314	0.1100	0.0902	0.0591	0.0314
Standard deviation	0.0284	0.0399	0.0872	0.0707	0.0511	0.0334
Min	0.0850	0.0300	0.0100	0.0200	0.0100	0.0100
Max	0.2000	0.2000	0.1700	0.2000	0.2000	0.1000
Number of observations	67	155	3	54	99	7

Source: CADE. Hardcore and softcore cartel cases are considered.

12. Thus, the Brazilian antitrust authority took another step towards transparency and legal certainty when it launched the Guide for Cartel Penalties, whose guidelines are:

- The gross turnover in the field of activity is considered the basis of calculation of the fine. According to the field of activity mentioned in CADE Resolution 3/2012, if the activity is found to be "grossly disproportionate", the authority may consider adapting that field, as in the year before CADE launched the Administrative Proceeding.[9]
- Impose the following effective tax rates for firms, according to the kind of conduct:
  - Bid rigging (Article 36, Paragraph 3, Item 1, Sub-item (d) of Law 12529/2011): 17%;
  - Hardcore cartels (Article 36, Paragraph 3, Item 1, Sub-items (a), (b), and (c) of Law 12529/2011): 15%;
  - Other kinds of concerted practices include softcore cartels: 8%.

---

8 CADE, *Guidelines: Cease and Desist Agreement for cartel cases (TCC)* (2016) (in Portuguese) <https://cdn.cade.gov.br/Portal/centrais-de-conteudo/publicacoes/guias-do-cade/guia-tcc-atualizado-11-09-17.pdf> accessed 26 September 2024.

9 CADE may also consider the total turnover of the company, as described in Article 37, paragraph 2 of Law 12529/2011, "CADE may consider the total revenues of the company or group of companies whenever information on the turnover linked to the field of economic activity in which the violation occurred, as defined by CADE, is unavailable or whenever the information presented is incomplete, not entirely clear or appropriate, or both".

- Adjust the effective tax rates, considering aggravating and mitigating factors, under CADE's case law.
- CADE recommends considering the differences in the duration of the respondent's participation in the conduct.

13. As an additional step to the development of the policy for fighting cartels, there is a simple econometric analysis of the data collected from CADE's case law. This procedure is used to foster discussions on possible improvements for fine calculation, mainly in references to adjust the tax rate, based on Items 3 and 4 of Law 12529/2011.

14. Therefore, there were linear regressions of the data related to the firms considering convictions for cartel cases and bid rigging (more robust samples). There were two models, as the variables "Long conduct period" and "Duration of the conduct (in months)" are not put together in the same regression to avoid multicollinearity issues[10] in the results. Thus, the following equations are used:

$$Tax\ rate_i = \alpha + \beta_1 Committed\ financial\ capacity_i + \beta_2 Leading\ role_i + \beta_3 Duration\ of\ the\ conduct_i + \varepsilon_i \quad 1$$

$$Tax\ rate_i = \alpha + \beta_1 Committed\ financial\ capacity_i + \beta_2 Leading\ role_i + \beta_3 Long\ conduct\ period_i + \varepsilon_i \quad 2$$

15. If the "Tax rate" is a decimal value, the "Committed financial capacity" takes up "value 1", regarding the economic difficulty of the respondent. The "Long conduct period" and the "Leading role" have unit values when they are mentioned as aggravating factors of the fine. The variable "Duration of the conduct" is defined based on the months of the conduct, whenever possible to identify it.

16. The results of the estimates confirm what is expected by antitrust authorities, β*'s* which are statistically significant, as seen below:

    $\beta 1 < 0$, as mitigating factors of the penalties, there is a negative effect in the tax rate.

    β_2 and $\beta_3 > 0$, as they are considered aggravating factors; therefore, the established tax rates were increased.

17. The results of the estimates suggest a standard tax rate for fines of firms that is about 13% in cartel cases and 15% for bid rigging from 2012–2022. Regarding the "Committed financial capacity" there is a reduction between 3.6–3.9pp.,[11] depending on the estimated model for cartels, and a reduction between 2.6–2.9pp. for bid rigging. In the case of the 'Leading role' for cartels, there is an improvement of 2.9–3.7pp. and 1.5pp. for bid rigging. Regarding the 'Duration of the conduct', whenever possible to estimate its duration in months, the results show that each month the conduct had an effect

10 Multicollinearity is the linear relationship between an explanatory variable and other variables. In this case, the coefficient of variance estimated is very high, in other words, the variance is overestimated.

11 The coefficients that follow dummy variables are interpreted as: *efeito* = (exp(β) − 1)*100.

of 0.011pp. for cartel cases and 0.02pp. for bid rigging. Thus, cartel cases and bid rigging lasting for 120 months, that is, 10 years, increased 1.32 and 2.4pp., respectively.[12] Whenever it was not possible to clearly identify the duration in months, but it was mentioned by the commissioners that there was a long period of practice as an aggravating factor of the fine calculation, the effect was 4.5pp. for bid rigging and 2.7pp. for cartels, respectively (Table 2).

Table 2. Results of regression analyses considering only fines imposed to legal persons in cases of cartel and bid rigging (2012–2022)

	Cartels		Bid Rigging	
	Model 1	Model 2	Model 1	Model 2
(Intercept)	0.12804***	0.12781***	0.15040***	0.14888***
	0.00367	0.00318	0.00619	0.00453
Committed financial capacity	-0.03665***	-0.04034***	-0.02656***	-0.02936***
	0.00695	0.00678	0.00680	0.00844
Leading role	0.03674***	0.02892***	0.01457*	0.01066
	0.00597	0.00636	0.00694	0.00792
Duration of the conduct (in months)	0.00011**		0.00020***	
	0.00003		0.00005	
Long conduct period		0.04444***		0.02739***
		0.00833		0.00602
R^2	0.37709	0.39344	0.46808	0.32148
Adj. R^2	0.36345	0.38139	0.43616	0.28917
Num. obs.	141	155	54	67
F) (statistical);	27.64562	32.64781	14.66630	9.94987
Breusch–Pagan Test	0.0009544	0.5954	0.1573	0.0109
Durbin Watson Test	1.476e-13	1.583e-13	2.328e-05	5.082e-08
Shapiro–Wilk Test	3e-04	0.0000	4e-04	0.3572
Kolmogorov–Smirnov Test	0.0056	0.0107	0.3092	0.2601

***$p < 0.001$; **$p < 0.01$; *$p < 0.05$; $p < 0.1$

Note: The tests mentioned above have the following null hypotheses: Breusch–Pagan Test: homoscedasticity; Durbin Watson Test: no serial correlation; Shapiro–Wilk and Kolmogorv–Smirnov Tests: normal distribution of residues. The p-values of the tests are reported in the table.
Source: CADE. Hardcore and softcore cartel cases are considered.

III. Why Should We Go Back to Basics?

18. Having kept up with discussions of antitrust authorities over the years, as well as those of various international bodies on competition, the authors sometimes wonder not only what the aims of the antitrust policy are, but mainly if the

12 (120*0.011) = 1.32 and (120*0.02) = 2.4

decisions of the antitrust authorities have had positive effects on society.[13] Our aim is not to discuss the objectives of the competition policy, but to reinforce the need for a continuous improvement of the policy of fighting against cartels, especially in Brazil.

19. An overview analysis of CADE's decisions from 2018–2023, as well as the fines imposed (Figures 5 and 6) shows the variety of the quantity of respondents and administrative proceedings adjudicated, and the total number of fines imposed per year in the decisions of the administrative proceedings related to fighting cartels.

Figure 5. Quantity of respondents adjudicated in the administrative proceedings for cartels divided by year, type, and decision (2018–2023)

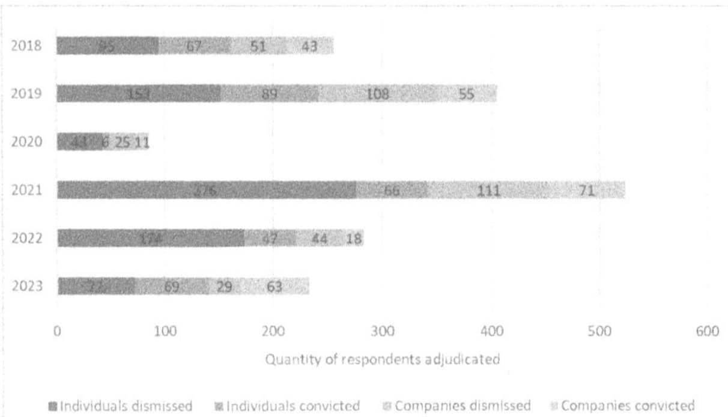

Source: CADE. Some of those were dismissed. They were dismissed due to lack of evidence, in compliance with the cease-and-desist agreements, or termination of penalty.

Figure 6. Quantity of administrative proceedings adjudicated and total value of the fines imposed in cases related to cartels per year (2018–2023)

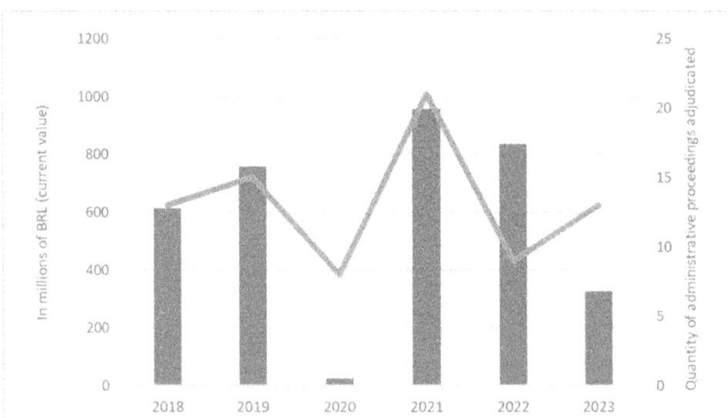

Source: CADE. The total value of the fines imposed per year can be different from the publications issued on the benefits of CADE's activities due to adjustments of the final value for a subsequent appeal.

13 OECD, *Advantages and Disadvantages of Competition Welfare Standards – Note by Brazil* (2023) <https://one.oecd.org/document/DAF/COMP/WD(2023)27/en/pdf> accessed 26 September 2024.

20. It is likely that a similar number of cases will be adjudicated, as in 2020 and 2022; however, there may be substantial differences in the number of parties represented and the total amount of fines imposed. Thus, a deeper analysis of the convictions is required to know the benefits expected from CADE's performance in the scope of suppression of cartel activities. Since 2020, the Department of Economic Studies (DEE) of CADE has been developing a study on the benefits of the authority's performance in cases related to anti-competitive practices and mergers,[14] based on the OECD's methodology.[15]

Figure 7. Development of benefits produced by CADE's performance in cartel cases (convictions and agreements), particularly in convictions and number of administrative proceedings adjudicated (2018–2023)

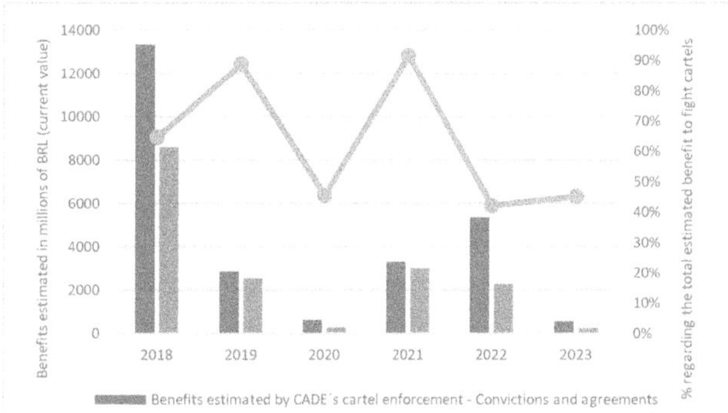

Source: CADE.

---

14 OECD, *Guide for helping competition authorities assess the expected impact of their activities* (2014) <www.oecd.org/daf/competition/Guide-competition-impact-assessmentEN.pdf> accessed 26 September 2024.

15 Guilherme M Resende et al., 'Mensuração dos benefícios esperados da atuação do Cade em 2018' (2020) CADE Working Paper 001/2020 (in Portuguese) <https://cdn.cade.gov.br/Portal/centrais-de-conteudo/publicacoes/estudos-economicos/documentos-de-trabalho/2020/documento-de-trabalho-n01-2020-mensuracao-dos-beneficios-esperados-da-atuacao-do-cade-em-2018.pdf> accessed 26 September 2024.

Guilherme M Resende and Thiago Luis dos Santos Pinto, 'Mensuração dos benefícios esperados da atuação do Cade em 2019' (2020) CADE Working Paper 007/2020 (in Portuguese) <https://cdn.cade.gov.br/Portal/centrais-de-conteudo/publicacoes/estudos-economicos/documentos-de-trabalho/2020/documento-de-trabalho-n07-mensuracao-dos-beneficios-esperados-da-atuacao-do-cade-em-2019.pdf> accessed 26 September 2024.

Guilherme M Resende, Thiago Luis dos Santos Pinto and Nicole Shama dos Santos, 'Mensuração dos benefícios esperados da atuação do Cade em 2020' (2021) CADE Working Paper 005/2021 (in Portuguese) <https://cdn.cade.gov.br/Portal/centrais-de-conteudo/publicacoes/estudos-economicos/documentos-de-trabalho/2021/Documento-de-Trabalho_Mensuracao-dos-beneficios-esperados-da-atuacao-do-Cade-em-2020.pdf> accessed 26 September 2024.

Guilherme M Resende, Thiago Luis dos Santos Pinto and Nicole Shama dos Santos, 'Mensuração dos benefícios esperados da atuação do Cade em 2021' (2022) CADE Working Paper 001/2022 (in Portuguese) <https://cdn.cade.gov.br/Portal/centrais-de-conteudo/publicacoes/estudos-economicos/documentos-de-trabalho/2022/DOC_001-2022_Mensuracao-dos-beneficios-esperados-da-atuacao-do-Cade-em-2021.pdf> accessed 26 September 2024.

Guilherme M Resende et al., 'Mensuração dos benefícios esperados da atuação do Cade em 2022' (2023) CADE Working Paper 001/2023 (in Portuguese) <https://cdn.cade.gov.br/Portal/centrais-de-conteudo/publicacoes/estudos-economicos/documentos-de-trabalho/2023/DT_001-Beneficios-de-atuacao-do-Cade-em-2022.pdf> accessed 26 September 2024.

Thiago L S Pinto, Nicole C Santos and Diandra Carolina O V da Rocha, 'Mensuração dos benefícios esperados da atuação do Cade em 2023' (2024) CADE Working Paper 001/2024 (in Portuguese) <https://cdn.cade.gov.br/Portal/centrais-de-conteudo/publicacoes/estudos-economicos/documentos-de-trabalho/2024/DT_001-Beneficios-de-atuacao-do-Cade-em-2023.pdf> accessed 10 October 2024.

21. The studies show an average benefit expected around BRL 3 billion from 2018–2023 for fighting cartels, considering only the concluded convictions. When the analysis is expanded, considering concluded agreements, this value is increased to more than BRL 4 billion in the same period. It is important to note that the methodology proposed by OECD considers three variables: (1) turnover of the companies in the affected market; (2) overprice removed or avoided; and (3) the expected duration of the price effect.

22. Finally, it is important to emphasise the phenomenal success of the agreement programmes of CADE, which can be observed in 2018 as a series of agreements related to the investigation of the Operation Car Wash (Lava Jato, in Portuguese),[16] on average, about 66% of the total benefits of fighting cartels are related to the penalties (convictions).

IV. Final Considerations

23. The fight against cartels is considered as the basic activity of antitrust policy. After creating a good structure of repression activities for collusive behaviour, the authorities might move on to a more advanced analysis step, based on merger control and repression of unilateral conduct. However, this development must be updated, especially with the strengthening of this large foundation. In fact, the development happens in a spiral way or in cycles with some feedback.

24. Therefore, it is possible to conclude that the Brazilian competition authority is attentive and developing several initiatives to improve competition policy. In the preventive role and in the repressive role of unilateral conducts, examples of these initiatives include the creation of a specific unit to review unilateral conduct, develop studies to improve antitrust remedies and a manual for trustees, and guidance for non-vertical practices, in addition to the release of a platform for the automation of mergers and acquisitions notification. However, it can be said that the Brazilian competition authority always goes back to basics. In other words, CADE has always worked on activities to fight cartels, not only in the investigation, but also in the punishment of violations, having released a Guide for Cartel Penalties recently.

25. Having said that, this work aims to contribute to the policy feedback with a simple econometric analysis of CADE's case law. This procedure is used to foster discussions on possible improvements for fine calculation in cartel cases, to adjust the tax rate based on aggravating and mitigating factors (leading role, duration of the conduct, and committed financial capacity). Regarding the "Committed financial capacity", there is a reduction between 3.6–3.9pp., depending on the estimated model for cartels, and a reduction

---

16 Cartels aiming to defraud government procurements of the Petrobras projects.

between 2.6–2.9pp. for bid rigging. For the aggravating 'Leading role', there is an improvement between 1.5 and 3.7 pp., depending on the models. Regarding the 'Duration of the conduct', whenever possible to estimate the duration of the violation in months, the results show that each month the conduct had an effect from 0.011pp. to 0.02pp. Whenever it was not possible to clearly identify the duration in months, but there was a conduct for a long period, the effect was 4.5pp. for bid rigging and 2.7pp. for cartels, respectively.

26. Finally, it is important to note that the estimated financial benefit of the policy to fight cartels in Brazil in the few past years, on average, was about BRL 3 million regarding convictions and BRL 5 million when adding the agreements signed.

Innovation Competition and Merger Policy: New? Not Sure. Robust? Not Quite![*]

Nicolas Petit[**]
European University Institute

1. In the last few years, the European Commission's (the Commission) assessment of horizontal mergers has been increasingly focused on innovation competition, particularly in mergers involving R&D intensive markets. In this context, the Commission's decision in *Dow/DuPont* of March 2017 continues to be the subject of much debate almost a year after its adoption[1]. The gist of this controversy consists in understanding whether the Commission has, in this case, intervened on the basis of a "*novel*" economic theory of harm in support of its finding that the merger created a risk of a significant impediment to effective innovation competition (SIEIC).

2. From a legal standpoint, the root cause of the controversy is one of process. Introducing new theories of harm during merger review is akin to experimenting with new surgical techniques… without peer validation (and anaesthesia). This line of critique does not preclude the Commission from changing merger policy. Instead, it suggests that it is malpractice to introduce new policy on the job. Policy changes should follow an open process of "*falsification*", so one can be sure that they are based on sound economic theory, backed by

---

* This article has been previously published in Concurrences, and it might have been edited for clarity and cohesion. Nicolas Petit, Innovation competition and merger policy: New? Not sure. Robust? Not quite!, May 2018, Concurrences N° 2-2018, Art. N° 86623, pp. 1-4.

** Professor of Law, University of Liege (ULiege), Liege Competition and Innovation Institute (LCII) Visiting Scholar at the Hoover Institution, Stanford University. Research Professor, University of South Australia (UniSA), Adelaide.

1 COMP/M.7932 – *Dow/DuPont*), para. 3297, available at http://ec.europa.eu/competition/mergers/cases/decisions/m7932_13668_3.pdf.

empirical evidence. This approach has been adopted time and time again in the past by the Commission. The debate that took place on minority shareholdings is a case in point.

3. From an economics perspective, the stir is more foundational. The theoretical relationship between firm size, market structure and innovation remains unsettled since Joseph Schumpeter and Kenneth Arrow[2]. Admittedly, some common ground was found around the idea that innovation thrives with contestability, appropriability and synergies[3]. However, those "*unifying*" economic principles – which denote that the relationship between concentration and innovation is essentially an empirical question – were called into question after *Dow/DuPont* when the Commission's chief economist declared – albeit in a personal capacity – that his team had developed a new model that showed that post-merger, the parties "*always*" decreased their innovation efforts[4]. Meanwhile, official statements from the Commission kept stressing that its assessment of innovation competition in *Dow/DuPont* belonged within ordinary garden variety unilateral effects analysis[5].

4. The official publication of the redacted version of the *Dow/DuPont* decision in late 2017 provides a unique opportunity to check whether the early concerns voiced by legal and economic practitioners were indeed valid. On close reading, it seems that *Dow/DuPont*'s SIEIC analysis marks a small but significant change to the Commission's merger policy in relation to innovation competition (Section I). At the same time, however, the economic model of unilateral effects underpinning SIEIC is based on several critical assumptions which are not robust for innovation competition (Section II).

I. SIEIC: A Small but Significant Change?

5. The Commission has traditionally examined the impact of mergers on innovation competition. Many cases in the pharmaceutical, chemical, industrial and financial sectors have been remedied on the grounds of a post-merger risk of decreased incentives to innovate. However, *Dow/ DuPont* strays from previous EU merger practice on three points.

---

2 J. Schumpeter, *Capitalism, Socialism and Democracy* (1942); K. J. Arrow, Economic Welfare and the Allocation of Resources for Invention, in *The Rate and Direction of Inventive Activity: Economic and Social Factors* (NBER, 1962), pp. 609–626.

3 C. Shapiro: Competition and Innovation. Did Arrow Hit the Bull's Eye?, in J. Lerner and S. Stern (eds), *The Rate and Direction of Inventive Activity Revisited*, 2012, pp. 361–410.

4 *See* EU merger control and innovation, *Competition policy brief*, 2016–01, April 2016, available at http:// ec.europa.eu/competition/publications/ cpb/2016/2016_001_en.pdf; G. Federico, G. Langus and T. Valletti, A Simple Model of Mergers and Innovation, *Economics Letters*, Vol. 157(C) (2017), pp. 136–140.

5 Dow/DuPont innovation concerns "not novel", EU insists, *MLex Insight*, *Competition merger brief*, Issue 2/2017, July, European Commission.

6. To start with, SIEIC extends the application of the standard unilateral effects model, which was previously used to assess pricing effects, to the assessment of innovation competition. *Dow/DuPont* is indeed the first case where the Commission explicitly relies on the unilateral effects framework in relation to innovation competition. In particular, SIEIC can be distinguished from the theory of "*cannibalisation*" developed earlier in *Novartis/GSK Oncology*[6].

7. In this case, the Commission's cannibalisation concerns related to clearly identified existing products. In contrast, the SIEIC theory developed in *Dow/DuPont* is "*broader*" since the harm to innovation applies to future products.[7]

8. The second change brought about by SIEIC is that it dispenses with the delineation of relevant markets. Instead, *Dow/DuPont* looks at competition in "*innovation spaces*", understood as "*the discovery targets*" over which firms compete[8]. This feature of SIEIC is unprecedented. In all merger cases involving the pharmaceutical and crop protection sectors that preceded *Dow/DuPont*, the Commission had focused its assessment of innovation competition on existing and pipeline products. The shift in analytical framework seen in *Dow/DuPont* seems to expand the scope of the merger review to early-stage R&D efforts, where products are several years away from reaching the market[9].

9. Third, *Dow/DuPont* clarifies that the competitive harm envisaged in an SIEIC is a scenario of exit by one of the merging parties from an innovation space. The decision repeatedly talks of an immediate post-merger "discontinuation, deferment or redirection of competing lines of research and early pipeline products". Admittedly, the idea of post-merger exit from lines of research and early pipeline products is not entirely new. For example, in *GE/Alstom*, the Commission found that GE had planned to discontinue parts of Alstom's 50 Hz turbines product offering and related R&D capabilities. However, in *GE/Alstom*, the Commission had specifically identified the products and related activities that the merged entity was likely to shut down. In contrast,

---

6 COMP M.7275 – *Novartis/GlaxoSmithKline Oncology Business*), available at https://ec.europa.eu/competition/mergers/cases/decisions/m7275_20150128_20212_4158734_EN.pdf.

7 Ibid., para. 2108:

> "(…) cannibalisation is often meant to refer to a diversion of sales from one or several existing products to an innovative product sold by the same firm. Innovation competition, instead, more broadly refers to the extent to which innovative products of one firm may divert sales and profits from both existing and other innovative future products of rival firms. (…). The Commission notes that its theory of harm rests on the broader notion of innovation competition rather than on the notion of cannibalisation".

8 COMP/M.7932 – *Dow/DuPont*), op. cit., para. 2168. The R&D undertaken in innovation spaces "generate[s] early pipeline products" (para. 2159).

9 For an early formulation of this point in a US context, see D. Wald and D. Feinstein, Merger Enforcement in Innovation Markets, *Antitrust Source* (2004) 1–11. In recent years, the Commission has increasingly taken into account early-stage pipeline products in its merger reviews. This is reflected in a number of cases in the pharmaceutical sector where the Commission's approach has diverged from its traditional method of focusing on phase III pipeline products. *See* for example *Novartis/ GlaxoSmithKline Oncology Business*, op. cit., and (COMP M.8041 – *J&J/Actelion*), available at http://ec.europa.eu/competition/mergers/cases/decisions/m8401_740_3.pdf.

in *Dow/DuPont*, the Commission concluded that the merger would give rise to an SIEIC even though it conceded that it "may not be able to identify precisely which early pipeline products or lines of research the parties would likely discontinue".

10. Taken together, those three inflections from previous practice denote a policy change. It may not be a "*quantum leap*", true[10]. But it surely is not "*business as usual*".

II. Is Unilateral Effects Theory Robust for Innovation Competition?

11. SIEIC predicts the exit of the merged firm from innovation spaces. The mechanics of exit from innovation spaces are similar to standard unilateral effects in price. As is well understood, in a merger between two close competitors X and Y, firm X will internalise the adverse effects on sales of price competition on firm Y. Hence, X has lower incentives to engage in price competition post-merger, and thus the merger gives rise to a significant impediment to effective competition. In an innovation setting, the assessment simply shifts its focus from post-merger price competition to R&D investments. X will internalise the adverse effects on (future) sales of R&D competition on firm Y. With reduced post-merger profits from innovation, X has lower incentives to engage in R&D competition, and the merger gives rise to an SIEIC.

12. But can one substitute price with R&D in the standard unilateral effects framework without further adjustments to the model? Put differently, are the critical assumptions of a standard unilateral effects model involving price effects robust when non-pricing decisions, and in particular R&D decisions, are considered? Three factors are relevant.

    - First, while prices and output can – to some extent – be adjusted in the short term, firms are unable to discontinue R&D programmes at the flick of a switch. This is because R&D capital is essentially composed of sunk and specific assets. In addition, the labour component of R&D programmes creates rigidity (besides labour market regulation, there may be industry-specific factors that create a need to retain scientists in pharmaceutical companies to oversee the registration and regulatory approval process). Moreover, strategic considerations, such as maintaining an R&D programme for defensive patenting purposes, may come into play. All this suggests that R&D programmes create exit barriers, much like fixed capacity, long-term contracts, etc.

10 See, for an early suggestion to that effect, N. Petit, Significant Impediment to Industry Innovation: A Novel Theory of Harm in EU Merger Control? 4 February 2017, available at SSRN: https://ssrn.com/abstract=2911597. Readers of that previous paper are asked to forgive me for use of the expression "quantum leap". At the time the Dow/DuPont decision had not been published. Given the modest numbers of downloads achieved by that earlier paper, I assume that its impact was insignificant.

- Second, even in the alternative exit scenario of a post-merger redirection of R&D programmes, it is not a given that an adverse impact on welfare will ensue. The welfare costs of reduced competition within one innovation space may well be outweighed by the welfare benefits brought about by the increased coordination ability of the merged entity to deploy its R&D resources across a higher number of innovation spaces. And while it is true that this empirical question cannot be answered in the abstract, this does not justify ignoring it entirely in the context of an SIEIC analysis.
- Third, SIEIC assumes away entirely the possibility that there may be post-merger intra-firm R&D competition in a same innovation space on account of the merged firms' organisational structure. This, in turn, is a limitation of SIEIC because firms' R&D structures are heterogeneous. There are varying degrees of centralisation both in terms of organisation structure – e.g., corporate-level v. business unit-level R&D labs – and decision-making for R&D funding – e.g., headquarter vetted v. business unit vetted R&D budgets[11]. For example, DuPont is often cited as an example of the decentralised R&D model where research is conducted at the divisional level or within business units (ibid.). In practice, an assessment of innovation competition should thus examine the merging parties' post-closing organisation plans.

13. With this background, it is clear that while intuitively appealing, the current formulation of SIEIC is incomplete. SIEIC pays no heed to several critical issues, such as the structural rigidity of R&D resources, the counterbalancing effect of intra-firm coordination across innovation spaces, or the organisational structure of R&D in a merged firm. Taken together, these factors can plausibly decrease the opportunity cost of innovation as well as outweigh the internalised cost of innovation cannibalisation. Short of their consideration, SIEIC remains a fragile basis for merger remediation.

III. Conclusion

14. In a "*forgotten paragraph*" of *Tetra Laval*[12], the Court of Justice of the EU has required the EU Commission to discharge a "*burden of persuasion*" in

---

11 N. Agyres and B. Silverman, R&D, organization structure, and the development of corporate technological knowledge, *Strategic Management Journal*, Vol. 25, Issue 8–9 (2004), p. 930.

12 Case C-12/03 P, *Commission v. Tetra Laval*, [2005] ECR I 987, para. 328, available at http://curia.europa.eu/juris/showPdf.jsf?text=&docid=49926&pageIndex=0&doclang=en&-mode=lst&dir=&occ=first&part=1&cid=630078; M. Jaeger, The Standard of Review in Competition Cases Involving Complex Economic Assessments: Towards the Marginalisation of the Marginal Review?, *Journal of European Competition Law & Practice* Vol. 2, No. 4 (2011), pp. 295–314.

relation to complex economic analysis[13]. Arguably, SIEIC falls within this category. Future cases will tell us if SIEIC can survive the test of accuracy, reliability, consistency and completeness required by the case law. Without prejudging on forthcoming improvements in merger analysis, a close reading of *Dow/DuPont* suggests, however, that in current formulation, SIEIC theory is too crude to produce empirical findings in relation to innovation competition[14].

13 This expression was coined by I. Liannos and C. Genakos, Econometric evidence in EU competition law: an empirical and theoretical analysis, in I. Lianos and D. Geradin (eds), *Handbook on European Competition Law: Enforcement and Procedure*, Edward Elgar Publishing (2013).

14 For more on the above, a comprehensive study of those issues can be found at https://papers.ssrn.com/sol3/papers.cfm?abstract_id=3113077.

Minority Interests and Joint Shareholding: A New Age of Enforcement?

ANNE WACHSMANN* AND MATTHIEU BLAYNEY**
Linklaters

1. Competition law is not different to other topics of academia, "hot topics" tend to come and go. This seeming frivolity requires modesty from trendsetters and taking a step back from commentators when discussing new subjects of interest.

2. The need to implement, or not, a means to review *non-controlling* minority shareholdings is one of those "*arlesiennes*" which has regularly come to the fore over the last twenty years, justifying its inclusion as an object of study in this publication.

I. Winter: The Exclusion of Non-Controlling Minority Shareholdings from Merger Control

3. Unlike the prohibition on cartels and abuses of dominant positions laid down in the Treaty of Rome, the introduction of merger control at European level did not originate in primary law.

4. The creation of such a mechanism was called for by the European Commission as early as the 1960s.

---

* Partner, Linklaters LLP. With thanks to Raphaël Wettasinghe, Associate, Linklaters LLP, for his help.
** Counsel, Linklaters LLP.

5. Reflecting a tension between, on the one hand, a partisan line of merger control that takes account of the imperatives of industrial policy, advocated by certain governments in particular with a view to creating national or European "champions", and, on the other hand, the advocates of a system based on an orthodox legal and economic framework centred on the protection of competition and consumer welfare, the Commission initially suffered a number of setbacks with its proposals in 1973, 1981 and 1984.

6. During this period, and despite the absence of mandatory merger control, the Commission occasionally resorted to Articles 85 and 86 of the Treaty establishing the European Economic Community (now Articles 101 and 102 TFEU) to oppose certain mergers, including for instance in the Philip Morris case[1] which many believed belonged to history, and which has very recently emerged again with the Court of Justice of the European Union's ruling of 16 March 2023 in the *Towercast* case. This control was upheld by the Court of Justice, notably in the famous *Continental Can* case of 21 February 1973.[2]

7. Merger control in Europe finally came to life with the adoption of Regulation 4064/89 of 21 December 1989 (Merger Regulation) introducing a system of compulsory and suspensive notification, if certain turnover thresholds are met, of mergers or acquisitions of "control of the whole or parts of one or more other undertakings" (Article 3.1(b)).

8. "Control" is defined pursuant to Article 3 of the Merger Regulation as the ability to exercise a "decisive influence" over an undertaking, in particular, through the existence of rights enabling to decide on the strategic commercial behaviour of an undertaking, either alone (sole control) or jointly (joint control). The restriction of merger control to "controlling" stakes was reaffirmed in Regulation 139/2004 of 20 January 2004 which replaced the 1989 Merger Regulation.[3] While most of minority shareholdings are not associated with such right and thus are not controlling, by exception it can occur that a minority shareholding suffices to provide sole[4] or joint control (de jure[5] or de facto).

---

1 Joined Cases 142/84 and 156/84 *British American Tobacco Co Ltd v Commission of the European Communities* ECLI:EU:C:1987:490; see European Court of Justice, "The EU Court of Justice states that letters addressed by the Commission rejecting complaints can be subjected to an action for annulment (British American Tobacco)" (1987) e-Competitions art. No. 106729.

2 Case 6/72 *Europemballage Corp v Commission of the European Communities* ECLI:EU:C:1973:22. See also, (Cases No IV/33.440 – *Warner-Lambert/Gillette and Others* and No IV/33.486 – *BIC/Gillette and Others*) Commission Decision 93/252/EEC [1993] OJ L116/21 where the Commission reviewed the acquisition of minority shareholding under Article 102 TFEU.

3 It should be remembered that not all minority shareholdings fall outside the Commission's control, as notification remains obligatory when the acquisition of a minority shareholding results in the exercise, alone or jointly, of decisive influence.

4 (Case COMP/M.7779 – *Trafigura / Nyrstar*) COM (2015) 9606 final.

5 (Case COMP/M.7270 – *Cesky Aeroholding/ Travel Service/ Ceske Aerolinie*) Commission Decision 18 December 2014.

9. As non-controlling minority shareholdings were never subject to merger control, they were subject to competition law rules, namely Articles 101 and 102 TFEU either as an agreement between undertakings or potentially as an abuse of dominant position.

II. Spring: The Inclusion of Non-Controlling Minority Shareholdings in the Substantive Analysis of Merger Control

10. This exclusion of non-controlling minority shareholdings from merger control does not mean, however, that the Commission does not consider that they cannot harm competition. On the contrary, theoretically, a shareholding, even a non-controlling one, can change the behaviour of the target company:

- The target company may wish to avoid antagonising the minority shareholder, in order to avoid undermining its financial support;
- The minority shareholder may discourage potential investors from acquiring the target (thereby making it more competitive).

11. In addition, a minority shareholding can change the behaviour of the company holding the shareholding:

- By changing its financial incentives to compete with the target if it is interested in the target's profits;
- By facilitating collusive behaviour if the holding company is represented, for example, on the target company's board of directors and can therefore access confidential and/or strategic information.

12. This is why, quite naturally in light of the above, the Commission takes into account the existence of minority shareholdings in its competitive analysis. It can occur that in the context of the notification of a main operation, existing minority shareholding are indirectly reviewed as part of the overall transaction. The acquisitions of Westinghouse by Toshiba in 2006,[6] of Telecom Italia[7] by Vivendi in 2017 and of TKR by Orange in 2021[8] illustrate this analysis by the Commission and the potential consequences for the parties.

---

6 (Case COMP/M.4153 – *Toshiba/Westinghouse*) Commission Decision 19 September 2006 [2007] OJ C10/1, see John Gatti and Mary Loughran, "The EU Commission conditionally clears a merger in the nuclear sector (Toshiba / Westinghouse / BNFL)" (2006) e-Competitions art. No. 38251.

7 (Case COMP/M.8465 – *Vivendi/Telecom Italia*) Commission Decision 30 May 2017, see European Commission, "The EU Commission clears a merger subject to remedies in the telecommunication market (Telecom Italia / Vivendi)" (2017) e-Competitions art. No. 84312.

8 (Case COMP/M.10153 – *Orange/ Telekom Romania Communications*) Commission Decision 28 July 2021, see European Commission, "The EU Commission approves an acquisition subject to conditions in the telecommunications sector (Telekom Romania / Orange)" (2021) e-Competitions art. No. 101854.

13. When Toshiba filed its acquisition of Westinghouse, the Commission took into account the non-controlling minority stake (24.5%) already held by Toshiba in GNF, a competitor of Westinghouse:

> "Toshiba could not only hamper or prevent its competitor GE from expanding its business by way of its existing veto rights. After the merger, Toshiba will, through its information rights and its representation in various Boards of GNF and its subsidiaries/joint ventures, also have the opportunity to obtain sensitive confidential information which might help Toshiba to make GE's expansion more difficult".[9]

14. Similarly, as part of the examination of Vivendi's acquisition of Telecom Italia, the Commission analysed the effect on competition of the minority stake (28.8%) already held by Vivendi in Mediaset, a competitor of a Telecom Italia subsidiary (Persidera) on the Digital Terrestrial Television market:

> "TIM's incentives to compete against Mediaset in DTT wholesale access will change as a result of the Transaction, since TIM's lost profits from raising prices or offering inferior conditions to TV channels wishing to broadcast over Persidera's MUXes would be recovered through Vivendi's minority shareholding in Mediaset. By worsening the conditions for access to Persidera's MUXes, Vivendi would financially benefit either directly (from higher prices charged for access to Persidera's MUXes) or indirectly from Mediaset's revenues (resulting from hosting additional third-party channels on its MUXes)".[10]

15. In consequence, the Commission cleared the acquisition subject to the divestment of Telecom Italia's stake in Persidera.

16. In 2021, the Commission conditioned Orange's acquisition of Telekom Romania on the divestiture of the latter's minority stake in Telekom Romania Mobile Communications (TRMC). This was justified by the fact that acquiring control of Telekom Romania would have also resulted in Orange acquiring a 30% minority stake in TRMC, the third largest Romanian mobile operator and a direct competitor of Orange. The Commission was concerned that Orange could have tried to limit TRMC's ability to effectively compete.

17. These examples highlight the paradoxical situation in which the Commission finds itself. The Commission does not have the power to control the acquisition of minority shareholdings as they do not allow the exercise of a "decisive influence", while at the same time taking account of these minority shareholdings in its substantive analysis when they appear in the context of

---

9 Case *Toshiba/Westinghouse* (n 6), para 92, see John Gatti and Mary Loughran, "The EU Commission conditionally clears a merger in the nuclear sector (Toshiba / Westinghouse / BNFL)" (2006) e-Competitions art. No. 38251.

10 Case *Vivendi/Telecom Italia* (n 7), para 75, see European Commission (n 7).

a notified operation and, if necessary, making its authorisation conditional on the disposal of these minority shareholdings. This results in a situation that is not necessarily optimal, since the Commission's possibility of control under merger control rules depends on external elements.

III. Autumn: The Aborted Attempt at ex-ante Control of Minority Shareholdings

18. While the 2001 Green Paper[11] on the revision of the Merger Regulation came out against the introduction of minority shareholding control,[12] the debate was started again in 2011 by Commissioner Almunia:

> "The issue of minority shareholdings, where we are probably looking at an *enforcement gap.*
>
> The Merger Regulation does not apply to minority shareholders, whereas some national systems - both in the EU and outside - make room for the review of such acquisitions. I have instructed my services to look into this issue and see whether it is significant enough for us to try and close this gap in EU merger control".[13] (emphasis added)

19. The Ryanair/Aer Lingus saga gave the Commission an opportunity to raise this *enforcement gap*. The Commission prohibited the acquisition of Aer Lingus by Ryanair by a decision of 27 June 2007.[14] Nevertheless, Ryanair had acquired a non-controlling minority stake in Aer Lingus. Aer Lingus demanded that the Commission order Ryanair to divest its non-controlling minority stake. The Commission's refusal, justified by its inability to control minority shareholdings, was upheld by the Court of the European Union.

20. Following a very broad public consultation, the Commission's 2014 White Paper, *Towards More Effective EU Merger Control* put forward two options: one to extend existing control to even minority stakes, the other consisting of a discretionary power of review by the Commission in the form of a "self-assessment" system operating on the basis of transparency and undertaking declarations.

---

11 European Commission, "Communication from the Commission of the European Communities" COM (2001) 745, Green Paper on the revision of Regulation (4064/89, 11 December 2001, see Stephen Ryan et al., "The EU Commission adopts a green paper on the review of the merger regulation" (2001) e-Competitions art. No. 38982.

12 The Green Paper states that only a few transactions involving the acquisition of minority shareholdings would raise competition concerns that could not be resolved by recourse to the former Articles 81 and 82 of the EC Treaty. Subjecting all acquisitions of minority shareholdings to ex-ante merger control would therefore be disproportionate (para 109) as it would have introduced too heavy an administrative burden for companies and the regulator by referring a large number of non-problematic transactions.

13 Speech by the Vice-President of the European Commission responsible for competition policy, Porter Elliott, "The EU Commission examines whether acquisitions of minority shareholdings should be subject to EU merger control" (2011) e-Competitions art. No. 41148.

14 (Case COMP/M.4439 – *Ryanair/Aer Lingus*) Commission Decision 11 October 2007 [2007] OJ C269/59.

21. Finally, the 2014 White Paper put forward a hybrid system whereby companies had to notify acquisitions of minority shareholdings with: (i) a vertical or horizontal link; and (ii) with a shareholding of around 20% or between 5–20% if accompanied by further enhanced rights such as a de facto blocking minority, a seat on the board of directors or access to confidential information of the target company. It was then up to the Commission to decide whether or not it wished to examine the transaction.

22. The proposal was widely criticised for significantly increasing the administrative burden on businesses.

23. This initiative was in any event firmly put aside by Commissioner Vestager, whose first term in office began in 2014 and who made public her strong doubts about the need for such a reform in 2016.[15]

IV. Summer: A Renaissance through Common Ownership?

24. At a time when minority shareholdings seemed destined to become a "has-been" concept, the Commission provided a new lifeline to the topic with the concept of common shareholding.

25. This issue was raised by the Commission on two occasions in the context of two transactions in the agrochemicals sector: the merger of Dow and DuPont in 2017[16] and the acquisition of Monsanto by Bayer in 2018.[17]

26. These two transactions raised important competition issues and were authorised after Phase 2 with heavy divestments notably in relations to concerns of reductions of innovation or innovation effort (such as R&D) following what many considered a "novel" theory of harm by the Commission. In analysing these two transactions, beyond the concerns related to innovation, the Commission questioned the impact of the significant level of common ownership in the agrochemicals sector. It indeed found in the Dow/Dupont case that 17 common investors each held between 21% and 36% of the shareholdings of the six leading companies in the sector and in the Bayer/Monsanto case that 29 institutional investors held between 26% and 39% of BASF, Bayer, Dow/Dupont and Monsanto.

27. The Commission considered that these so-called "passive" investors actually have a greater influence than their formal voting rights, particularly in that they can communicate with the board of directors and management in order

15 Remarks at the 2016 IBA Spring Meeting, Ron Knox, "Vestager: Minority shareholder reform may be unjustifiable" (*GCR*, 8 April 2016) <https://globalcompetitionreview.com/article/vestager-minority-shareholder-reform-may-be-unjustifiable> accessed 29 October 2024.

16 (Case COMP/M.7932 – *Dow/Dupont*) Commission Decision 27 March 2017, see Porter Elliott, "The EU Commission conditionally clears a merger in the chemical sector (Dow / DuPont)" (2017) e-Competitions art. No. 83819.

17 (Case COMP/M.8084 – *Bayer/Monsanto*) Commission Decision 29 May 2018 [2018] OJ C459/9.

to influence the company's strategy. It noted that it may reduce the probability for the companies to invest in R&D efforts, if this could harm the interests of competing firms also held in the investor portfolio. It also noted that the Herfindahl-Hirschman Index (HHI) index, which focuses on market shares, was not relevant in cases of common ownership. Despite its findings, the Commission nevertheless considered that common ownership did not call into question Bayer's independence but recognised more generally the existence of a debate on this issue.

28. These two cases seemed to herald a dynamic career for this new concept. But it was not to be.

29. In 2020, two studies, one commissioned by the European Parliament[18] and the other by DG-COMP,[19] came to the cautious conclusion that the existence of common ownership is associated with a high degree of market power, but that it is difficult to determine whether they constitute an infringement of competition. The question therefore remains open....

30. Nevertheless, a brief appearance in a 2023 judgment of the General Court is noteworthy as the Court referred to the Commission's conclusions in the Dow/Dupont and Bayer/Monsanto cases. The Court's approach seems measured, concluding that "even supposing that the reduction in competitive pressure on other competitors may result from a common shareholding, the effect of that reduction alone is not *in principle* sufficient to demonstrate a significant impediment to effective competition under a theory of harm based on non-coordinated effects"[20] (emphasis added), and therefore does not draw any conclusions regarding the presence of a common shareholding in this case.

V. Conclusion: The Renewal of the Control on the Basis of Articles 101 and 102 TFEU?

31. On 16 March 2023, the Court of Justice of the European Union reaffirmed the possibility of ex-post control of a merger on the basis of Article 101 and 102 TFEU in its *Towercast* judgment.[21] The Court ruled that a merger that

18 European Parliament, *Barriers to Competition through Joint Ownership by Institutional Investors* (2020) <www.europarl.europa.eu/RegData/etudes/STUD/2020/652708/IPOL_STU(2020)652708_EN.pdf> accessed 29 October 2024.

19 European Union, *Common Shareholding in Europe* (2020) <https://op.europa.eu/en/publication-detail/-/publication/eafd4226-02c9-11eb-8919-01aa75ed71a1/language-en> accessed 29 October 2024.

20 Case T-312/20 *EVH v European Commission* ECLI:EU:T:2023:252, para. 387, see General Court of the European Union, "The EU General Court rejects a claim alleging the Commission was mistaken to treat a complex merger involving several transactions separately and endorses the analysis and decision-making process (EVH / enercity / E.ON / RWE)" (2023) e-Competitions art. No. 112643.

21 Case C-449/21 *Towercast* ECLI:EU:C:2023:207, see Lucas Bettoni, "Merger below the thresholds: The Court of Justice of the European Union affirms that a merger with a non-European dimension may be subject to control at national level under the prohibition on abuse of a dominant position (Towercast)" (2023) 2 Concurrences 112742.

has not been notified because it falls below the notification thresholds is not immune from review on the grounds of abuse of a dominant position.[22]

32. It will be interesting to follow whether the possibility of controlling "concentrations" on the basis of antitrust rules will lead to a new trend of controlling minority shareholdings on the basis of Articles 101 and 102 TFEU.

33. Thus, after a long detour through merger control, the treatment of the control of minority shareholdings could potentially see a renewal by the classical application of Articles 101 and 102 TFEU.

22 See for an application in France, French Competition Authority, Case 24-D-05 *Meat Cutting* (2 May 2024) <www.autoritedelaconcurrence.fr/sites/default/files/integral_texts/2024-05/24d05.pdf> accessed 29 October 2024.

The Optimal Competition Guide Stars – Economic Rationality, Due Process

Abbott B. Lipsky*
GMU Antonin Scalia Law School

1. Within the domain of private commercial activity where antitrust rules govern, competition simply means striving for success. The framework for and boundaries of commercial activity are of course set by the government. The law of property, contract, tort, intellectual property, corporate/business organizations and securities, as well as other fields of law and regulation (federal, state and local) set the size, shape and other conditions of the "playing field" for trade and commerce. Within those constraints, a wide variety of business conduct is available to carry out productive activity – by individuals, business entities of various forms, as well as alliances involving distinct entities (e.g., supply, distribution, licensing and franchise arrangements, joint ventures, etc.). Analysis of historical evidence provides a few key insights regarding the character and value of competition.

2. First, the evidence is overwhelming that the primary source of improvements in the standard of living is innovation. Chose any realm of human activity – transportation, agriculture, communication, medical care – and consider its evolution over the last two centuries. In 1824, the comfort, convenience and speed of transportation were set by the capabilities of horses and wooden sailing vessels. Agriculture relied exclusively on human and animal labor

* Adjunct Professor, Antonin Scalia Law School, Arlington, Virginia. I have been devoted to antitrust for more than fifty years as a student, teacher, practitioner (government and private law firm as well as in-house at a leading global corporation) covering all facets of antitrust both US and international. The views expressed are solely those of the author, and do not intentionally represent those of any other individual or entity, including without limitation Antonin Scalia Law School and George Mason University.

before the invention of the mechanical reaper in 1831, after which farm productivity continuously rose based on mechanization, the use of power sources such as steam and internal combustion, chemical fertilization and many other innovations, including the "Green Revolution" of hybridization. Communication was primitive and slow before the invention of the telegraph in 1837, allowing immediate long-distance transmission of coded messages for the first time. Long-run improvements in the quality of medical care and in the character and performance of other economic sectors are equally striking over this time period.

3. Economists Robert Solow and Moses Abramovitz independently estimated that innovation could account for as much as 85 percent of real economic growth since the Industrial Revolution, although subsequent analysis suggests a lower figure. But it would take a mountain of persuasive evidence to contradict the conclusions that are obvious from measuring recent improvements in the conditions of life. World output went from $1.36 trillion (2017 prices) to $134.08 trillion in 2021. The global poverty rate has declined from 80 percent in the 1820's to less than 10 percent now, while world population has grown from roughly one billion to eight billion during the same period. Neither would have been possible without innovation.

4. Second, by contrast to the evidence on the importance of innovation, evidence on the relationship between competition and innovation is decidedly mixed. There is no doubt that competition is an effective spur to innovation, but beyond that the relationship is obscure. Long referred to as the "Schumpeter-Arrow" debate, there is a persistent difference in view as to whether large enterprises are somehow better able to engage in research and development, which often requires investing significant resources at high risk and waiting many years before realizing any tangible return. Whatever the intuitive appeal of this notion, there are plentiful examples of shoe-string operations that created new industries or totally disrupted others through innovations.

5. Consider the humble roots of Amazon, Apple, Facebook, Google, and Microsoft. Now the largest enterprises in history, it is worth reflection that each was launched on the basis of major innovations by one or a few individuals starting from scratch – Jeff Bezos in 1994, Steve Jobs, Steve Wozniak, and Ronald Wayne in 1976, Mark Zuckerberg and a few college friends in 2004, Larry Page and Sergey Brin in 1998, and Bill Gates and Paul Allen in 1975, respectively. There are numerous less well-known stories of equivalent and even greater success. In 1925 a teenage amateur radio operator, Arthur Collins, became a global celebrity as the leading innovator in radio communication. (At 16 years old, he was the first to engage in radio communication over long distances via short-wave radio – a feat that allowed him to communicate with a US Navy expedition to the Arctic at a time when no one else could do so.) In 1933 he founded the still-leading avionics firm Collins Radio, now the Collins Aerospace subsidiary of defense conglomerate RTX, successor to Raytheon. Then there is Shuji Nakamura, who worked alone and in defiance

of instructions from his employer, who saw no value in the project, to invent the blue LED. This device has made possible the inexpensive high-quality visual displays essential to billions of smartphones, computers, and TVs, as well as to a range of other important modern products, including light sources that can emit in any color, including white (which was not possible with only red and yellow LED). Nakamura shared the 2014 Nobel Prize in Physics for this accomplishment.

6. And then of course there were the justly famed Wright Brothers, bicycle mechanics working independently who won the race to invent the first powered, heavier-than-air manned aircraft. Their main competitor was a group which included Alexander Graham Bell – inventor of the telephone and fabulously wealthy owner of the Bell System, the largest telephone company in history – supported by a government grant (authorized by President McKinley and approved by then Assistant Navy Secretary Theodore Roosevelt), and assisted by Samuel P. Langley, astronomer, physicist, and Director of the Smithsonian Institution. The Wright Brothers' success is one of many examples that make it difficult to infer any simple causal connection between wealth, expertise, and/or government support on one hand and successful innovation on the other. This is not to say, however, that the larger resources are not helpful or even necessary to produce certain innovations, as illustrated by the many breakthroughs (e.g., transistor, solar cell) produced by the research arm of the Bell System, Bell Labs. Either way, dynamic competition is far more important in stimulating long-term economic growth – than other static measures of competition that do not fully incorporate intertemporal effects. Antitrust policy must be guided accordingly, and in the absence of any general expectation regarding the relationship between market structure or firm size and successful innovation, the circumstances of each case must be evaluated carefully and individually.

7. We also know that government administration of competition through economic regulation (limits on prices and other transaction terms, product quality, entry and exit) – especially agency regulation – is a seriously flawed model for successful competition and tends to suppress innovation, because the US has proven this over and over again. The first major public demands for US government control of business conduct arose after the American Civil War. New technologies and massive business organizations seeking to exploit those technologies emerged during this period in a variety of important industries – railroads, petroleum, steel – leading first to state "Granger Laws" limiting the prices and other terms for railroad transportation and grain storage. In 1887 intensifying grievances against the railroads led to passage of the Interstate Commerce Act, creating the first federal economic administrative agency, the Interstate Commerce Commission (ICC). The ICC eventually obtained comprehensive economic regulatory authority encompassing railroads and many other industries – transportation by motor carrier, inland waterway (barges), and petroleum pipelines. The ICC also obtained jurisdiction (for a brief time) to regulate radio communication and commercial aviation.

8. Other federal agencies modeled on the ICC were created to control other sectors: ocean shipping (by the US Shipping Board, later the Federal Maritime Commission), commercial aviation (Civil Aeronautics Authority, later Civil Aeronautics Board (CAB)), broadcasting and telecommunications (Federal Radio Commission, later Federal Communications Commission), and energy (Federal Power Commission, later Federal Energy Regulatory Commission). Many states created similar agencies and regulations. These ventures in agency control of competition were eventually discredited and severely cut back. The CAB was abolished in 1985, and the ICC was abolished in 1995. Other regulatory regimes were aggressively trimmed to reflect a more targeted assessment of their public value.

9. The antitrust agencies also sometimes attempted to impose broad and durable limitations on competitive practices within specific industries. A major antitrust effort undertaken by the Wilson Administration against the meatpacking industry led to the 1920 Meatpackers Decree, which imposed a variety of restrictions on simultaneous ownership of competitors in different segments of the trade until the Decree was terminated in 1981. An antitrust investigation of leading motion picture firms begun under Franklin Roosevelt led to the 1948 Paramount Decree that imposed restrictions generically similar to those of the Meatpackers Decree. That Decree lasted until terminated by a court in 2020. It turned out that long-running supervision of industry competition by antitrust agencies was not too dissimilar in its effects from economic regulation by administrative agency. Under the Paramount Decree, for example, the Antitrust Division authorized monopsony collusive bidding for motion picture exhibition rights by groups of competing theaters (so-called "splits") – a practice long (and correctly) regarded as per se illegal in other industries. During the Carter Administration the US Department of Justice was forced to litigate to reverse its own decree-enforcement policy and return to the accepted antitrust treatment of "splits" as collusive monopsony agreements.

10. The economic headwinds faced by the United States during the period of "stagflation" – late 1960's to 1980 – contributed to a broad reassessment of policy, including competition policy and the efficacy of regulated competition. New and more sophisticated legal and economic scholarship led ultimately to a broad consensus (among scholars, practitioners and other policy experts) that economic progress is best maintained by an intellectual property policy that respects the role of incentives in innovation, by a regulatory policy that recognizes both regulatory failure and market failure with equanimity, intervening only when clearly justified and even then to the minimum extent necessary, and by an antitrust policy that focuses on preservation of competition (rather than competitors) to maximize economic progress. In two merger cases in 1974 (*US v. General Dynamics*; *US v. Marine Bancorporation)*, and in a vertical restraints case (*Continental TV v. GTE Sylvania*), and a standing case (*Brunswick v. Pueblo Bowl-O-Mat*) in 1977, the Supreme Court implicitly overruled a 1972 precedent (*US v. Topco Associates*) rejecting and even

ridiculing the use of economics in antitrust. *Topco* capped an era (1937–1972) in which many competitive practices were declared per se illegal, and both mergers and dominant-firm conduct were heavily presumed illegal based on shallow and simplistic conceptions of competition.

11. Since that time the Supreme Court has consistently adhered to sound economics as its guide to antitrust-law interpretation. There is plenty of room for debate about the correct application of economic analysis to specific cases, but in general the Court has successfully emphasized the use of fact-based economic analysis, objective legal standards, and error-cost analysis. It has avoided the temptation to mix non-economic objectives into antitrust analysis, as was common prior to 1974. Since the advent of this economically rational antitrust approach, the US has consistently achieved growth and innovation beyond those of any other nation. Of course, antitrust can't be the whole story of this success. Intellectual property improvements and new macroeconomic policies – among many others – also had significant and generally helpful effects. But the other models available for antitrust policy do not offer much promise of superiority.

12. Economic regulation via administrative agency – the policy that began with creation of the ICC in 1887, before federal antitrust laws were first enacted – has been proven to suppress innovation and restrict competition, leading to poor economic performance. The administrative regulation approach has also proven extremely difficult to reform. The ICC itself, which was first recognized as an economic albatross by the Kennedy Administration, could not be eliminated until 1995 due to powerful interests that had ossified around the regulatory scheme. We now have another distinct antitrust model to compare to our own, established in 1957 by the creation of the European Economic Community (now the European Union). The competition rules originally contained in the Treaty of Rome that created the EEC are now embodied in Articles 101 and 102 (corresponding roughly to Sections 1 and 2 of the Sherman Act) of the Treaty on the Functioning of the European Union (TFEU). Since 1990, structural transactions having "Community dimension" are subject to mandatory prior notification and approval, as is common in many other jurisdictions. Thus, the EU relies on a long-standing, active and comprehensive but distinct system of competition rules that is roughly comparable to US law.

13. Substantively, the EU competition system relies on a more aggressively interventionist interpretation of antitrust. It recognizes non-competition objectives (i.e., creation of a Single Market, preservation of competitors for their own sake even at some economic cost), and its acceptance of fact-based economic analysis wavers at the edges. (A respected former Competition Commissioner was recently quoted as expressing some regret that he had endorsed the economic approach during his tenure.) European Union authorities observe a "precautionary principle," meaning they intervene against conduct that has some future possibility of ripening into something of public policy concern. This broad tendency, endorsed by the European courts, is reflected in the

Commission's apparent willingness to address competitive restraints even when the competitive risks are remote. Unlike the US rules on monopolization, EU rules on "abuse of dominance" explicitly confer authority on the competition agency to regulate "unfair" prices, terms or other conditions of trade adopted by dominant firms.

14. To complicate matters, this entire set of analytical concepts is embedded in a unique procedural system that offers limited rights of defense, which tends to exacerbate uncertainty and amplify interventionist temptations. Specifically, competition decisions are made only by the full EU College of Commissioners – appointed politicians without either specialized training in antitrust or detailed familiarity with the evidence in the administrative case record – but every other step in proceedings is the responsibility of an agency (the Directorate General for Competition) that has unitary control of investigation, case presentation, judgment and remedy, subject only to appeal to the EU courts. This unique combination – top-level approval by a political body and unitary case development, decision and remedy – produces decisions that tend to support broader EU objectives as distinct from careful and balanced economic assessment of probable competitive impact. There is some control of this tendency through judicial review, but such review is characteristically slow, deferential to the Commission and therefore somewhat marginal in ultimate effect.

15. Although this is hardly proof of the relative merits of the US and EU systems, it bears noting that the EU has lagged the US in economic growth and innovation over an extended period of time. The GDP of each (meaning for the EU side the EEC countries plus those that ultimately joined the EU) was roughly equivalent in Q1 1981 (about $3 trillion). By Q1 2020 US GDP reached $21 trillion while EU output was $15 trillion (all figures inflation adjusted). Perhaps some of this margin is attributable to the slower spread of active competition enforcement in Europe following the Treaty of Rome. But the EU essentially reached its present size and organic form in 1993, and the pattern has not significantly changed since that time.

16. In addition, the US leads substantially on any list of the most successful technology companies (measured by market capitalization), with 7 of the top 10 and 36 of the top 50, by one recent and typical count. The EU accounts for only 3 of the top 50. This perhaps explains why the EU has taken such aggressive steps to extend and even supplement its competition rules to control the behavior of the leading digital platforms (the so-called "gatekeeper" firms, which include all five of the US technology companies mentioned above, plus one Chinese company – but no European companies). Surveying the US–EU disparity in innovative performance with the new EU regulatory developments suggests to some extent that EU antitrust is being used for objectives more closely related to promotion of national champions and improving terms of trade, rather than to resolve bona fide questions about the effects of specific conduct on market competition.

17. In sum, analysis of historical experience provides several clear and fundamental guideposts for sound competition law and policy: ensuring they accord with economic rationality and with the overall objective of promoting economic progress, fully accounting for innovation and dynamic competitive effects, limiting the use of economic regulation (in any guise) to those rare instances where the predictable weaknesses of government administration are clearly less serious than those of the market, and ensuring that antitrust procedures efficiently produce accurate and impartial decisions. By these standards the US system has performed very well since the shift that began in 1974. At the least, the other obvious competitor systems – the EU, the administrative approach to economic regulation that pervaded US policy until the 1970's – have no basis for claims of superiority over the US system. Judged according to the lessons of historical performance, the current so-called "Neo Brandeisian" passion for approaches that echo the two other systems, as well as the discredited per se/presumptive illegality path taken by US antitrust from 1937–1972 – in addition to the remarkable procedural disadvantages placed upon those suspected or accused of anticompetitive conduct by current US agency practice – seems likely to lead the US down a cul-de-sac ending in serious economic failure.

“Policeman” or Arbitrator?*

Bruno Lasserre**

Commission for Access to Administrative Documents (CADA)

1. The Competition Authority is often described as the competition “policeman”, but it would be more accurate to describe it as an arbitrator. Because competition regulation is not limited to the exercise of the power to sanction anticompetitive practices or merger control, however much they contribute to the regulator’s visibility. The whistle and the cards are not everything: on the pitch, the referee also and perhaps above all ensures compliance with the rules by intervening in the interests of the game’s collective, the smooth running of the game, by ensuring that the players’ vigour is not impeded and by promoting *fair play* on the pitch. And those who are not indifferent to sport will agree that the game is never as good as when the teams play fairly.
2. In economic matters, this function of the regulator, which consists of promoting and teaching competition to the public authorities, companies and the general public, is commonly referred to as *advocacy*. It is essential to prevent restrictions of competition linked to regulations, to enlighten companies on the risks they run, to enable those who wish to do so to play the compliance card by understanding precisely the behaviours that comply or do not comply with competition law, and to develop sources of innovation and growth.
3. Without seeking to resolve the chicken-and-egg paradox here, we note in this respect that the acclimatization of our economy to the competition paradigm has gone hand in hand with the deepening and diversification of the Authority’s *advocacy* instruments.

---

* This article has been previously published in Concurrences, and it might have been edited for clarity and cohesion. Bruno Lasserre, “Policeman” or arbitrator?, September 2021, Concurrences N° 3-2021, Art. N° 101598, pp. 2-3.

** Commission for Access to Administrative Documents – CADA, Paris.

4. Its consultative function, a historical pillar of competition regulation which, in 1986, gave its name to the Competition Council, has thus been significantly expanded.

5. Nearly one-seventh of the Authority's referrals are now optional, given that the institutions that have this option have continued to diversify. And more and more government departments, not only the Ministry of the Economy, as well as members of parliament, are requesting competition analyses. Its opinions are sought, depending on the case, to analyse the concrete functioning of a market in order to provide input for the adoption of a regulation, to evaluate commercial practices and test the interest of a regulation for competitive reasons, to gather expertise on a draft law or decree, or finally to establish the competitive assessment of a regulation.

6. At the same time, the Autorité de la concurrence has made proactive use of the power of self-referral conferred on it by the Order of 13 November 2008. Intervening on a case-by-case basis, whether to negotiate commitments with a company or to impose a penalty, is not always the best solution: it is sometimes more strategic to look at the big picture, for example by examining a market as a whole and proposing, if necessary, solutions to improve its operation. A practice of sector inquiries inspired by the European Commission has thus been developed, which leads the Authority to deal with general competition issues and to target priorities, as it did, for example, in 2014, concerning long-distance passenger transport by coach, its recommendations having been largely taken up by the law of 7 August 2015 for growth, activity and equal economic opportunities.

7. Whether or not the AMF acts on its own initiative, its opinions have a structuring impact on the market, not only as a result of the change in operator behaviour and the resulting changes in standards, but also in terms of their impact on public debate, which contributes greatly to the dissemination of a competition culture. This dissemination is also helped by the increasing importance of competition analysis of draft legislation in impact studies and the many other educational tools developed by the regulator – computer graphics, thematic studies, guides, conferences and meetings – but it is difficult to disseminate in a country which, despite institutional changes, has remained marked by doubts about the virtues of competition and questions about its compatibility with a certain "French model".

8. This only makes the need for *advocacy* and the place it is to occupy in the Authority's activities even more obvious, if that were necessary. However, its progress will depend on the regulator's ability to deal with three unavoidable elements.

9. First, it is clear that *advocacy* is nothing, or not much, without a relevant and effective repressive policy. In this respect, it should be noted that the Authority's advisory function has only really come into its own when it has been combined with the other instruments of regulation, and that its opinions are only heard by economic operators to the extent of the binding powers it

holds. The defence of economic public order requires a regulator who walks on two legs, so *advocacy* cannot be thought of independently of its articulation with repression.

10. Second, *advocacy* is now necessarily part of the new jurisprudential framework that the Council of State is building step by step. The *Fairvesta* and *Numericable* decisions handed down on 21 March 2016 laid the foundations for judicial review of flexible law acts, a category that covers most *advocacy* instruments – opinions, press releases, position statements, replies to letters, etc. – which can now be challenged by way of recourse for misuse of powers. These can now be challenged on the grounds of misuse of power if they are likely to produce significant effects or are intended to have a significant influence on the behaviour of the persons to whom they are addressed. The decisions of *Ms. Le Pen* of 19 July 2019 and *GISTI* of 12 June 2020 then specified the litigation regime for these acts. This enshrinement of flexible law confirms the Authority's powers; at the same time, it places greater demands on it in terms of transparency, methodological rigour, accuracy and objectivity, which undeniably helps to improve its practices for the benefit of businesses.

11. Finally, the regulator's advisory activities, in particular sectoral investigations, must be carried out in accordance with the principle of fairness of evidence, which, as we know, tempers the rule of freedom of evidence that prevails in competition matters. Although the Authority, when it conducts such investigations, is not intended to find infringements, its analyses, conclusions and, above all, the information it requests from companies may be likely to be prejudicial to them, downstream, in a possible dispute. However, this is not and should not be their purpose, unlike the elements gathered in the context of the implementation of its investigative powers per se – a subject on which the Conseil d'État has just published a study, commissioned by the Prime Minister: it contains proposals aimed at ordering the particularly chaotic landscape of investigative and control powers entrusted to the administrations, by making their appropriateness to the ends they pursue a structuring criterion. While it is *ultimately* up to the judicial judge to specify the conditions under which such and such an element can legally serve as evidence, the Authority has everything to gain, upstream, by clearly stating the rules of the game to avoid surprises and foster the confidence of companies. Confidence is both a means and an end of its *advocacy*.

Enhanced Enforcement Across Instruments

CANI FERNÁNDEZ[*]
AND MARISA TIERNO[**]
National Commission for Markets and Competition (CNMC)

1. Competition agencies aim to advance their policy goals and compliance with competition law resorting to advocacy, guidance, influence and enforcement. Arguably, the latter constitutes their core activity, as they are invested with public authority for that purpose.

2. 'Enforcement' is a strong word, involving prompting, *forcing compliance* where necessary. The required *legitimacy to compel or cease actions* where appropriate and to impose *deterring sanctions* comes within a framework ensuring that rights of defence are guaranteed, as well as legal certainty and judicial scrutiny. In an administrative system like ours, the competition authority *oversees all sectors* of the economy and uses *an array of tools* to achieve those objectives. For instance, under *merger review* we produce decisions clearing mergers with or without structural or behavioural commitments and/or conditions, or we can prohibit mergers. When enforcing *antitrust rules* we resort to interim measures, infringement decisions with fines on companies and directors, public contracting ban and behavioural obligations, or decisions enforcing commitments, or we close files on substantive or on priority grounds. We have extensive *investigation powers,* and we actively prosecute companies in case of *gun-jumping, breaches of the duty to cooperate* with any sort of investigation *and failure to comply* with any of our decisions,

---

[*] President of the CNMC, President of the Board and Competition Chamber of the CNMC, the decision-making college.

[**] Former Director General for Competition of the CNMC, currently Head of the International Unit at DGCOMP, European Commission.

which are subject to systematic monitoring. A particular feature of the Spanish National Markets and Competition Commission (CNMC) (in its capacity as competition authority), is its additional *legal standing to challenge* in court regulations and administrative acts which restrict competition.

3. By 'enhancing enforcement across instruments' we mean combining: (1) a deliberate effort to address/prevent silo effects in competition investigations; (2) thoughtfully looking for spaces to deploy proactive enforcement interventions according to priorities and relevance, and (3) making conscious choices to tackle complexity

I. A Deliberate Effort to Address/Prevent Silo Effects in Competition Investigations

4. This requires purposely sharing and pooling knowledge, leads, momentum and synergies in assessing cases, triggering investigations, or deciding on priorities. Opportunities to do so derive from: (a) structural and inbuilt features, (b) joint endeavours, (c) multidisciplinary staff, and (d) management instructions.

5. Some of our *structural and inbuilt features* are helpful:

   - Out of the six operational units within the Directorate General for Competition (DG), three are *sectoral units*[1] *dealing with mergers, but also enforcing antitrust rules and unfair acts distorting competition*,[2] thereby ensuring cross-fertilisation and knowledge of the sectors and markets from different perspectives. Within those units, below deputy director-general level, there is one coordinator specialising in mergers, and another one in antitrust and unfair competition. However, they are experienced in both types of cases, and the rest of the staff can be assigned to the one or the other type of procedure depending on factors such as availability, sectoral knowledge and background. It is common practice to use the market knowledge gained in merger review when defining markets in antitrust proceedings.

   - *All sorts of CNMC's competition decisions are systematically monitored for compliance by the Monitoring Unit* created 10 years ago, which actively follows up and reports on the payment of fines, compliance with divestitures, behavioural commitments, conditions, obligations, interim measures…, irrespective of whether the decision concerned an antitrust or a merger case.[3] On 31 December 2023 we had

1 Industry and Energy, Information Society and Services.

2 Spanish Competition Act (Law 15/2007), art 3.

3 Exceptionally, compliance monitoring requiring very sophisticated sectoral knowledge is allocated to the relevant unit.

176 decisions subject to monitoring for compliance with CNMC's decisions. Having a dedicated unit is consistent with the legal consideration of non-compliance with CNMC's decisions as a very serious infringement (remedy violations are in the same category as an abuse of dominance or a cartel). By design, the Monitoring Unit cooperates with every other unit having investigated the relevant cases leading to such decisions, including the *Leniency and Cartels Unit*, which in turn may deal with cartels in any sector, and may *draw expertise from sectoral units*. Recently (the later in 2023) the Monitoring Unit has conducted inspections drawing resources from across the DG.[4]

– Finally, the *Economic Intelligence Unit* (EIU) is entrusted a.o. with applying artificial intelligence and data processing to advance *investigations of any of the other units*, as required. While performing that task, the EIU official is part of the relevant case team. In-house developed digital tools (eg gUIE.me, Brava) apply machine learning and artificial intelligence to enhance our capacity to find patterns, analyse and present data in any file to better inform our decision-making process, including some advanced tools for ex officio detection with special emphasis in bid-rigging and gun-jumping. The EIU is also in charge of the whistleblower facility, which has provided information and leads for any of the units and any of the instruments, originating three inspections since 2021.

6. *Joint endeavours* are commonplace:

– *Inspection teams typically consist of officials drawn from all units* of the DG, including the *Coordination and Support Unit* directly attached to the Director General, as well as computer specialists. These opportunities to build team spirit are manyfold, since in 2023 we carried out 9 inspections in 20 different locations,[5] hence forming over 20 inspection teams. We have conducted inspections concerning cartels and other horizontal infringements as well as abuses of dominance, but also regarding vertical restraints, and in the framework of files subject to monitoring for compliance with decisions.

– Beyond cases, the staff of the DG for competition take part in different internal *horizontal working groups across units* to deal with tasks, projects or subjects chosen to ensure consistency and regular updates on a variety of relevant procedural, substantive and practical matters.

4 CNMC, 'The CNMC is investigating several companies after detecting that possible anti-competitive practices persist in the market for transporting passengers and vehicles by sea between Algeciras and Ceuta' (20 December 2019) <https://www.cnmc.es/prensa/cnmc-inspeccion-navieras-20191220>; CNMC, 'The CNMC is investigating possible anti-competitive practices in the field of rail freight transport and railway traction services' (23 October 2023) <https://www.cnmc.es/prensa/inspeccion-sector-ferroviario-mercancias-20231027> accessed 11 October 2024.

5 If we add those assisting the European Commission, 11 cases.

- This, together with our *weekly staff gatherings,* ensures that colleagues have opportunities to update and learn from each other, and the same applies to the DG *coordination management meetings* every other week.

7. We have a *multidisciplinary staff*, counting not only many lawyers and economists (or both), but also an unusual rate of other professionals, such as pharmacists, engineers of different branches, data scientists, etc. This is essential for us to grasp swiftly, and in the necessary depth, the core issues and arguments relevant to very technical sectors within the stringent timing of our investigations. Although all officials are familiar with our procedures and with competition enforcement principles and law, their complementary backgrounds necessarily require collaboration to ensure compliance with legal standards and economic analysis.[6] We are subject to tight deadlines also in antitrust investigations,[7] the expiration of which triggers prescription.

8. All these factors, together with the *management instruction* to schedule cross-review of past cases and to have all instruments in mind when assessing ongoing cases and pondering ex officio efforts yield results:

   - At the time of writing, we have issued infringement decisions for *gun-jumping*[8] in 11 files since 2021 and there are others in the pipeline. Some of these were detected in other merger filings. A good example of this is the funerary sector, in which we *detected ex officio and reviewed five instances of gun-jumping*[9] when reviewing the merger case *Santa Lucia/Funespaña,*[10] imposing the corresponding fines.[11] Two additional *gun-jumping* cases[12] were detected in the healthcare sector for assisted reproductive treatments during the analysis of the merger case *KKR/IVI,*[13] urging the companies involved to file the mandatory notification to the CNMC and imposing the corresponding fines.

---

6 Eventually, we may consult the Legal Service and the Chief Economist team.

7 The deadline for antitrust proceedings has been extended from 18 to 24 months after the recent reform introduced by the Royal Law Decree 5/2023, of 28 June 2023.

8 Next to a traditional turnover threshold, mergers must be notified under the market share thresholds if the target's market share on a relevant market within Spain is of at least a 30%, unless the target's turnover in Spain is less then EUR 10 million, or irrespective of the target's turnover, if they result in an individual or joint market-share of at least 50% in a relevant market within Spain. Individual guidance is offered on the calculation of the market-share threshold prior to notification, as it is applied according to the market reality (in digital markets it can be devices, clicks, visits…).

9 Cases C/1267/22 *Funespaña/Funeraria San Vicente*; C/1271/22 *Albia / Tanatorio De Marin*; C/1155/20 *Funespaña/Alianza Canaria*; C/1167/21 *Albia / Tanatorios Mostoles.*

10 Case C/1086/19 *Santa Lucía / Funespaña.*

11 Cases Snc/Dc/086/22 *Albia/Tanatorio La Paz*; Snc/Dc/088/22 *Funespaña / San Vicente*; Snc/Dc/092/22 *Albia / Tanatorio De Marin*; Snc/Dc/014/21 *Funespaña / Alianza Canaria*; Snc/Dc/045/21 *Albia/Tanatorios Mostoles.*

12 Cases C/1431/23 *Generalife/ Gin*emed; C/1407/23 *Kkr/ Generalife.*

13 Case C/1321/22 *KKR/ IVI*, see Rafael Allendesalazar and Beatriz Sanchez-Ortiz, 'The Spanish Competition Authority fines two undertakings for respectively failing to notify the acquisitions of sole control, without prior notification to the Spanish competition authority (Generalife / Ginemed)' (29 May 2024) 3 Concurrences 120408 175-176.

- In the energy sector, the DG for Competition *detected two gun-jumping instances* when consulted by the 'sister' DG for Energy Regulation of the regulatory side of the CNMC in their own infringement proceedings. As a result, the two mergers were reviewed, and fines were imposed.[14] Similarly, *three possible abuse of dominance infringements* were detected leading to infringement decisions in cases *Enel Green*[15] and *Luminora.*[16] Proceedings are currently open concerning *Alfoz.*[17]
- In *Radiofármacos*,[18] a collusion case, some of the *suspicions leading to inspections* and an infringement decision derived from the merger review of successive acquisitions.[19]
- Our active monitoring of compliance with our CNMC's merger and antitrust decisions has resulted in 58 *remedy violation decisions* between 2008 and 2023. Since 2021, the CNMC has fined seven companies for *breach of merger commitments.*
- In 2023 we advised the competition community that we would be actively reviewing *restrictions not directly (or no-longer directly) related or necessary to mergers to identify non-poaching agreements and non-compete clauses.*

II. Thoughtfully Looking for Spaces to Deploy Proactive Enforcement Interventions According to Priorities and Relevance

9. Enhancing enforcement across instruments also implies giving some thought and direction to keep a balance between reactive and proactive interventions. A very substantial part of our work consists in discharging compulsory duties triggered by parties and other stakeholders, such as merger notifications or appeals. Since resources are always limited, agencies can surrender their initiative and be driven to limit their enforcement activity to the boundaries of notifications, complaints, submissions and legal duties. Instead, it is wise to diversify the sources of potential cases, thereby increasing enforcement choices

14 Cases SNC/DC/112/21 *Luxida Santa Clara*; SNC/DC/157/21 *Electra Alto Miño / Activos Arnoia.*

15 Case S/0022/20 *Enel Green Power España*, see Beatriz Sanchez-Ortiz and Rafael Allendesalazar, 'The Spanish Competition Authority imposes a fine on the operator of the national electricity network for abusing its dominant position in the electricity transmission network access market by self-referencing its own services (Enel)' (10 June 2022) 3 Concurrences 108365 215.

16 Case S/0003/23 *Luminora.*

17 Case S/0011/23 *Eólica Del Alfoz.*

18 Case S/0644/18 *Radiofármacos*, see Rafael Allendesalazar, 'The Spanish Competition Authority fines the two main suppliers of PET radiopharmaceuticals, in particular, 18F-FDG, a drug used in radiodiagnosis by positron emission tomography, as well as two of their managers, for sharing the market for supply contracts for this drug for at least four years (Radiofármacos)' (9 February 2021) 2 Concurrences 100612 225-226.

19 Case C/0591/14 *Iba Molecular / Molypharma.*

and scope for case selection and strategy, driving enforcement where it can be more useful, have wider impact or set the right precedent. Some practical examples come to mind:

- Since 2023 we have been able to discard some files on prioritisation grounds to deploy resources according to, eg relevance, efficiency and impact.
- An important part of our strategy in this regard is the CNMC's conscious investment in *ex officio detection*, particularly in the field of bid-rigging of public tenders. Almost 70% of our cartel decisions have been triggered by leads, public information, or complaints, rather than leniency, since 2018. Although in some cases there has been a leniency applicant for a reduction of fines supplying significant added probative value. Around 75% of our cartel decisions concern bid-rigging, mostly regarding public tenders.
- Our Economic Intelligence Unit:
    - o Combines in-house developed tools with artificial and business intelligence together with statistic software on datasets, including the public procurement database to identify and predict collusive patterns.
    - o Processes indicia of collusion in tenders which are reported by the tendering public procurement bodies and provides training to public tenderers on the detection of the relevant indicia.
    - o Centralises the anonymous whistleblowers' channel.
- Alternatively, investigations have also been prompted by international cooperation, by news, merger review (as already mentioned), or by the accidental finding of evidence of additional suspect behaviour during dawn raids.
- Finally, case teams are instructed to be proactive in *identifying procedural violations in ongoing investigations,* for instance by double checking the data and the methodologies used in replies to information requests or following up obstructions in inspections.

10. Such proactive means supplement and reinforce more traditional investigation triggers, such as complaints and a well-established leniency program for cartel cases applicable both to undertakings and their directors. Lately, some incentives have been added to the original leniency program, such as protecting leniency recipients from the ban from contracting with the public authorities attached to cartel (and other) infringements or extending immunity to criminal prosecution.[20] We have conducted a public consultation on our

20 Criminal immunity for immunity applicants was included in the Spanish Penal Code in 2022.

leniency program, identifying a.o. the need to include those new items in the existing leniency guidelines.

III. Making Conscious Choices to Tackle Complexity

11. *From 2021 to date*, we have deployed the full array of instruments at our disposal, *enforcing all legal prohibitions*:

- The CNMC's board has adopted 12 decisions[21] in the field of *cartels or bid-rigging*. The fact that 9 of those investigations started ex-officio, (immunity from fines was granted in 2 of these, leniency reduction was applied in 4 cases) was no obstacle to establishing 20 infringements and the liability of 82 companies and 36 individuals.[22] In the bid-rigging case *Public Works 2* (Obra Civil 2 of 2022), the authority imposed the third highest fine to date. Since 2021 to the time of writing, 70 decision proposals have been put forward by the CNMC's DG.

- The infringement decision concerning agreements between Amazon and Apple[23] in digital markets resulted in the highest fine imposed by the CNMC up to that date, but it was later surpassed by the fine in the recent infringement decision issued in July 2024, regarding an

21 Cases S/DC/0627/18 *Consultoras*, see Rafael Allendesalazar, 'The Spanish Competition Authority fines several consulting companies for colluding in local public tenders and imposes surprisingly low fines (Consultoras)' (11 May 2021) 3 Concurrences 101652210-211; S/0011/19 *Transporte Cántabro De Viajeros*; S/0013/19 *Conservación Carreteras*, Rafael Allendesalazar, 'The Spanish Competition Authority imposes fines on several companies for manipulating tenders for services of maintenance and management of the Spanish motorway network (Ferrovial servicios)' (17 August 2021) 4 Concurrences 103476 191-192; S/Dc/0614/17 *Seguridad Y Comunicaciones Ferroviarias*; S/0003/20 *Proptech*, see Rafael Allendesalazar, 'The Spanish Competition Authority fines seven real estate brokers and associations for imposing minimum fees in the real estate brokerage market (PROPTECH)' (25 November 2021) 1 Concurrences 105563 206-207; S/0012/19 *Chatarra Y Acero*, see Rafael Allendesalazar and Beatriz Sanchez-Ortiz, 'The Spanish Competition Authority fines three steel companies for participating in two exchanges of information on the scrap metal purchasing market (Chatarra y Acero)' (4 March 2022) Concurrences 106478 224-225; S/0002/21 *Bases De Datos Empresariales*, see Rafael Allendesalazar and Beatriz Sanchez-Ortiz, 'The Spanish Competition Authority fines a cartel between two of the main companies providing business information database services in Spain, which agreed to fix prices and share the market (BvD / Informa)' (4 July 2023) 4 Concurrences 115687 187; S/0008/21 *Licitaciones Material Militar*, see Rafael Allendesalazar and Beatriz Sanchez-Ortiz, 'The Spanish Competition Authority fines four manufacturers of military equipment, as well as their directives, for bid rigging in several tenders of the Spanish Ministry of Defence through two cartels (Comercial Hernando Moreno / Grupo de Ingeniería Reconstrucción y Recambios / Star Defence Logistics & Engineering / Casli)' (19 July 2023) 4 Concurrences 115709 190-191; S/0025/19 *Gestion De Archivos*; S/0021/20 *Obra Civil 2*, see Rafael Allendesalazar and Beatriz Sanchez-Ortiz, 'The Spanish competition authority (CNMC) imposes fines on the six main national construction companies for manipulating public infrastructure construction tenders (Acciona Construcción e.a.)' (5 July 2022) 4 Concurrences 109521 173-174; S/0016/21 *Suministro De Alimentos*.

22 The CNMC has imposed fines on 67 directors since 2018, out of which 4 have been granted immunity from fines, and 2 had their fines reduced.

23 Case S/0013/21 *Amazon / Apple Brandgating*, see Pablo Velasco Sanzo, 'The Spanish Competition Authority fines an e-commerce giant and a Big Tech company €194M for restricting inter and intra-brand competition in the online marketplace for electronic products in Spain (Apple / Amazon)' (2023) e-Competitions art. No. 114116.

abuse of dominant position by *Booking*[24] which established a new record.

- The CNMC's board has adopted 8 decisions finding 11 *abuses of a dominant position,*[25] including a.o. energy and pharma. The large majority concerned exclusionary conduct within a wide range of issues: *predatory pricing, margin squeeze, loyalty rebates, exclusivity clauses, tying, refusal to deal and sham litigation.* Exploitative conduct added another layer of complexity in the same period, assessing *excessive prices and unequitable conditions.* Up to 2024, several statements of objections or decisions proposals have been issued involving big technological companies.
- A decision established a unilateral infringement of the prohibition against *unfair acts distorting competition* (*Audax*[26]). The CNMC's DG has recently proposed to the Board the adoption of a decision finding both an infringement of that provision and an abuse of dominance and has issued a statement of objections combining it with an alleged collusion by an association of undertakings. These two cases would be the first in *combining Article 3 with antitrust provisions, including Articles 102 and 101 TFEU, respectively.*[27]
- *Behavioural obligations* were designed to end some infringements, such as facilitating access or eliminating exclusivities.

12. In the last two years, the CNMC has adopted *interim measures* in two abuse cases (one quarter of all interim measures since 2008). Reference has already been made to CNMC's decisions declaring *gun-jumping, procedural violations and monitoring decisions* and reports.

13. Since 2021, the CNMC has adopted 8 *commitment decisions enforcing voluntary undertakings* offered by the alleged infringer in three cases addressing

---

24 Case S/0005/21 *Booking.*

25 Case S/0041/19 *Correos 3*, see Rafael Allendesalazar and Beatriz Sanchez-Ortiz, 'The Spanish Competition Authority fines the public postal operator for abusing its dominant position in the traditional postal services market by applying exclusionary discounts for large customers (CORREOS 3)' (18 February 2022) 2 Concurrences 106474 223-224; S/0044/19 *Real Sociedad Canina De España*, see Rafael Allendesalazar and Beatriz Sanchez-Ortiz, 'The Spanish Competition Authority imposes a fine on the Spanish canine association for abusing its dominant position on the dog breed certification market by hampering the activity of rival associations and preventing judges from participating in competing events (Royal Canine Society of Spain)' (17 May 2022) 3 Concurrences 108367 214; S/0022/20 E*nel Green Power España*, see Rafael Allendesalazar and Beatriz Sanchez-Ortiz, 'The Spanish Competition Authority imposes a fine on the operator of the national electricity network for abusing its dominant position in the electricity transmission network access market by self-referencing its own services (Enel)' (10 June 2022) 3 Concurrences 108365 215; S/0026/19 *Merck Sharp Dome S.A*; S/0028/20 *Leadiant*, see Rafael Allendesalazar and Beatriz Sanchez-Ortiz, 'The Spanish Competition Authority imposes a fine for abuse of a dominant position in the market for the manufacture and supply of drugs based on chenodeoxycholic acid for the treatment of cerebrotendinous xanthomatosis in Spain (Leadiant Biosciences)' (10 November 2022) 1 Concurrences 111181 209-210; *Luminora* (n 16); S/0641/18 *Dama-Unison Rights Vs Sgae*; *Booking* (n 24).

26 Case S/0013/20 *Audax Renovables.*

27 Regulation (EC) 1/2003 of 16 December 2002 on the implementation of the rules on competition laid down in arts 81 and 82 of the Treaty (TFEU).

concerns: two in distribution networks[28] and one in tenders organised by a dominant company.[29]

14. When considering the inherent complexity of our analyses, attention should be paid as well to the fact that any infringement procedure of the Competition Act (collusion, abuses of a dominant position or unfair acts distorting competition) had to take place within 24 months[30] from the formal initiation of proceedings, with the subsequent intervention of two different bodies.[31] When it comes to procedural infringements, a decision is due within 3 months from the initiation of proceedings.[32]

15. In the field of *merger review*, between 2021 and 2023, the CNMC cleared 6 mergers in phase II, 15 mergers were approved subject to commitments (11 in phase I, 4 in phase II) and 2 mergers were for the first time subject to remedies imposed by the CNMC. While 2021 and 2022 were record years in terms of merger notifications, in 2023 there were more cases leading to closer scrutiny, which shows a relative increase in complexity (from 4 commitment decisions out of 103 in 2022, to 5 out of 70 in 2023).

16. Interestingly, in 2022, all merger cases cleared with remedies were captured by our market-share threshold, knowing that it applied in 64% of the merger deals we review, increasing to 80% of the digital mergers, which often implies deep, complex assessments. Although silence by the CNMC in merger cases would result in implicit authorisations, the CNMC systematically adopts decisions in merger cases, striving to provide legal certainty as soon as possible.

17. Competition authorities tackling complexity and creating some space for initiative and strategy may boost the relevance and impact of their enforcement efforts. Adopting concrete measures to prevent or address silo effects can assist them in cross-detecting infringements and in assessing markets and conduct, thereby balancing and enhancing their enforcement action across instruments.

---

28 Case S/0049/19 *Isdin*, see Rafael Allendesalazar and Beatriz Sanchez-Ortiz, 'The Spanish Competition Authority closes, by means of commitment decisions, two ongoing sanction proceedings in the market for the wholesale distribution of pharmaceutical products (SDIN)' (30 November 2022) 2 Concurrences 112522 204-206 and S/0006/20 *Maquinaria Garrido*.

29 Case S/0021/21 *Subastas De Ecoembes*, see Rafael Allendesalazar and Beatriz Sanchez-Ortiz, 'The Spanish Competition Authority closes by means of a commitments decision the infringement proceedings initiated against the manager of the sole Integrated Management System for plastic packaging waste in Spain for alleged abuse of a dominant position (Subastas de Ecoembes)' (13 December 2023) 1 Concurrences 116994 187-188.

30 The deadline has been extended from 18 months to 24 months since June 2023.

31 Only some short suspensions may apply, for instance in cases applying arts 101 and 102 TFUE, while the European Commission is being consulted. Within that deadline, first the DG for Competition, independently conducts the core of the investigation, adopts a statement of objections, ponders the parties' reply, proposes a draft decision to the Board; then the collegial Board considers the parties' reply to the DG's proposal, takes any other measure (eventually including an adversarial oral hearing), deliberates and adopts the final decision.

32 General Administrative Procedure Act, art 21.3.

State Aid Control Protects Competition from the Distortionary Effect of State Aid: But Does the Control of State Aid also Cause Distortions?

PHEDON NICOLAIDES[*]
University of Maastricht and the University of Nicosia

ALEXANDER ROSE[**]
Commercial and Competition DWF

I. Introduction

1. The core of the European Union is its internal market. The Commission Communication that launched the State Aid Modernisation in 2012 declared that "an effective internal market requires the deployment of two instruments: first, regulation to create one integrated market without national borders and, second, competition policy including State aid control to ensure that the functioning of that internal market is not distorted by anticompetitive behaviour of companies or by Member States favouring some actors to the detriment of others".[1]

---

* Professor at the University of Maastricht and the University of Nicosia.

** Partner in the Commercial and Competition team at DWF, UK.

1 European Commission, "Communication from the Commission to the European Parliament, the Council, the European Economic and Social Committee and the Committee of the Regions: EU State Aid Modernisation (SAM)" COM (2012) 0209 final, <https://eur-lex.europa.eu/legal-content/EN/ALL/?uri=CELEX%3A52012DC0209> accessed 25 October 2024.

2. Indeed subsidies alter the conditions of competition between undertakings, even where they aim to remedy market inefficiencies. Whether subsidies raise welfare depends, on the one hand, on the size of the benefits from the reduction of market inefficiencies and the costs from possible misallocation of resources, on the other. Therefore, as long as economies do not function perfectly or the market cannot allocate resources optimally, there should be no absolute prohibition of subsidies. It is for this reason that even though Article 107(1) TFEU declares subsidies that constitute State aid to be incompatible with the internal market, the principle of incompatibility of State aid is not absolute. State aid is or may be allowed for certain purposes and under certain conditions by the second and third paragraph of Article 107 and Articles 42, 93 and 106(2) TFEU.

3. But, if the case in favour or against State aid is conditional, it follows that its potential impact on competition must be assessed before it is granted. In the case of the EU, there is an additional reason for a system of ex-ante assessment of State aid. What is good for one Member State may be bad for another. In order to protect competition not just within a national market but also between different national markets, a supranational system State aid control appears to be indispensable.

4. Many studies have been carried out on the impact of State aid on competition.[2] Most of them conclude that State aid does distort competition, but it may also be an appropriate instrument for correcting market imperfections. Estimates and opinions vary on both the size of the distortion that can be caused and of the potential benefits that may be derived from State aid. Yet, there is hardly any study on the impact of the process of control of State aid on competition. Admittedly, it is exceptionally difficult to quantify that impact because no one knows the counterfactual situation without State aid control. It is also largely impossible to carry out any comparative analysis because no other jurisdiction has a State aid regime similar to that of the EU and the European Economic Area.

II. A Comparator: Subsidy Control in the UK

5. Yet, one of the silver linings of Brexit is that it is now possible to compare the provisions of the subsidy control system in the United Kingdom to those

---

2 See, for example, Bartosz Bartniczak, "Market Failures as Premises of Granting State Aid" (2017) 17 E&ES 475–489; Raffaello Bronzini and Paolo Piselli, "The Impact of R&D Subsidies on Firm Innovation" (2016) 45 RP 442–457; Caroline Buts and Marc Jegers, "The Effect of 'State Aid' on Market Shares: An Empirical Investigation in an EU Member State" (2013) 13 JIC&T 89–100; Mathias Dewatripont and Paul Seabright, "Wasteful Public Spending and State Aid Control" (2006) 4 J Eur EA 513–522; Marianne Fay, S Hallegatte and Adrien Vogt-Schilb, "Green Industrial Policies: When and How" (2013) SSRN Scholarly Paper 2346540 <https://papers.ssrn.com/sol3/papers.cfm?abstract_id=2346540> accessed 25 October 2024; Romualdas Ginevičius, Valentinas Podvezko and Šarūnas Bruzge, "Evaluating the Effect of State Aid to Business by Multicriteria Methods" (2008) 9 JBE&M 167–180; Justus Haucap and Ulrich Schwalbe, "Economic Principles of State Aid Control" (2011) DICE Working Paper 17; Nikoletta Poulou, Michael L Polemis and Aikaterina Oikonomou, "The Impact of State Aid on Economic Growth: Fresh Evidence from a Panel of 27 EU Countries" (2023) 19 Eur CJ 359–379; Dani Rodrik, Green Industrial Policy (2014) 30 Oxford Rev EP 469–491.

of the EU. This is even more so because one of the arguments in favour of the withdrawal of the UK from the EU was the allegedly bureaucratic nature of State aid control and the costs it imposed on both national administrations and companies.[3] Now the United Kingdom has its own system of State aid control that was established by the 2022 Subsidy Control Act (SCA).[4] It is, therefore, instructive to consider whether the UK system is less bureaucratic and less cumbersome for national authorities and companies.

6. According to the UK Government's explanatory notes[5] to the SCA, the UK's legislation aims to create a regime that:

> "a. Empowers local authorities, public bodies, the UK Government and the devolved administrations to design subsidies that deliver strong benefits for the UK taxpayer.
>
> b. Enables public authorities to deliver strategic interventions to support the UK's economic recovery and deliver priorities such as levelling up and achieving net zero.
>
> c. Provides certainty and confidence to businesses investing in the UK, by protecting against subsidies that risk causing distortive or harmful economic impacts, including to the UK internal market.
>
> d. Contributes to meeting the UK's international commitments on subsidy control, including its international commitments under the World Trade Organization Agreement on Subsidies and Countervailing Measures (ASCM), the Trade and Co-operation Agreement with the EU (TCA) and other free trade agreements".

7. Therefore, not only does the SCA aim to ensure the UK meets its commitments relating to subsidies that have been made in international trade agreements (including the UK–EU Trade and Cooperation Agreement (TCA)[6]) but also aims to avoid distortions arising to the UK's internal market as a result of subsidies.

8. The SCA lays down a definition of subsidies, rules on exemption of certain subsidies and rules on procedure and enforcement. In other words, in comparison to the EU regime, the SCA initially appears familiar, in that public

---

3 See the statements quoted in Thomas Pope and Alex Stojanovic, *Beyond State Aid: The Future of Subsidy Control in the UK* (Institute for Government September 2020) <www.instituteforgovernment.org.uk/sites/default/files/publications/beyond-state-aid.pdf> accessed 25 October 2024; Thomas Pope and Eleanor Shearer, *Taking Back Control of Subsidies: Replacing EU State Aid Rules in the UK* (Institute for Government May 2021) <www.instituteforgovernment.org.uk/sites/default/files/publications/taking-back-control-subsidies.pdf> both accessed 25 October 2024.

4 See The Subsidy Control Act (SCA) 2022 <www.legislation.gov.uk/ukpga/2022/23/enacted> accessed 25 October 2024.

5 See The Explanatory Notes to the SCA <www.legislation.gov.uk/ukpga/2022/23/notes/division/3/index.htm> accessed 25 October 2024.

6 The Trade and Cooperation Agreement between the United Kingdom of Great Britain and Northern Ireland, of the one part, and the European Union and the European Atomic Energy Community, of the other part Brussels and London (TCA) [2012] OJ L149/10. It was agreed on 30 December 2020 and published in the *Official Journal* on 30 April 2021.

authorities are obliged to determine the presence of subsidy and thereafter can lawfully make awards in line with routes which appear to broadly mirror treaty principles, block exemption regulations and guidelines on the compatibility of aid. Enforcement is achieved under procedural rules. However, there are also material differences.

9. The definition of a subsidy in Section 2 of the SCA appears substantially the same as that of State aid in the EU. However, the UK definition of subsidy is wider than the EU definition of State aid, encompassing measures which have purely domestic impact. Furthermore, the Competition Appeal Tribunal (CAT) in *The Durham Company Limited v Durham County Council*[7] decided that "no subsidy" arises "where a public authority gives financial assistance and has the same legal personality as the entity receiving it".[8] This goes contrary to the EU case law according to which a public authority can indeed grant State aid to itself when it acts as an undertaking, ie engaging in economic activities.[9]

10. There is also a difference in terms of how the definition must be applied. Under EU State aid law, Article 107(1) TFEU explicitly lays down the principle that State aid is incompatible with the internal market, unless certain conditions are met. The implication of this is that State aid measures must either comply with the provisions of block exemption regulation or be notified to the Commission in accordance with Article 108(3) TFEU. Under the SCA, public authorities must design their measures so that they are compatible with the routes within the SCA, however the presumption is that a measure is lawful unless it is challenged by an interested party (this being a competitor or the Secretary of State). Indeed, Section 12 SCA that sets out the basis upon which a decision of a public authority might be judicially reviewed, states that "a public authority: (a) must consider the subsidy control principles before deciding to give a subsidy, and (b) must not give the subsidy unless it is of the view that the subsidy is consistent with those principles".

11. Sections 15–23 and 27–19 SCA prohibit absolutely or conditionally certain subsidies such as unlimited guarantees and export subsidies or subsidies to providers of services of public economic interest. The UK has taken a different interpretation

7 *The Durham Company Limited v Durham County Council* [2023] CAT 50 [31] <www.catribunal.org.uk/cases/1577121323-durham-company-limited> accessed 25 October 2024; see Andrew Lidbetter et al., "The UK Competition Appeal Tribunal holds that it has jurisdiction to determine not only whether a subsidy is consistent with the "subsidy control requirements", but also to determine whether there is a 'subsidy' in the first place under the expedited dispute resolution process (Durham Company / Durham County Council)" (2023) e-Competitions art. No. 115427.

8 Department for Business and Trade, "Statutory Guidance for the United Kingdom Subsidy Control Regime" (2022) para 15.21, including fns 106 and 107 <https://assets.publishing.service.gov.uk/media/658025b295bf65000d719140/uk_subsidy_control_regime_statutory_guidance.pdf> accessed 25 October 2024.

9 For example, Case C-288/11 P *Mitteldeutsche Flughafen AG v European Commission* ECLI:EU:C:2012:821, clarified that in EU State aid law a public authority was capable of awarding itself State aid, when it used public resources to finance an economic activity, including the construction of airport infrastructure. The *Durham* case holds that the internal allocation of resources does not give rise to a legal commitment necessary for a subsidy to arise, see Bruno Stromsky, "Concept of undertaking: The Court of Justice rules that airport operators have to subsidise on their own resources the costs of the infrastructures which are the basis of their economic activity, if the activity of constructing is not linked, as such, to the exercise of State authority (Mitteldeutsche Flughafen and Flughafen Leipzig)" (19 December 2012) 1 Concurrences 50672 149–151.

of some of the points, for example Section 24 of the SCA reflects the TCA commitment[10] that: "Subsidies for restructuring an ailing or insolvent economic actor without the economic actor having prepared a credible restructuring plan shall be prohibited", but does not cover all subsidies to companies in difficulty, with the SCA Statutory Guidance clarifying: "There is no wider prohibition against giving subsidies that are not rescue or restructuring subsidies to ailing or insolvent enterprises. For example, an access to finance subsidy scheme open to small businesses generally does not constitute a rescue and restructuring subsidy even if one or more recipients (among many) may be ailing or insolvent".[11]

12. Like the EU regime, the SCA sets out different ways subsidies can be lawfully awarded. Some of these are similar to EU State aid rules. For example, the Minimal Financial Assistance regime at Section 36 of the SCA resembles that of the EU de minimis concept. Likewise, Services of Public Economic Interest at Section 29 (and for lower value awards, Section 38) broadly mirrors Services of General Economic Interest.

13. Whilst block exemptions can be created under Section 10 SCA, at the date of publication only three "streamlined routes" have been created. This appears to be a policy decision, because the UK authorities are eager for public authorities to make the most of the seven Subsidy Control principles listed at Schedule 1 of the Act, these being:

    1. subsidies should pursue a specific public policy objective in order to (a) remedy an identified market failure or (b) to address an equity rationale such as regional disadvantage, social difficulties or distributional concerns;

    2. subsidies should be proportionate to their specific public policy objective and limited to what is necessary to achieve it;

    3. subsidies should be designed to bring about a change of economic behaviour of the beneficiary. That change, in relation to a subsidy, should be (a) conducive to achieving its specific public policy objective, and (b) something that would not happen without the subsidy;

    4. subsidies should not normally compensate for the costs the beneficiary would have funded in the absence of any subsidy;

    5. subsidies should be an appropriate policy instrument for achieving their specific public policy objective and that objective cannot be achieved through other, less distortive, means;

    6. subsidies should be designed to achieve their specific policy objective while minimising any negative effects on competition or investment within the United Kingdom

10 UK–EU Trade and Cooperation Agreement art 367(3).

11 SCA Statutory Guidance (n 8) – paragraph 5.36

7. subsidies' beneficial effects (in terms of achieving their public policy objective) should outweigh any negative effects, including in particular negative effects on (a) competition or investment within the United Kingdom; (b) international trade or investment.

14. A public authority would need to demonstrate that it had reasonable grounds to conclude that the measure conformed with each of the principles, but only if a challenge was brought by an interested party within the "challenge period". The challenge period runs for one month from when relevant information about the subsidy is published on the UK's Subsidy Database.[12]

15. Subsidy schemes (frameworks that allow for future awards to be made) can also be created by public authorities. Again, a public authority would need to demonstrate that it had reasonable grounds to conclude that the scheme aligned with each of the principles, but only if a challenge was brought by an interested party.

16. Unlike the EU State aid regime, the UK's regulator, the Competition and Markets Authority (CMA) does not have the right to proactively investigate the compliance of subsidies. Rather, the UK regime contains a duty at Section 52 for public authorities to refer large and sensitive subsidies (classified as "Subsidies of Particular Interest") to the CMA prior to making the legal commitment of the subsidy. Section 31 prohibits the implementation of subsidies that must be mandatorily referred to the CMA for as long as the CMA has not published the required report.

17. The CMA is required to consider the referred subsidy setting out its views in a public report. The CMA's reports are not binding. Instead, under Section 59, the CMA provides feedback on the public authority's assessment outlining ways the measure can be improved. This is supposed to improve the decision making of public authorities awarding large subsidies. The CMA works to tight timescales. It has five working days, to determine whether a referral is satisfactory and is expected to publish its report within 30 working days.

18. Section 67 empowers the CMA to gather information for the purpose of preparing its reports on notified measures. However, it does not appear to enable the CMA to request information on non-notified measures.

19. Section 70 provides that any interested party who is aggrieved by a subsidy may petition the CAT. Under Section 74, the CAT may also make a recovery order. Please note that Section 74 does not oblige the CAT to make a recovery order if it finds that a subsidy does not comply with the principles laid down in the SCA. The decisions of the CAT may be appealed (Section 75). So far, there has only been one challenge against a UK subsidy under the SCA (the *Durham* case, cited above)[13].

---

12 Unless an interested party submits questions in line with SCA s 76, which extends the challenge period for one additional month from the information being provided (the public authority has 28 days to respond). See <https://searchforuksubsidies.beis.gov.uk/> accessed 25 October 2024.

13 With a second case, Mr Aubrey Weis v Greater Manchester Combined Authority, expected to be heard in 2025.

III. Does the UK Subsidy Control System Provide the Same Safeguards against Distortions as the EU State Aid Control System?

20. At first glance, the main features of the UK regime are similar to those of the EU system of State aid control. A measure that constitutes a subsidy must meet particular requirements to be safely awarded. Non-compliant awards, if found to be unlawful, could be recovered from the beneficiary. However, there are also substantive differences between the two systems. The UK system was described at its launch as being "more agile and flexible" than that of the EU.[14] This is reflected in the structure of the system, whereby measures are considered lawful, unless successfully challenged. Likewise, challenges may only be brought through the court system within a short challenge window, meaning interested parties must spot that a competitor has received a subsidy which causes concern and be willing to incur significant financial costs to launch proceedings.

21. Indeed, if one examines the details of the principles with which subsidies must comply, the thresholds of permissible subsidies and the categories of subsidies that are exempted from mandatory referral, one can find many differences with the corresponding EU provisions, which may seem small, but which could have significant implications.

22. For example, the CMA is not empowered to look into measures on its own initiative or to carry out ex-officio investigations. Nor can it stop a measure that it finds non-compliant with the principles of the SCA or order recovery. Indeed, CMA reports expressly state that the purpose of the report "is not to make a recommendation on whether the subsidy should be given, or directly assess whether it complies with the subsidy control requirements". A public authority that disagrees with the feedbac k of the CMA may still proceed to implement it until an interested party appeals to the CAT.

23. At the same time, all grants of over £10 million must be referred under the UK regime to the CMA and therefore undergo an external scrutiny process which examines the merit of the individual proposal against the SCA, at the end of which a public report is published. Contrast this with the EU State aid regime, where over 90% of awards proceed under the GBER, which allows grants of up to €150 million in certain circumstances on the basis of standardised aid intensity rates and thresholds.

---

14 See UK Government, Press Release, "New Subsidy System to Support UK Jobs and Businesses, Boost the Economy and Strengthen the Union" (30 June 2021) <www.gov.uk/government/news/new-subsidy-system-to-support-uk-jobs-and-businesses-boost-the-economy-and-strengthen-the-union> accessed 25 October 2024. See also the Impact Assessment that preceded the adoption of the SCA: "Subsidy Control: Designing a new approach for the UK Consultation Impact Assessment" (2021) <https://assets.publishing.service.gov.uk/government/uploads/system/uploads/attachment_data/file/961140/uk-subsidy-control-consultation-ia.pdf> accessed 25 October 2024.

IV. Comparison of the Two Systems

24. One has to be careful in comparing a nascent regime, which is bound to evolve, with a mature regime such as that of the EU that has already gone through multiple phases. Indeed, the interpretation of the UK substantive rules may evolve as interpretive regulations are issued, the UK case law develops and the SCA may be updated by Parliament.[15]

25. Yet, when considering the efficiency of the system of control itself and whether it generates distortions of its own, it is pertinent to ask whether the CMA's inability to stop or order the recovery of non-compliant subsidies makes the UK economy better or worse off in comparison to the EU's economy where the Commission is empowered to open ex-officio investigations, prohibit incompatible State aid and order its recovery. In other words, we need to ask whether reliance on judicial action by aggrieved parties is better, in whatever sense, than administrative action.

26. Before addressing this question, it is pertinent to recall, first, that the EU system is intended to manage subsidies awarded across 27 Member States. A central authority is indispensable in any system that lays down rules on State aid which apply in multiple counties.

27. Second, binding substantive rules are also indispensable in such a situation. It cannot be left to the granting authority to confirm, in a rule-free environment, that a subsidy has a net positive effect. That would be too abstract and vulnerable to creative interpretation and outright abuse.

28. Therefore, if it is necessary to have binding rules on what can be subsidised and by how much and to notify subsidy measures to a central authority before they are implemented, is there any extra value in empowering that central authority to examine non-notified measures, stop non-compliant measures or order the recovery of non-compliant subsidies? After all, if a measure is not notified or non-compliant, a competitor may initiate legal proceedings.

29. However, whether a competitor can initiate legal proceedings, depends, first, on whether it can detect a non-notified or non-compliant measure and, second, whether it has a sufficiently strong incentive to do so. With respect to the ease or difficulty of detection, a subsidy measure for which there is no prior CMA report is obviously non-notified and probably a competitor is more likely to detect such a measure than the CMA. The problem is when the granting authority claims that the implemented measure is not a subsidy. Then the competitor will have to prove that the measure fulfils all the criteria of a subsidy. This may not be easy, and brings us to whether a competitor would have sufficient incentives to lodge legal proceedings. Again, this depends on the information available to the competitor, the complexity of the measure,

15 Substantive and procedural provisions may be revised in the future, in light of the review of the TCA that is expected to happen in 2025.

whether a court has the requisite technical knowledge, the cost and duration of legal proceedings and the possible remedies. By contrast, the possibility of lodging a complaint with the CMA which has the expertise in assessing complex measures would be easier and cheaper.

30. Therefore, the combination of the right to submit complaints to the central authority with the right of that authority to investigate and stop or order the recovery of non-compliant measures appears to be a superior method of ensuring the proper functioning of a system of subsidy control than the mere reliance on judicial proceedings to protect the integrity of the system.

31. But, since any intervention can create distortions of its own, it is also necessary to consider the possible negative impact of a flood of frivolous complaints. The European Commission's experience suggests that unsubstantiated complaints can indeed be submitted. However, the Commission is also empowered to reject them.[16] Therefore, this risk can be mitigated.

32. Before, reaching any conclusions it is also necessary to consider whether the UK system counterbalances the limited powers of the CMA with lighter rules, creating in this way a less cumbersome notification procedure that is less costly for companies and public authorities than their counterparts in the EU.

33. Certainly, the SCA imposes on the CMA tighter deadlines than the EU's procedural regulation – Regulation 2015/1589. The fact that the CMA has to cope with tighter deadlines, might be seen as a positive effect for granting authorities and subsidy recipients but also creates a risk of incomplete, lenient or perfunctory assessment. Therefore, the positive effect of faster CMA decisions may be weakened by the risk of incomplete assessment. Even if we presume that the quality of CMA decisions is not compromised by the tight deadlines, the fact that notifications are processed faster does not in itself ameliorate the problem of the institutional weakness of the CMA in safeguarding the integrity of the UK system of subsidy control. It is, therefore, a matter of empirical appraisal whether in practice the benefits from faster decisions outweigh potential harm from reliance on competitors and the judicial system to disincentivise the granting of non-notified subsidies or the non-recovery of non-compliant subsidies.

34. Although it is too early to appraise empirically the actual impact of the UK rules, in November 2023, *The Economist* published an article [17]reporting that whereas the United Kingdom was once a frugal outlier on State aid, spending just 0.35% of GDP on supporting business, lagging far behind Germany's 1.35%, UK State aid had tripled to 1.13%. Indeed, the article concluded with

16 See Council Regulation (EU) 2015/1589 of 13 July 2015 laying down detailed rules for the application of Article 108 of the Treaty on the Functioning of the European Union (codification) [2015] OJ L248/9, art 24 <https://eur-lex.europa.eu/legal-content/EN/TXT/?uri=uriserv:OJ.L_.2015.248.01.0009.01.ENG> accessed 25 October 2024.

17 "Post-Brexit Britain is Splurging More on State Aid – New Figures Show That Britain Has Become More European" *The Economist* (London, 28 November 2023) <www.economist.com/britain/2023/11/28/post-brexit-britain-is-splurging-more-on-state-aid> accessed 25 October 2024.

the words: "Britain's post-Brexit system is designed to be permissive. In the EU the Commission must vet the largest subsidies before they are given. In Britain the regulator's advice to the government is non-binding; cash awards can be clawed back only after the fact by a court. Historically Britain was a frugal user of state aid. It is becoming more European".

35. If the UK regime is significantly more effective, one should expect to see evidence that there is an economic impact which has arisen due to this increased and more widely targeted spend. Perhaps such evidence will emerge in due course, but at this time it is not clear that the United Kingdom is seeing an economic return on its increased expenditure in subsidies.[18]

V. Conclusions

36. State aid or a subsidy is paid out of the public purse. It is well understood that raising revenue to finance public policies distorts the allocation of resources in an economy. It is also well understood that the enforcement of any system of rules is not only costly in terms of its funding requirements but can also cause distortions of its own.

37. The purpose of a system to control State aid is to prevent "bad" aid and allow "good" aid that remedies market failure and/or enables public authorities to achieve legitimate public policy objectives.[19] An effective system ensures that the positive effects of aid outweigh the negative effects. An efficient system achieves that without creating distortions of its own. But does the EU system of State aid control that protects the integrity of the internal market also create additional inefficiencies?

38. It is difficult to answer this question because it is not obvious what a counterfactual system could be. However, Brexit has created a possible comparator because the newly stablished subsidy control system in the UK was partly motivated by the belief that the EU system was too cumbersome and, consequently, the new UK system had to be lighter and more agile. This offers an opportunity to carry out a comparative analysis between the UK and EU systems.

39. There are many similarities between the two systems. There are also substantive and institutional differences. I expect that the UK substantive rules will evolve over time. The same may happen to the institutional architecture of the UK system. But, if one were to assess the design of the two systems with respect to their ability to prevent "bad" State aid or subsidies, the UK system appears to have weaker safeguards. At the same time, the procedure of notification of subsidies appears to be faster and therefore potentially less costly, although it is not clear whether it is also lighter in terms of information

---

18 HC Library, UK GDP (2024) <https://researchbriefings.files.parliament.uk/documents/SN02784/SN02784.pd>f accessed 25 October 2024.

19 See European Commission (n 1).

requirements. Whether the cost savings from faster procedures outweighs the weaker safeguards is an issue for empirical appraisal.

40. It follows from the comparison of EU and UK systems that the distortions that may be caused by EU procedural rules are inherent in a robust system of control and cannot be avoided. However, it may be possible to reduce them. Every expansion of the scope of block exemption regulations reduces the number of notifications and the corresponding administrative burden of compliance. It remains to be seen whether the Commission will be able to expand the scope of the General Block Exemption Regulation – Regulation 651/2014 – at the next revision which is due to happen in 2027.

Does Improved Market Contestability Imply Higher Consumer Surplus?

JORGE PADILLA* AND SALVATORE PICCOLO**
Compass Lexecon

I. Introduction

1. Consumer surplus is a fundamental economic concept. It represents the monetary gain people receive when purchasing a good or service at a price lower than the maximum amount they are willing to pay. Any price increase, be it driven by an anticompetitive conduct or increased market power, causes consumer surplus to decrease, either because every buyer who still purchases the product after the price increase pays a higher amount, or because fewer consumers can purchase the product due to the higher prices.

2. Another key economic concept is that of market contestability, which refers to the degree of competitiveness and ease with which new firms can enter or exit a market.[1]

3. This brief chapter discusses the relationship between the two notions, which is less obvious than is often assumed, especially by non-economists.

---

* Compass Lexecon and GW Innovation and Competition Lab, George Washington University.

** University of Bergamo and Compass Lexecon.

1 JOE STATEN Bain, Barriers to new competition, their character and consequences in manufacturing industries (Harvard Univ. Press 1956). Elizabeth Bailey & William Baumol, Deregulation and the Theory of Contestable Markets, 1 Yale J. Regul. 111 (1984). William J. Baumol et al., Contestable Markets: An Uprising in the Theory of Industry Structure: Reply, 73 Am. Econ. Rev. 491-496 (1983). William A. Brock, Contestable Markets and the Theory of Industry Structure: A Review Article, 91 J. Pol. Econ. 1055-1066 (1983). Marius Schwartz & Robert J. Reynolds, Contestable Markets: An Uprising in the Theory of Industry Structure: Comment, 73 AM. ECON. REV. 488-490 (1983).

4. It is well known that consumer surplus is maximized in a perfectly competitive market with many buyers and sellers and homogeneous products. In such an ideal setting, prices are driven down to marginal cost, and consumers capture the entire benefit of competition through lower prices. This result has led many to conclude that consumer welfare is maximized in the absence of market power and, therefore, that it is highest in markets where there are no barriers to entry and/or exit.

5. And yet, as is also well known, perfect competition is an idealized scenario. In the real world, economic factors – such as, economies of scale, product differentiation, and asymmetric information – and non-economic factors – such as legal and regulatory barriers to entry and exit – result in oligopolistic or monopolistic market structures characterized by the presence of market power, where consumer surplus is below its perfect-competition level.

6. The relevant and difficult question is whether in markets subject to economies of scale, product differentiation or asymmetric information, the elimination of barriers to entry and exit – i.e., the adoption of policies aimed at ensuring the contestability of markets – is necessarily aligned with the promotion of consumer welfare. Is it correct to think that maximizing market contestability necessarily leads to lower prices, greater output and, hence, higher consumer surplus.

7. Building on recent academic work, we explain why this presumption fails when there is cost heterogeneity within the industry and firms have private information about these cost differences. In these instances, an increase in market contestability may result in higher prices, lower quantity, and reduced consumer surplus. We then argue that settings with these features are not just theoretical curiosities, but are relevant from a practical point of view.

8. Assuming that consumer surplus maximization is equivalent to improved market contestability under these conditions might ultimately damage consumers. This is particularly the case when relatively inefficient firms enter a market with low barriers to entry but face high exit costs when adverse market conditions are realized. When firms are privately informed about their marginal production costs, the presence in the market of inefficient firms excessively reduces the production of their more efficient rivals, thereby inducing an inefficient allocation of market shares in the industry at the expense of consumers.

9. The rest of this chapter in organized as follows. In Section II, we explain the notion of market contestability and discuss its role in antitrust. Section III reviews traditional economic models showing that market contestability is not always good for "total welfare" – i.e., the sum of consumer welfare and industry profits. In Section IV, we explain the economic mechanism behind a recent academic article showing that increased market contestability may lower quantity, increase prices, and harm consumer surplus. Section V concludes.

II. Market Contestability in Antitrust

10. Antitrust laws are designed to protect and promote competition, deter anticompetitive practices, and ensure that markets operate efficiently for the benefit of consumers. While most antitrust analyses are fundamentally static, focusing on existing concentration levels, and in particular on the number of competitors, competition agencies increasingly incorporate dynamic considerations in their assessments, recognizing that market conditions and barriers to entry may evolve over time. This perspective takes into consideration the fact that even if a market appears concentrated today, it may become less so in the future, provided it is contestable.

11. A contestable market is characterized by no (or limited) barriers to entry and exit, creating an environment where existing firms face constant threats from potential entrants. High entry barriers such as significant capital requirements, regulatory hurdles, or proprietary technology, can reduce market contestability. The threat of entry is a key driver of competition, compelling firms to operate efficiently, innovate, and offer better prices and quality to attract and retain customers.

III. Contestability and Total Welfare

12. The presumption that unrestricted entry is conducive to social efficiency has dominated theoretical and policy paradigms for many years. However, several studies over time have challenged it, particularly in scenarios where firms face fixed set-up costs upon entry.

13. Notably, already in the 1970s and 1980s, when game-theory was starting to be applied in Industrial Organization, various authors showed that the link between entry and total welfare is far from obvious. Spence, and Dixit & Stiglitz found that in monopolistically competitive markets, where firms offer differentiated products, free entry could lead to an insufficient number of firms compared to the social optimum.[2] By contrast, von Weizsäcker, and Perry identified a tendency for excessive entry in markets with homogeneous products.[3]

14. In a seminal contribution, Mankiw & Whinston explained the complexity of the underlying economic mechanisms driving the link between entry and total welfare in oligopolistic markets.[4] They showed that in Cournot markets –

---

2 Michael Spence, Product Selection, Fixed Costs, and Monopolistic Competition, 43 Rev. Econ. Stud. 217-235 (1976). Avinash K. Dixit & Joseph E. Stiglitz, Monopolistic Competition and Optimum Product Diversity, 67 Am. Econ. Rev. 297-308 (1977).

3 C.C. von Weizsäcker, A Welfare Analysis of Barriers to Entry, 11 Bell J. Econ. 399-420 (1980). Martin K. Perry, Scale Economies, Imperfect Competition, and Public Policy, 32 J. Ind. Econ. 313-333 (1984).

4 N. Gregory Mankiw & Michael D. Whinston, Free Entry and Social Inefficiency, 17 RAND J. Econ. 48-58 (1986).

where firms competing by offering quantities of a homogeneous good and the market price clears the market – with entry costs and complete information, the elimination of all barriers to entry can result in excessive entry – there are more firms than the number of firms that maximize total welfare. In equilibrium all active firms break even, so that no other firm has an incentive to enter the market, and no active firm has an incentive to exit.

15. Entry by a firm steals business away from rivals. This occurs because the strategic response of the incumbents to the new entrant is to decrease their sales volume to accommodate entry, thus mitigating its price impact. The new entrant ends up "stealing business" from the incumbents. Another way to express this effect is that it occurs when the equilibrium output per firm diminishes with an increasing number of firms, which, as Mankiw & Whinston argued, occurs in most markets. Entrants fail to internalize this negative externality on their rivals when entering the market, which explains in part the divergence between their private incentives and total welfare.

16. More formally, total surplus, TS, is defined as the sum of the customers' surplus, CS, and industry profits Π.

$$TS = CS + \Pi.$$

17. Entry will cause a change in total surplus, ΔTS, equal to the sum of the change in customer's surplus, ΔCS, the change in the incumbents' profits, $\Delta \Pi^I$, and the change in the entrant's profits, $\Delta \Pi^E$. That is, $\Delta TS = \Delta CS + \Delta \Pi^I + \Delta \Pi^E$.

18. Entry takes place if the entrant does not incur in losses – i.e., its profits are non-negative: $\Delta \Pi^E > 0$ It follows then that a sufficient condition for entry to be desirable is that the change in costumers' surplus plus the change in the incumbents' profits has to be positive – i.e., if the Net Entry Effect (NEE), which equals $\Delta TS - \Delta \Pi^E = \Delta CS + \Delta \Pi^I$ is positive. Since entry will occur when $\Delta \Pi^E$ is non-negative, a positive NEE implies a positive change in total economic surplus. In that case, the social value of entry, ΔTS, exceeds its private value, $\Delta \Pi^E$. The opposite is true with a negative NEE.

19. In a Cournot market such as the one analyzed by Mankiw & Whinston, the change in customer surplus is positive since entry increases industry output and lowers prices to the benefit customers. Instead, the change in incumbents' profits is negative, since due to increased competition the incumbents' volumes and prices fall. If the "consumer welfare effect" dominates, the NEE is positive and entry has a positive result on total economic surplus. If, instead, the "business stealing effect" dominates, the NEE is negative, and a complex balancing exercise needs to be performed to determine whether the impact of entry on total economic surplus is positive or negative. Mankiw & Whinston explain that for a certain range of the fixed costs of operation in the market the NEE is negative and, therefore, entry is excessive from a social viewpoint.

20. In all these instances, raising entry barriers increases total welfare. However, the effect on consumer surplus is the opposite. That is, in their model, rising

entry barriers reduce consumer surplus. The reason is simple. Consumers do not internalize firms' entry costs and care only about aggregate quantity, which falls as entry barriers increase – i.e., the fewer firms in the market, the lower the aggregate quantity.

21. Following Mankiw & Whinston's insights, there has been some examination of the robustness of the excess-entry result under various sources of uncertainty. Creane considers an exogenous "failure" probability with which a firm, upon sinking the entry cost, cannot produce: insufficient entry may occur if this probability is high enough.[5] Silvers, supposes that entrants only observe a signal of their actual entry cost and finds that the expected number of excess entrants is minimal if this signal is uninformative.[6] In Deo & Corbett, the production process is characterized by yield uncertainty, and there is insufficient entry if the output variance is large enough.[7] Uncertain production costs, which are unknown to everyone at the entry stage but become common knowledge before production choices, exacerbate the excess-entry distortion in De Pinto & Goerke.[8]

22. In all these articles, excessive or insufficient entry is determined from a total welfare standpoint, because consumers unambiguously benefit from more entry. Hence, while this literature provides some warnings on the welfare desirability of increased contestability, it still points toward a positive link between reducing barriers to entry and consumer surplus. In the next section, we discuss new research that highlights the potential dark side of increasing market contestability.

IV. Contestability and Consumer Surplus

23. Recent academic work by Bisceglia et al., shows that the conclusion that market contestability is necessarily associated with higher consumer surplus crucially relies on the hypothesis of complete information and does not necessarily hold in Bayes-Cournot markets – i.e., in markets where firms have incomplete information on their rivals' costs.[9] In these instances, the authors show that raising entry costs – i.e., limiting market contestability – increases expected entrants' output and profits as well as overall industry output, and may also increase consumer surplus.

---

5 Anthon Creane, Note on Uncertainty and Socially Excessive Entry, 3 Int'l J. Econ. Theory 329-334 (2007).

6 Randy Silvers, Uncertain Entry Cost, Market Structure, and the Value of Public Information (Discussion Paper, 2018).

7 Sarang Deo & Charles J. Corbett, Cournot Competition Under Yield Uncertainty: The Case of the U.S. Influenza Vaccine Market, 11 Mfg. & Serv. Operations Mgmt. 563-576 (2009).

8 Marco De Pinto & Laszlo Goerke, Cost Uncertainty in an Oligopoly with Endogenous Entry, 74 Bull. Econ. Rsch. 927-948 (2022).

9 Michele Bisceglia et al., On Excessive Entry in Bayes-Cournot Oligopoly, RAND J. Econ. (forthcoming, 2023).

24. Incomplete information about rivals' costs is a common feature in many markets. There are good reasons to conclude that assuming private information about costs is more plausible than assuming complete information, including the high demand for benchmarking of costs in many industries.[10] The existence and significance of entrants' private information has been noted in recent empirical work on entry.[11]

25. Bisceglia et al., consider a linear-quadratic Bayes-Cournot market game, where firms are privately informed about their marginal production costs and must sink a set-up cost, whose amount is common knowledge, to enter the market. Firms compete by offering quantities of a homogeneous product and the market prices clears demand and supply.

26. They identify a new mechanism through which entry barriers affect output and welfare. With incomplete information, low entry barriers lead to an adverse selection of firms entering the market: some high-cost firms find it profitable to enter when they would not do so in a complete information world. Importantly, the possibility of entry by such high-cost firms will not only reduce incumbents' expected output, as in Mankiw & Whinston, but it can also reduce the expected output of the industry, leading to higher prices, and a reduction in consumer and total welfare. When that is the case, raising barriers to entry is consumer-welfare and total-welfare enhancing and it unambiguously constitutes optimal public policy.

27. The trade-offs shaping these results are easily illustrated in the simplest scenario where only one entrant faces competition from one or more incumbents that have already sunk their set-up costs. In this scenario, facilitating entry has two effects on the entrant's expected output. On the one hand, it increases the probability of entry, thus increasing the entrant's expected output. On the other hand, reducing the set-up cost raises the incumbents' expectation of the entrant's marginal cost of production – i.e., incumbents expect entry by firms with higher costs when the set-up cost is lower, which increases the cost of the entrant expected by the incumbents. This leads incumbents to produce higher quantity upon entry than they would if the set-up costs were higher, and since quantities are strategic substitutes, leads the entrant to produce less.

28. The optimal set-up cost that maximizes the entrant's expected output balances these two effects. Maximizing the entrant's expected output thus requires a positive level of set-up cost and some entry restrictions. The reason why the first effect does not always dominate the second can be understood by considering the limiting case where entry requires no set-up costs. In this scenario, even an entrant with marginal costs so high that it produces zero will enter the market.

10 *See, e.g.*, Xavier Vives, Private Information, Strategic Behavior, and Efficiency in Cournot Markets, 33 RAND J. Econ. 361-376 (2002).

11 Paul L.E. Grieco, Discrete Games with Flexible Information Structures: An Application to Local Grocery Markets, 45 RAND J. Econ. 303-340 (2014). Lorenzo Magnolfi & Camilla Roncoroni, Estimation of Discrete Games with Weak Assumptions on Information, 90 Rev. Econ. Stud. 2006–2041 (2022), https://academic.oup.com/restud/article/90/4/2006/6670639.

Its expected contribution to industry output is also zero. Yet, its possible presence in the market imposes a negative externality on more efficient entrants, since the incumbents will choose their quantities anticipating a relatively inefficient entrant. The incumbents' aggregate output does not depend on the entrant's actual cost but on its expected cost. Increasing the set-up cost slightly above zero leads incumbents to reduce that expected cost and reduce their aggregate output, which has a positive first-order effect on the entrant's expected output. Raising the set-up costs marginally increases the profitability of entry.

29. By a similar logic, entry restrictions can also increase expected industry output. Specifically, expected aggregate output falls post-entry if the entrant is relatively inefficient. In that case, it does not produce much, but its entry causes a disproportionate drop in the incumbents' aggregate output, given that they respond to the entrant's expected cost and not to its actual cost. This reaction is absent under complete information about costs.

30. The standard business-stealing logic implies that incumbents always favor entry restrictions. Yet, surprisingly perhaps, the entrant also benefits in expectation from market access restrictions. Although reducing the probability of entry and making entry more costly, a restrictive entry policy is de facto equivalent to an efficiency commitment, thereby inducing more accommodating behavior by the incumbents upon entry.

31. As for consumer surplus, Bisceglia et al., show that consumers are risk-loving: their expected utility is convex in aggregate output.[12] Therefore, in addition to valuing expected industry output, they also value output volatility, which increases as the range of possible entrant's costs rises. Hence, entry restrictions have two opposite effects on consumer surplus: a positive effect by increasing expected industry output and a negative impact by reducing expected output volatility. On the net, consumer welfare maximization does require entry barriers so long as, in expected terms, incumbents are relatively efficient compared with the entrant.

32. Conversely, total welfare is decreasing in the variance of industry output. Hence, even net of set-up costs, total welfare maximization requires restricting entry to increase expected output and reduce variance. Moreover, since firms are asymmetric, minimizing production costs requires more efficient firms to sell more, which again calls for entry restrictions.

V. Conclusion

33. Relying on recent work by Bisceglia et al., we have shown that the presumption that entry barriers – i.e., limits to market contestability – reduce expected output and consumer surplus is unwarranted when firms are privately informed

12 Frederick V. Waugh, *Does the Consumer Benefit from Price Instability?*, 58 Q.J. Econ. 602–614 (1944).

about their costs. We have explained that this assumption is reasonable in practice.

34. The implications of this finding for policy are significant, as it can no longer be presumed that policies – including industrial policy, regulatory policy and antitrust enforcement – aimed at increasing rivalry are necessarily aligned with consumer welfare. While the extant literature has demonstrated that free entry and exit could lead to inefficiency, in a world of incomplete information about costs, we now know that it can also harm consumers.

Why Antitrust? Antimonopoly in Europe

Barry Lynn[*]
Open Markets Institute

1. In 1950 French industrial administrator Jean Monnet made clear that the newly proposed European Coal and Steel Agreement required strong anti-monopoly provisions. A failure to eliminate monopolies, he said, would "result in the dominance of private interests in the place of the pursuit of common aims." Monnet also made clear that monopoly reduced prosperity. Competition, he said, provides "enterprises with a constant incentive" to drive "expansion" and "industrial progress."[1]

2. In targeting Europe's Nazi-era industrial structure, the French government did not act alone. Immediately after Germany's surrender in May 1945, US President Harry Truman ordered the US military to "effect a dispersion of ownership and control of German industry."[2] The US government also used the August 1945 Potsdam Agreement with the Soviet Union and Britain to demand the elimination of "cartels, syndicates, trusts and other monopolistic arrangements."[3]

3. Monnet would later call the Coal and Steel agreement the "first European anti-trust law." That international agreement also provided a policy framework for Germany's domestic post-war regulatory system. In February 1952, Chancellor Konrad Adenauer formally agreed to a wide-ranging and aggressive antitrust regime in West Germany, as part of a broader security arrangement that required his government to pledge not to build missiles, heavy ships,

---

* Barry C. Lynn is the director of the Open Markets Institute.

1 (116, 119)

2 (89).

3 (89)

or nuclear reactors.[4] Then in May 1952 the German government finalized the breakup of the infamous chemical monopoly IG Farben into an array of smaller components including such well-known manufacturers as BASF, Bayer, and Agfa.[5]

4. As they took these actions, two strong beliefs guided French and US policy-makers. First was that German industrial monopolists had helped to put Hitler into power and to keep him there. As French Marxist Daniel Guerin put it in a book that influenced American policy,[6] "heavy industry" sought "the aid of a dictatorial state" in order "to strengthen its economic hegemony." Second was that any return to the pre-war system of domestic monopoly and international cartels would limit Europe's ability to counter the Soviet military threat.

5. The democracy and security of post-war Europe, in short, stand on a foundation of antimonopoly principles and policies.

6. Today people around the world are once again debating the question: "Why Antitrust?" In the United States, Canada, and elsewhere, the result is a rush to rebuild and renew these tools. So too in Europe, where the EU Parliament in Brussels has passed a variety of new antimonopoly laws and regulations to address the threats posed by the online platform monopolists. Yet in Europe, when the law enforcers themselves talk of antitrust, it has become rare for anyone to speak of the role these laws play in protecting individual liberty, democracy, or the stability and security of international systems. On the contrary, most of Europe's competition policy leaders still insist that the main purpose of these laws is to promote the welfare of consumers through efficiency, choice, and sometimes, innovation.

7. The time has come for Europe to return to first principles on antimonopoly. Protecting democracy requires much more than shipping cash and missiles to Ukraine. It also requires wielding antitrust law and policy against any and all private corporations that pose threats to individual liberty, freedom of the press and of expression, and the industrial security of Europe and its allies. Antimonopoly law and enforcement – properly understood – is a first line of defense against the *political economic warpower* of both the private monopolist and the mercantilist state.

8. In doing so, Europeans will find themselves better equipped to continue to play a leading role in helping the United States and the world's other democracies with their own efforts to relearn and rebuild their ability to use antimonopoly to protect and strengthen democracy and human liberty, a project that remains dangerously incomplete and fragile.

---

4 (623 Acheson).

5 (94)

6 National Planning and Strategy: A working Bibliography for the Educational System of Officers of the Army (War Department Library 1946); Fascism in Action: A Documented Study and Analysis of Fascism in Europe (Library of Congress 1947).

I. Antimonopoly's European Roots

9. For most of modern antimonopoly's 400-year history, the political nature of these laws was never in question. From the first, European parliamentarians and other reformers viewed antimonopoly as essential to establishing a rule of law able to protect the political, intellectual, and moral independence of the individual.

10. This is clear, for instance, in the debates that shaped the founding period of modern democracy in Britain. The *Case of Monopolies* or (*Darcy v. Allen*) in 1601,[7] for instance, centered on claims by business owners that Queen Elizabeth's grants of monopoly to favored supporters threatened the "liberty" of her other subjects to do business with whom they "pleaseth."

11. We see this more broadly in the Statute of Monopolies in 1624. Today this act is remembered mainly for forcing King James to recognize Parliament's right to restrict his ability to interfere in the economy. But here again the case pivoted on the specific threat posed by a sovereign's attempt to establish private monopolies in the hands of whom he alone chose. Parliament made clear that such a license posed a threat to all private property, hence to the individual's freedom to speak one's own mind without fear of reprisal.

12. Remembering these origins of modern competition policy is useful for three other reasons. First, it reminds us of how antimonopoly principles and policies were originally forged in response to efforts by seventeenth-century sovereigns to build centralized states that concentrated all control in their own hands. In France, the antimonopolists ultimately failed, as Louis XIV established himself firmly atop French political and economic life. But in Britain and the Netherlands, antimonopoly played a key role in the early efforts to build systems designed to protect political and intellectual liberty.

13. Second, it reminds us of the foundational role that non-discrimination rules play in protecting the liberty of the individual. In recent years, discussions of antitrust law have tended to focus on whether to prevent a particular concentration or structure of power. Yet the goal of the Statute of Monopolies was to stop the King from being able to choose who wins and who loses. And it is here that we see the ultimate purpose of all antimonopoly law and regulation, which is to ensure equal treatment, equal access, and equal justice in the face of both public and private power.

14. Or as John Locke put it, "Freedom of men under government is to have a standing rule to live by, common to every one of that society… and not to be subject to the inconstant, uncertain, arbitrary will of another man."

15. Third, these origins remind us of how the British and European antimonopoly fights shaped the thinking of the founding generation in the United States. For thinkers such as John Adams and James Madison, the ultimate failure of

7 Darcy v. Allen 77 Eng. Rep. 1260 (K.B. 1603).

the Statute of Monopolies and the common law to prevent the rise of such dangerous eighteenth-century monopolies as the British East India Company meant that a far stronger system of control was necessary.

16. We see this thinking in the simple strong statement of goals in the Declaration of Independence: of nation from nation; of man from man. We see this thinking also in the system of checks and balances in the US Constitution, the single greatest antimonopoly document in human history.

17. Understood in this light, the subsequent history of American antimonopoly – from the "Bank War" to the Interstate Commerce Act, Sherman Act, Federal Reserve Act, Robinson Patman Act, and the American approach to "free trade" – should look a lot less exotic to a European audience. Rather than some weird concoction of the cowboy mind, antimonopoly in the United States appears more like a highly creative and ultimately successful effort to fully develop and perfect – over the course of two centuries – a European-born vision of human liberty, even while most European peoples were overwhelmed by war and the unrestrained powers of the centralized state and the private monopoly.

18. Thus, the post-war history of European antimonopoly also begins to look different. Rather than some sort of "Americanization" of Europe or the imposition of an "American model" of business – as some writers have phrased it[8] – antimonopoly is the restoration of a European vision of liberty that had been able to survive and thrive thanks largely to the security afforded by the Atlantic Ocean.

19. In other words, it is reasonable to view the American political economy of the mid-twentieth century – of the independent entrepreneur, independent farmer, and the independent community; of mass manufacture and vast prosperity; of the public university and democratic labor – as but the culmination of the dreams of the British, Dutch, French, and German middle classes of the Enlightenment.

II. The Monopolists' War on Democracy

20. The story of the weakening and subversion of antimonopoly law and policy is now broadly familiar. In the earliest days of the Reagan Administration a small group of radical pro-corporate scholars set out to redefine the most basic purposes and methods of political economic regulation. Rather than aiming at protecting liberty and democracy in the name of the citizen, they said antimonopoly law should instead focus on promoting economic efficiency, theoretically to produce more material wealth for "consumers."

21. To this end, they said law enforcers should welcome private monopoly, as long as the corporation in control of the monopoly promised to use its power to drive down prices. They also urged enforcers to abandon the ancient rules

8 Marie-Laure Djelic

requiring monopolies to treat all customers the same, here theoretically in the name of boosting the ability of the monopolist to redistribute wealth within society.

22. The radicals then buttressed their new system with an entirely new science of efficiency, in the form of a reimagined economics of industrial organization. Under traditional antimonopoly, the government set simple limits on the size, structure, and behavior of corporations. Under the new regime, specially trained economists were to use complex economic models to determine whether some particular acquisition would result in lower prices. If enforcers chose to challenge a deal, judges and juries were then expected to determine whose economic model was more accurate.

23. In the 1980s, the radicals assured the public that their new approach amounted to little more than some minor tweaking of the existing system. Yet in the United States, forty years on, it is clear that their project resulted in the most extreme concentration of power and control since the Civil War, to the point of subverting even the most basic of constitutional balances.

24. Four political effects especially stand out:

25. *The destruction of the free press and of free debate*, as Google, Facebook and other online communications platforms exploited the overthrow of non-discrimination law to build the world's most powerful systems for manipulating how people share news, art, and opinions with one another; and to divert most advertising dollars into their own pockets.

26. *The destabilization of the liberal international trading system*, through an extreme concentration of industrial capacity – most dramatically in China – in ways that increase the likelihood of conflict, war, and catastrophic industrial collapses.

27. *A revolutionary reordering of US society and politics*, as monopolists destroyed millions of family businesses in retail, farming, services, and light manufacturing, in ways that radicalized much of the middle class.

28. *The privatization and containment of innovation*, as monopolists used their power over entire industrial systems to block better technologies and techniques, including those that would reduce carbon emissions.

29. In Europe, the story is much the same. Into the 1990s, French chauvinism and the strong pro-democracy nature of the German post-war system largely succeeded at keeping Reagan-style corporate libertarian thinking out of European regulatory systems. The one big exception was the UK, where Margaret Thatcher and Tony Blair generally embraced the new pro-monopoly philosophy of the libertarians.

30. But around the turn of the millennium the resistance began to falter, especially in the European Commission. Perhaps the single most dramatic action came soon after September 11, 2001, when the Bush Administration took advantage of the attacks on New York and Washington to all but force Competition Commissioner Mario Monti to adopt the Consumer Welfare ideology.

31. In the years since, this philosophy took on the nature of gospel, especially in Brussels. In part this was due to the normal workings of the bureaucracies, with individual officials carefully learning the new rules and developing strict procedures with which to apply them, eventually without much thought or deviation. In part it is due to the influence of the new monopolists themselves, who continue to invest vast sums within Europe to promote and maintain the corporate libertarian philosophy.

32. And so in Europe today we see much the same political economic upheaval as in the United States. In Europe too we see a collapse of the free press and free debate. In Europe too we see a failure to prevent the physical concentration of vital industrial capacities in China. In Europe too we see the enclosure of the innovation commons. And – albeit at a slower pace – in Europe too we see a destruction of the political economic wellbeing of the independent entrepreneur, farmer, and worker, and a rise of right-wing rage and reaction.

III. A New Liberal Democratic Revolution?

33. Today the world's liberals stand stunned and confused, wondering what happened to the world we thought we had built. Hard right nationalism, even fascism, has pushed into our parliaments and state houses. Russia has launched a war in the heart of Europe, and in the seas around China we see the threat of a far more cataclysmic conflict. The corporate reaction against green policies grows stronger by the day.

34. Yet before we cede the future to the demagogues and their goons, and the great capitalists who often stand behind them, let's recognize that the responsibility for the collapse of liberal democracy lies on our shoulders. It was we the worlds liberals – and in using this term I include those Europeans who belong to most traditional conservative and democratic socialist parties – who largely forgot the first duty of the liberal. Which is to ruthlessly wield the power of the democratically controlled state to break or neutralize all concentrations of power at home and abroad that threaten the liberty of the citizen and the security of the nation and all democratic institutions.

35. We forgot that antimonopoly is how we extend constitutional checks and balances into our political economy; how we establish the laws and rules that govern the ways in which individuals and groups compete with and communicate with one another; how we harness the power concentrated in the corporation, the bank, the factory, and the transportation and communications network for constructive ends.

36. We forgot that antimonopoly is the sword we honed against fascism and autocracy, the sword we honed against the mercantilist and militarist, the sword we honed to protect peaceful cooperation among peoples. We forgot

that antimonopoly is the primary tool we use to architect a good society and a sustainable world. And to architect our own political and spiritual enlightenment.

37. We forgot that antimonopoly is both the language and the means of hope, and of faith in a better tomorrow.

38. Fortunately, we are at last awakening. Yes, the ideologues of right and left continue madly to scribble a vast new literature in which they imagine various "post-liberal" worlds. But we liberals are swiftly relearning how to wield our many weapons.

39. In President Biden's Executive Order on Competition, in the merger guidelines of the Department of Justice and Federal Trade Commission, in the visions of international trade presented by National Security Advisor Jake Sullivan and US Trade Representative Katherine Tai, we witness the restoration of traditional thinking and practice, and hear again the ancient language of liberty.

40. So too in the European Parliament's many important new legislative acts, and in the constancy with which the Members of the European Parliament move to further strengthen those laws. So too in the pioneering work of the Bundeskartellampt in Germany and the Competition Markets Authority in the UK.

41. But the debate at a recent conference in Brussels highlighted how many law enforcers within the European Commission stubbornly cling to key components of the libertarian philosophy and processes put into place at the turn of the century. In response to arguments urging the Commission to act more aggressively against the fast-growing threats to democracy and security, officials assured the public that they would continue to focus on promoting "the efficiencies" of the "competitive process."

42. European officials are correct when they contend their definition of "consumer welfare" is more wide-ranging than the definition that prevailed in the United States until Biden. What they fail to recognize is how the *terminology* of the consumer welfare ideology, and the *processes* designed to measure efficiency, *constrain* their ability to understand the full array of political goals intended by the founders of the post-war European system. And further, how this terminology serves to *hide* both the magnitude of the political threat posed by corporations such as Google and Facebook, and the full power of European laws to address these threats.

43. Every American should recognize with immense gratitude how European antimonopolists long stood alone against the power of big tech, often despite immense political pressure from the Bush, Obama, and Trump administrations to give way to the industrious young men of Silicon Valley. Americans should also fully recognize the fragility of our own achievements in the eight years since Senator Elizabeth Warren first warned of the political threats posed by the monopolization of our political economy. And Americans should be honest about our own continuing intellectual and policy failures, such as our

slowness to apply common carrier rules to the dominant online communications and commercial platforms.

44. But the time has come for Europeans to understand the value of the ideas, language, and spirit of today's antimonopoly movement in America, and to stake proper claim to these traditions. The time has come to remember, as the political economist Frederick Hayek put it in 1960, that our goal is to establish a "Constitution of Liberty" and to protect and "preserv[e] the conditions that make democracy workable."[9]

45. The latest Liberal Democratic revolution is at hand. Dare we lift the sword of liberty?

---

9 117

Towards a Manageable Concept of Abuse of Dominance in the EU*

Rupprecht Podszun**
Heinrich Heine University

1. What is an abuse of dominance in European competition law? Let's take a 2022 example from a first instance court in Frankfurt, Germany (case 2-03 O 58/22). It ruled on the application of an online seller of individualised number plates for cars to get an injunction against Google. Google had blocked ads by the seller on the basis of a Google-advertising directive. The Frankfurt court granted the injunction within three months, stating that the blocking of ads unfairly impeded the seller. The court cites a 1981 decision by the German Federal Supreme Court. Finding an infringement, the court says, "requires a comprehensive weighing of the individual interests of both parties, taking into account the objective of the [Competition Act], which is directed at the freedom of competition and requires non-discriminatory conduct based on objective considerations".

2. What follows is a weighing of concerns in seven paragraphs, about two pages long. These paragraphs are not very strong on economics or economic effects, but they contain plausible legal reasoning. The court takes the "special responsibility" of a dominant company into account and brings fundamental rights onto the scene.

3. This ruling is a standard example of an abuse case in private enforcement, which was – admittedly – based on Section 19 of the German Competition Act, the equivalent to Article 102 of the Treaty on the Functioning of the

---

* This article has been previously published in Concurrences, and it might have been edited for clarity and cohesion. Rupprecht Podszun, Towards a manageable concept of abuse of dominance in the EU, September 2023, Concurrences N° 3-2023, Art. N° 112966.

** Professor German and European competition law, Heinrich Heine University, Düsseldorf. Director, Institute of Antitrust Law (IKartR), Düsseldorf.

European Union (TFEU). The ruling neither represents a particularly well-crafted nor a particularly poorly reasoned decision. It is what normal judges can do within a couple of weeks.

4. Now, imagine the online seller had complained about Google to the European Commission instead of turning to a court. It may well have got a fully-fledged investigation – and a decision after several years that may have gone to court.

5. This is the reality of European competition law: a massive divergence between national private enforcement and public enforcement at the EU level, at least in cases involving abuse of dominance.

I. If Abuse Cases Are No Longer Manageable, the Answer Will Be Sector-Specific Regulation

6. The European Commission has now started the process of adopting new guidelines on Article 102 TFEU. The last time it tried this, it ended up in a debacle: Years of discussions left the Commission with enforcement priorities (instead of guidelines). The hapless and never-ending *Intel* saga and several blows in key cases severely damaged the Commission's enforcement record in the field. The new guidelines now need to close two gaps: They need to present a manageable approach that gives orientation for private enforcement as well as for more sophisticated public enforcement. They also need to take a position in the long-raging debate on the pros and cons of a "more economic approach".

7. It will not be particularly helpful to turn to what the courts say on abuse of dominance. The definition from the famous *Hoffmann-La Roche* (case 85/76) ruling in 1979, still seen as the standard textbook definition, operates with a reference to "normal competition". For competition fans who strive for innovation and energetic rivalry, "normal competition" sounds about as tedious as a game of Tetris. The lack of a good substantive definition made it important to describe the way or procedure to establish an abuse in a concrete case. *Servizio Elettrico Nazionale* (case C-377/20), the 2022 case of the Court of Justice, fails to describe this path in a conclusive manner – it takes up some of the language from times when a more structural approach was favoured, but it also leaves some room for proving effects.

8. Three aspects from *Servizio Elettrico Nazionale* seem noteworthy, though: First, conduct by a dominant undertaking is seen as abusive if "that practice is capable of impairing an effective competition structure". The court stays loyal to the protection of the competitive structure.

9. Second, it also reiterates that effects can relate to "among other things, price, choice, quality and innovation". This is broader than a narrow consumer welfare standard with economic models of output and price. Innovation-driven

concepts or the "consumer choice" approach could play a stronger role in the future.

10. Third, the court takes up thoughts from older rulings like *Roquettes Frères* (case C-94/00) and places the abuse provision into the larger context of the aims of the European Union: "Article 102 TFEU is part of a set of rules, the function of which is to prevent competition from being distorted to the detriment of the public interest, individual undertakings and consumers, which ensure well-being in the European Union".

11. Competition is not exclusively about protecting the final consumer – it serves the public interest, even individual undertakings, and well-being in the EU (whatever that may entail). This opens up the horizon, and is in line with the general tendency to take competition law out of its splendid isolation.

12. One of the most important aims for guidelines is that abuse of dominance becomes a manageable concept. It is a pillar of the European economic project that must not be damaged by overly lengthy and complicated investigations. The existing style of case-by-case analysis has not served well. Even lawmakers have reacted to the bad balance of costs and benefits in leading abuse proceedings: The Digital Markets Act is widely perceived as the result of the failure of antitrust to come to terms with the phenomena of the platform economy. When energy prices rose in the past year, the European Commission decided to use all kinds of regulatory instruments. But it was not DG Competition leading the fight with a quick remedy. If Article 102 TFEU is no longer manageable, competition law will lose its influence as the basic framework for business activities, and it will be replaced by more and more sector-specific regulation.

13. Getting the balance right will probably mean less economic effects analysis in individual cases – more Frankfurt, less *Intel*. Even determined advocates of law & economics distinguish between economic input in rulemaking (great!) and economic input in individual court cases (much harder!). This makes guidelines so important: They are the right place to lay down economic insights for the definition of naked restrictions, presumptions and key factors for assessing an abuse.

II. The Commission Needs to Be Bold and Go Beyond of What the Courts Have Said

14. The guidelines could draw up a scale for different patterns of corporate conduct: The scale runs from definitely unproblematic to definitely abusive for each group of cases. The guidelines could identify the aggravating and mitigating factors that move conduct from one end to the other of this scale. Market concentration, the duration of the practices, countervailing market power, financial means, the appreciability of the behaviour and other criteria may weigh in. Economists may tell the Commission what they see as indicators

for these factors, so this becomes a helpful tool for your daily judge in court and lawyers advising dominant companies that strive for compliance.

15. It will not suffice to summarise case law (as the Commission tends to do in guidelines). The Commission needs to be bold and put forward its own ideas for a methodology. This methodology needs to be future-proof – that is another lesson from the difficult attempts to enforce Article 102 TFEU in recent years: The rise of digital platforms produced new conduct that no one had thought of when the process of drafting guidelines was started twenty years ago. The 2005/2009 guidance discussed rebates – but did not know self-preferencing. New guidelines must foresee a way to deal with new phenomena that no one thinks about today. The Commission also needs an answer to the question of how new learnings can be integrated into the evolving case practice. Today, economists know much more about the "as-efficient-competitor test" than in 2005. What if some of the assumptions or ideas in guidelines are better understood or further developed? How can robust and tested tools be distinguished from others? It would be a seminal achievement to find mechanisms for speedy updates and revisions of guidelines. It is good and motivating news for competition experts: Law-making in such a dynamic field is an "open discovery procedure".

Who Guards the Guardians? The Role of Perception Surveys in Evaluating Competition Authorities

Felipe Irarrázabal*
CentroCompetencia (CeCo) of Universidad Adolfo Ibáñez

I. Introduction

1. I am grateful to Concurrences for the invitation to write a note for the book "Why Competition?" at a pivotal moment for the evolution of competition law and economics worldwide.
2. This note addresses the need for continuous evaluation of the performance of competition authorities, particularly as growing pressures call for more vigorous oversight of market activities.
3. I believe that performance of authorities can be efficiently and effectively measured through perception surveys, which were initially conducted by the Chilean authority and later by CentroCompetencia (CeCo) at Universidad Adolfo Ibáñez, surveying the main competition authorities in Latin America. A reverse exercise can also be performed: authorities evaluating the practitioners in their respective countries.
4. In my opinion, this approach is replicable in other jurisdictions.

---

* Felipe Irarrázabal Philippi is the Director of the CentroCompetencia (CeCo) and a senior fellow of Universidad Adolfo Ibáñez.

II. The Need to Evaluate Authorities

5. James Madison wrote a phrase in The Federalist Papers that remains relevant today: "If men were angels, no government would be necessary. If angels were to govern men, neither external nor internal controls on government would be necessary." This idea is complemented by another memorable quote from the same author: "Ambition must be made to counteract ambition."

6. We need to encourage entrepreneurial ambition, which arises when freedom of enterprise is granted. This is the fuel necessary for growth and allows us to aspire to a vibrant economy. However, such freedom cannot be absolute; it must be shaped to avoid infringing upon the freedoms of others. In terms of competition law, freedom cannot include collusion, abuse of market power, or selling our business to whomever we please. The role of setting and enforcing these rules belongs to the government. In other words, we need a watchman, but we also need to watch those guardians. Both private entities and the state can harm markets. Both are needed.

7. We should aspire public institutions to act in the general interest, ensuring that market oversight does not stifle them or replace the private sector with the public sector based on ideological views. One would also expect authorities to have a long-term perspective and understand markets without ideological bias.

8. We are all aware that an authority can become a "naked king," as in the tale by Hans Christian Andersen. It is not easy for the authority to know how well it is performing, or at least how the legal community – their counterparts – perceives their performance. An easy and conveniently anonymous way to find out is through a perception survey. This allows the authority to review its weaknesses and adjust its course if necessary. At the very least, it helps to avoid worsening the problem.

III. The Usefulness of Perception Surveys

9. Just as companies are measured by their profits, authorities should also strive to find methods to measure their performance and justify their budget.

10. The simplest way to review authorities is by looking at their levels of activity, that is, the cases they process and resolve. However, this output can lead to a short-sighted view. Additionally, since cases take time to resolve, especially when there are appeals to non-specialized bodies, this activity may end up being fruitless. Lawsuits can generate a lot of noise, but they may lead to nothing if they are lost.

11. For a competition agency's evaluation, it is essential to know the market's perception of its level of professionalism and performance. In other words, whether they are serious or not, whether they possess technical expertise and independence from purely political influences, and whether they are capable of

translating the most modern damage theories into the reality of their country, among many other factors.

12. A relatively simple way to assess how the authority is performing vis-à-vis the market is to ask those who deal with it daily: lawyers who litigate cases before the competition agency and advise clients on what can be done.

13. The fundamental purpose of these surveys is twofold. On the one hand, they allow the legal community to focus on evaluating key issues related to competition law. By answering specific questions – about 50 – the respondents become more aware of these aspects. On the other hand, they provide authorities with anonymous feedback on their performance, allowing them to identify areas for improvement and adjust their actions.

14. This is obvious: external evaluation is key to continuous improvement. Although receiving criticism can be uncomfortable (we know authorities tend to have thin skins), evaluations provide an opportunity to identify weak points, trends from previous surveys, and why not, foster healthy competition among authorities.

IV. Perception Surveys Conducted in Latin America

15. In 2012, Chile's National Economic Prosecutor's Office (FNE) commissioned Deloitte to conduct a perception survey of Chilean lawyers listed in well-known international rankings with significant experience before the Tribunal for the Defense of Free Competition of Chile (TDLC). The aggregated results were made public, and the same exercise was repeated in 2014 and 2016.

16. Later, CeCo at Universidad Adolfo Ibáñez took the lead and conducted the survey in 2020, 2022, and 2024. In early 2024, CeCo – with the assistance of George Washington University and six Latin American universities associated with CeCo – published the results of the latest survey, which included Argentina, Brazil, Chile, Colombia, Ecuador, Mexico, and Peru.

17. The same questions were asked, but different respondents and various authorities were analyzed, with each lawyer answering questions about their respective authorities. The 2024 survey was completed by 212 specialized antitrust lawyers from the region, all listed in *Chambers & Partners* and *The Legal 500*, with response rates exceeding 85 percent, except for Brazil and Mexico, which had response rates of 39 percent and 74 percent, respectively.

18. Additionally, in the 2024 survey, we asked the authorities to give aggregate scores to the lawyers in their respective countries, and a public Power BI software was released that allows the data to be broken down to encourage future academic research (see https://centrocompetencia.com/).

V. Main Findings of the 2024 Survey

1. Survey of Practitioners to Authorities

19. Below, I will summarize the main findings of the 2024 survey. More detailed information can be found on the CeCo website. The figures presented correspond to the averages obtained on a scale of 1 to 7, with 1 being the lowest score and 7 the highest.

A. *Deterrence*

20. In terms of deterrence generated by competition institutions, Chile, Peru, Brazil, and Mexico received the highest scores. This aligns with their strong performance in detecting cartels and unilateral abuses, and their ability to curb cartel formation.

21. In contrast, Argentina received the lowest ratings for both general deterrence and its effectiveness in detecting cartels and abuses.

B. *Political Independence*

22. Mexico and Chile ranked highest in terms of political independence, while Argentina performed the worst, particularly due to its specialized competition bodies. The Chilean TDLC was perceived as the most independent, with the least influence from non-competition factors.

Predictability

23. Peru, Mexico, and Argentina were rated the most predictable, with consistency between current and past decisions, especially in their specialized competition bodies. However, while Peru's institutions scored highly in predictability, they were also seen as more receptive to interests beyond competition law.

24. This contrasts with Chile's Supreme Court, which was perceived as the least predictable and the most susceptible to external factors such as material justice, media impact, and consumer protection.

Depth of Legal and Economic Analysis

25. The survey also examined the depth of legal and economic analysis. As expected, economic analysis was significantly stronger in specialized bodies compared to non-specialized ones. However, no major difference was observed in legal analysis across bodies.

26. The countries that performed best in terms of in-depth analysis – Peru, Chile, Mexico, and Brazil – were also perceived as being the most up to date with advances in comparative law and international standards. Notably, the Peruvian

National Directorate for the Investigation and Promotion of Free Competition stood out for its comprehensive legal analysis and the relevance of information it requested in investigations.

27. Despite these strengths, the valuation of economic expert opinions by authorities received low ratings overall, with an average score (3.8), indicating that economic reports are often not thoroughly analyzed. Chile's Tribunal for the Defense of Free Competition (TDLC) received the highest rating in this category (5.2), while Argentina's Secretary of Commerce was rated the lowest (2.0).

Due Process

28. In terms of safeguarding due process, non-specialized bodies were rated better than specialized ones, likely due to differences between judicial and administrative. Interestingly, the four countries with the best scores in due process – Mexico, Peru, Chile, and Brazil – also ranked highest in deterrence, political independence, transparency, and protection of confidential information.

Efficiency of Case Review

29. The speed of authorities in various procedural phases – investigative, sanctioning, and appeal – was generally rated low, with no country scoring higher than 4.1 in any phase.

Deference

30. Specialized bodies were seen as showing greater deference than non-specialized ones. The Superintendent of Industry and Commerce in Colombia was perceived as the most deferential (toward decisions of the Delegation for the Protection of Competition), while Chile's Supreme Court was seen as the least deferential (toward TDLC decisions).

Performance

31. Peru's National Directorate for the Investigation and Promotion of Free Competition ranked highest in overall performance (5.28), excelling in investigating anticompetitive behaviors, monitoring obligations, conducting market studies, overseeing concentration operations, and investigating collusive practices.

32. Notably, the authorities generally received low scores for their performance in investigating unilateral abuses, with Peru being the only country to score above 4. Ecuador's Superintendent of Economic Competition performed well in concentration operations (5.5).

Criteria for Initiating an Investigation

33. The survey also measured the clarity of the criteria used by authorities to initiate investigations. The highest clarity was observed in concentration operations (4.7), while unilateral abuses were perceived as less clear (3.7).

Merger Control

34. In Chile, Mexico, and Peru, there was broad consensus that the thresholds and requirements for notifying concentration operations are adequate.

35. However, in Colombia, more than half of the respondents felt that thresholds were inadequate and should be adjusted, though there was no consensus on whether they should be raised or lowered. In Argentina and Ecuador, a significant percentage of lawyers (36 percent and 37 percent, respectively) felt that thresholds should be less strict.

36. Peru's National Directorate for the Investigation and Promotion of Free Competition was the only body to score above 5 in terms of professionalism in negotiating mitigation measures or commitments in concentration cases.

37. Lawyers were also asked about the prohibition of concentration operations, specifically whether the current prohibitions were appropriate or if there should be more or fewer cases. In Chile, Mexico, Peru, Argentina, and Ecuador, the general consensus was that the prohibitions to date have been correct.

38. In contrast, a majority of lawyers in Brazil and Colombia felt that there should be more prohibitions, with at least half of the practitioners supporting this view.

Cartels

39. In terms of detecting collusion, no country scored higher than 5. Peru's INDECOPI, Chile's FNE, and Mexico's COFECE were the best-rated authorities in this category.

40. These three authorities were also rated highest in their overall performance in investigating collusion.

41. In Mexico, Brazil, Colombia, Argentina, and Ecuador, collusion was perceived as a "frequent" or "very frequent" occurrence, while a neutral perception prevailed in Chile and Peru.

42. Interestingly, over 75 percent of respondents in Mexico felt that collusion was frequent or very frequent, yet Mexico's competition institutions scored relatively well in deterrence (4.7).

43. When assessing the effectiveness of different measures to combat collusion, lawyers perceived administrative sanctions, criminal sanctions, and leniency programs as equally effective in destabilizing or preventing cartels. This suggests that criminal sanctions are not necessarily the most deterrent option.

44. Colombia, Ecuador, and Argentina received the lowest ratings for the deterrent effect of leniency programs, largely due to uncertainty surrounding competition agencies in these countries. In Chile, however, the main factor deterring the use of leniency programs was uncertainty surrounding the Supreme Court (82 percent).

Unilateral Abuses

45. The ability of competition authorities to detect unilateral abuses was rated low overall, with Peru's National Directorate for the Investigation and Promotion of Free Competition receiving the highest score (3.7).

46. Most practitioners felt that Latin American competition authorities were "reluctant" or "very reluctant" to investigate potential unilateral abuses.

Market Studies

47. No country scored above 5 for market studies, but Peru (4.7), Chile (4.2), and Mexico (4.1) received the highest evaluations. These countries were also rated highly for the depth of their economic analysis and the integration of comparative law and international standards.

48. The financial sector and digital markets were the most commonly suggested sectors for future market studies.

Litigation

49. In terms of litigation strategies, most lawyers in Chile and Peru perceived the administrative strategies of their authorities as "balanced-reasonable." In contrast, the administrative strategies of authorities in Colombia and Mexico were mostly viewed as "bold-risky."

50. Peru and Chile scored highest in professionalism in negotiating corrective measures or extrajudicial agreements, and these two countries (in reverse order) also performed best in economic analysis.

Monitoring of Authorities' Resolutions

51. Peru's National Directorate for the Investigation and Promotion of Free Competition was rated as the most effective in detecting non-compliance with resolutions, followed by Mexico's COFECE.

Compliance Programs

52. The general average for the depth of compliance programs was 4.8, with Colombia receiving the lowest score (4). The countries with the best-rated compliance programs – Peru, Mexico, Chile, and Brazil – were also perceived as having the strongest institutional deterrence overall.

53. Most lawyers agreed that the factor most likely to increase the implementation and monitoring of compliance programs was the "influence of foreign parent companies."

2. Survey of Authorities on Practitioners

54. The survey was completed by officials from the competition agencies of the countries involved in the study, with the exception of Colombia.

Level of Professionalism

55. In general, the level of professionalism among lawyers was perceived similarly across most countries, with scores ranging from 5 to 6. However, one official from CADE (Brazil) rated the professionalism of lawyers in their country with a score of 2.

56. It is worth noting that the same official from CADE consistently gave the lowest scores in nearly all areas of the survey.

Cooperation and Transparency

57. In terms of cooperation from practicing lawyers toward authorities, the highest rating (above 6) was given by the Public Official from INDECOPI (Peru). The official from INDECOPI also gave the highest score (6) in terms of transparency demonstrated by lawyers.

Honesty

58. With regard to the perception of lawyers' honesty, the highest scores (6) were awarded by the official from INDECOPI (Peru) and CNDC (Argentina). In contrast, the lowest scores (3) were given by two officials from Brazil.

Level of Specialization

59. In terms of the specialization of practicing lawyers in competition law, the two public officials from COFECE (Mexico) stood out, each rating this factor with a score of 7. On the other hand, lower scores were assigned by a CADE official in Brazil (3) and an official from SCE in Ecuador (4).

Adherence to Standards

60. Most authorities rated lawyers with scores above 5 when it came to staying up to date with advances in comparative law and international standards.

Legal and Economic Reports

61. The survey also asked authorities to evaluate the importance of legal and economic reports submitted by practicing lawyers. Six authorities rated the importance of independent legal reports with scores of 5 or higher. Exceptions included one official from CADE, who rated them with a score of 2, and another from SCE (Ecuador), who gave them a score of 4.

62. In contrast, the overall average for economic reports was 3.6 – one point lower than the average for legal reports – reflecting lower ratings from the authorities in Argentina (3) and Brazil (1).

Awareness of Rules by Practitioners

63. Authorities were also asked to assess the level of awareness among practitioners, market agents, consumers, and other state entities regarding competition rules.

64. For market agents, the authorities' ratings were generally low, with an average of 2.6, although results varied significantly. Regarding consumers, the overall average was 2.8, with less variation than for market agents, as six authorities rated this category with scores of 3 or lower. Finally, the average score for awareness among other state entities was 3.6, but there was considerable variation in the results.

VI. Final Remarks

65. A practical and insightful method for evaluating the performance of competition authorities is through detailed perception surveys conducted among the lawyers who interact with these agencies on a daily basis.

66. The 2024 survey commissioned by CeCo, with the participation of George Washington University, continues a long tradition of such surveys (conducted in 2012, 2014, 2016, and 2020, with the first three carried out by the same authority).

67. In our view, it accurately measures the performance of the authorities involved in the decision-making process of competition law. Additionally, this survey includes evaluations by the authorities themselves of the lawyers practicing in their respective countries.

68. CeCo at Universidad Adolfo Ibáñez will continue conducting perception surveys of competition authorities in Latin America, and I believe this exercise can be replicated by authorities in other parts of the world.

Form and Effects-Based Approaches: A Challenging Duality in the Application of Article 102 TFEU*

ARIEL EZRACHI**
University of Oxford

1. In recent years the debate on the soul of Article 102 TFEU and the effects-based approach have dominated the competition law landscape. While many would agree on the clear merit of introducing more carefully balanced analysis when establishing abuse, the practicalities of such an approach have been difficult to agree upon. The recent Guidance Paper on Enforcement Priorities in the Application of Article 102 TFEU, which stemmed from the public consultation, has further sparked the public debate in this area. Concerns were raised as to the scope of the effects-based variants in the Guidance Paper and the innovation it heralds – for example in the treatment of fidelity rebates and the use of the new proposed efficiency defence.

2. Beyond the substantive and conceptual complexities that an effects-based approach carries, its practical application has given rise to an interesting and somewhat disconcerting duality. On one hand, the European Court has not yet warmed to the effects-based approach. In its judgements, the Court, has by large, continued to hold that it is not necessary to demonstrate that the abuse in question had a concrete effect on the markets concerned. It has generally

---

* This article has been previously published in Concurrences, and it might have been edited for clarity and cohesion. Ariel Ezrachi, Form and effects based approaches: A challenging duality in the application of Art. 102 TFEU, May 2010, Concurrences N° 2-2010, Art. N° 31009.

** *Director, Oxford University Centre for Competition Law and Policy; Slaughter and May Lecturer in Competition Law, The University of Oxford.*

ignored the lively debate on the effects-based approach and even at times, the opinion of its own Advocate General.[1]

3. On the other hand, the Commission has pushed toward an effects-based analysis, not only in its Guidance Paper but also in its decision-making. In the *Prokent/Tomra* decision[2] the Commission noted that it has completed its analysis by considering the actual effects of the dominant company's practices and did not satisfy itself with the lower formalistic threshold established by the Court. Similarly, in *Intel Corporation*,[3] the Commission took the decision in line with the orientations set out in its Guidance Paper and considered the effects of the fidelity rebates. The Commission noted, however, that even with the absence of harmful effect, Intel's behaviour may be condemned under the formalistic analysis of abuse as applied by the Court, thus using a dual benchmark in its decision-making.

4. This form-based approach at the European Court and the effects-based approach as applied by the Commission, trigger apparent legal and business uncertainty. Arguably, this uncertainty is further amplified at national level where the duality of approaches may lead to the development of divergent case law. In this context, note that the Guidance Paper, being soft law, functions outside the precedent system and has no binding effect on national courts. Subsequently, while some national courts may take account of the effects-based variants, others may favour the traditional formalistic approach. When adding to this, the limited account of these concepts in the Guidance, and the varying capacity of national courts to engage in complex economic analysis, the scope for inconsistency is apparent.

5. While it is accepted that changes in the nature of legal analysis under Article 102 TFEU carry uncertainty in the interim period, its application at both national and Union levels necessitates a greater effort to instil clarity. Accordingly, the European Court's forthcoming decisions on appeal in the *Prokent/Tomra*, Intel Corporation, and other cases, should play a prominent role in shaping the boundaries of Article 102 TFEU. A full, or partial, endorsement by the Court of the effects-based approach will not only help crystallise the concepts at stake but would also transform them from soft law into binding law.

6. To be effective, judicial review in these cases will have to appraise the Commission's effects-based analysis and not satisfy itself with the formalistic benchmarks for abuse. In this respect, note however that while, on appeal, the Court undertakes a comprehensive review of the Commission's decision-making, it has traditionally limited its appraisal of complex economic and technical matters[4]. In the context of effects-base analyses, such self-imposed

---

1 See opinion of AG Dámaso Ruiz-Jarabo Colomer in Case C-468/06 *Sot. Lélos kai Sia E.E v Glaxosmithkline AEVE Farmakeftikon Proïonton ECLI:EU:C:2008:504.*

2 (COMP/E-1/38.113 – *Prokent/Tomra*) Commission Decision 29 March 2006 [2008] OJ C219/11.

3 (COMP/37.990 – *Intel*) Commission Decision 13 May 2009 [2009] OJ C227/7.

limitations may undermine effective judicial review. One would hope that the Court would seize the opportunity to shape and clarify the boundaries of Article 102 TFEU. Absent a proactive stance from the European Court, the interim period of uncertainty, which inevitably accompanies the Guidance Paper as it treads new ground, will extend beyond its natural scope.

The General Court of the European Union on the Move*

Laurent Truchot**
General Court of the European Union

1. What is the status of the reform of the European Union Tribunal?
2. Since it was adopted by regulation in 2015, the reform has followed the roadmap set out for it, which divided its course into three successive stages, to lead to the doubling of the number of judges.
3. The aim was to reduce, in the short term, both the volume of pending cases and the excessive length of proceedings before the Tribunal. This objective was gradually imposed under the constraint of a regular and hardly acceptable lengthening of the time taken to reach a decision in many areas, in particular in certain disputes of an economic nature, further supporting the observation that judicial time is not the time taken for cases.
4. In order to quickly clear the backlog of cases, twelve additional judges were to take office by the end of 2015, followed by the transfer of the seven judges' posts from the Civil Service Tribunal to the Tribunal in September 2016. Finally, the remaining nine judges were to take office in September 2019. This timetable has not been fully met. The projected number of judges has not been reached, due to delays in the appointment of some judges and the withdrawal of the United Kingdom from the European Union. However, since the entry into force of the Brexit, the European Union Tribunal is composed of 50 judges, with four judges yet to be appointed.

---

* This article has been previously published in Concurrences, and it might have been edited for clarity and cohesion. Laurent Truchot, The General Court of the European Union on the move, May 2021, Concurrences N° 2-2021, Art. N° 99628, pp. 2-4.

** General Court of the European Union, Luxembourg.

5. More than a year has passed since the Tribunal, in its new composition, began its work. It is true that it has been a singular year, marked by the pandemic. But it has been a year in which the European Union's court of first instance, even before organising itself to deal with this unexpected scourge, has undertaken a thorough review of its organisation and its mode of operation. Reform after reform, to take into account both the mechanical effects of this sharp increase in its productive forces and the need to continue the reflection, already begun, on the changes to be made in order to judge better and more quickly. This implied identifying and tracking down the factors that were slowing down the process and finding, in order to exploit them, the sources of productivity and ways of improving the quality of its decisions.

The Increase in the Number of Judges of the Tribunal Made It Necessary to Ensure That Its Mode of Operation Was More Flexible and That Its Jurisprudence Was Even More Consistent

6. The Tribunal first had to draw the inevitable consequences of the increase in the number of its members, for one cannot judge with 50 members as one judges with 28.

7. The first and not the easiest challenge arose from the legislator's decision not to accompany the doubling of the number of judges with a corresponding increase in the number of their staff. No additional referendaries or other staff could be recruited in the last phase, which ended in 2019. The Court of First Instance therefore had to reorganise the judges' chambers, which had long consisted of three legal secretaries, in order to reduce the number to two, while assigning to the Chambers themselves, and no longer to the judges, the surplus of these staff from the chambers already established. The "chamber legal secretaries", as they are now called, are now shared between the judges of a given chamber, being called upon to work alongside a judge of the chamber faced with an increase in workload, a complex case or an emergency. This has partly implemented the proposal made by the European Court of Auditors to the Court of Justice, with a view to improving case management, to introduce more flexibility in the assignment of legal secretaries.[1]

8. Even with a proportionately smaller number of staff and an unfinished doubling of the number of judges, such an increase in the number of judges cannot fail to create risks of divergence in its jurisprudence. Ten chambers of five judges have been established. In order to guarantee the consistency of the case-law, the Vice-President has been given a specific role of legal watch, consisting of systematically analysing the case-law of the Court of Justice and the Court of First Instance and organising on that basis an early warning system designed to prevent divergences.

---

1 Special Report No 14/2017, *Review of Case Management Performance at the Court of Justice of the European Union*, pt 98, C, p. 51, 2017.

It Was Equally Important to Add to the Reform of Its Composition, Completed In 2019, The Numerous Reforms of Its Organisation and Functioning That Would Reduce the Number of Pending Cases and the Length of Proceedings

9. The Tribunal then looked for ways to optimise the new forces assigned to it in order to limit its caseload, reduce the time taken to adjudicate cases and improve the quality of justice delivered.

10. Another major issue to be decided in this respect was the recurring question of the specialisation of the chambers, which has long been called for by the European legislator and the main players in European justice. It was a difficult decision to make. On the one hand, the judges of the Court of First Instance are recruited on the basis of their ability to exercise "high judicial functions" without any jurisdictional competence linked to experience in a specific legal field being required of them. On the other hand, there is no doubt that, in the judicial field as in others, intimate knowledge of a subject acquired through accumulated experience is a guarantee of efficiency, speed and quality of the work done. In order to reconcile these two concerns, it was therefore decided to resort to a partial specialisation of the chambers, at least for the time being. Thus, civil service cases and cases relating to intellectual property rights have been divided between two groups of Chambers, while the other litigation matters remain within the jurisdiction of all the Chambers.

11. The Court of First Instance is currently considering the possibility of further developing what might be termed "proactive" jurisdictional practice. This neologism refers to nothing other than the early examination of cases by the judge-rapporteur, without waiting for the written procedure to be completed, provided that this allows him or her to have sufficient knowledge of the language of the case and to be available to deal with cases that are already ready to be heard. This type of management increases the progressive and in-depth knowledge of the case file, while at the same time encouraging the anticipation of the measures of organisation of the procedure or of the investigation necessary for the efficient investigation of cases.

12. In order to reduce the time taken to deliver judgments, the Tribunal could not fail to re-examine the time limits which it sets for itself and on which its own assessment of the proper functioning of its chambers depends. In certain matters, it could thus soon be decided that the judges-rapporteur will have less time to hear the cases assigned to them.

13. Lastly, the groups of cases, which are adding to the portfolios of the Court's judges, often in the economic field (e.g. State aid, cartels, economic and monetary policy), warranted specific consideration. It is thus envisaged to assign cases belonging to the same group to several judge-rapporteurs within

the same bench and to ensure that they receive priority treatment and are dealt with in a "proactive" manner, while limiting the number of additional cases assigned to the judge-rapporteurs in order to reduce their workload.

14. The reduction of the time taken to render judgments is not an end in itself, but must be accompanied by a search for ways to improve the quality of the Tribunal's decisions.

15. The hearings, by deepening the knowledge of the facts and the legal issues they raise, fully contribute to the objective of improving the quality of the decisions. In the difficult context of the health crisis, the Tribunal has endeavoured to maintain the hearings already scheduled and to organise those that have been requested, if necessary by means of videoconferencing (38 hearings by this method, previously unheard of, out of a total of 227 hearings in 2020).

16. The use of expanded panels can also be considered a factor in improving the quality of justice rendered, as the cross-examination of a greater number of judges within a panel contributes to the deepening of judicial review. The decisions to refer cases to a five-judge formation, taken in the wake of the reform, have led to an increase in the number of cases decided by this type of formation, in the following proportions: 2018 (8.6%) and 2019 (6.7%), whereas between 2011 and 2015, on average only 1.8% of cases had been decided by a five-judge formation.[2] In 2020, the use of a five-judge bench increased substantially, with 14.8% of cases decided by this bench, while the proportion of cases decided by a three-judge bench, although still in the majority, fell to 75.3% of completed cases.

17. In its strictly legal aspect, having led to the doubling of the number of judges, the reform of the Tribunal has been completed since September 2019, even if it has still not met with 54 judges. Nevertheless, the reform remains, for some time to come, the work in progress for the many actions or methods that could improve its efficiency in the broadest sense.

The Volume of Pending Cases Is Still Too High

18. However, the first steps have begun to bear fruit.

19. It is true that, in terms of the volume of pending cases, no lasting downward trend has yet been observed. The stock of cases, equal to 1,267 in 2015, 1,486 in 2016 and 1,508 in 2017, after the transfer of the stock of cases from the Civil Service Tribunal (123 cases), fell significantly in 2019 (1,398), before rising again in 2020 (1,497). The implementation of the reform had been accompanied overall by an increase in the number of cases completed and had enabled the court to reach an all-time high of cases completed in 2018 (1,009), but, in the context of the health crisis, 2020 saw a sharp decline in these cases (748). This figure, which is obviously disappointing, can also be

2 Report provided for in Article 3(1) of Regulation (EU) 2015/2422, p. 35 and Tribunal statistics for 2020.

explained by a cyclical reason, relating to the volume of suspended cases, which of course cannot be closed until the reasons for suspension have disappeared. These cases alone account for almost 30 per cent of the Tribunal's caseload.

20. In 2020, an uneven evolution of the stock of competition cases (17 in 2015; 27 in 2020) and State aid cases (73 in 2015; 42 in 2020) could be observed, while the stock of IP cases remains stable, as does its share in the total number of cases brought, at around one third (302 in 2015; 282 in 2020).

21. The first effects of the reform can be seen in the time taken to reach a decision. The average time taken by the Court of First Instance to reach a decision, particularly in complex economic law cases involving infringements of EU competition or State aid rules, had been in excess of three or four years, without always being justified by the circumstances of the cases.

The Length of Time It Takes to Decide a Case Has Been Significantly Reduced

22. This time frame has begun to change significantly.

23. The overall duration of proceedings in 2019 was thus 16.9 months on average, a reduction of 3.7 months (-18.0%) compared to 2015. This decline is further confirmed in 2020, with the average duration having fallen by a further 1.5 months to 15.4 months (-9.0%).

24. In the field of economic litigation, efforts will have to be concentrated in the future on the length of time taken to process State aid cases, the downward trend in which still seems fragile (32.5 months in 2014; 17.4 months in 2015; 25.2 months in 2020).

25. In the same area, on the other hand, there has been a particularly marked reduction in the length of proceedings in competition cases (47.7 months in 2015; 30.2 months in 2020) and intellectual property cases (18.1 months in 2015; 12.5 months in 2020).

26. In short, although the trend is mixed, owing to the slowing effects of the implementation of the reform itself and the health crisis, it is nevertheless positive. The Tribunal will have to continue to work to consolidate and extend this trend to all its cases.

Leniency Policies in Anti-Cartel Enforcement: Critical Review Is Well Overdue*

Caron Beaton-Wells**
The Australia and New Zealand School of Government

1. The challenges associated with anti-cartel law enforcement have prompted the widespread adoption by competition authorities of a distinctive tool – the leniency policy (also referred to as an immunity policy or an amnesty policy). Providing the first eligible cartel member with full exemption from penalties and public proceedings, this is a tool employed only in respect of cartel conduct and generally not in relation to any other type of anticompetitive activity. It also appears to be unique to competition law enforcement. Equivalent weapons in the armoury of other law enforcement agencies are difficult to identify.
2. Based on the game theoretic model known in economic theory as the 'prisoner's dilemma', the use of a leniency policy in anti-cartel law enforcement is justified by authorities generally on the grounds that it is the most effective and least costly mechanism for detecting and prosecuting activity that is systematic, deliberate and covert.
3. It is also seen as contributing to the deterrence of cartel conduct. These benefits are regarded by governments and competition authorities as outweighing any

* This article has been previously published in Concurrences, and it might have been edited for clarity and cohesion. Caron Beaton-Wells, Leniency policies in anti-cartel enforcement: Critical review is well overdue, September 2015, Concurrences N° 3-2015, Art. N° 74084.

** Professor, University of Melbourne Law School. This foreword is a modified version of Caron Beaton-Wells, 'iLeniency Policies: Revolution or Religion?' in Caron Beaton-Wells and Christopher Tran (eds), *Anti-Cartel Enforcement in a Contemporary Age: Leniency Religion* (Hart Publishing, 2015), ch 1. Details of the book are available at <https://www.bloomsbury.com/uk/anticartel-enforcement-in-a-contemporary-age-9781782259428/> accessed 1 November 2024.

adverse effects in terms of lower penalties, and hence reduced general deterrence overall, as well as any adverse political, moral or other implications.

4. Over the last decade more than 50 jurisdictions have adopted some form of leniency policy in their anti-cartel enforcement program. At least on paper, there is a substantial high degree of similarity in the criteria for eligibility, processes for decision-making and outcomes provided for in such policies. There thus may be said to be a theoretical 'model' or orthodoxy in relation to the design and implementation of leniency policies around the world, based initially on the United States Department of Justice Antitrust Division's experience, followed closely by the experience of the European Commission and other jurisdictions, and reflected in the approach endorsed by international and regional organisations such as the Organisation for Economic Co-operation and Development, the International Competition Network and the European Competition Network.

Leniency Policies Are Seen as a Revolution in Anti-Cartel Enforcement

5. Enforcers are often zealous in their support for and advocacy of such policies, and at times defensive in the face of criticisms or perceived threats to their operation. At least traditionally there has also been a high degree of support for leniency policies amongst practising lawyers and economists, as well as amongst scholars and other commentators in competition law circles. Given their distinctiveness, proliferation and support, the adoption of leniency policies may be described as a 'revolution', a conceivably apt description in what has been referred to by enforcers as 'the war against cartels'.

6. In designing and reviewing the operation of a leniency policy there are fairly standard criteria seen by competition authorities as essential to ensuring 'optimal' effectiveness: namely severe sanctions; fear of detection and transparency and predictability in the policy's eligibility criteria, implementation and consequences. However, competition authorities rarely attempt to measure or assess the effectiveness of such instruments directly or systematically in light of the objectives of facilitating greater detection, prosecution and deterrence of cartel conduct than would otherwise be possible. Rather, the achievement of these objectives appears largely to be assumed, provided the policy fulfils the standard criteria.

7. Similarly, the approach taken by authorities (and many commentators) to leniency policy adoption and review tends to be inward-looking, focussed on the policy in a fairly discrete and isolated way and with a tendency to overlook or neglect deeper evaluation. More searching assessments of such policies would include consideration of the extent to which the policy has implications for or effects on other aspects of the overall system for enforcement and compliance (such as settlements, private actions for damages, advocacy and outreach activities and compliance programmes), as well as the extent

to which the policy is reconcilable with the competition authority's general approach to governance and its institutional values (such as transparency, consistency, proportionality and fairness).

8. There is a large body of theoretical and empirical economic research that has sought to establish the 'optimal' design of leniency policies and test for their 'success' in cartel detection, prosecution and deterrence. While valuable on its own terms, this research has acknowledged limitations relating to data availability and methodology. Moreover, it is often jurisdiction-specific and, even within a single jurisdiction, has produced mixed if not contradictory results.

9. More generally, the economic literature does not reveal how a leniency policy is actually perceived by the business sector in general, by leniency applicants or prospective applicants and their advisers and by competition authorities and their political masters. The economic research has also not explored the role and impact of leniency policies in a broader policy setting, in which other interconnected aspects of enforcement are at work and in which general considerations of agency governance are relevant.

10. There have been a number of published commentaries in recent years questioning the value of leniency policies, cautioning against over-reliance or myopia in their use, and drawing attention to the potentially deleterious effects of such policies on private enforcement, on criminal trials, and on engendering a culture of compliance amongst the business community. However, there is yet to be a systematic review or analysis that maps the emergence of the leniency phenomenon over the last two decades and interrogates its effects, both positive and negative, for contemporary anti-cartel enforcement. Without critical review and analysis of this nature, not just by independent commentators, but as if not more importantly, by the administrators and users of the leniency system, such policies might be seen as having as much the hallmarks of religion as they do the attributes of revolution.

11. Standing back and reflecting on the extensive body of research now available on leniency policies, as well as on the many years of practical experience with their development and application, several key themes emerge.

12. First, claims of leniency policy effectiveness in cartel detection and deterrence must be viewed conservatively. While competition authority anecdotes regarding leniency impact on enforcement programs and figures concerning the number of cartels detected through leniency applications are not be discounted, both empirical research and practical experience casts increasing doubt on the extent to which leniency policies are achieving cartel deterrence. Perhaps more disturbingly, a common theme emerging from the literature (including from empirical studies and published accounts of experienced practitioners) is that leniency policies are not only not deterring cartel activity but are in fact promoting it. Such policies are being seen as a strategic opportunity by cartelists to stabilise and enforce collusive arrangements.

13. Second, and conceivably relatedly, there is a clear discrepancy between the 'theory' of how leniency policy works and the reality of how it operates in practice. It is evident that competition authorities consistently recognise key principles that should underpin an effective leniency policy. However, it is also apparent that outside of the US, there is considerable divergence in the way in which such policies are in fact interpreted and applied. To some extent, the discrepancies need to be understood as a function of differences in legal and enforcement systems, institutions and cultures, and more generally in the political economy of competition law regimes. These differences suggest that while, superficially at least, the leniency policy trend may be geographically prolific, the manner in which it permeates individual enforcement regimes is best analysed on a jurisdiction-by-jurisdiction basis.

14. Moreover, there is disjuncture between the way in which leniency policies are theorised as affecting the perceptions and attitudes of cartelists and the way in which corporations and individuals in fact perceive and behave in response to such policies. There are good reasons to believe that leniency policy architects underestimate and over-simplify the decision-making task confronting prospective leniency applicants, both at corporate and individual levels. It is clear that this task cannot be reduced to a basic cost-benefit analysis. In part this is because many of the variables relevant to the analysis are either unknown or are unquantifiable.

15. However it also appears that what may be counted by some as reflecting the 'success' of the leniency policy phenomenon is tilting the equation against leniency applications. The proliferation of these policies across multiple jurisdictions makes it virtually impossible that an applicant will be 'first' in all places. Over-reliance on leniency at the expense of investment in other detection tools undermines the perceived threat of detection, independent of such policies. The growth in private actions for damages spurred by leniency-driven competition authority enforcement action has heightened the risks and disincentives weighed by potential applicants in connection with leniency decisions. These factors, amongst others, suggest caution at least is warranted in predicting the long-term sustainability and effectiveness of the leniency 'revolution'.

16. Third, the conception and administration of leniency policies has been too narrow and insular. While in some instances the relationship between leniency and other aspects of the enforcement system has been recognised, the discourse regarding the dynamics in and implications of these relationships has lacked sophistication and has often been one-sided, predominantly in favour of protecting leniency incentives.

17. In the case of criminal or penal sanctions for cartel conduct, much of the commentary has focussed on such sanctions as critical to the effectiveness of leniency policies. Relatively less attention has been given to what this means for the legitimacy and ultimately the effectiveness of the cartel criminalisation project. There are overlooked tensions and ambiguities in the coupling of

leniency policy and criminal sanctions, not least the retributive compromise and foreclosure inherent in a leniency-driven strategy of enforcement and the ways in which leniency policy underscores and may even reinforce the otherwise immoral (cheating) behaviour said to attract the moral opprobrium associated with criminal sanctions.

18. In the case of private actions for damages, much of the debate has centred on the threat that such actions pose to leniency policies. Yet, arguably, a more holistic assessment of the contributions that private enforcement and public enforcement (entailing, but not limited to enforcement based on leniency policy) can make respectively to the objectives of deterrence and compensation is called for, and the impact of private actions on leniency policies should be assessed in that broader context.

19. In the case of corporate compliance, the potential for leniency policies and compliance measures to be mutually reinforcing has been largely missing from the leniency discourse. While compliance training clearly bolsters leniency policies by increasing awareness by businesspeople of cartel laws and sanctions, leniency policies in turn could be drawn upon to strengthen compliance programs and culture. One way in which this could be done is through the assignment of credit for such programs in the context of penalty and sentencing decisions – an approach resisted by many competition authorities. Such resistance is at the expense of engendering a business culture in which ethical as well as legal values and behaviour are fostered.

20. The economic harmfulness of cartel conduct should not be questioned, nor should the challenges involved in its detection, prosecution or deterrence, nor even necessarily the justifications for and benefits of leniency policies in aiding the achievement of those ends. However, sound policy and effective public administration over the long term requires that the interaction and interdependencies between leniency policies and other facets of the overall enforcement system be acknowledged and carefully examined. This needs to be done even if the outcomes involve tempering the leniency policy faith.

Rating Agencies: How to Improve Them*

Nicolas Véron**
Bruegel

1. Rating agencies have long been part of the financial market landscape, but the financial crisis since 2007 has greatly increased their public visibility. Two sequences have been particularly striking. First, in 2007–08, the agencies were named among the main culprits in the subprime debacle in the United States, having assigned AAA ratings to structured products that did not deserve them because they failed to anticipate the possibility of a generalised decline in property prices throughout the United States. Second, over the past two years, the agencies have become the visible face of the sovereign securities markets in Europe, and are regularly denounced by political leaders for the irresponsibility they demonstrate in their downgrade decisions. Competition is an important dimension of the rating debate, since a dominant share of the market is in the hands of only two players, Standard & Poor's and Moody's; adding Fitch, the "big three" account for some 95% of the total market by most indicators. Combined with very high profit margins, these market shares explain the oligopoly qualification frequently applied to rating agencies, even if the existence of commercial agreements has not been identified so far.

2. It is undeniable that these agencies pose a problem: their fallibility, illustrated above all by the subprime episode, contrasts with the trust placed in their judgements by a large number of public regulations and commercial contracts. However, this problem needs to be seen in its true dimension. First, since

---

* This article has been previously published in Concurrences, and it might have been edited for clarity and cohesion. Nicolas Véron, Rating agencies: How to improve them?, February 2012, Concurrences N° 1-2012, Art. N° 41858.

** Economist, Bruegel, *Visiting Fellow, Peterson Institute, Washington, DC.*

agency ratings represent relative probabilities, their "errors" cannot strictly speaking be established on isolated cases but only on large samples using the law of large numbers. By this yardstick, their past mistakes have almost always been over-optimistic, which leads us to qualify the accusations of catastrophism that have been levelled at them in the context of the euro area crisis. Second, the claim that sovereign rating downgrades would have a major negative impact on sovereign credit markets deserves to be examined with some scepticism. In fact, rating downgrades are most often widely anticipated by investors, and their effects on markets are usually indirect through decisions taken by other actors, such as clearing houses (for rules governing margin calls) or investment banks (to determine "benchmark" indices that are then used as a reference by some investors). Moreover, their impact is generally far from mechanical, as was spectacularly illustrated in August 2011 when Standard & Poor's downgrade of the United States' sovereign credit rating resulted, apparently paradoxically, in a decline in US Treasury borrowing rates as a result of a simultaneous increase in general risk aversion. The impact of ratings is not fixed over time either, and it is likely that the influence that they have on investor decisions has actually declined in recent times, in light of the subprime episode and a political and legal environment that makes it increasingly difficult for the agencies to express a fully independent judgment.

3. Consequently, the rhetoric that portrays the agencies as a kind of supreme guide to the bond markets, and the enormous importance given to some of their decisions by the general media in several European countries, including France, appear disproportionate in view of the comparatively limited attention given to other dynamics that are at least as decisive, such as the (dys)functioning of the interbank market, or the issues of transparency and competition in the financial intermediation sector.

4. Nevertheless, the rating market, while not in itself significant in macroeconomic terms (its total worldwide turnover is less than EUR 4 billion), raises important competition issues. Lack of competition could contribute to poor quality ratings if agencies gain the impression that the lack of new entrants enables them to defend their market position even if their analysis is flawed. In principle, high profit margins could be reinvested in research capacity, but in practice the agencies have seemed to prefer to distribute them to their shareholders even at the cost of insufficient research, which was probably the case at least in the episode of US real estate structured products.

5. Moreover, the lack of competition could inhibit innovation, since the agencies would not consider it necessary to differentiate themselves by introducing new analytical techniques or new rating "products". However, the evolution of risk management techniques, with the exponential development of derivatives markets in particular, could make it necessary to review the very concept of credit rating, which was introduced in 1909 by journalist John Moody, the founder of Moody's, in a context of much more rudimentary financial techniques. Without satisfactory conditions of competition, the emergence of a "John Moody of the

twenty-first century" is unlikely, since such a person would be more likely to emerge outside the narrow circle of the "Big Three" than within one of them.

6. Government regulation of credit rating agencies is partly intended to address these challenges, but could also exacerbate them. In the United States, the registration process introduced in 1975 remained fairly non-intrusive for a long time, until a new supervisory regime was introduced in 2006. More importantly, the 2007–08 crisis led the G20 to recommend the introduction of similar regimes in most major economies. Regulation, however well-founded, tends to raise barriers to entry and discourage innovation, especially if it goes so far as to require the approval of new methodologies, as is currently being considered by the European Union. Moreover, the heterogeneity of national regulations could make it impossible for agencies to apply globally uniform methodologies, thereby significantly reducing the usefulness of ratings for investors and other economic actors.

7. So what can be done to remedy the shortcomings of the rating agencies? First, as in medicine, the first imperative is not to unnecessarily aggravate the situation. From this point of view, the European Union's most recent initiatives leave us perplexed, even if the good will of their promoters is hardly in doubt. The first Community regulation on CRAs was proposed by the European Commission in November 2008 and adopted one year later; the second, proposed in June 2010 and adopted in May 2011; a third regulation was proposed in November 2011 and will be examined by the Council and the European Parliament in 2012. While the first two regulations were justified by the G20 recommendations (themselves partly inspired by Europeans) and then by the change marked by the creation of the European Securities and Markets Authority (ESMA) in January 2011, the need for the third text is not self-evident at a time when uncertainty on the bond markets is reaching levels rarely seen in the past.

8. Second, any mechanical effects of agencies' decisions on market dynamics should be minimised as far as possible, since the limits of their judgement have been highlighted by the crisis. A number of initiatives have been taken to this end in Europe, the United States and at the global level, notably in the framework of the Financial Stability Board (FSB). However, it is not necessarily desirable that this objective should lead to the elimination of all references to agency ratings in public regulations and private contracts, since, in some cases at least, there may be no preferable alternative options. The experience of the United States is enlightening: the Dodd-Frank Act of July 2010 requires the federal public authorities to eliminate all references to agency ratings in prudential regulations, which was done in December 2011; but while applying the programme set for them by Congress, the federal authorities noted that the result was inferior to the previous situation in terms of regulatory efficiency. If the alternative is the discretionary judgement of another public or private actor, it may be as questionable as that of the agencies, or even more so if the actor in question is affected by political dependencies or commercial conflicts of

interest; relying on market prices increases the risks of manipulation and procyclical spirals. In such cases, reference to agency ratings is the worst solution.

9. Third, the most tangible antidote to the market impact of credit ratings is greater transparency of security issuers, so that the investment community can make better judgments without having to rely on rating agencies. From this point of view, much progress remains to be made. Sovereign issuers, including in the European Union, often suffer from obsolete accounting conventions that increase the opacity of their financial statements, to the detriment of their long-term financing conditions. Private issuers (companies and financial institutions) should not be allowed, as is currently the case, to provide agencies with information that they do not make available to the public; through their past mistakes the agencies have ceased to deserve this privilege of access to information. In the market for structured products, additional efforts to those made in recent years should also be made to enable investors to form their own judgement on the securities offered to them and to reduce their dependence on the judgement of the agencies. The issue of transparency, which concerns not only accounting information but also risk factors, especially those that can be the subject of quantitative information, now appears to be the most promising avenue for progress. From this perspective, the challenge for the public authorities is less to intervene in the agencies themselves than to reduce their status as a mandatory point of entry for the formation of investor opinions, through increased public transparency obligations, the implementation of which would be subject to more stringent controls than at present.

10. To sum up, there is no miracle solution to the problems posed by rating agencies, but these problems are not the most crucial in the current financial crisis. Many investors have begun to move towards a less exclusive focus on the agencies' decisions. Public initiatives must accompany this evolution and accelerate the desirable transition to a more diversified credit risk assessment landscape for better functioning financial markets.

PART IV

The Digital Age: Competition and Innovation

Current Approaches to Antitrust Are Not Delivering Robust Competition

Rod Sims*

Australian National University

1. A market economy is essential for productivity and prosperity. But I believe antitrust is not properly fulfilling its role in ensuring a market economy works as it should.

2. Adam Smith said: "It is not from the benevolence of the butcher, the brewer, or the baker that we expect our dinner, but from their regard to their own interest". These words were profound in 1776 and remain so.

3. Adam Smith, however, is usually quoted by those who believe that government and antitrust authorities should not intervene and that markets somehow self-correct. This is not what Smith was saying. As Heilbroner says, in his magnificent book *The Worldly Philosophers*:

> "But self-interest is only half the picture… a community activated only by self-interest would be community of ruthless profiteers. This regulator is competition, the conflict of the self-interested actors".
>
> "Adam Smith's laws of the market are basically simple… Specifically they show us how the drive of individual self interest in an environment of similarly motivated individuals will result in competition; and they

* Rod Sims AO is a Professor, Crawford School of Public Policy, at the Australian National University, Canberra; Chair of the Superpower Institute; Chair of Opera Australia; and Chair of Australia's National Data Advisory Committee. He, is on the Expert Advisory Panel to the Australian Treasury's Competition Review Taskforce and is an Expert Adviser to the UK's Competition and Markets Authority on digital platform issues. From 2011 to March 2022, he was Chair of The Australian Competition and Consumer Commission. Prior to that he had a range of senior corporate and government positions. From 1988 to 1990, he was the Principal Economic Adviser to Australia's Prime Minister Bob Hawke.

further demonstrate how competition will result in the provision of those goods that society wants, in the quantities that society desires, and at the prices society is prepared to pay".

"The great enemy to Adam Smith's system is... monopoly in any form".

4. This should all be obvious. If you are buying your meat, beer and bread from monopolies or duopolies "their regard to their own interest" would see you facing high prices and products of poor quality. For our market economies to work as intended they must be underpinned by robust competition.

5. My concern is that our current approaches to antitrust are not working as they should, and that the resulting lack of robust competition is damaging our societies. This should be of concern to all people who believe in the many benefits of market economies.

I. The Key Force Against Competition

6. The key force acting against competition in our market economies is, of course, companies themselves. Companies worked out long ago that the essence of corporate strategy is to gain and keep market power. Profits from "outrunning" many competitors from a common starting point are sufficient but often modest; profits from exercising market power can be large. Michael Porter's famous 1979 contribution made all this clear when he wrote his pivotal article that still underpins much of corporate strategy today.

7. Corporate strategy, said Porter, is about taking steps to reduce competition in your market, raise entry barriers to potential competitors, having dispersed suppliers and locking in consumers. Many antitrust theorists believe Porter's views are outdated. The problem is that the commercial world still works largely according to Porter; antitrust has increasingly become divorced from commercial reality.

8. Warren Buffet, for example, has repeatedly said that he only invests in companies that have "moats" around them. He means companies that are in significant ways protected from competition. This is logical; he wants to invest in companies that continually achieve returns above those attainable in competitive markets, and his track record is such that he has been successful in this.

9. Peter Theil is more direct when he says "competition is for losers"; he urges those starting businesses to aim for a monopoly position.

10. The growing economic literature shows that a lack of robust competition causes higher prices, poorer service, lower investment, less firm new entry and exit, lower productivity and increased inequality. Analysis of the data from our market economies shows that these outcomes from a lack of competition are playing out.

11. While this is not the place to go through this literature or data, one of the world's leading industrial organisation economists, Tommaso Valleti, who follows this literature closely, recently said:

> "Our (European) industries have become increasingly concentrated over the past thirty years. Margins, the ability of firms to set the price above the costs, have been going up, starting in the 1980s. Innovation is also more difficult than in the past: firms still leave the markets, still die, but they are not born at the same rate. The downside of these margins and profits ending up in fewer and fewer hands is that the workforce's share of the GDP gets smaller. So money is being made, but it is not trickling down in a uniform way, which perhaps also drives inequality. This is what economists have been finding recently. The initial response was: 'this is not true'. Every study was dissected and, as usual, no study is perfect. But if you put all the elements together, they always point in one direction and one direction only".

12. Others have even larger concerns. In the introduction to a 2019 book, Martin Wolf, the Chief Economics commentator for the London *Financial Times*, and widely recognised as one of the world's foremost economic thinkers, said:

> "Slowing growth and rising inequality have become a toxic combination in western economies, notably including the US. This combination now threatens the survival of liberal democracy itself. Why has this happened? Some blame an excess of free market capitalism… (but) the precise opposite is the case. What has emerged over the last 40 years is not free-market capitalism, but a predatory form of monopoly capitalism. Capitalists will, alas, always prefer monopoly".

13. Martin Wolf has now elaborated at length on these sentiments in his most recent book *The Crisis of Democratic Capitalism*. Wolf argues that "… a good part of what has gone wrong is what Adam Smith warned us against – the tendency of the powerful to rig the economic and political systems against the rest of society".

14. Antitrust success should not be measured in the outcomes from cases, however important these may be, but by the contribution antitrust is making to maintaining robust competition in our economies. Antitrust should seek to prevent market power gained by other than competition on the merits. In this, I believe, antitrust is not performing well.

15. So, what is not working in antitrust? I think five factors are important.

II. The Discipline of Commercial Strategy Seems to Be Ignored

16. On my very first day of corporate strategy training, yes a long time ago, I was told that while having good products, services and systems was necessary for commercial success it was by no means sufficient. Some form

of market power was needed. I was told that too much competition would harm returns, profits from a competitive market were insufficient, and high entry barriers were crucial (Warren Buffet's "moats"). Because this is simply common sense, at a high level it is as relevant today as it was then in terms of how so many businesspeople and their strategy advisers think and behave. The Porter model has been refined, but not in too many ways relevant to businesspeople.

17. What struck me on joining the Australian Competition and Consumer Commission (ACCC) was that competition lawyers and economists, particularly those working for companies alleged to have breached the law, and businesspeople wanting ACCC approvals, appeared to completely ignore commercial corporate strategy. It was as if in contemplating a merger the benefits of reduced competition never occurred to anyone. In my commercial strategy days, it was often an important driver of the transaction.

18. While I was at the ACCC, conversations with companies generally had an air of unreality about them.

19. Companies do wish to be in markets with less competition rather than more, they do seek to construct entry barriers, they want a dispersed range of suppliers, they do seek ways to lock in consumers, they will leverage market power from one market into another, and so on. All this behaviour is commercially rational. It is not, as seems often assumed, an aberration.

20. This is not to decry this behaviour, as it is part of what makes businesspeople and companies succeed. You cannot pick and choose how businesspeople seek to succeed.

21. What is striking, however, is the following:

    - First, absent difficult-to-get facts, suggestions that companies will act in a way fitting Porter's framework are often treated by the courts as "mere theory", "speculation" or, worse, "fanciful". Comments such as these appear naive to those from the commercial world.

    - Second, it is sometimes said that the competition agency's explanation for what drove certain behaviour is wrong and that there are good commercial reasons for what happened. But this suggests wanting to reduce competition or raise entry barriers is not commercial behaviour; it is indeed, however, the very essence of commercial behaviour.

22. The line between acting commercially and breaching the law can be quite thin. Corporate strategy and competition policy are often pulling in opposite directions.

23. This obvious point seems to be ignored in antitrust circles. It is as if any breach of antitrust laws by a company is an aberration, rather than part of a firm's commercial strategy.

III. We Have Raised the Evidentiary Burden on Enforcers

24. Over the last century the focus of antitrust has fluctuated from not wanting companies to become too large and influential, to wanting to maintain sound market structures given the likely consequences of unhealthy ones, then to the current dominant focus on the consumer welfare standard and an apparent disregard for market structure.

25. The history of economics, and public policy, is full of pendulum swings. Problems are found and, instead of simply being corrected, we see problems arise in the opposite direction. Concerns about too much focus on market failure, for example, and too little focus on government failure, saw concern with the latter come to dominate debate. Likewise, debate has moved backwards and forwards about how self-correcting markets are: consider Marshall, Keynes, and Friedman for a start.

26. This issue has profound significance in antitrust as we see with the pre- and post-Chicago school influence. The Chicago school, at its theoretical height, while bringing many important insights, got to the point where its belief in self-correcting markets was a triumph of hope over experience. Other fields of economics seemed to appreciate this faster than antitrust.

27. One concern with the consumer welfare standard is that it demands so much more than identifying harm to the competitive process; it wants considerable proof of harm to consumers. While there is logic to this, and it can encourage useful analysis, it raises issues of evidentiary burden.

28. In Australia we had a recent example where the Government of the State of New South Wales (NSW), in order to maximise the sale proceeds from the privatisation of the State-owned Sydney container port, entered into agreements that saw the port sold to a private company with effective financial prohibitions to there being a competitor container port established in NSW over the following 50 years. The ACCC launched court proceedings arguing the agreements substantially lessened competition. Among other things, the court found that the ACCC did not prove that a competitor port would be viable despite the owners of the Port of Newcastle (some 170 km from Sydney) saying they wanted to build a competitor container port and spending tens of millions of dollars in preparatory work, and even though the Port of Newcastle felt it needed to change its current focus over coming years from being the largest coal export port in the world due to climate change concerns.

29. The competitive process was clearly interfered with, another player was spending a lot of money wanting to compete and had strong reasons for doing so, but the court needed much more to rule the agreements anticompetitive.

30. In my view, debate about the focus of antitrust is closely linked to the issue of evidentiary burden. Should the focus of antitrust be to prevent harm to the competitive process? Of course, some level of harm to the trading parties on the other side of the market, usually but not always consumers, also needs to

be shown. This is to check the analysis of the effects of the conduct on the competitive process and to determine the materiality of the effect.

31. The question, however, is how much evidence of this harm should be needed once harm to the competitive process has been clearly demonstrated?

IV. We Are Trying Too Hard to Avoid Benign Conduct Wrongly Being Considered Illegal

32. Coming to the ACCC from over 15 years in the private sector I was surprised at how often concern was expressed about "chilling" investment or innovation. Often it seemed as if the speaker had never worked in the private sector; that is, in the room when business decisions are taken. Being a competition lawyer or economist consulting to the private sector may not count in this regard as often they come in when the business decision has been taken and the issue is how to gain regulatory approval.

33. The "animal spirits" mentioned by Keynes always seemed more apt. Businesspeople pursuing profit are not easily disturbed or dissuaded.

34. It therefore seemed to me that wrongly considering conduct illegal that turns out to be benign conduct, while to be avoided wherever possible, will rarely be disastrous for the business or the economy.

35. Allowing anticompetitive conduct to go unpunished, however, will more often do harm as market power is usually hard to unwind once gained. And businesspeople have every incentive and will work hard to ensure it is not unwound. Likewise, anticompetitive agreements or unilateral conduct can see competitors lost forever and new ones dissuaded.

36. There is another consideration. The cost of gaining competition agency approval is often trivial to businesses in comparison to the financial consequences of the issue at hand. Businesses can employ way more resources than the agency can on each specific matter, and there is often no limit to the per diems that can be afforded. These facts, all else equal, mean the system is more likely to generate situations where anticompetitive conduct goes unpunished than the reverse.

37. We should all aim always to arrive at the right answer. But if the objective is never stopping what turns out to be benign behaviour there will be under enforcement, which brings higher costs to the economy than over enforcement.

V. We Have a Problem with the Assessment of Mergers

38. I have always been struck by an anomaly. Antitrust seems very concerned to not block a merger that has a benign effect on competition, yet analysis by business academics shows that most mergers fail to meet their commercial

objectives. That is, antitrust seems to put more faith in mergers as an important element of economic dynamism than is in fact the case.

39. Assessing mergers is, I think, the most important work of a competition enforcer. Much better to stop anticompetitive mergers in the first place, than to deal with the effects of the resulting market power after the event. The problem is, however, that getting the evidence to act is harder for mergers than it is for other breaches of competition law. This is because the merger has not yet occurred.

40. The usual commercial logic, to which most businesspeople would adhere, is that some form of pricing power comes when there are less than four players in a market. Coordinated conduct is more likely to increase prices, and there is much less chance of one business seeking to gain share by reducing prices as they know this will only lead to retaliation, not extra share, and lower profits all round. Obviously, there are exceptions to this general rule, particularly in high fixed cost businesses.

41. Such well-accepted commercial logic, of course, appears to have no place in a courtroom. It is seen as "theoretical".

42. What makes all this more of a problem is that competition issues in the future are hard to prove with facts rather than commercial logic. Most businesspeople know not to write down the full commercial rationale for a merger lest it be used against them in court. Having to prove what has not yet happened loads the dice towards anticompetitive mergers gaining approval.

43. A key question is whether our economies are better off with merger laws with a strong structural presumption, based on commercial experience and logic, or an approach based on no starting presumption and detailed arguments in court each time trying to determine if competition will be substantially lessened?

44. Related to this is the enormous number of acquisitions undertaken by the large information companies. Small companies are constantly being purchased for a complex mix of reasons; to gain skill and ideas, to gain access to new markets, and to take out potential competitors early. Acquisitions of so-called nascent or potential competitors requires even more imagining by courts of what an uncertain future world would look like.

45. While the large digital platforms innovated their way to their initial success, for example, they have expanded and entrenched their market power through acquisitions which competition agencies have not been able to prevent except in the UK CMA's recent *Facebook (now Meta)/Giphy* case.

46. Where would Google be today without DoubleClick, Android, YouTube and so on, which were all acquired?

47. Competition agencies are struggling everywhere to deal with notions of "potential competition" from the continuing massive number of early acquisitions by the large information technology companies. Unless competition agencies can deal with issues of potential competition effectively then market structures may be entrenched as new entrants do not get the space to grow.

VI. We Are Being Ruled by Exceptions

48. As an economist by training, I have taken a particular interest in the role of competition economics and its difference from other areas of economics. Much competition economics comes from defences to allegations of anticompetitive behaviour. It often seeks to explain why, say, a three-to-two merger in a given market is not an issue, when usually it is. It is, therefore, not seeking to explain what usually happens, but why, with assumptions, what might seem like problematic behaviour is in fact in this particular case, benign.

49. Competition economics, in general, goes into considerable detail, which is a result of the case-driven workload. Such detailed analysis can bring benefits, but it also risks missing the bigger picture, can raise uncertainty, and increase the risk of not challenging anticompetitive behaviour.

50. I was in a meeting with agency head colleagues some months before I left the ACCC and the issue of structural presumptions in mergers was raised. One agency head surprised me by saying that economists would consider this bad economics. Why, I asked? There can be sound economic reasons for such an approach. Different economists will have a range of sensible views on this, but it is not inherently bad economics. Is competition economics so focused on case detail that it can miss the bigger picture?

51. My purpose here is to highlight some problems, not to come up with solutions. We need to discuss these issues and debate with open minds whether antitrust is working effectively. Those of us who want Adam Smith's "invisible hand" to keep guiding our societies have a real interest in this issue.

52. The good news is we do not need a revolution. Changes that bring different outcomes in a modest number of important commercial decisions can have a large effect.

Why Competition? Innovation

Aurelien Portuese*
The George Washington University

1. It is largely accepted that antitrust policy is designed to encourage innovation.[1] Those blaming lax antitrust enforcement policies argue that such policies stifle innovation.[2] Those blaming excessive antitrust enforcement policies equally argue that such policies stifles innovation.[3] Both camps are equally

---

* Research Professor and Founding Director of the GW Competition & Innovation Lab, George Washington University; Research Scholar, College de France, University of Paris (PSL); Special Editor of the Antitrust L.J.

1 Jonathan Baker, *Beyond Schumpeter vs. Arrow: How Antitrust Fosters Innovation*, 74 Antitrust L.J. 575–602 (2007) ("[…] U.S. competition policy as practiced today-antitrust doctrines and enforcement priorities taken as a whole-fosters innovation […]"); Richard Gilbert, Innovation Matters: Competition Policy for the High-Tech Economy 2 (MIT Press 2020): (stating that: "Antitrust agencies have taken steps to address innovation in their enforcement decisions" but advocating "to mov[ing] from price-centric to innovation-centric competition policies."); Aurelien Portuese, *Beyond Antitrust Populism: Towards Robust Antitrust*, 40 J. Econ. Aff. 237–258 (2020) (arguing for a greater focus on innovation in antitrust policy); Herbert Hovenkamp, *Antitrust and Innovation: Where We Are and Where We Should Be Going*, 77 Antitrust L.J. 749–756 (2011)

2 *See*, for instance, Tim Wu, *Taking Innovation Seriously: Antitrust Enforcement If Innovation Mattered Most*, 78 Antitrust L.J. 313–328 (2012) (arguing at 314 that "the Supreme Court's last two decades of jurisprudence, have, for example, generally made it more difficult to use the antitrust law to promote innovation, not easier."); Spencer Weber Waller & Matthew Sag, "*Promoting Innovation*, 100 Iowa L. Rev. 2223–2247 (2015) (advocating for "real Schumpeterian antitrust" that alters antitrust enforcement); Lina Khan, *The Separation of Platforms and Commerce*, 119 Colum. L. Rev. 973–1098 (2019) (considering that "the likely innovation harms stemming from platform appropriation and discrimination invite serious consideration of structural limits"); Amy Klobuchar, Antitrust. Taking Monopoly Power from the Gilded Age to the Digital Age (Alfred Knopf 2021), quoting former FTC Commissioner Rohit Chopra at 251 saying that: "Killer apps quickly become killer acquisitions. Immeasurable innovation has been lost because the government stopped preventing dominance from blocking disruption."); Sai Krishna Kamepalli, Raghuram Rajan & Luigi Zingales, *Kill Zone*, (Nat'l Bureau of Econ. Rsch., Working Paper No. 27146, May 2020), https://www.nber.org/papers/w27146 (revised May 2022) (arguing at 19 that innovation harms "could be deterred by an active antitrust authority, but the recent record on this front in the United States has been quite weak.")

3 J. Gregory Sidak & David J. Teece, *Dynamic Competition in Antitrust Law*, 5 J. Competition L. & Econ. 581–631 (2009) (concluding at 631 that "a wider appreciation of the importance of dynamic competition for innovation and consumer welfare may temper the hubris that the uninformed sometimes bring to antitrust analysis."); Portuese, *supra* note 1, (arguing that a robust antitrust policy grounded in innovation concerns); Aurelien Portuese, *Precautionary Antitrust: The Changing Nature of Competition Law*, 17 J. L. Econ. & Pol'y 548–634 (2022) (advocating to "overcome precautionary antitrust with innovation-based antitrust that best incentivizes dynamic competition."); Daniel Spulber, *Antitrust and Innovation Competition*, 11 J. Antitrust Enf't 5–50 (2022) (concluding that: "Antitrust should not evaluate competitive conduct and industry performance based solely on price competition and static technology. Antitrust also cannot abandon economic

concerned with innovation, but they cannot agree on which antitrust policy effectively promotes innovation. This fact is certainly because rarely, if ever, is *innovation* defined.[4]

2. What do we mean by innovation?[5] What is innovation from an antitrust perspective?[6] We propose a simple and operational definition of innovation for antitrust enforcers: Innovation is the commercialization of inventive ideas that successfully disrupt the set of consumer choices.

3. Why competition at all? The answer is innovation. Absent competition over scarce resources, the status quo and entrenchments of powerful actors prevent technological and social progress, leading to a regressive society. Indeed, there is competition, and competition policy correspondingly, because there is an imperative of rivalry over scarce resources.

4. There is a prevalent misconception that our world is abundant.[7] Nothing could be further from the truth. We are, always have, and always will live in a world of scarcity. The fundamental value – time – is scarce. Companies compete over consumers' time and attention. Also, consumer and business purchasing power is scarce: tradeoffs and arbitrages are incessantly made in an economically (ir)rational way. Information is scarce: despite being democratized, the level of available information remains highly limited: bounded willpower, choice fatigue, and inability to process the vast amount of information paradoxically reduce the level of available information creating reliance on intermediaries such as platforms and medias as filtering tools.

---

analysis just to chase after big firms in high-tech industries."); Hon. Douglas Ginsburg, *Wither The Consumer Welfare Standard?*, 46 Harv. J. L. & Pub. Pol'y 69–85 (2023) (raising concerns about ditching the consumer welfare standard at the cost of "higher prices, poorer quality, or foregone innovation […]"); Thomas M. Jorde & David J. Teece, *Innovation and Competition: Implications for Competition and Antitrust*, 4 J. Econ. Persp. 75–96 (1990) (proposing at 89 modifications to US antitrust law: "To insure that antitrust law is responsive to the needs of innovating firms and does not inhibit U.S. firms from competing effectively in global markets experiencing rapid technological change […]").

4 One of the few exceptions is Gilbert, *supra* note 1, ("By 'innovation,' I mean a new or improved product or process that differs significantly from previous products or processes. Innovation is more than invention, which is the act of discovering a new product or process, because innovation requires that an invention be put into active use or be made available for use by others.")

5 A definition is a challenging task given the multi-faceted nature of innovations. *See*, for instance, Stephen J. Kline & Nathan Rosenberg, *An Overview of Innovation*, in The Positive Sum Strategy: Harnessing Technology for Economic Growth 275–304 (Ralph Landau & Nathan Rosenberg eds., National Academy Press 1986) (arguing that "it is a serious mistake to treat an innovation as if it were a well-defined, homogenous thing that could be identified as entering the economy at a precise date – or becoming available at a precise point in time."); Jan Fegerberg, *Innovation: A Guide to the Literature*, in The Oxford Handbook of Innovation 1–27 (Jan Fagerberg, David C. Mowery & Richard R. Nelson eds., Oxford Univ. Press 2005): ("what we think of as a single innovation is often the result of a lengthy process involving many interrelated innovations.").

6 Antitrust authorities seldom assert that their actions systematically promote innovation. *See*, for instance, Address by Anne Bingaman, Assistant Attorney General at the DOJ's Antitrust Division, "Innovation and Antitrust" (Commonwealth Club of California, July 29, 1994), https://www.justice.gov/atr/speech/innovation-and-antitrust ("Antitrust actions in previous Administrations have been central in promoting innovation and growth in the U.S. economy.")

7 Deven R. Desai & Mark A. Lemley, *Editorial: Scarcity, Regulation, and the Abundance Society*, Frontiers (2023), https://www.frontiersin.org/journals/research-metrics-and-analytics/articles/10.3389/frma.2022.1104460/full (referring to the "technologies of abundance" and how IP creates artificial scarcity); Melanie Swan, *Philosophy of Social Robotics: Abundance Economics*, in Social Robotics 8th International Conference, ICSR 2016 900–908 (Arvin Agah et al. eds., Springer 2016); Brendan Sheehan, The Economics of Abundance: Affluent Consumption and the Global Economy (Edward Elgar 2010).

The antitrust implications of such limited information are considerable.[8] Time, money, and information are scarce and will forever remain scarce, contrary to those arguing that the information society and technological advancements have overcome scarcity.

5. Given the world of scarcity we live in, the absence of competition would mean the appropriation of few resources in the hands of those already having control of those resources – from Nomenklaturas in communist regimes to oligarchs in capitalist regimes. In the political realm, the absence of competition for, as an example, the role of heads of states means monarchies with families running as dynasties unless overthrown by disruptive revolutions or wars. In the economic realm, the absence of competition means entrenched market positions (often public monopolies granted by the political power rather than acquired) so that scarce resources held by capitalist oligarchs remain out of hand from potential competitors. Such absence of competition prevents rivalry for the control of these resources, not by force but by innovative ideas. Put simply, the lack of competition prevents contestants from challenging established positions through innovative means.

6. Competition means innovation – and the competitive process is a process of superior innovations that reward control of critical and scarce resources because of the economic welfare these innovative solutions generate to some or to many. Or at least it should be the case: the competitive process distorted by political forces may enable inferior solutions to prevail through protection from the competitive process or through the designation of the winner. The protection from the competitive processes is illustrated by the Uber taxi lobby weaponizing the political sphere to prevent ride-sharing apps from competing at the expense of economic welfare and consumers. The designation of the winner is illustrated by the rules laid down by natural monopolies or the oligarchs, winners of such privatizations. Either way, the lack of competition over scarce resources inhibits innovation and the rivalrous process of finding innovative and socially beneficial solutions to gain access to these resources.

7. But if the purpose of competition, in both the political and economic spheres, is innovation – what do we mean by *innovation*?

---

8 *See, e.g.*, Amanda P. Reeves & Maurice E. Stucke, *Behavioral Antitrust*, 86 IND. L.J. 1527–1586 (2011) (arguing that reliance by antitrust enforcers on the rational-choice theories fail to explain actual market behavior); Peter O' Loughlin, *Cognitive Foreclosure*, 38 GA. ST. U. L. REV. 1097–1174 (2022) (demonstrating how dominant platforms can cognitively foreclose competition); ANDREAS HEINEMANN, *Behavioural Antitrust: A "More Realistic Approach" to Competition Law*, in EUROPEAN PERSPECTIVES ON BEHAVIOURAL LAW AND ECONOMICS 211–242 (Klaus Mathis ed., Springer 2015). But see, Alan Devlin & Michael Jacobs, *The Empty Promise of Behavioral Antitrust*, 37 HARV. J. L. & PUB. POL'Y 1010–1063 (2010) (arguing that behavioral antitrust fails to provide a predictable comparable model to rational choice theories).

I. Defining Innovation and Its Antitrust Implications

8. Let's break down each element of this definition. Innovation differs from invention.[9] While inventing refers to a practically feasible idea that is imagined before being outlined, innovation on the other hand, refers to the throughput process of bringing this invention to the market.[10]

1. Innovation as Commercialized Inventions

9. That is why the patent system secures inventions but does not generate innovations, unless entrepreneurs commercialize patented ideas.[11] As Justice Kagan wrote in *Kimble*, because patents temporarily provide their holders with certain superpowers", Congress has balanced both objectives of "fostering innovation and ensuring public access to discoveries."[12] In that regard, the life sciences sectors and legacy industries such as aerospace, the petrochemical industry and other transport industries rely on patented inventions to innovate through their colossal corporate capabilities. Here, innovation means the commercialization of patented ideas, most of them being encouraged through in-house scientific efforts.

10. Although innovation emerges out of scientific and technological progress, innovation is the indirect result of such progress – invention being the immediate result of scientific progress and the cause of commercial innovations.[13] The difference explains why scientific and technological research needs massive subsidies (either in-house or public resources) to progress: unlike innovation, scientific and technological progress do not have a direct commercial use that make them financially sustainable. For antitrust purposes, large corporate subsidies of R&D are necessary in the hope that commercial innovations will emerge from corporations. Hence, Gilbert suggested that

---

9 This was made clear by Joseph Schumpeter in Business Cycles when he wrote that innovation "is not synonymous with 'invention'" because "invention does not necessarily induce innovation but produces of itself no economically relevant effect at all", in Joseph Schumpeter, Business Cycles. A Theoretical, Historical and Statistical Analysis of the Capitalist Process 59 (Porcupine Press 1989) (1939) (also noting at 60 that "the making of the invention and the carrying out of the corresponding innovation are two entirely different things.").

10 *See*, for instance, Joseph Schumpeter who defined innovation as the "carrying into effect" of inventions. *See id.* at 238.

11 Patents do not generate innovations but only two legal outcomes for the innovator – namely, the right to exclude against free-riders and a temporary property right. *See*, Aurelien Portuese, *Antitrust and Intellectual Property Rights: Toward a New Schumpeterian Approach*, J. Pat. & Trademark Off. Soc'y (forthcoming, 2024) (distinguishing between the corporate scale and the property lever to turn inventions into innovations); Stephen H. Haber & Naomi R. Lamoureux, *Introduction*, in The Battle over Patents. History and Politics of Innovation 1–26 (Stephen H. Harber & Naomi R. Lamoureux eds., Oxford Univ. Press 2021); Jonathan Barnett, Innovators, Firms, and Markets: The Organizational Logic of Intellectual Property (Oxford Univ. Press 2021) (demonstrating at 42 that IP regimes lead to either entrepreneurial innovations by independent firms, or hierarchical regimes by vertically integrated firms, or to bureaucratic innovations by governmental rewards).

12 Kimble v. Marvel Entm't, LLC, 135 S. Ct. 2401, at 2407 (2015). *See also*, Sears, Roebuck & Co. v. Stiffel Co., 376 U.S. 225 (1964).

13 But see, Hovenkamp who assimilate innovation with the "progress of science and useful arts". *See*, Hovenkamp, *supra* note 1, at 750.

we identify "innovation markets" where R&D capital intensity is particularly high and thus deserve specific antitrust protection (and encouragement) because of the considerable innovations that can emerge from these innovative efforts, but also because they epitomize escape-competition effect – namely, competing via innovation to differentiate the offerings from competitors. In that context, innovations are plausible bets that may never materialize due to the uncertainty of the outcome of scientific research but that need to be encouraged by the commercialization process – simply put, scientific research made possible with the prospect of eventual profitability and returns on investments.

11. Therefore, innovation occurs within an entrepreneurial dynamic, that is, a corporate incentive to invest in scientific research thanks to the profitability expectations from idealized returns. That is one fundamental aspect of the innovation dynamics – i.e., the incentive to incur massive costs and considerable bets in the hope of profitable recoupment. The other fundamental aspect of the innovation dynamics is the well-known spillover effect – namely, one innovation generates a considerable number of adjacent innovations that considerably benefit society via positive externalities. It is often said that innovators capture 2 percent of their innovations' commercial potential – the 98 percent is reaped out by society over generations.[14] Rarely does an innovation comes to the fore singularly. Oftentimes, an innovation generates what Schumpeter called "clusters of innovations" – the dynamics of innovation generates other entrepreneurs to commercialize adjacent and interoperable innovations atop the initial, more infrastructural innovation.

2. Innovations as Effective Means to Get Jobs Done

12. These innovation dynamics – or the cumulative effects of entrepreneurial incentives lured by the appropriability of innovation returns together with the clustering effects and positive externalities of innovation – constitute formidable engines of creative destruction that displace the status quo and encourage consumer-focused disruptions in the market. These innovation dynamics form the basis of the patent system whereby the expected monopolistic position generates the necessary incentives to massively invest in uncertain scientific and technological efforts whilst the publicity of the information secures the positive externalities of information dissemination for the benefit of society, via clustering of innovations and imitations.

13. The other, and most important, element of the innovation definition refers to a successful disruption in consumer choices. This is critical because commercialized inventions that fail cannot be considered as innovations from an economic perspective since they do not trigger the growth cycle inherent

14 *See*, the Solow Residual.

to innovation dynamics.[15] In other words, failed innovation is no innovation. But what makes a commercialized invention a successful innovation?

14. The answer is astonishingly simple: innovations get the job done. Indeed, the "jobs to be done" theory of innovation sits at the core of Clayton Christensen and his co-authors' book *Competing Against Luck*: innovation takes place when consumers effectively "hire" new products and services because they provide solutions that did not exist previously. Innovation is thus an entrepreneurial solution to consumer preferences that were so far unfulfilled, and that the innovator managed to capture by offering solutions that consumers hire. Consumers "hired" Uber drivers because they were more readily available and cheaper, consumers "hired" Google search engine because it was a solution to information gaps, and consumers "hired" Apple's iPhones because it provided a solution to multiple mobile devices (mobile phones, mobile browsing, mobile music) into a single device. Although innovations may emerge for high-spending customers, scale economies allow for a cheapening of disruptive innovations, leading to greater customer adoption by a "competing-down" process.[16] Innovation can take place either within the firm (through distributional capabilities of corporations) or within the market (through licensing and outsourcing of distributional capabilities).

3. The Antitrust Treatment of Innovation – The Rise of Dynamic Competition

15. In sum, "what is required for innovation is firm size, not market power per se."[17] The mass production enabled by organizational capabilities is a prerequisite for innovations to reach consumers.[18] Mass production together with mass distribution bring innovations to the markets and, should they perform the jobs for which they are "hired", these innovations can effectively disrupt incumbents.[19]

---

15 On innovation failures, see Clayton Christensen, The Innovator's Dilemma: When Technologies Cause Great Firms to Fail (Harvard Business Review Press 2016); Tao Wong, *Toward an Understanding of Innovation Failure: The Timing of Failure Experience*, 125 Technovation 1–10 (2023).

16 Joseph Schumpeter called in his earlier work the "competing down process" for what he will later refer as the "process of creative destruction", thereby emphasizing that the disruptive nature of innovations leads to a cheapening of goods and services thanks to scale economies and mass production which can be ruinous competition for the less efficient competitors. In other words, innovation as a process of creative destruction is the result of overproduction of popular and new products that push some competitors out of business. *See*, Joseph Schumpeter who defined innovation as the "carrying into effect" of inventions. *See*, Schumpeter, *supra* note 9, at 242–243 ("[C]osts probably differed widely and a competing-down process was running strongly. If this be true, it would follow that there was nothing in the general outcry about overproduction –those crying out, simply, who were not able to keep the pace and whose concerns were being made obsolete– although the surface presented a picture almost ideally conforming to the conceptions of the theory of overproduction.")

17 Richard R. Nelson & Sidney G. Winter, An Evolutionary Theory of Economic Change 280 (Harvard Univ. Press 1982).

18 Alfred Chandler best narrated the need for vertically integrated firms as the source of innovations. *See*, Alfred D. Chandler Jr., The Visible Hand: The Managerial Revolution in American Business (Harvard Univ. Press 1977); Alfred D. Chandler Jr., Scale and Scope: The Dynamics of Industrial Capitalism (Harvard Univ. Press 1990).

19 *See*, Chandler Jr., The Visible Hand, *supra* note 18 ("the basic difference between the coming of mass production and mass distribution lies, therefore, in technology. Mass distribution came primarily through organizational innovation and improvement, using the new forms in transportation and communication. Mass production, on the other hand, normally called for technological as well as organizational innovation.")

16. But what is scrutinized by antitrust enforcers is market power per se, not firm size. The disconnect between antitrust and innovation inextricably leads to an inevitable tension. Firm size is necessary to enjoy market power but is also equally important in delivering innovation. Antitrust authorities traditionally assume that market power is inferred from firm size. On the other hand, populist advocates are prompted to presume and equate (abuse of) market power with firm size as the "big-is-bad" motto encapsulates.[20]

17. In other words, innovation needs market imperfections. Imperfect competition with large corporations and oligopolistic market structures thus appears not to be a departure from dynamic competition but its very condition. The ability of firms to appropriate innovation returns determines innovation incentives, hence entrepreneurial dynamism. Appropriability of innovation returns is quite clear in the context of traditional sectors prone to innovate by relying on the patent system: transitory monopolistic returns constitute the necessary appropriability of innovation returns. But how does innovation take place in sectors where patents play a significantly less important role, such as in high-tech industries?

18. Again, firm size and appropriability capabilities through distributional restrictions enable entrepreneurs to capture innovation returns. But these distributional restrictions are likely to be considered as illegal restraints of trade for antitrust purposes. The courts have nevertheless provided some useful safeguards, implicitly building on the rationale underpinning the patent system which encourages innovation via temporary monopoly. Indeed, the U.S. Supreme Court was not shy in stating in *Trinko* that "the opportunity to charge monopoly prices – at least for a short period – is what attracts "business acumen" in the first place; it induces risk-taking that produces innovation and economic growth."[21] The Supreme Court went on to consider that to undermine the ability of an entrepreneur to recoup its investments by a mandatory sharing of resources would deter investments in those resources in the first place.[22] Innovation incentive matters

20 The populist "big-is-bad" motto is present in the literature but also in antitrust bills and the Digital Markets Acts where firm size, not market power, is the single criterion to regulate the companies on the assumption that size generates unfair competition. For the literature, see TIM WU, THE CURSE OF BIGNESS: ANTITRUST IN THE NEW GILDED AGE (Columbia Global Report 2018); Lina Khan, *The End of Antitrust History Revisited*, 133 HARV. L. REV. 1655–1682 (2020); ZEPHYR TEACHOUT, BREAK 'EM UP: RECOVERING OUR FREEDOM FROM BIG AG, BIG TECH, AND BIG MONEY (MacMillan 2020). *See*, U.S. antitrust bills: Journalism Competition and Preservation Act, S.673, (2022); Open App Markets Act, S.2710, (2021); American Innovation and Choice Online Act, S.2992, (2022); Platform Competition and Opportunity Act, S.3197, (2021); Competition and Transparency in Digital Advertising Act, S.4258, (2022). *See*, COMMISSION REGULATION 2022/1925 OF THE EUROPEAN PARLIAMENT AND OF THE COUNCIL OF SEPT. 14, 2022, ON CONTESTABLE AND FAIR MARKETS IN THE DIGITAL SECTOR AND AMENDING DIRECTIVES (EU) 2019/1937 AND (EU) 2020/1828 (DIGITAL MARKETS ACT), 2022, O.J. (L 265) 1. *See*, more generally, Aurelien Portuese. *Biden Antitrust: The Paradox of the New Antitrust Populism*, 29 Geo. Mason L. REV. 54 (2022).

21 Verizon Communs., Inc. v. Law Offices of Curtis V. Trinko, LLP, 540 U.S. 398 (2004).

22 *Id.* at 408 the Court stated that "To safeguard the incentive to innovate, the possession of monopoly power will not be found unlawful unless it is accompanied by an element of anticompetitive conduct. Firms may acquire monopoly power by establishing an infrastructure that renders them uniquely suited to serve their customers. Compelling such firms to share the source of their advantage is in some tension with the underlying purpose of antitrust law, since it may lessen the incentive for the monopolist, the rival, or both to invest in those economically beneficial facilities."

even if it comes at the market-imperfection price of possessing monopoly power and charging (temporarily) monopoly prices. *Trinko* remains the most innovation-focused and monopoly-tolerant decision by the U.S. Supreme Court so far and remains a controlling case.[23] *Trinko* frustrates the recent Neo-Brandeisian revolution agenda in antitrust.[24]

19. The tension lies in the fact that, as mentioned above, market power (let alone monopoly power) is not necessary to generate innovations: firm size along with large scale and scope are the prerequisites. In that regard, *Trinko* errs in asserting that monopoly prices are necessary.[25] But, on the other hand, what Justice Scalia meant by "monopoly prices" is not referring to the exercise of a market monopoly which antitrust laws prohibits but rather, referred to prices with profits (or apparently "excessive prices" in economic parlance) that depart from the neoclassical perfect competition model, whereby marginal prices equate marginal costs. This model is not only flawed but represents the single obstacle to innovation incentives. Therefore, *Trinko* is incorrect in assuming that "monopoly prices" are necessary to generate innovations but is correct in implicitly rejecting the notion of a perfectly competitive price derived from the misguided perfect competition model because that model, rejecting imperfect market structure with large firms, deters innovation. In other words, the drafting of *Trinko* may be inaccurate but its conceptual premise, rejecting perfect competition to focus on innovation incentives fostered by above marginal cost pricing and a right to exclude to capture returns on investments, is correct.

20. Consequently, dynamic competition – namely, today's imperfect competition for tomorrow's innovation gains – represents the imperfect competition with "uncompetitive" market structure. In that regard, dynamic competition is beneficial but its prerequisites (i.e., oligopolistic market structure, excessive pricing, and large firms) seems at odds with traditional antitrust thinking. In that vein, dynamic competition as an antitrust approach that preserves innovation incentives, encourages the process of creative destruction whereby

---

23 *See*, for instance, NCAA v. Alston, 141 S. Ct. 2141, (2021), see Alden Abbott, *The US Supreme Court upholds a District Court's injunction finding unlawful certain sports association rules limiting the education-related benefits schools may make available to student-athletes (NCAA / Alston)*, e-Competitions June 2021, art. No. 101238; Pac. Bell Tel. Co. v. linkLine Communs., Inc., 555 U.S. 438 (2009), see David Ernst, *The US Supreme Court rejects the price squeeze theory, noting that the upstream and downstream claims should be considered separately (Pacific Bell / linkLine)*, e-Competitions Feb. 2009, art. No. 26564; Steward Health Care Sys., LLC v. Blue Cross & Blue Shield of R.I., 311 F. Supp. 3d 468 (2018); Int'l Ass'n of Machinists & Aero. Workers, Local Lodge No. 1821 v. Verso Paper Corp., 80 F. Supp. 3d 247 (2015); Sterling Merch., Inc. v. Nestle, S.A., 724 F. Supp. 2d 245 (2010); Natchitoches Parish Hosp. Serv. Dist. v. Tyco Int'l, Ltd., 247 F.R.D. 253 (2008); La. Wholesale Drug Co. v. Shire LLC (In re Adderall XR Antitrust Litig.), 754 F.3d 128 (2014); Provepharm, Inc. v. Akorn, Inc., 2019 U.S. Dist. LEXIS 98719 (2019); N.Y. Mercantile Exch., Inc. v. IntercontinentalExchange, Inc., 323 F. Supp. 2d 559 (2004).

24 *See*, Jonathan Baker, *What about the Supreme Court? The Lurking Threat to US Antitrust Reform*, 11 J. Antitrust Enf't 154–161 (2023), (using *Trinko* as an illustration to argue that "successful antitrust reform must surmount a substantial obstacle: the non-interventionist perspective taken by today's Supreme Court."); Justin Lindeboom, *Two Challenges for Neo-Brandeisian Antitrust*, 68 Antitrust Bull. (2023) ("By emphasizing the inherent harm of domination, the Neo-Brandeisian antitrust reform agenda is the antithesis of this Schumpeterian perspective. Some antitrust doctrines indeed seem to take a Schumpeterian view. The U.S. Supreme Court's judgment in *Trinko*, in particular, clearly rejected" the Neo-Brandeisian viewpoint.)

25 Baker, *supra* note 24.

the replacement effect of superior products and technologies disrupt existing products and companies. That is why the antitrust treatment of innovation boils down to the preservation of the process of creative destruction or, as the Court said in *Novell, Inc. v. Microsoft Corp* in 2013, to "pursue an innovative replacement product of its own."[26] Therefore, innovation is an antitrust defense.[27]

21. Unsurprisingly, antitrust originalists such as Neo-Brandeisians can rely on dynamic competition as the bedrock for antitrust reforms by attacking the consumer welfare standard of overlooking the dynamic harms to innovation.[28] In the overall criticism of the price-centric nature of antitrust enforcement in general, and of the consumer welfare standard in particular, Schumpeterians and Neo-Brandeisians advocate for a concept of dynamic competition that would consider the broader range of "concerns" for Neo-Brandeisians or "constraints" for Schumpeterians in antitrust enforcement.

22. Neo-Brandeisians raise dynamic concerns such as the tendency of markets to tip and become monopolized,[29] the imbalance of market structure,[30] the concern on labor[31] and economic democracy,[32] and more generally any non-economic value that should be integrated in the antitrust analysis. Schumpeterians raise dynamic constraints such as the necessary ability to capture innovation rents from investments, the threat of entry from all sides of the markets and adjacent markets, the transitory aspect of market power, and the need to integrate competitiveness arguments into the antitrust analysis. Recent cases and enforcement policies side with Neo-Brandeisians: i.e., dynamic competition is generally interpreted as a modernized version of the incipiency doctrine whereby future, but hypothetical harms justify early antitrust interventions.

---

26 Novell, Inc. v. Microsoft Corp, 731 F.3d 1064, 1075 (10th Cir. 2013), see George Hay, *A U.S. Court of Appeal dismisses claims of monopolization against leading software company based on an alleged refusal to deal (Microsoft)*, E-COMPETITIONS Sept. 2013, art. No. 61086. *See also*, Viamedia, Inc. v. Comcast Corp., 951 F.3d 429, 52 (7th Circ. 2020) ("[…] what types of anticompetitive conduct are prohibited as illegally acquiring or maintaining monopoly power, rather than the kind of pro-competitive conduct the antitrust laws do not impede. The latter includes innovation resulting in superior products, the introduction of efficiencies reflecting superior business acumen, or even the luck of a firm that unwittingly stumbles into a monopoly position."). But see United States v. JetBlue Airways Corp., 2024 U.S Dist. Mass. LEXIS 7509 (2024) ("a reduction in product innovation resulting from an acquisition is a cognizable harm to competition.").

27 United States v. Grinnell Corp., 384 U.S. 563, 571, 86 S. Ct. 1698 (1966). *See also*, Viamedia, Inc. v. Comcast Corp., 951 F.3d 429, 52 (7th Circ. 2020) (citing Hovenkamp and Areeda to conclude that the procompetitive benefits typically recognized in antitrust law include evidence of higher output, improved product quality, energetic market penetration, successful research and development, cost-reducing innovations, and the like.)

28 *See*, for instance, Lina M. Khan, *The Separation of Platforms and Commerce*, 119 COLUM. L. REV. 973–1098 (2019) ("Insofar as platform conduct reduces investment and entrepreneurial activity by independent parties, any subsequent loss in innovation would – in a dynamic efficiency framework – constitute a harm to competition.")

29 C. Scott Hemphill & Tim Wu, *Nascent Competitors*, 168 U. PA. L. REV. 1879–1910 (2020),

30 Lina M. Khan & Sandeep Vaheesan, *Market Power and Inequality: The Antitrust Counterrevolution and Its Discontents*, 11 HARV. L. & POL'Y REV. 235–294 (2017).

31 Jose Azar et al., *Concentration in US Labor Markets: Evidence from Online Vacancy Data* 2, 4–7 (NAT'L BUREAU OF ECON. RSCH., Working Paper No. 24395, 2018); Diane Bartz, *U.S. Antitrust Official Says Competition in Labor Markets a Top Concern*, REUTERS (Oct. 1, 2021), https://www.reuters.com/world/us/us-antitrust-official-says-competition-labor-markets-top-concern-2021-10-01/.

32 Spencer Weber Waller, *Antitrust and Democracy*, 46 FLA. ST. U. L. REV. 807–860 (2019).

II. One View of Dynamic Competition: Atomized Innovation Markets

23. Even though innovation requires mass production and scale as discussed above, the antitrust approach to innovation via the concept of dynamic competition has departed from the traditional Schumpeterian perspective. The Brandeisian perspective of dynamic competition – and correspondingly innovation – as being preserved by ensuring atomized markets facilitating entry of new innovators is prevalent. This perspective underpins the Brandeisian agenda of atomized markets as opposed to oligopolistic markets whilst ensuring that the innovation dynamics constitute an obstacle to monopolization. In that regard, the incipiency doctrine of the Clayton Act is reassessed considering the Brandeisian perspective of dynamic competition. The new Merger Guidelines illustrate this use of dynamic competition to strive for atomized innovation markets.

24. Indeed, the 2023 Merger Guidelines[33] refer to the incipiency doctrine that emerged from the *Brown Shoe* case of 1962 where the U.S. Supreme Court considered that mergers "with probable anticompetitive effects were to be proscribed" and that "probabilities, not certainties" should justify blocking "incipient monopolies."[34] To determine whether there is such a threat to incipiency, the antitrust agencies will consider that "the likelihood of potential entry that could establish that a merger's effect 'may be'" to substantially lessen competition will generally not equal the likelihood of entry that would rebut a demonstrated risk that competition may be substantially lessened." In other words, the evidentiary threshold to prove that entry will not happen to challenge the merged firm, thus creating dynamically an incipiency threat, is much lower than the evidentiary threshold to prove that entry will happen to challenge the merged firm, thus effectively rebutting the reality of incipiency dynamics. This demonstrates alone that greater emphasis of the antitrust agencies on dynamically ensuring that entry is facilitated by blocking allegedly incipient monopolies formed by mergers. Additionally, the new Merger Guidelines reduce the post-merger change in the Herfindahl-Hirschman Index (HHI) that triggers a presumption of an illegal merger from 200 to 100 points.[35] In addition, the Final Guidelines deem

---

33 U.S. Dep't of Just. & Fed. Trade Comm'n, *2023 Merger Guidelines*, (Dec. 18, 2023), https://www.ftc.gov/system/files/ftc_gov/pdf/P234000-NEW-MERGER-GUIDELINES.pdf.

34 Brown Shoe Co. v. United States, 370 U.S. 294 (1962), at 323. *See also*, United States v. Philadelphia Nat. Bank, 374 U.S. 321 (1963); United States v. Aluminum Co. of America (Alcoa Rome), 377 U.S. 271 (1964); United States v. Penn-Olin Chemical Co., 378 U.S. 158, 170–71 (1964); United States v. Pabst Brewing Co., 384 U.S. 546 (1966); United States v. Von's Grocery, 384 U.S. 270 (1966); United States v. Marine Bancorp., 417 U.S. 602, 622 (1974). *See*, more generally, Peter C. Carstensen & Robert H. Lande, *The Merger Incipiency Doctrine and the Importance of "Redundant" Competitors*, Wis. L. Rev. 783–845 (2018); Keith N. Hylton, *Brown Shoe Versus the Horizontal Merger Guidelines*, 39 Rev. Indus. Org. 95–106 (2011); Robert H. Lande, *Resurrecting Incipiency: From Von's Grocery to Consumer Choice*, 68 Antitrust L.J. 875–898 (2001); Timothy J. Muris & Jonathan E. Nuechterlein, *First Principles for Review of Long-Consummated Mergers*, 5 The Criterion J. Innovation 29–48 (2020).

35 *See*, Herfindahl-Hirschman Index, https://ec.europa.eu/eurostat/statistics-explained/index.php?title=Glossary:Herfindahl_Hirschman_Index_(HHI)#:~:text=The%20Herfindahl%E2%80%93Hirschman%20Index%20(HHI,used%20to%20determine%20market%20competitiveness.

any transaction that leads to a combined market share above 30 percent and a change in the Herfindahl-Hirschman Index (HHI) exceeding 100 points as inherently illegal. In their efforts to atomize markets by blocking more mergers, antitrust agencies seem to assume that innovation will come from small and independent companies. As demonstrated above, inventions may come from such companies, but innovation will inevitably come from mass production enabled by corporate scale.

25. Again, the Merger Guidelines' approach is justified based on dynamic competition since the starting point of the agencies' merger analysis is now "to assess the risk of harm to competition in a dynamic and complex economy."[36] This is clear from the Merger Guidelines which accept rebuttal evidence only if entry is timely, likely, and sufficient to demonstrate that the merger does not create an incipient monopoly. Each of these element – timeliness, likelihood, and sufficiency – have hard thresholds since the agencies recognize that, for the first criterion of timeliness alone: "Entry in most industries takes a significant amount of time and is therefore insufficient to counteract any substantial lessening of competition that is threatened by a merger."[37] Interestingly, this one-sided view of the incipiency doctrine with extremely high evidentiary thresholds for rebuttal negates the importance of *General Dynamics*[38] as a controlling precedent where the Court held that if the existing market shares are not reliable predictors of future competitive dynamics due to capacity limitations, it is more appropriate to base the evaluation on a realistic assessment of future conditions rather than a static assessment of current situations. This statement acknowledges that in the context of the incipiency test, a decrease in concentration leads to a lower risk to competition. Although quoted in the Merger Guidelines, the *General Dynamics* case that applies the concept of dynamic competition in its duality – i.e., as proving an antitrust violation as well as rebutting evidence of such violation – does not curb the Brandeisian perspective of dynamic competition embedded in the new Merger Guidelines.

26. A similar perspective of the notion of dynamic competition was present in the *Meta/Within* case. The FTC believed that Meta was interested in purchasing a virtual reality fitness app – Within Unlimited – rather than developing its own, and it believed that the VR fitness industry would be more competitive if it did not acquire the app. Although the Court emphasized that "the harm to competition the doctrine aims to prevent is not the loss of present competition but rather the potential loss of a future competitor,"[39] the FTC lost its case. The FTC was unable to provide evidence of the merits of the case. However, the court acknowledged that if adequately demonstrated, both actual future competition and imagined potential competition by an

---

36 U.S. Dep't of Just. & Fed. Trade Comm'n, *supra* note 33, at 2.

37 *Id.* at 31.

38 United States v. General Dynamics Corp., 414 U.S. 486 (1974).

39 FTC v. Meta Platforms Inc., No. 22-cv-04325, 2022 WL 16637996, at *7 (N.D. Cal. Nov. 2, 2022)

acquirer in the market where a target company competes, could serve as valid grounds for allegations of injury to competition under Section 7 of the Clayton Act. Building on *Brown Shoe* and its peculiar notion of dynamic competition via assertive incipiency doctrine in light of uncertainties, the Court developed a "reasonable probability" standard and asked: "Is it reasonably probable that Meta would have entered the VR dedicated fitness app market *de novo* if it was not able to acquire Within?"[40] In assessing whether the company could have built instead of bought the app, the Court looked at how the merger allegedly dynamically undermined future competition instead of present competition.

27. More explicitly, the *Meta/Giphy*[41] case in the United Kingdom explicitly discussed the notion of dynamic competition to assess the effects on innovation of the envisaged merger. The acquisition by Meta of the Gif creation website, Giphy was effectively blocked by the Competition and Market Authority (CMA)'s order of 2021,[42] confirmed by the Competition Appeal Tribunal (CAT)'s judgment of 2022.[43] Interestingly, the CMA considered "the loss of dynamic competition" generated by the merger and explained that such loss does not "require that, absent the Merger, GIPHY would have become a meaningful competitor to Facebook in the future." In other words, the actual elimination of a "dynamic competitor" even if it is likely to fail can constitute a loss of dynamic competition leading to justification in blocking the merger. In that regard, dynamic competition does not mean future-effective competition but merely future-potential competition, echoing a similar reasoning in *Meta/Within* case in the US. Therefore, it is not so much the actual and potential competitive constraints that are protected against the merger but the structure of the market. Indeed, although acknowledging in its judgement that "identifying the criteria that are relevant for determining whether a state of dynamic competition exists and, if so, whether a merger weakens that competition, is extremely difficult,"[44] the CAT will confirm blocking the merger on the basis that the statutory text can be interpreted as prohibiting "a substantial lessening of competition arising through an impairment of dynamic competition"[45] when dynamic competition does not only mean a future impairment to competition but also an impairment to dynamic competition which is "a much more fluid form of competition between innovating firms."[46]

---

40 *Id.* at 43.

41 Facebook, Inc (now Meta Platforms, Inc) / Giphy, Inc merger inquiry. For a timeline of the procedure, see https://www.gov.uk/cma-cases/facebook-inc-giphy-inc-merger-inquiry (last visited Oct. 1, 2024).

42 Competition & Markets Authority, Completed acquisition by Facebook, Inc (now Meta Platforms, Inc) of Giphy, Inc., Final Report (Nov. 30, 2021), https://assets.publishing.service.gov.uk/media/61a64a618fa8f5037d67b7b5/Facebook__Meta__GIPHY_-_Final_Report_1221_.pdf

43 Meta Platforms Inc. v. Competition and Markets Authority, [2022] CAT 26, https://www.catribunal.org.uk/sites/cat/files/2022-06/20220614_1429_Judgment_FINAL%20%5B2022%5D%20CAT%2026.pdf

44 *Id.* at 37.

45 *Id.* at 39.

46 *Id.* at 34.

III. Conclusion

28. The "fluidity" of the notion of dynamic competition, as currently approached by the US antitrust agencies and courts but also in foreign jurisdictions, begs the question of the administrability of such notion, let alone the prevalent disregard for raising dynamic competition as an antitrust defense in favor of what appears to be an antitrust offense. Indeed, since the concept is barely defined and courts and agencies recognize the difficulty in assessing it, does it mean that any merger between innovative firms would constitute a harm to dynamic competition? The current practice seems to suggest so, although it is not a long-term solution given the inability of defendants to effectively demonstrate and convince on counterfactuals that are readily rejected as insufficient rebuttals.[47]

29. For instance, as the artificial intelligence (AI) sector is blossoming and disruptively innovative, does it mean that the concept of dynamic competition applied to the AI sector would lead to the blocking of mergers because the acquisition of a dynamic competitor, irrespective of its likelihood of success or entry in the market, would remove a competitor and would enable the acquirer not to build de novo products and services similar to those of the target company? It is true that applying the concept of dynamic competition as formulated in *Meta/Giphy* and as implicitly articulated in the new Merger Guidelines to the AI sector raises considerable regulatory risks for the acquirer and acquiree since they are both likely to be innovative companies in fast-changing markets where the agencies want to preserve the atomized structure of these innovation markets.

30. In that regard, ironically, the notion of dynamic competition initially meant to encapsulate innovation concerns in antitrust enforcement may very well end up slowing down innovation by delayed introduction of AI products and services to customers and a greater cost associated with AI startups exits, thus having a deterring effect on investments and venture capital in the sector. It is too late to improve the proportionality and administrability of the notion of dynamic competition to preserve the multifaceted nature of innovation that we have outlined.

31. In conclusion, a competition policy – and a dynamic competition approach specifically – is critically important for ensuring that the process of creative destruction, whereby scarce resources are efficiently allocated as a result of incessant rivalry between market actors, leads to social progress by disrupting status quos – all of them, i.e., both political and economic entrenchments.

---

47 *See*, U.S. Dep't of Just. & Fed. Trade Comm'n, *supra* note 33, at 30 et sub ("When assessing this [rebuttal] argument, the Agencies will not credit vague or speculative claims, nor will they credit benefits outside the relevant market that would not prevent a lessening of competition in the relevant market.")

KFTC's Response to Promote Competition in Digital Markets

HAN KI JEONG*
Korea Fair Trade Commission

I. Introduction

1. Now we are in the digital economy, where digital technologies shape the competitive landscape of a market determining a winner and a loser. How to respond to digital markets was a question we should prepare for only a few years ago, but now it is a question we should find an answer immediately as a competition authority. It has been almost a decade since Klaus Schwab argued that we are entering the fourth industrial revolution in 2015. Today, the key elements of the digital economy – e.g., platform ecosystem, big data and artificial intelligence – are playing a crucial role in almost all industries and businesses exercising enormous influence on market competition and consumer protection.
2. The most important driving force of digital markets is *innovation*. Innovation can only prosper in a highly competitive market. Competition motivates businesses to develop better products and services for customers, so in turn, broadens consumer choice and lowers price. Furthermore, competition in the digital economy facilitates development of new technology and business model that will drive the global market. This is why promoting competition has been a top priority for competition authorities across the world, including the Korea Fair Trade Commission. Assuming the responsibility of regulating business activity between business-to-business and business-to-consumer, the KFTC has been making ceaseless efforts to develop policies

* Han Ki Jeong was appointed as the 21st Chairperson of the Korea Fair Trade Commission.

that can promote competition profoundly and to respond to enforcement issues effectively, based on complete understanding of the digital economy and its unique characteristics.

3. In the following chapters, I would like to explain the KFTC's efforts to understand the digital economy and to promote competition in digital markets based on various research, law enforcement experiences, onsite communications with stakeholders and consumers and lively discussions between internal and external experts. The following chapters are <Characteristics of Digital Economy and KFTC's Responses>, <Key Enforcement Cases and Implications>, <Policy Efforts to Establish a Fair Competitive Order in the Platform Market> and <Other Important Issues>.

II. Characteristics of Digital Economy and KFTC's Responses

4. The speed of digital transformation in South Korea is one of the highest across the world. In such a rapid transformation, the KFTC has approached various digital market issues from a comprehensive perspective by considering both the big tech companies' behavior commonly witnessed in the global market and particularly witnessed in the Korean market. The characteristics of the digital economy and the KFTC's responses to the issues arising from digital markets are as follows.

5. The digital economy is mainly characterized by *cross-side network effects, free services, economies of scale* and *importance of data*. Firstly, cross-side effects, common in digital platforms, have become integral to the digital economy. Cross-side network effects occur when an increase in the number of users on one side of a platform enhances the benefits for users on the other side of the platform. For example, an increase of users in an app marketplace enhances the benefits for app developers on the marketplace, leading to an increase in the number of developers. As a result, users gain the ability to compare and purchase a wider variety of apps, which enhances user benefits and, in turn, attracts more users to the marketplace.

6. Secondly, a lot of digital services are offered *for free* to consumers in the digital economy. Free services give users greater access and convenience but less cost burden. However, they often require consumers to watch advertisements or allow data collection. For example, social networking service (SNS) platforms – e.g., Facebook, Instagram and KakaoTalk – provide users with free services but earn advertising revenues by capitalizing on vast amount of data collected from users.

7. Thirdly, economies of scale refer to the situation in which fixed costs of digital services are high, while additional costs associated with an increasing number of users are minimal – i.e., an increase in users translates into a

significant decrease in the average cost. A mobile OS, for example, would require substantial financial and human resources to develop and improve relevant technologies, but such cost does not increase in proportion with the increase in users. Therefore, the more users use the OS, the more cost effective the OS will be.

8. Lastly, the capability of collecting, maintaining and using data is key to a competitive edge in this digital economy, as data are put to use at every stage of business from production, distribution to promotion. A search engine, for example, can improve by studying users' search data and responding to their feedback, so more users and data will help gain an upper hand.

9. Given those key features of the digital economy, holding on to traditional way of enforcing laws and implementing policies will not help competition authorities fulfill their mission, i.e., promoting competition and innovation while protecting consumers from new consumer risks in digital markets. In this context, the KFTC has developed and improved relevant guidelines to enhance the existing law enforcement tools. In accordance with the guidelines, the unique characteristics of the digital economy will be fully considered in the case management process.

10. First of all, with regard to abuse of market dominance, the KFTC established the "Guidelines for Abuse of Dominance by Online Platforms" in January last year. The characteristics of digital platforms, identified through previous enforcement cases, were reflected in the Guidelines. This aims to set consistent enforcement standards for digital platforms making law enforcement more predictable for businesses. The Guidelines specify factors to consider when determining abuse of market dominance under the existing Monopoly Regulation and Fair Trade Act (hereinafter referred to as the "MRFTA"), which will make up for the limitations of the enforcement criteria established based on traditional industries. The Guidelines will ensure the unique characteristics of digital platforms are fully considered when the KFTC examines abuse of market dominance. Specific factors to be considered include – platforms' capability of data collection/maintenance and the gap in such capability between platforms; and criteria for calculating market share other than revenues (e.g., the number of users). Also, the major types of violations were explained: restriction of multi-homing, demand of most-favored-nation status, self-preferencing and tying. The Guidelines take an approach that balances the anticompetitive effects (e.g., market tipping) against the procompetitive effects (e.g., consumer benefits and innovation) of digital platforms.

11. Additionally, to ensure that the digital economy's characteristics are reflected in the merger review process, the KFTC revised the Merger Review Guidelines, which have been in effect since May of this year. The purpose of the revision is to modernize the existing merger review process and catch up with increasing demand for M&A driven by digital transformation. In the revised guidelines, for example, demand-side substitutability associated with quality

deterioration – other than prices – was suggested as a factor for market definition, given that many digital services are usually provided *for free* to consumers. *Network effects* are also supposed to be taken into account in analyzing anticompetitive effects according to the amendment. Furthermore, the updated guidelines ensure a balanced review process by covering both competition concerns and efficiency gains from mergers in the digital sector. Mergers can bring benefits to the economy and businesses: a merger may give rise to innovative services; startups can exit their businesses and recoup investment through a strategic acquisition; and this may leads to creation of a new startup.

12. In line with these efforts to improve the existing law enforcement tools, the KFTC has enhanced antitrust enforcement in domestic and foreign markets. Particularly, an amendment to the MRFTA is currently being pursued to regulate Big Tech platforms so that competition can be promoted effectively. The enforcement cases and the new legislation will be elaborated below.

III. Key Enforcement Cases and Implications

13. The KFTC has taken enforcement actions against abuse of dominant position by domestic and foreign companies under the MRFTA. In this chapter, two major cases will be reviewed in which the KFTC recently enforced the MRFTA in digital markets: (i) Google's abuse of dominance in the app store market and (ii) Kakao Mobility's abuse of dominance.

1. Google's Abuse of Dominance in the App Store Market

In April last year, the KFTC concluded that Google restricted competition by preventing mobile game developers from publishing apps on the competing app store and imposed remedies and a fine of KRW 42 billion and 56 million (EUR 29.6 million).

Taking a closer look at the case, Google forced a large game development company A to release their apps exclusively on Google Play in exchange for comprehensive promotion and marketing support, such as Google Play featuring and support for overseas product launches. Company A was planning to simultaneously release its blockbuster content via both Google Play and Google's rival app store to maximize its revenues, but Google persuaded company A to release the title on Google Play only. To secure the exclusive release, Google highlighted its leading position in the global market, and Google's high-level executives even came to Korea from the U.S. headquarters to have a meeting with company A in person.

Later in July 2016, Google further developed and expanded its strategy – providing support in exchange for an exclusive release – into the whole domestic market and fully implemented the strategy until April 2018. With the goal of foreclosing the competing app store, Google came up with a carefully-designed exclusive dealing strategy. Google classified game developers into tiers depending on factors like their revenues in terms of user spending, and possibility of publishing their titles via both Google Play and the rival app store simultaneously; set up a sub-strategy to respond to each tier; and selected important titles among newly released games and made sure they are exclusively released on Google Play. Knowing such exclusive agreements constitute a violation of competition law, Google tried to get rid of the evidence. Google informed developers of the terms and conditions as secretly as possible; required employers to delete emails that discussed exclusive agreements; and encouraged employees to have in-person meetings rather than online ones.

Due to the exclusive dealing conduct, many games, particularly large-scale ones from which most of the revenues come in the mobile game market, were distributed exclusively on Google Play. Therefore, the rival app store suffered a lot to launch new games, which led to negative network effects: less new games caused a decrease in paid users, and in turn, led to greater difficulties lunching new games again. Consequently, the competing app store saw a continuous decrease in revenues and lost more than half of its paid uses. On the other hand, Google Play's paid users increased by about 30% along with an increase in market share from about 80% in 2016 to more than 90% in 2018, which indicates Google's enhanced market power. When a game is distributed through multiple app stores, content itself and consumer benefits can be diversified spurring competition and broadening consumer choice in the market. In that sense, Google hurt consumer welfare and innovation in the mobile game market and app store market by preventing its rival from releasing new games.

In this case, the KFTC's enforcement action against Google has implications that the KFTC sanctioned abuse of market dominance by Google, a big tech platform company, and created a more competitive landscape in the app store market.

2. Kakao Mobility's Abuse of Dominance

In February 2023, the KFTC imposed remedies and a KRW 27.1 billion (EUR 19 million) fine on Kakao Mobility for abusing its market dominance: the company secretly manipulated its algorithm to give preferential treatment to drivers of Kakao T blue, run by Kakao's affiliates including its subsidiary.

Since Kakao Mobility started to run a franchise taxi-hailing service in March 2019, the company has implemented a passenger-driver matching algorithm designed to match passengers with drivers close to them with a short pick-up time until April 2020. However, the KFTC found the company gave priority to its own affiliated drivers over non-affiliated drivers if affiliated drivers can arrive within a certain time frame. Such preferential treatment to affiliated drivers was a sure method to scale up its business by increasing the number of affiliated cabs, and employees actively used the method in recognition of the effect.

And in mid-April 2020, KaKao Mobility made changes to the matching algorithm to prefer franchise drivers with a high ride acceptance rate to non-franchise drivers. Its AI-based system preferentially dispatched drivers to passengers with a ride acceptance rate over 40-50%, but the KFTC found the acceptance rate was designed in Kakao Mobility franchisees' favor, which resulted in a gap in acceptance rate between franchisees and non-franchisees averaging at 70-80% and 10%, respectively. Kakao Mobility deliberately took advantage of it, knowing that such gap between the two groups exists in the first place.

In addition, Kakao Moility excluded or reduced unprofitable short-distance rides when connecting affiliated drivers with passengers to maximize their profits. Affiliated drivers were excluded from short-distance rides of less than one kilometer from February 5 to mid-April in 2020, and later the AI system didn't even match them with ride-hailing requests of less than one kilometer.

As such, Kakao Mobility abused its overwhelming dominance in the general ride-hailing service market to prefer its own affiliated drivers. Kakao Mobility's dominance in the general ride-hailing service market was extended into the franchise ride-hailing service market; which limited competition the franchise ride-hailing market; and thereby competition was restricted in the general taxi-hailing market as well. As a result, Kakao T Blue's dominance was greatly enhanced in the franchise ride-hailing service market (market share in terms of the number of affiliated taxi drivers soared from 14.2% in 2029 to 73.7% in 2021), and concerns were raised that its competitors would suffer from securing franchise taxi drivers and be excluded from the market. Also, Kakao T Blue's dominance was maintained and intensified in the general ride-hailing market (market share in terms of the number of services intermediated increased from 92.99% in 2019 to 94.46% in 2021), which increased the possibility of raising fees for passengers and drivers.

The KFTC's ruling contributed to promoting competition and establishing fair practices in the general ride-hailing and the franchise ride-hailing markets, and also promoting innovative and dynamic growth of the mobility industry.

IV. Policy Efforts to Establish a Fair Competitive Order in the Platform Market

14. As we usher in the era of digital transformation, platform services has greatly contributed to boosting consumer welfare while reducing transaction costs. On the other hand, however, antitrust issues have been emerging one after another as only one or two monopolists monopolize a market. Monopolistic platforms with overwhelming power create the rules of the game on their own in a market, make other players follow the rule and even push rivals out of the playing field.

15. The KFTC has detected and taken action against monopolistic platforms that play against the rules under the existing MRFTA. The existing regulatory system, however, was not enough to restore market competition, as it has not kept pace with the rapid monopolization of the platform market and the agency was not able to act swiftly. In the aforementioned Google case as well, there is a tough challenge to restore the competitive landscape even though the company was hit with a KRW 42 billion (EUR 30 million) fine last year, because the rival app store has lost its competitiveness.

16. In consideration of the challenge, major competition authorities have vigorously pursued the improvement of their legal framework. The European Union (EU)'s Digital Markets Act (DMA), enacted in May last year and fully implemented on March 7 of this year, specifically targets big tech platforms.

17. Under the DMA, in addition to six giant platforms designated as "gatekeepers" in September last year – Apple, Alphabet, Meta, Amazon, Microsoft and ByteDance – Booking.com was added to the list in May of this year.

18. In Germany, the Act against Restraints of Competition (GWB) was revised to reflect the characteristics of the platform market and to make sure the regulatory framework effectively works in the market. The UK also enacted the Digital Markets, Competition and Consumers Act (DMCC) in May of this year. Similarly, Japan introduced the Smartphone Software Competition Promotion Act (SSCPA) in June, and the Indian government is reportedly in the process of drafting a Digital Competition Act.

19. Against this backdrop, the KFTC has moved to amend the MRFTA to promptly curb the anti-competitive practices of dominant platforms. In September of this year, the KFTC announced a legislative direction targeting platforms with overwhelming market influence, prohibiting key anti-competitive practices and imposing stricter burdens of proof. The plan also includes raising the upper limit for fines on identified anti-competitive behaviors and adopting an interim suspension order system to strengthen deterrence against violations. Subsequently, on October 28, a proposed amendment to the MRFTA reflecting these measures was introduced by lawmakers.

20. In addition to addressing the harms of monopolistic practices, the KFTC has also focused on establishing a fair trade order between platforms and their merchant partners. Recently, due to instances of some platforms failing to pay small and medium-sized merchants, the need for regulatory enhancements to strengthen protections for these merchants has come to light. In response, on October 18, the KFTC announced a proposed amendment to the Large Retail Business Act, imposing obligations – such as adherence to payment settlement deadlines – on second-hand online trading platforms above a certain size. Subsequently, on October 28, an amendment to the Large Retail Business Act reflecting these measures was introduced in the National Assembly.

21. It is hoped that the legislative processes for these two bills will be completed promptly, paving the way for a fair competitive order to be established in the platform market.

V. Other important Issues

22. Aside from the issues mentioned above, the KFTC has been paying close attention to so-called "Gap-Eul relationships", which refer to unfair power dynamics arising from bargaining power imbalances between parties in the platform ecosystem. To help the platform ecosystem continue to grow, quality products and services from vendors operating through platform businesses are essential; and the vendors can only prosper in a fair business environment where they receive the fair share they deserve.

23. To guarantee such fair environment, the agency has sought ways to promote fair practices between platforms and vendors based on self-regulation, particularly in food delivery apps, online marketplaces and hotel booking apps. Especially, the KFTC encourages them to improve contracting practices and dispute settlement system through consultations between the two parties so that platforms and vendors can achieve mutual growth by sharing burden.

24. Along with the issues between platforms and vendors, the KFTC has increased efforts to protect consumers from emerging harms in online spaces. The KFTC keeps a close eye on the harms caused by "dark patterns" in particular, which mislead or trick users and cause financial losses for them. The KFTC released a paper outlining the policy direction on dark patterns in April last year to explain major types of dark patterns and to promote self-regulation of the market, alongside the efforts to improve the existing legal framework. An amendment was made to the Telecommunications Business Act in this regard to regulate six dark patterns to which the Act could not apply: automatic subscription renewal, drip pricing, preselection, false hierarchy, roach motel and nagging. The Amendment will come into force in February next year.

25. Lastly, ushering in the era of "Artificial Intelligence", the agency is seeking ways to equip itself with capabilities to fulfill its mission – to promote competition and protect consumers – in the new environment. AI technologies

already have a significant impact on our day to day lives, industries and markets, and such impact will only grow going forward. AI technologies have numerous advantages that contribute to better productivity and accelerated innovation across various areas. However, on the other hand, concerns are constantly raised that they may contribute to market monopolization and lack of fairness/transparency. To address such concerns, the KFTC is working on Policy Paper on AI to lay the groundwork that can guarantee creative business activities and sustainable growth of relevant markets. The paper will explain competition/consumer issues involving AI and explore the overall approach to AI regulation. Conducted and published by the competition authority, the research will serve as a policy tool to proactively identify industry- or market-specific competition/consumer issues and to perform in-depth review. Working in partnership with overseas counterparts, the KFTC will cover international issues discussed with the OECD in the paper as well as giving full consideration to AI relevant policy trends in the US, UK and others.

VI. Conclusion

26. There is a saying in Korea that goes, "Even mountains and rivers change in a decade". It means everything will change as nothing can escape the decade-long time frame. Maybe now we should shorten the time frame of "a decade" in the saying, as change takes place at an increasingly fast pace, driven by digital transformation. It gives us shorter time frame to respond to competition issues and promote competition, so action should be taken more swiftly as well. Once a monopolistic market structure is established, it is hard to break up monopolies. That is why the KFTC has been making multifaceted efforts to address monopolies as aforementioned. The KFTC will remain committed to promoting competition in digital markets while keeping pace with rapid changes in the digital economy.

Artificial Intelligence Systems and Competition

Pierre Larouche[*]

University of Montreal

1. This short contribution explores how the use of Artificial Intelligence (AI) systems to corral massive amounts of data on consumer preferences can impact competitive markets, in the light of current theories about the nature and functioning of markets.

I. AI Systems and Markets: Effects on the Demand and Supply Sides

2. AI systems can be used to improve the understanding of the demand side of the market, i.e., to have a more precise and informed view of consumer preferences, down to the individual consumer. Some forms of AI systems are already implemented to that end, for instance in making individualized suggestions on Amazon, Netflix or YouTube, or in delivering personalized advertising on most digital platforms. For the purposes of this short chapter, we leave aside well-known controversies relating to privacy and data protection or to radicalization and fragmentation ("bubble" or "rabbit-hole" phenomena) in order to focus on the functioning of markets.

3. In market terms, tailoring offers to each consumer in line with an AI-driven assessment of their preferences, opens the door to extensive product differentiation and first-degree price discrimination, two related but distinct phenomena. In short, each consumer would receive a "unique" offer

---

[*] Professor of Innovation and Law, Faculty of Law, University of Montreal.

catering to their preferences (product differentiation), and presumably also matching exactly their willingness to pay for that offer (first-degree price discrimination).

4. As such, product differentiation is largely good for welfare, since consumers obtain a product whose characteristics (e.g., quality, user-friendliness, durability) track their preferences more closely. AI systems would help to reduce or remove informational barriers to product differentiation by producing granular data on consumer preferences. For most products, however, and especially for physical goods, organizational factors (notably production and administration costs) set a limit on how much differentiation is achievable, resulting in what is known as "mass customization." Mass customization relies on modularization and other techniques to achieve economies of scale and scope in production whilst allowing for as much differentiation as possible towards consumers. Accordingly, for most products, individual product differentiation is not possible and truly "unique" offers are illusory.

5. In parallel with differentiation, first-degree price discrimination – the ability to set prices according to the willingness to pay at individual consumer level – carries with it the risk that consumer surplus is entirely confiscated. Contrary to product differentiation, once informational barriers to ascertaining individual willingness to pay are overcome, no significant organizational constraints limit the ability of producers to engage in first-degree price discrimination.

6. Rather, in a standard market setting, well-known mechanisms would kick in to counter the confiscation of consumer surplus that follows from price discrimination. First, consumers could request competing offers, even if only for the sake of comparison (more on this later). In addition (or alternately), they could observe comparable transactions or peruse advertising to try to judge whether their personalized offer is acceptable or not. That latter mechanism is defeated in the context where most AI-driven individualized offers are made, namely online, where the consumer cannot easily witness other transactions or even see a price tag or sign, and the available advertising itself is likely to be personalized also.

7. Of course, technology can also come to the help of the consumer. Consumers can share information on their respective transactions, through social media or otherwise. Intermediaries could emerge, that shop around to try to obtain the best possible deal on behalf of the consumer. These phenomena can be observed in the airline industry, for instance, where algorithmic pricing by airlines faces off against sophisticated aggregator sites such as Kayak or Expedia that claim to work in the interest of consumers. Eventually, this could become a battle of AI systems on either side of the market. However, in contrast to other digital technology, AI systems generate not just large fixed costs, but also sizeable variable costs. Over time, consumer-side intermediaries might not be able to keep up with increasingly sophisticated AI systems on the producer side.

8. On balance, therefore, the use of AI systems to increase product differentiation and enable first-degree price discrimination could benefit producers (through confiscation of consumer surplus) more than consumers (through closer alignment with individual preferences). This imbalance would not be a significant issue if, as pointed out above, markets remain competitive, and consumers can obtain competing offers.

9. The use of AI systems to enhance product differentiation and implement first-degree price discrimination carries with it risks on the supply side too, however. As per the most recent OECD definition, an AI system is designed to "infer, from the input it receives, how to generate predictions, content, recommendations or decisions." Or as Agrawal, Gans & Goldfarb suggested, it is a "prediction machine." Irrespective of the underlying technology, AI systems will attempt to make the best possible prediction of consumer preferences and willingness to pay. Presumably, one or the other AI system will emerge as best-of-breed for that purpose, at least until another AI system improves upon its performance. On the assumption that such a best-of-breed AI system delivers significant benefits for a producer as compared to alternatives (AI or non-AI), the chances are that that AI system will become coveted by all producers, to power their commercial operations. Benchmarking exercises and consultancies will point every executive board in the direction of that AI system, without even any need for firms to conspire on this (within the meaning of competition law). The firm controlling that AI system could choose to license it to other firms, to turn into a platform that other firms will have to contract with or, on markets of its choosing, to ride it to market power, depending on its strategy.

10. Even if many producers would remain in competition with one another, they would then rely on the same AI system to drive their commercial policy and therefore would presumably present consumers with relatively similar "unique" individualized offerings. The main differentiation factor would be the data (input) that each producer feeds into that AI system, but one can doubt whether the datasets will differ all that much (especially since datasets can also be shared or licensed). By way of illustration, a similar convergence of competing offers around a best-of-breed standard has already occurred in investment funds, where index funds have emerged as the preferred offering across the industry.

11. In sum, in the light of current trends, broader use of increasingly sophisticated AI systems by producers in order to produce individualized offerings – as regards product characteristics and price – is bound to further affect the way markets work, above and beyond what can already be observed. On the demand side, AI systems could enable wide-ranging product differentiation (beneficial to consumers) coupled with first-degree price discrimination (detrimental to consumers). Since differentiation is subject to organizational constraints (as reflected in "mass customization" models) whereas price discrimination is not, consumers could lose in the trade-off. This is especially

true if – in an online environment – comparable transactions are not easily observable, and even truer if competing producers rely on the same best-of-breed AI system, trained on similar data, to produce individual offerings that are in fact closely converging.

II. A Simple Matrix of Market Theories

12. The lessons to be drawn from that scenario will vary depending on which market theory prevails. This short format only allows for a crisp – and by necessity oversimplified – overview of market theories. Two insights from von Hayek are used to structure this overview.

13. First of all, markets can be seen as a means to ensure the most *efficient* allocation of resources, with the perfect competition model as an abstract ideal. This conception is mostly static: market processes, even they have a time dimension, lead to a match between the supply and demand sides, so that the market "clears" and reaches an equilibrium. In contrast, as von Hayek and others pointed out, markets could also be seen more dynamically, perpetually trying to reach some elusive equilibrium, and generating useful information for market participants in the process. Under this conception, competitive markets are primarily a device for *discovering* information hitherto inaccessible or unearthed.

14. Second, the market can be considered either as a *construction* or a *spontaneous phenomenon*. In the former case, markets rest on ascertainable foundations, above all legal rules that enable them to function. Whether and how markets work depends on these rules. In the latter case, markets are a product of human evolution and constitute a basic element of human societies. They evidence some resilience. In such a naturalist perspective, the legal framework merely channels or conditions the working of markets, in a way that – depending on the author – either enhances or hinders their spontaneous or natural functioning.

15. The two conceptual pairs – efficiency or discovery, construction or spontaneity – can be combined in a simple two-by-two matrix and populated with rough versions of current theory and policy schools.

16. The upper-left corner is the realm of mainstream neo-classical economics, as expressed in public interest regulatory theory or post-Chicago antitrust. Markets serve the efficient allocation of resources, and they can be described and analyzed with sufficient accuracy that market failures can be identified and then remedied through proper legal or regulatory measures. In other words, the market is an instrument amenable to control.

17. The upper-right corner is where Chicago price theory, public choice theory and the Chicago school of antitrust would be located. Authors and policy-makers in that corner share with neo-classical economics the assumption that

markets foster the efficient allocation of resources. Yet they tend to take a more naturalist view of markets (which is not necessarily expressed in terms of spontaneity), as reflected in their view on the robustness of markets and the inability of public authorities to intervene effectively.

18. The Austrian school of economics, with its emphasis on the spontaneity of markets and their role as engines of information discovery through the price mechanism, fits in the lower-right corner. Even if its influence is widely felt, the Austrian school has few direct applications in the policy realm.

19. The lower-left corner would correspond to the tenets of ordoliberalism, which still exerts a powerful force on European competition and regulatory policy. Like the Austrian school, ordoliberalism posits that markets cannot be seen only as a means for the efficient allocation of resources at equilibrium; rather, competition is a value in and of itself, in that it reveals information and promotes entrepreneurship. However, markets are creations of the legal order and require constant supervision to work properly.

	Construction	**Spontaneity**
Efficiency	Neo-classical economics Post-Chicago antitrust school Public interest regulatory theory	Chicago price theory Chicago antitrust school Public choice regulatory theory
Discovery	Ordoliberalism Traditional EU competition/regulatory policy	Austrian school

20. The four quadrants are not watertight: depending on which of his writings is referred to and how it is read, von Hayek himself lies somewhere between the lower quadrants. Similarly, heterodox (neo-Schumpeterian or evolutionary) theories fit somewhere between the upper and lower rows, since they envisage that firms both seek to maximize efficiency within a specific market environment (in routine phases) and embark upon searches for new routines to deal with shocks to that environment (in upheaval phases).

III. AI Systems and Market Theories Based on Efficiency

21. At first glance, if markets are seen as tools to achieve efficiency (upper quadrants), increasing the use of AI systems in market transactions would improve the functioning of markets: individualized offerings will match consumer preferences more closely, and producers will be rewarded with higher profits (by appropriating consumer surplus). The upper-quadrant theories typically assume that information relating to consumer preferences and willingness to pay exists and can be secured. It is undisclosed, however, and must be

obtained by producers through search. Transaction costs and frictions arising from the need to search could be reduced, if not eliminated, by AI systems, thereby also increasing productive efficiency.

22. Accordingly, using more sophisticated AI systems to develop individualized offerings broadly fits with market theories based on efficiency, save for the confiscation of consumer surplus. Many authors will surely argue along these lines, and will downplay that confiscation as an unfortunate side-effect, perhaps even stating their confidence that robust markets will find a way to attenuate that side-effect.

23. In contrast to these authors, I would argue that the confiscation of consumer surplus through AI-enabled first-degree price discrimination is a significant downside. Much of the appeal of the equilibrium model that underpins the upper-quadrant theories lies in the presence of consumer surplus: not only do markets clear, but for most consumers, they deliver products at prices lower than their willingness to pay. A loss of some consumer surplus does not necessarily indicate a market failure. Here, however, it is the potential confiscation of the entire consumer surplus, without any say on the part of consumers, that is worrisome.

24. This would point to a weakness in the "Chicago" theories of the upper-right corner, which are dominant in US antitrust now. Markets may be more dependent on the legal environment than these theories envisage. Typically, spontaneous or naturalistic theories do recognize that markets need a solid private law foundation (property, contract, tort), but they stop at that. The presence of a marketplace, where suppliers and customers gather, where prices are not individualized and publicly posted and where transactions can be observed, remains an unstated assumption. That archetypical marketplace scarcely even exists anymore, but until recently it could still be used as an analogy or metaphor for the actual workings of the market. In the emerging age of dematerialized markets, however, nothing is left that could somehow be assimilated to a marketplace, thereby exposing some implicit assumptions of naturalistic theories.

25. Consumer surplus cannot be taken for granted: rather, as our analysis implies, its existence depends on the inability of producers to engage into first-degree price discrimination, which is in turn a consequence of the constraints imposed by search costs and the observability of transactions by consumers. Should these constraints be removed, maybe the legal environment ought to include measures that at least restore some consumer control over price discrimination (perhaps going as far as to push firms back to second- or third-degree discrimination). Obviously there, measures imply a trade-off against efficiency, but such trade-off might be desirable if it bolsters consumer sovereignty and more generally the legitimacy of market processes. Such measures would be in line with the more constructivist theories of the upper-left corner, where the legal environment plays a closer role in ensuring the functioning of markets.

26. Seen against that background, data protection and privacy laws, as well as legal provisions on price transparency and reference offers, would take on extra salience not just as consumer protection measures, but also as core components of the legal environment for AI-driven markets. The former obscure consumer data and can act as a cloak against first-degree discrimination. As for the latter, they enable consumers to observe other transactions.

IV. AI Systems and Market Theories Based on Discovery

27. Under market theories based on discovery, the introduction of refined AI systems has a fundamental, even existential impact. Indeed, the lower-quadrant theories rely on a strong assumption as to information distribution, best formulated in the mid-twentieth century by von Hayek in the course of a debate on central planning versus markets. Von Hayek argued that it is impossible to centralize relevant information about the preferences of individual market participants. Such information is inherently linked to the local circumstances of each participant. Collecting and compiling it, and then acting upon it, is beyond the capabilities of any central institution, be it the State or large firms. In contrast, markets enable such information to be distilled through the price mechanism and effectively revealed to other actors in a useable fashion. In the lower quadrants, lack of knowledge about consumer preferences is not just a feature (or a bug) that generates transaction costs and helps to sustain consumer surplus; it is the driving force behind markets and the source of their dynamism.

28. Should AI systems, combined with Big Data, reach a level of proficiency where information about the preferences of individual market participants is centrally available, then von Hayek's analysis is defeated. As far as lower-quadrant theories are concerned, this is the end of markets as we know them. Whether AI systems can ever achieve such proficiency is a question that cannot currently be answered, in my opinion, and in any event that answer will have to be supported by empirical evidence that does not exist yet. My intuition is that AI systems are not close to that point now and may never reach it. Market theories centered on information discovery still have some life to them.

29. A more interesting and more likely scenario is that, even if AI systems cannot disprove von Hayek's analysis, market actors would nonetheless come to believe, rightly or wrongly, that AI systems offer the best path towards ascertaining consumer preferences. As outlined above, producers could then converge around best-of-breed AI systems to guide their commercial policy, leading to adverse effects on competition.

30. Beyond the effect on competition, lower-quadrant theories would also predict an effect on entrepreneurship. Indeed, according to these theories, entrepreneurs base their ventures on a superior ability to understand, and discern

opportunities in, the localized data about consumer preferences, in connection with other information such as inventions. Successful entrepreneurs see their vision vindicated, and the stock of knowledge about consumer preferences increases. Entrepreneurs have a central role in bringing markets forward on the never-ending quest to reach equilibrium.

31. In the short term, AI systems can certainly help entrepreneurs in finding market openings. In the longer term, however, the picture is mixed, if and once AI systems become the go-to tool for entrepreneurs. AI systems are typically not geared to produce variety and question received wisdom; they rather seek to follow probabilities and identify correlations, with a view to optimization.

32. On the one hand, this could result in impoverished entrepreneurship, with less diversity. Entrepreneurial incentives could ultimately be reduced if a strong belief emerges that one cannot improve on AI systems.

33. On the other hand, maybe some entrepreneurs will seek and learn to exploit AI systems differently – almost subversively. Others will even dare to buck the AI trend and bet on their own reading of the market, and against AI systems. For these "superhero" entrepreneurs breaking from the rest of the entrepreneurial crowd, the rewards would become larger. In that case, AI systems could end up turbocharging entrepreneurship.

34. If entrepreneurship is influenced by the increased use of AI systems, innovation is likely to be affected as well. As set out above, AI systems are probabilistic; with similar datasets, they are likely to converge on the most probable prediction. If the term was not so politically charged, one could say that AI systems would lean conservative when used in support of efforts to innovate. In practice, this could tilt the balance towards sustaining innovation, i.e., innovation that fits within established value networks and product architectures. By implication, "superhero" entrepreneurs subverting or challenging AI would probably be steered, willingly or not, towards disruptive innovation.

35. In the end, as long as AI systems do not reach the point where von Hayek's analysis on the distribution of information is defeated (which they might never do), then the most important policy concern is to avoid that the widespread use of AI systems would dampen the diversity and the originality that drives the market process via entrepreneurship and innovation. Here as well, AI systems reveal vulnerabilities that the proponents of spontaneous market theories (Austrian school) might not have envisaged, including the possibility that information can be centrally held, or more realistically, the possibility that the belief would arise that AI systems can successfully unearth and collect the localized information on consumer preferences. As with efficiency-based theories, a more constructivist approach (lower-left corner) is more suitable in dealing with this concern.

36. Looking at AI systems through the lens of market theories based on discovery gives additional force to the conclusions reached earlier in the section on efficiency-based theories. The measures advocated to opacify consumer

preferences and promote the observability of transactions are useful not only to safeguard consumer surplus, but also to maintain some uncertainty and drive entrepreneurship. In addition, from a market-as-discovery angle, the risk of producer convergence around a best-of-breed AI system, on the supply side, becomes even more problematic as it could dampen entrepreneurship and innovation. There are few ready solutions to address that concern, however. One could put forward measures to align the perception of AI system proficiency with its real performance (through scientific research and benchmarking). Competition law could also be used to counter excessive circulation of, and reliance on, similar AI systems as between competing producers, using provisions and case law on information sharing between competitors.

V. Conclusion

37. The introduction of AI systems on competitive markets, in order to predict consumer preferences and willingness to pay, is bound to affect how markets work. It opens the door to increased product differentiation and first-degree price discrimination. More subtly, it also conjures the possibility that competing producers converge on a best-of-breed AI system and thereby end up with fairly similar "unique" offerings to each consumer.

38. At a deeper level, confronting this prospective analysis with current market theories (as arranged in a two-by-two matrix) reveals weaknesses in spontaneous or naturalistic theories, where the presence of some form of marketplace or the impossibility of centralizing localized consumer data is assumed to hold forever without the need for any support. Constructivist theories, where markets depend on their legal environment, appear better suited to deal with the impact of AI systems. On the other axis of the matrix, both efficiency-based and discovery-based theories complement each other in highlighting concerns arising from the use of AI systems. The confiscation of consumer surplus through first-degree price discrimination might be too high a price to pay for the increase in efficiency flowing from increased product differentiation via mass customization. Furthermore, even the mere belief that AI systems offer the best path to figuring consumer preferences and willingness to pay might undermine the discovery mechanism that drives markets, and thereby affect entrepreneurship and innovation.

39. In the end, legal remedies could help to avoid adverse scenarios. Data protection and privacy laws can act as a cloak to limit or even defeat first-degree discrimination. Consumer protection measures relating to price transparency and reference offers can offset the disappearance of genuine marketplaces. Finally, transparent assessment of AI system proficiency, combined with vigilant competition law enforcement regarding benchmarking and information exchange between competitors, can ensure that enough diversity and originality remains to feed the entrepreneurial drive and generate innovation.

From Cola to GAFAM: Defining Markets in Competition Law and Sector-Specific Regulations

Christian Bovet*
University of Geneva

I. Introduction

1. Probably all competition law professors around the world stress during their first classes the significance of market definition in this field of study. Some of them might use the cola beverage segment[1] in order to illustrate the various alternatives offered to consumers and producers in this sector and thus get their students to reflect on – and hopefully discuss – the possibilities open to them if they had to argue such a case before competition authorities. But as Bob Dylan sings in *The Times They Are A-Changin'*:

> "[...] admit that the waters
> Around you have grown [...].
> For the loser now will be later to win."[2]

---

* Hon. professor, University of Geneva.

1 European Commission, Former notice on the definition of relevant market for the purposes of Community competition law (Former Notice), O.J. 1997, (C 372) 5, § 18 (soft-drink bottlers). European Commission, Guidelines on the application of Article 81(3) of the Treaty, O.J. 2024, (C 101) 97, § 82 (carbonated soft drinks). *See also*, Mark A. Lemley and Mark P. McKenna, *Is Pepsi Really a Substitute for Coke? Market Definition in Antitrust and IP*, 100 Geo. L.J. 2055 (2012).

2 Lyrics available on Bob Dylan's official website: *https://www.bobdylan.com/songs/times-they-are-changin/* (last visited Oct. 15, 2024).

2. Indeed, methods and tests have evolved from rather traditional examples to technological ones. The entry into force of the Digital Market Act (DMA)[3] and the Digital Services Act (DSA)[4] and the adoption of the Artificial Intelligence Act (AI Act)[5] are supplementing the steps already taken thanks to the regulatory package liberalizing EU electronic communications services and networks as from January 1, 1998.[6]

II. Substitutability

3. Proper market definition covers a product and geographic dimension. This short chapter will focus on the former, and more particularly on the concept of substitutability or interchangeability. As the President of the UK Competition Appeal Tribunal put it in a 2022 judgment:[7]

> "…Suppose you are concerned about a competition abuse in the market for baked beans. It would be pretty stupid to start investigating the market for cough mixture in order to work out what the nature of the abuse was in baked beans, so there is a certain common sense as to where you look… But it becomes much harder if you are, let us say, looking at an abuse in the aspirin market and you might have a very hard question working out whether aspirin is the only product and it is the rival aspirin products that are only relevant or whether you need to look at paracetamol."[8]

4. Two groups of citations coming from both sides of the Atlantic and completing each other might help us to better understand a term sometimes qualified as

---

3 Regulation 2022/1925 of the European Parliament and of the Council of 14 September 2022 on contestable and fair markets in the digital sector and amending Directives 2019/1937 and 2020/1828 (Digital Markets Act), O.J. 2022, (L 265) 1.

4 Regulation 2022/2065 of the European Parliament and of the Council of 19 October 2022 on a single market for digital services and amending Directive 2000/31 (Digital Services Act), O.J. 2022, (L 277) 1. This text is, however, of no specific significance in the context of this contribution.

5 Regulation (EU) 2024/1689 of the European Parliament and of the Council of 13 June 2024 laying down harmonized rules on artificial intelligence and amending Regulations (EC) No 300/2008, (EU) 167/2013, (EU) 168/2013, (EU) 2018/858, (EU) 2018/1139 and (EU) 2019/2144 and Directives 2014/90/EU, (EU) 2016/797 and (EU) 2020/1828 (Artificial Intelligence (AI) Act) O.J. L Series. The definition of an "AI system" is rather broad since it "means a machine-based system designed to operate with varying levels of autonomy, that may exhibit adaptiveness after deployment and that, for explicit or implicit objectives, infers, from the input it receives, how to generate outputs such as predictions, content, recommendations, or decisions that can influence physical or virtual environments" (AI Act art. 3(1)). It might serve as a preliminary basis for market definition but will obviously need to be narrowed in order to encompass precisely the economic sector concerned by a competition restriction or a concentration.

6 After several revisions, various regulations governing electronic communications gave rise to Directive (EU) 2018/1972 of the European Parliament and of the Council of 11 December 2018 establishing the European Electronic Communications Code (Recast), O.J. 2018, (L 321) 36. See *id.* at art. 125 and *infra* notes 22 and 23.

7 UK Competition Appeal Tribunal, Judgment of Aug. 8, 2022, Case 1380/1/12/21, BGL (Holdings) Ltd. v. Competition & Mkt. Auth., [2022] CAT 36.

8 *Id.* at § 111.

"dangerous":[9] in *Brown Shoe Co. v. United States*,[10] the US Supreme Court stated that:

> "The outer boundaries of a product market are determined by the reasonable interchangeability of use or the cross-elasticity of demand between the product itself and substitutes for it. However, within this broad market, well-defined submarkets may exist which, in themselves, constitute product markets for antitrust purposes."[11]

5. In addition, both in the Former Notice and the February 2024 Revised Notice on market definition,[12] the European Commission pointed out that:[13]

Former Notice	**Revised Notice**
"A relevant product market comprises all those products *and/or services* which are regarded as interchangeable or substitutable by the *consumer*, by reason of the products' characteristics, their prices and their intended use."[14]	"*The* relevant product market comprises all those products that *customers* regard as interchangeable or substitutable to the product(s) *of the undertaking(s) involved*, based on the products' characteristics, their prices and their intended use, *taking into consideration the conditions of competition and the structure of supply and demand on the market*."[15]

6. The deletion of the word "services" in the draft Revised Notice is consistent with the terminology used in competition law, where the term "products" encompasses physical goods as well as services. To go back to cola, fountain-dispensed soft drinks may be deemed to constitute the relevant market and lead to consider the two companies as competitors,[16] although one might hesitate to consider the drinks themselves as belonging to the same relevant market.[17] Another example may be found in the Guidelines on

9 *Id.* at § 114: "The term 'market definition' is a dangerous one if it is understood to mean an attempt to grapple with, or state unambiguously, the notion of a market in a particular context."

10 Brown Shoe Co. v. United States, 370 U.S. 294 (1962). Fed. Trade Comm'n. & U.S. Dep't of Justice, *Merger Guidelines (2023)*, § 4.3 (Dec. 18, 2023), https://www.ftc.gov/system/files/ftc_gov/pdf/P234000-NEW-MERGER-GUIDELINES.pdf.

11 *See*, *Brown Shoe*, 370 U.S. 294 at 325.

12 Commission Notice on the definition of the relevant market for the purposes of Union competition law, O.J. 2024, C, (C/2024) 1645) (Revised Notice).

13 Most relevant changes are italicized.

14 Former Notice, *supra* note 1, at § 7.

15 Revised Notice, *supra* note 12, at § 12.

16 But see, Pepsi, Inc. v. Coca-Cola Co. 315 F.3d 101, 106-07 (2d Cir. 2002) (per curiam), where the court found that fountain-dispensed soft drinks were the relevant market and consequently treated the two companies as competitors.

17 For the European Commission, the market for the production and bottling of non-alcoholic beverages (NABs) should be further segmented into the production and bottling of carbonated soft drinks (CSDs) and non-carbonated soft drinks (NCSDs), which constitute two separate product markets. While the authority has not envisaged further potential segmentations within CSDs, it has considered, on the other hand, that, within NCSDs, water and ready-to-drink (RTD) teas belong to separate product markets. EU Commission, Decision of Jan. 24, 2022, Case M.10435, Refresco Group / Hansa-Heemann, at § 11 & 12 (with other references). The statistical reference to the economic activity based on NACE (acronym derived for the French title "*Nomenclature générale des Activités économiques dans les Communautés Européennes*") may also assist

vertical restraints.[18] Indeed, typically in case of single branding,[19] the type of product involved may play a role in the assessment of the risk of foreclosure at the wholesaling level: in a market where wholesaling can operate efficiently with only one product (e.g., ice cream), the manufacturer may have the ability and incentive, if necessary, to set up its own wholesaling system, in which case it is unlikely to be foreclosed from that market. By contrast, in a market where wholesaling requires a wide range of products (e.g., frozen foodstuffs), a manufacturer selling only one product would need to have access to established wholesalers, and the risk of foreclosure may therefore be higher, especially "if several suppliers tie most of the available wholesalers."[20] This is also a good illustration of the text added at the end of the excerpt of the draft Revised Notice, i.e., to take into consideration "the conditions of competition and the structure of supply and demand on the market." In the end, one could extend the statement made in *Brown Shoe* and retain not only that submarkets may constitute a specific and often narrower product market, but also that some markets may exist thanks to their relationship with a group of product markets.[21]

III. Digital Markets

7. The evolution towards digital markets was marked by the adoption of regulations governing the liberalization of what was identified as the "telecommunications" sector during the 1990s[22] and which rapidly became "electronic communications" in today's terminology.[23] While in competition law the concept of market definition applies to anticompetitive agreements, abuses of dominant positions and merger control, in electronic communications regulations this concept focuses on dominant positions. Indeed, according

---

the practitioner in its preliminary analysis; for instance, the above-mentioned case is referenced under "C.11.07 – Manufacture of soft drinks; production of mineral waters and other bottled waters." The current classification is NACE Rev.2.1. For more details, *see*, European Union, https://eur-lex.europa.eu/EN/legal-content/summary/statistical-classification-of-economic-activities-nace-revision-2-1.html (last visited Oct. 15, 2024).

18 European Commission, Guidelines on vertical restraints, O.J. 2022, (C 248) 1.

19 Single branding (*id.* at § 298): "Under the heading of 'single branding' fall those agreements which have as their main element the fact that the buyer is obliged or induced to concentrate its orders for a particular type of product with one supplier."

20 *Id.* at § 308.

21 Not all soft drinks dispensed through fountain-systems are substitutable, and not all frozen foodstuffs – and even ice creams – are deemed interchangeable by customers. However, see *supra* note 16.

22 See former Commission Directive 90/388/EEC of 28 June 1990 on competition in the markets for telecommunications services, O.J. 1990, (L 192) 10, and former Council Directive 90/387/EEC of 28 June 1990 on the establishment of the internal market for telecommunications services through the implementation of open network provision, O.J. 1990, (L 192) 1.

23 In particular, former Directive 2002/21/EC of the European Parliament and of the Council of 7 March 2002 on a common regulatory framework for electronic communications networks and services (Framework Directive), O.J. 2002, (L 108) 33, and former Directive 2002/19/EC of the European Parliament and of the Council of 7 March 2002 on access to, and interconnection of, electronic communications networks and associated facilities (Access Directive), O.J. 2002, (L 108) 7. For more information on this important regulatory step, see European Union, https://eur-lex.europa.eu/EN/legal-content/summary/a-new-framework-for-electronic-communications-services.html (last visited Oct. 15, 2024).

to Article 63(2) Directive (EU) 2018/1972 (Recast), "[a]n undertaking shall be deemed to have significant market power [SMP] if, either individually or jointly with others, it enjoys a position equivalent to dominance, namely a position of economic strength affording it the power to behave to an appreciable extent independently of competitors, customers and ultimately consumers." SMP is determined ex ante on the basis of three criteria set forth by Article 67(1) Directive (EU) 2018/1972 (Recast), i.e., the presence of high and non-transitory barriers to entry (a), a market structure non tending towards effective competition within a relevant time horizon (b), and insufficiency of competition law to address adequately the market failures identified (c). Since market definition plays a central role in this process, the Commission adopted a specific recommendation on this issue[24] in a manner consistent with "competition law principles,"[25] where it rightly stated that: "The definition of relevant markets may change over time as the characteristics of products and services available on such markets evolve and the possibilities for demand and supply substitution change due to technological, market and regulatory developments."[26]

8. Recital 5 of the DMA emphasizes that the scope of Articles 101 and 102 TFEU "is limited to certain instances of market power, for example dominance on specific markets and of anti-competitive behavior." Thanks to its ex ante mechanisms, the DMA "aims to complement the enforcement of competition law."[27] Indeed, undertakings meeting the qualitative and/or[28] quantitative size, gateway, and durability criteria of Article 3 DMA are to be designated as "gatekeepers" and subject to obligations independent from their behavior.[29] Despite these elements of distinction and even differentiation,[30] the DMA also contributes to a better understanding and definition of digital markets in competition law. In particular, the list of "core platform service[s]" provided for in Article 2(2) DMA[31] should

24 The first version of this Commission Recommendation on relevant product and service markets within the electronic communications sector susceptible to ex ante regulation was adopted on Feb. 11, 2003 (O.J. 2003, (L 114) 45). It was revised on Dec. 17, 2007 (O.J. 2007, (L 344) 65) and Oct. 9, 2014 (O.J. 2014, (L 295) 79). The current version is dated Dec. 18, 2020 (O.J. 2020, (L 439) 23), and its Annex identifies two markets which national regulatory authorities (NRAs) should analyze, i.e., wholesale local access provided at a fixed location and wholesale dedicated capacity (2020 Recommendation, conclusion 1). However, NRAs should also apply the tree-criteria test to markets listed in previous recommendations, in spite of the fact that these markets are no longer listed in the Annex to the 2020 Recommendation (2020 Recommendation, at § 45).

25 2020 Recommendation, *supra* note 24, § 5, 2nd sentence.

26 *Id.* at § 4, 1st sentence. *See also*, European Commission, Guidelines on market analysis and the assessment of significant market power under the EU regulatory framework for electronic communications networks and services, O.J. 2018, (C 159) 1.

27 Regulation 2022/1925, Recital 10.

28 In particular, see *id.* the mechanisms of arts. 3(2) and 3(8).

29 *Id.* or as Recital 11 puts it: "independently from the actual, potential or presumed effects of the conduct of a given gatekeeper [...] on competition on a given market."

30 For more details, see Georgios Gryllos, *The new digital landscape: Interaction between the DMA and rules of national and EU law governing the conduct of gatekeepers*, Concurrences No. 1-2024, art. No. 116827, 40, § 58 et seq., esp. 62.

31 For instance, online intermediation services (DMA, art. 2(2)(a) and art. 2(5)), online search engines (DMA art. 2(2)(b) and Article 2(6)), operating systems (DMA, art. 2(2)(f) and art. 2(10)), cloud computing services (DMA art. 2(2)(i) and art. 2(13)) or online advertising services (DMA, art. 2(2)(j)).

assist authorities and practitioners in the definition of markets concerned by "classic" anticompetitive behaviors. This is not really surprising since several of the services mentioned in Article 2(2) DMA were the subject of Commission investigations based on Article 101 and more frequently Article 102 TFEU.[32] One can therefore observe a real cross-fertilization between these two sets of rules.

9. The integration of digital markets in the Revised Notice constitutes a natural move, fully consistent with this evolution. Thus, digitalization is one the "significant developments of the past twenty years" which the Commission puts forward in its notice.[33] Three main consequences may be kept in mind:

- These types of markets belong to the categories where one should take into account "the expected changes in substitution possibilities resulting from the change in competitive dynamics."[34] Indeed, in the digital sector, "the introduction of new or newly developed products or processes, as well as technological or regulatory changes may lead to structural market transitions, which affect existing competitive dynamics and the general reactions to relative supply conditions."[35]

- Metrics other than merchant sales may be considered in order to assess an undertaking's market share in one of these business segments. In particular, one may think of the number of website visits, the quantity of streams, the number of downloads and updates, the number of active users, the number of interactions, time spent or audience numbers.[36] The Revised Notice also refers to "the number of interactions or the volume or value of transactions concluded over a platform," since it is common in digital markets to have services provided mainly at a zero monetary price.[37]

- The definition of "digital ecosystems" is inspired by the *Google Android* case where the General Court stated that in a system of this type: "the products or services which form part of the relevant markets that make up that ecosystem may overlap or be connected to each other on the basis of their horizontal or vertical complementarity."[38] This may lead to a situation where "a primary core product and several secondary (digital) products whose consumption is connected to the core product,

32 See for instance, recently, Case AT.40670, Google – Adtech and Data-related practices, Statement of objections, June 14, 2023, and Case AT.40684, Facebook Marketplace, Statement of objections, Dec. 19, 2022, for which the Commission identified inter alia as "economic activities" under the NACE classification, *supra* note 17 "J.63.12 – Web portals" and "J.63.1 – Data processing, hosting and related activities; web portals." Also, judgment of Sept. 14, 2022, Case T-604/18, Google Android, (appeal pending, Case C-738/22 P), and judgment of Nov. 10, 2021, Case 612/17, Google Shopping, (appeal pending, Case C-48/22 P).

33 Revised Notice, *supra* note 12, at § 3.

34 *Id.*, at § 55.

35 *Id.*, at § 55.

36 *Id.*, at § 108 (with other references).

37 *Id.*, at § 108.

38 Judgment of Sept. 14, 2022, Case T-604/18, Google and Alphabet v. Eur. Comm'n, at § 116.

for instance, by technological links or interoperability" (e.g., products built around a mobile operating system, including hardware, an application store and software applications).[39]

IV. Conclusion

10. The Former Notice was a rather clear, concise and pedagogical instrument; it constituted most of the time an excellent tool for practitioners and academics. The fact that it lasted almost 30 years without any amendment shows the quality of its elaboration. The revision of this document offered the possibility to adapt it to new technologies in the light of not only jurisprudence in competition law but also more broadly of new regulations. Questioning the validity and current value of policies and procedures is a necessity in a world where innovation – an essential component of competition policy – plays a central role in basically all economic sectors, although its intensity may vary depending on business specificities. Guidance should follow this trend. However, it should not lead to neglecting competition in "traditional" markets; the means and concepts developed for digital markets might even come useful also in the latter.

39 On the other hand, in its decision of July 18, 2018, Case AT.40099, Google Android, at § 299, the Commission concluded that the conditions for defining a system market comprising app stores and smart mobile operating systems had not been met.

Why Competition Matters (in Generative AI)?

NUNO CUNHA RODRIGUES*
Portuguese Competition Authority

I. Introduction

1. When asked about the advantages of competition, the Generative Artificial Intelligence (AI) application ChatGPT, developed by OpenAI,[1] recognizes its relevance and enumerates several benefits of promoting fair competition in the markets.

2. The elements listed include consumer welfare ("competition enforcement helps ensure that consumers have access to a variety of choices, competitive prices, and high-quality products or services"); innovation ("healthy competition encourages innovation as companies strive to differentiate themselves and gain a competitive edge. When market players are free to compete, they are more likely to invest in research and development, leading to the creation of new and improved products or services"); and efficient resource allocation ("competition enforcement prevents the formation of monopolies or cartels that can stifle competition and hinder efficient resource allocation. In competitive markets, resources are allocated based on market demand and supply, leading to optimal utilization").

---

* Nuno Cunha Rodrigues is President of the AdC from Mar. 13, 2023. With an academic career at the Faculty of Law of the University of Lisbon (FDUL), where he graduated, obtaining a Master's and a PhD in Legal and Economic Sciences, he is an Associate Professor at the Faculty of Law, Lisbon, holding a Jean Monnet Chair, awarded in 2018 by the European Commission. He has published books and scientific articles in Portugal and abroad and has been an invited speaker by several national and international universities. Before taking office at the AdC he was also a lawyer, legal consultant, and held non-executive positions in different companies.

1 Prompt used in ChatGPT (GPT-3 by OpenAI), (Jan. 26, 2024).

3. Generative AI is growing and has a disruptive effect on the economy. It can have a significant transformative impact across all economic sectors and on consumer habits, namely by increasing productivity, achieving large scale results, and driving innovation.[2] Not surprisingly, investment in AI – broadly speaking – has been steadily on the rise in recent years,[3] in multiple jurisdictions, including through public funding.[4]

4. Competition is crucial for maintaining a contestable, innovative, and efficient market environment that benefits consumers, businesses, and the overall economy. New economic sectors are not an exception. Therefore, risks of distortion of the competitive process need to be identified and prevented.

5. The prompt in ChatGPT is the same as the one we will address in this paper. Nonetheless, we will focus on the Generative AI sector in order to understand why competition matters in Generative AI.

6. First, we will start by briefly describing Generative AI; second, we will summarize the recent regulatory initiatives related to Generative AI, establishing possible interactions between them; finally, we will address the relevance of competition in Generative AI.

II. What is Generative AI?

7. There are many types of AI systems, uses, and different angles of analysis. In 2019, the European Parliament recognized AI as a strategic technology and a priority for the European agenda.[5] The EU sought a technology-neutral uniform definition for AI, establishing it as "the ability of a machine to display human-like capabilities such as reasoning, learning, planning and creativity."[6]

---

2 In the specific case of Generative AI, it is estimated that it may add up to 7 percent to world GDP in the next decade *Generative AI Could Raise Global GDP by 7%*, Goldman Sachs (2023), https://www.goldmansachs.com/insights/articles/generative-ai-could-raise-global-gdp-by-7-percent (last visited Oct. 28, 2024).

3 It is estimated that AI investment could approach 200 billion USD globally by 2025. *AI Investment Forecast to Approach $200 Billion Globally by 2025*, Goldman Sachs (2023), https://www.goldmansachs.com/insights/articles/ai-investment-forecast-to-approach-200-billion-globally-by-2025 (last visited Oct. 28, 2024).

4 *Welcome to the Era of AI Nationalism*, The Economist (Jan. 1, 2024), https://www.economist.com/business/2024/01/01/welcome-to-the-era-of-ai-nationalism?utm_medium=cpc.adword.pd&utm_source=google&ppccampaignID=18156330227&ppcadID=&utm_campaign=a.22brand_pmax&utm_content=conversion.direct-response.anonymous&gad_source=1&gclid=EAIaIQobChMI-c6JjKafiQM-VrIlQBh0Ycwv0EAAYASAAEgJ8d_D_BwE&gclsrc=aw.ds (last visited Oct. 28, 2024).

5 European Parliament resolution of 12 February 2019 on a comprehensive European industrial policy on artificial intelligence and robotics, 2020, O.J. (C 449) 37: "[AI] is one of the strategic technologies for the 21st century both globally and in Europe, bringing positive change for the European economy, enabling innovation, productivity, competitiveness and wellbeing"; "stresses the need for AI to be put on the agenda of existing institutions and organisations."

6 *See*, European Parliament, *What is Artificial Intelligence and How is it Used?*, https://www.europarl.europa.eu/topics/en/article/20200827STO85804/what-is-artificial-intelligence-and-how-is-it-used (last visited Oct. 21, 2024). A similar definition of "AI system" can be found in the Proposal for a Regulation of the European Parliament and of the Council Laying Down Harmonised Rules on Artificial Intelligence (Artificial Intelligence Act) and Amending Certain Union Legislative Acts (AI Act), art. 3(1), COM (2021) 206 final (Apr. 21, 2021).

8. Generative AI models do not possess conceptual knowledge of their own. These models learn patterns and structures within the data used for their training and produce new content similar to the training data (i.e., examples). This new content spans diverse types of data, including text, images, video, and audio. Each type of content requires specific statistical models, designed to generate it. A Generative AI model may combine different types of content (i.e., multimodal models).[7]

9. In general, the first step for development and deployment of Generative AI involves pre-training, in which the foundation model is developed. Foundation models, such as DALL-E or GPT-4, are trained on broad data that can be adapted to a wide range of downstream tasks.

10. The development of foundation models requires key inputs, such as large volumes of data, computing power, namely specialized hardware (for instance, specialized chips and cloud computer services), significant financial resources, and highly specialized know-how, particularly from the developers. In essence, these models are developed on a trial-and-error basis, requiring investment (human, financial, and time), data, and experimentation capacity.

11. Foundation models are generalized by nature. For that reason, it can be useful to fine-tune those models. That process involves additional training on a smaller, task-specific dataset to refine the model's capabilities for a particular application. For example, a fine-tuning model could be a chat service that answers questions, adapted from a large language model (i.e., the foundation model).

12. There are different types of Generative AI applications or tools, for instance standalone or interacting with other products or services. One example of the latter is the use of plugins. These are software components that may expand the features of Generative AI.[8] Plugins may be developed by third-parties or by the developer of the AI model.

13. At the end, Generative AI can have multiple uses – such as, optimization of customer support services, production of entertainment content, accelerating scientific research or identifying anomalies and fraud. It can be applied to a wide range of sectors and can have a positive impact on the economy.

III. Regulating AI

14. It is well known that digital markets and AI tools have great potential. But they also carry risks, especially for consumers. Some of the key concerns comprise privacy, security, and accuracy of information.

---

7 *See*, Portuguese Competition Authority, *Competition and Generative Artificial Intelligence*, (Nov. 2023), https://awards.concurrences.com/en/awards/2024/soft-laws-studies/competition-and-generative-artificial-intelligence.

8 *Ibidem*.

15. There have been several regulatory initiatives. Although the EU has taken a leading role, in what concerns, for instance, the proposal of the so-called EU AI Act it was complemented, at global level, by the G7's guiding principles and voluntary code of conduct for providers of AI systems.[9] On October 30, 2023, the same day of the G7 leaders' statement, President Biden issued an Executive Order on AI promoting fairness, civil rights, innovation, and competition, defending consumers and workers, and ensuring the safety of AI systems.[10]

16. In the case of the EU, it aims to ensure fair and open digital markets, as well as setting limits, guaranteeing safety and respecting fundamental rights, while encouraging business innovation.

1. The DMA

17. The Digital Markets Act (DMA) entered into force on November 1, 2022, reflecting the concerns of the EU institutions and legislators to keep up with the most recent developments in the tech industry and, consequently, presenting a strong and effective legal framework to handle its implications for markets and consumers.[11] In particular, in its initial proposal, the European Commission (EC) intended to reinforce the promotion and defense of competition in digital markets, by adapting its tools to the specific characteristics of the identified "gatekeepers" and respective risks they present to competition.

18. At the time of its publication, the DMA addressed large digital platforms, not having been specifically designed to deal with Generative AI. Notwithstanding this fact, it has been argued[12] that Generative AI services may fall within the scope of this Regulation, namely within Article 2(2)[13] or, specifically, under Article 2(12) of the DMA, in accordance with the definition of virtual assistants.[14]

19. Moreover, many obligations in the DMA, namely the ones set out in Article 5, refer to other services provided by the gatekeepers, which correspond to some of the major players in AI.[15] This said, it has also been argued that a

---

9 *See*, European Commission, *G7 Leaders' Statement on the Hiroshima AI Process*, (Oct. 30, 2023), https://digital-strategy.ec.europa.eu/en/library/g7-leaders-statement-hiroshima-ai-process.

10 *See*, The White House, *Executive Order on the Safe, Secure, and Trustworthy Development and Use of Artificial Intelligence*, (Oct. 30, 2023), https://www.whitehouse.gov/briefing-room/presidential-actions/2023/10/30/executive-order-on-the-safe-secure-and-trustworthy-development-and-use-of-artificial-intelligence/.

11 Regulation 2022/1925 of the European Parliament and of the Council of 14 September 2022 on contestable and fair markets in the digital sector and amending Directives 2019/1937 and 2020/1828 (Digital Markets Act), O.J. 2022, (L 265) 1.

12 *See*, European Parliament, Annual Report On Competition Policy 2023 (Dec. 18, 2023), https://www.europarl.europa.eu/doceo/document/A-9-2023-0427_EN.html, in particular ¶42, as well as the European Parliament, Report on Artificial Intelligence in a Digital Age (Mar. 22, 2022), https://oeil.secure.europarl.europa.eu/oeil/popups/printficheglobal.pdf?id=721501&l=en, in particular ¶¶65, 66 and 168, the latter broadly referring to the field of AI.

13 Mainly because of generative AI integration into existing core platform services.

14 According to DMA art. 2(12): "'virtual assistant' means a software that can process demands, tasks or questions, including those based on audio, visual, written input, gestures or motions, and that, based on those demands, tasks or questions, provides access to other services or controls connected physical devices."

15 A clear example of an obligation provided in DMA art. 5(2), is that gatekeepers obtain consent to combine personal data from a core platform service to any other service.

tailor-made regulatory framework was needed for Generative AI, especially considering its characteristics summarized above.

20. Overall, while it may be possible to apply the DMA to Generative AI services, given its specific scope, it may not be sufficient to fully cover the risks associated with the development and deployment of Generative AI. Therefore, some of these concerns were addressed in an autonomous regulation.

2. The AI ACT

21. The proposal for AI regulation (the EU AI Act) has been the subject of much anticipation.

22. After the Joint Declaration on the EU's legislative priorities for 2018–2019, from December 14, 2017,[16] the EC set up a group of experts, on March 9, 2018,[17] that proposed guidelines and recommendations aimed at regulating artificial intelligence based on a human-centric and trustworthy approach. It was therefore not surprising that, in April 2021, the EC presented a proposal for a regulation of AI based on the protection of fundamental rights and the functioning of the rule of law.[18]

23. The AI Regulation was then adopted by the European Parliament and the Council on June 13, 2024, having entered into force on August 1, 2024.[19]

24. The AI Act lays down the requirements and obligations of AI systems operating in the EU. It aims to provide a neutral definition of AI systems[20] and is grounded on a risk-based approach, in terms of the level of negative consequences that these systems represent to their users and society (from unacceptable AI practices to limited risk). The different levels of risk imply more or less obligations, in particular in terms of transparency, providing that if AI systems are deemed too harmful, they will be prohibited.[21]

---

16 The European institutions, namely the Council, the Parliament and the Commission agreed on the need to ensure "a high level of data protection, digital rights and ethical standards while capturing the benefits and avoiding the risks of developments in artificial intelligence and robotics," *see*, European Commission, *Joint Declaration on the EU's legislative priorities for 2018-19,* (Dec. 14, 2017), https://commission.europa.eu/publications/joint-declaration-eus-legislative-priorities-2018-19_en.

17 *See*, European Commission, Press Release, Artificial intelligence: Commission Kicks Off Work on Marrying Cutting-Edge Technology and Ethical Standards (Mar. 9, 2018), https://ec.europa.eu/commission/presscorner/detail/en/ip_18_1381.

18 In fact, the proposal ultimately placed the emphasis on the harmonization, risk management and transparency of AI. In this regard the legal basis chosen for the proposal was the Treaty on the Functioning of the European Union (TFEU) – harmonization art. 114. The reference to art. 16 of the same Treaty, which guarantees the right to the protection of personal data, was later added to the final text of the regulation.

19 Regulation (EU) 2024/1689 of the European Parliament and of the Council of 13 June 2024 laying down harmonised rules on artificial intelligence and amending Regulations (EC) 300/2008, (EU) 167/2013, (EU) 168/2013, (EU) 2018/858, (EU) 2018/1139 and (EU) 2019/2144 and Directives 2014/90/EU, (EU) 2016/797 and (EU) 2020/1828 (Artificial Intelligence (AI) Act), 2024, O.J. L Series.

20 According to AI Act art. 3(1): "'AI system' means a machine-based system that is designed to operate with varying levels of autonomy and that may exhibit adaptiveness after deployment, and that, for explicit or implicit objectives, infers, from the input it receives, how to generate outputs such as predictions, content, recommendations, or decisions that can influence physical or virtual environments."

21 Also, in the US, the Federal Communications Commission declared AI generated voices in robocalls illegal. *See*, FCC, *FCC Makes AI-Generated Voices in Robocalls Illegal*, (Feb. 28, 2024), https://docs.fcc.gov/public/attachments/DOC-400393A1.pdf.

25. Specifically, there are requirements for AI systems to disclose which content has been generated by AI and to publish information on the data used for its training.

26. This act aims to safeguard the public interest and to incentivize the development of reliable content; the application of security controls, and the creation of a reporting obligation to share information on incidents and malfunctions. It also foresees measures to support SMEs and start-ups, namely by reducing the regulatory burden on them.

3. The AI Value Chain

27. Security and transparency can be identified as cornerstone principles for the regulation of AI. There may also be concerns about the traceability of AI systems. The same principles can be found in the data strategy adopted by the EU.[22] Apart from the Data Governance Act,[23] the EU adopted the Data Act, which entered into force on January 11, 2024.[24] It focuses on fair and equitable data sharing, aiming to facilitate access to data, particularly large quantities of high-quality industrial data from the Internet of Things.

28. Another key parameter is the competitiveness of the markets. In this context, the EU has adopted the European Chips Act.[25,26] This aims to promote investment and capacity building in semiconductor ecosystem, strengthening the technological and strategic autonomy of the internal market.

IV. Competition and Generative AI

29. Notwithstanding the EU ex ante regulatory approach, competition rules continue to be applicable and competition enforcement shall complement the existent regulatory framework.

30. Therefore, it is not only important to understand these markets and acknowledge risks to competition, but also to identify the opportunities brought by them to the competitive process.

---

22 *See*, Communication from the Commission to the European Parliament, the Council, the European Economic and Social Committee and the Committee of the Regions a European Strategy for Data, COM (2020) 66 final.

23 Regulation (EU) 2022/868 of the European Parliament and of the Council of 30 May 2022 on European data governance and amending Regulation (EU) 2018/1724 (Data Governance Act), 2022, O.J. (L 152) 1, became applicable in September 2023.

24 Regulation (EU) 2023/2854 of the European Parliament and of the Council of 13 December 2023 on harmonised rules on fair access to and use of data and amending Regulation (EU) 2017/2394 and Directive (EU) 2020/1828 (Data Act), 2023, O.J. (L Series), becoming applicable in September 2025.

25 Regulation (EU) 2023/1781 of the European Parliament and of the Council of 13 September 2023 establishing a framework of measures for strengthening Europe's semiconductor ecosystem and amending Regulation (EU) 2021/694 (Chips Act), 2023, *O.J. (L 229) 1.*

26 In the US, President Biden signed the CHIPS and Science Act, Public Law No: 117-167 (Aug. 9, 2022) https://www.congress.gov/bill/117th-congress/house-bill/4346/text.

31. Generative AI reflects many of the challenges that digital markets present to competition. These markets have characteristics that make them prone to high levels of concentration.

32. These characteristics include strong scale effects, network effects, and a lack of multi-homing. As a result, digital incumbents and first movers may accumulate competitive advantages that can lead to entrenched market positions and potentially harmful competitive behavior.

33. Moreover, the optimization of Generative AI models also benefits from economies of scope in downstream markets, as these can be adapted to many different tasks (i.e., they are generalized by nature).

34. In addition, users will contribute to the adaptation, improvement of the performance, and wider application of models. As a result, the value of the model increases with the number of users, creating further network effects. Consequently, companies with more users have more information, which may give an advantage to their models, potentially allowing them to exclude competitors and impose unfair prices and conditions on the market.

35. Plugins may be another possible source of network effects and another factor of potential concentration in Generative AI markets. Plugins allow new markets to form. They connect users with suppliers. Generative AI with a greater number of plugins could have a wider range of features and be more attractive to end users.

36. On the one hand, these features will allow for fine-tuning and further customization of Generative AI models. On the other hand, they can, for instance, create high switching costs. If these become too high, there may be a significant cost to competition in the form of fewer and less versatile options for the downstream market.

37. In fact, there might be incentives for vertical integration, agreements, and partnerships. These can lead to efficiencies, such as guaranteed access to adjacent markets, computing infrastructures, creation of new products, and ecosystems. Nonetheless, they can also distort competition, for example through self-preferencing and the creation of barriers to new entrants.

38. Self-preferencing can be particularly worrying regarding foundation model owners that enjoy market power, given the ability and incentive to give their own Generative AI models privileged or preferential access downstream.

39. Therefore, access to foundation models plays a central role in the dynamics of competition in downstream markets for Generative AI. The format, type, size, speed, and scope of access to the foundation models are key features in the ability of downstream Generative AI service providers to compete.

40. Open-source models and the possibility of interoperability between them can be important in ensuring that new, versatile and complementary models emerge, creating further market options and the possibility of improving existing ones. However, the impact of open source in promoting competition

remains uncertain due to its lesser incentives for model development and potential constraints on monetization.

41. Among other factors, competition promotes the possibility for businesses and consumers not to be locked in a sole provider or ecosystem. Thus, it is important to incentivize access to the key elements for the development of Generative AI tools, spanning data, computing power, and know-how.

42. In fact, initiatives such as the EU Data Act, which aims to enable data portability and interoperability, and the European Chips Act, that promotes competitiveness and resilience in semiconductor technologies, may play a role in promoting competition in the Generative AI sector.

43. Another relevant initiative was announced by the EC, on January 24, 2024. It focuses on measures to support European start-ups and SMEs in the development of AI. These include not only financial support, but also access to computing power.[27]

44. Moreover, the performance of foundation models requires human talent. As with any other people-centric business, the labor market is another factor of concern. No-poaching or wage-fixing agreements may also be a source of relevant distortions in these markets.[28]

45. In addition, in the realm of opportunities, Generative AI in itself represents an opportunity for innovation and increased competitiveness in downstream markets. This positive contribution is not straightforward, however. The benefits will only be possible if there is no foreclosure in these markets. There needs to be investment and the possibility to develop multiple models, with different uses and capabilities.

46. Therefore, markets must remain contestable, open and fair to ensure that Generative AI tools continue to be developed and deployed overall to the benefit of the consumers.

47. The competition authorities are attentive, constantly monitoring the markets, and prepared to play their role in protecting competition in the market, both by providing relevant insights[29] and by conducting investigations.[30]

---

27 *See* European Commission, Press Release, Commission Launches AI Innovation Package to Support Artificial Intelligence Startups and SMEs (Jan. 24, 2024), https://ec.europa.eu/commission/presscorner/detail/en/ip_24_383.

28 *See*, Final Judgment, United States v. Adobe Systems, Inc., 75 Fed. Reg. 60820 (Oct. 1, 2010).

29 *See*, AdC, *supra* note 7, where the AdC mapped the key determinants of competition in Generative AI and identifies the main risks to competition in the sector. Following this Issues Paper, in Sept. 2024 the AdC publish the first paper of a new Short Papers Series, on Competition and Generative AI: Zooming in on Data. *See also*, the CMA, AI Foundation Models Initial Report (Apr. 16, 2024); the FTC, *Generative Artificial Intelligence and the Creative Economy Staff Report: Perspectives and Takeaways*, (2023). Moreover, the Hungarian enforcer has launched a "market analysis" to assess the effects of AI on competition and the Autorité de la concurrence (France) just issued an opinion on the competitive functioning of the sector. *See also*, European Commission, Press Release, Commission Launches Calls for Contributions on Competition in Virtual Worlds and Generative AI (Jan. 9, 2024), https://ec.europa.eu/commission/presscorner/detail/en/ip_24_85, having organized a workshop on the topic on June 28, 2024 and published a policy brief on competition in Generative AI in Sept. 2024.

30 In Sept. 2023, the Autorité de la concurrence (France) conducted inspections at the premises of a company suspected of having implemented anticompetitive practices in the graphics cards sector, more information, *see*, Autorité de la concurrence, Press Release, The General Rapporteur of the Autorité de la concurrence Indicates that an Unannounced Inspection was Carried Out in the Graphics Cards Sector (Sept. 27, 2023),

48. A lot of knowledge[31] has been generated in these areas and efforts have been made to identify the bottlenecks these markets may face.

49. For instance, the EC has launched in January 9, 2024, calls for contributions on the level of competition in virtual worlds (metaverses) and Generative AI. It has also sent requests for information to several large digital players, aiming to identify potential competition issues that may arise in these areas.

50. Overall, there is a strong focus on these markets. Compliance with competition rules minimizes harmful distortions and inefficiencies throughout the value chain, and effective monitoring and enforcement are essential to maintain competition.

V. Conclusion

51. Competition promotes positive outcomes and helps to realize the potential of the markets. It aims to prevent unduly distortions of the market dynamics, allowing businesses to grow and consumers to benefit from the best and most innovative products.

52. Effective competition will ensure that Generative AI markets are accessible and contestable, contributing to fully realize the potential of Generative AI and promoting its deployment across all sectors of the economy to the benefit of consumers. These markets require the right incentives, for instance by preventing foreclosure.

53. Competition authorities are vigilant and aware that competition is a driving force for the innovative and equitable development of Generative AI. In addition, the current regulatory framework also covers these concerns.

---

https://www.autoritedelaconcurrence.fr/en/press-release/general-rapporteur-autorite-de-la-concurrence-indicates-unannounced-inspection-was. Furthermore, after the Bundeskartellamt, which declared that the cooperation between Microsoft and OpenAI was, at the moment, not subject to merger control in Germany – *see*, Bundeskartellamt, Press Release, Cooperation between Microsoft and OpenAI Currently Not Subject to Merger Control (Nov. 15, 2023), https://www.bundeskartellamt.de/SharedDocs/Meldung/EN/Pressemitteilungen/2023/15_11_2023_Microsoft_OpenAI.html, the European Commission verified whether this Microsoft's investment would be reviewable under the EU Merger Regulation.

31 *See*, OECD, R*ecommendation on Artificial Intelligence 2019*, https://legalinstruments.oecd.org/en/instruments/oecd-legal-0449 (last visited Oct. 21, 2024), as well as OECD AI Policy Observatory and the OECD Artificial intelligence papers, https://www.oecd-ilibrary.org/science-and-technology/oecd-artificial-intelligence-papers_dee339a8-en (last visited Oct. 21, 2024). Moreover, *see*, World Economic Forum, *Artificial Intelligence as a Driving Force for the Economy and Society* was one of the four main themes from the World Economic Forum annual meeting, https://www.weforum.org/events/world-economic-forum-annual-meeting-2024/themes/artificial-intelligence-as-a-driving-force-for-the-economy-and-society/ (last visited Oct. 21, 2024). *See also*, IMF, *Artificial Intelligence: What AI Means for Economics*?, Fin. & Development (Dec. 2023), https://www.imf.org/en/Publications/fandd/issues.

Digital Markets Act and Services of Artificial Intelligence

Andreas Schwab*
European Parliament

I. Introduction

1. The famous scientist Stephen Hawking once said: "Success in creating effective AI could be the biggest event in the history of our civilization. Or the worst. We just do not know… Unless we learn how to prepare for, and avoid, the potential risks…".

2. One potential risk that is to be considered here could be the fact that services of artificial intelligence are not covered with the Digital Markets Act (DMA).[1] This is dangerous as the newly created regulation to deal with the fast-moving digital markets and their special risks of monopolies could fall apart when AI is used. And this even though the European Union embraced recently for a special law on artificial intelligence[2] to show to the world that we know how to deal with AI.

---

* Andreas Schwab is a Member of the European Parliament and a member of the European People's Party. He is the Chair for the Delegation for Northern cooperation and for relations with Switzerland and Norway and to the EU-Iceland Joint Parliamentary Committee and the European Economic Area (EEA) Joint Parliamentary Committee. He is also a member of the Committee on the Internal Market and Consumer Protection and a substitute for the Committee on Economic and Monetary Affairs.

1 Regulation (EU) 2022/1925 of the European Parliament and of the Council of 14 September 2022 on contestable and fair markets in the digital sector and amending Directives (EU) 2019/1937 and (EU) 2020/1828 (Digital Markets Act) [2022] OJ L265/1.

2 In March 2024, the European Parliament after reaching the agreement with the Council (trilogues) in December, adopted the AI Act's final text, European Parliament, "Artificial Intelligence Act: MEPs adopt landmark law" (13 March 2024) <www.europarl.europa.eu/news/en/press-room/20240308IPR19015/artificial-intelligence-act-meps-adopt-landmark-law> accessed 29 September 2024.

3. We do not explore here how the new law wants to ensure the respect of the rule of law and the full-scale application of fundamental rights when systems of artificial intelligence are brought into action. It is important that the new EU Artificial Intelligence (AI) Act aims to ensure safety, legal certainty and respect for fundamental rights.[3] The introduction of obligations based on the risks of different AI systems and establishment of efficient, but non bureaucratic governance structures for oversight and enforcement is the right way forward.

4. The question that has to be focussed on in this chapter is the economic consequences of artificial intelligence when AI is integrated into commercial systems. Therefore, it is about competition policy and AI. In this respect, it is noteworthy that Ursula von der Leyen, the President of the European Commission, underlined in September 2023[4] that the "DSA (Digital Services Act) and DMA are creating a safer digital space where fundamental rights are protected. And they are ensuring fairness with clear responsibilities for big tech. This is a historic achievement – and we should be proud of it. The same should be true for artificial intelligence.... But we also should not underestimate the very real threats". It's clear that the EU cares about the fundamental rights and rules and standards for both AI developers and users for "high-risk AI systems" (ie those that could have a significant impact on the rights and safety of people) as much as about economic power concerns.

II. AI is Penetrating Our Daily Life: What is at Stake

5. Rightly so, we are living in a world where AI is about to become an integral part of our daily lives, influencing various aspects of our society. Most recently the availability of large language models (LLMs) like ChatGPT has received a lot of attention, although the use of AI has long since penetrated not only into the use of everyday objects such as household appliances, cars, etc. but also in traditional public goods and services such as transport, healthcare, finance, public office services, etc. The use of AI makes these sectors "digitalised", with higher efficiency, automation and data-driven decision-making.

6. However, while there are many advantages to AI driven services, there can be no doubt about the concerns of this technology, especially from the antitrust point of view. First of all, its development requires access to three main components: computational resources, machine learning models and, of course, a database that only a few tech companies can provide. Therefore, different

---

3 Regulation (EU) 2024/1689 of the European Parliament and of the Council of 13 June 2024 laying down harmonised rules on artificial intelligence and amending Regulations (EC) No 300/2008, (EU) 167/2013, (EU) 168/2013, (EU) 2018/858, (EU) 2018/1139 and (EU) 2019/2144 and Directives 2014/90/EU, (EU) 2016/797 and (EU) 2020/1828 (Artificial Intelligence Act) [2024] OJ L series.

4 Margrethe Vestager Speech, "2023 State of the Union Address" (13 September 2023) <https://ec.europa.eu/commission/presscorner/detail/ov/speech_23_4426> accessed 30 September 2024.

partnerships between model developers and large cloud computing providers are emerging. This has then raised the debate on the concentration of resources for AI development resting in the hands of a few big tech companies; that may foster competition, but it could also lead to problematic practices such as tying.[5] Moreover, it may create barriers to access to this technology by smaller market players (SMEs and start-ups) but in particular, the risk of control remaining in the hands of a few large private players.

7. This leads to the need for regulation to avoid abuses of power and a weakening of our democracies. On this basis, early in 2024 the Commission launched two calls for contributions on competition in virtual worlds and generative artificial intelligence (AI) in order to assess the competition levels in these domains and to ensure market competitiveness.[6]

8. The need to regulate the risks that arise from these innovative and transformative opportunities potential of advanced AI systems[7] was also highlighted in the statement of the Hiroshima AI Process. This has led to the publication of the International Guiding Principles of the Hiroshima Process for Organisations Developing Advanced IA Systems and the International Code of Conduct of the Hiroshima Process for Organisations Developing Advanced IA Systems.[8] These initiatives will complement the rules contained in the regulation of the AI Act in the European Union.

9. Finally, the question remains as to which tool can be used to better tackle the behaviour of those (big) tech companies leading the innovation and development of the AI systems on the market and related competition concerns. Indeed, the complexity of AI may make it even more difficult to understand the logic of "self-preferencing" or "log-in-effects" that are characteristic of market dominance under Articles 101 and 102 TFEU. Much of the legal, political and ethical debate concerning AI has focused on the AI Act and its AI liability provisions, but I will explain here why the more comprehensive and effective regulatory constraints for this technology is contained in the DMA.

III. The Economic Logics of Digital Markets

10. The DMA as an ex-ante regulatory instrument aims to curb the market dominance or market power of large online platforms also known as gatekeepers for a more competitive and fairer market access. Therefore, the impact of

---

5 See the Partnership between Open AI and Microsoft, which at the moment is under scrutiny by the Commission.

6 See <https://ec.europa.eu/commission/presscorner/detail/en/ip_24_85>

7 "G7 Leaders' Statement on the Hiroshima AI Process" (30 October 2023) <www.mofa.go.jp/files/100573466.pdf> accessed 30 September 2024.

8 European Commission, "Hiroshima Process International Guiding Principles for Advanced AI System" (30 October 2023) <https://digital-strategy.ec.europa.eu/en/library/hiroshima-process-international-guiding-principles-advanced-ai-system#:~:text=Hiroshima%20Process%20International%20Guiding%20Principles,system%20%7C%20Shaping%20Europe's%20digital%20future> accessed 30 September 2024.

the DMA on AI systems is likely to be quite evident, as this regulation not only offers competitive opportunities in the market but also shapes the way gatekeepers and their competitors deal with AI systems.

11. It is sufficient to mention the provisions explicitly and specifically those regulating ranking and other gatekeeper AI applications. Given the importance of these applications for the development and implementation of gatekeeper technology, the rules and obligations contained in Articles 5, 6 and 7 of the DMA, will have an impact on the core systems of the digital economy.

12. Three of the main concerns that the DMA is addressing are: (1) self-preferencing; (2) data sharing; and (3) non-discrimination. All these three elements are basic principles of, among others, the rules laid down in Articles 5, and 6 of the DMA resulting from the many previous protracted EU competition law cases against the largest tech companies. These elements consist of a catalogue of proven anticompetitive practices that are automatically no longer permitted. In particular these rules will have an impact on the use and exploitation of certain services offered by big techs (or gatekeepers) based on artificial intelligence applications.

IV. Has the DMA Missed Out AI?

13. Although the specific term "artificial intelligence" is actually absent from the entire legislation text, the DMA focuses on regulating the use of data by gatekeepers and concerns about market concentration. The general approach of Article 2(2) DMA with so-called "core platform services" (CPS) allows the addition of new services if companies create a "new" service systemic tool.

14. Emerging generative AI models have already raised the question of whether this can be considered and then added as a CPS under the DMA. Their inclusion in the DMA would require a deep market investigation by the European Commission, and the collection of enough evidence before considering legislative changes to be proposed to the Parliament and the Council. However, before proceeding to analyse this option in detail, we need to assess whether the DMA already has an impact on this technology. In this regard, there are three areas in the DMA that would regulate certain AI systems: rules for fair ranking setting; information and transparency requirements for advertising; and data access and exploitation.

1. Fair Ranking Settings Article 6(5)

15. Indeed, ranking has become a prevalent aspect of users' lives, practically influencing their choices, especially in the digital realm, where online providers compete for consumer attention through the importance they attach to their offers and the way they present and organise search results. The large digital platforms therefore play an intermediary role in helping users

navigate this landscape of information and choice by sorting and prioritising the multitude of offers. In essence, ranking acts as the engine room of this new digital economy, shaping the demands, search habits and purchasing decisions of individuals.

16. Not surprisingly, many tech giants have diverted their business models towards ranking, using this as a key element of their competitive advantage. This advantage is even more pronounced when these entities not only act as intermediaries but also directly offer certain services or products, a concept known as vertical integration.

17. This dual role has long given gatekeepers the power to manipulate ranking in their favour, putting competitors at a disadvantage and distorting fair competition by engaging in the anticompetitive practice known today as self-preferencing.

18. Article 6(5) DMA has introduced a fundamental regulation of artificial intelligence-based rankings. This provision is probably one of the most comprehensive measures aimed at regulating applications of artificial intelligence by gatekeeper companies. It consists of three key elements:

   - Preventing self-preference: the gatekeeper is prohibited from giving preferential treatment to its own products or services in a ranking by including, thanks to the Parliament, also indexing and scanning, a broader scope than initially proposed by the Commission.

   - Transparency requirement: ranking must comply with a general transparency requirement.

   - Fairness and non-discrimination: ranking must also be fair and non-discriminatory (FRAND conditions).

19. In summary, Article 6(5) of the DMA establishes an articulated framework for regulating AI-based ranking, addressing issues of self-preference, transparency and fairness in the context of gatekeeper companies.

2. Data Access

A. *Data Access and Exploitation: Article 5(2)–6(2)*

20. Another area where the obligations of the DMA will have a significant impact on the way gatekeepers and their competitors can develop and use AI concerns restrictions on the use of specific datasets for their own purposes, particularly in the context of the development, training, validation and testing of AI models:

   - Article 5(2) DMA introduces several provisions on the cross-use of end-users' personal data. This restriction includes approaches such as "federated learning", in which data remain formally separate, but the resulting information is aggregated into a single AI model.

- Article 6(2) DMA introduces the corresponding prohibition on corporate user data (personal and non-personal), which is specifically aimed at gatekeepers. Indeed, gatekeepers may not use data (that are not already publicly accessible) that compete with corporate users and that the corporate users themselves or their end-users have generated or provided in the context of the core services of the platform. Consequently, for the first time, this restriction prevents the use of end-user or corporate data for AI-based inferences and prohibits its use in competition with corporate users.

B. *Access for Third Parties to Gatekeeper Data Sets: Articles 6(10)–6(11)*

- Article 6(10) DMA concerns the possibility of access to data provided or generated in the context of the use of gatekeepers' platform services. In this context, artificial intelligence could be particularly useful for predicting demand and optimising product design.
- Article 6(11) DMA remedies one of the most important search engine problems. Indeed, the quality of a search engine is mainly determined by the results provided. In particular, search engine operators are given the right to access gatekeeper data sets that operate the search engines themselves.
- Access to this classification, query, click and display data is to be provided according to the FRAND terms, which have already been outlined above, again with the aim of enabling business users to optimise their artificial intelligence models.

21. In addition, Article 6(11) DMA also stipulates that all personal data included in the classification, query, click and visualisation data must be offered anonymously. Consequently, it will be necessary for gatekeepers to use strong, state-of-the-art anonymisation strategies to comply with the requirements of the DMA and the GDPR.[9] Since, however, even strong anonymisation requires that a fair amount of data be removed or modified in the existing set, such measures may also lead to a reduction in the value of the dataset for AI training purposes. Thus, it is likely that gatekeepers will simply have to provide largely modified and anonymised datasets with limited practical use. As technology advances, however, so does the need for gatekeepers to provide datasets that are not only anonymised but also performance enabling through new state-of-the-art systems.

---

9 Regulation (EU) 2016/679 of the European Parliament and of the Council of 27 April 2016 on the protection of natural persons with regard to the processing of personal data and on the free movement of such data, and repealing Directive 95/46/EC (General Data Protection Regulation).

3. Transparency Requirements for Advertising Articles 5(9)–5(10) and 6(8)

22. These two articles concern obligations for gatekeepers in the advertising sector:

- Article 5(9)–(10) DMA imposes an obligation on gatekeepers to provide, upon request, the parameters used in the calculation of prices, commissions and fees for individual advertisements to both advertisers and publishers. This requirement is intended to promote price transparency and enable a fair comparison of offers between competing platforms. The world of advertisement and e-commerce encompasses a multitude of different parameters and companies are constantly striving to optimise these due to the significant impact on their business models.
- It is crucial to recognise that this disclosure obligation has substantial implications for gatekeepers, particularly given the very rapid and automated determination of advertising prices through real-time auctions supported by complex algorithms or machine learning techniques. Consequently, this obligation indirectly encourages gatekeepers and advertising technology networks to use explainable artificial intelligence systems, considering their importance in complying with the Regulation.
- Article 6(8) DMA likewise requires gatekeepers to disclose to advertisers and publishers the tools used to evaluate advertising performance. In cases involving artificial intelligence systems, these tools often include performance metrics such as predictive accuracy. In conclusion, given the critical role of AI applications in gatekeeper businesses, this regulation is expected to have a profound impact on the fundamental systems of the digital economy.

23. Finally, AI technology plays a central role in several operations such as search engines, language translation or interactive voice assistance that entails competitive advantage of the big platforms. These platforms rely on ranking and scoring models to offer customers customised lists of items in response to specific queries, attracting customers and advertisers. The success of these platforms therefore depends on the quality of the product offered, based on using advanced artificial intelligence models to effectively respond to queries. With the roll-out of a better cloud infrastructure and a growing number of high-speed processors in mobile technology, the big platforms will improve their services in an AI customised manner.

24. The DMA therefore stands as the tool by which to address all issues of market power and fairness, as it is the first case of explicit and precise regulation of services used by gatekeepers.

4. A Specific Provision for AI?

25. With the DMA we therefore have a powerful tool that can fully integrate AI services in a way to makes fair competition a reality in platforms with huge underlying data sets.

26. As gatekeepers are beginning to move into the area of generative AI applications, where generative AI is offered as a basic platform, the European Commission has to follow suit and act accordingly. As we saw, in some cases, some generative AI applications may indirectly fall under the purview of the DMA when gatekeepers incorporate own or third-party generative AI into their core platform services. Indeed, the Regulation already contains some provisions for specific CPS that apply artificial intelligence technologies.

27. However, the DMA's obligations for gatekeepers may not apply to their generative AI offerings when they are offered as stand-alone platform services. In this case the DMA offers in Article 19, a procedure for market investigation to evaluate the option to create a further CPS in Article 2(2). This would require the presentation of a legislative proposal that would amend the DMA Regulation. In this regard, Andreas Mundt spoke out in 2023, in favour of adding generative AI as a basic platform service in the Digital Markets Act.[10]

28. In the meantime, there are two potential short- medium-term solutions:

    - The newly emerging AI-based services could initially be included within the definition of other category of CPS, like the general category of online intermediation services or virtual assistants: this latter in particular draws interest when dealing with LLM machines as ChatGPT is at the moment. In fact, if we look at the definition of this category of SPC in Article 2 DMA, it states: "'virtual assistant' means a software that can process demands, tasks or questions, including those based on audio, visual, written input, gestures or motions, and that, based on those demands, tasks or questions, provides access to other services or controls connected physical devices". In this regard, the Commission may be interested in conducting a deep assessment.

    - For the most obvious cases where AI has an ancillary function to existing platform services, the Commission may adopt delegated acts that allow extension of the scope or to specify the modalities of implementation of the obligations set out in Articles 5, 6 and 7, as provided in Article 12 DMA. However, this mechanism, although flexible and faster, in the case where the AI application has a completely autonomous and separate platform function from those already listed in Article 2(2) DMA, can only be used as a short- to medium-term solution.

---

10 Ian Brown and Douwe Korff, "Data Protection and Digital Competition" (20 July 2023) <www.ianbrown.tech/2023/07/20/1426/> accessed 29 September 2024.

29. In this regard, the DMA proves to be a flexible and future-proof tool that offers an opportunity to address and deepen competitiveness and fairness issues of generative AI by, for example, considering adding specific AI software as new integral platform services and identifying certain developers as the new emerging gatekeepers. This option is functional for several reasons: not only does it imply an in-depth investigation of this new emerging market, but it also offers the possibility of addressing the challenges of this new technology in a proper and prompt manner, without jeopardising from the start the proper functioning of digital markets.

V. Conclusions

30. In conclusion, the Digital Markets Act stands out as the most effective legislative instrument currently available to regulate the growing development of generative AI in the market. This is especially significant given that the major developers of generative AI technologies are precisely the tech companies designated as gatekeepers under Article 3(2) DMA. The DMA's relevance is underlined by the limitations of traditional competition rules, which primarily offer an ex-post assessment of how operators exploit these technologies. Such rules fall short in addressing the proactive regulation required to navigate the complexities of AI development.

31. Moreover, the AI sector is still in its early stages, making it difficult to regulate comprehensively through a single piece of legislation such as the proposed AI Act. The DMA, however, provides a more adaptable and immediate framework. It is designed to tackle the substantial influence exercised by these powerful digital platforms right from the outset, ensuring that their control does not stifle competition or innovation.

32. By imposing obligations on gatekeepers, the DMA mitigates the risk of monopolistic practices and promotes a level playing field for emerging and smaller players in the AI market. It ensures that these dominant platforms cannot unfairly leverage their position to hinder the growth and development of new technologies. This proactive approach is crucial in maintaining a dynamic and competitive environment where innovation can flourish.

33. In essence, the DMA not only addresses current market imbalances but also anticipates future challenges in the digital landscape. Its enforcement mechanisms and regulatory oversight provide a robust safeguard against potential abuses of power by gatekeepers. By doing so, the DMA ensures that the development of generative AI remains aligned with the principles of fairness and competition, ultimately fostering a more innovative and equitable market for all stakeholders.

Competition and Regulation in Digital Markets – Key Considerations and Principles

KRISZTIAN KATONA*
Computer & Communications Industry Association (CCIA), Washington, DC

I. Introduction

1. In recent years, competition has become one of the most hotly discussed and debated areas of public policy and law enforcement globally. Much of the debate has focused on competition in digital or connected markets, with numerous articles, conference panels, studies, reports, and policy initiatives examining whether the existing tools are sufficient to address enforcement and policy challenges in these markets. Importantly, a key focal point of discussion has become whether regulation is necessary in the digital economy, and if so, what would be the right balance between ex-post competition enforcement and ex-ante regulation?

2. As competition agencies, regulators, and policymakers are actively considering ex-ante regulatory proposals for digital markets worldwide, it is worth noting how regulations may lead to intended but also unintended consequences that may significantly affect businesses, consumers, and the broader economy. Hence, before implementing any new regulation, it is paramount to closely examine the market characteristics and understand whether regulation would correspond to

---

* Krisztian Katona is Vice President of Global Competition and Regulatory Policy at the Computer & Communications Industry Association (CCIA) in Washington, DC. Prior to his current position, he served at the Federal Trade Commission (FTC) for fifteen years, including as Counsel for International Antitrust and as an attorney in the agency's Technology Enforcement Division.

the needs and priorities of a particular economy. With policy objectives such as promoting competition and innovation now intertwined with much broader and often moral goals such as fairness and equity, creating the right equilibrium between ex-ante regulation and ex-post competition enforcement may be a particularly delicate and challenging exercise for policymakers.

3. Why is competition so crucially important in the digital economy, and how can antitrust agencies and policymakers ensure that they continue to foster competition and innovation without curbing these vital policy objectives? This chapter will focus on these important questions by presenting an overview of the competitive dynamics in global digital markets and discussing principles that can be useful for legislators and regulators worldwide as they consider regulatory proposals in this area. Specifically, the chapter will explain: (i) the global digital regulatory context; (ii) the potential impact of digital regulation on the broader economy; and (iii) key principles that should be considered before implementing any ex-ante regulation.

II. The Global Digital Regulatory Context

4. Competition policy does not exist in a political vacuum. This is particularly true when one surveys recent international developments in the digital economy. Reviewing the complex interrelationship of competition and regulation in digital markets, it is fundamental to understand the global context and closely study the experience of jurisdictions that have been debating and considering new tools in this area, which also include ex-ante regulatory frameworks. Additionally, when examining international regulatory dynamics and convergence/divergence in digital markets, it is important to note how the regulated companies are often global, whereas regulators and competition agencies, as well as the laws and rules they apply, are national. This discrepancy and potential fragmentation of regulations is particularly significant amid current political sentiments of deglobalization and a heightened focus on national interests. Many national regulatory proposals are in response to broader political objectives and centrifugal forces, such as national technological sovereignty efforts, and the increased focus on national interests has resulted in policymakers coming under significant pressure to develop national digital programs and agendas.

5. In recent years, we have seen important digital competition and regulatory developments in a number of countries worldwide. These developments include regulatory and legislative reforms in some jurisdictions, such as the European Union's Digital Markets Act (DMA),[1] but also important

1 Regulation (EU) 2022/1925 of the European Parliament and of the Council of Sept. 14, 2022 on contestable and fair markets in the digital sector and amending Directives (EU) 2019/1937 and (EU) 2020/1828 (Digital Markets Act), 2022, O.J. (L 265) 1, https://eur-lex.europa.eu/legal-content/EN/TXT/?uri=uriserv%3AOJ.L_.2022.265.01.0001.01.ENG&toc=OJ%3AL%3A2022%3A265%3ATOC.

proposals and debates on this topic in countries such as Australia, Japan, Turkey, and South Africa.[2] However, even though there are different ex-ante digital regulatory proposals contemplated in a number of jurisdictions, so far, only two countries have actually created a new and fully operational ex-ante digital regulatory framework: Germany, through the 10th amendment of the German Competition Act (GWB)[3] and Section 19a of the GWB that went into effect in January 2021,[4] and the EU, where the DMA has been operational since March 2024.[5] In addition, the UK recently adopted the Digital Markets, Competition and Consumers Act (DMCCA),[6] and the Japanese Diet passed the Act of Promotion of Competition for Specified Smartphone Software,[7] both of which are expected to become fully operational in the near future.

6. Even though digital reforms are being considered in various countries, and some of them may be inspired by the EU's DMA,[8] there is no blueprint for jurisdictions that are contemplating these types of regulations. In fact, some national digital bills have just been proposed and have a long way to go to become law, if they go through the legislative process in the first place. For example, the US antitrust bills targeting a handful of technology companies, which were introduced during the previous Congress, raised numerous substantive concerns and do not seem to have political support to be adopted.[9] Other regulatory models, for example the UK's DMCCA and the proposals

---

2 *See, e.g.*, ACCC, Australia's Media and Digital Platforms Mandatory Bargaining Code, https://www.accc.gov.au/by-industry/digital-platforms-and-services/news-media-bargaining-code/news-media-bargaining-code (last visited Oct. 30, 2024); Japan's Ministry of Economy, Trade and Industry (METI), Japan's Transparency and Fairness Act, https://www.meti.go.jp/english/mobile/2021/20210423001en.html (last visited Oct. 30, 2024); Competition Commission of South Africa, Provisional Report of the Market Inquiry on Online Intermediation Platforms (2022), https://www.compcom.co.za/online-intermediation-platforms-market-inquiry-provisional-report/; Turkish Competition Authority, Draft Bill to Amend the Turkish Competition Law, https://www.rekabet.gov.tr/Dosya/sektor-raporlari/e-pazaryeri-si-raporu-pdf-20220425105139595-pdf (last visited Oct. 30, 2024).

3 See, *10th Amendment to the German Competition Act (GWB)*, 2021 Fed. L. Gazette 1 (Jan. 18, 2021), https://www.bgbl.de/xaver/bgbl/start.xav#__bgbl__%2F%2F*%5B%40attr_id%3D%27bgbl121s0002.pdf%27%5D__1730284105460.

4 *Id.* at § 19a ("The Bundeskartellamt may issue a decision declaring that an undertaking which is active to a significant extent on markets within the meaning of Section 18(3a) is of paramount significance for competition across markets.")

5 *Supra* note 1.

6 UK Government, Press Release, UK's Digital Markets, Competition and Consumers Act Receives Royal Assent (May 2024), https://www.gov.uk/government/news/digital-markets-competition-and-consumers-act-receives-royal-assent.

7 Japan Fair Trade Commission, Press Release, Regarding the Passage of the Act of Promotion of Competition for Specified Smartphone Software (June 12, 2024), https://www.jftc.go.jp/en/pressreleases/yearly-2024/June/240612.html#:~:text=As%20smartphones%20rapidly%20spread%20and,as%20%22Specified%20Software%22.

8 *See, e.g.*, Brazilian Government, *Brazil's Ministry of Finance Presents Proposals to Improve Competition Defense in the Digital Platform Environment*, (Oct. 10, 2024), https://www.gov.br/fazenda/pt-br/assuntos/noticias/2024/outubro/ministerio-da-fazenda-apresenta-propostas-para-aprimorar-a-defesa-da-concorrencia-no-ambiente-de-plataformas-digitais.

9 *See, e.g.*, Krisztian Katona, *AICOA's Data Security, Privacy, and Content Moderation Issues Call for Risk Assessment*, Project DisCo (June 7, 2022), https://project-disco.org/privacy/060722-aicoas-data-security-privacy-and-content-moderation-issues-call-for-risk-assessment/; see also, *AICOA's Failure and the Future of Competition Policy in Congress*, Project DisCo (Jan. 6, 2023), https://project-disco.org/competition/010623-aicoas-failure-and-the-future-of-competition-policy-in-congress/.

currently discussed in Australia, may introduce potential codes of conduct for companies.[10] Some commentators have highlighted that these models could potentially provide a more flexible and tailor-made regulatory approach; however, they also raise significant concerns regarding the regulator's overly broad authority.[11] Japan provides another international model by adopting its so-called Transparency Act in 2020,[12] which stipulates that designated digital platforms must take voluntary and proactive steps to ensure transparency and fairness under a so-called co-regulatory approach. All these international examples show that there is no one-size-fits-all digital regulation, even after the important question of whether regulation is actually *needed* in a particular country or economy.

7. Zooming in on the EU's experience with the DMA, it is important to consider that although its objective is to ensure that "markets, where gatekeepers are present, are and remain contestable and fair," it is also true that the effectiveness of the DMA as an innovative institutional experiment "hinges on the law's internal consistency and its application by the Commission in the years ahead."[13] In other words, the capacity of the DMA to effectively transform the digital market landscape still needs to be proven. Therefore, there is much less clarity about what the DMA would mean in practice, what practical results are expected from it, what would be considered success, and what its intended and unintended consequences will be down the road years from now, in addition to the numerous implementation challenges and expected litigation.[14] Despite this, many jurisdictions have been debating how to introduce ex-ante regulations for digital markets, some of which seem at least partially inspired by the DMA.

8. In this regard, it is important to consider some regulatory examples and historical lessons from other countries, including the United States' experience with the Interstate Commerce Commission (ICC) and the Civil Aeronautics Board's (CAB) regulatory experience in the transportation sector, which illustrate how *not to* regulate.[15] These regulations were brought under the concept of "fairness" and "non-discrimination," but it is widely accepted that, in fact, they distorted competition, reduced economic efficiency, and harmed the very

---

10 *See, e.g.*, CCIA, *Comments on the Australian Treasury's Consultation Document on the Australian Competition and Consumer Commission's Regulatory Reform Recommendations*, (Feb. 17, 2023), https://ccianet.org/wp-content/uploads/2023/02/CCIA-Comments-to-the-Australian-Treasury.pdf.

11 *See, e.g.*, CCIA, Press Release, CCIA Comments on the United Kingdom's "Digital Markets, Competition, and Consumer Bill" (July 18, 2023), https://ccianet.org/news/2023/07/ccia-files-comments-on-proposed-uk-regulation-regarding-competition-in-digital-markets/.

12 METI, Act on Improving Transparency and Fairness of Digital Platforms, (June 3, 2020), https://www.meti.go.jp/english/policy/mono_info_service/information_economy/digital_platforms/index.html.

13 Victor Oliveira Fernandes, *Lost in translation? Critically Assessing the Promises and Perils of Brazil's Digital Markets Act Proposal in the Light of International Experiments*, 52 Comput. L. & Sec. Rev. 105937 (2024), https://www.sciencedirect.com/science/article/abs/pii/S0267364924000049?via%3Dihub.

14 *Id.*

15 Jeffrey N. Shane, *The New DOT Takes on Transportation Regulatory Policy*, (Oct. 1980), https://www.transportation.gov/sites/dot.gov/files/docs/50/308721/regulatory-era.pdf.

consumers they were supposed to protect.[16] Now, the US experience with the ICC and CAB brings forward a few important lessons. First, provisions that sound simple in theory, such as a "fairness" or "non-discrimination" requirement, rarely prove simple in practice.[17] Second, effective regulation requires clarity, particularly regarding the three main questions of "what," "why," and "how." Specifically, "what" is the problem? Is there a systemic market problem that needs to be addressed? Then, "why" is this proposal the best way to solve it? And "how" may an agency regulate – and how may it not? This kind of clarity is needed not just at the outset, but also over time, as quickly changing market circumstances may lead to unintended consequences.[18]

9. Therefore, considering that ex-ante digital regulations are still being tested, avoiding rushing to adopt reforms reflecting international regulatory experiments and allowing some time to gauge how those are working or whether the reforms are harming consumers and innovation seems to be the best choice for a number of jurisdictions.[19] Given the extremely limited experience with these regulations, it is recommended for policymakers across the globe, particularly in emerging markets, to first learn from the experience in other jurisdictions and assess the more concrete results of those regulatory experiments. This, in turn, may help to inform some of the proposals and determine whether these regulatory examples could be applicable and even useful to adopt in other jurisdictions.

III. The Potential Impact of Ex-Ante Digital Regulation on the Economy

10. Ex-ante regulation may have a major impact on a country's consumers, entrepreneurship, and its broader economy. Overly complex, intrusive, or broad regulatory regimes are likely to deter entry and investment from companies, thereby significantly impacting competition.[20] Therefore, any ex-ante regulation

16 *See* Christine S. Wilson, *The Growing Nostalgia for Past Regulatory Misadventures and the Risk of Repeating These Mistakes with Big Tech* (2019), https://www.ftc.gov/news-events/news/public-statements/growing-nostalgia-past-regulatory-misadventures-risk-repeating-these-mistakes-big-tech.

17 *See* Christine S. Wilson, *Free Markets, Regulation, and Legislation: A Place for Everything, and Everything in Its Place* (2020), https://freestatefoundation.org/wp-content/uploads/2020/03/FTC-Commissioner-Christine-Wilson-Address-to-FSF-031020.pdf.

18 *Id.*

19 *See, e.g.*, Taiwan Fair Trade Commission, Press Release, White Paper on Competition Policy in the Digital Economy (2022), https://www.ftc.gov.tw/internet/english/doc/docDetail.aspx?uid=1942&docid=17352; Competition and Consumer Commission of Singapore, *Revised Guidelines on the Competition Act 2004* (2022), https://www.cccs.gov.sg/media-and-consultation/newsroom/media-releases/cccs-revises-competition-guidelines-for-greater-clarity-and-guidance.

20 *See, e.g.*, Philippe Aghion, Antonin Bergeaud & John Van Reenen, , *The Impact of Regulation on Innovation* (Banque de France, Working Paper No. 804, Jan. 16, 2023), https://papers.ssrn.com/sol3/papers.cfm?abstract_id=4325116; OECD, *Regulatory Reform and Innovation*, https://www.oecd.org/en/topics/policy-issues/regulatory-reform.html (last visited Oct. 30, 2024); William D. Eggers et al., *Regulation that Enables Innovation*, (Mar. 23, 2023), https://www2.deloitte.com/us/en/insights/industry/public-sector/government-trends/2023/regulatory-agencies-and-innovation.html.

needs to be introduced to address specific market failures, which is not the same as the mere existence of market power. Dynamic competition, which is particularly relevant in digital markets, comes forth as a natural way to resolve market failures by firms competing for the market and creating new and innovative products.[21]

11. Ex-ante regulation may very likely result in companies ending up investing less in their own research and R&D, potentially leading to a decrease in innovation expenditure in the impacted economy. Studies have found that the policy discussions around the DMA largely ignored competition and innovation models.[22] As a result, this type of ex-ante regulation could have larger spillover impacts on the broader economy, thereby potentially hurting employment, wages, and productivity.[23]

12. Looking further at the potential implications of ex-ante approaches to regulating the digital economy, this could also cause over-enforcement of competition laws by restricting a series of business practices (including bundling, tying, and self-referencing, among others) that are commonly found both offline and online, and that are often procompetitive or at least competitively benign.[24] This could significantly impact competition and innovation in the digital economy.

13. Therefore, when considering the impact of digital regulation on businesses, it is critical for policymakers to consider how the proposed additional costs of operation might hinder innovation and competition in a country's start-up ecosystem, and what the regulatory proposal's potential impact would be on digital businesses that have been able to thrive in an environment without this regulation in recent years.[25] In addition, it is important for policymakers to think more broadly and consider what an ex-ante regulation's impact would be on consumers and small and medium-sized businesses (SMBs) that have benefitted from the targeted digital products and services.

14. In addition, any country contemplating digital regulation should keep in mind that there is global competition for investment. Companies want to operate in jurisdictions and economies with transparent, predictable, and principle-based regulatory environments, without extreme regulatory obligations and excessive

---

21 Joseph A. Schumpeter, Capitalism, Socialism, and Democracy 81 (1942).

22 *See, e.g.,* Meredith Broadbent, *Implications of the Digital Markets Act for Transatlantic Cooperation*, CSIS (Sept. 15, 2021), at 6, https://www.csis.org/analysis/implications-digital-markets-act-transatlantic-cooperation; David J. Teece & Henry J. Kahwaty, *Is the Proposed Digital Markets Act the Cure for Europe's Platform Ills? Evidence from the European Commission's Impact Assessment*, BRG (Apr. 12, 2021), at 47, https://www.thinkbrg.com/insights/publications/digital-markets-act-eu-impact-assessment/.

23 *See* David J. Teece & Henry J. Kahwaty, *Is the Proposed Digital Markets Act the Cure for Europe's Platform Ills? Evidence from the European Commission's Impact Assessment*, BRG (Apr. 12, 2021), at 6.

24 *See, e.g.,* Felipe Florez Duncan, *How Platforms Create Value for Their Users: Implications for the Digital Markets Act*, Oxera (May 12, 2021), https://www.oxera.com/insights/reports/how-platforms-create-value/; D. Bruce Hoffman & Garrett D. Shinn, *Self-Preferencing and Antitrust: Harmful Solutions for an Improbable Problem*, (June 2021), https://www.clearygottlieb.com/-/media/files/cpi--hoffman--final-pdf.pdf; Sam Bowman & Geoffrey A. Manne, *Platform Self-Preferencing Can Be Good for Consumers and Even Competitors*, (Mar. 4, 2021), https://truthonthemarket.com/2021/03/04/platform-self-preferencing-can-be-good-for-consumers-and-even-competitors/.

25 *See, e.g.,* Sofia Kilmar & Guilherme Ribas, *Internet Regulation – Legislative Proposals in Brazil*, IBA (July 24, 2023), https://www.ibanet.org/internet-regulation-legislative-proposals-in-Brazil.

operating expenses.[26] If the compliance obligations involve significant fixed costs, then the effect of the regulation could be to create a moat around incumbent companies – this would reduce entry and startup activity, while also increasing costs for incumbents. This, in turn, could potentially decrease incumbent investment in R&D,[27] which may have a significant impact on the regional and global export competitiveness of national companies as well.

IV. Principles that Should Be Considered Before Implementing Ex-Ante Regulation

15. Global digitalization across numerous industries has provided consumers and businesses with tremendous benefits. Several studies have confirmed the many ways in which digital services and multi-sided business models create and stimulate competition in the economy. For example, the European Commission has stated that "alternative online distribution models such as online marketplaces have made it easier for retailers to access customers. By using these third-party platforms, small retailers may, with limited investments and effort, become visible to potential customers and sell products to a large customer base and in multiple Member States."[28] Platforms may also help their users create value through bundling and tying of different features and services. This, in turn, helps boost the efficiency of a market by reducing transaction costs, increasing choice for consumers, and helping businesses to achieve scale economies.[29]

16. Given the dynamic and innovative nature of digital markets, when proposing a digital regulation policymakers need to consider the wider potential implications for businesses, consumers, innovation, and the broader economy. Recognizing that an overly burdensome and heavy-handed regulation could significantly hinder innovation and economic growth, taking into consideration the following principles is crucial when designing any regulation for digital markets.

1. Cost and Benefit Analysis

17. Due to the significant economic impact of regulating digital markets, it is crucial for legislators and policymakers to engage with stakeholders in the development of any proposal for a new ex-ante regulatory regime.

---

26 *See, e.g.,* Christian M. Dippon & Matthew D. Hoell, *A Quantitative Evaluation: The Economic Costs of Structural Separation, Line of Business Restrictions, and Common Carrier Regulation of Online Platforms and Marketplaces*, CCIA (Mar. 18, 2022), https://ccianet.org/wp-content/uploads/2022/06/platform_regulation_quantitative__03_18_23.pdf; Engine and CCIA Research Center, *Tools to Compete Lower Costs, More Resources, and the Symbiosis of the Tech Ecosystem*, CCIA (Jan. 25, 2023), https://ccianet.org/research/reports/tools-to-compete/.

27 *Id.*

28 *See* European Commission, *Staff Working Document: Evaluation of the Vertical Block Exemption Regulation* (Sept. 8, 2020), at 32, https://competition-policy.ec.europa.eu/public-consultations_en.

29 Duncan, *supra* note 24.

Introducing new regulations is not costless, especially given the dynamic and innovative nature of digital markets. As a result, the ultimate objective of any new regime should be to promote and stimulate competition and innovation.

18. As the Organisation for Economic Co-operation and Development (OECD) and the International Competition Network (ICN) have underscored, to ensure that the cost of any new regulation does not outweigh its benefits, it should allow clearly procompetitive or competitively benign conduct, and recognize justifications for legitimate protections.[30] Without appropriate safeguards, a regulation may harm consumers and businesses, including SMBs that use and rely on digital services. Therefore, it is important for policymakers to thoroughly assess a regulatory proposal's potential impact, and whether the benefits of a proposed ex-ante digital regulation would outweigh its potential negative impact on consumers, businesses, and the broader economy.[31]

2. Balancing Competition Enforcement and Regulation in Digital Markets

19. Before contemplating an ex-ante regulation for digital markets, it is crucial to assess whether current enforcement and policy frameworks, including those for competition, consumer protection, and data privacy already offer more suitable methods to accomplish the desired policy goals.

20. Ex-ante regulation for digital markets, in the absence of a specific market failure that requires correction, would hinder not only the growth of companies in the digital and connected markets, but would also harm innovation and the competitive ecosystem, and thereby the overall economy.[32] Importantly, regulation of specific markets of the economy should only be considered when there is evidence of a sector-specific market failure that harms competition.

---

30 OECD Global Forum on Trade, *Key Issues in Digital Trade 2023*, at 13, https://www.oecd-ilibrary.org/trade/key-issues-in-digital-trade-review_b2a9c4b1-en#:~:text=Digital%20Trade%20Review-,OECD%20Global%20Forum%20on%20Trade%202023%20%E2%80%9CMaking%20Digital%20Trade%20Work,speed%20up%20the%20green%20transition. (last visited Oct. 30, 2024); OECD, *Maintaining Competitive Conditions in the Era of Digitalization*, (July 2018), at 4, https://www.oecd.org/en/about/oecd-and-g20.html; ICN Advocacy Working Group, *Framework of Competition Assessment Regimes*, (Apr. 2015), https://www.internationalcompetitionnetwork.org/wp-content/uploads/2018/09/AWG_FrameworkCompetitionAssessmentRegimes.pdf.

31 *See* OECD, Regulatory Policy Outlook (2021), https://www.oecd.org/en/publications/2021/10/oecd-regulatory-policy-outlook-2021_c5274577.html; OECD, Regulatory Impact Assessment (2020), https://www.oecd.org/en/publications/regulatory-impact-assessment_7a9638cb-en.html.

32 OECD, Directorate For Financial and Enterprise Affairs, Competition Committee, *Ex-Ante Regulation and Competition in Digital Markets*, (Dec. 2, 2021), Note by BIAC at 4, https://one.oecd.org/document/DAF/COMP/WD(2021)79/en/pdf; Badri Narayanan & Hosuk Lee-Makiyama, *Economic Costs of Ex-Ante Regulations*, ECIPE (Oct. 2020), https://ecipe.org/publications/ex-ante/; Fed. Trade Comm'n, Broadband Connectivity Competition Policy Staff Report 9 (June 2007), https://www.ftc.gov/sites/default/files/documents/reports/broadband-connectivity-competition-policy/v070000report.pdf (advising that "[i]n evaluating whether new proscriptions are necessary, we advise proceeding with caution before enacting broad, ex-ante restrictions in an unsettled, dynamic environment.").

3. Evidence-Based Approach

21. Finally, it is extremely important to review evidence and past experience and focus any proposed regulation on conduct that is demonstrably harmful to competition, rather than seeking to address theoretical or speculative harm. This would risk overregulation that could be particularly harmful to innovation and a country's start-up ecosystem. Now, clearly identifying the desired outcomes of any new regulation is a key element in determining policy goals. It is important to analyze to what extent any new regulation is directed towards the general purpose of competition – that is, promoting efficiency and consumer welfare. If there are economy-wide harms, they are better addressed by economy-wide reforms, rather than digital-specific regulation.

V. Conclusion

22. Legislators and policymakers across the globe should carefully examine the potential consequences of digital regulation and take into account the global and regional context to ensure that any regulatory proposal would align with the specific needs and priorities of their national economy. Importantly, promoting competition should remain the key policy objective in digital markets and the broader economy. A few jurisdictions, including Germany and the EU, have introduced ex-ante digital regulatory frameworks while other countries are debating and discussing similar proposals. While these frameworks, including the DMA, generally aim to foster fairness and contestability, they are still largely experimental, with their long-term effectiveness and impact on competition yet to be determined. Therefore, policymakers should carefully analyze the potential costs and benefits of digital regulation, while making sure that any regulatory proposal would address market issues specific to their own country's digital markets without implementing overly broad and complex regulatory regimes that risk deterring investments and stifling innovation. Furthermore, it is paramount to adopt an evidence-based approach since rushing to implement international regulatory experiments without thoroughly analyzing their suitability for the national market could lead to unintended economic consequences.

Opening Up Social Networks: Thinking Beyond the Current Framework

JEAN CATTAN*
French Digital Council

I. Opening Up Digital Spaces: The Historical Context and Role of Public Authorities in Digital Openness

1. When the Internet first arrived in our homes, it amazed us because it opened the door to many possibilities we thought were impossible, things we hadn't even thought of. These wonders are the result of several factors: open and decentralised protocols, but also a regulatory framework that allowed innovation. Let's not forget how much the emergence of a commercial internet is linked to the regulatory framework set up both in the United States and in Europe. Openness is not self-evident: public authorities open up ecosystems that otherwise tend to close off.

2. This was already the case with telecommunications networks. Public authorities intervened to open them up to third parties so that they could provide us with alternative phones, boxes, better customer services and much more affordable commercial offers. Then we identified internet service providers as undue gatekeepers, blocking innovation on markets such as VoIP, peer-to-peer and so many other services that could mobilise some additional bandwidth. This is what net neutrality is about. Public authorities make sure that telecom operators do not stifle innovation. Meanwhile, the European Commission has taken

* Jean Cattan, Secretary General of the French Digital Council.

action under competition law to open up the browsing market to competition. All this means that saying that the digital ecosystem is based on openness is partly true and partly false. True, the protocols tend towards and enable openness. But many predatory behaviours take place on this basis, and each time it is really up to the public authorities to ensure this openness remains.

3. Once the net neutrality guidelines were adopted at the European level, France's Electronic Communications, Postal and Print media distribution Regulatory Authority (Arcep) pushed the open internet philosophy one step further. If such logic were to be imposed on internet service providers, then it had to be extended to operating systems such as iOS and Android because they were the real access controllers. four years later, the European institutions put the Digital Markets Act (DMA) on the table, six years later this was adopted, and eight years later circumventing the AppStore is now deemed to be fully legit. This is the point of the whole story of European digital regulation: to ensure the openness of networks, devices, platforms, and markets.

4. The challenge at this stage is to know to what extent the DMA will achieve its objectives. This is a question that has been discussed at length since the start of the negotiations and one that will essentially be resolved in the ongoing implementation phase. The first steps seem shaky, but the task is significant. The European Commission opens a path that is likely twenty-five years long. As of today, we may regret that the text does not leave more room for national authorities to set priorities together and pool their analytical strengths. We may regret that it does not deal with business models as such, that it does not create a real capacity to understand the economic value of things and therefore what is at stake between the actors. But much will evolve as we move forward. Above all, the Commission is learning a new role as a market regulator, whereas so far it has just been the regulator of national regulators. In doing so, we shall make sure that it harnesses the power of national authorities and external groups. Let us ensure that it adopts the open and democratic regulatory model that will be needed while it is reshaping the global economy on a grand scale.

II. The One Thousand and One Possibilities Offered by the Opening of Social Networks

5. This brings us to the specific challenge of adapting the regulatory framework to the closed nature of certain digital ecosystems, particularly social networks. If we look closely, social networks are one of the few digital ecosystems that are completely closed to outside innovation. The fact that anyone can innovate on top of something else is what makes the digital economy so rich and wonderful. However, the current landscape of social networks paints a different picture. Here, innovation is stifled, confined to the whims of a few dominant players, often manifesting as mere imitation rather than genuine novelty. The vibrant innovation by the multitude is conspicuously absent. While it exists

in marginal social networks, it is notably absent in the dominant ones, each operating as a closed monopoly, entrapping its community.

6. The societal impact of current social network dynamics cannot be overstated. These platforms often find themselves precariously balancing the promotion of potentially harmful content with their moderation. The Digital Services Act (DSA) is a step towards ensuring this balance favours users' interests, marking a significant shift from a landscape of self-regulation to one underpinned by legislative oversight. Yet, relying solely on social networks for a variety of solutions is a narrow approach compared to the breadth of possibilities that could arise from a society-wide contribution. There lies a glaring missed opportunity to unlock a spectrum of innovations, thereby enhancing our collective ability to address these challenges effectively. Imagine a scenario where third-party entities could offer diverse curation and moderation solutions and enable users to tailor their online experience more precisely:

   – These solutions could range from integrated options within the application, akin to the Bluesky initiative that permits the use of alternative recommendation algorithms developed by users.

   – They might also include browser plug-ins that offer similar functionalities on a more experimental basis currently (see the Tournesol plugin or Youchoose). However, it is crucial to extend these innovations beyond legal uncertainty and into the mobile sphere, where most digital interactions occur.

   – Consider Mastodon, with its open code, its decentralised architecture, and its public open API fostering a thriving ecosystem of third-party applications. Open APIs were once a feature of platforms like Reddit and Twitter, but with the advent of generative AI technologies, there has been a trend toward restricting access through APIs.

   – Looking ahead, we must contemplate the evolving role of conversational agents such as ChatGPT. Could they become our primary interface with social networks and other digital services? Figures like Bill Gates believe this to be our future trajectory, a path arguably paved by OpenAI's GPT models. Technologies like Perplexity, focusing on specific sources such as YouTube and Reddit, and Large Action Models, enable this technical feasibility. The question remains: at what economical cost?

III. Social Interactions in the Age of Conversational Agents and Their Regulatory Implications

7. This very last evolution presents a mosaic of solutions to the plethora of challenges we face in our digital social spheres. In the future, content moderation might not just be a service provided by the networks themselves but could

be customised by users through simple, plain-text commands in one single conversational agent. Imagine being able to set specific content boundaries for a teenager across various platforms, or to filter out toxic content, or explore content popular among different political spectrums. The possibilities are as limitless as our imagination. Furthermore, this approach could address the overwhelming nature of endless scrolling, shifting the power from corporate algorithms to individual choice. Users would no longer be passive recipients of an unending stream of content, but active curators of their digital experiences. These perspectives make the DSA remediation tools look considerably pale and limited.

8. From an economic perspective, opening up social networks to external innovation could catalyse the growth of numerous markets. However, their potential is yet to be fully comprehended since these markets are still subject to social networks' monopoly (eg moderation on Twitter is a potential market, over which Twitter still exercises a monopoly). Currently, markets for services like moderation and curation are undeveloped, largely because social networks are viewed as monolithic entities, whereas in reality, they are aggregations of various functions. They pretend to be a whole, but they are only a sum. And in this case, the whole is certainly not greater than the sum of its parts. By not diversifying these functions, we are missing out on the wealth that could be generated in these markets.

9. Even social networks themselves could benefit from external contributions, similarly to how Apple thrived by leveraging the value created by others – without any abuse this time. This situation mirrors the unbundling of telecom networks, where incumbent networks were not just opened to competitors but were also subjected to a set of conditions, including technical and economic ones such as a monthly payment per line. This regulatory framework aimed to transform former monopolies into market leaders, fostering a competitive and innovative environment. And it worked.

10. Regulation in this context turns into a day-to-day exercise, as evidenced by the ongoing discussions about unbundling tariffs, even two decades after these regulations were adopted. For social networks, particularly as they shift from advertising to subscription-based models, setting fair transaction prices for users and third-party access becomes essential. This is the moment for public authorities to turn into market designers, and to assert users as clients, enjoying the freedom to choose from a wide range of external innovations.

11. Just as in the telecom sector, these potential social and technical benefits cannot occur without regulatory intervention. Beyond privacy and security, economic regulation is key to facilitating this transformation. If we envision conversational agents providing tailored access to social network content, an openness principle must be enforced. Conversely, to ensure the long-term prosperity of social networks, there must be a fair distribution of wealth along the value chain, achieved through a clear understanding of money flows, potentially a price-setting mechanism and a dispute resolution system. This aligns

with Maria Luisa Stasi's thesis: *Social media markets: A pro-competitive approach to free speech challenges*, that economic regulation can significantly enhance social regulation.

IV. Building Economic Regulation Starts with a Good Understanding of the Economic Landscape

12. As Joëlle Toledano suggests, the foundation of this forthcoming regulation would be a system that discerns the valuable from the non-valuable. Currently, our insights are predominantly based on data from large companies, with limited objective evidence. The interactions between the press and generative AIs are quite eloquent. Whilst Axel Springer negotiates with OpenAI for millions, the *New York Times* sues the firm for billions, and some others seek the right to opt-out. Before that, Reddit and Twitter limited the capacity of OpenAI to use their content by raising the fees of their APIs. The problem may be that some social networks or firms will provide access to their resources to some or one single AI creating new vertical silos. While this might be acceptable in contexts like football broadcasting rights, the stakes are considerably higher when it involves social networks, the press and the broader economy. To avoid a siloed economic structure, we must set a goal of general interconnection, necessitating a deep understanding of what holds value and what does not.

V. Navigating Current Legislative Frameworks: Is the Ark Definitely Lost?

13. What is the way forward, considering the existing legislative framework? We have several key texts at our disposal: the DMA, DSA, Data Governance Act, Data Act, and the Artificial Intelligence (AI) Act. However, none of these provide a comprehensive framework for opening up social networks. This oversight might stem from the fact that the social network issue has primarily been viewed through a societal lens, while the emergence of third-party applications in 2023 and generative AI at the end of 2022 has shifted the landscape.

14. The AI Act, for instance, does not provide any economic framework beyond the protection of intellectual property and the basic disclosure of resource usage. As to openness, it does not consider it as a goal. It simply sees open source as an exemption mechanism. Chapter 2 of the Data Act, conversely, focuses on data produced by connected products and does not cover any other intermediaries of the digital economy. It is a missed opportunity: this chapter of the Data Act provides the best framework so far to put the right

price on data to be shared among economic actors. Opening up its scope to data providers such as social networks would be a good solution. However, we cannot expect such a review before 2028.

15. The Data Governance Act offers a framework for data intermediation services but stops short of facilitating interconnection between different data sources, such as those of social networks and third-party applications. Besides, the European legislator remains faithful to the goodwill of data intermediaries where we need constraint.

16. The Digital Services Act introduces measures compelling very large online platforms, including dominant social networks, to mitigate systemic risks and provide a recommender system that is not based on profiling. However, these requirements fall short of the broader freedom and openness that is essential for a truly dynamic digital ecosystem. It barely scratches the surface of what could be achieved. A more visionary approach would be for the European Commission to consider including in Article 35 of the DSA remedies for the enablement of user-designed recommendation algorithms and the modification of terms of service to facilitate the integration of third-party applications. In its resolution on addictive interfaces from December 2023, the European Parliament invited the European Commission to examine the conditions for opening social networks. We can only wish that the European Commission's interpretation of Article 35 is in line with this encouragement.

17. Such a proactive stance would significantly enhance user agency and diversify the digital experience. However, a key limitation lies in the Commission's current lack of authority to impose specific remedies, except in urgent scenarios involving serious harm to end-users. This constraint reflects a broader issue with the DSA's underlying philosophy: it is more focused on making platforms accountable rather than cultivating the "wealth of networks".

18. The DSA's view of social networks as closed systems is a missed opportunity. By not fully embracing the potential for openness and innovation, the DSA limits how digital platforms can evolve and respond to user needs. If the DSA were to expand its scope to actively promote the integration of third-party services and user-generated content and algorithms, it could pave the way for a more adaptable, user-responsive and innovative online environment. Such changes would not only enhance user experience but could also spur new forms of digital creativity and entrepreneurship, enriching the digital economy as a whole.

VI. Evaluating the DMA's Potential Role in Social Network Innovation: Too Close to Fail

19. Last chance, in the DMA we find provisions that go in the right direction, but they will not enable us to fully exploit the potential of opening up social networks nor in ensuring that generative AI reaches its full potential. First of

all, the companies involved are not the right ones. We want to open up social networks but only a very small number of these are covered by the DMA. Regarding the obligations under the current framework, they do not align either with the goal of opening up social networks.

20. However, there is significant potential in the current obligations if they were to be further extended under the 2026 review mechanism or through the adoption of delegated acts (Article 12 DMA) at the initiative of either the European Commission (Article 19 DMA) or three Member States (Article 41 DMA). A prime example is Article 6.4, which, with a strategic amendment, could have far-reaching implications for social networks. Presently, the first phrase of this article mandates that:

> "The gatekeeper shall allow and technically enable the installation and effective use of third-party software applications or software application stores using, or interoperating with, its operating system and allow those software applications or software application stores to be accessed by means other than the relevant core platform services of that gatekeeper".

21. By simply integrating "social network" into this phrase, just after the reference to "operating system" we could catalyse a transformative change in the digital landscape.

22. This amendment would not only facilitate a diverse ecosystem of third-party applications tailored for social networks, each offering a unique array of features, but it would also pave the way for the innovative use of conversational agents and social networks. By doing so, we could open up a realm of possibilities where social networks are no longer monolithic, closed systems but vibrant, adaptable platforms. They would become spaces where creativity and technological innovation could flourish, driven by a multitude of contributors. This approach aligns with the broader vision of digital openness and user empowerment, significantly enhancing user choice and experience in the digital sphere.

23. Article 6.9 DMA framework offers promising avenues in terms of real-time data portability. It mandates that:

> "The gatekeeper shall provide end users and third parties authorised by an end user, at their request and free of charge, with effective portability of data provided by the end user or generated through the activity of the end user in the context of the use of the relevant core platform service, including by providing, free of charge, tools to facilitate the effective exercise of such data portability, and including by the provision of continuous and real-time access to such data".

24. This opens up exciting possibilities for third-party applications and conversational agents to access and utilise users' data in real-time. The focus should be on ensuring that the data available for portability is comprehensive and useful to the user. The next step should be to allow live data exchange with

the social network and not just the extraction of data from the social network. But this would mean imposing a form of interoperability that is not yet considered at this stage.

25. Article 7 DMA , which addresses the interoperability of online messaging services, hints at future expansion to include social networks in its 2026 review. However, the proposed interoperability is horizontal, focusing on cross-platform compatibility, rather than vertical, which would facilitate deeper integration and interaction with other types of players such as conversational agents. This distinction is vital, as vertical interoperability would allow for a more integrated and seamless user experience, promoting a richer and more diverse digital ecosystem.

26. Finally, Article 6.12 DMA, at first glance, appears to provide an appropriate framework for equitable access to social networks. It states: "The gatekeeper shall apply fair, reasonable, and non-discriminatory general conditions of access for business users to its software application stores, online search engines and online social networking services listed in the designation decision pursuant to Article 3(9)." However, a closer examination reveals a significant shortfall. Rather than ensuring that third-party companies can interact with social networks without discrimination, it is primarily focused on preventing discriminatory practices in publications, advertisements and application offerings. To truly unlock the potential of social networks and foster a more innovative landscape, the term "access" should be redefined as encompassing not just non-discriminatory practices in content and app offerings, but also the ability for third-party applications and services to interact directly with social network platforms.

27. Such a clarification or expansion in the legislation would bridge a significant gap, moving us closer to achieving genuine interoperability within social networks. It would enable a richer array of services and applications to flourish, ultimately enhancing user choice and fostering an environment ready for digital and social innovation. The goal should be to transform social networks from closed systems into open platforms where diverse applications and services can integrate seamlessly, creating a more vibrant digital ecosystem.

Competition Policy in the Digital Era*

DAVID BAILEY**
King's College London

1. *The Economist* has described digital data as the world's most valuable resource. Data is valuable for all of us as individuals and as consumers; it is valuable for businesses in terms of developing ever-more personalised advertising; and it is also valuable for societies as we seek to improve our understanding of the world around us. Not only is data inherently valuable, it is also voluminous. It has been predicted that the volume of data created will reach 180 zettabytes in 2025. Hence, the term "big data".

2. The value, size and use of data creates challenges and opportunities for competition policy. On the one hand, the virtue of digital data is its ability to help firms to develop new and better products, and to improve their "value proposition", since it can be tailored to the preferences of different consumers. On the other hand, the vice of digital data, especially big data, is that it may tip the market in favour of one firm that holds a genuine stranglehold over the market and makes it more difficult for new entrants to emerge.

3. Underlying this debate about virtues and vices is a profound disagreement about the likelihood of anti-competitive consequences and the risks of misdiagnosis. Those who advocate a much more restrained application of the competition rules maintain that the risks of anti-competitive outcomes are exaggerated, not least because the market will likely correct most short-term distortions. As one might expect, the advocates of a more interventionist approach under EU competition law and policy take issue with each of these points. They argue that the risks of anti-competitive foreclosure are significant

* This article has been previously published in Concurrences, and it might have been edited for clarity and cohesion. David Bailey, Competition policy in the digital era, February 2018, Concurrences N° 1-2018, Art. N° 85712.

** Visiting Professor, King's College London.

and the costs of permitting such conduct outweigh the costs of any constraint upon firms with substantial market power.

4. One way to examine the "virtuous" or "vicious" nature of digital data and cyber competition is by reference to two cases – a merger case and an abuse of a dominant position case – in the ICT sector. Both cases concerned the well-established theory of "leveraging" market power from a dominated market to a closely related market.

I. *Microsoft/LinkedIn*: Conglomeracy in the Digital Era

5. In 2016 Microsoft paid $26 billion to acquire LinkedIn. The purchase price was not for capital, brands or intellectual property. Rather, it was for user data and its revenue-earning potential. What is of interest for present purposes is the European Commission's investigation of a theory that the *Microsoft/LinkedIn* merger might have anti-competitive conglomerate effects. The Commission found that Microsoft/LinkedIn would have the technical ability and commercial incentive to pre-install LinkedIn with its ubiquitous Windows operating system. At the time of the merger, Microsoft had a market share of some 80%–90% of PC client operating systems in Europe, and 90% of productivity software solutions (i.e., Office). The Commission also found that this behaviour would be likely to significantly impede effective competition due to powerful network effects. Put shortly, the more professionals that use LinkedIn, the more valuable it becomes to other members of LinkedIn and the more attractive it becomes to non-members of LinkedIn. The Commission's concern was that a tipping point might be reached, where other competing professional social networking platforms would be unable to match the data-driven, competitive advantage of the merged firm. In the end, however, the merger was cleared because Microsoft gave behavioural remedies that promised not to do the very things that the Commission was worried about.

II. *Google Shopping*: Leveraging Market Power in the Digital Era

6. In June 2017 the Commission imposed a €2.42 billion fine on Google for giving its comparison shopping service an illegal advantage on its search engine results pages. Specifically, Google was found to have systematically given prominent placement to Google Shopping, its own comparison shopping service, while simultaneously demoting competing comparison shopping services in its search results. The decision has been appealed to the General Court of the European Union, and gives rise to a myriad of interesting questions.

One such question is the theory of harm that underpins the Commission's decision. In the absence of a public version of the decision, it appears that four theories might explain the decision.

7. The first is that Google's behaviour was not deemed not to be competition on the merits. As a general proposition, this conveys the sense of competition by reference to the "normal" parameters of price, quality and innovation that characterise competition in an unconcentrated market. Ultimately, however, the concept of "competition on the merits" may be too nebulous to provide an adequate explanation for the outcome of the case, and, in particular, does not explain how to deal with a dominant firm that may be dominant precisely because there are economic advantages to its scale which it would be counterproductive to require them to forego.

8. A second explanation of the Commission's conclusion is to characterise Google's conduct as being discriminatory, a theory and practice that applies as much in the offline as in the online worlds. The trouble with that explanation is discrimination might represent the malign exercise of market power, but, equally, it can represent the optimal way of recovering the firm's investment in the capital required to supply a product or service. Moreover, a theory of harm based on discrimination might imply that there is a duty on dominant firms not to discriminate at all, which could inhibit welfare-enhancing behaviour. From a consumer welfare perspective, discrimination has ambiguous effects; it cannot be classed as invariably good or bad.

9. A third theory of harm might be that the *Google Shopping* case is all about access to Google's flagship product: www.google.com. If that is right, then the Commission would have to show that Google's search engine is "indispensable" for comparison shopping services. The Court of Justice defined "indispensability" narrowly in *Bronner*, specifying that one would only exist where access to the facility is essential to an ability to compete on the secondary market and it is uneconomic to duplicate that facility. That definition reflects a policy concern that any refusal to supply an "essential facility" should be condemned with caution to avoid creating disincentives to investment. The Commission's Press Release does not refer to the decision treating Google's search engine as an essential facility, but this issue may be an important part of Google's appeal to the General Court.

10. A fourth and final explanation of the *Google Shopping* case might be the principle emanating from the Court of Justice's judgment in *Télémarketing*. That principle is that it is an abuse for a dominant firm to seek to reserve a secondary market to itself, and it might be suggested that Google had reserved the comparison shopping services market for itself. This is received wisdom in Europe, although it attracts criticism from those commentators who believe that it is based upon mistaken theories that a monopolist is able to increase its monopoly profit by extending the monopoly to a secondary market and, in doing so, sacrifices the dominant firm's legitimate objective to maximise the efficiency of its activities.

III. Conclusion

11. The publication of the non-confidential version of the Commission's decision in *Google* is eagerly awaited. In the meantime, there appears to be a compelling case for timely and judicious intervention under the competition rules in the digital world. There is also an urgent need to learn about what firms are doing online, how they distribute their products, which business models they choose, which is something the Commission did in its *E-commerce* sector inquiry.

12. The Commission's final report on that sector inquiry is essential reading for anyone interested in the evolution of online distribution and the way it is changing distribution systems and vertical restraints. It shows that it can sometimes be useful to listen and learn first, before deciding whether and when enforcement is appropriate. In the final analysis, it will be fascinating to see whether or not the digital world will be characterised by Joseph Schumpeter's "perennial gales of creative destruction" or will end up being dominated by a few, digital monopolies.

Are Market Investigations a Suitable Tool for the Analysis of Digital Markets?*

Alejandra Palacios Prieto
University of Southern California (USC)

1. This is a question that many competition authorities from different jurisdictions around the world and some competition experts are currently trying to answer. In fact, a salient discussion within the antitrust community around this question is related to the proposal to create the "new competition tool" by the European Commission,[1] as part of the search for a market analysis tool that allows an effective and timely enforcement intervention against the structural problems that the digital economy presents.[2]

2. In Mexico, market investigations are established in Article 94 of the Competition Law. Drawing from COFECE's experiences conducting market investigations, an exhaustive analysis of this tool was carried out by a small task force within the Commission to answer this specific question. My conclusion is that market investigations indeed could be effective in addressing the competition challenges that the digital era has brought to competition authorities, albeit with some challenges.

---

* This article has been previously published in Concurrences, and it might have been edited for clarity and cohesion. Alejandra Palacios Prieto, Are market investigations a suitable tool for the analysis of digital markets?, February 2021, Concurrences N° 1-2021, Art. N° 98391.

1 According to the European Commission, the new competition tool constitutes one of the three pillars through which more effective competition in the digital ecosystem is sought. When this text was being elaborated, the tool was in process of being issued. See https://ec.europa.eu/competition/consultations/2020_ new_comp_ tool/index_en.html.

2 As has been widely discussed, digital markets are often characterized by strong economies of scale and scope due to low production cost of digital services and the large number of customers served. Moreover, they are often multiple-sided and have strong network externalities, meaning that a digital technology will become more popular and convenient as more individuals use it. In addition, data collection and processing capabilities of a digital technology provide a digital supplier with a substantial competitive advantage.

3. This affirmation derives from three reasons. First, because of the intrinsic characteristics of our market investigations, it is possible to address structural competition problems that prevent a market from functioning properly. Second, this tool effectively allows for more holistic analyses, taking into account that the functioning of the market is explained not only by the behavior of the market players but also by other factors such as the behavior of consumers, as well as regulatory aspects. And third, the specific circumstances of digital markets that facilitate a dynamic that derives in market concentration, as well as a rapid decrease in competition, could be addressed with the type of remedies that this enforcement tool enables.

I. Article 94 of the Competition Law

4. COFECE's market investigations empower us to determine the existence of barriers to competition and to eliminate them, or the existence of an essential facility and to regulate its access.

5. Regarding barriers to competition, Article 94 allows the Commission to impose two types of remedies. First, there are behavioral remedies, which oblige economic agents to act in a specific way or to stop acts that distort the competitive process. There are also structural remedies, which allow modification of the structure of a market with the objective to create or restore competitive conditions. Moreover, we can also issue non-binding recommendations to authorities of any level of government to eliminate the regulatory barriers identified in a market investigation.

6. We can also determine the existence of essential facilities and, if deemed necessary, establish rules for their access and use by other economic agents when their existence is determined as a result of the market investigation.

7. Due to the aforesaid characteristics, Article 94 constitutes a hybrid competition and regulatory tool with the advantage that it allows to conduct a thorough market assessment employing all the Commission's investigative tools (among which are forensic analysis, screening, onsite searches, requests for information, depositions and international cooperation with other competition authorities). It also allows us to impose appropriate remedies even though competition problems are not directly related to traditional anticompetitive conducts.

8. Furthermore, this is a tool that is not intended for sanctioning anticompetitive practices carried out by an economic agent in particular, but rather to identify behavioral and structural problems present in the investigated market, and to order their correction through various remedies, including regulating the access to an essential facility.

II. COFECE's experience in market investigations

9. Thus far the Commission has opened seven market investigations into: (i) slot allocation at the Mexico City airport; (ii) local freight transportation in Sinaloa; (iii) barley production and distribution for beer factories; (iv) port services and transportation for bulk grains in Puerto Progreso in the state of Yucatan; (v) distribution and transportation of unprocessed milk in Chihuahua; (vi) norms and standards for evaluation of conformity assessment; and (vii) card payment systems.

10. Of these, three cases were closed by the Commission (barley, norms and standards, and port services) and one is still ongoing (payment systems). The cases related to freight transportation and milk determined that the competitive process was flawed because of the existence of regulatory barriers. In both cases, we issued non-binding recommendations to the local authorities in order to eliminate these barriers. In these cases, we learned that if we identify in advance that the main anticompetitive effects derive from regulatory barriers, and that the likely result of the market investigation will solely involve non-binding recommendations for public authorities to amend those regulations, then the outcome will be the same as our non-binding opinions. Hence, it does not make sense to devote too many enforcement resources to these types of cases.

11. Other salient experience we had with this tool derived from the airport slot allocation case, where we determined the existence of an essential facility. This case generated important lessons related to the Commission's scope to regulate access to an essential facility, since the Judiciary interpreted that COFECE's powers to regulate access to essential facilities have limits in the presence of a sectoral regulator, in this case the aeronautical authorities of the country. However, this judiciary precedent is not mandatory as case law. Additionally, as in other countries, no regulatory body for the digital economy exists in Mexico, so this allows COFECE to exercise its powers related to regulatory measures for essential facilities in said markets.

12. On the positive side, the experience with this tool has shown us that we are able to conduct deeper analyses of market structures, bringing to light elements which hinder competition but are usually unnoticed in the investigation of anti-competitive practices. Among these elements are behavioral biases, practices which affect competition but are not included in the Mexican catalogue of abuse of dominance practices, use of personal information, and the behavior of other competitors. The analysis of these elements is relevant in digital markets which exhibit characteristics that often result in high concentration, accumulation and control over large volumes of data, strong network effects, bundling of digital products or services, etc.

III. Applying Article 94 in the analysis of digital markets

13. The Commission's experience with market investigations has contributed identifying Article 94 as a possible mechanism for the analysis of digital markets and their intrinsic problems in at least four areas.

14. First, Article 94 facilitates the analysis and correction of behavioral barriers carried out by economic agents that do not necessarily enjoy at the present moment substantial market power, but that participate in markets with characteristics (i.e., network externalities, economies of scale and scope, etc.) that generate competition for the market. In this sense, the international discussion has warned that the intervention of competition authorities through traditional tools could happen too late, when the rest of the potential entrants can no longer compete with the consolidated platforms, even to offer improved or innovative features against dominant economic agents. In the competition jargon, this phenomenon is known as "tipped markets," which favor "winner-take-all" outcomes. Therefore, our market investigation tool can allow us to intervene at an early stage and establish behavioral or structural remedies that promote competitive processes.

15. Second, as I mentioned, Article 94 can also allow us to analyze practices that are not expressly found in the Mexican catalogue of abuse of dominance practices of Article 56 of the Competition Law. Some behaviors that have been identified in the international discussion as potential abuses of dominant position and do not necessarily fit in the list of abuse of dominance practices are self-preferencing or the imposition of abusive contract terms. These are likely to occur when a platform holds a gatekeeper position (that is to say, platforms that have control over distribution and/or entry channels to other lines of business and that benefit from network effects).

16. Third, with the use of Article 94 we could impose structural remedies such as:

    - Interoperability of data and protocols which could occur in different forms. For example, through compatible interoperability for third parties under discriminatory conditions, by making a protocol of one digital platform interoperable for competitors in the market. Or by establishing specific requirements to provide interoperability in relation to specific areas of a business model, and by generating interoperability in various related digital markets.

    - Data portability to allow the migration of each user's data from one platform to another, so it can be reused independently and without losing information previously created.

    - Establishment of codes of conduct applicable to dominant platforms in order to self-regulate the behavior of these agents and prohibit certain conducts (such as self-preferential practices or "abusive" contracts).

- Prohibition of discriminatory treatment or self-preferencing measures which could warrant diverse measures such as the application of an *ex ante* regulation to a vertically integrated digital platform that has a gatekeeper role.
- Divestiture and functional separation of digital platforms that have the ability to exercise market power and distort the competition process.

17. Fourth and last, as already mentioned, this mechanism can allow us to determine whether an economic agent possesses an essential facility and, if deemed necessary, to regulate its access. On the international level, discussions have focused on whether the data or databases in possession of certain economic agents, and even their processing capacity, could be considered as essential facilities. These can generate a competitive advantage that is difficult or impossible to achieve or replicate by their competitors.

IV. Final remark

18. Currently there are very few countries that have mechanisms that, independently of anticompetitive practices, allow to analyze and, when appropriate, correct market structures through remedies that favor the entry of new competitors and generate environments favorable to competition. Iceland, Greece, Mexico, South Africa and the United Kingdom are among the few countries that have mechanisms of this nature.

19. It is interesting to see how the characteristics of our market investigations and our experience with this tool have motivated the international community to turn its attention to the analysis of Article 94 in the search for answers to the question of its suitability to address competition problems arising in digital markets. When this provision was enacted in the 2014 Mexican Competition Act, it was largely criticized by various actors of the competition community. They considered it an unnecessary mechanism because we already had our abuse of dominance enforcement powers and because the Commission was not a regulator.

20. I believe that our experience and the four advantages described above can contribute positively to the international debate, and the accumulated knowledge from this debate will allow us, as a competition authority, to apply this tool in an effective manner. It corresponds to COFECE to assess in detail the application of Article 94 on a case-by-case basis. Our actions most certainly are going to be challenged by the investigated parties in the courts. But new challenges require new methods and new solutions that keep up with the times.

Should Digital Antitrust be Ordoliberal?*

Alexandre de Streel
University of Namur

1. History tells us that the concentration of economic power, what US Supreme Court Justice Louis Brandeis described as the curse of bigness, can be as dangerous as the concentration of political power, leading to social unrest and, if the state does not react appropriately and in a timely manner, to the weakening of liberal democracies or, at worst, the outbreak of wars. History also tells us that at the beginning of each industrial revolution, economic power tends to concentrate among the first few firms that master the new technologies. Indeed today, at the dawn of the fourth Industrial Revolution, few big digital conglomerates have accumulated not just important economic but also informational and quasi-regulatory powers. Europe should be particularly worried because most of those conglomerates are based in the US or in China.

2. As competition policy is one of the most powerful tools for controlling the concentration of private power, it comes as no surprise that there is now a fierce debate among academics on the role of antitrust in digital economy. Some, the neo-Brandeisians, claim that antitrust should go back to its roots and be as forcefully applied against big tech giants as it was against the barons of the second Industrial Revolution. Others, the neo-Schumpeterians, claim that the digital economy is very competitive, with rival products just "one click away" and new invention one garage away, hence markets should be left alone. Many antitrust agencies across the globe have done or commissioned reports on the adaptation of competition policy to the digital era and a consensus is emerging that more intervention is needed.

---

* This article has been previously published in Concurrences, and it might have been edited for clarity and cohesion. Alexandre de Streel, Should digital antitrust be ordo-liberal?, February 2020, Concurrences N° 1-2020, Art. N° 92610, pp. 2-4.

3. This debate is key for competition policy as it questions its fundamentals, in particular its objectives and underlying economic theories. It also goes beyond as *ex post* antitrust intervention is often the prelude to more comprehensive *ex ante* economic regulation. To advance the debate, we should first identify the main characteristics of the digital economy and then reflect on how those characteristics should shape the enforcement of competition law.

4. The characteristics of the digital economy are many and different across business models and digital platforms, but I see at least three characteristics that are key and common to most digital platforms.

   – The first characteristic is the market concentration due to the massive direct and indirect network effects as well as the different data feedback loops. The implications of market concentration on market power should be assessed case-by-case because network and feedback effects may be balanced by multi-homing but, often, the first effects are stronger than the latter. Concentration is horizontal within markets but is also "conglomeral" across markets. Indeed, "conglomeralism" is not a bug but a feature of the digital economy. This can be explained by a combination of supply-side and demand-side effects which reinforce each other. On the supply side, product development is often based on sharable modules, like Lego blocks, that can be used and reused to develop very different products or services. For instance, the same dataset may be reused to develop a search engine, a digital map or an autonomous car. This modular design product development generates economies of scope and reduces the costs of expansion across markets. On the demand side, customers often value the synergies within product ecosystems. For instance, many Apple customers value the smooth and secure interoperability between their iMac, iPad or Apple Watch. Those ecosystem synergies increase the benefits of expansion in different markets. Economies of scope and ecosystem synergies are not new but are very much amplified in the digital economy.
   – The second characteristic of the digital economy is the important and rapid pace of innovation. Most of the digital firms do not compete on the price (and surely not on the monetary price that is often absent) nor even on the quality of existing products and services. They compete on the innovation for the next product or service and, then, on its rapid take-up and scale up to reap the full benefit of the network and feedback effects and win the whole market. This is why the R&D spending ratio of the digital firms are higher than the average in the economy.
   – The third main characteristic is the high level of uncertainty of technology and market evolution. We know that it is difficult to make predictions, especially about the future. This is even more difficult in the digital economy. This is why Andy Grove, the iconic founder of Intel, famously wrote that only the paranoids survive or why Clayton Christensen warns firms about the risk of disruptive innovation. Indeed, digital innovation is not only sustaining within the value network of the

established firms, innovation is often disruptive and takes place outside the established value network by introducing a different package of attributes from the one mainstream customer historically value.

I. The three main characteristics of the digital economy – concentration, innovation and unpredictability – should shape the enforcement of competition policy in the 21st century

5. The relationship between those three characteristics are complex. On one side, the neo Schumpeterians claim that concentration is needed for innovation as it increases the appropriability of its benefits and, in any case, that innovation threat limits the market power effects of concentration. On the other side, the neo Brandeisians claim that concentration may slow down innovation as contestability is needed to stimulate it and that the concentration of innovation is, in any case, detrimental for the economy and the society. This debate, in particular the respective effects of appropriability and contestability, is very difficult to arbitrate, in particular when markets are unpredictable. However, the three main characteristics of the digital markets give some directions for the antitrust objectives, theories of harm, process and remedies in the 21st century.

6. As digital firms mainly compete in innovation, antitrust agencies should mainly aim at maintaining an "*innovation level playing field*" and ensure that a new innovator in a garage has the same chances as the big tech firms to develop and then diffuse her innovation. In other words, markets should remain contestable and contested. In addition, as the results of the digital innovation are often uncertain but also disruptive and unpredictable, agencies should look not only at the innovation outputs (the future products and services) but also at the innovation inputs – what David Teece calls the innovation capabilities. Those capabilities vary across industries and their innovation paths. In digital, they include data, computing power, computing skills or risky and patient capital. Thus, agencies should focus on the firms controlling the digital innovation capabilities and ensure that the key capabilities remain available to all. More controversially, antitrust agencies may also want to ensure a certain degree of diversity in the innovation field as evolutionary economics shows us that diversity may stimulate the level and the resilience of innovation.

7. The antitrust enforcers should then focus their attention on corporate behaviours that try to unlevel the innovation field. This is the case when big firms foreclose or limit access to key innovation capabilities. This was possibly the strategy of Twitter when it limited access to its data to PeopleBrowsr. Or when big firms combine their large users' base and important economies of scope to envelop their efficient but smaller and niche competitors. This may

have been the strategy of Alphabet using Google Search to envelop the competitors of Google Shopping. Or when big firms try to identify their potential competitors when they are small and then, with mergers or acquisitions, kill them while swallowing their innovation. This may have been the strategy of Facebook when it bought WhatsApp.

8. To be meaningful, those antitrust interventions should be sufficiently quick given the rapid pace of innovation and the possible irreversibility of market tipping. There may be a trade-off between the velocity and the quality of the process. To reduce this tension, authorities should increase their expertise and reduce their asymmetry of information vis-à-vis the digital firms. This is why the recent expert reports, the hiring of data scientists and AI experts and the increase transparency imposed by several new regulations, such as the recently adopted Platform-to-Business EU Regulation 2019/1150, are all welcome.

II. As most digital firms compete on innovation, antitrust agencies should maintain an innovation level playing field

9. This is also why a possible resurgence of the interim measures in the wake of the *Broadcom* case should be praised. In fact, the relevant EU rule on interim measures integrates the decision theory framework. Article 8 of Regulation 1/2003 provides that antitrust enforcer should impose interim measures when (i) there is a risk of serious and irreparable harm, i.e., the costs of type II errors (under-enforcement) are high, and (ii) when there is a prima facie case of finding an infringement, i.e., the risks of type I errors (overenforcement) are low. As several recent policy reports have shown, the costs of type II errors may be higher in the digital economy because of the possible irreversibility of market tipping while the risks of type I errors may be lower in the digital economy because of the high market concentration. So applying the legal rule, which is consistent with the insight of the economic theory under uncertainty, may lead to the imposition of more interim measures in the digital sector.

10. However, the most difficult issue for the antitrust enforcer is the choice of the appropriate remedies as the *Google Shopping* case illustrated. The choice of remedies has never been easy but given the rapid and unpredictable evolution of technology and markets as well as high information asymmetry between enforcers and firms, remedies design is particularly complex in the digital economy. This is probably where antitrust enforcers, with the support of the Courts, should be the most innovative. They could innovate in two directions. First, agencies may involve even more the parties, investigated firms and complaints alike, into the design of the remedies. In the same vein, Jean Tirole calls for a more "participatory antitrust". Second, the agencies may experiment different types of remedies and learn by doing. There is an obvious tension

between regulatory experimentation, which is necessary when uncertainty is high, and legal predictability, which is indispensable when a legal instrument is based on open norms and allows extensive remedies. Experimentation leads to long term benefits when the best solution is found but entails transitory costs until the solution is found. To reduce those transitory costs, experimentation may be limited to remedies which are behavioural (as they in general less costly for firms than structural remedies) and which have been co-designed with the parties involved. In any case, in the digital sector, behavioural access remedies are often preferable to structural separation remedies because the former keep the benefits of the economies of scope on the supply-side and ecosystem synergies on the demand-side.

11. In brief, contemporary antitrust should aim at ensuring innovation level playing field and possibly diversity. Agencies should focus on corporate behaviours that try to unlevel the innovation field by foreclosing access to key innovation capabilities, enveloping efficient but smaller and niche competitors or killing young potential competitors while swallowing their innovation. Agencies should do that quickly, when justified by imposing interim measures. Moreover, they should be more participatory and experimental in their remedies design.

III. As digital innovation is often unpredictable, the best objective for the antitrust agencies is to protect the competitive process

12. That leads us to a more fundamental question; what should be the normative framework for antitrust intervention in an economy that is more concentrated, innovative and unpredictable? The ordo-liberalism developed in the thirties by the Freiburg School as a reaction against the concentration of economic and political power in the Nazi Germany, may be a good place to start. Ordo-liberalism is not monolithic and has evolved over time but one of its main insights is the need to promote the competitive process and to protect the rivalry between firms. When competition in innovation is based on rivalry and future is very difficult to predict, it is probably better to pursue the competitive process as an objective in itself instead of focusing on the efficiency outcome. Uncertainty inevitably implies that competition authorities will make mistakes. Those should be minimized but, as puts by Jean Tirole, we should err on the side of competition. So yes, I suggest that the goal of competition policy in the digital era should have an ordo-liberal flavour and protect, as such, the competitive process and firms rivalry.

Reinforcing the Digital Markets Act: Merger Control and Structural Remedies*, **

Jens-Uwe Franck and Martin Peitz
University of Mannheim

1. Around the globe, there is growing discomfort about the market position of some large digital players that serve as matchmakers and gatekeepers, controlling entire ecosystems. In Europe and the U.S., "Big Tech" is associated with the names of Google (Alphabet), Amazon, Facebook (Meta), Apple, and Microsoft – now widely famous under the acronym "GAFAM" – and possibly a few others. Those Big Tech players are accused of, among other things, foreclosing or absorbing potential competitors, erecting barriers to entry, leveraging their entrenched market positions, and exploiting users. While the immediate effect of their actions on consumers is often difficult to assess, the claim is that there is long-term harm to innovation and consumers.

2. The European Commission has proposed the Digital Markets Act (DMA, COM(2020) 842 final) as a regulatory tool that is meant to complement EU competition law to guarantee contestable digital markets. However, from a policy point of view, self-restriction to behavioural remedies in competition law and merger control, as well as the focus on behavioural *ex ante* regulation via the DMA, is at best a half-hearted and at worst a misguided way to effectively address the Big Tech challenge.

---

* An earlier version of this opinion piece appeared as a blog entry on verfassungsblog. de. Jens-Uwe Franck has advised the German Federal Ministry for Economic Affairs on issues related to the DMA.

** This article has been previously published in Concurrences, and it might have been edited for clarity and cohesion. Martin Peitz, Jens-Uwe Franck, Reinforcing the Digital Markets Act: Merger control and structural remedies, February 2022, Concurrences N° 1-2022, Art. N° 104429.

3. We argue in favour of a competition law toolkit with extended options to use structural measures to tackle entrenched market dysfunctionalities: expanded and strengthened merger control; extended possibilities to respond to infringements of competition law and equivalent provisions with structural remedies; and the availability of forced divestiture, possibly after a market investigation.

I. The digital gatekeeper challenge

4. An increasing part of economic and social activity is facilitated by digital players and channelled through the internet, and a small number of firms have taken key "gatekeeper" positions. GAFAM have become private regulators dictating terms and conditions to participants in their ecosystems. Even if users are uncomfortable with those terms, there are often few viable alternatives to some of the services offered. Increasingly, GAFAM's position looks to have become entrenched for several services. Strong network effects increase the value of a digital service for consumers and business users, and because of coordination problems and inertia, switching to newcomers is unattractive. It might seem like Daniel Markovits's "Meritocracy Trap" (Penguin Press, 2019): Big Tech firms make more attractive value propositions and become more sophisticated in extracting rents, and challengers must overcome more and more hurdles.

II. The EU's regulatory response

5. What to do with firms enjoying a consolidated position of power relative to other businesses in a vertical relationship or entrenched market power? Regulation is a natural response and is indeed the EU's approach to ensure the functioning of digital markets. The EU lawmaker has established across-the-board transparency rules in its Platform-to-Business Regulation (EU) 2019/1150. These are meant to improve business users' position vis-à-vis the digital platforms. Through the DMA proposal, the EU lawmaker targets a small number of particularly powerful players with an entrenched market position and prohibits certain business practices when adopted by them. This approach is broadly suitable if the risks and economic harms of exploitation and foreclosure increase with the scope of operations and market entrenchment.

6. The proposed DMA specifically addresses gatekeeper platforms and seeks remedies that aim at keeping markets open or opening them up – both at the platform level and business user level – and prohibits certain business practices, but only for firms addressed by the DMA. For instance, a platform may oblige its business users not to offer lower prices elsewhere. Then, business users cannot divert consumers through price. This limits platforms'

incentives to compete on fees or other conditions they offer to their business users. End users may suffer from higher prices or lower quality. This concern goes beyond Big Tech and applies to other platforms in strong positions with respect to specific user groups, such as hotel booking platforms vis-à-vis independent hotels or event ticketing platforms vis-à-vis concert organisers. Thus, the rationale for singling out a few firms is not obvious in the case of some of the obligations and prohibitions in the proposed DMA, unless a convincing case can be made that traditional competition tools are often insufficient to deal with certain business practices of the targeted gatekeeper platforms, while they tend to be adequate for other firms.

III. Behavioural remedies and their shortcomings

7. At the EU level, we see, first of all, fines and behavioural remedies by the Commission based on findings of an infringement of Article 102 TFEU against Google (Alphabet)[2], as well as pending investigations against Apple[3], Amazon[4] and – again – Google[5]. Moreover, merger control may give the option to regulate market conduct via behavioural remedies so that combined resources (data) may not readily be used to erect new market barriers. In the *Google/Fitbit* merger proceedings (M.9660), the Commission made extensive use of this. For instance, Google had to commit to not using the health and wellness data collected from Fitbit devices for Google Ads (including search advertising and display advertising).

8. Lawyers tend to consider structural remedies – as opposed to behavioural remedies – to be the more intrusive measure. They may be seen as surgery instead of permanent drug treatment. Yet, structural remedies appear to be more in line with the idea that the state trusts market forces within an economic order it has formed, to guarantee the functioning of markets. Thus, in aggregate, "surgery" may be regarded as preferable, as it ultimately amounts to more economic freedom for all market players – including those that are subject to regulation due to their economic power.

9. The effectiveness of behavioural rules and remedies imposed on the large digital gatekeepers will always remain limited. Their drafting, monitoring, and sanctioning are (very) costly. The targeted gatekeepers will routinely find other ways to implement strategies that are meant to be prevented: For instance, there are many means by which Google can incentivize Android device manufacturers to prioritize Google Search.

---

2 *Google Shopping* – AT.39740, *Android* – AT.40099, and *AdSense* – AT.40411.

3 *App Store Practices (music streaming)* – AT.40437, *App Store Practices* – AT.40716, and *Apple Mobile Payments* – AT.40452.

4 *Amazon Marketplace* – AT.40462 and *Amazon – Buy Box* – AT.40703.

5 *Adtech and Data-related practices* – AT.40670.

10. One structural remedy that is hotly debated in the U.S. is the "breakup" of conglomerate digital structures. This is reflected by the Ending Platform Monopolies Act of 2021, which has been put forward by the House Judiciary Committee. According to this proposal, certain gatekeeper platforms will not be allowed to own or operate tied or vertically related activities to their core platform services. These activities will have to be stopped or divested. Sometimes, such forced divestitures simply correct a merger that has turned out to be problematic. While reinforced merger proceedings at the EU level could not repair the shortcomings of the past, they may avoid future competition problems. Thus, a discussion of structural remedies should start with *ex ante* merger control.

11. On 20 April 2021, the British Competition and Markets Authority (CMA), the Australian Competition and Consumer Commission (ACCC) and the Bundeskartellamt issued a Joint statement on merger control enforcement, stating that the "*increasing complexity of dynamic markets and the need to undertake forward-looking assessments require competition agencies to favour structural over behavioural remedies*." The CMA turned words into deeds: On 30 November 2021, rejecting the behavioural remedies offered by Meta (Facebook), the authority ordered the firm to reverse its acquisition of Giphy.

IV. EU merger policy for Big Tech

12. Big Tech has acquired many start-ups over the last decade. In digital markets, it is difficult to foresee how these start-ups would have developed if they had stayed independent or had been acquired by some other firm. Currently, to block a merger, the Commission must argue a case showing that the notified concentration will have anticompetitive effects. Given the uncertainties and the competition authorities' lack of information, this is often an almost impossible mission.

13. Strengthening competition authorities' power to prohibit mergers could mean lowering the required standard of proof or giving them the power to reverse the burden of proof regarding the expected effects on competition in clearly specified scenarios – for instance, if one of the merging firms has a powerful entrenched position. Such a position may be identified by a market investigation or by applying criteria as established in the proposed DMA or Section 19a of the German Competition Act. Furthermore, as pointed out, for instance, in the Furman report, merger assessment in digital markets – and in fact in all scenarios where potential competition and harm to innovation are of particular importance for merger analysis – must not solely focus on the likelihood that a certain harm to competition will occur, but also on the scale of this harm.

14. Various reform approaches point in this direction. In France, the Senate has approved a legislative initiative (Proposition de loi visant à garantir le libre choix du consommateur dans le cyberespace), currently pending

in the National Assembly, that would shift the burden of proof in merger cases involving (designated) large digital gatekeepers ("*entreprises structurantes*"): When the competition authority initiates an in-depth examination of a notified transaction, it is the undertaking that must provide evidence that the transaction is not likely to harm competition. Likewise, in the U.S., the House Judiciary Committee approved a bill (the Platform Competition and Opportunity Act of 2021) that would ban acquisitions by (designated) large digital platforms unless they can prove that the merger will not harm actual or potential competition. On 5 November 2021, U.S. Senators Klobuchar and Cotton introduced corresponding bipartisan legislation as a companion Senate bill.

15. In May 2021, the French, German, and Dutch governments (Friends of an Effective Digital Markets Act) have lamented that Article 12 of the DMA proposal lacked ambition. They demanded that the existing EU merger framework be modified for DMA gatekeepers: Acquisitions of low-turnover but high-value targets should be captured, and the substantive test should be adapted to more effectively address cases of "*potentially predatory acquisitions*." While this is water to our mill, the initiative did not command a majority within the EU Council. In November 2021, when setting their position for upcoming negotiations with the Commission and Parliament, the ministers did not endorse any proposal for tighter merger control under the DMA.

V. Market structure in digital

16. Ultimately, the choice over whether we live in an environment with a few firms controlling large ecosystems or a more fragmented digital world is political. Since innovations yet unknown will benefit unforeseen digital activities, our working hypothesis is that a more fragmented world is likely to deliver more innovation than a world with few ecosystems, controlled by heavily regulated firms.

17. Absent the ability to impose divestiture obligations and run a stricter merger policy, the DMA and its envisaged regulatory approach toward Big Tech may still help in opening space for new and independent digital players. By analogy, this happened in several regulated industries, for example telecommunications, in which privatized incumbent firms were subject to more stringent regulation than newcomers were.

18. Regulation via the DMA or, possibly, via behavioural remedies imposed on the occasion of merger proceedings, seems, at best, to be a very indirect way of achieving this outcome. Enabling the European Commission to impose divestiture obligations as the result of a market investigation and, looking forward, to block digital conglomerate mergers more easily is a more direct path to a healthier digital world. Considering institutional constraints, this may

be wishful thinking, but at least an open discussion in the Member States would be helpful. The option of stricter merger control and forced divestiture should not be taken off the table.

VI. Divestiture initiatives

19. Forced divestitures are not unheard of in Europe. In West Germany, after World War II, mandated unbundling, such as that of IG Farben, was a powerful beacon to herald the new paradigm of guaranteeing competition by means of regulatory intervention – if necessary, also by intervention in the market structure. This post-war period of competition law in West Germany was based on Allied decartelization laws inspired by U.S. antitrust law.

20. In the U.S., divestiture obligations are accepted as a legitimate remedy in the competition toolbox and its availability under Section 2 of the Sherman Act has been recognized by the U.S. Supreme Court. Certainly, this remedy is not exactly routinely used, but it is an option. In its complaint filed against Google on 20 October 2020 (case 1:20-cv-03010), the U.S. Department of Justice requested that the court "*[e]nter structural relief as needed to cure any anticompetitive harm.*" Moreover, politically, "unbundling Big Tech" is not seen as a far-fetched objective of competition policy. Rather, after recent debates in the House on a package of five tech-focused bills (including the Ending Platform Monopolies Act mentioned before), Dan Bishop, a Republican U.S. Representative for North Carolina, remarked, "*I will tell you, I'm not 100% there to break up Big Tech, but I'm close.*" (L. Feiner, House committee passes sweeping tech antitrust reforms, but their future remains murky, CNBC, 24 June 2021)?

21. Under German law, similar to EU law, structural remedies are hardly ever used, as they can only be imposed in case of competition infringements "*if there is no behavioural remedy which would be equally effective, or if the behavioural remedy would entail a greater burden for the undertakings concerned than the structural remedies*" (Section 32 of the Competition Act). Neither in the EU nor in Germany can divestiture be ordered as an (objective) instrument of market regulation. The last attempt to add such an instrument to the competition toolbox – initiated by the Federal Ministry of Economic Affairs and supported by the Monopoly Commission – got bogged down in 2010. The debate at the time focused on conceivable targets (remarkably, Big Tech was not really on the radar yet), on fundamental questions of competition policy, and on uncertainties about what leeway EU law and fundamental rights left to the German legislature.

22. Since 2010, however, the rise of the digital platform economy and of concentration within it has continued. With this ongoing fundamental transformation of our economy, it would seem careless not to have an open

mind to reconsidering structural instruments that were previously rejected as being too harsh for the addressees or too burdensome for the authorities to be implemented.

VII. What can we ultimately expect from the DMA?

23. In response to structural competition problems, it is only natural and indeed consistent to consider a serious strengthening of merger control, as well as structural remedies, including breakups of digital conglomerates. But who in the EU is willing to invest political capital to initiate a serious debate on strengthened merger control and forced divestitures as a regulatory instrument?

24. Hopes now rest on the European Parliament (EP). In its position adopted on 15 December 2021, it has endorsed three amendments that would make it easier to impose structural remedies as foreseen in Article 16 of the DMA proposal in case of systematic non-compliance: First, the standard for the imposition of a remedy should not be whether it is "*proportionate to the infringement committed*," but whether it is "*effective and necessary to ensure compliance*" with the DMA (Amendment 166). Secondly, the EP wants to eliminate that for structural remedies to be imposed, it would need to be shown that an "*equally effective behavioural remedy*" is either not available or "*more burdensome for the gatekeeper concerned*" (Amendment 168). Thirdly, the threshold for "*systematic non-compliance*" should be lowered from three to two non-compliance or fining decisions that must have been issued within a period of ten (instead of five) years.

25. These are certainly reasonable (albeit still cautious) moves to facilitate structural remedies. More startling is that, in the case of systematic non-compliance, the EP proposes to restrict gatekeepers for a certain period of time "*from making acquisitions in areas relevant to this Regulation*," which would include digital and data-related sectors. Thus, the Commission should have the option to impose such a ban either where it considers it proportionate and necessary to remedy damages caused by repeated infringements or "*to prevent further damage to the contestability and fairness of the internal market*" (Amendments 44 and 167). The logic behind the latter alternative could be: A digital firm that is not to be trusted to respect behavioural rules and remedies must be prevented from any step which could further strengthen its position as a gatekeeper.

26. While these proposals facilitate structural remedies, their effectiveness should not be overestimated. Also, the availability of an "acquisition ban" in response to non-compliance does certainly not make a reform of EU merger law and policy dispensable. In any case, at this point, it is unclear which of these proposals will become reality. That is why we fear that the EU will, in the end, continue to restrict itself to playing games of behavioural remedies and regulation.

27. Yet, some EU Member States may push for more. The new German coalition government announced in its programme that it will plead at the European level for an adjustment of merger control that prevents innovation-inhibiting acquisitions of potential competitors. This appears to us a much more promising initiative than opening doors for wannabe European champions.

State Support for Innovation: Time for Questions*

Jean Pisani Ferry
Bruegel

1. In fifteen years, public financial support for innovation has doubled in constant euros. According to the latest report by the National Commission for the Evaluation of Innovation Policies (CNEPI), it amounts to 10 billion euros, or half a point of GDP, financed by the State, the regions and the European Union. This is a considerable amount, for example, more than 25% higher than the budget for the justice system.

I. A consensual purpose

2. The decision to devote more and more resources to this policy has been maintained over the course of the political changeovers. The effort has been made in the service of a very explicit national ambition: to place the French economy on the technological frontier for the long term, to renew the drivers of its growth and to ensure its competitiveness by raising the range of goods and services produced. In the words of Philippe Aghion and Élie Cohen, the aim was to complete the transformation of our former "economy of imitation" into an "economy of innovation".

3. This choice can certainly be attributed to the fact that our governments have gradually become convinced that one of the best ways to stimulate economic growth was to focus on strengthening our research and innovation capacities.

* This article has been previously published in Concurrences, and it might have been edited for clarity and cohesion. Jean Pisani Ferry, State support for innovation: Time for questions, May 2016, Concurrences N° 2-2016, Art. N° 78529, pp. 5-7.

A key moment in this inflection, even if it was not the most significant financially, was in 2009 the Juppé-Rocard report, which gave birth to the first of the Investment Programs for the Future (IFP). A second PIA was launched in 2013 and a third is in preparation.

4. The objective is hardly questionable. Both the rapid rise of emerging countries and the economic and commercial successes of our partners who have been able to rely on novelty and quality confirm that, if an advanced country like ours wants to maintain its standard of living and defend its positions on international markets, it must play the innovation card.

5. However, several questions arise as to the means used to achieve this objective, the share of government financial support and the modalities of such support.

II. Why support innovation

6. Modern growth theories, which have developed considerably in recent decades, have incorporated innovation as a specific economic investment. They show that innovation is the result of risk-taking behaviour with a view to obtaining a return, and that its development depends first and foremost on the general environment in which the players – laboratories, companies, investors and the innovators themselves – operate.

7. The main determinants of innovation thus relate to the availability of resources (research, skilled work, infrastructure), the degree of investment in the maintenance and renewal of skills (which refers to the effectiveness of vocational training), but also to the nature of so-called economic institutions. These include the existence of long-term investors with a risk appetite, the intellectual property regime, bankruptcy law (which determines the cost of failure), taxation, the functioning of labour and product markets, *corporate governance*, and the depth, efficiency and liquidity of financial market segments that can contribute to project support.

8. The first of the innovation policies is for the State to mobilize resources in the areas for which it is responsible (education, research, infrastructure). It then needs to create a framework that is conducive to the development of the innovation activity of economic actors.

9. Even in an economy with institutions conducive to innovation activity, specific public action in its favour is nevertheless desirable. This has long been recognised in the case of research, because of the public-good nature of knowledge. The same argument applies, at least partly, to policies whose point of application is furthest downstream. For example, incentives for R&D are justified by its positive externalities. Similarly, policies to increase the density of innovation in a given territory – particularly in the context of competitiveness clusters – are justified by the important spatial interactions involved.

10. It is in this context that the effectiveness and efficiency of innovation support policies must be assessed. A number of discussions have arisen from their analysis.

III. Support or reform?

11. In the first place, it is important to bear in mind that direct or indirect support policies that mobilise public resources should always be assessed in the light of non-monetary reforms that would improve the functioning of the corresponding markets in order to create, without recourse to budgetary resources, conditions conducive to the renewal of products and processes. An economy's capacity for innovation depends at least as much on the quality of its economic and social regulations, the depth of its financial market, its tax system and, in short, the state of mind of its researchers, entrepreneurs and employees as on the direct financial effort of the national community.

12. Conversely, public support schemes are often justified by insufficient private investment or private financing mechanisms. It is necessary to identify the main reasons for these deficiencies and to examine whether they could not be addressed directly at the source, rather than through a multiplication of palliative mechanisms. Budgetary resources should be used as a priority where they have no substitutes, rather than being used to alleviate dysfunctions that can be remedied.

IV. Device inflation

13. It is in this spirit that we must analyse the French innovation support landscape. Today, it is characterised by a multiplicity of objectives, a profusion of instruments and an instability of systems. In 2000, the State and its operators managed nearly 30 national schemes. Their number has risen to 62, to which should be added those set up by local authorities. Their average size, excluding tax arrangements, rose from 126 to 39 million euros.

14. The specialisation of the devices makes it possible to precisely target market failures. But their multiplicity, especially if they are each small in scale, inevitably leads to a risk of inefficiency. A common rule of public policy is that you need as many instruments as you have objectives. In this case, it is hard to imagine that the government has set more than sixty different objectives. There is therefore, most certainly, a redundancy of instruments.

15. Moreover, national policy has been marked, over a relatively short period of time, by a high degree of instability in these arrangements. This inevitably affects the ability of the targeted beneficiaries to take full advantage of them. The profusion and instability of the instruments is likely to favour

those, companies or research actors, who invest in mastering administrative complexity, rather than supporting the most dynamic or innovative among them.

V. The emergence of two major players

16. However, a major institutional reorganisation has been carried out with the creation of two major players: the Commissariat général à l'investissement (CGI), which manages the PIAs, and the Banque publique d'investissement (Bpifrance), which supports and finances companies' innovation efforts. The PIA's innovation programmes represent 57% of direct support in annual flows and Bpifrance financing, in subsidy equivalent, 37% (including PIA actions managed by Bpifrance).

17. With this consolidation, we have, in fact, largely moved from a dominant principle of management of support mechanisms by the State to a growing delegation to agencies, whether it be the CGI, Bpifrance or the National Research Agency (ANR). These agencies (in fact, if not exactly in law) can select from among the schemes according to their suitability for a more general purpose.

18. In a way, therefore, institutional consolidation has compensated for the dispersion of arrangements. This does not make the situation satisfactory, however, because it has not been able to do so completely: even with an integrated operator, instrumental complexity remains a problem. Indeed, the agencies do not always have the latitude of choice that would allow them to disregard it. Hence the question as to the way forward: does the necessary simplification involve reducing the number of devices, or rather giving greater discretion to operators?

VI. The weight of the CIR

19. Tax incentives, mainly the Research Tax Credit (CIR), now account for more than 60% of total support, at 6.4 billion euros, compared with less than one-fifth in 2000.

20. Correlatively, direct aid, mainly in the form of subsidies, has been practically halved in real terms. They now account for 18% of support, compared with 81% in 2000.

21. This development has ensured simplified and undifferentiated access to the scheme for as many potential beneficiaries as possible. However, it also raises a question of purpose: the EIF has several targets and it is not clear how its effectiveness can be judged. Should it be assessed with regard to an objective of encouraging R&D, an objective of industrial competitiveness, or an objective of attractiveness of the territory? Is it a question of ensuring that

companies locate their R&D on French territory, or that they increase their spending on research and innovation? This measure, which the government has announced that it will remain in place until the end of the five-year period, has so far only been partially analysed.

22. The observations just made pose four questions for assessment: in what areas would direct action on economic institutions reduce the need for financial support? Should the number of support schemes be reduced? Should the agencies be given greater decision-making latitude? Finally, with regard to the EIF, against what objective should its effectiveness be examined?

23. Answering these questions is the purpose of the NCIPC. The philosophy that presided over its installation can be described as organic. Rather than the search for a *priori* rationality, it was given the mandate to contribute to rationalizations at the margin. In simple terms, it is a question of identifying which mechanisms provide evidence of effectiveness and which do not, in order to strengthen the former and reduce the means of the latter.

24. However, this is not an easy task. What microeconometric techniques can do well is to evaluate the devices one by one – based on natural experiments, for example. In this way, it is possible to determine the marginal efficiency of each device. But this is not really the question being asked, at least not the only one. It is difficult to isolate the effects of each device when a multiplicity of others target the same economic actors and pursue similar or identical goals. It can be misleading to evaluate a subsidy without questioning the institutions in which it is embedded. And even if these difficulties were overcome, there would be little point in simply assessing the marginal effectiveness of a range of support mechanisms on a case-by-case basis without questioning the effectiveness of the system as a whole.

25. These challenges are not unique to innovation support policies. In a number of other areas – housing policy, employment policy, business support or social aid – we have over the years accumulated incentives and other subsidies in the hope of responding to dysfunctions that we were unable or unwilling to address at the root. What can be called palliative spending has thus come to account for a significant proportion of public spending, with an effectiveness that, in terms of overall results, is admittedly limited. In a context of resource scarcity and the development of new priorities, it has become difficult to avoid sorting through the many mechanisms that have been put in place one after the other, in order to distinguish between expenditure that is indispensable and that which is not, a requirement that is difficult to circumvent.

PART V
Competition Policy as a Tool for Broader Societal Impact

Using Consumer Protection Law to Achieve Competition Policy Goals

DARREN BUSH*
University of Houston Law Center

SPENCER WEBER WALLER**
Loyola University Chicago School of Law

1. Institutional design matters in competition and consumer protection enforcement. In the United States, only one agency, the Antitrust Division of the Justice Department, can enforce both criminal and civil antitrust matters. In contrast, the United States Federal Trade Commission (FTC), can enforce virtually all civil antitrust matters, as well as consumer protection matters. It is highly unusual to have two different agencies doing antitrust in the same jurisdiction as in the United States. Internationally, there are many different models of agencies, some that work exclusively on competition matters and others that have both competition and consumer protection powers to varying degrees. There is an ongoing, and probably unsolvable, debate about which model is best in the abstract and what is desirable for any given jurisdiction.[1]

---

* Leonard B. Rosenberg Professor of Law, University of Houston Law Center. Copyright 2023 by the authors. This chapter is part of a larger project on the issues of institutional design and the better integration of competition, consumer protection, and data privacy enforcement powers.

** John Paul Stevens Chair in Competition Law, Loyola University Chicago School of Law. In 2022, Professor Waller served as a Senior Adviser to the Chair of the United States Federal Trade Commission and worked on matters related to the subject matter of this chapter. This contribution reflects only the personal views of the authors. All matters discussed in this chapter are based only on publicly available information about the work of the FTC or the other competition agencies mentioned.

1 OECD, *The Optimal Design, Organisation and Powers of Competition Authorities*, (Dec. 4, 2023), https://web-archive.oecd.org/temp/2024-01-16/665480-optimal-design-organisation-and-powers-of-competition-authorities.htm; Spencer W. Waller, *Antitrust Marathon: With Authority*, 2010 EUR. COMP. J. 503 (symposium exploring how best to integrate competition and consumer protection enforcement).

2. This chapter examines one largely ignored aspect of this debate. We argue that agencies with integrated competition and consumer protection powers can resolve market failure problems by using their consumer protection powers to achieve results in the real world that also help solve competition issues. We use the pending separate FTC consumer protection and antitrust complaints against Amazon as an example of the potential of this approach and to urge other integrated enforcement agencies to consider such a two-pronged approach where appropriate.

I. The Two Sides of Section 5 of the FTC Act

3. The FTC's basic enforcement powers are spelled out in Section 5 of the Federal Trade Commission (FTC Act).[2] The FTC derives its competition powers from the portion of the FTC Act that prohibits unfair methods of competition (UMC).[3] The FTC's consumer protection powers stem from additional language in Section 5 that also prohibits unfair or deceptive acts and practices (UDAP).[4] Over the years, Congress has passed dozens of other statutes granting the FTC enforcement authority over specific industries and practices.[5]

4. US courts agree that the FTC's UMC authority covers all violations of the letter of the Sherman and Clayton Acts, as well as some set of "incipient" violations of the antitrust laws and conduct that violates the "spirit" of the antitrust laws.[6] In 2022, the FTC issued the first comprehensive agency policy statement interpreting the meaning of unfair methods of competition under Section 5.[7] These guidelines would be subject to court review in any specific rulemaking or enforcement proceeding involving competition matters.

5. In contrast, Congress has amended the UDAP portion of Section 5 defining unfairness by statute. It requires that any consumer protection conduct deemed "unfair" in consumer protection cases must cause, or is likely to cause, substantial injury to consumers which is not reasonably avoidable by the consumers and not outweighed by any positive effects of the conduct in question.[8] There are separate agency guidelines as to when conduct can be deemed "deceptive" under the UDAP prong of Section 5.[9]

---

2 15 USC § 45.

3 *Id.* at § 45(a)(1).

4 *Id.*

5 *See generally*, 2 Stephanie Kanwit, Federal Trade Commission (2024).

6 FTC v. Sperry & Hutchinson Co., 405 U.S. 233 (1972).

7 *FTC Policy Statement Regarding the Scope of Unfair Methods of Competition Under Section 5 of the Federal Trade Commission Act*, File No. P221202, (Nov. 10, 2022), https://www.ftc.gov/system/files/ftc_gov/pdf/P221202Section5PolicyStatement.pdf.

8 15 U.S.C. § 45(n). *See also, FTC Policy Statement on Unfairness, December 17, 1980, appended to International Harvester Co.*, 104, 949, 1070 (1984), https://www.ftc.gov/legal-library/browse/ftc-policy-statement-unfairness.

9 *FTC Policy Statement on Deception, October 14, 1983, appended to Cliffdale Associates, Inc.*, 103, 110, 174 (1984), https://www.ftc.gov/system/files/documents/public_statements/410531/831014deceptionstmt.pdf.

II. Contemporary Emphasis on Outcomes and Solving Problems

6. The FTC is an independent regulatory agency and not part of the Executive Branch of the United States government. Nonetheless, it stands to benefit from a new whole-of-government approach to competition problems that has the potential to break down silos within agencies and between executive branch departments and independent agencies with overlapping tools and jurisdiction.

7. In July 2021, the Biden Administration issued an Executive Order on Promoting Competition in the American Economy (Biden EO).[10] The Biden EO requires a whole-of-government approach to persistent market failures, some of which can be thought of as traditional competition law problems, while others sound more like consumer protection problems. These range from the persistence of excessive and poorly disclosed junk fees imposed by airlines, hotel chains, and financial institutions, restrictions on the right of repair, and unduly high prices for such goods as hearing aids and insulin. Such an approach envisions creativity and cooperation within, and between, the executive branch and independent agencies. More importantly, such an approach requires accountability, regular reporting, and problem solving in the real world, rather than just the use of traditional enforcement powers by a competition or consumer protection agency.

8. Agencies are being asked: how do we solve this market problem in the real world? What powers do we have to solve this problem lawfully and creatively? What partners, if any, do we need to achieve the desired outcome?

III. The Promise and Perils of Combined UMC and UDAP Enforcement by the FTC

9. The FTC has a unique role to play in this type of approach to market failure. It has two distinct powers that can be used to investigate and challenge conduct that violates the two halves of Section 5 of the FTC Act. A UMC case and a UDAP case can be investigated together, or separately, and challenged in two separate cases or as two counts of a single case against the same respondent. The FTC can also cooperate (or defer to) other agencies that may have better enforcement powers over the same conduct.

10 The White House, *Executive Order on Promoting Competition in the American Economy*, (July 9, 2021), https://www.whitehouse.gov/briefing-room/presidential-actions/2021/07/09/executive-order-on-promoting-competition-in-the-american-economy/; Executive Order on Promoting Competition in the American Economy, Fact Sheet (July 9, 2021), https://www.whitehouse.gov/briefing-room/statements-releases/2021/07/09/fact-sheet-executive-order-on-promoting-competition-in-the-american-economy/.

10. The FTC has a number of challenges to implement this broader, more flexible approach, on how to attack problems in the real world. Historically, the FTC has separate Bureaus of Competition and Consumer Protection that are highly siloed.[11] Matters traditionally are investigated and litigated separately by different staff with expertise in either UMC or UDAP cases and typically have only limited experience with the other side of the agency's jurisdiction.

11. Fortunately, this is changing. The Chair of the FTC has publicly spoken of the need to better integrate both sides of the Section 5 fence.[12] The agency has instituted a new honors hiring program where new attorneys will rotate between both Bureaus in their early years.[13]

12. The FTC has begun to use its UDAP powers to challenge conduct that also could potentially be challenged as unfair methods of competition but that fit more naturally as a consumer protection UDAP violation. While such matters as commercial surveillance by websites, restrictions on rights to repair, and privacy violations could potentially be shoehorned into antitrust violations and unfair methods of competition, consumer protection theories are often a better fit for theories of liability and remedies that also help restore competition in the real world (or at least lower barriers to effective competition). It then becomes a matter of agency discretion and resources whether to bring two separate cases or one combined case against the respondent.

13. This combined approach may also help alleviate many of the practical and political constraints the FTC faces from a generally conservative and hostile judiciary, defense bar, and business press. The scope of the FTC's consumer protection powers generally is less contested than its antitrust powers. FTC rulemaking authority in consumer protection matters is also less subject to legal challenge.

14. Unfortunately, such a whole-of-agency approach by itself will not address all the pending administrative and constitutional law challenges to the FTC structure and authority as part of a more general conservative effort to dismantle the administrative state.[14] But in a legal world where there are many paths to the Buddha, it matters less what path you take, if you can achieve total enlightenment.[15]

---

11 There is also a separate Bureau of Economics that supports the work of both the BC and BCP.

12 FTC Chair, Memorandum from: Chair Lina M. Khan to Commission Staff and Commissioners re: Vision and Priorities for the FTC (Sept. 22, 2021), https://www.ftc.gov/system/files/documents/public_statements/1596664/agency_priorities_memo_from_chair_lina_m_khan_9-22-21.pdf.

13 FTC, Honors Attorney Program: Cross-Bureau Entry-Level Opportunity, https://www.ftc.gov/about-ftc/bureaus-offices/bureau-competition/legal-careers-bureau-competition/entry-level-attorneys/ftc-honors-attorney-program-cross-bureau-entry-level-opportunity (last visited Oct. 30, 2024).

14 *See generally*, Jack M. Beermann, *The Never-Ending Assault on the Administrative State*, 93 Notre Dame L. Rev. 1599 (2018).

15 Caddyshack (Orion Pictures 1980) ("…on your deathbed, you will receive total consciousness. 'So I got that goin' for me, which is nice.'").

IV. How Consumer Protection Can Help Achieve More Competitive Markets in a Hostile Legal/Political Antitrust Environment

15. We turn now toward the alternative paths available to the FTC using its UDAP authority. We highlight the value of combining different causes of actions, different remedies, and a mixture of rulemaking and enforcement actions to achieve better results in the real world.

1. Different Causes of Action

16. Section 5 of the FTC Act states that "unfair or deceptive acts or practices in or affecting commerce... are ... declared unlawful."[16] Deceptive acts or practices require a "material representation, omission or practice that is likely to mislead a consumer acting reasonably in the circumstances."[17] An act or practice is "unfair" if it "causes or is likely to cause substantial injury to consumers which is not reasonably avoidable by consumers themselves and not outweighed by countervailing benefits to consumers or to competition."[18] While the agency is charged with enforcement of a plethora of other statutory provisions within a variety of different acts, this is the gist of the consumer protection game.[19]

17. While the "countervailing benefits" language might suggest something akin to the full-blown rule of reason in UMC cases, it is not the case. First, there is no need to define the relevant market, nor to have a myriad of economists debate it. Second, there is no need to discuss issues of entry or offsetting efficiencies. The question is instead the net benefit or harm of the behavior. Conversely, alleging a UMC violation may pose difficult legal and factual questions, but it does not require showing actual deception or unfairness.[20]

2. Better Remedies

18. The ability of the FTC to attack harm arising under its consumer protection arm has been tested. While its available remedies have been under attack in recent years, the FTC still wields substantial ability to prohibit unfair or deceptive acts or practices. The FTC may issue a cease-and-desist order.[21]

---

16 15 U.S.C. § 45(a)(1).

17 *See*, *FTC Policy Statement on Deception*, https://www.ftc.gov/about-ftc/mission/enforcement-authority#:~:text=Policy%20Statement%20on%20Deception (last visited Oct. 30, 2024).

18 15 U.S.C. § 45(n).

19 *See generally*, FTC, Legal Library Statutes, https://www.ftc.gov/legal-library/browse/statutes (last visited Oct. 30, 2024).

20 However, deception may be part of an antitrust or UMC violation. *See generally*, Maurice E. Stucke, *When a Monopolist Deceives*, 76 ANTITRUST L.J. 823 (2010); FTC Policy Statement, *supra* note 7, at 9.

21 15 U.S.C. § 45(b).

It may also obtain injunctive and other equitable relief in court. It may also impose civil penalties on repeat offenders and non-respondents where "the violator had "actual knowledge that such act or practice is unfair or deceptive and is unlawful."[22]

19. It may also, in some limited circumstances, obtain disgorgement and restitution in consumer protection cases. However, since the Supreme Court's decision in *AMG*, it appears more difficult for the FTC to approach this path.[23] Nonetheless, as the Supreme Court noted, some exceptions apply:

> "Further, the structure of the Act beyond § 13(b) confirms this conclusion. Congress in § 5(*l*) and § 19 gave district courts the authority to impose limited monetary penalties and to award monetary relief in cases where the Commission has *issued cease and desist orders, i.e.*, where the Commission has engaged in administrative proceedings. Since in these provisions Congress explicitly provided for "other and further equitable relief," 15 U. S. C. § 45(*l*), and for the "refund of money or return of property," § 57b(b), it likely did not intend for § 13(b)'s more cabined "permanent injunction" language to have similarly broad scope."[24]

20. It is FTC's UDAP rulemaking authority that has made, perhaps, the largest difference. In terms of common consumer experiences, wash and dry labels, insulation R values, octane ratings for gasoline, funeral prices, eyeglasses, auto fuel ratings, used cars, energy ratings, door-to-door sales, identity theft, free credit report, contact lenses and eyeglasses, and child protection are a few examples of rules that are broad in reach.[25] We turn toward FTC's UDAP rulemaking authority next.

3. An "Easier" Path to Rulemaking

21. The most recent unfair method of competition rulemaking attempt by the FTC,[26] the noncompete agreement NPRM, suggests much hesitancy toward that path. Despite prior use of rulemaking in this context and older precedent,[27] there are larger questions raised about the future of such rulemaking before any court. The FTC, even under optimal UMC rulemaking, would most likely not receive any substantial form of Skidmore[28] or *Auer*[29] deference with respect to

---

22 15 U.S.C. § 45(a)(1) and 15 U.S.C. § 45(m)(1)(B).

23 "We must conclude, however, that § 13(b) [of the FTC Act] as currently written does not grant the Commission authority to obtain equitable monetary relief." AMG Cap. Mgmt., LLC v. Fed. Trade Comm'n, 593 U.S. 67 (2021).

24 AMG Cap. Mgmt., LLC 593 U.S. 67, 77.

25 *See generally*, 16 C.F.R. pt. 408 et. seq. See, e.g., 16 C.F.R. pt. 422 (Octane Standards); 16 C.F.R. part 453 (Funeral Rule); 16 C.F.R. pt. 429 (Door to Door Sales); 16 C.F.R. pt 456 (Eyeglass Rule); 16 C.F.R. pt. 460 (Insulation); 16 C.F.R. pt. 455 (used cars).

26 FTC, Non-Compete Clause Rulemaking, https://www.ftc.gov/legal-library/browse/federal-register-notices/non-compete-clause-rulemaking (last visited Oct. 30, 2024).

27 16 C.F.R. pt. 423 (Tailoring rule); Nat'l Petroleum Refiners Ass'n v. F.T.C., 482 F.2d 672 (D.C. Cir. 1973).

28 Skidmore v. Swift & Co., 323 U. S. 134, 140 (1944).

29 Auer v. Robbins, 519 U.S. 452 (1997).

such rulemaking even before Loper Bright.[30] Moreover, challenges to UMC rulemaking will likely mean that any such action is delayed, if not halted completely. In particular, critics question whether such rulemaking would be barred under the major questions doctrine.[31]

22. Two other paths to rulemaking exist for the agency. In many instances, the FTC must undertake Magnuson-Moss rulemaking. While most agencies must engage in some form of Administrative Procedure Act informal rulemaking, Congress imposed additional steps upon the FTC. First, the FTC must provide an advanced notice of proposed rulemaking to its oversight committees in Congress.[32] Second, the FTC may engage in its notice of proposed rulemaking similar to other agency processes, including providing notice and receiving public comment. However, the FTC must provide opportunity for oral hearing if so requested and must provide additional information with its proposed rulemaking. These requirements extend the time and cost of rulemaking.[33] The triggering of a request for oral testimony compels the presence of a presiding officer and other procedures in the event of such testimony.[34] Beyond that, promulgation of any rule will likely lead to petitions for judicial review, as well as applications for exemptions to such rule. While the FTC Magnuson-Moss path is still filled with delays and pitfalls, it is a more familiar and accepted path than the UMC rulemaking path.[35]

23. The FTC can bypass Magnuson-Moss when authorized by Congress. For example, Dodd-Frank provided for the ability of the FTC to promulgate rules for auto dealers under its usual APA-related processes.[36]

24. We turn now to an important recent example where the FTC has separately challenged certain conduct by Amazon as a UDAP consumer protection violation and other conduct as an UMC antitrust violation and how the successful resolution of either part of the case will help achieve real world benefits regardless of the legal labels used by the agency or the courts.

---

30 *See*, Justin Hurwitz, *Chevron and the Limits of Administrative Antitrust,* 76 U. Pitt. L. Rev. 209, 212 (2014) ("Indeed, there is widespread consensus within the antitrust bar that Chevron does not apply to FTC interpretations of Section 5."). See Loper Bright Enterprises v. Raimondo, 603 US _ (2024), available at https://www.supremecourt.gov/opinions/23pdf/22-451_7m58.pdf, overturning Chevron, U.S.A., Inc. v. Nat. Res. Def. Council, Inc., 467 U.S. 837 (1984).

31 *See generally*, FDA v. Brown & Williamson Tobacco Corp., 529 U.S. 120, 159-60 (2000); King v. Burwell, 576 U.S. 473 (2015).

32 16 CFR § 1.10.

33 *See*, 16 CFR § 1.11.

34 16 CFR § 1.13.

35 Apart from the recent noncompete rulemaking, the only other instance the authors can recall is the tailored clothing rule. See FTC, *Discriminatory Practices in Men's and Boys' Tailored Clothing Industry*, 16 CFR Pt. 412 (1968), https://tile.loc.gov/storage-services/service/ll/cfr/cf/r1/99/20/51/-T/16/CI/P4/12/cfr1992051-T16CIP412/cfr1992051-T16CIP412.pdf.

36 "Section 1029 of the Dodd-Frank Act authorizes the FTC to prescribe rules with respect to unfair or deceptive acts or practices by motor vehicle dealers, and to do so pursuant to the Commission's authority under the FTC Act and in accordance with the Administrative Procedure Act (APA)." *See*, FTC, *Motor Vehicle Dealers Trade Regulation Rule*, 6 CFR Pt. 463 (2022), https://www.federalregister.gov/documents/2022/07/13/2022-14214/motor-vehicle-dealers-trade-regulation-rule.

V. There Are Many Paths to the Buddha – An Amazon Example

25. The FTC's antitrust complaint against Amazon alleges several issues that could be the basis of an unfair and deceptive acts claim. For example, the FTC's antitrust complaint alleges that Amazon prevents merchants from steering customers to a lower-cost platform – that is, a platform that charges a lower take rate – by offering discounts off the price it charges on Amazon. Amazon threatens merchants' access to the Buy Box if merchants are caught charging a lower price outside of Amazon, a variant of a most favored-nation (MFN) restriction. In other words, Amazon won't allow merchants to share any portions of its savings with customers as an inducement to switch platforms; doing so would put downward pressure on Amazon's take rate, which has climbed from 35 to 45 percent since 2020.[37]

26. The complaint also alleges that Amazon ties its fulfillment services to access to Amazon Prime. Given the importance of Amazon Prime to survival on Amazon's Superstore, Amazon's policy is effectively conditioning a merchant's access to its Superstore on an agreement to purchase Amazon's fulfillment, often at inflated rates. Meanwhile, many suppliers would prefer "multi-homing:"

> "[Multihoming is] simultaneously offering their goods across multiple online sales channels. Multihoming can be an especially critical mechanism of competition in online markets, enabling rivals to overcome the barriers to entry and expansion that scale economies and network effects can create. Multihoming is one way that sellers can reduce their dependence on a single sales channel."[38]

27. Finally, the Complaint alleges that Amazon gives its own private label brands preference in search results. The complaint states:

> "Amazon further degrades the quality of its search results by buying organic content under recommendation widgets, such as the "expert recommendation" widget, which display Amazon's private label products over other products sold on Amazon."[39]

28. A potential remedy for such conduct might well be to break Amazon up or something more innovative.[40] Or to leave it intact as an essential facility.[41]

---

37 *See*, Stacy Mitchell, *The Amazon Monopoly Tollbooth in 2023*, (Sept. 21, 2023), https://ilsr.org/articles/amazonmonopolytollbooth-2023/.

38 Complaint, FTC v. Amazon.com, Inc., No. 2:23-cv-01495 (Sept. 26, 2023), at ¶ 28, https://www.ftc.gov/system/files/ftc_gov/pdf/1910129AmazoneCommerceComplaintPublic.pdf (FTC Antitrust Complaint)

39 *Id.* at ¶ 241.

40 See Peter Carstensen & Darren Bush, *How to Break Up Amazon* (U. Wis. Legal Stud. Rsch., Paper No. 1789, Oct. 30, 2023), https://www.thesling.org/how-to-break-up-amazon/.

41 Brett Frischmann & Spencer Weber Waller, *Revitalizing Essential Facilities*, 75 Antitrust L.J. 1 (2008).

However, judicial reticence to such approaches might leave intact the problem without much in the way of supervision, such as a decree lasting a few years with minimal oversight.

29. FTC enforcement or rulemaking under its consumer protection umbrella could serve to perhaps more effectively remedy such issues, even more broadly than just Amazon. What follows is some speculation as to how it could do so, with analogies from existing rules.

30. Under consumer protection rulemaking, one might envision the conduct as a variant of a junk fee (which is the subject of current rulemaking by the FTC and other agencies), if the prices on both platforms match, but are enhanced on the competing platform due to the MFN clause.

31. The tying of delivery and sale (the multi-homing problem) could be viewed as similar to the contact lens and prescription glasses problem. The purchase takes place at the portal and compels the delivery via the same owner, assuring higher prices. Prior to the glasses rule, a prescription was obtained at the optometrist and the glasses were compelled to be delivered by the same entity.

32. The "expert recommendation" issue is perhaps the strongest consumer protection claim. For if the basis of the recommendation is payment, it would indeed appear deceptive. The FTC has begun rulemaking on the issue of paid reviews and other methods used to deceive consumers.[42]

33. Beyond rulemaking, the FTC could also halt behavior that is more patently problematic. The FTC also brought a separate UDAP complaint against Amazon shortly before the broader antitrust/UMC case. This complaint alleges Amazon "knowingly duped millions of customers" into enrolling in Amazon Prime, all the while making it exceptionally difficult to cancel. In some instances, customers could be enrolled in Amazon Prime without making a purchase.[43]

34. This complaint was brought under the UDAP arm of the FTC and the Restore Online Shoppers' Confidence Act (ROSCA).[44] The complaint seeks an injunction barring the practices, civil penalties, and other relief. A win in this consumer protection case has the potential to lower barriers to exit for customers who might otherwise buy a product on another platform, thus lowering barriers to entry for multi-homing.

---

42 *See* FTC, *Trade Regulation Rule on the Use of Reviews and Endorsements*, 16 CFR Pt. 465 (2022), https://www.federalregister.gov/documents/2022/11/08/2022-24139/trade-regulation-rule-on-the-use-of-reviews-and-endorsements. Compare with FTC Antitrust Complaint, *supra* note 38, at ¶ 246: Rather than competing to secure recommendations based on quality, Amazon intentionally warped its own algorithms to hide helpful, objective, expert reviews from its shoppers. One Amazon executive reportedly said that "[f]or a lot of people on the team, it was not an Amazonian thing to do," explaining that "[j]ust putting our badges on those products when we didn't necessarily earn them seemed a little bit against the customer, as well as anti-competitive."

43 FTC Antitrust Complaint, *supra* note 38, at ¶ 40.

44 15 U.S.C. §§ 8401-8405.

35. It "just doesn't matter"[45] that the UDAP case was brought separately or whether it was brought as an additional count in the larger antitrust/UMC complaint. Either is substantively and procedurally correct. What does matter is how the FTC can use the full array of its statutory powers to remedy harm in the real world.

VI. Conclusion: One Theory of Dharma, Many Paths

36. We do not suggest that integration of consumer protection remedies to mitigate antitrust harms is a panacea. We suggest here some commonality of issues arising in both the consumer protection and the antitrust context. To the extent that the harms arise from similar sources, the more expedient path to remedy would also be the most beneficial.

37. Antitrust is undergoing a renaissance in the United States. But we are painfully aware that such a path forward may be temporary. It is also filled with many traps and barriers to success, laid forth by the courts and advocated by pro-concentration academics. While there are many paths to the Buddha, they do not need to directly confront all such impediments.

45 Meatballs (Paramount Pictures 1979) (Camp counsellor played by Bill Murray exhorting his team in preparation for competition against bigger, stronger, better resourced opponent).

Is it the Advent of Fairness?*

MARC IVALDI AND CONNIE LEE
Toulouse School of Economics, NERA

I. Fairness is everywhere in the DMA

1. Fairness has emerged as a central theme in the European Commission's Digital Markets Act (DMA) and is increasingly visible in policy discussions regarding digital markets.

2. The DMA claims that "*market processes are often incapable of ensuring fair economic outcomes with regard to core platform services*," (recital 5) and sets forward a definition for gatekeepers in the digital markets. The Commission describes its concerns this way: "[gatekeeper features are] *likely to lead, in many cases, to serious imbalances in bargaining power and, consequently, to unfair practices and conditions for business users, as well as for end users of core platform services provided by gatekeepers, to the detriment of prices, quality, fair competition, choice and innovation in the digital sector*." (recital 4)

3. Notably, the closest the DMA comes to describing what is fair is in stating, "*unfairness should relate to an imbalance between the rights and obligations of business users where the gatekeeper obtains a disproportionate advantage*." (recital 33) Interestingly, end users (i.e., consumers) are not part of this definition. While the DMA describes how end users fit into the digital markets setting, they are nowhere to be seen where it sets forward a theory of harm and a framework for intervention. Instead, the principles of contestability and fairness take center stage.

---

* This article has been previously published in Concurrences, and it might have been edited for clarity and cohesion. Marc Ivaldi, Connie Lee, Is it the advent of fairness?, September 2023, Concurrences N° 3-2023, Art. N° 113069.

4. Given Margrethe Vestager's focus on fairness since her term in office began, this is not surprising. Many have noticed a clear increase in the use of the words "fair" and "unfair" in Vestager's speeches, and some have voiced concerns about getting lost in the moral or "romantic" ideas of fairness. As we discuss below, fairness is a principle that can be defined in many ways on economic grounds, and when it comes time to implement rules, we have to be careful not to apply contradicting definitions of fairness.

II. Fairness has always been present in competition law and policy

5. While some say the resurgence of fairness is a step away from the economic approach to competition enforcement, this is not the full picture.

6. The concept of fairness is deeply ingrained in the history of antitrust. Since the beginning of the 20th century – when Standard Oil was accused of abusing its market dominance with unfair business practices – experts have evoked notions of fairness. A debate among legal professionals and economists on the goals of antitrust policy resulted in a convergence on the consumer welfare standard and Chicago School principles of economic efficiency. Crucially, this is a manifestation of fair principles, not an independent concept of fairness. The consumer welfare standard puts the consumer at the heart of the definition of fairness and, essentially, represents a consensus on the basis for applying fairness.

7. In the EU, fair principles have been present in the Treaty on the functioning of the European Union (TFEU) since its inception. Article 102 prohibits "unfair trading conditions" and "unfair prices," and Article 101(1) refers to assessing whether consumers receive "a fair share." Furthermore, non-discrimination is a central theme in EU law. Again, the consumer welfare standard has been the standard used to guide these fair principles.

III. Why is fairness so present in digital markets?

8. Today, the broader theme of fairness is returning once more, pushing the limits of the consumer welfare standard. This is particularly evident in digital markets as digital platforms have emerged with new market characteristics that do not fit into the existing framework. Digital platforms are often characterized by significant size asymmetries, zero-price services, network effects, weak IP protection, and more.

9. The internet has been credited with enhancing access to information and lowering barriers to entry for small businesses. This means businesses on the web can reach more consumers, but they are also in competition with more

businesses. As the online web is so widely cast, the removal of one business from a platform means there are multiple other options to take its place. This has caused discontent among parties such as marketplace sellers and news publishers as they feel their asymmetric bargaining positions leave them subject to "unfair" terms or cause them to lose out on a "fair share" of the return.

10. In addition, a fundamental principle of the open web is that it is "open." Consumers can access it freely and at zero price. Some may say the price consumers pay is the data they provide, but a precise methodology to measure this has not yet been established. This turns the consumer welfare principle on its head as the consumer surplus, in its traditional sense, is already maximized.

11. The effects of any purported harmful practices will not be captured in a pass-through to prices. Therefore, the traditional methods of evaluation are ineffective.

12. Instead, consumers may be affected by non-price factors such as quality or product variety or, alternatively, more social factors such as privacy and information access for democratic reasons. Further, nobody denies that digital platforms are innovative and have generated huge gains for society; however, the effect on innovation in adjacent areas may not be fully internalized.

13. These effects on consumers are fundamentally more difficult to quantify and, therefore, potential harms are more difficult to measure. Since antitrust enforcers are concerned about type II errors, the difficulty in measuring effects on consumers has led to more theories of harm that stop short at the first step, with businesses. Even though businesses were already included in antitrust policy, the previous guiding principle was how that would then affect consumers. Now that the effect on consumers is more ambiguous, various parties are turning to fairness arguments for themselves and losing sight of consumers.

IV. The difficulties of defining fairness

14. While the concept of fairness has a positive connotation among the broader population, when it comes to setting rules based on fairness, many issues emerge. What is "fair" can vary in the eye of the beholder. As George Stigler pointedly put it, justice is "*a suitcase full of bottled ethics from which one freely chooses to blend his own type of justice*."[1]

15. The well-known cake-cutting exercise is an analogy that illustrates this challenge. What is the fairest way to cut a cake? One could cut the cake into equal slices, but how should one determine the people to share the cake between? Another distribution could be based on the value people have for cake, such that people who like cake get a larger slice than people who

1 J. Stigler, The Law and Economics of Public Policy: A Plea to the Scholars; (1972).

don't like cake as much. The cake could also be distributed based on subgroups. For instance, a fair distribution could split equal parts of the cake between men and women. Another distribution strategy could be based on equality of opportunity. This could be implemented by giving everyone a fork and letting them dig in at the same time. It could also be implemented as a raffle where everyone has an equal probability of winning, but the cake would only go to one person.

16. As this analogy makes clear, different outcomes can be considered fair depending on the basis used. Operationalizing the concept will require answering questions such as "Fairness for who? And on what basis?" Equality, equity, equal opportunity, efficiency, etc., imply different outcomes, and using the term "fair" without a common definition will create the risk of conflicting effects.

V. How should fairness be implemented in practice?

17. The typical question of how to fairly allocate the gains created by the actions of all, or a set of, players is the central question of cooperative game theory. Assuming all players explicitly or implicitly agree to cooperate, the object of cooperative game theory is to provide solution concepts that define and determine the allocation each player receives. These solutions are not self-enforcing. They must be enforced by external forces or contracts.

18. The DMA, as well as many experts, considers that the outcomes – in terms of industrial organization – generated by the characteristics of the digital sector as summarized above (e.g., for core platform services) create situations of strong imbalances in bargaining power. Therefore, they require enforcement of fair allocations. This is why the concept and tools of cooperative game theory are called in.

19. In this context, a fair allocation is one that allows a player to get a revenue at least as high as its contribution to the overall wealth generated by the actions of all players. Although it is an intuitive way to define fairness, implementing and enforcing this fair allocation is not an easy task for the regulator, the agency, or the intermediary since it requires the observation of information such as the costs and revenues of each player.

20. One solution is to let the players enter a Nash bargaining agreement in which they must decide how to share the payoffs of the game. In a world of asymmetric information, it is not clear that this will end in a legally stable situation. Moreover, nothing guarantees that the outcome of such an agreement corresponds to the highest social welfare one could expect from the working of all individuals and firms in the economy.

21. Clearly, the fairness objective strongly put forward in the DMA has opened Pandora's box.

Universities, Competition, and Academic Values

PHILIP E. OGDEN
Queen Mary University of London

I. Expansion, State, and Market

1. Keith Thomas, one of the most distinguished historians of his generation with a long academic career behind him, recently listed among his major concerns "the notion that universities, instead of collaborating in the framework of their common mission, should compete and, with private providers, sell their services in a market where students are considered not as partners in a joint enterprise of teaching and learning but as 'consumers' seeking the cheapest offerings that will enable them to graduate with the highest salary claims."

2. It is the recent changes in funding for higher education and long-term concerns about the impact of the rapid expansion of the university system in the UK that have motivated this public reaction, as well as those from other leading intellectuals. The role of universities in the economic, cultural, and intellectual life of many countries has evolved drastically over the last few decades – a development that is particularly noticeable in the UK.

II. What is the Purpose of Competition?

3. Now, nearly 50% of an age cohort attends university, and the number of universities has increased from about fifty in the 1980s to over 150, through a process involving both the creation of new institutions and the rebranding of existing ones. The title of "university" now covers a wide range of varied and quality missions. Large universities have become complex organizations (some provocatively use

the term "businesses"), with an annual turnover exceeding half a billion pounds and a reach that extends well beyond the borders of the UK. These institutions are in open competition in terms of reputation and brand image for research funding and recruitment of staff and students, both nationally and internationally.

4. Once highly selective institutions that were relatively directly funded by public funds twenty-five years ago, modern British universities now depend on a variety of revenue sources, a diversity that calls for sustained vigilance to ensure institutional stability. Nevertheless, universities remain dependent on a certain level of public funding, and thus on the subtleties of government directives – especially regarding the funding of studies and research – which tend to be as numerous as they are inconvenient and inconsistent.

5. The very terms "brand image," "competition," "market," and "business," which now slip so easily from our lips in this context (as is particularly true for me as a recently appointed academic administrator of an institution), are, as some assert, symptomatic of a profound malaise that has overwhelmed the system during this period of intense expansion and change. It is clear that a strong tension has emerged between, on one hand, the benefits of growth regarding student participation, the international reputation of British research, and the contributions of universities to both the national economy and local communities, and, on the other hand, the consequences of a market-driven competitive approach on the intellectual health and values of universities.

6. Thus, Brown and Carasso (2013) as well as McGettigan (2013) focus particularly on the role of money and markets. At the same time, Stefan Collini (2013), from the University of Cambridge, has also recently delivered a scathing critique: "The enormous gamble being taken with higher education in England constitutes an unprecedented ideologically tinged experiment, the consequences of which even its authors are unable to predict or control." He raises an interesting question in passing: "Future historians (&) will find it very difficult to explain the curious fact that, while the record of British businesses is extremely mixed (…). And while the overwhelming majority of publicly funded fully competitive institutions such as museums and art galleries, the BBC, and universities have an excellent record (…) it remains that over the past three decades politicians have relentlessly attempted to force the second type of institutions to change to resemble the first as closely as possible."

III. International Competition

7. A part of the context in which this debate has taken place consists of the ambition of British universities to achieve global leadership status. International competition has essentially taken three forms. The first is the place held in university rankings, especially regarding research and the establishment of globally significant institutional "brands." The three main international rankings (the Times Higher Education World University Ranking; the Academic

Ranking of World Universities by Shanghai Jiao Tong University; and the QS World University Ranking) testify to the strength of the British system on a global scale: in the rankings of the world's top one hundred universities, the UK holds second place behind the United States in all three rankings despite some methodological differences. Table 1 shows the first of these rankings, which identifies the top ten countries ranked by the number of universities appearing in the top 100 worldwide.

8. The significance of these rankings has been widely debated (and their value strongly questioned), not least given the fact that some aspects of government policy (for research, for example, as will be seen later) find their justification in maintaining or enhancing the international competitiveness of the UK. Bekhradnia (2013) interestingly notes that these successes are based, at least in part, on recruiting talented researchers from abroad: about 48% of postgraduate students are not from the UK.

Table 1 : Universities ranked in the top 100 globally, by country, 2013-14

Country	%
United States	46
United Kingdom	11
Netherlands	8
Germany	6
Australia	5
Canada	4
France	3
South Korea	2
Switzerland	3
Belgium	2

Source: Times Higher Education, World University Ranking 2013-14

9. The second is the competition to attract high-tuition international students to study in the UK. The number of students from non-EU countries has increased from 175,000 to 300,000 over the past ten years, with 67,000 coming from China. Table 2 shows the strength of the UK's position in the global market. Representing about 1 in 6 students, this constitutes a significant revenue stream and a source of highly talented youth that has led to intense competition, reinforced by substantial marketing investments. A remarkable related trend has recently emerged with British universities establishing small campuses in London as part of their initiatives to attract foreign students, particularly in fields such as business, management, and law. The third is the desire to establish campuses abroad and encourage partnerships, official or otherwise, with foreign universities. The models for conducting operations abroad vary widely, but despite some high-profile failures, many universities have successfully expanded internationally, thus

opening themselves to new sources of revenue and bolstering their claims to be "international" institutions. International partnerships are also viewed as an effective means to strengthen research ties.

Table 2 : Global market share percentage of international students
Top ten countries, 2013

Country	%
United States	16.4
United Kingdom	13.0
Germany	6.2
France	6.1
Australia	6.0
Canada	4.6
Russia	4.0
Japan	3.7
China	1.9
New Zealand	1.8

Source: adapted from Bekhradnia, 2013, p. 14, based on OECD data

IV. Research: Funding Race and Challenges to Intellectual Practices

10. The notion of "competition" among British universities, and the ensuing debate regarding its impact, is particularly visible in the assessment and funding of research. Since 1986, a series of national assessments of research quality have been conducted for each discipline and have become an indispensable tool for the allocation of public funds. Conducted every four to six years, this exercise, later known as the Research Assessment Exercise (RAE) and subsequently the Research Excellence Framework (REF), has seen its methodology evolve progressively. However, it has remained based on the same fundamental principle, namely an assessment of research quality by discipline ("units of assessment") based on the publications and other "outputs" of individual staff members and on more general considerations such as postgraduate students, research funding, and the research environment. The last exercise, REF 2014, during which 52,000 researchers working in 36 disciplines were evaluated, was complemented by a new dimension: measuring the "impact" of research through a series of case studies. The ratings are based on the perceived quality of research nationally and internationally on a descending scale of 4*, 3*, 2*, and 1*, where only the top two categories qualify for funding (in proportion to the number of individuals submitted for assessment). The overall ranking is based on "outputs" (65%), "impact" (20%), and "environment" (15%).

11. The allocation of public funds resulting from this "competition" reveals two interesting, albeit somewhat contradictory, outcomes. Firstly, high-quality research, even if sometimes limited in scope, is relatively widely distributed across the overall university system. Thus, in 2008, of the 135 universities that submitted staff for evaluation, very few had no research rated at the highest level (4*). Nevertheless, the association between the number of researchers and quality has resulted in a very high concentration of research funding allocated. In 2013-2014, of the £1.6 billion distributed, nearly 60% of research funding determined by this selective competition was awarded to the top 12 universities, and this funding exceeded the amount of public funds allocated to teaching in only 26 cases. This pattern is further reinforced by the distribution of other research funds – from UK Research Councils, charities, and the private sector

12. If almost everyone agrees that some form of attribution mechanism is essential, that the exercises have generally led to an improvement in the overall quality of research for British universities (as evidenced by the rankings mentioned earlier), and that the national rankings produced for each discipline have been relatively rarely challenged, it remains true that the process has attracted numerous criticisms regarding both its methods and its long-term impact. For example, it has been alleged that this ranking generates intense but dangerous competition among universities for recruiting "star" researchers; that it encourages universities and individuals to prioritize research over teaching; that the relatively short periods between exercises impose an inflexible rhythm that hinders large-scale projects, especially in the humanities; that it discourages risk-taking and intellectual innovation; and that it has led many universities to be completely deprived of public funding. Some argue that it has completely perverted the very nature of academic research: "It has generated a large quantity of premature publications and an even greater quantity of useless publications by those who have nothing to say at that precise moment, but who are forced to 'churn out copy,' however confused their ideas may be" (Thomas, 2011).

13. There is no doubt that the overall effect of these policies has been to generate intense competition among universities, whether for acquiring funds or prestige, which can be boasted by those that succeed in maximizing research quality. While some elements attest to a form of collaboration (for example, regional alliances like Exeter, Bristol, Bath, and Cardiff to coordinate investment in research facilities for the most expensive disciplines), the emphasis remains on ruthless competition.

V. Students: Funding, Recruitment, and Participation

14. The number of students in British universities increased by about 320% between 1979 and 2011, and the funding of their studies has undergone

unprecedented upheaval: a system that was free of all fees for British students and granted them a certain level of public assistance for living expenses has been replaced by a regime of high fees, financed by public loans granted on a case-by-case basis, complemented by a variety of scholarships and special grants. Among the many twists and turns of the political path, the underlying goal has always been to create a market where competition is supposed to promote quality, but a market nonetheless largely determined and strictly regulated by government policy.

15. The first phase of university expansion during the 1980s and 1990s relied on a reduction in the amounts spent by the state per student (from a base of 100 in 1976, the figures fell to 79 in 1989 and to 60 in 1994). However, it quickly became clear that if the participation rate in higher education was to reach 50% of the age cohort (according to a famous statement by Tony Blair in the late 1990s), then public funding modes would necessarily have to change. Tuition fees were part of the response: introduced in 1998 at £1,000 per year, they were tripled in 2004, and then, following the Browne Report of 2010 (which recommended not capping fees), universities were allowed to charge up to £9,000 per year (effectively limiting competition and the market) borrowed by each student through the state. This represented a fundamental change, as it meant the withdrawal of a large part of the state funding that supported teaching, and its complete abandonment for the humanities and social sciences. In reality, most universities immediately chose to charge the maximum amount of fees. To counter the inherent lack of competition in this mechanism, the government then turned to manipulating the number of students that universities were allowed to recruit, ultimately proposing in 2013 the complete removal of national controls starting in 2015. This undoubtedly generated a new wave of intense competition to attract the most qualified students, where universities' eagerness to achieve good scores in national student satisfaction surveys (which publicly funded universities are obliged to participate in) played a significant role.

16. Two other aspects of the impact of these new funding rules deserve commentary. First, an important aspect of the introduction of new fees is their potential impact on the participation in higher education of less advantaged social groups. While the expansion of universities has generally largely favored the middle classes, and less advantaged groups tend to concentrate in more recent institutions primarily focused on teaching, there is no decisive evidence to date suggesting that the new fee regime encourages students to apply or exacerbates social disparities (even if it is clear that it does nothing to reduce them). Secondly, as part of an approach aimed once again at diversifying the sector and strengthening competition, the government allowed that university status be granted to entirely private institutions, which consequently acquire the title, as well as, for example, the right for their students to take out government-funded loans to cover their costs.

VI. Conclusions

17. This brief article provides some markers to get an idea of the rapid evolution of higher education in the UK and the biases through which competition underpins much of the current activity. Universities are undoubtedly flourishing – record numbers of both domestic and international students, strong international recognition of research activities, vast construction programs, expansion abroad, and, despite pressures, sustained autonomy of institutions to "maintain control over the most important aspects of their activities and operations" (Bekhradnia 2013). Nonetheless, today's university is radically different from the smaller, largely state-funded institutions of thirty years ago. The term "university" covers a wide range of quality, reputation, and size. Financial diversity poses the challenge of sustainability and raises concerns about the risk that the "commodification" of higher education and the encouragement of competition will erode the core values of the impartial pursuit of knowledge, intellectual integrity, and the public good.

Beyond Competition: What Is Needed to Make Markets Work Well?

ALEXIS WALCKIERS*

E.CA Economics

I. Introduction

1. Competition between companies makes markets work better. As consumers, we have all experienced that competition fosters better behaviour on the side of producers of goods and services. This experience is often more perceivable in the absence of competition: when we do not have the choice between suppliers, our provider takes our customership for granted, and the price we pay, the quality of service or the choice we get often disimproves.

2. But while competition is an essential ingredient for well-functioning markets, what is the role of competition law enforcement and competition policy more broadly? And what are the limits, if any, of what can be achieved by competition agencies? Competition policy cannot deliver well-functioning markets in a vacuum; other market-friendly economic policies are required. This article describes some of these wider market-friendly economic policies.

3. This short contribution is organised as follows. I will first try and define how well-functioning markets can be recognised by what they deliver to consumers. In essence, this is elasticity of supply: increasing demand can be met, without significant price shifts. Section III discusses the role of competition policy and competition enforcement, along with more demand-side policies such as consumer protection. Section IV considers the role of institutions, such as democracy,

---

* I thank Brecht Boone for useful discussions on these subjects and a careful review of an earlier draft. The author is a Director at E.CA Economics, teaches economics at the Université libre de Bruxelles and at the Université de Namur, and is an Assessor of the Belgian Competition Authority.

but also fair and efficient courts and administrative processes. Section V argues that asset reallocation towards growing or better organised firms is key to well-functioning markets for goods and services, and to meet long-term challenges such as the digitalisation of the economy, ageing of the population, reshoring of production and transition to a net-zero economy. This reallocation of assets requires well-functioning capital markets. Section VI concludes on the role of competition authorities in asset reallocation, arguing that mergers can play a key role in helping markets function well. While competition authorities' role is crucial in reviewing mergers of firms with market power, they would be well advised to encourage merger activity of firms without market power.

II. When Do Markets Function Well?

4. Well-functioning markets deliver high-quality, diverse and innovative products and services at fair prices. And, as demand for some products and services evolves (or for some categories or features of products and services), well-functioning markets will adapt and match new market demand, without significant price evolutions.

5. In economic terms, well-functioning markets are characterised by an elastic supply function. In other words, the supply function should be relatively flat: when demand increases, the additional demand should be delivered at slightly higher prices and, when demand decreases, prices should not drop sharply. The additional demand can be matched by existing suppliers that expand their production, or by newcomers on the market. Similarly, when demand decreases, supply reduction can come from a production reduction of current suppliers, or from market exit. Obviously, there will be significant variations across markets. Supply is more elastic in some markets than in others for technical reasons, but other things being equal, supply will be more elastic in well-functioning markets.

6. Economic models usually focus on price as a strategic variable, but prices are only one of the possibly relevant choice variables. In some cases, price might not be the most relevant variable. It could be that some feature of a good becomes more relevant for consumers. For instance, consumers may suddenly wish (or need) more powerful batteries or better cameras on their mobile phones. Well-functioning markets are able to adapt and deliver these features, without significant price increases.

III. Role of Competition and Consumer Protection Laws

7. It will not come as a surprise to the competition law community (which is the target audience of this volume) that competition law enforcement (and

competition policy more broadly) play a key role in fostering well-functioning markets. Indeed, abuses of dominance, cartels and anticompetitive mergers have the capacity to reduce the provision of high-quality products at low prices, which is often their main objective. In some cases, dominant firms can use demand shifts strategically to segment markets and discriminate, for example by offering the required quality or features (powerful batteries or better cameras in our earlier example) at higher prices, while still supplying basic products at lower prices, to extract more consumer surplus. Such discrimination requires market power, because in sufficiently competitive markets, competitors would compete away additional profits on premium phones.

8. Next to competition law, which mainly focuses on the supply-side of the market, the enforcement of consumer protection laws also plays an important role. Consumer protection laws are key to helping consumers make the best choice for themselves. They can help consumers access relevant information to make their choices and act accordingly. And active customer choice is key to incentivising producers to market products and services that fit consumer requirements and preferences: why would producers try and satisfy consumers, if they do not purchase these products and services? There is a feedback loop between demand and supply, whereby active consumer choice plays a crucial role in fostering supply-side innovation, and producers' attention to demand evolution depends on customers' readiness to opt for the option that best fits their requirements or desires. This is also the reason why many countries have chosen to delegate the enforcement of competition law and consumer protection to a single institution.

9. In some regulated sectors, regulators play a key role in organising and policing the competitive process on the market. While many instruments can be used by regulators, from price setting to market design, and many forms of less coercive incentives, they often try and foster competition between regulated firms to achieve their objectives. And competition agencies have a role to play here as well.

IV. Well-Functioning Institutions

10. Well-functioning markets require well-functioning institutions. The Sveriges Riksbank Prize in Economic Sciences in Memory of Alfred Nobel has recently been awarded to Daron Acemoglu, Simon Johnson and James Robinson for demonstrating the relevance of well-functioning institutions for a country's prosperity. They have, in particular, shown that countries with a poor rule of law and institutions that exploit the population do not generate growth. There are obviously examples of growing developing economies with weak institutions, but, particularly for developed economies, it is generally agreed that institutions are crucial. Stable and fair institutions ensure that investors can keep their assets and reap the benefits of their investments, even

when the time-horizon of the investment is (very) long. Often, market entry requires decisions with very long-term implications – and investment horizons. Therefore, predictable economic policies are important in fostering entry and, more broadly, well-functioning economic markets.

11. Well-functioning and stable institutions rely in particular on access to courts (and justice). Companies must be able to enforce their contracts in a predictable way and while enforcement in court is often the last resort mechanism, it is crucial that it is accessible, when necessary. This requires that the decisions of the courts are predictable, timely and that the cost of the process is reasonable. Beyond courts, competition agencies, regulators and administrative agencies should be impartial, non-corrupt and should decide impartially in a timely and predictable manner.

12. While democratic institutions have advantages and disadvantages, and while it has often been argued that large corporations can curb democratic processes to their advantage, non-democratic processes are often worse. An example would be, large Chinese corporations recently targeted by the Chinese authorities, where a combination of lack of democratic political structures and of independent courts, left them with few options to defend themselves. In autocracies, rulers can make the life of companies better or worse, in a way that is very hard to predict. The lack of predictability of the political and judicial processes makes market entry and expansion more uncertain, and therefore less likely. In most western democracies most teachers, policemen, judges and civil servants do not take bribes, which means that the level of corruption is relatively low (note that we are not trying to argue here that corruption does not exist), and corruption does not play a primary role in business.

13. More generally, well-functioning markets require a pro-competitive market environment. What this means in practice varies across markets. Market-friendly laws can take the form of easing access to professions or fair and timely urban planning, or access to other assets and resources. Similarly, especially in small countries, well-functioning markets require input from foreign companies, and therefore openness to international trade is key.

V. Asset Reallocation and Well-Functioning Capital Markets

14. As was explained in Section II, well-functioning markets for products and services require expansion and reduction of supply, when demand expands or reduces. Such expansion and reduction can come from existing suppliers, but often it requires entry into or exit from the market. This, in turn, requires a reallocation of resources and assets, which often requires well-functioning capital markets.

15. First, supply expansion requires access to additional productive assets. In some sectors, when the extent of the expansion required is not too great, existing

suppliers can meet the additional demand. They will often need additional input, employees and sometimes additional lines of production. These cannot always be financed based on retained profits, and companies will often require additional financing.

16. When demand shifts are more significant, market demand will often also be met by new entrants. These can be homegrown firms (including startups), relying on readily available or disrupting technologies, or on subsidiaries of established foreign competitors. Most of these firms will require access to outside finance.

17. When customer demand shifts towards new functionalities of products and services, well-functioning capital markets are even more important. And when companies cannot purchase these new functionalities from third parties, but should innovate to bring them to the market, this is even more the case. Indeed, innovation often requires very substantial and risky investments, with long and unpredictable investment horizons. Financial intermediaries that are willing to engage in these types of risky investments take very specific risks. They therefore need to have a good understanding of the innovation processes they engage in and rely on funds from investors who themselves comprehend the risks they face.

18. Second, in well-functioning markets, when consumer demand decreases, producers adapt their supply accordingly, without significant price moves. In some markets, the supply of products and services can be adapted by existing producers, who can reduce their inputs and personnel to reduce production. This is especially the case when the extent of demand reduction is limited.

19. Well-functioning markets also allow for a reallocation of assets to national or international companies, where necessary. For example, a reallocation of assets may be desirable if there is a strong shift in demand, such as e.g., long-term evolutions such as the digitalisation of the economy, ageing of the population, reshoring of production and transition to a net-zero economy (for simplicity I will refer in what follows to an *efficient* firm as a firm that better uses its assets is able to lower its costs, or makes better use of digital, greener or any other comparative or absolute advantage). Indeed, maintaining underused or less efficient assets on the market increases the overall cost structure, which influences prices paid by consumers (at least in the medium term). Ideally, productive assets should be reallocated to companies that use them best whenever this is possible. But, in practice, less efficient companies often stay in the market and serve part of the demand. There are many reasons for less efficient companies to stay in the market, such as sunk costs for instance. When an entrepreneur has invested in productive assets, it can be profitable to stay in the market, because part of the investment will not be recovered. Also, many entrepreneurs have studied and developed expertise in their trade, and they may not want to move to another line of business. They can also wait and hope for better market conditions to materialise.

20. Mergers are powerful instruments of asset reallocation, enabling compensation to the current owners of the assets. As competition experts, we are mostly exposed to mergers where competition concerns could be raised, but we must remind ourselves that most mergers are very healthy for the economy. They enable assets to be reallocated to more efficient companies. That is why the acquirer values the assets more than the seller, which also makes it possible that this asset reallocation benefits both parties.

21. Mergers also enable more efficient companies to grow their client base and serve more customers, which again enables a larger part of the market to be served by more efficient producers. In contrast to growth based on the development of a firm's own assets, mergers enable the acquirer to increase the size of its operations by quantum growth and serve a larger client base more speedily (often the acquirer brings in client contacts along with productive assets). It therefore brings the products and services of the more efficient company to a broader client base quicker. That is not only good for the firm, but also for the clients.[1]

22. In some extreme cases, when demand decreases sharply, some producers file for insolvency. Like mergers, efficient insolvency proceedings can play a crucial role in asset reallocation towards more efficient companies.

23. In short, demand shifts, i.e., market expansion but also market reduction not only require access to a variety of inputs including workers, but also often requires access to outside financial resources. In particular, the reallocation of assets is desirable (and made possible), because the assets are worth more when owned (and managed) by an efficient firm than when they are owned by an inefficient firm. But while future profits make the assets more valuable, financing the acquisition requires access to the necessary funds today, meaning that the swift reallocation of productive assets often requires access to capital. These resources can be made available provided that capital markets work well. And, as argued in Section IV of this contribution, capital markets themselves build on stable and predictable institutions.

24. These additional financial resources can come from various sources. Depending on the sector and on the size of companies involved, additional financial resources can be supplied by banks and other financial institutions, state-backed financial institutions, private equity operators or financial markets. These intermediaries help funnel consumer savings and state funding to the most promising projects. They therefore need to gain deep knowledge of sectors and countries to identify the projects where funds are most likely to be usefully deployed. Each type of financial intermediary may have its comparative advantage, depending on the size of the companies involved, the need for

---

1 Mergers have other advantages that are not discussed in this chapter. In particular, mergers can enhance the efficiency of the acquirer, because they provide an opportunity to reorganise the company (specifically for larger firms, when they acquire substantial firms). Through mergers, companies can also for instance complement their product offering, achieve lower (average or variable) costs because of economies of scale and achieve better prices from their suppliers.

innovation, the risks involved and the time-horizon of the investment, etc., but the presence of a healthy combination of these financial intermediaries with sufficient access to capital is key.

VI. Asset Reallocation and Competition Policy

25. Antitrust and merger control are designed as a policy instrument to control the reorganisation and recombination of assets by firms with market power. The focus of competition authorities is therefore on the largest deals, with the bulk of mergers not being subject to merger control.

26. As mentioned above, with some exceptions, mergers are good for the economy, as they tend to reallocate assets to more efficient companies and contribute to the better functioning of markets. One would therefore expect that competition authorities embrace merger activity insofar as it concerns mergers that are not subject to merger control.

27. However, over the last decade, some commentators have expressed concerns about mergers in relation to the increased concentration in markets in the economy. Some base their comments on (excellent) economic research[2] that highlights the economy-wide increase in margins and concentration across the economy. It is not possible nor the aim here to summarise this literature, its conclusions or its shortcomings in this chapter, but even assuming that concentration has increased and harmed consumers through higher margins (there is no unanimous agreement on this point),[3] the role of mergers (in unconcentrated industries) on the evolution of concentration and margins in general is unclear. Given the effect of mergers on the reallocation of assets described above, I think that competition authorities (and commentators) should not oppose mergers in general, but on the contrary, this does not mean that merger control should not play its role in concentrated industries.

28. Relatedly, a number of decisions by the courts and by European policymakers have reinvigorated merger control under the merger thresholds and added additional filings (for instance concerning foreign direct investment (FDI)). In particular, the European Court of Justice's *Towercast* judgment[4] confirms that the prohibition on abuse of a dominant position laid down in Article 102 TFEU allows a merger to be reviewed a posteriori. It is beyond the scope of this chapter to examine the pros and cons of this jurisprudence, but in effect

2 See for instance, Jan de Loecker, Jan Eeckhout and Gabriel Unger, "The Rise of Market Power and the Macroeconomic Implications" (2020) 135 QJ Economics 561–644.

3 See for instance Nathan Miller's presentation Nathan Miller, "Industrial Organization and The Rise of Market Power" (2023) <www.nathanhmiller.org/miller_marketpower_slides.pdf> accessed 27 September 2024.

4 Judgment of 16 March 2023 in Case C-449/21 *Towercast* ECLI:EU:C:2023:207; see Marie Cartapanis, *Notification thresholds: The Court of Justice of the European Union restores the Continental Can judgment and holds that Article 102 TFEU is capable of applying to a non-notifiable merger (Towercast)*, Concurrences, No. 2-2023, art. No. 112511, 78–82.

it shifts the criterion for merger review from turnover to market share. While there is no doubt that turnover is an imperfect criterion, it is (reasonably) easy for merging firms to estimate. Defining the relevant product and geographic markets is much more complicated and estimating market shares with some degree of certainty requires access to competitors' detailed sales data, which, with a few exceptions, is not available.

29. Beyond the additional uncertainty for merger transactions brought by the *Towercast* jurisprudence, merging firms must now also consider Article 22 EC Merger Regulation referrals,[5] FDI screening and some provisions of the Digital Markets Act (DMA).[6] All of these require additional paperwork and put supplementary risks on merging parties, thus also for mergers that contribute to the better functioning of markets (which is the lion's share of mergers), this may decrease the incentive to merge, which in turn may harm the functioning of markets and – ultimately – consumers, especially in sectors that require significant reallocation of assets because of major economic changes, such as the transition to a net-zero economy, digitalisation, ageing society and the reshoring of production.

---

5 Council Regulation (EC) 139/2004 of 20 January 2004 on the control of concentrations between undertakings [2004] OJ L24/1 (the EC Merger Regulation), art 22.

6 Council Regulation (EU) 2022/1925 of the European Parliament and of the Council of 14 September 2022 on contestable and fair markets in the digital sector and amending Directives (EU) 2019/1937 and (EU) 2020/1828 [2022] OJ L 265/1 (Digital Markets Act).

Why Competition Policy is Relevant to the Fight against Climate Change and a Sustainable Future: What is the Problem and What Are We Doing About It?

Simon Holmes*

Competition Appeal Tribunal

1. This chapter is divided into four parts. The first part explains why competition policy is relevant to the fight against climate change and a sustainable future. It will highlight why competition policy is holding back vital cooperation by business in this area (with some real-life examples). It will then explain (in non-technical terms) why this need not be the case. Part two will give an overview of what has been done so far and show how this gives the green light for business to do much more than it has done so far – again with some real-life examples. Part three will summarise what more can and must be done. Part four concludes.

* Simon Holmes advised businesses on competition law for some 35 years before joining the UK Competition Appeal Tribunal as a judge. He was latterly head of competition law at SJ Berwin and then King & Wood Mallesons – first in the UK and Europe and then on a global basis. He is a Visiting Professor at Oxford University where he teaches competition law. He is also an adviser to the NGO, ClientEarth; Chair of the Sustainability and Competition Taskforce of the International Chamber of Commerce (ICC); a member of the international advisory board of the IDC (Instituto de derecho de la competencia); an associate member of the UCL Centre for Law, Economics, and Society (CLES); and president of the advisory board of the Inclusive Competition Forum. He writes and speaks regularly on competition and regulatory issues and has a particular interest in the relationship between climate change, sustainability and competition law. He is co-editor of a book on this subject: Simon Holmes, Dirk Middelschulte and Martiyn Snoep (eds), *Competition Law, Climate Change and Environmental Sustainability* (Concurrences 2021).

I. Part One: What is the Problem and What is the Solution?

2. You may wonder what competition law has to do with action to fight climate change or, indeed, to build a more sustainable world? Perhaps surprisingly the answer is, quite a lot!

3. Competition to produce more sustainable products and services is obviously good. However, competition can also drive companies (often against their best intentions) to use less sustainable inputs and have less sustainable production processes – simply because they have to do things as cheaply as possible in order to compete and stay in business. Furthermore, conventional competition policy and accounting principles do not take account of many of the "true" costs of production – for example pollution generated or toxic waste dumped into the sea are treated as so-called "externalities" – i.e. costs for society that never appear in the profit and loss statements of corporations. It is therefore important that competition policy helps, rather than hinders, companies to take steps to make their businesses more sustainable.

4. Of course, in many instances, regulation is the answer (minimum environmental standards, etc). Unfortunately, regulation is often lacking, is too slow in coming, is limited to particular jurisdictions, or frankly, it is hopelessly limited in scope and ambition. If the world could agree a realistic carbon price, carbon taxes, or a proper phase out of fossil fuels, the discussion of competition policy would probably not arise. However, in the real world, this is not going to happen any time soon (you only need to look at the recent COPs).

5. Of course, companies can, and should where they can, compete to produce more sustainable products. However, more sustainable production processes, or more sustainable inputs, may be more expensive (at least in the short term) giving rise to a competitive disadvantage (a "first mover dis-advantage"). Furthermore, even if some goods can be produced both profitably and sustainably, this is often limited to niche sectors of the market, and we need to put whole sectors of our economy on a sustainable footing-and as quickly as possible.[1]

6. Companies therefore need to work together to transform their industries at the necessary scale and pace. This is where competition law comes in. Companies have (quite rightly) learnt they should compete rather than collaborate with their competitors, and this instinct is inhibiting the sort of cooperation between businesses which we need if we are to fight climate change at scale and pace. I have experience of this in industries ranging from fishing to fast fashion, and

---

1 The failings of regulation and of the competitive process described here ae sometimes referred to as "market failures" or "regulatory failures" and one might add "climate change failures".

from deforestation in Amazonia to efforts to reduce plastic use and increase recycling in UK supply chains.[2]

7. However, in most cases projects such as these can go ahead without infringing competition law. Until recently, the position was uncertain but writers such as myself (and others) have explained how a modern competition policy can take into account sustainability considerations, and thus help, rather than hinder, efforts to fight climate change.[3] The competition authorities have listened and responded accordingly.[4]

8. Having highlighted the problem, we now turn to the solution. In fact, in most cases, this is relatively easy, and most competition laws in the world are probably capable of incorporating sustainability considerations.

9. In this short chapter space does not allow detailed discussion, but I and others have written extensively on this subject.[5] For now, I would make three general points:

10. First, sustainability is widely recognised as an aspect of quality and/or innovation which are key parameters of competition. Agreements which improve quality or innovation are, prima facie procompetitive, not anticompetitive.

11. Second, if a sustainability agreement is, on the face of it, caught by a prohibition on anticompetitive agreements, it is often capable of being exempted. Again, this is not the place for detailed analysis, but to give you a flavour of this the first condition for an exemption under EU law (and most European states, including the United Kingdom), is that the agreement must "contribute to improving the production *or* distribution of goods, *or* to promoting technical *or* economic progress". (emphasis added). One does not need to be a competition expert to appreciate that many (or perhaps most) sustainability agreements are likely to fall within one or more of the four limbs of this condition (for example, an agreement to use less polluting inputs; less polluting technology or to share logistics).

---

2 For real-life examples of where fear of competition law (whether well founded or not) is inhibiting progress in the fight against climate change see the paper produced by the ICC's Sustainability and Competition Taskforce for COP 27, ICC, "When Chilling Contributes to Warming. How Competition Policy Acts as a Barrier to Climate Action" (2022) <https://iccwbo.org/wp-content/uploads/sites/3/2022/11/when-chilling-contributes-to-warming-2.pdf> accessed 29 October 2024.

3 See for example my publications on this subject, Simon Holmes, OUP, <www.law.ox.ac.uk/people/simon-holmes> accessed 29 October 2024. There are also excellent papers by many academics and practitioners on this such as: Maurits Dolmans, "Competition 'Noble Co-Opetition', and the Climate Change Example" (2022) <www.clearygottlieb.com/news-and-insights/publication-listing/competition-overdose-noble-coopetition-and-the-climate-change-example> accessed 29 October 2024; and Maurits Dolmans et al., "Competition Overdose: Exploring the Limitations, searching for the treatment" (February 2022) <www.clearygottlieb.com/-/media/files/competition-overdose-exploring-the-limitations-searching-for-the-treatment.pdf> accessed 29 October 2024. There are also excellent contributions coming out of organisation like the OECD such as the paper by Cristina Volpin, "Environmental Considerations in Competition Enforcement: Legal Assessment" (2021) Background Paper by the Secretariat <https://one.oecd.org/document/DAF/COMP(2021)4/en/pdf> accessed 29 October 2024. See also Holmes, Middelschulte and Snoep (eds), *Competition Law, Climate Change & Environmental Sustainability* (Concurrences 2021) (a collection of 40 essays) and a collection of 8 essays by Marjolein De Backer et al., *Sustainability and Competition Policy* (February 2023) 1 Concurrences 111069.

4 See further Part Two below.

5 See (n3) and Simon Holmes, "Climate Change, Sustainability, and Competition Law" (2020) 8 JAE 354–405 <https://academic.oup.com/antitrust/article/8/2/354/5819564?login=true> accessed 29 October 2024.

12. Third, while my focus has been largely on the EU and UK competition law, the competition laws of most countries around the world are capable of reaching very similar conclusions. For example, Australia has a "public interest" test, but has approved sustainability agreements in circumstances where European states or the EU could have come to essentially the same conclusion.[6]

II. Part Two: Where Have We Got To?

13. Great progress has been made over the last few years with key jurisdictions producing guidelines/guidance on how to incorporate sustainability into modern competition policy and ensuring that competition policy is not an obstacle to vital agreements to fight climate change. As the UK Competition and Markets Authority (CMA), put it when publishing its guidance "the CMA is keen to help businesses take action on climate change and environmental sustainability, without undue fear of breaching competition, law".[7]

14. The following part identifies or summarises some of the key developments.

1. New Guidelines etc

15. Perhaps the most important of these new guidelines are those published by the European Commission in June 2023 on "Sustainability Agreements"[8] and those published by the CMA referred to above, the "Green Agreements Guidance" (which is probably the most advanced in the world at the moment). This sort of guidance helps businesses, understand:

> Which agreements are unlikely to be caught by competition law (eg because they fall within a "safe harbour" for standards); and
>
> Which agreements might benefit from an exemption from competition law (very broadly because the benefits outweigh the anticompetitive effects[9]).

---

6 An example is ACCC, "Battery Stewardship Scheme" (2020) <www.accc.gov.au/public-registers/authorisations-and-notifications-registers/authorisations-register/battery-stewardship-council> accessed 29 October 2024.

7 CMA, "Green Agreements Guidance 185" (12 October 2023) <https://assets.publishing.service.gov.uk/media/6526b81b244f8e000d8e742c/Green_agreements_guidance_.pdf> accessed 29 October 2024.

8 See European Commission, "Guidelines on Horizontal Agreements" (1 June 2023) ch 9. See also, Simon Holmes, "Sustainability and Competition Policy in Europe: Recent Developments" (2023) 14 JECLAP 448–456.

9 To benefit from an exemption under EU law (Article 101(3) TFEU), or the national equivalents, an agreement must give rise to certain benefits (as discussed at the end of Part one above); consumers must get a "fair share" of those benefits; it must be no more restrictive than necessary (the "indispensability" test); and it must not eliminate(effective) competition completely.

16. Several of the guidelines produced also:
    - Invite companies to speak to the competition authority informally about potential projects (an "open door" policy); and
    - Provide considerable protection from enforcement action/fines if the principles of the guidance are adhered to, or the parties have discussed the matter with the authority.

17. The UK guidance also includes a "more permissive approach" for "climate change agreements". Without going into the technicalities, "climate change agreements" are a sub-set of environmental sustainability agreements which contribute to combating climate change. Obvious examples are agreements which reduce greenhouse gases, such as carbon dioxide and methane, emitted from the production, distribution or consumption of goods and services. The "more permissive approach" involves taking a more inclusive approach to the consumers which are recognised to benefit from the agreement in question.[10]

18. Many other countries have also produced guidelines, draft guidelines, reports and statements all designed to show how sustainability and competition policy can go hand in hand.[11] These include:
    - Within Europe notable examples are the Dutch, Greek, French and German competition authorities (with others being under consideration – eg in Portugal).
    - Beyond Europe there are new initiatives in countries as diverse as Japan, India, Mexico, New Zealand and Brazil – with more in the pipeline (eg draft guidelines in Singapore and guidance in preparation in Australia).

2. Practical Guidance

19. However helpful general guidelines may be, there is also a need for more specific guidance on particular projects. Obviously, this helps the companies in question. However, it also helps other companies get a better idea of what they can or cannot do and helps develop the understanding of the competition authorities – which can, in turn, help them give better guidance and update their guidelines.

---

10 Under the EU Commission's approach, the basic stance is that the benefits of the agreement must outweigh any negative effects on consumers in the relevant market. The CMA recognises that in the case of climate change agreements it will take account of the benefits accruing to all UK consumers (see the CMA Guidance (n 8), s 6. In many cases this may ensure that the polluter (or the consumer whose demand is causing the pollution) pays for pollution in accordance with the fundamental principle of the "polluter pays" (on which see Maurits Dolmans, "Sustainable Competition Policy and the 'Polluter Pays' Principle" in Holmes, Middelschulte and Snoep (n 3))

11 For fuller reviews of these see the paper produced by the ICC Sustainability and Competition Taskforce for COP 28, ICC, "Taking the Chill Factor Out of Climate Action: A Progress Report on Aligning Competition Policy with Global Sustainability Goals" (2023) <https://iccwbo.org/wp-content/uploads/sites/3/2022/11/2023-ICC-Progress-report-on-aligning-competition-policy-with-global-sustainability-goals.pdf> accessed 29 October 2024; and "Sustainability and competition policy in Europe: recent developments", 21, October, 2024. https://academic.oup.com/jeclap/advance-article/doi/10.1093/jeclap/lpae063/7828941?searchresult=1

20. Many competition authorities are encouraging businesses to come forward with practical examples, and some have published the guidance which they have given so far (subject to important confidentiality considerations).[12]

21. Examples include:

- The UK CMA has now published guidance in two cases:
  - Guidance to the Fairtrade Foundation regarding an agreement which encourages more sustainable farming practices; and
  - Guidance to WWF regarding a commitment by leading UK supermarkets to reduce greenhouse gas emissions in their supply chains.
- The Dutch competition authority (the ACM) has published short decisions on cooperation arrangements as diverse as:
  - Cooperation between waste collectors to stimulate recycling;
  - A joint agreement between soft drink suppliers to discontinue plastic handles;
  - An agreement between Shell and TotalEnergies regarding the storage of CO2 in empty North Sea gas fields; and
  - Arrangements between garden centres to curtail the use of illegal pesticides.
- The French competition authority has published an opinion in the animal nutrition sector designed to harmonise and improve methods of calculating the environmental footprint of products.
- The German competition authority (BKA) has indicated that it will not take enforcement action in relation to a number of sustainability initiatives in areas as varied as Cocoa, animal welfare and bananas.
- The Belgian competition authority has ruled on a cooperation agreement concerning "living wages" in the banana industry (notable because this is taking a wider view of sustainability, beyond environmental sustainability).
- Again illustrating, how all parts of the economy are affected by sustainability considerations, the Brazilian competition authority (CADE) approved a joint venture in the agricultural commodity sector concerning a B2B software platform tracking and standardising sustainability metrics.

22. I should add in this Part that there have also been cases where the authorities have (quite rightly) used competition law as a "sword" to attack agreements which unjustifiably restrict competition on environmental aspects. Perhaps the

---

12 For a fuller review see the ICC, Taking the Chill Factor Out of Climate Action (n 11).

best example is the decision of the European Commission in July 2021 to fine five German car manufacturers some €875 million for restricting competition in emission cleaning for new diesel passenger cars.[13]

23. Finally, although beyond the scope of this chapter, competition law can also be used to attack abusive and unsustainable practices by dominant companies. It can also be a factor (positive or negative) when competition authorities are assessing a merger.[14]

III. Part Three: What Remains to Be Done?

24. Whilst a great deal has been achieved in the last few years to take account of sustainability considerations (and the fight against climate change, in particular) in modern competition policies, much work remains to be done. I would highlight four key issues.

1. The Guidelines Are Work in Progress

25. New guidelines such as the EU guidelines on sustainability and horizontal agreements (or the CMA's Green Agreements Guidance) provide a good framework by which businesses can enter into agreements on such things as green production, phasing out the use of dirty fuels and sourcing inputs on a more sustainable basis.

26. However, these guidelines do not (and could not) provide the answers to all the questions that businesses and others will have on what they can and cannot do in this area. However, these authorities have reaffirmed their "open door" principle, emphasising, that they are willing to provide "informal guidance" on individual sustainability agreements. What we now need is more cooperation between the private sector and the authorities to define and develop what the guidelines mean in practice. This will improve both legal certainty for businesses and help the authorities develop their decisional practice.

27. A specific example of this is to work out how we can ensure that the Commission's view that the "overall effect [of an agreement] on consumers in the relevant market is at least neutral" does not undermine our ability

---

13 European Commission, Decision of 8 July 2021 relating to a proceeding under Article 101 of the Treaty on the Functioning of the European Union and Article 53 of the EEA Agreement (Case AT.40178 – *Car Emissions*) [2021] OJ C458/16 (the so-called *AdBlue* case). This is discussed in Holmes (n 8), Pt V.A. (1) and more fully in Simon Holmes, "Cartels harming Sustainability (and those that don't) in Europe" in Julian Nowag (ed), *Research Handbook on Sustainability and Competition Law* (Edward Elgar 2024), Pt 1.

14 These issues are discussed in Holmes (n 5) and in Simon Holmes and Michelle Meagher, "A Sustainable Future: How Can Control of Monopoly Power Play a Part?" (2023) 1 ECLR <https://static1.squarespace.com/static/65c9daef199ea70aa66592fe/t/65ee9ab3029a7371cd2ce65f/1710135994092/A-sustainable-future_Parts-I-to-III-1.pdf> accessed 29 October 2024. See also four chapters on these topics in "Competition Law, Climate Change and Environmental Sustainability" (n 3). For a short summary see Simon Holmes, "Competition Policy: A Powerful Sword and Shield to Fight Climate Change" (Green European J (1 August 2024) <www.greeneuropeanjournal.eu/competition-policy-a-powerful-sword-and-shield-to-fight-climate-change/> accessed 29 October 2024.

to develop those agreements that will have the greatest impact on climate change – such as phasing out support (eg insurance and finance) for new fossil fuel projects. I believe that this can be done. The CMA's "more permissive approach" to "climate change agreements" is one possibility.

2. Biodiversity

28. We also need to lift our sights beyond climate change and focus on another existential threat to humanity: biodiversity loss. Whilst this falls within the definition of "sustainability", it is not (yet) eligible for the UK CMA's "more permissive approach", which currently only applies to "climate change agreements". The CMA says that this more permissive approach is "justified by the fact that climate change represents a special category of threat: the sheer magnitude of the risk that climate change represents, the degree of public concern about it, and the binding national and international commitments that successive UK governments have entered into". All these points apply equally to agreements to fight biodiversity loss and ecosystems degradation. It is therefore imperative that this more permissive approach be applied to such agreements. On a positive note, the CMA is keeping this approach under review.

3. Moving Beyond Europe

29. To date, the greatest progress on integrating sustainability into modern competition policies has been in Europe. However, climate change is a global threat and many agreements to combat it will need to be consistent with the competition laws of many countries around the world. A priority therefore is to bring this issue up the agendas of other non-European competition authorities. Whilst some progress has been made on this (see above), much remains to be done. Although outside the scope of this chapter a particular issue is the politically motivated opposition to "woke ESG" antitrust currently emanating from certain Republican states in the US. Steps must be, and are, being taken to combat this.[15] It would also be helpful if the Chines competition authorities were to produce guidelines and guidance in this area.[16]

4. Moving Beyond Sustainability Cooperation Agreements

30. The focus so far has been (quite rightly) on ensuring that competition policy does not unduly inhibit vital action to fight climate change: ie it has largely

15 See Dolmans, Hollis, Lin: "Sustainability and Net Zero Climate Agreements – A Transatlantic Perspective" (2023) 8 CLPD <www.elgaronline.com/view/journals/clpd/8/2/article-p63.xml> accessed 29 October 2024; and Maurits Dolman's blog as to why accusations by some members of the US House Judiciary Committee of antitrust violations make no sense, Maurits Dolmans, "The Need to Integrate Externalities, Market Failures, and Collective Action Problems in Antitrust Analysis" (*NYU*, 2024) <https://wp.nyu.edu/compliance_enforcement/tag/maurits-dolmans/> accessed 29 October 2024. See also Colombia Center on Sustainable Development and Sabin Center report, *Antitrust and Sustainability: A Landscape Analysis* (26 July 2023) <https://ccsi.columbia.edu/sites/default/files/content/docs/Antitrust-Sustainability-Landscape-Analysis.pdf> accessed 29 October 2024.

16 On which see further ICC, Taking the Chill Factor Out of Climate Action (n 11), Pt 2.

focused on the prohibition on anticompetitive agreements in Article 101 TFEU and its national equivalents.

31. However, sustainability is relevant to all areas of competition policy: state, aid, public procurement, mergers, abuse of dominance and anticompetitive agreements. At the end of Part Two I touched on the abuse of dominance provisions – which can also be relevant where sustainability considerations are in play – but more work needs to be done both in this area and others such as how to take account of sustainability considerations in merger control.[17]

IV. Part Four: Some Conclusions

32. I hope the above has explained why competition policy is relevant to the fight against climate change, and a sustainable future. Part one showed that any modern competition policy can (and must) incorporate sustainability considerations into its analysis. Part two illustrated how recent efforts have given the green light to cooperation between businesses to fight climate change and Part three identified some of the things which remain to be done.

33. I hope it is clear from this that competition policy is in no way the answer to climate change, but we need to use all tools and policies available in this fight and competition policy can, and must, play its part. To this extent competition policy may cease to be "part of the problem" and be "part of the solution".

34. Competition policy is a compliment, not a substitute, to regulatory action and competitive action by individual companies.

35. Furthermore, for the most part, we are not asking competition authorities to fight climate change.[18] For the most part, we are only asking them to provide guidance and help so that businesses understand better how they can work together to fight climate change and ensure a sustainable future.

---

17 See sources cited in (n 14).

18 Although there is scope for them to use competition tools as a "sword" to attack agreements restricting competition on sustainability where it is a parameter of competition or where dominant companies engage in unsustainable abusive practices (see the end of Part Two above and the *AdBlue* case (n 13), and the articles cited in (n 14).

The Multiple Objectives of Competition Law: Juggling Between Law and Politics

MARC VAN DER WOUDE*
General Court of the European Union

I. A Few Provisions, Much Law

1. In most jurisdictions around the world, the competition rules are limited to a few provisions dealing with restrictive agreements, the conduct of monopolies or dominant firms and concentrations. In the EU these rules are essentially contained in Articles 101, 102 TFEU and Article 2 of Regulation 139/2004. Despite their apparent simplicity, these three provisions are at the basis of an impressive body of rules and case law.

2. Indeed, they lay down very open norms that lend themselves to various interpretations and hence to various policies. These policies are embedded in implementing rules, such as Regulation 1/2003 and interpretative notices, adopted by the EU legislator or the Commission and have lead over the years to many decisions and case law of the EU courts. EU competition law is not only applied by the Commission, but also by National Competition Authorities (NCAs) that operate together with the Commission in a European-wide network (European Competition Network, ECN) and the decisions of which are subject to review by national courts. In addition, national courts can apply Articles 101 and 102 TFEU even in the absence of administrative enforcement decisions. Indeed, companies and customers can seek judicial protection directly before these courts to enforce the rights that these rules confer upon

* President of the General Court of the European Union, Luxembourg.

them. Finally, a large group of legal practitioners, consultants, legal scholars, and economists further contributes to foster and comment this ever-growing area of the law. This growth, which has been spectacular over the last two decades, raises at least two interacting questions, one concerning the various roles played by these actors and, a second one, relating to the consequences of this diversity on the definition of the objectives, which the EU competition law system is supposed to pursue.

II. Many Actors with Different Roles

3. First, which authority decides in which direction EU competition law should evolve? Is it the EU legislator, the Commission, the ECN or the Court of Justice? There is no straightforward answer to this question, because each of these players has their own specific role to play in the system. Setting up the procedures and conferring enforcement powers are matters for the EU legislator, which includes, according to the subject matter and the hierarchy of norms, the Council and the Parliament.[1] This legislative framework is binding on the other actors in the system. The EU legislator interacts in its turn with other actors, in particular the EU Member States, which are represented in the Council. Therefore, when the Commission proposes new legislation, it has to take account of the position of the Member States. These national positions often reflect those of the NCAs represented in the ECN. Moreover, procedures and formal powers laid down in EU legislation are not necessarily indicative of the way they will be applied. The Commission and the NCAs, in and outside the ECN, take the enforcement decisions in individual cases and set their enforcement priorities. Finally, the EU legislator, the Commission and the NCAs must respect the rules of the Treaty. On that point, the Court of Justice has the final say, either when it rules on appeal against judgments of the General Court reviewing Commission decisions or when it answers to preliminary reference questions from national courts pursuant to Article 267 TFEU.

III. Many Actors Pursuing Different Objectives

4. It follows that there are a multitude of actors determining the evolution of EU competition law.

5. This finding is also important when dealing with the second question referred to above. What is the driving force of this evolution? Do the actors pursue a common objective to that effect? As with the first question, there is no

1 The EU Legislator can also empower the Commission to take implementing regulations and block-exemption regulations.

unequivocal answer. All actors in the system probably agree on the important role that competition plays in a market-based economy in which scarce resources are allocated through the laws of supply and demand. To put it differently, all actors share in one way or another the insights of neoclassical economic theory. In consequence, they are, as a rule, opposed to cartels and monopolies that prevent the market forces from fulfilling their wealth enhancing function and that may have worrying spill-over effects on our freedom, as we see today in the field of digital services. I guess, however, that this is probably where the consensus stops. There are very different perceptions as to which goods and services should be subject to market forces and, hence, to what the limits of competition should be. Similarly, there are many diverging views as to both the concept of wealth and its societal importance, in particular against the backdrop of an environmental crisis. Defining the limits of competition and weighing its benefits against other policy considerations is essentially a political question, to which the various actors in the system of EU competition law have different approaches reflecting their different roles, as will be discussed below.

6. Enforcement authorities, such as the Commission and the NCAs, are the first in line to determine which cases they will pursue, what the level of sanctions should be to repress conduct that they consider to be harmful to society or, conversely, to offer guidance as to the categories of authorized conduct. Setting enforcement priorities and giving guidance are the backbone of the EU competition law system, as illustrated by the many notices published by the Commission and the NCAs or as reflected in the various speeches of the persons in charge of these agencies. These policy considerations very often seek to address urgent societal questions, such as the need to combat unemployment and inflation or to protect the environment, all matters on which the Commission and other members of the ECN may sometimes have diverging views.

7. Another level of policy consideration concerns the legislative toolbox. If the procedures and powers granted to the enforcement authorities no longer suffice to deal efficiently with the problems they encounter, the legislative framework needs to be revised or complemented. Such revisions are relatively rare. The adoption of Regulation 1/2003 after 40 years of Regulation 17 and the adoption of Regulation 139/2004 revising the EU system of concentration control after 15 years offer typical examples of such landmark changes. Both reforms were necessary to adjust and modernize the system of EU competition law. The Digital Markets Act (DMA) offers a more recent example.[2] Since the existing toolbox no longer sufficed to control in an efficient and timely manner the behemoths of the digital world, the EU legislator conferred new

2 Regulation (EU) 2022/1925 of the European Parliament and of the Council of Sept. 14, 2022 on contestable and fair markets in the digital sector and amending Directives (EU) 2019/1937 and (EU) 2020/1828 (Digital Markets Act), 2022, O.J. (L 265) 1.

powers on the Commission allowing it to subject these entities to a kind of ex-ante conduct control.[3]

8. The Court of Justice has yet another approach in defining the evolution of EU competition law or rather in setting the limits to this evolution. This approach, which I would qualify as constitutional, has two limbs.

IV. The Legal Limits to Policy Making

9. First, the Court of Justice must ensure that the other actors in the system stay within the limits set by the Treaties. These limits not only concern classical questions regarding the use of the appropriate legal basis for EU action, but also more philosophical questions as to whether that action is in line with the objectives pursued by EU competition law.[4] Before the adoption of the Lisbon Treaty, these objectives were listed in the EC Treaty itself and in particular in Article 3 thereof. It stated that the activities of the Community shall include "a system ensuring that competition in the internal market is not distorted". With the adoption of the Treaty of Lisbon, the structure of the founding treaties changed. Neither the overarching EU Treaty nor the Treaty on the functioning of the EU contain a list of action points similar to the one of Article 3 EC. Article 2 of the TEU lists the fundamental values and rights, whereas Article 3 TEU specifies the impact of these values in the various policy areas of the EU, including the setting up of an internal market. No reference is made, however, to the competition rules. Even so, Protocol 27, attached to the Treaties, provides "that the internal market as set out in Article 3 of the Treaty on the European Union includes a system ensuring that competition is not distorted". Although some commentators feared that this restructuring would degrade the importance of the competition rules in the EU system, the Court of Justice soon recalled in its case law "the vital nature of the Treaty rules on competition" as "the expression of one of the essential tasks with which the European Union is entrusted."[5] The objectives pursued under the Treaty of Lisbon remain those pursued by the Treaty of Rome.

10. These objectives matter. Indeed, when the Court of Justice interprets a provision of EU law, it not only considers its wording, but also the context in which it occurs, and the objectives pursued by the rules of which it is part.[6] This interpretation method can work in two ways: either the act under the

---

3 *See also*, Regulation (EU) 2022/2560 of the European Parliament and of the Council of 14 December 2022 on foreign subsidies distorting the internal market, 2022, O.J. (L 330) 1.

4 *See*, Giuliano Amato, Antitrust and the Bounds of Power; The Dilemma of Liberal Democracy in the History of the Market (Hart Publishing 1997).

5 Case C-496/09, Eur. Comm'n v. Italian Republic, ECLI:EU:C:2011:740, ¶ 60 and Case C-52/09, Konkurrensverket v. TeliaSonera Sverige AB, , ECLI:EU:C:2011:83, see Thomas Graf, *The EU Court of Justice holds a decision on margin squeezes in the telecommunications sector addressing the issue of indispensability (TeliaSonera)*, e-Competitions Feb. 2011, art. No. 35312.

6 Case C-17/10, Toshiba Corp v. Urad pro ochranu hospodarske souteze, ECLI:EU:C:2012:72, ¶ 73, see *The EU Court of Justice rules on parallel enforcement under Regulation 1/2003 while declining to redefine ne bis in idem within the ECN (Toshiba)*, e-Competitions Feb. 2012, art. No. 49475.

Court's scrutiny is compatible with the objectives or it is not. In most, if not all cases, the Court has followed a flexible and extensive interpretation of the scope and thrust of the competition rules. In the very early years of the European Economic Community, it confirmed that the cartel prohibition also applies to vertical agreements.[7] A decade later, it approved the Commission's initiative to apply Article 86 EEC (now Article 102 TFEU) to acquisitions made by dominant firms. The teleological interpretation method followed by the Court of Justice is worth quoting in this respect:

> "... [I]f Article 3 (f) provides for the institution of a system ensuring that competition in the Common Market is not distorted, then it requires a fortiori that competition must not be eliminated. This requirement is so essential that without it numerous provisions of the Treaty would be pointless. Moreover, it corresponds to the precept of Article 2 of the Treaty according to which one of the tasks of the Community is 'to promote throughout the Community a harmonious development of economic activities'. Thus the restraints on competition which the Treaty allows under certain conditions because of the need to harmonize the various objectives of the Treaty, are limited by the requirements of Articles 2 and 3. Going beyond this limit involves the risk that the weakening of competition would conflict with the aims of the Common Market."[8]

11. In *Gencor*, the General Court followed a similar type of reasoning when ruling that Article 2 of the Regulation on Concentration Control also relates to the creation or strengthening of collective dominant positions.[9]

12. Starting in the late seventies until the end of the nineties, the Court of Justice conferred to the objectives of EU competition law a new dimension. Articles 101 and 102 TFEU not only apply to undertakings, but they are also relevant for Member States when they enact rules that may run counter these objectives by undermining the practical effect of the competition rules.[10] This new string of case law was particularly relevant to open certain sectors of the economy, such as civil aviation in particular, to competition.[11] This lost its practical relevance when the internal market project was getting closer to completion during the nineties.

13. From the early days to date, the Court of Justice has always favored an extensive interpretation of the competition rules allowing them to adjust to

7 Case 32/65, Italy v. Eur. Comm'n, ECLI:EU:C:1966:42.

8 Case 6/72, Europemballage Corp v. Comm'n Eur. Comtys, ECLI:EU:C:1973:22, *see also*, Case C-449/21, Towercast, EU:C:2023:207 for a revival of the Continental Can case law in a national context, see Catherine Gordley, *The EU Court of Justice confirms the ex post application of abuse of dominance rules to non-notifiable mergers (Towercast)*, e-Competitions Mar. 2023, art. No. 112151.

9 Case T-102/96, Gencor Ltd v. Comm'n Eur. Comtys, EU:T:1999:65, ¶ 148 to 151, see Philip Owen, *The EU General Court confirms the Commission's decision prohibiting a merger in the platinum and rhodium markets (Impala Platinum / Gencor / Lonrho)*, e-Competitions Mar. 1999, art. No. 39345.

10 Case 13/77, GB-INNO-BM NV v. Vereniging van de Kleinhandelaars in Tabak, ECLI:EU:C:1977:185.

11 Joined Cases 209/84 to 213/84, Ministere Public v. Asjes, ECLI:EU:C:1986:188 and Case 66/86, Ahmed Saeed Flugreisen v. Zentrale zur Bekampfung Unlauteren Wettbewerbs eV, ECLI:EU:C:1989:140.

societal needs. It resisted attempts to limit the scope of the objectives to certain currents of economic thinking, such as the suggestion that consumer welfare consideration would be their main purpose:

14. "… Article 81 EC aims to protect not only the interests of competitors or of consumers, but also the structure of the market and, in so doing, competition as such. Consequently, for a finding that an agreement has an anti-competitive object, it is not necessary that final consumers be deprived of the advantages of effective competition in terms of supply or price…"[12]

15. This open approach also transpires from more recent case law. In case *Servizo Elettrico Nazionale*, the Italian Council of State asked the Court of Justice whether the applicability of Article 102 TFEU to certain conduct depends on the capability of that practice to affect an effective competition structure or its capability to affect the well-being of consumers. The Court of Justice focused on the first alternative, but specified at the same time that the dominant firm may escape that prohibition by showing that the exclusionary effect resulting from that practice is counterbalanced by positive effects for consumers.[13] The objective remains the proper functioning of effective competition, but consumer welfare theories may play a role in the context of the burden of proof.[14]

16. This open attitude, which is favored by the vague terms of Protocol 27, does not exclude however that the Court of Justice occasionally readjusts its case law, in order to allow other policy considerations to play a role. The case law offers various examples. The Court may decide to modulate the confines of the concept of undertaking as initially defined in *Höfner*.[15] It can also state that competition is not always a relevant parameter or find ad hoc solutions when competition is not necessarily desirable.[16] Occasionally, the Court of Justice also backpedals when its earlier statements turn out to be too wide

12 Case C-501/06 P, GlaxoSmithKline Services Unlimited v. Comm'n Eur. Comtys, ECLI:EU:C:2009:610, ¶ 63, see Anne Wachsmann et al., *The EU Court of Justice confirms that the Commission must assess whether an agreement to limit parallel trade in medicines has pro-competitive benefits (GlaxoSmithKline)*, E-COMPETITIONS Oct. 2009, art. No. 41281.

13 Case C-377/20, Servizio Elettrico Nazionale SpA v. Autorita Garante della Concorrenza e del Mercato, ECLI:EU:C:2022:379, see Anne Wachsmann, Nicolas Zacharie & Daniel Green, *Notion d'abus : La Cour de justice de l'Union européenne précise les critères à retenir pour qualifier l'exploitation abusive d'une position dominante caractérisée par des pratiques d'éviction (Servizio Elettrico Nazionale)*, CONCURRENCES No. 3-2022, art. No. 108170, 88–90.

14 *See also*, Case C-413/14 P, Intel Corp Inc v. Eur. Comm'n, ECLI:EU:C:2017:632 and Case C-209/10, Post Danmark A/S v. Konkurrenceradet, ECLI:EU:C:2012:172, see Wessel Geursen, *The EU Court of Justice endorses an effects-based approach on the assessment of low pricing policy under Article 102 TFEU (Post Danmark)*, E-COMPETITIONS Mar. 2012, art. No. 57395.

15 Case C-41/60, Höfner v. Macrotron GmbH, ECLI:EU:C:1991:161; Case C-413/13, FNV Kunsten Informatie en Media v. Netherlands, EU:C:2014:2411 and Case C-492/21 P, Casa Regina Apostolorum della Pia Società delle Figlie di San Paolo v. Eur. Comm'n, EU:C:2023:354, see Raphaël Vuitton, *Absence d'aide : La Cour de justice de l'Union européenne confirme l'arrêt du Tribunal rejetant un recours dirigé contre une décision de la Commission rejetant une plainte alléguant l'octroi d'une aide illégale aux hôpitaux publics dans la région italienne du Latium (Casa Regina Apostolorum della Pia Società delle Figlie di San Paolo)*, CONCURRENCES No. 3-2023, art. No. 113803, 125–126.

16 Case C-222/98, Van der Woude v. Stichting Beatrixoord, ECLI:EU:C:2000:475 and Case C-309/99, Wouters v. Algemene Raad van de Nederlandse Orde van Advocaten, ECLI:EU:C:2002:98.

or unsuitable to address new issues.[17] The Court's approach is not dogmatic, but pragmatic in nature.

17. It follows that the boundaries of antitrust, as defined by the Court of Justice, are relatively flexible and adjustable. It is conscious of the need to leave the other actors in the system of EU competition law sufficient space to develop their policies and make the system evolve. Policies are developed within the limits of the law and may ultimately crystallize into law, but there is a line to be drawn between the application of the law and the law itself.

V. The Legal Limits to Decision Making

18. The Court of Justice' constitutional role not only relates to the policymaking of the other actors in the EU competition law system by ensuring that they stay within the limits of the Treaties, but also to decision-making in individual cases. This second function concerns the right to a fair trial as guaranteed by Article 6 ECHR and Article 47 of the Charter. When it comes to enforcing the competition rules, the Commission (and the NCAs) may impose heavy fines. In such a quasi-criminal area of law, the rule of law, which the EU Courts must guarantee pursuant to Article 19 TEU, commands that the accused have access to independent courts with full jurisdiction, as both the ECHR and the Court of Justice made clear in, respectively, *Menarini* and *Chalkor*.[18] These powers allow the EU Courts not only to control the legality of the Commission's action, but also to assess whether the fine is appropriate. Seen from this angle, the EU Courts can overrule the Commission, even if the contested decision is not vitiated by an illegality.[19]

19. This judicial power constrains the Commission's discretion in setting fines. However, this power is limited to individual cases and does not prevent the Commission or the EU legislator from defining the parameters and criteria pursuant to which the gravity of the sanctions will be set. In the current system, the fining policy remains a matter for the Commission.[20] Even if

17 Case C-7/97, Oscar Bronner GmbH & Co KG v. Mediaprint Zeitungs- und Zeitschriftenverlag GmbH & Co KG, ECLI:EU:C:1998:569 versus Case C-152/19 P, Deutsche Telekom AG v. Eur. Comm'n, EU:C:2021:238, see European Court of Justice, *The EU Court of Justice holds that a media company's refusal to include a newspaper in its home-delivery service does not constitute an abuse dominance since essential facilities doctrine does not apply due to the existence of alternative means (Bronner / Mediaprint)*, e-Competitions Nov. 1998, art. No. 108303, see Maria-Olga Papadopoulou, *The EU Court of Justice dismisses the appeals brought by two telecommunications companies and rules that the indispensability requirement does not apply to conduct that falls short of an outright refusal to supply (Slovak Telekom) (Deutsche Telekom)*, e-Competitions Mar. 2021, art. No. 100833.

18 Menarini v. Italy, Eur. Ct H.R. (43509/08) (2011) and Case C-386/10 P, Chalkor AE Epexergasias Metallon v. Eur. Comm'n, ECLI:EU:C:2011:815, Pascal Cardonnel, *Art. 6, § 1 CEDH : La Cour EDH examine les modalités du contrôle juridictionnel sur les décisions en matière de cartel (Menarini Diagnostics)*, Concurrences No. 4-2011, art. No. 40019, 166–168, and Richard Burton, *The EU Court of Justice upholds General Court judgment in copper industrial and plumbing tubes cartel cases (KME / Chalkor)*, e-Competitions Dec. 2011, art. No. 58853.

19 Case C-137/92 P, Comm'n Eur. Comtys v. BASF, ECLI:EU:C:1994:247.

20 Joined Cases 101 to 103/80, Musique Diffusion Francaise SA v. Comm'n Eur. Comtys, ECLI:EU:C:1983:158.

the EU Courts enjoy full jurisdiction as regards the appropriate level of the fine in an individual case, this policy will be relevant for their assessment, especially where EU Courts must ensure equal treatment when deciding on the appropriate level of the fine in similar or related cases.

VI. Final Comments

20. The EU competition law system relies on a few substantive provisions, laid down in the Treaties and Article 2 of the Regulation 139/2024. This limited basis contrasts with the wide body of legislation, notices, decisions, and case law to which the application of these provisions has given rise, both at EU and national level. This dynamic and organic growth results from the action of various players in the EU competition law system that each play different roles. Even if they probably all adhere to the basic insights of neoclassical economic theory, they have differing views on societal questions and pursue differing objectives. Moreover, these views change over time. This buoyant whole must, however, stay within the limits set by the Treaty. It is the role of the Court of Justice to protect these limits. When exercising this task, it takes account of the objectives of EU competition law, as laid down in Protocol 27. It does so in a flexible and pragmatic manner allowing the various actors to pursue a variety of policy objectives. By contrast, it is and must be rigorous when offering judicial protection in individual cases. In short and blunt, nobody really runs the show, but the Court sets the scene.

The Multidimensional Impact of Competition Advocacy for the Creation of a Culture of Free and Fair Competition

MARÍA ELENA VÁSQUEZ TAVERAS*
National Commission for the Defense
of Competition (Pro-Competencia)

I. Introduction

1. Competition authorities play crucial roles beyond the imposition of sanctions for anticompetitive practices, encompassing the promotion of competition and the defense of competitive principles. The effectiveness of these functions depends on a broad and multidisciplinary understanding of competition law, the complexity of which often hinders its understanding among the public and professionals, especially in developing countries.

2. This leads us to reflect on whether enough has been done to make competition law understandable in all areas. This challenge is accentuated by the limited formal education on the subject and the need to simplify its communication. Thus, the importance of competition promotion and advocacy as essential means to foster a culture of competition, beneficial for economic growth and general welfare, is highlighted.

---

* President of the Board of Directors of the National Commission for the Defense of Competition (Pro-Competencia), Dominican Republic.

II. Competition Policy and Advocacy

3. Competition policy refers to the set of rules, regulations, and government policies aimed at promoting effective competition in markets, preventing monopolistic behavior, protecting consumers, and ensuring a fair distribution of resources. In other words, the legal scaffolding that a State provides for the regulation of competition issues.

4. Regarding this, Enrique Vergara Vial,[1] former president of the Chilean Court for the Defense of Free Competition, states that: "[C]ompetition policy comprises two lines of action: on the one hand, its promotion, and, on the other hand, the application of the law, its compliance, (…) we will not have a society more aware of the importance of this public policy only with punishments… it is also necessary to educate, especially in a matter as complex as this one."

5. Vergara Vial stresses that, in addition to the traditional sanctioning application of competition policy, known as *antitrust enforcement*, which focuses on penalizing anticompetitive practices, it is essential to recognize and value other methods that foster a culture of competition. Competition promotion and advocacy emerge as key components, extending the vision of competition policy beyond the mere reaction to market distortions to a preventive and multidimensional approach.

6. This new approach, as Craig Conrath argues, seeks to ensure that competition policy does not wait for events that harm competition, but rather that competition policy serves to foster a competitive environment in markets, which, in turn, generates competition, and is not only aimed at preserving it.[2]

7. Competition advocacy has been defined by the Advocacy Working Group (AWG)[3] of the International Competition Network (ICN), as the activities carried out by competition authorities related to the promotion of the importance of free and fair competition for economic activity, mainly through relations with other bodies, the preparation of recommendations on economic regulation to public authorities, and educational activities aimed at creating "competition awareness," with the *particularity that these actions do not mean an application of the law in its enforcement character*.[4]

8. This last aspect has been a criterion of discussion, since the application and powers of advocacy vary greatly depending on the jurisdiction that applies. In most developed countries with mature competition law and authorities, this only applied to private economic agents, and not much importance has been

1 Enrique Vergara Vial, *Creating a Culture of Competition*, Diario Financiero (Nov. 9, 2011, at 05:00 AM), https://www.df.cl/opinion/columnistas/enrique-vergara/creando-cultura-de-la-competencia.

2 Craig W. Conrath, Practical Handbook of Antitrust Law Enforcement for Economies (2003).

3 ICN, Advocacy Working Group (AWG), https://www.internationalcompetitionnetwork.org/working-groups/advocacy/ (last visited Oct. 21, 2024).

4 Emphasis added.

given to competition advocacy.[5] Hence, the idea was created that competition advocacy, as such, is not law enforcement.

9. However, as competition law expanded, different jurisdictions, mainly in developing countries, established that its rules also reached public authorities, with special emphasis on regulators,[6] which, in the words of Kovacic,[7] makes competition advocacy a direct application of competition law, and an important factor in competition authorities, mainly in nascent competition authorities.

10. From this point on, competition authorities began to use competition advocacy in the following actions: (i) recommendation actions aimed at public entities (mostly regulators) with the objective of influencing the creation of a regulatory framework that does not distort competition, and (ii) dissemination and promotion of competition, through education on free and fair competition; which translates into creating a culture of free competition in public and private economic agents and consumers on the *benefits of competition and its importance for the economy.*

III. Competition Advocacy: Day-To-Day Enforcement of Competition Laws, the Formation of a Competition Culture and its Impact on Small Competition Authorities

11. As Kovacic points out[8] competition authorities in transition should dedicate their first efforts to the development of competition advocacy, and gradually open space for enforcement. This is because in most cases, competition authorities do not have the human, technical or monetary resources to properly investigate anticompetitive practices.[9] This is aggravated by a lack of knowledge or competition culture on the part of public and private entities, and leaves the competition authorities with no margin of action on enforcement, since the information required to investigate these practices is of a private nature.

12. Competition advocacy is essential in the day-to-day function of regulatory authorities and is not limited to entities in transition but to all in general. This practice does not rely exclusively on the voluntary cooperation of entities to

5 Such is the case in the United States, where the strength of the Competition Advocacy as part of the FTC's competition policy dates back to the years 2001–2005.

6 *See*, Federal Law on Economic Competition of Mexico 1992; Law on the Promotion of Competition and Effective Consumer Protection of Costa Rica 1994; Law No. 22,262 on the Defense of Competition of Argentina 1980 and General Law on the Defense of Competition of the Dominican Republic, Law No. 42-08 2008.

7 William E. Kovacic, *Getting Started: Creating New Competition Policy Institutions in Transition Economies*, 23 Brooklyn J. Int'l L. 403 (1997), https://brooklynworks.brooklaw.edu/cgi/viewcontent.cgi?article=1682&context=bjil.

8 *Id.*

9 ICN, Competition Advocacy (2002), https://www.cofece.mx/wp-content/uploads/2018/05/abogacia.pdf.

provide information but on the use of public data, and active competition advocacy. It encompasses a crucial political dimension, making it easier for authorities to explain their importance to State bodies. The routine activities of a competition authority, such as issuing reports, guides, regulatory recommendations, market studies, and opinions, are fundamental and often more frequent than investigations and sanctions for anticompetitive practices.

13. Undoubtedly, competition advocacy is the implementation of the application of competition law, allowing the development of its multidimensional character, which with its continuous application would lead to the creation of a true competition culture in the economic sectors and for consumers. As an example of this impact, the following aspects can be highlighted.

1. Impact on Public Administration

14. The impact of competition advocacy in the process of regulation formation not only increases public officials' awareness of the importance of not creating barriers to entry, avoiding the abuse of dominant positions, and creating a pro-competitive legal and regulatory framework, but it also promotes a public management philosophy that is more in line with the purposes of the State paradigm and the nature of the economy assumed by the country in question. Hence, Khemani and Dutz,[10] state that an effective competition policy must include the power of the competition authority to take measures to promote competition, which translates, in the words of Professor José Miguel de la Cole Restrepo, that the advocacy plays a role of "fostering the culture of free competition within the State," vital for the maintenance and strengthening of the competition policy itself.

15. At Pro-Competencia, we have observed a remarkable impact on public administration, as a result of an intensive competition advocacy agenda during the last two years. This agenda has included the issuance of almost 30 opinions through recommendation reports to regulatory entities, the publication of Methodological Guides for the analysis of State Aid from a competition perspective and a series of training processes on antitrust matters. This effort has generated a growing interest in administrative institutions on the relevance of free competition in the elaboration of legislative proposals, manifested in an increase of requests for prior review of regulatory proposals by Pro-Competencia, and in jurisdictional decisions related to competition.[11]

---

10 R. Shyam Khemani & Mark Dutz, Competition Law and Policy : Challenges in South Asia 14-15 (World Bank, 2007), https://documents1.worldbank.org/curated/en/216041468101344634/pdf/452810WP0Box334059B01PUBLIC1.pdf.

11 Judges are important actors in antitrust models that, like the Dominican model, respond to the *concurrent administrative model*, in which there is an administrative authority responsible for investigating and submitting the possible concurrence of anticompetitive practices and another in charge of studying and sanctioning the conduct. In this type of model, judges have an essential role as the bodies responsible for closing the conflict, the ultimate interpreters of the competition law. In the experience of the Dominican Republic, it has been possible to verify a greater understanding of judges in competition matters at the time of ruling on the review of a resolution of the competition authority. This followed training processes that Pro-Competencia has provided to judges on matters of free and fair competition.

2. Impact on Corporate Culture

16. As noted above, in developing economies and with competition authorities in transition, awareness of competition, even among private agents, is minimal. The adoption of free competition as part of the business culture represents one of the key benefits of an effective competition advocacy strategy. Fostering a culture of competition is an essential tool, especially in a context where citizens demand a more active and participatory role vis-à-vis the State. As the culture of free competition develops, prosecutions and penalties will be reduced as companies themselves adopt good competitive practices as part of their management philosophy.

17. This impact of the promotion of competition in the business sector transforms companies from simple *regulated subjects* or *key players* in the consolidation of this culture of free competition, moving from a passive to an active role, thus benefiting the climate of free competition in the country. Indeed, as Curiel Leindez[12] points out, "the active role of the business community should reinforce the presence of elements of competition in the design of policies that affect it.*" In this* way, the promotion of a business philosophy that incorporates good pro-competitive business practices is initiated,

18. This approach not only transforms companies from being mere regulated subjects to proactive players in promoting competition, but also improves the competitive environment in the country. According to Curiel Leindez, the active commitment of the business community should strengthen competition in the design of policies that affect them.

3. Social Impact of Competition

19. The importance of free and fair competition in the social and economic fabric of a nation is undeniable, especially in terms of its ability to positively influence the reduction of poverty and inequality. Free competition not only stimulates innovation and efficiency among businesses, but also ensures that the benefits of a healthy market extend to all strata of society, contributing significantly to overall well-being.

20. Competition agencies and international cooperation organizations play a crucial role in this area. Their collaboration is essential to generate a broad and deep knowledge of the positive effects of competition, placing it in a position of relevance that it deserves. This effort should focus on three fundamental axes:

    (1) The creation of accessible educational materials and initiatives on the importance of free and fair competition.

    (2) Creation of tools to quantify the benefits of competition advocacy activities.

    (3) Creation of data to establish the impact of free competition in the fight to reduce poverty.

---

12 Claudia Curiel Leindez, Design of a Competition Advocacy Model in the Context of the Implementation of Competition Policies in Latin America 40 (UNCTAD, 1996), https://unctad.org/publication/developing-competition-advocacy-model-context-introduction-competition-policies-latin.

21. The need for tools to measure the benefits of competition is equally critical. These tools should facilitate the evaluation of how competition policies contribute to the overall implementation of effective economic policies, including the involvement of government institutions in promoting a competitive market environment.

22. In the case of the Dominican Republic, the social impact of competition law is articulated around the promotion of an equitable and efficient market, which serves as a fundamental pillar for the sustainable economic and social development of the country. This is enshrined in Article 217 of the Constitution,[13] recognizing free competition as a guiding principle of the Dominican economic regime; the Constitution reflects this vision, emphasizing human development and social justice as the foundations of the economic regime. Free competition, therefore, is not only a mechanism for economic growth but also a crucial component for sustainable development and the realization of a more just and equitable society.

23. Consequently, at Pro-Competencia, we have consolidated an approach that highlights the relevance of competition law and its significant social impact. This approach has materialized in the implementation of various advocacy initiatives designed to promote a greater understanding and appreciation of the principles of free and fair competition, and to have a social impact. These initiatives include the analysis of regulatory standards with a marked social impact, materialized through the issuance of recommendation reports; the publication of a Methodological Guide for the analysis of State aid from a competition perspective; and the development of promotional activities aimed at fostering a culture of competition among citizens. In this last aspect, the essay contest: "Writing for Competition," aimed at encouraging the participation of university students, and the implementation of training specifically aimed at strengthening the capacities of small- and medium-sized companies in the field of competition.[14] These actions reflect our commitment to promoting a competitive environment that benefits all of Dominican society, reinforcing our belief that free and fair competition benefits everyone.

IV. The Relationship between Competition Advocacy and Communication: Impact and Outcomes of Competition Policy

24. For John Clark, the competition advocacy actions of competition authorities would be further strengthened if the authorities have the following institutional scaffolding: (i) organizational autonomy, (ii) adequate financial resources, and

13 Dominican Republic's Constitution 2015 art. 217

14 *See*, Pro-Competenci, https://procompetencia.gob.do/atribuciones/ (last visited Oct. 21, 2024).

(iii) a reputation for effectiveness and neutrality. Of these characteristics, I will focus on the latter as an essential part of strengthening competition authority through competition advocacy.[15]

25. The relevance of competition advocacy in the development of a competitive culture and its multidimensional effect on the various social sectors has been evidenced. However, adequate communication of these actions is crucial to strengthen the perception of the effectiveness of the competition authority and, therefore, to foster a competition culture.

26. To this end, it is necessary for competition authorities, through their competition advocacy powers, to implement policies aimed at raising awareness of the impact and results of competition policies for the economy, and how this is reflected in their daily lives. This effective communication of the competition authority's efforts would enable the authorities to demonstrate the tangible benefits of their interventions. To ensure this, it is necessary for competition authorities to examine the quantification of the benefits of competition and its actions on people and to communicate these facts over time.

27. As an illustration, the Organisation for Economic Co-operation and Development (OECD),[16] in a recently published study in 2023, stated that: "Competition policy can help combat income inequality and should also be considered in this light, especially in developing countries where the fight against poverty becomes a pressing priority amidst a landscape of scarce public resources (…)." *This* means that competition can have a distributive impact on consumers. For Gutmann and Voigt,[17] countries that have competition policy legislation have GDP growth between 2 and 3 percent higher compared to those that do not. Likewise, Andrés Aradillas-López et al.,[18] states that free competition encourages the participation of entrepreneurs and small and medium SMEs, a phenomenon that would not be possible if the markets had companies with abuse of dominant positions.

28. These data reflect the fact that the defense of free competition has direct effects on people's lives, and is fundamental to stimulating innovation, improving market efficiency, and offering more options and better prices to consumers. The effectiveness of competition policy depends not only on its rigorous implementation, but also on public perception of its effectiveness, fairness, and its role in economic democracy. This is achieved primarily through a competition advocacy strategy aimed at educating consumers about the benefits of free and fair competition.

---

15 John Clark, *Competition Advocacy: Challenges for Developing Countries*, (Sept. 27, 2005), https://www.oecd-ilibrary.org/governance/competition-advocacy_clp-v6-art10-en

16 OECD, Latin American and Caribbean Competition Forum, *Competition and Poverty*, (Sept. 28–29, 2023), https://one.oecd.org/document/DAF/COMP/LACCF(2023)15/en/pdf.

17 Jerg Gutmann & Stefan Voigt, *Lending a Hand to the Invisible Hand? Assessing the Effects of New Competition Laws*, J. Inst. L. & Econ. (Feb. 8, 2014), https://papers.ssrn.com/sol3/papers.cfm?abstract_id=2392780.

18 Andrés Aradillas-López et al., Poder de Mercado y Bienestar Social (COFECE, 2018), https://www.cofece.mx/wp-content/uploads/2018/10/Libro-CPC-PoderyBienestar-ver4.pdf.

V. Conclusions

29. Competition advocacy focused on promoting a culture of free competition and defending this right through advocacy, plays a crucial role in the economic and social development of any country. Competition advocacy has a significant impact on public management, preventing anticompetitive practices that distort the economy, promoting innovation, efficiency, and consumer welfare. This approach not only fosters a business culture of excellence and creativity, but also ensures that ethics and legality prevail in the actions of economic agents, contributing to long-term reputational strength.

30. In addition, competition advocacy provides technical tools and raises the political cost for those who seek to impose regulations that limit competition, convincing stakeholders of the benefits of maintaining a competitive marketplace. At the same time, it establishes important legal precedents that guide economic behavior and ensure informed judicial decisions aligned with competition principles.

31. These multidimensional efforts are fundamental to strengthening competition advocacy, positively influencing business culture, governance, and the judiciary, and contributing to the eradication of poverty. The goal is for society as a whole, including governments and businesses, to understand the importance of free competition, recognizing its direct impact on general welfare and economic competitiveness.

32. In conclusion, competition advocacy is a powerful tool that radiates significant benefits through its ability to educate consumers, influence policy formulation, and provide a technical and ethical framework for market players. It is essential that all sectors understand and value these impacts to ensure inclusive and sustainable economic development.

Justice for All: The Role of Competition Law Beyond Consumer Protection

SAMUEL CHAN*
Hong Kong Competition Commission

1. This short contribution does not seek to delve into the ongoing debate regarding whether consumer protection or consumer welfare should be the central focus of competition law and policy.

2. Instead, drawing on the author's experience as a lawyer who has had the privilege of engaging with various regulatory and advisory bodies in Hong Kong for the past two decades, the following discussion aims to offer insights into the distinctive role of competition law in delivering justice to numerous individuals, going beyond merely providing legal remedies post-adjudication.

3. While the importance of understanding the central role of competition law is not discounted, it is essential to identify and comprehend the underlying policy objectives that inform its framework. As the Antitrust Law Section of the American Bar Association (ABA) pointed out in its *Report on Antitrust Policy Objectives* submitted to the Federal Trade Commission and the US Department of Justice in 2003:

4. "The policy objectives that underlie the application and enforcement of antitrust or competition laws are important for several reasons and are not simply of academic interest:

   1. They inform the enforcement and application of the law.
   2. They help identify and explain differences in legal standards and outcomes in individual cases.

---

* Chairman, Competition Commission, Hong Kong.

3. They increase transparency and facilitate reasoned debate to the extent that they make explicit the rationales for decisions in individual cases".

5. Four years after the publication of the ABA's *Report on Antitrust Policy Objectives*, in a report prepared by the Unilateral Conduct Working Group of the International Competition Network (ICN) for the 6th Annual Conference 2007, thirty-five member agencies and fourteen non-governmental advisors responded to a questionnaire and identified ten objectives of unilateral conduct laws, regulations and policies as follows:
   - Ensuring an effective competitive process;
   - Promoting consumer welfare;
   - Enhancing efficiency;
   - Ensuring economic freedom;
   - Ensuring a level playing field for small and mid-sized enterprises;
   - Promoting fairness and equality;
   - Promoting consumer choice;
   - Achieving market integration;
   - Facilitating privatisation and market liberalisation;
   - Promoting competitiveness in international markets.

6. Almost two decades have elapsed since then, yet a consensus remains elusive regarding the precise interpretations of these identified objectives. For instance, when referencing "consumer welfare", does it pertain solely to consumer protection in a narrow context, or does it extend to considerations of "total welfare"?

7. Similarly, when delving into the concepts of "fairness and equality", shall we encompass moral dimensions, and if so, to what extent should they be factored into the discourse? These unresolved questions underscore the ongoing complexity in understanding and applying these goals within the realm of competition law and policy.

8. Under the sway of the neoclassical economic school of thought, antitrust analysis is often considered to be concerned primarily with economic efficiency. This perspective was eloquently articulated by Professor Maurice Stucke, a former attorney at the Antitrust Division of the US Department of Justice:

   "Since terms like "morality" and "evil" are judgmental, not descriptive, they are deemed outside the discourse of economic theory's self-described positivism. Reducing antitrust to normative morality judgments would represent, for Richard Posner and others, antitrust's descent into 'a weak field, a field in disarray, a field in which consensus is impossible to achieve in our society'".[1]

9. If competition law is solely centred on allocative efficiency and is devoid of moral considerations, the question arises regarding the treatment of hard-core cartels. These cartels are typically deemed unlawful per se and may even incur severe criminal penalties in certain jurisdictions. This juxtaposition prompts an examination of how competition law navigates the intersection of economic efficiency and ethical considerations when addressing these anticompetitive behaviours.

10. It is interesting to note that in an unrelated survey conducted in 2000 regarding perceptions of white-collar crime, more than twice as many respondents considered the embezzler as the more serious criminal compared to the street thief (56% compared to 27%).[2]

11. It would be audacious to embark on an exploration of jurisprudential ideologies concerning "law and morality" within the confines of this brief chapter. Policy objectives that hold significance in certain jurisdictions may not carry the same weight in others, given the disparities in economic, social or cultural landscapes. Drawing from over three decades of legal practice experiences and recent first-hand encounters with the effects of competition law on the lives of millions in a vibrant and bustling international metropolis, the author ventures to offer observations that aim to spark curiosity and encourage deeper reflection.

12. The relevance of social morals in tackling the problem of bid-rigging in Hong Kong is a useful case study or illustration of whether, and if so to what extent, ethical considerations and societal values should be factored in.

13. Under the Competition Ordinance in Hong Kong, bid-rigging is classified as one of the four categories of "serious anticompetitive conduct", alongside price-fixing, market-sharing, and output limitation. Treating bid-rigging as a grave violation in Hong Kong is not only natural but also commendable in the eyes of legislators and the general public, given its widespread presence in various sectors, notably the local building maintenance and renovation market.

14. Quite apart from undermining fair competition and causing detrimental effects to market dynamics and consumer welfare, rigging bids in building maintenance and renovation projects is seen by most if not all homeowners as particularly egregious. Under the statutory scheme for better management of multi-storey buildings – many of which are high-rise developments housing hundreds or even thousands of households in the same estate – flat owners

---

1 Maurice E Stucke, "Morality and Antitrust" (2006) 3 Columbia Bus L Rev <https://journals.library.columbia.edu/index.php/CBLR/article/view/2992> accessed 29 October 2024, citing Richard A Posner, "Law and Economics Is Moral" (1990) 24 Valparaiso U L Rev 163, 166 <https://chicagounbound.uchicago.edu/cgi/viewcontent.cgi?article=2901&context=journal_articles> accessed 29 October 2024.

2 ibid 500.

have no choice but to shoulder their respective shares of the renovation contractor's hefty bill once the building or estate has gone through an open tender exercise. Individual owners' legal obligation to foot the bill is both personal and collective, and in some cases the financial burden amounts to hundreds of millions of dollars.

15. Home ownership in Hong Kong is notoriously expensive, with property prices ranking among the highest in the world. The soaring real estate market, limited land supply and high demand all play a role in the exorbitant cost of purchasing a home in this bustling metropolis. The dream of owning an apartment is a prevalent aspiration for many residents in the city, particularly young families. There is also a legitimate expectation of tranquillity for the elderly or retired individuals who have fully settled their home mortgage loan. Any additional and unreasonable financial burdens associated with the mandatory maintenance of residential buildings would understandably provoke strong reactions from society.

16. In these circumstances, one would be hard pressed to argue that bid-rigging in relation to buildings renovation projects should be solely viewed through the lens of economic theories, divorced from moral considerations. The ethical dimension of such practices cannot be overlooked, as bid-rigging not only distorts market competition but also raises profound questions about integrity, fairness and social responsibility in the business environment.

17. Likewise, should the discussion turn to the consideration of imposing more draconian criminal penalties for bid-rigging in Hong Kong, such as the imprisonment of the responsible directors or controllers of companies, can one genuinely suggest that broader policy objectives beyond consumer welfare and economic efficiency, including moral and social considerations, should be disregarded in the pursuit of a fair and principled approach?

18. While some legal scholars may argue that law and morality are distinct realms, the practical realities of legal practice often reveal a more nuanced connection between the two. Advocates who have appeared in the courts over long periods can attest to the influence of moral considerations on judicial decision-making, as judges often rely on their intuitive sense of right and wrong when interpreting and applying the law. This intersection of law and morality in the courtroom underscores the role of conscience and ethical principles in shaping legal outcomes, as evidenced by notions such as "the conscience of the court being shocked" in certain legal systems.

19. Indeed, if various branches of the law have acknowledged the significance of moral considerations, even in civil matters, there is a compelling argument for enforcers, policymakers and stakeholders in competition law to broaden their perspectives beyond traditional analyses centred solely on consumer welfare or economic efficiency. Embracing a more holistic approach that encompasses moral judgments can lead to a more nuanced understanding of the implications of anticompetitive practices and guide the development of a

regulatory framework that prioritises integrity, fairness, and the well-being of society as a whole.

20. Touching upon or even shocking the conscience with ethical considerations can lead to a deeper understanding and acceptance of the principles underlying competition law. Clear and unambiguous policy formulation is indeed paramount for regulators, whether in enforcement actions or advocacy efforts. By avoiding overly technical or unappealing language and presenting concepts in a relatable manner, regulators may engage stakeholders effectively and foster broader interest and understanding in the realm of competition law and policy.

Governance and Competition – The Case of Sports

Damien J. Neven*
Graduate Institute of International and Development Studies

Petros C. Mavroidis**
Columbia University

I. Introduction

1. The objective of this short chapter is to discuss the extent to which the enforcement of competition rules can affect the internal governance of Sports Governing Bodies.

2. Some Sport Governing Bodies (SGBs), and in particular FIFA and UEFA, have well-documented governance issues.[1] To illustrate, FIFA experienced rampant governance issues that have culminated in the period 2010–2015. In the context of the choices for the attribution of hosting the 2018 and 2022 World Cups (that eventually went to Russia and Quatar), two FIFA officials were banned from participating in the vote because of misconduct. Jack Warner (the then chairman of the Confederation of North, Central American and Caribbean Association Football (CONCACAF) and member of FIFA executive committee was found to have channeled payments to some of the CONCACAF members from Mohamed bin Hammam of

* Graduate Institute of International and Development Studies, Geneva, Compass Lexecon and CEPR

** Columbia Law School, New York.

1 On FIFA, see for instance, Sahiba Gill, Edouard Adelus & Francisco de Abreu Duarte, *Whose Game? FIFA, Corruption and the Challenge of Global Governance*, 30 Eur. J. Int'l L. 1041–1066 (2019), who provide a summary and discussion of the evidence reported in five books on corruption at FIFA leading to the raids 2015 and indictments of officials.

Qatar (another member of the executive committee) shortly before the latter ran for president against Sepp Blatter. In May[2] and December 2025, the US Department of Justice indicted 29 erstwhile and former FIFA officials for corruption (including racketeering, wire fraud and money laundering). The indictment found "rampant, systemic, and deep-rooted corruption" that spanned "at least two generations of soccer officials who, as alleged, have abused their positions of trust to acquire millions of dollars in bribes and kickbacks." Almost all of those indicted either pleaded guilty of were convicted. Sepp Blatter himself was banned from football for six years in relation to a payment to Michel Platini, the then president of the Union of European Football Associations (UEFA).

3. Following the events, FIFA embarked in a process of reform of its internal procedures that was meant to establish greater transparency, avoid conflicts of interests and establish independent oversight. The process however turned out to be short lived. One of the key elements of the reform was to remove the responsibility for appointing (and firing) members of the newly established Governance Audit and Compliance Committee,[3] as well as the existing Ethics Committee from the Executive Committee, and assign it to the wider membership. This power was however soon returned, without explanation, to the FIFA Council, the successor of the FIFA Executive Committee, which is subject to much greater control by the president.[4]

4. In response, the chair of the Audit and Compliance Committee resigned, FIFA ousted the chairman of the Governance Committee and the chairmen of the investigatory and adjudicatory chambers of the Ethics Committee, which prompted several other Governance Committee members to resign as well. Maduro and Weiler[5] who were chair and member of the Governance Committee respectively, provide a vivid first-hand account of this episode and the overarching governance problems in FIFA. In their account, governance issues in FIFA appear to run deep – with a culture which does not sufficiently recognize the need to avoid conflicts of interest, the need for an independent oversight (isolated from pressure from the executive), and the need to ensure a commitment to the implementation of rules. They describe FIFA as "political cartel with a high concentration of power at the top" which is no longer subject to checks and balances.

---

2 US Dep't. of Justice, Press Release, Nine FIFA Officials and Five Corporate Executives Indicted for Racketeering Conspiracy and Corruption (May 27, 2015), https://www.justice.gov/opa/pr/nine-fifa-officials-and-five-corporate-executives-indicted-racketeering-conspiracy-and.

3 The Governance Audit and Compliance Committee is the current name, and this committee was created through the merger of two committees, the Audit and Compliance, and the Governance Committees.

4 The FIFA Council comprises 37 members only and is headed by the FIFA President, https://inside.fifa.com/about-fifa/organisation/fifa-council (last visited Oct. 8, 2024). The FIFA counts 211 members in total.

5 Miguel Poiares Maduro & Joseph H.H. Weiler, *'Integrity', 'independence' and the internal reform of FIFA. A view from the trenches*, *in* Good Governance in Sport, Critical Reflections (Arnout Geeraert & Frank van Eekeren eds., 2021). *See also*, Navi Pillay, Miguel Poiares Maduro & Joseph H.H. Weiler, *Our Sin? We Appeared to Take Our Task at FIFA Too Seriously*, The Guardian (Dec. 21, 2017, at 19:50 PM GMT), https://www.theguardian.com/football/2017/dec/21/our-sin-take-task-fifa-seriously.

5. This and similar incidents[6] raise the question of whether competition (and competition enforcement in particular) can affect the governance of SGBs or at least alleviate its negative consequences. Our analysis starts from the twin observations that competition can be a substitute for effective governance mechanisms, and that SGBs are subject to limited competitive constraints.

6. Economic analysis has indeed long emphasized the role of competition in disciplining the behavior of decision-makers within organizations.[7] Competition across firms will lead managers to take efficient decisions (rather than for instance decisions that suit their personal interest) because failing to do so would lead to a loss of profit, poor returns for stakeholders, job losses, and possibly their dismissal. There is also a large empirical literature which tends to validate the role of competition as substitute for effective governance mechanisms.[8] One of the findings is that institutions that are faced with competition may have poor governance structures but those no longer matter for performance as competition provides the necessary discipline.

7. However, the activities of SGBs like UEFA and FIFA are often not subject to competitive constraints. They are (self-appointed) monopolists. Even though both FIFA and UEFA operate in the football market, they do not feel the competitive constraints of each other because of the geographic market division that they have agreed to.[9] It is undeniable that some of their activities are best performed by a single entity in a monopoly position.[10] Think for instance of the enactment of sporting rules (such as the size of the pitch or the length of a game). However, some of the main activities of SGBs which relate to the organization of tournaments, and their main source of income, could potentially be subjected to competition.

8. Nevertheless, the matter is delicate as competition needs to be introduced without jeopardizing the activities of the SGBs that are best left to a monopoly/regulator. More generally, because of the idiosyncratic features of sport as an economic activity, and in particular the need to maintain competitive balance, some restriction of competition may be warranted. Even

---

6 The choice of the host for the 2034 world cup, which went to Saudi Arabia, has also drawn attention. It appears that FIFA gave candidates two weeks to present interest in hosting the world cup. As North America (host 2026) Europe, Africa and Latin America (Morocco, Spain and Portugal jointly hosting 2030; with two games going Latin America) has no realistic chance, the host would have to come from Asia or Oceania. According to press report, Australia was keen to prepare a bid but could not provide one within the deadline of two weeks (and was not granted an extension). Saudi Arabia however had a bid ready and turned out to be the only bidder. *See*, https://www.nytimes.com/2023/11/15/world/middleeast/saudi-arabia-fifa-world-cup.html (last visited Oct. 8, 2024).

7 *See*, for instance, Oliver D. Hart, *The Market Mechanism as an Incentive Scheme*, BELL J. ECON. 14, 366–382 (1983) or David S. Scharfstein, *Product-Market Competition and Managerial Slack*, RAND J. ECON. 19, 147–155 (1988).

8 *See*, for instance, Julia Chou et al., *Product Market Competition and Corporate Governance*, REV. DEV. FIN. 1, 114–130 (2011).

9 Even if this picture might change in the near future, as a result of FIFA's resolve to introduce its own clubs' competitions. Still, even in this scenario, their overlapping activities will be of very limited nature indeed.

10 Pablo Ibáñez-Colomo, *Competition Law and Sports Governance: Disentangling a Complex Relationship*, WORLD COMPETITION 45, 323–350 (2022).

in those areas in which competition is introduced, it may be appropriate to maintain some form of coordination among competitors. For instance, when clubs simultaneously participate in an open or a closed league (as in the case of basketball in Europe with FIBA and EuroLeague), competitive balance within each of the tournaments will be affected by the design of both competitions; the transfers that a club obtains to maintain competitive balance in one tournament will also affect its position in another. Some coordination may also be required with respect to the calendar of events. Hence, the way in which competition is introduced and its precise scope, might matter. There is clearly some potential for competition enforcement to deteriorate rather than to improve the outcome.

9. Overall, competition, and competition enforcement in particular, potentially have a role to play in providing a discipline on SGBs. Short of prompting changes in their governance structure, competition might at least alleviate the consequences of poor governance. Still, much will depend on how competitive constraints are introduced and whether the existing enforcement framework is up to the task. If this policy proves difficult, the only alternative will be a direct regulation (presumably at the EU level).

10. A comprehensive discussion of this issue is much beyond the scope for this chapter. Our ambition is simply to consider recent developments, in particular recent court judgments and highlight some features that may be relevant to this discussion. We will consider in particular the discipline that is developing on SGBs and their ability to justify restrictions of competition. We will tentatively observe that the current framework might need further refinement in order to allow for an effective development of competitive constraints on SGBs.

II. The Role of Competition Enforcement in Challenging SGBs

11. There are two main areas in which competition enforcement has progressively eroded the ability of SGB to extract rents. First, by restricting the circumstances in which TV rights can be sold exclusively (in part by allowing Member States wide discretion in defining protected events whose rights cannot be sold exclusively[11]) and by restriction their ability to exclude competitors. The three judgments of December 2023 are particularly meaningful in this respect.[12]

---

11 *See*, Stephen Weatherill, Principles and Practice in EU Sports Law (Oxford Univ. Press 2017), for a discussion.

12 Case C-124/21 P, ISU v. European Commission, ECLI:EU:C:2023:1012, see Paschalis Paschalidis, *The EU Court of Justice rules that the holding of an unfettered power that does not comply with non-discriminatory obligations under EU law constitutes a restriction by object and abuse of dominance (International Skating Union)*, e-Competitions Dec. 2023, art. No. 116686; Case C-333/21, ESL v. FIFA/UEFA, ECLI:EU:C:2023:1011; Case C-680/21, Royal Antwerp v. URBSFA & UEFA, ECLI:EU:C:2023:1010, see

12. Following these judgments,[13] when a measure involves a restriction by object, no legitimate objective can be invoked to ensure that it would fall outside the scope of Article 101 TFEU (Treaty on the Functioning of the European Union), according to the Wouters doctrine. Furthermore, if the challenged measure involves a restriction by effect, SGBs can invoke a legitimate objective to ensure that it falls outside the scope of Article 101 TFEU, but they cannot invoke Article 165 TFEU to this effect, as this provision is addressed to the EU institutions only. Finally, there is an additional discipline imposed on SGBs that are in a position to affect entry in a market that is similar to the discipline imposed through Article 106 TFEU in circumstances where EU Member States have granted entities special and/or exclusive rights. The December 2023 judgments saw an extension of this discipline to those SGBs that can act as "gatekeepers." Consequently, the December 2023 judgments have imposed a significant discipline on SGBs and have equally restricted their opportunities to justify restrictions.

1. Restriction Inspired by Article 106 TFEU

13. By drawing inspiration from Article 106 TFEU, the CJEU effectively imposed on SGBs the obligation to regulate their own conduct with respect to the authorization of entry in such a way as to eliminate the risk of an abuse. The imposition of a self-discipline on (quasi-)regulators with respect to requirements regarding the authorization of entry, implies that the question of whether restrictions on entry can be justified through invocation of legitimate objectives (or efficiencies) has become irrelevant.

14. The approach of the CJEU implies that the system of prior authorization needs to eliminate the risk of an abuse (or that of restriction of competition). There is by construction no scope for keeping the restriction outside the scope of Article 101 TFEU or a conduct outside the scope of Article 102 TFEU (because of the pursuit of a legitimate objective) simply because the ex-ante system of authorization should have eliminated the occurrence of such events in the first place.

15. Formally, the Court has only imposed constraints inspired from Article 106 TFEU with respect to measures authorizing entry. However, one would expect

---

Anne-Sophie Choné-Grimaldi, *Association of undertakings: The Court of Justice of the European Union delivers three landmark rulings that provide numerous clarifications on the classification and possible exemptions of a concerted practice ruling on the applicability of the competition rules to sporting activities (ISU; ESLC; Royal Antwerp)*, Concurrences No. 2-2024, art. No. 118651, 70–73.

13 *See*, Jan Zglinski, *Can EU Competition Law Save Sports Governance?*, Int' Sports L.J. (2024), https://doi.org/10.1007/s40318-024-00258-9; Petros C. Mavroidis & Damien J. Neven, *Legitimate Objectives in Antitrust Analysis, The FIFA regulation of agents and the right to regulate football in Europe*, Concurrences No. 1-2024, art. No. 117382; Mark James & Antoine Duval, *Another Bosman Moment? The decisions of the court of justice of the European Union on 21 December 2023 and the future of transnational sports governance*, Int' Sports L.J. (2024), https://doi.org/10.1007/s40318-024-00268-7 or Stephen Weatherill, *Football Revolution: how do the Court's rulings of 21 December 2023 affect UEFA's role as a 'gatekeeper'?*, EU L. Analysis (2024), https://eulawanalysis.blogspot.com/2024/01/football-revolution-how-do-courts.html, for a discussion of these rulings.

that the discipline would also apply to other conducts which effectively foreclose competitors' access to the market.

2. Efficiency Benefits Under Article 101(3) TFEU

16. For conducts which are not subject to a discipline inspired by Article 106 TFEU but involve a restriction of competition by object, SGBs will have to argue as per Article 101(3) TFEU, that their conduct brings efficiency benefits.

17. The test under Article 101(3) TFEU is quite demanding. It involves four cumulative conditions, namely that: (i) efficiencies understood as involving the improvement of the production or distribution of products or the promotion of technical or economic progress need to be proven; (ii) consumers need to have a fair share of the resulting benefit (this implies that the net effect of the restrictions and the efficiencies is positive); (iii) efficiencies cannot be achieved in another way (the restrictions are indispensable to achieve them); and finally (iv) there is no elimination of competition.

18. The test can be applied in the most straightforward fashion when resulting efficiencies directly affect the magnitude of harm suffered by consumers. If efficiencies reduce marginal cost, prices will be reduced so that even if the measure increases margins, consumers can be better off. The efficiencies directly affect the dimension (price) in which harm is occurring.

19. In principle, this test allows consideration of the consequences of agreements which affect consumers in other dimensions than those in which restrictions occur. The Commission has provided further guidance on such circumstances in the Guidelines adopted in 2023.[14] The Commission is explicitly allowing for the consideration of external effects (that are particularly relevant for agreements that have an impact on the environment). The requirement to operate a balance between effects that harm consumers and those that bring benefits still requires a common metric. This inevitably restricts the range of efficiency benefits, and hence the other objectives that can be taken into account.

20. For instance, an argument that a restriction of competition leads to an improvement in competitive balance and hence increases the quality (value) of competition could presumably be considered under Article 101(3) TFEU. However, consider an argument to the effect that a restriction of competition (e.g., the prevention of entry or restrictions on the players' rosters) enhances the sporting achievement as a value or enhances cohesion and thereby brings societal benefits. It is not clear whether such effects could be taken into account under Article 101(3) TFEU, considering also that, as reemphasized by the recent guidelines, the customers affected by the restrictions and those affected by the efficiencies need to be substantially the same (no cross-market efficiencies).

---

14 European Commission, Guidelines on the applicability of Article 101 of the Treaty on the Functioning of the European Union to horizontal co-operation agreements, C(2023) 3445.

3. The Wouters-Test

21. The Wouters Test under Article 101(1) TFEU[15] does not involve balancing between positive and negative effects, but instead involves: (i) the recognition of a legitimate public policy objective; and (ii) a proportionality test.

22. We understand that when applying a proportionality test in this context, the CJEU is for all practical purposes engaging in an assessment of alternative means to achieve the stated objective. The test asks whether a recognized public policy objective can be achieved to the same extent by alternative means which involve fewer restrictions of competition. It is different from a balancing test properly understood, to the extent that it does not involve an assessment of the resulting net benefit.[16] From this perspective, it is also more deferential to the public policy objectives pursued. The objectives need not be considered commensurable to the effects of restrictions of competition.

23. The extent to which the Wouters approach could be applied to sport depends on the objectives that can be recognized as legitimate. It is also potentially seriously constrained by the recent judgements such that it cannot be applied to restrictions of competition by object. We consider both these issues in turn below.

24. With respect to an objective that can be considered legitimate, there is so far only a negative answer (Article 165 TFEU and the European sport model is not a legitimate objective that UEFA/FIFA can invoke) and a positive answer (preventing doping is appropriate following the *Meca-Medina* judgment[17]). There is no clear framework to determine more generally what objective can be considered legitimate. We have argued that legitimate objectives should flow from an explicit delegation provided by a public authority.[18] We also find that the case law of the Court of Justice is broadly consistent with this perspective. Still some greater clarity from the Courts or the Commission on what objectives can be deemed legitimate in the context of the Wouters doctrine would be useful.

25. In the *ESL* judgment,[19] the Court was clear that the Wouters approach does not apply to restrictions of competition by object or unilateral conduct which "by its very nature" infringes Article 102 TFEU. However, the CJEU did not

---

15 *See*, Mavroidis & Neven, *supra* note 13, for an application to sports.

16 *See*, Case 104/75, Officier van Justitie v. De Peijper, ECLI:EU:C:1976:67, for a discussion of the difference between proportionality and balancing.

17 Case C-519/04 P, Meca-Medina v. Comm'n of the European Communities, ECLI:EU:C:2006:492; see Marc van der Woude, *Antidoping rules: The ECJ holds that the CFI gave a too narrow definition of the scope of the competition rules, but rejects the application in view of the legitimate objective pursued by the contested rules (Meca-Medina)*, CONCURRENCES No. 4-2006, art. No. 12548, 68.

18 Mavroidis & Neven, *supra* note 13.

19 ESL v. FIFA/UEFA, *supra* note 12, at ¶ 186. The Wouter doctrine "does not apply in situation involving conduct which, far from merely having the inherent effect of restricting competition, at least potentially, by limiting the freedom of action of certain undertakings, reveals a degree of harm in relation to that competition that justifies a finding that it has as its very object the prevention, restriction or distortion of competition". *Id.* at ¶ 185–186.

provide a detailed reasoning to support this important finding.[20] This ruling is puzzling at least if, following *Cartes bancaires*,[21] one understands a restriction of competition by object as one which "reveals in itself a sufficient degree of harm to competition" for it to be considered that it is not necessary to assess its effects. If one adopts this approach, the ruling of the Court could be understood as saying that restrictions of competition by object involve such a magnitude of harm that it can never be compensated. This could be appropriate in the context of a balancing test in which harm triggered by the restriction of competition is assessed against efficiency benefits under a common metric. It is potentially less suitable in the context of the proportionality test which involves considering less restrictive alternatives.[22]

26. Admittedly, if instead of following *Cartes bancaires*, one emphasizes the purpose of an agreement as the decisive feature of whether it restricts competition by object, there may indeed be little room to advance legitimate objectives: an agreement which strives to restrict competition risks not being compatible with the pursuit of a legitimate objective. This is for instance, the perspective taken by Ibañez-Colomo.[23]

III. Afterthought

27. In this chapter we have developed the argument that the current enforcement framework could be refined to allow for the recognition of sport specificities in an efficient way. It may still very well be that an explicit regulation would be preferable but a discussion along these lines is beyond the scope of this note.

28. This contribution has also taken the perspective that competition can contribute to good governance or at least alleviates the nefarious consequences of mismanagement. Whether this principle applies in the case of SGBs might however deserve further consideration. One reason is possibly that the root cause of dysfunctional governance in SGBs cannot be addressed exclusively through competition. Competition among teams requires a high level of coordination/cooperation and the maintenance of competitive balance requires

---

20 The Court refers in ¶ 185 to ¶ 53 of its Motoe judgment (Case C-49/07, Motosykletistiki Omospondia Ellados NPID (MOTOE) v. Greece, ECLI:EU:C:2008:376) where, ostensibly, this approach was "already implicitly but necessarily apparent". Motoe concerned the organization of motorcycle races and involved a potential conflict of interest: Motoe was both authorizing the organization of motorcycling events and organizing them itself. The conditions for authorizing events organized by other entities had not been clearly spelled out. In its conclusion, the Court affirmed positively that Article 102 TFEU applies, so it implicitly ruled out the possibility of appealing to legitimate objectives. It is, of course, a stretch to extend this approach beyond the specific circumstances of the case. This case involved a blatant incentive to restrict entry.

21 *See*, Case C-67/13, Groupement des cartes bancaires (CB) v. Eur. Comm'n , ECLI:EU:C:2014:2204 and opinion of AG Wahl, ECLI:EU:C:2014:1958. *See also*, Case C-228/18, Gazdasagi Versenyhivatal v. Budapest Bank Nyrt, ECLI:EU:C:2020:265, at ¶ 37, see Yves Botteman & Camille Keres, *The EU Court of Justice AG Bobek publishes his opinion on the concept of restriction of competition by object or by effect (Gazdasági Versenyhivatal / Budapest Bank)*, E-COMPETITIONS September 2019, art. No. 92036.

22 Unless there is an irrefragable presumption that there is always a less restrictive alternative to a restriction by object. But it is not clear what could support this.

23 Ibañez-Colomo, (2023).

some transfers (such that some clubs are taxed and others are subsidized), or some constraints on teams expenditures and investments . In this context, even if all teams benefits from the maintenance of competitive balance, they will disagree on their respective contributions to this objective.

29. This is illustrated by the emergence of the Super League, which arose at least in part out of the dissatisfaction of some large teams regarding the share of the rents from European competitions that would accrue to them. Competing tournaments might shift the allocation of rents but are unlikely to address the underlying divergence of interest and its consequences in terms of dysfunctional governance. A specific set of rules that can be credibly enforced may be required for that. If the experience of the absence of meaningful internal reform at FIFA offers guidance here, these rules might also have to be imposed exogenously.

The Agricultural Bermuda Triangle: A Tale of Three Market Failures

MARTIJN SNOEP*
The Netherlands Authority for Consumers and Markets (ACM)

I. Introduction

1. Why are so many farmers angry, struggling, and without much hope for a better future for themselves or their successors? Why is it so hard to reduce the devastating impact of farming on our environment? What can be done about this, and how can the government and authorities like the Authority for Consumers and Markets (ACM) help? There are obviously no easy answers here, but through a concerted effort along three avenues a happy ending is possible.

2. First, let me clarify that not all farmers are struggling and angry. Some are actually making a very decent and happy living with an innovative and future-proof business. Also, it is important not to focus on one year only, as a farmer's income may vary annually. The weather, pests, and global market developments impact their income. And there is no such thing as the average farmer. Dairy farmers face different challenges than tomato farmers, which in turn are different from pig farmers. So, an adequate comparison would require a multi-year, product-by-product analysis.

II. The Agricultural Food Supply Chain

3. Any market analysis should start with laying out the structure of the supply chain. Most supply chains resemble pyramids. Concentration levels are high

---

* Chairman, Authority for Consumers and Markets, The Hague, The Netherlands.

at the top (raw materials) and low at the bottom (consumers). But a stylized agricultural food supply chain has an exceptional hourglass shape. At the top, concentration levels are low due to the many small- and mid-sized farmers who produce a wide variety of agricultural commodities on the land they own. They have little or no individual bargaining power towards the next level in the supply chain.

4. This level consists of the big commodity traders and well-known processors such as dairy companies, slaughterhouses, vegetable packers, and potato chips factories, who purchase agricultural commodities directly or indirectly from farmers. The market for commodity trading in cereal grains (wheat, corn) and oil seeds (soybeans, rapeseed) is highly concentrated and global in nature. Processors of other agricultural commodities (milk, meat, potatoes, sugar beets) tend to source more regionally due to transportation costs and perishability. Supermarkets form the next concentrated level of the supply chain. Retailers predominantly source imported or domestically processed agricultural products – sometimes directly from farmers – at a national level to be able to cater to national consumer preferences. They typically sell these products at a local level, in competition with only a handful of other supermarket chains. At the bottom of the agricultural supply chain are the consumers, typically a heterogeneous group of price-sensitive buyers with no individual bargaining power.

III. Market Failure: Purchasing Power

5. There are three major market failures in this supply chain. First, there is purchasing power at the trader/processor and retailer levels. This is a problem, especially because barriers to exit for farmers are high, as they are tied to the land they own, not only financially, but also culturally, and emotionally. This makes them an easy target for exploitation by processors through: (i) purchasing prices that barely cover short term marginal costs, and (ii) one-sided purchasing conditions that push the downside risk to the farmer (weather, pests), while keeping much of the upside potential (shortages). Hence the saying that farmers live poor and die rich, (due to the value of the land).

6. Still, most processors only benefit marginally from their purchasing power over farmers, because the next level in the supply chain, retailers, have purchasing power towards them. At the same time, contrary to popular belief, many supermarkets do not benefit from this purchasing power. Net margins for retailers on many fresh agricultural products are small, especially compared to margins on durable, branded products. Fresh agricultural products are often used as loss leaders to draw in consumers. So ultimately, it is the consumer who benefits from low prices of agricultural products. Indeed, food prices for consumers have never been so low historically relative to income, even despite the price hikes of the last years.

IV. Market Failure: Negative Externalities

7. The second market failure lies in negative externalities that come with agricultural production. Monoculture, nitrogen emissions, pesticides, freshwater depletion, to name a few, all negatively affect our habitat and biodiversity. The direct and indirect costs of these impacts are passed on to citizens, next generations, and ecosystems. In efficient markets, all direct and indirect costs plus a reasonable profit margin are included in prices along the supply chain. Negative externalities should be mitigated by regulation and as a result this will lead to higher prices. However, as a result of regulatory failure, these negative externalities remain largely intact. The most important reason is that "true prices," that include the real costs of farming, would make agricultural products more expensive and out of reach for a significant part of the population, at least in the quantities consumers are used to now. I'll return to that later.

V. Market Failure: Information Asymmetry

8. The third market failure relates to information asymmetries. Many consumers are willing to pay more for agricultural products if they are produced more sustainably and farmers receive a fair price that allows for a decent living. But how can consumers know that this actually happens? More sustainable products often look and taste the same as regular products and whether the farmer received a fair price or not cannot be checked by consumers. One has to trust retailers that what they are claiming on sustainability and fair prices is true. And other retailers must trust that competitors will not be able to make false claims about this. Free riders will quickly eliminate every incentive for retailers to offer more sustainable food products and smother a systemic shift in agricultural production.

VI. A Possible Happy Ending?

9. So how to get out of this Bermuda Triangle of market failures that harms farmers as well as our planet? What is the role of the government and, in particular, that of an integrated competition and consumer protection authority, like the ACM. Is there a happy ending possible, anyway? Yes, there is. There are three avenues that need to be followed in parallel.

1. Protection against Purchasing Power

10. The first avenue starts with protecting farmers against purchasing power and exploitation. They need to get a fair price for their products and should not bear the entire economic risk. But this needs to be done without resorting

to the classic price interventions of the past – recall the "milk oceans" and "butter mountains" of the past. Protection against exploitation can be achieved by laws prohibiting unfair practices; such laws exist at the EU level in the form of the Directive on Unfair Trading Practices in the Agri-Food supply chain. In a number of countries, including the Netherlands, the competition authority is entrusted with enforcement.

11. The justification for protecting farmers in their business-to-relationships against powerful traders and processors is that they cannot be treated like any other entrepreneur. Their barriers to exit from the market are extraordinarily high. Farming is not only a business, but also a way of life for farmers and their families. A "rational entrepreneur" would already have exited the market. Also, farming is part of the cultural identity of most European countries. There is strong public support for farmers, even if they block roads with their big tractors and protest violently. It is too early to tell whether these rules will make a difference, but the ACM provided extensive guidance and brought the first two cases, against Vion (meat processor) and Lactalis (dairy processor). To be effective, further evaluations and updates of the rules are of course called for.

12. Also, in regular industries, producers often merge to create efficiencies and protect their position against powerful buyers. But most farmers want to maintain full ownership over their farm, including production and sales. That's perfectly fine, but it shouldn't have to be so expensive for them. Therefore, EU exemptions from the competition laws allow them to cooperate with other farmers without giving up their entire autonomy. In particular, for sustainable farming, this exemption is broad for all levels in the supply chain. To the ACM's surprise, few farmers seem to make use of the exemptions despite general and individual guidance by the ACM. We need to better understand why these exemptions do not seem to make a difference and how they can be improved.

13. Finally, competition authorities should be vigilant against further consolidation of traders, processors, and supermarkets that increase their already powerful purchasing positions. Traditionally, competition authorities focus on downstream selling power and largely ignore purchasing power on the basis of a "trickle down" price theory. Purchasing power should lead to lower prices that will be passed on to the consumer. Lower purchasing prices should lead to incentives for producers to create economies of scale and to produce more efficiently. And there is a market exit for those who cannot keep up. However, this theory does not take into account the actual barriers to exit for farmers, to the detriment of themselves, their animals, and the environment. In the social market economy that the EU aims to be, these factors should be taken into account. An independent competition authority entrusted with enforcement of the competition laws and the laws against unfair trading practices is well-positioned to find the proper balance

between competition and protection of farmers as it is immune to political and vested interest lobbying.

2. Another Inconvenient Truth

14. That first avenue was the easy bit. The second avenue is harder and probably the most challenging in the current political climate, but it is inevitable. Far more stringent environmental regulations are needed so that negative externalities are reduced to a minimum and the race to the bottom among farmers is stopped. In the EU, with its open agricultural market, this must be carried out by the EU legislature. Leaving aside the influence of interest groups who will try to protect exports outside the EU that will become more expensive, we also face the inconvenient truth that the resulting "true" prices will increase food prices for EU citizens. A larger part of a household's income will need to be spent on food to the detriment of other spending, assuming there will be no miraculous growth in other areas. This change will lead to political unrest, friction and, therefore, it will take many years to reach a new status quo. In the meantime, income support at the national level for low-income consumers will be needed, probably in combination with a gradual change of the European consumers' diet – more vegetable proteins instead of animal proteins – which is also healthier. It will be a very hard sell for EU and national politicians to be reelected on a program that will increase food prices and change diets, but it is the only route out of the agricultural Bermuda Triangle. It will require brave and skilled politicians, compromises and patience to follow this second avenue. There is only so much that competition and consumer protection authorities can contribute. However, their deep market knowledge and independent position make them ideal truth-tellers in separating myths from realities.

VII. Protection Against Greenwashing

15. On the third avenue out of the agricultural Bermuda Triangle, integrated competition and consumer protection authorities have a clear role to play. Especially during the transition phase, there are already and will be more initiatives from farmers, processors, and supermarkets to come to more sustainable farming without exploiting consumers willing to pay a fair price, possibly after some gentle nudging. But these consumers need to be able to trust claims about sustainability and fair incomes for farmers made by processors and supermarkets. That requires clear rules against greenwashing. Fortunately, such rules are in place at the EU level. The ACM plays a role not only in enforcement but also through general guidance for businesses and awareness campaigns for consumers. Because of its role in the bigger food transition, it is well-positioned to put these rules in that broader perspective,

finding the right balance against greenwashing while avoiding greenhushing. Retailers will have to be able to use the power of persuasion to lead consumers in the transition without misleading them. So, there are three avenues or, better still, long and winding roads that need to be followed in concert to get to the happy ending of this tale. It will not be easy, but it is the only way forward for a future-proof and revitalized European agricultural food chain. The ACM is ready to play its part.

Competition Law: Solving or Dissolving the Social Question?*

Jean-Pascal Chazal
Sciences Po

1. The origins of competition law lie in the desire to resolve the social question, that is, the problem that arises in a democratic society when the majority of the people participate in the creation of wealth but are excluded, for the most part, from its distribution. We are at the end of the 19th century in the United States, a time when the unprecedented increase in inequality (with the appearance of the first very large companies and the first billionaires) threatens not only the cohesion of American society and the republican form of its government, but also the American dream itself of a citizen living with dignity from the fruits of his independent work. The Anti-Trust Act of 1890 was thus intended, in a bipartisan consensus, to dismantle monopolies and prohibit excessive concentrations of wealth and economic power. Competition was not considered an end in itself, in that it would produce a state of social well-being, because many thought that it was also mortifying (a "*cut-throat competition*"). The aim was to preserve the existence of small entrepreneurs by allowing them to make a fair profit from their activity and by preventing a minority from extorting the wealth produced and exercising, to their detriment, an oppressive tyranny.[1]

---

* This article has been previously published in Concurrences, and it might have been edited for clarity and cohesion. Jean-Pascal Chazal, Competition law: Solving or dissolving the social question?, February 2023, Concurrences N° 1-2023, Art. N° 110544.

1 The expressions "*extorted wealth*" and "*grinding tyrannies*" can be found in the debates in Congress.

This is why, despite the divisions and nuances, the debates focused more on the idea of "*fair* competition" than on free and unfettered competition.

2. Certainly, from a historical point of view, it cannot be said that the Anti-Trust Act resolved the social question. After refusing to apply the Act to production activities, on the grounds that they were not commerce,[2] while accepting its use to sanction concerted union action,[3] the Supreme Court finally abandoned its restrictive interpretation[4] and dismantled the oil and tobacco refining monopolies.[5] However, in these two resounding decisions, the Supreme Court doubly distorted the Anti-Trust Act: on the one hand, by introducing the famous rule of reason (which had previously been rejected) and, on the other hand, by considering that what was illicit was not the size of the company and the domination of a market that it allowed, but the wrongful behaviour of the managers. In his dissenting opinion, Justice Harlan criticized this reversal and recalled that the 1890 legislature had designed a legal weapon to prevent the economic enslavement of the people. Without being able to elaborate on this, I suggest that this development is largely explained by the contradiction between the fight against monopolies and the protection of private property and freedom of contract.

3. This struggle continued with very mixed success during the 20th century (with a notable inflection during the New Deal), only to undergo a radical change in philosophy from the 1980s onwards. Gradually, competition was no longer conceived as a means of combating concentrations of wealth, but as an order that had to be legally regulated in order to allow the market to function freely.

4. Thus, competition law has contributed to the dissolution of the social question. This development is usually attributed to neo-liberalism, which, from the 1930s onwards in Europe, promoted a theory often referred to as "market fundamentalism", according to which the market would be self-regulating and the play of free and undistorted competition would create an optimal equilibrium. The reality of neoliberal thinking is much more complex, for alongside the theory idealizing the efficiency of markets, there is a more pessimistic neo-liberalism which considers that competition is imposed because of the limits of human knowledge, which disqualify any action by the state to direct the economy. The state should therefore confine itself to providing a legal framework for the market to enable it to form prices and thus send signals to economic agents. Beyond the divergences, both conceptions lead to the same conclusion: the need to constitutionalize the rules of free competition in order to place it beyond the reach of public authorities, which might be tempted, under the pressure of universal suffrage, to disrupt the supposedly

---

2 *E.C. Knight Co*, 1895.

3 *In Re Debs*, 1895, and *Loewe v. Lawlor*, 1908.

4 *Trans-Missouri Freight Association*, 1897.

5 *Standard Oil and American Tobacco*, 1911.

natural allocation of wealth by imposing redistribution policies. The state must therefore both ensure the constitution and preservation of the "competitive *order*", to use F. Hayek's expression, while refraining from intervening in its functioning. In this perspective, state action is legitimate only insofar as it guarantees the functioning of a free market economy.

5. This is precisely what is meant by the term "social market economy" (coined by A. Müller-Armack, a Nazi convert to post-war neo-liberalism), which was eventually introduced by the Lisbon Treaty, which completed the unravelling of the compromise found in the Treaty of Rome between German ordo-liberalism (even if this program was never applied in Germany before the beginning of the 21st century) and the French mixed economy. The effect, if not the purpose, of the competition law thus constitutionalized is to disqualify political power from dealing with questions of inequality and injustice in the distribution of wealth. The concentration of wealth in the hands of a minority is no longer an evil in itself, nor a threat to democracy, but a mark of success. It is only at the margins that the correction will take place, namely when the one who has a dominant position abuses it.

6. However, it would be an exaggeration to say that neoliberals have ignored the social question, but they have undeniably minimized it. For them, the main cause of poverty lies in the "illiberal" interventions of the state in the redistribution of wealth (the "*welfare state*" and dirigisme) and the harmful influence of the workers' unions, which disrupt the competitive order, the functioning of which should be sufficient to generate prosperity for most people. All that remains to be dealt with is residual poverty,[6] for which the solutions are not consensual: the idea of a minimum living wage proposed by F. Hayek was far from being consensual, while M. Friedman's proposal to introduce a tax on the income of the poor was not. Friedman's proposal to introduce a negative tax to eradicate poverty met with hostility from his colleagues in the Mont Pelerin Society both on the means (M. Allais) and on the end (Hayek saying: "*I doubt that I would dare to put the phrase 'eliminate poverty' in my program as a liberal*", speech of April 8, 1947). Basically, neo-liberalism does not abandon a certain humanism, even humanitarianism, based on the realistic observation that a competitive order cannot by itself make poverty disappear. But this is no longer a central issue, only a marginal one, in the sense that state intervention is only legitimate in the margins of poverty left by the free market.

7. This is how the State has been put at the service of the markets (let us understand speculators, speculation being one of the blind spots of neoliberal thinking) and the law at the service of competition, thus making the social question disappear from the debate by transforming it into a question about assistance and social aid. Thus dissolved, the question of inequalities has become a political unthinkable, even though their deepening over the last

6 M. Friedman evoked the "*sub-marginal workers*".

thirty years has brought most Western countries back to the level that existed at the beginning of the 20th century.[7] To those who think that the wage gap between a worker and the head of a company is disproportionate (the average salary of CAC 40 executives is 239 SMIC) or who wonder why a footballer earns several million euros a month and a hospital nurse barely 1,700 euros (i.e. about the median salary in France), many reply that this kind of questioning is irrelevant. Like our Minister of the Economy, who claims not to know what a "super profit" is (in order to dismiss the idea of additional taxation, while public companies accumulate annual profits that can be counted in tens of billions of euros or dollars), neo-liberal thinking does not admit that the question of the social utility of economic activities and their level of remuneration should be democratically decided. And for good reason, these matters are taken care of by the (alleged) law of supply and demand presiding over the setting of prices and thus over the distribution of wealth: if some people receive large remunerations, it is because there are others in the market who are willing to pay them. This is exactly the opinion of L. Von Mises when he explained that, although under the "*reign of competition*", the market exercises rigorous control over economic agents, the latter nonetheless retain decision-making power through the use of their money: "*each penny plays the role of a ballot paper*".

8. How can we fail to see that the system in which power is thus conferred on the richest is not a democracy (which implies a right to vote distributed equally among all citizens, regardless of their level of income or wealth), but a plutocracy?

7 Cf. the work of T. Piketty.

8 Art. L 335-2 Code de la Propriété Intellectuelle.

Corporate Funding for Antitrust Academics can be a Problem[*]

CYRIL RITTER[**]
European Commission

1. The topic of corporate funding for academic articles – and the possibility of academic bias – has been the subject of many recent press articles, blog posts, reports, and academic articles[1].

2. This debate is playing out on both sides of the Atlantic, mostly in the areas of antitrust, intellectual property, privacy, and internet regulation.

---

* This article has been previously published in Concurrences, and it might have been edited for clarity and cohesion. Cyril Ritter, Corporate funding for antitrust academics can be a problem, February 2018, Concurrences N° 1-2018, Art. N° 86396.

** These are my personal views. This is a slightly revised version of a blog post that first appeared on medium.com. More generally, on the challenge of maintaining integrity in the academic community despite sometimes perverse incentives, see M. Edwards and S. Roy, Academic Research in the 21st Century: Maintaining Scientific Integrity in a Climate of Perverse Incentives and Hypercompetition, Environmental Engineering Science, Vol. 34, No. 1, 2017, pp. 51–61; and P. Roelofs and M. Gallien, Clickbait and Impact: How Academia has been Hacked, blogs.lse.ac.uk, 19 September 2017.

1 B. Mullins and J. Nicas, Paying Professors: Inside Google's Academic Influence Campaign, *Wall Street Journal*, 14 July 2017; J. Eisinger and J. Elliott, These Professors Make More Than a Thousand Bucks an Hour Peddling Mega-Mergers, *ProPublica*, 16 November 2016; P. Ibáñez Colomo, What drives academic writings in competition law and economics?, chillingcompetition.com, 23 January 2017; P. Ibáñez Colomo, On companies funding legal research: beyond the sound and the fury, chillingcompetition.com, 14 July 2017; D. Crane, Setting the record straight on WSJ Google "Paying Professors" Article, profdancrane.com, 12 July 2017; N. Petit, On bias and conflicts of interest in antitrust academia, medium.com, 14 July 2017; Google-Funded Speakers Dominate Policy Conferences, googletransparencyproject.org, 15 August 2016; New Report Reveals Google's Extensive Financial Support for Academia, campaignforaccountability.org, 11 July 2017; J. Deparle, Goals Reached, Donor on Right Closes Up Shop, *New York Times*, 29 May 2005; W. Wils, The Judgment of the EU General Court in Intel and the So-Called 'More Economic Approach' to Abuse of Dominance, *World Competition: Law and Economics Review*, Vol. 37, No. 4, 2014, pp. 405–434; J. Broulík, Economics in Antitrust Enforcement and the Private Benefit of Scholarly Commentators, *TILEC Discussion Paper* No. 2017-1, January 2017; A. Ezrachi, Sponge, *Journal of Antitrust Enforcement*, Vol. 5, Issue 1 April 2017, pp. 49–75; L. Zingales, Preventing Economists' Capture, in D. Carpenter and D. Moss (eds.), *Preventing Regulatory Capture: Special Interest Influence and How to Limit it*, Cambridge University Press, 2013; and R. Feldman, M. A. Lemley, J. Masur, and A. K. Rai, Open Letter on Ethical Norms in Intellectual Property Scholarship, 29 *Harvard Journal of Law & Technology*, pp. 1–14 (2016).

3. Corporate funding has been linked to ethical issues in medical research, climate science, food safety and nutrition, financial regulation, and other fields. There is no reason to believe that antitrust law and economics are necessarily immune to such concerns.

4. The response from some antitrust academics has been to make a series of arguments that are not particularly consistent with each other: (a) the funding does not matter, only the ideas and arguments matter; (b) the campaign for better disclosure of corporate funding is itself driven by corporate funding from the "other side," with a particular agenda in mind; (c) there is no evidence of academic bias; (d) there is no bias when academics express their sincere views; (e) all academic writing is biased, as it seeks to advance the author's personal interests (including when the author is a government official); and (f) at the same time, let's aim for better disclosure of funding – but not all types of funding.

5. To be fair, antitrust agencies sometimes have relationships with academics as well, either as advisers or to produce studies, or by hiring academics in part-time or short-term positions. And corporate funding for academics can take place on both sides of an argument (antitrust defendants and antitrust complainants, licensors and licensees, content providers and platforms, infrastructure owners and "over-the-top" providers, etc.).

6. However, the one constituency which is systematically under-represented in academic debates is consumers. This is probably another manifestation of the collective action problem: more concentrated interests are better at defending themselves, while larger groups – whose members have more diffuse interests – have more difficulty organising and financing efforts to push their interests[2].

7. Moreover, given that many European academics' salaries are paid by taxpayers, one would expect them to work in the public interest, instead of working for particular corporate interests (I am indebted to Ioannis Lianos for this idea).

I. Corporate funding artificially amplifies certain views

8. Certainly, every idea deserves to be discussed, regardless of its motives or sponsors (except for hate speech). Equally, identifying the funding behind certain ideas does not automatically discredit such ideas.

9. But corporate funding can "push" an idea very effectively through different channels, such as law journals, newspapers, and conferences. This happens not only through funding for articles, but also through other means: journal editors controlling the contents of their journals, awards for academic articles,

2 M. Olson, *The Logic of Collective Action: Public Goods and the Theory of Groups*, Harvard University Press, 1965.

and firms buying speaking slots on conference panels, for example. This can create the false impression that certain ideas are more prevalent than they really are. Corporate funding distorts the competition of ideas by essentially buying a large number of channels and spokespersons.

10. Furthermore, after reaching critical mass, an artificially created view can achieve a kind of self-propelling effect. This works especially well when this view is portrayed as the "modern" view. This effect is compounded when the proponents of a particular idea support their argument by referring to the "consensus" or dominant view in the literature (indeed EU antitrust case-law is replete with parties' arguments making references to "the literature"). This is a way to cut short the debate, rather than to foster debate.

11. Not only does corporate funding seek to influence EU antitrust law, but it also seeks to replace some EU antitrust law notions with its artificially constructed consensus. For example, there is a view that the notion of "restriction by object" should include only those restrictions recognised as such in the "consensus" – that is, the consensus which is influenced by corporate funding. When the corporate-funded consensus argues that the law should reflect the corporate-funded consensus, we have come full circle.

II. Corporate funding changes the tone of academic discourse

12. Corporate funding moves the centre of gravity of academic debate from basic research to discussions of specific cases, often while those cases are still pending, and sometimes before there is even a decision to discuss. Is it a problem if the debate moves from the court room to the public arena? Not necessarily. But it can be a problem if ongoing cases are discussed in a superficial way, without reference to evidence, because there is no published decision (or even no decision adopted by the Commission). Debating a case in a superficial and confrontational way is a recipe for increasing polarisation. I am not sure the academic world should wish to be drawn towards this trend.

13. Moreover, corporate funding replaces more neutral and reflective pieces by more argumentative, one-sided pieces. Again, it is always good to debate ideas, but the point of academic literature is also to provide objective, reliable surveys of particular issues (even if an article can also put forward a thesis or personal opinions). By contrast, reading a piece influenced by corporate funding is a different mental exercise: it requires extra gymnastics to spot the gaps and find the "other side of the story." It is the difference between academic discourse and litigation. I cannot imagine that academics want their articles to be treated with the same degree of scepticism as written pleadings or lobbyists' memos.

III. Corporate funding also produces more subtle effects

14. There are different types of corporate funding, from "restricted" and "unrestricted" financing for articles, to indirect funding (endowments, scholarships and sponsoring for departments, research centres and conferences), to ongoing relationships, for example when an academic regularly provides expert testimony to a client. When an academic is also employed by a law firm or has a long-standing relationship with that firm, one may wonder whether he or she is truly independent from the interests of the firm's clients. The problem is even more acute for people who are primarily law firm lawyers but who also write with their academic "hats" on.

15. All such types of funding should be disclosed, and efforts in that direction are welcome[3]. This could be subject to some appreciability threshold and subject to the confidentiality of client names where necessary (e.g., to maintain lawyer-client confidentiality or the confidentiality of arbitration proceedings; in such cases it would be enough to disclose funding from a client "with an interest in the discussion"). We could also consider disclosing not only ongoing funding, but all such funding over the last few years. Going further, authors could also disclose whether the document at issue (whether an academic article, a press article, or a speech or presentation) has been shared with its sponsors before publication.

16. But disclosure does not solve the more "*subtle*," "*insidious*," and "*subconscious*" types of corporate funding[4].

    – When an antitrust academic is looking to supplement his or her revenues with consulting work or funded articles, it becomes clear pretty quickly that there is more money in supporting corporate views. So the expectation of working for corporate clients can already "pull" an academic in a particular direction before such work even begins. The evidence on this point is difficult to collect, but the ability and incentives are there.

    – When a lawyer or academic has already completed some work for a corporate client but there is an expectation or possibility of further work for the same client, this is an ongoing relationship which is liable to impair objectivity. Speaking out against the former client's interests is likely to rule out further work for that client.

    – Moreover, previously published corporate-funded views can make it harder for an academic to publicly change his or her mind. In other words, corporate funding can make some academics path-dependent. This can be even more problematic when someone makes the jump

3 P. Ibáñez Colomo and G. De Stefano, Protecting the Integrity and Reputation of Legal Research: JECLAP's New Rules on Disclosure, *Journal of European Competition Law & Practice*, 2017, pp. 623-624; N. Petit, On bias and conflicts of interest in antitrust academia, medium.com, 14 July 2017.

4 See Feldman and others' "Open Letter on Ethical Norms in Intellectual Property Scholarship", cited above.

from a position as a lawyer in private practice or academic to a position in an antitrust agency or as a judge. In that new position, he or she may want to remain consistent with previously published positions. When those positions were influenced by corporate funding, such funding can effectively influence the public sector for years.

17. To be sure, there is no place for stigmatising individuals; everyone must be respected and heard; and (almost) all ideas deserve to be discussed. Academics provide invaluable services to their fields. The aim here is neither to "*demonise all corporate-funded research*"[5] nor to prohibit corporate funding, nor to demand perfect objectivity. But perhaps we should aim to make some progress in terms of transparency and awareness of these issues – at least as a service to readers of academic articles.

5 P. Ibáñez Colomo, On companies funding legal research: beyond the sound and the fury, chillingcompetition.com, 14 July 2017.

Competition: A Catholic Perspective[*]

Étienne Perrot
Jesuit priest

1. The Catholic Church's social teachings categorize competition under "liberalism." The Center for Research and Social Action (Ceras) does the same: the entry "competition" links directly to "liberalism"[1]. Liberalism in its three dimensions – moral, political, and economic – has long been opposed by the Church. Although the Church eventually accommodated, if not embraced, liberal democracy, with adherence to freedom of conscience and human rights becoming central to Catholic social discourse, liberal capitalism still faces criticism. This critique is grounded in the intertwining of economic and social elements, as Catholic doctrine seeks not to separate the efficiency of production driven by competition from the pitfalls of a market system governed solely by individual preferences.

I. Social Concerns of Unchecked Competition

2. Against the social effects of unregulated competition, the Church's official bodies have increasingly recognized the need for at least establishing equality among contracting parties, without which the market breeds inequity, as Pope Paul VI highlighted in his encyclical *Populorum Progressio* in 1967 (§58). This observation is echoed in *Caritas in Veritate* by Benedict XVI in 2009 (§35). Between these, in 1991, John Paul II outlined the dilemma in

---

* This article has been previously published, in French, in Concurrences' book *À quoi sert la concurrence*, it has been translated and edited for clarity and cohesion.

1 *The Social Discourse of the Catholic Church: From Leo XIII to Benedict XVI, the Major Texts of Catholic Social Teaching Compiled and Presented, with a Thematic Index*, Bayard, Montrouge, 2009, 1055 pages. An updated, in-depth presentation is available at www.ceras-projet.org.

Centesimus Annus: "It seems that, within each country as well as internationally, the free market is the most suitable instrument for allocating resources [implying productive resources] and responding effectively to needs" (§34).

3. In 2012, echoing the concept of a social market economy as outlined in the Lisbon Treaty, the Commission of the Bishops' Conferences of the European Community (COMECE) reiterated the key principles of doctrine[2]. The third chapter, titled "Market Economy and Competition," recognizes the positive effects of competition and its resource efficiency while warning against its excesses, calling for public regulation and even "clear rules with sanctions" in the monetary and financial sectors. "Competition is not a natural phenomenon that arises simply from economic freedom" (§6).

4. Between the extremes of regulation and unbridled competition, Catholic doctrine has developed a unique view of humanity in society. Beneath contradictory values lies a dual requirement: personal discernment supported by the most rigorous scientific approach.

II. Contradictory Values

5. The COMECE document, like election speeches, juxtaposes conflicting values. The dual cultural heritage – combining the individualistic legalism of Roman law with biblical personalism – creates a sort of hybrid that merges law with spirituality, leading to practical ambiguity regarding human nature.

6. For instance, private property, which is a condition for individual freedom and competition, is defined in the Napoleonic Code as the right to use and dispose of property as long as it is not used in a manner prohibited by law. However, the Church's social doctrine regards private property[3] as a "natural right." Are these the same property rights? No, as the revolutionary notion is grounded in individualistic anthropology from Roman law, while the Church's view opens onto the social responsibility of the owner, introducing the concept of a "social mortgage" attached to property in recognition of humanity's "social" nature.

7. The pair of solidarity and responsibility carries similar ambiguities. Is solidarity universal, reflecting charity without borders, or limited by political authority, as in the European focus in COMECE? It is clear that responsibility, expressed through the moral (not legal) value of subsidiarity, varies greatly depending on the extent of solidarity.

8. The freedom and justice pair is equally uncertain. As Lord Acton, in the Christian tradition, put it: "(…) freedom is not the power to do what we want but the right to be capable of doing what we should." Or is freedom simply

---

2 *COMECE, 2012, A European Community of Solidarity and Responsibility: Declaration of the Bishops of COMECE on the Aim of a Competitive Social Market Economy in the Treaty of the European Union*, original in German, www.comece.org.

3 "Even the means of production," specifies Pope John XXIII in 1961, §109 of *Mater et Magistra*.

the absence of public constraint, as advocated by Ludwig von Mises, for whom price evaluations, like all moral values, only reflect individual preferences? "The terms society and state, as used by modern socialists, planners, and proponents of social control over all individual activities, signify a deity. The priests of this new religion attribute to their idol all the attributes that theologians assign to God: omnipotence, omniscience, infinite goodness, etc."[4].

9. Thus, the justice referenced in Catholic social doctrine goes beyond commutative justice governing individual exchanges; it also encompasses distributive justice, which seeks to equip individuals to fulfill their personal and social responsibilities, and legal justice, representing everyone's duties to the community. This limits the free space left to competition.

III. Seriousness of Science

10. The Church's social doctrine has long grappled with the distinction held by classical economists of the 19th century: on one side, economic science, tasked with efficiently organizing wealth creation via the competitive market; on the other, the "moral and political sciences," entrusted with distributing wealth according to justice. This classic division removes distribution from economic science, placing it in the more subjective corrective interactions of social relations. Yet this overlooks how distribution shapes production, a point which demands rigorous scientific study. Economic and social history defies simplistic scientism stemming from Karl Marx's view that production techniques generate social relations, which then express themselves through legal, ideological, and religious superstructures. More seriously, as Max Weber's dialectic in *The Protestant Ethic and the Spirit of Capitalism* illustrates, social and cultural constraints influence production methods as much as production techniques shape wealth distribution and its ideological justification.

11. Avoiding the naive separation of economy and society, the contemporary Catholic discourse reconnects with Schumpeter's scientific insight: "Social events are a whole. They form a great current from which the researcher's ordering hand forcefully extracts economic facts. Calling a fact economic is an abstraction, the first of many abstractions that technical necessities impose on our thinking when it seeks to reproduce reality"[5]. This observation explains that economic laws – which must be followed for efficient production – are both ephemeral and limited in scope. Rather than dismissing them, we should support those that most effectively serve social goals. Efficiency, even toward extra-economic aims, is not morally optional, and competition remains a means to be valued and applied case by case.

---

4 *Human Action*, Paris, PUF, 1985, p. 159.

5 *The Theory of Economic Development*, Paris, Dalloz, 1935, p. 1.

12. Competition is not a stable state of the liberal economic system. Like in sports competition, each participant develops relative strengths; the aim is not to mimic others but to leverage specific advantages. Economists acknowledge that in a competitive system, the quest for rents (technological, climatic, social, regulatory, financial) is the true driver of economic development, eventually leading to monopolies that negate the benefits of competition. Thus, competition is a communal good that must be continually reclaimed.

IV. The Role of Public Regulation

13. Public regulation alone cannot enforce this reclamation. The COMECE document asserts (§6): "It is up to those who set the political framework to ensure real competition in the market. Monopolies, cartels, price-fixing agreements, and distortions of competition through economic power abuses or public subsidies must be actively fought and prevented by EU legislators and executives." Since competition is not a natural and stable state, it is naive to deny the need for regulation to promote it. Yet it is equally naive to rely solely on public regulation for two reasons: first, regulation doesn't create competition but merely supports it – competition is created by entrepreneurs taking business risks. The economic risk, often ignored in Church and anti-liberal discourses, is inherent to competition. Second, as Karl Marx observed, regulation is always reactive, addressing scandals post-facto through broad generalizations that never cover every case. Moreover, it promotes formal rule compliance at the expense of social objectives.

V. Conclusion

14. By emphasizing "the revision of our values" (§7), "the conscientiousness of leaders" (§8), "the culture of decency, whose development cannot be left solely to politics" (same §), and in general, "the ethical choice" underlying the social market economy, the COMECE document aligns with the heart of Catholic social doctrine: the irreplaceable role of personal discernment, a prerequisite for responsibility that cannot be delegated to any institution, no matter how well-organized. Institutions, by nature, respond to problems arising from constantly evolving socioeconomic realities. Discernment requires continuous adjustments to competition rules. As Benedict XVI reminds us in *Caritas in Veritate* (2009): "Solidarity means, first and foremost, feeling responsible for everyone; it cannot, therefore, be delegated solely to the state" (§38).

Competition in Judaism or the Balance of Hopes*

Haim Korsia
Chief Rabbi of France

1. Is there room for everyone on Earth? Is each of us destined for a specific place here? When I create a business, am I within my rights, or am I infringing on someone else's? What is my neighbor's vital space? Does starting a business necessarily come at someone else's expense, or can it create value?

2. Since the beginning of the world and the start of social life, the question of the legitimacy of opening a business, setting up a workshop, or creating a company near an existing one has always concerned those who value respect for others and uphold laws that protect the vulnerable, not just those in power. The Talmud, in *Baba Batra 21b*, shares the views of two sages, Rav Huna and Rav Huna son of Yehoshua. The former suggests that a miller established on a street can prohibit another from setting up a mill on the same street, arguing, "You have cut off my livelihood; the customers who used to come to me will now turn to you." The latter, however, defends the right to free competition and allows for a second mill, but only if established by a resident of the same street. The new resident could argue, "As you worry about your sustenance, so I must worry about mine. Each customer will go where they wish, and each of us will earn what Heaven has allocated for us."

3. There is still a restriction on absolute free enterprise, as another operator can set up shop only if they reside on the street. The rule (*Choshen Mishpat 156, 2*) supports this second view, thus allowing competition between two people residing on the same street while forbidding an outsider from building a second mill there. But in our contemporary "small world," what does the notion of

---

* This article has been previously published, in French, in Concurrences' book *À quoi sert la concurrence*, it has been translated and edited for clarity and cohesion.

"the same street" mean? One decision-maker views the entire city as a shared space where any resident can open a business where they please. For outsiders, however, it is forbidden to compete in a city not their own, as the two sages agree, regardless of their interpretive differences, on this argument: "You are coming from outside our social group to take away my livelihood."

4. One finds the origin of this restriction in the verse: "You shall not move your neighbor's boundary marker, set by your predecessors, in the inheritance you shall receive" (Deuteronomy 19:14). While the Bible seems to prohibit only the theft of land, this concept has been extended to include those who would encroach on a neighbor's livelihood. This prohibition of "Hassagat Gvul" – literally, encroaching on another's territory – is used by contemporary authorities to denote the prohibition of unfair competition. In fact, one of the most prominent contemporary decision-makers, American Rabbi Moshe Feinstein, used this logic when considering the case of someone wishing to open a new synagogue in an area already served by several.

5. Some rabbis argue that unchecked competition is a form of theft; others see it as pure malice to open a business directly opposite an existing store. But this seems only to apply to outsiders. According to Jewish law, however, anyone paying local taxes is considered a full city resident, with all associated rights, including free establishment. Contributing to city finances, therefore, entitles a person to full civic privileges. Market days, for example, allow all merchants, without exception, to offer their goods, as these events draw clients from all around. On other days, only jewelry and perfume vendors – today we would call these luxury items – are allowed from outside, as Ezra permitted so that the city's daughters would always look their best!

6. This ethical tension exists between, on one side, the desire to freely undertake not just for economic productivity but as an inalienable right, and, on the other, the protection of an established economic system, even if it involves indirect risk or harm. This balance, set out in *Baba Metzia 60*, notes that Rabbi Yehuda believed that one shouldn't sell below competitors' prices because it attracts all customers, affecting rivals' livelihoods. Other rabbis disagreed, believing that lowering prices benefits consumers. This millennia-old debate persists today, such as with the arrival of a fourth telecom operator that lowered prices but reduced sector margins, possibly impacting 5G investments. Should we prioritize merchant margins, ensuring prosperity and reinvestment, or favor consumer interests?

7. Interestingly, Torah teachers have a special status under the Talmudic principle: "Competition among sages benefits the advancement of wisdom" (*Baba Batra 21a*), thus allowing religious teachers to settle freely, enhancing educational quality. This underscores the idea that competition generally improves service quality.

8. Furthermore, Jewish law allows merchants to lower prices, provided they don't sell at a loss, which would harm both competitors and themselves. Our

current commercial laws only reflect the practical wisdom of Talmudic laws, where commerce was already seen as a signal of trust in the future.

9. Our financial and commercial systems revolve around entrepreneurial freedom. Laws strictly punish monopolies, unlawful agreements, and practices that hinder competition, which is expected to benefit consumers and bring market honesty. Supply and demand alone determine a fair product price, but the Talmud's insight lies in having the community decide on acceptable pricing ranges or business placements, as *Baba Batra 8b* explains: "The inhabitants of a town can determine commercial measures and product prices and impose sanctions against those who disregard these rules."

10. Throughout history, sages have worked to regulate local commerce in their communities through rabbinic decrees to protect merchants without disadvantaging consumers. These decrees are frequently found in records of ancient communities, where offenders could be ostracized or even excommunicated.

11. In our time, when cutthroat competition has become the norm, it is good to remember the questions posed by King David: "Who may stay in your tent? Who may live on your holy mountain? One who has not wronged their neighbor" (Psalms 15:1–3). The Talmud specifies: "It is someone who has never harmed their neighbor's work" (*Makot 24a*). The Maharam of Rothenburg (Responsa, 677) explains that this person is not merely one who followed strict competition laws but someone who refrained from harming their neighbor's livelihood, even when allowed.

12. Avoiding greed to protect another's subsistence – or better, their dignity – demonstrates a complete faith in the Almighty to provide daily bread and opens the path to paradise. Jewish law forbids interest-bearing loans because they disrupt time, favoring lenders as time pressures the borrower; they transfer all risk to the borrower, and ultimately, they break fraternity. Economy, and at its heart, competition, must not disregard the hope of fraternity.

13. A just person is one who finds the fine line between their freedom and that of others, between their right to prosper and the right of others to do the same. This may be the real challenge of contemporary society: to achieve this miracle first within our nation, then across Europe, and eventually across all of humanity, fostering healthy competition that never undermines the dream of fraternity.

PART VI

Sector-Specific Insights and Emerging Trends

Why Competition in Food Markets? An Analysis of Recent Trends

Teresa Moreira
Senior Competition expert

Rodrigo Cárcamo-Díaz*
Senior Economist and Commodities expert

I. Introduction

1. Competition policy is critical for the effective functioning of good and service markets, regardless of countries' level of development.

2. Competition law and policy has spread widely across the world in the last 40 years since the introduction of the United Nations Set of Multilaterally Agreed Equitable Control of Restrictive Business Practices (UN Set of Principles and Rules on Competition), adopted by the United Nations General Assembly in 1980.[1] The UN Set of Principles and Rules on Competition recognized the importance of competition law and policy for development, acknowledging that developing countries could enact and implement this legislation according to their specific circumstances (development dimension)[2] and established a framework for international cooperation, conferring a central role to UN Trade and Development (UNCTAD)[3] in this field.

---

* The findings, interpretations and conclusions expressed in this document are exclusively those of the authors and do not necessarily reflect the views of the United Nations or its officials or Member States.

1 *See*, UNGA, *Resolution 35/63 Control of Restrictive Business Practices*, (Dec. 5, 1980), https://unctad.org/system/files/official-document/tdrbpconf10r2.en.pdf.

2 *Id. Multilaterally agreed equitable principles for the control of restrictive business practices, point (iii) Preferential or differential treatment for developing countries*, at § C.

3 *Id. International measures* and G. *International Institutional Machinery*, at § F.

3. Over 140 countries, including many developing countries and some least developed countries, have adopted competition law and set up enforcement institutions, while several regional economic organizations are also active in this area at the regional level.[4]
4. Despite the progress observed since 1980, many new and small competition authorities in developing countries today still face a steep learning curve for the successful implementation of their competition mandates, while also facing severe resource constraints. However robust ongoing policy dialogue efforts on competition law and policy among international (UNCTAD[5]) and regional organizations and academia provide the former with a steady flow of advice, technical cooperation and support at bilateral, regional, and international levels.
5. Since the Covid-19 pandemic outbreak in early 2020, competition authorities were at the forefront of the public response to its negative impact on markets, by closely monitoring market conditions and strongly enforcing law, as well as demonstrating flexibility on procedural requirements and merger control when necessary. This allowed the supply of key consumer goods, including personal protective equipment and essential products, and research and development (R&D) cooperation projects and coordination between SMEs in certain sectors through specific exemptions. Competition advocacy also supported more balanced and equitable national economic recovery packages, clearly demonstrating the important contribution of competition law and policy as a valuable public policy instrument in times of crisis.[6]
6. Finally, the cascading negative economic shocks on developing countries that followed since 2022 including the war in Ukraine and geopolitical tensions in the world, leading to high food (and fuel) prices,[7] paved the way for this reflection on the role of competition policy in global food markets, adding to other recent work on this topic.[8]

---

4 For example, ASEAN (Association of Southeast Asian Nations), CARICOM (Caribbean Community and Common Market); COMESA (Common Market for Eastern and Southern Africa); Eurasian Economic Union; WAEMU (West African Economic and Monetary Union); and SIECA (Central American Economic Integration System), see Teresa Moreira *International cooperation in competition law enforcement: Is regional cooperation the best option for developing countries?*, CONCURRENCES No. 3-2021, art. No. 101384.

5 UNCTAD focuses on assisting developing countries in all areas under its vast mandate, including competition policy. *See*, UNCTAD activities on Competition and Consumer policies here: https://unctad.org/Topic/Competition-and-Consumer-Protection; and the latest report, see UNCTAD, REVIEW OF CAPACITY-BUILDING IN AND TECHNICAL ASSISTANCE ON COMPETITION AND CONSUMER PROTECTION LAWS AND POLICIES (2024), https://unctad.org/system/files/official-document/ciclpd76_en.pdf.

6 *See*, secretariat background notes, UNCTAD, *Competition Advocacy during and in the Aftermath of the COVID-19 Crisis*, (Apr. 2021), https://unctad.org/system/files/official-document/ciclpd58_en.pdf; UNCTAD, *Rethinking competition law enforcement Lessons learned from the pandemic, particularly in socially important markets – Challenges and opportunities for an effective response during the pandemic and economic recovery in the post-pandemic period*, (May 2022), https://unctad.org/system/files/official-document/ciclpd63_en.pdf; UNCTAD, *Interaction between competition and industrial policies*, (Apr. 2023), https://unctad.org/system/files/official-document/ciclpd69_en.pdf. Also see, World Bank, *Tracker of Subsidies and State Aid to Mitigate COVID-19 Effects,* https://dataviz.worldbank.org/views/AID-COVID19/Overview?%3Aembed=y&%3AisGuestRedirectFromVizportal=y&%3Adisplay_count=n&%3AshowAppBanner=false&%3Aorigin=viz_share_link&%3AshowVizHome=n (last visited Oct. 20, 2024).

7 See the briefs and other publications: https://unctad.org/global-crisis (last visited Oct. 20, 2024).

8 Two excellent recent examples are Roberts, S. (2023), "Competition, trade, and sustainability in agriculture and food markets in Africa", Oxford Review of Economic Policy, Vol. 39(1), pp. 147-161.and, for a book-length treatment of this topic, Lianos, I., Ivanov, A. and Davis, D. editors (2022), Global Food Value Chains and Competition law, Cambridge: Cambridge University Press, 2022.

II. The Importance of Agricultural Value Chains for Developing Countries and the Role of Competition Policy

7. Agriculture is a key sector for developing countries in their development path. Not only does it provide income to entrepreneurs and employment opportunities all along the value chain, but agriculture can also be an important generator of public revenue and foreign exchange (through exports), and a key provider of inputs for the agro-industrial sector. Additionally, a healthy food sector plays a key role in ensuring food security and in boosting health and nutrition in the population.

8. Food insecurity continues to be a serious problem around the world. During the period 2020–2022, 460 million people[9] were estimated to experience severe food insecurity, with a very high incidence in Africa (297 million), followed by Asia (97 million) and the Americas (53 million). For the average country around the world,[10] the percentage of people affected by severe food insecurity is 12.3 percent, but there are very large differences across countries, linked to their level of development. While across the group of least developed countries this value was 26.6 percent, in other developing countries it was 10.7 percent, while in the group of developed countries, the average was 2.4 percent. In terms of regional distribution, African countries as a group had the largest average share of people who were severely food insecure, with 25.6 percent. Additionally, in 34 countries, 28 of which are in Africa, more than 1 in 4 people face severe food insecurity, and in 10 of these countries, the percentage rises to more than one-third of the population.

9. In recent years, the discussion about the role of increased competition in strengthening the competitiveness of agricultural value chains (AVCs) in developing countries has become more urgent. In addition to increasing welfare by maximizing economic efficiency in a dynamic way,[11] boosting innovation and strengthening employment, public and private revenue, and export roles of AVCs, competition policy can also contribute to reducing poverty by lowering markups in food prices, improving food security, and reducing inequality in view of the significant role that expenditure in food plays in consumers consumption in developing countries. For these reasons, among others, competition law enforcement in AVCs across developing countries has become a priority in recent years, in particular in larger and higher-income jurisdictions.

---

9 Authors' calculations using FAOSTAT data for 110 countries, downloaded July 19, 2024. Among the countries with no data were China and India. *See*, FAOSTAT, https://www.fao.org/faostat/en/#data

10 Authors' calculations using FAOSTAT data for 143 countries, downloaded July 19, 2024. Among the countries with no data were China and India. The available data on national shares of severely food-insecure people were used to calculate world and regional averages.See FAOSTAT, https://www.fao.org/faostat/en/#data

11 This means the belief of the authors that efficiency needs to be understood not in a static way, but also incorporating a dimension of economic, environmental, and social sustainability.

III. Competition Challenges in Agricultural Value Chains

1. Market Concentration

10. In general, market power in agricultural markets is de facto the norm rather than the exception even in developed countries.[12] Concentration in segments of AVCs, including food processing, trading and retail, either through mergers or the expansion of large firms into new markets, is common. Concentration in post-farmgate segments of these value chains can be driven, among other things, by the reduction in transaction costs for buyers or sellers that result from having fewer and larger suppliers or customers. Spot or auction-type market transactions have often been replaced by vertical contracts, in a context of increasing differentiation along different dimensions of "quality". For agricultural products, quality is a multi-dimensional construct which can include (depending on the product and geographic market) assorted characteristics, notably including food safety as well as the sustainability of the product along its environmental, social, and economic dimensions.[13]

11. The structure and dynamics of AVCs around the world are heterogeneous. On the one hand, the "mid-stream" segments of these value chains (including processing, storage, sales intermediaries and aggregators, and logistics) have become increasingly important, also in developing countries, while modern large supermarket chains have come to play a large role in urban centers as retailers of food.[14] On the other hand, several AVCs in different developing countries involve a myriad of stakeholders, including intermediaries of various sizes, and often different sizes of vendors (e.g., wholesale, retail, micro-retail), between producers and final consumers.[15] In several AVCs in developing countries, imperfect input markets, large fixed and variable transaction costs (e.g., search costs), and other issues result in the continued use of mechanisms such as "interlinked transactions," where intermediaries provide credit to farmers and other intermediaries, and where the price of transacted agricultural products is part of a bundle together with inputs provided at credit.[16]

---

12 *See* Sexton, R. J. (2012), "Market Power, Misconceptions and Modern Agricultural Markets", American Journal of Agricultural Economics, Vol. 95 (2), pp. 209-219.

13 The sustainability dimensions of agricultural product quality are becoming increasingly important around the world. For example, increasing stock-taking about the role of land use change for agriculture in explaining a significant part of deforestation has led consumers and the authorities of importing countries to increasingly demand that the agricultural products that they buy come from fully traceable AVCs.

14 *See* Reardon, T. (2015), "The hidden middle: the quiet revolution in the midstream of agrifood value chains in developing countries", Oxford Review of Economic Policy, Vol. 31 (1), pp. 45 – 63.

15 *See* Fafchamps, M. (2004), Market Institutions in Sub-Saharan Africa: Theory and Evidence, (Cambridge, MA: The MIT Press, 2004).

16 Many studies have empirically documented in developing countries the bundling of credit provision, often in the form of farm inputs like seeds, agrochemicals, and fertilizers, together with buying agricultural produce at harvest time. For example, UNCTAD (2020) found that out of a survey of 175 maize farmers in three provinces in north Lao PDR, 35 percent of farmers received credit from traders (often in inputs), but the

12. The high market concentration in different segments of AVCs, both in input and output markets, in some cases leads to abuse of market power towards farmers, which are often small- and medium-sized companies, or even sole proprietors. In input markets, such as fertilizers and seeds, farmers are often dependent on a few dominant suppliers, and could face exploitative pricing or experience unfair trading terms. In output markets, large distributors and retailers have significant buyer power with respect to farmers and this bargaining power could result in unfavorable payment terms or conditions (discussed below) for the latter.[17]

13. In many different developing countries, promoting competition in agricultural products and input markets may increase economic efficiency along these value chains, and boost economic activity.

14. However, many competition authorities in developing countries often cannot easily access and analyze granular data on an economic sector (at the transaction level), including sales volumes, prices, investment, installed capacity, fixed and variable costs and other variables that are key for merger assessment. It may also be difficult to detect and stop cartels or to prevent dominant firms from implementing exclusionary practices. Particularly in the least developed countries, limited capacity, and commitment are pervasive, referring in the first case to the insufficient resources available to the regulators, both financial and qualified human resources, and a weak competition culture. And in the second case, to the extent to which competition authorities are independent and capable of neutrally enforcing their pro-competition mandate, in particular in the presence of concentrated economic and political interests.[18] Higher rents often originate in insufficient competition.[19]

2. Cartelization and Collusion

15. Over the last two decades, competition authorities and other regulators have identified a number of cartels operating at different times in developing countries, including in agriculture. However, it is possible that the number of cartels detected is significantly smaller than those operating, as favorable conditions often exist across different agricultural input product markets (including fertilizers, seeds, and agrochemicals),[20] such as the very high concentration of

---

prevalence of this bundling practice by traders varied by province. *See* UNCTAD (2020), "Characterizing the Maize Value Chain for Export in Lao People's Democratic Republic", UNCTAD, UNCTAD/DITC/COM/MISC/2020/2, available at. https://unctad.org/publication/analyzing-maize-value-chain-export-lao-peoples-democratic-republic.

17 *See*, Ioannis Lianos & Dmitry Yurevich Katalevsky, *Economic Concentration and the Food Value Chain - Legal and Economic Perspectives*, *in* GLOBAL FOOD VALUE CHAINS AND COMPETITION LAW 118-171 (Ioannis Lianos et al. eds., 2022).

18 *See* Estache, A. and Wren-Lewis, L. (2009), "Toward a theory of regulation for developing countries: Following jean-jacques laffont's lead", *Journal of Economic Literature*, Vol. 47(3), pp. 729- 770.

19 *See* Ades, A. and Di Tella, R. (1999), "Rents, competition, and corruption", *American Economic Review*, Vol. 89(4), pp. 982-993.

20 Studies like Vilakazi and Roberts (2024) show the factors behind past collusion practices in fertilizer markets in S&E Africa. See Vilakazi, T. and Roberts, S., (2024), Cartels as 'fraud'? Insights from collusion in southern and East Africa in the fertiliser and cement industries. In Capitalism and Economic Crime in Africa (pp. 37-54). Routledge; and

international suppliers of inputs like fertilizers, and seeds, both in terms of firms and country of origin.[21]

16. In the case of seeds and agrochemicals, these sectors are very intensive in terms of investments in R&D in the development and testing of new products, often with a significant element of risk, leading to very large economies of scale which result in high concentration. The firms operating in these markets are often global players, with most R&D and product development concentrated in a few developed countries and some large middle-income, food-exporting developing countries.

17. In the case of fertilizers, the concentration of the ownership of large mineral deposits of key fertilizers such as potash and phosphate rock is high, as well as ownership of import or storage facilities, and networks of distributors facilitate implicit or explicit coordination among incumbent firms by increasing the barriers to entry, and by reducing the size asymmetry among market players operating in each country.[22]

3. Merger Control

18. Structural market changes have also been intense in recent years, highlighting the paramount importance of adequate ex ante merger assessments.[23] This is particularly important in view of the research indicating that cartel breakdown (by natural causes or official action) often results in increased merger activity.[24]

19. This challenge becomes especially important when the level of complexity of a merger is significant and when there is a large imbalance between the resources available to the merging entities, and those available to the competition authorities. For example, when two merging agricultural multinationals with operations in a developing country have minority stakes in other competitors, ex ante merger assessment needs to go beyond estimating the unilateral effects of a merger, as the merger might facilitate post-merger coordinated effects. Competition authorities in developed countries have in recent years been increasingly concerned with post-merger potential coordinated effects, as shown by Guideline 3 of the 2023 version of the

---

21 High concentration of fertilizer and seed markets are analyzed, respectively, in Hernandez, M.A. and Torero, M. (2013), "Market concentration and pricing behavior in the fertilizer industry: a global approach", Agricultural Economics, Vol. 44(6), pp. 723-734; Deconinck, K. (2020), "Concentration in seed and biotech markets: Extent, causes, and impacts", Annual Review of Resource Economics, Vol. 12(1), pp. 129-147; Bonny, S. (2017), "Corporate concentration and technological change in the global seed industry", Sustainability, Vol. 9(9), pp. 16-32; and Srinavasan, C. S. (2003), "Concentration in Ownership of Plant Variety Rights: Some Implications for Developing Countries", Food Policy, Vol. 28 (5-6), pp. 519-546.

22 *See* Compte, O., Jenny, F. and Rey, P. (2002), "Capacity Constraints, Mergers and Collusion", European Economic Review, Vol. 46 (1), pp. 1-29.

23 For example, recent large international mergers in agricultural input markets include Bayer-Monsanto and Dow-Dupont, which were closely assessed by different competition policy authorities, in some cases leading to substantial required structural remedies.

24 See Davies, S., Ormosi, P.L. and Graffenberger, M. (2015), "Mergers after Cartels: How Markets React to Cartel Breakdown", Journal of Law and Economics, Vol. 58, pp. 561-583.

Horizontal Merger Guidelines by the US Department of Justice and the Federal Trade Commission.[25]

20. Another challenge for developing countries is that mergers of agricultural input firms can have an impact on their agricultural sectors even if they do not have operations in the country, depending on the functioning of the import, logistic, distribution, and retail segments of the agricultural inputs value chains. While a perfectly competitive domestic part of these value chains would fully transfer a price change in inputs like fertilizers, in the presence of market power domestically the domestic price change would be expected to be smaller.[26]

21. It is clear that in these highly concentrated AVC segments, the cross-border dimension of mergers and acquisitions involving multinational companies needs to be addressed through international and regional cooperation between competition authorities even though there are no "one-size-fits-all" regime across the world.

4. Abuse of Dominance and Vertical Issues[27]

22. Agriculture is no stranger to the use of vertical restrictions by firms, and practices such as abuse of market power, exclusive dealing, and tying that may have harmful effects on competition in different stages of the AVCs. In this regard, developing countries share concerns with developed countries.

23. As concentration in the wholesale and retail segments of AVCs is very high in different countries, farmers and other suppliers who have less negotiating power (including few possible alternative buyers) may receive a lower price for their products than would be the case in a more competitive market, or experience unfair trading terms, due to stronger buyer power of distributors and retailers. For example, the Competition Authority of Kenya recently found that a large supermarket chain engaged in practices constituting an abuse of

---

25 Another example is the report by the Competition Bureau of Canada to the Ministry of Transport indicating that the proposed merger between Bunge and Viterra "…is likely to result in substantial anti-competitive effects in agricultural markets in Canada, and a significant loss of rivalry between Bunge and Viterra in a number of markets". Specifically concerning coordinated effects when buying grains, the Competition Bureau indicated that "Bunge has the ability to materially influence G3 and receives commercially sensitive confidential information from G3. Bunge's acquisition of G3's largest rival will provide Bunge additional incentive to use this influence and access to confidential information to the detriment of competition in agricultural markets in Canada, particularly given evidence suggesting that G3 is a particularly aggressive rival for the purchase of grain. This has the potential to result in harm to farmers who would otherwise benefit from competition between G3 and Viterra when they sell their grain." *See*, Competition Bureau Canada, Report to the Minister of Transport and the Parties to the Transaction Pursuant to Subsection 53.2(2) of the Canada Transportation Act (2024), https://competition-bureau.canada.ca/how-we-foster-competition/education-and-outreach/report-minister-transport-and-parties-transaction-pursuant-subsection-5322-canada-transportation-act.

26 *See*, Von Cramon-Taubadel & Goodwin (2021) for a survey of models of price transmission in agricultural products. See Von Cramon-Taubadel, S. and Goodwin, B. (2021), "Price Transmission in Agricultural Markets", Annual Review of Resource Economics, Vol. 13, pp. 65-84.

27 Unfair trading practices have also become a concern of competition authorities in this and other markets, such as digital markets, leading to more active use of relevant provisions or even legal amendments in some jurisdictions, as illustrated by UNCTAD, *Global Competition Law and Policy Approaches to Digital Markets*, (Mar. 22, 2024), https://unctad.org/publication/global-competition-law-and-policy-approaches-digital-markets; and secretariat note, UNCTAD, *Enforcing Competition Law in Digital Markets and Ecosystems: Policy Challenges and Options*, (Apr. 24, 2024), https://unctad.org/system/files/official-document/ciclpd74_en.pdf.

buyer power, by applying and collecting rebates, including demanding the payment of listing fees to access stores.[28]

24. In recent years, policymakers have become increasingly interested in the challenges posed by the relational nature of contracting, both formal and informal, as contracting relationships of different types are increasingly common in AVCs. In these value chains in developed countries and an increasing number of developing countries, a powerful driver for the strengthened role of relational contracts has been the increasing importance of product differentiation and "quality" issues in agricultural products, notably also in food.[29] In many developing countries, in AVCs where producers are largely smallholders, e.g., of coffee or cocoa, an additional strong driving force is the role played by interlinked transactions and by "relations" in a context dominated by high search costs, asymmetric information, network externalities, high sunk costs of establishing reputation, the "experience" and "credence" good nature of agricultural products,[30] and other characteristics of agricultural markets in developing countries.

25. In a number of these value chains, contracts are oral and implicit (instead of written and explicit, including prices or quantities), "quality" is endogenous to the transaction and possibly state-contingent (i.e., it might depend on international prices or other reference prices for the relevant product), large fixed and variable costs (including search, transaction and transport costs) resulting in persistent buyer–seller relationships that are based on reputation, with smallholder sellers often having a reduced number of buyers.[31]

26. For these value chains, where inputs are often provided on credit by buyers to farmers as part of a bundle and pricing and quality are (probably endogenously) not transparent, dynamic efficiency of the value chain is an important consideration. In particular, there are different dimensions of the issue.

27. Stakeholders have varying degrees of bargaining power, but that may or may not result in the abuse of the weaker party (e.g., smallholder farmers). For example, Casaburi and Reed present a model where traders provide credit to cocoa farmers they buy from, and using data from Sierra Leone, they find limited evidence of market power when counting the provision

28 *See*, Competition Authority Kenya, Press Release, The Competition Authority of Kenya Sanctions Majid Al Futtaim Hypermarkets Limited (Carrefour) for Abuse of Buyer Power (Dec. 19, 2023), https://cak.go.ke/sites/default/files/2024-01/PRESS%20RELEASE%20-%20CAK%20Sanctions%20Carrefour%20for%20Abuse%20of%20Buyer%20Power.pdf.

29 See Sexton (2012), *op. cit.*

30 "*Credence qualities are those which… cannot be evaluated in normal use. Instead, the assessment of their value requires additional costly information*" (Michael R. Darby & Edi Karni, *Free Competition and the Optimal Amount of Fraud*, 16 J.L. & Econ. 68-69 (1973)). Phillip Nelson, *Information and Consumer Behavior*, 78 J. Pol. Econ. 311-329 (1970) introduced the concepts of *search* and *experience* characteristics of goods, learned before and after purchase, respectively.

31 For example, using survey data on 175 maize farmers in three provinces in Lao PDR, an UNCTAD study (n 16) found that 76 percent of farmers reported only one trader buying maize from them, while less than 10 pe cent reported. selling to more than two traders. The median duration of the relationship reported by surveyed farmers was 3 years and a mean of 5.6 years (but substantial heterogeneity across provinces). Most surveyed farmers were smallholders, as the median farm size for the whole sample was 3.7 hectares.

of credit.[32] However, empirical evidence from different value chains and countries indicates that the interest rates are often "high" by comparison with the prices they receive for their products or their yearly income. For example, an UNCTAD study found that in a survey of 175 maize farmers in three provinces in northern Lao PDR, the median yearly income was US$ 3,622 and the 18 percent of surveyed farmers who specified the rate of interest they paid for credit from traders buying their produce indicated paying a median interest rate of 2.5 percent per month, which matched the rate reported by surveyed traders.[33] However, many smallholder farmers lack collateral[34] and credit histories, while creditors face the possibility of side-selling and strategic default by farmers at harvest time. Therefore, identifying whether risk-adjusted credit costs are "excessive" in each value chain, geographic market (at the subnational level or smaller), and time period, can be de facto extremely challenging.

28. In general, dynamic efficiency of such AVCs requires intertemporal sustainability. This means that production, intermediation, marketing, and other functions carried out by each stakeholder need to be sustainable over time alongside the economic, environmental, and social dimensions. While relationship-based AVCs have the potential to internalize long-term sustainability, this is not guaranteed.[35] Hence, while taking into consideration the issues mentioned, competition policy may have a role to play in complementing other policies boosting transparency within ACVs.

IV. Strengthening Competition in Food Markets

29. Competition rules usually apply to all economic sectors and all enterprises, either private or public, involved in "commercial activities."

30. However, agriculture at different times has been granted a special status in terms of competition law. For example, in the early days of the European Communities, the objectives of the Common Agriculture Policy (CAP) – "increasing productivity of agricultural production, ensuring a fair standard of living for agricultural communities, stabilizing markets, assuring supplies and ensuring reasonable prices for the consumer" (Article 39 TFEU), justified a specific competition regime applicable to agricultural products (Article 42 TFEU). More recently, however, the European competition authorities have

32 See Casaburi, L. and Reed, T. (2022), "Using individual-level randomized treatment to learn about market structure", American Economic Journal: Applied Economics, Vol. 14(4), pp. 58-90.

33 For more details, see UNCTAD (n 16).

34 In many cases in developing countries, farmers do not have clear titles to their land, making it unusable as collateral.

35 For an analysis of the importance of reputational capital and persistent relationships in agricultural value chains, see Boudreau, L., Cajal-Grossi, J. and Macchiavello, R. (2023), "Global value chains in developing countries: a relational perspective from coffee and garments", Journal of Economic Perspectives, Vol. 37(3), pp. 59-86.

been monitoring the food sector from a competition perspective, for example within the European Competition Network in 2012, following an increase in food prices and concerns about the functioning of the overall food supply chain in the European Union after mid-2007.[36]

31. In some developed countries, competition concerns in food markets have often been raised in relation to price-fixing agreements in different segments of AVCs. Also, while not globally considered as an anticompetitive practice, some jurisdictions prohibit unfair trade practices such as abuse of a superior bargaining position[37,38] and refusal to deal, which are closely related to the buyer power of big retailers.[39]

32. Other concerns about the imbalances in bargaining power between suppliers and buyers of agricultural products later led to the adoption of the Directive on Unfair Trading Practices 2019 in business-to-business relationships in AVCs[40] to improve the protection of farmers and small-, medium- and mid-range sized suppliers, providing mandatory rules that outlaw certain unfair trading practices. The directive, which "...... aims to stop larger businesses exploiting small and medium-sized suppliers because of their weaker bargaining position, and to avoid the costs of such practices being passed on to primary producers," was already transposed to the European Union Member States' national legislation, being enforced by their national competition authorities in many cases, but also by ministries of agriculture and economy bodies, illustrating different options but possibly also leading to overlapping competences among regulators.

33. In particular since 2022, the mentioned increases in food prices and their volatility led some competition authorities to undertake sectoral enquiries, market studies, and price monitoring exercises, seeking to better understand

---

36 *See*, ECN, Report on Competition Law Enforcement and Market Monitoring Activities by European Competition Authorities in the Food Sector (2012), https://competition-policy.ec.europa.eu/antitrust-and-cartels/european-competition-network_en.

37 *See*, ICN, Working Group Market Studies information store: Sector Groceries (food and drink) (updated July 2020), https://internationalcompetitionnetwork.org/wp-content/uploads/2021/05/AWG_MktStudies_Groceries2020.pdf.

38 For example, Japanese competition law ("Act on Prohibition of Private Monopolization and Maintenance of Fair Trade (Act No. 54 of April 14, 1947)" prohibits abuse of superior bargaining position as one of the unfair trade practices. Article 2(9)(v): "engaging in any act specified in one of the following by making use of one's superior bargaining position over the counterparty unjustly, in light of normal business practices: (a) causing the counterparty in continuous transactions (including a party with whom one newly intends to engage in continuous transactions; the same applies in (b) below) to purchase goods or services other than those to which the relevant transactions pertain (b) causing the counterparty in continuous transactions to provide money, services or other economic benefits (c) refusing to receive goods in transactions with the counterparty, causing the counterparty to take back such goods after receiving them from the counterparty, delaying payment to the counterparty or reducing the amount of payment, or otherwise establishing or changing trade terms or executing transactions in a way disadvantageous to the counterparty." (https://www.jftc.go.jp/en/legislation_gls/AMA.pdf).Also, Korea's Competition Law (art. 45(1)6. prohibits "[m]aking transactions with the other party to the transaction by unfairly taking advantage of the bargaining position of the business entity itself" as one of the categories of unfair trade practices.

39 *See*, UNCTAD, *Competition Issues in the Food Chain: Possible Measures to Address Buyer Power in the Retail Sector* (Discussion Paper, 2014), https://unctad.org/system/files/non-official-document/tdb61_c01_UNCTAD.pdf; and secretariat note, UNCTAD *Enforcement of Competition Policy in the Retail Sector: Competition Issues in the Food Retail Chain*, (Aug. 17, 2016), https://unctad.org/system/files/official-document/ciclpd38_en.pdf.

40 Directive (EU) 2019/633 of the European Parliament and of the Council of 17 April 2019 on unfair trading practices in business-to-business relationships in the agricultural and food supply chain, 2019, O.J. (L 111) 59-72.

these markets' structure and functioning. This complemented a vigilant law enforcement stance against identified abuses of market power, and collusive practices, including merger control, and advising governments on regulatory measures and reforms when necessary.

34. In October 2023, the International Competition Network's (ICN) "Special project on competition concerns in agriculture and food markets" was launched, led by the South African Competition Commission and the Competition Authority of Kenya, and motivated by the high food inflation experienced by developing and developed countries, in view of "the transnational nature of (agricultural) businesses, the increasing use and current vulnerabilities of global value chains, and the importance of international markets such as for agriculture inputs."[41] International workshops and conferences in different countries have also been held to monitor and analyze food and agricultural market competition issues from the national and regional perspectives.[42]

35. The widely shared interest around competition in food markets demonstrates that, in the current context of high concentration in different segments of ACVs, aggravated by factors like high barriers to entry, the increasing importance of network externalities, the relational nature of links within ACVs and their endogenous nature, competition policy must strengthen ongoing efforts to address anticompetitive practices and boost market efficiency and transparency. High market concentration, abuse of dominance, exclusionary practices, and collusion, all require competition authorities to resort to all tools available in favor of the procompetitive market and consumer welfare. This includes law enforcement, sectoral enquiries, market monitoring, advocacy to government on legislative and regulatory measures, and others as necessary, further engaging with their peers within regional and international frameworks as it is of the utmost importance regarding cross-border challenges.

---

41 *See*, ICN Brief, *Working Group and Special Steering Group projects for ICN year 2024–2025*, https://www.internationalcompetitionnetwork.org/wp-content/uploads/2024/07/ICN-in-brief-2024-2025.pdf (last visited Oct. 20, 2024).

42 For example, the BRICS Competition Law and Policy Center, in cooperation with the Egyptian Competition Authority and the Federal Antimonopoly Service of the Russian Federation, held an international workshop: Global Food Value Chains: Focus on the Global Grain Trade (Feb. 2024), https://www.bricscompetition.org/events/68. The International Competition Network annual conference – ICN SAUIPE 2024 included a plenary session dedicated to: Interaction between Global Markets and Local Needs in Agriculture and Food Markets – Competition Concerns in Agriculture and Food Markets and a breakout session on: Competition enforcement in Agriculture and Food Markets: Reflections on Pro-Active Research, Monitoring, and Price Observatories (2024), https://icn2024sauipe.cade.gov.br/program/. UNCTAD fifteenth meeting of its Research Partnership Platform included a session on: Global Food Markets and Competition and Consumer Policies Challenges https://unctad.org/meeting/fifteenth-meeting-unctad-research-partnership-platform(July 2024). The COMESA Competition Commission in collaboration with the University of Johannesburg's Centre for Competition Regulation and Economic Development (CCRED) on the African Market Observatory (AMO) have produced research studies in the agriculture and food markets, such as on fertilizer markets and vegetable oils, COMESA, Competition, Concentration, and Market Outcomes in Fertiliser Markets In East And Southern Africa (Apr. 18, 2024), https://comesacompetition.org/resources/publications/competitionconcentrationand-market-outcomes-in-fertiliser-markets-in-east-and-southern-africa/; and COMESA, Concentration, Market Structure And Barriers To Entry In The Vegetable Oil Value Chain In East And Southern Africa (Apr. 18, 2024), https://comesacompetition.org/resources/publications/concentrationmarket-structure-and-barriers-to-entry-in-the-vegetable-oil-value-chain-in-east-and-souther-africa/.

36. The competition authorities of several developing countries, in particular newer and smaller ones, should aim to complement and enhance their limited available resources and experience by fully exploring the potential of regional and international cooperation. This could occur either within the framework of formal arrangements or under informal settings, including through joint research and investigations to address transnational issues in agriculture markets, such as those involving inputs or others mentioned above.

37. Similarly, there is a need for strengthened coordination between competition policy and other policies affecting agricultural value chains, such as international trade (including market access trade barriers, namely non-tariff measures and export restrictions), agricultural sectorial policies (such as those seeking to strengthen domestic food security, diversification, value addition and policies targeted to reduce rural inequality), and consumer protection[43] (including improving access to food for all people and all countries, improving food security, controlling speculative practices, informing and educating consumers on nutrition and food adulteration[44]).

38. This requires a holistic policy approach that boosts not only static but also dynamic competition and innovation in an economically, environmentally, and socially sustainable way.

V. Conclusion

39. Global food markets are extremely important for people, the planet, and prosperity. Attaining Sustainable Development Goal 2 – End Hunger, achieving Food Security and improved Nutrition and promoting Sustainable Development[45] by 2030, has been seriously at risk since 2015 due to the compounding impacts of the Covid-19 pandemic, conflicts, climate change, and growing inequalities.[46] Achieving this goal will require a multifaceted approach, including ensuring global market access to nutritious food through international trade and cross-border cooperation, and reducing price volatility.[47]

---

43 Consumers International, the world federation of consumer organizations, has been working on Fair Food Prices. See the reports: CONSUMERS INTERNATIONAL, CONSUMERS IN CRISIS: AN ACTION AGENDA FOR FUTURE FOOD SYSTEMS (2022), https://www.consumersinternational.org/media/547573/agenda-for-future-food-systems-report.pdf; and UNLOCKING CONSUMER ACTION FOR FOOD SYSTEMS TRANSFORMATION (2024), https://www.consumersinternational.org/media/552304/consumer-action-for-food-systems-transformation.pdf.

44 *See*, UNCTAD, *United Nations, Guidelines for Consumer Protection*, Guideline 44(a) (2015), https://unctad.org/system/files/official-document/ditccplpmisc2016d1_en.pdf.

45 United Nations, Sustainable Development Goals, https://www.un.org/sustainabledevelopment/hunger/ (last visited Oct. 20, 2024).

46 UNITED NATIONS, THE SUSTAINABLE DEVELOPMENT GOALS REPORT (2023), https://unstats.un.org/sdgs/report/2023/The-Sustainable-Development-Goals-Report-2023.pdf.

47 UNCTAD, *International Trade in Open and Transparent Markets May Help Alleviate the Effects of Shocks and Ensure Food Security*, https://sdgpulse.unctad.org/trade-agriculture-biotrade/ (last visited Oct. 20, 2024).

40. Competition policy, coordinated with trade, agriculture, and consumer protection policies in a consistent way, can improve the functioning of food markets, increasing people's access to affordable food and providing opportunities for small- and medium-sized businesses. Competition authorities may combine tools and measures to address markets' structure and functioning issues, taking advantage of international cooperation opportunities to work together in addressing common challenges.

41. Cooperation with international and regional organizations, academia, and civil society organizations can contribute to expanding and deepening research and analysis on taxing competition challenges affecting agricultural value chains, including the impact of intellectual property rights, the role of technology, and the increasing importance of economic and environmental sustainability issues.

42. Multi-disciplinary policy efforts on commodities, competition, and consumer policies, trade analysis and trade agreements, trade and environment, and trade logistics, as UNCTAD offers under its wide mandate on all issues related to economic and sustainable development, are required to assist developing countries to identify the best policy options at their disposal to tackle agricultural value chain structural and behavioral challenges in partnership with numerous counterparts.

Generative AI, Pyramids and Legal Institutionalism*

THIBAULT SCHREPEL
Vrije University of Amsterdam

1. Baseball's Yogi Berra once observed that "*it is difficult to make predictions, especially about the future*." Scholars, policymakers, computer engineers, practitioners and others will surely agree that legal rules and standards for generative AI ("genAI") should not be based on mere speculations. They should be based on facts. That said, legal institutions may also have a role to play in maintaining dynamism in the space, which entails developing policies and enforcement actions based on reasonable anticipations. These anticipations can be informed by an analysis of the factors that define the dynamics of generative AI. As Yogi also said, "*You can observe a lot by watching*." I suggest we do just that.

I. Emerging Competitive Dynamics

2. Generative AI, which I define as AI that can generate text, images, and other output, has at least four distinct layers. These layers form a pyramid that informs emerging competitive dynamics and, as we shall see, the role and importance of legal institutions.

3. The first is the infrastructure layer. Companies like Nvidia, Qualcomm, and Amazon Web Services (AWS) provide the computing power, chips, and storage capacity critical to the creation and training of all things generative AI.

---

* This article has been previously published in Concurrences, and it might have been edited for clarity and cohesion. Thibault Schrepel, Generative AI, pyramids and legal institutionalism, November 2023, Concurrences N° 4-2023, Art. N° 113962.

The second layer is that of AI foundation models. Companies like OpenAI, Google, Hugging Face, Midjourney, and Anthropic build and train these models using the first layer infrastructures, often with billions of parameters. Their models underpin the third layer, which comprises all generative AI applications. At the time of this writing, ChatGPT, DALL·E 2, Midjourney, and GitHub Copilot are popular applications that generate text, pictures, and code. Last, companies and individuals are using generative AI to reduce their costs, speed up processes, be more creative, etc. Early estimates (Goldman Sachs, 2023) predict a 1.4 percentage points increase in global GDP thanks to generative AI.

Figure

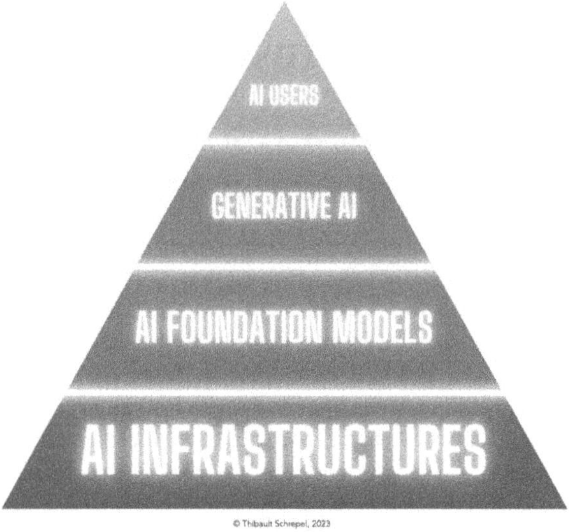

4. As Sandy Pentland and I cover in a working paper entitled "Competition between AI Foundation Models: Dynamics and Policy Recommendations" (https://ssrn.com/ abstract=4493900), these four layers are interconnected. To take a couple of examples, the cost of compute impacts the ability to train AI foundation models. OpenAI spent $540 million on the development of GPT-4 in 2022 alone. The same company reportedly spends $700,000 per day running ChatGPT (mostly to compute all the prompts). Moving one layer up, competitive dynamics between AI foundation models influences quality, diversity, price and access conditions. The more dynamic, the more generative AI applications, and thus, the greater the adoption at the end layer.

5. In reverse order, the more users, the easier it is to attract venture capital ("VC") funding. VCs have already increased their investments in AI start-ups from $408 million in 2018 to $4.5 billion by 2022. The more applications, the more AI foundation models will be developed, thus increasing the incentive to compete at the infrastructure layer. Nvidia, whose shares are up 200% year-to-date, claims that using its GPU has reduced the price

of training foundation models from $10 million to just $400,000 in 2023. Since there is little doubt that these layers will remain interconnected, it seems that future analyses of competitive issues in this space will need to build on their interdependence.

II. Policies for a Dynamic Ecosystem

6. Policymakers and regulators are showing a strong inclination to intervene in the field of generative AI, if only to demonstrate that they will not be left behind. Conveniently, they have a critical role to play in ensuring dynamism between the different layers of the pyramid. In what follows, I outline what I think a reasonable policy agenda could look like.

7. Starting with the target of regulation, the interdependence of all layers underscores the need to focus on the pyramid foundations. To put it bluntly, there is no generative AI without computing power. Similarly, there will be no continuous flourishing of applications without a dynamic foundation model layer. If one company were to control the dominant model with little competitive pressure (e.g., thanks to anticompetitive practices that reduce the increasing returns of the main alternatives), the conditions of access would be such that incentives to develop genAI applications would be greatly diminished. Bottom layers are therefore critical and should be at the forefront of competition policy.

8. In terms of policies, policymakers and regulators can avoid an ecosystem freeze by ensuring that new laws do not favor the big players. I take two examples. First, we see that open source ("OS") AI foundation models and applications are being vilified. I expect they will be increasingly so, as they do not offer the same level of centralized control as proprietary alternatives. On the social front, OS solutions are labeled as anti-democratic because they promote freedom of speech to a degree that is commonly disputed. On the economic front, OS is described as unfair because underlying models are often trained on data without providing compensation. As we are already seeing, large corporations are pushing for licenses and royalties to be paid to content providers whose publications are used for AI training. Conveniently, large companies can afford these costs, while smaller and OS competitors often cannot. New legislation and court rulings in this area will have a major impact on the competitiveness of OS solutions.

9. Second, it appears that the upcoming regulatory burden resulting from the AI Act will not be distributed proportionately. As it stands, all companies putting a high-risk AI system on the market will have to produce technical documentation showing that their system is in line with the "*values, fundamental rights and principles*" of the European Union (see AI Act, p. 1 and Art. 11). I doubt that companies with a handful of employees will be able to produce such "technolegal" documentation without having to cut back

on R&D spending. I suggest that the AI Act follows the same logic as the Digital Services Act, which imposes fewer obligations on companies with a limited number of users.

10. Policymakers can also encourage dynamism by ensuring that existing laws do not favor large players. For example, Japan's Minister of Education, Culture, Sports, Science and Technology, Keiko Nagaoka, recently gave her blessing (https://go2senkyo.com/seijika/122181/ posts/685617) to AI models trained on proprietary data. This interpretation of Japanese intellectual property law allows small players, who are unable to pay expensive licensing fees, to compete with larger companies. In other words, the bending of copyright laws appears critical to the competitiveness of generative AI. Similarly, I propose introducing antitrust exemptions for open-source and open-access companies. Antitrust agencies could allow these companies to pool their resources in joint ventures without having to notify the operation. They could allow strategic alliances without calling them cartels. And they could expand the scope of the EU's R&D exemption beyond the current market share thresholds and competing efforts criteria. If they do not, I can think of at least one other country that will.

11. In short, policymakers and regulators have an important role to play in supporting the short-, medium-, and long-term dynamism of generative AI. But if generative AI highlights the importance of legal institutionalism, I sometimes fear that it may also reveal its danger in a world where regulation can be captured by private and public actors alike.

A Consumer View of EU Competition Law: What's Working, What Isn't, and How This Can Be Fixed

AGUSTIN REYNA AND VANESSA TURNER
The European Consumer Organisation (BEUC)

I. Introduction

1. In recent times, competition law, including in the EU, has faced criticism, highlighting the need for improvements. Long and complex procedures can lead to delayed decisions, legal uncertainties and lack of effectiveness. Additionally, EU and national cases too often lack input from civil society, limiting transparency, accountability and evidence gathering, thereby exposing regulators to one-sided narratives. While current shortcomings need to be improved, these do not negate the overall value of EU competition law. Nor do they require a fundamental recast of its legal foundation.

2. EU competition policy remains vital for maintaining competitive markets, protecting consumers and addressing emerging concerns. EU competition law's adaptability demonstrates its ongoing relevance in today's ever-changing social and economic landscape. In the last few years, competition policy has been aligned with broader European Union priorities, including the green and digital transitions – both in antitrust and merger control.

3. Competition policy is essential in ensuring that businesses compete fairly in developing and offering more sustainable goods and services.[1] It can act against greenwashing cartels and to encourage innovation in sustainable technologies. It could also be considered in relation to green abuses of dominance (eg pollution by a dominant undertaking to gain a competitive advantage). By promoting competition in clean energy, and eco-friendly products, consumers are presented with more choices that can support a more sustainable lifestyle.

4. In the field of digitalisation, European and national competition authorities have been active in keeping digital markets open and competitive. In this process, it was also possible to identify the complementarity between competition law and regulation, with the adoption of the Digital Markets Act.[2] As the digital economy continues to grow, competition policy should contribute to fostering a more dynamic and consumer-focused digital marketplace.[3] This will also require the ability to review mergers falling below current turnover thresholds where these could further strengthen the unparalleled market power of big tech ecosystems.[4]

5. EU competition law has been able to address multiple objectives such as the protection of consumer wellbeing,[5] consumer welfare,[6] efficiency,[7] effective

---

1 OECD, "Sustainability and Competition" (1 December 2020) Note by BEUC <https://one.oecd.org/document/DAF/COMP/WD(2020)72/en/pdf> accessed 29 October 2024.

2 Regulation (EU) 2022/1925 of the European Parliament and of the Council of 14 September 2022 on contestable and fair markets in the digital sector and amending Directives (EU) 2019/1937 and (EU) 2020/1828 (Digital Markets Act) [2022] OJ L265/1.

3 BEUC, *The Role of Competition Policy in Protecting Consumers' Well-being in the Digital Era* (2019) <www.beuc.eu/reports/role-competition-policy-protecting-consumers-well-being-digital-era> accessed 29 October 2024.

4 OECD, "Start-ups, Killer Acquisitions and Merger Control" (11 June 2020) Note by BEUC <https://one.oecd.org/document/DAF/COMP/WD(2020)30/en/pdf> accessed 2 April 2024.

5 Case C-377/20 *Servizio Elettrico Nazionale SpA v Autorita Garante della Concorrenza e del Mercato* ECLI:EU:C:2022:379, para 46 "the well-being of both intermediary and final consumers must be regarded as the ultimate objective warranting the intervention of competition law", see Lesley Hannah and Ginevra Bicciolo, "The EU Court of Justice delivers a ruling which sheds more light on non-price abuses under Article 102 TFEU in relation to conduct which constitutes an abuse of dominance and the interpretation of the concept of "competition on the merits" (Servizio Elettrico Nazionale)" (2022) e-Competitions art. No. 106948.

6 Case C-501/06 P *GlaxoSmithKline Services Unlimited v Commission of the European Communities* ECLI:EU:C:2009:610, para 63; Case C-8/08 *T-Mobile Netherlands BV v Raad van Bestuur van de Nederlandse Mededingingsautoriteit* [2009] ECLI:EU:C:2009:343, paras 31, 36, 38–39, see Anne Wachsmann et al., "The EU Court of Justice confirms that the Commission must assess whether an agreement to limit parallel trade in medicines has pro-competitive benefits (GlaxoSmithKline)" (2009) e-Competitions art. No. 41281 , and see Michel Debroux, "Potentiality of anticompetitive object: The ECJ rules that a practice of exchange of information between competitors, even limited in scope, can have an anticompetitive object and that the causality presumption is a substantive rule, not a procedural rule (T-Mobile Netherlands)" (4 June 2009) 3 Concurrences 28166 70–71.

7 European Commission, Guidance on the Commission's enforcement priorities in applying Article 82 of the EC Treaty to abusive exclusionary conduct by dominant undertakings [2009] OJ C45/7, paras 1, 5–7; European Commission, "Guidelines on Vertical Restraints" [2022] OJ C248/1, para 10.

competition structure,[8] the protection of input providers,[9] fairness,[10] plurality in a democratic society,[11] the functioning of the internal market[12] and market integration.[13] In essence, EU competition law is about protecting the competitive process[14] in a way that can ultimately benefit consumers and citizens in terms of prices, choice, quality and innovation.

6. Naturally, no law can be pursued in isolation and without reference to the legal, economic, political and social context. Tackling changes in the global economic landscape today, however, does not mean that the EU's standard of intervention should be replaced. EU competition law, with its flexible standard, by and large has the necessary ability to adapt to deal with today's context,[15] with different market failures and priorities. It is, much more so than the US antitrust law standard, equipped to cater also for non-price issues such as quality and innovation. There is therefore no need, and it would rather be counterproductive, to attempt to change or widen this tried and tested standard to ostensibly accommodate current political priorities such as industrial policy or to serve European or other vested interests.

---

8 *Servizio Elettrico Nazionale SpA* (n 5), para 44; Case C-322/81 *Nederlandsche Banden Industrie Michelin NV v Commission of the European Communities* ECLI:EU:C:1983:313, para 57 holding that the dominant undertaking has a "special responsibility not to allow its conduct to impair genuine undistorted competition on the common market"; Case 6/72 *Europemballage Corp v Commission of the European Communities* ECLI:EU:C:1973:22, para 26; Case C-95/04 P *British Airways Plc v Commission of the European Communities* ECLI:EU:C:2007:166, para 106; Case T-340/03 *France Telecom SA (formerly Wanadoo Interactive SA) v Commission of the European Communities* ECLI:EU:T:2007:22, para 266; Case C-52/09 *Konkurrensverket v TeliaSonera Sverige AB* ECLI:EU:C:2011:83, para 24; Joined Cases C-468 to 478/06 *Sot Lelos kai Sia EE v GlaxoSmithKline AEVE Farmakeftikon Proionton (formerly Glaxowellcome AEVE)* ECLI:EU:C:2008:504, para 68; Case C-280/08 P *Deutsche Telekom AG v European Commission* ECLI:EU:C:2010:603, para 176, see Anne-Lise Sibony, "Compression des marges - Ciseau tarifaire : La Cour de Justice de l'Union européenne rend son premier arrêt sur l'abus par compression de marge et confirme que le ciseau tarifaire constitue un abus même lorsque l'un des éléments du tarif de l'entreprise en position dominante a été approuvé par le régulateur sectoriel (Deutsche Telekom)" (14 October 2010) 1 Concurrences 34038 91–95.

9 (Case COMP/C.38.281/B.2 – *Raw Tobacco Italy*) Commission Decision 20 October 2005 [2005] OJ L353/45; Joined Cases C-264/01, C-306/01, C-354/01 and C-355/01 *AOK Bundesverband v Ichthyol Gesellschaft Cordes* ECLI:EU:C:2004:150, see Alain Ronzano, "Notion d'entreprise : La CJCE dit pour droit que des caisses d'assurances maladie ne peuvent pas être considérées comme des entreprises au sens du droit de la concurrence (AOK-Bundesverband e.a.)" (16 March 2004) 1 Concurrences 55798.

10 Case 26/75 *General Motors Continental NV v Commission of the European Communities* ECLI:EU:C:1975:150; Case 27/76 *United Brands Co v Commission of the European Communities* ECLI:EU:C:1978:22; Case C-177/16 *Autortiesibu un Komunicesanas Konsultaciju Agentura/Latvijas Autoru Apvieniba v Konkurences Padome* ECLI:EU:C:2017:689; (Case COMP/C-1/36.915 – *Deutsche Post AG*) Commission Decision 2001/892/EC [2001] OJ L331/40.

11 The General Court explicitly recognised the importance of consumer choice "to ensure plurality in a democratic society". Case T-604/18 *Google LLC v European Commission (Google Android)* ECLI:EU:T:2022:541, para 1028.

12 *Servizio Elettrico Nazionale SpA* (n 5), para 42.

13 BEUC, *The Role of Competition Policy* (n 3); European Commission, Press Release, "Keynote of EVP Vestager at the European Competition Law Tuesdays: A Principles Based approach to Competition Policy" (25 October 2022) <https://ec.europa.eu/commission/presscorner/detail/en/SPEECH_22_6393> accessed 29 October 2024, "EU competition policy is able to pursue multiple goals, such as fairness and a level-playing field, market integration, preserving competitive processes, consumer welfare, efficiency and innovation, and ultimately plurality and democracy".

14 European Commission, "Guidelines on the Application of Article 81(3) of the Treaty" [2004] OJ C101/97, para 105 "in other words, the ultimate aim of Article 101 is to protect the competitive process".

15 BEUC, *The Role of Competition Policy* (n 3); European Commission, *XXIInd Report on Competition Policy* (1992) 13.

7. What should, however, be changed to strengthen its effectiveness, is the way that competition law is enforced and the tools it has at its disposal. Ideas on how to achieve this are outlined below.

II. How to Improve the Application of EU Competition Law

8. From the consumer perspective, there are several ways to optimise the application of competition law (both antitrust and merger control) to the benefit of consumers. These include reassessing the role of economic analysis in competition cases, broadening and upgrading evidence gathering for a more empirical approach to cases, increasing the breadth of agencies' resources, developing a less siloed approach across regulators, more effective remedies in mergers and in bringing antitrust law infringements to an end, and finally to generate restorative justice for consumer victims of competition law violations.

1. Upgrading the Evidence Used in Competition Law Enforcement

9. In the early 2000s, the enforcement of competition law took a new direction (in response to some notable judgments of the European Court[16]) with the introduction of the "more economic approach" or the "effects-based approach". While introducing more economics was undoubtedly beneficial, looking at the way that this trend has developed over the last 20 years, there are good arguments that the use of industrial organisation economics has gone too far to the extent that it is seen as the only useful economic evidence.

10. Input-output analysis (IO) economics is not empirical evidence but is often based on applying theories to datasets with these theories having changed overtime to reflect the latest fashionable idea. Certainly, some of these theories have been helpful in the analysis of mergers, abuse of dominance and so on. However, this has been at the cost of ignoring empirical evidence from other disciplines. In the interests of effective and timely competition law enforcement,[17] the balance must be redressed as recognised in the recent

---

16 Case T-342/99 *Airtours Plc v Commission of the European Communities* ECLI:EU:T:2002:146; Case T-5/02 *Tetra Laval BV v Commission of the European Communities* ECLI:EU:T:2002:264; Case T-310/01 *Schneider Electric SA v Commission of the European Communities* ECLI:EU:T:2002:254, see Kay Parplies, Mary Loughran and Roosmarijn Schade, "The EU Court of Justice annuls the Commission's decision to prohibit a merger between two UK based holiday tour operators (Airtours / First Choice)" (2002) e-Competitions art. No. 38925, see General Court of the European Union, "The EU General Court annuls a Commission decision prohibiting a merger in the packaging industry for insufficient evidence in the examination of the potential leveraging methods (Tetra Laval / Sidel)" (2002) e-Competitions art. No. 93625.

17 See also "Spamming the Regulator" and the effect on effective enforcement of a surfeit of economic "evidence". Marlene Jugl et al., "Spamming the Regulator: Exploring a New Lobbying Strategy in EU Competition Procedures" (2023) 12 JAE <https://academic.oup.com/antitrust/article-abstract/12/1/7/7128249?redirected From=fulltext> accessed 29 October 2024.

case law of the European Court.[18] Competition authorities' evidence-gathering practices and procedures must be reviewed to ensure that they are fit for purpose.[19] This implies considering other disciplines that can provide useful evidence and approaches.

11. Greater use should be made of evidential tools such as behavioural economics (or behavioural insights) and financial analytics, as well as data, computer, and AI science inputs.

12. In relation to behavioural economics, from the competition law perspective, the behaviour of consumers matters because it can affect companies' ability to retain existing customers and steer new ones away from rivals.[20] Human beings do not always behave in the way that economic theories predict. Competition law analysis must be based on realities not theories. How consumers react to information presented to them can be tested in experiments and field trials. Companies can undermine competition by taking advantage of consumers' actual behaviours. This has been recognised by the Commission and the European Court, most recently in the *Google Shopping* and *Google Android* cases.[21] Behavioural insights also have a significant role to play in ensuring that remedies are effective in consumer-facing markets, considering the significant effect consumer behaviour can have on the success of a remedy.[22]

13. Economic evidence should furthermore be broadened out to other expertise beyond industrial organisation economics to include financial evidence analysis, (including of analysis of statutory accounts, financial reporting, communications to shareholders and investors, published financial performance and targets, etc) to better understand company incentives and to test theories against actual financial data. Much can be learned from "following the money".

---

18 Case C-680/20 *Unilever Italia Mkt Operations Srl v Autorita Garante della Concorrenza e del Mercato* ECLI:EU:C:2023:33, para 58; *Servizio Elettrico Nazionale SpA* (n 5), para 81; Case C-333/21 *European Superleague Company SL v Federation internationale de football association (FIFA)* ECLI:EU:C:2023:1011, para 130, see Paschalis Lois, "The EU Court of Justice issues a decision on the imputation of liability and treatment of exclusivity under the EU prohibition on abuse of dominance (Unilever Italia)" (2023) e-Competitions art. No. 110872, see Anne Wachsmann, Nicolas Zacharie and Daniel Green, "Notion d'abus : La Cour de justice de l'Union européenne précise les critères à retenir pour qualifier l'exploitation abusive d'une position dominante caractérisée par des pratiques d'éviction (Servizio Elettrico Nazionale)" (12 May 2022) 3 Concurrences 108170 88–90.

19 BEUC, "Evaluation of the Framework for Antitrust Enforcement of Articles 101 and 102 TFEU, BEUC's Response to the Public Consultation in Relation to the Evaluation of Regulation 1/2003" (2022) <www.beuc.eu/sites/default/files/publications/BEUC-X-2022-102_Evaluation_of_the_framework_for_antitrust_enforcement_of_articles_101_and_102_TFEU.pdf> accessed 29 October 2024.

20 OECD, "Integrating Consumer Behaviour Insights in Competition Enforcement" (24 June 2022) Note by BEUC <https://one.oecd.org/document/DAF/COMP/WD(2022)55/en/pdf> accessed 29 October 2024.

21 (Case AT.40099 – *Google Android*) Commission Decision 18 July 2018 [2019] OJ C402/19; (Case AT.39740 – *Google Search (Shopping)*) Commission Decision 27 June 2017 [2018] OJ C9/11; T-612/17 *Google LLC v European Commission (Google Shopping)* ECLI:EU:T:2021:763; *Google LLC v European Commission (Google Android)* (n 11).

22 BEUC, Evaluation of the Framework for Antitrust Enforcement (n 19).

2. Increasing Agencies Resources and Analytical Capability

14. There is a need to increase the resources and analytical capabilities of competition agencies in Europe. The increasing complexity of modern markets, the digital transformation, and the asymmetry of resources between regulators and infringing firms have placed unprecedented demands on enforcers. To effectively enforce competition law and safeguard consumer interests, agencies must have access to additional resources to broaden their expertise. This includes dealing with emerging fields such as data privacy, artificial intelligence, and sustainability, as well as behavioural economics and financial analysis expertise. By cultivating a broader knowledge base, competition agencies can gain a more comprehensive understanding of complex markets, enabling them to detect anticompetitive practices more effectively and adapt to the evolving economic landscape thereby safeguarding consumer interests.[23] This expertise is a pre-condition for more effective interventions and remedies.

3. Out-of-Silo Cooperation

15. There are clear advantages to cooperation between the European Commission and other authorities such as data protection authorities, consumer protection bodies and sector-specific regulators in competition law enforcement. This is, however, not possible under the existing EU legal framework. For the European Commission to be able to formally consult other authorities in the context of specific cases it would require amendments to Regulation 1/2003. For example, Articles 11 and 12 of Regulation 1/2003 on cooperation with other competition authorities could be extended to cooperation with other types of regulators where appropriate to enable consistent, non-siloed enforcement. This approach would allow the European Commission (DG-Comp) to exchange information in specific cases with the European Data Protection Board and the Consumer Protection Cooperation Network, better applying the principle of sincere cooperation embedded in the Treaty on the European Union (TEU).[24] This could be particularly useful when considering and articulating different theories of harm for which the expertise of data protection and consumer bodies could be of significant value for DG-Comp as well as for the design of remedies, both in mergers and in the context of a prohibition decision or commitment procedures in antitrust proceedings.[25]

---

23 This has been recognized recently by the International Competition Network (ICN). ICN, "Building Digital Capacity to Strengthen and Support Law Enforcement Agencies" (25–26 March 2024) <www.internationalcompetitionnetwork.org/wp-content/uploads/2024/03/ITF-Digital-Capacity-Building-messaging-2024.pdf> accessed 29 October 2024.

24 Case C-252/21 *Meta Platforms Inc v Bundeskartellamt* ECLI:EU:C:2023:537, para 53.

25 BEUC, Evaluation of the Framework for Antitrust Enforcement (n 19).

4. Developing More Effective Remedies

16. What is the purpose of intervening in markets if this does not have a beneficial effect in practice? Effective remedies do not always appear to have been front of mind in competition law enforcement however.[26] The effectives of remedies could be improved in particular through a number of procedural adjustments.[27]

17. In antitrust, the process of designing remedies should first and foremost not be solely in the hands of the infringing company which has no interest in effectively terminating an infringement that it has pursued for its own advantage. Therefore, remedy design should systematically involve the consultation of third parties, including consumer representatives in consumer-facing markets.[28] Third parties who are intended to benefit from or be part of the remedy design will likely be better placed than even the regulator to assess the effectiveness and viability of remedies proposed by the infringing company. While third-party consultation may take some time, the delay caused would be minimal compared to the delay caused if ineffective remedies need correction to actually bring an infringement to an end years later, after subsequent third-party input.[29]

18. Second, the Commission should systematically review and amend any remedy which proves to be unsuited to "effectively bring an infringement to an end". That this is within its powers was recognised in the *Ufex*[30] and *Microsoft* cases.[31]

19. In some cases, in addition to requiring the conduct to be terminated, the Commission may need to require restorative steps to be taken to re-introduce or restore effective competition in a market in light of the gravity and/or duration of an infringement, as recognised in the case law.[32]

---

26 EOCD, "Abuse of Dominance in Digital Markets" – (8 December 2020) <https://one.oecd.org/document/DAF/COMP/GF/WD(2020)1/en/pdf> accessed 29 October 2024.

27 These could be explicitly included in any revision of Regulation 1/2003. BEUC, Evaluation of the Framework for Antitrust Enforcement (n 19).

28 A formal consultation procedure on remedies under Regulation 1/2003 art 7 does not exist for prohibition decisions, unlike under art 9.

29 *Google Android* (n 21), see Stephanie McAree Mirrow, "The EU Commission fines a tech company for illegal tying in the market for third-party mobile device manufacturing (Google Android)" (2018) e-Competitions art. No. 89343.

30 Case C-119/97 P *Union Francaise de l'Express (UFEX) v Commission of the European Communities* ECLI:EU:C:1999:116, para 94, see Ann-Christin Richter and Merlin Gömann, "The EU Court of Justice holds that National Competition Authorities may consider violations of data protection laws during abuse of dominance assessments (Meta)" (2023) e-Competitions art. No. 114093.

31 Case T-201/04 *Microsoft Corp v Commission of the European Communities* ECLI:EU:T:2007:289, para 1265, see Catherine Prieto, "Saga Microsoft : Le Tribunal de première instance des Communautés européennes rejette le recours formé par Microsoft condamné pour un double abus de position dominante (Microsoft)" (17 September 2007) 4 Concurrences 14477 78–83.

32 *Google Android* (n 21), see Nicholas Levy et al., "The EU General Court partially annuls the Commission's decision against a Big Tech company for non-price-based abuses of dominance (Google Android)" (2022) e-Competitions art. No. 109329. (Case AT.39530 – *Microsoft (Tying)*) Commission Decision 6 December 2009 [2010] OJ C36/7, see Thomas Kramler et al., "The EU Commission renders legally binding commitment offered by U.S. software undertaking concerning web browsers (Microsoft)" (2009) e-Competitions art. No. 34882.

20. In mergers, if there are doubts about the remedy's effectiveness, the default position should be that the merger cannot be cleared, especially in industries with a history of ineffective remedies.[33]

III. Compensating Consumer Victims of Competition Law Violations

21. Private damages actions are meant to ensure compensation for victims of competition law violations for the harm caused to them. The EU Damages Directive[34] aims at facilitating private actions but is in reality of little practical help to consumers as it does not include collective actions, the only realistic way for consumers to obtain redress. This contrasts with other areas of EU law which are covered by the Representative Actions Directive (the RAD).[35] From the consumer perspective there is, therefore, a gap in EU competition law enforcement in terms of their ability to obtain any form of financial redress or corrective justice for competition law violations which cause them harm. This could be remedied in a number of ways.

1. Revision of the EU Damages Directive

22. Including collective actions in a revision of the Damages Directive, or potentially adding Regulation 1/2003 to the RAD, could contribute to remedying the current unsatisfactory situation. In addition to enabling consumer victims to be compensated, damages actions would contribute to deterring anticompetitive behaviour, as recognised in the case law.[36]

2. Restitution (Financial Contributions)

23. In the absence of or in addition to a revision of the Damages Directive, victims could obtain some level of redress in settlement and commitment cases by including a requirement to make a voluntary financial contribution

---

33 Bundeskartellamt, "IKK 2024 – Margrethe Vestager, Executive Vice-President and European Commissioner for Competition" (29 February 2024), (22nd International Conference on Competition, Berlin, Q&A with Rikard Jermsten, Director General, Swedish Competition Authority) <www.youtube.com/watch?v=XIhSoGtbZIA> accessed 29 October 2024. EVP Vestager comments expressing reservations on the effectiveness of slot remedies in airline mergers.

34 Directive 2014/104/EU of the European Parliament and of the Council of 26 November 2014 on certain rules governing actions for damages under national law for infringements of the competition law provisions of the Member States and of the European Union [2014] OJ L349/1.

35 Directive (EU) 2020/1828 of the European Parliament and of the Council of 25 November 2020 on representative actions for the protection of the collective interests of consumers and repealing Directive 2009/22/EC [2020] OJ L409/1.

36 Case C-453/99 *Courage Ltd v Crehan* ECLI:EU:C:2001:465, para 26. "The full effectiveness of Article 85 of the Treaty and, in particular, the practical effect of the prohibition laid down in Article 85(1) would be put at risk if it were not open to any individual to claim damages for loss caused to him by a contract or by conduct liable to restrict or distort competition. Indeed, the existence of such a right strengthens the working of the Community competition rules and discourages agreements or practices, which are frequently covert, which are liable to restrict or distort competition. From that point of view, actions for damages before the national courts can make a significant contribution to the maintenance of effective competition in the Community".

to consumer or other civil society representatives of the victims. This kind of approach has been taken in the past in cases at both European Commission[37] and national competition authority (NCA) level.[38]

3. Fines Fund

24. Finally, where fines are imposed by competition authorities on companies violating competition law, part of these fines could be used to help establish funds to finance projects that seek to improve the protection of consumer rights, including under competition law. Earmarking a proportion of fines for funding such projects would contribute to a form of "corrective justice" for competition law breaches and create a stronger link between competition law enforcement and consumers.[39]

IV. Beyond Articles 101 and 102 TFEU: New Powers for DG Competition and the NCAs

25. So far, this contribution has covered how to improve the enforcement of Articles 101 and 102 Treaty on the Functioning of the European Union (TFEU) and merger control. However, European[40] and national legislators[41] should also consider the introduction of a "new competition tool" or market investigation tool to deal with market failures that cannot be tackled effectively under abuse of dominance and anticompetitive agreements rules. Such market failures include systemic market failures that go beyond the conduct of a particular market player, specific structural features such as high concentration and barriers to entry, tacit collusion and demand-side failures, such as lack of consumer switching.

V. Conclusion

26. EU competition law has served consumers in Europe well, but important changes need to be made to improve its enforcement to ensure more competitive, fair and sustainable markets for consumers.

---

37 DG-COMP Ángel Pena Castellot "Commission Settles Allegations of Abuse and Clears Patent Pools in the CD Market" (2003) 3 Competition Policy Newsletter <https://op.europa.eu/en/publication-detail/-/publication/769abdd3-b1aa-11e9-9d01-01aa75ed71a1/language-de> accessed 29 October 2024.

38 BEUC, Evaluation of the Framework for Antitrust Enforcement (n 19).

39 Such an idea of financing consumer projects with a contribution from competition fines has been implemented in Portugal. Parliament Law No 17/2022 of 17 August 2022 which transposed Directive (EU) 2019/1 of the European Parliament and of the Council of 11 December 2018 to empower the competition authorities of the Member States to be more effective enforcers and to ensure the proper functioning of the internal market (ECN+ Directive) [2019] OJ 11/3 art 35, para 8.

40 European Commission, "Impact Assessment for a Possible New Competition Tool" (2020) <https://competition-policy.ec.europa.eu/public-consultations/2020-new-comp-tool_en> accessed 29 October 2024. The Commission should revive its idea of the New Competition tool as set out in its 2020 consultation.

41 Competition authorities, notably in the UK, Greece, Iceland and as of recently in Germany and Italy have such a tools Others, ie Denmark, Norway, Sweden, Czechia and the Netherlands are actively considering introducing comparable market investigation tools.

Competition: Economics, Evidence, Policy and Ethics

Darren Brady Nelson*
Center for Freedom and Prosperity

I. Introduction

1. I wrote specifically about competition[1] for a lay audience, where I made the following points, which are pertinent as an introduction here: "Almost everybody, including the progressively political ESPN, understands the importance of genuine competition on the fields, courts, rinks and links. This will come as a huge surprise to most, but competition in sports is nothing like competition in the economy. The former is win-lose, whilst the latter is win-win."

II. Competition Economics

2. My Master's law essay, regarding the Account of Profits[2] remedy under Australian IP law,[3] largely summed up the mainstream economics of competition in the diagram below. Competition leads to lower prices (P), higher quantities (Q) and normal profit (π). Monopoly leads to higher P, lower Q and supernormal π. Free-market economics shows that monopoly is only

---

* *Associate Scholar, Center for Freedom and Prosperity, Washington DC USA.*

1 Darren Brady Nelson, *New Data Shows Competition Is Making America Great Again*, (2018), https://www.pc.gov.au/__data/assets/pdf_file/0010/382186/sub013-competition-analysis.pdf.

2 IP Australia, *Account of profits*, (June 2024), https://www.ipaustralia.gov.au/manage-my-ip/someone-is-using-my-ip/escalate-to-court#:~:text=Account%20of%20profits,made%20from%20using%20your%20IP.

3 IP Australia, *Understanding intellectual property (IP)*, (June 2024), https://www.ipaustralia.gov.au/understanding-ip/types-of-ip.

sustainable by government intervention and that this usually requires monopoly investment (I) in getting and protecting that over time. Christian economics is a mix.

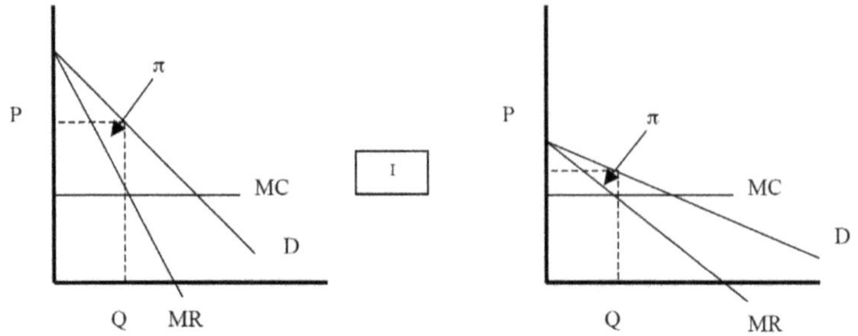

1. Mainstream Economics

3. Mainstream economics largely provides the foundation for Australian competition law.[4] The Competition Policy Reform Act 1995[5] states: "2. The object of this Act is to enhance the welfare of Australians through the promotion of competition[.]" The Competition and Consumer Act 2010[6] adds: "4E. For the purposes of this Act, market includes goods or services that are substitutable for, or otherwise competitive with, the first-mentioned goods or services."

4. As I wrote in my Master's law thesis at UNSW: "The importance of market competition is not as an end in itself, but as a means to an end. This end is removing monopoly power and thus increase the economic welfare – ie the living standards – for all people in the community. Market competition does this by providing the incentives ('carrot') and discipline ('stick') that ensures that goods and services are provided in a way that is efficient, effective and equitable."

5. I further wrote: "Structure-Conduct-Performance Paradigm (SCP);[7] Five Forces (FFs);[8] and Market Continuum (MC).[9] SCP asserts that market performance, like welfare, is determined by market conduct which is, in turn, determined by market structure. The FFs of conduct are: market rivalry; market entry; product substitutability; supplier power; and buyer power.

---

4 ACCC, *Competition and Anti-Competitive Behaviour*, (June 2024), https://www.accc.gov.au/business/competition-and-exemptions/competition-and-anti-competitive-behaviour.

5 Competition Policy Reform Act 1995, (June 2024), https://www.legislation.gov.au/C2004A04938/asmade/text.

6 Competition and Consumer Act 2010, (June 2024), https://www.legislation.gov.au/C2004A00109/latest/text.

7 Matthew T. Panhans, *The Rise, Fall, and Legacy of the Structure-Conduct-Performance Paradigm*, (2023), https://ipl.econ.duke.edu/seminars/system/files/seminars/3754_paper.pdf.

8 *See*, *Porter's Five Forces Explained and How to Use the Model*, Investopedia (2024), https://www.investopedia.com/terms/p/porter.asp.

9 *See*, *Perfect Competition: Examples and How It Works*, Investopedia (2024), https://www.investopedia.com/terms/p/perfectcompetition.asp.

MC ranges from natural monopoly to cooperating and rivalry cartels to perfect competition."

2. Free-Market Economics

6. Adam Smith famously observed in *The Wealth of Nations*:[10] "Every individual necessarily labours to render the annual revenue of society as great as he can. He generally neither intends to promote the public interest, nor knows how much he is promoting it. He intends only his own gain, and he is, in this, as in many other cases, led by an invisible hand to promote an end which was not part of his intention." In a nutshell, that "invisible hand" is market competition.

7. Friedrich Hayek wrote about *The Meaning of Competition*:[11] on the supply-side, "competition is essentially a process of the formation of opinion"; and, on the demand-side, "the function of competition is...precisely to teach us who will serve us well." He concluded: "The practical lesson of all this...is that we should worry much less about whether competition in a given case is perfect and worry much more whether there is competition at all."

8. Milton Friedman in *Free to Choose*,[12] however, warned about political competition: "There is, as it were, an invisible hand in politics that operates in precisely the opposite direction to Adam Smith's invisible hand. Individuals who intend only to promote the general interest are led by the invisible political hand to promote a special interest that they had no intention to promote." This is what Public Choice Theory[13] calls "government failure" in contrast to "market failure."

3. Christian Economics

9. Shawn Ritenour in his book, *Foundations of Economics: A Christian View*,[14] wrote: "The fall greatly magnified scarcity, [thus humanity] must take advantage of social cooperation through the division of labor [and] exchange. Competition reduces the indeterminate range for the price actually charged for the good exchanged. As long as a market is free, meaning as long as private property rights are secure, an economy will manifest true competition."

---

10 Adam Smith, The Wealth of Nations (1776), https://www.amazon.com/Wealth-Nations-Adam-Smith/dp/1614278814.

11 Friedrich A. Hayek, *The Meaning of Competition*, (1946), https://competitionandappropriation.econ.ucla.edu/wp-content/uploads/sites/95/2018/06/HayekMeaningOfCompetition.pdf.

12 Milton Friedman & Rose Friedman, Free To Choose: A Personal Statement (1973), https://periferiaactiva.wordpress.com/wp-content/uploads/2019/07/free-to-choose_-a-personal-statement.pdf.

13 Eamonn Butler, *Public Choice – A Primer*, IEA (Mar. 25, 2012), https://iea.org.uk/publications/research/public-choice-a-primer.

14 Shawn Ritenour, Foundations of Economics: A Christian View (2015), https://www.amazon.com/Foundations-Economics-Christian-Shawn-Ritenour-ebook/dp/B013XTFF5Y/.

10. Thomas Woods in his book, *The Church and the Market: A Catholic Defense of the Free Economy*,[15] penned: "The [market] process is driven by the profit motive, which leads business continually to search for new and improved products and to cut costs in order to earn premium profits. Competition then serves to pass on the quality improvements and cost cuts on to the consumers, who obtain progressively more and better products at lower and lower real prices."

11. R.C. Sproul Jr. in his book, *Biblical Economics: A Commonsense Guide to Our Daily Bread*,[16] scribed: "One man's profit is another man's loss-that was the myth that [once] blinded me. Profit rest[s] on the subjective nature of value. In [an] exchange both profit. They each get what they value more in exchange for what they value less. If this were not so, the exchange simply would not take place. In a free market, competition forces the greedy to reduce prices."

12. Jay Richards in his book, *Money, Greed, and God: The Christian Case for Free Enterprise*,[17] scrawled: "To prosper, a market economy needs not just competition, but rule of law and virtues like cooperation, stable families, self-sacrifice, a commitment to delayed gratification, and a willingness to risk based on a future hope. These all fit nicely with the Christian worldview. The key source of material wealth in a modern market economy is immaterial. It's spiritual."

13. Gary North in his book, *Christian Economics: Student's Edition*,[18] opined: "Competition in economics is always based on an offer: 'Buy this from me, not from someone else.' Out of this system of competition – sellers vs. sellers, buyers vs. buyers – comes an array of [auction] prices. It is analogous to marriage: 'Marry me, not someone else.' Competition is not based on power. It is based on ethics. Might does not make right. Right eventually makes might."

III. Competition Evidence

14. High and rising prices over time are prima facie evidence of uncompetitive markets. Low and falling, or at least flat, prices over time are prima facie evidence of competitive markets. Thus, the first and last place to look for competition evidence is in prices. And the first and easiest place to start is the Consumer Price Index (CPI). However, CPI is an index and not prices themselves plus there are other price indexes such as for: assets, imports, producers, and wages.

---

15 Thomas E. Woods, Jr., The Church and the Market: A Catholic Defense of the Free Economy (2015), https://www.amazon.com/Church-Market-Catholic-Defense-Economics-ebook/dp/B00U4MXO1G/.

16 R.C. Sproul, Jr., Biblical Economics: A Commonsense Guide To Our Daily Bread (2010), https://www.amazon.com/Biblical-Economics-Commonsense-Guide-Daily-ebook/dp/B003ZDO2HQ/.

17 Jay W. Richards, Money, Greed, and God: The Christian Case for Free Enterprise (2019), https://www.amazon.com/Money-Greed-God-10th-Anniversary-ebook/dp/B07D6MT923/.

18 Gary North, Christian Economics: Student's Edition (2017), https://www.garynorth.com/public/16567.cfm.

1. Price Evidence

15. The book, *Forty Centuries of Price Controls*,[19] documents when government interventions, rather than free-market competition, tries to "regulate" prices: "In all times and in all places they have just as invariably failed to achieve their announced purposes. With the advent of the 19th century the Western world was blessed by a happy period of relative peace and prosperity. History (as it sometimes does) has come full circle [in the 20th and 21st centuries]."

16. Christopher Casey made the following key points in an article for the Mises Institute about Deflating the Deflation Myth:[20] "There is nothing inherently dangerous or damaging about deflation [or falling prices]. We see this every day in the computer/electronics industry[.] Twice, while experiencing sustained and significant economic growth, the American economy 'endured' deflationary periods of [53%, from 1815 to 1860, and 48%, from 1865 to 1900]."

17. My 2024 submission[21] to the Productivity Commission's (PC's) analysis[22] of a potential reboot of National Competition Policy (NCP) from 1995–2005[23] summarized: "Unsurprisingly, those [products] that have the highest and growing CPI are those that also have the greatest and heaviest government intervention. For example: alcohol and tobacco, which are highly taxed; utilities, which are highly protected; education and health, which are highly government provided, regulated and/or subsidized; and housing, which is highly restricted."

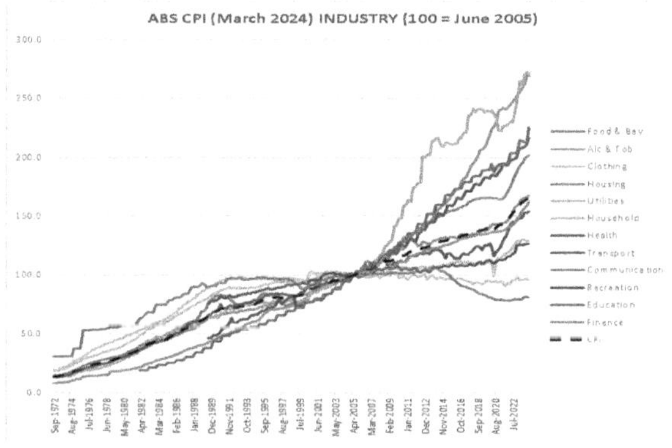

---

19 Robert L. Scheuttinger & Eamonn F. Butler, Forty Centuries of Wage and Price Controls: How Not to Fight Inflation (1978), https://mises.org/library/book/forty-centuries-wage-and-price-controls-how-not-fight-inflation.

20 Christopher Casey, *Deflating the Deflation Myth*, Mises Inst. (2014), https://mises.org/mises-daily/deflating-deflation-myth.

21 Darren Brady Nelson, *National Competition Policy Analysis (NCP 3.0)*, (Submitted May 2024), https://www.pc.gov.au/__data/assets/pdf_file/0010/382186/sub013-competition-analysis.pdf.

22 Productivity Commission (PC), National Competition Policy analysis, (Mar. 2024, forthcoming), https://www.pc.gov.au/inquiries/current/competition-analysis#report.

23 NCC, National Competition Policy (NCP), (Oct. 1992), http://ncp.ncc.gov.au/.

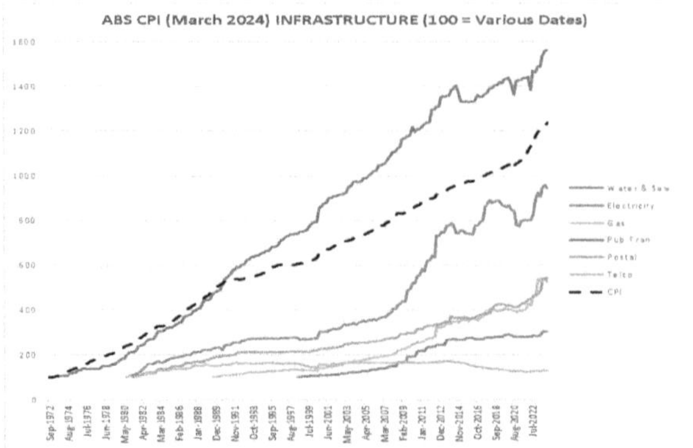

2. Policy Evidence

18. The PC's 1999 NCP Impact Inquiry[24] report estimated: "Real GDP of 2.5% above what would otherwise occur in the absence of the reforms. This is equivalent to almost one year's average annual growth of the Australian economy. The estimated annual gain in real household consumption is 2.8%. In contrast to the 1995 estimates, more of the gains accrue to households because the estimated increase in government revenue is assumed to lower income taxes."

19. The PC's 2005 NCP Impact Inquiry[25] report calculated "real service-price changes in NCP-related infrastructure activities over the 1990s" as follows: "Electricity" fell 3%; "Gas" rose 1%; "Urban water and sewerage" fell 4%; "Urban rail transport" rose 17%; "Urban road transport" rose 30%; "Urban water transport" rose 32%; "Ports" fell 35%; "Rail freight" fell 25%; and "Telecommunications" fell 22%. The "Urban" ones had prices well below costs.

20. My 2020 paper *How to Fix America's Crumbling Infrastructure: Lessons from Australia*[26] found: "There was a massive net-benefit (benefits over costs) from NCP ie competition performance above competition payments. The sowing of AU$5.5 billion in taxpayer payments during the NCP decade conservatively reaped more than AU$1 trillion in additional benefits for Australian families, gained from productivity and price changes observed over the 1990s in the electricity, gas, urban water, telecommunications, urban transport, ports and rail freight sectors. This economic return was of biblical proportions, well over a hundred-fold."

---

24 PC, Impact of competition policy reforms on rural and regional Australia (Oct. 1999), https://www.pc.gov.au/inquiries/completed/competition-policy/report.

25 PC, Review of National Competition Policy arrangements (Apr. 2005), https://www.pc.gov.au/inquiries/completed/national-competition-policy.

26 Darren Brady Nelson, *How to Fix America's Crumbling Infrastructure: Lessons from Australia*, Heartland Inst. (May 13, 2020), https://heartland.org/publications/policy-brief-how-to-fix-americas-crumbling-infrastructure-lessons-from-australia/.

3. Other Evidence

21. The PC's third Productivity Insights[27] paper of 2020 highlighted: "The micro-economic policy reforms of the 1980s and [NCP 1.0 of the] 1990s likely contributed to an MFP boom in the 1990s, in which Australia's productivity grew at its fastest rate in the two decades before or after. Australian businesses facing fiercer competitive pressures were given greater freedom. The resulting increase in domestic and international competition encouraged a more efficient allocation of resources and a more vigorous pursuit of productivity improvement."

Figure 20 **The 1990s saw a surge in MFP growth ...**
Average MFP growth[a] by decade

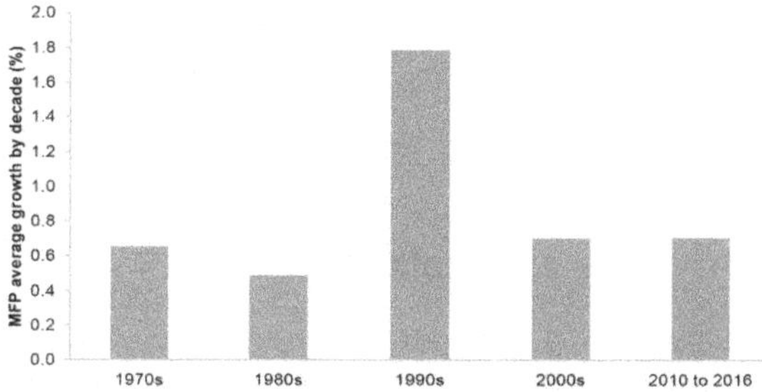

Figure 21 **... which helped Australian GDP growth outpace other advanced economies**
Real GDP per capita indices (constant PPP) from 1990 to 2018

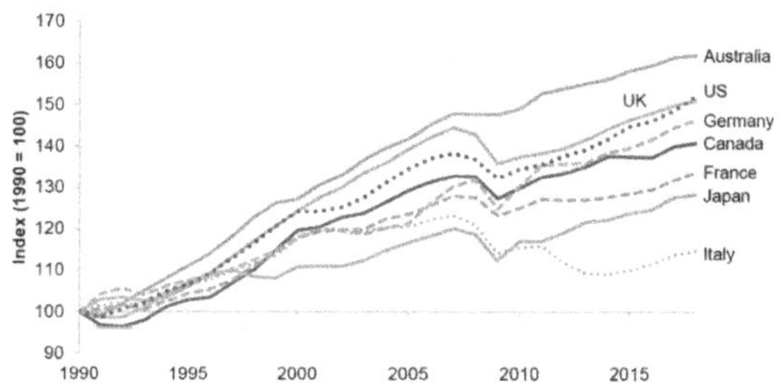

22. The Fraser Institute's 2023 Economic Freedom of the World[28] report states: "The cornerstones of economic freedom are personal choice, voluntary exchange, open markets, and property rights." Australia underperforms mainly due to the "Size of Government" with a ranking now of 122 out of 165 nations. From 2000 to 2021: "Transfers and subsidies" increased by 27% and "Regulatory burden" increased by 41%; whilst "Freedom to compete" reduced by 7%.

---

27 PC, Productivity Insights (ISSN 2652-5461 | No.3/2020) (Nov. 2020), https://www.pc.gov.au/ongoing/productivity-insights/long-term/productivity-insights-2020-long-term.pdf.

28 Fraser Institute, Economic Freedom of the World (Sept. 2023), https://www.fraserinstitute.org/sites/default/files/economic-freedom-of-the-world-2023.pdf.

23. In 2018, I observed in my *Advance Australia Fair*[29] reforms study that: "The reference to 'free' and 'wealth for toil' [in Australia's national anthem] reflects the many [free-market competition] reforms under Prime Ministers Hawke, Keating and Howard from the mid-1980s to mid-2000s. Unfortunately, from the late-2000s to the present, Australia has largely stalled. Both major political parties share the credit until the mid-2000s, as well as the blame since."

IV. Competition Policy

24. Competition policy should be about removing government interventions that intentionally or unintentionally reduce free-market competition. Government has three powers: force, money, and persuasion. Regulatory policy is the force of command and control. Fiscal policy is taxing, spending, and borrowing money. Monetary policy is printing, and lending fiat money. Politicians, bureaucrats, and cronies try to persuade about market but never government failure.

1. Regulatory Policy

25. My 2020 *Concurrences* foreword entitled, *Antitrust, Anticompetition: Lessons from Economics*,[30] observed: "If [antitrust] laws were originally meant to protect less efficient business organizations from competition rather than to promote the interests of consumers, then from that perspective, antitrust regulation is just another historical example of protectionist rent-seeking legislation, the overall effect of which is to lessen economic efficiency."

26. My 2015 MasterResource article, about *Regulation of Public Utilities as a Pseudo Tax*,[31] stated: "The little-known history of natural monopoly teaches that there was plenty of effective competition prior to the less effective competitors lobbying for market protection regulation. [And if truly] natural (ie could produce at a lower total cost than all others, actual and potential) it would not be in need of all of the other types of regulations preventing market entry."

27. Roy Cordato argued in his 2004 essay *Toward an Austrian Theory of Environmental Economics*:[32] "If a pollution problem exists then its solution must be found in either a clearer definition [or in the stricter enforcement] of property rights to the relevant resources. This shifts the perspective on

---

29 Darren Brady Nelson, *Advance Australia Fair: reforms from the past, challenges for the future*, (July 2018), https://www.pc.gov.au/__data/assets/pdf_file/0010/382186/sub013-competition-analysis.pdf.

30 Darren Brady Nelson, *Antitrust, Anticompetition: Lessons from Economics*, Concurrences No. 1-2020, art. No. 92528.

31 Darren Brady Nelson, *Regulation of Public Utilities as a Pseudo Tax*, MasterResource (July 2, 2015), https://www.masterresource.org/public-utility-regulation/regulation-of-public-utilities-as-a-pseudo-tax/.

32 Roy Cordato, *Toward an Austrian Theory of Environmental Economics*, (Spring 2004), https://cdn.mises.org/qjae7_1_1.pdf.

pollution from one of market failure, where the free-market is seen as failing, to [government] failure where the market process is prevented from proceeding efficiently."

2. Fiscal Policy

28. In my 2024 paper for the Heartland Institute, *CPI-X: A Novel Method to Decrease Spending and the National Debt*,[33] I demonstrate: "Reckless [government] spending is the primary driver of unsustainable deficits, an ever-increasing national debt, endless taxes, mounting red tape, and inflationary money printing. This reduces [competitive] supply of goods and services, increases unproductive demand, and blurs the lines between the private and public sectors."

29. My unpublished 2023 legislative testimony for Maine on a Local Option Sales Tax[34] reminded: "A sure-fire way to get less of something [including competition] is to tax more. Small businesses [and consumers] take a hit [50/50 to 80/20], including a pass-backward in the supply chain. [Plus], at first, raising tax rates tend to grow government revenues but, not long after, these revenues tend to shrink at least in relative terms. This is called the Laffer Curve[35] effect."

30. Bob Murphy warns in his 2011 textbook *Lessons for the Young Economist*:[36] "[Government] debt is the cumulative result of all previous deficits and surpluses. Government deficits divert real resources away from private-sector investment [, supply and competition], and result in a smaller inheritance for future generations. [And] government deficits allow [a central bank] to purchase more Treasury bonds, a practice that is inflationary [, reducing competition further]."

3. Monetary Policy

31. My 2023 Spectator Australia article on the Reckless Bank of Australia[37] highlighted: "The RBA's money monopoly was established under the Reserve Bank Act 1959.[38] Inflation was, is, and always will be inflation of the money supply. The Aussie money supply starts with RBA 'printing and lending' and ends with big banks 'lending and printing'. Two standard measures of

33 Darren Brady Nelson, CPI-X: A Novel Method to Decrease Spending and the National Debt (Jan. 2024), https://heartland.org/wp-content/uploads/2024/02/2024-CPIX-final.pdf.

34 Darren Brady Nelson, Testimony: Local Option Sales Tax (LDs 996 & 1298) (Jan. 2024), https://mainepolicy.org/a-lost-cause-the-local-option-sales-tax/. (NB: different report, same topic.)

35 Daniel J. Mitchell, *A Primer on the Laffer Curve*, Int'l Liberty (Aug. 13, 2020), https://danieljmitchell.wordpress.com/2020/08/13/a-primer-on-the-laffer-curve/.

36 Robert P. Murphy, Lessons for the Young Economist (2011), https://mises.org/library/book/lessons-young-economist.

37 Darren Brady Nelson, *The RBA (reckless bank of Australia) needs a radical, not reserved, review*, Spectator AU (Mar. 3, 2023), https://www.spectator.com.au/2023/03/the-rba-reckless-bank-of-australia-needs-a-radical-not-reserved-review/.

38 Reserve Bank Act 1959, (June 2024), https://www.legislation.gov.au/C1959A00004/latest/text.

these are M1 and M3, [and] are 'eye wateringly' showing increases in the tens of thousands."

32. My 2023 Mises Institute piece on Fractional Reserve Banking (FRB)[39] quotes the Bank of England (BoE):[40] "The reality of how money is created today differs from the description found in some economics textbooks: Rather than banks receiving deposits when households save and then lending them out, bank lending creates deposits. At that moment, new money is created. For this reason, some economists have referred to bank deposits as 'fountain pen money'."

33. Gary North shows, in his 2015 book *Honest Money*,[41] that competitive businesses react to government fiat money and crony credit inflation by: "1. Same price, same product: get stuck. 2. Doubled price, same product: lose sales. 3. Same price, reduced quality: [shrinkflation]. Competitors [2] make more profits, and [1] honest ones eventually go out of business, or [3] begin to imitate the corruption [against the unenforced] law of honest weights and measures."

V. Competition Ethics

34. This section is based entirely on Gary North's 2017 book, *Christian Economics: Student's Edition*,[42] as: "He began this project in 1973 [and] finished it in 2012. No one before him had ever attempted anything like this [and he] doubt[s] that anyone else will. His arguments are based on detailed exegesis of biblical texts." And importantly note: "[Humanist] economics begins with the axiom of purposeful action. Christian economics begins with God's purpose."

1. Creation Ethics

35. *Ownership*: "God is the Creator [of the heavens and universe,] therefore, He owns it. He has delegated the ownership of the earth to mankind. God issued the command to be fruitful and multiply, and to exercise dominion across the face of the earth [as well as] to serve as God's steward. God established the [economic] laws by which the creation operates. Without sanctions, there are no laws. This makes Christian economics a matter of ethics primarily."

36. *Stewardship*: "God doesn't directly control the earth apart from those He has chosen to manage His property, because man is made in the image of God. Families, individuals and organizations act as stewards, meaning legal

---

39 Darren Brady Nelson, *The Bank of England: Money Creation in Their Own Words*, Mises Inst. (Mar. 2023), https://mises.org/mises-wire/bank-england-money-creation-their-own-words.

40 Bank of England (BoE), *Money creation in the modern economy*, (Mar. 2014), https://www.bankofengland.co.uk/quarterly-bulletin/2014/q1/money-creation-in-the-modern-economy.

41 Gary North, Honest Money (2011), https://mises.org/library/book/honest-money.

42 North, *supra* note 18.

representatives of God and also as economic representatives of God. Ownership is both individual and collective. There is judicial and eternal equality but temporal economic inequality: to whom much is given, much is expected."

37. *Property*: "God placed a judicial/covenantal boundary around [the tree of the knowledge of good and evil]. Ethics is a series of boundaries [and, these,] in the field of economics centers on the issue of property rights. If [an owner] allocates [property] to one use, he cannot allocate it to a competing use at the same time. [Such] specialization is an aspect of economic efficiency. The civil government's guarantee of property increases the willingness of people to specialize."

38. *Imputation*: "In the field of economics, imputation means 'to attribute value to.' This scale of values is ordinal: first, second, third, etc. Economic value is subjective. A person then decides what he is willing and able to bid to purchase or rent [and] others also make bids. The result of these competing bids is an objective price. This is how value and price are related in the free market. This is a conclusion on Jesus' parable of the pearl of great price (Matthew 13:45–46)."

39. *Inheritance*: "The Bible teaches the concept of linear time [which] is progressive because of the concept of dominion. Dominion is through inheritance [which] is established through economic growth [from] capital creation. [The latter] takes thrift, less spending than income, [and] also entrepreneurship, the wisdom to imagine enough about future economic conditions so as to invest wisely. This is [reflected] in Jesus' parable of the talents (Matthew 25:14–30)."

2. Fall Ethics

40. *Chance*: "[Humanist] economics is an unstable mixture of randomness, meaning 100% incoherence, and omniscience, meaning 100% understanding by humans. Humanist economics teaches that randomness or chance is the test of any theory. Proverbs 16:33 is clear: there is no such thing as chance. But men do not believe this [and] gamble. These are what economists call zero-sum games. Winners win at the expense of losers. There is no net increase of wealth."

41. *Autonomy*: "Humanistic economics has no theory of a sovereign God who providentially brings all things to pass. If God is not God, then man is. But man is plural, not just a single species: lots of competing gods, each seeking to impose his order on the rest of humanity. Sometimes the gods cooperate [such as, decreasingly, in the positive-sum free market]. Usually, the gods [are] at war with each other [such as, increasingly, in the zero-sum political market]."

42. *Theft*: "Original sin was an act of theft [and this] placed economics at the center of ethics. Theft is not productive. It does not create wealth. It reduces wealth. The gains of the thief come from the loss to the victim [zero-sum]. They do not accept the legitimacy of wealth distribution performed in competitive markets. The most serious crimes against property are committed by

civil governments [fiscal, regulatory and monetary]. This undermines trust in government."

43. *Bureaucratization*: "Bureaucrats act on the basis of self-interest, just as everyone else does. This is an ancient insight. But it was long ignored by economists. It led in the final third of the twentieth century to a specialized field of economics: public choice theory. [Bureaucracy has] no system of competition through pricing. It continues to extend its power into the economy whenever politicians extend the jurisdiction of the [fiscal, regulatory and monetary] state."

44. *Disinheritance*: "Inheritance necessarily involves disinheritance, just as [competition] sanctions are both positive and negative. [Heirs'] wealth is based on market competition. But they maintain wealth that they gained through [that] by means of political competition. Humanistic elitists [or false heirs] want a smaller state with respect to taxation and a stronger state with respect to protection. They cannot achieve both. The result is decapitalization."

3. Redemption Ethics

45. *Providence*: "Are there economic laws? Yes, because these laws are manifestations of the providence of God [which includes] the regularities that we see in nature, including human nature. But apart from God's providence, defenders of the free market cannot show logically that the auction's competition benefits society, which is a collective concept. God's providence teaches that the results of the private property system are beneficial to individuals and society."

46. *Service*: "Socialists always said this: 'There should be cooperation, not competition.' This meant that they wanted politically appointed central planners. This system of allocation invariably led to tyranny: monopoly control by political elite. It also led to falling production and widespread poverty. In [a competitive] free market social order, consumers possess final economic authority. The free-market economy is a gigantic system of mutual service."

47. *Leasehold*: "God's dominion covenant had to be modified after the fall of man. This transformed private property into what we call a leasehold. A leasehold agreement has this crucial goal: to keep the tenant from exploiting the property that has been transferred to him. Because of Adam's sin [including Eve's as 'one flesh'], all humans occupy for temporary time."

48. *Entrepreneurship*: "Economists distinguish between risk and uncertainty. Risk is subject to the law of large numbers [and insurance]. Uncertainty is not. An entrepreneur deals mainly with uncertainty. A manager deals mainly with risk. The free market rests on the decisions of entrepreneurs who specialize in forecasting future supply and demand [in competition, for pure profit, not wages]. Without entrepreneurs, most of us would die [or] live in extreme poverty."

49. *Compounding*: "Beginning around 1800, steady economic growth at 2% or 3% per capita per year has completely transformed the world. Economic historians have no agreed-on explanation. The possibility of long-term economic

growth and population growth first appears in ancient literature in Leviticus 26 and Deuteronomy 28. Christian economics is authoritative because God still imposes [individual and communal] sanctions in terms of His law."

4. Covenant Ethics

50. "[We] are under the terms of four covenants, in addition to the dominion covenant: individual, family, church, and state." Each of these four are, in turn, discussed below by Gary North.

51. *Individual*: "The Bible teaches this: 'You shall not steal' (Exodus 20:15). It does not say this: 'You shall not steal, except by majority vote.' There are always special-interest groups that seek subsidies from the state. They often justify these subsidies in the name of social justice. These payments are political pay-offs: money for having enough votes to grab it. These handouts are funded by taxation, by government debt, and by central bank monetary inflation. There is no third source. Stop [asking for, taking and/or] voting for government handouts of any kind."

52. *Family*: "The family is the primary welfare institution in every society. It is bound by law and love. Because people are sinners, they are always looking for ways to compel other people to pay for the expenses of their families. [Unlike the church,] the state has the power to force a redistribution of wealth. It therefore has the economic capacity to replace the family [and the 'ethical' capacity to replace the church] in many areas of life."

53. *Church*: "Churches should not accept money from [the] civil government [lest] it becomes dependent on that institution. Pastors should preach against the idea that tax exemption is an indirect subsidy from the state. This pernicious idea rests on a philosophy of civil government that says that the state owns everything in principle. Such an idea places the state above the church in terms of its authority and lawful jurisdiction. The church is the bride of Christ."

54. *Civil*: "Biblical law made a provision for [civil government], and had placed [them] under tight restrictions (Deuteronomy 17). Today, in the West, total taxation is in the range of 50% of national income. In order for the West to return to the tyranny of Pharaoh's regime, there would have to be a 60% tax cut [and] to return to the tyranny [of King Saul's regime], an 80% tax cut. Yet Christians [and humanists both] regard themselves as living in free societies."

VI. Conclusion

55. The following points, from my 2018 competition[43] article, are pertinent as a conclusion here: "Obviously, in sports each game [with some exceptions] and season has the one winner. Far less obviously, is the inherent win-win

43 Nelson, *supra* note 1.

nature of competition in the market. There are a number of reasons for this. A really important, but neglected, one is that all businesses and consumers get to 'free ride,' as it were, on the ever-decreasing prices and ever-increasing innovation that competition makes possible. Such competition is essentially a bottom-up 'discovery process.' It is far more effective, efficient and peaceful than that of the top-down process of government 'command-and-control.' The government process, regardless of how democratic or not, is all about monopoly [and cartels]. This is a win-lose process, like sports. Not initially for the 'Bootleggers and Baptists'[44] though. [Thus,] competition is the only true [market] regulator."

44 Susan E. Dudley, *Bootleggers & Baptists: The Experience of Another Regulatory Economist* (Geo. Wash. U., Working Paper, 2018), https://regulatorystudies.columbian.gwu.edu/sites/g/files/zaxdzs4751/files/downloads/WorkingPapers/GW%20Reg%20Studies%20-%20Bootleggers%20and%20Baptitsts%20Working%20Paper%20-%20SDudley.pdf.

The Role of State Aid Rules in Ensuring a Level Playing Field, and the Impact of Recent Crises

NICOLE ROBINS*
Oxera Consulting

1. State aid rules were designed to ensure a level playing field within the EU and to avoid a subsidy race between Member States, which could undermine the internal market. The Covid-19 pandemic and the subsequent energy crisis led to substantial changes to State aid rules, with unprecedented amounts of aid granted by Member States to support their economies. In this chapter, we explore how the level playing field has been affected by the State aid rules that were introduced in both crises. More recently, legislation introduced by third countries, such as the Inflation Reduction Act (IRA) in the US, has contributed towards a greater focus in the EU on industrial policy with the aim of ensuring its competitiveness. At the same time, the EU has introduced the Foreign Subsidies Regulation (FSR), which is designed to tackle the impact of distortive subsidies provided by third countries on the internal market. We explore the impact of both on the level playing field.[1]

I. Introduction

2. State aid rules were designed to ensure a level playing field in the EU and to avoid state support for certain undertakings triggering retaliatory support

* Nicole Robins is a Partner at the economics and finance consultancy Oxera Consulting LLP, and leads Oxera's State aid and Subsidy control practice. She is based in Brussels.

1 Regulation (EU) 2022/2560 of the European Parliament and of the Council of 14 December 2022 on foreign subsidies distorting the internal market (Foreign Subsidies Regulation) [2022] OJ L330/1. US Inflation Reduction Act 2022 Public Law No: 117–169.

from other Member States, which could result in a 'subsidy race'.[2] The concept of a level playing field, whereby all economic actors are bound by the same set of rules and conditions to ensure fair competition, has been a core foundation of economic integration within the EU and has governed economic interactions between Member States.[3] State aid control aims to protect the level playing field by ensuring that the positive effects of subsidies are not outweighed by their negative effects in terms of creating undue distortions to competition and trade.[4]

3. State aid rules have been reformed significantly over time, most notably in 2005 and then again in 2012 following the economic and financial crisis.[5] These reforms were designed to facilitate aid that fosters growth and efficiency, and also introduced common economic principles for State aid control in order to balance the benefits of government intervention against its distortions, as well as to focus enforcement on the larger, more distortive cases.[6]

4. Following the onset of the Covid-19 pandemic in March 2020, the Commission quickly introduced a new State aid framework – the Temporary Framework, which enabled Member States to support companies that were adversely affected by the crisis.[7] Following the start of the energy crisis triggered by Russia's invasion of Ukraine, in March 2022 the Commission introduced the Temporary Crisis Framework (TCF) which outlined the tools that could be used by Member States to support companies that were struggling in light of the crisis.[8]

5. At the same time, third countries, including the US, have introduced significant support packages, with the IRA representing the largest ever investment by the US Government in climate and energy.[9] Meanwhile, there has been a renewed focus in the EU on industrial policies for ensuring its competitiveness and autonomy.[10] In February 2023, the Commission introduced its 'Green Deal Industrial Plan for the Net-Zero Age'.[11] As a result, in March 2023 the TCF

---

2 Kelyn Bacon, *European Union Law of State Aid* (3rd edn, OUP 2017), para 1.04.

3 Fabian Zuleeg, 'The End of the Level Playing Field?' Commentary, (*European Policy Centre*, 1 October 2020) <www.epc.eu/en/Publications/The-end-of-the-level-playing-field~377b20> accessed 18 October 2024.

4 Joanna Piechucka, Lluís Saurí-Romero and Ben Smulders, 'Industrial Policies, Competition and Efficiency: The Need for State Aid Control' (2023) JCLE, 19:4 < https://academic.oup.com/jcle/article-abstract/19/4/503/7334444> accessed 27 October 2024.

5 European Commission, 'State Aid Action Plan, Less and Better Targeted State Aid: A Roadmap for State Aid Reform 2005–2009' COM (2005) 107 final; and European Commission, 'Communication from the Commission to the European Parliament, the Council, the European Economic and Social Committee and the Committee of the Regions, EU State Aid Modernisation (SAM)' COM (2012) 209 final.

6 Ibid.

7 European Commission, 'The State Aid Temporary Framework' <https://competition-policy.ec.europa.eu/state-aid/coronavirus/temporary-framework_en> accessed 18 October 2024.

8 European Commission, 'Temporary Crisis and Transition Framework' <https://competition-policy.ec.europa.eu/state-aid/temporary-crisis-and-transition-framework_en> accessed 18 October 2024.

9 The White House, 'Inflation Reduction Act Guidebook' (28 November 2023) <www.whitehouse.gov/cleanenergy/inflation-reduction-act-guidebook/> accessed 18 October 2024.

10 European Council, 'EU Industrial Policy' <www.consilium.europa.eu/en/policies/eu-industrial-policy/#:~:text=The%20EU's%20industrial%20policy%20aims,The%20importance%20of%20EU%20industry> accessed 18 October 2024.

11 Ibid; European Parliament, 'General Principles of EU Industrial Policy' <www.europarl.europa.eu/factsheets/en/sheet/61/general-principles-of-eu-industrial-policy> accessed 18 October 2024.

evolved into the Temporary Crisis and Transition Framework (TCTF), which outlines measures to be used by Member States to support sectors that are key to the transition to a net-zero economy.[12]

6. Against the backdrop of an increase in subsidies provided by third countries to their domestic industry, in July 2023 the FSR began to apply, which enables the Commission to assess certain subsidies granted by third countries to companies operating in the EU.[13] The FSR contributes towards the EU's objective of ensuring its strategic autonomy.[14] In line with this objective, the Commission introduced the European Chips Act in September 2023 with the aim of ensuring the EU's strategic autonomy in the design and manufacture of semi-conductor chips.[15]

7. In this chapter, we firstly consider the effectiveness of State aid rules in preserving the level playing field during the Covid-19 crisis and the subsequent energy crisis. We then assess the implications of the greater focus on industrial policy within the EU, through measures such as the European Chips Act, and we discuss how the FSR might help to ensure the level playing field within the internal market.

II. State Aid Rules during the Covid-19 and Energy Crises, and Their Impact on the Level Playing Field

1. State Aid Rules during the Covid-19 Pandemic

8. In March 2020, the Commission responded exceptionally quickly to the onset of the Covid-19 pandemic by altering State aid rules through the introduction of a Temporary Framework, which enabled Member States to provide short-term liquidity support to companies adversely affected by the containment measures that were introduced in light of the pandemic.[16] As the impact of the crisis deepened, the Temporary Framework evolved through the introduction of measures to support the solvency of undertakings, including recapitalisation aid.[17]

---

12 European Commission, Press Release, 'Remarks by Executive Vice-President Vestager on the proposal for a State aid Temporary Crisis and Transition Framework' (1 February 2023) <https://ec.europa.eu/commission/presscorner/detail/en/SPEECH_23_527> accessed 18 October 2024.

13 Regulation (EU) 2022/2560 (FSR) [2022] OJ L330/1.

14 Regulation (EU) 2022/2560 (FSR) [2022] OJ L330/1, para 7.

15 European Commission, Press Release, 'Digital Sovereignty: European Chips Act Enters into Force Today' (21 September 2023) <https://ec.europa.eu/commission/presscorner/detail/en/ip_23_4518> accessed 18 October 2024.

16 European Commission, 'Competition Policy, The State Aid Temporary Framework' <https://competition-policy.ec.europa.eu/state-aid/coronavirus/temporary-framework_en> accessed 18 October 2024.

17 European Commission, 'Communication from the Commission, Temporary Framework for State Aid Measures to Support the Economy in the Current COVID-19 Outbreak' s 3.11 <https://competition-policy.ec.europa.eu/document/download/44e43fe8-b02b-478d-8605-68456154295a_en?filename=TF_consolidated_version_amended_3_april_8_may_and_29_june_2020_en.pdf> accessed 18 October 2024.

9. Member States intervened on a significant scale with support measures to tackle the economic impact of the crisis, with around €3.1 trillion of aid being approved by the Commission following the start of the pandemic up to late 2021.[18] However, there were substantial differences in the amount of aid provided by Member States, with Germany, France, Italy and Spain granting more than 80% of all Covid-19-related aid in the EU.[19] The asymmetry in the response to the crisis across Member States, combined with the size of some aid measures, led to concerns being raised about their distortive effects on competition and the potential for the aid to artificially support non-productive (zombie) companies.[20] The depth of the recession in 2020 and the speed of recovery in 2021 and 2022 varied significantly across Member States, with those Member States with more limited fiscal capacity recovering more slowly from the pandemic.[21]

10. During the pandemic, Member States provided an unprecedented amount of aid to companies in the aviation sector, particularly flag carriers, with the aim of avoiding the adverse economic and social consequences of the failure of 'strategically important' airlines, with some commentators highlighting that certain legacy carriers were deemed 'too big to fail'.[22] The OECD highlighted that the risk that government interventions would negatively affect productivity was particularly acute in the aviation sector, given the substantial variability in profitability and productivity across the sector prior to the pandemic.[23]

11. Under the Temporary Framework, remedies were required for certain types of aid that are more distortive – specifically, for recapitalisation aid in excess of €250 million granted to beneficiaries with significant market power (SMP) in at least one of the relevant markets in which they operate, in order to 'preserve effective competition'.[24] However, as illustrated by the *Lufthansa* case discussed below, there are question marks over the effectiveness of the remedies in limiting distortions to competition.

---

18 European Commission, Press Release, 'Remarks by Executive Vice-President Vestager on the Communication on a Competition Policy Fit for New Challenges' (18 November 2021)) <https://ec.europa.eu/commission/presscorner/detail/en/speech_21_6115> accessed 18 October 2024.

19 European Commission, 'Looking back at the State aid COVID Temporary Framework: The Take-Up of Measures in the EU' (State Aid Brief, October 2022) 3 <https://competition-policy.ec.europa.eu/system/files/2022-11/state_aid_brief_3_2022_kdam22003enn_coronavirus.pdf> accessed 18 October 2024.

20 Banque de France, 'Les aides d'État dans la crise Covid-19: un dilemme européen' (November/December 2021) 238(3) *Bulletin de la Banque de France* 3 <https://publications.banque-france.fr/sites/default/files/medias/documents/bulletin-banque-de-france_238-3_aides-d-etat.pdf> accessed 18 October 2024; and 'La fin des aides d'Etat l'an prochain s'annonce périlleuse' (*Les Echos*, 26 December 2021) <www.lesechos.fr/monde/europe/la-fin-des-aides-detat-lan-prochain-sannonce-perilleuse-1374879> accessed 18 October 2024.

21 European Commission, *European Economic Forecast, Autumn 2020* (2020) 18 <https://economy-finance.ec.europa.eu/system/files/2020-11/ip136_en_2.pdf> accessed 18 October 2024; and European Central Bank, *Financial Stability Review, November 2020* (ECB, 2020) <www.ecb.europa.eu/press/financial-stability-publications/fsr/html/ecb.fsr202011~b7be9ae1f1.en.html> accessed 18 October 2024.

22 Tania Pantazi, 'State Aid to Airlines in the Context of Covid-19: Damages, Disturbances, and Equal Treatment' (2021) 13 JECLP 6.

23 OECD, 'COVID-19 and the Aviation Industry: Impact and Policy Responses' (15 October 2020) 6.

24 European Commission (n 17), para 72.

12. In the *Lufthansa* case, the remedies took the form of slot divestments at slot-constrained airports where the airline had a base and was deemed to have SMP.[25] The Commission concluded that Lufthansa had SMP at Frankfurt and Munich airports, and agreed with Germany's proposal to require Lufthansa to divest up to 24 slots per day at each airport.[26] According to the Commission, the purpose of the commitments was to ensure effective competition in the longer term at these airports.[27]

13. In Ryanair's appeal of the Commission's decision that approved the aid to Lufthansa, Ryanair argued that the divestment of 24 slots per day at each airport was insufficient to preserve effective competition, as the reduction implied in terms of the number of flights to be operated by Lufthansa was 'insignificant'.[28] The General Court, however, concluded that the slots to be divested by Lufthansa were sufficient to maintain effective competition, as the divestments would amount to approximately 2–3% of the total slots at each airport, which was similar to that of the beneficiary's competitors at each airport.[29] However, as Lufthansa had a share of slot holdings of up to 60% at Frankfurt Airport and up to 55% at Munich Airport on average, with much higher shares at peak times, a competitor with only a 2–3% share of the slots was unlikely to impose a competitive constraint.[30] Therefore, while the remedies could, in principle, help to preserve effective competition, in the Covid-19 recapitalisation aid cases there are question marks over their effectiveness.

14. Some research has indicated that the amount of aid provided by Member States during the Covid-19 pandemic was not proportionate to the adverse effects of the crisis on particular sectors, including the transport sector, and that the more flexible application of State aid rules during the pandemic could distort the level playing field.[31] While EU funding has helped, initiatives such as the Recovery and Resilience Facility (RRF) may only partly mitigate the impact of the asymmetry of the response during the Covid-19 pandemic. In particular, some of the main recipients of funding under the RRF were Spain, Italy France and Germany, which are among the Member States that provided the

25 European Commission, 'State Aid SA.57153 (2020/N) – Germany – COVID-19 – Aid to Lufthansa' COM (2020) 4372 final, paras 172–219.

26 Ibid paras 221–230.

27 Ibid para 221.

28 Judgment of the General Court, Joined Cases T-34/21 and T-87/21 *Ryanair v European Commission (Lufthansa; COVID-19)* ECLI:EU:T:2023:248, para 442 <https://curia.europa.eu/juris/liste.jsf?nat=or&mat=or&pcs=Oor&jur=C%2CT%2CF&num=T-34%252F21&for=&jge=&dates=&language=en&pro=&cit=none%252CC%252CCJ%252CR%252C2008E%252C%252C%252C%252C%252C%252C%252C%252C%252C%252Ctrue%252Cfalse%252Cfalse&oqp=&td=%3BALL&avg=&lgrec=en&lg=&page=1&cid=3842735> accessed 18 October 2024.

29 Ibid paras 453–454.

30 European Commission (n 25), ss 3.3.6.4.1 and 3.3.6.4.2.

31 European Parliament, *Impact of State Aid on Competition and competitiveness during the COVID-19 Pandemic: An Early Assessment* (2020) <www.europarl.europa.eu/RegData/etudes/STUD/2020/658214/IPOL_STU(2020)658214_EN.pdf> accessed 18 October 2024; and Holtan Lakså, 'Proportionality of the Sectoral Application of the Covid-19 Temporary Framework' (2023) 22 ESALQ 356–370 <https://estal.lexxion.eu/article/ESTAL/2023/4/3> accessed 18 October 2024.

highest amounts of aid (as a percentage of their respective GDP) during the Covid-19 pandemic.[32]

2. State Aid Rules in Response to the Energy Crisis

15. Following Russia's invasion of Ukraine in March 2022, the Commission adopted the TCF, which sets out the tools available to Member States to provide funding to companies to mitigate the wider economic effects of the invasion.[33]

16. As in the case of the Covid-19 pandemic, there have been significant differences across Member States in terms of the amount of aid provided under the TCF, with less indebted countries, such as Germany and France, providing greater subsidies to households and businesses.[34]

17. Under the TCF, Member States could recapitalise companies facing solvency issues, subject to certain conditions, including compensatory measures in line with the Rescue and Restructuring Aid Guidelines.[35] As illustrated by the case involving recapitalisation aid granted by Germany to the energy company Uniper, the remedies were more extensive than those required under the Covid-19 Temporary Framework.

18. In June 2022, following Russia's decision to significantly reduce gas supplies to the EU, Uniper was forced to replace its supplies from Russia in the open market at very high replacement costs, which led to Uniper experiencing financial difficulties.[36] The recapitalisation aid that was granted to Uniper by Germany was accompanied by a number of remedies, including divestments of power plants, which led to Uniper exiting the Hungarian and Latvian markets altogether, significantly reducing its capacity in other markets, and becoming subject to behavioural commitments, including a cap on the amount of natural gas that Uniper could sell to business-to-business customers in the EU.[37] The Commission noted that the calibration of the remedies took into account the significant amount of aid, its non-repayable nature as a direct equity investment, and the scope of Uniper's activities.[38]

---

32 European Commission, 'Recovery and Resilience Scoreboard' <https://ec.europa.eu/economy_finance/recovery-and-resilience-scoreboard/country_overview.html?lang=en. > accessed 18 October 2024; and European Commission (n 19).

33 European Commission (n 8).

34 Elisabetta Cornago and John Springford, 'Europe Needs Both Fiscal and Energy Solidarity' (*Centre for European Reform*, 2023) 2 <www.cer.eu/sites/default/files/pbrief_energy_solidarity_EC_JS_14.3.23.pdf> accessed 18 October 2024; European Commission, 'The Use of Crisis State Aid Measures in Response to the Russian Invasion of Ukraine' (State Aid Brief, July 2023) 2 <https://competition-policy.ec.europa.eu/system/files/2023-07/state_aid_brief_1_2023_kdam23001enn_TCTF_survey_0.pdf> accessed 18 October 2024; and S Fleming, A Hancock and J Espinoza, 'Can the EU Keep Up with the US on Green Subsidies?' *Financial Times* (London, 1 February (2023) <www.ft.com/content/85b55126-e1e6-4b2c-8bb2-753d3cafcbe5> accessed 18 October 2024.

35 European Commission (n 8), para 32(e).

36 European Commission, 'State Aid SA.103791 (2022/N) – Germany – Recapitalisation of Uniper' COM (2022) 9985 final, paras 23 and 36.

37 Ibid paras 92–98, 103–105, and 187.

38 Ibid para 179.

19. While the structure of the gas market is different from the structure of the aviation market, the remedies were still significantly more extensive in this case than in the cases of Covid-19 recapitalisation aid, and there was a clearer basis for their calibration.

III. State Aid and Industrial Policy

20. The various crises have led to a greater focus on industrial policy in the EU in order to strengthen the external competitiveness of the EU, particularly in light of geopolitical tensions.[39] In this section, we discuss the TCTF and the European Chips Act, and their possible implications for the level playing field.

21. While there are some advantages of a strengthened industrial policy, such as improved public control over the green transition, it is also associated with some downsides.[40] One of the main critiques against industrial policy has traditionally been that it could lead to picking winners in a sub-optimal way, contributing towards an inefficient allocation of resources.[41]

1. The Temporary Crisis and Transition Framework

22. The introduction of the IRA in the US, which provides up to $369 billion of subsidies for green investments if the products are manufactured mainly in North America, led to a debate about whether the EU should introduce a more active industrial policy.[42] Some Member States advocated for a stronger industrial policy with enhanced EU funding, while others have been more sceptical.[43] Following the introduction of the IRA, and with high energy prices in the EU contributing to the risk that companies might relocate

39 European Commission, 'European Industrial Strategy' <https://commission.europa.eu/strategy-and-policy/priorities-2019-2024/europe-fit-digital-age/european-industrial-strategy_en> accessed 18 October 2024.

40 For further discussion, see Réka Juhász, Nathan Lane and Dani Rodrik, 'The New Economics of Industrial Policy' (2023) NBER Working Paper 31538 <www.nber.org/papers/w31538 accessed 18 October 2024; and Piechucka, Saurí-Romero and Smulders (n 4), 13.

41 Ruchir Agarwal, 'Industrial Policy and the Growth Strategy Dilemma' (*IMF*, 21 March 2023) <www.imf.org/en/Publications/fandd/issues/Series/Analytical-Series/industrial-policy and the growth-strategy-trilemma-ruchir-agarwal accessed 18 October 2024.

42 The White House, 'Building A Clean Energy Economy: A Guidebook To The Inflation Reduction Act's Investments In Clean Energy And Climate Action' (2023) 5 <www.whitehouse.gov/wp-content/uploads/2022/12/Inflation-Reduction-Act-Guidebook.pdf> accessed 18 October 2024; Dave Keating, 'The EU is Offering as Much Green Funding as the US IRA. So Why Aren't Innovators Getting It?' (*Energy Monitor*, 25 October 2023) <www.energymonitor.ai/policy/green-deals/eu-green-funds-match-us-ira-but-harder-to-access/> accessed 18 October 2024; and European Parliament, 'EU's Response to the US Inflation Reduction Act (IRA)', (2023) Briefing requested by the ECON Committee.

43 Ferdi De Ville, 'The Return of Industrial Policy in the European Union' (2023) <www.ugent.be/ps/politiekewetenschappen/gies/en/research/publications/gies_papers/2023-global-energy-crisis/the-return-of-industrial-policy-in-the-european-union#_edn2> accessed 18 October 2024 and Mlex, 'Relaxation of EU's State Aid Rules Might Jeopardize Single Market, Sweden, Poland and others say' (1 March 2024).

outside the EU, a new State aid framework – the TCTF – was introduced by the Commission in March 2023.[44]

23. Under the TCTF, if there is a significant risk that investments in key sectors required for the green transition could be diverted away from the EU, Member States can provide the amount of support that the beneficiary could receive for an equivalent investment in the alternative location outside the European Economic Area (EEA) (known as 'matching aid'), subject to certain conditions.[45] The introduction of matching aid could therefore affect a company's decision about where to locate its investment both relative to third countries and within the EU, although there are safeguards that prevent a company from receiving aid to relocate within the EU, and the TCTF also favours pan-European projects.

24. Commissioner Vestager has acknowledged the potential for matching aid to create 'a serious risk to competition and the integrity of the Single Market',[46] and has explained: '[t]hat's why we need to make this possibility temporary, well targeted in size and scope, and pending real benefits for people and the European economy at large'.[47]

25. It is noticeable that, in its impact assessment of the FSR, the Commission considered systematic matching aid as a response to foreign subsidies to be ineffective and likely to be distortive, with the potential to lead to a harmful subsidy race.[48] Indeed, research suggests that a subsidy race triggered by the IRA could entail significant welfare losses for both the US and the EU.[49] Commentators have also highlighted that higher energy prices in the EU than in the US are likely to have a greater impact on the relative attractiveness of the EU than the IRA, highlighting the importance of developing energy infrastructure in the EU alongside expanding renewable energy.[50]

---

44 European Commission, Press Release, 'State aid: Commission adopts Temporary Crisis and Transition Framework to further support transition towards net-zero economy' (9 March 2023) <https://ec.europa.eu/commission/presscorner/detail/en/ip_23_1563> accessed 18 October 2024.

45 The amount of aid must be less than the funding gap, defined as the minimum amount needed to incentivise the beneficiary to locate the investment within the EEA; investments must take place in assisted areas or investments must occur cross-border with a significant element taking place in at least two assisted areas; the beneficiary should use state-of-the-art production technology from the perspective of environmental emissions; and the aid cannot trigger the relocation of investments between Member States. See European Commission, Press Release (n 12); and European Commission, Press Release (n 44).

46 European Commission, Press Release (n 12).

47 Ibid.

48 European Commission, 'Commission Staff Working Document, Impact Assessment Accompanying the Proposal for a Regulation of the European Parliament and of the Council on Foreign Subsidies Distorting the Internal Market' SWD (2021) 99 final, 42.

49 German Council of Economic Experts, 'How Should Europe Respond to the Inflation Reduction Act?' (14 July 2023) <www.sachverstaendigenrat-wirtschaft.de/en/media/details/policy-brief-inflation-reduction-act-pressrelease.html>; and CEPR, 'The US Inflation Reduction Act: How the EU is Affected and How It Should React' (17 October 2023) <https://cepr.org/voxeu/columns/us-inflation-reduction-act-how-eu-affected-and-how-it-should-react> accessed 18 October 2024.

50 German Council of Economic Experts (n 49); Walburga HemetsBerger, 'Delivering the Ambition of the Green Deal Industry Plan for Solar PV' (*SolarPower Europe*, 22 May 2022) <https://api.solarpowereurope.org/uploads/Solar_Power_Europe_NZIA_letter_May_2022_6a59e60336.pdf?updated_at=2023-05-19T13:47:20.624Z> accessed 18 October 2024; and 'Record-low Solar PV Prices Risk EU's Open Strategic Autonomy' (*Solar Power Europe*, 11 September 2023) <https://api.solarpowereurope.org/uploads/Solar_Power_Europe_Price_Crisis_Letter_11_September_2023_16ce4c88fa.pdf?updated_at=2023-09-11T08:02:41.696Z> accessed 18 October 2024.

26. Given the challenges of responding to geopolitical developments such as the IRA, and with some industries arguing that the TCTF is not sufficiently far-reaching to ensure the long-term competitiveness of EU industry, it is difficult to strike an appropriate balance between providing additional subsidies and avoiding distortions to the level playing field.[51]

2. The European Chips Act

27. Under the European Chips Act, which represents an important element of the EU's industry policy, the EU aims to 'mobilise' more than €43 billion of 'policy-driven' public and private investments in the chips industry in the EU to achieve Europe's 'strategic autonomy' in semiconductor technologies.[52] The target is to double the EU's share of the global semiconductor market from less than 10% as of 2023 to 20% by 2030.[53] The Commission's Vice-President for Values and Transparency has stated that '[t]he global race for leadership in chips is a fact and Europe must secure her active part in it'.[54]

28. At the same time, a number of other countries are also providing support to strengthen their domestic production of semiconductor chips, including China, Japan, Taiwan and the US.[55] As a result, commentators have highlighted the gap in funding being provided in the EU compared with countries such as the US, and some of the challenges in the EU in relation to the availability of skilled labour.[56]

29. Although it is not explicitly stated in the Chips Act Communication, the similarities between aid granted under the Chips Act and that granted under other State aid frameworks, such as the Regional Aid Guidelines (where, in the absence of aid from an EU Member State, a company may locate production outside the EEA), indicate that the possibility of granting matching aid might also be available under the Chips Act.[57] As with the matching aid clause under the TCTF, this possibility could affect a company's decision about where to locate investment.

---

51 ERT, 'Appraisal of Recent EU Initiatives Aimed at Improving European Competitiveness' (2023) European Round Table for Industry Expert Paper 12 <https://ert.eu/wp-content/uploads/2023/06/ERT-Appraisal-of-EU-initiatives-on-competitiveness.pdf> accessed 18 October 2024.

52 European Commission, 'European Chips Act' <https://commission.europa.eu/strategy-and-policy/priorities-2019-2024/europe-fit-digital-age/european-chips-act_en> accessed 18 October 2024.

53 European Commission, Press Release (n 15).

54 Ibid.

55 European Commission, Press Release, 'European Chips Act – Questions and Answers' (30 November 2023) <https://ec.europa.eu/commission/presscorner/detail/en/qanda_23_4519> accessed 18 October 2024; Reuters, 'US to Announce Billions in Subsidies for Advanced Chips – WSJ' (*Reuters*, 28 January 2024) <www.reuters.com/markets/us/us-announce-billions-subsidies-advanced-chips-wsj-2024-01-27/ accessed 18 October 2024; and ICC, *ICC 2023 Trade Report: A Fragmenting World* (2023) <https://iccwbo.org/news-publications/policies-reports/icc-2023-trade-report-a-fragmenting-world/> accessed 18 October 2024.

56 L Li, 'The Global Microchip Race: Europe's Bid to Catch Up' *Financial Times* (London, 13 December 2022) <www.ft.com/content/b31e27fd-0781-4ffd-bb69-9af985abff41> accessed 18 October 2024.

57 European Commission, 'Communication from the Commission, Guidelines on Regional State Aid' [2021] OJ C153/1, para 97.

30. However, in terms of the compatibility of aid, a more detailed assessment appears to have been undertaken by the Commission of the possible distortions to competition created by the aid than in some other areas of State aid control.[58] Furthermore, under the European Chips Act, a clawback mechanism may also be required to limit the amount of aid, whereby the beneficiary is required to make payments to the State if the profitability of the project exceeds the level expected at the time of the notification of the aid to the Commission.[59]

31. While it may be challenging to find an appropriate balance between ensuring self-autonomy for the EU and affecting companies' decisions about where to locate investment, the balancing of the positive effects of aid against their negative effects under State aid rules can help to mitigate the risks.

IV. Conclusions

32. The greater role for the State during crises inevitably creates some tensions in terms of maintaining a level playing field. Both the Covid-19 crisis and the energy crisis have highlighted asymmetries in the responses by Member States, with differences in Member States' ability to grant State aid leading to questions about how to maintain the level playing field. During these crises, to an extent, Member States have needed to decide which companies are strategically important and hence should receive aid. The crises have placed a spotlight on some of the issues that have subsequently arisen in the industrial policy debate.

33. Certain crisis measures have recognised that aid can be distortive and that the most distortive forms of aid should be accompanied by remedies to preserve the level playing field. However, the precise objective of the remedies in terms of what they are intended to achieve has not always been as clear as it could be.

34. Following the crises, there has been an increased emphasis on industrial policy in the EU, particularly in light of geopolitical risks, which could have implications for ensuring the level playing field. The FSR can help in terms of tackling subsidies granted by third countries that could unduly distort the level playing field in EU. However, in light of policies such as the IRA in the US, there is likely to be a greater need for incentives to both retain and attract companies into the EU. As a result, it is plausible that there might be a greater willingness to accept competitive distortions on the internal market in order to ensure the competitiveness of the EU vis-à-vis third countries.

---

58 European Commission, 'State Aid SA.103083 (2022/N) – Italy RRF: STMicroelectronics – New Silicon Carbide Substrates Plant in Catania' COM (2022) 7165 final, s 3.3.3.2.5.

59 European Commission, 'Communication from the Commission to the European Parliament, The Council, The European Economic and Social Committee and the Committee of the Regions: A Chips Act for Europe' COM (2022) 45 final, fn 57.

35. However, due to the level of market integration in the EU, responding to such geopolitical developments requires coordinated policy interventions across Member States.[60] Going forward, the design of appropriate industrial policy will be key to avoid unduly distorting competition. However, the greater the degree of coordination that can be maintained at the EU level, the lower the likelihood of distortions to the level playing field.[61]

60 For further discussion, Piechucka, Saurí-Romero and Smulders (n 4) accessed 18 October 2024 and Mlex (n 43).

61 German Council of Economic Experts (n 49); and De Ville (n 43).

Recent Trends at the Court of Justice of the European Union*

Nils Wahl**
Court of Justice of the European Union

1. In this foreword, three recent trends of antitrust litigation at the Court of Justice of the European Union shall be identified and discussed.

2. The first is a structural/systemic one. To put this into proper context, please allow me to jump back in time: one hundred years, to be precise. Indeed, the year 2018 is the centennial of Woodrow Wilson's "Fourteen Points" speech. Nine months after the United States had entered World War I, President Wilson appeared before Congress to outline his plan for a postwar peace. In just over 1,200 words, his speech contributed to changing the world. In particular, he suggested ending secret treaties, ensuring freedom of the seas, promoting reciprocal and free trade and creating "a general association of nations" in order to guarantee the "political independence and territorial integrity of great and small states alike." President Wilson, however, did not succeed in winning general support for that project at the time. It would take another world war and another US president before his ideas would eventually prevail both domestically and abroad.

3. President Wilson's ideas found particularly fertile ground in Europe after the end of World War II. The founding fathers of the then European Economic Community (now, the European Union) decided to establish a community of states with the primary objective of creating lasting peace. This was done, at least as the first step of the process was concerned, by progressively integrating

---

* This article has been previously published in Concurrences, and it might have been edited for clarity and cohesion. Nils Wahl, Recent trends at the Court of Justice of the European Union, November 2018, Concurrences N° 4-2018, Art. N° 88071.

** Advocate General, Court of Justice of the European Union, Luxembourg.

the economies of the various European states. Put simply, the key idea was to turn former enemies into business partners. To do so, an internal market had to be created in order to ensure the free circulation of goods, services, capitals and workers within Europe. In that context, a body of pan-European antitrust rules also had to be enacted. What was the point of removing state-made obstacles to trade if companies could basically re-create them by dividing the market?

4. Antitrust was, accordingly, a key policy for the first 4–5 decades in the life of the European Union. The Court of Justice of the European Union had, in those years, to deal with numerous high-profile EU antitrust rules. Judgments such as *Consten and Grundig* (56/64 and 58/64), *Société Technique Minière* (56/65), *Wilhelm v. Bundeskartellamt* (14/68), Dyestuffs (48/69), *Continental Can* (6/72), *United Brands* (27/76), *Hoffmann-La Roche* (85/76), *Hoechst* (46/87 and 227/88), *Delimitis* (C-234/89), *Woodpulp II* (C-89/85, C-104/85, C-114/85, C-116/85, C-117/85 and C-125/85 to C-129/85), and *Tetra Pak II* (C-333/94 P) were eagerly awaited by the institutions, economic operators and not least the academic community.

5. However, the interest generated by these antitrust cases decided by the Court has progressively, but clearly, diminished over the last three decades and I believe there are at least three reasons for that development.

6. The process towards a declining interest probably started in 1988, when the Court of First Instance (now, the General Court) was set up, in order to assist the Court of Justice, which was faced with an ever-growing number of cases. The new court was intended to deal in particular with antitrust cases: they were numerous and often raised a variety of factual, legal and economic issues which – it was thought – deserved dedicated and highly specialized staff. The Court of Justice (i.e., the body at the apex of the judicial structure) thus would be enabled to concentrate more on its constitutional role.

7. The second reason seems to be the completion of the European Single Market on January 1, 1993. As from that date, goods, services, capital and workers were free to move across the EU. It was the achievement of the long-term plan conceived by the founding fathers. After that moment, the focus of the integration process gradually shifted. The EU was given new areas of competence such as foreign and security policy, environment, energy, justice – thereby evolving from being a primarily economic organization to something close to a federation of states. This inevitably affected the number and types of cases which were brought before the Court, which then had to venture into new (and often sensitive) fields of law. Antitrust as a consequence progressively lost its central importance.

8. Third, with the reform introduced by Regulation (EC) No. 1/2003, a significant part of the enforcement of EU competition rules has been decentralized towards the national competition authorities (NCAs) and courts of the Member States. In particular, having acquired more powers and more resources, the NCAs have, over time, become more proactive (and bold!). For its part, the Commission seems more concerned with developing competition law by

focusing on a few bigger cases raising novel issues (the recent *Google* decisions are a good example). More routine cases are often dealt with by way of settlement or commitment decisions.

9. This means that the EU courts, both the General Court and the Court of Justice, receive by way of direct actions significantly fewer cases than before. For example, according to a recent study, the number of judicial proceedings for cartel- related cases dropped by a margin of 20 to 55 percent due to the introduction of the settlement procedure alone[1].

10. While the three factors just mentioned might point to a relatively diminishing importance of antitrust cases before the EU courts, there are then again also developments pointing in a different direction. As a direct consequence of the decentralization of the application of the antitrust rules to NCAs and courts, more cases than in the past come before the Court indirectly, via the preliminary ruling procedure. Indeed, national courts hearing appeals against decisions rendered by the NCAs may have doubts concerning the scope of Articles 101 and 102 TFEU in specific circumstances and thus are more likely to turn to the Court for assistance. Cases such as *AKKA/LAA* (C-177/16, on excessive prices), *APVE* (C-671/15, on the application of competition rules to the agricultural sector) and *Coty Germany* (C-230/16, on internet sales bans) illustrate this well. These cases, which attracted considerable attention, allowed the Court to provide important clarifications as regards the reach of EU competition rules.

11. Turning now to the second trend which I have identified as being substantive in nature.

12. Until fairly recently, faced with questions regarding the alleged anticompetitive nature of a given conduct, the EU courts have frequently relied on presumptions developed on the basis of the legal and economic analyses carried out in past case law, especially in some landmark cases of the 1970s and 1980s. For that reason, the EU courts have been criticized for their reluctance to carry out any in-depth assessment of the cases brought before them, even when the most recent economic theories appeared to cast doubts on certain presumptions. More recently, however, there seems to be a renewed interest – especially by the Court of Justice – to analyze the concrete effects on the market of a conduct alleged to be anticompetitive, or at least to verify the presumed harmfulness of a conduct by examining it in the light of all the relevant circumstances. In particular, in *Cartes Bancaires* (C-67/13 P), the Court of Justice faulted the General Court for adopting too broad a concept of "restrictions by object" for the purposes of Article 101 TFEU. It held that the first instance court could not validly conclude that the pricing measures adopted by the economic interest grouping set up by the main French banks had as "their object" the restriction of competition. Similarly, in *Intel* (C-413/14 P),

---

1 M. Hellwig, K. Hüschelrath, and U. Laitenberger, Settlements and Appeals in the European Commission's Cartel Cases: An Empirical Assessment, ZEW, Discussion Paper No. 16-010, January 2016

the Court of Justice dismissed the per se approach that had been adopted by the General Court: the latter should have verified whether the loyalty rebates granted by Intel to four computer manufacturers were capable of restricting competition. In *AKKA/LAA*, the Court indicated that for high prices charged by a dominant company to be considered "*unfair*" for the purposes of Article 102 TFEU those prices must be "significantly and persistently" higher than the competitive prices, and that the analysis by the authorities must be based on "objective, appropriate and verifiable criteria" and carried out "on a consistent basis." In *Coty Germany*, the Court held that a supplier of luxury goods can, in principle, prohibit the authorized distributors of a selective distribution network from selling those goods on a third-party internet platform (such as Amazon). The Court found that, when imposed uniformly and not applied in a discriminatory fashion, such a measure is appropriate to preserve the luxury image of the products at issue and does not go beyond what is necessary to achieve that aim.

13. However, also within this trend one can find indications of a different and, perhaps, more conservative or rigid approach. In particular, in *Hoffmann-La Roche* (C-179/16), the Court held that an arrangement between two undertakings marketing two competing medicinal products, which consists in the dissemination, in a context of scientific uncertainty, of misleading information relating to adverse reactions resulting from the off-label use of one of those products with a view to reducing the competitive pressure it exerts on the other product, constitutes a restriction of competition "by object."

14. Unlike the first and second trends, the third trend, I would like to emphasize, is a procedural one.

15. For quite some time the EU system (with the Commission as investigating authority and the courts tasked with verifying the legality of the former's decisions) has been criticized not only for resorting to a much too frequent reliance on presumptions, but also for being too lenient in tolerating the far-reaching investigative powers of the Commission. However, a number of recent cases have given the EU courts the opportunity to provide important clarifications as regards the scope of the Commission's powers of investigation under Regulation No. 1/2003. In those cases, the EU courts, and in particular the Court of Justice, have given substance to the fundamental rights invoked by the undertakings affected by the investigative measures, censuring the unlawful use of the Commission's powers. In *Nexans* (C-37/13 P), *Prysmian* (T-475/14) and (very recently) *České dráhy* (T-325/16), the EU courts have partly annulled decisions ordering companies to submit to an *in loco* inspection on the ground that the statement of reasons provided in the decisions in question was too broad, covering also products, services or forms of conduct for which the Commission had no element to justify an inspection. In *Deutsche Bahn* (C-583/13 P), the Court censured what was, in part, a "fishing expedition": immediately before a (regularly authorized) inspection at the premises of Deutsche Bahn, the Commission staff was informed about

another, unrelated, possible infringement by the same company. During the raid, the Commission officials did find documents concerning the new alleged infringement and informed their colleagues in Brussels, which prompted the Commission to adopt second and third inspection decisions, which then also covered the new suspected infringement. The Court observed that the information given to the Commission's officials on the second alleged infringement could not be viewed as part of the general background information on the first alleged infringement. The Court concluded that the Commission's conduct had infringed the right of defense of the undertaking concerned and annulled the second and third inspection decisions. Some months later, in four almost identical judgments, the Court annulled requests for information sent by the Commission to companies active in the cement industry (C-247/14 P; C-248/14 P; C-267/14 P; and C-268/14 P). The Court found the statement of reasons provided in the decisions at issue to be excessively brief, vague, generic and, in some respects, also ambiguous. In particular, the decisions did not set out, with the minimum degree of clarity required, the subject matter of the investigation, the alleged infringements, and the suspicions that the Commission intended to investigate. Such a statement of reasons could not justify requests for information which, furthermore, were sent more than two years after the first inspections and after the Commission had already sent a number of requests for information. Here it is interesting to note that the questionnaire sent by the Commission comprised nearly 100 pages and multiple sets of questions and sub-questions. The questions posed were extraordinarily numerous and covered very diverse types of information, some of which concerned a ten-year period. Furthermore, the information had to be provided in a very specific and rigid format.

16. Just as for the other two trends, also when it comes to this one, there are cases pointing in a different direction. In *Intel* the Court did criticize the Commission for failing to comply with its duty to record statements made during interviews of natural or legal persons, but did not view that as a breach of an essential procedural requirement capable of justifying the annulment of the challenged decision. The facts were as follows: during the investigations, the Commission held a meeting with a senior executive of a computer manufacturer without, however, recording the meeting. When Intel asked about that meeting, the Commission first denied that such a meeting had taken place. Only at a later stage did the Commission admit to the existence of the meeting and sent Intel a non-confidential version of an internal note on that meeting. The confidential version of that note was communicated to Intel only during the first instance proceedings. On appeal, the Court of Justice rejected the Commission's argument that a distinction could be made, under Regulation No. 1/2003, between formal and informal interviews. The interview in question thus should have been properly recorded. In addition, the Court rejected the argument that, by making available to Intel during the administrative procedure the non-confidential version of the internal note, the Commission

had remedied the omission. That said, the Court pointed out that Intel had not managed to prove that the breach committed by the Commission could influence, to Intel's detriment, the course of the proceedings and, ultimately, the content of the Commission's decision. The Court thus rejected Intel's request to annul the challenged decision.

17. The three trends I have identified (one structural/ systemic, one substantive and one of a procedural nature) are, as indicated before, only trends. In other words, the picture emerging from a complete analysis of the recent case law of the EU courts is not always and entirely homogeneous and unambiguous. One can easily find decisions which seem to go against the flow or that are blurring the picture. I would dare say that looking at the whole picture, it is more modern art rather than figurative art. Just like a cubist painting, the case law of the EU courts needs to be de-codified in order to be understood, explained and, where appropriate, criticized. As a member of the Court of Justice I am ill-suited to judge the quality of that case law. Naturally, as transpires from this contribution, I too find certain decisions more convincing, sound or clear than others.

18. Overall, however, I am of the view that two of the mentioned trends are clearly positive. First, the EU courts appear more ready to concretely verify the alleged anti-competitiveness of certain forms of conduct which, in the past, were considered harmful almost by definition. The Court of Justice, in particular, is not insensitive to more recent legal and economic theories: presumptions are an inevitable tool for judges, but their soundness and, in any event, their applicability to a specific set of circumstances need to be verified. Second, a number of cases show the EU courts' willingness to censure the Commission for an improper, excessive or abusive use of its powers of investigation, thereby strengthening the right to effective judicial protection of the companies subject to an investigation. This is a crucial development, especially in the light of the level of fines imposed in the most recent Commission decisions. True, the Court has adopted a rather lenient approach in *Intel*, but perhaps that may be explained by its desire to rule on the substantive issues concerning the rebates.

19. That said, whether the progressive decrease in the quantity of cases brought directly before the EU courts is to be regarded as a positive trend is an open question. From the perspective of the enforcer, I understand the rationale of the new Commission policy: it frees resources that may then be employed in the most complex cases. However, when I look at it from the perspective of the companies that decide to settle, I am more doubtful. May that be explained by the fact that companies see no added value in going before the EU courts? If that is so, I would hope that the increased stringency of the EU courts with regard to the Commission (which I just outlined) may in the future change that attitude. In that context, I would point out that the recent reform of the General Court has doubled the number of judges. Presumably, more resources are now available to carry out an in-depth and comprehensive review of the

challenged decisions. It is also true that, in these last years, a larger number of cases land before the Court through the preliminary ruling procedure. Yet, antitrust is a particularly technical field of law and the specificities of each case are often of crucial importance to rule on the lawfulness or unlawfulness of a given form of conduct. As I see it, requiring the Court to provide an answer to an abstract question of law in this field may, at times, be neither straightforward for the Court of Justice nor satisfactory for the referring national court.

20. To conclude, I think that it can be safely said that the "association of nations" established in Europe after World War II has successfully achieved the objective of creating lasting peace on the continent, protecting the territorial integrity of large and small European states. It also greatly contributed to increasing the welfare of those countries.

21. Today, the European Union must face new challenges, which often also have a global dimension: terrorism, climate change, illegal immigration, the financial crisis, etc. The Court of Justice of the European Union, also in those fields, has to fulfill its mission to ensure the rule of law. In that regard, antitrust policy may have lost, to some extent, the preeminence it once enjoyed when the European project was more focused on economic integration. However, as a key instrument to ensure the genuine freedom of markets, its present and future importance should not be overlooked. Paraphrasing Austro- American economist Ludwig von Mises: we should not forget that basic freedoms such as "freedom of speech, of thought, of the press, freedom of religion, freedom from imprisonment without trial" can never be preserved in the absence of economic freedoms. In a system where there is no free market, "all those other freedoms become illusory, even if they are made into laws and written up in constitutions."

Competition Law Institutions and Future Challenges

IMELDA MAHER AND MINA HOSSEINI*
UCD Sutherland School of Law

1. Competition Law is classically seen as prohibiting conduct that is inimical to markets, the market being seen as the main device through which innovation and ultimately consumer or total welfare will be achieved.[1] Thus breaches of prohibited conduct are reviewed retrospectively, save for mergers which are reviewed prospectively. Two key questions arise as to how to achieve this end: (1) who enforces competition law and (2) where? These questions are common to all competition regimes irrespective of how the core prohibitions are articulated in law. In this brief chapter, we first address these two questions before exploring the key challenges posed by digital technology to authorities and the crises of Covid and climate change.

I. Who Polices Competition Law?

2. The most common answer to this question is an independent agency established by law. Independence is seen as critical but in turn raises two questions: why independent and from whom? For competition authorities to be the guardians of competition, they need to be independent from government.[2] This ensures

* Dr Mina Hosseini is an Adjunct Research Fellow and Marie Skłodowska-Curie Alumna at UCD Sutherland School of Law, Dublin. Professor Imelda Maher is the Sutherland Full Professor of European Law at UCD Sutherland School of Law, Dublin.

1 There is much debate about application of the consumer welfare standard and its relationship with total welfare in competition law see eg Joseph Farrell and Michael L Katz, 'The Economics of Welfare Standards in Antitrust' (2006) 2 *Competition Policy International* 3.

2 The degree of independence varies even among EU Member States. For an explanatory analysis see Mattia Guidi, 'Delegation and Varieties of Capitalism: Explaining the Independence of National Competition Agencies in the European Union' (2014) 12 *Journal of Common Market Studies* 343.

competition law enforcement is largely immune from the electoral cycle so the very wide discretion as to enforcement priorities[3] remains free from party politics and lobbying.[4] Such independence remains within constitutional limits imposing procedural obligations, fundamental rights considerations and other constitutional concerns on competition agencies.

3. However, even if the agency is independent, the scope of the legislation may place limits on its activities from the outset. In general, competitive neutrality – whereby all firms have a level playing field with respect to a state's ownership, regulation or activity in the market – is recommended as far as practicable by the OECD.[5] Important sectors of the market may be excluded eg professions initially could apply for their rules to be immune from British competition law;[6] agriculture in the EU under which the competition rules only apply indirectly through legislation.[7] Exclusions can undermine the enforcement activity and effectiveness of the agency. Indirectly, agencies can be subject to resource constraints that inhibit the effective performance of their functions eg through limitations on budgets, staff recruitment and even office space.

4. In liberal democracies there is another necessary caveat on independence and that is accountability. The exercise of public power ultimately must be accountable to elected representatives. This arises directly, usually through an annual reporting obligation to parliament and government, and through the courts. Internationally, a soft form of accountability for the state can arise through framework reviews of competition regimes such as those carried out by the OECD.[8] And participation in agency networks where there is information sharing can lead to transparency between peers and peer review.[9]

5. The degree of independence varies between jurisdictions, but the principle of independence is broadly accepted. Internationally, the EU model of a single powerful agency rather than the more complex, bifurcated US model seems to be preferred.[10]

---

3 Or Brook and Katalin J Cseres, 'Priority Setting as the Blind Spot of Administrative Law Enforcement: A Theoretical, Conceptual, and Empirical Study of Competition Authorities in Europe' (17 April 2024) MLR <https://onlinelibrary.wiley.com/doi/10.1111/1468-2230.12881> accessed 16 October 2024.

4 Imelda Maher, 'The Institutional Structure of Competition Law' in Michael W Dowdle, John Gillespie and Imelda Maher (eds), *Asian Capitalism and the Regulation of CUP* (CUP 2013).

5 OECD, Council Recommendation on Competitive Neutrality (31 May 2021).

6 Competition Act 1998, sch 4, appealed under the Enterprise Act 2002.

7 TFEU art 42 and Regulation (EU) 1308/2013 of the European Parliament and of the Council of 17 December 2013 establishing a common organisation of the markets in agricultural products and repealing Council Regulations (EEC) 922/72, (EEC) 234/79, (EC) 1037/2001 and (EC) 34/2007, pt IV [2013] OJ L347/671, art 2, (as amended) see <https://competition-policy.ec.europa.eu/sectors/agriculture_en> accessed 16 October 2024. Katalin J Cseres, '"Acceptable" Cartels at the Crossroads of EU Competition Law and the Common Agricultural Policy: A Legal Inquiry into the Political, Economic, and Social Dimensions of (Strengthening Farmers') Bargaining Power' (2020) 65 *The Antitrust Bulletin* 401.

8 OECD, 'Country Reviews of Competition Policy Frameworks' <https://web-archive.oecd.org/temp/2024-06-27/657175-countryreviewsofcompetitionpolicyframeworks.htm> accessed 16 October 2024.

9 Imelda Maher and Oana Stefan, 'Competition Law in Europe: The Challenge of a Network Constitution' in Dawn Oliver, Tony Prosser and Richard Rawlings (eds), *The Regulatory State: Constitutional Implications* (OUP 2010) 192.

10 Anu Bradford et al., 'The Global Dominance of European Competition Law Over American Antitrust Law' (2019) 16 *Journal of Empirical Legal Studies* 731.

6. There are also other institutions involved in competition enforcement. Most notably, courts are part of the enforcement apparatus. There can be a full appeal of an agency decision, judicial review, hearings for damages, or in those jurisdictions with criminal sanctions for breach of competition laws, a criminal trial. There may be a specialist tribunal with members from fields beyond law such as economics and accounting[11] or competition appeals may be heard by a specially designated judge/court[12] or in the ordinary civil or criminal courts either at first instance, or on appeal.[13] Competition law issues can be addressed through arbitration with arbitration clauses often found in commercial contracts eg in the EU, such decisions are subject to appeal on competition grounds.[14]

7. Competition law enforcement is shared often with regulators eg in telecoms, energy. Such concurrent jurisdiction per se does not compromise independence provided there are mechanisms in place to ensure consistency and to reduce the risk of regulatory capture.[15] Regulatory powers can also be added to the competition authority's duties most notably in relation to consumer protection see eg the Australian Competition and Consumer Commission which has held both competition and consumer protection responsibilities since its creation in 1995.[16] Government ministers may also retain residual powers eg in relation to approval of mergers and acquisitions for public policy reasons such as national security or media plurality.[17]

II. Where? Where Competition Law is Enforced: National Boundaries and Beyond

8. In this multipolar world, with large multinationals, competition law enforcement remains fragmented across national boundaries. The main exception is the EU where the European Commission and Courts and national competition agencies and courts from 27 Member States enforce the EU competition laws

11 For example, the UK Competition Appeals Tribunal see Enterprise Act 2002, s 12 and sch 2.

12 For example, there is a designated competition law judge in Ireland see, <www.courts.ie/rules/competition-proceedings> accessed 16 October 2024.

13 For contrasting critiques of courts and competition see the chapters by Javier Tapia et al., *The Global Limits of Competition Law* (Stanford University Press 2013).

14 Case C-126/97 *Eco Swiss China Time Ltd v Benetton International NV* ECLI:EU:C:1999:269; James Segan, 'Arbitration Clauses and Competition Law' (2018) 9 *Journal of European Competition Law & Practice* 423.

15 Niamh Dunne, *Competition Law and Economic Regulation: Making and Managing Markets* (CUP 2015), chs. 4 and 5.

16 Set up in 1995. See Amanda Smullen and Catherine Clutton, 'The ACCC: Guardian of Viable Markets and Consumer Rights' in Arjen Boin, Lauren A Fahy and Paul 't Hart (eds), *in Guardians of Public Values: How Public Organizations become and remain Institutions* (2021).

17 Adelaida Afilipoaie and Heritiana Renaud Ranaivoson, 'Assessing Media Merger & Acquisitions: The Power Pyramids of regulatory cooperation' (2022) 15(1) Journal of Media and Policy 7.

(with national competition laws also in place).[18] With a now moribund WTO,[19] and a failed attempt to introduce competition norms at the WTO level,[20] common transnational rules have given way to transnational cooperation on enforcement, through bilateral, regional and international agreements.[21] As well as international bodies such as the OECD and UNCTAD that focus on technical support, voluntary regime reviews and soft law statements, there are also a plethora of competition agency networks, the largest of which is the International Competition Network.[22] Preferential trade agreements can contain competition sections and such sections commonly contain cooperation provisions.[23] Finally, the extraterritorial application of competition rules is also an increasingly common feature of competition law and is no longer the preserve of US antitrust law.[24]

9. Common and profound challenges arise transnationally for competition authorities from crises that are either long term and directly (digital markets) or indirectly (sustainability and climate crisis) connected to competition law or are episodic disruptors (Covid-19). One issue is how agencies prepare for, are shaped by and respond to those challenges.

III. The Key Challenge for Competition Authorities

10. The digital sector is a big part of the global economy, and the role of digital and AI innovations in the short, medium, and long term for economies worldwide will be considerable. One peculiarity of digital markets is the complementary nature of competition and regulation. For example, the EU has made impressive attempts to regulate digital platforms in recent years. Some new initiatives, such as the Digital Markets Acts (DMA), the Digital Service Act (DSA), the Data Act, and the AI Act, are all critical pieces

---

18 European Commission, 'European Competition Network (ECN)' <https://competition-policy.ec.europa.eu/antitrust-and-cartels/european-competition-network_en> accessed 16 October 2024. See also the creation of regional CAs under the Chinese Anti-Monopoly Law 2022, s 12 and the network of Attorneys General under US law (although they enforce state rather than federal law).

19 Robert Howse and Joanna Langille, 'Continuity and Change in the World Trade Organization: Pluralism Past, Present, and Future' (2023) 117 *The American Journal of International Law* 1.

20 Josef Drexl, 'International Competition Policy after Cancun: Placing a Singapore Issue on the WTO Development Agenda' (2004) 27 *World Competition* 419. WTO law has some relevance to competition law see Chris Noonan, *The Emerging Principles of International Competition Law* (OUP 2008), ch. 11.

21 See the OECD, Competition Cooperation Database <https://data-explorer.oecd.org/> accessed 16 October 2024, arising from the OECD–ICN, *Report on International Co-operation in Competition Enforcement 2021* (2021) <https://web-archive.oecd.org/temp/2023-09-18/576983-oecd-icn-report-on-international-cooperation-in-competition-enforcement-2021.htm> accessed 16 October 2024.

22 ICN, International Competition Network <www.internationalcompetitionnetwork.org/> accessed 16 October 2024. In general, see Imelda Maher, 'The Networked (Agency) Regulation of Competition' in Peter Drahos (ed), *Regulatory Theory Foundations and Applications* (ANU Press 2017).

23 Anu Bradford and Adam Chilton, 'Regulating Antitrust through Trade Agreements' (2021) 84 *Antitrust Law Journal* 103.

24 UNCTAD, *Developing Countries' Experience with Extraterritoriality in Competition Law* (2021). Marek Martyniszyn, 'Extraterritoriality in Competition Law: Changing Frictions' in Austen Parrish and Cedric Ryngaert (eds), *Research Handbook on Extraterritoriality in International Law* (Edward Elgar 2023).

of regulation[25] that now operate alongside and supplement competition law enforcement. Enforcement of the DMA resides with the Commission with a number of bodies with policy coordination and roles to straddle the competition and regulation divide.[26] Within the Commission itself, a joint team in the Directorates-General for Competition (DG-Comp) and Communications Networks, Content and Technology (Connect) is responsible for the implementation and enforcement of the Act.[27] Hence, while competition enforcement remains distinct, it is inextricably now bound up with regulation of digital markets.

11. Competition law authorities have a proven track record of successful enforcement over a century in the US, six decades in the EU, and a considerable history in other parts of the world, such as Japan and Canada. As Cremer de Montjoye and Schweitzer[28] emphasised, competition is still the best way to ensure consumer interests and some key authorities have increased scrutiny of the digital sector.[29] Microsoft,[30] Google Android,[31] and the ongoing Meta cases (regarding tying),[32] the Google Shopping case,[33] and Amazon's Marketplace and Buy Box cases[34] (regarding self-preferencing), as well as the investigation into 'Apple Pay' and App Store rules for music streaming

---

25 European Commission, 'A Europe Fit for the Digital Age' <https://commission.europa.eu/strategy-and-policy/priorities-2019-2024/europe-fit-digital-age_en> accessed 16 October 2024. See Regulation (EU) 2022/1925 of the European Parliament and of the Council of 14 September 2022 on contestable and fair markets in the digital sector and amending Directives (EU) 2019/1937 and (EU) 2020/1828 (Digital Markets Act) [2022] OJ L265/1. Regulation (EU) 2022/2065 of the European Parliament and of the Council of 19 October 2022 on a Single Market for Digital Services and amending Directive 2000/31/EC (Digital Services Act) [2022] OJ L277/1. Regulation (EU) 2023/2854 of the European Parliament and of the Council of 13 December 2023 on harmonised rules on fair access to and use of data and amending Regulation (EU) 2017/2394 and Directive (EU) 2020/1828 (Data Act) [2023] OJ L Series. Regulation (EU) 2024/1689 of the European Parliament and of the Council of 13 June 2024 laying down harmonised rules on artificial intelligence and amending Regulations (EC) 300/2008, (EU) 167/2013, (EU) No 168/2013, (EU) 2018/858, (EU) 2018/1139 and (EU) 2019/2144 and Directives 2014/90/EU, (EU) 2016/797 and (EU) 2020/1828 (Artificial Intelligence Act) [2024] OJ L Series.

26 Imelda Maher, 'Regulatory Design in the EU Digital Markets Act: No Solo Run for the Commission' (2024) *Journal of Antitrust Enforcement* 1.

27 See European Commission, The Digital Markets Act <https://digital-markets-act.ec.europa.eu/index_en> accessed 16 October 2024

28 Crémer, Jacques, Yves-Alexandre de Montjoye and Heike Schweitzer, 'Competition Policy for the Digital Era' (2019) Working Paper No. 6, 39.

29 Collectively called GAFAM Google, Apple, Facebook, Amazon and Microsoft.

30 Case COM/37.792 – *Microsoft*, 24 March 2004 (Commission decision), see James Killick, 'The EU Commission condemns leading US software company for abuse of a dominant position in the market for client PC operating systems, ordering to grant compulsory license to competitor (Microsoft / Sun Microsystems)' (2004) e-Competitions art. No. 37126.

31 Case AT. 40099–*Google Android*, 18 July 2018. See also Case T-604/18 *Google and Alphabet v Commission (Google Android)* EU:T:2022:541, General Court, see Cristina Caffarra, 'The EU General Court confirms that a Big Tech company abused its dominance by tying its operating system with the app store suite (Google Android)' (2022) e-Competitions art. No. 108801.

32 European Commission, Press Release, 'Antitrust: Commission sends Statement of Objections to Meta over abusive practices benefiting Facebook Marketplace' (19 December 2022).

33 Case AT. 39740–*Google (Shopping)*, 27 June 2017. See also, Case T-612/17 *Google and Alphabet v Commission (Google Shopping)* EU:T:2021:763 General Court, see Dimitrios Katsifis, 'The EU General Court delivers a judgment which confirms the Commission's decision and finds a Big Tech company guilty of abuse of dominance by favouring its own comparison shopping services on its general result pages (Google Shopping)' (2021) e-Competitions art. No. 108828.

34 Case AT. 4046–*Amazon Marketplace* and Case AT 4073–*Amazon Buy Box*, 20 December 2022.

providers[35] are some examples of the European Commission's actions against big tech companies. Similar antitrust enforcement has happened against these companies in the US,[36] India, China, and South Korea.[37]

12. AI is another emerging topic in competition law enforcement with Ezrachi and Stuck setting out different scenarios in which AI can help implement, conceal, or create anticompetitive agreements. For example, AI can help with autonomous coordination between undertakings, algorithmic manipulation, or autonomous collusion through self-learning algorithms.[38] Competition authorities can find it challenging to detect and address the emerging anti-competitive practices employed by AI deployers in the digital era. Yet some agencies have already begun to investigate these practices. For example, in the US, the Department of Justice (DOJ) and Federal Trade Commission (FTC) announced on June 6, 2024, that they would launch investigations into potential anticompetitive practices by major AI companies. NVIDIA, the leading manufacturer of AI chips, faced scrutiny over allegations that it used tactics to lock customers into exclusively using its proprietary chip designs. Simultaneously, the joint investigation targeted Microsoft's partnership with OpenAI amid concerns about potential tying arrangements.[39]

13. Enforcement of competition law in the digital sector is difficult and complex. These complexities are changing established competition law concepts and impact the forms and effects of anticompetitive practices. Defining relevant markets is rendered more complex with the rapid change in AI technology disrupting various industries, making it more difficult to determine the boundaries of relevant markets.[40] The new Commission Notice[41] and new concepts emerging in the courts and in academic literature such as 'ecosystem'[42] point

---

35 European Commission, Press Release, 'Antitrust: Commission sends Statement of Objections to Apple over practice regarding Apple Pay' (2 May 2022), and European Commission, Press Release, 'Antitrust: Commission sends Statement of Objections to apple clarifying concerns over App Store rules for music streaming providers' (28 February 2024).

36 See for example: *Federal Trade Commission v Meta Platforms, Inc.*, No. 191 0134 (DDC filed 17 November 2021), *United States v Apple* (2024) see Julie Grangeon, 'United States: The Department of Justice and sixteen states sue big tech player for illegal monopoly (Apple)' (22 March 2024) 2 Concurrences 118694 220-222, United States v. Google LLC, 1:20-cv-03010m, United States v. Apple Inc., 952 F. Supp. 2d 638 (S.D.N.Y. 2013), USA and Plaintiff States v. Apple Inc., filed on March 21, 2024 (Case No. 2:24-cv-04055 in the District of New Jersey)

37 For an overview of the antitrust enforcement in the digital sector in 19 jurisdictions See: ICC, *Global Report on Antitrust Enforcement in the Digital Economy* (2023) <https://iccwbo.org/news-publications/policies-reports/global-report-on-antitrust-enforcement-in-the-digital-economy/> accessed 16 October 2024.

38 Ariel Ezrachi and Maurice E Stucke, 'Artificial Intelligence & Collusion: When Computers Inhibit Competition' (2017) *University of Illinois Law Review* 1775.

39 David McCabe, 'U.S. Clears Way for Antitrust Inquiries of Nvidia, Microsoft and OpenAI' *NY Times* (5 June 2024) <www.nytimes.com/2024/06/05/technology/nvidia-microsoft-openai-antitrust-doj-ftc.html> accessed 16 October 2024.

40 Crémer, de Montjoye and Schweitzer (n 28), 47.

41 European Commission, Notice on the definition of the relevant market for the purposes of Union competition law, [2024] OJ C/2024/1645.

42 T-604/18 Google (Android) v. Commission ECLI:EU:T:2022:541 (on appeal) at para. 116 "Thus, in a digital 'ecosystem', which brings together several categories of supplier, customer and consumer and causes them to interact within a platform, the products or services which form part of the relevant markets that make up that ecosystem may overlap or be connected to each other on the basis of their horizontal or vertical complementarity. Taken together, the relevant markets may also have a global

to an evolving context where change is already happening in concepts with the emergence and advancement of digital technologies (which started with digital markets but continues with AI). The concept of 'market power' in the digital economy is also different because of network effects, and although the network effect is more related to platforms, it is also relevant in AI. AI companies' dominance directly relates to the amount of data (also the quality of data). There are serious ethical concerns about the datasets used for AI training. These data could be gender-biased, racially biased, or contain misinformation and disinformation, yet collaboration between competitors to clean the data could be considered anticompetitive.[43]

14. Competition law enforcement is affected by crises. The issue of how competition law enforcement takes account of sustainability in the context of the climate crisis is much debated.[44] During the Covid-19 pandemic, EU competition authorities used a flexible approach to competition law enforcement (including state aid[45]), and this approach was justified because of public policy and public health objectives[46] and was followed in similar cases, such as the Ukraine–Russia war.[47] As Evans[48] argues, crises can incentivise firms to engage in anticompetitive practices, and the chaos of the catastrophic situation can lead to a lower speed in competition law enforcement. The Covid-19 pandemic highlights the risk of crises raising the question of how competition authorities should prepare.

15. These different crises: the long term but now rapidly intensifying climate crisis; the increasingly rapidly developing innovative tech sector which is creating and redefining markets and wider society, and the immediate, sudden and traumatic pandemic, all pose challenges for competition authorities along three main axes: expertise, resources and cooperation.

---

dimension in the light of the system that brings its components together and of any competitive constraints within that system or from other systems." See also Ioannis Lianos, Klaas Hendrik Eller and Tobias Kleinschmitt 'Towards a Legal Theory of Digital Ecosystems' (27 May 2024) Faculty of Laws University College London Law Research Paper No. 16/2024 <https://papers.ssrn.com/sol3/papers.cfm?abstract_id=4849340> accessed 16 October 2024. Recently, several competition law works have mentioned and discussed this concept. See also, Ioannis Lianos, 'Reorienting Competition Law' (2022) 10 *Journal of Antitrust Enforcement* 1.

43 See Rajmund Molski, 'Competition Law and Artificial Intelligence–Challenges and Opportunities' (2021) 14 *Teka Komisji Prawniczej PAN Oddział w Lublinie* 339.

44 The ICN announced its first sustainability workshop held in July 2024 see ICN, 'Workshop on Competition and Sustainable Development' (2024) <www.internationalcompetitionnetwork.org/featured/sustainability-workshop/> accessed 16 October 2024. Simon Holmes, Dirk Middelschulte and Martijn Snoep, *Competition Law, Climate Change & Environmental Sustainability* (Concurrences 2021).

45 Communication from the Commission, Temporary Framework for State aid measures to support the economy in the current COVID-19 outbreak OJ C 91I, 20.3.2020, p. 1. See also discussions around competition law and the fiscal crises in the EU, Michael Reynolds, Sarah Macrory and Michelle Chowdhury, 'EU Competition Policy in the Financial Crisis: Extraordinary Measures' (2010) 33 *Fordham International Law Journal* 1670.

46 Maciej M Sokołowski, 'Regulation in the COVID-19 Pandemic and Post-Pandemic Times: Day-Watchman Tackling the Novel Coronavirus' (2021) 15 *Transforming Government: People, Process and Policy* 206.

47 See 'Competition Law in Times of War: Response to the Russian Invasion of Ukraine' (*Kluwer Competition Law Blog*, 2022) <https://competitionlawblog.kluwercompetitionlaw.com/2022/04/04/competition-law-in-times-of-war-response-to-the-russian-invasion-of-ukraine/> accessed 16 October 2024.

48 David S Evans, 'Planning for Catastrophes' (2020) 8 *Journal of Antitrust Enforcement* 273.

16. The complexity of digital markets, AI, and the systemic risks posed by crises require adequate and competent personnel with appropriate expertise in well-resourced authorities, to address these concerns effectively. The competition authority's job is to ensure the competitiveness of markets for today and tomorrow and in doing so, it should have a forward-looking vision to successfully face and manage ongoing and unforeseen crises. As Majcher and Robinson[49] argue, having a 'Strategic Foresight' plan and even a Unit (such as the OECD's Strategic Foresight Unit[50]) to constantly plan for the future and face the evolving nature of digital transformation could help face these challenges.

17. For competition authorities to manage the consequences of AI challenges they need to develop new analytical tools that can be an important resource for enforcement.[51] Training on sector-specific data that can help competition authorities scan and use large amounts of data, analyse the information, and predict a potential competition law breach by a firm could be an effective tool for enforcers.[52] For example, the Italian NCA (Autorità Garante della Concorrenza e del Mercato) has initiated an experimental programme that leverages data analysis, AI and machine learning tools to explore the algorithms and practices of some online platforms (such as Amazon).[53] Some authorities have already implemented data-based solutions, such as using data scientists in their teams to analyse digital market players' behaviours and impact on platform ecosystems. For example, in a special unit designed for 'Forensic Investigation Detection', the Greek Competition Authority uses several data scientists as part of their enforcement team.[54]

18. Finally, coordination between regulators and competition authorities will be important as seen for example in the design of the EU DMA. The role of networks, international cooperation, and harmonisation in competition law enforcement will continue to be crucial. One example of such cooperation is the US DOJ (Antitrust Division), FTC, and the European Commission's cooperation in the 'US–EU Joint Technology Competition Policy Dialogue'.

---

49 Klaudia Majcher and Viktoria HSE Robertson, 'Strategic Foresight and EU Competition Law' (2024) Working Paper <https://papers.ssrn.com/sol3/papers.cfm?abstract_id=4710206> accessed 16 October 2024.

50 OECD, *OECD Scenarios for Digital Transformation* (2018) <https://web-archive.oecd.org/2022-05-30/632953-Scenarios_for_Digital_Transformation.pdf> accessed 16 October 2024.

51 See FTC, 'Generative AI Raises Competition Concerns' (*Technology Blog*, 2023) <www.ftc.gov/policy/advocacy-research/tech-at-ftc/2023/06/generative-ai-raises-competition-concerns> accessed 16 October 2024, see also: Richard May, Artificial Intelligence, Data and Competition, (2024) OECD Artificial Intelligence Papers No. 18 <www.oecd-ilibrary.org/science-and-technology/artificial-intelligence-data-and-competition_e7e88884-en accessed> 16 October 2024.

52 Antonio Capobianco, 'Artificial Intelligence, Data and Competition – Background Note by the Secretariat' (2024) 52.

53 Isabella Lorenzoni, 'Why do Competition Authorities need Artificial Intelligence?' (2022) 15 *Yearbook of Antitrust and Regulatory Studies* 37.

54 OECD, 'Data Screening Tools in Competition Investigations – Background Note by the Secretariat' (2022) 24 <https://one.oecd.org/document/DAF/COMP/WP3(2022)5/en/pdf> accessed 16 October 2024.

These dialogues are mostly about regulating the big tech companies and AI.[55] Such cooperation can facilitate harmonising competition policies, guidelines, and enforcement practices.

IV. Conclusion

19. Independence remains the key to institutional design for competition authorities, but independence is not and never can be absolute with authorities operating within a constitutional context and subject to constraints of scope and resources. Competition authorities are not the only institutions involved in competition law enforcement with jurisdiction shared with most notably courts but also regulators and ministers. One of the major constraints on any authority is jurisdiction, addressed through the now well-established principle of extraterritoriality and in the absence of an international competition regime, enforcement cooperation is realised through international bodies, bi and multilateral agreements, competition provisions in trade agreements and through agency networks.

20. There are several major challenges facing competition enforcement: climate change and sustainability; digital markets; and unforeseen crises such as Covid. These have tested and stretched well-established concepts in competition law and have highlighted the need for forward planning for future crises and how competition regimes can work to support necessary societal responses. These crises have also shown the ongoing need for expert and competent personnel adequately resourced and the continuing importance of coordination between competition authorities and regulators and in enforcement internationally.

55 European Commission, 'EU-US Hold Fourth Joint Technology Competition Policy Dialogue' (2024) <https://ec.europa.eu/commission/presscorner/detail/en/ip_24_1952> accessed 16 October 2024.

The Growing and Worrying Trend of Global Geopolitical Protectionism

IOANNIS KOKKORIS*
Queen Mary University of London

I. Introduction

1. In the context of global markets, the notion of economic nationalism refers to the measures that can be adopted to protect national economies from foreign economic interests.[1] Nations have adopted a wide range of policies including controlling imports and direct foreign investment, and strengthening state-owned companies.[2] Friedrich List, the 19th-century thinker whose ideas influenced the rise of economic nationalism, proclaimed that the only way to attain prosperity was industrialization, and to that end it was necessary to protect domestic industry against foreign competition.[3] These protectionist policies have been adopted with vigour throughout history, particularly during the Great Depression (1929-1934) – when a policy oriented to replacing goods which were formerly imported with domestically produced, known as import substitution,[4] was introduced in the 1930s across Asia, Africa and

---

*

1 Sam Pryke, 'Economic Nationalism: Theory, History and Prospects' (2012) 3(3) Global Policy 281; Anthony D. Smith, *Nationalism and Modernism: A Critical Survey of Recent Theories of Nations and Nationalism* (Routledge 1998) 49.

2 Pryke (n 1) 285.

3 Jeromin Zettelmeyer, 'The Return of Economic Nationalism in Germany' (March 2019) Peterson Institute for International Economics Policy Briefs 19-4, https://www.piie.com/publications/policy-briefs/return-economic-nationalism-germany accessed 15 September 2023.

4 For an interesting background and discussions about import substitution see Werner Baer, 'Import Substitution and Industrialization in Latin America: Experiences and Interpretations' (1972) 7(1) Latin American Research Review 95; Albert O. Hirschman, 'The Political Economy of Import-Substituting Industrialization in Latin America' (1968) 82(1) The Quarterly Journal of Economics 1; David Felix, 'Import Substitution and Late Industrialization: Latin America and Asia Compared' (1989) 17(9) World Development 1455.

Latin America (sometimes accompanied by expropriation of foreign companies and sequestration)[5] – and the financial crisis of 2008-2009.[6] It seems that these protectionist measures are accentuated in times of crisis, which in present times can be identified as the Covid-19 pandemic and the exponential expansion of the Chinese investment abroad. Although it has been recognised that now the importance of market integration may resist a strengthening of protectionism policies, there is an increasing number of stakeholders advocating for renewed emphasis on nationalist policies in relation to FDI and in particular to M&A assessment, especially from sovereign wealth funds and state-owned enterprises.[7]

2. Figures 1 and 2 illustrate the average FDI stocks and flows, respectively, to and from the EU, the UK, the US, China, Russia, Japan, India and South Africa between 2013–2022.

Figure 1. FDI stocks as % of GDP in several jurisdictions (2013–22 average)

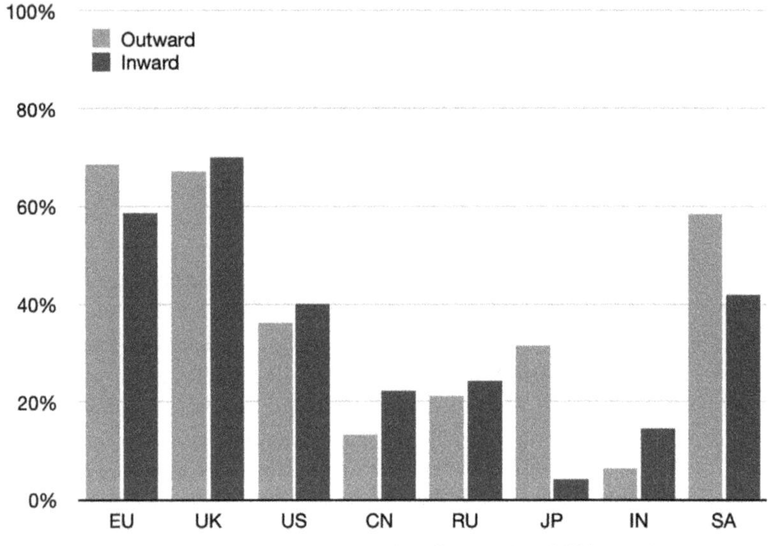

Author's elaboration based on OECD, 'FDI Stocks' https://data.oecd.org/fdi/fdi-stocks.htm

5 Geoffrey Jones, *Multinational Companies and Global Capitalism* (Oxford University Press 2005) 244.

6 For further analysis see Pryke (n 1) 285-289.

7 This analysis draws from Kokkoris I., Merger Control, National Security, and Foreign Direct Investment Screening: A Comparative Perspective, Oxford University Press (c 160000 words) forthcoming 2024.

Figure 2. FDI flows as % of GDP in several jurisdictions (2013–22 average)

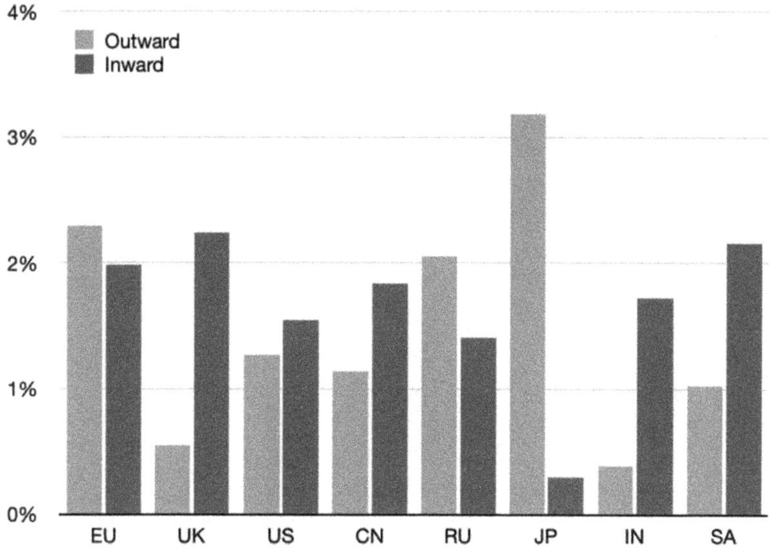

Author's elaboration based on OECD, 'FDI Flows' https://data.oecd.org/fdi/fdi-flows.htm

3. More recently, the COVID-19 pandemic has reinvigorated the debate about the need to reassess the global trade model. The outbreak made governments reflect on the merits of globalised supply chains and the security of supply.[8] In response to the pandemic, several jurisdictions seeking to protect their economic sovereignty either introduced or updated screening regimes for foreign investment on national security grounds.

4. Indeed, the UNCTAD's World Investment Report 2021 indicated that in 2020, 67 countries adopted policy measures related to foreign investment, most of which took place in developed economies, largely as a response to the pandemic and mainly restrictive.[9] The report noted that the number of restrictive policy measures in reaction to the pandemic superseded those that were adopted during the financial crisis of 2008-2009.[10] It also outlined that even if the vast majority of FDI measures have been generally adopted

---

8 Philip Lowe, Adam Kidane, and Alec Burnside, 'Industrial Policy and EU Merger Control: Finding the Right Tools' in Ioannis Kokkoris and Nicholas Levy (eds), *Research Handbook on Global Merger Control* (Edward Elgar 2023) 273; Ioannis Kokkoris, 'EU Merger Control and National Security Assessment: A Moving Target', in Ioannis Kokkoris and Nicholas Levy (eds), *Research Handbook on Global Merger Control* (Edward Elgar 2023) 328; Fountoukakos K, Roberts V and Allen R, 'Addressing National Security Concerns in the Merger Context', in Ioannis Kokkoris and Claudia Lemus (eds), *Research Handbook on the Law and Economics of Competition Enforcement* (Edward Elgar 2022) 217.

9 United Nations Conference on Trade and Development (UNCTAD), 'World Investment Report 2021: Investing in Sustainable Recovery' 109 https://unctad.org/system/files/official-document/wir2021_en.pdf accessed 15 September 2023.

10 Ibid.

by developed economies (81 per cent), an important number of developing and emerging economies are mirroring the movement.[11]

5. Figure 3 shows the OECD assessment of FDI restrictiveness for the UK, the US, China, Russia, Japan, India, South Africa, Germany, Spain, France, and Italy. The OECD defines restrictiveness based on 'four main types of restrictions: foreign equity restrictions; discriminatory screening or approval mechanisms; restrictions on key foreign personnel and operational restrictions' and assigns a score between 0 (open) and 1 (closed).

Figure 3. OECD FDI Restrictiveness Indicator (2020)

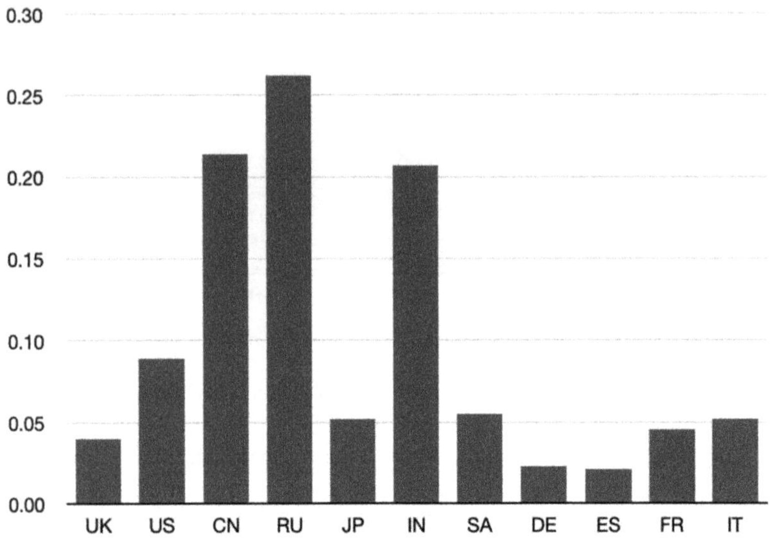

Author's elaboration based on OECD, 'FDI Restrictiveness' (indicator) https://data.oecd.org/fdi/fdi-restrictiveness.htm

6. *There was no data available for the EU. Germany, Spain, France, and Italy were used as proxy instead.*

7. The types of measures vary from country to country: some are temporary and others are permanent, some have lowered the thresholds that trigger intervention, some have expanded the prior approval requirements for FDI, and others have established strategic sectors where the special power regime is applied strictly.[12]

8. FDI has both economic and security implications. The concept of national security varies considerably from one jurisdiction to the other. There is wide diversity of what jurisdictions consider to be national security. The concept of national security differs from one legal system to the other: some jurisdictions use a narrow

11 Ibid, 109, 111.

12 See UNCTAD (n 9) 111-113.

definition, while others use an open and vague definition of what national security considerations entail. There is no exact definition of what national security is, and, therefore, the interpretation is left to the relevant authority.

II. The approach to the assessment of national security in the European Union

9. The EU has been recognised as a leading recipient of Foreign Direct Investment (FDI)[13] and as one of the most open investment regimes in the world.[14] This approach derives from the notion that FDI stimulates the emergence of capital, the transference of technology, the integration of societies, the improvement of employment conditions, and the advance in research and product development.[15] The referred openness tendency was bolstered with the entry into force of the Lisbon Treaty, in which Article 207(1) TFEU incorporated FDI into the EU's common commercial policy (CCP),[16] translating the elimination of restrictions on international trade and investments in a constitutional obligation for the EU's common commercial policy.[17] As a result, the number of cross-border mergers and acquisitions (M&As), through FDI, has gradually increased in the EU by attracting the attention of US investors during the 1960s, later during the 1990s from Japanese and Korean firms, and most recently from the People's Republic of China (PRC).[18]

10. It has been argued that the flow of Chinese FDI was also prompted by the financial crisis that afflicted the globe in 2008-2009, accompanied by the sovereign debt crisis in Europe.[19] The statistics show that Chinese

13 According to the OECD, a direct investment is *"a category of cross-border investment made by a resident in one economy (the direct investor) with the objective of establishing a lasting interest in an enterprise (the direct investment enterprise) that is resident in an economy other than that of the direct investor. The motivation of the direct investor is a strategic long-term relationship with the direct investment enterprise to ensure a significant degree of influence by the direct investor in the management of the direct investment enterprise. The 'lasting interest' is evidenced when the direct investor owns at least 10% of the voting power of the direct invest enterprise."* See OECD, Benchmark Definition of Foreign Direct Investment (BMD4) (4th edition, 2008) https://www.oecd.org/investment/fdibenchmarkdefinition.htm accessed 15 September 2023. M&A are a form of FDI in which companies either associate operations or where one company acquires stakes in another company. See Dustin Tingley and others, 'The Political Economy of Inward FDI: Opposition to Chinese Mergers and Acquisitions' (2015) 8(1) Chinese Journal of International Politics 27, 28.

14 See OECD, FDI Regulatory Restrictiveness Index (2018) https://www.oecd.org/investment/fdiindex.htm accessed 16 August 2023; European Commission, Communication 'Towards a Comprehensive European International Investment Policy' COM (2010) 343 final, 3-4.

15 European Commission, 'Reflection Paper on Harnessing Globalisation' (2017) 8, https://commission.europa.eu/publications/reflection-paper-harnessing-globalisation_en accessed 15 September 2023.

16 Catherine Titi, 'International Investment Law and the European Union: Towards a New Generation of International Investment Agreements' (2015) 26(3) European Journal of International Law 639.

17 Stephan W. Schill, 'The European Union's Foreign Direct Investment Screening Paradox: Tightening Inward Investment Control to Further External Investment Liberalization' (2019) Amsterdam Law School Legal Studies Research Paper No. 2019-17, 10-11; see also Articles 119 and 206 TFEU.

18 Carlos Esplugues, 'Towards a Common Screening System of Foreign Direct Investment on National Interest Grounds in the European Union' (2018) 11(2) Culture, Media and Entertainment Law 3, https://ssrn.com/abstract=3267386 accessed 15 September 2023.

19 Sophie Meunier, '"Beggars Can't Be Choosers": The European Crisis and Chinese Direct Investment in the European Union'(2014) 36(3) Journal of European Integration 283, 284.

investment expanded by 155 per cent between 2009 and 2011. By 2012 China became one of the most important investors in Germany and by 2012 Europe was the most attractive destination for Chinese outbound FDI.[20] This staggering surge raised concerns among different stakeholders, who were suspicious that this foreign control would compromise the national security of the member states and their degree of control over key sectors.[21] In response, some member states introduced some measures aiming to interfere with Community dimension transactions, a reaction that was described as a "renaissance of protectionism."[22] Under the EC merger Regulation (EUMR), the European Commission (hereafter the Commission or the EC) has exclusive jurisdiction to review Community dimension transactions,[23] which correspond to those that satisfy the thresholds indicated in Article 1(2)[24] or (3) EUMR[25] or referred to the Commission pursuant Article 4(5)[26] or 22[27] EUMR. Notably, Article 21(3) EUMR provides that *"No Member State shall apply its national legislation on competition to any concentration that has a Community dimension,"* (known as the "exclusivity principle") which contrasts with the competence that member states enjoy with regard to concentrations that do not have a Community dimension.[28] This Community dimension or supranational jurisdiction was adopted under the presumption that it would offer some benefits to the firms operating in the European single market, such as a one-stop shop, the prevalence of long-term policy objectives rather than the short-term

20 Ibid.

21 Alison Jones and John Davies, 'Merger Control and the Public Interest: Balancing EU and National Law in the Protectionist Debate' (2014) 10(3) European Competition Journal 453, 455.

22 Neelie Kroes, 'European competition policy facing a renaissance of protectionism – which strategy for the future?' (St Gallen International Competition Law Forum, St Gallen, 11 May 2007) https://ec.europa.eu/commission/presscorner/detail/en/SPEECH_07_301 accessed 15 September 2023.

23 Article 21(2) EUMR, states that the Commission 'shall have sole jurisdiction' to control the compatibility of concentrations of a Community dimension.

24 Article 1(2) EUMR indicates that a concentration has a Community dimension where: (a) the combine aggregate worldwide turnover of all the undertakings concerned is more than EUR 5,000 million, and (b) the aggregate Community-wide turnover of each of at least two of the undertakings concerned is more than EUR 250 million.

25 Article 1(3) EUMR provides that a concentration that does not meet the thresholds laid down in paragraph 2 has Community decision where: (a) the combined aggregate worldwide turnover of all the undertakings concerned is more than EUR 2500 million; (b) in each of at least three Member States, the combined aggregate turnover of all undertakings concerned is more than EUR 100 million; (c) in each of at least three Member States included for the purpose of point (b), the aggregate turnover of each of at least two of the undertakings concerned is more than EUR 25 million; and (d) the aggregate Community-wide turnover of each of at least two of the undertakings concerned is more than EUR 100 million. Unless each of the undertakings concerned achieves more than two-thirds of its aggregate Community-wide turnover with one and the same Member State (known as the 'two-thirds rule').

26 Article 4(5) EUMR refers to a mechanism for merging parties to make a reasoned submission that the Commission should review the concentration which does not have a Community dimension, and which is capable of being examined under the national competition laws of at least three Member States.

27 Article 22 EUMR gives power to the Commission to examine a concentration without Community dimension when one or more Member States request the Commission to examine any concentration as defined in Article 3 that does not have a Community dimension within the meaning of Article 1 but affects trade between Member States and threatens to significantly affect competition within the territory of the Member State or States making the request.

28 Article 21(1) EUMR. As a general rule, the national law only applies to concentrations which do not have Community dimension.

inclinations of Member States, and the fact that a supranational institution would develop capacity expertise in a more quick and efficient manner, among others.[29]

11. In the EU regime, Article 21 of the EU Merger Regulation allows Member States to adopt, with regard to concentrations with an EU dimension, measures to protect certain interests other than competition, as long as these measures are necessary and proportionate to their aim and compatible with EU law. Article 21 EUMR distinguishes between "recognised interests" – namely security of supply, plurality of the media, and prudential rules, all of which are considered prima facie legitimate – and "other public interests", which require an ex ante review by the Commission.

12. Examples of Member States attempting to intervene under Article 21 in the Commission's review of a proposed merger include the following:

    - Spain cited Article 21 as justification for imposing certain conditions on E.ON's bid for Endesa (*Case COMP/M.4110*), as well as on Enel and Acciona's bid for Endesa (*Case COMP/M.4685*), although both transactions had already been cleared unconditionally by the Commission.

    - Poland imposed divestment conditions on the *Unicredito/HVB* merger (*Case COMP/M.3894*) under Article 21, despite the fact that the full transaction had already been authorised by the Commission.

    - Italy cited Article 21 as justification for refusing to authorise the *Abertis/Autostrade* merger (*Case COMP/M.4249*), based on public concerns unrelated to competition law. This occurred during the Commission's review of the transaction, which was subsequently cleared.

13. Almost all Member States[30] have screening mechanisms in place or have initiated the introduction of screening mechanisms (except Cyprus and Bulgaria) to assess non-competition law considerations of concentrations. Moreover, the existing screening mechanisms are characterised by differences in scope and procedure: some operate ex-ante, some ex-post; notification can be voluntary or mandatory; general/sectoral coverage; companies/assets; applicable to investments from other Member States and third countries or third countries only, etc.[31]

14. The Commission published a Regulation in 2021 in order to establish a framework for the Member States, and in certain cases the Commission, to screen foreign direct investments in the European Union, while allowing Member States to take into account of their individual situations and national

29 Michael Harker, 'Cross-Border Mergers in the EU: The Commission v the Member States' (2003) 3(2) European Competition Journal 503, 507.

30 European Commission, Staff Working Document accompanying the Proposal for a Regulation establishing a framework for screening of foreign direct investments in the European Union, SWD (2017) 297, 2.

31 Ibid.

circumstances.[32] The Regulation provides that the Commission may carry out a screening on grounds of security and public order, in case where a foreign direct investment may affect projects or programmes of Union interest.

15. In addition, an EU Commission has taken further concrete steps to screen certain foreign direct investments into the EU.[33] It accompanies a proposal for the abovementioned Regulation that establishes a framework to screen foreign direct investments from third countries on grounds of security and public order in the EU, together with a cooperation mechanism among Member States as well as a framework for screening at the EU level.

III. The approach to the assessment of national security in the United Kingdom

16. In the UK, prior to the entry into force of the Enterprise Act, mergers were reviewed under a broad public interest test. With the adoption of the Enterprise Act in 2002, two significant changes took place. Firstly, the primacy of a competition-based test was stated. Secondly, a list of public interest considerations that could be taken into account in merger assessment was included in the Act. The UK merger control regime allows for intervention in mergers by the Secretary of State on national security and media plurality grounds; also, there is a safeguard procedure, under which ministers can give notice of an additional public interest ground, if it happens to arise in a particular case, and seek the approval of the parliament to use it. The Secretary of State can also intervene in a very limited number of cases on public interest grounds where the jurisdictional thresholds are not met.

17. In one of the most recent cases where national security considerations were, Hytera's proposed acquisition of digital radio manufacturer Sepura invoked a public interest intervention notice on national security grounds. There have been six more such interventions on national security grounds including defence mergers General Dynamics/Alvis, Finmeccanica/ AgustaWestland, Finmeccanica/BAE Systems, Lockheed Martin/Insys and General Electric/Smiths Aerospace under the

---

32 The specific objectives to be achieved are the following:

- provide a coherent framework to screen foreign direct investment in the EU on grounds of security or public order, without impinging on Member States' national prerogatives;
- facilitate close and systematic cooperation among Member States and between Member States and the Commission with regard to the screening of certain foreign direct investment when these raise security or public order concerns, including strengthened exchange of information;
- increase transparency of foreign direct investment that may have an impact on security or public order;
- effectively address cases of foreign direct investment raising security or public order concerns in relation to projects or programmes of Union interest;
- prevent circumvention of national foreign direct investment screening mechanisms.

33 European Commission, Communication 'Welcoming Foreign Direct Investment while Protecting Essential Interests' COM (2017) 494 final.

pre existing national security regime. Those transactions were ultimately cleared by the Office of Fair Trading after the parties offered remedies.

18. In a recent significant legislative development,[34] the UK government has expanded its national security regime. It followed the example of other developed countries and make more substantive changes to how it scrutinises the national security implications of foreign investment. The reforms have a particular focus on ensuring adequate scrutiny of whether significant foreign investment in critical businesses raises any national security concerns and providing the ability to act in circumstances where this might be the case. The expectation is that the need to act would be relatively rare, but the risk that this can turn into a tool to implement industrial policy considerations does exist.

19. The reforms are concerned only with national security, and arguably are designed to be focused and proportionate in their scope and application. The reforms in the UK regime include:

   - an expanded version of the 'call-in' power, modeled on the existing power within the Enterprise Act 2002, to allow Government to scrutinise a broader range of transactions for national security concerns within a voluntary notification regime and/or;
   - a mandatory notification regime for foreign investment into the provision of a focused set of 'essential functions' in key parts of the economy. Mandatory notification could also be required for new projects that could reasonably be expected in future to provide essential functions and/or foreign investment in specific businesses or assets.

IV. The approach to the assessment of national security in United States of America

20. The Committee on Foreign Investment in the United States (CFIUS) is an inter-agency committee authorized to review transactions that could result in the control of a U.S. business by a foreign person in order to determine the effect of such transactions on the national security of the United States. During the review period, CFIUS members examine the transaction in order to identify and address, as appropriate, any national security concerns that arise as a result of the transaction. CFIUS can decide within an initial 30-day review period but in certain circumstances CFIUS may initiate a subsequent investigation,

34 Department for Business, Energy and Industrial Strategy (BEIS), 'National Security and Infrastructure Investment Review: The Government's Review of the National Security Implications of Foreign Ownership or Control' (October 2017) https://www.gov.uk/government/uploads/system/uploads/attachment_data/file/652505/2017_10_16_NSII_Green_Paper_final.pdf accessed 15 September 2023.

which must be completed within 45 days.[35] These deadlines affect the timing of the approval of transactions.

21. If CFIUS finds that the covered transaction does not present any national security risks or that other provisions of law provide adequate and appropriate authority to address the risks, then CFIUS will advise the parties in writing. If CFIUS finds that a covered transaction presents national security risks and that other provisions of law do not provide adequate authority to address the risks, then CFIUS may enter into an agreement with, or impose conditions on, parties to mitigate such risks or may refer the case to the President for action.

22. Where CFIUS has completed all action with respect to a covered transaction or the President has announced a decision not to exercise his authority with respect to the covered transaction, then the parties receive a "safe harbor" with respect to that transaction.

V. The approach to the assessment of national security in China

23. Since the Chinese Antimonopoly law (AML) came into force in 2008, the Ministry of Commerce (MOFCOM, which changed to the State Administration for Market Regulation, SAMR now) has reviewed over 750 merger cases. Separate to the AML and to merger control enforcement by SAMR, all foreign investment in China is subject to discretionary approval by MOFCOM or one of its local branches. In some sectors, special regulatory approvals may be required by other administrative agencies as well. Foreign investment is also regulated on a sector-by-sector basis by MOFCOM as outlined in the Foreign Investment Industrial Guidance Catalogue, which has periodically been revised in recent years. Under the Foreign Investment Industrial Guidance Catalogue, some sectors are closed to foreign investment or subject to foreign ownership restrictions, while foreign investment in certain industries is encouraged through preferential policies.[36]

24. The approval that needs to be considered under the national security review regime, is relevant if the transaction involves the military sector (including enterprises located near key and sensitive military facilities and other enterprises active in connection with national defence), key agricultural products, as well as sectors involving key energy infrastructure, transport, technology and equipment manufacturing, and the transaction will result in the acquisition of 'actual control' by the foreign investor over the Chinese domestic business. If a transaction needs to be reviewed on national security grounds,

35 CFIUS may also refer a transaction to the President for decision and the President has to announce a decision with respect to a transaction within 15 days of CFIUS's completion of the investigation.

36 Yuxin Shen and others, 'The Foreign Investment Regulation Review: China' (The Law Reviews, 21 October 2022) https://thelawreviews.co.uk/title/the-foreign-investment-regulation-review/china accessed 15 September 2023.

it will be conducted by an inter-Ministerial Committee, which will be led by the National Development and Reform Commission (NDRC) as well as MOFCOM (the Committee).

25. The following four main types of structures are caught:

- A foreign investor acquires equity interests in a non-foreign-invested enterprise in China («Domestic Enterprise»), or subscribes for an increase in the registered capital of a Domestic Enterprise, thereby converting the Domestic Enterprise into an FIE.
- A foreign investor acquires the equity interests of the Chinese shareholder in an foreign-invested enterprise ("FIE") in China, or subscribes to an increase in the capital of such enterprise.
- A foreign investor establishes an FIE and agrees by contract to acquire and operate the assets of a Domestic Enterprise through such FIE; or the foreign investor acquires equity interests in a Domestic Enterprise through such FIE.
- A foreign investor directly acquires the assets of a Domestic Enterprise and uses such assets to invest in, and establish, an FIE to operate said assets.

26. In addition, the Rules on Mergers with and Acquisitions of Domestic Enterprises by Foreign Investors (the M&A Rules) also require a notification to MOFCOM where a transaction will result in a foreign investor obtaining a controlling equity interest in a domestic Chinese enterprise under any of the following circumstances:

- the domestic target operates in a 'key industry';
- the transaction has an impact on state 'economic security'; or
- the domestic target possesses a well-known trademark or established Chinese brand.

27. Under the Security Review Circular,[37] whether a proposed M&A transaction constitutes a threat to national security will be determined by looking at its potential impact on the following:

- The production and supply of products and services and the relevant facilities necessary for national defence within China;
- National economic stability;
- Order within society;
- China's ability to research and develop key technologies relating to national security.[38]

---

37 General Office of the State Council of China, Circular on Security Review System of Merger and Acquisition by Foreign Investors (3 February 2011) https://investmentpolicy.unctad.org/investment-laws/laws/229/china-circular-on-security-review-system-of-merger-and-acquisition-by-foreign-investors accessed 15 September 2023.

38 Lehman Brown, 'China's New National Security Review Procedures for Mergers and Acquisitions Involving Foreign Investors' (18 March 2011) https://www.lehmanbrown.com/wp-content/uploads/2014/12/Insights-2011-4.pdf accessed 15 September 2023.

28. The national security review is conducted in two phases: a 'general review' (Phase I), which lasts up to 30 working days and a 'special review' (Phase II), which lasts up to 60 working days. Where the Committee cannot reach consensus, the transaction may be referred to the State Council for final determination, for which there is no time limit for a decision. Where the Committee determines that a transaction gives rise to national security concerns, parties may be required to abandon or (in cases where completion has already occurred) unwind the transaction, or to put in place remedial measures to address the concern.

VI. The approach to the assessment of national security in other jurisdictions: Japan, India, Russia, South Africa

29. These jurisdictions are pertinent case studies as their unique characteristics offer us the opportunity to provide some reflections. For instance, the collapse of the Soviet Union was a watershed moment for liberal thinkers, who have sought to keep governments separated from business. Despite the expectations, the Russian regime has seen in the FDI rules a right tool to advance it. Like other countries, Japan has expanded the scope of review by lowering the thresholds from 10 per cent to 1 per cent and by including more than 500 companies in 12 industries as relevant to national security. Unlike most jurisdictions, Japan has incorporated some foreign investment screening exemptions. India has crafted its national security measures grounded on land borders. This tactic was devised to protect its companies from opportunistic takeovers during the pandemic. In South Africa, a screening mechanism of foreign investments was introduced in 2018 but is not yet in force.

30. The world has experienced the effects of economic globalization, a trend once seen as irreversible.[39] Progressively this tendency that once was fervently embraced under the presumed notion that it would spur worldwide prosperity,[40] is facing increased opposition. The first signs of this wave against globalization and free markets emerged when the financial crisis of 2007-2009 hit the global economy.[41] This upheaval casted doubt on whether liberalized businesses without government oversight was a safe approach. Hence, in a synchronised manner governments responded implementing different regulations

39 Gao Shangquan, 'Economic Globalization: Trends, Risks and Risk Prevention' (2000) CDP Background Paper No. 1 https://www.un.org/en/development/desa/policy/cdp/cdp_background_papers/bp2000_1.pdf accessed 15 September 2023.

40 See Adam Smith, *An Inquiry into the Nature and Causes of the Wealth of Nations* (first published 1776, Oxford University Press 2008). In his work, Smith explains that in integrated world markets there is a better division of labor, an essential factor for technological progress that promotes global prosperity.

41 Anjan V. Thakor, 'The Financial Crisis of 2007-2009: Why Did It Happen and What Did We Learn' (2015) 4(2) Review of Corporate Finance Studies 155.

to prevent future financial crises.[42] Most recently, the debate about the virtues of globalisation have been refuelled by developed economies. As an illustration, Donald Trump during his election campaign pledged that he would raise trade barriers, withdraw from some trade agreements, limit imports, among other measures, arguing that globalization helped "the financial elite," while leaving "millions of our workers with nothing but poverty and heartache."[43] In the UK, Brexit was a clear sign that globalisation was no longer perceived as a panacea[44] and, having left the European Union, the UK sought to protect its companies from unattractive foreign investors by widening the national security rules.[45] The Covid pandemic fuelled additional protectionism especially in relation to sensitive supply chains. Similar concerns arose in countries such as Russia, South Africa, India and Japan.

VII. Some Concerns as a Conclusion

31. Protectionism is not new in trade and investment. Governments have felt compelled to intervene in the economy, specially, in times of crisis, war or pandemics. Even if there have been periods in which governments have tried to retreat from intervening and allow the markets to function freely, as during the 1990s, it is almost inevitable that they find a reason to embrace policies oriented to protect their domestic economies.

32. The line between intrusive policies and independent review of foreign M&As and FDI is now blurring. Governments and enforcement agencies have got accustomed to using restrictions on FDI based on national security concerns as an effective way to deal with geostrategic concerns and as an indirect means to promote unclear and non-transparent in some cases industrial strategy. However, it is also likely that they come to learn that they have interfered with free trade at their peril. What is needed is transparency and an adequate degree of legal certainty that will benefit all stakeholders involved.

42 For an interesting analysis of the fragmented regulatory responses see Sumit Agarwal and others, 'Inconsistent Regulators: Evidence from Banking' (2014) 129 Quarterly Journal of Economics 889.

43 Nick Corasaniti, Alexander Burns and Binyamin Appelbaum, 'Donald Trump Vows to Rip Up Trade Deals and Confront China' (New York Times, 28 June 2016) https://www.nytimes.com/2016/06/29/us/politics/donald-trump-trade-speech.html accessed 15 September 2023.

44 For a good discussion about why most British people voted for Brexit see Harold D. Clarke, Matthew Goodwin, and Paul Whiteley, *Brexit: Why Britain Voted to Leave the European Union* (Cambridge University Press 2017).

45 Liz Alderman, 'Its Eye on China, Britain Pushes Back on Foreign Takeovers' (New York Times, 24 July 2018) https://www.nytimes.com/2018/07/24/business/uk-china-takeovers-national-security.html accessed 15 September 2023. For a comprehensive overview of the legal framework that was adopted to tighten the foreign direct investment rules in the UK; and Ioannis Kokkoris, 'National Security as a Public Interest Consideration in UK Merger Control' (2021) Journal of Strategic Security 14(2) 47.

Why Competition? Voices from the Antitrust Community and Beyond

Gina Cass Gottlieb[*]
Australian Competition & Consumer Commission

I. Introduction

1. It is both an exciting and challenging time to be leading the Australian Competition and Consumer Commission (ACCC). The Australian Government and community expect the agency to be a bold and effective champion of competition and protector of consumers and small business. At the same time business expects that compliance should come without undue burden. Key to meeting their high expectations are:
   - An appreciation of the advantages and limitations of competition as a means to enhance economic efficiency and consumer welfare;
   - A focus on effective ways of working to harness the forensic strength of competition law and economics to advance the agency's objective; and
   - Periodic review and refinement of competition policy and law to ensure it remains relevant and useful for achieving economic, social and political objectives.

---

[*] Chair of the Australian Competition and Consumer Commission.

II. Competition: Its Advantages and Limitations

2. At its core competition is the process of rivalry between individual sellers to win and retain customers[1] on their merits. It is a powerful force that promotes economic efficiency and consumer welfare by aligning the profit seeking behaviour of firms with the interests of consumers.

3. In markets where competition is effective, firms pursue profits by beating rivals to supply the products and services that consumers need and want at the best price. Firms with price-product-service offerings that best meet consumers' preferences tend to prosper, while those that do not may be taken over or forced to exit if they do not improve. This spurs firms to innovate to develop new and better products and production methods in a quest to obtain a temporary advantage over rivals.

4. Absent effective competition, there may not be significant adverse consequences for firms that are not highly responsive to customers' needs and wants. Without the constraining influence of rivals, a firm may be able to profitably raise prices, restricting output, or invest less in the development of new and better products and production methods.

5. Australian competition law protects and promotes competition, not as an end in itself, but as a means to enhance the welfare of Australians.[2] Part IV of the Australian Competition and Consumer Act 2010 (CCA) deals with various restrictive trade practices that harm competition. It prohibits cartel conduct (price fixing, market sharing, output restrictions and bid-rigging) and resale price maintenance per se. It prohibits various other conduct[3] that has the purpose or effect, or would be likely have the effect, of substantially lessening competition in a market. And it prohibits mergers and acquisitions that would have the effect, or be likely to have the effect, of substantially lessening competition.

6. The ACCC is an independent statutory authority responsible for enforcing the CCA, including its competition provisions. We take this responsibility very seriously. Our concern is to preserve and promote competition on its merits across the economy. We take action where we consider that conduct or mergers are likely to substantially harm the competitive process, including by creating, protecting or extending market power. And we advocate for reforms to enhance our ability to promote competition to advance the welfare of Australians.[4]

---

1 Or between buyers to acquire from suppliers.

2 Australian Competition and Consumer Act 2010 (CCA) s 2.

3 For example, ibid s 45 is directed at contracts, arrangements or understandings between competitors that restrict dealings or affect competition not dealt with by cartel provisions, s 46 targets misuses of market power, s 47 addresses exclusive dealing, and s 48 considers resale price maintenance.

4 While the CCA does not prescribe a particular welfare standard, the ACCC typically adopts a broad interpretation of "welfare of Australians" when carrying out its functions. For example, when assessing applications for exemption of conduct or mergers from competition law under CCA Pt VII (n 8), or when recommending remedies to address market failure problems identified in market studies, we take into account factors that are commonly considered under a consumer welfare standard – eg impact on price, product

7. Core to the ACCC's work is the belief that informed and confident consumers benefit and are benefited by effective competition. Competition benefits consumers by encouraging new and better products and services, cost-reflective pricing and more choice for consumers. In turn, the purchasing decisions of well-informed consumers, acting in their own self-interest, enhance the effectiveness of competition by rewarding the firms that best meet consumers' needs and budgets.

8. We recognise that there are occasions when the competitive process, left to its own devices, may fail to maximise efficiency and consumer welfare. This can happen, for example, due to the presence of market power[5], insufficient or asymmetric information in the marketplace, positive or negative externalities[6], or public goods[7]. Any of these forms of market failure can cause misalignment between profit seeking behaviour of firms and the welfare interest of consumers.

9. The ACCC contributes to the amelioration of market failure in three important ways. First, we strive to limit the creation, entrenchment or exercise of substantial market power through mergers or business conduct captured by the CCA. Second, we grant exemptions[8] from prosecution for breaches of competition law for conduct that requires cooperation between competitors to address market failure problems where we are satisfied that the conduct is not likely to substantially lessen competition or is likely to confer public benefits that outweigh public detriment from a lessening of competition. Finally, through our market studies work we cast light on the nature and sources of market failure in various markets and identify potential solutions for consideration by government.

---

quality, product range, level of service and innovation in the relevant market(s) – as well as wider economic and social costs and benefits likely to be conferred by the conduct, merger or potential policy intervention. Enforcement of CCA Pt IV (competition) provisions requires application of a substantial lessening of competition (SLC) test, unless conduct is prohibited per se. While this test typically does not take into account wider economic and social impacts, the ACCC has discretion to not litigate conduct that we consider is likely to substantially lessen competition but nevertheless enhance the welfare of Australians.

5 A firm has market power if it can profitably raise price above the competitive level. This depends on the extent to which customers can substitute other products or sources of supply.

6 Negative externalities exist where production or consumption of a good or service imposes additional costs on others that are not captured in the decision of how much to consume or produce (eg environmental damage). Positive externalities exist where production or consumption of a good or service confers additional benefits to others that are not taken into account in the decision of how much to produce or consume (eg environmental improvement).

7 These goods are characterised by their non-excludability (ie individuals cannot easily be prevented from accessing) and non-rivalry (ie use by one person does not limit use by others). They are usually funded or provided by government (eg national defence).

8 CCA Pt VII empowers the ACCC to grant exemptions from prosecution for breaches of competition law if the agency is satisfied that the conduct or merger either is not likely to substantially lessen competition or is in the public interest because it is likely to confer public benefits that outweigh the public detriment caused by a substantial lessening of competition.

III. Alignment of Agency Objective with Ways of Working

10. The ACCC's objective mirrors that of Australian competition and consumer law: to enhance the welfare of Australians through the promotion of competition and fair trading and through the provision of consumer protection.[9]

11. My approach to fulfilling this objective and appreciation of its critical importance is inspired by the work and insights of the late Professor Maureen Brunt, first Australian woman professor of economics in 1967 and one the great early framers, decision-makers and teachers of competition law and economics in Australia and New Zealand. She was a foundation member of the Trade Practices Tribunal (now Australian Competition Tribunal) and High Court of New Zealand in competition cases.

12. Professor Brunt exhorted us "to keep our eyes on the ultimate objective, namely the protection of the consumer by means of an efficient competitive process".[10]

13. Professor Brunt stressed the importance of distinguishing between conduct that is part of the competitive process and conduct that interferes with that process. She urged investigations and judicial decision makers to ask: "What is going on here?" when faced with an allegation of anticompetitive conduct or a merger.[11] This is now a common refrain within the ACCC.

14. The ACCC has a strong CCA enforcement focus. We recognise the importance of enforcement outcomes in achieving specific and general deterrence of conduct prohibited by the CCA and in ensuring that consumers, businesses and the wider community continue to have confidence in our market economy.

15. Consistent with Professor Brunt's teachings, we take a harm-based approach to work prioritisation and decision-making. We use theories of harm to focus and inform our in-depth investigation and assessment of conduct that has the potential to substantially lessen competition. Theories of harm are a succinct and economically coherent explanation of how the conduct or merger under investigation could adversely impact competition in a relevant market. They are a hypothesis to be tested and refined through the collection and assessment of evidence by the investigating team, assisted by in-house legal and economic advisors.

16. In many cases we assess that the conduct or merger under investigation is not problematic. However, when the evidence indicates that substantial competitive harm has occurred, or is likely to occur, we take legal action. Our first

---

9 Australian Competition and Consumer Act 2010 (CCA) s 2.

10 Maureen Brunt, "Economic Essays on Australian and New Zealand Competition Law" (2003) 8 Kluwer L International 270, reprinted from 1992 *International Antirust Law and Policy Fordham Corporate Law Institute* (Barry Hawk ed., Juris Publishing).

11 For example, ibid 358.

priority is always to achieve the best possible outcome for the community and to manage risk proportionately. We are willing to test the limits of Australian competition law in court to challenge conduct that we consider substantially lessens competition and reduces welfare.

17. In some cases, we may have a competition concern but insufficient evidence or agency resources to take action. In such cases the ACCC usually will engage with business executives to inform them of our concerns. In our experience they often choose to cease or modify the conduct to remove harm so as to avoid the distraction and reputational consequences of ACCC scrutiny.

18. Like many modern competition agencies, our toolkit has evolved beyond traditional competition law enforcement and merger assessment so that we may advocate more widely and effectively for competition and foster awareness of how business conduct may harm competition. In addition to expertise in competition law and economics, this requires skills in critical thinking, public policy formulation, data analytics and different styles of communication. It also requires openness to criticism and better ideas.

IV. Ensuring Competition Policy and Law Remains Relevant and Useful

19. For competition policy and law to remain relevant and useful in achieving economic, social and political objectives it must be flexible and evolve to address revealed shortcomings and meet new challenges. This requires periodic review of the effectiveness of existing competition policy and law, pre-emptive identification of looming challenges, and design of effective solutions and refinements that do not unnecessarily compromise the benefits of competition.

20. Some of the largest and most complex challenges we face today in Australia, and globally, stem from generational shifts in our economy and society, such as the move to a more environmentally sustainable future, continuing expansion of digital platforms and use of artificial intelligence, and increased demand for care and support services that are more responsive to the needs of recipients.

21. Past reviews of competition policy and law in Australia have resulted in significant and enduring reforms to harness the benefits of competition. For example, the 1993 Hilmer Review resulted in reform to apply nationally consistent competition conduct rules to market participants regardless of ownership and legal structure, established a national access regime for essential infrastructure, bound governments to the provision of competition law as if they were carrying on a business, and introduced the welfare object clause into Australian competition law. It also brought different levels of government together to agree how they would work together to remove unnecessary regulatory barriers to competition and implement other reforms. The 2015 Harper Review resulted in various refinements to simplify and improve competition

law, including amendments to misuse of market power and concerted practices provisions.

22. In August 2023, the Australian Government announced a further review to advise government on how to improve competition across the economy. A taskforce has been established within the Australian Department of Treasury to conduct the review over two years. Initial issues to be considered by the Taskforce include merger reform, the net zero transformation, and the care economy.[12] Reforms to protect and promote competition in digital markets are being dealt with in a separate process. The ACCC is an active contributor to these processes.

1. The Need for Reform of Merger Laws in Australia

23. A strong and effective merger regime is essential for the maintenance of competitive markets. It protects the underlying conditions necessary for competition to thrive, while allowing for business renewal and reinvigoration.

24. Most mergers do not raise significant competition concerns and can be beneficial to the extent that they allow firms to achieve efficiencies, diversify risk or enter new markets. However, some have the potential to significantly alter the competitive process in ways that reduce economic efficiency and consumer welfare.

25. The ACCC is concerned that existing merger laws do not allow the agency to properly scrutinise and, when necessary, prevent mergers that are likely to substantially lessen competition. This may be contributing to increased market concentration and market power in Australia. Recent research indicates that Australia is experiencing an overall increase in industry concentration[13] that is correlated with increasing firm mark-ups.[14] The research suggests that the higher mark-ups are more likely to be caused by a decline in competition than the increased stature of more efficient firms.[15] This is a concerning development as it suggests – to paraphrase Professor Brunt – that firms in these more concentrated markets are able to give less and charge more but still retain their grip on the market.

26. Unlike many other jurisdictions, in Australia there is no legal requirement for merger parties to notify the ACCC of proposed mergers and acquisitions or to wait for ACCC clearance before completing the transaction. In instances where

12 Australian Treasury Portfolio Ministers, Press Release, "A More Dynamic and Competitive Economy" (23 August 2023) <https://ministers.treasury.gov.au/ministers/jim-chalmers-2022/media-releases/more-dynamic-and-competitive-economy#:~:text=The%20review%20will%20look%20at,of%20living%20and%20boost%20wages> accessed 24 January 2024.

13 Sasan Bakhtiari, "Trends in Market Concentration of Australian Industries" (2021) 54 Australian Economic Rev 57–75 <https://www.industry.gov.au/sites/default/files/2019-09/trends-in-market-concentration-of-australian-industries.pdf> accessed 24 January 2024.

14 Jonathan Hambur, "Product Market Power and its Implications for the Australian Economy" (2021) Treasury Working Paper 2021/3 <https://treasury.gov.au/sites/default/files/2021-06/p2021-177591_product_market_power_implications_0.pdf> accessed 24 January 2024.

15 Ibid.

the ACCC considers a merger to be anticompetitive, and the merger parties do not voluntarily abandon the transaction or offer remedies that address the ACCC's competition concerns, the agency must take action in the Federal Court to seek orders to prevent or unwind the transaction. This places a high burden of proof on the competition regulator. Since merger law is forward looking, to prove a breach of competition law we must establish in court that the merger is likely to have the effect of substantially lessening competition in the future. The future is inherently uncertain. In situations where there is significant uncertainty about the future, markets are dynamic and there are complex commercial considerations, the ACCC can find it very difficult to positively prove a breach.

27. In our assessment, the weaknesses inherent in a voluntary system with enforcement through court action are increasingly evident.

28. First, when merger parties do not notify the ACCC it is difficult for the agency to take a harm-based approach that prioritises preserving competitive market structures and promoting competition in markets where there is a high risk of entrenching market power.

29. Second, we are increasingly finding that businesses that voluntarily notify the ACCC of proposed transactions are providing late, incomplete or incorrect information. More are threatening to complete their transaction before we have finalised our review. Increasingly we are put in the position of having to negotiate with the merger parties to obtain sufficient information and time to conduct our review. In global transactions we find that the merger parties will often prioritise filings and engagement with regulators in other jurisdictions with mandatory clearance regimes over our voluntary regime.

30. Third, in situations where there is great uncertainty about the future and difficulties in positively proving in court that a merger is anticompetitive, the default position becomes to permit, or not to oppose the merger. In our view, the balance under the current regime is shifted too much toward avoiding the risk of opposing a benign merger at the expense of increased risk of enabling anticompetitive mergers. It is the public rather than the merger parties that bear this risk.

31. We have made submissions to government proposing that Australia's current merger regime be replaced with a formal clearance model, where merger parties must demonstrate to the satisfaction of the ACCC (or the Australian Competition Tribunal on review) that their transaction is not likely to substantially lessen competition before they can proceed. We also propose that the government make it mandatory for merger parties to notify the ACCC of mergers above specified thresholds, require transactions to be suspended from completion without ACCC clearance, and introduce compulsory upfront information requirements. We envisage that merger parties should still have the option to apply for clearance on public interest grounds, as they can under the current regime, if they are not able to

first satisfy the ACCC or Tribunal that the transaction can be cleared on competition grounds.[16]

2. Ex-ante Regulation in Digital Markets to Protect and Promote Competition

32. There are great opportunities and challenges as the global economy moves forward in the digital age. Existing markets are rapidly transforming and new markets are continually emerging. In this dynamic environment we observe a variety of business practices and conduct that are shaping the structure of digital markets and the nature of future competition.

33. Through our enforcement work and five-year Digital Platform Services Inquiry, the ACCC has gained deep insight into the state of competition in markets for the supply of digital platform services, including online private messaging services, app marketplace services, web browser services, search engine services, general online retail marketplace services, social media services and data broking services.

34. We have documented concerning increases in market concentration and business practices that may be conferring enduring market power in these markets that is not in the interest of consumers. These practices include anticompetitive self-preferencing, unnecessary restrictions on interoperability, exclusive pre-installation agreements, poor information disclosure to consumers, practices that limit consumers' ability to switch between services or devices and denial of competitor access to essential technological infrastructure.

35. In 2022 we formed the view that current competition and consumer law in Australia is not, by itself, well suited to addressing these issues and called for stronger safeguards to minimise harm and promote trust and confidence. To address competition issues, the ACCC recommended that government introduce mandatory codes of conduct for designated digital platforms. We recommended that:

    – Codes should be based on legislated principles to allow flexibility to tailor obligations to address the competition issues relevant to each service as they change over time.

    – Decisions about which digital platforms should fall within the scope of these codes should have regard to the platform service provider's market power, number of Australian users, and Australian and/or global revenue.

    – Codes should include specific obligations to address anticompetitive tying, exclusive pre-installation and default agreements that hinder

16 This article was prepared in January 2024. In April 2024, the Australian Government announced a policy decision supporting reform to the Australian merger control system and introduced legislation into the Parliament to implement this reform. As of 6 November 2024 we await passage of the legislation through Parliament.

competition, impediments to consumer switching, impediments to interoperability, data-related barriers to entry and expansion (where privacy impacts can be managed), lack of transparency, unfair dealings with business users (particularly in respect of intellectual property), and anticompetitive exclusivity and price parity clauses in contracts with business users (eg clauses preventing businesses from selling through other channels or at different prices).

– Codes should also take into account any potential reasons why such conduct occurs, including how, in some circumstances, it may provide a net benefit to consumers.

36. The Australian Government has recently released a statement[17] that it supports these recommendations in principle and the Treasury Department is undertaking consultation on potential reforms.

3. Protecting and Promoting Competition during the Transition to an Environmentally Sustainable Future

37. Consumers are increasingly factoring the environmental credentials of suppliers and products into their purchasing decisions and are often willing to pay more for sustainable practices.

38. False, misleading and vague claims about sustainability credentials can cause the competitive process to break down by enabling firms to earn higher profit without contributing to more sustainable environmental outcomes and undermining consumer trust in the integrity of sustainability claims. Both reduce incentives for firms to participate in the transition to become a more sustainable economy.

39. We recently conducted an internet sweep of sustainability claims by businesses, which highlighted several problems in the way some businesses are marketing their environmental credentials. We found that 57% of businesses reviewed in the sweep made concerning claims about their environmental credentials. The cosmetic, clothing and footwear, and food and drink industries were found to have the highest proportion of concerning claims among the industries targeted in the operation.

40. Our focus on sustainability issues extends beyond greenwashing. We closely monitor for collusion and other anticompetitive conduct as the green transition unfolds to prevent such practices from distorting market incentives and investment signals. We undertake careful assessment of mergers in industries transitioning to more environmentally sustainable outcomes to ensure that they benefit from competition. And on occasions where it is likely to be

17 Assistant Treasurer and Minister for Financial Services (Stephen Jones) and Minister for Communications (Michelle Rowland), Joint Press Release, "Government's response to the ACCC's major competition and consumer recommendations for digital platforms" https://ministers.treasury.gov.au/ministers/stephen-jones-2022/media-releases/governments-response-acccs-major-competition-and accessed 24 January 2024.

more efficient and effective for firms to work together to pursue sustainability initiatives – for example, to overcome first mover disadvantage and free rider problems which otherwise could result in underinvestment in sustainability initiatives from society's perspective – we can exempt such cooperation from prosecution for breach of competition law if satisfied that it confers public benefits that outweigh public detriment associated with a loss of competition.

V. Conclusion

41. The ACCC plays a key role in protecting and promoting competition because competitive markets are important for the welfare of all Australians. We use the forensic strength of competition (antitrust) economic and legal analysis to cast light on the competitive conditions in markets and the harms caused by business conduct and mergers and inform the design of remedies to help address the critical economic, social and political issues we face. In the words of Professor Maureen Brunt:

42. "In my view the path to wisdom in antitrust work lies in recognising and emphasising the essential character of antitrust law as economic law. If antitrust is to be relevant and socially useful, the very fabric of the law must have mixed economic-legal content, with due attention given to both terms… most obviously antitrust law is a type of regulatory law directed to achieving economic and associated social and political objectives…".[18]

---

18 Brunt (n 10) 354.

Competition in Troubled Times*

Jonathan Faull**
Brunswick Group

1. It has become a commonplace and an understatement that competition policy today faces new challenges, opportunities and dangers. I will focus in what follows on competition policy in the broad sense as it is understood in Europe, encompassing antitrust, mergers and state aid. The digital economy, climate emergency, Brexit, populism, trade tensions and now Covid-19 all come together to shake the foundations of a consensus carefully established over the last fifty years.
2. While there have always been schools of thought, paradoxes, ruptures and disagreements in this field, it does seem that intellectual ferment, political impatience and questioning of the traditional roles of key protagonists (institutions, courts, lawyers, economists) are reaching a crescendo unprecedented in recent times.[1]
3. In the European Union, and I expect in other jurisdictions with which I am less familiar too, there has never been a uniform view about the purposes and details of competition policy. Courts, authorities, practitioners and academics have always had to take account of political mood changes expressed, in democracies, through the mechanisms of accountability, institutional interactions and appointments. One does not need to be a legal archaeologist to identify traces of yesterday's battles in today's treaty articles, regulations and other provisions. To name but a few:
4. What does "technical or economic progress"[2] mean in 2020, whatever it meant in 1957?

---

* This article has been previously published in Concurrences, and it might have been edited for clarity and cohesion. Jonathan Faull, Competition in troubled times, September 2020, Concurrences N° 3-2020, Art. N° 95098.

** Chair, European Public Affairs, Brunswick Group, Brussels. Former Director General, European Commission, Brussels. Writing in a personal capacity.

1 See, e.g., R. Pitofsky, The Political Content of Antitrust, 127 *University of Pennsylvania Law Review* 1051–1075 (1979); T. Calvani and J. Stewart-Teitelbaum, Introduction, 65(2) *The Antitrust Bulletin* 199–207 (2020).

2 Article 101(3) TFEU.

5. In today's and tomorrow's world, what is an undertaking "entrusted with the operation of services of general economic interest"?[3]

6. What is "aid to promote the execution of an important project of common European interest or to remedy a serious disturbance in the economy of a Member State"?[4] Who decides on the common interest and what constitutes a serious disturbance?

7. In the EU Merger Regulation, the familiar but still elusive words "technical and economic progress"[5] are included among the criteria of which the Commission must take account in its "appraisal of concentrations": "the development of technical and economic progress provided that it is to consumers' advantage and does not form an obstacle to competition". Why is the EU Merger Regulation (Article 24) so concerned about "relations with third countries" that it requires that "[t]he Member States shall inform the Commission of any general difficulties encountered by their undertakings with concentrations (…) in a third country" and sets up a reporting mechanism on such difficulties?

8. Why is that concern still prevalent in 2020, thirty years after the Merger Regulation entered into force? The Commission's 2020 Work Programme announced: "We also need to ensure fair competition and the level playing field in the global market. A White Paper on an Instrument on Foreign Subsidies will reflect on possible new tools to address the distortive effects of foreign subsidies in the single market. This will help prepare the ground for a legislative proposal in 2021".

9. As European Commission Vice-President and Competition Commissioner Margrethe Vestager said in a recent speech, "right now, we're working on new powers to protect fair competition – powers that would allow us to deal, for example, with the harm that foreign subsidies and state ownership can do to competition in Europe. By the end of June, we plan to publish a White Paper, to get input on our ideas for how these new powers could work".[6]

I. Competition Here or There?

10. One such "distortive" effect may occur when a subsidised, state-owned or state-backed foreign company seeks to acquire a European company. This is not an entirely novel consideration and it applies even when both companies involved in a merger are foreign. Thus, in 1997, when the European Commission scrutinised Boeing's purchase of McDonnell Douglas, it paid close attention to the advantages the merged entity would have as a result

---

3 Article 106(2) TFEU.

4 Article 107(3)(b).

5 Note that the conjunction "*or*" has been replaced by "*and*".

6 Keeping the EU competitive in a green and digital world, College of Europe, Bruges, 2 March 2020.

of "much greater access to R&D which is funded by the US Department of Defense (DoD), the National Aeronautics and Space Administration (NASA) or other public bodies". The Commission approved the merger once it had secured commitments relating to licensing of government-funded patents and transparency of research and development funding.[7]

11. Given the interplay between law, politics, economics and trade, it is not surprising that there is no science of competition policy ready to be handed over to artificially intelligent algorithms fed with rules and case law, armed with theories of harm and the econometrics needed to apply them. Equally unsurprisingly, calls to change competition law are met with dire warnings about the time it could take to prise open Pandora's box and the dangers lurking inside it, coupled with reassuring references to the flexibility of the language of the law.

12. Some issues are specific to individual jurisdictions and their particular laws and politics, while others are of universal concern. Among the latter is the age-old question of market definition. Peering into the microscope, we adjust the focus until we see clearly who is competing with whom (or is foreseeably likely to do so soon) and where they are doing it (or are foreseeably likely to be doing it soon). Then we can begin our analysis of the effect of whatever we are investigating on the competitive space we have identified.

13. Is that market definition method flexible enough to bear the strain of the policy it serves or to respond to the concerns some wish to associate with the policy? A frequent argument here is the relevance or otherwise of competitive advantages, including subsidies and entry barriers, in the separate, usually foreign, market from which one of the parties comes. This, as seen above with reference to Article 24 of the EU Merger Regulation, is not a novel concern. A Martian company seeks to merge with a Belgian one. The initial focus is rightly on Belgium. But what's happening back on Mars? How relevant is that? If the roles were reversed, could the Belgian company enter the Martian market? Does the Martian company have support from its government bolstering its domestic position and giving it the firepower to maraud on other planets? Should the competition authorities responsible for what happens in Belgium worry only about the prices offered to Belgian consumers or add concerns about where what they consume is made, opportunities for Belgian companies in foreign markets and the sovereignty of Belgium or the European Union to which it belongs? In other words, is it legitimate to oppose a merger or subject its approval to conditions on the grounds that a foreign party's home market is impenetrable? Or that the domestic party's activities are deemed "strategic" and must remain located in the domestic territory? If the competition authorities take a narrow view of their responsibilities, to whom are they accountable and what other authority can deal with wider issues?

7 OJ L336, 8.12.1997, pp. 16–47, paras. 83, 114 et seq.

14. In addition to the legal and economic analyses which underpin competition policy, we also need an understanding of political science and the incentives and interests of agencies and professions involved in enforcement and administration. Why did the European Commission use competition law to deal with telecom liberalisation, airline deregulation, taxation of the tech sector, transfer pricing and bank resolution? Why did some other competition authorities not follow suit? Why are courts prominent in some jurisdictions and less so in others? What is the role of parliaments in competition policy? Merely to make the laws and then sit back and watch them being applied, or to set parameters for enforcement of the rules? To whom are competition authorities accountable?

II. Into the Breach

15. Should competition authorities step into breaches left open by other policy inadequacies or the lack of requisite regulatory power at what they judge to be the relevant level of authority? Does it matter whether the competition authority is or is not independent of other government structures?

16. To take a recent example, if bank resolution rules are missing, should state aid rules be used to approve state support with conditions resembling those for which legislation might have been provided had it been enacted in time? In the absence of tax rules at EU level, should a country's favourable tax arrangements for a company in return for local investment be dealt with as a distortion of competition within the EU's "single" market?

17. These considerations go beyond arguments about what parameters of competition should be included in the traditional analysis of competitive effects. Output, price, research and development, innovation, nipping future competitors in the bud, predatory behaviour and foreclosure are all legitimate concerns. Can new theories of harm be developed to deal with concerns about competitiveness as they emerge, or re-emerge, into political consciousness?

18. We are in a time of flux in which answers to these questions are urgently needed and will not be the same in 2025 as they would have been in 2015. Competition policy will have an important role to play in the sustainable reconstruction of post-confinement economies.

19. It is not possible to bring protagonists from all over the world together to debate these issues at the moment. Learned journals open to all relevant disciplines should encourage debate as a matter of urgency. A paradigm shift will be welcomed by some, feared by others: a greater danger is the adoption of different paradigms in different jurisdictions, encouraging fragmentation and protectionism.

Is it Time for Competition Authorities to Modernize Their Vision of the Consumer?*

FRANÇOIS LÉVÊQUE
Mines-ParisTech University PSL

1. Is it not time to modernize and make more complex the competition authorities' vision of the consumer? To follow in the footsteps of economic theory, whose conceptions now go far beyond the figure of the consumer *homo œconomicus*?

2. The implementation of competition law gives priority to the consumer's interest. To do so, it relies on various concepts and models of economic analysis: demand function, heterogeneity of preferences, estimation of consumer surplus, etc. These instruments are very useful but correspond to a limited vision of consumer behavior, that of an economic agent sovereign in his tastes, looking at the market and the market. These instruments are very useful, but they correspond to a limited vision of consumer behavior, that of an economic agent who is sovereign in his tastes, who looks far ahead, weighs the risks and relentlessly maximizes his satisfaction. His only constraint is budgetary. He can never make bad choices; he can never make decisions that harm him.

* This article has been previously published in Concurrences, and it might have been edited for clarity and cohesion. François Lévêque, Is it time for competition authorities to modernize their vision of the consumer?, May 2022, Concurrences N° 2-2022, Art. N° 106117.

I. Behavioral economics and the economics of happiness

3. For more than half a century, however, economic analysis has not ceased to revise this conception of a perfect consumer and to broaden its horizons in order to understand behaviours that do not fit with the neoclassical theory of consumer choice. Let us mention a few names and works: Herbert Simon, the only double winner of the equivalent of the Nobel Prize in economics and the Turing Prize in computer science, and his model of bounded rationality (1955), a model that takes into account the limited nature of human cognitive capacities; Daniel Kahneman and Amos Tversky highlighting the biases of our appreciation of risks (1974) and the notion of utility based on experience; Richard Thaler proposing a positive theory of consumer choice (1983). Economic analysis has thus gradually opened up to psychology, particularly experimental psychology. It now allows it to detect and understand consumer behaviour that is closer to reality, whether it is seen as an anomaly in the model of perfect rationality or whether perfect rationality itself is finally considered an exception.

4. In another vein, let us also mention the work of the economics of happiness, a branch of economics that developed from the 1970s onwards. In simpler terms, this subdiscipline proposes a measure of subjective well-being by asking individuals whether they are satisfied with their lives on the whole, for example on an increasing satisfaction scale from 0 to 10. It then seeks to establish how this index varies according to the wealth of the country and the individual's income, and then also according to numerous other variables such as age, level of education, family situation, number of friends, etc. The economics of happiness has highlighted the lack of self-control of individuals, a lack that prevents the correct consideration of the long-term effects of their decisions. It allows for a better understanding of many phenomena of overconsumption, such as the excessive amount of time spent watching television or other screens, an overconsumption that ultimately reduces individual well-being.

5. I feel that taking into account these advances in economic analysis could be useful in a number of decisions by competition authorities - those, of course, primarily involving companies that deal with final consumers. Taking into account consumer failures could undoubtedly allow for a better delimitation of relevant markets, a better assessment of the effects of a concentration of personal data following a merger, or a better evaluation of the harm to consumers. On this last point, it is important to stop automatically considering that offering more choice to consumers is always better for them, and that less choice is necessarily harmful to them. Happiness economists have shown, for example, that access to a greater number of television channels reduces the well-being of heavy consumers of television programs. Similarly, when it comes to the provision of information to consumers, more transparency does

not automatically improve their well-being. Less product information is not always bad for consumers. Behavioral economists know that a label stating that a product contains a potentially harmful ingredient, or that it is free of harmful ingredients, triggers decisions far removed from those predicted by rational consumer choice theory.

II. The imperfect consumer, a new reference?

6. The application of competition law has been able to take into account progress in the economic analysis of imperfect competition, its various sources and its various effects. I believe that the same trend regarding imperfect consumption should be encouraged, as it is likely to improve the quality of the decisions rendered by the competition authorities. The debate deserves to be opened. It seems to me to be at least as important as the question of whether and how the objective of competition law should be extended beyond the sole interest of consumers.

State Aids, Banking Resolution and Quantitative Easing*

ELIE COHEN

National Centre for Scientific Research (CNRS)

1. The Italian banking crisis in the summer of 2016 (risk of bankruptcy of Europe's oldest bank, Monte Paschi di Siena MPS) is unprecedented in that it mobilises the tools of competition policy (state aid), banking regulation (resolution) and monetary policy (quantitative easing). There are three ways to describe this crisis, to understand its drivers and to sketch out its outcome.

2. The first one could be told like this. Once upon a time there were three small banks that were victims of the country's sluggish growth, their bad risks, and the nonchalant management of their executives. To their misfortune, their difficulties will continue into 2016 when a new European directive prohibits bailouts by the State *(bail out)* and requires creditors to contribute *(bail in)*. Victims of aggressive sales advisors, retirees have lost their savings imprudently invested in bank bonds presented as being as safe as deposits. A bankrupt pensioner then puts an end to his life, forcing the political authorities to intervene, especially as contagion threatens and a major bank, the MPS, which had already received aid over the previous two years (8 billion euros), is once again in need of help.

3. The second is a case of a school of government by rules (Resolution Directive and State aid doctrine) implemented by independent authorities (DGComp and ECB) and designed to avoid moral hazard by preserving taxpayers' money. The spread of the crisis and the scale of the problem to be solved (the whole Italian banking sector is involved) are such that the new rules on *leases in*

* This article has been previously published in Concurrences, and it might have been edited for clarity and cohesion. Elie Cohen, State aids, banking resolution and quantitative easing, November 2016, Concurrences N° 4-2016, Art. N° 81338, pp. 1-3

force since 1/1/2016 must apply. The European Commission and the ECB are legitimately resisting the demands of a hard-pressed political power that can only denounce the tyranny of unelected bodies and strongly claim the discretionary choices it intends to make to protect its citizens.

4. The third underlines the rare combination of the problems of state aid, systemic risk prevention and eligibility for the ECB's quantitative easing policy of securitised loans in a turbulent European political context since Brexit and at a time when Mr Renzi is facing a perilous referendum. It is difficult to reduce the complexity of the issue to discretionary or pre-settled, to intervention by the monetary authorities when the stakes are ultimately budgetary, to the disruptive effects of *lease-in* (ruin of creditors) and to the rejection of the (fiscal) consequences of *lease-out*.

5. Unravelling this story today means, beyond the specificity of the Italian banking crisis or the domestic policy issues which are not our objects here, understanding the construction of a practical solution to a problem of MPS insolvency with a plurality of standards raising as much macro-prudential risks as competition under acute political constraints.

6. Indeed, in a representative democracy, which is additionally threatened by populist risk, the Government cannot be indifferent to the plight of aggrieved savers, and it cannot therefore accept that the rules of *tenancy* apply to investors who have imprudently put their money into bonds issued by banks that have become insolvent. On the other hand, the European Commission cannot accept that public aid should be paid to banks in difficulty which by their easy credit policy have led to unfair competition with their competitors. Finally, the ECB cannot accept that the Directive on the resolution as soon as it is adopted be emptied of its meaning. How, then, can we reconcile these contradictory demands, bearing in mind that MPS is the underside of the iceberg of bad risks borne by the entire Italian banking system?

7. The solution invented by JPMorgan at the request of Mr. Renzi is worth recalling.

8. Ten years of economic stagnation have weakened the entire Italian banking system and deteriorated credit quality. The IMF estimates Italian banks' bad loans at EUR 360 billion. At the end of the stress tests conducted by the European Banking Authority, one bank is designated as unable to cope with the adverse scenario tested, namely MPS, despite the aid already paid out following two recapitalisation operations. The portfolio of bad risks is evaluated at €50 billion, i.e. 1/3 of its portfolio. The company has to be recapitalised again. A private solution, involving neither direct public aid, prohibited by the European Resolution Mechanism, nor participation of creditors and depositors in the restructuring, prohibited by the political context, must therefore be sought. JPMorgan thus proposes a solution that is elegant on paper and reconciles incompatible constraints.

9. The planned operation will be carried out in three stages.

10. 27,7 billion of doubtful loans were first removed from MPS's balance sheet by means of a sale to a hive-off vehicle (SecCo) which in turn securitises, tranches and sells these doubtful loans on the market. The mechanics are simple and have been tried and tested with subprimes: doubtful loans reduced to a value of EUR 9.2 billion are securitised in three tranches of decreasing risk.

11. The junior tranche will be guaranteed by the shareholders of MPS ('1.6 billion for a nominal value of 4.8). The mezzanine tranche (€1.6 billion taken over by the Atlante Fund (Unicredit Intesa for €300m Generali and Cassa Depositi and Prestiti + pension funds). The third so-called "senior" tranche of €6 billion and 18 in nominal value is guaranteed by the State through the GAGS fund. Thus it is the new shareholders of a restructured and recapitalised MPS that guarantee SecCo's losses. It is an investment fund that brings together Italian finance, public pension funds and the Italian Caisse des Dépôts that guarantee the mezzanine tranche. It is a public body that guarantees the senior tranche, the one that a priori will sell the best, thus avoiding the need to call in a state guarantee.

12. The recapitalisation of MPS is therefore crucial and must be carried out by private investors. JPMorgan has made a strong commitment to secure this capital increase with its partners (Credit Suisse, Bank of America, Deutsche Bank Santander and Citigroup. The planned recapitalisation is €5 billion, the amount of the loss recorded between the sale price of the receivables and their balance sheet value. This operation is conditional on the success of the previous one, i.e. the sale on the market of the three packages of securitised receivables.

13. If all operations are completed, the new shareholders of MPS will sell their shares on the market, pocketing the profits in the process.

14. To sum up: this private operation blessed by the regulators will involve the State at each stage of the assembly. For the least risky senior tranche, the State guarantee should be called since the price paid by SecCo is 40% higher than the market value. ... But the investor benefits from a second guarantee, that of the ECB which buys MBS! As long as Italy and its banks are solvent, debt securities traded on the secondary market are eligible for repurchases by the ECB under the quantitative easing policy. We can see from this example that central bank financing can be a substitute for budgetary and therefore fiscal financing.

15. For the mezzanine tranche, public bodies guarantee the investment.

16. 5 billion recapitalisation of MPS depends on the success of this operation of securitised and sliced loans, as the investor shareholders intend to sell a restructured bank.

17. All in all, it is the Italian State which, through its intervention, financially guarantees the operation and keeps up appearances because the BRRD Directive is inapplicable in all its rigour. As for the ECB, if it repurchases the securitised loans (MBS) it will in fact accept to carry part of the credit risk on its balance sheet, something which the German economist Werner Sinn has constantly denounced.

18. What conclusions can be drawn from the MPS case?

19. The first concerns the sustainability of the solution found. Everything is done as if the markets were going to favour the arrangement by buying securities that do not reflect the intrinsic value of the underlying, which will allow private investors to finance the arrangement and the State not to be called as collateral. While the solution found may be politically feasible, it is not necessarily viable. If the process derails, which cannot be ruled out, a new mechanism will have to be invented based on the same set of constraints.

20. The second is that, faced with a perceived political imperative, here the populist threat and the political fate of Matteo Renzi, there are no rules powerful enough to impose themselves even when the case in question suffers little discussion.

21. Generalizing *lease-in* solutions, preserving taxpayers' money, sending the right signals to the banks by putting an end to the reign of *too big to fail* is legitimate. It is also legitimate to enshrine these principles in binding rules. At the same time political power cannot abolish rules in the name of exercising sovereignty. In Europe we have long lived under a regime of voluntary and mutually self-limiting sovereignties.

22. The third concerns the degree of political discretion used to make the application of the rules politically acceptable. As long as the *lease in* rules do not apply mechanically and attempts are made to sort out among bank bondholders between those who are ill-informed and who should be compensated and those who are enlightened investors and who should take their losses, there is a considerable risk of arbitrariness. The solution found in Italy is not to sort it out, which considerably weakens the *lease-in* rule.

23. The fourth concerns state aid. Is it possible, for reasons relating to the economic argument of preventing moral hazard and for classic competition reasons, to prohibit State aid in a situation of financial distress of a bank and automatically switch to a *lease-in* scheme. The answer is clearly no. The shortcomings in consumer protection regimes, in the financial traditions of the various countries and, all in all, the incompleteness of the Banking Union make it impossible for the common rule to apply automatically. It was inevitable that the Government would come to the aid of investors who had been cheated by sellers who had not properly informed them of the dangers of bank bonds.

24. The fifth relates to the sustainability of the solution found and thus the durability of the banking union and in particular its resolution mechanisms. Here again, the answer is clearly no, the UB in its current functioning is not sustainable. The episode reveals what we already knew, namely that as long as the bad risks and debts of the past have not been cleared, we cannot expect mutualisation mechanisms to work, recourse to national solutions will continue to be necessary. What happens then if a country cannot cope with a banking crisis that is beyond its capacity to intervene? The solution then lies in the mechanisms that have been tried and tested in the Greek, Portuguese, Irish and Spanish cases, i.e. intervention by European funds.

25. All in all, the MPS case illustrates the difficulties of rule-discretion arbitration, the very notion of state aid when quantitative easing policies are implemented, and the failure in incomplete federations of independent authorities designed to tie the hands of politicians.

Politics, Digital Innovation, Intellectual Property and the Future of Competition Law*

JOSEF DREXL
Max Planck Institute for Innovation and Competition

1. We live in highly political times. While multilateralism, economic globalization and convergence of economic policies characterized the era at the turn to the new millennium, today's world seems to drift apart. Resurgent ideologies and populism, economic nationalism and new trade wars have become part of the political agenda of many governments. Even in the field of competition law, voices get stronger that claim exceptions from standard application to favour national champions.
2. The rise of economic nationalism coincides with the digital transformation, which is not only fundamentally changing the way firms are doing business, but also how individuals work, consume, interact and behave as citizens. Currently, digital transformation makes jurisdictions around the globe rethink the rules that define the relationship between firms, citizens and the state.
3. Competition law is just one field of the law that is now under scrutiny. In several jurisdictions, such as the EU, the UK, Germany and Australia, expert groups most recently delivered reports with new ideas on adapting competition policy and law to address the challenges in the digital sector. These reports discuss whether competition law enforcement has so far allowed too many false negatives, whether the traditional role of market definition and market

* This article has been previously published in Concurrences, and it might have been edited for clarity and cohesion. Josef Drexl, Politics, digital innovation, intellectual property and the future of competition law, November 2019, Concurrences N° 4-2019, Art. N° 91838, pp. 2-5.

dominance should be reconsidered and whether new theories of harm are needed to address more appropriately restraints of competition in the digital sector.

I. In the digital era, competition law cannot ignore the fundamental changes of how firms do business.

4. A strengthening of competition law enforcement would especially target the digital platform giants originating from the US. These firms do not sell simple brick-and-mortar products. In various ways, they put personal data of customers at the centre of their business models. They drag consumers into digital ecosystems where big data analytics is used to make predictions on individual preferences and where automated decision-making by connected devices replaces autonomous decisions of consumers. It is clear that competition law cannot ignore such fundamental changes of how firms do business. In addition, the much wider range of diverse interests that the new business models affect explains the urgent need to think about the goals of competition law and its relationship with other fields of the law, including data protection law, media law and consumer protection laws in particular. The character of the reforms jurisdictions are now envisaging with relation to the data economy is therefore of a highly political and even constitutional nature. They are about future society, about how we want to communicate and act as both economic agents and citizens. It is clear that jurisdictions will not make a uniform choice. Especially China, the US and the EU will pave very different roads, and other jurisdictions of the world will probably choose one of these roads as the model for their legislation.

5. What does this mean for competition law more specifically? A debate has started about controlling and regulating the power of digital giants. Although protecting democracy against the economic power of big firms was a major motivation to adopt a competition law in many jurisdictions, this law should not lose its credibility as the centrepiece of legislation that protects competition across different sectors of the economy according to uniform standards. In this regard, competition law should continue to focus on guaranteeing the fundamental benefits that competition can provide to society.

6. This is where the goal of innovation comes into the picture. Competition appears as the most important driver of digital innovation. Even in traditional fields of manufacturing, firms are nowadays investing heavily in the digitization of their products to remain in the market; digital giants constantly develop their business models out of the fear that future disruptive digital applications could exclude them from the market. But firms can also act strategically to create market entry barriers for potential innovators or decrease incentives for innovation of competitors. To protect innovation competition should therefore be recognized a major task of competition policy in the field.

7. Yet integrating innovation as a goal into competition law has never been easy. This is also mirrored by the mentioned reports on reforming competition law for the digital sector. They generally acknowledge the importance of innovation as a goal and more specifically focus on the need to protect innovation competition against killer acquisitions of start-ups. But a common understanding of how innovation should be integrated in the competition law analysis in the digital sector is still missing.

8. One focal point of the innovation dimension of competition law is its application to intellectual property (IP). In this regard, it is noteworthy that the recent reports are largely silent on IP. Only the British Furman Report notes that competition policy should be concerned about patent thickets and extending patent rights to the digital sector where they are currently not available. This critical view on patents is astonishing, on the one hand. With variations across different jurisdictions, competition law has generally accepted patent law as a major incentive system for innovation. On the other hand, the Furman Report confirms that patents can also create barriers to entry for new firms.

II. The US DOJ sent out a clear signal in favour of strengthening IP rights against antitrust law by starting to implement the "New Madison" approach.

9. Taking into account the central role of digitization for future innovation, the question has to be asked in which direction competition law should move at the interface to intellectual property law. In this regard, it has to be noted that the US DOJ sent out a clear signal in favour of strengthening IP rights against the application of antitrust law when it formally withdrew its consent to the 2013 Joint DOJ-PTO Policy Statement on Remedies for Standards-Essential Patents in December 2018. Makan Delrahim, assistant attorney general for antitrust at the US DOJ, thereby moved to implement his strongly advocated "New Madison" approach. Going back to the times of the drafting of the US Constitution, Delrahim identifies James Madison, the drafter of the Constitution, as the true father of the US patent law who convinced Thomas Jefferson about the particular benefits of patents for society. According to Delrahim, Jefferson changed his mind on patents and finally supported the so-called patent and copyright clause in the Constitution, while initially he wanted to preserve competition against all monopolies. Based on the Constitutional history, Delrahim argues against the use of US antitrust law to enforce FRAND commitments made by holders of standard-essential patents (SEPs).

10. Indeed SEPs play a major role in the innovation system. To the extent that they relate to mobile telecommunications technology, these patents protect the major infrastructure technology on which digital transformation and especially the Internet of Things have to rely. But this does not automatically mean that

the "New Madison" approach is a useful guiding post for the future application of competition law in the digital sector. One day, Delrahim may be successful in convincing the Supreme Court judges, who increasingly like to interpret the Constitution in the "original" way the fathers of the Constitution understood its wording. Yet the historical debate on which Delrahim relies took place in a completely different technological and economic context. Therefore, it should not influence competition policy and law in the US nor in other parts of the world. Still, in the United States, Delrahim's approach will remain of limited practical effect. There, the exclusivity of SEPs is controlled by courts based on other legal regimes and doctrines, namely, the limited availability of patent law injunctions as an equitable remedy as well as contract law. In other jurisdictions, and especially on the EU level, such alternatives are not available to the same extent, making competition law the primary legal regime to address the adverse effects of the strategic use of SEPs on innovation.

III. Against the backdrop of the digital transformation there are several reasons why IP rights should now be looked at more critically.

11. Even more, in the context of digital transformation, competition concerns regarding IP should not be limited to the issue of controlling the use of SEPs. In fact, there are several reasons why IP rights should now be looked at more critically against the backdrop of the digital transformation. There are several general reasons for this:

- The first reason has already been mentioned. The current digital transformation primarily seems to be driven by competition and not intellectual property. This already is an indication that innovation competition in the digital sector is not necessarily in need of a strengthening or extension of IP rights.

- Secondly, data as the most important assets that firms hold are not protected by clearly defined IP rights and are not in need of such protection. Firms use data in various ways, for instance, as customer data to succeed in competition among different digital ecosystems or as valuable training data for artificial intelligence applications. So far, the recent and intensive debate on the future intellectual property regime that is necessary to drive the digital economy in the EU has not come up with any convincing arguments for the introduction of new economic ownership rights in data. Indeed, firms can protect their business models based on de facto data control and technological protection measures. Supported by potentially available trade secrets protection, this is sufficient for firms to license their data for use in secondary markets. Beyond this, impediments for data transactions are much more likely to be caused by technical problems, such as the lack of data interoperability, than the absence of legal protection of data. This is why the current debate is now focusing much more on the need for promoting data access. In this regard, the debate on data access rights that help overcome data lock-ins of customers addresses a major competition-related issue.

– The third reason is arguable the most important and maybe still least noted one. The digital revolution may require a complete reassessment of the intellectual property regime as it has developed so far. Digitization is not only a game changer for markets as they have traditionally worked; digitization is also changing the innovation processes in practically all fields of technology. In particular, machine learning algorithms, representing a field of rapid digital innovation within AI technologies that does not seem to have to rely a lot on intellectual property either, are about to become major innovation tools, thereby increasingly substituting humans as inventors. For the future, facilitated access to data and broad availability of artificial intelligence research tools may well raise the question whether and to which extent intellectual property regimes, including patent law, can still be justified, or to which extent they are in need of an adjustment. The problem, however, is that it is particularly difficult to reform established intellectual property systems. State institutions administering IP systems will prefer to do business as usual, instead of questioning the system as such. Large groups of rightholders benefit from the existing system and can rely on economic and political power. They will happily welcome the "New Madison" approach, which reflects an almost ideological belief that IP rights will always promote innovation. In such circumstances, competition law enforcement may well have to address new challenges, especially if "outdated" intellectual property law creates additional possibilities for strategic behaviour of rightholders to restrict access to data or, as the Furman Report warns, patent law further expands to the digital field.

12. The risk of dysfunctional IP can be illustrated by the potential adverse effects of database rights within the EU. The European Commission was assessing the working of the Database Directive 96/9/EC for the modern data economy in 2018. While the results of the assessment and, even more so, legal researchers hinted at the risk that courts on the national and maybe even the EU level may recognize database rights regarding data collected by connected devices, the Commission has announced to refrain from proposing a reform of the Directive. Without such reform, and before the CJEU gets a chance to interpret the Directive in a pro-competitive way, data holders could therefore strategically rely on potentially available *sui generis* database rights for years to counter competition law claims for access to data.

13. In sum, this shows that there is a dual task for the future: reforming IP law and adjusting competition law for the digital sector. To use competition law with the objective to restrict the exclusivity of unjustified IP rights will only be the second-best solution. Yet EU law is not badly placed to fulfil its role in this regard. Following *Magill*, which was indeed a judgment on excessive copyright protection restricting access to essential information, and *Microsoft*, which was a case on a refusal to grant access to data at best protected as trade secrets, the EU can rely on competition case law as a platform to promote free flow of data in all sectors of the economy. But competition law has to develop further, since the threshold for application of Article 102 TFEU especially to refusals to license intellectual property is very high. The *Huawei* judgment marks a very much needed step to overcome an overly narrow reading of the "cumulative" theory recognized by the CJEU in *IMS Health*. In the future, the CJEU would be well advised to make clear that, beyond leveraging cases, the *Huawei* holding should also apply to SEP holders that are not active in the downstream product markets. This is most important in the era of the Internet of Things, where it will be the rule rather than the exception that SEP holders do not compete in the numerous markets for connected devices in which their technologies are implemented.

IV. In the digital era, intellectual property may well be losing its role as a most important system for innovation.

14. The most important insight is, however, of a general nature. Intellectual property may well be losing its traditional role as a most important incentive system for innovation. Innovation will be much more driven by very short and disruptive innovation cycles and competition. This does not mean that exclusive intellectual property rights will no longer be needed. The challenge consists more in redefining the positive role intellectual property can and has to play as part of an integrated legal system that aims at promoting innovation as a paradigm of competition. For fulfilling this task, competition law enforcers will need to be at the forefront of understanding the economic impact of new and quickly changing technologies.

15. The fathers of the US Constitution were certainly very wise men. But referring to them today, at the time of a fundamental digital transformation, to insulate IP against competition law application is nothing else than a political agenda that serves the economic interests of a few. From a global perspective, the "New Madison" approach is a poisoned bread offered by the US government to the world to preach strong IP protection in the interests of US rightholders. It thereby makes a nice addendum to modern US economic nationalism.

PART VII

Personal Reflections and Regional Experiences

Why Competition?

Calvin S. Goldman[*]
Calvin Goldman Law

1. I am pleased to contribute this relatively brief summary on the subject of "Why Competition?" My perspective on this important subject is based on over 40 years of experience in addressing competition law and policy issues. While most of that time has been spent in advising private sector entities as well as engagement in public policy issues from a private sector perspective, I've also had the direct experience of enforcing the Canadian Competition Act as the first head of the Competition Bureau following the enactment of that legislation, coupled with my experience as an assistant special prosecutor and special counsel for the Attorney General of Canada on two significant case matters which were heard by the Supreme Court of Canada. The Competition Act, which was enacted in June 1986, brought into force an entirely new set of merger review provisions; Canada was the second nation, following upon the United States, to enact competition law pertaining to proposed mergers and related remedial provisions.

2. My experience over the years also has included participating in many fora that have taken place at the Organisation for Economic Co-operation and Development (OECD) Competition Committee since the late 1980s (when I was both Vice-Chair of that OECD Committee and the lead representative of Canada on that Committee) and participating in various International Competition Network working groups since its formation as a Non-Government Advisor (ICN-NGAs). I've also had experience over the years in the leadership of the Canadian Bar Association's Competition Law Section and the American Bar Association's Antitrust Law Section, as well as other private

* Calvin S. Goldman is a principal at The Law Office of Calvin Goldman Calvin S. Goldman Cal Goldman's practice encompasses Canadian and international matters before the Competition Bureau, as well as foreign investment reviews under the Investment Canada Act.

sector organizations such as the Business and Industry Advisory Committee (BIAC) and the International Chamber of Commerce (ICC) Competition Commission. All of those institutions have provided considerable case and policy groundwork for this summary.

3. A primary objective of competition law and policy is directed toward encouraging markets to operate fairly and efficiently in a manner unimpeded by barriers to entry and expansion. Such barriers may be established by public sector regulatory provisions or by private sector entities which have attained market power. In many instances, such barriers to entry may impede the ability of firms in the relevant market, including but not limited to new entrants, to grow and compete effectively. Barriers to entry also are likely to constrain choice and competitive pricing to purchasers.

4. Other conduct that reflects market power, for example in cases of abuse of dominance, almost inevitably constrains fair and competitive pricing as well as innovation, which otherwise would lead to enhanced quality and choice for consumers and other purchasers of products.

5. Effective enforcement of competition law has been proven repeatedly to bring about opportunities for a wider range of business entities to enter and expand in relevant markets in a competitive manner, thereby leading to fairer prices for purchasers, greater choices, enhanced innovation, and expansion of and growth of competitors, both domestically and internationally.

6. In sum, effective competition law and policy has been proven to allow markets to operate efficiently in a manner unimpeded by private or public sector constraints. When markets are allowed to work efficiently, there are considerably more benefits to consumers and a wide range of business entities operating in that market, compared to when markets are constrained by unnecessary barriers or regulation by the public sector.

7. The potential benefits of effective competition law and policy also are important in encouraging transborder and a wider range of international investment, including foreign direct investment by entities prepared to enter the market. That encompasses proposed mergers and acquisitions, which may pertain to more than one country and be subject to antitrust law review by competition law authorities in more than one jurisdiction. In this respect, in addition to barriers to entry, experience has shown that system frictions between jurisdictions can discourage such proposed investments and overall growth in markets both domestically and internationally.

8. This is where the ongoing work of international bodies such as the OECD Competition Committee and the ICN has important mandates, directed toward encouraging parallel standards for competition law review, which may be particularly applicable to transborder mergers and acquisitions. An important consideration in the decision-making process of corporate entities that are considering proposed mergers and acquisitions in the context of transborder markets is having reasonable certainty of the issues that it may be

necessary to address before the respective competition authorities as well as the relevant considerations applicable to the assessment of those regulatory issues. Experience has shown that when there is relative uncertainty as to the manner in which the competition assessment in a particular jurisdiction takes place, there is a significant risk of discouraging such investment. One paramount consideration when counsel are advising senior business executives and boards in relation to proposed mergers and acquisitions is to make every reasonable effort to ensure there are "no surprises" in the applicable regulatory reviews both from a procedural and substantive perspective. That objective may become significantly more challenging when there are material system frictions between two or more jurisdictions that may review a proposed transaction; in other words, inconsistency between jurisdictions in the applicable competition law assessment standards also discourages transborder investments.

9. Similarly, case experience has shown that the reduction of system frictions also enhances cooperation between and among competition authorities, thereby leading to more effective competition law enforcement in relation to transborder cases. Such cooperation is not limited to proposed mergers and acquisitions; experience has shown it also may be applicable to the enforcement of other areas of competition law such as addressing international cartel conduct and parallel abuse of dominance cases. Therefore, the ongoing work of the OECD Competition Committee and the ICN has continued to lessen potential system frictions, as well as encouraging transborder investments and growth in multiple jurisdictions across the globe. That ongoing work has led to more effective enforcement by competition authorities in relation to parallel competition reviews in a wide range of transborder cases.

10. One current example of outdated government regulation is illustrated by the quite significant restrictions on foreign direct investment that are applicable at this time in relation to the telecommunications and airlines sectors in Canada. These restrictions severely disincentivize even US-based telecom competitors (such as AT&T and Verizon) from entering Canada on any sufficient scale. There are similar significant limitations which restrict the ability of foreign-based airlines to operate routes within Canada. Without the doors being opened in Canada to foreign competition, even from entities based in other Five Eyes (FVEY) intelligence allies of Canada (the US, Britain, Australia, and New Zealand) and other trusted countries, Canadian consumers and businesses are not likely to see substantial competitive choice or competitive pricing. Innovation and long-term growth are also potentially undermined. Canadians are likely to continue to pay among the highest prices in the world in these sectors. This was the subject of a recent Business Commentary/Op-Ed, that I co-authored with Thomas Mathews, which was published in Canada's *Globe and Mail* newspaper on January 26, 2024. That built on earlier commentaries including the C.D. Howe Institute Intelligence Memo that I co-authored with Larry Schwartz and Richard Taylor, which was published in March 2023.

In addition, an even more recent Op-Ed on February 22, 2024, by Andrew Coyne, who is a business commentator with the *Globe and Mail* newspaper, conveyed similar points quite effectively pertaining to the need for greater competition in Canada's telecom and airline sectors. As reflected in those three writings, Canada should significantly enhance its competitive markets by opening the doors to investment in these two sectors from businesses based in Canada's trusted allies.

11. One example of significant uncertainties pertaining to the applicability of fundamental principles of jurisdiction for merger review arises from the relatively recent assertion of jurisdiction by the European Commission in relation to Illumina Inc's proposed acquisition of GRAIL, Inc. While that proposed acquisition did not trigger the merger review thresholds in the EU or in any Member State, the Commission applied its interpretation of Article 22 of the EUMR as a basis for its assertion of jurisdiction. I participated together with Frank Montag (Freshfields, Brussels) and John Pecman (Fasken, Ottawa) in the drafting of a Statement of Concerns pertaining to this assertion of jurisdiction; we then conferred with a number of very experienced individuals who formerly held domestic and international leadership positions in competition law and policy. This led to the publication in Concurrences in September, 2023 of the "Statement of Concerns regarding the jurisdictional issues arising in the European Commission's position in relation to the Illumina/GRAIL transaction." That Statement of Concerns, which was signed by 12 distinguished individuals (including three former European Court judges and two former Chairs of the International Competition Network's Steering Group, among others), took the position that this assertion of jurisdiction in this matter is inconsistent with fundamental principles of jurisdiction, including principles of international law and international recommendations made unanimously at the OECD and the ICN. Legal certainty on principles of jurisdiction is of fundamental importance for merger control cases, both for competition authorities and for the private sector.

12. By letting markets work without unnecessary barriers to entry, or other unnecessary domestic sectoral regulations, and by reducing system frictions between jurisdictions as well as unnecessary uncertainty pertaining to the issues to be addressed by the respective competition authorities, consumers and business entities can realize maximum potential benefits while competition authorities can work more effectively together in protecting those markets for the benefit of overall economic growth. That, in a nutshell, is why competition law and policy is so fundamental to economic prosperity.

My Personal Competition Law Journey

BARRY J. RODGER*
University of Strathclyde

1. I stumbled upon competition law by chance, switching to that subject from legal theory (which was an elective at the relatively modern Law School at Strathclyde University) at the start of the third year of my LLB Degree in 1986. John Aristotle Kapranos (JAK) Huntley (father of Alex Kapranos, lead singer in Franz Ferdinand!) was way ahead of his time in developing a stand-alone Competition Law elective in the early 1980s, when in most (if not all) UK academic institutions, competition law featured (if at all) as a part of EU law, or as a sideshow in commercial law teaching. I had already been taught about Hoffman La Roche's nasty commercial tactics and United Brands' banana strategy by Professor Akos Toth in EU law. Akos had famously escaped Hungary, long before its EU membership, as a young man with his wife and with all their savings hidden in a traditional Hungarian cake which the border guards didn't think to search... John fostered my interest in competition law, albeit the class (in the period before the cartel focus and big fines at the EU level) concentrated more on UK competition law, with ready cooked breakfast cereals and contraceptive sheaths featuring prominently!! John was a big fan of Sunderland FC (having been sent from Greece as a boy to live with relatives in Sunderland) and I remember fondly one question in the class multiple choice test asking the year in which Sunderland won the FA Cup? Inevitably, as a football obsessive I knew it was 1973 but it always surprised me why other students didn't also choose that option given that it was the year of the primary UK competition legislation at that time – The Fair Trading Act 1973 – a mischievous but rather easy

* Professor, Chair and co-organiser of the Competition Law Scholars'.

question to answer! The 1973 Act was predicated on the "public interest" a broad, all-encompassing test for assessing markets and mergers, not simply focused on efficiency and/or increased competitiveness but a wide range of other "non-competition" factors. Younger readers should be aware that competition law debates on the inclusion of wider policy objectives in any competition law enforcement system are cyclical and not exclusive to contemporary debates about environmental sustainability or about data protection/privacy concerns in aspects of the business practices of certain big players in the digital economy. I always suggest that anyone interested in competition law should read the wonderful book by Stephen Wilks, *In the Public Interest, Competition Policy and the Monopolies and Mergers Commission* (Oxford University Press 1999) – a tour de force history of a key institutional player, the Monopolies and Mergers Commission (MMC) in UK competition law development and the concomitant role of the public interest in UK competition law. The link between competition law, politics and the political economy was clear to me (competition law and policy in my view is difficult to equate with a technocratic function) and exercised my interest in particular in the early years of my competition law learning.

2. In my final (Honours) year at Strathclyde, I decided to undertake my dissertation (20,000 words!) on a competition law topic – inspired by the recent takeover of a leading Scottish drinks and pharmaceuticals business, The Distillers Company Ltd., by Guinness. The deal was not referred to the UK MMC for consideration under the Fair Trading Act 1973 although Guinness had reneged on a key promise to relocate headquarters of the combined business to Edinburgh. In my dissertation I explored the role of the public interest, and in particular, that of the regional policy criterion which was an express part of the statute's public interest test (Section 84(1)(d) of the 1973 Act required the MMC to have regard to "the balanced distribution of industry and employment in the UK") , in a series of takeovers involving important Scottish businesses which would have produced detrimental impacts on the Scottish economy. The key aspects of my dissertation were later published in revised form, when I was a relatively young academic, in the *European Competition Law Review* in 1996 under the title: "Reinforcing the Scottish 'Ring-Fence'; a critique of UK Mergers Policy vis-à-vis the Scottish Economy". Merger control was at that stage aptly recognised as an aspect of industrial policy and the relevant government minister had the final say on decisions to refer mergers for review by the MMC and in taking any decisions on their final reports. My view at the time was that there should be a requirement, absent in the legislation, for the Secretary of State to be required to have regard to the public interest test in all its glory in making these important decisions. (The Guinness/Distillers merger was not referred on the basis it raised no "competition" grounds…)

3. After Strathclyde I was fortunate to gain a place on the BCL at Oxford University in 1989–90 where I first met a youthful Richard Whish and

developed my understanding of competition law in a much deeper way, using the 2nd edition of his *Competition Law* text, which is now co-authored with David Bailey and in its 11th edition. Richard remains the competition law guru in the UK (and way beyond), identifying trends and challenges in enforcement and policy and sharing his insights with academics, policymakers and practitioners alike. Richard was inspirational in seminars and was joined by resident Oxford academic, Paul Craig, legendary public lawyer who had just returned from a summer stint in Chicago and provided seminars with a constant "devil's-advocate" Borkian point of view. This inspired my first reading of Bork – utterly brilliant, compelling but wrong. Of course, better basketball players get paid more, but that sporting analogy doesn't really translate well to the commercial world, and the consumer welfare test advocated by Bork seemed not only counter-intuitive but also misleading in my view.

4. Oligopoly and the theory of oligopolistic interdependence were de rigeur, and when I was halfway through my legal traineeship in a small law firm in Glasgow following the BCL, I applied for the LLM programme at the European University Institute in Florence. My LLM thesis proposal was based on the recent *Italian Flat Glass* case and looked at oligopoly and the concept of collective dominance from a comparative perspective. I turned up at the interview with my Collins Spanish dictionary ready to discuss "*el problema del oligopolio*" but thankfully all discussion continued in English. The LLM was an amazing year of preparation for being an academic: reading, thinking and attending seminars in a glorious setting overlooking Florence. I had two wonderful supervisors, neither competition law-centric but both incredible academics with sage advice: Francis Snyder ("you should read Carl Harlow") and Christian Joerges ("you should think about economic constitutionalism…"). I still hadn't finished my thesis when I returned to Glasgow in the summer of 1993, with my mind still full of vespas, Fiorentina, café corretto and oligopolies. I had contemplated returning to the legal profession, with a vague long-term plan of going to the Bar to be an advocate (Scottish term for barrister). This never came to pass, and in the meantime, I was in urgent need of a job to pay the bills at least until the thesis submission deadline date at the end of February 1994.

5. I met with the Strathclyde Head of Law School to discuss any tutoring availability – he asked if I knew about competition law and if I could teach the whole class and tutorials as John Huntley had become the Vice-Dean of Research and had been relieved of teaching duties. Of course I agreed, and the rest is history – call it luck… serendipity but ever since I've always urged students to recognise that it is difficult to plan your career to the nth degree and to pursue interests and grasp whatever opportunities come your way. The academic world was a different place 30 years ago in 1993; more relaxed, less pressure to publish, never mind the need to deliver knowledge exchange and impact. But change was coming in UK academia, with a justifiable drive to greater accountability, and in particular for academic institutions including

law schools to demonstrate their contribution to academic knowledge and the wider impact of their academic work and publications. This is now known as the REF–Research Excellence Framework, and it drives much of what goes on in the academic sector and is used in ranking law schools. At this point I was mentored informally by two law (not competition law) academics who became very influential in the development of my academic career, and also great personal friends – Professors Kenny Miller and Gerry Maher; the latter sadly passed away in January 2023. They pressed on me the need to publish- "just get your work out there Baz" and consequently my academic career got a nice kickstart when I split my 50,000 word LLM thesis on the comparative treatment of the oligopoly issue in the EU, US and UK into three articles, published respectively in the *European Competition Law Review*, *Legal Issues of European Integration* and the *Columbia Journal of European Law*. Various male professors were clearly significant in my competition law journey, but along the way I've met a number of incredible and inspirational female competition law colleagues, to name but a few: Eleanor Fox, Brenda Sufrin, Rosa Greaves, Mary Catherine Lucey, Pinar Akman, Arianna Andreangeli, Kati Cseres, Magali Eben and Or Brook. There are so many more, and thankfully, academia generally, and competition law in particular, now has many more inspirational female role models for Undergraduate and PhD students to follow.

6. When I started teaching competition law 30 years ago, perhaps because of the nature of UK competition law at that time before the major transformation brought around by the Competition Act 1998, my teaching focused on public enforcement of EU and UK competition law, and particularly around the goals of competition law and the intersection between competition policy and other broader public policies; the big debates about the role and scope of competition law in society to which we have returned again more recently. The shifting sands of competition law and the recurring themes in competition law debates and enforcement, are also reflected in the revised structure and content of the various editions of my competition law student textbook co-authored with Angus MacCulloch, a competition law academic at Lancaster University. I had taught Angus competition law in his LLM at Strathclyde during my first year of teaching at Strathclyde and we have remained good friends since – the competition law community is a good place to develop lifelong friends. Richard's textbook, albeit brilliant, had become very dense and we wanted to provide a textbook as an accompaniment to a one-semester competition law UG class, and the book has been fairly successful, published first in 1999 and now in its 6th edition, *Competition Law and Policy in the EU and UK* (Routledge 2021). The book has developed with changing substantive law and enforcement trends, notably now including chapters on private enforcement, market investigations and cartel enforcement which did not appear in the first edition. The book and the teaching of the subject has changed for various reasons in the last 25 years. Some key trends are

observable, notably the transformed landscape of UK competition law since the introduction of the Competition Act 1998. This was the first time the UK had a system of prohibitions and sanctions, enforced by a competition authority (formerly the OFT and now the CMA) with investigative powers mirroring those of the European Commission. The old system of market investigations (formerly monopoly investigations) remains but the prohibitions are a new area of enforcement activity to follow and teach, albeit there has been justifiable criticism of the rather limited infringement enforcement generally in the UK and in particular in relation to the abuse of dominance prohibition. Brexit has of course also proved to be a challenge and opportunity for the UK competition enforcement system (see Barry Rodger and Andreas Stephan, *Brexit and UK Competition Law* (Routledge 2022).The second key trend I will mention here is the focus on cartel activity at the EU level – of course this seems obvious now, but it was less so 25 years ago and beyond when the EU prioritised resources on dealing with vertical restraints and the potential impact they may have had on European market integration. These two trends also support my opening gambit for third year UG students new to the subject who have grown up in an era where society has tended to idolise big-name brands. "Business and business-people do bad things"! They charge excessive prices, collude and rip consumers off. And its clear that they continue to do so despite years of increased awareness of the role and impact of antitrust rules and work on enhancing compliance commitment to those rules. I did some empirical research in the early noughties on awareness and compliance in the UK business community and the results were worrying. Of course, the central fault-line for any effective competition law enforcement system is the potential for conflict with the commercial focus on profit-maximisation and returns for shareholders. If the shareholder interest in profit-maximisation were to be limited, many competition law problems would diminish, though that is a simplistic view I accept.

7. Academics can approach and teach competition law from a range of perspectives: the public law perspective stressing the role of and limitations on governmental agencies; from a commercial perspective, looking at how competition law regulates and limits commercial freedom of action; from a criminal law perspective, focusing on the sanctions available, and in particular penal sanctions directed at individuals in certain jurisdictions, including the UK; and from a private law perspective, emphasising the rights and obligations created by competition law and how this impacts relations between private parties and potentially in any legal disputes between them. Although originally attracted to competition law from a political lens and the politicised public interest underpinning of competition law in the UK at least, my academic research over the last 20 years has focused on enforcement of competition law generally, and primarily in private enforcement of competition law, reflecting my other academic research and teaching interests in private law and private international law. This research has developed from early work

where I looked at all the case-law in the UK courts over periods of time, to work focusing on the preliminary reference procedure (including a project where we sought to ascertain, with some limited success, what happened to rulings back in the national courts, see Barry Rodger, *Competition Law and Article 234: An Analysis* (Kluwer Law 2008)), to more recent work which seeks to be international, collaborative, comparative and empirical in nature. Various comments are merited here. First, empirical research and the gathering and analysis of data on aspects of competition law enforcement, is incredibly important – it really is crucial in helping to understand what is really going on and to help to inform policy decision-making, and through various projects I have sought to make a contribution to a really growing and significant field of academic literature here (e.g., see www.mappingcomplawreview.com/). Empirical work is of course fraught with difficulty, in particular in relation to obtaining access to all relevant information. In my first empirical project in this area, suggested to me by Richard Whish, I sought to uncover information about competition litigation settlements in the UK over a period of time (2000-2005, {2008] ECLR 29(2) 96-116; and later 2008-2012, [2015] GCLR 8(3) 89-108). Some interesting and significant information was unearthed but there remained a reluctance among certain members of the legal profession to disclose information, even on a confidential and anonymous basis – and I would urge the profession in future to collaborate with academic researchers, who will be working on the basis of strong institutional ethical codes in dealing with sensitive and confidential information.

8. It is also really important to develop comparative projects, which can help us to understand distinctive approaches and how different legal systems tackle the same issue, and how divergent these approaches can be even when dealing with the same set of issues under the "same" EU legal system (see www.mappingcomplawreview.com/). International and comparative projects can of course only work effectively and with full appreciation of the rules and context, when academics or specialists, being native language speakers, from that particular legal system, contribute and we have found that engaging specialists across all legal systems can be difficult, in terms of locating experts and ensuring uniformity of approach. Nonetheless, work done with long-term competition colleagues and friends, Professors Paco Marcos and Miguel Sousa Ferro, was successful in providing a comparative analysis of the implementation of the Antitrust Damages Directive in the EU (*The EU Antitrust Damages Directive, Transposition in the Member States* (Oxford University Press 2018)). Moreover, my most recent (and ongoing) comparative and empirical EU-wide project, albeit in the public enforcement context, co-led with Dr Or Brook, and also involving Paco Marcos, Maciej Bernatt and Annalies Outhuijse (*Judicial Review of Competition Law Enforcement in the EU* Member States and the UK, Kluwer Law International, 2024), has delivered a fascinating story of divergent systems and practices and experience across the EU in relation to judicial review of the enforcement action

of NCAs, involving their role in enforcing EU competition law. Probably my most interesting contribution here in terms of competition law tales of intrigue, suspense and outcome, is my edited collection entitled *Landmark Cases in Competition Law: Around the World in Fourteen Stories* (Kluwer Law 2012), basically doing what it says on the tin!

9. The final comment here is about the recent focus of my work on consumers, access to justice and ways of enhancing collective redress. Competition law has the consumer interest at its heart and yet, at least in European legal systems, for a long time the focus has only been on public enforcement, sanctions and fines recovered by the State authorities, whether EU or national. Of course, this has changed with private enforcement being encouraged and facilitated at the EU and UK levels, but I have been more interested recently in examining the developments in consumer redress, both on a comparative basis, and in particular in the UK, following the Consumer Rights Act 2015 and the significant introduction of a new opt-out collective redress scheme to facilitate "class actions". On a positive note, the more recent period in the UK evidences a real change, following the 2015 Act, to more large-scale consumer redress claims, utilising the opt-out model advantages allied with the availability of third-party litigation funding. This has apparently encouraged and facilitated multiple mass stand-alone collective claims, in relation to abuse of dominance, and again this has featured significantly in relation to very big business players in various tech and digital markets, for instance Alphabet and Apple. This leads to my final observation that current conversations around the digital economy, and for instance environmental sustainability, challenge the more formalistic, legalistic nature of rules based on the notion of "pure competition" alone, and we are witnessing a cyclical return to debates about the wider role of the public interest in competition law, and this may make it more difficult to litigate certain competition issues before the courts. Finally, these points lead to my central thesis that competition law is about calling companies to account for their market behaviour – both politically at a macro level to society generally, and privately, at a micro level, to individual consumers for the harm they have suffered as a consequence of anticompetitive conduct.

Why Has Competition Policy Played Such an Important Role in the EU for So Long?

JEAN-FRANÇOIS BELLIS*
Van Bael & Bellis

1. From the outset, the post-war European project has attached particular importance to competition law. Provisions on competition rules were already included in the Treaty of Paris of 18 April 1951, which established the European Coal and Steel Community (ECSC).

2. Yet competition law is not a European invention. Before the Second World War, Europe was best known for its cartels. These were tolerated, even encouraged, by public authorities which viewed them as a legitimate tool for rationalising industrial production.

3. As we all know, it was in the United States that competition law originated, with the 1890 enactment of the Sherman act which prohibited anticompetitive agreements and monopolisation practices. In his memoirs, Jean Monnet explains that the task of drafting the articles on competition law in the ECSC Treaty was entrusted to a young American professor, Robert Bowie. These are the provisions that served as the basis for the competition law articles eventually incorporated into the Treaty on the Functioning of the European Union (TFEU) in force today.

4. Unlike other European policies, competition policy and its enforcement were placed in the hands of the European Union's executive branch, the European Commission. From the early days of the European Economic Community, set

* Founding partner, Van Bael & Bellis, Brussels. Professor,Institute for European Studies, Université Libre de Bruxelles (ULB).

up by the Treaty of Rome in 1957, the Commission has enjoyed extensive supranational investigative and decision-making powers that have enabled it to conduct investigations into anticompetitive practices anywhere in the European Union and to penalise with increasingly severe financial penalties any breach of the European competition rules.

5. The Commission has used these significant powers to develop an original form of European competition law that differs from the classic antitrust law applied in the United States. In the sense that it was put at the service of the overriding policy objective of creating a common market among European states. For several decades since the early 1960s, the Commission has attacked all forms of agreement that erected obstacles to the free movement of products and services within the European market, such as, for example, clauses in distribution contracts that prohibited the sale of a product outside the national territory granted to a distributor. That emphasis on prohibiting vertical restrictions that hampered parallel trade within the EU put EU competition law more and more at odds with the Chicago School antitrust approach increasingly applied in the US since the 1980s. For the Chicago School what mattered was conduct that restricted horizontal competition. Vertical restrictions were viewed as innocuous forms of partial integration that were of no concern in themselves.

6. Despite the emphasis on practices that were inconsistent with the common market policy objective, European competition law in the last decades of the twentieth century had in common with US antitrust enforcement the notion that cartels needed to be severely sanctioned. In contrast with the attitude of US antitrust enforcers at the time, the Commission also developed a strong policy on abuses of a dominant position which led to a number of infringement decisions directed at US companies operating in Europe.

7. Compared to other antitrust enforcers around the world, the Commission was at a serious disadvantage until the early 1990s. There was a very significant gap in the legislative arsenal available to the Commission. The drafters of the Treaty of Rome had not seen fit to give to the Commission the power to exercise prior control over merger plans. The reason for this choice was that there was a broad consensus in Europe at the time about the vital need to encourage mergers and acquisitions in order to make European industry more competitive with its powerful international competitors, especially from the US. In his famous essay "The American Challenge", published in 1967, Jean-Jacques Servan Schreiber warned that "within fifteen years, the third industrial power in the world, after the United States and the USSR, could well be not Europe but American industry in Europe". This perception at the time of European industry being too weak to compete effectively in world markets explains why the Rome Treaty deliberately did not contain any provision allowing the Commission to act against industrial concentration at the European level.

8. Riding the wave of enthusiasm that accompanied Jacques Delors' project to relaunch the single market, the famous "1992 objective", the Commission finally succeeded in convincing the European Council of Ministers to adopt in 1989 a merger control regulation. That regulation set up a procedure of compulsory and suspensive notification to the Commission of any proposed mergers if certain worldwide and European turnover thresholds were reached. That regulation came into force in 1990.

9. It was then that European competition policy had its finest hour. The post of Competition Commissioner became one of the most sought-after positions within the European Commission. Whoever held that post was sure that they would enjoy instant international recognition. No other Commission Member, except perhaps the President, would dream of having such international notoriety.

10. Competition policy is indeed the only area in which the Commission has direct enforcement powers which it can exercise without having to obtain the approval of the Member States. The Commission's decisions on European competition law breaches make headlines in the international press. This media interest is due to the spectacular nature of many of the decisions adopted against world-renowned companies, often of American origin, which have been subjected to some of the highest antitrust fines in the world.

11. The first European Competition Commissioner to fully benefit from the international aura of European competition law at the end of the last century was Karel Van Miert, from Belgium, whom the international press described as the "the most powerful man in Europe".

12. In 1997, Karel Van Miert distinguished himself in particular by his relentless fight against the merger between the aircraft manufacturer Boeing and its competitor MacDonnell Douglas. Despite the purely American nature of this merger, the European Commission took the view that it could prohibit it because of its impact on competition in the European market for certain types of aircraft. This claim provoked a wave of indignation in the United States, where the transaction was allowed by the Federal trade Commission (FTC). A long list of retaliatory measures, including, for example, the abolition of Air France's landing rights in the United States, was even drawn up within the US Congress. This case could have resulted in a trade war between Europe and the United States. But, in the end, there was no trade war because, instead of prohibiting the merger outright, the Commission limited itself to requiring Boeing to enter into a series of commercial commitments that provided certain competitive benefits to Airbus. A one-hour documentary film shot by the Arte TV channel describes the many twists and turns of this affair. The final scene shows the press conference at which Karel Van Miert proudly announces the final concessions won from Boeing in the course of the previous night.

13. The terms of office of the Competition Commissioners who succeeded Karel Van Miert were also punctuated by epic battles with the largest and most prestigious American companies.

14. It was with two of these giants that Commissioner Mario Monti from Italy crossed swords: General Electric, then at its peak, whose merger with Honeywell was prohibited by the Commission in 2002, even though it had been authorised by the American antitrust authorities, and Microsoft, condemned in 2004 for two abuses of a dominant position.

15. The skirmishes with Microsoft continued during the tenure of Commissioner Neelie Kroes from the Netherlands, who succeeded Mario Monti. But the high point of her tenure was the Commission's decision in 2009 to impose on US semiconductor producer Intel the highest individual fine in the world at the time, namely €1.06 billion, for having committed an abuse of a dominant position. The main elements of this decision were annulled in 2022 by the General Court of the European Union following a very long procedure.

16. After the more discreet interlude of the Spanish Commissioner Joaquín Almunia, Margrethe Vestager, the current Competition Commissioner from Denmark, has taken up the torch in the fight against the big American companies accused of abuse of dominance in the digital sector, with no less than three successive infringement decisions against Google in 2017, 2018 and 2019, accompanied by fines totalling more than €8 billion euros.

17. Over time, the European Commission has come to be recognised as the most important competition authority not only in Europe but also in the world. Its decisions, which are often bolder than those of its American counterparts, particularly in the area of abuse of a dominant position, have set precedents around the world. It was from the European competition law system that China drew inspiration to draft its own antitrust legislation in the 2000s.

18. Having achieved such a level of international recognition, will European competition policy be able to maintain this leading role?

19. In the system of an increasingly deregulated market economy that triumphed at the turn of the new millennium, European competition policy shone particularly brightly because it was one of the rare forms of public intervention in the market at European level. The Commission acted as a police force of the market economy seeking to contain the most serious abuses.

20. But the world has changed. The new geopolitical challenges facing Europe now require new, more interventionist European public policies. It will not be possible to ensure the ecological and digital transition, encourage the re-industrialisation of Europe and protect it against the intensification of international competition, sometimes fuelled by subsidies from third countries, by merely bringing cases against competition law infringements.

21. We are witnessing the revival of a concept that had become taboo at European level, that of industrial policy. In the area of state aid granted by European Union Member States, which is an integral part of European competition law, the Commission has already relaxed its policy to allow Member States to match the public support offered to strategic industries by third countries such as the United States or China.

22. The consequence of all this will be that competition policy will necessarily take second place to the new geopolitical objectives pursued by the European Union, and that it will above all have to take care not to thwart them.

23. This is not to say that European competition law will no longer be important. On the contrary, it will continue to play a major role which companies operating on the European market could only ignore at their peril.

24. But it will probably no longer occur to anyone to say that the European Competition Commissioner is the most powerful person in Europe.

Is Competition Everything? The UK Experience

Peter Freeman*
Competition Appeal Tribunal

I. Introduction – The Virtue of Competition

1. There is general acceptance amongst industrialised economies that competition policy is a key instrument bringing economic benefits of many kinds. For consumers, there is more choice and lower prices, new and innovative products and services; for industry there is greater efficiency, access to new markets and pressure to innovate; for the economy as a whole there is increased productivity and growth. But this may be difficult to translate into practical terms and measurable results and some commentators appear puzzled by what competition policy is trying to achieve. This short chapter examines the challenges facing UK competition policy in the light of recent problems in enforcement, and suggests a way forward.

II. Contrasting Views

2. Some recent press comments accuse the authorities of intervening too much, others take the opposite view. *The Times*, commenting on a recent decision of the UK authorities, said: 'recent evidence suggests that the balance has swung too far towards intervention' and that' '… competition policy… is now subject too much to the discretion of regulators and is insufficiently

---

* Peter Freeman CBE KC (Hon) is a Senior Adviser (Policy) at the Competition Appeal Tribunal. All views expressed are personal to the author.

sensitive to the needs of an open, trading economy…'.[1] *The Economist*, in a thoughtful article on the issue of scale and antitrust,[2] observed that: 'Zealous trustbusting carries its own risks…'. By contrast, only a few weeks later, *The Times*' own Financial Editor wrote: 'Weakening the interpretation of competition rules will in the long run harm the British economy, not help it'.[3] So what is going on? Is competition policy at some new crossroads? Or is it just being misapplied? Let us first examine how we got to where we are.

III. From Theory to Practice – the UK Context

3. Turning competition theory into practice requires a clear policy, effective laws and competent enforcement in a proper institutional framework. It is also important that enforcement activity takes account of state action, as well as that of businesses and citizens.

4. In the UK, competition policy has been endorsed by successive governments for at least the past three decades. A 1988 policy review[4] stated: '(I)t is the promotion of competition which is at the heart of the government's economic philosophy'. In 2001, another review[5] asserted: 'Vigorous competition between firms is the lifeblood of strong and effective markets…Competition is a central driver for productivity growth in the economy….'. In 2016 a further review said:[6] 'Effective competition is central to ensuring a well-functioning economy. Competition supports productivity and growth'. The most recent review[7] puts the commitment as follows: 'Well-functioning markets encourage competition to drive down prices, offer increased choice, and maintain high consumer standards'. Whilst successive governments may play around with the wording, the overall commitment to promoting competition, as a key element of economic policy, does not appear to be in doubt.

5. In terms of laws, in 1998 the UK adopted the EU prohibition framework covering agreements and abuse of dominant position, overseen by the Office of Fair Trading (OFT) but retained, in a reconstituted form, administrative

1 See *The Times* view on competition: 'Closed for Business' *The Times* (London, 5 June 2023); and 'Britain's Competition Regime Must Not Be So Stringent as to Deter Investment' *The Times* (London, 16 October 2023).

2 'How Bad Is Being Big?' *The Economist* (London, 15 July 2023) 55.

3 Patrick Hosking, 'Loosening Competition Rules Is No Cure for Problems in the Economy' *The Times* (London, 15 August 2023) 35, (corrected text).

4 Department of Trade and Industry, *The Liesner Review* (Cm 331, 1986).

5 Department of Trade and Industry, *Productivity and Enterprise – A World Class Competition Regime* (Cm 5233, 2001).

6 Department for Business, Innovation and Skills, 'Consultation: Options to Refine the UK Competition Regime' (26 May 2016) <https://assets.publishing.service.gov.uk/media/5a80511ae5274a2e87db91e1/bis-16-253-options-to-refine-competition-regime.pdf> accessed 31 October 2024.

7 Department for Business, Energy, and Industrial Strategy, Consultation: Reforming Competition and Consumer Policy' July 2021 (Ministerial Foreword) <https://assets.publishing.service.gov.uk/media/60f5d5b1e90e0764ccfbd820/CCS001_CCS0721951242-001_Reforming_Competition_and_Consumer_Policy_E-Laying.pdf> accessed 31 October 2024.

control by the OFT and the Competition Commission (CC) of markets and mergers. Although these regimes can overlap, problems have largely been avoided in practice.

6. The UK institutional structure was again reformed in 2013, with the creation of the Competition and Markets Authority (CMA). This authority combined the functions of the former OFT and CC giving a structure within which to operate the two systems described above. In particular, for so called 'phase 2' merger and market investigations, the CMA operates a panel system very similar to that of the former CC.

7. The present structure was conceived as an 'independent agency' model. Ministers, who had previously been extensively involved, 'stepped back' and decision-making for all parts of the regime was allocated to the newly empowered authorities.[8] This broadly reflected the position in comparable jurisdictions (the 2001 White Paper referred to a 'world-class' system) but it was major change for the UK.

8. Having independent authorities make decisions and Ministers stepping back meant a greater role for the courts in holding authorities to account. In 2003 a specialised Competition Appeal Tribunal (CAT) was also set up to hear appeals from authority decisions. The CAT has grown in stature and authority over the past two decades, although there remains some uncertainty over the intensity of its scrutiny of authority decisions.[9]

9. Since 2020, the regime has operated outside the EU legal framework, with the result that more, and more important, cases fall to be considered by UK authorities. The main consequence so far is an increase in UK merger cases.

IV. Expanding the Reach of Competition Law

10. It remains unclear how far competition should extend to sectors of the economy where the State was the main player, either as participant or regulator. In the enthusiastic atmosphere of two decades ago, financial services, public health and higher education appeared to be fruitful areas for intervention. There has since been something of a reaction, with competition in retreat.

11. In financial services, where the state played a major regulatory role, possible adverse effects on prudential requirements of introducing greater competition were probably under-estimated, particularly in banking. The resulting over-extension and under-capitalisation of some major financial institutions was

---

8 Subject to powers to safeguard specific public interest concerns and, recently, national security interests.

9 See eg Department for Business, Energy, and Industrial Strategy, 'Reforming Competition and Consumer Policy: Government Response' (April 2022) 50 <www.gov.uk/government/consultations/reforming-competition-and-consumer-policy/outcome/reforming-competition-and-consumer-policy-government-response> accessed 31 October 2024 'Overall, government is not minded to change the standard by which the Tribunal determines appeals against infringement decisions *at this time*'. (emphasis added).

central to the 2008 financial crisis. The recommendations (for ring-fencing and increased capitalisation) of the specially constituted Independent Banking Commission represented a decisive re-assertion by government of prudential regulation rather than greater competition.

12. In public health, a succession of reforms introduced market-type arrangements (and a regulatory body with competition powers) to the provision of primary and secondary healthcare, as well as bringing NHS hospital mergers within the scope of merger control. These policies have now been largely reversed, as being too costly and unrealistic in a sector under intense resource pressure where, it is argued, many tasks require collaboration under central direction.

13. In higher education, block grants to universities were largely replaced by student fees funded by a government loan scheme. It was intended that universities would compete on price to attract students, who would benefit from a competitive market with increased choice. In practice, price competition was not widespread, and most universities charged the maximum amount permitted for UK students, whilst overall numbers remained capped. This experiment has not yet run its course but does not appear to have achieved its main objective of reducing State funding and increasing choice for students and is unlikely to continue without major reform.

14. It would seem from these examples that introducing competition into complex administrative contexts may not, on its own, bring the results intended and that other policy considerations may take precedence. It also remains difficult to apply standard competition principles to sectors where the State is itself an active player.

V. Other Challenges

15. Competition policy has also had to face external challenges greater even than the 2008 financial crisis. These include the Covid-19 pandemic, the recent energy crisis, and the growth of the so-called 'big tech' industry.

16. The Covid-19 pandemic was a largely unforeseen shock, in the UK as elsewhere, to public health, to the economy and to society as a whole. The nature of the challenge was twofold.

17. First, the economy did not seem well prepared for events of this kind. It seemed there were large gaps in the UK's pharmaceutical and health care production capability. How far these were the result of the application of competition policy is debatable[10] but the promotion of sovereign capacity was clearly not one of the priorities.[11]

---

10 The supply of pharmaceuticals to the NHS is subject to detailed, partly voluntary, regulation.

11 Other gaps, for example in public health laboratory capacity, were a more direct result of government policies.

18. The second aspect was in responding to the pandemic. As the UK Government acknowledged:[12] 'It is clear that the pandemic has had a more profound impact on the way business and the economy functions than anything else in recent history'. Competition enforcement was less relevant in the face of this upheaval, with companies having to co-operate rather than compete and the CMA concentrating on short-term price hikes and shortage of supply of key items.

19. In the energy sector, in particular gas supply, competition appeared ineffective if not irrelevant in the face of supply shortages following the war in Ukraine and sanctions imposed on Russia. UK regulatory policy for energy, emphasising retail competition, assumed easy and plentiful access to international supply at the wholesale level. When supply was restricted, wholesale prices rose drastically, making retail price caps (already controversial) of little use.

20. In these major, albeit very different, external shock situations, competition appeared largely irrelevant to any solution; competition policy had to defer to more important considerations of capacity, security and national control.

VI. The Big Tech Challenge

21. The challenge presented by what is loosely called 'big tech' is different as it is not external to the economy, but rather a result of its operation. 'Antitrust' law has always faced challenges from new, emerging, powerful industrial sectors. Conceived in the 1890s in response to railroad 'trusts', the law was challenged in turn by the oil companies[13] and later by the communications industry.[14] These challenges emerged in slightly differing forms in other competition regimes, particularly the EU,[15] as information technology emerged as another powerful industrial force.

22. The rise of 'big tech' represents a significant challenge in several important respects. First, the companies involved are, by definition, very large and well-funded, and operate internationally, if not globally, A national or even a regional authority, however well resourced, is therefore at a disadvantage.

23. Second, the firms' organisation and practices, whether as platforms or intermediaries, by the amassing of information and data, by vertical integration,

---

12 Department for Business, Energy, and Industrial Strategy (n 7), 8.

13 *Standard Oil Co of New Jersey v United States* 221 U.S. 1 (1911).

14 *United States v American Telephone & Telegraph Co* Civil Action no 74-1698 (DDC 1974).

15 See the cases brought by the European Commission in 1973 against IBM (settled in 1984 (Bull EC 10-1984) and in 2000 against Microsoft (Case 201/04 *Microsoft Corp v Commission of the European Communities* [2007] ECR II-3601) see Fin Lomholt, 'The EU Commission monitors remedies offered by software company in an abuse of dominant case (IBM)' (1984) e-Competitions art. No. 39382 and Catherine Prieto, 'The Microsoft Saga: The Court of First Instance upholds the Commission's finding that Microsoft had abused its dominant position in the PC operating system market (Microsoft)' (17 September 2007) 4 Concurrences 14478 78-83.

by the acquisition of potential competitors, or by a combination of any of these, challenge some established competition law assumptions. Some argue that their activities fall largely outside the scope of competition law.

24. The standard competition policy measures of adverse effect on price and choice are hard to apply, as most 'big tech' companies offer services to consumers that are innovative and useful, and 'free' to the consumer. Consumer detriment has to be shown in other, more indirect, ways – such as loss of control over personal data. This can seem to put competition policy at odds with the preferences of the actual consumer.

25. Faced with this, competition authorities have sought to apply traditional measures more flexibly, to look for hidden costs and detriments, and to prevent the build-up of market power by extending merger control to cover potential, future, threats to competition. This is not a straightforward exercise, although there is no inherent reason why competition theory should not adapt to accommodate new forms of market power and abuse. Practices such as favouring in-house suppliers and unfair tying practices have already been examined under traditional competition law, and merger control has never been set in stone.

26. Nevertheless, the preferred method, both in the EU and the UK, of confronting 'big tech' is through regulation rather than competition. In the UK this will be by enacting a new legal framework[16] to empower a Digital Markets Unit (DMU) within the CMA to apply rules and codes of practice to designated companies, (in practice the major 'big tech' companies) and require compliance under pain of financial penalty or further measures.

27. It is significant that in this important industrial and technical sphere, regulation has been preferred to competition enforcement, despite the UK already having a powerful market investigation regime. In justification it is said that digital markets regulation supplements but does not replace the competition regime; ex-post enforcement can be slow and cumbersome; regulation is better fitted to keeping up with technological advance; and competition enforcement remains available as a last resort.

28. These arguments do not necessarily convince. In practice it may be difficult to operate the two public enforcement systems in parallel, whatever the intention, and operating the regulatory system may not be easy.

29. The assumption appears to be that the companies subject to this form of regulation will be willing to cooperate with the DMU in making the regulatory regime work. That is one ground put forward for having appeals from DMU decisions being by way of judicial review rather than, as with most competition appeals, 'on the merits'.[17]

16 Digital Markets, Competition and Consumers Act 2024 ch 13. The Digital Markets, Competition and Consumer Bill was introduced in Parliament in March 2023 and became law in May 2024.

17 The UK Government has proposed making appeals against penalties on the same merits basis as in competition cases.

30. Whether or not this assumption is correct, private enforcement actions against 'big tech' companies are increasing in number and importance, offering a separate stream of enforcement outside the scope of the digital regulation system. Private actions are necessarily considered by the CAT 'on the merits'.

31. In facing this challenge, the UK authorities, after the UK's departure from the EU, stand alone, at least in a formal sense. They are not unique in this, but the UK's separation is recent and deliberate. In practice, however, the UK will cooperate and act in co-ordination with other authorities, principally in the US and EU. But being formally outside the EU's competition enforcement structure, however close the cooperation, will hardly help the UK authorities' ability to regulate a possibly unwilling international group.

VII. Assessment

32. These considerations suggest that although great care must be taken when extending competition to new sectors where other policy considerations may be more important, the main benefits of the policy itself are not in serious doubt. What matters more is that competition enforcement must be realistic and pragmatic.

33. Applying competition to sectors such as public health and higher education has caused difficulties. When applied with greater emphasis to banking and some financial services, it may have operated in conflict with other important policies, even to the detriment of the consumers.

34. Faced with the recent major external shocks in public health and energy supply, both competition policy and its enforcement have appeared to be ineffective and even irrelevant.

35. Finally, the rise of 'big tech' has put in question whether competition policy is the preferred means of control and, if so, how it should best be applied. Government has opted for a regulatory regime rather than traditional competition enforcement, on the grounds that regulation is more robust and agile in this sector.

36. Is competition policy therefore no longer seen as central to economic performance? Although expectations cannot be as high as they were two decades ago, the central importance of competition policy is not seriously in doubt. But care is needed to ensure that applying it unthinkingly, or enforcing it over zealously, do not damage the broad consensus on which the acceptance of competition policy depends.

37. It is highly desirable that competition policy should continue to play a central role in the economy. Despite the difficulties and criticisms, no realistic alternative solution has been offered. Regulation, state control and central

planning, other than in time of war (or possibly a pandemic), have a poor record in terms of producing improved economic performance. But a realistic and pragmatic approach to enforcement is needed.

VIII. Independence and Relevance

38. Two other factors play an important role in enhancing this pragmatic approach. They are, first, freedom for the authorities from political interference and, second, the need to make the competition policy and its enforcement understandable to its 'stakeholders' – that is politicians, business, the media and the consumer.

39. Independence of the authorities has looked increasingly fragile under pressure of recent events. Of course, it was never the case that agencies entrusted with such an important function would be entirely free from political influence. The question is one of degree. As with economic regulation, where regulators have fallen increasingly back under governmental direction, the danger of competition authorities being subject to excessive interference is also not to be underrated.

40. What is important is to preserve operational independence, ie the ability for an authority to make the decisions it wants to make free from political pressure. On the other hand, the authorities will recognise that they exercise their powers in a political and legislative context in which government, through parliament, is inevitably the master. Authorities must therefore be politically aware and be sensitive to political currents, without necessarily giving way to them.

41. In return, government, having out-sourced much of its expertise in the field of competition policy, must re-equip itself with the necessary ministerial and administrative expertise and resources. This will enable government and competition authorities to have better mutual understanding and to avoid surprises and mishaps, remaining conscious of their clearly-defined respective roles.

42. Second, and crucially, competition must appear relevant and understandable to the consumer and to the business community; to the media and to those in government and parliament.

43. Making policy understandable and appreciated by the public (in the broad sense) is an essential part of good administrative practice which applies in the competition field as in any other. The best way to do this is to make enforcement decisions understandable. This requires careful choice of cases to take forward and clear presentation of the result in plain language. Over time, this not only brings public recognition but also a realisation that competition can make a difference to everyday life and work. The authorities are well aware of this and already use the media widely and to considerable effect. But, given the challenges we have outlined, they surely need to redouble their efforts.

IX. Conclusion

44. To return to the title of this short piece, and with apologies to Professor Krugman,[18] competition may not be everything, but in the long run it is almost everything. It must be applied with a pragmatic sense of what will work and what will not. It must be made understandable and its relevance to the needs and interests of business, consumers and politicians properly communicated. Approaching things in this way will help to ensure that competition policy remains central to a successful economy.

18 Paul Krugman, *The Age of Diminishing Expectations* (MIT Press 1994) 'Productivity isn't everything, but in the long run it is almost everything'.

Competition as Mechanism for Fostering a Cohesive and Effective Commercial System

DEBORAH HEALEY*
The University of New South Wales

I. What is Competition?

1. This chapter considers aspects of competition in the context of competition law and policy generally, and in Australia.

2. 'Competition' exists as a concept throughout global society: for example, in sport, in social settings, between individuals, and in business. General dictionary definitions for 'competition' include 'event or contest in which people take part in order to establish superiority or supremacy in a particular area';[1] 'the action of endeavouring to gain what another endeavours to gain at the same time'; 'the striving of two or more for the same object'.[2]

3. While the general idea behind competition is consistent and linked to the above definitions, as with many words, different contexts substantially change the meaning. As was noted long ago by the Trade Practices Tribunal (now the Australian Competition Tribunal), 'Competition is a very rich concept… Competition may be valued for many reasons as serving economic, social

---

* Professor and Director China International Economic Law Centre (CIBEL) Faculty of Law and Justice, University of New South Wales.

1 Oxford Languages, <https://languages.oup.com/google-dictionary-en/> accessed 12 October 2024.

2 *Oxford English Dictionary*, <www.oed.com/?tl=true> accessed 12 October 2024.

and political goals'.[3] In sport, for example, competition is linked to physical activity. People may compete against other people or teams in a game or an event, or compete against the clock, or compete to complete a particular task. The distinction between the meaning of the word in this context and in a competition law context was noted in one seminal Australian competition law case involving football, where the judge cautioned against confusion between the two usages.[4] There the judge said:

> "The word 'competition' when used in a commercial or economic sense is not to be confused with the word 'competition' when used in a sporting sense when the word has a different meaning. Sporting teams compete with each other to win a sporting event. Football teams engage in matches. They compete against each other to win a premiership. In the present case, care must be taken to ensure that the use of the word 'competition' does not cause confusion. In social settings, competition may be linked to measurement of esteem or achievement in particular contexts".

4. But why do we value competition? The judge's words above recognise that in an economic and commercial context, competition has developed a more specific meaning, and in both economic and legal terms, the pursuit of competition is of itself important in delivering the wants and needs of society.

5. In these contexts, competition is 'rivalrous market behaviour'. It has 'an economic role as a device for controlling the disposition of society's resources... it is a mechanism... for firms discovering the kinds of goods and services the community wants and the manner in which these may be supplied in the cheapest way... firms disregard these signals at their peril'.[5] It is an economic regulator in the public interest.[6] This rivalry may be as a supplier or an acquirer. Restrictions on competition reduce the incentive for firms to compete on price, quality or innovative features and ultimately disadvantages consumers (who may be other businesses or individuals).

6. Market power is the antithesis of competition, parties with market power having the ability to reduce output or capacity, to raise prices or to reduce quality or choice or to reduce or stifle innovation. The assessment of market power requires the assessment of competition.

7. The area in which entities compete is known as a market. Market definition delineates the area of transactions in which products or services compete, as to products or services and as to functional level and geography. Appropriate market definition is one of the key issues in determining the impact of likely

---

3 *Re Queensland Co-operative Milling Association Limited and Defiance Holdings (Re QCMA)* 1976FLR 169, 187. Many seminal comments on competition and markets are contained in this case, which is oft quoted at all court levels and is still very influential in Australia, despite its age.

4 *Adamson v West Perth Football Club* Inc (1979) 39 FLR 199, (Northrop J) 64.

5 ibid.

6 Bruce G Donald and John D Heydon, *Trade Practices Law* (Law Book Company 1978) vol 1, 78.

anticompetitive conduct: too broad a market dilutes the impact of the conduct, but too narrow a market enhances it.

8. But in all cases, the purpose of the analysis is the assessment and measurement of the state of rivalry or market power of participants to ascertain the level of competition in the market, usually by comparison with the position with and without the subject conduct. And competition is a dynamic process which means that the analysis will consider the market at the current time and into the future before reaching a conclusion. To consider the impact of particular conduct, the state of the market going forward with and without the proposed conduct is assessed.

II. Competition as an Economic Concept in Competition Law

9. The identification or concept of a law as a 'competition law' requires the identification of its focus and how it is to be interpreted. Why do we have competition law? This is relevant to its application and interpretation. The goals or objects of an individual competition law may differ in established and newer jurisdictions.[7] There are some 'standard approaches ' and other newer views on what is important in drafting and interpreting a competition law. Goals of competition law have also changed over time with changing economic ideologies. Among developing economies, different approaches to development and different conceptions of what competition law can do may affect the goals and scope of competition law. But against all of this, 'the most commonly stated objective of competition policy is the promotion and protection of the competitive process'.[8] Competition is thus valued because it results in efficiency and delivers consumer welfare. And as an examination of the objects of various competition law shows, competition policy 'is an expression of the current values and aims of society and is as susceptible to change as political thinking generally'.[9]

III. Competition and Markets

10. Competition law was originally designed as a 'creature of the industrial era'.[10] The rise of concentration in the last century meant that competition law was focused on the existence and behaviour of oligopolies. These entities were arguably inclined to collude, and the focus of competition law was on collusion and exclusionary conduct. Tools such as product and services substitution tests

---

7 As to the issue of goals generally, see Deborah Healey, 'The Ambit of Competition Law: Comments on its Goals' in Deborah Healey, Michael Jacobs and Rhonda Smith (eds), *Research Handbook on Methods and Models of Competition Law* (Edward Elgar 2020) 12.

8 ASEAN, *Regional Guidelines on Competition Policy* (2010) paras 2.1.2, 2.2.1, <www.asean.org/wp-content/uploads/images/2012/publications/ASEAN%20Regional%20Guidelines%20on%20Competition%20Policy.pdf> accessed 12 October 2024, discussed in Healey (n 7) 16.

9 Richard Whish and David Bailey, *Competition Law* (9th edn, OUP 2018) 19.

10 Pablo Ibáñez Columo, *The New EU Competition Law* (Hart Publishing 2023) 31.

based on price sensitivity defined markets in which behaviour of market participants could be tested. But market rivalry was not so relevant to markets which were natural monopolies containing bottlenecks at higher or lower functional levels. The traditional assumptions did not work so well in network industries or in markets inhabited by digital platforms. Price sensitivity tests did not work in two sided markets where acquirers did not pay for services (or paid in other ways such as giving over information which the acquirer could subsequently use). Particularly in digital markets, incumbent platforms engaged in competition in new ways. Behaviours such as 'anticompetitive self-preferencing, tying and bundling practices, [creation of] barriers to switching', and 'lack of access to third party applications on a platform or service' are all relatively new types of conduct (or old conduct in very different contexts) which require a different approach to competition law assessment.[11] Coupled with consumer problems such as unconstrained use of consumer data, difficulties with data portability, business practices such as unfair trading, inadequate reporting and compliance mechanisms,[12] the rise of digital platforms has required new approaches to competition regulation. These are based on the multiple endemic issues around market power, critical timing and cost problems with traditional enforcement methods, unbridled use of consumer data and the extremely dynamic nature of digital markets. To ensure that consumers and other businesses are protected from rising costs and capture, new digital industry competition regulation has been passed in a number of jurisdictions globally and this trend is likely to continue.[13]

IV. Competition in Australian Competition Law

11. The object of the Competition and Consumer Act 2010 (CCA) in Australia is fairly simple in the scheme of things. It is 'to enhance the welfare of Australians through the promotion of competition and fair trading and provision for consumer protection'.[14] This provision was introduced in 1995, but before this it was always understood that 'competition' should be given its economic meaning, in terms of preferencing efficient market performance. In an Australian context, it was clear even before the addition of this provision that competition law does not protect a group such as small business, for example, unless they are efficient performers likely to be damaged by anticompetitive conduct.

---

11 See ACCC, *Digital Platform Services Inquiry Final Report – Issues Paper* (Report forthcoming 2025) 4.

12 ibid.

13 See, for example, Regulation (EU) 2022/1925 of the European Parliament and of the Council of 14 September 2022 on contestable and fair markets in the digital sector and amending Directives (EU) 2019/1937 and (EU) 2020/1828 (Digital Markets Act) [2022] OJ L 265/1; Regulation (EU) 2022/2065 of the European Parliament and of the Council of 19 October 2022 on a Single Market For Digital Services and amending Directive 2000/31/EC (Digital Services Act) [2022] OJ L 277/1. and various other regulations. Germany amended the German Competition Act with the GWB Digitalisation Act 2021. India, draft Digital Competition Bill 2024. Japan Improving Transparency and Fairness of Digital Platforms Act 2020. South Korea, draft Act on the Promotion of Platform Competition, 2023. UK, Digital Markets, Competition and Consumers Act 2024. These examples are listed in the ACCC *Final Report* (n 11).

14 Competition and Consumer Act 2010 (CCA), s 2introduced in 1995.

12. Aside from the objects clause, there is a definition of competition in Section 4 of the CCA, but it is an inclusive definition only and is really an application provision, put there to indicate that the CCA covers competition from imports and potential imports of goods and services which are capable of being rendered in Australia.[15]

13. Competition 'is a process rather than a situation'.[16] This was further described in an evocative way by French J. J in a merger case, where he stated:

> "Competition in a market is not assessed by a snapshot view of participant behaviour at a particular time. The theatre of competition is a theatre of real actors and shadow actors. The shadows are cast by the potential for new entry. The competitive process is informed by the rivalry of the participants and the potential rivalry of potential participants. Competition so understood is conceptually distinct from the idea of the market and the elements of market structure which may constrain or facilitate it".[17]

14. At its most extreme, the nature of vigorous competition has been described in the following way by the Australian High Court, in an influential judgment delivered before the addition of the objects clause to the Act:

> "Competition by its very nature is deliberate and ruthless. Competitors jockey for sales, the more effective competitors injuring the less effective by taking sales away. Competitors almost always try to 'injure' each other in this way… these injuries are the inevitable consequence of the competition [the Act] is designed to foster".[18]

15. So, Australia recognises that competition will be dynamic and may be ruthless in nature. Potential competition has always been an important part of the competitive process and an important part of analysis in Australia.[19] Traditional methods for assessing competition in markets have applied in Australia. Market as the place where competition occurs has been defined using price sensitivity tests. The impact of particular conduct on markets has been determined using a 'future with and without test' which recognises that a market is not a static construct.[20]

16. But in Australia as in other jurisdictions digital platforms have presented novel and growing problems for competition. This was recognised in 2019 when the Australian Government commissioned the Digital Platforms Inquiry

---

15 ACCC *Final Report* (n 11).

16 See (n 3).

17 *Australian Gas Light Company v Australian Competition and Consumer Commission (No 3)* [2003] FCA 1525, 350. Recognition of the role of entrants and their role in facilitating competition of more recent times has been a focus when assessing mergers involving start-ups and nascent competitors by digital platform businesses.

18 *Queensland Wire Industries v BHP*, (1989), 167 CLR 177, 24.

19 ibid.

20 *Outboard Marine Australia Pty Ltd v Hecar Investments (No 6) Pty Ltd* 1982) 66 FLR 120; *Stirling Harbour Services Pty Ltd v Bunbury Port Authority* [2000] FCA 38.

following concerns about the impact of digital platforms on privacy, media and journalism, consumer protection and choice. The inquiry focused on search engines, social media platforms and other digital content aggregation platforms, and three user groups: advertisers, media content creators and consumers.[21]

17. The resulting report was influential, and the government gave the competition regulator, the Australian Competition and Consumer Commission (ACCC), funding for five years to examine specific questions on the competitive impact of aspects of digital platforms, with the final report due in 2025.[22] The ACCC has examined and reported on online private messaging, app marketplaces, search defaults and choice screens, product ecosystems and data brokers. The ACCC has made many recommendations on amendments to merger law to address digital mergers.[23] Mandatory codes of conduct for specific mandated platforms and specific services have been recommended and the proposal accepted in principle by the government.[24] This is somewhat similar to the EU Digital Markets Act (DMA) and enforceable under the CCA, although the mode is intended to provide more flexibility. A final report is currently in draft form and open for comment.[25]

V. Is Competition an End in Itself or Should Other Issues be Considered Where There Is Overriding Public Benefit Despite Less Competition?

18. The goals of competition law are primarily focused on the economic, but may in some jurisdictions diverge to consider fairness, equality and other issues.[26] But what of the question of overriding public benefit? The Australian system recognises that 'competition is not an end in itself'.[27] It has since its inception contained a unique system of administrative permission called authorisation' for conducwhich may substantially lessen

21 ACCC *Final Report* (n 11).

22 ibid.

23 This is in the context also of major proposals to reform the current Australian merger review system: see Australian Government, 'Mergers and acquisitions' <https://treasury.gov.au/review/competition-review-2023/mergers> accessed 12 October 2024. Draft merger laws are currently subject to submissions.

24 ACCA, *Digital Platform Services Inquiry Interim Report 2022*, (2022) <www.accc.gov.au/inquiries-and-consultations/digital-platform-services-inquiry-2020-25/september-2022-interim-report> accessed 12 October 2024.

25 ACCC *Final Report* (n 11).

26 See Healey (n 7) generally. There are other laws which allow non-competition issues to override competition analysis. See, for example, Ioannis Kokkoris and Nicholas Levy (eds), *Research Handbook on Global Merger Control* (Edward Elgar 2023) 35.

27 Rod Sims and Graeme Woodbridge, 'The Continuing Journey to Protect Competition: The ACCC's Perspectives on Part IV' in Michael Gvozdenovic and Stephen Puttick (eds), *Current Issues in Competition Law, Volume II Practice and Perspectives* (The Federation Press 2021) 37.

competition but has overriding public benefit. This has been described in the following way:

> "To the extent that protecting the competitive process does not promote economic efficiency in a particular market, or where other policy goals conflict with economic efficiency and required some trade-off to be made, exemptions from the general rules should also be granted through those exemption mechanisms, such as authorisation".[28]

19. The process is thus a direct mechanism for resolving conflicts between the competitive process and other policy goals where[29] applications are made by the parties to the ACCC in relation to a specific arrangement or other conduct including a merger outlining the anticompetitive impacts of the conduct and any public benefits arising[30]. Put simply, if the public benefits outweigh the anticompetitive detriment, the conduct may be authorised for a specific period of up to five years. Conditions may be imposed. The views of any interested or affected parties are considered. The grant is reviewed after five years. The authorisation can be revoked at any time for change of circumstances, although the parties are able to contest this. The parties may appeal the determination to the Australian Competition Tribunal.

20. This process has worked well in Australia and provided a significant degree of flexibility during Covid-19 to override competition in emergency circumstances for short periods of time.[31]

VI. Is Competition the Same as Competitiveness?

21. Some might argue that 'competition' and 'competitiveness' are the same or similar aspects of the same thing, but competitiveness is not the same thing as competition. While the OECD has stated that competitiveness is 'an inherently nebulous concept without an agreed definition',[32] ultimately the OECD distinguishes 'competitiveness' and 'competition' in the following way: competitiveness as 'the relevant position (ie the strength or weakness) of a firm vis-à-vis other firms in a market'; while competition 'refers to the state of

---

28 Report by Independent Committee of Inquiry, *National Competition Policy AGPS Canberra 1993* (Hilmer Report 1993) 26 <http://ncp.ncc.gov.au/docs/National%20Competition%20Policy%20Review%20report,%20The%20Hilmer%20Report,%20August%201993.pdf> accessed 12 October 2024.

29 ibid 28–29.

30 Authorisation was recently granted, for example, to a merger on public benefit grounds linked to sustainability outcomes: ACCC, 'Brookfield LP and MidOcean proposed acquisition of Origins Energy Limited' (5 June 2023) <www.accc.gov.au/public-registers/mergers-registers/merger-authorisations-register/brookfield-lp-and-midocean-proposed-acquisition-of-origin-energy-limited> accessed 12 October 2024. For the relevant provisions, see Part VI of the CCA.

31 ACCC Chair Rod Sims, 'Managing the Impacts of COVID-19 Disruption on Consumers and Business Speech' (8 April 2020) <www.accc.gov.au/about-us/news/speeches/managing-the-impacts-of-covid-19-disruption-on-consumers-and-business-speech> accessed 12 October 2024.

32 Paul Davidson, Celine Kauffmann and Marie-Gabrielle de Liedekerke, 'How Do Laws and Regulations Affect Competitiveness: The Role for Regulatory Impact Assessment' (2021) OECD Regulatory Policy Working Papers 15, 9.

the market, ie the level of competition'.[33] Analysis of competitiveness over time has ranged from a simple cost and price analysis to a wider focus using factors having social and environmental dimensions.[34]

22. Globally, 'competitiveness' is consistently used 'synonymously with productivity, competition, comparative advantage and exchange rate' and can be applied to different economic actors, such as a business, a region or a country.[35] It means different things depending on context. But most definitions focus on the notion of *international* competition rather than competition within a jurisdiction. Michael Porter's works focused on factors linked to international competitiveness of companies and nations.[36] In Ireland, for example, 'competitiveness' is defined as ' the ability to achieve success in international markets leading to better standards of living for all'. The EU states that a competitive economy 'is an economy whose sustained rate of productivity is able to drive growth and, consequently, income and welfare' and notes that economic competitiveness 'has long been one of the key political priorities of the European Union (EU)'.[37] In Australia, the Productivity Commission uses the term competitiveness as a synonym of both comparative advantage and productivity, depending on the context.[38]

23. Policy makers need to consider both competition and competitiveness. But competition law (and policy), the subjects of this current volume, generally focus on competition in the narrower sense of the actual degree of competition in a particular market.

---

33 Department of the Taoiseach, *Revised RIA Guidelines: How to conduct a Regulatory Impact Analysis*, (2009) <https://publicspendingcode.per.gov.ie/wpcontent/uploads/2012/07/Revised_RIA_Guidelines_June_20091.pdf> 13, cited in OECD ibid 25.

34 OECD fn 32, 15

35 ibid 12.

36 See, for example, and generally, Michael E. Porter, *The Competitive Advantage of Nations* (MacMillan Press 1990); and *On Competition* (Harvard Business Review Book 2008).

37 European Union, 'Competitiveness' <https://eur-lex.europa.eu/EN/legal-content/glossary/competitiveness.html> accessed 12 October 2024.

38 OECD (n 32) 69.

Competing To Be Competitive

Sir Philip Lowe*
Oxera Consulting

1. Unlike probably the majority of contributors to this volume, I did not begin my career in the hallowed world of antitrust law. It has become an acquired and much appreciated taste....

2. Studying economics at Oxford nevertheless brought me into contact with ideas and theories about markets and how they worked and naturally the generally accepted assumption that a market could only really work if there was sufficient competition. I was intrigued by the concept of competition.

3. Competition between suppliers meant that those buying a good, a service had a choice and could then choose the best offer. 'Perfect' competition could theoretically exist if no new competitors had the incentive to enter the market and no existing competitors wanted to leave it. In this perfect world, price could also reach an equilibrium in which, as Pareto argued, no one could become better without someone else being worse off.

4. I personally found this world of perfect competition and equilibrium theory particularly arid. It suits mathematicians who can play around with the parameters of price, supply and demand and impress us with complicated equations. But it does not seem to reflect the reality of how markets work, except perhaps for commodities like potatoes and wheat.

5. Competition on a defined market for a good or service is not only about price. Competing firms can vie with each other to provide better quality, more attractive packaging, faster delivery or better after-sales service. This is obviously a good thing for consumers and for society and is a good enough reason to say that we should promote competition. Naturally, we cannot assume that having more than one supplier automatically creates competitive rivalry. There

---

* *Sir Philip Lowe, Former Director* General *for Competition, European Commission; Partner, Oxera Consulting.*

are many markets where suppliers don't make a serious effort to compete with each other because they are all content with the margins they earn, and the market share they have obtained and there is no urgency for them to be more proactive. There is also the phenomenon of consumer inertia. Sometimes people don't do anything to get a better deal when it is staring them in the face. But it is a good start if no supplier has a monopoly of a market. Monopoly doesn't have a good record in delivering better results for consumers or society as a whole.

6. In looking for ways in which markets can work better, I have on balance been more attracted by the work of Joseph Schumpeter,[1],who talked about the destructive forces of competition, and the dynamism and change which resulted from entrepreneurship and innovation. After all, it is disruption and discontinuity which tend to make a market significantly more competitive, not slow progression along preordained demand and supply curves.

7. Dynamism and innovation don't necessarily imply transforming the market completely. It may simply be limited to more efficient and effective ways of delivering goods and services based on existing technologies. But more radical innovations can mean that suppliers are not just competing on the market but also competing to create new markets and to open new opportunities for consumers, whether they are individuals, households or businesses. At this end of the spectrum, the benefits of competition become much more visible. I therefore find it encouraging that Mario Draghi, in addressing the challenges to European competitiveness,[2] has placed considerable emphasis on innovation in his recommendations on the future of European competition policy. He even proposes that some otherwise problematic mergers could be allowed to go ahead if they strengthen a firm's capacity to innovate.

8. More broadly, any analysis of competition between individuals, between firms or between countries confirms a more dynamic view of how markets can work. The incentive to compete successfully, and reap the rewards from it, is to have a new idea or to have an old idea which no one has ever exploited effectively. And to do it quickly so that you get the reward before others can catch up.

9. This may sound like condoning monopoly. No. The competitive advantage which innovation gives a supplier must at least be sustainable in the short term so that one obtains some benefit from it. The incentive to innovate, to get better results, will not be there unless people have an incentive to produce a step change in how the markets work rather than plodding on along trodden ways which benefits no one. Michael Porter's 'five forces model'[3] reflects this: anticipating the threat of new entrants and of new substitute products,

---

1 Joseph Schumpeter, *History of Economic Analysis* (Allen & Unwin 1954).

2 Mario Draghi, *The Future of European Competitiveness: A Competitiveness Strategy for Europe* (European Commission, September 2024) <https://commission.europa.eu/document/download/97e481fd-2dc3-412d-be4c-f152a8232961_en?filename=The%20future%20of%20European%20competitiveness%20_%20A%20competitiveness%20strategy%20for%20Europe.pdf&prefLang=sv> accessed 25 October 2024.

3 Michael E Porter, 'How Competitive Forces Shape Strategy' (1979) 57 Harvard Business Rev 137–145.

confronting the potential bargaining power of buyers or of suppliers, and engaging in the competitive rivalry which can emerge between suppliers. His book *The Competitive Advantage of Nations*[4] also underlines the reality that dynamic competition is equally a feature of the global success of individual countries. As he wrote 'a nation's competitiveness depends on the capacity of its industry to innovate and upgrade'.

10. This is of course the positive side of the coin of competition and competitiveness. Those who innovate and upgrade become ultimately more prosperous and those who fall behind lose out or have to catch up if they are to stay alive.

11. I started my career during the 1970's in the UK in manufacturing industry where many firms were producing goods of good quality and were inventing new things, but where they failed to exploit their innovations and failed to control costs. Instead of being the winners in industrial innovation in sectors such as cars and domestic appliances, they lost out to foreign competition which was more attuned to what consumers wanted and which was more ruthless in the control of costs.

12. But, if this was the end of the story about competition and competitiveness, things would be simple. There are many roadblocks on the road to promoting more competition and competitiveness which are not linked to a lack of dynamism and innovation. Competitive markets may satisfy producers and consumers, but they may not deliver the outcomes which we as citizens (and collectively, society) want. Governments and public agencies often need to intervene, as many competition authorities and regulators say, 'to make markets work'. As a result, there is no lack of regulation and antitrust law throughout the world which aims to do that.

13. The first check to be applied to effective competition is that aggressive competition on a market can result in private benefits but social costs. For example, competition to sell more and more cars driven by internal combustion engines can result in excessive CO2 emissions and frustrate efforts to halt climate change. Competition to provide more attractive packaging for products can result in an unacceptable increase in non-degradable waste. Expansion of competitively priced cheap air flights can result in excessive CO2 emissions, noise pollution and road congestion. Competition to induce children to eat more and more sugar-based products can result in a deterioration of their fitness and health.

14. All these examples point to the reality that there are limits to be placed on how firms compete. Only a cursory look at the mass of regulation on safety and health issues is enough to confirm that unbridled competition has to be subject to some restraints.

15. In addition, no government or parliament can ignore the distributional impact of the competitive process. In some countries, it is generally accepted that the management and workforce of failing companies should simply withdraw from

4 Michael E Porter, *The Competitive Advantage of Nations* (Free Press1990, rev edn 1998).

the market concerned and start again somewhere else. But in other countries, this is not politically acceptable: their governments are often under pressure either to support the failing firms which are no longer competitive or to put in place schemes for re-employment of redundant workers in other sectors.

16. Another more problematic distributional issue related to competition and competitiveness is the reality that economic and social conditions in the various countries where companies are competing against each other are often radically different. It's difficult for example for a supplier in a country which has poor road and telecommunications infrastructure and only a few skilled workers to compete with suppliers in other countries where developed infrastructures and a trained workforce already exist. Some countries are also rich in mineral resources and others have none.

17. On the other hand, people in emerging and developing countries who are much poorer than in developed countries will be willing to work for wages that are significantly lower than in developed countries. The consequence is that workers elsewhere consider this as unfair competition and condemn it as 'social dumping'. The protectionist movements in the US and Europe, which are linked to the loss of jobs in traditional industries, are an obvious consequence of these developments. In order to allow competition to be effective and fair, there is no alternative except to work towards international trade and cooperation agreements which are mutually beneficial for poorer and richer countries.

18. In the last thirty years, there has been sufficient global consensus for growth in trade between the US, Europe, China, India and Africa that has been globally positive on both sides of the prosperity divide. However, in the current climate of geopolitics, that consensus is unlikely to be sustained sufficiently to allow any further market integration beyond the situation today. What progress is being made is on the basis of bilateral trade agreements despite the fact that in principle, many markets for goods and services are already regional, if not global.

19. Even within the EU, which is in principle a single internal market, with freedom of movement of people, capital, goods and services, there is only a reluctant acceptance of relocation of industries to lower income Member States. Yet how can firms in the EU's poorer countries and regions be expected to compete in the single EU market when they don't have facilities and skill to do so? Thirty years ago, their leaders argued persuasively that there was no level playing field for them and they needed assistance. As a result, the creation of the EU's internal market was made conditional on Member States' parallel commitment to a programme of support to 'economic and social cohesion' which initially took concrete form in substantial aid to Ireland, Greece and Spain, as well as may poorer regions of bigger Member States. Political leaders of opposing ideologies, such as Margaret Thatcher and Jacques Delors, signed up to the twin objectives of a single competitive European market on the one hand but a commitment to economic and social cohesion on the

other. That political compact has continued and the programme of support to poorer countries and regions has been reinforced following the expansion of the EU to the East and South-East of the continent.

20. So, in order to be able to promote competition and achieve international competitiveness, there has to be some agreement on what free and fair competition is. This is why the notion of a level playing field and the common recognition of some rules of the game are as essential for competitive markets as they are for competitive sport.

21. However, a second roadblock to competition, and the competitiveness which competition promotes, is the reality that businesses don't always want to compete freely and fairly. Once firms have gained sufficient market power through innovation and organic growth, the tendency is often for them to want to hold on to it by whatever means. They will be jealous to maintain the stream of revenue and profits they have enjoyed in their period of innovation and growth.

22. There are several well-tried ways of holding on to market power. Forming a cartel with your competitors is one. Acquiring one or more of your competitors is another. Trying to extend the life of a patent beyond its authorised term is also a frequently used device to avoid competition without the need to compete and innovate. Use of restrictive contractual clauses to keep out competitors is also a frequent occurrence.

23. So, it is not surprising that anti-cartel enforcement, merger control, and control of abuse of market power have come to prominence and are the core activities of competition agencies. How can we extol the virtues of competition if it is continually being undermined by competitors who should be competing?

24. A third roadblock on the competition road is the way in which government sets the framework for markets to function. Government intervention into markets has been proven over time to be sometimes good, sometimes bad and sometimes ugly.

25. The provision of infrastructures (in energy, telecoms, transport) across a country should in principle be good for the economy and the competitiveness of a country. But if a state-owned company takes monopoly ownership of the infrastructures (which are so-called 'natural monopolies') and also has a monopoly of the supply of the services using these infrastructures, then there is unlikely to be any competitive pressure on it and no likelihood of it being very innovative.

26. It is now probably in the realm of pre-history, but I am certainly not the only consumer who had to wait almost a year for the state telecoms monopoly to connect a fixed line telephone connection to my house.

27. Since the early 1980's, practically all jurisdictions in the world have struggled with this issue. The most common solution has been for the downstream market to be opened up to more competitors and for the investment in and management of infrastructure networks, whether publicly or privately owned, to be monitored closely by sectoral regulators. At least these arrangements

create a solid framework for competition to take place, although they do not necessarily guarantee a sufficient level of dynamism on the market. Nor do they eliminate a proportion of retail prices which is not determined by the market. For example, regulated network charges account for about a third of final energy prices.

28. A second and crucially important role for governments in supporting competition and competitiveness is to put in place a framework of regulation which genuinely ensures a level playing field between competitors. Crucial areas are product standards, regulations on employment, environmental protection, safety and patent protection. And the more that markets become global, the more important it is for regulation to be applied across national borders under international agreements.

29. A third role that governments have played in relation to the goal of competitiveness is to support investments which are regarded by private operators as too risky to finance on their own, but which are judged to be essential in preserving the competitiveness of the country or of a sector. Typical examples here are the support given by the French Government in the 1960's and 1970's to the nuclear industry and to the development of high-speed trains. Investments in strategically important sectors under state control such as defence and cybersecurity may also have positive spillover effects in related commercial activities. The initial and rapid development of the internet is arguably due to the support provided by US Federal agencies. in addition, there is some justification, on the grounds of national security, for public support to the creation of domestic industries in order to avoid situations where a country might become overly dependent on foreign imports.

30. The key challenge in this area is to ensure that the state support provided is really necessary and that it doesn't have the effect of distorting competition on the market, including where subsidies given by one government have a potentially negative impact on competitors in another country. State aid control in the EU, as well as its Regulation on Foreign subsidies, aim to limit the effect of distortive subsidies. WTO rules have similar goals and a global reach, but it has been recently difficult to obtain international consensus on their enforcement.

31. Nevertheless, some government interventions have uglier features from a competition point of view. One of these is to give support to firms which are uncompetitive and are unlikely to retain their competitiveness even with government support. There are plenty of examples in Europe, in digital and in aviation, of public money going down the drain in lost causes of this kind.

32. Another plague on competition is the introduction of legislation which deliberately discriminates against foreign firms in order to protect domestic firms. Protectionist measures of this kind may have superficial justification in industrial policy but often find their origin in populist promises which offer the vain hope of countries being competitive but do not face up to the challenge

of creating a framework in which firms can become competitive on a long-term basis (education and training, solid infrastructures, good regulation…).

33. A final roadblock to ensuring a sufficient dynamic of competition in markets is the facility or difficulty which firms have in accessing capital. Research and development efforts may need to be substantial, with uncertain results. Investment in production facilities usually needs to be amortized of a long period. Revenue streams from new investments may only begin to flow after several years. It is not therefore surprising that investors scrutinise carefully the prospects for returns on the capital they provide and review equally carefully the profile of the firms and institutions to which they extend support. And it is equally unsurprising that the cost of capital suppliers of goods and services who are active on the same markets may be different. So, competing effectively depends not only on marketing and pricing strategies and control of operating costs but also on sourcing capital at competitive rates.

34. There are therefore a series of important preconditions in order to ensure that competition functions fairly and effectively in markets and that it can have a durable impact on competitiveness. Having assessed these preconditions (or roadblocks as I have described them above) I think we should be fairly cynical about the frequently heard call to 'let the market work'. The sort of dynamic competition which will lead to a genuine increase in a firm's or a country's competitiveness will only emerge on the basis of good regulation at national and international level, on taking account of social as well as private costs, on sound enforcement of merger and antitrust laws, on strong government support to improve infrastructures and skills, on selective but proportionate state support to key economic sectors, on effective access to capital markets, and above all on a political consensus at national and international level that competition can result, at least in the short term, in the reality that some firms or some countries will perform less well and will lose out unless they take measures to improve their performance. If the underlying conditions (prosperity, infrastructures, skills…) are holding them back, there is a strong case for public intervention at national and international level. But if you are uncompetitive, the logic of competition is either that you improve your performance rapidly or you leave the market you are in and start again somewhere else. The benefits to society of competition therefore translate into greater economic efficiency and substantial benefits to consumers and individual citizens. It is hard to find any system of market organisation which is more efficient in achieving these results than competition.

Table of Contents

PART I: Foundations and Philosophical Insights on Competition

PART II: Global Competition Challenges and Opportunities

PART III: Enforcement and Market Regulation

PART V: Competition Policy as a Tool for Broader Societal Impact

PART VII: Personal Reflections and Regional Experiences

Concurrences Review

Concurrences is a print and online quarterly peer reviewed journal dedicated to EU and national competitions laws. It has been launched in 2004 as the flagship of the Institute of Competition Law in order to provide a forum for academics, practitioners and enforcers. Concurrences' influence and expertise has garnered contributions or interviews with such figures as Christine Lagarde, Bill Kovacic, Emmanuel Macron, Antonin Scalia and Magrethe Vestager.

Contents

More than 15,000 articles, print and/or online. Quarterly issues provide current coverage with contributions from the EU or national or foreign countries thanks to more than 2,500 authors in Europe and abroad.

Format

In order to balance academic contributions with opinions or legal practice notes, Concurrences provides its insight and analysis in a number of formats:

- Forewords: Opinions by leading academics or enforcers
- Interviews: Interviews of antitrust experts
- On-Topics: 4 to 6 short papers on hot issues
- Law & Economics: Short papers written by economists for a legal audience
- Articles: Long academic papers
- Case Summaries: Case commentary on EU and French case law
- Legal Practice: Short papers for in-house counsels
- International: Medium size papers on international policies
- Books Review: Summaries of recent antitrust books
- Articles Review: Summaries of leading articles published in 45 antitrust journals

Boards

The Scientific Committee is headed by Laurence Idot, Professor at Panthéon Assas University. The International Committee is headed by Frederic Jenny, OECD Competition Comitteee Chairman. Boards members include Douglas Ginsburg, Benoît Cœuré, Howard Shelanski, Richard Whish, Wouter Wils, Joshua Wright, etc.

Online version

Concurrences website provides all articles published since its inception, in addition to selected articles published online only in the electronic supplement.

Write for Concurrences

Concurrences welcome spontaneous contributions. Except in rare circumstances, the journal accepts only unpublished articles, whatever the form and nature of the contribution. The Editorial Board checks the form of the proposals, and then submits these to the Scientific Committee. Selection of the papers is conditional to a peer review by at least two members of the Committee. Within a month, the Committee assesses whether the draft article can be published and notifies the author.

www.ingramcontent.com/pod-product-compliance
Ingram Content Group UK Ltd.
Pitfield, Milton Keynes, MK11 3LW, UK
UKHW021816051026
15470UKWH00025B/347